# NATIONAL REGISTER OF PSYCHOTHERAPISTS 2004

# NATIONAL REGISTER OF PSYCHOTHERAPISTS 2004

United Kingdom Council for Psychotherapy

Routledge
Taylor & Francis Group
LONDON AND NEW YORK

UKCP
UK Council for Psychotherapy

First published 2004 by Brunner-Routledge

Published 2020 by Routledge
2 Park Square, Milton Park, Abingdon, Oxon OX14 4RN
605 Third Avenue, New York, NY 10017

*Routledge is an imprint of the Taylor & Francis Group, an informa business*



*British Library Cataloguing in Publication Data*
A catalogue record for this book is available from the British Library

ISSN 1461-0175

ISBN 13: 978-1-58391-701-5 (pbk)
ISBN 13: 978-1-138-46313-4 (hbk)

# Table of Contents

# Foreword

Each year, in the opening line of this foreword, we repeat the phrase that it is now so many years since the Foster Report proposed that psychotherapy become a regulated profession. It is as though we need to constantly remind ourselves of where we have come from. More important, it reminds us of where we are going.

This year has been a significant one in the life of the Registration Board. Next year has the possibility of an even greater significance.

This year saw us finally make some progress on debates that have bogged us down for the last few years. Decisions were taken concerning what some of our registrants ought to be allowed to call themselves. This may sound trivial, but there were questions about identity, custodianship of standards, and, not least, status, at the heart of the debate. Inevitably, these issues inflamed feelings, and inhibited careful decision-making.

In order to make these decisions, we had to reach a place of relative calm. A way of doing this was to develop a 'due process' – a term that was broadly accepted and understood, but whose meaning was rather unspecific. We spent a good deal of time developing a process, and engaged in thorough going consultations that were probably unprecedented in the field of psychotherapy.

The results are generally known: we agreed that it was acceptable for appropriately trained registrants in the Humanistic and Integrative Psychotherapy Section to call themselves 'Integrative Child Psychotherapists'. Their stance was supported by many, but opposed principally by the Association of Child Psychotherapists, who felt, (and feel), with some passion, that their specifically psychoanalytic approaches to psychotherapy warranted their monopoly over that particular juxtaposition of words: 'Child' and 'Psychotherapist'.

We also agreed that although we accepted that the Psychoanalytic and Psychodynamic Section had made a good case in opposing the monopoly (in Britain, at least) of the term 'psychoanalyst', they had not made it clear how they proposed to identify the difference between a 'psychoanalyst' and a 'psychoanalytic psychotherapist'. The Board also wondered whether we should not specifically just be talking about 'psychotherapists', and that, if we were not, then we should consider the creation of a separate section in the Register for people who wanted to be termed 'psychoanalyst', and who were appropriately qualified. So although we turned down the Section's request to be allowed to use the label, we began a consideration of whether we should, in fact, have a separate Section in the register for those who wish to call themselves 'psychoanalyst'.

That piece of work proceeds.

The decisions have not ended the debate, but they have allowed us to move on. The world, as we know it, has not come to an end, even though there have been some re-alignments. We have gathered confidence in our ability to lead and to make tough decisions. There were inevitably some who were extremely upset about our decisions, but we continue to keep in dialogue with them. There were inevitably flaws in our process, but we are able to acknowledge and learn from them.

So what of the future?

This will be the last year that the UKCP Register is produced in just this format. We are planning to make the Register more widely available than its current printed form: to produce it on CDs and make it available to a wider section of the public. We also intend to make clearer to the public what the information in it means: what all the terms like 'Jungian Analyst', 'Core Process Psychotherapist' for example, actually means; whether the practitioners named in the Register are actually available for consultation.

This is part of much wider and more root and branch changes that we, in partnership with the UKCP Governing Board, hope to unfold over the next period, to March 2005. For we need to separate out the regulatory functions of the UKCP from the non-regulatory. We need to move to a place where there is more consistency across our member organisations and institutions about how we accredit and re-accredit our registrants; about how we deal with disciplinary matters and complaints from the public.

In short, we are still mindful of the Foster report, and, even though government regulation is still a distance away, we have the chance to improve our self-regulation. This will mean, we hope, that when statutory regulation does eventually come, it will not come as a trauma.

Finally, it seems important to say this: this document, the National Register of Psychotherapists, is, to a large extent, self-referential. It contains terms and descriptors in it, which may mean a lot to many psychotherapists, but are unhelpful to the public. We are moving in the direction of more transparency and more accountability. We will of course strive to find ways of doing that without losing the freshness and originality of new forms of psychotherapy, and without losing our respect for what we call our 'modalities' – the different kinds of thinking that inform the eight sections of the UKCP.

Andrew Enever

Andrew Enever
Chair, Registration Board

January 2004

# Using the Register

The National Register of Psychotherapists is designed to make it easy to find and contact a psychotherapist in your area. The names, addresses, and telephone numbers of registered psychotherapists are listed alphabetically within geographical areas. Each entry includes a brief description of the type of psychotherapy offered and a code denoting the organisation(s) to which the psychotherapist belongs. A list of these codes and the organisations they relate to appears on page xiv. The Register also lists practitioners under the organisation(s) to which they belong.

Each of the eight sections of UKCP has a Flag Statement outlining its purpose and distinguishing it from the other sections. The Flag Statements and a list of organisations belonging to each section appear on pages xi-xiii.

*One asterisk beside the Organisation Code of members of the Confederation of Analytical Psychologists indicates that these psychotherapists belong to either the Society of Analytical Psychology (SAP) or the British Association of Psychotherapists (BAP) or both. The BAP and the SAP were founding Member Organisations of the UKCP. Since 1999 they are no longer members.

Users of the Register may inquire of the UKCP office as to whether a named practitioner is currently listed on the UKCP database. We hope that you will find this Register easy to use and that you will write with your comments to:

**United Kingdom Council for Psychotherapy**
167-169 Great Portland Street
London W1W 5PF

Tel: 020 7436 3002

Fax: 020 7436 3013

Email: ukcp@psychotherapy.org.uk

http://www.psychotherapy.org.uk

The information contained in the Register reflects the membership of the Registration Board at 31st December 2003. The UKCP cannot however accept responsibility for any inaccuracies in the data provided by the Member Organisations. Additions and deletions to the Register are published biannually in the UKCP newsletter: *The Psychotherapist*. The UKCP database of the *National Register of Psychotherapists* is continually updated.

# Governing Board

# Registration Board

| | |
|---|---|
| **Andrew Enever** | Chair |
| **Marj Thoburn** | Vice Chair |
| **David Campbell** | Institutional Member |
| **Richard Cleminson** | Humanistic and Integrative Psychotherapy Section |
| **Alex Coren** | Institutional Member |
| **Martin Weaver** | Experiential Constructivist Therapies Section |
| **Claudia Herbert** | Behavioural and Cognitive Psychotherapy Section |
| **To be confirmed** | Psychoanalytically Based Therapy with Children Section |
| **Nigel McBride** | Psychoanalytic and Psychodynamic Section |
| **Peter Nevins** | Psychoanalytic and Psychodynamic Section |
| **Bracha Newman** | Analytical Psychology Section |
| **Bernard Roberts** | Special member |
| **Charlotte Sills** | Humanistic and Integrative Psychotherapy Section |
| **To be confirmed** | Psychoanalytic and Psychodynamic Section |
| **To be confirmed** | British Psychological Society |
| **To be confirmed** | Hypno Psychotherapy Section |
| **Ken Evans** | Humanistic and Integrative Psychotherapy Section |

# Ethical Guidelines

## of the United Kingdom Council for Psychotherapy

### 1. Introduction

1.1 The purpose of a Code of Ethics is to define general principles and to establish standards of professional conduct for psychotherapists in their work and to inform and protect those members of the public who seek their services. Each organisation will include and elaborate upon the following principles in its Code of Ethics.

1.2 All psychotherapists are expected to approach their work with the aim of alleviating suffering and promoting the well-being of their clients. Psychotherapists should endeavour to use their abilities and skills to their clients' best advantage without prejudice and with due recognition of the value and dignity of every human being.

**1.3 All psychotherapists on the UKCP Register are required to adhere to the Codes of Ethics and Practice of their own organisations which will be consistent with the following statements and which will have been approved by the appropriate UKCP Section.**

### 2. Codes Of Ethics

Each Member Organisation of UKCP must have published a Code of Ethics approved by the appropriate UKCP Section and appropriate for the practitioners of that particular organisation and their clients. The Code of Ethics will include and elaborate upon the following ten points to which attention is drawn here. Al psychotherapists on the UKCP Register are required to adhere to the Codes of Ethics of their own organisations.

2.1 **Qualifications:** Psychotherapists are required to disclose their qualifications when requested and not claim, or imply, qualifications that they do not have.

2.2 **Terms, Conditions and Methods of Practice:** Psychotherapists are required to disclose on request their terms, conditions and, where appropriate, methods of practice at the outset of psychotherapy.

2.3 **Confidentiality:** Psychotherapists are required to preserve confidentiality and to disclose, if requested, the limits of confidentiality and circumstances under which it might be broken to specific third parties.

2.4 **Professional Relationship:** Psychotherapists should consider the client's best interest when making appropriate contact with the client's GP, relevant psychiatric services, or other relevant professionals with the client's knowledge. Psychotherapists should be aware of their own limitations.

2.5 **Relationship with Clients:** Psychotherapists are required to maintain appropriate boundaries with their clients. They must take care not to exploit their clients, current or past, in any way, financially, sexually, or emotionally.

2.6 **Research:** Psychotherapists are required to clarify with clients the nature, purpose and conditions of any research in which the clients are to be involved and to ensure that informed and verifiable consent is given before commencement.

2.7 **Publication:** Psychotherapists are required to safeguard the welfare and anonymity of clients when any form of publication of clinical material is being considered and to obtain their consent whenever possible.

2.8 **Practitioner Competence:** Psychotherapists are required to maintain their ability to perform competently and to take necessary steps to do so.

2.9 **Indemnity Insurance:** Psychotherapists are required to ensure that their professional work is adequately covered by appropriate indemnity insurance.

2.10 **Detrimental Behaviour:**

(i) Psychotherapists are required to refrain from any behaviour that may be detrimental to the profession, to colleagues or to trainees.

(ii) Psychotherapists are required to take appropriate action in accordance with Clause 5.7 with regard to the behaviour of a colleague which may be detrimental to the profession, to colleagues or to trainees.

### 3. Advertising

Member Organisations of UKCP and individual psychotherapists are required to restrict promotion of their work to a description of the type of psychotherapy they provide. Psychotherapists are required to distinguish carefully between self-descriptions, as in a list and advertising seeking enquiries.

### 4. Code of Practice

Each Member Organisation of UKCP will have published a Code of Practice approved by the appropriate UKCP Section and appropriate for the practitioners of that particular organisation and their clients. The purpose of general principles established in the Code of Ethics of the organisation and the practical application of those principles. All psychotherapists on the UKCP Register will be required to adhere to the Codes of Practice of their own organisations.

### 5. Complaints Procedure

Each Member Organisation of UKCP must have published a Complaints Procedure, including information about the acceptability or otherwise of a complaint made by a third party against a practitioner, approved by the appropriate UKCP Section and appropriate for the practitioners of that particular organisation and their clients. The purpose of a Complaints Procedure is to ensure that practitioners and their clients have clear information about the procedure and processes involved in dealing with complaints. All psychotherapists on the UKCP Register are required to adhere to the Complaints Procedure of their own organisation.

5.1 **Making a complaint:** A client wishing to complain shall be advised to contact the Member Organisation.

5.2 **Receiving a complaint:** A Member Organisation receiving a complaint against one of its psychotherapists shall ensure that the therapist is informed immediately and that both complainant and therapist are aware of the Complaints Procedure.

5.3 **Appeals:**

(i) After the completion of the Complaints Procedure within an organisation, provision must be made for an appeal, stating time limits, grounds and procedures.

(ii) After the completion of all procedures in an organisation, an appeal may be made to the UKCP Professional Conduct Committee.

5.4 **Reports to UKCP Section:** Where a complaint is upheld the Section shall be informed by the organisation.

5.5 **Reports to the UKCP Registration Board.** Member Organisations are required to report to the UKCP Registration Board the names of members who have been suspended or expelled.

5.6 **Complaints upheld and convictions:** Psychotherapists are required to inform their Member Organisations if any complaint is upheld against them in another Member Organisation, if they are convicted of any notifiable criminal offence or if successful civil proceedings are brought against them in relation to their work as psychotherapists.

5.7 **Conduct of colleagues:** Psychotherapists concerned that a colleague's conduct may be unprofessional should initiate the Complaints Procedure of the relevant Member Organisation.

5.8 The resignation of a member of an organisation shall not be allowed to impede the process of any investigation as long as the alleged offence took place during the person's membership.

## 6. Sanctions

Psychotherapists who are suspended by, or expelled from, a Member Organisation are automatically deleted from the UKCP Register.

## 7. Monitoring Complaints

7.1 Member Organisations previously reported to the Registration Board annually concerning the number of complaints received, the nature of the complaints and their disposition. This function is being transferred to the Professional Conduct Committee.

7.2 The Professional Conduct Committee shall report annually to the Governing Board on the adequacy of Member Organisations' disciplinary procedures.

# Sections and Flag Statements

## ANALYTICAL PSYCHOLOGY SECTION

This stems from the work of C.G.Jung. The central idea is that what we do and feel, how we think of ourselves and other people, depend upon forces and processes we are not aware of – the 'unconscious'. These may be part of our common human nature of particular to the individual.

The analytical psychologist (also known as a Jungian analyst) tries to understand these unconscious elements in what the patient says and the dreams they report. Particular attention is given to how the patient regards the analyst and vice versa. It can be beneficial for a patient to understand how this 'transference' mirrors the early family situation, enabling them to take conscious control. Jungian analysts believe that we are all highly capable of healing ourselves and taking charge of our lives.

Analytical psychologists treat people suffering from emotional disorders or problems with relationships, but can also help 'normal' people who are discontented with themselves or have lost a sense of direction in their lives. So it is not necessary to be 'ill' to benefit from Jungian analysis, since self-discovery and the exploration of the inner world are valuable in themselves.

Analytical psychology also has much to say about society and culture, showing how unconscious processes affect the groups and institutions we belong to.

**Organisations**

| | |
|---|---|
| Association of Jungian Analysts | **AJA** |
| Confederation of Analytical Psychologists | **CAP** |
| The Independent Group of Analytical Psychologists | **IGAP** |

## BEHAVIOURAL & COGNITIVE PSYCHOTHERAPY SECTION

Behavioural and Cognitive Psychotherapies are psychological approaches which are based on scientific principles and which research has shown to be effective for a wide range of problems. Clients and therapists work together to identify and understand problems in terms of the relationship between thoughts, feelings and behaviour. The approach usually focuses on difficulties in the here and now, and relies on the therapist and client developing a shared view of the individual's problem. This then leads to the identification of personalised, time-limited therapy goals and strategies which are continually monitored and evaluated. Behavioural and Cognitive Psychotherapists work with individuals, families and groups. The approaches can be used to help anyone irrespective of ability, culture, race, gender or sexual preference.

Behavioural and Cognitive Psychotherapists are usually health professionals such as nurses, psychologists, doctors, social workers, counsellors etc. Whilst all behavioural and cognitive psychotherapists share the above principles, individual therapists may call themselves Cognitive Psychotherapists, Behavioural Psychotherapists, Cognitive Behavioural Psychotherapists or Rational Emotive Behaviour Therapists. These different titles often reflect the preference and training of individual therapists for specific techniques which address problematic thoughts, assumptions and beliefs directly (Cognitive Psychotherapists), address behaviour directly (Behavioural Psychotherapists) or a combination of techniques aimed at addressing thoughts and behaviour (Cognitive Behavioural Psychotherapists, Rational Emotive Behaviour Therapists). Whatever title they use, the approach is commonly referred to as CBT. Most importantly, all therapists aim to help clients achieve desired change in the way they think, feel and behave.

**Organisation**

| | |
|---|---|
| Association for Rational Emotive Behaviour Therapists | **AREBT** |
| British Association for Behavioural and Cognitive Psychotherapies | **BABCP** |

## EXPERIENTIAL CONSTRUCTIVIST THERAPIES SECTION

These therapies are based on the assumption that our world is not just given to us complete, but that we construct our individual picture of it from our own experiences. Then, what we do, what we believe, what we feel is largely dictated by this picture, or model. For a person badly treated, the world may be seen as cruel or unreliable, whereas for one well treated, it may appear a good place. We are constantly modifying our models in the light of experience.

The first task in therapy is to help the client clarify the models they use, consciously or not, to represent the world to themselves. They will need to explore and try out different ways of constructing their model and living within it, with no suggestion that any particular model is the 'correct' one. Changes may come in a small way in different behaviour or more extensively in revision of values, beliefs and identity.

These therapies often have a specific focus and expect to effect positive changes in the short term, as well as dealing with the underlying issues, which may require longer term therapy. The setting may be one-to-one or in a group. A wide range of methods is used, imaginatively tailored to the individual, who is involved at every stage. The process, depending on mutual respect between therapist and client, is designed to enable the client to take better charge of their life.

**Organisations**

| | |
|---|---|
| Neuro Linguistic Psychotherapy Counselling Association | **NLPtCA** |
| PCP Education & Training | **PCP** |
| Society for Existential Analysis | **SEA** |

## FAMILY, COUPLE, SEXUAL & SYSTEMIC THERAPY SECTION

The members within this group of organisations share an assumption that individual's problems cannot adequately be understood without considering the wider relevance of the families and groups which form each individuals' past and present wider context. Information about this wider system may be elicited within therapy sessions with individuals, couples or family groups. Some systemic psychotherapists also consult to organisational and business systems.

Therapy aims to identify and explore the patterns of belief and behaviours in roles and relationships (including sexual relationships) which seem to have become set over time, and to enable people to decide where change would be desirable and to facilitate the process of establishing new and more fulfilling patterns.

Systemic psychotherapists, whilst often actively intervening in client systems, strive to maintain a non-blaming and neutral position, respecting differences of culture, race, gender, sexual orientation etc. Therapists may work in teams, using live consultation or as sole practitioners using retrospective consultation in order to draw upon other perspectives to their practice. Therapy is often relatively short-term.

**Organisations**

| | |
|---|---|
| Association for Family Therapy | **AFT** |
| British Association for Sexual and Relationship Therapy | **BASRT** |
| The Family Institute Cardiff | **FIC** |
| Institute of Family Therapy | **IFT** |
| Kensington Consultation Centre | **KCC** |

## HUMANISTIC & INTEGRATIVE PSYCHOTHERAPY SECTION

This Section includes different psychotherapies which approach the individual as a whole person including body, feelings, mind and spirit. Members welcome interdisciplinary dialogue and an exploration of different psychological processes with particular emphasis on integration within the Section. Organisation in this Section practice approaches compatible with the following:

**Humanistic psychotherapy** is an approach which tries to do justice to the whole person including mind, body and spirit. It represents a broad range of therapeutic methods. Each method recognises the self-healing capacities of the client. The humanistic psychotherapist works towards an authentic meeting of equals in the therapy relationship.

**Existential psychotherapy** aims at enabling clients to find constructive ways of coming to terms with the challenges of everyday living. The focus is on the client's concrete, individual experience of anxiety and distress leading to an exploration of their personal beliefs and value system, in order to clarify and understand these in relation to the specific physical, psychological and socio-cultural context. The experience and influences of the past, present and future are given equal emphasis. The questioning of assumptions and facing up to the possibilities and limitations of living is an important part of this interactive, dynamic and direct approach.

**Transpersonal/Psychospiritual psychotherapy** can be defined by its orientation which includes the spiritual dimension rather than the content of therapy. It views the human psyche as having a central core Self or Soul as the centre of identity as well as a personal ego. Psychotherapists draw on a wide range of therapeutic methods towards the uncovering of past psychological material within a context of the individuals potential based on spiritual insight and experience. Within this perspective there is both a movement of the personal centre to the Self and a movement of the Self to manifest its nature through and in the personal centre. Thus therapy includes both repair and individuation.

**Integrative therapy** can be distinguished from eclecticism by its determination to show there are significant connections between different therapies, which may be unrecognised by their exclusive proponents. While remaining respectful to each approach, integrative psychotherapy draws from many sources in the belief that no one approach has all the truth. The therapeutic relationship is the vehicle for experience, growth and change. It aims to hold together the dual forces of disintegration and integration, as presented by the psychologically distressed and disabled. The integrative therapeutic experience leads towards a greater tolerance of life's experiences and an increase of creativity and service.

**Organisations**

| | |
|---|---|
| Association for Cognitive Analytic Therapists | **ACAT** |
| Association of Humanistic Psychology Practitioners | **AHPP** |
| Bath Centre for Psychotherapy and Counselling | **BCPC** |
| British Psychodrama Association | **BPA** |
| Centre for Counselling and Psychotherapy Education | **CCPE** |
| Centre for Transpersonal Psychology | **CTP** |
| Chiron Centre for Body Psychotherapy | **CCBP** |
| Gestalt Centre, London | **GCL** |
| Gestalt Psychotherapy Training Institute | **GPTI** |
| Guild for Analytical Psychology & Spirituality | **GAPS** |
| Institute of Psychosynthesis | **IPS** |
| Institute of Transactional Analysis | **ITA** |
| Institute for Arts in Therapy and Education | **IATE** |
| Karuna Institute | **KI** |
| London Association of Primal Psychotherapists | **LAPP** |
| London School of Biodynamic Psychotherapy | **LSBP** |
| Metanoia Institute | **MET** |
| Minster Centre | **MC** |
| Northern Guild for Psychotherapy | **NGP** |
| Psychosynthesis and Education Trust | **PET** |
| School of Psychotherapy and Counselling Regent's College | **SPCRC** |
| Re-Vision | **RE.V** |
| Scarbrough Psychotherapy Training Institute | **ScPTI** |
| Sherwood Psychotherapy Training Institute | **SPTI** |
| Spectrum | **SPEC** |

## HYPNO-PSYCHOTHERAPY SECTION

Hypno-psychotherapy is the branch of psychotherapy which uses hypnosis. It rests on an extensive body of work and publications over the last three hundred years, leading to that of Milton, Erickson and those influenced by him. It understands that we have a learned model of the world which can restrict the way we feel, what we understand, our attitudes and behaviour. Hypnosis is a state of relaxation which people enter voluntarily, during which there occurs an altered state of conscious awareness. The therapist can intervene to draw the individual's attention to new possibilities, to alternative patterns of thought, emotions and behaviour. The methods and strategies used in therapy are designed to make use of the resources and capabilities that reside within all people, and do not require the individual to fit into a standardised pattern. Hypnotherapy may be invaluable for anyone seeking to resolve specific problems, or for personal development.

**Organisations**

| | |
|---|---|
| British Autogenic Society | **BAS** |
| Centre Training International School of Hypnotherapy and Psychotherapy | **CTIS** |
| National College of Hypnosis and Psychotherapy | **NCHP** |
| National Register of Hypnotherapists and Psychotherapists | **NRHP** |
| National School of Hypnosis and Psychotherapy | **N-SHAP** |

## PSYCHOANALYTIC & PSYCHODYNAMIC SECTION

These therapies are based on psychoanalytic theory and practice. They may take place one-to-one or in a group. They may be of long or short duration. The central principle is that much distress has been caused by events in early life which we are no longer aware of. The therapy offers a reliable setting for the patient to explore free associations, memories, fantasies, feelings and dreams, to do with past and present. Particular attention is given to the interaction with the therapist, through which the patient may relive situations from their early life, the 'transference'. In these ways the patient may achieve a new and better resolution of longstanding conflicts.

**Organisations**

| | |
|---|---|
| Arbours Association | **ARBS** |
| Association for Group and Individual Psychotherapy | **AGIP** |
| The Association of Independent Psychotherapists | **AIP** |
| British Association of Psychoanalytic and Psychodynamic Supervison | **BAPPS** |
| Cambridge Society for Psychotherapy | **CSP** |
| Centre for Attachment Based Psychoanalytic Psychotherapy | **CAPP** |
| Centre for Freudian Analysis and Research | **CFAR** |
| Canterbury Consortium of Psychoanalytic Psychodynamic Psychotherapists | **CCOPPP** |
| Forum for Independent Psychotherapists | **FIP** |
| Foundation for Psychotherapy and Counselling | **FPC** |
| Group Analysis South West | **GASW** |
| Guild of Psychotherapists | **GUILD** |
| Hallam Institute of Psychotherapy | **HIP** |
| Institute of Group Analysis | **IGA** |
| Institute of Psychotherapy and Social Studies | **IPSS** |
| Liverpool Psychotherapy Diploma Organisation | **LPDO** |
| NAFSIYAT | **NAFSI** |
| North West Institute for Dynamic Psychotherapy | **NWIDP** |
| Philadelphia Association | **PA** |
| Severnside Institute for Psychotherapy | **SIP** |
| Site for Contemporary Psychoanalysis | **SITE** |
| Society of Couple Psychoanalytic Psychotherapists | **SCPP** |
| South Trent Training in Dynamic Psychotherapy | **STTDP** |
| Tavistock Marital Studies Institute | **TMSI** |
| Vaughan Association of Psychodynamic Psychotherapists | **VAPP** |
| West Midlands Institute of Psychotherapy | **WMIP** |
| Westminster Pastoral Foundation | **WPF** |
| Women's Therapy Centre | **WTC** |
| Yorkshire Association for Psychodynamic Psychotherapy | **YAPP** |

## PSYCHOANALYTICALLY-BASED THERAPY WITH CHILDREN

Therapists in this Section work with children who have problems beyond the resources of parent or school. Psychoanalytic theory is used to understand what the children have to say, consciously or unconsciously, in conversation, play, drawings and educational tasks. The aim is to restore the child to the stage of development appropriate to their age. This is done by observing the child within a reliable setting and interpreting their behaviour, including how they relate to the therapist and how they use materials supplied. As children depend on adults and the environment they provide, the work often includes contact with parents and families and treatment of them.

**Organisations**

| | |
|---|---|
| The Caspari Foundation for Educational Therapy and Therapeutic Teaching (formerly FAETT) | **CFET** |

## INSTITUTIONAL MEMBERS

A category of full membership of UKCP open to those psychotherapy organisations whose large size and complexity make it inappropriate for their membership to be confined to any individual Section. Institutional Members have 2 seats on the Governing Board.

**Organisations**

| | |
|---|---|
| Association for Counsellors & Psychotherapists in Primary Care | **CPC** |
| Tavistock Clinic | **TAVI** |
| Universities Psychotherapy & Counselling Association | **UPCA** |

## SPECIAL MEMBERS

Two organisations, of unique importance to the profession of psychotherapy and encompassing other related disciplines, have retained this special category of full membership. Each has a seat on the Governing Board. (This is not an open category of membership and cannot be applied for)

**Organisations**

| | |
|---|---|
| British Psychological Society | **BPS** |
| Royal College of Psychiatrists | **RCPsych** |

## FRIEND OF THE COUNCIL

A non-voting category for organisations closely associated with UKCP but not seeking full membership.

**Organisation**

| | |
|---|---|
| British Association for Counselling & Psychotherapy | **BACP** |

# Organisation Codes

| Code | Organisation |
|---|---|
| **ARBS** | Arbours Association |
| **AFT** | Association for Family Therapy |
| **AGIP** | Association for Group and Individual Psychotherapy |
| **ACP** | Association of Child Psychotherapists |
| **ACAT** | Association for Cognitive Analytic Therapists |
| **AHPP** | Association of Humanistic Psychology Practitioners |
| **AIP** | Association of Independent Psychotherapists |
| **AJA** | Association of Jungian Analysts |
| **AREBT** | Association of Rational Emotive Behaviour Psychotherapies |
| **BCPC** | Bath Centre for Psychotherapy and Counselling |
| **BABCP** | British Association for Behavioural and Cognitive Psychotherapies |
| **BACP** | British Association for Counselling & Psychotherapy |
| **BAPPPS** | British Association for Psychoanalytic and Psychodynamic Psychotherapy Supervision |
| **BASRT** | British Association for Sexual and Relationship Therapy |
| **BAS** | British Autogenic Society |
| **BPA** | British Psychodrama Association |
| **BPS** | British Psychological Society |
| **CSP** | Cambridge Society for Psychotherapy |
| **CAPP** | Centre for Attachment-Based Psychoanalytic Psychotherapy |
| **CCPE** | Centre for Counselling & Psychotherapy Education |
| **CFAR** | Centre for Freudian Analysis and Research |
| **CFET** | Caspari Foundation |
| **CPC** | Association for Counsellors & Psychotherapists in Primary Care |
| **CCOPPP** | Canterbury Consortium of Psychoanalytic & Psychodynamic Psychotherapists |
| **CTP** | Centre for Transpersonal Psychology |
| **CTS** | Centre Training International School for Hypnotherapy and Psychotherapy |
| **CCBP** | Chiron Centre for Body Psychotherapy |
| **CAP** | Confederation of Analytical Psychologists |
| **FIC** | Family Institute, Cardiff |
| **FIP** | Forum for Independent Psychotherapists |
| **FPC** | Foundation for Psychotherapy and Counselling |
| **GAPS** | Guild for Analytical Psychology and Spirituality |
| **GCL** | Gestalt Centre, London |
| **GPTI** | Gestalt Psychotherapy Training Institute |
| **GASW** | Group Analysis South West |
| **GUILD** | Guild of Psychotherapists |
| **HIP** | Hallam Institute of Psychotherapy |
| **IGAP** | Independent Group of Analytical Psychologists |

| Code | Organisation |
|---|---|
| **IATE** | Institute for Arts in Therapy and Education |
| **IFT** | Institute of Family Therapy |
| **IGA** | Institute of Group Analysis |
| **IPS** | Institute of Psychosynthesis |
| **IPSS** | Institute of Psychotherapy and Social Studies |
| **ITA** | Institute of Transactional Analysis |
| **KI** | Karuna Institute |
| **KCC** | Kensington Consultation Centre |
| **LAPP** | London Association of Primal Psychotherapists |
| **LPDO** | Liverpool Psychotherapy Diploma Organisation |
| **LSBP** | London School of Biodynamic Psychotherapy |
| **MET** | Metanoia Institute |
| **MC** | Minster Centre |
| **NAFSI** | NAFSIYAT |
| **NCHP** | National College of Hypnotherapists & Psychotherapists |
| **NRHP** | National Register of Hypnotherapists & Psychotherapists |
| **NSHAP** | National School of Hypnosis & Psychotherapy |
| **NGP** | Northern Guild for Psychotherapy |
| **NLPtCA** | Neuro Linguistic Psychotherapy Counselling Association |
| **NWIDP** | North West Institute for Dynamic Psychotherapy |
| **PA** | Philadelphia Association |
| **PCP** | PCP Education and Training |
| **PET** | Psychosynthesis & Education Trust |
| **RE.V** | Re.Vision |
| **RCPsych** | Royal College of Psychiatrists |
| **ScPTI** | Scarbrough Psychotherapy Training Institute |
| **SPCRC** | School of Psychotherapy and Counselling Regent's College |
| **SIP** | Severnside Institute for Psychotherapy |
| **SITE** | Site for Contemporary Psychoanalysis |
| **SEA** | Society for Existential Analysis |
| **STTDP** | South Trent Training in Dynamic Psychotherapy |
| **SPEC** | Spectrum |
| **SCPP** | Soceity of Couple Psychoanalytic Psychotherapists |
| **TAVI** | Tavistock Clinic |
| **TMSI** | Tavistock Marital Studies Institute |
| **UPCA** | Universities Psychotherapy & Counselling Association |
| **VAPP** | Vaughan Association of Psychodynamic Psychotherapists |
| **WMIP** | West Midlands Institute of Psychotherapy |
| **WPF** | Westminster Pastoral Foundation |
| **WTC** | Women's Therapy Centre |
| **YAPP** | Yorkshire Association for Psychodynamic Psychotherapy |

# Geographical Listing

## LONDON CENTRAL

**ADAMS-LANGLEY**, Stephen
**Integrative Psychotherapist**
33 Molyneux Street
London
W1H 5HW
☎ 020 7724 3493
slangley@xtrabox.com
SPCRC

**ANDREWS**, Ulla
**Transpersonal Psychotherapist**
c/o CCPE
Beauchamp Lodge
2 Warwick Crescent
London
W2 6NE
☎ 01923 229240
☎ 07787 511777
ulla@Andrews.uk.net
CCPE

**ANTONAS**, Vassilis
**Integrative Psychotherapist**
Counselling & Psychotherapy Associates
4 Wimpole Street
London
W1G 9SH
☎ 020 7637 7763
☎ 020 7226 1900
info@counselling.org or
v.antonas@therapyconnections.com
AHPP

**ASHWIN**, Mary
**Integrative Psychotherapist**
9 Nottingham Mansions
Nottingham Street
London
W1U 5EN
☎ 020 7486 3574
maryashwin@btopenworld.com
SPCRC

**ATKINSON**, Debbee
**Transpersonal Psychotherapist**
c/o CCPE
Beauchamp Lodge
2 Warwick Crescent
London
W2 6NE
☎ 020 7266 3006
☎ 07905 021 911
CCPE

**BARNES**, Tricia
**Sexual and Relationship Psychotherapist**
♿ 21F Devonshire Place
London
W1G 6HZ
☎ 020 7935 0113
☎ 020 8241 1201
tbapractice@aol.com
BASRT

**BARTY**, Alison
**Gestalt Psychotherapist**
♿ SOAS
Thornhaugh St
Russel Square
London
WC1H OXG
☎ 020 7354 2175
alisonbarty@aol.com
GPTI

**BASHARAN**, Harika
**Transpersonal Psychotherapist**
Central London
☎ 020 8 995 3836
Hbasharan@aol.com
CCPE

**BENTOVIM**, Dr Arnon
**Family & Systemic Psychotherapist**
♿ 97 Harley Street
London
W1G 6AG
☎ 020 7435 2255
☎ 020 7224 2800
bentovim@lcfcs.co.uk
IFT

**BERNARD**, Beverley
**Transpersonal Psychotherapist**
c/o CCPE
Beauchamp Lodge
2 Warwick Crescent
London
W2 6NE
CCPE

**BHATIA**, Pushan
**Transpersonal Psychotherapist**
CCPE
Warwick Crescent
London
W2 6NE
☎ 020 88610595
CCPE

**BIRCHARD**, Thaddeus
**Sexual and Relationship Psychotherapist**
Medical Suite
Bentinck Mansions
Bentinck Street
London
W1U 2ER
☎ 020 7372 3155
thaddeus@birchard.co.uk
BASRT

**BLEDIN**, Kenneth
**Group Analyst**
Psychology Department
Hunter Street Health Centre
8 Hunter Street
London
WC1N 1BN
☎ 020 7530 6800
ken.bledin@candi.nhs.uk
IGA

**BOSWOOD**, Bryan
**Group Analyst**
The Group Analytic Practice
88 Montagu Mansions
London
W1U 6LF
☎ 020 7935 3103
boswood@gapractice.org.uk
IGA

**BOZOVIC**, Zoran
**Group Analyst**
The Group Analytic Practice
88 Montagu Mansions
London
W1U 6LF
☎ 020 7935 3103
IGA

**BRAYNE**, Mark
**Transpersonal Psychotherapist**
c/o CCPE
Beauchamp Lodge
2 Warwick Crescent
London
W2 6NE
☎ 07711 888682
mark.brayne@virgin.net
CCPE

**BROUGHTON**, Helen
**Transpersonal Psychotherapist**
c/o CCPE
Beauchamp Lodge
2 Warwick Crescent
London
W2 6NE
☎ 020 7266 3006
☎ 020 8770 2187
CCPE

**BROWN**, Ian B
**Psychoanalytic Psychotherapist**
4
Wimpole Sreet
London
W1G 9YB
☎ 02074 868 914
post@counselling.org
IPSS

**CAHILL**, Pauline
**Humanistic Psychotherapist**
c/o AHPP
BCM AHPP
London
WC1N 3XX
☎ 07958 533135
Pauline.Cahill@uwe.ac.uk
AHPP

**CAIN**, Dennis
**Transpersonal Psychotherapist**
Centre for Counselling &
Psychotherapy Education
2 Warwick Crescent
London
W2 6NE
☎ 020 8 491 7077
CCPE

**CAMERON**, Michael John
**Cognitive Behavioural Psychotherapist**
60 Bloomsbury Street
London
WC1B 3QT
☎ 020 8445 1369
BABCP

**CANETE**, Maria
**Group Analyst**
Dept. of Psychology, University
College Hospital
4th Floor, Cecil Flemming House
Grafton Way, Gower Street
London
WC1E 6AU
☎ 020 7387 9300 x8553
IGA

**CANTELO**, Frances
**Transpersonal Psychotherapist**
CCPE
2 Warwick Crescent
London
W2 6NE
☎ 020 8 749 5974
francantelo@yahoo.com
CCPE

**CASEY**, Jan
**Transpersonal Psychotherapist**
99 St Mary's Mansions
Park Place Villas
Little Venice
London
W2 1SY
☎ 07850 354339
☎ 020 7723 4406
jan@jancasey.co.uk
CCPE

**CHARLES MA**, Debbie
**Transpersonal Psychotherapist**
c/o CCPE
Beauchamp Lodge
2 Warwick Crescent
London
W2 6NE
☎ 020 8441 5457
☎ 07952 06 49 94
dd.charles@virgin.net
CCPE

**CLARK**, Corah
**Transpersonal Psychotherapist**
c/o CCPE
Beauchamp Lodge
2 Warwick Crescent
London
W2 6NE
☎ 020 7266 3006
corah_c@hotmail.com
CCPE

**CONSTANTINOU**, Daniel
**Cognitive Behavioural Psychotherapist**
♿ 10 Harley Street
London
W1G 9PF
☎ 020 7467 8360
daniel.constantinou@virgin.net
BABCP

**CROSBY**, Simon
**Personal Construct Psychotherapist**
4 Sandringham Court
Dufour's Place
London
W1
☎ 01342 824 545
Simon@scapegoat.demon.co.uk
PCP

**CROWE**, Michael
**Sexual and Relationship Psychotherapist**
21 Wimpole Street
London
W1G 8GG
☎ 020 7637 0146
mjcrowe65@hotmail.com
AFT, BABCP, BASRT, IFT

**CUMMINS MA**, Kate
**Transpersonal Psychotherapist**
c/o CCPE
Beauchamp Lodge
2 Warwick Crescent
London
W2 6NE
☎ 020 7266 3006
CCPE

**CUTTERIDGE**, Simon
**Systemic Psychotherapist**
Covent Garden Counselling
23 Bedfordbury
London
WC2N 4BL
☎ 020 7240 1911
KCC

**D'COSTA**, Fjona
**Transpersonal Psychotherapist**
66 Star Street
London
W2 1QG
☎ 020 7262 9597
fjona@btinternet.com
CCPE

**DACHY**, Vincent
**Lacanian Analyst**
LONDON
W1
☎ 020 7580 9708
CFAR

**DALE**, Tim
**Transpersonal Psychotherapist**
c/o CCPE
Beauchamp Lodge
2 Warwick Crescent
London
W2 6NE
☎ 01622 725 302
timothy_dale@hotmail.com
CCPE

**DAVIES**, Hilary
**Family & Systemic Psychotherapist**
♿ Dept of Psychological Medicine
Great Ormond Street Hospital
Great Ormond Street
London
WC1N 3JH
☎ 020 7829 8679
IFT

**DEAHL**, Kieron
**Neurolinguistic Psychotherapist**
Ability
29 Crawford Street
London
W1H 1PL
☎ 02074 199 657
kierondeahl@yahoo.com
NLPtCA

**DEAVILLE**, Debra
**Transpersonal Psychotherapist**
c/o CCPE
Beauchamp Lodge
2 Warwick Crescent London
W2 6NE
☎ 07802 210 981
☎ 0207 266 3006
CCPE

**DENNEHY**, Carmel
**Transpersonal Psychotherapist**
CCPE
2 Warwick Crescent
London
W2 6NE
☎ 020 7372 9922
CCPE

**DENNISON**, Nishah
**Humanistic Psychotherapist, Integrative Psychotherapist**
7 Bryanston Mews East
London
W1H 2DB
☎ 020 7224 8031
Free@nishah.fsnet.co.uk
AHPP

**DIAMOND**, Vera
**Autogenic Psychotherapist**
10 Sherwood Court
Seymour Place
London
W1H 5TH
☎ 020 7723 2184
vera.diamond@lineone.net
BAS

**DILLON WESTON**, Marisa
**Group Analyst**
♿ 91 Bedford Court Mansions
Bedford Avenue
WC1 3AE
☎ 020 8994 6749
eng.lang@btinternet.com
IGA

**DOVE**, Rabbi Jonathan
**Integrative Psychotherapist**
Suite 3
41 Wimpole Street
London
W1M 7AF
☎ 07966 134 838
jdconsulting@cwcom.net
MET, SPCRC

**DOWN**, Gwynneth
**Family & Systemic Psychotherapist**
♿ Dept. of Psychological Medicine
Great Ormond Street Hospital for Sick Children
Great Ormond Street
WC1N 0HH
☎ 020 7405 9200 x0273
IFT

**DRANEY**, Sue
**Psychoanalytic Psychotherapist**
Flat 1
Clare Court
Judd Street
London
WC1H 9QW
☎ 020 7833 4156
suzie@draney.fsnet.co.uk
GUILD

**DRYDEN**, Windy
**Cognitive Behavioural Psychotherapist, Rational Emotive Behaviour Therapist**
136 Montague Mansions
London
W1U 6LQ
☎ 020 7486 3034
windy@thedrydens.clara.net
BABCP, AREBT

**EHLERS**, Hella
**Psychoanalytic Psychotherapist**
Flat 12
Byron Court
26 Mecklenburgh Square
London
WC1N 2AF
☎ 020 7278 2212
ARBS

**EVANS**, Sandra
**Group Analyst**
♿ Bloombury Therapy Centre
80A Southampton Row
London
WC1
☎ 02078 317 924
IGA

**FARLEY**, Nancy M.
**Cognitive Behavioural Psychotherapist**
London Medical Centre
144 Harley Street
London
W1N 4AH
☎ 020 7935 0023
BABCP

**FERGUSON**, Joyce
**Transpersonal Psychotherapist**
407 Grenville House
Dolphin Square
London
SW1V 3LP
☎ 020 7 798 8073
j.ferguson4@ntlworld.com
CCPE

**FINNIGAN**, Cathy
**Family & Systemic Psychotherapist**
31 Pembroke House
Hallfield Estate
London
W2 6HG
☎ 020 7723 1408
AFT

**FITZGERALD-KLEIN**, Marianne
**Transpersonal Psychotherapist**
CCPE
2 Warwick Crescent
London
W2 6NE
☎ 01223 438 181
mariannefk@hotmail.com
CCPE

**FLOWER**, Charles
**Transpersonal Psychotherapist**
c/o CCPE
2 Warwick Crescent
London
W2 6NE
☎ 020 7266 3006
CCPE

**FORSSANDER**, Jennifer
**Analytical Psychologist-Jungian Analyst, Transpersonal Psychotherapist**
27 Bathurst Mews
London
W2 2SB
☎ 020 7402 0290
☎ 01935 825 869
jenniforssander@aol.com
AJA, CCPE

**FRANCIS**, Gabriela
**Systemic Psychotherapist**
♿ 10 Harley Street
London
W1G 9PF
☎ 020 7467 8472 or 07946 516 343
☎ 020 7720 7301
KCC

**FREDMAN**, Glenda
**Systemic Psychotherapist**
♿ Department Child and Adolescent Psychological Services
North House Middlesex Hospital
Cleveland Street
W1N 8AA
☎ 020 7380 9086
glenda.fredman@ntlworld.com
KCC

**FREEMAN**, Linda
**Analytical Psychologist-Jungian Analyst**
23 Chilworth Mews
London
W2 3RG
☎ 020 7402 2204
l.freeman@britishlibrary.net
IGAP

**FREEMAN**, Martin
**Psychoanalytic Psychotherapist**
2 Clarendon Place
London
W2 2NP
☎ 020 7262 3693
m.freeman@mf.homechoice.co.uk
FIP

**FRIZE**, Graham
**Cognitive Behavioural Psychotherapist**
Clinical Health Psychology Dept.
Clarence Wing
St Mary's Hospital
Praed Street
London
W2 1NY
☎ 020 7886 1658
graham.frize@st-marys.nhs.uk
BABCP

**GANN**, Sandra Y
**Sexual and Relationship Psychotherapist**
♿ Department of Social Work
St. Bartholomew's Hospital
West Smithfield
London
EC1A 7BE
☎ 020 7601 8718
sandra.gann@corpoflondon.gov.uk
BASRT

**GERRA**, Stephanie
**Psychosynthesis Psychotherapist**
37 Knolly's House
Tavistock Place
London
WC1H 9SA
☎ 02073 835 083
☎ 02078 376 737
stephanie.gerra@virgin.net
IPS

**GINKELL**, Andreas
**Psychoanalytic Psychotherapist**
Flat 3
Dean House
116 Great Titchfield Street
London
W1W 6SP
a-ginkel@dircon.co.uk
ARBS

**GLENN**, Liza
**Group Analyst**
The Group-Analytic Practice
88 Montagu Mansions
London
W1U 6LF
☎ 020 7935 3103
members@gapractice.org.uk
IGA

**GOLDMAN**, John
**Sexual and Relationship Psychotherapist**
22 De Walden Street
London
W1G 8RN
☎ 020 7486 5148
therapist@lineone.net
BASRT

**GREEN**, Brian
**Psychoanalytic Psychotherapist**
91 Bedford Court Mansions
Bedford Avenue
London
WC1B 3AE
☎ 020 7225 3514
FPC

**GREENBERG**, Maurice
**Group Analyst**
The Group Analytic Practice
88 Montagu Mansions
W1U 6LF
☎ 020 7935 3103
mauricegreenberg@gapractice.org.uk
IGA

**GREENE**, Alice
**Autogenic Psychotherapist**
86 Harley Street
London
W1G 7HP
☎ 020 7580 4188
BAS

**GREW**, Lesley
**Hypno-Psychotherapist**
11 Clare Court
Judd Street
London
WC1H 9QW
☎ 02078 379 772
NRHP

**GRUBER**, Angela
**Transpersonal Psychotherapist**
CCPE
Beauchamp Lodge
2 Warwick Crescent
London
W2 6NE
☎ 020 7266 3006
☎ 01462 635027
CCPE

**HAGENBACH**, Keith
**Transpersonal Psychotherapist**
CCPE
2 Warwick Crescent
London
W2 6NE
☎ 01342 823461
kk.hagenbach@virgin.net
CCPE

**HAMILTON**, Nigel
**Transpersonal Psychotherapist**
Beauchamp Lodge
2 Warwick Crescent
London
W2 6NE
☎ 020 7 266 3006
CCPE

**HANMAN**, Elke
**Transpersonal Psychotherapist**
c/o CCPE
Beauchamp Lodge
2 Warwick Crescent
London
W2 6NE
☎ 020 7266 3006
CCPE

**HANNA**, Gilli
**Transpersonal Psychotherapist**
London W2
London EC3
☎ 07771 766 055
gilli@lifework.org.uk
CCPE

**HARREL**, Julia
**Transpersonal Psychotherapist**
CCPE
Beauchamp Lodge
2 Warwick Crescent
London
W2 6NE
☎ 020 7266 3006
☎ 07753 659 952
juliaharrel@yahoo.co.uk
CCPE

**HARRIS**, Jonathan
**Transpersonal Psychotherapist**
CCPE
2 Warwick Crescent
London
W2 6NE
☎ 07000 Counsel
☎ 01908 282 427
CCPE

**HARVEY**, Angelia
**Transpersonal Psychotherapist**
c/o CCPE
Beauchamp Lodge
2 Warwick Crescent
London
W2 6NE
☎ 020 7266 3006
CCPE

**HASSAIN**, Alan
**Transpersonal Psychotherapist**
c/o CCPE
Beauchamp Lodge
2 Warwick Crescent
London
W2 6NE
☎ 07941 281025
alanhassain@hotmail.com
CCPE

**HAUPTS**, Brigitta
**Cognitive Analytic Therapist**
Kensington Gardens Square
Bayswater
London
W2
☎ 020 7221 2501
brigitte.haupts@virgin.net
ACAT

**HAY-BURNS**, Jean
**Transpersonal Psychotherapist**
Beauchamp Lodge
2 Warwick Crescent
London
W2 6NE
☎ 07909 620905
☎ 020 76252014
nurjehan@amserve.net
CCPE

**HAYES**, Susan
**Transpersonal Psychotherapist**
c/o CCPE
2 Warwick Crescent
London
W2 6NE
☎ 020 7 266 3006
CCPE

**HEARN**, Julie
**Transpersonal Psychotherapist**
c/o CCPE
Beauchamp Lodge
2 Warwick Crescent
London
W2 6NE
☎ 020 7266 3006
juliehearn@tiscali.co.uk
CCPE

**HETHERTON**, Jacquie
**Cognitive Behavioural Psychotherapist**
B.K.C.W.
Paterson Centre for Mental Health
20 South Wharf Road
London
W2 1PD
☎ 01784 444 049
☎ 07976 621 020
jacquiehetherton@hotmail.com
BABCP

**HILES**, David
**Transpersonal Psychotherapist**
c/o CCPE
W2
☎ 0116 212 8194
drhiles@ntlworld.com
CCPE

**HODGES**, Jill
**Child Psychotherapist**
Dept. of Psychological Medicine
Great Ormond Street Hospital
Great Ormond Street
London
WC1N 3JH
☎ 020 7829 8888 X 557
☎ 020 8809 2834
ACP

**HODGSON**, Phillip A. J.
**Transpersonal Psychotherapist**
c/o CPPE
Beauchamp Lodge
2 Warwick Crescent
London
W2 6NE
☎ 01684 572 938
☎ 07779 026 113
philip@transpersonalemergence.com
CCPE

**HORMASJI**, Faridoon
**Hypno-Psychotherapist**
♿ 10 Harley Street
London
W1G 9PF
☎ 08701 676 667
☎ 02074 678 300
faridoonh@aol.com
NRHP

**IBISON**, Janet M.
**Cognitive Behavioural Psychotherapist**
♿ 10 Harley Street
London
W1G 9PF
☎ 020 7467 8360
☎ 07779 646 533
BABCP

**IKKOS**, George
**Group Analyst**
♿ The Group Analytic Practice
88 Montagu Mansions
London
W1U 6LF
☎ 020 7935 3103
gikkos@hotmail.com
IGA

**INGRAM**, Sonia
**Group Analyst, Sexual and Relationship Psychotherapist**
5 Albert Mansions
Luxborough Street
London
W1M 3LN
IGA

**KAFTON**, Maggie
**Transpersonal Psychotherapist**
Beauchamp Lodge
2 Warwick Crescent
London
W2 6NE
☎ 020 7266 3006
140 Harley Street
London
W1G 7LB
CCPE

**KENDAL**, Susan J.
**Cognitive Behavioural Psychotherapist**
♿ Counselling Psychologist
St Philips Medical Centre
London School of Economics
Houghton Street, London
WC2A 2AE
skendal@kendal.homechoice.co.uk
BABCP

**KERR**, Anna
**Psychoanalytic Psychotherapist**
8 Hanson Street
London
W1W 6TY
☎ 020 7580 2628
annakerr8@aol.com
GUILD

**KNOWLES**, Jane
**Group Analyst**
The Group Analytic Practice
88 Montagu Mansions
W1U 6LF
☎ 020 7935 3103
IGA

**KORN**, Susan
**Transpersonal Psychotherapist**
CCPE
Beauchamp Lodge
2 Warwick Crescent
London
W2 6NE
☎ 07985 129642
☎ 01923 263355
CCPE

**L'ESTRANGE**, Jeanette
**Transpersonal Psychotherapist**
C.C.P.E.
Beauchamp Lodge
2 Warwick Crescent
London
W2 6NE
CCPE

**LAUT**, Susan
**Transpersonal Psychotherapist**
c/o CCPE
Beauchamp Lodge
2 Warwick Crescent
London
W2 6NE
CCPE

**LEADER**, Darian
**Lacanian Analyst, Psychoanalytic Psychotherapist**
Flat 2
5 Bulstrode Street
London
W1U 2JB
☎ 020 7487 5415
CFAR

**LEBON**, Marsha
**Psychoanalyst**
55 Great Titchfield Street
London
W1W 7PT
☎ 020 7580 9518
marsha.lebon@virgin.net
SITE

**LILLIE**, Francis
**Cognitive Behavioural Psychotherapist**
27a Harley Place
London
W1G 8LZ
☎ 020 7323 2370
francis@francislillie.com
BABCP

**LIPSITH**, Josie
**Sexual and Relationship Psychotherapist**
♿ Jane Wadsworth Sexual Function Clinic
St Mary's Hospital
Praed Street
Paddington, London
W2 1NY
☎ 01202 709 155
☎ 020 7722 9397
josie.lipsith@virgin.net
BASRT

**LIVINGSTON**, Christine
**Transpersonal Psychotherapist**
CCPE
Beauchamp Lodge
2 Warwick Crescent
London
W2 6NE
☎ 020 8946 3110
☎ 07767 244 977
christine.livingston@livingstonconsulting.co.uk
CCPE

**LOOSE**, Judith Green
**Child Psychotherapist**
6 Montagu Square
London
W1H 1RA
☎ 020 7224 6028
☎ 020 7935 0802 t/f
ACP

**LOWDEN**, Barbara
**Transpersonal Psychotherapist**
CCPE
Beauchamp Lodge
2 Warwick Crescent
London
W2 6NE
☎ 020 8854 4074
☎ 020 7266 3006
CCPE

**LUCIANI**, Dorothy
**Child Psychotherapist**
17 Wimpole Street
London
W1M 7AD
☎ 020 7436 1144
ACP

**LYNSEY**, Paul
**Cognitive Analytic Therapist**
40 Tonbridge House
Tonbridge Street
London
WC1H 9PB
☎ 07930 481 041
☎ 020 7916 3203
plynsey@aol.com
ACAT

**MAGAGNA**, Jeanne
**Child Psychotherapist**
Dept. of Psychological Medicine
Great Ormond Street Hospital
Great Ormond Street
London
WC1N 3JH
☎ 020 7405 9200 ext. 5578
mgagi@gosh.nhs.uk
ACP

**MAGUIRE**, Anne
**Analytical Psychologist-Jungian Analyst**
23 Harley Street
London
W1N 1DA
☎ 020 7436 5262
☎ 01254 59910
IGAP

**MARATOS**, Jason
**Group Analyst**
The Group Analytic Practice
88 Montagu Mansions
W1U 6LF
☎ 020 7935 3103
jm@gapractice.org.uk
IGA

**MARGRIE**, Paul
**Transpersonal Psychotherapist**
c/o CCPE
Beauchamp Lodge
2 Warwick Crescent
London
W2 6NE
☎ 07766 024 263
☎ 020 8977 1560
paulmargrie@hotmail.com
CCPE

**MARKOVIC**, Desa
**Family & Systemic Psychotherapist**
Covent Garden Counselling
23 Bedfordbury
London
WC2N 4BN
☎ 020 7240 1911
desamarkovic@btinternet.com
IFT

**MARTIN**, Sheila
**Transpersonal Psychotherapist**
c/o CCPE
Beauchamp Lodge
2 Warwick Crescent
London
W2 6NE
☎ 020 7266 3006
CCPE

**MAYER-JOHNSON**, Jessica
**Group Analyst**
91 Bedford Court Mansions
Bedford Avenue
London
WC1B 3AE
☎ 020 7359 4925
ragjohnson@aol.com
IGA

**MCDERMOTT**, Paul
**Transpersonal Psychotherapist**
140 Harley Street
London
W1N 1AH
☎ 07957 392340
☎ 020 7482 4296
CCPE

**MCEWAN**, Geraldine
**Neurolinguistic Psychotherapist**
1a Upper Wimpole Street
London
W1G 6LD
☎ 02074 862 122
☎ 07967 361 375
geraldinemcewan@btconnect.com
NLPtCA

**MEDICE**, Pauline
**Transpersonal Psychotherapist**
c/o CCPE
Beauchamp Lodge
2 Warwick Crescent
London
W2 6NE
☎ 07958 538 412
pmedice@cksweb.net
CCPE

**MENEZES**, Ray
**Transpersonal Psychotherapist**
c/o CCPE
Beauchamp Lodge
2 Warwick Crescent
London
W2 6NE
☎ 020 7 266 3006
CCPE

**MEREDITH**, Judith
**Transpersonal Psychotherapist**
CCPE
Beauchamp Lodge
2 Warwick Crescent
London
W2 6NE
☎ 01424 777 985
☎ 01252 628 428
CCPE

**MITCHELL**, Richard
**Individual and Group Humanistic Psychotherapist**
140 Harley Street
London
W1N 1AH
☎ 01727 861 468
☎ 020 7224 3387
richard-mitchell@ntlworld.com
AHPP

**MITTWOCH**, Adele
**Group Analyst, Psychoanalytic Psychotherapist**
The Group Analytic Practice
88 Montagu Mansions
London
W1U 6LF
☎ 020 7935 3103
am@gapractice.org.uk
IGA

**MOJSA**, Jan
**Transpersonal Psychotherapist**
c/o CTP
101 Crawford St.
London
W1
☎ 01373 824 314
☎ 07940 937 267
CTP

**MORRIS**, Clare
**Personal Construct Psychotherapist**
CANDID
Dementia Research Group
8-11 Queen Square
London
WC1N 3BG
☎ 020 7829 8772
c.morris@candid.ion.ucl.ac.uk
PCP

**MUIR**, Kate
**Psychosynthesis Psychotherapist**
44 Carroll House
Craven Terrace
London
W2 3PR
☎ 020 7706 4357
PET

**MURDIN**, Lesley
**Psychoanalytic Psychotherapist**
Flat 11
115 Westbourne Terrace
W2
☎ 020 7361 4853
☎ 01223 312 848
murdin@compuserve.com
FPC, SITE

**MURPHY**, Alan
**Transpersonal Psychotherapist**
42 Georgiana Street
London
NW1 0EB
☎ 020 7 485 0358
CCPE

**MYERS**, Carole
**Existential Psychotherapist**
10 Harley Street
London
W1G 9PF
☎ 020 7467 8437
carole@mr-psychology.co.uk
SEA

**NIPPODA**, Yuko
**Humanistic and Integrative Psychotherapist, Psychoanalytic Psychotherapist**
Beauchamp Lodge
2 Warwick Crescent
London
W2 6NE
☎ 07958 213 456
yuko.nippoda@virgin.net
AHPP, NAFSI

**NITSUN**, Morris
**Group Analyst**
The Group Analytic Practice
88 Montagu Mansions
W1U 6LF
☎ 020 7935 3103
member@gapractice.org.uk
IGA

**NUTTALL**, Caryn
**Integrative Psychotherapist**
12a/13 Cumberland Mansions
George Street
London
W1H 5TE
☎ 020 7724 0660
caryn@carynnuttall.co.uk
SPCRC

**O RUAIRC**, Micheál
**Transpersonal Psychotherapist**
c/o CCPE
Beauchamp Lodge
2 Warwick Crescent
London
W2 6NE
☎ 020 8208 0920
☎ 0771 917 9419
m.or@btinternet.com
CCPE

**O'DWYER**, Annegret
**Integrative Psychotherapist**
Alpha Clinics
21a Devonshire Place
London
W1
☎ 01372 465039
www.annegretodwyer.co.uk
MET

**OLDMAN**, David
**Couple Psychoanalytic Psychotherapist**
The Counselling Partnership
5 Albert Mansions
Luxborough Street
London
W1U 5BQ
☎ 020 7487 3766
☎ 01737 844 079
david@oldmanonline.me.uk
SCPP

**OPIK**, Urve
**Transpersonal Psychotherapist**
c/o CCPE
Beauchamp Lodge
2 Warwick Crescent
London
W2 6NE
☎ 0775 409 4717
urveopik@hotmail.com
CCPE

**PACEY**, Susan
**Sexual and Relationship Psychotherapist**
Medical Suite
Bentinck Mansions
Bentinck Street
London
W1U 2ER
☎ 020 7916 7055
susanpacey@yahoo.com
BASRT

**PAGE-HANSON**, Paul
**Existential Psychotherapist**
42 Blomfield Villas
London
W2 6NQ
☎ 02072 661 203
peepers@page-hanson.freeserve.co.uk
UPCA

**PERRING**, Dr Michael
**Integrative Psychotherapist, Sexual and Relationship Psychotherapist**
♿ 19 Milford House
7 Queen Anne Street
London
W1G 9HN
☎ 020 7436 7713
PracticeManager@OptimalHealth.org.uk
BASRT, MET

**PIMENTEL**, Allan
**Transpersonal Psychotherapist**
c/o CCPE
2 Warwick Crescent
London
W2 6NE
☎ 020 7 266 3006
CCPE

**PINES**, Malcolm
**Group Analyst**
♿ 5 Carisbrooke Court
65 Weymouth Street
London
W1G 8NZ
☎ 020 7935 1923
malpines@aol.com
IGA

**PINTO**, Luca
**Integrative Psychotherapist**
Mayfair Counselling & Psychotherapy
63 Wigmore Street
London
W1U 1BQ
☎ 01712 074 663
luca@dircon.co.uk
MET

**PRESS**, Joanne
**Transpersonal Psychotherapist**
CCPE
W2
☎ 0786 799 6176
☎ 020 8866 5773
CCPE

**QUINN**, Asher
**Transpersonal Psychotherapist**
Little Venice
London
W2
☎ 077331 13428
CCPE

**RAESIDE**, Dominic
**Family & Systemic Psychotherapist**
♿ The Family Law Consortium
2 Henrietta Street
Covent Garden
London
WC2 8PS
☎ 020 7420 5000
dr@tflc.co.uk
AFT

**RAMAGE**, Margaret
**Sexual and Relationship Psychotherapist**
4 Bentinck Mansions
Bentinck Street
London
W1N 2ER
☎ 020 7935 0616
mpramage@patnertherapy.com
BASRT

**READ**, Elizabeth J.
**Family & Systemic Psychotherapist**
♿ Dept of Psychological Medicine
Great Ormond Street Hospital
NHS Trust
Great Ormond Street
WC1N 3JH
☎ 02078 298 657
IFT

**REILLY**, Nicole S.
**Transpersonal Psychotherapist**
CCPE
Beauchamp Lodge
2 Warwick Crescent
London
W2 6NE
☎ 01903 203533
CCPE

**REINISCH**, Lili
**Integrative Psychotherapist**
20 Prince Edwards Mansion
Moscow Road
London
W2 4WA
☎ 020 7792 6973
☎ 020 7243 0993
SPCRC

**REYNOLDS**, Francois
**Neurolinguistic Psychotherapist**
The Alexander Street Practice
33a Alexander Street
London
W2 5NU
☎ 02072 214 940
NLPtCA

**RICHARDSON**, Ann
**Transpersonal Psychotherapist**
CCPE
Beauchamp Lodge
2 Warwick Crescent
London
W2 6NE
☎ 020 8 994 5964
ann@onlychild.icom43.net
CCPE

**RIGNELL**, John
**Psychoanalytic Psychotherapist**
Flat 9
Napier House
51, Riding House Street
London
W1
☎ 01273 204314
john.rignell@amserve.net
FPC

**ROBERTS**, Jeff
**Group Analyst**
The Group Analytic Practice
88 Montagu Mansions
London
W1U 6LF
☎ 020 7935 3103
members@gapractice.org.uk
IGA

**ROBERTSON**, Donald
**Hypno-Psychotherapist**
Transpersonal Excellence
10 Harley Street
London
W1G 9PF
☎ 0800 195 9809
admin@ukhypnosis.com
NRHP

**ROBSON**, Annie
**Psychoanalytic Psychotherapist**
The Counselling Partnership
5 Albert Mansions
Luxborough Street
London
W1U 5BQ
☎ 020 7487 3766
☎ 020 8853 8770
CCOPPP

**ROGERS**, Cynthia
**Group Analyst**
The Group Analytic Practice
88 Montagu Mansions
London
W1U 6LF
☎ 020 7935 3103
cynthia@groupanalyst.com
IGA

**SEGAL**, Barbara
**Child Psychotherapist**
Department of C&A Psychological Services
Middlesex Hospital
North House, Cleveland Street
London
W1N 8AA
☎ 020 7380 9089
ACP

**SIGNORA**, Susanna Jamila
**Transpersonal Psychotherapist**
c/o CCPE
Beauchamp Lodge
2 Warwick Crescent
London
W2 6NE
☎ 01483 720 587
ssignora@aol.com
CCPE

**SIMON**, Gail
**Systemic Psychotherapist**
♿ The Pink Practice
16-19 Southampton Place
Holborn
London
WC1 2AJ
☎ 07020 955 512
☎ 01535 661 531
KCC

**SIMPSON**, David
**Existential Psychotherapist**
♿ 10 Harley Street
London
W1G 9PF
☎ 07736 444 165
davidsimpsonuk@aol.com
UPCA

**SINASON**, Valerie
**Child Psychotherapist**
10 Harley Street
London
W1G 9PF
☎ 020 7794 1655
☎ 020 7467 8436
VSinason@aol.com
ACP

**SLIW**, Mrs Regina
**Sexual and Relationship Psychotherapist**
4 Wimpole Street
London
W1G 9SS
☎ 020 8958 9013
BASRT

**SOMERFIELD**, Lynn
**Transpersonal Psychotherapist**
CCPE
Beauchamp Lodge
2 Warwick Crescent
London
W2 6NE
☎ 020 8740 0984
☎ 07762 738 238
CCPE

**SOUTHWELL**, Clover
**Biodynamic Psychotherapist**
3 Bulstrode Street
London
W1M 5FS
☎ 02079 355 107
clovers@onetel.net.uk
LSBP

**SPEYER**, Josefine
**Integrative Psychotherapist**
Neal's Yard Therapy Rooms
2 Neal's Yard
Covent Garden
London
WC2D 9DP
☎ 020 8208 0670
josefine@waitrose.com
AHPP, CCBP

**SPITZ**, Shirley
**Integrative Psychotherapist**
Flat 1
15 Hyde Park Gardens
London
W2 2LU
☎ 020 7262 3807
SPTI

**STANNARD**, Marie
**Transpersonal Psychotherapist**
c/o CCPE
Beauchamp Lodge
2 Warwick Crescent
London
W2 6NE
☎ 020 7266 3006
☎ 07767 698966
CCPE

**STEDMAN**, Maire
**Systemic Psychotherapist**
University of London
Faculty of Continuing Education
26 Russell Square
London
WC1
☎ 020 8469 0975
☎ 020 7631 5505
mairestedman@eircom.net
IFT

**STONE**, Marie Clare
**Transpersonal Psychotherapist**
c/o CCPE
Beauchamp Lodge
2 Warwick Crescent
London
W2 6NE
☎ 020 7266 3006
☎ 07860 483 598
stonemc@aol.com
CCPE

**SWATTON**, Richard
**Transpersonal Psychotherapist**
c/o CCPE
Beauchamp Lodge
2 Warwick Crescent
London
W2 6NE
☎ 020 7627 8509
CCPE

**TAYLOR**, Alison
**Transpersonal Psychotherapist**
140 Harley Street
London
W1
☎ 07778 023192
alisontaylor@hotmail.com
c/o CCPE
Beauchamp Lodge
2 Warwick Crescent
London
W2 6NE
CCPE

**TAYLOR**, Sajada Katalin
**Transpersonal Psychotherapist**
c/o CCPE
Beauchamp Lodge
2 Warwick Crescent
London
W2 6NE
☎ 020 7 266 3006
CCPE

**TOTSUKA**, Yoko
**Family & Systemic Psychotherapist**
332 Russell Court
Woburn Place
London
WC1H 0NG
☎ 020 7813 3239
y.totsuko@virgin.net
AFT

**TROWBRIDGE**, Louise
**Transpersonal Psychotherapist**
c/o CCPE
Beauchamp Lodge
2 Warwick Crescent
London
W2 6NE
☎ 020 7266 3006
CCPE

**TUGENDHAT**, Julia
**Systemic Psychotherapist**
♿ Basement Flat
35 Westbourne Park Road
London
W2 5QD
☎ 020 7221 9036
KCC

**VIBERT**, Eva
**Integrative Psychosynthesis Psychotherapist, Transpersonal Psychotherapist**
Flat 9, Devonshire Court
26a Devonshire Street
London
W1G 6PJ
☎ 020 7486 8747
evavibert@aol.com
CTP, RE.V

**VICK**, Philippa
**Transpersonal Psychotherapist**
44 Gloucester Place Mews
London
W1H 3PL
☎ 020 7935 2294
☎ 01225 445 532
CTP

**WALLER, MA**, Charlotte
**Transpersonal Psychotherapist**
c/o CCPE
Beauchamp Lodge
2 Warwick Crescent
London
W2 6NE
☎ 020 8877 1464
CCPE

**WALSH**, Eileen
**Neurolinguistic Psychotherapist**
1 Harley Street
London
W1
☎ 020 7385 8914
☎ 07776 237852
E.Walsh@btinternet.com,
www.ewalsh.co.uk
NLPtCA

**WARD**, Sharron
**Transpersonal Psychotherapist**
c/o CCPE
2 Warwick Crescent
London
W2 6NE
☎ 020 7286 8184
www.Ah-ha.org.uk
CCPE

**WELLINGS**, Nigel
**Psychoanalytic Psychotherapist**
44 Gloucester Place Mews
London
W1M 3PL
☎ 01225 445 532
☎ 020 7935 2294
AGIP, AIP

**WEST**, Alison
**Transpersonal Psychotherapist**
c/o CTP
101 Crawford Street
London
W1H 2HP
☎ 020 8878 7574
☎ 07798 938 910
CTP

**WHITELEY**, Christopher M.
**Cognitive Behavioural Psychotherapist**
14 Devonshire Place
London
W1G 6HX
☎ 020 7503 2365
BABCP

**WIGRAM**, Penny
**Psychoanalytic Psychotherapist**
2 Clarendon Place
London
W2 2NP
☎ 020 7723 8925
pa.wigram@virgin.net
FIP, FPC

**WILLIAMS**, Chris
**Gestalt Psychotherapist**
63 Wigmore Street
London
W1U 1BD
☎ 020 7924 0344
☎ 020 7935 8608
bradwill@clara.co.uk
GPTI

**WILSON**, Peter
**Group Analyst**
The Group Analytic Practice
88 Montagu Mansions
London
W1U 6LF
☎ 020 7935 3103
IGA

**WOOTTON**, Julie
**Integrative Psychotherapist**
1st Floor
6 Porter Street
Baker Street
London
W1
☎ 07710 086 019
jhwootton@btinternet.com
MC

**WRIGHT**, Laurie Jo
**Attachment-based Psychoanalytic Psychotherapist**
16 Bingham Place
London
W1U 5AZ
☎ 020 7486 2608
ljwright@btinternet.com
CAPP

**YOUNG**, Sabine
**Transpersonal Psychotherapist**
CCPE
Beauchamp Lodge
2 Warwick Crescent
London
W2 6NE
☎ 020 8 876 2439
Sabineyoung@blueyonder.com
CCPE

**VON BRITZKE**, Michaela
**Integrative Psychotherapist**
28F Leinster Square
London
W2 4NQ
☎ 020 7221 2107
101503.3273@compuserve.com
SPCRC

## LONDON EAST

**ADAMS**, Martin
**Existential Psychotherapist**
84 Middleton Road
London
E8 4LN
☎ 020 7254 2707
adamsmc@regents.ac.uk
SPCRC

**AGGETT**, Percy
**Systemic Psychotherapist**
69 Glenarm Road
London
E5 0LY
☎ 020 8533 0594
☎ 020 7445 7800
Percy.aggett@lineone.net
Child & Family Consultation Service
York House
411 Barking Road
London
E13 8AL
IFT

**AKSOY ROBINS**, A Asu
**Group Analytic Psychotherapist**
19 Independent Place
London
E8 2HE
☎ 020 7923 2928
a.aksoy@gold.ac.uk
UPCA

**ARORA**, Alka
**Systemic Psychotherapist**
661 Barking Road
Plaistow
London
E13 9BX
☎ 020 8472 0528
alkarora@hotmail.com
KCC

**ATKINSON**, Francis
**Integrative Psychotherapist**
123 Matlock Road
Leyton
London
E10 6DJ
☎ 020 8558 6926
☎ 07960 645654
fnatkinson@aol.com
277-279 Bethnal Green Raod
London
E2 6AH
MET

**BAJER**, Maryse
**Existential Psychotherapist**
♿ 77 Malford Grove
South Woodford
London
E18 2DH
☎ 02089 895 868
marysebajer@hotmail.com
UPCA

**BANNISTER**, Gill
**Psychoanalytic Psychotherapist**
78 Lichfield Road
Bow
London
E3 5AL
☎ 020 8981 2244
FPC

**BARBER**, Keith
**Integrative Psychosynthesis Psychotherapist**
The Gables
17 Holland Road
East Ham
London
E6 2EW
☎ 020 8586 7513
keith@gaybles.demon.co.uk
RE.V

**BARTLETT**, Sheila
**Integrative Psychosynthesis Psychotherapist**
17c Towpath Walk
Homerton
Hackney
London
E9 5HX
☎ 020 8985 8820
RE.V

**BASKERVILLE**, Victoria
**Transactional Analysis Psychotherapist**
Maynard Rd
Walthamstow
London
E17 9JF
☎ 02085 203 244
baskervillevictoria@hotmail.com
ITA

**BENDER**, Helen
**Child Psychotherapist**
Child & Family Consultation Service
Royal London Hospital
Whitechapel
London
E1 1BB
☎ 020 7377 7390
☎ 020 8445 4798
ACP

**BICKERTON**, Tricia
**Psychoanalytic Psychotherapist**
86 Eleanor Road
Hackney
London
E8 1DN
☎ 020 7 249 2770
GUILD

**BLAIR**, George
**Integrative Psychotherapist**
Sundance
British Waterways
420 Manchester Road
London
E14 9SD
☎ 020 7963 7614
☎ 07876 744 753
george.blair@tns-global.com
CCBP

**BOND**, Lesley
**Transpersonal Psychotherapist**
59 Godwin Road
Forest Gate
London
E7 0LF
☎ 020 8 555 8869
lesleybond23@hotmail.com
CCPE

**BOND**, Sharon
**Systemic Psychotherapist**
Chiron Consultation & Therapy Services
153-159 Bow Road
London
E3 2SE
☎ 020 8257 7915
chi_ron1997@yahoo.co.uk
KCC

**BRION**, Marion
**Neurolinguistic Psychotherapist**
4 Bedford Road
South Woodford
London
E18 2AQ
☎ 02085 308 480
NLPtCA

**BUCKLEY**, Nicky
**Psychoanalytic Psychotherapist**
c/o directlink
37 Maynard Road
London
E17 9JE
☎ 020 8521 4539
ARBS

**BURGESS**, Shanti
**Hypno-Psychotherapist**
64 Queenswood Gardens
Wanstead
London
E11 3SF
☎ 02085 304 413
NSHAP

**BURLINGTON**, Maggie
**Psychosynthesis Psychotherapist**
♿ 56 Gordon Road
Wanstead
London
E11 2RB
☎ 020 8518 8699
maggieburl@aol.com
PET

**BYERS**, Angela
**Group Analytic Psychotherapist**
59 Brooke Road
London
E17 9HH
☎ 02086 826 236
angieb@crystal.demon.co.uk
UPCA

**CAIN**, Dennis
**Transpersonal Psychotherapist**
Psychotherapy & Counselling Unit
Eastwood Medical Centre
Eastwood Road
South Woodford
E18 1BN
☎ 020 8 491 7077
CCPE

**CHAPMAN**, Sandy
**Analytical Psychologist-Jungian Analyst**
♿ 148 Millfields Road
London
E5 0AD
☎ 020 8986 3792
sandychapman@blueyonder.co.uk
CAP, FIP *

**CHESNER**, Anna
**Psychodrama Psychotherapist**
Institute of Action Methods
64 Manchester Road
Isle of Dogs
London
E14 3BE
☎ 020 7515 6342
chesnera@aol.com
BPA

**CLARKE**, Simon
**Hypno-Psychotherapist**
16 Skipworth Road
Hackney
London
E9 7JH
☎ 02085 250 418
☎ 02085 037 794
Simon.Clarke2@btinternet.com
The Health Works
111a Hoe Street
Walthamstow
London
E17 4RX
NRHP

**COOPER**, Rebecca
**Humanistic Psychotherapist**
5 Sutton Place
London
E9 6EH
☎ 020 8880 6606
☎ 020 8985 0803
rebecca.cooper@excite.com
The Crypt
St John on Bethnal Green
London
E2 9PA
AHPP

**COPSEY**, Nigel
**Humanistic Psychotherapist**
4 Hawksmoore Close
Beckton
London
E6 5SL
N.Copsey@btopenworld.com
AHPP

**CORBETT**, Martyn
**Group Analyst**
♿ 21 Malvern Road
London
E8 3LP
☎ 020 7923 4549
corkel@vossnet.co.uk
IGA

**CRAWFORD**, Joan
**Integrative Psychosynthesis Psychotherapist**
56 Gordon Road
London
E11 2RB
☎ 020 8518 8699
Jocrawf@aol.com
RE.V

**CREEDY**, Katherine
**Family & Systemic Psychotherapist**
♿ 3 Brownsea Court
160 Clarence Road
London
E5 8EF
☎ 020 8985 6948
katecreedy@email.com
AFT

**DANIEL**, Catherine
**Educational Therapist**
11b Grosvenor Road
London
E11 2EW
☎ 020 8530 4866
CFET

**DELVE**, Stuart
**Family & Systemic Psychotherapist**
33 Sherrard Road
London
E7 8DN
☎ 020 8471 7498
AFT

**DENVIR**, Hazel
**Transpersonal Psychotherapist**
Pennethorne Close
Victoria Park Road
London
E9
☎ 020 8986 6344
☎ 01524 263 147
Hazeldenvir@mac.com
CCPE, RE.V

**DOSANJH**, Charanjit
**Body Psychotherapist, Integrative Psychotherapist**
118 Pearcroft Road
Leytonstone
London
E11 4DR
☎ 020 8556 5454
CCBP

**EISEN**, Susan
**Psychoanalytic Psychotherapist**
♿ 1 Lingwood Road
London
E5 9BN
☎ 020 8 806 8313
☎ 020 8 806 8703
sueeisen@hotmail.com
GUILD

**EL-HADI**, Ali
**Psychoanalytic Psychotherapist**
18 Colworth Road
Leytonstone
London
E11 1HY
☎ 020 8924 6301
☎ 020 8539 5496
a.el-hadi@ntworld.com
FIP

**FRENCH**, Anne
**Integrative Psychotherapist**
58 Cheneys Road
Leytonstone
London
E11 3LN
☎ 020 8503 0481
annefrench2000@hotmail.com
SPCRC

**FROSHAUG**, Ann
**Analytical Psychotherapist**
196 Queensbridge Road
London
E8 4QE
☎ 020 7254 4041
☎ 07985 082 117
FIP

**GAL**, Oshrat
**Psychoanalytic Psychotherapist**
7 Artillary Lane
London
E1
☎ 020 8431 4456
☎ 020 8 455 5333
GUILD

**GAWLER-WRIGHT**, Pamela
**Hypno-Psychotherapist**
Beeleaf House
34 Grove Road
London
E3 5AX
☎ 020 8983 9699
☎ 020 8981 1017
pam@beeleaf.com
NLPtCA, NSHAP

**GIBSON**, Jenny
**Transactional Analysis Psychotherapist**
Stepney Green
London
E1
☎ 02077 904 784
ITA, MET

**GLENDINNING**, Laura
**Family & Systemic Psychotherapist**
28 Hampton Road
Forest Gate
London
E7 0PB
☎ 020 8555 5977
lauraglendinning@tiscali.co.uk
AFT

**GOLDBERG**, Henia
**Family & Systemic Psychotherapist**
24 Fletching Rd
London
E5 9QP
☎ 020 7682 1139
heniagoldberg@hotmail.com
AFT

**GOOD**, Elizabeth
**Psychoanalytic Psychotherapist**
14 Belgrave Road
Wanstead
London
E11 3QN
☎ 020 8989 6529
☎ 020 7794 3377
AGIP

**GOOD**, Simon
**Psychoanalyst**
14 Belgrave Road
London
E11 3QN
☎ 020 8518 8887
☎ 020 8989 6529
GUILD

**GOODES**, Deborah
**Psychoanalytic Psychotherapist**
Leytonstone
London
E11
☎ 020 8926 0797
ARBS

**GOODING**, Kim
**Integrative Psychotherapist**
213 St Stephens Road
Bow
London
E3 5JW
☎ 020 8981 8477
SPCRC

**GOTI**, Itsaso
**Group Analytic Psychotherapist**
E. London & City NHS Trust
Older Adult Psychology Service
Mile End Hospital
Bancroft Rd, London
E1 4DG
☎ 02073 777 000 ext 7848
i_goti@hotmail.com
UPCA

**GRAHAM**, Judith
**Gestalt Psychotherapist, Humanistic Psychotherapist**
Healthy Living
282 St. Paul's Road
London
E1 1LH
☎ 020 7354 2240
☎ 020 7704 6900
jugrfrog@dircon.co.uk
AHPP

**GRAY**, Kati
**Psychoanalytic Psychotherapist**
30 Skelton Road
London
E7 9NJ
☎ 020 8471 8016
GUILD, SITE

**GREALLY**, Brid
**Psychoanalytic Psychotherapist**
81 Diana Road
Walthamstow
London
E17 5LE
☎ 020 8527 9980
bgreally@fields1.demon.co.uk
FPC

**GRIFFIN**, Susanne
**Family & Systemic Psychotherapist**
♿ Wellington Way Child & Family Consultation
1a Wellington Way
Bow
London
E3 4NE
☎ 020 8981 9283
☎ 020 7388 3877
AFT

**GRIFFITHS**, John
**Cognitive Behavioural Psychotherapist**
♿ Dept of Clinical Psychology
E London & The City MH NHS Trust
50-52 Clifden Road
London
E5 0LJ
☎ 020 8510 8661
BABCP

**HARBER-KELLY**, Andrea
**Transpersonal Psychotherapist**
London
E10
☎ 020 8503 7794
☎ 07812 988 926
aharber@yahoo.com
The Health Works
111a Hoe Street
Walthamstow
London
E17 4RX
CCPE

**HARDING**, C.
**Psychoanalytic Psychotherapist**
36 Richmond Road
Leytonstone
London
E11 4BU
☎ 020 8556 5089
FPC

**HARRINGTON**, Finola
**Cognitive Behavioural Psychotherapist**
36 Calvin Street
London
E1 6NW
☎ 020 7377 7530
☎ 07802 934 771
BABCP

**HASLAM**, Deirdre
**Humanistic Psychotherapist**
85 Rushmore Road
London
E5 0EX
☎ 020 8986 3051
☎ 01245 493 131 x4982
deirdre@haslam1.co.uk
AHPP

**HAWKES**, Bernadette
**Psychoanalytic Psychotherapist**
32 Canning Road
Walthamstow
London
E17 6LT
☎ 020 8509 1484
hawkes92@msn.com
IPSS

**HAYES**, Cheryl
**Sexual and Relationship Psychotherapist**
♿ 25 St Mary Grace's Court
Cartwright Street
E1 8NB
☎ 020 7481 4007
cheryl.hayes@btopenworld.com
BASRT

**HENDERSON**, John
**Child Psychotherapist**
Newham Child & Family Consultation Service
York House
409/411 Barking Road
London
E13 8AL
☎ 020 7445 7800
idh@dircon.co.uk
ACP

**HOANG**, Astrid
**Group Analytic Psychotherapist**
40 Spruce Hills Road
Walthamstow
London
E17 4LD
☎ 020 8527 7258
sprucehills@ntlworld.com
FPC

**HUDSON**, Pauline
**Systemic Psychotherapist**
Emanuel Miller Child & Family Consultation Service
11 Gill Street
London
E14 8HQ
☎ 020 8883 7662
☎ 020 7515 6633
hudsonple@aol.com or
husdonp@elcmht.nhs.uk
KCC

**HUGHES**, Gillian
**Systemic Psychotherapist**
118 Greenwood Road
Dalston
London
E8 1NE
☎ 020 7241 0938
☎ 020 7445 7777
gillianhughes@gn.apc.org
Newham Psychology & Counselling Service
Community House
430 Barking Road
Plaistow, London
E13 8HJ
KCC

**HUSON**, Richard
**Psychosynthesis Psychotherapist**
Flat 7
Sugar Loaf Walk
London
E2 0JQ
☎ 02089 812 428
IPS

**JACK**, Sarah
**Attachment-based Psychoanalytic Psychotherapist**
♿ 69 Turner Road
Walthamstow
London
E17 3JG
☎ 020 8509 9751
CAPP

**JONES**, Dave
**Humanistic Psychotherapist**
8 Forest Glade
Leytonstone
London
E11 1LU
☎ 020 8989 6565
davidjones5@cwctv.net
AHPP

**KANE**, Ros
**Psychoanalytic Psychotherapist**
♿ 15 Matcham Road
London
E11 3LE
☎ 020 8 555 5248
GUILD

**KEAL**, Susan
**Integrative Psychotherapist**
6 Shaftesbury Road
London
E17 9BP
☎ 020 8521 6722
suekeal@btopenworld.com
SPCRC

**KEANE**, Agnes
**Transpersonal Psychotherapist**
29 Dunton Road
Leyton
London
E10 7AF
CCPE

**KELLY**, Ann
**Family & Systemic Psychotherapist**
89 Mildenhall Road
London
E5 0RT
☎ 02089 856 955
ak@sabs.demon.co.uk
IFT

**KIRKLAND**, Margot
**Psychosynthesis Psychotherapist**
Ashwin Street Practice
The Print House
18 Ashwin Street
London
E8 3DL
☎ 02072 549 202
margot_kirkland@hotmail.com
IPS

**LEACH**, Victoria
**Attachment-based Psychoanalytic Psychotherapist**
28 Queens Road
London
E11 1BB
☎ 020 8925 8034
torivleach@aol.com
CAPP

**LESADD**, Jenny
**Psychoanalytic Psychotherapist**
56 Brunswick Street
Walthamstow
London
E17 9NB
☎ 020 8520 1779
IPSS

**LUCA**, Maria
**Integrative Psychotherapist**
67 Middleton Road
London
E8 4EE
☎ 020 7249 8050
lucam@regents.ac.uk
SPCRC

**MALLEY**, Maeve
**Systemic Psychotherapist**
12 Drysdale Dwellings
Dunn Street
London
E8 2DH
☎ 07940 598 341
m.mal@virgin.net
IFT

**MANGLANI**, Dona
**Psychoanalytic Psychotherapist**
72 Elderfield Road
London
E5 0LF
☎ 0778 865 217
donamanglani@btopenworld.com
IPSS

**MARSH**, Jeanette
**Transpersonal Psychotherapist**
The Phoenix Centre
Bressey Lodge
Bressey Grove
London
E18 2HP
☎ 020 8530 8198
jeanette@counsel-therapy.freeserve.co.uk
CCPE

**MASON**, Christina
**Integrative Psychotherapist**
47 Rosebank Gardens
Bow
London
E3 5EF
☎ 0208 980 4124
cmason@stjh.org.uk
MET

**MCWILLIAM**, Jill
**Educational Therapist**
93 Crofton Road
Plaistow
London
E13 8QT
☎ 020 7476 1777
jillmcwilliam@aol.com
CFET

**MILLARD**, Lorraine
**Transpersonal Psychotherapist**
31 Barrett Road
London
E17 9ES
☎ 020 8520 4159
CCPE

**MULLER**, Nina
**Psychodynamic Psychotherapist**
888 Lea Bridge Road
London
E17 9DW
☎ 020 8597 3628
christina.muller1@virgin.net
AIP

**NAOR**, Lillie
**Integrative Arts Psychotherapist**
8 Lansdowne Road
Walthamstow
London
E17 8QU
☎ 020 8509 0224
lillietherapy@hotmail.com
IATE

**NASH**, Sue
**Psychoanalytic Psychotherapist**
8 Godwin Road
Forest Gate
London
E7 0LE
☎ 020 8536 1536
suenash@supanet.com
IPSS

**NESBIT**, Judith
**Psychoanalytic Psychotherapist**
32 Thornby Road
London
E5 9QL
☎ 020 8986 5286
nesbit@dircon.co.uk
AGIP

**O'BRIEN**, Jackie
**Systemic Psychotherapist**
♿ Child & Family Consultation Centre
York House
411 Barking Road
Plaistow
E13 8AL
☎ 020 7445 7800
☎ 01708 453 665
KCC

**O'CARROLL**, Madeline
**Cognitive Behavioural Psychotherapist**
City University
Philpot Street
London
E1 2EA
☎ 020 7505 5815
M.O'Carroll@city.ac.uk
BABCP

**O'KEEFFE**, Tim
**Psychoanalytic Psychotherapist**
60 St Mary Road
Walthamstow
London
E17 9RE
☎ 020 8520 3766
AGIP

**OMODIAGBE**, Kemi
**Integrative Psychotherapist**
♿ Stratford Advice Centre
107-109 The Grove
Stratford
E15
☎ 07946 255 298
☎ 020 8558 0957
info@djembeproject.co.uk
MET

**PAPADOPOULOS**, Renos K
**Analytical Psychologist-Jungian Analyst, Family & Systemic Psychotherapist**
20 Woodriffe Road
London
E11 1AH
☎ 020 8556 3180
renos@essex.ac.uk
AFT

**PATTON**, Jane
**Gestalt Psychotherapist**
158 Swaton Road
Bow
London
E3 4ER
☎ 020 7515 4756
GCL

**PEARMAIN**, Dr Rosalind
**Integrative Psychotherapist, Psychoanalytic Psychotherapist**
69 Gordon Road
Wanstead
London
E11 2RA
☎ 020 8989 4941
rosalind.pearmain@virgin.net
GUILD, SPCRC

**PEARSON**, Eileen
**Psychoanalytic Psychotherapist**
7 Northumberland Avenue
London
E12 5HF
☎ 020 8989 3070
eileen.pearson@ntworld.com
FIP

**PERKINS**, Kevin
**Integrative Psychotherapist**
80 Greenway Avenue
Walthamstow
London
E17 3QW
☎ 02085 203 460
MET

**PHILBIN**, Mairead
**Psychosynthesis Psychotherapist**
♿ St. Joseph's Hospice
Mare Street
Hackney
London
E8 4SA
☎ 02089 862 285
IPS

**PIXNER**, Stefanie
**Integrative Psychotherapist**
94 Colvestone Crescent
Hackney
London
E8 2LJ
☎ 020 7254 6216
MC

**PRENDEVILLE**, William
**Psychoanalytic Psychotherapist**
191 Sebert Road
Forest Gate
London
E7 0NP
☎ 02085 198 521
GUILD

**PRIEST**, Caroline
**Systemic Psychotherapist**
Leyton Green NHS
180 Essex Road
Leyton
London
E10 6BT
☎ 020 8341 6488
☎ 020 8556 6902
carolinepr@aol.com
KCC

**QUALTROUGH**, Heather
**Systemic Psychotherapist**
44 Arnold Road
Bow
London
E3 4NU
☎ 020 8981 3636
☎ 020 7445 7777
haqualtrough@aol.com
Newham Psychology and
Counselling Service
Community House
430 Barking Road
London
E13 8HJ
KCC

**RAO**, Ms Varija
**Attachment-based Psychoanalytic Psychotherapist, Psychoanalytic Psychotherapist**
40 Walton Road
Plaistow
London
E13 9BP
☎ 020 8552 7289
raovarija@hotmail.com
CAPP, NAFSI

**ROBERTS**, Laurence
**Psychoanalytic Psychotherapist**
40 Boleyn Road
Upton Lane
Forest Gate
E7 9QE
☎ 020 8 472 2430
referrals@citytherapies.org.uk
GUILD, SITE

**ROBERTSON**, Eileen
**Integrative Psychotherapist**
57 Lansdowne Drive
Hackney
London
E8 3EP
☎ 0207 249 7186
eileen.robertson@btinternet.com
MC

**ROBERTSON**, Jo
**Attachment-based Psychoanalytic Psychotherapist**
♿ 59 Wilton Way
London
E8 1BG
☎ 020 7249 6871
CAPP

**SALES**, Sally
**Psychoanalyst**
76a Lauriston Road
London
E9 7HA
☎ 020 8986 5889
SITE

**SANDELSON**, Jennifer
**Sexual and Relationship Psychotherapist**
9 Meynell Crescent
London
E9 7AS
☎ 020 8525 0772
jennysandelson@yahoo.com
BASRT

**SCOTT**, Tricia
**Individual and Group Humanistic Psychotherapist**
8 Shrubland Road
London
E8 4NN
☎ 02072 544 490
tricia.scott@btinternet.com
AHPP, UPCA

**SHEARMAN**, Christine
**Gestalt Psychotherapist, Integrative Psychotherapist, Transactional Analysis Psychotherapist**
♿ London
E11
☎ 02089 895 206
christine.shearmann@virgin.net
GPTI, ITA, MET

**SHENG**, Rosemary Hui
**Psychoanalytic Psychotherapist**
51 Washington Avenue
Manor Park
London
E12 5JA
☎ 07764 682 035
☎ 02077 291 557
NAFSI

**SHEPPARD**, Jan
**Existential Psychotherapist**
14 Landon's Close
Prestons Road
London
E14 9QQ
☎ 07742 423 222
shebaddi@yahoo.co.uk
SEA

**SHETLAND**, Ilrich
**Psychoanalyst**
76A Lauriston Road
London
E9 7HA
☎ 020 8986 5889
Sallyand.Ilric@virgin.net
IPSS, SITE

**SHUTTLEWORTH**, Alan
**Child Psychotherapist**
Walthamstow Child & Family Consultation Service
Shernhall Street
London
E17 3EA
☎ 020 8509 0424
☎ 020 8883 7908
ACP

**SHUTTLEWORTH**, Caroline
**Group Analytic Psychotherapist**
20 Ellesmere Road
Bow
London
E3 5QX
☎ 020 8981 4227
wetherick@fish.co.uk
FPC

**SLADE**, John
**Integrative Psychotherapist**
86 Clifden Road
London
E5 0LN
☎ 020 8533 0022
johnslade@blueyonder.co.uk
MC

**SMART**, Tanya
**Systemic Psychotherapist**
♿ Kingsmead School
Kinsmead Way
London
E9 5PP
☎ 020 8985 5779
☎ 020 8438 1770
tanyasmart42@hotmail.com
KCC

**SMITH**, Alexander
**Existential Psychotherapist**
10 Hampstead Walk
London
E3 2JN
☎ 020 8981 9250
☎ 020 7487 7555
smithx@regents.ac.uk
SEA

**SMITH**, Gerrilyn
**Family & Systemic Psychotherapist**
P O Box 6568
London
E5 0XD
☎ 020 8985 8081
gerrilyn.smith@virgin.net
IFT

**SMITH**, Heather
**Psychosynthesis Psychotherapist**
91 Ashfield Street
Whitechapel
London
E1 2HA
☎ 020 7924 3924
☎ 020 7377 5873
dilsha@jsa-london.com
PET

**SOMERVILLE**, Gwynnedd
**Psychoanalytic Psychotherapist**
23 Mornington Grove
Bow
London
E3 4NS
☎ 020 8983 1085
grsomerville@dsl.pipex.com
FPC

**ST JOHN**, Frances
**Family & Systemic Psychotherapist**
♿ Newham Child and Family Consultation Service
York House
411 Barking Road
London
E13 8AL
☎ 020 7445 7800
frances.stjohn@newhampct.nhs.uk
IFT

**STAINES**, John
**Family & Systemic Psychotherapist**
CFCS
Lower Clapton Road
London
E5 0PQ
☎ 02089 867 351
j.staines@tiscali.co.uk
IFT

**STEPHENS**, Sally
**Family & Systemic Psychotherapist**
Behavioural & Education Support Team (BEST)
The Bungalow, McEntee School
Billet Road
Walthamstow, London
E17 5DP
☎ 020 8527 8091
IFT

**STIASNY**, Jennifer
**Child Psychotherapist**
Newham Child & Family Consultation Service
York House
409/411 Barking Road
London
E13 8AL
☎ 020 7445 7800
ACP

**SUTHERLAND**, Elisabeth
**Psychosynthesis Psychotherapist**
50 Blondin Street
Bow
London
E3 2TR
☎ 020 8981 1553
lissutherland@clara.co.uk
PET

**TAYLOR**, Sheena
**Integrative Psychotherapist**
Flat 8
James Hilton House
23 Woodford Road
London
E18 2EL
☎ 02089 895 458
sheenamtaylor@yahoo.co.uk
MET

**THUMMEL**, Uwe
**Group Analyst**
62 Millfields Road
London
E5 0SD
☎ 020 8533 2120
IGA

**TRISTRAM**, Sue
**Body Psychotherapist, Integrative Psychotherapist**
231 Glyn Road
London
E5
☎ 020 8986 4923
sjtristram@hotmail.com
CCBP

**URWIN**, Catherine
**Child Psychotherapist**
Emanuel Miller Centre
The Health Centre
11 Gill Street
London
E14 8HQ
☎ 020 7515 6633
☎ 020 8802 8593
cathy.urwin@ukgateway.net
ACP

**VAS DIAS**, Susan
**Attachment-based Psychoanalytic Psychotherapist, Child Psychotherapist**
♿ 69 Gordon Road
London
E18 1DT
☎ 020 8559 1244
ACP, CAPP

**VIBHAKAR**, Lopa
**Systemic Psychotherapist**
♿ Psychology Department
St Clements Hospital
2a Bow Road
London
E3 4LL
☎ 020 8514 7641
☎ 020 7377 7969
IFT

**VINCENT**, David
**Group Analyst**
Suite 8, 1st Floor Hollywell House
Wanstead Passge
Wanstead
London
E11 2AL
☎ 020 8530 8749
IGA

**VIRTANEN**, Helena
**Family & Systemic Psychotherapist**
64 Goldsmith Road
Walthamstow
London
E17 6AW
☎ 020 8527 5460
helena@virtanen.freeserve.co.uk
IFT

**VOGEL**, Ludwig
**Neurolinguistic Psychotherapist**
3 Dycer House
Wick Road
London
E9 5AS
☎ 02085 335 314
NLPtCA

**WILLIAMS**, Gwen
**Psychoanalytic Psychotherapist**
♿ 226 Twickenham Road
Leytonstone
London
E11 4BH
☎ 02085 394 992
gwen@soulcom.fsnet.co.uk
IPSS, WTC

## LONDON EAST CENTRAL

**ALTMAN**, Michelle M
**Cognitive Behavioural Psychotherapist**
♿ 262 Shakespeare Tower
Barbican
London
EC2Y 8DR
☎ 020 7628 9719
BABCP

**AMBROSE**, Tony
**Gestalt Psychotherapist, Integrative Psychotherapist**
The Gestalt Centre
1st Floor
62 Paul Street
EC2A 4NA
☎ 020 8542 5930
☎ 07905 117 718
GCL

**AMUNDSEN**, Paul
**Gestalt Psychotherapist**
Gestalt Centre
62 Paul Street
London
EC2A 4NA
☎ 07766 711 729
☎ 020 8519 3435
paulamun@yahoo.co.uk
GCL

**ASHMORE**, Tom
**Systemic Psychotherapist**
♿ Department of Psychotherapy
William Harvey House
St Bartholomew's Hospital
61 Bartholomew Close, Lon
EC1 A7B
☎ 020 7735 3927
☎ 020 7601 8107
tomashmore@bigfoot.com
KCC

**BEECHER-MOORE**, Naona
**Humanistic Psychotherapist, Psychosynthesis Psychotherapist**
3 Temple Gardens
Middle Temple Lane
London
EC4 9AU
☎ 020 7353 2101
naonabm@aol.com
AHPP, PET

**BOND**, Frank W
**Cognitive Behavioural Psychotherapist**
Department of Psychology
City University London
Northampton Square
London
EC1V 0HB
☎ 020 7040 8484
F.W.Bond@city.ac.uk
BABCP

**BURCH**, Nigel
**Psychoanalytic Psychotherapist**
29a Northampton Square
London
EC1V 0ES
☎ 020 7253 7798
nigelburch@tiscali.co.uk
ARBS

**CROSS**, Malcolm C
**Personal Construct Psychotherapist**
Department of Psychology
City University
Northampton Square
London
EC1V 0HB
☎ 020 7477 8531
m.c.cross@city.ac.uk
PCP

**DALY**, Kevin
**Cognitive Behavioural Psychotherapist**
49 Queen Victoria Street
London
EC4N 4SA
☎ 020 7431 1794
BABCP

**DARDENNE**, Patricia
**Sexual and Relationship Psychotherapist**
♿ Institute of Psychotrauma
William Harvey House
61 Bartholomew Close
London
EC1A 7BE
☎ 020 7601 7019
patricia.dardenne@elmht.nhs.uk
BABCP, BASRT, BPS

**GEORGE**, Evan A H
**Systemic Psychotherapist**
Brief Therapy Practice
7 - 8 Newbury Street
London
EC1A 7HU
☎ 020 7600 3366
evangeorge@brieftherapy.org.uk
IFT

**GLADSTONE**, Guy
**Humanistic and Integrative Psychotherapist**
The Open Centre
188 Old Street
London
EC1V 9FR
☎ 020 7272 6672
AHPP, IPSS

**HOLDEN**, John
**Psychoanalytic Psychotherapist**
4 Foster lane
London
EC2V 6HH
☎ 020 7606 1863
FPC

**IVESON**, Chris
**Family & Systemic Psychotherapist**
The Brief Therapy Practice
7-8 Newbury Street
London
EC1A 7HU
☎ 020 7600 3366
Chrisiveson@brieftherapy.org.uk
IFT

**MARSH**, Jane
**Attachment-based Psychoanalytic Psychotherapist**
The Gestalt Centre
62 Paul Street
London
EC2A 4NA
☎ 01494 837 482
janemarsh@compuserve.com
CAPP

**MYCROFT**, Jessica
**Psychoanalytic Psychotherapist**
♿ 26 Northampton Square
London
EC1V 0ES
☎ 02072 536 963
☎ 02072 533 765
jessica-mycroft@citypsych.freeserve.co.uk
IPSS, WTC

**RANDALL-VINING**, Morgan
**Cognitive Behavioural Psychotherapist**
Blossoms Inn Medical Centre
21-26 Garlick Hill
London
EC4V 2AU
☎ 020 8397 6820
☎ 020 7489 9292
BABCP

**RATNER**, Harvey
**Systemic Psychotherapist**
Brief Therapy Practice
7 - 8 Newbury Street
London
EC1A 7HU
☎ 020 7600 3366
harveyratner@brieftherapy.org.uk
IFT

**ROBERTS**, Laurence
**Psychoanalytic Psychotherapist**
City Consultation Service
Fenchurch Street
London
EC3
☎ 020 8 472 2430
referrals@citytherapies.org.uk
GUILD, SITE

**ROSS**, Mo
**Psychoanalytic Psychotherapist**
ICC
7 Artillery Lane
London
EC1 7LP
☎ 020 8806 4263
kymet@waitrose.com
AGIP

**SHORROCK**, Andrew
**Psychosynthesis Psychotherapist**
Lomard Street
London
EC1
☎ 020 7231 8016
Aanda@ndirect.co.uk
PET

**WEAVER**, Stephen
**Transpersonal Psychotherapist**
London
EC4
☎ 0793 9393 567
☎ 020 8780 1668
stephenweaver@btopenworld.com
CCPE

**WHITNEY**, Glenn
**Integrative Psychotherapist**
62 Britton Street
London
EC1M 5UY
☎ 020 7253 2507
gwhitney@ecdinsight.com
SPCRC

**WILSON**, Peter
**Child Psychotherapist**
Young Minds
2nd Floor
102-108 Clerkenwell Road
London
EC1M 5SA
☎ 020 7336 8445
☎ 020 8883 6370
ACP

## LONDON NORTH

**ABELES**, Margi (Margaret)
**Systemic Psychotherapist**
London
N2
☎ 02083 740 634
KCC

**ABLACK**, Joanne
**Body Psychotherapist, Integrative Psychotherapist**
71 Burghley Road
London
N8 0QG
☎ 020 8888 6010
JoanneAbl@aol.com
CCBP

**ABRAHAMS**, Elizabeth M
**Integrative Psychotherapist**
57 Holdenhurst Avenue
Finchley
London
N12 0JA
☎ 020 8 346 7104
MC

**ABRAM**, Vicky
**Humanistic Psychotherapist**
77 Wood Vale
London
N10 3DL
☎ 020 8883 2771
Vicky@theabrams.co.uk
AHPP

**ABSE**, Susanna
**Couple Psychoanalytic Psychotherapist**
17 Muswell Avenue
London
N10 2EB
☎ 020 7447 3818
☎ 020 8883 5746
susannaabse@hotmail.com
TMSI, SCPP

**ADAMS**, Kathryn
**Psychoanalytic Psychotherapist**
58 Finsbury Park Road
London
N4 2JX
☎ 020 7226 1977
enquiries@fppc.org
GUILD

**ADAMS**, Sue
**Humanistic and Integrative Psychotherapist**
Flat 4
30c Alexandra Road
Hornsey
London
N8 0PP
☎ 020 8889 9524
BCPC

**ADEMA**, Rachel
**Psychoanalytic Psychotherapist**
22 Harcourt Road
LONDON
N22 7XW
☎ 020 8888 5136
☎ 020 8888 5136
rachelaf@blueyonder.co.uk
FIP

**AIRD**, Eileen
**Psychoanalytic Psychotherapist**
♿ Flat 8, Fortior Court
100 Hornsey Lane
London
N6 5LD
☎ 02072 725 738
WTC

**AKGUN**, Shirley
**Cognitive Analytic Therapist**
Counsellor & Psychotherapist, Family Health Care C
Somerset Gardens
4 Creighton Road
London
N17 8NW
☎ 0774 243 2044
ACAT

**AL-JARRAH**, Nadina
**Psychoanalytic Psychotherapist**
12 Regina Road
Islington
London
N4 3PP
☎ 02076 863 887
ihooper@london213.freeserve.co.uk
NAFSI

**ALBRECHT**, Gisela
**Psychoanalytic Psychotherapist**
45 Ashley Road
London
N19 3AG
☎ 020 7281 1265
gisela.albrecht@virgin.net
FPC

**ALEKSIC**, Sonya
**Attachment-based Psychoanalytic Psychotherapist**
5 Crossfield Road
Tottenham
London
N17 6AY
☎ 020 8376 3262
CAPP

**ALEXANDER**, Zelda
**Integrative Psychotherapist**
Finchley
London
N3
☎ 020 8343 3528
SPCRC

**ALFEROFF**, Tamara
**Transpersonal Psychotherapist**
London
N19 3BG
☎ 020 7272 3589
tamara@counselling.com
CCPE

**ALLSOP**, Paul
**Gestalt Psychotherapist, Humanistic and Integrative Psychotherapist**
Spectrum
7 Endymion Road
London
N4 1EE
☎ 020 8341 2277
☎ 020 8883 3246
paul@louperail.demon.co.uk
SPEC

**ALPHONSE**, Jenny
**Systemic Psychotherapist**
Multi Cultural Counselling Centre
Claremont Centre
24-27 White Lion Street
London
N1 9PD
☎ 020 7837 3303
j.alphonse@btopenworld.com or
multicult@hotmail.com
KCC

**AMIAS**, David
**Family & Systemic Psychotherapist**
60 Clifton Road
Finchley
London
N3 2AR
☎ 020 8346 2121
davidamias@hotmail.com
IFT

**AMIEL**, Olivia
**Psychoanalytic Psychotherapist**
16 Elms Avenue
London
N10 2JP
☎ 020 8 442 0753 (t/f)
GUILD

**ANDERSON**, Liz
**Psychoanalytic Psychotherapist**
1 Fairbridge Road
London
N19 3EW
☎ 020 7272 7013
☎ 07801 495 471
AGIP

**ANDRY**, Robert
**Group Analyst, Psychoanalytic Psychotherapist**
Highgate
London
N6
IGA

**ANTONAS**, Vassilis
**Integrative Psychotherapist**
55 Northampton Park
Canonbur
Islington
London
N1 2PP
☎ 020 7637 7763
☎ 020 7226 1900
info@counselling.org or
v.antonas@therapyconnections.com
AHPP

**ARIEL**, Seema
**Psychoanalytic Psychotherapist**
19 Great Bushey Drive
Totteridge
London
N20 8QN
☎ 020 8369 5811
Bra.2020@btinternet.com
AGIP

**ARNOLD**, Katherine
**Child Psychotherapist**
57 Cecile Park
Crouch End
London
N8 9AX
☎ 020 8340 2922
ACP

**ARNOLD**, Rosemary
**Psychoanalytic Psychotherapist**
3 Stanmore Road
London
N15 3PR
☎ 020 8 889 7335
GUILD

**ASHERI**, Shoshi
**Body Psychotherapist, Integrative Psychotherapist**
22b Uplands Road
Crouch End
London
N8 9NL
☎ 020 8340 7168
shoshAsh@aol.com
CCBP

**ASHTON**, Barbara
**Attachment-based Psychoanalytic Psychotherapist**
♿ 22 Bishop's Court
10 Mathias Road
London
N16 8QZ
☎ 020 7690 9305
ba015f0606@blueyonder.com
CAPP

**AZGAD**, Racheli
**Contemporary Psychoanalyst**
67 Dollis Road
London
N3 1RD
☎ 020 8346 1525
izziazgad@aol.com
SITE

**BAILEY**, David
**Systemic Psychotherapist**
44 Corinne Road
London
N19 5EY
☎ 020 7607 8017
☎ 01923 470 610
david.bailey@hpt.nhs.uk
KCC

**BAKER**, Adrienne
**Integrative Psychotherapist**
16 Sheldon Avenue
Highgate
London
N6 4JT
☎ 020 8340 5970
bakera@regents.ac.uk
SPCRC

**BALICK**, Aaron
**Integrative Psychotherapist**
Islington
London
N1
☎ 020 7688 0529
therapy@n1psychotherapy.co.uk
SPTI

**BALOGH HENGHES**, Tessa
**Child Psychotherapist**
92 Highgate Hill
London
N6 5HE
☎ 020 8348 7731
ACP

**BARKER**, Gina
**Attachment-based Psychoanalytic Psychotherapist**
50 Burma Road
London
N16 9BJ
☎ 020 7275 8002
CAPP

**BARRY**, Anne
**Integrative Psychotherapist, Psychoanalytic Psychotherapist**
43 Dukes Avenue
Muswell Hill
London
N10 2PX
AGIP

**BARTY**, Alison
**Gestalt Psychotherapist**
18 Canning Road
London
N5 2JS
☎ 020 7354 2175
alisonbarty@aol.com
GPTI

**BATCHELOR**, Sue
**Integrative Psychotherapist**
5 Coleridge Road
London
N8 8EH
☎ 0208 442 9242
sue@batchelor.com
MC

**BEAUMONT**, Mia
**Educational Therapist, Psychoanalytic Psychotherapist**
13 Highbury Terrace
London
N5 1UP
☎ 020 7226 8103
mia-beaumont@talk21.com
CFET, GUILD

**BEBER**, Ray
**Group Analytic Psychotherapist**
16 Grasmere Road
London
N10 2DJ
☎ 02088 834 737
beber@btinternet.com
UPCA

**BECKER**, Amely
**Gestalt Psychotherapist, Individual and Group Humanistic Psychotherapist**
15a Langdon Park Road
Highgate
London
N6 5PS
☎ 020 8348 6253
amely@globalnet.co.uk
AHPP, GCL

**BEDDINGTON**, Jenny
**Analytical Psychologist-Jungian Analyst**
39 Waterlow Road
Highgate Hill
London
N6 5NJ
☎ 020 7263 3551
jennybeddington@aol.com
CAP *

**BEHR**, Harold
**Group Analyst**
The North London Centre for Psychotherapy
138 Bramley Road
Oakwood
London
N14 4HU
☎ 020 8440 1451
nlcent@aol.com
IGA

**BENTLEY**, Patrick
**Systemic Psychotherapist**
♿ 44 Sydney Road
Muswell Hill
London
N10 2RL
☎ 020 8883 9943
☎ 020 8354 8030
KCC

**BERESFORD**, Marie
**Psychosynthesis Psychotherapist**
153c Brecknock Road
Tufnell Park
London
N19
☎ 02072 843 015
IPS

**BERGER**, Sue
**Attachment-based Psychoanalytic Psychotherapist**
11Archibald Road
London
N7 0AN
☎ 020 7609 3661
syberger@aol.com
CAPP

**BERKE**, Joseph H
**Psychoanalytic Psychotherapist**
5 Shepherd's Close
London
N6 5AG
☎ 020 8348 4492
jhberke@aol.com - www.jhberke.com
ARBS

**BERRY**, Sally
**Psychoanalytic Psychotherapist**
♿ 11 Cecile Park Road
London
N8 9AX
☎ 020 8340 5161
ARBS, SITE, WTC

**BEVERIDGE**, John
**Attachment-based Psychoanalytic Psychotherapist**
53 Eburne Road
London
N7 6AU
☎ 020 7561 0715
JJBeveridge@aol.com
CAPP

**BHATT**, Vibha
**Psychoanalytic Psychotherapist**
85 Sydney Road
London
N8 0ET
☎ 020 8 348 9313
GUILD

**BIANCO**, Vicky
**Family & Systemic Psychotherapist**
Child & Family Consultation Service
St Leonards Primary Care Trust
Nuttall Street
London
N1 5LZ
☎ 020 7301 3414
IFT

**BIERSCHENK**, John Henry
**Analytical Psychologist-Jungian Analyst**
♿ 58 Queen's Avenue
London
N10 3NU
☎ 020 8883 3567
bierschenk@jbierschenk.freeserve.co.uk
AJA

**BILDER**, Tessa
**Transpersonal Psychotherapist**
61 Huntingdon Road
London
N2 9DX
☎ 020 8444 5289
CCPE

**BLACKWELL**, Frances
**Psychoanalytic Psychotherapist**
♿ 28 Kirkstall Avenue
Tottenham
London
N17 6PH
☎ 020 8 880 9553
frances_blackwell@hotmail.com
IPSS

**BLAIR**, Dana-Jane
**Psychoanalytic Psychotherapist**
♿ 11 Fieldway Crescent
Highbury
London
N5 1PU
☎ 02076 092 969
bairdj@tiscali.co.uk
IPSS

**BLENCH**, Graeme
**Integrative Arts Psychotherapist**
c/o Centre for Child Mental Health
2-18 Britannia Row
London
N1 8PA
☎ 07814 856 809
IATE

**BOWMAN**, Heather
**Integrative Psychotherapist**
9 Leadale Road
Stamford Hill
London
N16 6BZ
☎ 020 8 800 8476
bowman@stamhill.freeserve.co.uk
MC

**BOWNAS**, Jo
**Systemic Psychotherapist**
4 Clyro Court
Tollington Park
London
N4 3AQ
☎ 020 7263 1897
KCC

**BOYDEN**, Tina
**Hypno-Psychotherapist, Neurolinguistic Psychotherapist**
69 Goddard Place
off Monnery Road
London
N19 5GT
☎ 02072 819 663
tina@tba.globalnet.co.uk
NLPtCA, NSHAP

**BRATERMAN**, Eleanor
**Hypno-Psychotherapist**
36E Portland Rise
London
N4 2PP
☎ 02088 029 206
NSHAP

**BRATLEY**, Mary
**Family & Systemic Psychotherapist**
4 The Gables
Fortis Green
Muswell Hill
London
N10 3EA
☎ 020 8444 3094
AFT

**BRAUNER**, Rita
**Integrative Psychotherapist, Psychoanalytic Psychotherapist, Transactional Analysis Psychotherapist**
Upper Flat,
69 Rectory Road
London
N16 7PP
☎ 02072 411 477
rita.firaseika@virgin.net
ITA, MET, NAFSI

**BRAVESMITH**, Anna
**Analytical Psychologist-Jungian Analyst**
59 Holmesdale Road
Highgate
London
N6 5TH
☎ 020 8340 9137
☎ 020 8340 9037
anna@jar59.fsnet.co.uk
CAP *

**BREATHNACH**, Eibhlin (Eileen)
**Psychoanalytic Psychotherapist**
110 Brecknock Road
London
N7 0DB
☎ 020 7700 5430
eibhlin@onetel.net.uk
AGIP

**BRENNAN**, Damian
**Personal Construct Psychotherapist**
81 Sperling Road
Tottenham
London
N17 6UJ
☎ 020 8808 2205
☎ 020 8969 8636
PCP

**BROWN**, Mo
**Psychoanalytic Psychotherapist**
The Burma Road Practice
50 Burma Road
London
N16 9BJ
☎ 02072 267 047
☎ 08454 589 290
45 Grosvenor Avenue
Islington
London
N5 5NN
NAFSI

**BROWN**, Sara
**Psychoanalytic Psychotherapist**
6 Carlingford Road
Turnpike Lane
London
N15 3EH
☎ 020 8889 3464
☎ 020 8889 8536
sara111155@hotmail.com
1 Fairbridge Road
London
N19 3EW
AGIP

**BURGOYNE**, Bernard
**Lacanian Analyst**
5 Stanmore Road
London
N15 3PR
☎ 020 8889 5925
CFAR

**BURGOYNE**, Vivien
**Lacanian Analyst, Psychoanalytic Psychotherapist**
5 Stanmore Road
London
N15 3PR
☎ 020 8 889 5925
v.burgoyne@tiscali.co.uk
CFAR, GUILD, WTC

**BURROUGHES**, Christopher Henry
**Family & Systemic Psychotherapist**
143 Kyverdale Road
London
N16 6PS
☎ 020 8806 3577
chris.burroughes@bigfoot.com
AFT

**BURY**, Dennis R.
**Cognitive Behavioural Psychotherapist, Personal Construct Psychotherapist**
47 Mayfield Road
Hornsey
London
N8 9LL
☎ 020 8348 9181
☎ 07889 884 081
pscidu@globalnet.co.uk
BABCP, PCP

**BUSS-TWACHTMANN**, Christel
**Couple Psychoanalytic Psychotherapist**
Flat 1
75 Cromwell Avenue
London
N6 5HS
☎ 020 7435 7111
☎ 020 8341 1358
TMSI, SCPP

**BYRING**, Carola
**Biodynamic Psychotherapist**
32 Rosemary Avenue
London
N3 2QN
☎ 020 7343 0255
carolabyring@aol.com
LSBP

**CAMERON**, Anna
**Psychoanalytic Psychotherapist**
37 Orpington Road
Winchmore Hill
London
N21 3PD
☎ 020 8482 0787
ARBS

**CAMERON**, Michael John
**Cognitive Behavioural Psychotherapist**
3A Thyra Grove
Finchley
London
N12 8HD
☎ 020 8445 1369
BABCP

**CAMERON**, Roderick
**Psychoanalytic Psychotherapist**
37 Orpington Road
Winchmore Hill
London
N21 3PD
☎ 020 8482 0787
☎ 01483 443 683
rodcameron@blueyonder.co.uk
ARBS

**CAMPBELL**, David
**Family & Systemic Psychotherapist, Systemic Psychotherapist**
5 Tivoli Road
London
N8 8RE
☎ 020 8340 3404
IFT

**CANTWELL**, Maureen
**Analytical Psychologist-Jungian Analyst, Analytical Psychotherapist (Jungian)**
7 Phoenix House
Waverley Road
London
N8 9QU
☎ 020 8482 5943
mhecantwell@onetel.net.uk
IGAP, GAPS

**CARROLL**, Pennie
**Psychosynthesis Psychotherapist**
38 Ridgeway Gardens
Hornsey Lane
Highgate
London
N6 5XR
☎ 02072 812 300
IPS

**CARUANA**, Charles Victor
**Psychoanalytic Psychotherapist**
1 Fairbridge Road
London
N19 3EW
☎ 020 7277 7402
AGIP

**CASIMIR**, Anne
**Educational Therapist**
50 Brookfield
Highgate West Hill
London
N6 6AT
☎ 020 8340 6655
CFET

**CATHIE**, Sean
**Psychoanalytic Psychotherapist**
23 Brookfield Mansions
Highgate West Hill
London
N6 6AS
☎ 020 8347 7050
scathie@waitrose.com
FPC

**CHAMLEE-COLE**, Laurena
**Neurolinguistic Psychotherapist**
38 Middle Lane
London
N8 8PG
☎ 02083 408 156
NLPtCA

**CHANDLER**, Philip
**Psychoanalytic Psychotherapist**
31 Huntingdon Road
London
N2 9DX
☎ 020 8 444 7690
pchandler@orange.net
GUILD, UPCA

**CHILD**, Rachel
**Psychoanalytic Psychotherapist**
99 Albert Road
Alexandra Park
LONDON
N22 7AG
☎ 020 8888 0457
ARBS

**CHINA**, Jacques
**Psychoanalytic Psychotherapist**
54 Compton Road
London
N1 2PB
☎ 020 7 354 1533 (t/f)
GUILD

**CHIPPERFIELD**, Dianne
**Body Psychotherapist, Integrative Psychotherapist**
32a Coppetts Road
Muswell Hill
London
N10 1JY
☎ 020 8444 2881
☎ 07764 422 059
diannechip@aol.com
CCBP

**CHOPIN**, Mathias
**Sexual and Relationship Psychotherapist**
74 Seaford Road
London
N15 5DT
☎ 020 8802 4803
therapyN15@hotmail.com
BASRT

**CHRISTIE**, Rose
**Psychoanalytic Psychotherapist**
The Maya Centre
131B St. Johns Way
N19 3RQ
☎ 020 8942 3835
rose@christie.intonet.co.uk
FPC

**CHRISTOPHER**, Elphis
**Analytical Psychologist-Jungian Analyst**
♿ 35 Wood Vale
London
N10 3DJ
☎ 020 8883 0085
CAPP, FIP

**CLANCY**, Pauline
**Psychoanalytic Psychotherapist**
23 Ashley Road
London
N19 3AG
☎ 020 7272 5107
ARBS

**CLIFFORD**, Jennifer
**Psychoanalytic Psychotherapist**
10 Alwyne Place
London
N1 2NL
☎ 020 7354 3930
jaclifford@blueyonder.co.uk
FPC

**COHEN**, Maggie
**Child Psychotherapist**
Neonatal Intensive Care Unit
Whittington Hospital
Highgate
London
N19 5NF
☎ 020 7288 5530
☎ 020 7485 4999
ACP

**COHEN**, Sylvia
**Psychoanalyst**
11 Clifton Avenue
London
N3 1BN
☎ 020 8343 4097
sylviac@clara.co.uk
GUILD, SITE

**CONOLLY**, John
**Lacanian Analyst, Psychoanalytic Psychotherapist**
48 Beresford Road
London
N8 0AJ
☎ 020 8340 6044
jmpconolly@callnetuk.com
CFAR

**COOK**, Alice
**Integrative Psychotherapist**
2a St John's Grove
London
N19 5RW
☎ 02072 721 590
alice2.cook@virgin.net
MC

**COOPER**, Howard
**Psychoanalytic Psychotherapist**
37 Lansdowne Road
Finchley
London
N3 1ET
☎ 020 8349 3891
hcooper@waitrose.com
AGIP

**COOPER**, Jill
**Existential Psychotherapist**
24 Rocliffe Street
London
N1 8DT
☎ 020 7253 1651
jcooper@psynet.freeserve.co.uk
SEA

**COOPER**, Sara
**Psychoanalytic Psychotherapist**
37 Lansdowne Road
London
N3 1ET
☎ 020 8 349 3891
GUILD

**COOPER**, Terry
**Humanistic Psychotherapist, Somatic Emotional Therapist**
Spectrum
7 Endymion Road
London
N4 1EE
☎ 020 8341 2277
terrycooper@spectrumtherapy.co.uk
SPEC

**CORSO**, Teresa
**Existential Psychotherapist**
36 Burgoyne Road
London
N4 1AD
☎ 020 8347 9597
☎ 07950 331 533
teresacorso@hotmail.com
SEA

**CORTI**, Lucia
**Lacanian Analyst, Psychoanalytic Psychotherapist**
work
N19 5BJ
☎ 020 8341 6953
lu@luciacorti.fsnet.co.uk
4b Elder Avenue
Crouch End
London
N8 9TH
CFAR

**COUZYN**, Jeni
**Psychoanalytic Psychotherapist**
♿ 30 Chestnut Avenue
London
N8 8NY
☎ 020 8 340 5697
jeni@firelizard.co.uk
GUILD

**COWAN-JENSSEN**, Susan
**Integrative Psychotherapist, Primal Psychotherapist**
West Hill House
6 Swains Lane
Highgate
London
N6 6QU
☎ 02072 679 616
☎ 02074 824 212
sue@lapp.org
LAPP

**CRACE**, Gay
**Analytical Psychotherapist**
♿ 125 Ashurst Road
North Finchley
London
N12 9AD
☎ 02084 461 251
gaycrace@lineone.net
AIP, WTC

**CRAWFORD**, Stephen
**Psychoanalytic Psychotherapist**
29 Cromwell Close
East Finchley
London
N2 0LL
☎ 020 8444 8570
FPC

**CRITCHLEY**, Bill
**Gestalt Psychotherapist, Integrative Psychotherapist**
1 Northolme Road
London
N5 2UZ
☎ 020 7354 0745
billcritchley@yahoo.co.uk
GPTI, MET

**CROFTON**, Sue
**Humanistic Psychotherapist, Integrative Psychotherapist**
Spectrum
7 Endymion Road
London
N4 1EE
☎ 020 8904 6433
sue.crofton@btinternet.com
SPEC

**CROWLEY**, Julia
**Psychoanalytic Psychotherapist**
5 Inkwell Close
Woodside Grove
Finchley
London
N12 8QQ
☎ 020 8 446 5161
julia.c@amserve.net
FPC

**CROWTHER**, Catherine
**Analytical Psychologist-Jungian Analyst**
50 Leconfield Road
London
N5 2SN
☎ 020 7226 3112
c.s.crowther@talk21.com
CAP *

**CURTI-GIALDINO**, Francesca
**Family & Systemic Psychotherapist**
29 Parolles Road
London
N19 3RE
☎ 020 7281 3861
AFT

**D**, Niki
**Existential Psychotherapist**
13b Darville Road
Stoke Newington
London
N16 7PT
☎ 07901 926 400
UPCA

**DACRE**, Winnie
**Psychoanalytic Psychotherapist**
11 Finsbury Park Road
London
N4 2LA
☎ 020 7354 0769
AGIP

**DALAL**, Farhad
**Group Analyst**
North East London Psychotherapy & Counselling Asso
24 Kyverdale Road
Stoke Newington
London
N16 7AH
☎ 020 7502 7536
fd@groupanalyticnetwork.co.uk
IGA

**DANIELS**, Orpa
**Couple Psychoanalytic Psychotherapist**
4 Shortgate
Woodside Park
London
N12 7JP
☎ 020 8922 5223
apro_dan@hotmail.com
Flat 1
75 Cromwell Avenue
Highgate
N6 5HS
SCPP

**DANIELS**, Susan
**Psychoanalytic Psychotherapist**
4 Finsbury Park Road
London
N4 2JZ
☎ 020 7 503 8154
scdaniels@talk21.com
IPSS

**DAR**, Limor
**Integrative Arts Psychotherapist**
112 North View Road
London
N8 7LP
☎ 02083 404 929
limordar@ukonline.co.uk
IATE

**DAVENPORT**, Marie-Laure
**Group Analyst, Psychoanalytic Psychotherapist**
♿ 28 Onslow Gardens
London
N10 3JU
☎ 02084 444 695
☎ 02084 510 070
PA, WTC

**DAVIDE**, Adele
**Analytical Psychologist-Jungian Analyst**
5 Raleigh Street
Islington
London
N1 8NW
☎ 020 7226 5250
AJA

**DAVIS**, Susan
**Psychosynthesis Psychotherapist**
8 Perth Road
London
N4 3HB
☎ 0207 281 3799
sld.8@virgin.net
PET

**DAVIS**, Wendy
**Integrative Psychotherapist**
22 Mountfield Road
London
N3 3NE
☎ 020 8349 4178
AHPP

**DAVY**, Rosalind
**Psychoanalytic Psychotherapist**
11 Collingwood Avenue
Muswell Hill
London
N10 3EH
☎ 020 8444 3986
redary@waitrose.com
IPSS

**DAWSON**, Neil K
**Family & Systemic Psychotherapist**
24 Compton Terrace
London
N1 2UN
☎ 020 7704 6112
IFT

**DIANIN**, Gianni
**Psychoanalytic Psychotherapist**
24 Morley Avenue
Wood Green
London
N22 6LY
☎ 020 7377 7976
☎ 020 8888 7338
gianni.dianin@bluebell0.demon.co.uk
ARBS, FIP

**DOBBS**, Wendy
**Psychoanalytic Psychotherapist**
2 Giesbach Road
London
N19 3EH
☎ 020 7272 4207
AGIP, FIP

**DODGE**, Elizabeth
**Family & Systemic Psychotherapist**
♿ The Phoenix Wing
St Ann's Hospital
St Ann's Road
London
N15 3TH
☎ 020 8442 6387
IFT

**DOMB**, Yair
**Child Psychotherapist**
1 Coleraine Cottages
London
N2 9HJ
☎ 020 8883 7694
ACP

**DORRIAN**, Maeve
**Integrative Psychotherapist**
19a Mount Pleasant Villas
Hornsey
London
N4 4HH
☎ 020 7263 0750
maevedorrian@clara.co.uk
SPCRC

**DOUST**, Gill
**Humanistic and Integrative Psychotherapist**
1 Duckett Road
London
N4 1BJ
☎ 020 8341 9168
☎ 020 8341 2277
gilldoust@spectrumtherapy.co.uk
Spectrum
7 Endymion Road
London
N4 1EE
SPEC

**DOWLING**, Emilia
**Family & Systemic Psychotherapist**
29 Lynmouth Road
London
N2 9LR
☎ 020 8444 6795
☎ 020 7435 7111
emilia@dowling29.freeserve.co.uk
IFT

**DRIVER**, Christine
**Psychoanalytic Psychotherapist**
71 Umfreville Road
Harringay
London
N4 1RZ
☎ 020 8340 3324
FPC

**DUTTON**, Jane
**Systemic Psychotherapist**
97 Foulden Road
London
N16 7UH
☎ 020 7249 3993
IFT

**EFSTRATIOU**, Alida
**Integrative Arts Psychotherapist**
69 Blake Road
London
N11 2AG
☎ 020 8361 4845
IATE

**EGERT**, Susan
**Psychoanalytic Psychotherapist**
136 Winston Road
London
N16 9LJ
☎ 020 7254 0526
GUILD

**EINHORN**, Sue
**Group Analyst, Psychoanalytic Psychotherapist**
18 Mount Pleasant Villas
London
N4 4HD
☎ 02072 817 184
sue.einhorn@talk21.com
IGA, SITE

**ELEFTHERIADOU**, Zack
**Integrative Psychotherapist, Psychoanalytic Psychotherapist**
9 Woodside Avenue
London
N6 4SP
☎ 02084 444 042
zack@dircon.co.uk
NAFSI, SPCRC

**ELLIOTT**, Lois
**Psychoanalytic Psychotherapist**
112 Nelson Road
London
N8 9RN
☎ 020 8348 8419
ARBS

**ELLIS**, Mary Lynne
**Psychoanalytic Psychotherapist**
78 Huddleston Road
London
N7 0EG
☎ 020 7687 2206
SITE

**EMANUEL**, Louise
**Child Psychotherapist**
52 Inderwick Road
London
N8 9LD
☎ 020 8348 7032
ACP

**ENDER**, Beckett
**Psychosynthesis Psychotherapist**
124b North View Road
London
N8 7LP
☎ 02089 055 937
☎ 02083 409 423
beckettender@aol.com
IPS

**ENDER**, Dorry
**Psychosynthesis Psychotherapist**
36 Heysham Road
London
N15 6HL
☎ 0207 349 996
☎ 02088 096 061
therapeutics@blueyonder.co.uk
IPS

**EPSTEIN**, Bunny (F.C)
**Integrative Psychotherapist**
156 Gladesmore Road
London
N15 6TH
☎ 020 8802 0761
SPCRC

**EPSTEIN**, June
**Integrative Psychotherapist**
1 Cyprus Gardens
London
N3 1SP
☎ 020 8346 6082
j.epstein@btopenworld.com
SPCRC

**ERNST**, Sheila
**Group Analyst**
53 Manor Road
Stoke Newington
London
N16 5BH
☎ 020 8800 7371
sheila.ernst@btinternet.com
IGA

**ESSENHIGH**, Caroline
**Child Psychotherapist**
114 De Beauvoir Road
London
N1 4DJ
☎ 020 7241 1361
ACP

**EVANS**, Caron
**Psychoanalytic Psychotherapist**
♿ Focus ICTP
6 Swains Lane
London
N6 6QU
☎ 020 7482 3505
☎ 020 7383 5696
caron@evans3752.fsnet.co.uk
IPSS

**FAGAN**, Margaret
**Psychoanalytic Psychotherapist**
76 Twyford Avenue
London
N2 9NN
☎ 020 8883 9095
ARBS

**FAGIN**, Dee
**Psychoanalytic Psychotherapist**
9 Wormesley Road
Crouch End
London
N8 9AE
☎ 020 8340 0879
dfagin@blueyonder.co.uk
AGIP

**FARELL**, Em
**Integrative Psychotherapist**
26 Freegrove Road
London
N7 9RQ
☎ 020 7609 0507
emfreegrove@aol.com
SPCRC

**FARLEIGH**, Laura
**Integrative Arts Psychotherapist**
35 Windermere Avenue
London
N3 5SR
☎ 020 8346 5507
IATE

**FARRELL**, Em
**Integrative Psychotherapist**
26 Freegrove Road
London
N7 9RQ
☎ 020 7609 0507
emfreegrove@aol.com
SPCRC

**FELDMAN**, Wendy
**Child Psychotherapist**
5 Cholmeley Crescent
Highgate
London
N6 5EZ
☎ 020 8340 0878
ACP

**FERGUSON MA**, Peter
**Transpersonal Psychotherapist**
3A Fitzroy Lodge
The Grove
Highgate Village
London
N6 6LH
☎ 020 8348 0331
peter.ferguson@virgin.net
CCPE

**FERGUSON**, Geoffrey
**Psychoanalytic Psychotherapist**
20 Mayfield Avenue
London
N14 6DU
☎ 020 7428 5955
☎ 020 8847 5955
geoff.ferguson@casa.org.uk
FIP

**FINCH**, Helen
**Group Analytic Psychotherapist**
21 Etheldene Avenue
London
N10 3QG
☎ 02088 830 392
helen.finch@btconnect.com
UPCA

**FISHER**, Jinny
**Psychoanalytic Psychotherapist**
27 Leicester Road
East Finchley
London
N2 9DY
☎ 020 8883 5125
jinny@fisherlevine.plus.com
GUILD, WTC

**FISHER**, Kim
**Existential Psychotherapist**
50 Buckmaster House
London
N7 9SB
☎ 020 7687 6913
☎ 07788 776 012
kim@fisher4433.fsworld.co.uk
UPCA

**FITZGERALD**, Jim
**Analytical Psychologist-Jungian Analyst, Analytical Psychotherapist (Jungian)**
30 St. John's Road
London
N15 6QP
☎ 020 8802 6395
jfitzger3o@hotmail.com
IGAP, GAPS

**FLATT**, Raymond
**Psychoanalytic Psychotherapist**
89 Swain's Lane
Highgate
London
N6 6PJ
☎ 020 8341 9407
raymondflatt@lineone.net
FPC

**FOGEL**, Vivienne
**Psychosynthesis Psychotherapist**
♿ 105a Rathcoole Gardens
Crouch End
London
N8 9PH
☎ 020 8374 7224
vivwynant@lineone.net
PET

**FORSTER**, Sally
**Humanistic Psychotherapist**
141 Hemingford Road
London
N1 1BZ
☎ 020 7700 7285
AHPP, MC

**FORTI**, Laura
**Psychoanalytic Psychotherapist**
♿ 38 Berkeley Road
Crouch End
London
N8 8RU
☎ 020 8348 6933
ARBS

**FOX**, Loretta
**Psychosynthesis Psychotherapist**
♿ 1 Helen Court
Hendon Lane
Finchley
London
N3 3SX
☎ 020 8349 0448
PET

**FOX**, Su
**Humanistic Psychotherapist**
50 Burma Road
London
N16 9BJ
☎ 020 7275 8002
sufox@blueyonder.co.uk
AHPP

**FRAWLEY**, Thomas Oliver
**Existential Psychotherapist**
33c Bouverie Road
Stoke Newington
London
N16 0AH
☎ 020 8809 0211
☎ 07890 207 252
SEA

**FRAZER**, Diane
**Psychoanalytic Psychotherapist**
AGIP
1 Fairbridge Road
London
N19 3EW
☎ 020 7272 7013
AGIP

**FREEDMAN**, Jax
**Humanistic and Integrative Psychotherapist**
Spectrum
7 Endymion Road
London
N4 1EE
☎ 020 7732 9353
☎ 07989 080 271
janejax@bt.openworld.com
SPEC

**FREEMAN**, Catherine
**Psychoanalytic Psychotherapist**
AGIP
1 Fairbridge Road
London
N19 3EW
☎ 020 7272 7013
☎ 020 8881 3883
catherinederenn@blueyonder.co.uk
AGIP

**FREEMAN**, Sue
**Psychoanalytic Psychotherapist**
5a Winchester Road
Highgate
London
N6 5HW
☎ 020 8348 8889
SJF4@hotmail.com
FPC

**GALLAGHER**, Teresa
**Integrative Psychotherapist**
ICAP
79 1/2 Tollington Park
London
N4 3AG
teresa@icap.org.uk
SPCRC

**GELBERG**, Gilla
**Integrative Psychotherapist**
52 Park Avenue
North London
N8 7RT
☎ 02083 485 756
☎ 07879 693 847
ggjw@btinternet.com
MC

**GLANTZ**, Robert
**Psychoanalytic Psychotherapist**
♿ 75 Huddleston Road
London
N7 OAE
☎ 020 7609 3330
robertglanz@hotmail.com
IPSS

**GLYNN**, Tania
**Psychoanalytic Psychotherapist**
Flat 1
159 Stapleton Hall Road
London
N4 4QS
☎ 020 8348 1337
tglynn@dircon.co.uk
GUILD

**GOODRICH**, Diana
**Psychoanalytic Psychotherapist**
16 Clifton Road
Crouch End
London
N8
☎ 020 8374 0968
☎ 020 8374 0968
FPC, GUILD, WPF

**GORDON**, Elizabeth
**Analytical Psychologist-Jungian Analyst, Analytical Psychotherapist (Jungian)**
68 Hornsey Lane
London
N6 5LU
☎ 020 7263 7266
elizabeth_gordon@onetel.net.uk
IGAP, GAPS

**GORRELL BARNES**, Gill
**Family & Systemic Psychotherapist**
♿ 89 Southwood Lane
Highgate
London
N6 5TB
☎ 020 8348 9029
gilbarnes@fam.org.com
IFT

**GOSLETT**, Kate
**Psychoanalytic Psychotherapist**
83 Axminster Road
London
N7 6BS
☎ 020 7 272 8322
IPSS

**GOW**, Marion
**Psychoanalytic Psychotherapist**
N8
☎ 02083 478 748
Bema@RMplc.co.uk
GUILD, SITE, WTC

**GRAHAM**, Anthony
**Systemic Psychotherapist**
Upper Street Multi Cultural
Counselling Centre
24-27 White Lion Street
London
N1 9PD
☎ 02078 373 303
multicult@hotmail.com
KCC

**GRAHAM**, Judith
**Gestalt Psychotherapist, Humanistic Psychotherapist**
12 Almeida Street
London
N1 1TA
☎ 020 7354 2240
☎ 020 7704 6900
jugrfrog@dircon.co.uk
AHPP

**GRANOWSKI**, Margaret
**Integrative Psychotherapist**
191 Brecknock Road
London
N19 5AB
☎ 020 7 485 5274
gronski@lineone.net
MC

**GRANT**, Rosamund
**Psychoanalytic Psychotherapist**
146 Maryland Road
London
N22 5AP
☎ 020 8889 6814
rosamund.grant@virgin.net
GUILD

**GRANVILLE**, Julia
**Family & Systemic Psychotherapist**
4 Quernmore Road
London
N4 4QU
☎ 07947 611 025
IFT

**GREEN**, Brian
**Psychoanalytic Psychotherapist**
Alwyne Road
Islington
London
N1
☎ 020 7225 3514
FPC

**GREENSMITH**, Katherine
**Group Analytic Psychotherapist**
29 Limes Avenue
London
N12 8QN
☎ 020 8446 2055
FPC

**GROSS**, Stephen
**Analytical Psychologist-Jungian Analyst**
5 Barnard Hill
Muswell Hill
London
N10 2HB
☎ 020 8444 0598
stephengross37@hotmail.com
AIP

**GROSS**, Vivienne
**Family & Systemic Psychotherapist**
5 Barnard Hill
Muswell Hill
London
N10 2HB
☎ 020 8444 0598
vivgross@hotmail.com
IFT

**GURION**, Michal
**Child Psychotherapist**
28 Princes Avenue
London
N22 4SA
☎ 020 8881 0026
michi@gurion.demon.co.uk
ACP

**GÜNGÖR**, Dilek
**Group Analytic Psychotherapist**
7 Palace Gates Road
Woodgreen
London
N22 7BW
☎ 020 8881 1921
☎ 020 7686 8666
DILEKFridaKahlo@aol.com
Family Welfare Association
Hackney Well Family
Woodbury Down Community Primar
Woodbury Grove, London
N4 1SY
NAFSI, UPCA

**HABERLIN**, Jane
**Psychoanalytic Psychotherapist**
♿ 73 Huddleston Road
Tufnell Park
London
N7 0AE
☎ 07961 355 792 (voicemail)
☎ 02083 660 505
JaneHaberlin@yahoo.co.uk
ARBS, WTC

**HADARY**, Gideon
**Child Psychotherapist**
8 Highgate Edge
Great North Road
London
N2 0NT
☎ 020 8374 8295
ACP

**HALL**, Guy
**Psychoanalytic Psychotherapist**
13 Falkland Avenue
London
N3 1QR
☎ 020 8343 0069
rabbi@beeb.net
FIP

**HALL**, Kirsty
**Psychoanalytic Psychotherapist**
134 Dukes Avenue
London
N10 2QB
☎ 020 8883 9681
kirsty@freudian11.demon.co.uk
SITE

**HALTON**, William
**Child Psychotherapist**
10 Lincoln Road
London
N2 9DL
☎ 020 8444 7497
ACP

**HAMILTON**, Dorothy
**Psychoanalytic Psychotherapist**
AGIP
1 Fairbridge Road
London
N19 3EW
☎ 020 7272 7013
AGIP

**HAMROGUE**, Tom
**Group Analyst**
♿ North London Cetre for Group Psychotherapy
138 Bramley Road
Oakwood
London
N14
☎ 020 8888 6315
☎ 020 7431 2693
IGA

**HANCOCK**, Maureen
**Gestalt Psychotherapist**
233 Biddestone Road
Islington
London
N7 9UE
☎ 020 7700 3298
GCL

**HANNON**, Letizia M
**Educational Therapist**
53 Bethune Road
London
N16 5EE
☎ 020 8802 3430
CFET

**HARGREAVES**, Judy
**Humanistic Psychotherapist**
Spectrum
7 Endymion Road
London
N4 1EE
☎ 020 8749 1964
☎ 020 8341 2277
judyhargreaves@spectrumtherapy.co.uk
SPEC

**HARPER**, Anita
**Transpersonal Psychotherapist**
62 Highgate Hill
London
N19 5NQ
☎ 020 7 263 2005
anita@123harper.freeserve.co.uk
CCPE

**HARPER**, Eric
**Psychoanalytic Psychotherapist**
35 Alexandra Road
London
N4 2LQ
☎ 07815 731 701
eric.harper@btopenworld.com
SITE

**HARRIS**, Mary
**Integrative Psychotherapist**
126b St. Paul's Road
London
N1 2LP
☎ 020 7288 2546
marry.harris@blueyonder.co.uk
SPCRC

**HARRIS**, Tirril
**Psychoanalytic Psychotherapist**
♿ 6 Tufnell Park Road
London
N7 0DP
☎ 020 7928 9292 ext6905
☎ 020 7272 3073
tirril.harris@kcl.ac.uk
FIP

**HARTMAN**, Wendy
**Psychoanalytic Psychotherapist**
19 Baalbec Road
Highbury Fields
London
N5 1QN
☎ 020 7226 4775
Wendyjoyhartman@aol.com
FPC

**HARVEY**, Trudy
**Psychoanalytic Psychotherapist**
♿ 58 Park Hall Road
London
N2 9PX
☎ 02084 445 456
WTC

**HARWARD**, Matthew
**Psychoanalytic Psychotherapist**
214 Middle Lane
Crouch End
London
N8 7LA
☎ 01223 720863
☎ 07808 612 777
matthew.harward@ntlworld.com
ARBS

**HASKINS**, Nicola
**Transpersonal Psychotherapist**
Highbury
London
N5
☎ 020 7226 6680
CCPE

**HAUGH**, Sheila
**Integrative Psychotherapist**
♿ 101 Albert Road
Alexandra Palace
London
N22 7AG
☎ 0790 996 5136
shaugh@compuserve.com
SPCRC

**HAZELTON**, Sally
**Integrative Psychotherapist**
10 Glaserton Road
London
N16 5QX
☎ 020 7502 8129
SPCRC

**HEARST**, Liesel
**Group Analyst**
♿ The North London Centre for Group Therapy
138 Bramley Road
Oakwood
N14 4UH
☎ 020 8440 1451
nlcent@aol.com
IGA

**HEISMANN**, Elisabeth
**Systemic Psychotherapist**
81 - 83b Arlington Avenue
London
N1 7BA
☎ 020 7226 3946
KCC

**HEMMING**, Judith
**Gestalt Psychotherapist**
79 Ronalds Road
London
N5 1XB
☎ 020 7359 3000
jfwhemming@dial.pipex.com
GPTI

**HENDERSON**, David
**Analytical Psychotherapist**
90b Harberton Road
London
N19 3JP
☎ 02072 816 219
henderson@dial.pipex.com
AIP, UPCA

**HERTZMANN**, Leezah
**Attachment-based Psychoanalytic Psychotherapist**
West Hill House
6 Swaine Lane
London
N6 6QS
☎ 07956 670 410
☎ 01923 833 620
CAPP

**HEWISON**, David
**Analytical Psychologist-Jungian Analyst, Couple Psychoanalytic Psychotherapist**
2 Lincoln Road
East Finchley
London
N2 9DL
☎ 020 7435 7111
☎ 020 8442 2601
mail@davidhewison.com
CAP, TMSI, SCPP

**HEWITT**, Amanda
**Family & Systemic Psychotherapist**
♿ Home Farm
Totteridge Green
London
N20 8PH
☎ 020 8445 7882
AFT

**HEWITT**, Rosalind
**Sexual and Relationship Psychotherapist**
Highgate
N6
☎ 020 8340 4824
☎ 07904 228 283
rosalind.hewitt@btinternet.com
BASRT

**HIGH**, Helen
**Educational Therapist**
7 Hillside Gardens
Highgate
London
N6 5SU
☎ 020 8340 7037
helen@highandwatt.com
CFET

**HILDER**, Alison
**Child Psychotherapist**
7 Quick Street
London
N1 8HL
☎ 020 7278 2088
ACP

**HIRST**, Sue
**Psychoanalytic Psychotherapist**
1 Fairbridge Road
London
N19 3EW
☎ 020 7272 7013
AGIP

**HOLLAND**, Stevie
**Attachment-based Psychoanalytic Psychotherapist**
♿ 7 Cheverton Road
Upper Holloway
London
N19 3BB
☎ 020 7263 4184
CAPP

**HOLLINGS**, Avril
**Humanistic Psychotherapist**
West Hill House
6 Swains Lane
Highgate
London
N6 6QU
☎ 020 8444 0670
avril.hollings@ukonline.co.uk
AHPP

**HOLLOWS**, Belinda
**Existential Psychotherapist**
Flat 4
334-338 Essex Road
London
N1 3PB
☎ 02073 545 871
☎ 07789 430 841
belindahollows@hotmail.com
UPCA

**HOLT**, Alexandra
**Psychoanalytic Psychotherapist**
Stoke Newington
London
N16
☎ 020 7254 2162
ARBS

**HOPE**, Francis
**Psychosynthesis Psychotherapist**
♿ 4 Highbury Terrace Mews
London
N5 1UT
☎ 02072 269 798
☎ 02072 264 900
fhope@globalnet.co.uk
IPS

**HOQUE**, Rumman
**Psychoanalytic Psychotherapist**
20 Canning Road
Highbury
London
N5 2JS
NAFSI

**HORSMAN**, Val
**Psychoanalytic Psychotherapist**
3 Carysfort Road
London
N16 9AA
☎ 020 7249 7846
GUILD

**HOWELL**, Carolyn
**Transpersonal Psychotherapist**
36A Mildmay Road (Basement Flat)
London
N1 4NG
☎ 020 7275 8715
CCPE

**HUDSON**, Alan
**Family & Systemic Psychotherapist**
6 Redston Road
Hornsey
London
N8 7HJ
☎ 020 8340 9145
☎ 020 7854 5890
Alan.Hudson@rbkc.gov.uk
IFT

**HUDSON**, Inge
**Group Analyst, Psychoanalytic Psychotherapist**
♿ Stroud Green
London
N4
☎ 02072 811 710
inge.hudson@virgin.net
IGA, UPCA, WTC

**HUDSON**, Pauline
**Systemic Psychotherapist**
68 Tetherdown
London
N10 1NG
☎ 020 8883 7662
☎ 020 7515 6633
hudsonple@aol.com or
husdonp@elcmht.nhs.uk
KCC

**HUMPHRIES**, Harold W A
**Psychoanalytic Psychotherapist**
1 Fairbridge Road
London
N19 3EW
☎ 01453 757 900
AGIP

**HUNNEYBELL**, Darrel
**Psychosynthesis Psychotherapist**
36 Heysham Road
London
N15 6HL
☎ 02088 096 061
IPS

**HURST**, Hannah
**Attachment-based Psychoanalytic Psychotherapist**
55 Maury Road
London
N16 7BT
☎ 020 8806 1909
hannah@oakhurt1.freeserve.co.uk
CAPP

**HUTCHINSON**, Sylvia
**Group Analyst**
♿ North London Centre for Group Therapy
138 Bramley Road
Oakwood
N14 4HU
☎ 020 8440 1451
nlcent@aol.com
IGA

**INLANDER**, Antonia
**Psychoanalytic Psychotherapist**
AGIP
1 Fairbridge Road
London
N19 3EW
☎ 020 7272 7013
AGIP

**ISAKSSON-HURST**, Gun I.E.
**Integrative Psychotherapist, Transactional Analysis Psychotherapist**
344 Alexandra Park Road
Muswell Hill
London
N22 7BD
☎ 0208 881 4266
allhurst@msn.com
MET

**IVESON**, Diana
**Family & Systemic Psychotherapist**
77 Muswell Avenue
London
N10 2EH
☎ 020 8883 5731
Chrisiveson@brieftherapy.org.uk
IFT

**JACKSON**, Eve
**Analytical Psychologist-Jungian Analyst**
54 Eade Road
London
N4 1DH
☎ 020 8800 1418
unus.mundus@blueyonder.co.uk
IGAP

**JACKSON**, Maureen
**Hypno-Psychotherapist**
Phoenix House
12 Overton Road
Oakwood
London
N14 4SY
☎ 02083 607 019
maureen-jackson@tiscali.co.uk
NRHP

**JAMES**, Jessica
**Group Analyst, Psychoanalytic Psychotherapist**
♿ 26 Kyverdale Road
London
N16 7AH
☎ 02088 064 820
jessicaj@blueyonder.co.uk
IGA, WTC

**JARVIS**, Charlotte
**Child Psychotherapist**
Open Door
12 Middle Lane
London
N8 8PL
☎ 020 8348 5947
ACP

**JEFFERIES**, Alison
**Integrative Psychotherapist**
16 Summerlee Gardens
East Finchley
London
N2 9QN
☎ 0208 883 3070
Alison.Jefferies@Brunel.ac.uk
MC

**JENSSEN**, Einar D.
**Integrative Psychotherapist, Primal Psychotherapist**
West Hill House
6 Swains Lane
Highgate
London
N6 6QU
☎ 02072 679 616
☎ 02074 824 212
einar@lapp.org
LAPP

**JOHANSSON**, Birgitta
**Psychoanalytic Psychotherapist**
♿ 45 Ashley Road
London
N19 3AG
☎ 020 7 281 9567
big.jssn@virgin.net
GUILD

**JOHN-BAPTISTE**, Louisa
**Psychoanalytic Psychotherapist**
62A Kingsdown Road
London
N19 4LW
☎ 020 7272 6541
louisa@traininglink.org.uk
IPSS

**JOHNSON**, Kay
**Lacanian Analyst, Psychoanalytic Psychotherapist**
89 Grosvenor Avenue
London
N5 2NL
☎ 020 7354 0651
CFAR

**JONES**, Alan
**Integrative Psychotherapist**
85 Finn House
Bevenden Street
London
N1 1BL
☎ 020 7566 0043
SPCRC

**JONES**, Annvirginia
**Systemic Psychotherapist**
31 Elmhurst Avenue
East Finchley
London
N2 0LT
☎ 020 8365 3849
North London Hospice
47 Woodside Avenue
Finchley
N12 8TF
KCC

**KAUR**, Manshant Rani
**Psychoanalytic Psychotherapist**
11 Holbrooke Court
Tufnell Park Road
London
N7 0PW
☎ 020 7607 6273
☎ 020 7687 0410
arnilaxmi@yahoo.co.uk
IPSS

**KEANE**, Barry
**Psychoanalytic Psychotherapist**
2a St George's Avenue
Tufnell Park
London
N7 0HD
☎ 020 7609 7313
FPC

**KEEDY-LILLEY**, Ray
**Hypno-Psychotherapist**
28 Finsbury Park Road
London
N4 2JX
NSHAP

**KELLY**, Michael
**Psychoanalytic Psychotherapist**
132 Stapleton Hall Road
London
N4 4QB
☎ 020 8340 9597
ARBS, IGA

**KENDAL**, Susan J.
**Cognitive Behavioural Psychotherapist**
♿ 6 Queenswood Park
London
N3 1UN
skendal@kendal.homechoice.co.uk
BABCP

**KENNY**, Angela
**Psychoanalytic Psychotherapist**
128 Nevill Road
Stoke Newington
London
N16 0SX
☎ 020 7254 8558
a.l.kenny@tesco.net
AGIP

**KENNY**, Miranda H.
**Psychoanalytic Psychotherapist**
63 Maury Road
Stoke Newington
London
N16 7BT
☎ 020 8806 9202
mhk@mirandakenny.fsnet.co.uk
CAPP, FIP

**KERBEKIAN**, Rosalie
**Child Psychotherapist**
Flat 3
West Hill Court
Millfield Lane
London
N6 6JJ
☎ 020 8348 8575
ACP

**KIDD**, Lee
**Psychoanalytic Psychotherapist**
13 Brambledown Mansions
Crouch Hill
London
N4 4SA
☎ 020 7281 3435
lee@leekidd.com
FPC

**KOPPELMAN**, Liora
**Couple Psychoanalytic Psychotherapist**
135 Southwood Lane
Highgate
London
N6 5TA
☎ 020 8455 3092
michaelk@wkoppelman.freeserve.co.uk
SCPP

**KOSTIC**, Jasna
**Integrative Psychotherapist, Primal Psychotherapist**
West Hill House
6 Swains Lane
Highgate
London
N6 6QU
☎ 02072 679 616
☎ 02074 824 212
LAPP

**KRAJNOVIC**, Valentina J
**Group Analyst**
The Manor House Centre for Psychotherapy and Counselling, 80 East End Road
London
N3 2SY
☎ 020 8371 0180
IGA

**KRAMER**, Claudia
**Psychoanalytic Psychotherapist**
69 Fallowcourt Avenue
London
N12 0BE
☎ 020 7938 0939
☎ 020 8445 1952
ckramer@onetel.net.uk
FIP

**KREEGER**, Angela
**Psychoanalyst**
5 Russell Road
Bowes Park
London
N13 4RS
☎ 020 8888 8329
akreeger@waitrose.com
SITE

**KRZOWSKI**, Sue
**Psychoanalytic Psychotherapist**
39A Axminster Road
London
N7 6BP
☎ 020 7 272 6379
GUILD

**L'ESTRANGE**, Jeanette
**Transpersonal Psychotherapist**
London
N3
CCPE

**LALLAH**, Regine
**Psychoanalytic Psychotherapist**
2 Greville Lodge
40 Avenue Road
London
N6 5DP
☎ 020 8340 9943
FPC

**LANDAW**, John
**Attachment-based Psychoanalytic Psychotherapist**
10 Kingsley Place
Highgate
London
N6 5EA
☎ 020 8245 3758
john@landaw.com
CAPP

**LANDI**, Donatella
**Attachment-based Psychoanalytic Psychotherapist**
56 Queen's Avenue
London
N10 3NU
☎ 020 8374 2553
CAPP

**LANG**, Richard
**Integrative Psychotherapist**
87B Cazenove Road
London
N16 6BB
☎ 02088 063 710
☎ 07968 845 825
headexchange@gn.apc.org
MC

**LATHAM**, Valerie
**Transpersonal Psychotherapist**
London
77 The Grove
N13 5JS
☎ 020 8367 7463
valerielatham@aol.com
CCPE

**LAVILLE**, Vicki
**Psychoanalytic Psychotherapist**
3c Pemberton Gardens
London
N19 5RR
☎ 02072 815 257
NAFSI

**LAWLEY**, James
**Neurolinguistic Psychotherapist**
9 Southwood Lawn Road
Highgate
London
N6 5SD
☎ 02083 411 062
james@cleanlanguage.co.uk
NLPtCA

**LAZARUS**, Myrna
**Family & Systemic Psychotherapist**
30 Jackson's Lane
Highgate
London
N6 5SX
☎ 020 8348 2886
1@myrnalazarus.fsnet.co.uk
AFT

**LEDERMAN**, Tsafi
**Biodynamic Psychotherapist**
15 Harberton Road
London
N19 3JS
☎ 02072 638 551
LSBP

**LEE**, Simone
**Existential Psychotherapist**
50 Wentworth Avenue
London
N3 1YL
☎ 020 8349 9889
hermeneutic@hotmail.com
SPCRC, SEA

**LEPPER**, Georgia
**Analytical Psychologist-Jungian Analyst**
92 Red Square
Carysfort Road
London
N16 9AG
☎ 020 7503 4483
georgia@lepper.co.uk
CCOPPP

**LESLIE**, Tina
**Integrative Arts Psychotherapist**
103 Frobisher Road
London
N8 0QU
☎ 020 8347 9396
tinakinsgate@hotmail.com
IATE

**LEVENS**, Mary
**Psychodrama Psychotherapist**
12 Edmunds Walk
Hampstead Garden Suburb
London
N2 0HU
☎ 020 8444 5869
mlevens@btopenworld.com
BPA

**LEVITT**, Olga
**Systemic Psychotherapist**
"Normandy"
Northcliffe Drive
London
N20 8JX
☎ 020 8446 1313
olga@levitt.co.uk
KCC

**LEWIS**, Jacqueline
**Existential Psychotherapist**
17 Woodside Avenue
London
N6 4SP
☎ 020 8444 9457
☎ 07930 442 630
jackylewis@blueyonder.co.uk
SEA

**LEYGRAF**, Bernd C
**Humanistic and Integrative Psychotherapist, Sexual and Relationship Psychotherapist**
♿ Flat 3
7 Wedmore Street
London
N19 4RU
☎ 020 7281 5324
☎ +34 958 270 334
leygraf@aol.com
AHPP, BASRT, UPCA

**LIEBLING**, Lauren
**Biodynamic Psychotherapist**
6 Crescent Street
Barnsbury
London
N1 1BT
☎ 020 7700 3995
laurendarling:care4free.net
LSBP

**LIPMAN**, Amanda
**Integrative Psychotherapist**
35 Lavers Road
London
N16 0DU
☎ 020 7254 0863
azlipman@lineone.net
SPCRC

**LISTER**, Patricia Anne
**Cognitive Behavioural Psychotherapist**
23 Wray Crescent
Islington
London
N4 3LN
☎ 020 7686 2849
BABCP

**LODRICK**, Michael
**Group Analyst, Psychoanalytic Psychotherapist**
2c Ronalds Road
London
N5 1XH
☎ 020 7609 9112
☎ 01986 896 419
lodrick@ukonline.co.uk
FPC, IGA

**LOUSADA**, Olivia
**Psychodrama Psychotherapist**
♿ 14 Allerton Road
London
N16 5UJ
☎ 020 8802 5284
olivia_lousada@boysgirlstwins.org
BPA

**LOUW**, Francois
**Integrative Psychotherapist**
Flat 2 88 Cromwell Avenue
Highgate
London
N6 5HQ
☎ 020 8342 5212
francois.louw@cnwl.nhs.uk
SPTI

**LOVEGROVE**, Sherine
**Neurolinguistic Psychotherapist**
8 Cascade Avenue
Muswell Hill
London
N10 3PU
☎ 02084 442 249
sherine@bluetarn.com
NLPtCA

**LYNCH**, Monica
**Systemic Psychotherapist**
♿ The Northern Health Centre
580 Holloway Road
London
N7 6LB
☎ 020 7445 8150
monica.lynch@nhs.net
IFT

**LYNDON**, Barbara
**Educational Therapist, Psychoanalytic Psychotherapist**
Agip
1 Fairbridge Road
London
N19 3EW
☎ 020 7372 8009
barbaralyndon@talk21.com
AGIP, CFET

**MACADAM**, Gregor
**Attachment-based Psychoanalytic Psychotherapist**
19 Belmont Avenue
Turnpike Lane
London
N17 6AX
☎ 020 8888 1626
CAPP

**MACLEAN**, Annie
**Integrative Psychotherapist**
Garden Flat
31 Navarino Road
Hackney
London
E8 1AD
☎ 020 7241 3794
MET

**MACNICOL**, Fred
**Body Psychotherapist, Integrative Psychotherapist**
66 Dumont Road
London
N16 0NJ
☎ 020 7254 8282
fred.macnicol@virgin.net
CCBP

**MALKIN**, Julius
**Cognitive Behavioural Psychotherapist**
♿ Basement Flat
20 Ashlay Road
London
N19 3AE
☎ 020 7591 7793
☎ 0061 9810 6586
BABCP

**MALKIN**, Marion
**Integrative Psychotherapist, Psychoanalytic Psychotherapist**
1 Fairbridge Road
London
N19 3EW
☎ 020 7272 7013
☎ 07815 122 048
AGIP, SPCRC

**MALONEY**, Chris
**Psychoanalytic Psychotherapist**
13 Barbauld Road
London
N16 0SD
☎ 020 7241 9700
☎ 020 7249 5751
chrismaloney@doctors.org.uk
Somerford Grove Practice
Somerford Grove
London
N16 7UA
FIP, UPCA

**MARCUS-JEDAMZIK**, Deena
**Psychosynthesis Psychotherapist**
37 The Grove
Finchley
London
N3 1QT
☎ 02089 226 241
deena@cryosystem.com
IPS

**MARKS**, Susannah
**Child Psychotherapist**
Hornsey Rise Child & Family Consultation Service
Hornsey Rise Health Centre
London
N19 3YU
☎ 020 7530 2940
ACP

**MARSHALLSAY**, Nicholas
**Analytical Psychologist-Jungian Analyst**
10 Wavel Mews
Park Avenue South
Crouch End
London
N8 8LQ
☎ 020 8340 0169
nm@macace.net
CAP *

**MARTIN**, Stephen
**Child Psychotherapist**
22 Blythwood Road
London
N4 4EU
☎ 020 7272 5090 (t/f)
stephenmartin@freeserve.co.uk
ACP

**MASON**, Dr Barry
**Family & Systemic Psychotherapist**
21 Manor Road
Stoke Newington
London
N16 5BQ
☎ 020 8802 9165
barry@bmason.demon.co.uk
IFT

**MASSIL**, Ros
**Integrative Psychotherapist**
Archway
London
N19
☎ 020 7281 5269
SPCRC

**MASTERS**, David
**Systemic Psychotherapist**
♿ 50 Park Hill
London
N8 8SU
☎ 020 7435 5492
☎ 020 8348 8325
KCC

**MAY**, Catriona
**Integrative Psychotherapist**
♿ 54 Plimsoll Road
London
N4 2EL
☎ 07786 393 284
cat@bearcomm.com
SPCRC

**MAYER**, Robert
**Family & Systemic Psychotherapist**
♿ 44 North Hill
London
N6 4QA
☎ 020 8340 6628
☎ 020 8340 4712
robertmayer@onetel.net.uk
36 Park Avenue South
London
N8 8LT
IFT

**MAZURE**, David
**Integrative Psychotherapist**
169 Avenue Mews
London
N10 3NN
☎ 020 8365 3545
davidmazure@hotmail.com
MC

**MCATEER**, Catherine
**Psychoanalytic Psychotherapist**
AGIP
1 Fairbridge Road
London
N19 3EW
☎ 020 7272 7013
cath@timandcath.com
AGIP

**MCCANN**, Linda
**Family & Systemic Psychotherapist**
Flat 2
14 Clifton Road
Crouch End
London
N8 8HY
☎ 020 8347 8460
linda.mccann@tiscali.co.uk
IFT

**MCELDOWNEY**, Dennis
**Psychoanalytic Psychotherapist**
♿ 76-80 Isledon Road
London
N7 7LB
☎ 020 7700 7458
☎ 020 8 993 1559
dennis@mcel.fslife.co.uk
IPSS

**MCGEE**, Colin
**Psychoanalytic Psychotherapist**
24 Palace Road
Crouch End
London
N8 8QJ
☎ 020 8348 1848
☎ 07951 160309
cmcgee1499@aol.com/Website: avoiceforchange.co.uk
IPSS

**MCKENZIE**, Maggie
**Humanistic Psychotherapist**
Spectrum
7 Endymion Road
London
N4 1EE
☎ 020 8341 2277
m.mckenzie@spectrumtherapy.co.uk
SPEC

**MCKEON**, Mary
**Psychoanalytic Psychotherapist**
219 Fox Lane
Palmers Green
London
N13 4BB
☎ 020 8886 0766
FPC

**MCNEIL**, Delcia
**Humanistic and Integrative Psychotherapist**
Flat 2
56 Queens Avenue
London
N10 3NU
☎ 01539 562 420
☎ 020 8442 0391
delcia.mcneil@virgin.net
SPEC

**MEAD**, Betty
**Psychoanalytic Psychotherapist**
Basement Flat, 13 St. Mark's Mansions
60 Tollington Park
London
N4 3QZ
☎ 020 7263 5822
Bdm@onetel.net.uk
AGIP

**MELLOWS**, David
**Psychoanalytic Psychotherapist**
34 Curzon Road
London
N10 2RA
☎ 07956 370 111
☎ 020 8883 6230
dave.mellows@virgin.net
FIP

**MELLOWS**, Hilary
**Psychoanalytic Psychotherapist**
34 Curzon Road
London
N10 2RA
☎ 01707 655 512
☎ 020 8883 6230
FIP

**MERRICK**, Bozena
**Transpersonal Psychotherapist**
Finchley
London
N12
☎ 07931 340 669
CCPE

**MESSENT**, Philip
**Family & Systemic Psychotherapist**
73 Duckett Road
London
N4 1BL
☎ 020 8340 7915
philip.messent@ntlworld.com
IFT

**METHUEN**, Oriel
**Gestalt Psychotherapist, Humanistic Psychotherapist**
Spectrum
7 Endymion Road
London
N4 1EE
☎ 020 8341 2277
☎ 020 8883 3246
orielmethuen@spectrumtherapy.co.uk
SPEC

**MEZA**, Ann L.
**Transpersonal Psychotherapist**
25 Crane Grove
London
N7 8LD
☎ 020 7607 6805
CCPE

**MICHAEL**, Jess
**Attachment-based Psychoanalytic Psychotherapist**
8 Perth Road
Finsbury Park
London
N4 3HB
☎ 020 7281 1871
CAPP

**MILLER**, Jean
**Sexual and Relationship Psychotherapist**
40 Grosvenor Road
Muswell Hill
London
N10 2DS
☎ 020 8374 2074
jean.miller@lineone.net
BASRT

**MILLER**, Penny
**Attachment-based Psychoanalytic Psychotherapist**
3 Carysfort Road
Stoke Newington
London
N16 9AA
☎ 020 7249 7846
☎ 020 7249 7846
CAPP

**MILLER**, Riva
**Family & Systemic Psychotherapist**
24 Wood Lane
Highgate
London
N6 5UB
☎ 020 8340 3548
IFT

**MILLICHAMP**, Stacey
**Psychosynthesis Psychotherapist**
4 Pembroke Mews
Muswell Hill
London
N10 2JL
☎ 020 8444 2670
staceymillichamp@aol.com
PET

**MILLWARD**, Christopher
**Transpersonal Psychotherapist**
Flat 2
29 Bishops Road
Highgate
London
N6 4HP
☎ 020 8341 2723
CCPE

**MILROY**, Rachel
**Psychoanalytic Psychotherapist**
6 Church Lane,
Crouch End,
London
N8
ARBS

**MILTON**, Alison
**Family & Systemic Psychotherapist**
MHCOP A13, Charterhouse Building
Archway Campus
Wittington Hospital
London
N19 5NF
☎ 020 7530 2317
alison.milton@ccndi.nhs.uk
AFT

**MONTERO**, Isabel
**Psychoanalytic Psychotherapist**
♿ 23 River Avenue
London
N13 5RX
☎ 02088 821 618
ARBS, WTC

**MORAVIA KESSEL**, Inge
**Humanistic and Integrative Psychotherapist**
♿ 96 Winston Road
London
N16 9LR
☎ 020 7690 0966
BCPC

**MORDECAI**, Aslan
**Psychoanalytic Psychotherapist**
Dukebury House
76 Grove Avenue
Muswell Hill
London
N10 2AN
☎ 020 8883 9665
aslan@rakesmordecai.co.uk
FIP

**MORDECAI**, Kay
**Psychoanalytic Psychotherapist**
Dukebury House
76 Grove Avenue
Muswell Hill
London
N10 2AN
☎ 020 8883 9665
kay@rakesmordecai.co.uk
FIP

**MORGAN**, Mary
**Couple Psychoanalytic Psychotherapist**
95 Wilberforce Road
Finsbury Park
London
N4 2SP
☎ 020 7359 0238
m.e.morgan@virgin.net
TMSI, SCPP

**MORLEY**, Elspeth
**Psychoanalytic Psychotherapist, Couple Psychoanalytic Psychotherapist**
43 Highbury Place
London
N5 1QL
☎ 020 7359 2282
elspethmorley@btopenworld.com
FIP, SCPP

**MORLEY**, Robert
**Psychoanalytic Psychotherapist, Couple Psychoanalytic Psychotherapist**
43 Highbury Place
London
N5 1QL
☎ 020 7359 2282
☎ 020 7288 0265
robertmorley@dunelm.org.uk
FIP, SCPP

**MORRIS**, Allan
**Family & Systemic Psychotherapist**
127 Mount View Road
London
N4 4JH
☎ 020 8341 9238
allan.morris@blueyonder.co.uk
IFT

**MORRIS**, Shosh
**Psychoanalytic Psychotherapist**
23C Milner Square
London
N1 1TL
☎ 020 7 359 0258
shosh.morris@virgin.net
GUILD

**MORTON**, Gillian
**Educational Therapist**
17 Haslemere Road
London
N8 9QP
☎ 020 8340 5686
CFET

**MULHERN**, Alan
**Analytical Psychologist-Jungian Analyst**
♿ 30 Danvers Road
London
N8 7HH
☎ 020 8347 6910
☎ 020 8348 9809
A.Mulhern@kingston.ac.uk
AJA

**MUSIC**, Graham
**Child Psychotherapist, Integrative Psychotherapist**
90 Huddlesdon Road
London
N7 0EG
☎ 020 7281 1989
graham.music@onetel.net.uk
ACP, MC

**NAISH**, Julia
**Humanistic Psychotherapist**
Spectrum
7 Endymion Road
London
N4 1EE
☎ 020 8341 2277
julianaish@spectrumtherapy.co.uk
SPEC

**NAVARRO**, Trinidad
**Psychoanalytic Psychotherapist**
154 Downhills Park Road
London
N17 6BP
☎ 020 8888 4217
trini6000@aol.com
ARBS

**NEHMAD**, Annie
**Cognitive Analytic Therapist**
London
N16 0EA
☎ 07957 232 906
ACAT

**NEIVA**, Judith
**Psychoanalytic Psychotherapist**
1 Fairbridge Road
London
N19 3EW
☎ 020 7272 7013
AGIP

**NEUMANN**, Anton
**Psychoanalytic Psychotherapist**
26 Orchard Road
London
N6 5TR
☎ 020 8348 5472
antonneumann@excite.com
AGIP

**NEVINS**, Peter
**Psychoanalytic Psychotherapist**
♿ 45 Queen's Head Street
Islington
London
N1 8NQ
☎ 020 7272 6797 (t/f)
☎ 020 7354 9430
p.nevins@netmatters.co.uk
PA, SITE

**NEWMAN**, Bracha
**Analytical Psychologist-Jungian Analyst**
46 Torrington Park
London
N12 9TP
☎ 020 8343 7510
newmans@compuserve.com
IGAP

**NGAH**, Zah
**Child Psychotherapist**
47 Pentoville Road
London
N1 9LP
☎ 020 7278 8018 (t/f)
bangah@portables1.ngfl.gov
ACP

**NICOLAUS**, Georg
**Integrative Psychosynthesis Psychotherapist**
7 Stanhope Gardens
Highgate
London
N6 5TT
☎ 020 8340 6751
RE.V

**NOACK**, Amelie
**Analytical Psychologist-Jungian Analyst, Group Analyst**
70 Graham Road
London
N15 3NJ
☎ 020 8826 0080
amelienoac@aol.com
AJA, IGA

**NOBLE**, Jane
**Psychoanalytic Psychotherapist**
54 Redston Road
London
N8 7HE
☎ 020 8 348 2801
GUILD

**NODELMAN**, Marsha
**Integrative Psychotherapist, Primal Psychotherapist**
West Hill House
6 Swains Lane
Highgate
London
N6 6QU
☎ 02074 824 212
☎ 02072 679 616
LAPP

**O'CONNOR**, Ann
**Integrative Psychosynthesis Psychotherapist**
31A Highgate High Street
Highgate Village
London
N6 5JT
☎ 020 8348 5721
oconnoranne@compuserve.com
RE.V

**O'CONNOR**, Noreen
**Psychoanalytic Psychotherapist**
78 Huddleston Road
London
N7 0EG
☎ 020 7687 2206
GUILD, SITE

**O'KEEFFE**, Mandy
**Psychoanalytic Psychotherapist**
♿ 67 Avenell Road
London
N5 1BT
☎ 020 7288 2359
okeeffe@onetel.net.uk
AGIP

**O'MALLY**, Gerry
**Analytical Psychotherapist**
Flat 12
10 Cromartie Road
London
N19 3SJ
☎ 020 7281 6829
gerryomalley@cromartie.fsnet.co.uk
SITE

**OAKLEY**, Sanja
**Existential Psychotherapist**
22 Cavendish Road
London
N4 1RT
☎ 020 8348 3484
☎ 07966 463 454
Sanja@sanja.fsnet.co.uk
UPCA

**OHENE**, Margaret D.
**Systemic Psychotherapist**
♿ 16 Wilton Road
Muswell Hill
London
N10 1LS
KCC

**OLIVER**, Mandy
**Integrative Psychotherapist**
13 Oakeshott Avenue
Highgate
London
N6 6NT
☎ 020 7419 0573
SPCRC

**OLIVER**, Rosamund
**Core Process Psychotherapist**
29 Beversbrook Road
Islington
London
N19 4QQ
☎ 020 7 272 3666
KI

**OWENS**, Patti
**Humanistic and Integrative Psychotherapist**
♿ 98 Church Lane
East Finchley
London
N2 0TB
☎ 020 8365 4621
contact@pattiowens.co.uk
AHPP

**PALAMOUNTAIN**, Alan
**Integrative Psychotherapist**
144 Warwick Road
Upper Edmonton
London
N18 1RT
☎ 020 8884 0881
alanp144@yahoo.co.uk
SPCRC

**PANETTA-CREAN**, Simona
**Analytical Psychologist-Jungian Analyst**
15 Landrock Road
London
N8 9HR
☎ 020 8374 9234
☎ 020 8374 9556
simonapanetta@tiscali.co.uk
AIP, CAP *

**PARKER**, Rosie
**Psychoanalytic Psychotherapist**
17 Archibald Road
London
N7 0AN
☎ 020 7700 2097
rozsika.parker@virgin.net
FPC, SITE

**PARKS**, Val
**Psychoanalytic Psychotherapist**
18 Rosemary Avenue
Finchley
London
N3 2QN
☎ 020 8346 6188
valparks@lineone.net
FPC

**PARSONS**, Kathy
**Existential Psychotherapist**
55a Stoke Newington Church Street
London
N16 0AR
☎ 020 7249 6122
kathy@kathyparsons.co.uk
77 Clissold Crescent
London
N16 9AR
UPCA

**PATEL**, Gita
**Psychoanalytic Psychotherapist**
113 Ferme Park Road
London
N8 9SA
☎ 0208 341 3502
NAFSI, WTC

**PATTERSON**, Anna
**Humanistic Psychotherapist**
Spectrum
7 Endymion Road
London
N4 1EE
☎ 020 8341 2277
annapatterson@spectrumtherapy.co.uk
SPEC

**PAULSON**, Diana
**Family & Systemic Psychotherapist**
♿ Islington Child & Family Consultation Service
Northern Health Centre
580 Holloway Road
London
N7 6LB
☎ 020 7445 8150
☎ 020 7267 4857
IFT

**PAYNE**, Lizzi
**Psychoanalytic Psychotherapist**
C/O Arbours Association
6 Church Lane
London
N8 7BU
☎ 07950 933907 (M)
ARBS

**PEARCE**, Gerald
**Integrative Psychotherapist**
♿ 1 Golfers View
54 Finchley Park
London
N12 9JX
☎ 02084 451 867
MET

**PEARCE**, Peter
**Integrative Psychotherapist**
Flat D
90 Hillfield Avenue
Crouch End
London
N8 7DN
☎ 02083 419 525
peter.pearce1@virgin.net
MET

**PENALOSA-CLARKE**, Adriana Lucia
**Systemic Psychotherapist**
28 Fortismere Avenue
London
N10 3BL
KCC

**PENGELLY**, Paul
**Couple Psychoanalytic Psychotherapist**
103 Tottenham Road
London
N1 4EA
☎ 020 7249 7816
paul.pengelly@virgin.net
SCPP

**PENTECOST**, David
24 Evesham Road
London
N11 2RN
☎ 020 8361 5686
davidpentecost@bigfoot.com
AFT

**PEPELI**, Hara
**Lacanian Analyst, Psychoanalytic Psychotherapist**
10 The Avenue
Hornsey
London
N8 0JR
☎ 020 8888 7104
haroulapepeli@hotmail.com
CFAR

**PERICLEOUS**, Christine
**Psychoanalytic Psychotherapist**
47 Ecclesbourne Gardens
London
N13 5JD
☎ 020 8372 8760
christinepericleous@hotmail.com
ARBS

**PERRY**, Ann
**Psychoanalytic Psychotherapist**
35 Huntingdon Street
London
N1 1BP
☎ 020 7609 3378
ann_perry@btopenworld.com
AIP

**PETKOVA**, Petia
**Family & Systemic Psychotherapist**
♿ 99A Balfour Road
London
N5 2HE
☎ 020 7226 5661
petia@tesco.net
AFT

**PHILIP**, Debra
**Systemic Psychotherapist**
11 Bedford Road
London
N15 3BL
KCC

**PHILO**, Judith
**Analytical Psychologist-Jungian Analyst**
194 Tufnell Park Road
London
N7 0EE
☎ 020 7263 1952
CAP *

**PICKSTOCK**, Keith
**Psychosynthesis Psychotherapist**
105 Clissold Crescent
Stoke Newington
London
N16 9AS
☎ 020 7254 4975
keith@pickstock35.freeserve.co.uk
PET

**PIKE**, Joanna
**Psychoanalytic Psychotherapist**
1 Fairbridge Road
London
N19 3EW
☎ 020 7272 7013
jopike@onetel.com
AGIP

**PIMENTEL**, Edna Barreto
**Humanistic and Integrative Psychotherapist**
41 Springcroft Avenue
London
N2 9JH
☎ 020 8883 0511
edna@couto.demon.co.uk
AHPP

**POLLARD**, James
**Attachment-based Psychoanalytic Psychotherapist**
58B Crayford Road
London
N7 0ND
☎ 01223 514 917
james@pollardj.fsnet.co.uk
CAPP

**PRASAD**, Vijaya
**Hypno-Psychotherapist**
Hillcrest Gardens
Finchley
London
N3 3EY
☎ 02083 493 201
vijay@prasad.fsbusiness.co.uk
NRHP

**PRESANT**, Fern
**Integrative Psychotherapist**
22 Osbaldeston Road
London
N16 7DP
☎ 020 8806 8119
FPRB@globalnet.co.uk
MC

**PRESTON**, Kay
**Group Analytic Psychotherapist**
53 Curzon Road
Muswell Hill
London
N10 2RB
☎ 020 8883 9051
020 8883 9051
FPC

**PRIEST**, Caroline
**Systemic Psychotherapist**
83a Uplands Road
London
N8 9NH
☎ 020 8341 6488
☎ 020 8556 6902
carolinepr@aol.com
KCC

**PUDDY**, Jane
**Gestalt Psychotherapist**
80 Hungerford Road
London
N7 9LP
☎ 020 7609 1826
kahan@dircon.co.uk
GCL

**QUOILIN**, Michelle
**Biodynamic Psychotherapist**
98 Malborough Road
Wood Green
London
N22 8NN
☎ 02088 885 307
LSBP

**RADLETT**, Marty
**Existential Psychotherapist**
46 Noel Road
London
N1
☎ 020 8868 5836
martyr@panoslondon.org.uk
SPCRC

**RAIMES**, Peter
**Group Analytic Psychotherapist**
129 Shakespeare Walk
Stoke Newington
London
N16 8TB
☎ 020 7923 1355
☎ 02089 376 320
pete.raimes@nhs.net
UPCA

**RAINSFORD**, Helena
**Group Analytic Psychotherapist**
c/o 6 Church Lane
Hornsey
London
N8 7BU
☎ 020 8 341 9524
UPCA

**REA**, Judith
**Psychoanalytic Psychotherapist**
11 Anson Road
London
N7 0RB
☎ 020 7 607 0546
GUILD

**REBUCK**, Alexandra Jane
**Systemic Psychotherapist**
Ivy House
3 Hendon Avenue
Finchley
London
N3 1UL
☎ 020 8349 3626
☎ 07074 262 626
alex@rebuck.net
The North London Hospice
47 Woodside Avenue
London
N12 8TF
KCC

**REEVES**, Richard
**Psychoanalytic Psychotherapist**
5 Cedars Road
Winchmore Hill
London
N21 3HB
☎ 020 8360 0761
☎ 07940 075 018
richardreeves@reevesrh.freeserve.co.uk
FIP

**REGUIS**, Marie-Christine
**Psychoanalytic Psychotherapist**
c/o Arbours Association
6, Church Lane
N8 7BU
ARBS

**REID**, Elizabeth
**Lacanian Analyst, Psychoanalytic Psychotherapist**
376 Hornsey Road
Islington
London
N19 4HT
☎ 020 8346 0945
☎ 07946 653263
SITE

**REILLY**, Philip
**Integrative Psychotherapist**
7 Baron Close
Friern Barnet
London
N11 3PS
☎ 02083 689 027
philip@biotholm.org.uk
MC

**RENOUX**, Martine
**Integrative Psychotherapist**
107 Sylvan Avenue
London
N22 5JB
☎ 020 8889 9980
renouxbowler@tiscali.co.uk
MC

**RHIND**, Sue
**Psychosynthesis Psychotherapist**
♿ 35 Long Lane
Church End
Finchley
London
N3 2PS
☎ 02089 220 661
suefoxpsych@aol.com
IPS

**RICHARDS**, Val
**Analytical Psychotherapist**
28 Ravensdale Avenue
London
N12 9HT
☎ 020 8446 8449
☎ 020 8445 6120
farin@dircon.co.uk
AGIP, AIP, GUILD, IPSS

**RIDDELL**, Jenny
**Attachment-based Psychoanalytic Psychotherapist**
15 Park Avenue South
Crouch End
London
N8 8LU
☎ 020 8341 3124
riddells@onetel.net.uk
57 Cecile Park
Crouch End
London
N8
CAPP

**RITCHIE**, Sheila
**Group Analytic Psychotherapist, Psychoanalytic Psychotherapist**
167 Whittington Road
Bowes Park
N22 8YP
☎ 020 8365 7602
AGIP, UPCA, WTC

**ROBERTSON**, Ruth
**Educational Therapist**
♿ 14 Sanford Terrace
London
N16 7LH
☎ 020 7254 6408
ruth-robertson@yahoo.com
CFET

**ROMISCH-CLAY**, Liza
**Integrative Psychotherapist**
7 Rookfield Close
London
N10 3TR
☎ 020 8883 6575
SPCRC

**ROSE**, Kevin
**Psychoanalytic Psychotherapist**
♿ 76-80 Isledon Road
London
N7 7LB
☎ 020 8 455 5936 (t/f)
kevinrose@freeola.com
IPSS

**ROSENTHALL**, Joanna
**Couple Psychoanalytic Psychotherapist**
64 Sotheby Road
London
N5 2YT
☎ 020 7435 7111
☎ 020 7704 1174
101576.2651@compuserve.com
TMSI, SCPP

**ROSS**, Mo
**Psychoanalytic Psychotherapist**
♿ 46 Jenner Road
London
N16 7SA
☎ 020 8806 4263
kymet@waitrose.com
AGIP

**ROTH**, Jenner
**Humanistic Psychotherapist**
Spectrum
7 Endymion Road
London
N4 1EE
☎ 020 8341 2277
jennerroth@spectrumtherapy.co.uk
SPEC

**ROWAN**, Alan J
**Lacanian Analyst, Psychoanalytic Psychotherapist**
113 Lichfield Grove
Finchley
London
N3 2JL
☎ 020 8346 3599
CFAR

**ROWE**, Dorothy
**Personal Construct Psychotherapist**
The Garden Flat
40 Highbury Grove
London
N5 2AG
☎ 020 7 354 3498
DRowe6@compuserve.com
PCP

**ROZENBERG**, Rosette
**Psychoanalytic Psychotherapist**
26 Orchard Road
London
N6 5TR
☎ 020 8348 5472
r.rozenberg@blueyonder.co.uk
1 Fairbridge Road
London
N19 3EW
AGIP

**RYAN**, Jane
**Attachment-based Psychoanalytic Psychotherapist**
36a Mildmay Road
London
N1 4NG
☎ 020 7254 2323
CAPP

**RYAN**, Joanna
**Psychoanalytic Psychotherapist**
44 Lordship Road
London
N16 0QT
☎ 020 8802 1641
joannaryan@onetel.net.uk
SITE

**RYAN**, Tom
**Psychoanalytic Psychotherapist**
11 Cecile Park
London
N8 9AX
☎ 020 8292 8908
thomasjryan@blueyonder.co.uk
ARBS, SITE

**RYZ**, Patsy
**Child Psychotherapist**
36 Essex Park
London
N3 1NE
☎ 020 8349 2263
ACP

**SABBADINI**, Andrea
**Psychoanalytic Psychotherapist**
38 Berkeley Road
Crouch End
London
N8 8RU
☎ 020 8 340 2936
a.sabbadiini@macunlimited.net
ARBS

**SALISBURY**, Claire
**Gestalt Psychotherapist, Humanistic Psychotherapist**
119 Maidstone Road
London
N11 2JT
☎ 020 8361 6146
☎ 020 7485 2316
clairesalisbury@lineone.net
35A Croftdown Road
London
N11 2JT
AHPP

**SALLES**, Miriam
**Biodynamic Psychotherapist**
38 Onslow Gardens
London
N10 3JU
☎ 020 8883 9698
LSBP

**SAMUELS**, Andrew
**Analytical Psychologist-Jungian Analyst**
148 Mercers Road
London
N19 4PX
☎ 020 7272 1292
andrew.samuels@virgin.net
CAP, FIP *

**SAMUELS**, Jocelyne
**Integrative Arts Psychotherapist**
148 Mercers Road
Tufnel Park
London
N19 4PX
☎ 020 7272 1812
jocelynesamuels@aol.com
IATE

**SAVILLE**, Sue
**Psychoanalytic Psychotherapist**
25a Woodland Gardens
Muswell Hill
London
N10 3UE
☎ 020 8444 4826
sue.saville@talk21.com
FPC

**SCHMITT-CASTILLA**, Maria
**Existential Psychotherapist**
23 New Trinity Road
London
N2 8EE
☎ 020 8444 2393
schmittcastilla@hotmail.com
SPCRC

**SCHONFIELD**, Tamar
**Psychoanalytic Psychotherapist**
71 Woodland Rise
London
N10 3UN
☎ 020 8372 2168
tschon@blueyonder.co.uk
ARBS

**SELBY**, Marilyn
**Educational Therapist**
34 Arden Road
London
N3 3AN
☎ 020 8349 2507
CFET

**SENGUN**, Seda
**Group Analyst, Psychoanalytic Psychotherapist**
♿ Womens Therapy Centre
10 Manor Gardens
Holloway
N7 5JS
☎ 02072 637 860
sedasengun@ukonline.co.uk
IGA, WTC

**SERFATY**, Marc A.
**Cognitive Behavioural Psychotherapist**
♿ Senior Lecturer & Consultant
Grovelands Priory Hospital
The Bourne
Southgate
N14 6RA
☎ 020 8882 8191
marc@rfhsm.ac.uk
BABCP

**SEYMOUR**, Charlotte
**Family & Systemic Psychotherapist**
65 Muswell Road
London
N10 2BS
☎ 020 8245 0712
cseymour@blueyonder.co.uk
AFT

**SHAPIRO**, Adella
**Integrative Psychotherapist**
41a Fairmead Road
London
N19 4DG
☎ 020 7272 5868
Adella@waitrose.com
MC

**SHARIFI**, Pury
**Analytical Psychologist-Jungian Analyst**
27 Fortismere Avenue
London
N10 3BN
☎ 020 8444 8234
CAP *

**SHARP**, Belinda
**Psychoanalytic Psychotherapist**
54 Park Drive
Winchmore Hill
London
N21 2LS
☎ 020 8351 8774
belindas@blueyonder.co.uk
FPC

**SHAW**, Elizabeth
**Cognitive Behavioural Psychotherapist**
♿ Psychology Service
St. Ann's Hospital
St. Ann's Road
London
N15 3TH
☎ 020 8442 6458
BABCP

**SHEARER**, Ann
**Analytical Psychologist-Jungian Analyst**
9 Shepherd's Close
London
N6 5AG
☎ 020 8340 6524
ann.shearer@ukgateway.net
AIP, IGAP

**SHIVANATH**, Suhith
**Transactional Analysis Psychotherapist**
5 Roseberry Gardens
London
N4 1JQ
☎ 02088 090 332
suhithshivanath@onetel.net.uk
MET

**SILLS**, Ros
**Psychoanalytic Psychotherapist**
1 Fairbridge Road
London
N19 3EW
☎ 020 7272 7013
☎ 020 7278 3434
rossils@aol.com
AGIP

**SILVER**, Anna-Mae
**Psychoanalytic Psychotherapist**
AGIP
1 Fairbridge Road
London
N19 3EW
☎ 020 7272 7013
☎ 020 8455 0431
annamation@aol.com
AGIP

**SILVER**, Claire
**Psychoanalytic Psychotherapist**
103 Richmond Road
London
N15 6QA
☎ 020 8800 2272
clairesilver100@hotmail.com
IPSS

**SIMMONS**, Gloria
**Family & Systemic Psychotherapist**
♿ Flat 22 Henderson Court
88 Holden Road
Woodside Park
London
N12 7EL
☎ 020 8445 6025
simmonsconex@onetel.net.uk
AFT

**SIMMONS**, Kevin
**Family & Systemic Psychotherapist**
♿ CNWL Family Therapy
Substance Misuse Service, Unit 5
1-31 Elkstone Road
London
N8 8LD
☎ 020 8960 0880
☎ 020 8341 3273
kevin.simmons@cnwl.nhs.uk
21 Farrer Road
London
N8 8LD
IFT

**SIMMONS**, Ruth
**Psychoanalytic Psychotherapist**
87 Hawthorn Road
London
N8 7LY
☎ 020 8341 9987
GUILD

**SIMPSON**, Catherine
**Integrative Psychotherapist**
31a Bewdley Street
Islington
London
N1 1HB
☎ 020 7607 8186
kssimpson2@hotmail.com
SPCRC

**SINGER**, Iris
**Attachment-based Psychoanalytic Psychotherapist**
♿ 99 Nether Street
North Finchley
Barnet
London
N12 7NP
☎ 020 8446 6406
☎ 020 8446 9925
irrisinger@btinternet.com
CAPP

**SMITH**, Jonathan
**Psychoanalytic Psychotherapist**
59 Holmesdale Road
London
N6 5TH
☎ 020 8 340 9137
jdsmith@jar59.fsnet.co.uk
IPSS

**SMITH**, Maggie
**Systemic Psychotherapist**
40 Vallance Road
Wood Green
London
N22 7UB
KCC

**SMITH**, Sue
**Integrative Psychotherapist**
497 Archway Road
Highgate
London
N6 4HX
☎ 02083 408 470
suesmith.340@virgin.net
MC

**SMOSARSKI**, Lizzie
**Integrative Arts Psychotherapist**
47 Crescent Road
Alexandra Park
London
N22 7RU
lizzie@smosarski.fsnet.co.uk
IATE

**SOLEMANI**, Hannah
**Psychoanalytic Psychotherapist**
82 Cecile Park
London
N8 9AU
☎ 020 8374 6950
☎ 020 8341 1612
ARBS

**SOLOWAY**, Clare
**Integrative Psychotherapist**
100 Sydney Road
Muswell Hill
London
N10 2RN
☎ 020 8442 0928
claresoloway@mac.com
AHPP

**SPADA**, Marcantonio
**Cognitive Behavioural Psychotherapist**
♿ Dept. of Psychology
London Metropolitan University
Ladbroke House 62-66
Highbury Grove, London
N5 2AD
☎ 020 7423 0000 x5047
☎ 020 7736 4643
m.spada@londonmet.ac.uk
BABCP

**SPITZER**, Shayne
**Analytical Psychologist-Jungian Analyst**
42 Priory Avenue
London
N8 7RN
☎ 020 8341 7031
AJA

**STAPLEHURST**, Carron
**Integrative Psychotherapist**
32 Church Crescent
Muswell Hill
London
N10 3NE
☎ 020 8444 2438
MC

**STEIN**, Yvonne
**Family & Systemic Psychotherapist**
48 Finchley Park
North Finchley
London
N12 9JL
☎ 020 8446 4913
AFT, SPCRC

**STEVENSON**, Kate
**Systemic Psychotherapist**
12 Hampstead Lane
Highgate
London
N6 4SB
☎ 020 8342 9391
☎ 020 7720 7301
kate.stevenson@virgin.net
KCC

**STEYN**, Angela
**Group Analytic Psychotherapist**
Highgate Counselling Centre
Tetherdown Halls
Tetherdown
London
N10 1ND
☎ 020 8458 1214
angela.steyn@virgin.net
FPC

**STOGDON**, Mark
**Systemic Psychotherapist**
70 Corbyn Street
London
N4 3BZ
☎ 020 7281 4570
mark.stogdon@virgin.net
IFT

**STONE**, Anthony
**Humanistic and Integrative Psychotherapist**
Spectrum
7 Endymion Road
London
N4 1EE
☎ 020 8455 0794
anthony.stone4@btconnect.com
SPEC

**STONE**, Judith H
**Group Analytic Psychotherapist**
13 Lordship Park
London
N16 5UN
☎ 02088 093 811
stonejud@aol.com
UPCA

**STROMBERG**, Marla J
**Cognitive Behavioural Psychotherapist**
Priory Hospital North London
Grovelands House
The Bourne, Southgate
London
N14 6RA
☎ 020 8882 8191 x366/523
marla.joy@attglobal.net
BABCP

**SULLIVAN**, Gerald
**Lacanian Analyst**
52 Park Hall Road
London
N2 9PX
☎ 00353 1454 4304
CFAR

**SUNDERLAND**, Margot
**Gestalt Psychotherapist, Integrative Arts Psychotherapist**
'Terpsichore'
70 Cranwich Road
London
N16 5JD
☎ 020 7704 2534
☎ 020 8809 5866
IATE, MET

**SWAN**, Adrienne
**Psychoanalytic Psychotherapist**
♿ Priory Hospital North London,
Grovelands House,
The Bourne,
Southgate, London
N14 6RA
☎ 020 8882 8191
☎ 020 8350 9699
132 New River Crescent
Palmers Green
London
N8 5RJ
ARBS

**SWYNNERTON**, Richard
**Existential Psychotherapist**
11 Links View
Dollis Road
Finchley Central
London
N3 1RN
☎ 020 8371 0443
richard.swynnerton@virgin.net
SPCRC

**SYMONS**, Judith Jane
**Psychoanalytic Psychotherapist**
1 Fairbridge Road
London
N19 3EW
☎ 020 7272 7013
judithjane@handbag.com
AGIP

**SÜNKEL**, Sue
**Psychoanalytic Psychotherapist**
1 Foxham Road
Tufnell Park
London
N19 4RR
☎ 020 7 281 5193 (t/f)
suesunkel@aol.com
IPSS

**TAPANG**, Peter
**Family & Systemic Psychotherapist**
♿ Community Mental Health Centre
305-309 Fore Street
Edmonton
London
N9 0PD
☎ 020 8220 7757
☎ 020 8887 0606
P.Tapang@btopenworld.com
IFT

**TAYLOR**, Alan
**Analytical Psychotherapist**
8 Victoria Mansions
135 Holloway Road
London
N7 8LZ
☎ 020 7607 0210
alantaylor135@mac.com
AIP

**TAYLOR**, Harvey
**Psychoanalytic Psychotherapist**
AGIP
1 Fairbridge Road
London
N19 3EW
☎ 020 7272 7013
☎ 020 8349 9792
AGIP

**TAYLOR**, Karen
**Existential Psychotherapist**
36 Oakdale
Southgate
London
N14 5RE
☎ 02083 680 309
UPCA

**TAYLOR**, Mary
**Systemic Psychotherapist**
♿ GP Practice
Killick Street Health Centre
75 Killick Street
Kings Cross
N1 9RH
KCC

**TAYLOR**, Shirley
**Integrative Psychosynthesis Psychotherapist**
St Joseph's Retreat
Highgate Hill
London
N19 5NE
☎ 020 7561 0518
☎ 07801 350 904
stjoseph@waitrose.com
RE.V

**THOMAS**, Mark
**Gestalt Psychotherapist**
♿ 54 Windus Road
London
N16 6UP
☎ 020 8806 4055
GPTI

**TICKTIN**, Stephen
**Existential Psychotherapist**
55 Tufnell Park Road
London
N7 0PS
☎ 020 7687 1628
sjticktin@hotmail.com
SPCRC

**TILLETT**, Penny
**Educational Therapist**
2 The Drive
Fordington Road
London
N6 4TD
☎ 020 8444 7073
CFET

**TOMPKINS**, Penny
**Neurolinguistic Psychotherapist**
9 Southwood Lawn Road
Highgate
London
N6 5SD
☎ 02083 411 062
penny@cleanlanguage.co.uk
NLPtCA

**TREVOR DAVIES**, Helen
**Group Analyst**
♿ The North London Centre for Group Therapy
138 Bramley Road
Oakwood
London
N14 4HU
☎ 020 8440 1451
nlcent@aol.com
IGA

**TURNBULL**, Dheeresh Charles
**Cognitive Behavioural Psychotherapist**
Therapy Services
Priory Hospital North London
Grovelands House
The Bourne, London
N14 6RA
☎ 020 8882 8191 x 523
BABCP

**TUTTON**, Catherine
**Integrative Psychosynthesis Psychotherapist**
33 Lausanne Road
London
N8 0HJ
☎ 020 8967 7056
catherine.tutton@macmillan.org.uk
RE.V

**USHER**, Margaret Christine
**Family & Systemic Psychotherapist**
Garden Flat
205 Church Street
Stoke Newington
London
N16 9ES
☎ 020 7249 2834
AFT

**USISKIN**, Judith
**Child Psychotherapist**
110 Chanctonbury Way
London
N12 7AB
☎ 020 8445 5671
ACP

**UTTING**, Julia
**Psychoanalytic Psychotherapist**
15 Dagmar Road
Wood Green
London
N22 7RT
☎ 020 8 881 3200
IPSS

**VALENTINE**, Marguerite
**Psychoanalytic Psychotherapist**
39 Womersley Road
London
N8 9AP
☎ 020 8341 2761
marguerite@f25.com
ARBS

**VALENTINE**, Victoria
**Integrative Psychotherapist**
21 Thorpedale Road
London
N4 3BH
☎ 02072 632 518
MET

**VAN GOGH**, Mark
**Integrative Psychosynthesis Psychotherapist**
Garden Flat
71 Anson Road
London
N7 0AS
☎ 020 7609 8526
mvangogh@waitrose.com
RE.V

**VEALE**, Maurice
**Gestalt Psychotherapist**
148 Corbyn Street
Finsbury Park
London
N4 3DB
☎ 020 7263 4079
info@abod.co.uk
AHPP, GCL

**VERNON**, Paul
**Psychoanalytic Psychotherapist**
47 Cazenove Road
London
N16 6PA
☎ 020 8806 6046
pfvernon@blueyonder.co.uk
FIP

**WADDY**, Melanie
**Psychoanalytic Psychotherapist**
39 Cranley Gardens
London
N10 3AB
☎ 020 8815 0073
ARBS

**WARWICK**, Kate
**Child Psychotherapist**
Islington Child & Family Consultation Service
The Northern Health Centre
594 Holloway Road
London
N7 6LB
☎ 020 7445 8150
☎ 020 8809 7791
ACP

**WATERFIELD**, Hilary
**Psychoanalytic Psychotherapist**
160 Albion Road
London
N16 9JS
☎ 020 7690 9048
ARBS

**WEAVER**, Ziva
**Body Psychotherapist, Integrative Psychotherapist**
226c Brecknock Road
London
N19 5BG
☎ 020 7697 9426
zivaweaver@hotmail.com
CCBP

**WEERAMANTHRI**, Tara
**Family & Systemic Psychotherapist**
12c Petherton Road
London
N5 2RD
☎ 020 7226 2731
tarabw@btopenworld.com
AFT

**WHITBY**, Susan
**Psychoanalytic Psychotherapist**
1A Windsor Road
Finchley Central
London
N3 3SZ
☎ 020 8 346 1698[t/f]
whitby.s@virgin.net
IPSS

**WHITE**, Jean
**Psychoanalytic Psychotherapist**
Flat 5
77 Sunnyside Road
London
N19 3SL
☎ 020 7 263 7417
GUILD

**WHITE**, Nuala
**Gestalt Psychotherapist**
10 Alexander Road
Holloway
London
N19 3PQ
☎ 020 7263 7403
nualawhite@hotmail.com
GCL

**WHITTLE**, Sonia J
**Psychoanalytic Psychotherapist**
44b Priory Road
Hornsey
London
N8 7EX
☎ 020 8348 6303
ARBS

**WHYTE**, Miranda
**Transpersonal Psychotherapist**
Flat 5, 14 Clifton Road
Crouch End
London
N8 8HY
☎ 020 8348 1825
CTP

**WIELAND**, Christina
**Psychoanalytic Psychotherapist**
50 Fernleigh Road
London
N21 3AL
☎ 020 8882 9531
☎ 020 7272 7013
1 Fairbridge Road
London
N19 3EW
AGIP

**WIESELBERG**, Huguette
**Family & Systemic Psychotherapist**
8 Broughton Avenue
London
N3 3ER
☎ 020 8349 9780
mwieselberg@compuserve.com
IFT

**WILKINSON**, Linda
**Psychoanalytic Psychotherapist**
12 The Green
Southgate
LONDON
N14 7EH
☎ 020 8882 0124
LMBWilkinson@aol.com
FIP

**WILLIAMS**, Timothy
**Psychosynthesis Psychotherapist**
32 Noel Road
London
N1 8HA
☎ 020 7359 5473
PET

**WILLMOTT**, Susan
**Humanistic and Integrative Psychotherapist**
London
N15
☎ 020 8374 8728
susan.willmott@blueyonder.co.uk
SPEC

**WILSON**, Carol
**Integrative Psychotherapist**
88 Talbot Road
Highgate
London
N6 4RA
☎ 020 8348 1988
carolwilsoncounsellor@hotmail.com
SPCRC

**WILSON**, Janet
**Hypno-Psychotherapist**
♿ 29 Danvers Road
London
N8 7HH
☎ 02083 476 696
janewilson35@hotmail.com
NSHAP

**WILSON**, Jilian
**Child Psychotherapist**
Department of Child & Adolescent Psychiatry
North Middlesex Hospital
Sterling Way
London
N18 1QX
☎ 020 8887 4231
☎ 020 8883 6370
ACP

**WILSON**, Shula
**Integrative Psychotherapist**
♿ 50 Mayfield Avenue
London
N12 9JD
☎ 020 8445 7541
shulawilson@dial.pipex.com
SPCRC

**WINGFIELD**, Rachel
**Attachment-based Psychoanalytic Psychotherapist**
39 Selbourne Road
London
N22 7TH
☎ 020 8352 0878
rlwingfield@blueyonder.co.uk
CAPP

**WINSHIP**, Gary
**Group Analytic Psychotherapist**
117 Beresford Road
London
N8 0AG
☎ 01189 561 250
☎ 02083 408 284
gwinship@aol.com
UPCA

**WOOD**, Philip
**Integrative Psychotherapist**
32 Church Crescent
Muswell Hill
London
N10 3NE
☎ 020 8444 2438
philip.wood@cwcom.net
MC

**WOOD**, Rob
**Psychoanalytic Psychotherapist**
19 Baalbec Road
Highbury Fields
London
N5 1QN
☎ 020 7226 4775
robwoodlondon@aol.com
FPC

**WOODHEAD**, Louise
**Psychoanalytic Psychotherapist**
26 Ripon Road
London
N17 6PP
☎ 020 8 885 5958
GUILD

**WOODS**, William
**Transpersonal Psychotherapist**
London
N1
☎ 020 7837 7288
☎ 07759 342 428
billwoods80@hotmail.com
CCPE

**WORRALL**, Chrysoula
**Psychoanalytic Psychotherapist**
15 Gresley Road
London
N19 3LA
☎ 020 7272 4133
chrysoulaworrall@aol.com
GUILD

**WRIGHT**, Jason
**Analytical Psychotherapist, Transpersonal Psychotherapist**
237 Gladstone Avenue
London
N22 6LD
☎ 020 8352 0020
☎ 020 7258 3031
jw015a2286@blueyonder.co.uk
AIP, CTP

**WYNTER-PHILP**, Lloyd
**Existential Psychotherapist**
21 Sandringham Road
Wood Green
London
N22 6RB
☎ 020 8376 8083
lloydphilippsych@msn.com
UPCA

**YARE**, Brinley
**Existential Psychotherapist**
Unit 9
6 Rufus Street
London
N1 6PE
☎ 07970 157 012
UPCA

**YATES**, Tony
**Group Analytic Psychotherapist**
27 Toyne Way
London
N6 4EG
☎ 020 8374 9788
FPC

**YOUNG**, Dianne
**Integrative Psychotherapist**
72 Ockendon Road
Islington
London
N1 3NW
☎ 020 7704 1876
dianneyoung@hotmail.com
SPCRC

**YOUNG**, Robert
**Psychoanalytic Psychotherapist**
26 Freegrove Road
London
N7 9RQ
☎ 020 7607 8306
robert@rmy1.demon.co.uk
FIP, UPCA

**YOUSRY**, Menis
**Family & Systemic Psychotherapist**
5 Birchwood Avenue
London
N10 3BE
☎ 02088 835 852 / 07956 278 186
☎ 02083 836 125
menis.yousry@virgin.net
IFT

**ZANE**, Helen
**Psychoanalytic Psychotherapist**
14 Friern Mount Drive
Whetstone
London
N20 9DN
☎ 020 8445 6796
FIP

**ZIMMERMAN**, Frankie
**Family & Systemic Psychotherapist**
♿ 2 Elm Gardens
East Finchley
London
N2 0TF
☎ 020 8444 6388
frankiez561@aol.co.uk
AFT

**DE BOTTON**, Susan
**Integrative Psychotherapist**
15 Sussex Gardens
Highgate
London
N6 4LY
☎ 07989 307 575
suedebotton@hotmail.com
SPCRC

**DEL STROTHER**, Sybil
**Psychoanalytic Psychotherapist**
50 Leconfield Road
Highbury
London
N5 2SN
☎ 07768 224 101
FPC

## LONDON NORTH WEST

**ABSE**, Susanna
**Couple Psychoanalytic Psychotherapist**
♿ Tavistock Marital Studies Institute
Tavistock Centre
120 Belsize Lane
London
NW3 5BA
☎ 020 7447 3818
☎ 020 8883 5746
susannaabse@hotmail.com
TMSI, SCPP

**ACQUARONE**, Stella
**Child Psychotherapist**
27 Frognal Street
London
NW3 6AR
☎ 020 7794 2521
acquarone@aol.com
ACP

**ADLER**, Phyllis
**Integrative Psychotherapist**
23 College Crescent
London
NW3 5LL
☎ 07979 603 313
Phyllis.Adler@btinternet.com
SPCRC

**ALAYARIAN**, Aida
**Psychoanalytic Psychotherapist**
55 Cumbrian Gardens
London
NW2 1ED
☎ 020 7272 2565
☎ 020 8465 1433
aidaalayarian@yahoo.co.uk
NAFSI

**ALI-KHAN**, Farra
**Systemic Psychotherapist**
33 Snowdon Drive
Welsh Harp Village
London
NW9 7RF
☎ 07957 504 819
Farraukcp@aol.com
IFT

**ALLEN**, Anita
**Psychoanalytic Psychotherapist**
167 Sumatra Road
London
NW6 1PN
☎ 02077 941 433
anita.allen@mail.com
NAFSI

**ALLEN**, Dorothy
**Transpersonal Psychotherapist**
20 Fleetwood Road
Dollis Hill
London
NW10 1ND
☎ 020 8830 6434
CTP

**ALTSCHULER**, Jenny
**Systemic Psychotherapist**
♿ Tavistock Clinic
120 Belsize Lane
London
NW3 5BA
☎ 020 8458 4193
altschuler@compuserve.com
AFT

**ALVAREZ**, Anne
**Child Psychotherapist**
Tavistock Child & Family Department
120 Belsize Lane
LONDON
NW3 5BA
☎ 020 7435 7111
ACP

**ANDERSON**, Linda
**Group Analyst**
London
NW10
☎ 020 8965 5872
linda.anderson@talk21.com
IGA

**ANKER**, Ofra
**Psychosynthesis Psychotherapist**
65a Watford Way
London
NW4 3AU
☎ 020 8275 0463
ofra@btinternet.com
IPS

**ANTHONY**, Monica
**Transpersonal Psychotherapist**
Violet Hill Studios,
6 Violet Hill
London
NW8 9EB
☎ 020 7232 2562
CTP

**ANTONIS**, Phyllis
**Child Psychotherapist**
7 Rodborough Road
London
NW11 8SA
☎ 020 8455 9009
ACP

**ARAM**, Eliat
**Gestalt Psychotherapist**
Choice Psychotherapy & Consulting
18a Heriot Road
London
NW4
☎ 020 8202 1023
☎ 020 7272 8807
e.1.Aram@herts.ac.uk
Choice
18a Heriot Road
London
NW4
GPTI, MET

**AUSTIN**, Lesley
**Integrative Psychotherapist**
48 Carlton Hill
St.Johns Wood
London
NW8 0ES
☎ 020 7624 6862
lesley.portner@virgin.net
SPCRC

**AUSTIN**, Susan
**Psychoanalytic Psychotherapist**
♿ 50 Abbey Gardens
St John's Wood
London
NW8 9AT
☎ 02073 286 640
WTC

**BAILEY-SMITH**, Yvonne A
**Family & Systemic Psychotherapist**
110 Brondesbury Park
London
NW2 5JR
☎ 020 8459 6579
ybailey_smith@hotmail.com
AFT

**BALL**, Rebekah
**Attachment-based Psychoanalytic Psychotherapist**
43 Parliament Hill Mansions
Lissenden Gardens
London
NW5 1NA
☎ 020 7267 6303
CAPP

**BARKER**, Sally
**Psychoanalytic Psychotherapist**
The Hillside Practice
One Hillside
Highgate Road
London
NW5 1QT
☎ 020 7482 3293
☎ 07833 376 7026
sallybarker@hotmail.com
GUILD

**BARNETT**, Madeleine
**Integrative Psychotherapist**
29 Dollis Hill Avenue
London
NW2 6EU
☎ 0208 452 7345
MC

**BARNETT**, Ruth
**Psychoanalytic Psychotherapist**
♿ 73 Fortune Green Road
London
NW6 1DR
☎ 020 7431 0837
RuthLBarnett@aol.com
FIP

**BARTELS-ELLIS**, Phillida
**Psychoanalytic Psychotherapist**
12 Blenheim Gardens
London
NW2 4NS
☎ 02084 504 048
NAFSI

**BATHAI**, Parizad
**Psychodynamic Psychotherapist**
Flat C
85 Melrose Avenue
London
NW2 4LR
☎ 020 8208 1095
FIP

**BATTERSBY**, Audrey
**Psychoanalytic Psychotherapist**
22 Belsize Square
London
NW3 4HT
☎ 020 7435 4627
GUILD

**BECK**, Orit
**Psychoanalytic Psychotherapist**
♿ 167 Sumatra Road
London
NW6 1PN
☎ 02089 224 928
oritsvirsky@another.com
IPSS, WTC

**BENJAMIN**, Haydene
**Child Psychotherapist**
7 Turners Wood
London
NW11 6TD
☎ 020 8455 2065
ACP

**BENSIMON**, Marlene
**Psychoanalytic Psychotherapist**
32 Leighton Road
Kentish Town
London
NW5 2QE
☎ 02084 445 878
m.bensimon@usa.net
IPSS

**BENTOVIM**, Dr Arnon
**Family & Systemic Psychotherapist**
♿ 12 Falcon Lodge
Oakhill Park
London
NW3 7LD
☎ 020 7435 2255
☎ 020 7224 2800
bentovim@lcfcs.co.uk
IFT

**BERDASCO**, Lourdes
**Family & Systemic Psychotherapist**
♿ Medical Foundation
Star House
104-108 Grafton Road
London
NW5 4BD
☎ 02078 139 999
IFT

**BERGEL**, Edith
**Psychoanalytic Psychotherapist**
21 Pembroke Hall
Mulberry Close
London
NW4 1QW
☎ 02082 021 300
LPDO

**BERGESE**, Rebecca
**Child Psychotherapist**
c/o ACP
120 West Heath Road
London
NW3 7TU
☎ 020 7301 3414
ACP

**BICKERS**, Adrian
**Psychosynthesis Psychotherapist**
Institue of Psychosynthesis
65a Watford Way
Hendon
London
NW4 3AQ
☎ 01462 734 188
01462 734 188
IPS

**BILDER**, Tessa
**Transpersonal Psychotherapist**
73 Eyre Court
Finchley Road
London
NW8 9TX
☎ 020 8444 5289
CCPE

**BLACK**, David
**Psychoanalytic Psychotherapist**
30 Cholmley Gardens
London
NW6 1AG
☎ 020 7435 9192
dmbalck@clara.co.uk
FPC

**BLAIR**, Margaret
**Analytical Psychotherapist (Jungian)**
80 Dyne Road
London
NW6 7DS
☎ 020 7372 7864
margaretblair@onetel.com
GAPS

**BLANDY**, Evanthe M
**Child Psychotherapist, Psychoanalytic Psychotherapist**
♿ 2 Montrose Avenue
Queens Park
London
NW6 6LB
☎ 020 8964 3813
eblandy@dircon.co.uk
ACP, GUILD

**BODGENER**, Sue
**Gestalt Psychotherapist**
9 Brownlow Road
Harlesden
London
NW10 9QN
☎ 020 8961 2763
☎ 020 7485 1945 (W)
MET

**BOND**, Frank W
**Cognitive Behavioural Psychotherapist**
7 Lisson Grove
Marylebone
London
NW1 6SH
☎ 020 7040 8484
F.W.Bond@city.ac.uk
BABCP

**BOR**, Prof. Robert
**Family & Systemic Psychotherapist**
♿ Royal Free Hospital
Psychology Unit - 10th Floor
Pond Street
London
NW3 2QG
☎ 020 7830 2152
Robert.bor@royalfree.nhs.uk
IFT

**BORSIG**, Su
**Integrative Psychotherapist**
90 Harvist Road
London
NW6 6HL
☎ 020 8964 2719
SuBorsig@aol.com
MET

**BOYSAN**, Zehra
**Psychodynamic Psychotherapist**
17 Neville Court
8 Abbey Road
London
NW8 9DD
☎ 020 7286 4165
zboysan@aol.com
BPS, HIP

**BRADLEY**, Catrin
**Child Psychotherapist**
Greenland Road Children's
4 Greenland Road
NW1 OAS
☎ 020 75304823
☎ 020 8444 4733
ACP

**BRADLEY**, Jonathan
**Child Psychotherapist**
Adolescent Dept.
Tavistock Clinic
120 Belsize Lane
London
NW3 5BA
☎ 020 7447 3781
jbradley@tavi-port.nhs.uk
ACP

**BROWN**, Lesley
**Gestalt Psychotherapist, Integrative Psychotherapist, Integrative Psychosynthesis Psychotherapist**
97 Brondesbury Road
Queens Park
London
NW6 6RY
☎ 01932 220 590
GPTI, MET, RE.V

**BROWN**, Malcolm
**Integrative Psychotherapist**
♿ c/o Respond
3rd Floor
24-32 Stephenson Way
London
NW1 2HD
mcrt.brown@btinternet.com
SPCRC

**BUNGENER**, Janet
**Child Psychotherapist**
107 Greencroft Gardens
London
NW6 3PE
☎ 020 7372 8707
ACP

**BURCK**, Charlotte
**Family & Systemic Psychotherapist**
Tavistock Clinic
120 Belsize Lane
London
NW3 5BA
☎ 020 7447 3804
cburck@tavi-port.nhs.uk
IFT

**BURNS**, Alex
**Psychoanalytic Psychotherapist**
♿ Flat 26
119 Haverstock Hill
Belsize Park
London
NW3 4RS
☎ 020 7 586 7076
☎ 01788 536446
alexburns@nwlpc.co.uk
IPSS

**BURTT**, Lucy
**Neurolinguistic Psychotherapist**
147 Bathurst Gardens
Kensal Green
London
NW10 5JJ
☎ 02089 649 843
NLPtCA

**BUSS-TWACHTMANN**, Christel
**Couple Psychoanalytic Psychotherapist**
♿ Tavistock Marital Studies Institute
Tavistock Centre
120 Belsize Lane
London
NW3 5BA
☎ 020 7435 7111
☎ 020 8341 1358
TMSI, SCPP

**BYNG-HALL**, John
**Family & Systemic Psychotherapist**
24 Shirlock Road
London
NW3 2HS
☎ 020 7485 6602
jbynghall@mistral.co.uk
AFT

**CAMPBELL**, Elizabeth
**Psychoanalytic Psychotherapist**
2 Provost Road
London
NW3 4ST
☎ 020 7 722 7573
GUILD

**CAMPHER**, Rosemary
**Integrative Psychotherapist**
Flat 15
119 Haverstock Hill
London
NW3 4RS
☎ 020 7722 8992
rosemarycampher@hotmail.com
SPCRC

**CANNING**, Miles
**Psychoanalytic Psychotherapist**
31 Priory Road
West Hampstead
London
NW6 4NN
☎ 07760 110 999
mcanning@usa.net
IPSS

**CARDELLE MARTINEZ**, Raquel
**Systemic Psychotherapist**
♿ Brent Child and Family Clinic
Warranty House
Dudden Hill Lane
Neasden, London
NW10 1DL
☎ 020 8208 7200
KCC

**CARLSON**, Theresa
**Transpersonal Psychotherapist**
18 Chalcot Crescent
Primrose Hill
London
NW1 8YD
☎ 020 7 722 2317
CCPE

**CARROLL**, Roz
**Body Psychotherapist, Integrative Psychotherapist**
68 Lynton Avenue
London
NW9 6RY
☎ 020 8205 2253
☎ 07980 340 481
thinkbody@lineone.net
CCBP

**CAVE**, Prue
**Psychoanalytic Psychotherapist**
Top Flat
41 Buckland Crescent
London
NW3 5DJ
☎ 020 7722 2589
pruecave@hotmail.com
ARBS

**CHANDWANI**, Lilian
**Psychoanalytic Psychotherapist**
18 Park Drive
London
NW11 7SP
☎ 020 8 458 8204
chandwani@btinternet.com
IPSS

**CHAPPELL**, Claire
**Transpersonal Psychotherapist**
46 Princess Road
London
NW1 8JL
☎ 020 7722 9716
CTP, CFET

**CHINA**, Giselle
**Psychoanalytic Psychotherapist**
24B South Hill Park Gardens
London
NW3 2TG
☎ 020 7 435 6361
glchina@btopenworld.com
IPSS

**CLARKE**, Colin
**Existential Psychotherapist**
♿ 69 Camden Mews
London
NW1 9BY
☎ 02072 670 327
colin.clarke6@virgin.net
UPCA

**CLULOW**, Christopher
**Couple Psychoanalytic Psychotherapist**
♿ Tavistock Marital Studies Institute
Tavistock Centre
120 Belsize Lane
London
NW3 5BA
☎ 020 7435 7111
☎ 01727 868 108
TMSI, SCPP

**COHEN**, Nomy
**Family & Systemic Psychotherapist**
47 Wykenham Road
London
NW4 2SS
☎ 020 8203 8415
☎ 07973 416 314
KCC

**COLAHAN**, Mireille
**Family & Systemic Psychotherapist**
9 Lyme Street
London
NW1 0EH
☎ 020 7482 0303
m.colahan@virgin.net
AFT

**COOPER**, Hilary
**Psychoanalytic Psychotherapist**
♿ 14 Dartmouth Road
London
NW2 4EU
☎ 020 8208 0600
☎ 020 8208 3349
cooperate@bigfoot.com
PA

**COPPENS**, Arnoldus
**Integrative Psychotherapist**
12 Mowbray Road
Kilburn
London
NW6 7QU
☎ 020 8451 1676
coppens@coppens.com
MET

**CORBETT**, Gemma
**Integrative Psychotherapist**
83 St. Gabriels Road
London
NW2 4DU
☎ 020 8830 5064
gemma.corbett@virgin.net
SPCRC

**CORNISH**, Ursula
**Systemic Psychotherapist**
39 Chalcot Square
London
NW1 8YP
☎ 020 7586 2582
IFT

**COSTELLO**, Marie
**Psychoanalytic Psychotherapist**
Maresfield Gardens
London
NW3
☎ 020 7431 8159
marie.c@virgin.net
FPC

**COUSINS**, Jan
**Child Psychotherapist**
107c Bartholomew Road
London
NW5 2AR
☎ 020 7482 4923
ACP

**CREGEEN**, Simon
**Child Psychotherapist**
c/o ACP
120 West Heath Road
London
NW3 7TU
☎ 0151 670 0031
ACP

**CUDMORE**, Lynne
**Child Psychotherapist, Couple Psychoanalytic Psychotherapist**
♿ T.M.S.I.
Tavistock Centre
120 Belsize Lane
London
NW3 5BA
☎ 020 7435 7111
☎ 020 8993 1534
seancudmore802@hotmail.com
ACP, TMSI, SCPP

**CUMMINGS**, Celia
**Child Psychotherapist**
c/o ACP
120 West Heath Road
London
NW3 7TU
☎ 020 7586 8881
ccatarc@aol.com
ACP

**CUMMINS MA**, Kate
**Transpersonal Psychotherapist**
London
NW10
☎ 020 7266 3006
CCPE

**DALE**, Barbara Janet
**Systemic Psychotherapist**
♿ Child & Family Dept
Tavistock Clinic
120 Belsize Lane
London
NW3
☎ 020 7435 7111
IFT

**DAUM**, Minna
**Family & Systemic Psychotherapist**
The Anna Freud Centre
21 Maresfield Gardens
London
NW3 5SD
☎ 020 8930 1801
minnadaum@cwcom.net
AFT

**DAVIDS**, Jennifer
**Child Psychotherapist**
Flat 2
16 Priory Terrace
London
NW6 4DH
☎ 020 7794 2313
☎ 020 7372 3403
ACP

**DAVIES**, Judy
**Attachment-based Psychoanalytic Psychotherapist**
39 Goldhurst Terrace
London
NW6 3HB
☎ 020 7624 3908
judy_davies@btopenworld.com
CAPP

**DAVIS**, Diana
**Psychoanalytic Psychotherapist**
39 Eton Hall
Eton College Road
London
NW3 2DP
☎ 020 7586 4876
dfdavis@btinternet.com
IPSS

**DAVIS**, Helen
**Integrative Psychotherapist**
♿ 17 Mapesbury Road
Willesden
London
NW2 4HU
☎ 020 8450 4401
☎ 020 8450 3311
MC

**DAVIS**, Paul E.
**Cognitive Behavioural Psychotherapist**
Department of Psychology
St. James House
108 Hampstead Road
London
NW1 2LS
☎ 020 7530 3057
Paul.Davis@btinternet.com
BABCP

**DAVIS**, Wendy
**Integrative Psychotherapist**
33 Crofton Road
London
NW5
☎ 020 8349 4178
AHPP

**DAWSON**, Liz
**Integrative Psychotherapist**
70 Rucklidge Avenue
Harlseden
London
NW10 4PS
☎ 020 8961 6840
lizdawson@ukcp.net
MET

**DE MARE**, Patrick
**Group Analyst**
5 Holly Place
London
NW3 6QU
☎ 020 7794 3171
IGA

**DECO**, Sarah
**Group Analyst**
Institute of Group Analysis
1 Daleham Gardens
London
NW3 5BY
☎ 020 7431 2693
sarah.deco@igalondon.org.uk
IGA

**DELL**, Judith
**Psychoanalytic Psychotherapist**
45 Litchfield Way
London
NW11 6NU
☎ 020 8458 7893
jsdell@aol.com
FIP

**DENT**, Carey
**Integrative Psychotherapist**
71a King Henry's Road
Primrose Hill
London
NW3 3QU
☎ 020 7722 9565
SPCRC

**DIMCOVIC**, Nada
**Personal Construct Psychotherapist**
Department of Clinical Psychology
Colindale Hospital
Colindale Avenue
London
NW9 5H
☎ 020 8440 2169
☎ 020 8952 2381 ext 3761
nada@dimcovic.fsnet.co.uk
PCP

**DIYALJEE**, Angeli
**Hypno-Psychotherapist**
Flat 6
346 Finchley Road
Hampstead
London
NW3 7AJ
☎ 02074 314 943
NRHP

**DOGMETCHI**, Geri
**Psychoanalytic Psychotherapist**
♿ 18 Spencer Rise
London
NW5 1AP
☎ 020 7 485 2883
IPSS

**DOORLEY**, Damien
**Analytical Psychologist-Jungian Analyst**
75 Goldhurst Terrace
London
NW6 3HA
☎ 020 7624 6524
ballyliffin@aol.com
AJA

**DOVER**, Jennifer
**Educational Therapist**
11 Gainsborough Gardens
London
NW3 1BJ
☎ 020 7794 6510
jennydover@blueyonder.co.uk
CFET

**DOWLING**, Emilia
**Family & Systemic Psychotherapist**
♿ Child & Family Dept
Tavistock Clinic
London
NW3 5BA
☎ 020 8444 6795
☎ 020 7435 7111
emilia@dowling29.freeserve.co.uk
IFT

**DOWNES**, Celia
**Psychodynamic Psychotherapist**
17 Provost Road
London
NW3 4ST
☎ 020 7722 0561
cdpach@aol.com
FIP

**DU PLOCK**, Simon
**Existential Psychotherapist**
School of Pyschotherapy & Counselling
Regent's College
Inner Circle
London
NW1 4NS
☎ 020 7487 7680
duplocks@regents.ac.uk
SPCRC

**DU RY**, Marc
**Lacanian Analyst**
1 Manor Mansions
Belsize Park Gardens
London
NW3 4NB
☎ 0770 888 116
CFAR

**DUBINSKY**, Helene
**Child Psychotherapist**
Tavistock Child and Family Department
NW3
☎ 020 7435 7111
☎ 020 7794 5047
ACP

**DUCKWORTH**, Moira
**Analytical Psychologist-Jungian Analyst, Psychoanalytic Psychotherapist**
24 Achilles Road
West Hampstead
London
NW6 1EA
☎ 020 7431 0811
moirad@dircon.co.uk
AJA, FPC

**DUNBAR**, Gill
**Analytical Psychologist-Jungian Analyst, Psychoanalytic Psychotherapist**
NW2
☎ 020 8201 9062
gilldunbar@aol.com
CAP, FPC *

**DUNN**, Nicola
**Integrative Psychotherapist**
53 Shirlock Road
London
NW3 2HR
☎ 020 7 267 4106
MC

**DYCZKOWSKA**, Ania
**Psychosynthesis Psychotherapist**
The London Psychosynthesis Clinic
65A Watford Way
Hendon
London
NW4 3AQ
☎ 02085 791 979
☎ 02082 024 525
IPS

**EASTER**, Judith
**Psychoanalytic Psychotherapist**
77 Torbay Road
London
NW6 7DU
☎ 020 7 328 6250
GUILD

**EDWARDS**, Dagmar
**Gestalt Psychotherapist**
28 Blenheim Gardens
London
NW2 4NS
☎ 020 8208 1235
dagmaredwards@btinternet.com
MET

**EISENHAUER**, Gary
**Integrative Psychotherapist**
80 Ashburnham Road
Kensal Green
London
NW10 5SE
☎ 020 8968 4568
garye@aol.com
SPCRC

**EKDAWI**, Isabelle
**Systemic Psychotherapist**
MH COP
2nd Floor, North East Building
St Pancras Hospital
London
NW1 0PE
☎ 020 7530 3369
KCC

**ELLIS**, Michael
**Gestalt Psychotherapist**
♿ 1 Hillside
Highgate Road
London
NW5 1QT
☎ 020 7281 9443
☎ 020 7482 3293
michael.aellis@btopenworld.com
GCL

**EMANUEL**, Ricky
**Child Psychotherapist**
Dept. of Child & Adolescent Psychiatry
Royal Free Hospital
Pond Street
London
NW3 2QG
☎ 020 7830 2931
☎ 020 8348 7032
email@remanuel.freeserve.co.uk
ACP

**ENDER**, Beckett
**Psychosynthesis Psychotherapist**
186 North End Road
Golders Green
London
NW11 7PH
☎ 02089 055 937
☎ 02083 409 423
beckettender@aol.com
IPS

**ENEVER**, Andrew
**Attachment-based Psychoanalytic Psychotherapist**
Flat B
27 Greenland Road
London
NW1 0AX
☎ 020 7482 2106
aenever@myself.com
CAPP

**ESLAVA**, Carlota
**Family & Systemic Psychotherapist**
Flat 3
50 Priory Road
South Hampstead
London
NW6 3RE
☎ 020 7625 4042
aesla01@students.bbk.ac.uk
AFT

**ESTERHUYSE FALCK**, Sonja
**Psychoanalytic Psychotherapist**
Hampstead
London
NW3
☎ 020 7435 6806
sonja.falck@btinternet.com
PA

**EVANS**, Caron
**Psychoanalytic Psychotherapist**
7 St Anthony's Flats
Aldenham Street
London
NW1 1SA
☎ 020 7482 3505
☎ 020 7383 5696
caron@evans3752.fsnet.co.uk
IPSS

**EVANS**, Joan
**Psychosynthesis Psychotherapist**
Institute of Psychosynthesis
9 Burroughs Gardens
Hendon
London
NW4 3AQ
☎ 020 8202 4525
joanevans@psychosynthesis.org
IPS

**EVANS**, Roger
**Psychosynthesis Psychotherapist**
Institute of Psychosynthesis
9 Burroughs Gardens
Hendon
London
NW4 3AQ
☎ 02082 024 525
revans@clc.co.uk
IPS

**FALK**, Helen
**Analytical Psychologist-Jungian Analyst**
6 Reeds Place
London
NW1 9NA
☎ 020 7267 5435
AJA

**FALLOWES**, Diana
**Child Psychotherapist**
ACP
120 West Heath Road
London
NW3 7TU
☎ 0121-788-8852
diana.fallowes@solihull-pct.nhs.uk
ACP

**FANNING**, Alexandra
**Psychoanalytic Psychotherapist**
167 Sumatra Road
London
NW6 1PN
☎ 02077 944 010
Alexandra@psychotherapist.demon.co.uk
FIP, UPCA

**FARAH**, Paula
**Family & Systemic Psychotherapist**
3 Westbere Road
West Hampstead
London
NW2 3SP
☎ 01895 256 521
paulafarah@hotmail.com
IFT

**FARHI**, Nina
**Psychoanalytic Psychotherapist**
11 North Square
London
NW11 7AB
☎ 020 8 455 5329
☎ 020 8 731 6109 (f)
farhi@clara.net
GUILD

**FARZIM**, Pari
**Family & Systemic Psychotherapist**
♿ 52 Teignmouth Road
London
NW2 4DX
☎ 020 8452 3585
PFarzim@aol.com
IFT

**FENTIMAN**, John
**Transpersonal Psychotherapist**
Flat 1
62 Canfield Gardens
London
NW6 3EB
☎ 020 7 328 7083
jfentiman@onetel.net.uk
CCPE

**FESTENSTEIN**, Geraldine
**Group Analyst**
Flat 3
18 Acol Road
London
NW6 3AG
geeteefest@yahoo.co.uk
IGA

**FICARRA**, Berthe
**Psychoanalytic Psychotherapist**
7 Estelle Road
London
NW3 2JX
☎ 020 7 482 3399
GUILD

**FITZPATRICK**, Marion
**Integrative Psychotherapist**
18 Kings Road
London
NW10 2BL
☎ 02084 594 285
☎ 07939 145 030
MC

**FLOWER**, Annie
**Family & Systemic Psychotherapist**
♿ 91 South Hill Park
London
NW3 2SP
☎ 020 7794 4398
AFT

**FRANKLYN**, Frank
**Psychoanalytic Psychotherapist**
♿ 26 Sydney Grove
Hendon
London
NW4 2EH
☎ 0208 202 7546
ffranklyn@tiscali.co.uk
IPSS

**FREUDENBERG**, Susan
**Group Analyst**
♿ Adult Dept.
The Tavistock Centre
120 Belsize Lane
London
NW3 5BA
☎ 020 7447 3739
IGA

**FRIEDMAN**, Debbie
**Psychosynthesis Psychotherapist**
1189a Finchley Road
London
NW11 0AA
☎ 02084 585 760
friedman@btinternet.com
IPS

**FRIEDMAN**, Joe
**Psychoanalytic Psychotherapist**
Top Flat
41 Buckland Crescent
London
NW3 5DJ
☎ 020 7722 5077
PA

**FRISVOLD**, Tove
**Psychoanalytic Psychotherapist**
22, Princess Road
London
NW1 8JJ
☎ 01608 810412
tove@amberbridge.co.uk
IPSS

**GAL**, Oshrat
**Psychoanalytic Psychotherapist**
54a Woodstock Avenue
London
NW11 9RG
☎ 020 8431 4456
☎ 020 8 455 5333
GUILD

**GASTER**, Yishai
**Body Psychotherapist, Integrative Psychotherapist**
5 Shakespeare Road
Mill Hill
London
NW7 4BA
☎ 07976 853 267
ygaster@tiscali.co.uk
CCBP

**GAVSHON**, Audrey
**Child Psychotherapist**
Anna Freud Centre
21 Maresfield Gardens
London
NW3 5SH
☎ 020 7794 2313
☎ 020 8348 0276
ACP

**GESSERT**, Astrid
**Lacanian Analyst**
Consulting rooms
167 Sumatra Rd
London
NW6 1PN
☎ 01297 560 497
astnd@gessert.fsnet.co.uk
CFAR

**GIBSON**, Glen
**Psychosynthesis Psychotherapist**
♿ 21 Rossendale Way
Camden Town
NW1
☎ 020 7916 1342
IPS

**GIBSON**, Walter
**Integrative Psychotherapist**
12 Parkfield Road
Willesden
London
NW10 2BJ
☎ 0208 537 2302
WalterGibson@mac.com
MC

**GILBERT**, Gillie
**Biodynamic Psychotherapist**
Violet Hill Studios
Violet Hill
St Johns Wood
NW6
☎ 02084 458 424
gilliegilbert@onetel.com
LSBP

**GILBERT**, Kate
**Psychoanalytic Psychotherapist**
♿ Flat A
4 Frognal
London
NW3 6AJ
☎ 020 7419 1984
☎ 07767 655 316
gilbertkate@hotmail.com
PA

**GILDEBRAND**, Katarina
**Transactional Analysis Psychotherapist**
17 Midland Terrace
London
NW2 6QH
☎ 02084 506 896
Katarina@dircon.co.uk
ITA

**GLOSSOP**, Miranda
**Psychoanalytic Psychotherapist**
4 Marty's Yard
17 Hampstead High Street
London
NW3 1QW
☎ 07973 154 552
☎ 020 7722 1438
PA

**GODINHO**, Bernadette
**Systemic Psychotherapist**
24 Ulysses Road
London
NW6 1EE
KCC

**GOLD**, Bonnie
**Group Analyst**
52a Charlbert Court
Mackennal Street
London
NW8 7DB
☎ 020 7586 1963
bonniegold@totalise.co.uk
IGA

**GOLDENBERG**, Harriet
**Existential Psychotherapist**
31a Buckland Crescent
London
NW3 5DJ
☎ 020 7722 2510
stranger@land.demon.co.uk
SPCRC

**GOMEZ**, Lavinia
**Humanistic Psychotherapist**
21 Mill Lane
London
NW6 1NT
☎ 020 7794 5308
lavinia.gomez@bigfoot.com
AHPP, FIP

**GOOD**, Elizabeth
**Psychoanalytic Psychotherapist**
Flat 2
308 Finchley Road
Hampstead
London
NW3
☎ 020 8989 6529
☎ 020 7794 3377
AGIP

**GOODMAN**, Diana
**Psychodynamic Psychotherapist**
22 Fitzjohns Avenue
London
NW3 5NB
☎ 020 7435 1079
dianagoodman@onetel.net.uk
AIP

**GORDON**, Paul
**Psychoanalytic Psychotherapist**
74 Victoria Road
London
NW6 6QA
☎ 020 7624 3053
psgordon@talk21.com
PA

**GORODENSKY**, Arlene
**Integrative Psychotherapist**
♿ North End Road Practice
18B North End Road
Golders Green
London
NW11 7PH
☎ 020 8958 7021
ARLENE@Psych2001.freeserve.co.uk
SPCRC

**GRANT**, Iona
**Psychoanalytic Psychotherapist**
♿ 75 Fleetwood Road
Dollis Hill
London
NW10 1NR
☎ 020 8452 4479
ARBS

**GRAY**, Dennis
**Group Analytic Psychotherapist**
♿ 1 Daleham Gardens
London
NW3 5BA
☎ 020 7681 8773
denniswgray@yahoo.com
FPC

**GRAY**, Elizabeth
**Family & Systemic Psychotherapist**
11 Well Road
London
NW3 1LH
☎ 020 7435 9228
AFT

**GREAVES**, Sarah
**Psychoanalyst**
23 College Crescent
London
NW3 5LL
☎ 01223 354 526
sarah.greaves@virgin.net
CSP, GUILD

**GREEN**, Viviane
**Child Psychotherapist**
Anna Freud Centre
21 Maresfield Gardens
London
NW3 5SH
☎ 020 7794 2313
☎ 020 7435 4960
viviane@viviane.freeserve.co.uk
ACP

**GREENWOOD**, Lynn
**Integrative Psychotherapist**
8a Lady Margaret Road
London
NW5 2XS
☎ 020 7428 0902
lynn.greenwood@btopenworld.com
SPCRC

**GROOCOCK**, Pamela
**Systemic Psychotherapist**
17 Marlborough Mansions
Cannon Hill
London
NW6 1JR
KCC

**GROSS**, Erwin
**Family & Systemic Psychotherapist**
Ashbourne House
Alberon Garden
London
NW11 0BN
☎ 07811 451 576
e.gross@btinternet.com
IFT

**GUILFOYLE**, John Francis
**Sexual and Relationship Psychotherapist**
40 Brooksville Avenue
Queens Park
London
NW6 6TG
☎ 020 8969 7856
jfguilfoyle@tiscali.co.uk
BASRT

**GUILLEMOT**, Yves
**Integrative Psychotherapist**
51 Oxgate Gardens
London
NW2 6EA
☎ 02084 524 432
yves@dircom.co.uk
MC

**HACKER**, Margaret
**Psychosynthesis Psychotherapist**
46 Hodford Road
London
NW11 8NN
☎ 02084 553 785
IPS

**HACKER**, Roger
**Psychoanalytic Psychotherapist**
5 Chalcot Gardens
London
NW3 4YB
☎ 020 7 586 4144
RogerJ.Hacker@AOL.com
ARBS

**HAGENBACH**, Kitty
**Transpersonal Psychotherapist**
Viveka
27a Queens Terrace
London
NW8 6EA
☎ 020 7483 3788
☎ 01342 823461
kitty@kittyh.demon.co.uk
CCPE

**HAINE**, Stephen R
**Psychoanalytic Psychotherapist**
Flat C 96 Fortess Road
Kentish Town
London
NW5 2HJ
☎ 020 7813 9069
stephenhaine@aol.com
AGIP

**HALL**, Albyn
**Integrative Psychotherapist**
41a Lady Somerset Road
London
NW5 1TY
☎ 020 7482 3197
albyn65@yahoo.com
SPCRC

**HALL**, Francesca
**Integrative Arts Psychotherapist**
54d Belsize Avenue
Belsize Park
London
NW3 4AE
☎ 020 7435 2961
IATE

**HAMROGUE**, Tom
**Group Analyst**
Institute of Group Analysis
1 Daleham Gardens
London
NW3 5BY
☎ 020 8888 6315
☎ 020 7431 2693
IGA

**HARDING**, Michael
**Existential Psychotherapist**
24 Birchington Court
West End Lane
London
NW6 4PB
☎ 020 7487 7694
☎ 020 7328 1823
hardingm@regents.ac.uk
SPCRC, SEA

**HARRIS**, Rita
**Family & Systemic Psychotherapist**
♿ Child and Family Depertment
Tavistock Clinic
120 Belsize Lane
London
NW3 5BA
☎ 020 7447 3779
rharris@tavi-port.org
AFT

**HARVARD-WATTS**, Olivia
**Psychoanalytic Psychotherapist**
44 Woodsome Road
London
NW5 1RZ
☎ 020 7 424 0233
☎ 020 7 485 6582
GUILD

**HARVEY**, Natasha
**Psychoanalytic Psychotherapist**
Flat 5
130 Fellows Road
London
NW1 5BL
☎ 020 7483 4649
☎ 020 8341 9513
FPC

**HAUSSMAN**, Rochelle
**Educational Therapist**
NW11
☎ 020 8209 0423
CFET

**HAY-BURNS**, Jean
**Transpersonal Psychotherapist**
♿ 4 Andover Place
London
NW6 5EF
☎ 07909 620905
☎ 020 76252014
nurjehan@amserve.net
CCPE

**HENRY**, John
**Attachment-based Psychoanalytic Psychotherapist**
♿ 27 Elm Grove
London
NW2 3AE
☎ 020 8452 8865
john@henrysun.plus.com
CAPP

**HERING-JOSEFOWITZ**, Pauline
**Child Psychotherapist**
C/O ACP
NW3
☎ 00 41 22 349 1230
ACP

**HERST**, Edward
**Analytical Psychologist-Jungian Analyst**
9 Fitzroy Road
London
NW1 8TU
☎ 020 7722 1661
CAP *

**HESELTINE**, Lynne
**Systemic Psychotherapist**
April House
45b Maresfield Gardens
Hampstead
London
NW3 5TE
☎ 020 7435 1900
☎ 020 7720 7301
lynneh@cybase.co.uk
KCC

**HEWISON**, David
**Analytical Psychologist-Jungian Analyst, Couple Psychoanalytic Psychotherapist**
♿ T.M.S.I.
The Tavistock Centre
120 Belsize Lane
London
NW3 5BA
☎ 020 7435 7111
☎ 020 8442 2601
mail@davidhewison.com
CAP, TMSI, SCPP

**HICKEY**, Alaco
**Psychosynthesis Psychotherapist**
Institute of Psychosynthesis
65a Watford Way
Hendon
London
NW4 3AQ
☎ 02084 490 465
alacohickey@hotmail.com
IPS

**HILDEBRAND**, Judy
**Family & Systemic Psychotherapist**
43 Oak Village
London
NW5 4QL
☎ 020 7267 2910
judy@jhildebrand.demon.co.uk
IFT

**HILL**, Finella
**Family & Systemic Psychotherapist**
♿ Willesden Centre for Psychological Treatment
Pound Lane Health Centre
Pound Lane
London
NW10 2HH
☎ 01494 471 739
☎ 020 8438 1770
IFT

**HILL**, Philip
**Lacanian Analyst**
The Hillside Practice
1 Hillside
Highgate Road
London
NW5 1QT
☎ 020 8340 9941
phfh@philiphill.com
CFAR

**HOLDEN**, Maxine
**Transpersonal Psychotherapist**
8A Lymington Road
London
NW6 1HY
☎ 020 7431 8757
CTP

**HOLLAND**, Ray
**Integrative Psychotherapist**
25 Greenhill Road
Harlesden
London
NW10 8UD
☎ 020 8838 3424
☎ 07812 480 947
rsholland@btinternet.com
CCBP

**HOLM**, Kirsti
**Hypno-Psychotherapist**
♿ 48 Shirehall Park
London
NW4 2QX
NSHAP

**HOPPER**, Earl
**Group Analyst**
11 Heath Mansions
The Mount
Heath Street
London
NW3 6SN
☎ 020 7435 2053
earlhopper@btinternet.com
IGA

**HORNE**, Ann
**Child Psychotherapist**
Portman Clinic
8 Fitzjohns Avenue
London
NW3 5NA
☎ 020 7794 8262
annie@linnet.1.demon.co.uk
ACP

**HOUSTON**, Gaie
**Gestalt Psychotherapist**
8 Rochester Terrace
London
NW1 9JN
☎ 020 7485 9265
gaiehouston@btconnect.com
GCL

**HOWARD**, Angela
**Psychoanalytic Psychotherapist**
1 Tower Close
Lyndhurst Road
London
NW3 5TB
☎ 020 7 431 6410
angehow@aol.com
GUILD

**HUGHES**, Rose
**Cognitive Analytic Therapist**
55 Brookfield Avenue
Mill Hill
London
NW7 2DB
☎ 020 8906 0055
ACAT

**HUMPHREY**, Anna
**Integrative Psychotherapist**
17 Grafton Road
London
NW5 3DX
☎ 020 7485 1167
MC

**HURRY**, Anne
**Child Psychotherapist**
Anna Freud Centre
21 Maresfield Gardens
London
NW3 5SH
☎ 020 7794 2313
☎ 020 7794 1762
ACP

**ILJON FOREMAN**, Elaine
**Cognitive Behavioural Psychotherapist**
Freedom to Fly
EIF Consulting Rooms
21A Dean Road
London
NW2 5AB
☎ 020 8459 3428
free2fly@dial.pipex.com
BABCP

**ITTEN**, Theodor
**Psychoanalytic Psychotherapist**
57 Fitzroy Road
London
NW1 8TP
☎ +41 71 244 2121
info@ittentheodor.ch
PA

**JAAX**, Stepahnie
**Lacanian Analyst, Psychoanalytic Psychotherapist**
19 King Henry Road
London
NW3 3QP
☎ +32 474 902 653
☎ +32 346 7383
stefanie.jaax@wannado.be
CFAR

**JACKSON**, Diana
**Integrative Psychotherapist**
26 Willifield Way
London
NW11 7XT
☎ 020 8458 5791
dianajackson5791@hotmail.com
SPTI

**JACOBS**, Joe
**Child Psychotherapist**
Flat 3
50 Well Walk
London
NW3 1BT
☎ 020 7433 1927
AJJJJA@aol.com
ACP

**JOFFE**, Riva
**Psychoanalytic Psychotherapist**
♿ 6 Peploe Road
Queen's Park
London
NW6 6EB
☎ 020 8 969 0288 (t/f)
☎ 07775 636642
riva@upwardspiral.demon.co.uk
IPSS

**JOHNSON**, Avril
**Psychoanalytic Psychotherapist**
15 New Court
Flask Walk
Lutton Terrace
London
NW3 1HD
☎ 020 7431 5873 [t/f]
avril.johnson@bigfoot.com
IPSS

**JOLLES**, Pamela
**Integrative Psychotherapist**
110 Regent's Park Road
London
NW1 8UG
☎ 020 7586 2841
SPCRC

**JOLLIFFE**, John
**Attachment-based Psychoanalytic Psychotherapist**
2 Chiltern Gardens
Cricklewood
London
NW2 1PX
☎ 020 8731 7301
johnjolliffe@onetel.net.uk
CAPP

**JORDAN**, Hazel
**Integrative Psychotherapist**
♿ 55 Fortress Road
Kentish Town
London
NW5 1AD
☎ 020 8341 3861
MET

**JORDAN**, Susan
**Core Process Psychotherapist**
181c Fordwych Road
London
NW2 3NG
☎ 020 8452 4174
KI

**JUKES**, Adam
**Group Analyst**
7 Hylda Court
3/5 St Albans Road
London
NW5 1RE
☎ 020 7267 8713
adejuk@aol.com
IGA

**KAHR**, Brett
**Attachment-based Psychoanalytic Psychotherapist, Integrative Psychotherapist**
Suite 6
4 Marty's Yard
17 Hampstead High Street
Hampstead, London
NW3 1QW
CAPP, SPCRC

**KAPLAN**, Myron R
**Psychoanalytic Psychotherapist**
1 Clarence Gate Gardens
Glentworth Street
London
NW1 6AY
☎ 020 7724 3062
dearuwang@aol.com
AGIP

**KARBAN**, Barbara
**Existential Psychotherapist**
Flat 3
15 Alma Square
London
NW8 9QA
☎ 020 7286 0019
SPCRC

**KARP**, Marcia
**Psychodrama Psychotherapist**
69 Fordwych Road
London
NW2 3TL
☎ 020 8452 3448
☎ 07710 481 017
mkarp11444@aol.com
BPA

**KATZ**, Andy
**Integrative Arts Psychotherapist**
London
NW11
☎ 020 8455 1878
IATE

**KATZMAN**, Stewart
**Analytical Psychologist-Jungian Analyst**
70 Oakley Square
London
NW1 1NJ
☎ 020 7387 0680
☎ 020 7387 5655
katzman@bluecarrots.com
CAP *

**KELLY**, Caro
**Gestalt Psychotherapist**
CHOICE Psychotherapy Practice
18a Heriot Road
Hendon
London
NW4 2DG
☎ 020 8202 1023
☎ 020 8223 0680
caro.kelly@btinternet.com
GPTI

**KENNEDY**, Michael
**Lacanian Analyst**
c/o Suite 56
571 Finchley Road
London
NW3 7BN
☎ 020 7639 8289
michael@cfar.demon.co.uk
CFAR

**KERNOFF**, Marilyn
**Psychosynthesis Psychotherapist**
Flat 3
64 Aberdare Gardens
London
NW6 3QD
☎ 020 7624 0587
mkern@globalnet.co.uk
PET

**KESHET-ORR**, Judi
**Individual and Group Humanistic Psychotherapist, Sexual and Relationship Psychotherapist**
181 Hampstead Way
London
NW11 7YA
☎ 020 8455 4511
judiko@ulfie.demon.co.uk
AHPP, BASRT, UPCA

**KHAN**, Sacha
**Hypno-Psychotherapist**
69 Marlborough Place
St Johns Wood
London
NW8 0PT
☎ 02073 286 224
NRHP

**KISCH**, Marlies
**Psychodynamic Psychotherapist**
2 Rona Road
London
NW3 2DA
☎ 020 7267 8356
marlieskisch@hotmail.com
FPC

**KITSEN**, Jane
**Attachment-based Psychoanalytic Psychotherapist**
♿ 48 Roe Lane
Kingsbury
London
NW9 9BD
☎ 020 8204 8480
therapy@janekitsen.co.uk
YAPP

**KLOEPFER**, Irene
**Psychoanalytic Psychotherapist**
40 Bell Lane
Hendon
London
NW4 2AD
☎ 020 8203 4584
Kloepfer40@aol.com
AGIP

**KNIGHT**, Michael
**Cognitive Analytic Therapist**
♿ Swiss Cottage
London
NW3
☎ 020 7586 5626
mj.knight@ukonline.co.uk
ACAT

**KNOTT**, Louise
**Psychoanalytic Psychotherapist**
44C Falkland Road
London
NW5 2XA
☎ 020 7284 4931
☎ 07909 542717
laknott@hotmail.com
IPSS

**KOHON**, Valli
**Child Psychotherapist**
NW3
☎ 020 8455 4173
ACP

**KOPPELMAN**, Liora
**Couple Psychoanalytic Psychotherapist**
60 Corringham Road
London
NW11 7BX
☎ 020 8455 3092
michaelk@wkoppelman.freeserve.co.uk
SCPP

**KRISTAL**, Barbie
**Existential Psychotherapist**
Flat A
95 Constantine Road
London
NW3 2LP
☎ 020 7794 3751
barbiekristal@aol.com
SPCRC

**LA TOURELLE**, Maggie
**Neurolinguistic Psychotherapist**
70a Caversham Road
Kentish Town
London
NW5 2DS
☎ 02074 854 215
info@maggielatourelle.co.uk
NLPtCA

**LAFFY**, Cabby
**Humanistic Psychotherapist**
10b Modbury Gardens
London
NW5 3QE
☎ 020 7482 6371
cabbylaffy@yahoo.co.uk
AHPP

**LAMPSHIRE**, Julia
**Neurolinguistic Psychotherapist**
7 Woodside
Hampstead
Garden Suburb
London
NW11 6HH
☎ 02082 090 654
julia@jlampshire.freeserve.co.uk
NLPtCA

**LAPORT-STEUERMAN**, M.
**Child Psychotherapist**
34 Ornan Road
London
NW3 4QB
☎ 020 7435 4376
ACP

**LAU**, Annie
**Family & Systemic Psychotherapist**
Loxford Hall
Loxford Lane
Ilford
☎ 020 8478 7211
IFT

**LAUNER**, John
**Family & Systemic Psychotherapist**
♿ Child and Family Department
Tavistock Clinic
120 Belsize Lane
London
NW3 5BA
☎ 020 7447 3763
jllauner@tavi-port.nhs.uk
AFT

**LAWLOR**, Virginia
**Integrative Psychotherapist**
43 Shirlock Road
London
NW3 2HR
☎ 01277 364 744
ginnielawlor@hotmail.com
SPCRC

**LAYTON**, Clare
**Core Process Psychotherapist**
44b Frognal
London
NW3 6AG
☎ 020 7431 1867
KI

**LE QUESNE**, Susan
**Psychoanalytic Psychotherapist**
32A Llanvanor Road
London
NW2 2AP
☎ 020 7435 3151
☎ 020 8922 7102
susanlequesne@uk2.net
FIP, FPC

**LEDER**, Catherine
**Integrative Psychotherapist**
♿ 12a Ravenshaw Street
London
NW6 1NN
☎ 020 7794 2995
cleder@ukonline.co.uk
AHPP

**LEDERMAN**, Tsafi
**Biodynamic Psychotherapist**
33 Croftdown Road
London
NW5
☎ 02072 638 551
LSBP

**LEHRER**, Pam
**Psychoanalytic Psychotherapist**
32 Wildwood Road
London
NW11 6XB
☎ 020 8 458 8750
hyam.lehrer@talk21.com
IPSS

**LEVITSKY**, Jackie
**Psychoanalytic Psychotherapist**
95 Willifield Way
London
NW11 6HY
☎ 020 7467 8301
☎ 020 8455 6413
FIP

**LEVY**, Colette
**Psychoanalytic Psychotherapist**
St Johns Wood
London
NW8
☎ 020 7289 5044
FPC

**LIKIERMAN**, Meira
**Child Psychotherapist**
Tavistock Child & Family Department
NW3
☎ 020 7435 7111
☎ 020 7435 9888
ACP

**LINDEN**, Roger
**Psychoanalytic Psychotherapist**
14 Boscastle Road
Dartmouth Park
London
NW5 1EG
☎ 020 7485 2292
r.linden@virgin.net
FPC

**LINDSEY**, Dr Caroline
**Family & Systemic Psychotherapist**
♿ Child & Family Department
The Tavistock Clinic
120 Belsize Lane
London
NW3 5BA
☎ 020 7447 3808
☎ 020 8455 2882
clindsey@tavi-port.nhs.uk
23 Gresham Gardens
London
NW11 8NX
IFT

**LININGTON**, Mark
**Attachment-based Psychoanalytic Psychotherapist**
167 Sumatra Road
London
NW6 1PN
☎ 020 7372 3394
CAPP

**LOCK**, Gillian
**Integrative Psychotherapist**
22 Park Avenue
London
NW11 7SJ
☎ 020 8905 5692
☎ 07769 908 778
gillianlock@tesco.net
SPCRC

**LOCK**, Josephine
**Integrative Psychotherapist**
Flat 3
26 Minster Road
London
NW2 3KB
☎ 02084 522 116
MC

**LOW**, James
**Cognitive Analytic Therapist, Integrative Arts Psychotherapist, Psychoanalytic Psychotherapist, Sexual and Relationship Psychotherapist**
78b Princess Road
London
NW6 5QX
☎ 020 7328 4450
ACAT, BASRT, IATE, PA

**LUMBIS**, Gerald
**Integrative Psychotherapist**
21c Bramshill Gardens
Dartmouth Park
London
NW5 1JJ
☎ 020 7281 6605
lumbisg@yahoo.co.uk
SPCRC

**LYNDON**, Barbara
**Educational Therapist, Psychoanalytic Psychotherapist**
8 Honiton Road
London
NW6 6QE
☎ 020 7372 8009
barbaralyndon@talk21.com
AGIP, CFET

**MACGREGOR**, Catherine
**Psychosynthesis Psychotherapist**
24 Harley Road
Hampstead
London
NW3 3BN
☎ 02077 226 067 / 07808 856 829
☎ 02073 510 217
IPS

**MACKENNA**, Christopher
**Analytical Psychologist-Jungian Analyst, Analytical Psychotherapist**
St Marylebone Parish Church
17 Marylebone Road
London
NW1 5LT
☎ 020 7486 9363
☎ 020 7935 5066
cmackenna@stmarylebone.org
CAP *

**MACHADO**, Danuza
**Lacanian Analyst**
14 Eton Hall
Eton College Road
London
NW3 2DW
CFAR

**MADDOX**, Chris
**Existential Psychotherapist**
23 College Crescent
Swiss Cottage
London
NW3
☎ 02083 310 078
cgmaddox@teci.fsnet.co.uk
UPCA

**MAGRIEL**, Nicolas
**Body Psychotherapist, Integrative Psychotherapist**
Flat 8
118 Haverstock Hill
London
NW3 2BA
☎ 020 7722 6072
nm49@soas.ac.uk
CCBP

**MAITRA**, Begum
**Analytical Psychologist-Jungian Analyst**
38 Nant Road
London
NW2 2AT
☎ 020 8986 7351
☎ 020 8458 2510
AJA

**MALIK**, Rabia
**Systemic Psychotherapist**
Marlborough Family Service
38 Marlborough Place
London
NW8 0PJ
☎ 02076 248 605
r.malik@uel.ac.uk
IFT

**MALKIN**, Marion
**Integrative Psychotherapist, Psychoanalytic Psychotherapist**
67 Sumatra Road
West Hempstead
London
NW6 1PN
☎ 020 7272 7013
☎ 07815 122 048
AGIP, SPCRC

**MANDER**, Gertrud
**Psychoanalytic Psychotherapist**
24 Chalcot Crescent
London
NW1 8YD
☎ 020 7722 0033
g.mander@virgin.net
FPC

**MANDIN**, Philippe
**Family & Systemic Psychotherapist**
Marlborough Family Service
38 Marlborough Place
London
NW8 0PJ
☎ 020 7624 8605
philippe.mandin@cnwl.nhs.uk
IFT

**MANZI**, Christine
**Group Analyst**
7 Raeburn Close
Hampstead Garden Suburb
London
NW11 6UG
Cmanzi@aol.com
IGA

**MARKOVIC**, Desa
**Family & Systemic Psychotherapist**
Institute of Family Therapy
24-32 Stephenson Way
London
NW1 2HX
☎ 020 7240 1911
desamarkovic@btinternet.com
IFT

**MARTIN**, Christine
**Child Psychotherapist**
South Brent Child & Family Clinic
Warranty House
Dudden Hill Lane
London
NW10 1DL
☎ 020 8208 7200/1
cmm@chipsy.demon.co.uk
ACP

**MARX**, Philippa
**Group Analytic Psychotherapist**
Queens Park
NW6
☎ 020 8450 3385
FPC

**MASTERS**, David
**Systemic Psychotherapist**
Couple Therapy
London
NW3
☎ 020 7435 5492
☎ 020 8348 8325
KCC

**MAY**, Ian
**Transpersonal Psychotherapist**
♿ Central London
NW1
☎ 07939 043759 (mobile)
ianmay@excite.com
CCPE

**MAYO**, Rosalind
**Psychoanalytic Psychotherapist**
4 Marty's Yard
17 Hampstead High Street
London
NW3 1QW
☎ 01553 760 978
☎ 07811 480 310
rosalindmayo@aol.com
PA

**MCBRIDE**, Nigel
**Attachment-based Psychoanalytic Psychotherapist**
54 Grafton Terrace
London
NW5 4HY
☎ 020 7267 0594
nigelp.mcbride@virgin.net
CAPP

**MCEVOY**, Patricia Elaine
**Systemic Psychotherapist**
31 Cholmley Gardens
Aldred Road
London
NW6 1AG
☎ 020 7435 6597
☎ 020 7449 1296
pat@expatusa.demon.co.uk
The American School in London
1 Waverley Place
London
NW8 0NP
KCC

**MCGEE**, Colin
**Psychoanalytic Psychotherapist**
8 South Villas
Camden
London
NW1
☎ 020 8348 1848
☎ 07951 160309
cmcgee1499@aol.com/Website:
avoiceforchange.co.uk
IPSS

**MCKENZIE-SMITH**, Bryce
**Psychoanalytic Psychotherapist**
34 Dudley Court
Finchley Road
London
NW11 6AE
☎ 020 8731 6861
AGIP, AIP

**MCKEOWN**, Andy
**Integrative Psychotherapist**
Choice
18A Heriot Road
Hendon
London
NW4 2DG
☎ 01373 812237
☎ 020 8202 1023
andy.mckeown@talk21.com
MET

**MCLEAN**, Julienne
**Analytical Psychologist-Jungian Analyst**
Flat 21 Christchurch Court
171 Willesden Lane
London
NW6 7XF
☎ 020 8451 5255
juliennemclean@btinternet.com
AJA

**MEAKINS**, Elizabeth
**Psychoanalytic Psychotherapist**
The Hillside Practice
1 Hillside
Highgate Road
London
NW5 1QT
☎ 020 7482 3293
☎ 020 7485 1160
elizabeth.meakins@blueyonder.co.uk
GUILD

**MENDELSOHN**, Annette
**Child Psychotherapist**
Department of Child & Adolescent Psychiatry
Royal Free Hospital
Pond Street
London
NW3 2QG
☎ 020 7830 2931
☎ 020 7794 8708
amendelsohn@hotmail.com
ACP

**MEREDITH-OWEN**, William
**Analytical Psychotherapist**
Courtyard Flat
6 Holly Mount
London
NW3 6SG
WMIP

**MILLER**, Ann
**Family & Systemic Psychotherapist**
♿ Marlborough Family Service
38 Marlborough Place
London
NW8 OPJ
☎ 020 7624 8605
Ann.Miller@cnwl.nhs.uk
IFT

**MILLER**, John Andrew
**Integrative Psychotherapist, Psychoanalytic Psychotherapist**
22 Fitzjohn's Avenue
London
NW3 5NB
☎ 020 7435 1079
☎ 020 8905 5937
johnandrewmiller@onetel.net.uk
18B North End Road
London
NW11 7PH
AGIP, MET

**MILLER**, Lisa
**Child Psychotherapist**
Tavistock Child & Family Department
NW3
☎ 020 7435 7111
ACP

**MILLINGTON**, Malcolm
**Couple Psychoanalytic Psychotherapist**
T.M.S.I.
The Tavistock Centre
120 Belsize Lane
NW3 5BA
☎ 020 7435 7111
TMSI, SCPP

**MOJA-STRASSER**, Lucia
**Existential Psychotherapist**
144A Abbey Road
London
NW6 4SR
☎ 020 7372 6407
strassel@regents.ac.uk
SPCRC

**MOORE**, Julia
**Integrative Psychotherapist**
126 College Road
London
NW10 3PE
☎ 02089 692 726
moore.julia@talk21.com
MC

**MOORHEAD**, Michael
**Systemic Psychotherapist**
♿ The Vicarage
3 Station Road
Harlesden
London
NW10 4UJ
☎ 020 8965 4988
mike@dmoorhead.freeserve.co.uk
KCC

**MORRIS**, Patricia
**Psychoanalytic Psychotherapist**
17 Tanza Road
Hampstead
London
NW3 2UA
☎ 02074 310 896
patricia@trishmorris.demon.co.uk
NAFSI

**MOSS**, Valerie
**Existential Psychotherapist**
21 Estelle Road
London
NW3 2JX
☎ 020 7482 5350
☎ 07768 082 232
valerie@mossv.freeserve.co.uk
SEA

**MOURATOGLOU**, Vassilis
**Family & Systemic Psychotherapist**
♿ 90 Grove End Gardens
Grove End Road
St John's Wood
London
NW8 9LP
☎ 020 7286 3126
vm@psy.org
AFT

**MOUTSOU**, Christina
**Psychoanalytic Psychotherapist**
8 St Mark's Crescent
London
NW1 7TS
☎ 020 7209 2439
☎ 020 7383 3361
cmm22@cus.cam.ac.uk
PA

**MUFFET**, Ruth
**Analytical Psychologist-Jungian Analyst**
Flat 3
39 Belsize Square
London
NW3 4HL
☎ 020 7794 5303
☎ 020 7794 9854
CAP *

**MUIR**, Kate
**Psychosynthesis Psychotherapist**
Belsize Park
London
NW3
☎ 020 7706 4357
PET

**MYERS**, Philip
**Family & Systemic Psychotherapist**
♿ 68B Queens Crescent
Camden
London
NW5 4EE
☎ 020 7428 0892
philmyers27@hotmail.com
AFT

**NABARRO**, Elizabeth
**Psychoanalytic Psychotherapist**
58 Croftdown Road
London
NW5 1EN
☎ 020 7485 3597
☎ 07761 334 753
libnabarro1@aol.com
GUILD

**NEAL**, Charles
**Humanistic and Integrative Psychotherapist**
♿ 23 Rossendale Way
Elm Village
Camden
London
NW1 0XB
☎ 020 7387 6758
Charles.Neal@bigwaves.demon.co.uk
23 Rossendale Way
Camden
London
NW1 0XB
SPEC

**NELSON**, Sandy
**Integrative Psychotherapist**
80 Ashburnham Road
London
NW10 5SE
☎ 020 8968 4568
snelson145958742@aol.com
MC

**NICOLAUS**, Georg
**Integrative Psychosynthesis Psychotherapist**
Re-Vision
97 Brondesbury Road
London
NW6 6RY
☎ 020 8340 6751
RE.V

**NIELSEN**, Claudia
**Integrative Psychotherapist**
38 Denning Road
London
NW3 1SU
☎ 020 7431 1177
claudia@cnielsen.demon.co.uk
SPCRC

**NORBURN**, Veronica
**Psychoanalytic Psychotherapist**
18a Tanza Road
London
NW3 2UB
☎ 020 7 794 8697 (t/f)
veronica.norburn@o2.co.uk
IPSS

**NORTON**, Prue
**Integrative Psychotherapist**
9 Boscastle Road
London
NW5 1EE
☎ 0207 485 1860
pruenorton@hotmail.com
MC

**O'CALLAGHAN**, Lesley
**Integrative Psychotherapist**
53 Okehampton Road
London
NW10 3EN
☎ 020 8830 1912
MC

**O'DRISCOLL**, David
**Integrative Psychotherapist**
Respond
3rd Floor
24-32 Stephenson Way
London
NWI 2HD
☎ 020 7387 0700
☎ 0808 808 0700
david.odriscoll@respond.org.uk
www.respond.org.uk
SPCRC

**O'GORMAN**, Mary Pat
**Integrative Psychotherapist**
17 Lambolle Road
London
NW3 4HS
☎ 020 7794 8800
mpog@onetel.net.uk
MC

**OAKLEY**, Haya
**Psychoanalyst**
♿ 62 Upper Park Road
London
NW3 2UX
☎ 020 7722 1628
hayaoakley@freenetname.co.uk
GUILD, SITE

**OAKLEY**, Madeleine
**Family & Systemic Psychotherapist, Psychoanalytic Psychotherapist**
♿ Camden,City,Islington and Westminster Bereavement
295-299 Kentish Town Road
London
NW5 2TS
☎ 020 8883 4179
madeleineoakley@yahoo.co.uk
AFT, IPSS

**OAKLEY**, Sanja
**Existential Psychotherapist**
Regent's College
Inner Circle
Regent's Park
London
NW1 4NS
☎ 020 8348 3484
☎ 07966 463 454
Sanja@sanja.fsnet.co.uk
UPCA

**ODGERS**, Andrew
**Attachment-based Psychoanalytic Psychotherapist**
27 Ravensworth Road
Kensal Green
London
NW10 5NP
☎ 020 8969 3340
CAPP

**OLEY**, Mary
**Psychoanalytic Psychotherapist**
18b Huddlestone Road
London
NW2 5DN
☎ 020 8451 0196
23 College Crescent
London
NW3
ARBS

**ORBACH**, Susie
**Psychoanalytic Psychotherapist**
♿ 2 Lancaster Drive
London
NW3 4HA
☎ 02077 948 226
susieorbach@blueyonder.co.uk
WTC

**ORFORD**, Eileen
**Child Psychotherapist**
30 Regents Park Road
London
NW1 7TR
☎ 020 7485 4012 (t/f)
ACP

**ORLANS**, Vanja
**Gestalt Psychotherapist**
28 Blenheim Gardens
London
NW2 4NS
☎ 020 8208 1235
VanjaOrlans@btinternet.com
GPTI, MET

**PACEY**, Susan
**Sexual and Relationship Psychotherapist**
♿ Kentish Town Health Centre
James Wigg Practice
2 Bartholomew Road
London
NW5 2BX
☎ 020 7916 7055
susanpacey@yahoo.com
BASRT

**PALMER**, Jane
**Integrative Psychotherapist**
31B Wroltesley Road
Harlesden
London
NW10 5UT
☎ 020 8961 8076
jeprek@btinternet.com
MC

**PARISSIS**, Maria
**Integrative Psychotherapist**
24 Oxford Road
London
NW6 5SL
☎ 020 7328 9430
mariaparissis@hotmail.com
SPCRC

**PARK**, James
**Attachment-based Psychoanalytic Psychotherapist**
13 Streatley Road
London
NW6 7LJ
☎ 020 7328 3284
jamespark@pop3.poptel.org.uk
CAPP

**PARKINS**, Yvonne
**Core Process Psychotherapist**
Yew Tree Lodge
10 Tudor Close
Mill Hill
Ldonon
NW7 2BG
☎ 020 8906 0468
KI

**PAULSON**, Diana
**Family & Systemic Psychotherapist**
34 Alma Street
London
NW5 3DH
☎ 020 7445 8150
☎ 020 7267 4857
IFT

**PAWSON**, Chris
**Biodynamic Psychotherapist**
33 Croftdown Road
Highgate
NW5 1EL
☎ 01442 862029
LSBP

**PAYNE**, Christopher
**Integrative Psychosynthesis Psychotherapist**
6A Egbert Street
London
NW1 8LJ
☎ 0207 722 6874
RE.V

**PEARSON**, Jenny
**Psychoanalytic Psychotherapist**
2 Modbury Gardens
London
NW5 3QE
☎ 020 7482 1817
jenny.pearson-rycroft@virgin.net
AIP, FPC

**PECOTIC**, Branka
**Child Psychotherapist**
1 West Heath Lodge
Branch Hill
London
NW3 7LU
☎ 020 7433 1940
mpecotic@compuserve.com
ACP

**PETERS**, Linda
**Psychoanalytic Psychotherapist**
6 Sandwell Crescent
West Hampstead
London
NW6 1PB
☎ 020 7794 0836
FPC

**PHILLIPS**, Asha
**Child Psychotherapist**
c/o ACP
NW3
☎ 020 8954 4909
ashoop@blueyonder.co.uk
ACP

**PIKE**, Joanna
**Psychoanalytic Psychotherapist**
Studio E
49 The Avenue
London
NW6 7NR
☎ 020 7272 7013
jopike@onetel.com
AGIP

**PLANT**, Victoria
**Cognitive Analytic Therapist**
20 Bramston Road
London
NW10 5TU
☎ 07752 591 061
victoriaplant1@yahoo.co.uk
ACAT

**PLATT**, Sue
**Integrative Psychotherapist**
6 Marion Road
Mill Hill
London
NW7 4AN
☎ 02089 596 560
sue@platt.nitdram.co.uk
MC, WTC

**PLUNKETT**, Eileen
**Integrative Arts Psychotherapist**
St.Mary's Abbey Lodge
The Ridgeway
Mill Hill, London
NW7 4HX
☎ 020 8959 1364
IATE

**POLDEN**, Anne
**Psychoanalytic Psychotherapist**
Flat 10
111 Fordwych Road
West Hampstead
London
NW2 3NJ
☎ 020 8868 9429
IPSS

**PORTER**, Christine
**Child Psychotherapist**
c/o ACP
NW3
☎ 020 7262 4289
ACP

**POWELL**, Angela
**Psychoanalytic Psychotherapist**
♿ 167 Sumatra Road
London
NW6 1PN
☎ 01923 352 731
☎ 02077 941 433
ARBS, WTC

**POWER**, Teresa
**Child Psychotherapist**
c/o ACP
NW3
ACP

**PRALL**, Werner
**Integrative Psychotherapist**
61 Riffel Road
Willesden Green
London
NW2 4PG
☎ 02084 529 438
wprall@onetel.net.uk
MET

**PREISINGER**, Kristiane
**Humanistic Psychotherapist,**
**Integrative Psychotherapist**
14 Richborough Road
London
NW2 3LU
☎ 020 8452 6703
k_preisinger@onetel.net.uk
AHPP, CCBP

**PROKAYEVA-ROSS**, Tatiana
**Integrative Psychotherapist**
1 Huson Close
Swiss Cottage
London
NW3 3JW
☎ 02075 864 066
tatiana@prokayeva.freeserve.co.uk
MET

**PURPURA**, Davide
**Integrative Psychotherapist**
47 Asmuns Place
London
NW11 7XE
☎ 020 8731 8249
d.purpura@btinternet.com
SPCRC

**RABIN**, Judith
**Existential Psychotherapist**
33 West Heath Drive
London
NW11 7QG
☎ 020 8458 1007
SPCRC, SEA

**RAPHAEL-LINCOLN**, Francesca
**Psychoanalytic Psychotherapist**
Flat 4
58 Teignmouth Road
London
NW2 4DX
☎ 020 8452 5516
16 Aldershot Road
London
NW6 7LG
AGIP

**RAPP**, Hilde
**Integrative Psychotherapist,**
**Psychoanalytic Psychotherapist**
21 Priory Terrace
London
NW6 4DG
☎ 02076 254 287
rapp.biip@blueyonder.co.uk
IPSS, MET, UPCA

**RAVENSDALE**, Verity
**Psychoanalytic Psychotherapist**
2 Gloucester Crescent
London
NW1 7DS
☎ 020 7485 4514
☎ mobile: 07785 926358
Florence Nightingale Hospitals,
11-19 Lisson Grove
London
NW1 6SH
ARBS

**RAWSON-JONES**, Elizabeth
**Hypno-Psychotherapist**
18 North End Road
Golders Green
London
NW11
☎ 01923 824 755
NRHP

**RAYNER**, Mark
**Integrative Psychotherapist**
♿ Flat 1
143 West End Lane
London
NW6 2PH
☎ 020 7624 2706
serenity@pro-net.co.uk
SPCRC

**REDLER**, Leon
**Psychoanalytic Psychotherapist**
c/o Diorama Centre for Art, Therapy
& Technology
34 Osnaburgh Street
London
NW1 3ND
☎ 020 7916 5191
leonredler@blueyonder.co.uk
PA

**REID**, Susan
**Child Psychotherapist**
Tavistock Child & Family Department
NW3
☎ 020 7435 7111
☎ 020 7435 0467
ACP

**RENTON**, Mirjana
**Child Psychotherapist**
24 Silsoe House
50 Park Village East
London
NW1 7QH
☎ 020 7388 5689
ACP

**RICHARDS**, Diana
**Psychoanalytic Psychotherapist**
71 The Avenue
Brondesbury Park
London
NW6 7NS
☎ 02084 593 180
NAFSI

**RIDLEY**, Elizabeth
**Hypno-Psychotherapist**
58 Cumberland Terrace
London
NW1 4HJ
NSHAP

**ROBERTS**, Philip
**Family & Systemic Psychotherapist**
127 Olive Road
London
NW2 6UT
☎ 020 8450 6243
AFT

**ROBERTSON**, Chris
**Integrative Psychosynthesis Psychotherapist**
Re.Vision
97 Brondesbury Road
London
NW6 6RY
☎ 020 8357 8881
☎ 020 8451 2165
re-vision@ntlworld.com
RE.V

**ROBERTSON**, Ewa
**Integrative Psychosynthesis Psychotherapist**
Re.Vision
97 Brondesbury Road
London
NW6 6RY
☎ 020 8357 8881
☎ 020 8451 2165
RE.V

**ROBINSON**, Martin
**Analytical Psychologist-Jungian Analyst**
Studio E
49 The Avenue
London
NW6 7NR
☎ 0208 459 5442
☎ 01258 817 301
AJA, SIP

**ROEMMELE**, Caroline
**Integrative Arts Psychotherapist**
42 Willes Road
London
NW5 3DL
☎ 020 7284 3649
☎ 07956 934 024
IATE

**ROMERO**, Maria Jose
**Gestalt Psychotherapist**
Ground Floor Flat
83 Riffel Road
London
NW2 4PG
☎ 020 8452 9417
mariajromero@btopenworld.com
GPTI, MET

**ROSE**, Kevin
**Psychoanalytic Psychotherapist**
37 Ashbourne Avenue
London
NW11 ODT
☎ 020 8 455 5936 (t/f)
kevinrose@freeola.com
IPSS

**ROSENTHALL**, Joanna
**Couple Psychoanalytic Psychotherapist**
T.M.S.I.
Tavistock Centre
120 Belsize Lane
London
NW3 5BA
☎ 020 7435 7111
☎ 020 7704 1174
101576.2651@compuserve.com
TMSI, SCPP

**ROSSOTTI**, Nicole
**Personal Construct Psychotherapist**
Department of Clinical Psychology
Silkstream Unit
Colindale Hospital
Colindale Avenue, London
NW9 5GH
☎ 020 8952 2381 ext 3578
☎ 01582 792 970
n.rossotti@mtlworld.com
PCP

**ROTH**, Priscilla
**Child Psychotherapist**
12 Parkhill Road
London
NW3 2YN
☎ 020 7485 4038
☎ 020 7284 3331
PriscillaRoth@compuserve.com
ACP

**ROTH**, Ruth
**Humanistic and Integrative Psychotherapist**
♿ 16 Oman Avenue
London
NW2 6BG
☎ 020 8452 7376
ruth.roth@tiscali.co.uk
BCPC

**ROYLE**, Anthony
**Integrative Psychotherapist**
4 Denning Road
Hampstead
London
NW3 1SU
☎ 020 7435 4798
Anthony.J.Royle@btinternet.com
SPCRC

**RYZ**, Patsy
**Child Psychotherapist**
Bishop Harvey Family Service
6 Egerton Gardens
London
NW4 4BA
☎ 020 8349 2263
ACP

**SACHS**, Adah
**Attachment-based Psychoanalytic Psychotherapist, Integrative Psychotherapist**
♿ 81 Bartholomew Road
London
NW5 2AH
☎ 020 7267 1831
CAPP, SPCRC

**SAUNDERS**, Sonia
**Autogenic Psychotherapist**
201 Haverstock Hill
London
NW3 4QG
☎ 020 7431 2828
SSaunders@interfis.com
BAS

**SAWYERR**, Alice A A
**Family & Systemic Psychotherapist**
♿ The Marlborough Family Service
38 Marlborough Place
St. John's Wood
London
NW8 0PJ
☎ 020 7624 8605
a.a.a.sawyerr@rhul.ac.uk
AFT

**SAYAMA**, Kinko
**Analytical Psychologist-Jungian Analyst**
547 Finchley Road
London
NW3 7BJ
☎ 020 7431 1992
kinko.sayama@btinternet.com
IGAP

**SCARLETT**, Jean
**Psychoanalytic Psychotherapist**
3 Byron Villas
Vale of Health
London
NW3 1AR
☎ 020 7435 2362
FIP

**SCHATZMAN**, Morton
**Psychoanalytic Psychotherapist**
♿ 35 Croftdown Road
London
NW5 1EL
☎ 020 7267 0304
mortonschatzman@cs.com
ARBS

**SCHERZER**, Andrea
**Integrative Psychotherapist**
Basement Flat
47a Canfield Gardens
London
NW6 3JL
☎ 07947 004 703
andrea@seymour.u-net.com
SPCRC

**SCHIEMANN**, Margot
**Group Analyst, Integrative Psychotherapist**
17b Frognal
London
NW3 6AR
☎ 020 7431 1810
schiemann@globalnet.co.uk
IGA, MC

**SCHNEIDER**, Evelyne
**Group Analyst**
Garden Flat
8 Belsize Park
London
NW3 4ET
☎ 020 7794 8834
stevelyne@aol.com
IGA

**SCHNURMANN**, Anneliese
**Child Psychotherapist**
Flat 5
11 Netherall Gardens
London
NW3 5RN
☎ 020 7435 9315
ACP

**SCHWARTZ**, Joseph
**Attachment-based Psychoanalytic Psychotherapist**
2 Lancaster Drive
London
NW3 4HA
☎ 020 7794 8226
☎ 07946 301 227 Messages
CAPP

**SEGLOW**, Ruth M.
**Child Psychotherapist**
c/o ACP
NW3
☎ 020 8340 9145
ACP

**SELWYN**, Ruth
**Child Psychotherapist**
2 Edis Street
London
NW1 8LG
☎ 020 7722 2558
ruthselwyn2000@yahoo.co.uk
ACP

**SEU**, Bruna Irene
**Psychoanalytic Psychotherapist**
♿ 40 King's Road
London
NW10 2BP
☎ 020 8 459 3423
b.seu@bbk.ac.uk
ARBS

**SHACKLE**, Shahrukh Husain
**Psychoanalytic Psychotherapist**
♿ 29 Winchester Avenue
London
NW6 7TT
☎ 02076 246 324
husainshackle@msn.com
NAFSI

**SHAPIRO**, Philip
**Child Psychotherapist**
c/o ACP
NW3
☎ 020 8789 1295
ACP

**SHERIFF**, Farida
**Psychoanalytic Psychotherapist**
9 Belsize Crescent
London
NW3 5QY
☎ 02074 352 632
NAFSI

**SHERMAN**, Arthur
**Analytical Psychologist-Jungian Analyst**
4 Springfield Court
41 Eton Avenue
London
NW3 3ER
☎ 020 7431 1175
asher@ouvip.com
AIP

**SHINE**, Sharon
**Child Psychotherapist**
c/o ACP
NW3
☎ 020 7301 3414
ACP

**SHIVAKUMAR**, H.
**Analytical Psychologist-Jungian Analyst**
14B Portsdown Avenue
London
NW11 0ND
☎ 020 8731 7181
AIP, CAP *

**SHMUKLER**, Diana
**Integrative Psychotherapist**
23a Bracknell Gardens
London
NW3 7EE
☎ 020 7431 9031
diana.shmukler@virgin.net
ITA, MET, SPTI

**SILVER**, Anna-Mae
**Psychoanalytic Psychotherapist**
1 Arcade House
Hampstead Way
London
NW11 7TL
☎ 020 7272 7013
☎ 020 8455 0431
annamation@aol.com
AGIP

**SILVERMAN**, Carl M.
**Analytical Psychologist-Jungian Analyst**
1 Thurlow Terrace
London
NW5 4JB
☎ 020 7485 2877
AJA

**SILVESTER**, Keith
**Psychosynthesis Psychotherapist**
65a Watford Way
Hendon
London
NW4 3AQ
☎ 02075 864 146
k.silvester@virgin.net
10 Kings College Court
Primrose Hill
London
NW3 3EA
IPS

**SIMMONDS**, Tina
**Integrative Psychotherapist**
14 Park Avenue
London
NW11 7SJ
☎ 020 8455 9102
mail@tinasimmonds.freeserve.co.uk
MC

**SIMPSON**, Richard
**Sexual and Relationship Psychotherapist**
North/Central London
☎ 020 7428 0260
☎ 07768 838 526
psychotherapist@blueyonder.co.uk
BASRT

**SINGER**, Dani
**Integrative Psychotherapist**
167 Sumatra Road
London
NW6 1PN
☎ 020 7586 3125
113443.145@compuserve.com
SPCRC

**SINGH**, Reenee
**Family & Systemic Psychotherapist**
The Asian Service
Tavistock Clinic
120 Belsize Lane
London
NW3 5BA
☎ 020 7447 3800
reeneesingh@hotmail.com
AFT

**SLESS**, Deborah
**Integrative Psychotherapist, Transactional Analysis Psychotherapist**
23 Patshull Road
London
NW5 2JX
☎ 02074 852 664
deborah@wisdomsense.com
ITA, SPTI

**SLIW**, Mrs Regina
**Sexual and Relationship Psychotherapist**
♿ The Ravenscroft Suite
166a Golders Green Road
London
NW11 8BB
☎ 020 8958 9013
BASRT

**SMART**, Tanya
**Systemic Psychotherapist**
♿ Willesden Centre for Psychological Treatment
Proud Lane
London
NW10 2HH
☎ 020 8985 5779
☎ 020 8438 1770
tanyasmart42@hotmail.com
KCC

**SMITH**, Alison
**Personal Construct Psychotherapist**
61b Cambridge Road
London
NW6 5AG
☎ 020 8960 0880
☎ 020 7624 2597
PCP

**SMITH**, Carole
**Psychoanalytic Psychotherapist**
86 Canfield Gardens
London
NW6 3EE
☎ 020 7624 5271
rockpool@dircon.co.uk
IPSS

**SOULTANI**, Effie
**Sexual and Relationship Psychotherapist**
114a Braemar Avenue
Neasden
London
NW10 0DP
☎ 020 8450 0258
☎ 07790 485 453
effie@soultani.fsnet.co.uk
BASRT

**SOUTHGATE**, John
**Attachment-based Psychoanalytic Psychotherapist**
12 Nassington Road
London
NW3 2UD
☎ 020 7435 2663
CAPP

**SPECTERMAN**, Liz
**Psychosynthesis Psychotherapist**
26 Priory Terrace
West Hampstead
London
NW6 4DH
☎ 020 7624 8569
PET

**SPEYER**, Josefine
**Integrative Psychotherapist**
Chiron Centre
90 Harvist Road
Queens Park
London
NW6 6HL
☎ 020 8208 0670
josefine@waitrose.com
AHPP, CCBP

**SPURLING**, Laurence
**Psychoanalytic Psychotherapist**
4 Marty's Yard
17 Hampstead High Street
London
NW3 1PX
☎ 020 7 431 5471
GUILD

**SPYER**, Natalie
**Psychoanalytic Psychotherapist**
38 Temple Fortune Lane
London
NW11 7UD
☎ 020 8 455 3050 (t/f)
spyer@dircon.co.uk
IPSS

**STADLEN**, Anthony
**Existential Psychotherapist, Psychoanalytic Psychotherapist**
64 Dartmouth Park Road
London
NW5 1SN
☎ 020 7485 3896
stadlen@aol.com
AIP, SPCRC

**STADLEN**, Naomi
**Existential Psychotherapist**
64 Dartmouth Park Road
London
NW5 1SN
☎ 02074 853 896
stadlen@aol.com
UPCA

**STEELE**, Miriam
**Child Psychotherapist**
Anna Freud Centre
21 Maresfield Gardens
London
NW3 5SH
☎ 020 7794 2313
ACP

**STEVENSON**, Bruce
**Body Psychotherapist, Integrative Psychotherapist**
20 Goodhall Street
London
NW10 6TU
☎ 020 8961 7802
Bruce.Stevenson@Tesco.net
CCBP, MET

**STEWART**, John
**Psychoanalytic Psychotherapist**
51 Hendale Avenue
Hendon
London
NW4 4LP
☎ 020 8203 9079
johnastewart@btopenworld.com
FPC

**STOBEZKI**, Yael
**Transpersonal Psychotherapist**
Flat E
46 Fairhazel Gardens
London
NW6 3SJ
☎ 020 7328 9015
CCPE

**STONE**, Anthony
**Humanistic and Integrative Psychotherapist**
7 Westholm
London
NW11 6LH
☎ 020 8455 0794
anthony.stone4@btconnect.com
SPEC

**STONE**, Martin
**Analytical Psychologist-Jungian Analyst**
Consulting Room, Flat 1
62 Rosslyn Hill
London
NW3 1ND
☎ 020 7794 8445
marstone@dircon.co.uk
AJA

**STONE**, Miriam
**Psychoanalytic Psychotherapist**
Garden Flat
2 Strathray Gardens
London
NW3 4NY
☎ 020 7435 6072
FIP, FPC

**STONE**, Sandra
**Child Psychotherapist**
31 Alma Square
London
NW8 9PY
☎ 020 7286 3331
ACP

**STRASSER**, Freddie
**Existential Psychotherapist**
99 West Heath Road
Hampstead
London
NW3 7TN
☎ 020 8455 0118
strasser@btopenworld.com
SPCRC

**SUEKE**, Minoo
**Psychoanalytic Psychotherapist**
London Centre for Psychotherapy
32 Leighton Road
London
NW5 2QE
☎ 020 7435 6958
FIP

**SULLIVAN**, Anita
**Humanistic Psychotherapist**
143 Melrose Avenue
London
NW2 4LY
☎ 020 8450 2107
Anita.Sullivan@bigwig.net
AHPP

**SULLIVAN**, Christopher
**Psychosynthesis Psychotherapist**
143 Melrose Avenue
London
NW2 4LY
☎ 020 8830 5662
☎ +46 820 0054
christophersullivan@compuserve.com
PET

**SUMMER**, Jennifer
**Family & Systemic Psychotherapist**
♿ Marlborough Family Service
38 Marlborough Place
St Johns Wood
London
NW8 0PJ
☎ 020 7624 8605
IFT

**SUTTERS**, Amabel
**Integrative Psychotherapist**
140 Iverson Road
London
NW6 2HH
☎ 020 7372 1329
MC

**SWABEY**, ffiona
**Analytical Psychologist-Jungian Analyst**
46 Lambolle Road
London
NW3 4HR
☎ 01608 676 928
☎ 020 7794 5061
ffiona@chilson.freeserve.co.uk
IGAP

**SYZ**, Ann
**Child Psychotherapist**
Tavistock Adolescent Department
120 Belsize Lane
London
NW3 5BA
☎ 020 7722 2121
☎ 020 7435 7111
ACP

**TAUBE**, Idonea
**Educational Therapist**
15 Church Row
London
NW3 6UP
☎ 020 7431 4543
CFET

**TAYLOR**, Mary
**Systemic Psychotherapist**
39 Dartmouth Park Road
London
NW5 1SU
KCC

**TAYLOR-THOMAS**, Caroline
**Psychoanalytic Psychotherapist**
9 Hayland Close
London
NW9 0LH
☎ 020 8200 1609
FPC

**THOMPSON**, Michael Guy
**Psychoanalytic Psychotherapist**
c/o Philadelphia Association
4 Marty's Yard
17 Hampstead High Street
London
NW3 1QW
☎ 020 7794 2652
michaelguy@aol.com
PA

**THOMPSON**, Thea
**Attachment-based Psychoanalytic Psychotherapist**
54 Roderick Road
London
NW3 2NL
☎ 020 7485 2837
thea.vigne@virgin.net
CAPP

**THOMSON**, Jean
**Analytical Psychologist-Jungian Analyst**
♿ 1 Beatty Street
London
NW1 7LN
☎ 020 7388 5508
thomson@agnes-j.fsnet.co.uk
CAP, FIP *

**TIBBLES**, Paul
**Family & Systemic Psychotherapist**
Child & Family Dept.
The Tavistock Clinic
120 Belsize Lane
London
NW3 3BA
☎ 020 7435 7111
ptibbles@tavi-port.nhs.uk
AFT

**TOTMAN**, Maria
**Psychosynthesis Psychotherapist**
34 Asnaburgh Street
london
NW1 3ND
☎ 01322 334139
IPS

**TOUBKIN**, Rita
**Psychosynthesis Psychotherapist**
77 Hampstead Way
London
NW11 7LG
☎ 02084 587 571
☎ 02084 554 515
IPS

**TOUTON-VICTOR**, Patricia
**Psychoanalytic Psychotherapist**
♿ 63 Cholmley Gardens
West Hampstead
London
NW6 1AJ
☎ 020 7435 4251
☎ 07968 539 008
ptv@btinternet.com
PA

**TOWER**, Rupert
**Transpersonal Psychotherapist**
♿ 25 Langland Gardens
Hampstead
London
NW3 6QE
☎ 020 7433 3640
CTP

**TOWNLEY**, Judy Rifkin
**Child Psychotherapist**
3 North Square
London
NW11 7AA
☎ 020 8455 8934
ACP

**TREVATT**, David
**Child Psychotherapist**
c/o ACP
NW3
☎ 020 7224 6028
ACP

**TURKIÉ**, Janine
**Psychodrama Psychotherapist**
32 Well Walk
Hampstead
London
NW3 1BX
☎ 020 7794 8887
janine@turkie.freeserve.co.uk
BPA

**TURNER**, Vivien
**Cognitive Analytic Therapist**
38 North Gate
Prince Albert Road
London
NW8 7EG
☎ 020 7722 3171
Jturner747@hotmail.com
ACAT

**TURP**, Maggie
**Psychoanalytic Psychotherapist**
Bell Number 5
4. Marty's Yard
off Hampstead High Street
London
NW3 1QW
☎ 020 7461 0134
maggieturp@aol.com
IPSS

**VETERE**, Arlene
**Family & Systemic Psychotherapist**
♿ Child & Family Department
Tavistock Centre
120 Belsize Lane
London
NW3 5BA
☎ 020 7435 7111
a.l.vetere@reading.ac.uk
AFT

**WALKER**, Clare
**Psychosynthesis Psychotherapist**
65a Watford Way
North London - Hendon
NW4 3AU
☎ 01206 303 345
☎ 02083 404 874
IPS

**WALTERS**, Cheryl
**Psychoanalytic Psychotherapist**
51 Gloucester Crescent
Primerose Hill
London
NW1 7EG
☎ 020 7722 2312
cherylwalters@lblueyonder.co.uk
FPC

**WATSON**, Lindsay
**Lacanian Analyst, Psychoanalytic Psychotherapist**
95 Parliament Hill Mansions
Lissenden Gardens
London
NW5 1NB
☎ 020 7485 1274
CFAR

**WAYGOOD**, Rob
**Transpersonal Psychotherapist**
9 Grove Road
Willesden Green
London
NW2
☎ 01865 247 851
CTP

**WEIDER**, Bilha
**Family & Systemic Psychotherapist**
♿ 4 Cranbourne Gardens
London
NW1 0HP
☎ 020 8455 6668
j.weider@howardkennedy.com
AFT

**WEINRICH**, Hildegard
**Analytical Psychologist-Jungian Analyst**
38 Cranhurst Road
London
NW2 4LP
☎ 020 8450 0537
akh.weinrich@virgin.net
IGAP

**WEISENSEL**, Karin
**Integrative Psychotherapist**
Regents College
NW1
☎ 020 7589 0023
SPCRC, SEA

**WEISZ**, Janet
**Psychoanalytic Psychotherapist**
74A Grove End Road
St Johns Wood
London
NW8 9ND
☎ 020 7722 8515
JanWeisz@aol.com
FPC

**WELLS**, Lindsay James
**Psychoanalytic Psychotherapist**
130 Walm Lane
London
NW2 4RT
☎ 020 8208 1567
AGIP, AIP

**WHITE**, Kate
**Attachment-based Psychoanalytic Psychotherapist**
12 Nassington Road
London
NW3 2UD
☎ 020 7433 1263
CAPP

**WILKE**, Gerhard
**Group Analyst**
London
NW2
☎ 020 8450 0469
gerhard@gerhardwilke.com
IGA

**WILLIAMS**, Gianna
**Child Psychotherapist**
Tavistock Child and Family Department
NW3
☎ 020 7435 7111
☎ 020 8455 5682
ACP

**WILLIAMS**, Ruth
**Integrative Psychotherapist**
1 Hillside
Highgate Road
London
NW5 1QT
☎ 07958 711 151
☎ 020 7515 2012
RuthWilliams@msn.com
MC

**WINDLE**, Ruth
**Analytical Psychologist-Jungian Analyst**
Studio E
49 The Avenue
London
NW6
☎ 020 8459 5442
☎ 01373 467 661
AJA

**WINE**, Noga
**Lacanian Analyst**
3 Hampstead Way
London
NW11 7JA
☎ 020 8455 1177
noga@wine4.freeserve.co.uk
CFAR

**WINTER**, Rachel
**Psychoanalytic Psychotherapist**
167 Sumatra Road
London
NW6 1PN
☎ 020 7624 7431
AGIP, FIP

**WISE**, Penny
**Psychoanalytic Psychotherapist**
17 Lisburne Road
London
NW3 2NS
☎ 020 7 485 0005
IPSS

**WOLF**, Darren
**Integrative Psychotherapist**
School of Psychotherapy & Counselling
Regent's College
Inner Circle
London
NW1 4NS
☎ 020 7790 1835
darren.wolf@virgin.net
SPCRC

**WOODCOCK**, Therese
**Child Psychotherapist**
c/o ACP
120 West Heath Road
London
NW3 7TU
☎ 020 8458 1609
tmyw@globalnet.co.uk
ACP

**WOODROFFE**, Roe
**Integrative Psychosynthesis Psychotherapist**
c/o Re.Vision
97 Brondesbury Road
London
NW6 6RY
☎ 020 8357 8881
☎ 0798 912 5065
RE.V

**WORRELL**, Michael
**Existential Psychotherapist**
83 Riffel Road
Willesden Green
London
NW2 4PG
☎ 020 8452 9417
☎ 020 8453 2306
michael.worrell@btinternet.com
SEA

**WRIGHT**, Jason
**Analytical Psychotherapist, Transpersonal Psychotherapist**
The CORE Trust
Lisson Cottages
35a Lisson Grove
London
NW1 6UD
☎ 020 8352 0020
☎ 020 7258 3031
jw015a2286@blueyonder.co.uk
AIP, CTP

**YANDOLI**, Dennis
**Family & Systemic Psychotherapist**
♿ 10 North Villas
London
NW1 9BJ
☎ 020 7482 3163
☎ 020 8960 0880
dennis.yandoli@cnwl.nhs.uk
IFT

**YASS**, Marion
**Couple Psychoanalytic Psychotherapist**
5a Templewood Avenue
London
NW3 7UY
☎ 020 7794 2221
mryass@aol.com
SCPP

**YENTOB**, Linda
**Integrative Psychotherapist**
18 Cumberland Terrace
London
NW1 4HS
☎ 07776 296 280
lyentob@aol.com
SPCRC

**ZAPHIRIOU WOODS**, Marie
**Child Psychotherapist**
21 Hillfield Road
London
NW6 1QD
☎ 020 7794 6276
☎ 020 77942313
ACP

**ZEFF**, Paula
**Psychoanalytic Psychotherapist**
45 Hollycroft Avenue
London
NW3 7QJ
☎ 020 7435 9918
p.zeff@virgin.net
GUILD

**DE LASZLO**, Alexandra
**Systemic Psychotherapist**
The Therapy Rooms
68-70 Chalk Farm Road
London
NW1 8AN
☎ 020 7267 0110
KCC

**DE SAMAIO CAMPOS**, Claudia
**Biodynamic Psychotherapist**
Upstairs Flat
149 Queens Crescent
Kentish Town
London
NW5 4ED
☎ 02074 859 473
LSBP

**VAN HEEL**, Carlien
**Biodynamic Psychotherapist**
Flat 4
1a Laurier Road
London
NW5 1SD
☎ 02074 852 922
carlienvanheel@copperstream.co.uk
LSBP

## LONDON SOUTH EAST

**ABABIO**, Baffour Senkyere
**Psychoanalytic Psychotherapist**
12 Lammas Green
Sydenham Hill
London
SE26 6LT
☎ 02082 996 618
☎ 07956 436 379
bababio@hotmail.com
NAFSI

**ADAMS**, Tessa
**Psychoanalytic Psychotherapist**
122 Erlanger Road
London
SE14 5TJ
☎ 020 7358 0018
tessa@adamsnx.freeserve.co.uk
GUILD, SITE

**ADAMSON**, Niki
**Psychosynthesis Psychotherapist**
92-94 Tooley Street
London Bridge
London
SE1 2TH
☎ 01435 872 789
☎ 07799 866 640
niki@solutions-inc.co.uk
PET

**AHERN**, Geoffrey
**Integrative Psychotherapist**
14 Ewelme Road
Forest Hill
London
SE23 3BH
☎ 020 8699 6042
geoffreyahern@onetel.com
SPCRC

**ALABASTER**, Nigel
**Family & Systemic Psychotherapist**
♿ Oxleas NHST CAMHS
Highpoint House
Shooters Hill Road
London
SE18 3RZ
☎ 020 8855 3770
nigel.alabaster@oxleas.nhs.uk
AFT

**ALLEYNE**, Aileen
**Psychoanalytic Psychotherapist**
35 Pellatt Road
East Dulwich
London
SE22 9JA
☎ 02086 934 159
aileen@kisskadee.ukf.net
FIP, NAFSI

**ALWARD**, Susanna
**Integrative Psychotherapist**
27 Shooter's Hill
London
SE18 4LG
☎ 020 8856 4404
☎ 020 8856 6666
anna.alward@lineone.net
SPCRC

**ANTHONY**, Monica
**Transpersonal Psychotherapist**
43 Gomm Road
London
SE16 2TY
☎ 020 7232 2562
CTP

**ANTRICAN**, James Gray
**Psychoanalytic Psychotherapist**
9 Underhill Road
East Dulwich
London
SE22 0BT
☎ 020 8299 3971
IPSS

**ARNOLD-BAKER**, Claire
**Existential Psychotherapist**
Royal Waterloo House
51-55 Waterloo Road
London
SE1 8TX
☎ 07957 154 621
Claire@nspc.org.uk
UPCA

**ATTIAS**, Sandra
**Transpersonal Psychotherapist**
17 Halifax street
sydenham
London
SE26 6JA
☎ 020 8314 4183
☎ 020 8 766 0101
sandra.attias@btopenworld.com
CCPE

**ATTWOOD**, Peter
**Family & Systemic Psychotherapist**
317b Upland Road
East Dulwich
London
SE22 0DL
☎ 020 8299 3014
☎ 020 8252 3070
peter.attwood@freeserve.co.uk
South London & Maudsley NHS Trust
Lewisham Young People's & Children
Old School House, Leahurst Roa
London
SE13 5LS
IFT

**AUDLEY**, Matthew
**Psychosynthesis Psychotherapist**
16 Sears Street
London
SE5 7JL
☎ 020 7642 3694
PET

**AUST**, Frank
**Family & Systemic Psychotherapist**
♿ Child & Adolescent Mental Health Service
William Geoffrey House
35 Black Prince Road
London
SE11 6JJ
☎ 02074 114 140
IFT

**AYLWARD**, Peter
**Psychoanalytic Psychotherapist**
30 Glenshiel Road
Eltham
London
SE9 1AQ
☎ 020 8859 0617
aylwardpj@hotmail.com
FPC

**AYO**, Yvonne
**Systemic Psychotherapist**
North Southwark Community Child
&
Family Service
151 Blackfriars Road
London
SE1 8EL
KCC

**AYRES**, Anthony
**Psychoanalytic Psychotherapist**
37 Donaldson Road
London
SE18 3JZ
☎ 020 8 856 1542
GUILD

**BARFRED-DIXON**, Ameyo Katharina
**Integrative Psychosynthesis Psychotherapist**
Flat 357, Block 15
Devon Mansions
Tooley Street
London Bridge
SE1 2XG
☎ 07905 034 101
☎ 020 8943 3163
RE.V

**BARNEY**, Lesley
**Educational Therapist**
43A Longton Avenue
Sydenham
London
SE26 6RE
☎ 020 8291 5512
elbarney@zoom.co.uk
CFET

**BARRETT**, Jean
**Psychoanalytic Psychotherapist**
8 Meadowcourt Road
London
SE3 9DY
☎ 020 8297 8599
GUILD

**BARTER**, Ruth
**Child Psychotherapist**
29 Colfe Road
London
SE23 2ES
☎ 020 8291 1675
ACP

**BATESON**, Fiona
**Psychosynthesis Psychotherapist**
92 Tooley Street
London
SE1 2TH
☎ 020 8877 1683
fiona_bateson@msn.com
PET

**BEARD**, Hilary
**Cognitive Analytic Therapist, Psychoanalytic Psychotherapist**
4 Grangewood Terrace
Grange Road
South Norwood
London
SE25 6TA
☎ 020 8771 4475
☎ 020 7928 9292 x2272
St Thomas' Psychotherapy Unit
Lower Ground Floor, Block8, South W
St Thomas' Hospital
Lambeth Palace Road, Lon
SE1 7EH
ACAT, GUILD

**BELL**, Christine
**Humanistic Psychotherapist, Integrative Psychotherapist**
♿ 49 Shell Road
Ladywell
London
SE13 7DF
☎ 020 8692 5076
christine@bellcj.demon.co.uk
AHPP

**BELL**, Frances
**Analytical Psychologist-Jungian Analyst**
296 Commercial Way
Peckham
London
SE15 1QN
☎ 020 7732 9709
AJA

**BENNETT**, Lesley
**Psychoanalytic Psychotherapist**
167 Brockley Rise
Forest Hill
London
SE23 1NL
☎ 020 8 690 7537
lesley@bennett167.freeserve.co.uk
IPSS

**BISHOP**, Elizabeth
**Group Analytic Psychotherapist**
I.P.T.S.
York Clinic
47 Weston Road
London
SE1 3RR
☎ 02079 554 901
bishopeliza@aol.com
UPCA

**BISHOP**, Patricia
**Psychoanalytic Psychotherapist**
No 2, Spencer House
23 Dartmouth Row
Greenwich
London
SE10 8AW
☎ 020 8 691 9800
IPSS

**BLACK**, Judith
**Hypno-Psychotherapist**
Flat 2
64 Lowther Hill
London
SE23 1PY
NSHAP

**BLACK**, Sandra
**Psychoanalytic Psychotherapist**
112 Friern Road
Dulwich
London
SE22 OAX
☎ 020 8 693 7524
☎ 07947 029 132
sblack.312@ntlworld.com, www.ipss-psychotherapy.org/sblack
IPSS

**BLACKIE**, Suzanne
**Analytical Psychologist-Jungian Analyst**
7 Balcaskie Road
Eltham
London
SE9 1HQ
☎ 020 8850 0633
i.blackie@btinternet.com
CAP *

**BLAKELOCK**, Pamela
**Educational Therapist**
303 Upland Road
London
SE22 0DL
☎ 020 8693 3722
pamblakelock@yahoo.co.uk
CFET

**BLOCKLEY**, Kate
**Transpersonal Psychotherapist**
28a Wellmeadow Road
Hither Green
London
SE13 6TB
☎ 07799 533 520
CCPE

**BLOMFIELD**, Valerie
**Psychosynthesis Psychotherapist**
12 Woodlands Park Road
Greenwich
London
SE10 9XD
☎ 020 8853 0772
vblomfield@aol.com
PET

**BORONSKA**, Teresa .W
**Group Analytic Psychotherapist**
9C Crystal Palace Park Road
Sydenham
London
SE26 6EG
☎ 02087 782 326
tboro@waitrose.com
Goldsmiths College
New Cross
London
SE14 6NW
UPCA

**BRENNAN**, Sue
**Psychoanalytic Psychotherapist**
341 Grange Road
London
SE19 3BY
☎ 020 8771 1657
s.brennan@tinyonline.co.uk
GUILD

**BRIGHT**, Jenifer A
**Cognitive Behavioural Psychotherapist**
Maudsley Psychologist Centre
Maudsley Hospital
Denmark Hill
LONDON
SE5 8AZ
☎ 020 8877 9853
☎ 020 7919 2194
jeniferbright@hotmail.com
BABCP

**BRINER**, Wendy
**Systemic Psychotherapist**
♿ London Centre of Complementary Healthcare
137 Greenwich South Street
London
SE10 8PP
KCC

**BRITTAIN**, Charlie
**Group Analytic Psychotherapist, Transpersonal Psychotherapist**
120 Sandyhill Road
London
SE18 7BA
☎ 020 8316 4907
bristark@compuserve.com
CCPE, UPCA

**BROOKS**, Beverly
**Cognitive Analytic Therapist**
15 Cibber Road
Forest Hill
London
SE23 2EF
☎ 020 8291 1245
bev.brooks@virgin.net
ACAT

**BUCHAN**, Ian
**Sexual and Relationship Psychotherapist**
158 New Kent Road
London
SE1 4YS
☎ 020 7708 3773
☎ 07801 334 854
buchan158@btopenworld.com
BASRT

**BUCKINGHAM**, Linda
**Child Psychotherapist, Psychoanalytic Psychotherapist**
8 Meadowcourt Road
London
SE3 9DY
☎ 020 8297 0276
ACP, GUILD

**BURCH**, Rosemary
**Group Analytic Psychotherapist**
19 Grove Park
Camberwell
London
SE5 8LH
☎ 020 7733 9057
☎ 020 7928 9292 x3864
rosemary.burch@gstt.sthames.nhs.uk
St Thomas' Hospital
London
SE1 7EH
FPC

**BURGESS**, Mary
**Cognitive Behavioural Psychotherapist**
The New Medical School Building
Kings College Hospital
Denmark Hill
London
SE5 9RS
☎ 07957 469 118
☎ 020 7346 3363
mary.burgess@slam.nhs.uk
BABCP

**CAHILL**, Pauline
**Humanistic Psychotherapist**
East Dulwich
London
SE22
☎ 07958 533135
Pauline.Cahill@uwe.ac.uk
AHPP

**CANTY**, Josephine
**Group Analyst**
For Private Practice
125 Taunton Road
Lee
SE12 8PA
☎ 020 8301 9428
☎ 020 8318 9023
IGA

**CARTER**, Mary Hope
**Family & Systemic Psychotherapist**
46 Greenwich South Street
London
SE10 8UN
☎ 020 8692 2573
☎ 020 7955 4583
mhc@totalise.co.uk
Bloomfield Centre
Guys Hospital
St Thomas Street
London
SE1 9RT
IFT

**CHAPMAN**, Trudy
**Psychoanalytic Psychotherapist**
29 Faversham Road
London
SE6 4XE
☎ 020 8690 4120
GUILD

**CHAVUNDUKA**, Gladys
**Psychoanalytic Psychotherapist**
Flat 8
18/20 Rosendale Road
West Dulwich
London
SE21 8DX
☎ 02087 668 140
NAFSI

**CHESSELL**, Karen
**Psychoanalytic Psychotherapist**
329 Upland Road
London
SE22 0DL
☎ 020 8 299 2890
k.chessell@virgin.net
IPSS

**CLOUGH**, Andrea
**Psychosynthesis Psychotherapist**
37 Harefield Road
Brockley
London
SE4 1LW
☎ 020 8 691 5303
IPS

**COETZEE**, Kotie
**Integrative Psychotherapist**
8 Benson Road
London
SE23 3RJ
☎ 020 8699 8663
kotiecoetzee@kcmm.demon.co.uk
SPCRC

**COHEN**, Clare
**Integrative Psychotherapist**
62 Lilford Road
Camberwell
London
SE5 9HR
☎ 02072 747 341
MC

**COLLARD**, Patrizia C
**Cognitive Behavioural Psychotherapist**
45 Lowther Hill
LONDON
SE23 1PZ
☎ 07941 544 958
contact@stressminus.co.uk
BABCP

**COLVIN**, Naomi
**Attachment-based Psychoanalytic Psychotherapist**
2 Jowett Street
Peckham
London
SE15 6JN
☎ 020 7233 9993
CAPP

**COMBES**, Ann
**Group Analytic Psychotherapist**
53 South Norwood Hill
South Norwood
London
SE25 6BX
FPC

**COMINS**, Jayne
**Analytical Psychologist-Jungian Analyst**
3 Foxwood Road
London
SE3 9HT
☎ 020 8852 1667
jcomins@btopneworld.com
CAP *

**CORNECK**, Sue
**Psychoanalytic Psychotherapist**
41 Creek Road
London
SE8 3BU
☎ 020 8694 0221
sue@corneck.freeserve.co.uk
AGIP

**CORRALES**, Iris
**Systemic Psychotherapist**
♿ Braidwood Centre
Elmcourt Road
London
SE27 9BZ
☎ 020 7244 0197
☎ 020 7926 0445
iriscorrales@yahoo.com
KCC

**COTTER**, Angela
**Analytical Psychotherapist (Jungian)**
194 Algernon Road
Ladywell
London
SE13 7AN
☎ 02083 141 003
acotter@cotlea.u-net.com
GAPS

**COWMEADOW**, Pauline
**Cognitive Analytic Therapist**
45 Beauval Road
Dulwich
London
SE22 8UG
ACAT

**CREAMER**, Mary
**Transpersonal Psychotherapist**
21 Archery Road
Eltham
London
SE9 1HF
☎ 020 8 850 8357 (t/f)
CCPE

**CULLIFORD**, Penny
**Psychoanalytic Psychotherapist**
Badgers Oak
12 Chinbrook Road
Grove Park
London
SE12 9TH
☎ 020 8857 6525
penny_culliford@hotmail.com
AJA, FPC

**CUMBERBATCH**, Andrea
**Systemic Psychotherapist**
40c Talfour Road
Peckham
London
SE15 5NY
☎ 020 7708 4498
acumbi@onetel.net.uk
KCC

**CURRAN**, Anna Lee
**Cognitive Analytic Therapist**
West Norwood
London
SE27
☎ 020 8761 2836
ACAT

**CURTIS**, Debra
**Sexual and Relationship Psychotherapist**
Ground Floor
250 Leahurst Road
Hither Green
London
SE13 5LT
☎ 020 8318 0029
debra@debracurtis.co.uk
BASRT

**CYBULSKA**, Dr Beata Adriana
**Sexual and Relationship Psychotherapist**
♿ Sex and Relationship Problems Clinic
York Clinic
Guy's Hospital
London
SE1
☎ 020 7955 2881
☎ 020 7702 0263
beata@doctors.org.uk
BASRT

**CZUBINSKA**, Grazyna
**Psychoanalytic Psychotherapist**
2 Greenwich Park Street
Greenwich
London
SE10 9AA
☎ 020 8853 0156
gczubinska@hotmail.com
FPC

**DABOR**, Thelma
**Cognitive Behavioural Psychotherapist, Rational Emotive Behaviour Therapist**
19 Ridgeway
Central Hill
Upper Norwood
London
SE19 1EH
☎ 020 8766 6258
thelmadabor@hotmail.com
The Cassel Centre
4 Waldram Park Road
London
SE23 2PN
BABCP, AREBT

**DAVIES**, Stephen
**Cognitive Behavioural Psychotherapist**
♿ Community Mental Health Team
3rd Floor Ladywell Unit
University Hospital Lewisham
Lewisham High Street, Lo
SE13 6LH
☎ 020 8333 3000 x. 8212
☎ 07919 534 956
daviesstephen@yahoo.co.uk
BABCP

**DAVIS**, Brenda
**Cognitive Behavioural Psychotherapist**
Child and Adolescent Service
Wooden Spoon House
Mary Sheridan Centre
Dugard Way, London
SE11 4TH
☎ 020 7414 1479
brenda.davis@slam.nhs.uk
BABCP

**DAWSON**, Peter
**Transpersonal Psychotherapist**
8A Peabody Buildings
Camberwell Green
London
SE5 7BD
☎ 020 7 708 5399
CCPE

**DENFORD**, Lindsey D.
**Cognitive Behavioural Psychotherapist**
Section of Psychiatric Nursing
Institute of Psychiatry
De Crespigny Park
London
SE5 8AF
☎ 020 7848 0505
l.denford@iop.kcl.ac.uk
BABCP

**DERES**, Mebrat
**Systemic Psychotherapist**
8(b) Ulverstone Road
West Norwood
London
SE27 0AJ
☎ 020 8670 8438
mebrat.deres@lineone.net
KCC

**DOBB**, Cornelia
**Transpersonal Psychotherapist**
The Family Natural Health Centre
106 Lordship Lane
East Dulwich
London
SE22 8HF
☎ 07905 212 774
☎ 020 8693 5515
CCPE

**DONAGHY**, Miriam
**Existential Psychotherapist**
44 Halstow Road
Greenwich
London
SE10 0LD
☎ 02084 882 111
m.donaghy@virgin.net
UPCA

**DOWBER**, Hilary
**Psychoanalytic Psychotherapist**
4 Waldram Park Road
Forest Hill
London
SE23 2PN
☎ 020 8 694 2408
☎ 020 8 291 3436
IPSS

**DRAYCOTT**, Christine
**Cognitive Behavioural Psychotherapist**
19 Avondale Road
Mottingham
London
SE9 4SN
☎ 020 8857 7465
☎ 01622 723 813
chris.draycott@lineone.net
BABCP

**DUCKWORTH**, Rosemary
**Psychoanalytic Psychotherapist**
14 Ashton Heights
51 Horniman Drive
London
SE23 3BS
☎ 020 8 291 2916
IPSS

**DUDLEY**, Jane M
**Group Analytic Psychotherapist**
Goldsmiths College
New Cross
London
SE14 6NW
☎ 02086 601 402
Jane.Dudley@down21.freeuk.net
UPCA

**DUNN**, Mark
**Cognitive Analytic Therapist**
♿ Bridge Psychotherapy & Counselling Service
30 Borough High Street
London
SE1 1XU
☎ 02074 077 879
☎ 02073 783 264
bridgepsych@aol.com
The Munro Centre
Guys Hospital
66 Snowfields
SE1 3SS
ACAT, UPCA

**DUNN**, Sophia
**Cognitive Analytic Therapist**
The Bridge:Psychotherapy & Counselling Services
30 Borough High Street, Top Floor F
London Bridge
London
SE1 1XU
☎ 020 7407 7879
☎ 07973 673 168
sophia@bridgepsych.com
ACAT

**DUNSTAN**, Julie Leger
**Integrative Psychotherapist**
79 Chesnut Road
London
SE27 9LD
☎ 02086 701 582
leger-dunstan@virgin.net
MC

**DUPUY**, Alan
**Personal Construct Psychotherapist**
Flat 16
Dominic Court
43 The Gardens
Dulwich, London
SE22 9QG
☎ 020 8693 5769
alandupuy1@aol.com
PCP

**ECONOMIDOU**, Nitsa
**Transpersonal Psychotherapist**
92-94 Tooley Street
London Bridge
London
SE1 2TH
☎ 020 8 788 5687
☎ 07957 346972
CCPE

**EDGE**, Jon
**Psychoanalytic Psychotherapist**
'Clovelly'
29 Rosenthal Road
London
SE6 2BX
☎ 020 8698 3205
GUILD

**EGERT**, Stella
**Family & Systemic Psychotherapist**
♿ Rosendale Family & Couple Consultation Service
183 Rosendale Road
West Dulwich
London
SE21 8LW
☎ 020 8670 3417
IFT

**EISLER**, Ivan
**Family & Systemic Psychotherapist**
♿ The Institute of Psychiatry
Psychotherapy Section. PO73
DeCrespigny Park, Camberwell
London
SE5 8AF
i.eisler@iop.kcl.ac.uk
IFT

**EISLER**, Z
**Sexual and Relationship Psychotherapist**
London
South East
SE26
☎ 020 8699 7328
BASRT

**EKDAWI**, Isabelle
**Systemic Psychotherapist**
♿ 66 Ruskin Walk
Herne Hill
London
SE24 9LZ
☎ 020 7530 3369
KCC

**ELLIOTT**, Sandra A.
**Cognitive Behavioural Psychotherapist**
♿ MAPPIM Perinatal MHS, Adamson Centre
St Thomas Hospital
Lambeth Palace Road
London
SE1 7EH
☎ 020 7960 5805
☎ 020 7928 5485
Sandra.Elliott@slam.nhs.uk
The Consulting Rooms
York House
199 Westminster Bridge Road
London
SE1 7UT
BABCP

**ELLIOTT**, Victoria
**Child Psychotherapist**
Plumstead Child Guidance Unit
Plumstead Health Centre
Tewson Road
London
SE18 1BH
☎ 020 8855 9254
☎ 020 8244 4732
ACP

**FAIRWEATHER**, Cassandra
**Group Analytic Psychotherapist**
101 Algernon Road
Lewisham
London
SE13 7AP
☎ 020 8690 9434
UPCA

**FARQUHAR-STANTON**, Kate
**Psychoanalytic Psychotherapist**
♿ 169 Peckham Rye
London
SE15 3HZ
☎ 07768 345 414
☎ 020 7732 9431 - 020 7277 6890
kate.ontherye@virgin.net
CFAR, FIP

**FINDLAY**, David Alistair
**Integrative Psychotherapist**
207 Waller Road
London
SE14 5LX
☎ 020 7639 9732
RE.V

**FINN**, Peter
**Group Analyst**
c/o The Peper Harow Foundation
Station House
150 Waterloo Road
London
SE1 5SB
☎ 02079 287 388
p.finn@peperharow.org.uk
IGA

**FISHER**, Linda
**Cognitive Behavioural Psychotherapist**
CFS Research Unit
The New Medical School
Bessemer Road
London
SE5 9PJ
☎ 020 7346 3363
☎ 07787 502 111
spdplfi@iop.kcl.ac.uk
BABCP

**FLANAGAN**, Eileen
**Psychoanalytic Psychotherapist**
London
SE1
☎ 01908 613 533
☎ 07710 411 765
FPC

**FLEMING**, Robert W.K.
**Child Psychotherapist**
29 South Croxted Road
West Dulwich
London
SE21 8AZ
☎ 020 8670 0019 (t/f)
ACP

**FLETCHER**, Joan
**Humanistic and Integrative Psychotherapist**
171 Algernon Road
Lewisham
London
SE13 7AP
☎ 020 8690 8987
joan2@uel.ac.uk
SPEC

**FOX**, Catherine
**Psychosynthesis Psychotherapist**
♿ 95a Herne Hill
London
SE24 9LY
☎ 020 7924 0369
catherinejifox@hotmail.com
92-94 Tooley Street
London
SE1 2TH
PET

**FREEDMAN**, Jax
**Humanistic and Integrative Psychotherapist**
6 Arbuthnot Road
New Cross
London
SE14 5NP
☎ 020 7732 9353
☎ 07989 080 271
janejax@bt.openworld.com
SPEC

**GARDINER**, Margaret
**Psychoanalytic Psychotherapist**
44 Granville Park
Lewisham
London
SE13 7DX
☎ 020 8318 3303
☎ 020 7848 2613
AGIP, FIP

**GEORGE**, Dorothy
**Integrative Psychotherapist**
♿ RM 603
The Chandlery
50 Westminster Bridge Road
London
SE1 7QY
☎ 020 7586 8862
SPCRC

**GEORGOPOULOU**, Victoria
**Systemic Psychotherapist**
Flat 8
Sycamore Court
7-9 Silverdale
London
SE26 4SD
☎ 07929 081 827
victoria07uk@yahoo.co.uk
KCC

**GERAGHTY**, Wendy
**Family & Systemic Psychotherapist**
33 Wicham Road
Brockley
London
SE4 1PW
☎ 020 8692 4329
wendy.geraghty@lewisham.gov.uk
AFT

**GINSBORG**, Robby
**Analytical Psychologist-Jungian Analyst**
84 Thornlaw Road
London
SE27 0SA
☎ 020 8761 3607
☎ 020 8670 4184
ginsborg@thornlaw.u-net.com
IGAP

**GOODMAN**, Susan
**Analytical Psychologist-Jungian Analyst**
114 Court Lane
Dulwich
SE21 7EA
☎ 020 8693 9926
CAP *

**GOTTSCHALK**, Margaret
**Integrative Psychotherapist**
21 Marsden Road
London
SE15 4EE
☎ 0207 277 9528
MC

**GRAY**, Rebecca
**Sexual and Relationship Psychotherapist**
72a Wicham Road
Brockley
London
SE4 1LS
☎ 01903 884 251
☎ 020 8694 0189
rg.ds.doz@virgin.net
BASRT

**GREENGRASS**, Carol
**Psychoanalytic Psychotherapist**
18 West Square
London
SE11 4SN
☎ 020 7793 1305
carolgreengrass@aol.com
IPSS

**GREENWOOD**, Anthony
**Group Analytic Psychotherapist**
19 Brunswick Quay
Rotherhithe
London
SE16 7PU
☎ 02072 314 309
UPCA

**GREGORY**, Marilyn
**Family & Systemic Psychotherapist**
Lewisham Child & Therapy Centre
78 Lewisham Park
London
SE13 6QT
☎ 020 8690 1086
AFT

**GREY**, David
**Psychoanalytic Psychotherapist**
♿ 93 Alleyn Park
London
SE21 8AA
☎ 020 8299 9918
davidgrey@spin1.fsnet.co.uk
IPSS

**GRIFFIN**, Dr M
**Sexual and Relationship Psychotherapist**
♿ The Amarant Centre
Gainsborough Clinic
80 Lambeth Road
London
SE1
☎ 020 7401 3855
☎ 07956 461 940
BASRT

**GURNEY**, Paul
**Psychoanalytic Psychotherapist**
♿ 76 Macclesfield Road
London
SE25 4RX
☎ 020 8656 5032
PA, SITE

**HADDINGTON**, Janet
**Psychoanalytic Psychotherapist**
2a Bromar Road
Camberwell
London
SE5 8DL
☎ 020 7326 1332
☎ 020 7641 3469
FIP

**HANCHEN**, Tomasz
**Neurolinguistic Psychotherapist**
♿ 55 Cressingham Road
Lewisham
London
SE13 5AQ
☎ 02083 183 102
tommyhanchen@hibrid.waitrose.com
NLPtCA

**HANCOCK**, Pauline
**Psychosynthesis Psychotherapist**
♿ Flat 1
194 Peckham Rye
East Dulwich
London
SE22 9QA
☎ 020 8299 1767
pfh@ukf.net
PET

**HARDING**, Valentine
**Psychoanalytic Psychotherapist**
11 Portal Close
London
SE27 0BN
☎ 02087 610 260
☎ 02075 156 144
newt1127@aol.com
NAFSI

**HARGADEN**, Helena
**Integrative Psychotherapist, Transactional Analysis Psychotherapist**
43 Brockley Park
Forest Hill
London
SE23 1PT
☎ 020 8690 3175
helenahargaden27@hotmail.com
ITA, MET

**HARGRAVE**, Annie
**Psychoanalytic Psychotherapist**
Interhealth
157 Waterloo Road
London
SE1 8US
☎ 020 790 2900
annieh@interhealth.org.uk
CSP

**HARRIOT**, Juanita
**Psychoanalytic Psychotherapist**
19a Bovill Road
Forest Hill
London
SE23 1HB
☎ 020 8291 5605
IPSS

**HARRIS**, Lynn
**Integrative Psychotherapist**
8 'Springfield' Avenue Road
South Norwood
London
SE25 4ED
☎ 02087 681 697
MET

**HARRIS**, Tirril
**Psychoanalytic Psychotherapist**
Academic Department of Psychiatry
St. Thomas' Hospital
Lambeth Palace Road
London
SE1 7EH
☎ 020 7928 9292 ext6905
☎ 020 7272 3073
tirril.harris@kcl.ac.uk
FIP

**HARRISON**, Simon
**Psychosynthesis Psychotherapist**
17A Fox Hill
London
SE19 2UX
☎ 020 8653 4644
slcharrison@hotmail.com
PET

**HAUKE**, Christopher
**Analytical Psychologist-Jungian Analyst**
♿ 1b Maidstone Buildings
74-76 Borough High Street
London Bridge
London
SE1 1GD
☎ 0781 805 1571
☎ 020 8301 5886
chauke@blythehill.u-net.com
CAP *

**HEAPHY**, Grace
**Systemic Psychotherapist**
♿ Michael Rutter Centre for Children and Young People
Maudsley Hospital
Denmark Hill
SE5 8AZ
☎ 020 7919 2619
☎ 020 7241 0448
gracehea@aol.com
KCC

**HEDGES**, Fran
**Systemic Psychotherapist**
213 New Cross Road
London
SE14 5UH
☎ 020 8392 3632
☎ 020 7358 0518
f.hedges@roehampton.ac.uk
KCC

**HENDRY**, Evelyn R.
**Cognitive Behavioural Psychotherapist**
York Clinic
Guy's Hospital
London
SE1 1NP
BABCP

**HINDMARCH**, Dorothea
**Group Analyst**
♿ Kings College Hospital
Denmark Hill
London
SE5 9RS
☎ 020 7346 3524
thea.hindmarch@kingsch.nhs.uk
IGA

**HODGKISS**, Andrew
**Lacanian Analyst**
♿ The Consulting Rooms
199 Westminster Bridge Road
London
SE1 7UT
☎ 02079 605 735
CFAR, UPCA

**HOGARTH**, Susy
**Systemic Psychotherapist**
49 Brockwell Park Gardens
London
SE24 9BJ
☎ 020 8674 8250
KCC

**HOPKINS**, Kathleen
**Psychosynthesis Psychotherapist**
Cenacle
142a Rodney Road
Walworth
London
SE17 1RA
☎ 020 7708 3541
kathleenhopkins@btopenworld.com
PET

**HOPPING**, Geoff
**Transactional Analysis Psychotherapist**
♿ 22-24 Chapter Road
London
SE17 3ET
☎ 020 7820 0268
geoff@streathamhillsw2.fresserve.co.uk
ITA, MET

**HOTCHKIES**, Lynsey
**Group Analytic Psychotherapist**
35 Dalmore Road
London
SE21 8HD
☎ 020 8244 8292
lynseyhotchckies@hotmail.com
UPCA

**HOWARD**, Heather
**Psychoanalytic Psychotherapist**
83 Blackheath Park
London
SE3 0EU
☎ 020 8 852 6564
IPSS

**HUDSON**, David
**Integrative Psychotherapist**
72 Hurley House
Cotton Gardens Estate
Kennington Lane
London
SE11 4PD
☎ 07890 056 309
dhudsontherapist@yahoo.co.uk
SPCRC

**HUNTER**, Margaret
**Child Psychotherapist**
Clinical Manager
Bloomfield Centre, Guys Hospital
St Thomas Street
LONDON
SE1 9RT
☎ 020 7955 4583 ext 4947
ACP

**JACOBS**, Dr Brian William
**Family & Systemic Psychotherapist**
♿ 8 Maberley Road
Upper Norwood
London
SE19 2JB
☎ 020 8771 0342
bJacobs@iop.kcl.ac.uk
IFT

**JEFFORD**, Adam
**Group Analytic Psychotherapist**
Intensive Psychological Treatment Service
York Clinic
47 Weston Street
London
SE1 3RR
☎ 02079 554 901
UPCA

**JENKINS**, Hugh
**Systemic Psychotherapist**
♿ 83 Hurstbourne Road
Forest Hill
London
SE23 2AQ
☎ 020 8291 4791
IFT

**JENNINGS**, Peter
**Integrative Psychotherapist**
55 Ravensbourne Park Crescent
Catford
SE6 4YG
☎ 020 8690 1839
quotidiansemaphore@yahoo.co.uk
SPCRC

**JIAH**, Hildah
**Cognitive Behavioural Psychotherapist**
♿ The Sainsbury Centre for Mental Health
Maya House
134-138 Borough High Street
London
SE1 1LB
☎ 020 8691 3237
☎ 020 8761 4554
70 Casewick Road
West Norwood
London
SE27 0SZ
BABCP

**JONES**, Kevin
**Psychoanalytic Psychotherapist**
35 Whatman Road
Forest Hill
London
SE23 1EY
☎ 020 7919 7239
k.jones@gold.ac.uk
IPSS

**JONES**, Merryn
**Group Analytic Psychotherapist**
8 Broadwall
London
SE1 9QE
☎ 020 7401 2393
FPC

**JUDE**, Julia
**Group Analytic Psychotherapist**
24 Canadian Avenue
Catford
London
SE6 3AS
☎ 02086 908 900
UPCA

**JURY**, Lorraine
**Psychosynthesis Psychotherapist**
Top Floor Flat
Unity Wharf
Mill Street
London
SE1 2BH
☎ 020 7237 8660
☎ 07702 415 241
lorrainejury@aol.com
PET

**KALITOWSKI**, Matthew
**Hypno-Psychotherapist**
c/o 13
153 Fawnbrake Avenue
London
SE24 08G
☎ 00612 9665 8284
NSHAP

**KERR**, Anna
**Psychoanalytic Psychotherapist**
61 Humber Road
London
SE3 7LR
☎ 020 7580 2628
annakerr8@aol.com
GUILD

**KERRIDGE**, Jack
**Psychoanalytic Psychotherapist**
96 Langton Way
London
SE3 7JU
☎ 020 8 305 1287
GUILD

**KING**, Christine
**Hypno-Psychotherapist**
St Johns Park
Blackheath
London
SE3 7JP
☎ 02083 052 317
NRHP

**KLEINOT**, Pamela
**Psychoanalytic Psychotherapist**
♿ 13 Russell Lodge
24 Spurgeon Street
Southwark
London
SE1 4YJ
☎ 02074 035 584
ARBS, WTC

**KNIGHT**, Elaine
**Transpersonal Psychotherapist**
Norfolk Cottage
89 Riverdale Road
Plumstead
London
SE18 1PD
☎ 020 8854 7835
☎ 07905 973 964
CTP

**KOEPPELMANN**, Marianna
**Psychosynthesis Psychotherapist**
73 Lawnside
Blackheath
London
SE3 9HL
☎ 020 8318 0792
PET

**KOWSZUN**, Graz
**Humanistic Psychotherapist**
♿ 127 Kinveachy Gardens
Charlton
London
SE7 8EQ
☎ 020 8854 0604
Graz.k@btopenworld.com
AHPP, MET

**LANGDON**, Monica
**Psychoanalytic Psychotherapist**
6 Upwood Road
Lee
London
SE12 8AA
☎ 020 8318 0110
monica@langdon119.freeserve.co.uk
AGIP

**LANYADO**, Monica
**Child Psychotherapist**
30 Brookway
Blackheath
London
SE3 9BJ
☎ 020 8463 0638
ACP

**LASK**, Judith
**Family & Systemic Psychotherapist**
Flat 9
25 Broadwall
London
SE1 9PL
☎ 020 7771 7679
j.lask@iop.kcl.ac.uk
AFT

**LAYFIELD**, Elly
**Systemic Psychotherapist**
Conan Doyle House
12 Tennison Road
London
SE25 5RT
☎ 07977 121 871
elly-layfield@msn.com or
elly@kingscrest.demon.co.uk
KCC

**LEACH**, Mark J
**Sexual and Relationship Psychotherapist**
♿ Dept. of Secual Health
The Caldecot Centre
King's Healthcare NHS Trust
15-22 Caldecot Road, London
SE5 9RS
☎ 01708 445 156
☎ 020 7346 4535
BASRT

**LEE**, Joan Mary
**Analytical Psychologist-Jungian Analyst**
69 Beaconsfield Road
Blackheath
London
SE3 7LG
☎ 020 8858 3133
CAP *

**LEEMING**, Gareth
**Psychoanalytic Psychotherapist**
Flat 8
82 Wickham Road
Brockley
London
SE4 1LS
☎ 020 8469 0666
FPC

**LESSEM**, Pauline Joey
**Cognitive Analytic Therapist**
c/o 92-94 Tooley Street
London Bridge
London
SE1 2TH
☎ 01342 823 291
☎ 07050 098 785
jlessem@btopenworld.com
ACAT

**LIPSEDGE**, Catherine
**Cognitive Behavioural Psychotherapist**
♿ Priory Clinic
Kents House
24-26 St Thomas Street
London
SE1 9RS
☎ 07770 853 320
cbaptiste-cyrous@cwctv.net
BABCP

**LIVANOU**, M.
**Cognitive Behavioural Psychotherapist**
Section of Trauma Studies
Institute of Psychiatry
38 Carver Road
London
SE24 9LT
☎ 020 7738 4967
m.livanou@iop.kcl.ac.uk
BABCP

**LONGHURST**, Martin
**Systemic Psychotherapist**
10 Tomson House
Saint Saviors Estate
London
SE1 3DJ
☎ 07867 762 981
KCC

**LONGLEY**, Joan
**Psychoanalytic Psychotherapist**
Lavender Cottage
9b Tudor Road
Upper Norwood
London
SE19 2UH
☎ 020 8768 0224
joan.longley@btinternet.com
AGIP

**LOVE**, Derek
**Group Analyst**
The Vale Practice
64 Grove Vale
London
SE22 8DT
☎ 020 8299 9798
IGA

**LOWDEN**, Barbara
**Transpersonal Psychotherapist**
99A Griffin Road
Plumstead
London
SE18 7QE
☎ 020 8854 4074
☎ 020 7266 3006
CCPE

**LYON**, Josephine
**Hypno-Psychotherapist**
33 Herald's Place
Renfrew Road
London
SE11 4NP
☎ 020 7735 0462
NSHAP

**LYONS**, Kathleen
**Psychosynthesis Psychotherapist**
Cenacle Sisters
142a Rodney Road
Walworth, London
SE17 1RA
☎ 020 7708 3541
kathlyons@btinternet.com
PET

**MACDONALD**, Laurie
**Neurolinguistic Psychotherapist**
♿ 24 Robinscroft Mews
Greenwich
London
SE10 8DN
☎ 02086 916 513
☎ 02086 916 517
NLPtCA

**MACKINTOSH**, Peri
**Gestalt Psychotherapist**
♿ i-U Therapy Services
92-94 Tooley Street
London
SE1 2TH
☎ 07947 369 990
peri@i-u.org
GPTI, MET

**MADDOX**, Chris
**Existential Psychotherapist**
62 Ennis Road
Plumstead
London
SE18 2QT
☎ 02083 310 078
cgmaddox@teci.fsnet.co.uk
UPCA

**MANICOM**, Hilary
**Systemic Psychotherapist**
17 Rommany Road
West Norwood
London
SE27 9PY
☎ 020 8651 5611
KCC

**MARSH**, Jennifer
**Psychoanalytic Psychotherapist**
96 Elfindale Road
Herne Hill
London
SE24 9NW
☎ 020 7 274 3467
GUILD

**MARSHALL**, Eamonn
**Gestalt Psychotherapist**
London
SE4
☎ 07941 410 554
therapeia@lineone.net
GPTI

**MASSARA**, Catharina
**Integrative Psychotherapist**
Flat 16
46 Renfrew Road
London
SE11 4NA
☎ 020 7711 9481
SPCRC

**MASSIL**, Dr Helen
**Sexual and Relationship Psychotherapist**
♿ Department of Reproductive Health
St Giles
St Giles Road
London
SE5 7RN
☎ 020 7771 3330
BASRT

**MASTERS**, Alison
**Analytical Psychologist-Jungian Analyst**
71 Walcot Square
Kennington
London
SE11 4UB
☎ 020 7735 4600
ammasters@btinternet.com
CAP *

**MAUNDER**, Brian
**Psychoanalytic Psychotherapist**
Badgers' Oak
12 Chinbrook Road
Grove Park
London
SE12 9TH
☎ 020 8851 5702
brian_maunder@hotmail.com
FPC

**MCAULAY**, Ruth
**Psychosynthesis Psychotherapist**
5 Montpelier Row
Blackheath
London
SE3 0RL
☎ 020 8318 9926
frances.marling@btinternet.com
Psychosynthesis & Education Trust
92-94 Tooley Street
London
SE1
PET

**MCBRIDE**, Marie
**Family & Systemic Psychotherapist**
♿ The Bloomfield Centre
Guys Hospital
London
SE1 9RT
☎ 020 7955 4583
marie.mcbride@slam-tr.nhs.uk
IFT

**MCCABE**, Jennifer
**Group Analytic Psychotherapist**
♿ The Bridge
30 Borough High Street
London
SE1 1XU
☎ 02088 764 702
jennifermccabe@aol.com
UPCA

**MCCOMBE**, Brian
**Group Analytic Psychotherapist**
♿ 125 Manor Park
Lewisham
London
SE13 5RQ
☎ 02088 525 056
brianmc@onetel.net.uk
UPCA

**MCCUTCHEON**, Moira
**Child Psychotherapist**
Camberwell Child Guidance Centre
Lister Health Centre
1 Camden Square
Peckham Road, London
SE15 5LA
☎ 020 7701 7371
ACP

**MCKENZIE**, Thomas
**Transpersonal Psychotherapist**
Flat 4
64 Thicket Road
London
SE20 8DR
☎ 020 8659 6909
CTP

**MCKENZIE-MAVINGA**, I
**Psychoanalytic Psychotherapist**
10 Wallbutton Road
London
SE4 2NX
☎ 02076 521 361
talk2mavinga@aol.com
NAFSI

**MCMAHON**, Gladeana
**Cognitive Behavioural Psychotherapist**
11 Streetfield Mews
Blackheath Park
London
SE3 0ER
☎ 020 8852 4854
gladeana@dircon.co.uk
BABCP

**MCMILLAN**, Penny
**Attachment-based Psychoanalytic Psychotherapist**
32 Congers House
Bronze Street
London
SE8 3DT
☎ 020 8691 7199
pennymac@dial.pipex.com
CAPP

**MILES**, Natalie
**Integrative Psychotherapist**
7 The Lane
Blackheath
London
SE3 9SL
☎ 020 8318 3423
info@nataliemiles.fsnet.co.uk
SPCRC

**MILLAR**, Gerry
**Psychosynthesis Psychotherapist**
Psychosynthesis & Education Trust
92-94 Tooley Street
London
SE1 2TH
☎ 02076 357 754
☎ 02077 326 396
gerry.millar@lineone.net
1 Greenstreet Hill
Drakefell Road
London
SE14 5SR
IPS

**MILNER-JONES**, Cassandra
**Psychoanalytic Psychotherapist**
56 Foxes Dale
Blackheath
London
SE3 9BQ
☎ 020 8852 3753
FPC

**MINIHANE**, Anna
**Integrative Psychotherapist**
Lower Flat
30 Padua Road
Penge
London
SE20 8HF
☎ 020 8776 5946
☎ 01303 257 659
amvm@ukgateway.net
MET

**MONTICELLI**, Wendy
**Psychoanalytic Psychotherapist**
19 Brunswick Quay
Rotherhithe
London
SE16 1PU
☎ 020 7231 4309
FPC

**MOOREY**, Stirling
**Cognitive Psychotherapist**
♿ Psychotherapy Unit, Outpatients Dept
Maudsley Hospital
Denmark Hill
London
SE5 8AZ
☎ 020 7919 2389
☎ 020 7919 2382
stirling.moorey@slam-tr.nhs.uk
BABCP

**MORGAN**, Guy
**Cognitive Behavioural Psychotherapist**
♿ Meridian Mental Health Centre
68 The Heights
Charlton
London
SE7 8JH
☎ 020 8921 2423
guy.morgan@oxleas.nhs.uk
BABCP

**MORIN (MS)**, Terry
**Gestalt Psychotherapist**
97 Fawnbrake Avenue
London
SE24 0BG
☎ 020 7737 2173
terry.morin@virgin.net
MET

**MORINO**, Yuriko
**Family & Systemic Psychotherapist**
2 Mylis Close
Sydenham
London
SE26 6JL
☎ 020 8699 7839
yuriko@morino.freeserve.co.uk
AFT

**MORLEY**, Jane
**Group Analytic Psychotherapist**
11 Tylney Avenue
London
SE19 1LN
☎ 02072 502 316
UPCA

**MUIR**, Adeola
**Psychoanalytic Psychotherapist**
89A Lorrimore Road
London
SE17 3LZ
☎ 02072 771 488
☎ 079456 895 094
rmuir57974@aol.com
NAFSI

**MUKUMA**, Diana
**Gestalt Psychotherapist**
Flat 3
194 Kennington Lane
London
SE11 5DL
☎ 020 7735 5442
GPTI, MET

**MUMVURI-ELLIS**, Gladys
**Systemic Psychotherapist**
♿ Child Adolescent Eating Disorders Service
Michael Rutter Centre, The Maudesle
De Crespigny Park Road
London
SE5
☎ 020 8597 0623
☎ 020 7919 3464
Gladys.Ellis@slam.nhs.uk
IFT

**MURPHY**, Sue
**Integrative Psychotherapist**
4 Egremont Road
London
SE27 0BH
☎ 020 8670 6139
smurphy@sghms.ac.uk
SPCRC

**MURRAY**, Christine
**Integrative Psychotherapist**
50 Ormiston Road
Greenwich
London
SE10 0LN
☎ 020 8858 7350
christinemurray@malicity.com
MET

**MUTTI**, Derek
**Psychosynthesis Psychotherapist**
44 Wood Vale
Forest Hill
London
SE23 3EE
☎ 020 8693 7314
derek_mutti@onetel.net.uk
PET

**MYERS**, Dania
**Psychodynamic Psychotherapist**
4 Elliscombe Road
London
SE7 7PY
☎ 020 8858 1722
AIP

**NANCARROW**, Kiya
**Core Process Psychotherapist**
11 Bridge House
47 Adelaide Avenue
London
SE4 1LF
☎ 020 8801 7233
KI

**NEVILL**, Stuart
**Psychoanalytic Psychotherapist**
42 Elsinore Road
Forest Hill
London
SE23 2SL
☎ 020 8699 1287
nevillstuart@hotmail.com
ARBS

**NEWBIGIN**, Alison
**Analytical Psychotherapist**
48 Surrey Square
London
SE17 2JX
☎ 020 7703 9544
alison@anewbegin.fsnet.co.uk
AIP, MC

**NEWNS**, Kerri
**Systemic Psychotherapist**
50 Eversley Road
Charlton
London
SE7 7LD
☎ 020 8305 9842
☎ 01322 299 900
kerri@globalnet.co.uk
KCC

**NICHOLLS**, John
**Group Analytic Psychotherapist**
43 Athenlay Road
Nunhead
London
SE15 3EN
☎ 02076 402 715
☎ 02078 348 494
jnicholls55@hotmail.com
UPCA

**O'BRIEN**, Celia
**Cognitive Analytic Therapist**
36a Tressillian Road
Brockley
London
SE4 1YB
☎ 020 8692 9937
☎ 07803 904 247
Munro Centre
Guy's Hospital
Snowfields
SE1 3SS
ACAT

**O'CALLAGHAN**, Diane
**Psychoanalytic Psychotherapist**
16 Colwell Road
East Dulwich
London
SE22 8QP
☎ 020 8516 5906
AGIP

**O'GRADY**, Margaret
**Psychoanalytic Psychotherapist**
♿ 265 Bellenden Road
London
SE15 4DQ
☎ 020 7639 6702
☎ 020 8299 9798
margaretogrady@yahoo.co.uk
The Vale Practice
64 Grove Vale
London
SE22 8DT
AGIP

**O'KELLY**, Marie
**Psychosynthesis Psychotherapist**
Flat 357
Devon Mansions
Tooley Street
London
SE1 2XG
☎ 020 7357 6967
marieo'kelly@eircom.net
PET

**O'LOUGHLIN**, Brenda
**Systemic Psychotherapist**
89 Mount Pleasant Road
Lewisham
London
SE13 6RG
☎ 020 8314 5688
KCC

**OPIK**, Urve
**Transpersonal Psychotherapist**
London
SE13
☎ 0775 409 4717
urveopik@hotmail.com
CCPE

**PALGRAVE**, Lesley
**Cognitive Analytic Therapist**
85 Heathlee Road
Blackheath
London
SE3 9HS
☎ 020 8852 4674
☎ 07855 638 442
lesleypalgrave@btopenworld.com
ACAT

**PALMER**, Stephen
**Cognitive Behavioural Psychotherapist, Rational Emotive Behaviour Therapist**
Centre for Stress Management
156 Westcombe Hill
Blackheath
London
SE3 7DH
☎ 020 8318 4448
palmer@managingstress.com
BABCP, AREBT

**PARKINSON**, Judy
**Psychoanalytic Psychotherapist**
Newlands Park Natural Health Care Centre
48 Newlands Park
Sydenham
Sydenham
SE26 5NE
☎ 020 8659 5001
FPC

**PAWSEY**, Jack
**Psychoanalytic Psychotherapist**
20 Addington Square
London
SE5 7JZ
jack@addpaw.fsnet.co.uk
FPC

**PAYNE**, Christopher
**Integrative Psychosynthesis Psychotherapist**
London SE1
Near London Bridge and Tower Bridge
SE1
☎ 0207 722 6874
RE.V

**PETERS**, Sheila
**Hypno-Psychotherapist**
102A Holmesdale Road
South Norwood
London
SE25 6JF
☎ 02086 534 242
sheila102a@aol.com
NRHP

**PLOWS**, Barbara
**Group Analytic Psychotherapist**
Forest Hill
London
SE23
☎ 020 8244 3251
barbara.plows@ntworld.com
FPC

**POVER**, Jane S E
**Group Analytic Psychotherapist**
Kings College
James Clerk Maxwell Building
57 Waterloo Road
London
SE1 8WA
☎ 02078 483 582
☎ 01732 887 346
jane.pover@kcl.ac.uk
UPCA

**PRICE**, Susan
**Psychoanalytic Psychotherapist**
♿ 15 Boyne Road
London
SE13 5AL
☎ 02083 184 410
susanprice@clara.co.uk
The Lind Clinic
James Lind House
Grove Street
London
SE8 3RA
GUILD, WTC

**PUCKETT**, Jane
**Hypno-Psychotherapist**
Nunhead Grove
Nunhead
London
SE15 3DF
☎ 07930 615 014
jane@puckett21.freeserve.co.uk
NRHP

**RAILTON**, Ja'far
**Psychoanalytic Psychotherapist**
87 Stansfeld House
Longfield Estate
London
SE1 5PN
☎ 02072 318 937
railton@ukgateway.net
NAFSI

**RANCE**, Christopher
**Group Analyst**
43 Rosendale Road
Dulwich
London
SE21 8DY
☎ 020 8670 5023
ckrance@btclick.com
IGA

**RENOUF**, Johanna
**Psychoanalytic Psychotherapist**
70 St Julians Farm Road
West Norwood
London
SE27 0RS
☎ 020 8670 2745
johrnouf@aol.com
FPC

**RIBEIRO-NELSON**, Caroline
**Existential Psychotherapist**
83a Sunderland Road
Forest Hill
London
SE23 2PS
☎ 020 8699 7902
☎ 07951 016 133
SEA

**RICHARDS-GRAY**, Susan
**Educational Therapist**
11 Homeleigh Road
London
SE15 3EE
☎ 020 7732 2214
datsuncherry@supanet.com
CFET

**RIGBY**, Yvonne
**Gestalt Psychotherapist**
10 Ravensbourne Road
London
SE6 4UX
☎ 020 8690 1411
GCL

**RIMER**, Penelope Ann
**Cognitive Analytic Therapist**
♿ South London and Maudsley Hospital NHS Trust
Maudsley Hospital
Denmark Hill
London
SE5 8AZ
ACAT

**RIMMER**, Annie
**Integrative Psychotherapist, Transactional Analysis Psychotherapist**
♿ 10 Mount Ash Road
Sydenham
London
SE26 6LZ
☎ 02082 914 091
annie.rimmer@breathemail.net
ITA, MET

**ROBERTS**, Jennifer
**Body Psychotherapist, Integrative Psychotherapist**
208 Camberwell New Road
London
SE5 0RR
☎ 020 7582 5932
☎ 07971 864 225
jenniferakaj@hotmail.com
CCBP

**ROBERTS**, Rosemarie
**Family & Systemic Psychotherapist**
♿ Southwark Community Child & Family Service
South London & Maudsley NHST
151 Blackfriars Road
London
SE1 8EL
☎ 020 7620 0923
rosemarie.roberts@slam.nhs.uk
AFT

**ROBERTSON**, Judith
**Psychoanalytic Psychotherapist**
76 Crawthew Grove
London
SE22 9AB
☎ 020 8516 1173
judith@psychotherapy-london.co.uk
IPSS

**ROBINSON**, Ferga
**Cognitive Behavioural Psychotherapist**
♿ 44 Brockwell Park Gardens
Herne Hill
London
SE24 9BJ
☎ 020 8674 2359
BABCP

**ROBSON**, Annie
**Psychoanalytic Psychotherapist**
100 King George Street
Greenwich
London
SE10 8PX
☎ 020 7487 3766
☎ 020 8853 8770
CCOPPP

**RODGER**, Catherine
**Family & Systemic Psychotherapist**
Lewisham Community Child & Family Service
The Old School House
Leahurst Road, Hither Green
London
SE13 5LS
☎ 020 8852 3070 x 229
IFT

**RUDDELL**, Peter
**Cognitive Behavioural Psychotherapist, Rational Emotive Behaviour Therapist**
Centre for Rational Emotive BehaviourTherapy
156 Westcombe Hill
Blackheath
London
SE3 7DH
☎ 020 8318 4448
ruddell@managingstress.com
BABCP, AREBT

**RUMNEY**, Boris
**Psychoanalytic Psychotherapist**
1 Foxes Dale
London
SE3 9BD
☎ 020 8 852 9015
GUILD

**RUSHFORTH**, Catherine
**Systemic Psychotherapist**
♿ London Centre of Complementary Healthcare
137 Greenwich South Street
Greenwich
London
SE10 8PP
☎ 020 8305 6778
info@holistic_healing.org.uk
KCC

**RYLEY**, Brigitte
**Humanistic and Integrative Psychotherapist**
Flat 1
39a Glengarry Road
London
SE22 8QA
☎ 020 8693 6953
AHPP

**SALMON**, Gillian
**Educational Therapist**
57 Kennington Road
London
SE1 7PZ
☎ 020 7401 8169
gilliansalmon@whsmithnet.co.uk
CFET

**SANDERS**, Julie
**Transpersonal Psychotherapist**
♿ 38 Dunblane Road
Eltham
London
SE9 6RS
☎ 020 8265 8080
CCPE

**SCHMIDT**, Martin
**Analytical Psychologist-Jungian Analyst**
71 Ivanhoe Road
London
SE5 8DH
☎ 020 7274 3758
martinalanschmidt@yahoo.com
CAP *

**SHORROCK**, Andrew
**Psychosynthesis Psychotherapist**
14 Lovell Place
London
SE16 6QQ
☎ 020 7231 8016
Aanda@ndirect.co.uk
PET

**SHYAM-ANSARI**, Dr Shakir
**Cognitive Analytic Therapist**
♿ York Clinic
Guy's Hospital
St Thomas' Street
London
SE1 9RT
☎ 020 8301 9421
ACAT

**SIEDERER**, Carol
**Gestalt Psychotherapist**
76 Erlanger Road
London
SE14 5TH
☎ 020 7787 2813
CarolSiederer@aol.com
GCL

**SIGALAS**, Anthony
**Psychoanalytic Psychotherapist**
25 The Green House
Burbage Close
London
SE1 4EG
☎ 02074 035 933
sigalasgr@yahoo.co.uk
NAFSI

**SILVERTON**, Stephen
**Core Process Psychotherapist**
6 Orchard Grove
London
SE20 8DZ
☎ 020 8676 9247
KI

**SIMPSON**, Ian
**Group Analyst**
♿ Psychotherapy Unit
Adamson Centre
St Thomas Hospital
London
SE1 7EH
☎ 020 7928 9292 x 2272
IGA

**SINGHAM**, Stephanie
**Cognitive Analytic Therapist**
♿ Diabetes Day Centre
3rd Floor Lambeth Wing
St Thomas' Hospital
London
SE1 7EH
☎ 020 7928 9292 x3786
stephanie.singham@gstt.sthames.nhs.uk
ACAT

**SIRET**, Rachel E
**Group Analytic Psychotherapist**
28 Bromley Road
London
SE6 2TP
☎ 07889 471110 (mob)
☎ 020 8690 6672
UPCA

**SMETHURST**, Philippa
**Integrative Psychotherapist**
168 Manor Park
London
SE13 5RH
☎ 02083 183 268
MET

**SMITH**, Juliet
**Integrative Psychotherapist**
52 Pilgrimage Street
London Bridge
London
SE1 4LL
☎ 02074 035 497
MET

**SMITH**, R.L
**Cognitive Behavioural Psychotherapist**
♿ Mental Health Advice Centre
1 Southbrook Road
Lee
London
SE12 8LH
☎ 020 8318 1339
☎ 020 8333 3030 x8117
SMITH1815@HOTMAIL.COM
BABCP

**SMITH**, Ruthie
**Psychoanalytic Psychotherapist**
♿ 2a Banning Street
Greenwich
London
SE10 9PH
☎ 020 8281 1710
ruthie@ruthiesmith.demon.co.uk
WTC

**SMITH**, Trevor E.L.
**Cognitive Behavioural Psychotherapist**
22 Pleydell Avenue
Upper Norwood
London
SE19 2LP
☎ 020 8653 0924
☎ 020 8993 7892
BABCP

**SOOD**, Punam
**Body Psychotherapist, Integrative Psychotherapist**
12 Ospring House
Wootton Street
Waterloo
London
SE1 8TP
☎ 020 7261 9886
CCBP

**SOUTA**, Marie Ludmila
**Transpersonal Psychotherapist**
25 Point Hill
Greenwich
London
SE10 8QW
☎ 020 8692 0628 (t/f)
mjreeve@dial.pipex.com
CCPE

**SPALDING**, John
**Psychoanalytic Psychotherapist**
1 Southbrook Road
Lee
London
SE12
☎ 020 8466 2500
☎ 020 8464 8292
jpespalding@yahoo.co.uk
AGIP

**SPENCE**, Mary
**Systemic Psychotherapist**
88 St John's Park
London
SE3 7JW
KCC

**SPINELLI**, Ernesto
**Existential Psychotherapist**
69 Oglander Road
East Dulwich
London
SE15 4DD
☎ 020 8693 9332
spinelle@regents.ac.uk
SPCRC

**STANIER**, Graham
**Hypno-Psychotherapist**
The London Television Centre
Upper Ground
London
SE1 9LT
☎ 02089 775 638
saunier@lineone.net
NRHP

**STEDMAN**, Maire
**Systemic Psychotherapist**
11 Lamerton Street
Greenwich
London
SE8 3PL
☎ 020 8469 0975
☎ 020 7631 5505
mairestedman@eircom.net
IFT

**STEEL**, Marion
**Integrative Psychotherapist**
♿ 9a Piermont Road
East Dulwich
London
SE22 0LN
☎ 020 8299 9863
SPCRC

**STEVENSON**, Bruce
**Body Psychotherapist, Integrative Psychotherapist**
Garden Flat
13 Park Hill Road
London
SE21 8EH
☎ 020 8961 7802
Bruce.Stevenson@Tesco.net
CCBP, MET

**SULLIVAN**, Jill
**Group Analyst**
Southbrook CMHT
1 South Brook Road
London
SE12 8LH
☎ 020 8318 1339
jsullivan@nhs.co.uk
IGA

**TANNER**, Claire
**Cognitive Analytic Therapist**
26 Vancouver Road
Forest Hill
London
SE23 2AF
☎ 020 8699 7996
ctanner@another.com
ACAT

**TAYLOR**, Dee
**Family & Systemic Psychotherapist**
182A Devonshire Road
London
SE23 3TB
☎ 020 8291 3584
Dee.Taylor@gp-G85095.nhs.uk
IFT

**TENN**, Linda
**Hypno-Psychotherapist**
Woolstone Road
Forest Hill
London
SE23
☎ 01761 311 327
lindatenn@hotmail.com
NRHP

**THOMAS**, Kim
**Psychoanalytic Psychotherapist**
35 Broxholm Road
London
SE27 0NA
☎ 02086 700 285
akimathomas@ukonline.co.uk
NAFSI

**THOMAS**, Mary R.
**Psychoanalytic Psychotherapist**
16 Colwell Rd
East Dulwich
London
SE22 8QP
☎ 020 8693 8316
FPC

**THORNDYCRAFT**, Bill
**Group Analytic Psychotherapist**
South London and Maudsley NHS Trust
c/o Psychotherapy Department
Adamson Centre, Block 8
St Thomas' Hospital
SE1 7EH
SOCBJ@RBKC.gov.uk
FPC

**TOPLISS**, Nick
**Family & Systemic Psychotherapist**
162 Kilmorie Road
Forest Hill
London
SE23 2SR
☎ 020 8244 0284
IFT

**TOREY**, Sharon
**Psychoanalytic Psychotherapist**
31 Whidborne Close
St John's Vale
London
SE8 4DL
☎ 02086 914 338
☎ 02079 231 982
NAFSI

**VINCENT**, Christopher R
**Systemic Psychotherapist**
Lewisham Community Child & Family Service
The Old School House
Leahurst Road
Hither Green
SE13 5LS
☎ 020 8852 3070
☎ 020 8695 6236
Sure Start Bellingham
Sure Start Centre
109a Randlesdown Road
Bellingham
SE6 3BT
KCC

**VOLLUM**, Dorothy
**Integrative Psychotherapist**
Flat 1
15 St Germans Place
London
SE3 0NN
☎ 02088 583 741
MET

**WACH**, Karin Marie
**Psychoanalytic Psychotherapist**
2 Pottery Street
Cherry Garden Pier
London
SE16 4PH
☎ 020 7252 3947
ARBS

**WADDINGTON**, Louise
**Cognitive Behavioural Psychotherapist**
♿ Henry Wellcome Psychology Building
Institute of Psychiatry
De Crespigny Park
London
SE5 8AF
☎ 020 7848 0594
l.waddington@iop.kcl.ac.uk
BABCP

**WAINWRIGHT**, Claire Stephanie
**Systemic Psychotherapist**
107 Troughton Road
Charlton
London
SE7 7QF
☎ 020 8488 4212
☎ 020 8592 4445
clairewainwright60@hotmail.com
KCC

**WALLER**, Diane E
**Group Analytic Psychotherapist**
Goldsmiths College
Psychotherapeutic Studies
23 St James
London
SE14 6AD
☎ 01273 685 852
diane.waller@virgin.net
UPCA

**WALSH**, Carys
**Integrative Psychotherapist**
88 Ashburnham Grove
Greenwich
London
SE10 8UJ
☎ 07931 750526
carys.walsh@btinternet.com
MC

**WARDLEY**, Jean
**Cognitive Behavioural Psychotherapist**
♿ Suite 7
Woodrow Business Centre
Woodrow
London
SE18 5DH
☎ 020 8854 1819
BABCP

**WAY**, Patsy
**Systemic Psychotherapist**
72 Alleyn Road
Dulwich
London
SE21 8AH
☎ 020 8670 5315
☎ 020 8768 4587
patsy.way@virgin.net
Candle Project St Christopher's Hospice
51-59 Lawrie Park Road
Sydenham
London
SE26 6DZ
KCC

**WEINBERG**, Jane
**Integrative Psychosynthesis Psychotherapist**
6 Arbuthnot Road
New Cross
London
SE14 5NP
☎ 020 7358 9721
RE.V

**WELA NKUMANDA**, Rachel
**Psychoanalytic Psychotherapist**
6 Kelso Court
94 Anerley Park
Penge
London
SE20 8NZ
☎ 02087 782 929
rachelacaps@yahoo.co.uk
MET, NAFSI

**WELLS**, Charles
**Existential Psychotherapist**
28b Hamlet Road
Crystal Palace
London
SE19 2AW
☎ 020 8768 1875
charles@kodot.co.uk
UPCA

**WIGHAM**, Avril
**Psychosynthesis Psychotherapist**
Psychosynthesis and Education Trust
92-94 Tooley Street
London Bridge
London
SE1
☎ 01303 263 118
☎ 07855 063 554
avrilw@btconnect.com
PET

**WILCE**, Gillian
**Psychoanalytic Psychotherapist**
26 Wilson Grove
London
SE16 4PJ
☎ 020 7394 1002
G_Wilce@hotmail.com
GUILD

**WILLIAMS**, Diana
**Transpersonal Psychotherapist**
17 Chestnut Road
London
SE27 9EZ
☎ 020 8670 1035
CTP

**WILLIAMS**, Pat
**Integrative Psychotherapist**
79 Ermine Road
Lewisham
London
SE13 7JJ
☎ 02086 907 731
pw6@onetel.net.uk
MC

**WINDERS**, Suzanne
**Psychoanalytic Psychotherapist**
21B Holmdene Avenue
London
SE24 9LB
☎ 020 7274 7517
SUZANNE.WINDERS@lineone.net
FPC

**WOOD**, Morag
**Integrative Psychotherapist**
♿ 92 Inchmery Road
London
SE6 2ND
☎ 020 8698 9332
morag.wood@virgin.net
SPCRC

**WOODLEY**, Ermine
**Psychoanalytic Psychotherapist**
40 Siddons Road
Forest Hill
London
SE23 2JQ
☎ 02082 913 185
E.V.Woodley@City.ac.uk
IPSS

**WOOSTER**, Frances
**Psychoanalytic Psychotherapist**
28 Holly Grove
London
SE15 5DF
☎ 020 7 635 0448
GUILD

**WUEBBELER**, Hartmut
**Biodynamic Psychotherapist**
5 Kenbury Mansions
Kenbury Street
London
SE5 9BU
☎ 02073 265 324
hartmut@biodynamic.uk.net
LSBP

## LONDON SOUTH WEST

**ADAMS**, Marie
**Integrative Psychotherapist**
31B Rush Hill Road
London
SW11 5NW
☎ 020 7207 9156
mariead@aol.com
MET

**AFFORD**, Peter
**Psychosynthesis Psychotherapist**
8 Rudloe Road
Clapham
London
SW12 0DS
☎ 020 8673 1860
pjafford@dircon.co.uk
PET

**AGUIRREGABIRIA**, Ana
**Psychodrama Psychotherapist**
40B Althea Street
London
SW6 2RY
☎ 020 7384 2059
Ana@cpsychol.demon.co.uk
BPA

**AKINBORO-COOPER**, Bobbie
**Child Psychotherapist**
21 Lower Common South
London
SW15 1BP
☎ 020 8788 1642
ACP

**AKSOY ROBINS**, A. Asu
**Analytical Psychotherapist (Jungian)**
More House
53 Cromwell Road
London
SW7 2EH
☎ 020 7225 1088
mgabrielrobin@btinternet.com
GAPS

**ALLAWI**, Nadia
**Psychoanalytic Psychotherapist**
Woolborough House
40 Roedean Crescent
Roehampton
London
SW15 5JU
☎ 020 8 876 4182
☎ 07831 776615
nadsallawi@aol.com
IPSS

**ALLSOP**, Pamela
**Transpersonal Psychotherapist**
68 Redcliffe Square
London
SW10 9BN
☎ 020 7373 0891
CTP

**ANTHONY**, Paul
**Systemic Psychotherapist**
Adolescent Service
32 York Road
Battersea
London
SW11 3QJ
KCC

**ASHMORE**, Tom
**Systemic Psychotherapist**
72 Claylands Road
London
SW8 1NZ
☎ 020 7735 3927
☎ 020 7601 8107
tomashmore@bigfoot.com
KCC

**ASTOR**, Bronwen
**Psychoanalytic Psychotherapist**
43 Ranelagh Grove
London
SW1W 8PB
☎ 020 7730 7856
bronwenastor@aol.com
AGIP

**BAKER**, Kathy
**Psychoanalytic Psychotherapist**
51 Ryfold Road
Wimbledon Park
London
SW19 8DF
☎ 020 8946 3957
IPSS

**BARNES**, Tricia
**Sexual and Relationship Psychotherapist**
7 Grange Park Place
Thurstan Road
Wimbledon
London
SW20 0EE
☎ 020 7935 0113
☎ 020 8241 1201
tbapractice@aol.com
BASRT

**BARTLETT**, Neill
**Psychoanalytic Psychotherapist**
66d Lillie Road
Fulham
London
SW6 1TH
☎ 07940 212 703
neill.bartlett@btopenworld.com
ARBS

**BATESON**, Fiona
**Psychosynthesis Psychotherapist**
Flat 21
Prospect Quay
98 Point Pleasant
London
SW18 1PR
☎ 020 8877 1683
fiona_bateson@msn.com
PET

**BENNIS**, Jackie
**Transpersonal Psychotherapist**
33 Elm Grove Road
Barnes
London
SW13 0BU
☎ 020 8878 9344
CCPE

**BERESFORD**, Lucy
**Integrative Psychotherapist**
9 West Warwick Place
Pimlico
London
SW1V 2DL
☎ 07957 388 623
SPCRC

**BERGER**, Jocelyn
**Integrative Psychotherapist**
London SW
SW18
☎ 020 8874 0763
SPCRC

**BIBBY**, Keith
**Hypno-Psychotherapist**
49 Klea Avenue
Clapham Common
London
SW4 9HG
☎ 02086 736 311
bibbyk@globalnet.co.uk
NSHAP

**BIRKETT**, Diana
**Psychoanalytic Psychotherapist**
95 Elspeth Road
London
SW11 1DP
☎ 020 7652 6749
☎ 020 7652 6101
FIP

**BLOWERS**, Colin M.
**Cognitive Behavioural Psychotherapist**
The Priory Hospital
Priory Lane
Roehampton
London
SW15 5JJ
☎ 020 8876 8261
☎ 01273 504 980
BABCP

**BOAKES**, Janet
**Group Analyst, Psychoanalytic Psychotherapist**
Department of Psychotherapy
Harewood House
Springfield Hospital, Glenbour
Tooting, London
SW17 7DJ
☎ 020 8682 6681
jboakes@swlstg-tr.nhs.uk
IGA

**BOLL**, Antonia
**Analytical Psychologist-Jungian Analyst**
51 Coniger Road
London
SW6 3TB
☎ 020 7736 0226
AJA

**BORGES**, Sheila
**Integrative Psychotherapist**
♿ 67 Mantilla Road
London
SW17 8DY
☎ 020 8767 6595
MC

**BOWDERY**, Sally
**Humanistic Psychotherapist**
132 Babington Road
London
SW16 6AH
☎ 020 8769 5298
bowdery@boltblue.net
AHPP

**BOYLE**, Alexander
**Psychosynthesis Psychotherapist**
6 Foxbourne Road
London
SW17 8EW
☎ 02086 723 140
Westminster Health Centre
34-36 Warwick Way
London
SW1
IPS

**BRADSHAW**, Thomas Owen
**Psychoanalytic Psychotherapist**
27 Hemberton Road
Stockwell
London
SW9 9LF
☎ 020 7274 2976
tombradshaw1@btopenworld.com
ARBS

**BRADY**, Kate
**Integrative Psychosynthesis Psychotherapist**
239 Balham High Road
London
SW17 7BE
☎ 020 8769 0675
akbrady@blueyonder.co.uk
RE.V

**BREITENSTEIN**, Dorrit
**Integrative Psychotherapist**
82 Bronsart Road
Fulham
London
SW6 6AB
☎ 020 7610 3239
dorrit@breitenstein.freeserve.co.uk
MET

**BRIGHT**, Jenifer A
**Cognitive Behavioural Psychotherapist**
54 Ellerton Road
Wandsworth Common
LONDON
SW18 3NN
☎ 020 8877 9853
☎ 020 7919 2194
jeniferbright@hotmail.com
BABCP

**BRITTON**, Julia
**Child Psychotherapist**
Department of Child & Adolescent Mental Health
Chelsea & Westminster Hospital
369 Fulham Road
London
SW10 9NH
☎ 020 7263 7558
ACP

**BROOKS**, Cynthia M
**Group Analytic Psychotherapist**
50 Madeira Road
Streatham
London
SW16 2DE
☎ 02086 967 130
UPCA

**BRYAN**, Agnes
**Gestalt Psychotherapist**
3 Streatham Place
London
SW2 4PY
☎ 07956 905 191
GCL

**BUCKLEY**, Marie-Noël (aka Billie)
**Psychoanalytic Psychotherapist**
6 Trevor Place
Knightsbridge
London
SW7 1LA
☎ 020 7581 3987
bb51@bigfoot.com
FPC

**BUCKLEY**, Miranda
**Cognitive Analytic Therapist**
47 Bury Walk
London
SW3 6QE
☎ 020 7589 9799
ACAT

**BUFFERY**, Elli
**Systemic Psychotherapist**
The KCC Foundation
2 Wyvil Court
Trenchold Street
London
SW8 2TG
☎ 01892 511 468
KCC

**BURNARD**, Linda
**Integrative Psychotherapist**
♿ 76 Ryecroft Road
London
SW16 3EH
☎ 020 8670 9400
jlt@burnardjl.fsnet.co.uk
SPCRC

**BURNHAM**, John
**Systemic Psychotherapist**
♿ The KCC Foundation
2 Wyvil Court
Trenchold Street
London
SW8 2TG
☎ 0121 243 2000
☎ 020 7720 7301
burnham1@aol.com
KCC

**BUTLER SMITH**, Catherine
**Personal Construct Psychotherapist**
30 Cleveland Gardens
London
SW13 0AG
☎ 020 8 878 3017 (t/f)
catherine.butlersmith@virgin.net
PCP

**BUTLER**, John
**Autogenic Psychotherapist, Hypno-Psychotherapist, Integrative Psychotherapist**
37 Orbain Road
Fulham
London
SW6 7JZ
☎ 020 7385 1166
john.butler@kcl.ac.uk
BAS, NRHP, UPCA

**BYERS**, Angela
**Group Analytic Psychotherapist**
Arts Therapies Department
Springfield Hospital
61 Glenburnie Road
London
SW17 7DJ
☎ 02086 826 236
angieb@crystal.demon.co.uk
UPCA

**CAMPBELL**, Christine
**Integrative Psychotherapist**
33 Montpelier Walk
London
SW7 1JG
☎ 020 7581 3374
campbellcotter@aol.com
SPCRC

**CHANCER**, Anne
**Psychoanalytic Psychotherapist**
53 Westfields Avenue
London
SW13 0AT
☎ 020 8 876 1523
GUILD

**CHILD**, Melanie
**Family & Systemic Psychotherapist**
Flat C
61 Winchester Street
London
SW1V 4NU
☎ 07850 137 793
melaniechild@hotmail.com
AFT

**CHILDS**, Margaret
**Systemic Psychotherapist**
45 Becmead Avenue
Streatham
London
SW16 1UJ
5 Collingham Gardens
London
SW5 0HR
KCC

**CHURCH**, John
**Cognitive Behavioural Psychotherapist**
Balham Health Centre
120 Bedford Hill
Balham
London
SW12 9HS
☎ 020 8715 4547
☎ 07958 651322
johnchurch@thecounsellingconcern.freeserve.co.uk
BABCP

**CLAY**, Lorna
**Psychosynthesis Psychotherapist**
40 Galveston Road
London
SW15 2SA
☎ 020 8871 9408
lclayscapes@aol.com
PET

**CLERY**, Cairns
**Family & Systemic Psychotherapist**
♿ 50 Girdwood Road
Southfields
London
SW1 5QS
☎ 020 8333 8400
AFT

**CLIFTON**, Elaine
**Integrative Psychotherapist**
Flat 3
55 Onslow Square
London
SW7 3LR
☎ 020 7581 0387
onslowsquare@tach21.com
MET

**COCKERSELL**, Peter
**Psychoanalytic Psychotherapist**
♿ 82a Fentiman Road
London
SW8 1LA
☎ 02075 821 739
peter@intapsych.org
NAFSI

**COLES**, Walter
**Educational Therapist**
18 Spencer Road
London
SW18 2SW
☎ 020 7738 2455
CFET

**COLLINGS**, Sarah
**Humanistic Psychotherapist, Sexual and Relationship Psychotherapist**
SW10
☎ 020 7349 9623
☎ 07808 281 336
psyc1sar@aol.com
AHPP, BASRT, UPCA

**COLLINS**, Ann
**Transpersonal Psychotherapist**
Putney
London
SW15 1DR
☎ 020 8788 5315
CCPE

**COLVIN**, Naomi
**Attachment-based Psychoanalytic Psychotherapist**
123 Wilton Road
Victoria
London
SW1V 1JZ
☎ 020 7233 9993
CAPP

**CONNELL**, Anne
**Integrative Psychotherapist, Transpersonal Psychotherapist**
71 Smeaton Road
Southfields
London
SW18 5JJ
☎ 020 8265 8315
CTP

**CORONAS**, Ita
**Humanistic Psychotherapist**
37 Barkston Gardens
London
SW5 OER
☎ 020 7373 3989
AHPP

**CORRALES**, Iris
**Systemic Psychotherapist**
♿ Flat 1
120 Cromwell Road
London
SW7 4ET
☎ 020 7244 0197
☎ 020 7926 0445
iriscorrales@yahoo.com
KCC

**COSTELLO**, John J
**Analytical Psychologist-Jungian Analyst, Analytical Psychotherapist (Jungian)**
122 Lupus Street
London
SW1V 4AN
☎ 020 7834 1708 (t/f)
jjcostello@clara.co.uk
IGAP, GAPS

**COTTEN**, Naomi
**Psychoanalytic Psychotherapist**
14 The Chase
Clapham Common
London
SW4 0NH
☎ 020 7 720 6466
cotten@dircon.co.uk
IPSS

**COUMONT GRAUBART**, Valerie
**Integrative Psychotherapist**
18 Laitwood Road
Balham
London
SW12 9QL
☎ 0208 265 5504
MC

**COVERDALE**, Sally
**Group Analytic Psychotherapist**
21 Spencer Walk
Putney
London
SW15 1PL
☎ 020 8789 2207
☎ 07710 524 959
sally@coverdale7288.freeserve.co.uk
UPCA

**CRASTER**, Helen
**Integrative Arts Psychotherapist**
30 Veronica Road
Balham
London
SW17 8QL
IATE

**CRAWLEY**, Barbara
**Psychosynthesis Psychotherapist**
1 Winifred Road
Old Merton Park
London
SW19 3AS
☎ 020 8540 7679
bklcrawley@hotmail.com
PET

**CULLIS**, Andrew
**Psychoanalytic Psychotherapist**
23 Amesbury Avenue
Streatham Hill
London
SW2 3AE
☎ 020 8 671 0732
andy@culliss.co.uk
IPSS

**CUSACK**, Anne
**Body Psychotherapist, Integrative Psychotherapist**
32 Webbs Road
London
SW11 6SF
☎ 020 7585 0653
☎ 077962 72823
acusack7@onetel.co.uk
CCBP

**DANN**, Lois
**Transpersonal Psychotherapist**
1 The Clockhouse
Windmill Road
Wimbledon
London
SW19 5NQ
☎ 020 8947 2176
CCPE

**DARE-BRYAN**, Arminal
**Psychoanalytic Psychotherapist**
15 Melrose Road
Southfields
London
SW18 1ND
☎ 020 8874 3138
☎ 01935 872 111
FPC

**DAVIDSON**, Steve
**Psychoanalytic Psychotherapist**
6, Lansdowne Gardens
Stockwell
London
SW8 2EG
☎ 020 7 978 2663
IPSS

**DAVIS**, Cascia
**Attachment-based Psychoanalytic Psychotherapist**
9a Glasford Street
London
SW17 9HL
☎ 020 8672 9189
CAPP

**DAVIS**, Emerald
**Attachment-based Psychoanalytic Psychotherapist**
64 Lyndhurst Avenue
Norbury
London
SW16 4UF
☎ 020 8764 6740
EDavis5072@aol.com
CAPP

**DEBENHAM**, Jane
**Analytical Psychotherapist**
12 Stratford Grove
London
SW15 1NV
☎ 020 8789 7491
AIP

**DENMAN**, Cara
**Analytical Psychologist-Jungian Analyst**
23 Lawrence Street
London
SW3 5NF
☎ 020 7351 7336
yemanja@dircon.co.uk
IGAP

**DENNIS**, Suzanne
**Integrative Psychosynthesis Psychotherapist**
Streatham
London
SW16
☎ 020 8679 3572
suzanne.dennis@lineone.net
RE.V

**DENNISON**, Paul
**Analytical Psychologist-Jungian Analyst**
9 Mossbury Road
London
SW11 2PA
☎ 020 7924 5601
napaul@ntlworld.com
CAP *

**DEWSBERY**, Sarah
**Psychoanalytic Psychotherapist**
12 Clapham Court
Kings Avenue
SW4 8DU
☎ 020 72747390
sarah@dewsbery.demon.co.uk
ARBS

**DIGHTON**, Rosemary
**Sexual and Relationship Psychotherapist, Systemic Psychotherapist**
The Elm Therapists
45a High Street
Wimbledon Village
London
SW19 5AU
☎ 020 8946 1097
BASRT, KCC

**DOE**, Anthony J
**Psychoanalytic Psychotherapist**
31 Lower Belgrave Street
London
SW1W 0LS
☎ 020 8964 3800
anthonydoe@Avila-demon.co.uk
AGIP

**DOHERTY**, Jackie
**Transpersonal Psychotherapist**
♿ 28 Mansel Road
Wimbledon
London
SW19 4AA
☎ 01843 834 843
☎ 07721 853 824
Jackie233@yahoo.co.uk
CCPE

**DONALDSON**, Kathy
**Family & Systemic Psychotherapist**
♿ 44 Fernwood Avenue
London
SW16 1RD
☎ 020 7228 6680
☎ 020 8677 5590
AFT

**DONINGTON**, Laura
**Core Process Psychotherapist**
42 Hillier Road
London
SW11 6AU
☎ 020 7585 0909
me@lauradonington.demon.co.uk
KI

**DORMANDY**, Ruth
**Psychosynthesis Psychotherapist**
56 Tatchbrook Street
London
SW1V 2NA
☎ 020 7834 0929
ruthdorm@connectfree.co.uk
PET

**DREW**, Philippa
**Systemic Psychotherapist**
♿ 4 Kingwood Road
Fulham
London
SW6 6SR
☎ 020 7386 5048
philippadrew@yahoo.co.uk
Edith Carvell Practice
41 Streatham Hill
London
SW2 4TP
KCC

**DRUMMOND**, Lynne M
**Cognitive Behavioural Psychotherapist**
Behavioural Cognitive Psychotherapy
Top floor, White Lodge
Springfield Hospital
Glenburnie Road, London
SW17 7DJ
☎ 020 8682 6961
☎ 020 8725 5561
l.drummond@sghms.ac.uk
St.Georges Hospital Medical School
Department of Psychiatry
Cranmer Terrace, Tooting
London
SW17 0RE
BABCP

**EDINGTON**, Jane
**Integrative Arts Psychotherapist**
7 St Simon's Avenue
London
SW15 6DU
☎ 020 8788 1729
IATE

**EGLIN**, Patricia
**Integrative Psychotherapist**
36 Turret Grove
London
SW4 0ET
☎ 020 7978 1180
pat@eglin.net
SPCRC

**EILES**, Clive
**Psychoanalytic Psychotherapist**
21 Trelawn Road
Brixton
London
SW2 1DH
☎ 020 7274 8142
clive.eiles@ukgateway.net
FIP

**ELEFTHERIOU-BARWELL**, Despina
**Cognitive Analytic Therapist**
Wimbledon
London
SW19
☎ 07961 152 938
ACAT

**ELLIOT**, Patricia
**Psychosynthesis Psychotherapist**
4 Denmark Avenue
London
SW19 4HF
☎ 020 8 947 6059
PET

**ELVIN**, Gill R
**Group Analytic Psychotherapist**
69 Muncaster Road
London
SW11 6NX
☎ 02075 853 025
UPCA

**EMELEUS**, Frances
**Sexual and Relationship Psychotherapist**
♿ 303 Duncan House
Dolphin Square
London
SW1V 3PW
☎ 020 7931 0248
frances.emeleus@virgin.net
BASRT

**ENDER**, Dorry
**Psychosynthesis Psychotherapist**
♿ Chelsea Harbour
1-4 Harbour Yard
London
SW10
☎ 0207 349 996
☎ 02088 096 061
therapeutics@blueyonder.co.uk
IPS

**ESTERHUYZEN**, Alex
**Analytical Psychotherapist (Jungian)**
Drake Field Centre
239 Balham High Road
London
SW17 7BE
☎ 01342 836 588
☎ 07770 471 975
alexe@btinternet.com
IGAP

**FENWICK**, John
**Family & Systemic Psychotherapist**
♿ Prudence Skynner Family Therapy Clinic
Springfield University Hospital
Harewood House, 61 Glenburnie
London
SW1 7DJ
☎ 020 8682 6195
AFT

**FERRAIOLO**, Stefano
**Integrative Psychotherapist**
Flat 4
22 Redcliffe Square
London
SW10 9JY
☎ 020 7373 1030
sferraiolo@aol.com
SPCRC

**FIELDMAN**, George
**Cognitive Behavioural Psychotherapist**
Barnes
London
SW13
☎ 020 8748 1923
☎ 020 8715 5452
gf@george-fieldman.co.uk
BABCP

**FINN**, Walter
**Psychoanalytic Psychotherapist**
17 Colin Court
Woodfield Avenue
London
SW16 1LJ
☎ 020 8769 6410
GUILD

**FISCHER**, Michael
**Group Analyst, Psychoanalytic Psychotherapist**
Centre for Public Service Organisations
The Business School
Imperial College London
South Kensington Campus,
SW7 2AZ
☎ 02075 947 380
michael.fischer@imperial.ac.uk
IGA, NWIDP

**FISHER**, Jonathan
**Existential Psychotherapist**
The Alma Practice
10-12 Exhibition Road
London
SW7 2HF
☎ 07887 932 473
☎ 020 7584 5700
jonathanfisher@fsmail.net
UPCA

**FLATT**, Deborah
**Transactional Analysis Psychotherapist**
Bramwell
95a Earlsfield Road
London
SW18 3DA
☎ 02088 702 821
debbie_psych@hotmail.com
ITA, MET

**FLOWER**, Michael
**Systemic Psychotherapist**
26 Keildon Road
London
SW11 1XH
☎ 020 7223 6166
☎ 07779 156 028
michaelflower26@yahoo.co.uk
The KCC Foundation
2 Wyvil Court
Trenchold Street
London
SW8 2TG
KCC

**FOWLIE**, Heather
**Transactional Analysis Psychotherapist**
♿ 264 Cannon Hill Lane
Raynes Park
London
SW20 9HN
☎ 020 8543 8106
solutionsHF@aol.com
ITA, MET

**FRANCIS**, Gabriela
**Systemic Psychotherapist**
♿ The KCC Foundation
2 Wyvil Court
Trenchold Street
London
SW8 2TG
☎ 020 7467 8472 or 07946 516 343
☎ 020 7720 7301
KCC

**FRIEDRICH**, Michael
**Psychoanalytic Psychotherapist**
♿ 20 Milton Road
London
SW19 8SE
☎ 020 8544 1266
☎ 020 8544 1266
GUILD

**FRIEDRICH**, Stephen
**Analytical Psychologist, Transpersonal Psychotherapist**
16 Holmesdale Avenue
Mortlake
London
SW14 7BQ
☎ 020 8878 9939
AIP, CTP

**GAD**, Gabriele
**Biodynamic Psychotherapist**
25c Vauxhall Grove
London
SW8
☎ 02077 354 513
therapy@gabriellegad.co.uk
LSBP

**GAIRDNER**, Wendy
**Family & Systemic Psychotherapist**
17 Larpent Avenue
London
SW1 6UP
☎ 020 8788 7953
wendy@gairdner.fsnet.co.uk
AFT

**GANDY**, Rus
**Biodynamic Psychotherapist**
5 Avenue Mansions
Battersea
London
SW11 5SL
☎ 020 7223 4269
rus@sadhippo.com
LSBP

**GARCIA-LLAVONA**, Cristina M
**Cognitive Behavioural Psychotherapist**
The Priory Hospital
Priory Lane
Roehampton
London
SW15 5JQ
☎ 020 7792 9372
☎ 020 8392 4215
cgllavona@hotmail.com
BABCP

**GARDINER**, Brenda
**Cognitive Behavioural Psychotherapist**
35 Cicada Road
London
SW18 2NN
☎ 020 8870 6988
BABCP

**GEE**, Stephen
**Psychoanalytic Psychotherapist**
6 Arlingford Road
London
SW2 2SU
☎ 020 8265 8305
gee@orpheus.fsworld.co.uk
SITE

**GILL**, Richard
**Attachment-based Psychoanalytic Psychotherapist**
Consulting Rooms
122a Wilton Road
London
SW1V 1JZ
☎ 020 7931 0767
CAPP

**GOLDBERGER**, Danny
**Integrative Psychotherapist**
27 Kynance Mews
London
SW7 4QR
☎ 020 7937 1329
dzgoldberger@hotmail.com
SPCRC, SEA

**GORDON**, Inger
**Systemic Psychotherapist**
♿ The KCC Foundation
2 Wyvil Court
Trenchold Street
London
SW8 2TG
☎ 01892 771 225
inger.gordon@virgin.net
KCC

**GORMAN**, Susan
**Group Analyst, Psychoanalytic Psychotherapist**
♿ 19b Handforth Road
Oval
London
SW9 0LL
☎ 02075 827 565
☎ 07879 622 883
susanigorman@msn.com
IGA, WTC

**GOWER**, Barry
**Sexual and Relationship Psychotherapist**
105 Narbonne Avenue
London
SW4 9LQ
☎ 020 8673 8193
BASRT, UPCA

**GRAHAM FULLER**, Victoria
**Group Analyst**
10 Onslow Gardens
London
SW7 3AP
☎ 020 7584 7939
graham@vgf.demon.co.uk
IGA

**GRAHAM**, Nancy H
**Family & Systemic Psychotherapist**
54 Heythorp Street
Southfields
London
SW18 5BN
☎ 020 8870 0399
Nhalegraham@aol.com
IFT

**GREEN**, Roberta
**Group Analyst, Psychoanalytic Psychotherapist**
41 Woodlawn Road
Fulham
London
SW6 6NQ
☎ 020 7385 3408
roberta.green41@btopeworld.com
IGA

**GREENWOOD**, John
**Psychoanalytic Psychotherapist**
98 White Hart Lane
London
SW13 0QA
☎ 020 8286 3533
johngreenwood@blueyonder.co.uk
ARBS, FPC

**GUNDRY**, Caroline
**Psychoanalytic Psychotherapist**
15 Genoa Avenue
Putney
London
SW15 6DY
☎ 020 8785 1550
FPC

**HADFIELD**, Chris
**Integrative Arts Psychotherapist**
45 Herondale Avenue
Wandsworth Common
London
SW18 3JN
☎ 020 8870 1582
christopher.hafield@dsl.pipex.com
IATE

**HARDY**, Jo
**Core Process Psychotherapist**
6 Stanton Road
London
SW13 0EX
☎ 07905 493 956
KI

**HART**, Robin
**Cognitive Behavioural Psychotherapist**
45 Sloane Gardens
London
SW1W 8ED
☎ 020 7259 9739
☎ 020 7259 9743
hart.hart@btinternet.com
BABCP

**HEADON (PH D)**, Christopher F
**Sexual and Relationship Psychotherapist**
Albany Trust
239a Balham High Road
London
SW17 7BE
☎ 020 8767 1827
BASRT

**HEDGES**, Fran
**Systemic Psychotherapist**
Roehampton University of Surrey
Counselling Service
Grove House, Froebel College
Roehampton Lane, London
SW15 5PJ
☎ 020 8392 3632
☎ 020 7358 0518
f.hedges@roehampton.ac.uk
KCC

**HELLER**, Fawkia
**Group Analytic Psychotherapist**
1 Dungarvan Avenue
Putney
London
SW15 5QU
☎ 02084 875 809
☎ 07968 239 196
ffheller@aol.com
UPCA

**HENNY**, Lindy
**Group Analytic Psychotherapist**
Colne Denton
106 Cheyne Walk
London
SW10 0DG
☎ 020 7352 3977
lindy@effect.fsnet.co.uk
FPC

**HENRIQUES**, Marika
**Humanistic Psychotherapist, Psychoanalytic Psychotherapist**
♿ 54 Campbell Court
Gloucester Road
London
SW7 4PD
☎ 020 7584 9793
AHPP, GUILD

**HERALALL**, Ellen
**Integrative Psychotherapist**
93 Barcombe Avenue
Streatham Hill
London
SW2 3BQ
☎ 020 8671 5204
SPCRC

**HERSHKOWITZ**, Annie
**Group Analytic Psychotherapist**
14 Wynter Street
Battersea
London
SW11 2TZ
☎ 02088 747 881
Alassart@aol.com
UPCA

**HESELTINE**, Lynne
**Systemic Psychotherapist**
♿ The KCC Foundation
2 Wyvil Court
Trenchold Street
London
SW8 2TG
☎ 020 7435 1900
☎ 020 7720 7301
lynneh@cybase.co.uk
KCC

**HEWITT**, Philip
**Psychoanalytic Psychotherapist**
Westminster School
17 Dean's Yard
London
SW1P 3PB
☎ 020 7963 1099
☎ 020 8402 2984
philipjhewitt@yahoo.co.uk
FIP

**HIPPS**, Hilary
**Integrative Psychotherapist**
21 Malbrook Road
London
SW15 6UH
☎ 020 8 785 6707
MET

**HIRIGOYEN**, Sarah
**Integrative Psychotherapist**
311B Fulham Palace Road
London
SW6 6TQ
☎ 020 7731 4905
sarah.hiri@virgin.net
SPCRC

**HOGARTH**, Susy
**Systemic Psychotherapist**
43 Hans Place
London
SW1X 0JL
☎ 020 8674 8250
KCC

**HOLDEN**, Sarah
**Group Analyst**
♿ Art Therapies Department
Springfield Hospital
Glenburne Road
London
SW17 7DJ
☎ 020 8682 6246
sarah.holden@swlstg-tr.nhs.uk
IGA

**HOOKER**, Dennis
**Transactional Analysis Psychotherapist**
63 Warren Road
London
SW19 2HY
☎ 020 8542 1835
ITA

**HOOPER**, Rosanne
**Integrative Psychosynthesis Psychotherapist**
83c Erpingham Road
London
SW15 1BJ
☎ 020 8788 6268
☎ 020 8741 9264
RE.V

**HORNE**, David C
**Existential Psychotherapist**
Flat 3
10 Bernay's Grove
London
SW9 8DF
☎ 020 7733 0944
dc.horne@virgin.net
SPCRC

**HORROCKS**, Roger
**Humanistic Psychotherapist**
83c Erpingham Road
London
SW15 1BJ
☎ 020 8788 6268
rahorrocks@hotmail.com
AHPP

**HOWARD**, Gloria
**Psychoanalytic Psychotherapist**
53 Mount Road
Wimbledon
London
SW19 8ES
☎ 07967 635 617
gloria.howard@totalise.co.uk
FPC

**HOWELL**, Sylvia
**Transpersonal Psychotherapist**
♿ River House
Nassau Road
Barnes
London
SW13 9QE
☎ 020 8563 2691
CCPE

**HUGHES**, Janet
**Integrative Psychotherapist**
72 Elms Crescent
Clapham Common
London
SW4 8QX
☎ 020 7720 6205
janet.hughes@virgin.net
MET

**HUNT**, Jill
**Transactional Analysis Psychotherapist**
Flat 4
24 Upper Tachbrook Street
London
SW1V 1SW
☎ 02075 920 059
jillshunt@aol.com
ITA

**IRVING**, Susan
**Psychoanalytic Psychotherapist**
33 Greyhound Lane
Streatham Common
London
SW16 5NP
☎ 020 8769 7988
FIP

**JARVIS**, Eileen
**Systemic Psychotherapist**
7b Ellerton Road
Wandsworth
London
SW18 3NG
☎ 020 8870 0037
KCC

**JONES**, David
**Humanistic Psychotherapist**
8 Arundel Close
London
SW11 1HR
☎ 020 7223 7020
davidjonesmail@aol.com
AHPP

**KEANE**, Pamela
**Transpersonal Psychotherapist**
♿ 8 Thurstan Road
Wimbledon
London
SW20 0EB
☎ 020 8 946 8522
CCPE

**KEMMIS BETTY**, Sally
**Systemic Psychotherapist**
♿ Counselling & Family Therapy Service
30 Lillian Road
London
SW13 9JG
☎ 020 8563 7909
KCC

**KENDALL**, Tim
**Psychoanalytic Psychotherapist**
Royal College of Psychiatrists
Research Unit
83 Victoria Street
London
SW1H 0HW
☎ 0114 271 8710
☎ 0114 271 6715
tim.kendall@sct.nhs.uk
UPCA

**KERRY**, Sue
**Transpersonal Psychotherapist**
Flat 2, 42 Streathbourne Road
London
SW17 8QX
☎ 07815 532045
☎ 020 8 672 6573
apairoftrainers@fsbdial.co.uk
CCPE

**KIND**, Gillian
**Analytical Psychologist-Jungian Analyst**
12 Daisy Lane
London
SW6 3DD
☎ 020 7736 3140
IGAP

**KIRBY**, Babs
**Humanistic Psychotherapist**
194 Ferndale Road
London
SW9 8AH
☎ 020 7733 2748
babskirby@aol.com
AHPP

**KIRBY**, Steve
**Existential Psychotherapist**
88 Horseferry Road
London
SW1 2EE
☎ 07905 913 448
☎ 02086 714 084
steve.kirby3@btinternet.com
37 Lycett House
Clapham Park Estate
New Park Road
Brixton
SW2 4UZ
UPCA

**KNIGHT**, Elaine
**Transpersonal Psychotherapist**
Balham Therapy Rooms
156 Balham High Road
London
SW12 9BN
☎ 020 8854 7835
☎ 07905 973 964
CTP

**KOLB**, Peter John
**Cognitive Behavioural Psychotherapist**
White Lodge, BCPU
Springfield Hospital
Glenburnie Road
Tooting, London
SW17 7DJ
☎ 020 8672 9911 x. 42961
BABCP

**KOLBUSZEWSKI**, Marianne
**Integrative Psychotherapist**
187 Latchmere Road
Battersea
London
SW11 2JZ
☎ 020 7228 1560
marianKolb@aol.com
MC

**KUJAWSKI**, Pedro
**Analytical Psychologist-Jungian Analyst**
Flat 4
25 Longridge Road
London
SW5 9SB
☎ 020 7373 7897
IGAP

**LANG**, Peter
**Systemic Psychotherapist**
♿ The KCC Foundation
2 Wyvil Court
Trenchold Street
London
SW8 2TG
☎ 020 7720 7301
KCC

**LANG**, Susan
**Systemic Psychotherapist**
♿ The KCC Foundation
2 Wyvil Court
Trenchold Street
London
SW8 2TG
☎ 020 7720 7301
☎ 020 7720 7302
KCC

**LEE**, John
**Group Analyst**
C.A.A Cowley House
9 Little College Street
Westminster
London
SW1P 3SH
☎ 020 7898 1898
john.lee@c-of-e.org.uk
IGA

**LEMA**, Juan Carlos
**Systemic Psychotherapist**
Flat 7
171 New Kings Road
London
SW6 4JN
☎ 020 7371 7419
☎ 020 7352 1155
juanc@lema.datanet.co.uk
West London Action for Children
Ashburnham Community Centre
Tetcott Road
London
SW10 0SB
KCC

**LEON**, Sara
**Integrative Arts Psychotherapist**
17 Josephine Avenue
Brixton
London
SW2 2JX
☎ 020 8674 3074
IATE

**LEWIS**, Joan
**Systemic Psychotherapist**
111 Gleneagle Road
Streatham
London
SW16 6AZ
☎ 020 8769 6736
☎ 020 8392 3636
Reohampton University of Surrey
Counselling Service, Grove House
Froebel College, Roehampton L
London
SW15 5PJ
KCC

**LEWIS**, Richard
**Integrative Psychotherapist**
182 MacMillan Way
London
SW17 6AU
☎ 02086 725 035
richlew@aol.com
MC

**LITTLE**, Martin
**Systemic Psychotherapist**
♿ The KCC Foundation
2 Wyvil Court
Trenchold Street
London
SW8 2TG
☎ 020 7720 7301
KCC

**LOBB-ROSSINI**, Karen
**Sexual and Relationship Psychotherapist**
Wimbledon
SW20
☎ 07799 778 840
karen@rossini.info
BASRT

**LOEWENTHAL**, Del
**Psychoanalytic Psychotherapist**
70 Kenilworth Avenue
Wimbledon
London
SW19 7LR
☎ 01483 683 143
☎ 02089 477 085
D.Loewenthal@surrey.ac.uk
PA, UPCA

**LOUDEN**, Penny
**Systemic Psychotherapist**
♿ Counselling & Family Therapy Service
30 Lillian Road
London
SW13 9JG
☎ 020 8563 7909
KCC

**MACGREGOR**, Catherine
**Psychosynthesis Psychotherapist**
11 Redcliffe Gardens
London
SW10 9BG
☎ 02077 226 067 / 07808 856 829
☎ 02073 510 217
IPS

**MACLAREN**, Ian
**Existential Psychotherapist**
6 Weir House
Weir Road
London
SW12 0NG
☎ 020 8673 1338
encounter@btopenworld.com
UPCA

**MAGLO**, Dorothy
**Existential Psychotherapist**
6 Narbonne Avenue
London
SW4 9JS
☎ 02087 729 530
dmaglo@hotmail.com
UPCA

**MAGUIRE**, Marie
**Psychoanalytic Psychotherapist**
♿ 6 Stockwell Park Road
London
SW9 0AJ
☎ 02078 201 344
GUILD, WTC

**MAHAFFEY**, Helen
**Systemic Psychotherapist**
1a Sydney Close
London
SW3 6HN
KCC

**MANN**, James
**Psychoanalyst, Psychoanalytic Psychotherapist**
Flat 2
24-28 Nelson's Row
Clapham
London
SW4 7JT
☎ 020 7622 8700
☎ 01227 273 681
SITE

**MARCUS**, Marietta
**Analytical Psychologist-Jungian Analyst**
16 Sunbury Avenue
East Sheen
London
SW14 8RA
☎ 020 8876 1040
CAP *

**MARLING**, Frances
**Psychosynthesis Psychotherapist**
6 Kenilworth Avenue
Wimbledon
London
SW19 7LW
☎ 020 8946 4063
frances.marling@btinternet.com
PET

**MARRIOTT**, Marcia
**Integrative Psychotherapist**
103 Pathfield Road
Streatham
London
SW16 5PA
☎ 020 8769 6922
marciam@onetel.net.uk
SPCRC

**MARSDEN**, Patricia
**Psychoanalytic Psychotherapist**
48 Wandle Road
London
SW17 7DW
☎ 020 8767 0563
pmarsden@sghms.ac.uk
FPC

**MARSHALL**, Jill
**Hypno-Psychotherapist**
♿ The Putney Natural Therapy Clinic
11 Montserrat Road
Putney
London
SW15
☎ 02085 465 793
☎ 02087 892 548
jill.marshall@virgin.net
NRHP

**MATADEEN**, Dev' Yasdeo
**Psychoanalytic Psychotherapist**
77 Grand Drive
Raynes Park
London
SW20 9DW
☎ 020 8395 6483
☎ 020 8255 3391
dev.matadeen@london.probation.gsx.gov.uk
CCOPPP

**MATHERS**, Carola
**Analytical Psychologist-Jungian Analyst**
63 Briarwood Road
London
SW4 9PJ
☎ 020 7720 5681
☎ 020 8296 4182
carolamathers@yahoo.com
CAP *

**MATHERS**, Dale
**Analytical Psychologist-Jungian Analyst**
63 Briarwood Road
Clapham
London
SW4 9PJ
☎ 020 7720 5681
dalemathers@yahoo.co.uk
AJA

**MCADAM**, Elspeth
**Systemic Psychotherapist**
♿ 49 Elm Quay Court
Nine Elms Lane
London
SW8 5DF
☎ 020 7622 2732
elspeth_mcadam@compuserve.com
KCC

**MCCARRY**, Nicola
**Systemic Psychotherapist**
♿ Child & Adolescent Eating Disorder Service
Harewood House Springfield Hospital
Glenburnie Road
London
SW17 6DJ
☎ 020 8682 6195
nicolamccarry@blueyonder.co.uk
KCC

**MCMANUS**, Gaynor
**Systemic Psychotherapist**
35 Sutherland Street
London
SW1V 4JU
☎ 020 7834 3113
gaynormcmanus@onetel.net.uk
KCC

**MEADEN**, Rosaleen
**Psychoanalytic Psychotherapist**
78 Ringford Road
London
SW18 1RR
☎ 020 8355 9569
rmeaden@skepic.homechoice.co.uk
FPC

**MENDENHALL**, Marybeth
**Systemic Psychotherapist**
♿ 4 Dover Park Drive
London
SW15 5BG
KCC

**MENDOZA**, Hilda
**Integrative Arts Psychotherapist**
Pysiotherapy & Psychotherapy Surgery
1-4 Harbour Yard
Chelsea Harbour
London
SW10
☎ 020 7603 0845
☎ 020 7349 9996
mendozadenham@yahoo.co.uk
IATE

**MERZ**, Juliet
**Cognitive Analytic Therapist**
♿ 93 Clarence Road
Wimbledon
London
SW19 8QB
☎ 020 8542 4482
ACAT

**MICCIARELLI**, Felicia
**Systemic Psychotherapist**
84 Engadine Street
London
SW18 5DA
☎ 020 8870 2793
☎ 07751 420 627
University of Surry Roehampton
Frebel Institute
Counselling Service Department
Roehampton Lane, London
SW15 5PU
KCC

**MILLAR**, Wilma
**Body Psychotherapist, Integrative Psychotherapist**
52 Finborough Road
London
SW10
☎ 020 7351 4830
CCBP

**MILLARD**, Maureen
**Rational Emotive Behaviour Therapist**
Consulting Rooms
88 Horseferry Road
London
SW1P 2EE
☎ 07960 977 128
maureen.millard@whsmithnet.co.uk
BABCP

**MILLIER**, Sylvia
**Psychoanalytic Psychotherapist**
♿ 18 Mercier Road
Putney
London
SW15 2AR
☎ 02087 889 016
sylvia.mary@ukgateway.net
FPC, WTC

**MILTON MSC**, Sylvia
**Sexual and Relationship Psychotherapist**
♿ The Priory Hospital
Priory Lane
Roehampton
☎ 07801 441 240
☎ 020 8290 1241
sylvia@masteryandchange.freeserve.co.uk
9a Wilbraham Place
Sloane Square
London
SW
BASRT

**MITCHELL**, Ruth
**Sexual and Relationship Psychotherapist**
41 Nassau Road
London
SW13 9QF
☎ 020 8748 3978
woomit@hotmail.com.uk
BASRT

**MORANTE**, Flavia
**Psychoanalytic Psychotherapist**
24 Kynance Mews
London
SW7 4QR
☎ 020 7937 8371
IPSS

**MURPHY**, Dennis
**Group Analyst**
♿ Forsenic Department
108 Landor Road
Stockwell
London
SW9 9NT
☎ 020 7411 6575
drdjmurphy@aol.com
IGA

**NAPPEZ**, Sue
**Transpersonal Psychotherapist**
♿ 147 The High
Streatham High Road
London
SW16 1HD
☎ 020 8 769 5101
CCPE

**NEAL**, (Ms) Lalage
**Psychoanalytic Psychotherapist**
2 Rossdale Road
Putney
London
SW15 1AD
☎ 020 8780 3171
ljvneal@hotmail.com
FPC, WPF

**NEATE**, Patricia
**Systemic Psychotherapist**
♿ 2 Daylesford Avenue
Putney
London
SW15 5QR
☎ 020 8876 1902
patricia.neate@btinternet.com
KCC

**NETZER-STEIN**, Antje
**Child Psychotherapist**
40 Ryecroft Road
London
SW16 3EQ
☎ 020 8766 0406 (t/f)
ACP

**NICHOLLS**, John
**Group Analytic Psychotherapist**
66 Lupus Street
London
SW1V 3EQ
☎ 02076 402 715
☎ 02078 348 494
jnicholls55@hotmail.com
UPCA

**NIELD**, Carolyn
**Cognitive Analytic Therapist**
♿ Goodman Crescent
London
SW2 4NR
☎ 07736 713 516
neil.cal@virgin.net
ACAT

**NOLAN**, Michael A
**Group Analytic Psychotherapist**
10 Turret Grove
London
SW4 0EU
☎ 02076 222 870
tnolan1@compuserve.com
UPCA

**NOONAN**, Mairead
**Systemic Psychotherapist**
♿ Medaille House
Landguard Road
Shirley
Southampton
SW15 5DL
KCC

**NORTH**, Bindy
**Psychoanalytic Psychotherapist**
Side Entrance
10B Kirkstall Road
London
SW2 4HF
☎ 020 8678 6518
FPC

**NTARILI**, Kassandra-Maria
**Cognitive Behavioural Psychotherapist**
26 Chapel Stree
Belgravia
London
SW1X 7DA
☎ 07957 507 236
kdarili@hotmail.com
BABCP

**NUTTALL**, Serena
**Cognitive Analytic Therapist**
49 Felden Street
London
SW6 5AE
☎ 020 7736 6740
ACAT

**O'CALLAGHAN**, Jean
**Integrative Psychotherapist**
School of Psychology & Therapeutic Studies
University of Surrey
Roehampton
London
SW15 3SN
☎ 020 8392 3624
j.ocallaghan@roehampton.ac.uk
MET

**O'NEILL**, James
**Psychoanalytic Psychotherapist**
Flat 2
24-28 Nelson's Row
London
SW4
☎ 020 7622 0101
☎ 020 7622 0607
PA

**O'SULLIVAN**, Elizabeth
**Existential Psychotherapist**
1 Kingsley House
Beaufort Street
London
SW3
☎ 07747 108 157
☎ 020 8534 9956
lizzy.o@virgin.net
SEA

**OLIVER**, Christine
**Systemic Psychotherapist**
♿ 3 Beverley Gardens
Barnes
London
SW13 0LZ
☎ 07803 987 940
oliver@madeleybarnes.u-net.com
KCC

**OWUSU-HIRSCH**, Mary
**Psychoanalytic Psychotherapist**
56 Vineyard Hill Road
London
SW19 7JH
☎ 02074 003 636
☎ 02072 877 004
maowusuhirsch@yahoo.co.uk
NAFSI

**PALLENBERG**, Sue
**Sexual and Relationship Psychotherapist**
Langham Mansions
10 Warwick Road
Earls Court
London
SW5 9UH
☎ 01727 832 403
BASRT

**PARIKH**, Prakash
**Family & Systemic Psychotherapist**
218 Mitcham Lane
London
SW1 6NT
☎ 020 8769 8708
prakash.parikh@swistg-tr.nhs.uk
AFT

**PARKER**, Mary
**Humanistic and Integrative Psychotherapist**
♿ 66 Brixton Water Lane
London
SW2 1QB
☎ 020 7274 6531
maryparker_online@hotmail.com
AHPP

**PARKIN**, Gwendolyn
**Integrative Psychotherapist**
♿ 26 Clareville Street
London
SW7 5AW
☎ 020 7370 1855
wparkin@netcomuk.co.uk
SPCRC

**PARKINSON**, Phil
**Transpersonal Psychotherapist**
Welham Road
London
SW16
☎ 020 8677 8440
CCPE

**PARTRIDGE**, Karen
**Systemic Psychotherapist**
♿ South Kensington & Chelsea Mental Health Unit
1 Nightingale Place
London
SW10 9NG
☎ 020 8549 1815
☎ 020 8846 6051
karenpartridge@blueyonder.co.uk
KCC

**PAVINCICH**, Lesley
**Psychoanalytic Psychotherapist**
20 Rydal Road
London
SW16 1QN
☎ 020 8769 4473
ARBS

**PEACOCK**, Anne
**Hypno-Psychotherapist**
83 St. George's Square Mews
Pimlico
London
SW1V 3RZ
☎ 02079 765 352
NSHAP

**PHILLIPS**, Amanda
**Integrative Psychotherapist**
88 HORSEFERRY ROAD
VICTORIA
LONDON
SW1 P2E
☎ 02089 916 690
amanda@apconsulting.co.uk
MET

**PICK**, Geoffrey
**Psychoanalytic Psychotherapist**
♿ 78 Aylward Road
Merton Park
London
SW20 9AF
☎ 020 8408 2975
ARBS

**PICK**, Rachel
**Child Psychotherapist**
Imperial College Health Service
South Side,Watt's Way
Prince's Gardens
London
SW7 1LU
☎ 020 7584 6301
☎ 020 7724 5990
ACP

**PICKELIN**, Ulrike
**Cognitive Behavioural Psychotherapist**
38A Elm Road
East Sheen
London
SW14 7JQ
☎ 020 8878 8787
rikki.p@virgin.net
BABCP

**PICKLES**, Penny
**Analytical Psychologist-Jungian Analyst**
2 Marmion Road
London
SW11 5PA
☎ 020 7228 9161
☎ 020 7228 2384
penny.pickles@btinternet.com
CAP *

**PIDD**, Gregory
**Cognitive Behavioural Psychotherapist**
♿ 44 Cannon Hill Lane
Merton Park
London
SW20 9ES
☎ 020 8715 6410
BABCP

**PINTO**, Luca
**Integrative Psychotherapist**
5 Norfolk House
Rushcroft Road
London
SW2 1JX
☎ 01712 074 663
luca@dircon.co.uk
MET

**POLLITZER**, Juliette
**Transactional Analysis Psychotherapist**
Flat 5
64 Rutland Gate
London
SW7 1PJ
☎ 02075 844 951
ITA

**POWER**, Anne
**Attachment-based Psychoanalytic Psychotherapist**
Flat 9
Neate House
Lupus Street
SW1V 3EG
☎ 020 7821 0223
CAPP

**PRIESTLEY**, John
**Analytical Psychologist-Jungian Analyst**
29 Ryde Vale Road
London
SW12 9JQ
☎ 020 8675 0280
☎ 020 8296 0030
CAP *

**QUAINE**, Mary
**Group Analytic Psychotherapist**
7 Harwood Terrace
Fulham
London
SW6 2AF
☎ 020 7736 4606
FPC

**QUINN**, Asher
**Transpersonal Psychotherapist**
Putney
London
SW15
☎ 077331 13428
CCPE

**RADZISZEWICZ**, Tina
**Integrative Psychotherapist**
Tooting
London
SW17
SPCRC

**RAGIADAKOS**, Nikolas
**Group Analytic Psychotherapist**
Flat 55
Effra Court
Brixton Hill
London
SW2 1RB
☎ 07968 782 997
nragiadakos@yahoo.co.uk
UPCA

**RANI**, R S
**Cognitive Behavioural Psychotherapist**
Behavioural/Cognitive Psychotherapy Unit
White Lodge
Springfield Hospital
61 Glenburnie Rd., London
SW17 7DJ
☎ 020 8682 6548
BABCP

**RATCLIFFE**, Susan
**Hypno-Psychotherapist**
176a Arthur Road
London
SW19 8AQ
☎ 07977 156 149
☎ 02083 984 333
sue@susanratcliffe.com
NSHAP

**RAZZAQ-BAINS**, Saira
**Integrative Psychotherapist**
8 Waldermar Road
Wimbledon
London
SW19 7LJ
Sairarb@aol.com
MET

**REARDON**, Paula
**Integrative Psychotherapist**
28 Seaton Close
Lynden Gate
Portsmouth Road
Putney Heath, London
SW15 3TJ
☎ 020 8788 7020
reardop@richmond.ac.uk
SPCRC

**RENSHAW**, Julia
**Cognitive Behavioural Psychotherapist**
♿ Stockwell Group Practice
107 Stockwell Road
LONDON
SW9 9TJ
☎ 020 7274 3225
BABCP

**REUVID**, Jennie
**Autogenic Psychotherapist**
♿ 26 Birley Street
Battersea
London
SW11 5XF
☎ 020 7223 9236
reuvid@clara.co.uk
BAS

**RIDDY**, Paula
**Integrative Psychotherapist**
8 Princess Court
The Downs
Wimbledon
London
SW20 8HP
Paula@Riddy.com
SPCRC

**ROSE**, Wendy
**Transpersonal Psychotherapist**
Southfields
London
SW18
☎ 020 8 870 2446
☎ 07801 233296 (mobile)
wrose@dircon.co.uk
CCPE

**RUSSELL**, Julian
**Neurolinguistic Psychotherapist**
PPD Consultancy Ltd
31A St James's Square
London
SW1Y 4JR
☎ 02076 651 677
pace@ppdconsulting.com
NLPtCA

**RYAN**, Frank
**Cognitive Behavioural Psychotherapist**
The London Institute
Earls Court Square
10 Warwick Road
London
SW5 9UH
☎ 07808 7996 000
Frankryan@changebehaviour.to
BABCP

**RYAN**, Geraldine
**Psychoanalytic Psychotherapist**
27 Hemberton Road
London
SW9 9LF
☎ 020 7274 2976
ARBS, WTC

**SABATH**, Martin Edmund Francis
**Psychoanalytic Psychotherapist**
93 Pulborough Road
Southfields
London
SW18 5UL
☎ 020 8874 3636
☎ 07958 078 005
martinsabath@hotmail.com
ARBS

**SALM**, Anne Marie
**Group Analyst**
The Eden Medical Centre
63a Kings Road
London
SW3 4NT
☎ 020 7881 5800
amsalm@aol.com
IGA

**SAMPSON**, Gill
**Integrative Psychotherapist**
Flat 18
69/71 St Georges Drive
Victoria
London
SW1V 4DB
☎ 07931 868 972
samsongill@hotmail.com
MET

**SAMUEL**, Irene
**Integrative Psychotherapist**
17 Roskell Road
Putney
London
SW13 1DS
☎ 02088 785 209
Isamuel@compuserve.com
MET

**SANDERS**, Gill
**Sexual and Relationship Psychotherapist**
18 Southside Quarter
38 Burns Road
SW11 5GY
☎ 020 7924 1243
gasanders@ukonline.co.uk
BASRT

**SAUNDERS-WARD**, Pam
**Rational Emotive Behaviour Therapist**
45 Sloane Gardens
London
SW1
☎ 01621 816 837
pam@fhr-services.co.uk
AREBT

**SAYYAH**, Shahrzad
**Existential Psychotherapist**
Flat 6
116 Queens Gate
London
SW7 5LP
☎ 020 7581 5228
SPCRC

**SCHILD**, Maureen
**Psychosynthesis Psychotherapist**
Chelasea Harbour
1-4 Harbour Yard
London
SW10 0XD
☎ 01684 561 229
☎ 02073 499 996
PPSeminars101@aol.com
IPS

**SCHOFIELD**, Lynn-Ella
**Psychoanalytic Psychotherapist**
105 Warwick Way
London
SW1V 1QL
☎ 020 7834 0518
☎ 020 7 821 1012
The Acupuncture & Osteopathy
34 Alderney Street
London
SW1V 4EU
GUILD

**SCOTT STEWART**, Mog
**Cognitive Analytic Therapist**
13a Abbeville Road
London
SW4 9LA
☎ 020 8673 8503
mog.johnstone@virgin.net
ACAT

**SEDDON**, Hester
**Psychosynthesis Psychotherapist**
Physiotherapy and Psychotherapy Practice
1-4 Harbour Yard
Chelsea Harbour
London
SW10 0XD
☎ 02073 287 769
☎ 02073 499 996
hseddon@waitrose.com
IPS

**SEYMOUR**, Jane
**Sexual and Relationship Psychotherapist**
4 Chelsham Road
Clapham
London
SW4 6NP
☎ 020 7720 1162
jane@1seymour.fsnet.co.uk
BASRT

**SILVER-LEIGH**, Vivienne
**Transpersonal Psychotherapist**
♿ 64B Princes Way
London
SW19 6JF
☎ 020 8 788 5291 (t/f)
Vsilverl@aol.com
CCPE

**SIMMONDS-JONES**, Arlene
**Attachment-based Psychoanalytic Psychotherapist**
123 Wilton Road
London
SW1V 1JZ
☎ 07946 421 003
CAPP

**SINGH SEHMI**, Harjinder
**Group Analyst**
Faculty of Health and Social Care Sciences Kingsto
St George's Medical School
Granmer Terrace
London
SW17 8RE
☎ 02087 250 116
hsehmi@swlstg-tr.nhs.uk
IGA

**SMAIL**, Mary
**Integrative Psychosynthesis Psychotherapist**
151 Elm Park
London
SW2 2EE
☎ 07931 348 052
☎ 020 8671 8092
RE.V

**SMAIL**, Richard
**Cognitive Behavioural Psychotherapist**
The Good Practice
Clinical Psychology & Psychotherapy
409 King's Road
London
SW10 0LR
☎ 020 7351 1766
r.smail@btinternet.com
BABCP

**SMALLWOOD**, Imogen
**Integrative Psychotherapist**
98 Bonneville Gardens
London
SW4 9LC
☎ 020 8675 6836
SPCRC

**SMITH**, Amanda
**Integrative Psychotherapist**
88 Horseferry Road
Victoria
London
SW1P 2EE
☎ 07966 254 433
MET

**SMITH**, Anne
**Psychoanalytic Psychotherapist**
39 Dornton Road
Balham
London
SW12 9NB
☎ 020 8 675 3098
GUILD

**SMITH**, Heather
**Psychosynthesis Psychotherapist**
♿ Cancer Resource Centre
20-22 York Road
London
SW11 3QE
☎ 020 7924 3924
☎ 020 7377 5873
dilsha@jsa-london.com
PET

**SMITH**, Steven
**Integrative Psychotherapist**
9 Walham Grove
Fulham
London
SW6 1QP
☎ 02073 851 348
MET

**SMITH-PICKARD**, Paul J
**Existential Psychotherapist**
16 Seldon House
Stewarts Road
London
SW8 4DP
☎ 02077 203 413
☎ 07739 559 541
psmithpickard@ukonline.co.uk
UPCA

**SNOW**, Randa
**Psychoanalytic Psychotherapist**
41 Breer Street
London
SW6 3HE
☎ 020 7736 0146
randa.snow@virgin.net
FPC

**SPADA**, Marcantonio
**Cognitive Behavioural Psychotherapist**
♿ Cognitive Therapy Cntr Prob. Drinking
P.O Box 649
28 Old Brompton Road
London
SW7 3SS
☎ 020 7423 0000 x5047
☎ 020 7736 4643
m.spada@londonmet.ac.uk
BABCP

**SPENCER**, Janet W
**Analytical Psychologist-Jungian Analyst**
7a Carlton Drive
London
SW15 2BZ
☎ 020 8785 0390
☎ 020 8789 3727
IGAP

**STEFFENS**, Dorothy
**Analytical Psychologist-Jungian Analyst**
156 Hurlingham Road
London
SW6 3NG
☎ 020 7384 2251
CAP, FPC *

**STEVENSON**, Kate
**Systemic Psychotherapist**
♿ Kensington Consultation Centre
2 Wyvil Court
Trenchold Street
London
SW8 2TG
☎ 020 8342 9391
☎ 020 7720 7301
kate.stevenson@virgin.net
KCC

**STEWART**, Richard
**Transpersonal Psychotherapist**
Top Flat
23 Lewin Road
London
SW16 6JZ
☎ 020 8769 6549
CCPE

**STIFFELL**, Gilly
**Psychoanalytic Psychotherapist**
9a Wilbraham Place
Sloane Square
SW1X 9AE
☎ 01206 845 602
gilly.stiffell@ntlworld.com
FPC

**STOKES**, Jean
**Psychoanalytic Psychotherapist**
Southfields
London
SW18
☎ 020 8874 6631
stokeshazell@hotmail.com
AJA

**STOLEAR**, Meir
**Rational Emotive Behaviour Therapist**
88 Horseferry Road
Victoria
London
SW1P 2EE
☎ 01438 364 638
☎ 07900 258 207
meir1@mac.com
BABCP

**STRACEY**, Amarilla
**Body Psychotherapist, Integrative Psychotherapist**
22 Elms Crescent
London
SW4 8RA
☎ 020 7720 4601
CCBP

**STRAULI**, Ursula
**Psychosynthesis Psychotherapist**
49 Basuto Road
London
SW6 4BL
☎ 020 7736 3929
strauliu@aol.com
PET

**STRAUPMANIS**, Helen
**Attachment-based Psychoanalytic Psychotherapist**
123 Wilton Road
London
SW1V 1JZ
☎ 07957 460 708
CAPP

**SWATTON**, Richard
**Transpersonal Psychotherapist**
♿ Clapham
London
SW4
☎ 020 7627 8509
CCPE

**TAGGART**, John
**Psychoanalytic Psychotherapist**
♿ 6 Norfolk Mansions
Prince of Wales Drive
London
SW11 4HL
☎ 020 7787 9841
john1tagg@aol.com
FPC

**TANDY (PILBROW)**, Alannah
**Psychosynthesis Psychotherapist**
25 Lamont Road
London
SW10 0HR
☎ 020 7352 9540
alannahtp@classicfm.net
PET

**TANGUAY**, Daniel
**Biodynamic Psychotherapist**
Flat 1
Langley Mansions
Langley Lane
London
SW8 1TJ
☎ 020 7582 4287
dttanguay@onetel.net.uk
LSBP

**TAUSSIG**, Maggie
30 Bathgate Road
Wimbledon
London
SW19 5PJ
☎ 020 8879 7437
maggie-taussig@hotmail.com
MET

**TAYLOR**, Jackie
**Transpersonal Psychotherapist**
Streatham
London
SW16
☎ 020 8677 9212
jackie@jptaylor.freeserve.co.uk
Southfields
London
SW18
CCPE

**TAYLOR**, Jennifer
**Integrative Psychotherapist**
26 Thorparch Road
London
SW8 4RU
☎ 020 7652 6754
jennytay@hotmail.com
SPCRC

**TAYLOR**, Louise
**Humanistic Psychotherapist**
83 Grand Drive
Raynes Park
London
SW20 9DW
☎ 020 8543 5839
louisetaylor@psychotherapy-counselling.co.uk
AHPP

**TAYLOR**, Mrs Jane
**Sexual and Relationship Psychotherapist**
♿ 136 Sutherland Grove
Southfields
London
SW18 5QN
☎ 020 8780 9890
BASRT

**THOLSTRUP**, Margaret
**Integrative Psychotherapist**
10 Parkmead,
Roehampton
London
SW15 5BS
☎ 02087 890 090
margaretholstrup@aol.com
MET

**THOMAS**, Marcia
**Gestalt Psychotherapist**
25 Guildersfield Road
Streatham
London
SW16 5LS
☎ 02086 794 338
MET

**THOMAS**, Tinu
**Existential Psychotherapist**
26 Westbourne House
Ebury Bridge Road
Victoria
London
SW1P 8SJ
☎ 020 7730 6869
olezonetherapy@yahoo.co.uk
SEA

**TODD**, Janet
**Psychosynthesis Psychotherapist**
Flat 3
114 Lower Richmond Road
Putney
London
SW15 1LN
☎ 020 8785 2750
PET

**TOMLINSON**, Sharn
**Systemic Psychotherapist**
♿ The KCC Foundation
2 Wyvil Court
Trenchold Street
London
SW8 2TG
☎ 01438 355 215
sharntomlinson@compuserve.com
KCC

**TOWNSEND**, Anne
**Psychoanalytic Psychotherapist**
89E Victoria Drive
London
SW19 6PT
☎ 020 8785 7675
GUILD

**TOWNSEND**, Hugo
**Personal Construct Psychotherapist**
46 Sefton Street
Putney
London
SW15 1LZ
☎ 020 8789 0937
h@townsix.co.uk
PCP

**TROMBACCIA**, Francesca R
**Family & Systemic Psychotherapist**
7 Astwood Mews
London
SW7 4DE
☎ 020 7565 7131
ftrombaccia@yahoo.co.uk
AFT

**TUBY**, Molly
**Analytical Psychologist-Jungian Analyst**
Flat D
60 Stanhope Gardens
London
SW7 5RF
☎ 020 7373 0892
IGAP

**TUFNELL**, Jane
**Transpersonal Psychotherapist**
9 Snowbury Road
Fulham
London
SW6 2NR
☎ 020 7610 9382
☎ 020 7731 2424
CCPE

**TURNER**, Annie
**Family & Systemic Psychotherapist**
81 Pendle Road
London
SW16 6RX
☎ 020 8677 5026
IFT

**VAN HEESWYK**, Paul
**Child Psychotherapist**
58 Briarwood Road
Clapham Park
London
SW4 9PX
☎ 020 7622 6493
ACP

**VANESSE**, Connie
**Psychoanalytic Psychotherapist**
London
SW18
☎ 020 8870 0282
FPC

**WAINWRIGHT**, Richard
**Analytical Psychologist-Jungian Analyst**
4 Ormonde Road
East Sheen
London
SW14 7BG
☎ 01707 285 335 Tues/Thurs
☎ 020 8876 4325
WainwrightR@aol.com
AJA

**WALLACE**, Patti
**Integrative Psychotherapist**
Lavender Hill Clinic
33 Ilminster Gardens
Clapham Junction
London
SW11 1PJ
☎ 020 7978 4519
P.Wallace@roehampton.ac.uk
SPCRC

**WALLINE**, Sandra
**Analytical Psychologist-Jungian Analyst**
26 Disraeli Road
London
SW15 2DS
☎ 020 8785 9647
swalline@aol.com
CAP *

**WALSH**, Aine (Anne)
**Psychoanalytic Psychotherapist, Analytical Psychotherapist (Jungian)**
56c Sarsfeld Road
Balham
London
SW12 8HN
☎ 020 8767 8997
FPC, GAPS

**WARBURTON**, Geoff
**Gestalt Psychotherapist**
70 Forthbridge Road
London
SW11 5NY
☎ 02072 284 837
MET

**WARNER**, Barbara
**Family & Systemic Psychotherapist**
32 Lewin Road
East Sheen
London
SW1 8DR
☎ 020 8878 6505
barwara@aol.com
AFT

**WEAVER**, Stephen
**Transpersonal Psychotherapist**
London
SW15
☎ 0793 9393 567
☎ 020 8780 1668
stephenweaver@btopenworld.com
CCPE

**WEBSTER**, Anne
**Psychoanalytic Psychotherapist**
92 Rossiter Road
Balham
London
SW12 9RX
☎ 020 8675 1397
FPC

**WEINSTEIN**, Jeremy
**Gestalt Psychotherapist**
♿ 21 Parklands Road
London
SW16 6TB
☎ 020 8677 6869
☎ 07870 410 932
jeremy.weinstein@care4free.net
GCL

**WEST**, Virginia
**Cognitive Analytic Therapist, Psychoanalytic Psychotherapist**
14 Heslop Road
Wandsworth Common
London
SW12 8EG
☎ 020 8673 5508
ACAT, AGIP

**WHITTON**, Eric
**Humanistic Psychotherapist**
31 Ovington Street
Chelsea
London
SW3 2JA
☎ 020 7584 8819
haldewit@aol.com
AHPP

**WHYTE**, Prue
**Group Analytic Psychotherapist**
17 Commondale
Putney
London
SW15 1HS
☎ 020 8789 7395
prue_whyte@hotmail.com
FPC

**WIDLAKE**, Bernard C.
**Psychodrama Psychotherapist**
210 Tildesley Road
Putney
London
SW15 3BG
☎ 020 8788 4794
beju@globalnet.co.uk
BPA

**WILDING**, Vicky
**Group Analytic Psychotherapist**
The Wimbledon Guild
30-32 Worple Road
Wimbledon
London
SW9 4EF
☎ 020 8296 0030
☎ 020 8547 3143
vicky@macunlimited.net
FPC

**WILKINSON**, Gill
**Integrative Psychotherapist**
181 Putney Bridge Road
London
SW15 2NZ
☎ 02088 746 433
mail@gillwilkinson.co.uk
MC

**WILKINSON**, Heward
**Integrative Psychotherapist**
♿ 1 Quinton Street
London
SW18 3QR
☎ 020 8947 5167
☎ 07710 100 181
hewardwilkinson@aol.com
ScPTI

**WILKINSON**, Joan
**Integrative Psychotherapist**
60a Kenilwrith Avenue
Wimbledon
SW19 7LW
☎ 02089 476 478
MC

**WILLIAMS**, Averil
**Analytical Psychologist-Jungian Analyst**
78 Kenilworth Avenue
London
SW19 7LR
☎ 020 8946 6857
averil@brickyard70.freeserve.co.uk
CAP *

**WILLIAMS**, Chris
**Gestalt Psychotherapist**
Tunstall Studios
34/44 Tunstall Road
Brixton
London
SW9 8DA
☎ 020 7924 0344
☎ 020 7935 8608
bradwill@clara.co.uk
GPTI

**WILSON**, Catherine
**Analytical Psychologist-Jungian Analyst**
21 Trelawn Road
London
SW2 1DH
☎ 020 7326 0084
CAP *

**WILSON**, Dawn
**Cognitive Analytic Therapist**
122a Wilton Road
Victoria
London
SW1V 3EE
☎ 020 8801 7665
ACAT

**WILSON**, Norman
**Sexual and Relationship Psychotherapist**
16 Lower Common South
Putney
London
SW15 1BP
☎ 020 8785 7895
nw16rcs@talk21.com
BASRT

**WILSON**, Teresa
**Systemic Psychotherapist**
♿ The Elm Therapists
55 Cloudesdale Road
London
SW17 8ET
☎ 020 8675 7848
☎ 020 8946 1097
teresa.wilson@btopenworld.com
The Elm Therapists
45a High Street
Wimbledon Village
London
SW19 5AU
KCC

**WORTHINGTON**, Anne
**Psychoanalytic Psychotherapist**
47A Upper Tulse Hill
London
SW2 2SQ
☎ 020 8671 5684
aeworthington@btopenworld.com
GUILD, SITE

**YAZAR**, Jale
**Psychoanalytic Psychotherapist**
♿ 116 Pullman Court
London
SW2 4SU
☎ 02086 717 644
IPSS, NAFSI, WTC

**YOUNG**, Sabine
**Transpersonal Psychotherapist**
284 Cowley Mansions
Mortlake High Street
London
SW14 8SL
☎ 020 8 876 2439
Sabineyoung@blueyonder.com
CCPE

**YOUNG**, Sarah
**Integrative Psychotherapist**
21 Broomhouse Road
London
SW6 3QU
☎ 020 7736 1343
SPCRC

**ZAGORSKA**, Joan Krystyna
**Cognitive Behavioural Psychotherapist**
29 Glebe Place
London
SW3 5LD
☎ 020 7352 5315
BABCP

**DE MARQUIEGUI**, Dr Asun
**Sexual and Relationship Psychotherapist**
Clapham Common Clinic
151 - 153 Clapham High Street
London
SW4 7SS
☎ 020 7627 8890
☎ 020 7622 4382
asun@claphamcommonclinic.co.uk
BASRT

## LONDON WEST

**ABDULEZER**, Tania
**Neurolinguistic Psychotherapist**
Bushmaster Natural Health Practice
204 Uxbridge Road
London
W12 7JD
☎ 07768 278 654
tania.abdulezer@virgin.net
NLPtCA

**ADDISON**, Ann
**Analytical Psychologist-Jungian Analyst**
53 Faroe Road
London
W14 0EL
☎ 020 7603 8417
annaddison@callnetuk.com
CAP *

**AIZENBERG**, Eldad
**Psychoanalytic Psychotherapist**
74 Ealing Park Gardens
London
EALING
W5 4EU
☎ 020 8847 5395
aizenberg@lineone.net
IPSS

**ANDERSON**, Eleanor
**Systemic Psychotherapist**
♿ Psychology Department
Older Adult Mental Health Services
St Charles Hospital
Exmoor Street, London
W10 6DZ
☎ 01923 775 993
☎ 020 8962 4362
moneyhill@ntlworld.com
KCC

**ARBIA**, G. Nicoletta
**Transpersonal Psychotherapist**
Flat 4
79 Randolph Avenue
Maida Vale
London
W9 1DW
☎ 020 7266 5701
narbia@yahoo.com
CCPE

**ARCHUTOWSKA**, Jane
**Transpersonal Psychotherapist**
27 Denmark Road
Ealing
London
W13 8RQ
☎ 020 8567 7787
☎ 07958 251 742
archutowska@breathe.com
CCPE

**ARMSTRONG**, Caroline
**Biodynamic Psychotherapist**
22 Bolton Road
London
W4 3TB
☎ 02089 940 951
cg.armstrong@btinternet.com
LSBP

**ARNOLD**, Lynn
**Integrative Psychotherapist**
296 Westbourne Park Road
London
W11 1EH
☎ 020 7 727 0688
MC

**ARZOUMANIDES**, Yiannis
**Integrative Psychotherapist**
218D Randolph Avenue
London
W9 1PF
☎ 020 7328 8955
yiannis@arzou.freeserve.co.uk
SPCRC

**ASSEILY**, Alexandra
**Neurolinguistic Psychotherapist**
13 Addison Road
London
W14 8DJ
☎ 02076 021 402
alexandra.a@innocent.com
NLPtCA

**AYO**, Yvonne
**Systemic Psychotherapist**
♿ 28 Chatsworth Gardens
London
W3 9LW
KCC

**BABARIK**, Anthony
**Integrative Psychotherapist**
106 Sutherland Avenue
London
W9 2QP
☎ 020 7286 8154
tonybabarik@aol.com
SPCRC

**BAKER**, Jan
**Integrative Psychotherapist**
30 Beaconsfield Road
Ealing
London
W5 5JE
☎ 020 8 840 3849
janbaker@ntlworld.com
MC

**BAMBER**, James
**Analytical Psychologist-Jungian Analyst, Group Analyst**
115 Ladbroke Grove
Notting Hill
London
W11 1PG
☎ 020 7727 6368
AJA, IGA

**BARKER**, Elizabeth
**Biodynamic Psychotherapist**
82 Esmond Road
Chiswick
London
W4 1JF
☎ 01672 551051
☎ 020 8995 7031
liz.barker@amservice.net
LSBP

**BARRY**, Ruth
**Integrative Psychotherapist**
73 Ealing Park Gardens
London
W5 4ET
ruthwbarry@aol.com
SPCRC

**BARTLETT**, Beatrice
**Psychoanalytic Psychotherapist**
31 Finstock Road
London
W10 6LU
☎ 020 8969 0092
bebconsult@ukonline.co.uk
FPC

**BARWICK**, Kay
**Hypno-Psychotherapist**
19 Mervyn Road
London
W13 9UW
☎ 02088 400 387
☎ 07798 806 248
rkayb@onetel.net.uk
NSHAP

**BASHARAN**, Harika
**Transpersonal Psychotherapist**
9 Fletcher Road
Chiswick
London
W4 5AT
☎ 020 8 995 3836
Hbasharan@aol.com
CCPE

**BENTLEY**, Radhe
**Family & Systemic Psychotherapist**
♿ 28a Ashchurch Grove
Shepherds Bush
London
W12 9BU
☎ 020 8740 4462
AFT

**BENWELL**, Jennifer
**Analytical Psychologist-Jungian Analyst, Psychoanalytic Psychotherapist**
20 Sinclair Gardens
London
W14 0AT
☎ 020 7602 1986
jenny@jbenwell.demon.co.uk
CAP, FPC *

**BISHOP**, Beata
**Transpersonal Psychotherapist**
27 Waldeck Road
Strand-on-the-Green
London
W4 3NL
☎ 020 8994 8895
beatabishop@clara.co.uk
CTP

**BLASS**, David
**Analytical Psychologist-Jungian Analyst**
22 Meon Road
London
W3 8AN
☎ 020 8992 6443
mail@dblass.co.uk
IGAP

**BOENING**, Joachim
**Integrative Psychotherapist**
1 Studley Grange Road
Hanwell
London
W7 2LU
☎ 020 8 579 2993
CCBP

**BOENING**, Michaela
**Body Psychotherapist, Integrative Psychotherapist**
1 Studley Grange Road
Hanwell
London
W7 2LU
☎ 020 8579 2993
CCBP

**BONNER**, David C
**Hypno-Psychotherapist**
♿ 26 Compton Crescent
Chiswick
London
W4 3JA
☎ 02089 945 520
david.bonner@blueyonder.co.uk
NRHP

**BOWERS**, Petina
**Integrative Psychotherapist**
Bliss
333 Portobello Road
London
W10 5SA
☎ 020 8969 3331
SPCRC

**BOYESEN**, Gerda
**Biodynamic Psychotherapist**
15 The Ridgeway
Acton
London
W3 8LW
☎ 020 8992 5435
LSBP

**BRENINEK**, Andrea
**Cognitive Behavioural Psychotherapist**
Dept of Clinical Psychology
2 Wolverton Gardens
London
W6 7DY
☎ 020 8846 7765
BABCP

**BRENNAN**, Damian
**Personal Construct Psychotherapist**
c/o Kensington&Chelsea Mind
47/49 Chesterton Road
London
W10 6ES
☎ 020 8808 2205
☎ 020 8969 8636
PCP

**BROWNE**, Margaret
**Integrative Psychotherapist**
♿ 28 West Lodge Avenue
Acton
London
W3 9SF
☎ 020 8896 1046
m.browne@amserve.com
SPCRC

**BROWNE**, Maureen
**Body Psychotherapist, Integrative Psychotherapist**
16 Cavendish Avenue
Ealing
London
W13 0JQ
☎ 020 8998 1168
CCBP

**BUIRSKI**, Diana
**Transpersonal Psychotherapist**
First Floor Flat
3 Essendine Road
London
W9 2LS
☎ 0207 289 9368
☎ 0208 940 2770
Psychdiney@lineone.net
CCPE

**BYRNE**, Patricia
**Transpersonal Psychotherapist**
Hammersmith/Chiswick
London
W6
☎ 020 8748 7043
CCPE

**CALEB**, Ruth
**Integrative Psychotherapist**
31 Emlyn Road
Stamford Brook
London
W12 9TF
☎ 020 8354 0987
Ruth.Caleb@brunel.ac.uk
SPCRC

**CANTELO**, Frances
**Transpersonal Psychotherapist**
London
W12
☎ 020 8 749 5974
francantelo@yahoo.com
CCPE

**CARDWELL**, Amynta
**Systemic Psychotherapist**
♿ Parkside Clinic Child & Adolescent Mental Health Clinic
63-65 Lancaster Road
London
W11
☎ 020 8383 6123
acardwell@inter-logics.net
KCC

**CASATELLO**, Giovanna
**Integrative Psychotherapist**
Holland Park
Kensington
London
W11
giovannacasatello@hotmail.com
MET

**CASEMENT**, Ann
**Analytical Psychologist-Jungian Analyst**
5 Kensington Park Gardens
London
W11 3HB
☎ 020 7727 8218
AJA

**CHARLERY**, Lydia
**Psychoanalytic Psychotherapist**
The Forward Project
Black Mental Health Resource Centre
15 Coverdale Road, Shepherd's
London
W12 8JJ
☎ 020 8749 8747
charlery@boltblue.com
IPSS

**CHATAWAY**, Carola
**Systemic Psychotherapist**
80 Maida Vale
London
W9 1PR
☎ 020 7624 4052
KCC

**CHEETHAM**, Brian
**Transactional Analysis Psychotherapist**
♿ 28 Rosemont Road
Acton
London
W3 9LY
☎ 0208 993 2514
bcheetham@elixir.demon.co.uk
ITA, MET

**CHERRY**, Chris
**Integrative Psychotherapist**
33 Ennismore Avenue
London
W4 1SE
☎ 02089 643 996
MC

**CHISHOLM**, Lisa
**Analytical Psychotherapist**
♿ 45 Woodhurst Road
London
W3 6SS
☎ 02089 933 035
l.chisholm@virgin.net
AIP, WTC

**CHOUDREE**, Sangamithra U.D.
**Cognitive Analytic Therapist**
72 Cardross Street
London
W6 0DR
ACAT

**CLANCY**, Catherine
**Psychoanalytic Psychotherapist**
Chiswick
West London
W4
☎ 020 8747 9202
catherineclancy@amserve.com
FPC

**CLARE**, John
**Psychoanalytic Psychotherapist**
15 Waldeck Road
Chiswich
London
W4 3NL
☎ 020 8 747 9424
john.e.clare@ukgateway.net
IPSS

**CLIFFORD MA**, Barry
**Transpersonal Psychotherapist**
Fulham Palace Road
Hammersmith
London
W6
☎ 020 8741 0834
☎ 07759 466 788
15 Dorville Crescent
London
W6 0HH
CCPE

**COUTTS**, Melody
**Psychoanalytic Psychotherapist**
Chesson Therapy Centre
Chesson Road
London
W14 9QS
☎ 07754 765 101
mcoutts@attglobal.net
FPC

**COWARD**, Roger
**Transpersonal Psychotherapist**
52 Brook Green
London
W6 7BJ
☎ 01597 851 929
☎ 020 7603 9692
roger.coward@dial.pipex.com
CTP

**CROCKATT**, Gabrielle
**Child Psychotherapist**
Parkside Clinic
63-65 Lancaster Road
London
W11 1QG
☎ 020 7221 4656
ACP

**CUDMORE**, Lynne
**Child Psychotherapist, Couple Psychoanalytic Psychotherapist**
70 Mill Hill Road
London
W3 8JJ
☎ 020 7435 7111
☎ 020 8993 1534
seancudmore802@hotmail.com
ACP, TMSI, SCPP

**DAINTRY**, Penelope
**Gestalt Psychotherapist**
83 Stile Hall Gardens
Chiswick
London
W4 3BT
☎ 020 8995 4531
penny.daintry@virgin.net
GPTI, MET

**DALAL**, Caroline
**Systemic Psychotherapist**
♿ Child & Family Consultation Centre
West London Mental Health Trust
1 Wolverton Gardens
London
W6 7DY
☎ 020 8846 7806
caroline.dalal@wlmht.nhs.uk
KCC

**DALEY**, Morica
**Integrative Psychotherapist**
♿ Metanoia Institute
13 North Common Road
Ealing
London
W5 2QB
☎ 0207 534 6697
☎ 07833 593 876
moricad@aol.com
MET

**DALTON**, Peggy
**Personal Construct Psychotherapist**
20 Cleveland Avenue
Chiswick
London
W4 1SN
☎ 020 8994 7959
dalton@pcped.talk21.com
PCP

**DANIEL**, Barbara
**Psychoanalytic Psychotherapist**
Kensington & Chelsea SSD
c/o Children's Resource Team
2a Wallinford Avenue
London
W10 6QB
☎ 020 8986 6374
bedaniel@freeuk.com
GUILD

**DANKS**, Alan
**Psychoanalytic Psychotherapist**
♿ 33 Park Road
Chiswick
London
W4 3EY
☎ 020 8994 3131
alan.danks@dial.pipex.com
FPC

**DAVIDGE**, Maggie
**Gestalt Psychotherapist**
36 Newburgh Road
Acton
London
W3 6DQ
☎ 020 8993 0868
mdavidge_s@hotmail.com
GCL, MET

**DAVIES**, Valentine
**Integrative Psychotherapist**
30 Aynhoe Road
London
W14 0QD
☎ 020 7602 8639
SPCRC

**DAVIS**, Joyce
**Analytical Psychologist-Jungian Analyst**
♿ 66 South Edwardes Square
London
W8 6HL
☎ 020 7602 6348
joyce-davis@ntlworld.com
IGAP

**DAWSON**, Liz
**Integrative Psychotherapist**
48a Overdale Road
Northfields
London
W5 4TT
☎ 020 8961 6840
lizdawson@ukcp.net
MET

**DEFRIES**, Nicky
**Psychoanalytic Psychotherapist**
3 Whitehall Gardens
London
W3 9RD
☎ 01753 869 755
☎ 020 8723 2598
GUILD, SITE

**DENIFLEE**, Ursula
**Biodynamic Psychotherapist**
Brackenbury Health Centre
30 Brackenbury Road
London
W6 0BA
☎ 02074 013 582
u_deniflee@onetel.net.uk
LSBP

**DHILLON STEVENS**, Harbrinder
**Integrative Psychotherapist**
♿ Metanoia Institute
13 Nort Common Road
Ealing
London
W5 2QB
☎ 01932 874902
harbrinder.dhillonstevens@virgin.net
MET

**DINWOODIE**, John
**Neurolinguistic Psychotherapist**
68 Fielding Road
Chiswick
London
W4 1HL
☎ 02089 950 384
☎ 07711 306 549
john.dinwoodie@clearcutpictures.com
NLPtCA

**DIVAC**, Aleksandra Sanya
**Systemic Psychotherapist**
25 Ayr Court
Monks Drive
London
W3 0EA
KCC

**DOLPHIN**, Eve
**Integrative Psychotherapist**
♿ Laburnum Cottage
17 Stamford Brook Road
London
W6 0XJ
☎ 020 8741 9474
evedolphin@aol.com
SPCRC

**DYCZKOWSKA**, Ania
**Psychosynthesis Psychotherapist**
22 Dane Road
Ealing
London
W13 9AQ
☎ 02085 791 979
☎ 02082 024 525
IPS

**EICHELBERGER CLEESE**, Alyce Faye
**Child Psychotherapist**
43 Holland Park Mews
London
W11 3SP
☎ 020 7229 6344
ACP

**EIDEN**, Bernd
**Body Psychotherapist, Individual Humanistic Psychotherapist**
26 Eaton Rise
Ealing
London
W5 2ER
☎ 020 8997 5219
chiron@chiron.org
AHPP, CCBP

**ELLIOTT**, Dena
**Integrative Psychotherapist**
9 Flanchford Road
Stamford Brook
London
W12 9ND
☎ 0795 7291467
☎ 020 8 735 2853
CCBP

**ELTON WILSON**, Jenifer
**Integrative Psychotherapist**
♿ Metanoia Institute
13 North Common Road
Ealing
London
W5 2QB
☎ 07971 627 804
jenifer_bakehouse@lineone.net
MET

**ENCKE**, Jochen
**Body Psychotherapist, Individual and Group Humanistic Psychotherapist**
♿ 23 Whitehall Gardens
Acton
London
W3 9RD
☎ 020 8992 9514
jochen@encke.waitrose.com
AHPP

**ERRINGTON**, Meg
**Psychoanalytic Psychotherapist**
21 Hanover Court
197 Uxbridge Road
London
W12 9EP
☎ 020 8740 1981
FPC

**EVANS-STICKLAND**, Deborah
35d Bassett Road
London
W10 6LB
☎ 0208 968 3478
LSBP

**FELL**, Angela
**Analytical Psychologist-Jungian Analyst**
87 Rothschild Road
London
W4 5NT
☎ 020 8994 6206
afell@nildram.co.uk
CAP *

**FRASER**, Sonia
**Transpersonal Psychotherapist**
London
W4
☎ 020 8742 1639 t/f
CCPE

**FRIEDRICH**, Brigitte
**Existential Psychotherapist**
London
W4
☎ 020 8747 9448
SPCRC

**FRY**, Caroline
**Psychoanalytic Psychotherapist**
5 Ranelagh Mews
Ealing
London
W5 5RN
☎ 020 8567 3071
☎ 020 8997 7293
caroline.fry@virgin.net
GUILD

**GARCIA-LLAVONA**, Cristina M
**Cognitive Behavioural Psychotherapist**
Studio Flat
20 Norland Square
London
W11 4PU
☎ 020 7792 9372
☎ 020 8392 4215
cgllavona@hotmail.com
BABCP

**GENOVA**, Jacqueline
**Psychosynthesis Psychotherapist**
39 Addison Gardens
London
W14 0DP
☎ 020 7602 3782
jackiegenova@lineone.net
PET

**GIBSON**, Melanie
**Psychoanalytic Psychotherapist**
♿ 99 Vicarage Court
Vicarage Gate
Kensington
London
W8 4HQ
☎ 020 7937 6280
FPC

**GILBERT**, Maria
**Gestalt Psychotherapist**
35 Bradley Gardens
West Ealing
London
W13 8HE
☎ 020 8997 6062
☎ 07973 432831
maria@fluffy.dircon.co.uk
GPTI, ITA, MET

**GLANVILLE**, Tony
**Gestalt Psychotherapist**
39 Spring Grove
London
W4 3NH
☎ 020 8995 8929
tonyglanville@aol.com
GPTI

**GLYN**, David R
**Group Analytic Psychotherapist**
48 Godolphin Road
London
W12 8JF
☎ 02087 492 373
☎ 07905 780 428
davidglyn@onetel.net.uk
UPCA

**GLYNN**, Paul
**Integrative Psychotherapist**
17 Jeddo Road
Shepherds Bush
London
W12 9EB
☎ 020 8749 0783
Pglynn1056@aol.com
AHPP

**GRACE**, Carole
**Existential Psychotherapist**
♿ 170 Valetta Road
Acton
London
W3 7TP
☎ 020 8743 8096
caroleg2001@yahoo.co.uk
SPCRC

**GRACIE**, Judith
**Psychoanalytic Psychotherapist**
10 Ravenscourt Place
London
W6 0UN
☎ 020 8748 8959
IPSS

**GRANT**, Bob
**Psychoanalytic Psychotherapist**
72 Sinclair Road
London
W14 0NJ
☎ 020 7 603 0529
ARBS

**GRIFFITHS**, Pamela
**Transpersonal Psychotherapist**
10 Livingstone Mansions
Queens Club Gardens
London
W14 9RW
☎ 020 7 385 8937
CCPE

**HALL**, Keven
**Analytical Psychologist-Jungian Analyst**
3 Roman Close
Avenue Gardens
London
W3 8HE
☎ 020 8752 0543
kevenhall@hotmail.com
AJA

**HAMILTON**, Susan
**Transpersonal Psychotherapist**
♿ 40 Finstock Road
London
W10 6LU
☎ 020 8969 5715
CCPE

**HARGREAVES**, Judy
**Humanistic Psychotherapist**
34 Bassein Park Road
London
W12 9RZ
☎ 020 8749 1964
☎ 020 8341 2277
judyhargreaves@spectrumtherapy.co.uk
SPEC

**HAUSER**, Susan
**Biodynamic Psychotherapist**
20 Goldsmith Road
Acton
London
W3 6PX
☎ 02089 924 110
susan@susanhauser.plus.com
LSBP

**HEAP**, Maggie
**Transpersonal Psychotherapist**
London
W4
☎ 020 8994 1458
☎ 07802 888 164
maggieheap@beeb.net
London
W5
CCPE

**HENDERSON**, Andrew
**Integrative Psychotherapist**
178 Lancaster Road
London
W11 1QU
☎ 020 7229 6790
MET

**HEUER**, Gottfried
**Analytical Psychologist-Jungian Analyst**
♿ 13 Mansell Road
London
W3 7QH
☎ 020 8749 4388
gottfried.heuer@virgin.net
AJA

**HIRST**, Diane Zervas
**Analytical Psychologist-Jungian Analyst, Analytical Psychotherapist (Jungian)**
19 Avondale Park Gardens
London
W11 4PR
☎ 020 7792 1654
☎ 020 7603 0767
zervashirst@clara.co.uk
IGAP, GAPS

**HOBART**, Angela
**Psychodynamic Psychotherapist**
Flat 3
25 Stanley Crescent
London
W11 2NA
☎ 02072 212 935
UPCA

**HOLMES**, Lynne
**Body Psychotherapist, Integrative Psychotherapist**
21 Woodfield Crescent
London
W5 1PD
☎ 020 8997 0942
☎ 020 8998 9159
CCBP

**HOOPER**, Rosanne
**Integrative Psychosynthesis Psychotherapist**
Brackenbury Health Clinic
30 Brackenbury Road
London
W6 0BA
☎ 020 8788 6268
☎ 020 8741 9264
RE.V

**HUDSON**, Alan
**Family & Systemic Psychotherapist**
♿ Family Resource Project
2a Wallingford Avenue
London
W10 6QB
☎ 020 8340 9145
☎ 020 7854 5890
Alan.Hudson@rbkc.gov.uk
IFT

**HUMPHRY**, Alexis
**Psychoanalytic Psychotherapist**
Knightsbridge House
229 Acton Lane
London
W4 5DD
☎ 020 8742 2212
☎ 020 8892 5103
alexis@humphry.cc
FPC

**JARVIS**, Cecilia
**Psychosynthesis Psychotherapist**
11 Walmer Gardens
Ealing
London
W13 9TS
☎ 020 8567 1331
cfjarvis@zoom.co.uk
PET

**JORDAN**, Elizabeth
**Humanistic Psychotherapist**
183 Linden Court
Brunswick Road
Ealing
London
W5 1AL
☎ 01494 605 018
☎ 020 8998 5739
Elizabeth.jordan@bcuc.ac.uk
AHPP

**JOYCE**, Philip
**Gestalt Psychotherapist**
2 Richmond Road
Ealing
London
W5 5NS
☎ 020 8567 9217
j@redshark.demon.co.uk
GPTI, MET

**KARAN**, Alexandra
**Psychoanalytic Psychotherapist**
47 Lanark Road
London
W9 1DE
☎ 020 7 286 7090
alexkaran@aol.com
GUILD

**KARDOUCHE**, Amanda
**Systemic Psychotherapist**
♿ 172 Oakwood Court
Abbostbury Road
London
W14 8JE
☎ 020 7603 2776
akardouche@hotmail.com
KCC

**KAUFMANN**, Mickey
**Psychosynthesis Psychotherapist**
8 St Quintin Gardens
London
W10 6AS
☎ 020 8354 2988
m.kaufmann@ntlworld.com
IPS

**KAVNER**, Ellie
**Family & Systemic Psychotherapist**
51a Faraday Road
London
W10 5SF
☎ 020 8968 0510
emanel@dircon.co.uk
IFT

**KEARNS**, Anne
**Gestalt Psychotherapist, Integrative Psychotherapist**
83 Stile Hall Gardens
Chiswick
London
W4 3BT
☎ 020 8995 4531
ap.kearns@virgin.net
GPTI, MET

**KEGERREIS**, Susan
**Child Psychotherapist**
67 Addison Gardens
London
W14 0DT
☎ 020 7603 9609
ACP

**KEGGEREIS**, Duncan
**Group Analyst**
London
W14
☎ 020 7603 9609
☎ 020 7603 9603
s.keger@virgin.net
IGA

**KENNETT-BROWN**, Wendy
**Psychoanalytic Psychotherapist**
♿ 30 Amherst Road
Ealing
London
W13 8LT
☎ 020 8997 2975
wendy@kennett-brown.fsnet.co.uk
AGIP

**KIDD**, Vicky
**Body Psychotherapist, Integrative Psychotherapist**
98 Adelaide Road
Ealing
London
W13 9EB
☎ 020 8567 3573
vicky@kidd-chrysalis.freeserve.co.uk
CCBP

**KINDER**, Diana
**Group Analyst, Psychoanalytic Psychotherapist**
23 Woodville Gardens
Ealing
London
W5 2LL
☎ 020 8997 1207
diana@jkinder.co.uk
CPP, IGA

**LAVENDER**, Lesley
**Transpersonal Psychotherapist**
Ealing Friends Meeting House
17 Woddville Road
London
W5 2SE
☎ 020 8998 0992
CCPE

**LAWLEY**, Mike
**Integrative Psychotherapist**
31 Shakespeare Road
Hanwell
London
W7 1LT
☎ 020 8567 4943
mike.lawley@lineone.net
MET

**LEADER MAYNARD**, Carol
**Psychoanalytic Psychotherapist**
24 Kenilworth Road
Ealing
London
W5 3UH
☎ 020 8840 9417
caroll@freeuk.com
AGIP

**LEE**, Graham
**Psychoanalytic Psychotherapist**
Flat 8
32-34 Gratton Road
London
W14 OJX
☎ 01753 887 047
☎ 07703 300 336
potentialspace@hotmail.com
AGIP

**LEE**, Jan
**Psychoanalytic Psychotherapist**
85 Speldhurst Road
London
W4 1BY
☎ 020 8 994 1430
GUILD

**LETLEY**, Emma
**Psychoanalytic Psychotherapist**
♿ 11, Pottery Lane,
London
W11 4LY
☎ 020 7229 1398
emma@letley24.freeserve.co.uk
24, Princedale Road,
London
W11 4NJ
ARBS

**LEVEQUE**, Brigitte
**Integrative Psychotherapist**
30 Atwood Road
London
W6 0XH
☎ 020 8748 9656
brigittelvq@btopenworld.com
SPCRC, SEA

**LITTLE**, Ray
**Transactional Analysis Psychotherapist**
16 Hatfield Road
London
W4 1AF
☎ 02089 942 905
ITA

**LUCAS**, Pauline
**Humanistic and Integrative Psychotherapist**
♿ 7 Wellesley Road
Chiswick
London
W4 4BJ
☎ 020 8742 0982
SPEC

**LUDE**, Jochen
**Body Psychotherapist, Individual and Group Humanistic Psychotherapist, Integrative Psychotherapist**
26 Eaton Rise
Ealing
London
W5 2ER
☎ 020 8997 5219
chiron@chiron.org
AHPP, CCBP

**LYNN-EVANS**, Julie
**Child Psychotherapist, Transpersonal Psychotherapist**
12 Boscombe Road
London
W12 9HP
☎ 020 8743 6850
CTP

**MAKGOBA**, Sindi
**Systemic Psychotherapist**
♿ Family Resource Project
2a Wallingford Avenue
London
W10 3TU
☎ 020 7854 5880
☎ 020 7624 8605
Marlborough Family Service
38 Marlborough Place
London
W9
KCC

**MANOJLOVIC**, Jelena
**Systemic Psychotherapist**
3 St Mary's Place
London
W8 5UE
☎ 020 8940 3331
jelenamanojlovic@onetel.net.uk or
jelena.manojlovic@swlstg-tr.nhs.uk
KCC

**MARTELLO**, Liza
**Psychoanalytic Psychotherapist**
261B Ladbroke Grove
London
W10 6HF
☎ 020 8968 4747
IPSS

**MASOLIVER**, Chandra
**Psychoanalytic Psychotherapist**
Flat 15
Argyll Mansions
Hammersmith Road
London
W14 8QG
☎ 020 7602 1525
ARBS

**MATADEEN**, Dev' Yasdeo
**Psychoanalytic Psychotherapist**
143 Notting Hill Gate
London
W11 3LE
☎ 020 8395 6483
☎ 020 8255 3391
dev.matadeen@london.probation.gsx.gov.uk
CCOPPP

**MATTHEWS**, Carol
**Psychoanalytic Psychotherapist**
122 St. Albans Avenue
Chiswick
London
W4 5JR
☎ 020 8987 8786
FPC, SIP

**MAY**, Ian
**Transpersonal Psychotherapist**
♿ London W12 & W2
W12
☎ 07939 043759 (mobile)
ianmay@excite.com
CCPE

**MCCREANOR**, Teresa
**Group Analytic Psychotherapist**
65a Randolph Avenue
London
W9 1DW
☎ 020 7286 6435
FIP

**MCELDOWNEY**, Dennis
**Psychoanalytic Psychotherapist**
♿ 39 Leythe Road
Acton
London
W3 8AW
☎ 020 7700 7458
☎ 020 8 993 1559
dennis@mcel.fslife.co.uk
IPSS

**MCGLASHAN**, Judy
**Integrative Psychotherapist**
21 Hollingbourne Gardens
Ealing
London
W13 8EN
☎ 020 8998 8724
judy.mcglashan@virgin.net
MET

**MCGUINNESS**, Mark
**Hypno-Psychotherapist**
The Life Centre
15 The Edge Street
London
W8 7PN
☎ 02072 078 942
NSHAP

**MEAD**, Christine
**Psychosynthesis Psychotherapist**
41 Cromwell Grove
London
W6 7RQ
☎ 07745 346 003
IPS

**MENDOZA**, Hilda
**Integrative Arts Psychotherapist**
16 Brook Green
London
W6 7BL
☎ 020 7603 0845
☎ 020 7349 9996
mendozadenham@yahoo.co.uk
IATE

**MENSINGA**, Vera
**Transpersonal Psychotherapist**
Flat2, 37 Bristol Gardens
London
W9 2JG
☎ 01342 823006
veramensinga@compuserve.com
CCPE

**MICHAELS**, Ruth
**Integrative Psychotherapist**
♿ 11 St Dunstans Road
London
W7 2EY
☎ 02088 407 316
MET

**MILLER**, Juliet
**Analytical Psychologist-Jungian Analyst**
60 Grove Park Terrace
Chiswick
London
W4 3QE
☎ 020 8742 2322
☎ 020 8994 5724
juliet_e.miller@virgin.net
AJA

**MIQUEU-BAZ**, Christine
**Integrative Psychotherapist**
Medicare
3 Harrington Gardens
London
SW7 4JJ
☎ 020 8960 8632
christine.m@virgin.net
SPCRC

**MITSON**, Catherine
**Attachment-based Psychoanalytic Psychotherapist**
44 Warwick Avenue
Maida Vale
London
W9 2PU
☎ 020 7286 9107
catherine@catherinemitson.com
CAPP

**MOORE**, Joan
**Transactional Analysis Psychotherapist**
90 Cumberland Road
Hanwell
London
W7 2EB
☎ 02088 403 087
joanmoore24@hotmail.com
ITA

**MORGAN**, Natasha
**Gestalt Psychotherapist**
5 Arminger Road
London
W12 7BA
☎ 020 8743 2509
natasha@morganna.freeserve.co.uk
Bushmaster Natural Health Practice
204 Uxbridge Road
Shepherds Bush
London
W12
GPTI

**MORIARTY**, Leigh
**Systemic Psychotherapist**
♿ St Vincent's Family Centre
118 Mayfield Gardens
Hanwell
London
W7 3RD
☎ 020 8578 6378
☎ 020 8801 4625
KCC

**MORLEY**, Myriel
**Transpersonal Psychotherapist**
9 Denbigh Road
Notting Hill
London
W11 2SJ
☎ 020 7221 7126
rebalance@btopenworld.com
CCPE

**MORRIS**, Clare
**Personal Construct Psychotherapist**
65 Braybrook Street
London
W12 0AL
☎ 020 7829 8772
c.morris@candid.ion.ucl.ac.uk
PCP

**MURPHY**, Katherine
**Integrative Psychotherapist, Transactional Analysis Psychotherapist**
48A Overdale Road
Ealing
London
W5 4TT
☎ 020 8810 0291
kmurphks@aol.com
ITA, MET

**MURRAY**, Jane
**Integrative Psychotherapist**
48a Overdale Road
Ealing
London
W5 4TT
☎ 01344 626366
☎ 07762 389 050
MET

**NADIRSHAW**, Zenobia
**Cognitive Behavioural Psychotherapist**
Psychology Department
Parkside Community Health NHS Trust
20 Kingsbridge Road
London
W10 6PU
☎ 020 8746 5858
BABCP

**NIEBOER**, Sarah
**Transpersonal Psychotherapist**
8 Kinnoul Road
London
W6 8NQ
☎ 020 7 385 7123
sarahnieboer@virgin.net
CCPE

**O'HAGAN**, Judith
**Transpersonal Psychotherapist**
32a Berrymede Road
London
W4 5JD
☎ 01458 252 236
☎ 020 8995 2250
johagan@dircon.co.uk
CTP

**OPIENSKI**, Jacek
**Gestalt Psychotherapist**
36 Brentham Way
Ealing
London
W5
☎ 07949 333 105
jho@abelgratis.com
GPTI, MET

**OWEN**, Mike
**Family & Systemic Psychotherapist**
♿ Sanabitur Behavioural Healthcare
11 Stowe Road
London
W12 8BQ
☎ 020 8740 0603
mikeowen2002@btopenworld.com
AFT

**PALMER**, Ede
**Psychoanalytic Psychotherapist**
♿ 4 Campden Terrace
Linden Gardens
London
W4 2EP
☎ 020 8994 5574
☎ 020 8995 5168
ede palmer@hotmail.com
69 Linden Gardens
London
W4 2EW
IPSS

**PHILLIPS**, Adam
**Child Psychotherapist, Psychoanalytic Psychotherapist**
Flat 2, 99 Talbot Road
London
W11 2AT
☎ 020 7221 9237
ACP, GUILD

**PHILLIPS**, Amanda
**Integrative Psychotherapist**
28 Woodfield Avenue
Ealing
London
W5 1PA
☎ 02089 916 690
amanda@apconsulting.co.uk
MET

**PICTET**, Dariane
**Existential Psychotherapist, Analytical Psychotherapist (Jungian)**
1 Lampton Place
Westbourne Grove
London
W11 2SH
☎ 020 7243 0732
dariane@dircon.co.uk
SPCRC, GAPS

**PLOTEL**, Angela
**Hypno-Psychotherapist**
Shepherds Bush
London
W12
☎ 02087 404 674
angela.plotel@virgin.net
NRHP

**PONOMAREVA**, Nadejda
**Integrative Psychotherapist**
47 Queensdale Road
London
W11 4SD
☎ 020 7723 0588
SPCRC

**POPE**, Alan
**Psychoanalytic Psychotherapist**
38 Greenside Road
London
W12 9JG
☎ 020 8749 9745
alphapop@aol.com
SITE

**PRONER**, Barry D
**Child Psychotherapist**
83 Strand on the Green
London
W4 3PU
☎ 020 8995 8319
ACP

**PUGH**, Gabrielle
**Systemic Psychotherapist**
♿ 5 Ravenscourt Road
London
W6 0UH
☎ 020 8748 2281
☎ 020 8846 7806
gabriellepugh@yahoo.co.uk
West London Mental Health Trust
Child & Family Consultation Centre
1-3 Wolverton Gardens
London
W6 7DY
KCC

**RANSLEY**, Cynthia
**Integrative Psychotherapist**
♿ 3 Binden Road
London
W12 9RJ
☎ 02087 407 580
☎ 07951 115 150
cynthiaransley@onetel.net.uk
MET

**RAPHAELY**, Mary
**Group Analytic Psychotherapist**
81 Gunterstone Road
London
W14 9BT
☎ 020 7603 7491
mary@raphnet.dircon.co.uk
FPC

**RAPLEY**, Catherine
**Family & Systemic Psychotherapist**
♿ 20 Castlebar Park
Ealing
London
W5 1BX
☎ 020 8998 0775
IFT

**RATTIGAN**, Bridget
**Integrative Psychotherapist**
18 Blossom Close
London
W5 4YF
☎ 020 8567 9923
bridget@grhouse.freeserve.co.uk
MET

**READ**, Jane
**Sexual and Relationship Psychotherapist**
16 Hatfield Road
Chiswick
London
W4 1AF
☎ 020 8994 2905
BASRT

**REED**, Keith
**Analytical Psychologist-Jungian Analyst**
8 Wilton Avenue
London
W4 2HY
☎ 020 8994 3978
agare@legend.co.uk
CAP *

**REVELLI**, Simona
**Existential Psychotherapist**
150b Lancaster Road
London
W11 1QU
☎ 07944 758 805
simonarevelli@btinternet.com
SPCRC, SITE

**RICHARDSON**, Ann
**Transpersonal Psychotherapist**
Chiswick
London
W4
☎ 020 8 994 5964
ann@onlychild.icom43.net
CCPE

**ROBINSON**, Sue
**Family & Systemic Psychotherapist, Psychoanalytic Psychotherapist**
7 Richford Street
Shepherd's Bush
London
W6 7HJ
☎ 020 8740 1120
Sue@richford.demon.co.uk
AFT, GUILD

**ROGERS**, Maggie
**Psychoanalytic Psychotherapist**
137 Fielding Road
Chiswick
London
W4 1DA
☎ 020 8 994 3580
Maggie@art-at-the-studio.freeserve.co.uk
IPSS

**ROSS**, Suzanne
**Transpersonal Psychotherapist**
Bedford Park Surgery
55 South Parade
Chiswick
London
W4
☎ 020 8891 3234
CCPE

**RUSSELL**, Olivia
**Analytical Psychotherapist (Jungian)**
Flat 3
30 Brunswick Gardens
London
W8 4AL
☎ 020 7727 0978
☎ 020 7229 7365
oliviarussell@clara.co.uk
GAPS

**RYAN**, Frank
**Cognitive Behavioural Psychotherapist**
CNWL Mental Health Trust
5 Wolverton Gardens
Hammersmith
London
W6 7DY
☎ 07808 7996 000
Frankryan@changebehaviour.to
BABCP

**SAABOR**, Geraldine
**Transpersonal Psychotherapist**
8 Johnson Lodge
Admiral Walk
Carlton Gate
London
W9 3TJ
☎ 020 7286 6772
CTP

**SANDERS**, Susie
**Group Analyst, Transpersonal Psychotherapist**
Flat D
30 Royal Crescent
London
W11 4SN
☎ 020 7 584 5251
CCPE, IGA

**SCHAIBLE**, Monika
**Body Psychotherapist, Integrative Psychotherapist**
31 Berrymead Gardens
Acton
London
W3 8AA
☎ 020 8752 0246
developchi@aol.com
CCBP

**SCOTT**, Janice
**Gestalt Psychotherapist**
2 Oak Cottages
Green Lane
Hanwell
London
W7 2PE
☎ 020 8840 4886
GPTI, MET

**SELL**, Patrick
**Body Psychotherapist, Humanistic Psychotherapist, Integrative Psychotherapist**
5 Shalimar Road
London
W3 9JD
sell@globalnet.co.uk
AHPP, CCBP

**SHAMPAN**, Linda
**Psychoanalytic Psychotherapist**
11 Aylmer Road
London
W12 9LG
☎ 020 8932 0165
griggshampan1@ukonline.co.uk
IPSS

**SHAND**, Belinda
**Couple Psychoanalytic Psychotherapist**
61 Wallingford Avenue
London
W10 6PZ
☎ 020 8968 0020
belinda.shand@tiscali.co.uk
SCPP

**SHARMA**, Meera
**Transpersonal Psychotherapist**
4 Bridge Avenue
Hanwell
London
W7 3DJ
☎ 020 8578 3331
☎ 07811 383 707
Msharma669@aol.com
CCPE

**SHARMAN**, Geoffrey
**Cognitive Analytic Therapist**
209 Hammersmith Grove
London
W6 0ND
☎ 07771 783 775
GOEFFALANS@aol.com
ACAT, BPS

**SHARMAN**, Juliet
**Psychoanalytic Psychotherapist**
209 Hammersmith Grove
London
W6 0NP
☎ 020 8749 0270
FPC

**SHERIDAN**, Dolores
**Transpersonal Psychotherapist**
53 Matlock Court
Kensington Park Road
Notting Hill
London
W11 3BS
☎ 020 7 221 0331
dolores.sheridan@talk21.com
CCPE

**SHREEVES**, Rosa
**Humanistic and Integrative Psychotherapist, Integrative Arts Psychotherapist**
24 Strand-on-the-Green
London
W4 3PH
☎ 020 8995 5904
SPEC

**SHUTTLEWORTH**, John
**Gestalt Psychotherapist**
Bushmaster Natural Health & Healing Centre
204 Uxbridge Road
London
W12 7DJ
☎ 01293 442 290
☎ 020 8749 3792
john@jshuttleworth.fsnet.co.uk
GPTI

**SICHEL**, David
**Integrative Psychotherapist**
194 Sutton Court Road
Chiswick
London
W4 3HR
☎ 020 8995 7175
davidsichel@lycos.co.uk
MC

**SILLS**, Charlotte
**Integrative Psychotherapist, Transactional Analysis Psychotherapist**
Rectory Lawn
2 Richmond Road
Ealing
London
W5 5NS
☎ 02085 679 217
charlottes@metanoia.ac.uk
ITA, MET

**SIM**, Camilla
**Integrative Psychotherapist**
18 Clifton Avenue
London
W12 9DR
☎ 020 8743 3251
camillasim@hotmail.com
SPCRC

**SIMPSON**, Steve
**Psychosynthesis Psychotherapist**
13a Bridge Avenue
London
W6 9JA
☎ 020 8 741 2839 (t/f)
IPS

**SLADE**, Laurie
**Psychoanalytic Psychotherapist**
71 Netheravon Road
London
W4 2NB
☎ 020 8 995 0528
GUILD

**SMILJANIC**, Slobadanka
**Systemic Psychotherapist**
Child & Family Consultation Centre
1 Wolverton Gardens
Hammersmith
London
W6 7DY
KCC

**SMITH**, Alison
**Personal Construct Psychotherapist**
NWL Mental Health NHS Trust
Solution Based Family Service
Unit 5,1-31 Elkstone Road
London
W10 5NT
☎ 020 8960 0880
☎ 020 7624 2597
PCP

**SMITH**, Jonathan
**Gestalt Psychotherapist, Humanistic Psychotherapist**
36 Newburgh Road
London
W3 6DQ
☎ 020 8993 0868
AHPP, GCL

**SMOLAR**, Monika
**Integrative Psychotherapist**
61 Dorset Road
Ealing
London
W5 4HX
☎ 020 8840 5351
msmolar@talk21.com
SPCRC

**SMOLIRA**, David
**Hypno-Psychotherapist**
114 Mount Street
London
W1K 3AH
☎ 02075 294 815
☎ 02074 990 285
drssj@lineone.net
AFT, NSHAP

**SOMERFIELD**, Lynn
**Transpersonal Psychotherapist**
Flat 2
237 Uxbridge Road
London
W12 9DL
☎ 020 8740 0984
☎ 07762 738 238
CCPE

**SPURLING**, Laurence
**Psychoanalytic Psychotherapist**
Psychotherapy Department
Charing Cross Hospital
Fulham Palace Road
London
W6 8RF
☎ 020 7 431 5471
GUILD

**STANG**, Pamela
**Psychoanalytic Psychotherapist**
♿ 3 Irving Mansions
Queens Club Gardens
London
W14 9SL
☎ 020 7385 4476
pam.stang@virgin.net
FPC

**STEEDS**, Leila
**Integrative Psychotherapist**
228c Ladbroke Grove
London
W10 5LT
☎ 020 8962 0658
leila.steeds@ic24.net
SPCRC

**STEYN**, Angela
**Group Analytic Psychotherapist**
Westminster Pastoral Foundation
23 Kensington Square
London
W8 5HN
☎ 020 8458 1214
angela.steyn@virgin.net
FPC

**SUTCLIFFE**, Pauline
**Family & Systemic Psychotherapist**
52a Oxford Gardens
London
W10 5UN
IFT

**SYRETT**, Karin
**Analytical Psychologist-Jungian Analyst**
27 Royal Crescent
London
W11 4SN
☎ 020 7602 0864
AJA

**SZOPA**, Miriam
**Transpersonal Psychotherapist**
Help Advisory Centre
57 Portobello Road
London
W11 3DB
CCPE

**SZYMANSKA**, Kasia (Y.L.C)
**Cognitive Behavioural Psychotherapist**
48 Lynton Avenue
Ealing
London
W13 0EB
☎ 07770 478880
kasia.s@tinyonline.co.uk
BABCP

**THACKRAY**, Dayle
**Analytical Psychologist-Jungian Analyst**
52 Elliot Road
Chiswick
London
W4 1PE
☎ 020 8995 8607
CAP *

**THOMAS**, Graham
**Hypno-Psychotherapist**
56 Biddulph Mansions
Elgin Avenue
Maida Vale
London
W9 1HT
☎ 02072 860 887
graham@gtconsult.co.uk
NSHAP

**THOMAS**, Kerry
**Analytical Psychologist-Jungian Analyst**
93 Blenheim Crescent
London
W11 2EQ
☎ 020 7727 8572
k.thomas@open.ac.uk
CAP, FIP *

**THOMAS**, Lennox
**Psychoanalytic Psychotherapist**
♿ 63 Church Path
Chiswick
London
W4 5BH
☎ 02089 954 362
☎ 07811 333 425
NAFSI

**THOMAS**, Tim
**Group Analyst**
London
W11
☎ 020 7229 3851
IGA

**THORPE**, Carola
**Psychoanalytic Psychotherapist**
♿ Flat 10, Old Court House
24 Old Court Place
London
W8 4PD
☎ 020 7937 3030
AGIP

**TILLMAN**, Linda
**Integrative Psychotherapist**
34 Oliver Close
Chiswick
London
W4 3RL
☎ 02089 944 392
MET

**UPHOFF-CHMIELNIK**, Andrea
**Integrative Psychotherapist**
Flat 2
17 Newburgh Road
Acton
London
W3 6DQ
☎ 07789 240 828
andreauphoff@hotmail.com
SPCRC

**WADLAND**, Elisabeth
**Family & Systemic Psychotherapist**
4 Selby Rd
Ealing
London
W5 1LX
☎ 020 8998 1839
wadland@lizbryan.freeserve.co.uk
AFT

**WALLSTEIN**, Richard S
**Gestalt Psychotherapist**
15 Lena Gardens
London
W6 7PY
☎ 020 7602 2053
richard@field-work.co.uk
GPTI, MET

**WARD**, Sharron
**Transpersonal Psychotherapist**
93d Elgin Avenue
Maida Vale
London
W9 2DA
☎ 020 7286 8184
www.Ah-ha.org.uk
CCPE

**WASTELL MA**, Karen
**Transpersonal Psychotherapist**
Maida Vale
London
W9
☎ 020 7624 6262
kwastell@aol.com
CCPE

**WATERMAN**, Zak
**Transpersonal Psychotherapist**
16 Bradiston Road
London
W9 3HN
☎ 07779 115179
☎ 020 8969 4077
zakw@demon.co.uk
CCPE

**WEATHERLEY**, Paul
**Systemic Psychotherapist**
30 St Stephen's Road
Ealing
London
W13 8HH
☎ 020 8462 1453
pj.weatherley@ntlworld.com
KCC

**WEAVER**, Martin
**Neurolinguistic Psychotherapist**
♿ 13 Chiswick Village
London
W4 3BY
☎ 02085 809 712
health@martinweaver.co.uk
NLPtCA

**WEISENSEL**, Karin
**Integrative Psychotherapist**
11b Albert Place
London
W8 5PD
☎ 020 7589 0023
SPCRC, SEA

**WENHAM**, Jane
**Psychoanalytic Psychotherapist**
♿ 1 Dale Street
Chiswick
London
W4 2BJ
☎ 020 8995 8426
FPC

**WOOD**, Mary
**Transpersonal Psychotherapist**
2 Augustine Road
London
W14 0HZ
☎ 020 7602 0862
mary.wood@dial.pipex.com
CTP

**WREN**, Gillian
**Psychosynthesis Psychotherapist**
31 Goldsmith Avenue
Acton
London
W3 6HR
☎ 02089 929 118
gillwren@aol.com
IPS

**WRIGHT**, James
**Psychoanalytic Psychotherapist**
Chesson Therapy Centre
59a Chesson Road
London
W14 9QS
☎ 01394 450 497
☎ 020 7385 6279
FPC

**YANDOLI**, Dennis
**Family & Systemic Psychotherapist**
♿ Family Therapy Service
Unit 5
1 - 31 Elkstone Road
London
W10 5NT
☎ 020 7482 3163
☎ 020 8960 0880
dennis.yandoli@cnwl.nhs.uk
IFT

**YAWETZ**, Mrs Christine
**Sexual and Relationship Psychotherapist**
2 Aubrey Road
Campden Hill
London
W8 7JJ
☎ 020 7727 6121
☎ 07836 653 562
BASRT

**ZARBAFI**, Ali
**Psychoanalytic Psychotherapist**
30 Magnolia Road
Strand-on-the-Green
Chiswick
London
W4 3QW
☎ 020 8 747 0408
azarbafi@aol.com
IPSS

**ZIN**, Shoshi
**Family & Systemic Psychotherapist**
51 Essendine Rd
London
W9 2LX
☎ 020 7289 9226
shoshi.zin@btinternet.com
AFT

**ZINOVIEFF**, Nicholas
**Existential Psychotherapist**
London
W4
☎ 020 8996 9029
SPCRC

**DE LEON**, Heather
**Psychoanalytic Psychotherapist**
11 Whitehall Gardens
London
W4 3LT
☎ 020 8741 0661
☎ 020 8994 2930
PA, SITE

## AVON & SOMERSET

**GROVES**, Stephanie
**Integrative Psychotherapist**
The Landing
10 High Street
Glastonbury
☎ 01458 830 677
22 Merioneth Street
Bristol
BS3 4SL
BCPC

**SCHOLEFIELD**, Miranda
**Humanistic and Integrative Psychotherapist**
♿ Cedar Cottage
Barrow Lane
Pilton
Somerset
BA4 4BH
☎ 0845 458 8263
miranda@antipole.co.uk
Combe Down Branch Surgery
Sulis Manor Road
Odd Down
Bath
BA2 2AL
BCPC

## BATH

**BARCLAY**, Elizabeth
**Transpersonal Psychotherapist**
Mulberry House
Sion Hill
Bath
BA1 2UL
☎ 01225 424 868
CTP

**BEBBER**, Gillian
**Psychoanalytic Psychotherapist**
22 Church Street
Bathford
Bath
BA1 7TU
☎ 01225 858 490
gillian@bebber.fsnet.co.uk
SIP

**BROUGHTON**, Vivian
**Gestalt Psychotherapist**
Room 1, The Obelisk Rooms
4 Chapel Row
Bath
BA1
☎ 01749 850 661
☎ 07813 812 852
vivian@ordinarypeople.org.uk
GPTI

**CAIRNS**, Samantha
**Psychosynthesis Psychotherapist**
Openings
Bluecoat House
Sawclose
Bath
BA1 7ES
☎ 01225 859 015
samantha@jcairns.fsnet.co.uk
IPS

**CATTON**, Derek
**Humanistic and Integrative Psychotherapist**
Lower Ground Floor
24 Gay Street
Bath
BA1
☎ 01225 469 238
☎ 01225 462 157
derek_catton@yahoo.com
BCPC

**CHESHIRE**, Jane
**Psychoanalytic Psychotherapist**
74 Wells Road
Bath
BA2 3AR
☎ 01225 482 283
jane.cheshire@ukonline.co.uk
SIP, WMIP

**COTTMAN**, Barbara
**Psychoanalytic Psychotherapist**
Hillview Lodge
Royal United
Bath
BA1 3NG
☎ 01225 825 361
barbara.cottman@awp.nhs.uk
SIP

**FEILDEN**, Tish
**Integrative Psychotherapist**
♿ Sheephouse Farm
Warleigh
Bathford
Bath
BA1 8EE
☎ 01225 858 301
feilden@sheephouse.demon.co.uk
BCPC

**FISHER**, Anstice
**Psychosynthesis Psychotherapist**
9 Eastville
Claremont Road
Bath
BA1 6QN
☎ 01225 445 653
RE.V

**GABRIEL**, Jill
**Humanistic and Integrative Psychotherapist**
Langridge House
Langridge
Bath
Avon
BA1 9BX
☎ 01225 318 834
jill.gabriel@btopenworld.com
SPEC

**GRAHAM**, Margaret
**Humanistic and Integrative Psychotherapist**
18 The Tyning
Widcombe
Bath
BA2 6AL
☎ 01225 443 793
margaretegraham@mac.com
BCPC

**GRANT**, Núala
**Sexual and Relationship Psychotherapist**
No 4 Chapel Road
Bath
BA1 1HN
☎ 07803 882 062
☎ 01225 312 232
nuala_grant@hotmail.com
21 Catherine Place
Bath
BA1 2PS
BASRT

**GREEN**, Sylvia
**Psychoanalytic Psychotherapist**
Third Floor
1 John Street
BATH
BA1 2JL
☎ 01225 482 326
SIP

**HARWOOD**, Matthew
**Analytical Psychologist-Jungian Analyst**
1 Battlefields House
Lansdown
Bath
BA1 9DD
☎ 0117 932 9204
matthew.harwood@virgin.net
IGAP

**HAWDON**, Sheila
**Psychoanalytic Psychotherapist**
3 Warleigh Manor
Bathford
Bath
BA1 8EE
☎ 01225 852 900
SIP

**JAMES**, Glenys
**Psychoanalytic Psychotherapist**
Flat 1
20 The Belmont
Lansdown
Bath
BA1 5DZ
☎ 01225 463 324
SIP

**KINGSTON**, Breda
**Psychoanalytic Psychotherapist**
Psychotherapy Services Network
Hillview Lodge
Royal United Hospital
Combe Park, Bath
BA1 3NG
☎ 01225 825 361
SIP

**KUHN**, Sue
**Cognitive Analytic Therapist**
13 Belgrave Crescent
Bath
Avon
BA1 5JU
☎ 01225 465 846
Sue.kuhn@virgin.net
ACAT

**LACY-SMITH**, Jo
**Humanistic and Integrative Psychotherapist**
Openings
Bluecoat House
Sawclose
Bath
BA1 1EY
☎ 0117 944 5127
JoLacySmith@aol.com
BCPC

**LE BRUN**, Christine
**Integrative Psychotherapist**
4 Walmesley Terrace
Camden
Bath
BA1 6DW
☎ 01225 480 548
christinelebrun@onetel.net.uk
SPCRC

**MARLOWE**, Martin
**Cognitive Analytic Therapist**
♿ Bath North CMHT
Bath NHS House
Newbridge Hill
Bath
BA1 3QE
☎ 01225 731 642
ACAT

**MCLOUGHLIN**, Brendan
**Psychoanalytic Psychotherapist**
14 Cork Terrace
Bath
BA1 3BE
☎ 01225 481 297
bmaclock@bathresolve.fslife.co.uk
FPC

**MELLETT**, Jane
**Humanistic and Integrative Psychotherapist**
♿ The Chiropractic clinic
207 London Road
Batheaston
Bath
BA1 7NB
☎ 01225 742 163
AHPP, BCPC

**MILLS**, Christopher
**Humanistic and Integrative Psychotherapist**
6B Hanover Street
Bath
BA1 6PP
☎ 01225 445 237
c.a.mills@bath.ac.uk
BCPC

**PATTERSON**, Linda
**Psychoanalytic Psychotherapist**
10 Brookleaze Buildings
Larkhall
Bath
BA1 6RA
☎ 01225 463 054
SIP

**SAYERS**, Jacqui
**Family & Systemic Psychotherapist**
Child & Family Therapy
Royal United Hospital
Combe Park
Bath
BA1 3NG
☎ 01225 825 075
jaqui-sayers@awp.nhs.uk
FIC

**SELBY**, Anne
**Humanistic and Integrative Psychotherapist**
Prospect House
4 Prospect Place
Beechen Cliff Road
Bath
BA2 4QP
☎ 01225 428 826
☎ 01225 311 399
anne.selby1@virgin.net
BCPC

**SLATTERY**, David
**Humanistic and Integrative Psychotherapist**
♿ 6b Hanover Street
Bath
BA1 6PP
☎ 01453 832 215
☎ 01225 445 237
dnslattery@blackbird6.freeserve.co.uk
BCPC

**SMITH**, Gill
**Integrative Psychotherapist**
18 Govenors House
Stuart Place
Bath
BA2 3RG
☎ 01225 334 624
gill@nfli.fsbusiness.co.uk
MC

**STALLARD**, Paul
**Cognitive Behavioural Psychotherapist**
♿ Dept. Child & Family Psychiatry
Royal United Hospital
Combe Park
Bath
BA1 3NG
☎ 01225 825 075
BABCP

**VALENTINE**, Christine
**Humanistic and Integrative Psychotherapist**
42 Millmead Road
Oldfield Park
Bath
BA2 3JP
☎ 01225 337 372
BCPC

**VAUGHAN**, Victoria
**Humanistic and Integrative Psychotherapist**
Flat 2
6 Grosvenor Place
Bath
BA1 6AX
☎ 01225 333 543
victoriavaughan@amserve.com
BCPC

**VICK**, Philippa
**Transpersonal Psychotherapist**
18 Richmond Place
Bath
BA1 5PZ
☎ 020 7935 2294
☎ 01225 445 532
CTP

**WELLINGS**, Nigel
**Psychoanalytic Psychotherapist**
18 Richmond Place
Bath
BA1 5PZ
☎ 01225 445 532
☎ 020 7935 2294
AGIP, AIP

**WHITFIELD**, Erica
**Core Process Psychotherapist**
Old Mill Cottage
42 Northend
Bath
BA1 7ES
☎ 01225 858 791
KI

**WILLIAMS**, Ruth M.
**Cognitive Behavioural Psychotherapist**
♿ Flat 38
Pitman Court
Gloucester Road
Bath
BA1 8BD
☎ 01225 330 312
ruthwilliams@lineone.net
BABCP

**WILSON**, Alexandra
**Psychoanalytic Psychotherapist**
Flat 7, Abbey House
Abbey Green
Bath
BA1 1NR
☎ 01225 336 591
wilson@macunlimited.net
SIP

**WOOD**, Mrs L M
**Sexual and Relationship Psychotherapist**
♿ Batheaston Medical Centre
Coalpit Road
Batheaston
BA1 7NP
☎ 01225 858 128
☎ 07986 955 025
Linda5wood@aol.com
BASRT

## BEDFORDSHIRE

**BARLOW**, Sanchia
**Psychoanalytic Psychotherapist**
Honey House
19 High Street
Harrold
Bedford
MK43 7DQ
☎ 01234 310 241
☎ 01234 720 433
sanchia.barlow@btinternet.com
Clinical Psychology and Psychotherapy
Bedford Hospital North Wing
3 Kimbolton Road
Bedford
MK40 2NU
FIP

**BICKERS**, Adrian
**Psychosynthesis Psychotherapist**
Hitchin Natural Therapy Centres
3-4 High Street
Hitchin
SG5 1BH
☎ 01462 734 188
01462 734 188
IPS

**BROWN**, Mavis
**Systemic Psychotherapist**
♿ Child & Family Consultation Service
24 Grove Place
Bedford
MK44 3JT
☎ 01234 310 800
KCC

**BUCKROYD**, Julia
**Psychoanalytic Psychotherapist**
58 Chruch Road
Willington
Bedfordshire
MK44 3PU
☎ 01727 841 007
GUILD

**CHADWICK**, Philip
**Systemic Psychotherapist**
♿ Family Consultation Clinic Service
5-7 Rush Court
Bedford
MK40 3JT
☎ 01234 310 670
philip.chadwick@sbchc-tr.anglox.nhs.uk
KCC

**CLACKSON**, Suzanne
**Psychoanalytic Psychotherapist**
♿ 21 Bradgate Road
Bedford
MK40 3DE
☎ 01234 356996
GUILD

**CLARE**, Louise
**Psychoanalytic Psychotherapist**
11 Warden Abbey
Bedford
MK41 0SW
☎ 01234 267405
GUILD

**COX**, Keith Frederick
**Family & Systemic Psychotherapist**
♿ CAMHS Trend House
Dallow Road
Luton
LU1 1LY
☎ 01582 708 140
keith.cox@sbchc-tr.anglox.nhs.uk
AFT

**DIXON**, John
**Sexual and Relationship Psychotherapist**
♿ 74 Honeysuckle Way
Bedford
MK41 0TF
☎ 01234 273 282
☎ 07879 438 743
johnabdixon@ntlworld.com
Relate
6 St Paul's Square
Bedford
MK40 1SQ
BASRT

**DUTTON**, Andrew
**Psychoanalytic Psychotherapist**
6 Adelaide Square
Bedford
MK40 2RW
☎ 01234 267 903
GUILD

**EDGE**, Andrew
**Systemic Psychotherapist**
♿ CAMH (Mid-Bedfordshire)
Looked After Children Team
24 Grove Place
Bedford
MK40 3JJ
☎ 01908 510 723
andrew.edge@talk21.com
KCC

**FAUSSET**, Ann
**Systemic Psychotherapist**
♿ 21 Royal Oak Lane
Pirton
Hitchin
SG5 3QT
☎ 01462 712 343
KCC

**FRANKE**, Christine
**Psychoanalytic Psychotherapist**
♿ 14 Old Station Court
Blunham
Bedford
MK44 3PN
☎ 01767 640 863
☎ 01767 640 345
frankecm@aol.com
AGIP

**HAMILTON**, Doreen
**Systemic Psychotherapist**
♿ Familyl Consultation Clinic
Trend House
Dallow Road
Luton
LU4
☎ 01582 708 162
☎ 01582 708 140
KCC

**HANNAH**, Chris
**Systemic Psychotherapist**
♿ 5 Millfield
Bromham
MK43 8LR
☎ 01234 823 098
channah@btinternet.com
KCC

**HANNAH**, Clare
**Systemic Psychotherapist**
♿ Family Consultation Clinic
5-7 Rush Court
Bedford
MK42 3JT
KCC

**HICKMAN**, Sue
**Systemic Psychotherapist**
11 Colchester Way
Bedford
MK41 8BG
☎ 01234 343 506
☎ 01234 273 894
Barford Avenue Centre
29 Barford Avenue
Bedford
MK42 0DS
KCC

**KATZ**, Janice
**Psychoanalytic Psychotherapist**
29 King Street
Luton
Beds
LU1 2DW
☎ 01582 482 220
jan@dlhjnk.fsnet.co.uk
FIP

**KRAUSE**, Inga-Britt
**Family & Systemic Psychotherapist**
4 The Coach House
Bromham Hall
Bromham
Bedford
MK43 8HH
☎ 01234 823 880
ingabrittkrause@hotmail.com
AFT

**MCALLISTER**, Christopher
**Cognitive Behavioural Psychotherapist**
255 New Bedford Road
Luton
LU3 1LW
☎ 01582 876 800
BABCP

**MCKAY**, Barbara
**Systemic Psychotherapist**
♿ Quince Cottage
54 Wood End Road
Wood End
Kempston
MK43 9BD
☎ 01234 854 457
KCC

**MCLURE**, Elizabeth
**Group Analytic Psychotherapist**
20 Aquila Road
Leighton Buzzard
Bedfordshire
LU7 8XD
☎ 01525 378 007
egmmac@aol.com
UPCA

**MOORE**, Maria
**Integrative Psychotherapist**
52 Tring Road
Dunstable
LU6 2PT
☎ 01582 609 191
SPTI

**MOORE**, Rosemary
**Psychoanalytic Psychotherapist**
147 Dudley Street
Bedford
MK40 3SY
☎ 01234 344736
GUILD

**MORGAN**, Barbara
**Gestalt Psychotherapist**
Hitchin Natural Therapy Centre
3-4 High St
Hitchin
Herts
SG5
☎ 01462 459020/01767 601259
☎ 01462 733267
Barbara@stotfold89.freeserve.co.uk
GCL

**MOULDING**, Sara
**Systemic Psychotherapist**
25 Station Road
Oakley
MK43 7RB
☎ 01234 825 242
KCC

**O'BRIEN**, Gillian
**Integrative Psychotherapist**
391 Turnpike Drive
Luton
Bedfordshire
LU3 3RE
☎ 01525 751133
gillobrien@aol.com
MET

**PAPÉ**, Maureen
**Sexual and Relationship Psychotherapist**
296 Kimbolton Road
Bedford
MK41 8AG
☎ 01234 349 223
Maureen.pape@btinternet.com
BASRT

**PARAMOUR**, Annabelle
**Psychoanalytic Psychotherapist**
8 The Grove
Bedford
MK40 3JN
☎ 01234 345 553
CSP

**PEARCE**, Gerald
**Integrative Psychotherapist**
♿ 13 George Street West
Luton
Beds
LU1 2RD
☎ 02084 451 867
MET

**PEART**, Mary
**Psychosynthesis Psychotherapist**
3 School House Mews
High Street
Silsoe
Bedfordshire
MK45 4DY
☎ 01525 862139
IPS

**READ**, Linda
**Sexual and Relationship Psychotherapist**
♿ Harrold Medical Centre
Peaches Close
Harrold
☎ 01234 720 225
☎ 01234 711 344
BASRT

**RICHARDSON**, Miriam Ann
**Systemic Psychotherapist**
River House
Bromham Park
Bedford
MK43 8HH
☎ 01234 310 670
☎ 01234 825 512
miriam@river18.freeserve.co.uk
Family Consultation Clinic
5-7 Rush Court
Bedford
MK40 3JT
KCC

**ROGERS**, Anne
**Psychoanalytic Psychotherapist**
32a Church End
Renhold
Bedfordshire
MK41 0LU
☎ 01234 771 595
annerogers32a@aol.com
AGIP, FIP

**SHERNO**, Peggy
**Gestalt Psychotherapist**
♿ 22 Garden Row
Hitchin
Herts
SG5 1QD
☎ 01462 432 439
peggy.sherno@idnet.co.uk
GCL

**SLATER**, Joan
**Integrative Psychotherapist**
♿ 3 Ditmas Avenue
Kempston
MK42 7DR
☎ 01234 840 562
slaterjoan@aol.com
SPCRC

**STOW**, Doug
**Sexual and Relationship Psychotherapist**
♿ The Lodge
4 George Street West
Luton
LU1 2BJ
☎ 01582 511 034
☎ 01908 609 307
dougL@sstow.fsnet.co.uk
AHPP, BASRT

**SWEET**, Patricia
**Systemic Psychotherapist**
♿ 16 Arbroath Road
Sundon Park Road
Luton
LU3 3LA
☎ 01582 708 370
patsweet@tiscali.co.uk
KCC

**TENWICK**, Stephanie
**Systemic Psychotherapist**
6 Brittains Close
Lower Stondon
Honlow
SG16 6JT
☎ 01462 850 415
steffenwick@hotmail.com
KCC

**THORMAN**, Chris
**Personal Construct Psychotherapist**
69 Startpoint
Downs Road
Luton
LU1 1XN
christhorman@hotmail.com
PCP

**TRUSTAM**, Gillian
**Psychoanalytic Psychotherapist**
86 High Street
Oakley
Beds
MK43 7RH
☎ 01234 822 985
AGIP

**WEBB**, Ann
**Systemic Psychotherapist**
30 Royal Oak Lane
Pirton
Hitchin
SG5 3QT
☎ 01462 712 304
annwebb@btopenworld.com
KCC

**WILLIAMS**, Sherly
**Psychoanalytic Psychotherapist**
Mill Cottage
The Green
Harrold
Bedford
MK43 7DB
☎ 01234 721 835
FPC, VAPP, WMIP

**WOODHEAD**, Judith M
**Analytical Psychologist-Jungian Analyst**
21 Devon Road
Bedford
MK40 3DJ
☎ 01234 330 829
☎ 07957 467 598
judith.woodhead@virgin.net
CAP *

## BERKSHIRE

**ADAMS**, Janet
**Attachment-based Psychoanalytic Psychotherapist**
24 Stone Street
Reading
Berkshire
RG30 1HU
☎ 01189 676 500
CAPP

**ADSHEAD**, Gwen
**Group Analyst**
Psychotherapy Department
Broadmoor Hospital
Crowthorne
Berks
RG45 7EG
☎ 01344 754 396
rak@wlmht.nhs.uk
IGA

**ALLEN**, Lynne
**Biodynamic Psychotherapist**
Willow Cottage
off Wokingham Road
Hurst
Berks
RG10 0RU
☎ 0118 934 2843
c.allen12@ntlworld.com
LSBP

**ARMSON**, Simon
**Cognitive Analytic Therapist**
Broad Oak
Hurley
Maindenhead
SL6 5LW
☎ 01628 824 322
☎ 07788 186 339
armson@btinternet.com
ACAT

**ARNOLD-BAKER**, Claire
**Existential Psychotherapist**
1 Hill House Cottages
Reading Road
Streatley
Reading
RG8 9JN
☎ 07957 154 621
Claire@nspc.org.uk
UPCA

**ATKINS**, Lorna
**Family & Systemic Psychotherapist**
The Charter House
12a Rectory Road
Wokingham
Berks
RG4 1DH
☎ 0118 977 2429
lornaatkins@btopenworld.com
AFT

**AUFFLICK**, Julia
**Systemic Psychotherapist**
26 Grove Close
Old Windsor
SL4 2LY
☎ 01753 859 388
KCC

**BOOTH**, Philip
**Systemic Psychotherapist**
The Cardinal Clinic
Oakley Green
Windsor
Berkshire
SL4 5UL
☎ 01753-869 755
☎ 01865 721 597
pbooth@netshark.demon.co.uk
FIC

**BURCH**, Jean
**Sexual and Relationship Psychotherapist**
♿ The Peppers
Mustard Lane
Sonning
RG4 6GH
☎ 0118 969 8363
jean@burchj.freeserve.co.uk
BASRT

**BURDEN**, Michele A
**Group Analytic Psychotherapist**
44 New Road
Twyford
Berkshire
RG10 9PT
☎ 01189 344 491
Michele_Burden@hotmail.com
UPCA

**CALLEA**, Tamara
**Autogenic Psychotherapist, Humanistic Psychotherapist**
♿ Woodside
7 Kiff Green
Caversham, Upper Woolahampton
Reading
RG7 5TN
☎ 0118 971 3537
AHPP, BAS

**CALVERT**, Harriet B.
**Child Psychotherapist**
Cardinal Clinic
Oakley Green
Windsor, Berks
SL4
☎ 01753 631021
harrietcalvert@compuserve
ACP

**CARROLL**, Victoria
**Integrative Psychotherapist**
Sutherland House
Devenish Road
Sunninghill
Ascot
SL5 9PE
☎ 01344 628 630
martin.carroll@talk21.com
SPCRC

**CARTER**, Clare
**Attachment-based Psychoanalytic Psychotherapist**
The Old Post House
Crazies Hill
Wargrave
Berkshire
RG10 8LU
☎ 01189 403 437
☎ 07811 119 154
CAPP

**CASEY**, Aideen
**Psychoanalytic Psychotherapist**
♿ Winterbourne House
53/55 Argyle Road
Reading
RG1 7YL
☎ 01189 561 250
CCOPPP

**CHALCRAFT**, Helen
**Sexual and Relationship Psychotherapist**
Camden House
53 New Street
Henley-on-Thames
Oxon
RG9 2BP
☎ 01491 574 405
☎ 01189 864 621
hchalcraft@tinyworld.co.uk
Family Planning Service
7 Craven Road
Reading
RG1 5LE
BASRT

**CLAPHAM**, Miles
**Psychoanalytic Psychotherapist**
♿ Huntercombe Manor Hospital
Huntercombe Lane
South Taplow
Maidenhead
SL6 0PQ
☎ 01628 667 881
☎ 01225 422 354
miles.clapham@btinternet.com
PA

**COLLINS**, Jane
**Sexual and Relationship Psychotherapist**
♿ Magnolia House Surgery
Sunningdale
Ascot
SL5 0QJ
☎ 01344 637 800
BASRT

**COOPER**, Janette
**Family & Systemic Psychotherapist**
5 Buckhurst Way
Earley
Reading
RG6 7RL
☎ 0118 962 6095
jl.cooper@online.co.uk
AFT

**COSTA**, Beverley
**Psychodrama Psychotherapist**
12 College Road
Reading
Berkshire
RG6 1QB
☎ 01189 666 159
beverleycosta@hotmail.com
BPA

**COXWELL-WHITE**, Jenny
**Integrative Psychotherapist**
113 New Road
North Ascot
Berkshire
SL5 8PZ
☎ 01344 884 142
CCBP

**CUFF**, Jenny
**Autogenic Psychotherapist**
153 Northcourt Avenue
Reading
RG2 7HG
☎ 0118 986 6987
BAS

**DEFRIES**, Nicky
**Psychoanalytic Psychotherapist**
♿ Cardinal Clinic
Bishops Lodge
Oakley Green
Berks
SL4 5UL
☎ 01753 869 755
☎ 020 8723 2598
GUILD, SITE

**DENMAN**, Dido
**Transpersonal Psychotherapist**
Life Story
Therapeutic Centre
17 Eldon Square
Reading
RG1 4DP
☎ 0118 971 4663
1 Nuttage Gate Cottages
Peasehill
Bucklebury
Reading
RG7 6RS
CTP

**EATON**, John
**Hypno-Psychotherapist**
Waterloo House
158 London Road
Newbury
Berkshire
RG14 2AX
☎ 0163 544 444
dr.john.eaton@virgin.net
NSHAP

**ECONOMAKIS**, Tara
**Hypno-Psychotherapist**
Upper Valley Stud
Crooked Soley
Chilton Foliat
Hungerford
RG17 0TW
☎ 01672 540 321
tarabecon@hotmail.com
NSHAP

**ENGLAND**, David
**Psychosynthesis Psychotherapist**
48 Trenchard Road
Holyport, Maidenhead
Berkshire
SL6 2LR
☎ 01628 778 820
☎ 01628 639 313
david@inner-leadership.com
IPS

**FOSKETT**, Julia
**Family & Systemic Psychotherapist**
♿ CAMHS Team
The Cottage
St Marks Hospital
Maidenhead
SL6 6DU
☎ 01753 638 467
IFT

**HAIGH**, Rex
**Group Analyst**
♿ Winterbourne House
53-55 Argyle Road
Reading
Berkshire
RG1 7YL
☎ 0118 956 1250
☎ 0118 933 2205
(W) rex.haigh@virgin.net, (H) rex@haighfamily.freeserve.co.uk
IGA, UPCA

**HAMMOND**, Tania
**Integrative Psychotherapist**
The Consulting Room
50 High Street
Hungerford
RG17 0NE
☎ 01488 684 993
help@theconsultingroom.co.uk
SPCRC

**HARRIS**, Sue
**Integrative Arts Psychotherapist**
30 St Leonards Road
Windsor
SL4 3BU
☎ 01753 858 239
sue.harris@sueharris.co.uk
IATE

**HODGSON**, Diane
**Gestalt Psychotherapist**
♿ 87 Old Wokingham Road
Crowthorne
Berkshire
RG45 6LJ
☎ 01344 750 903
dianehodgson@genesis2K.fsnet.co.uk
GPTI, MET

**HOLT**, Joan
**Family & Systemic Psychotherapist**
20 Wallingford Road
Goring
Reading
RG8 0AY
☎ 01895 438 657
☎ 07879 822 880
joan@holt611.fsnet.co.uk
AFT

**HUTTON**, Margaret
**Group Analytic Psychotherapist**
The Life Story Therapeutic Centre
17 Eldon Square
Reading
RG1 4DP
☎ 0118 976 1165
☎ 0772 009 5895
margaret.hutton@btinternet.com
FPC

**KELLEY**, Linda
**Transactional Analysis Psychotherapist**
Bracknell
RG12
☎ 01344 642 616
linda.j.kelley@dial.pipex.com
ITA

**KLEIN**, Wendy T
**Family & Systemic Psychotherapist**
12 St. James Close
Pangbourne
RG8 7AP
☎ 0118 984 2856
wendy@wklein.freeserve.co.uk
AFT

**MADDEN**, Felicity W.
**Psychoanalytic Psychotherapist**
♿ Willow House
Stanford Dingley
Reading
RG7 6LX
VAPP, WMIP

**MAY**, Caroline
**Integrative Psychotherapist**
47 Coley Avenue
Reading
Berkshire
RG1 6LQ
☎ 01189 594 345
caroline.may@ntlworld.com
MC

**MCGREGOR**, Tony
**Hypno-Psychotherapist**
127 Kingsley Close
Shaw
Newbury
Berkshire
RG14 2EB
☎ 01635 34231
NRHP

**MELTON**, Jane
**Cognitive Analytic Therapist**
46 Clifton Road
Wokingham
Berkshire
RG41 1NB
☎ 0118 977 1409
ACAT

**MURRAY**, Jane
**Integrative Psychotherapist**
5 Chieveley Mews
London Road
Sunningdale
Berks
SL5 0UD
☎ 01344 626366
☎ 07762 389 050
MET

**NEWMAN**, Adam
**Analytical Psychologist-Jungian Analyst**
98 Norcot Road
Tilehurst
Reading
Berkshire
RG30 6BT
☎ 0118 942 2348
☎ 07748 76 78 25
ad.newman@btinternet.com
CAP *

**O'CONNELL**, Patrick
**Group Analytic Psychotherapist**
♿ Berkshire Psychotherapy Service
53-55 Argyle Road
Reading
RG1 7YL
☎ 01256 420 048
☎ 0118 956 1250
p.oconnell1@ntlworld.com
FPC

**PARKER**, Christopher
**Child Psychotherapist**
6B Church Street
Reading, Berks
RG1 2SB
☎ 0118 9566043
ACP

**PATTERSON**, Sharon
**Family & Systemic Psychotherapist**
3 Fulmer Close
Earley
Reading
RG6 5UR
☎ 0118 986 0935
sharon@thepattersons.freeserve.co.uk
AFT

**PLOUMAKI**, Sophia
**Group Analytic Psychotherapist**
17 Shepherd's Lane
Bracknell
Berkshire
RG42 2BN
☎ 07718 914 296
☎ 01344 452 519
ploumaki@aol.com
UPCA

**PODOLSKA**, Sue
**Hypno-Psychotherapist**
♿ 12 Pennypiece
Goring on Thames
Oxon
RG8 9BY
☎ 01491 874 130
sue.podolska@demon.co.uk
NRHP

**POLLOCK**, Jo
**Sexual and Relationship Psychotherapist**
The Haven
7 King Street
Mortimer
RG7 3RS
☎ 0118 933 1746
counsellorjsp@hotmail.com
BASRT

**RAWLINSON**, David
**Group Analytic Psychotherapist**
Winterboune House
52-55 Argyle Road
Reading
Berkshire
RG1 7YL
☎ 01189 561 250
sue.clarke@berkshire.nhs.uk
UPCA

**RENZ**, Johanna
**Systemic Psychotherapist**
♿ Upsticks Ltd
P O Box 2311
Ascot
SL5 8WE
☎ 01344 875 095
info@upsticksandgo.com
KCC

**RICHARDS**, Janet
**Psychoanalytic Psychotherapist**
38A Priest Hill
Caversham
Reading
Berks
RG4 7RY
☎ 0118 9269545
GUILD

**ROBERTS**, Alison
**Systemic Psychotherapist**
♿ Huntercombe Manor Hospital
Huntercombe Land South
Taplow
Maidenhead
SL6 0PQ
☎ 01296 630 256
☎ 01628 667 881
robertsathome@yahoo.co.uk
KCC

**ROWAN**, Cathy
**Transpersonal Psychotherapist**
81 Donnington Road
Reading
Berkshire
RG1 5NE
☎ 0118 926 1568
☎ 0118 958 0806
cathyrowan@freeuk.com
Life Story
17 Eldon Square
Reading
Berks
RG1 4D
CCPE

**RUDGLEY**, Lisa
**Family & Systemic Psychotherapist**
♿ CAMHS
88 Newton Road
Newbury
Berkshire
RG1 7BT
☎ 01635 45888
rudgley@supanet.com
AFT

**SAWERS**, Martin
**Humanistic and Integrative Psychotherapist**
109 Stafford Avenue
Slough
Berks
SL2 1AP
☎ 0117 909 8196
☎ 01735 673 765
martinsawers@ukonline.co.uk
BCPC

**SCOVELL**, Janet
**Integrative Psychotherapist**
25 The Grove
Reading
Berks
RG1 4RB
☎ 0118 956 1976
pjhersco@clara.co.uk
MC

**SHORT**, Patricia
**Systemic Psychotherapist**
Psychology Department
Broadmoor Hospital
Crowthorne
RG45 7EG
☎ 01344 754 582 or 80
patshort@wlmht.nhs.uk
KCC

**STAFFORD**, Amanda
**Psychoanalytic Psychotherapist**
Forelands, 2 The Avenue
Mortimer
Reading
Berks
RG7 3QY
☎ 0118 9561 250
☎ 0118 9474 860
amandajstafford@yahoo.com
Winterbourne House
53-55 Argyle Road
Reading
Berks
RG1 7YL
FIP

**TAMPIN**, Jill
**Integrative Psychotherapist**
Dodbrook House
Altwood Bailey
Maidenhead
Berkshire
SL6 4PQ
☎ 01628 781 076
jilltampin@hotmail.com
MET

**TAYLOR**, Diana
**Integrative Psychotherapist**
47 Cheviot Road
Sandnurst
Berkshire
GU47 8NE
☎ 01344 774 861
dt1864875@aol.com
MET

**TYTEL**, Laurie
**Psychoanalytic Psychotherapist**
♿ 101 Chiltern Road
Caversham
Reading
Berkshire
RG4 5HS
☎ 0118 947 0625
laurietytel@hotmail.com
The Camellias
Birds Lane,Midgham
Reading
BERKSHIRE
RG7 5UL
FIP

**WAGSTAFF**, Susan
**Family & Systemic Psychotherapist**
♿ Berkshire Adolescent Unit
Wokingham Hospital
41 Barkham Road
Wokingham
RG4 2RE
☎ 0118 949 5019
susan.wagstaff@berkshire.nhs.uk
AFT

**WALKER**, Bridget
**Integrative Arts Psychotherapist**
Winterbourne House
53-55 Argyle Road
Reading
Marlborough
RG1 7YL
☎ 01189 561 250
bridget.walker@virgin.net
IATE

**WARD**, Hilary
**Transpersonal Psychotherapist**
Blair Villa
Wokefield Row
Mortimer
Berkshire
RG7 3AL
☎ 0118 933 3006
☎ 07879 634 641
Hilaryward1@aol.com
CCPE

**WILLIAMS**, K.A.
**Cognitive Behavioural Psychotherapist**
29 Lockstile Way
Goring-on-Thames
Reading
RG8 0AL
☎ 01491 872 072
☎ 01189 473 686
38A Priest Hill
Caversham
Reading
RG4 7RY
BABCP

**WINSHIP**, Gary
**Group Analytic Psychotherapist**
Psychotherapy Department Berkshire NHS
53-55 Argyle Road
Reading
Berks
RG1 7YL
☎ 01189 561 250
☎ 02083 408 284
gwinship@aol.com
UPCA

**WRIGHT**, Shelagh
**Family & Systemic Psychotherapist**
♿ Huntercombe Manor Hospital
Huntercombe Lane South
Taplow
Maidenhead
SL6 0PQ
☎ 01628 607 404
shelagh.wright@fshc.co.uk
AFT

**VON BUHLER**, J M A Herbert Pardo
**Sexual and Relationship Psychotherapist**
♿ The Cardinal Clinic
Bishop's Lodge
Oakley Green
Windsor
SL4 5UL
☎ 07973 442 143
☎ 01753 869 755
jvbuhler@buhler.demon.co.uk
BASRT

## BOURNEMOUTH

**BENNETT**, Gerald A.
**Cognitive Behavioural Psychotherapist**
♿ Community Drug Team
Park Lodge
Gloucester Road
Bournemouth, Dorset
BH7 6JF
☎ 01202 397 003
BABCP

**CLARKE**, Susan Elizabeth
**Cognitive Analytic Therapist, Cognitive Behavioural Psychotherapist, Cognitive Psychotherapist**
♿ Intensive Psychological Therapies Service
Branksome Clinic
51a Layton Road
Parkstone, Poole
BH12 2BJ
☎ 01202 584 120
☎ 01202 734 092
ACAT, BABCP

**CODD**, Anne Marie
**Psychoanalytic Psychotherapist**
59 Grand Avenue
Southbourne
Bournemouth
Dorset
BH6 3TA
☎ 01202 428 548
AGIP

**FITZGERALD-POOL**, Zoe
**Existential Psychotherapist**
85 Curzon Road
Bournmouth
London
BH1 4PR
☎ 01202 396 830
☎ 07818 445 742
fitzoe@yahoo.com
UPCA

**GREGORY**, Peter
**Sexual and Relationship Psychotherapist**
♿ Broad-Reach Clinic
56 Alum Chine Road
Westbourne
BH4 8DZ
☎ 023 80 617 990
☎ 01202 769 976
BASRT

**JORDAN**, Ruth
**Integrative Psychotherapist**
85 Watcombe Road
Southburne
Bournemouth
BH6 3LX
☎ 01202 771 926
rjordan@bournemouth.ac.uk
MC

**LONG**, Jennifer
**Cognitive Behavioural Psychotherapist**
♿ Dept. of Psychological Therapies
16-18 Tower Road
Boscombe
Bournemouth
BH1 4LB
☎ 01202 304 634
BABCP

**OSTLER**, Dorothy
**Systemic Psychotherapist**
Shelley Clinic
Boscombe Community Hospital
11 Shelley Road
Boscombe, Bournemouth
BH1 4JQ
☎ 01202 443 011
FIC

**VENKI**, Malathi
**Cognitive Behavioural Psychotherapist**
11 William Road
Queens Park
Bournemouth
Dorset
BH7 7BB
☎ 01202 246 719
malvenki@yahoo.co.uk
BABCP

**WALLACE-SMITH**, Nigel
**Sexual and Relationship Psychotherapist**
♿ The Broad Reach Clinic
56 Alum Chine Road
Westbourne
BH4 8DZ
☎ 01202 738052
bmtherapy@aol.com
BASRT

**WILTSHIRE**, Gill
**Cognitive Behavioural Psychotherapist**
61 Lowther Road
Bournemouth
Dorset
BH8 8NW
☎ 01202 398 233
BABCP

**WITHERS**, Jacqueline M.J.
**Cognitive Analytic Therapist, Cognitive Behavioural Psychotherapist**
♿ Psychology Dept.
16-18 Tower Road
Boscombe
Bournemouth
BH1 4LB
☎ 01202 304 634
ACAT, BABCP

## BRIGHTON AND HOVE

**ACKET**, Marijke
**Psychosynthesis Psychotherapist**
55a Grantham Road
Brighton
BN2 6EF
☎ 01273 884 966
m.acket@ntlworld.com
IPS

**ALDRIDGE**, Felicity
**Humanistic Psychotherapist**
3 Bigwood Avenue
Hove
East Sussex
BN3 6FP
☎ 01273 884 256
☎ 01273 729 365
felicity.aldridge@ntlworld.com
The Whitehouse
54 New Church Road
Hove
East Sussex
BN3
AHPP

**ALEXANDER**, Gail
**Analytical Psychologist-Jungian Analyst**
47 Rugby Place
Kemp Town
Brighton
BN2 5JB
☎ 01273 600 307
FIP

**BARNETT**, Mary
**Psychoanalytic Psychotherapist**
♿ Specialist Psychotherapy Service
Hove Polyclinic
Nevill Avenue
Hove
BN3 7HY
☎ 01273 242017
☎ 01273 506258
mary.barnett@southdowns.nhs.uk
GUILD

**BAZZARD**, Helen
**Transpersonal Psychotherapist**
152 Carden Avenue
Patchman
Brighton
BN1 8NH
☎ 01273 243 780
☎ 01273 700 581
CTP

**BERRY**, Julia
**Integrative Arts Psychotherapist**
♿ c/o Room 6
Royal Sussex Hospital
Eastern Road
Brighton
BN2 5BE
☎ 01273 696 955 x7620
IATE

**BEST**, Richard
**Family & Systemic Psychotherapist**
CAMS Southdown NHS MH
St Stephen House
45a Borough Street
Brighton
BN1 3BJ
☎ 01273 327 221
richard.a.best@talk21.com
AFT

**BLUNDEN**, Jane
**Cognitive Analytic Therapist**
♿ Consultant Psychisatrist in Psychotherapy
Specialist Psychotherapy Service
Hove Polyclinic, Neville Avenu
Hove
BN3 7HY
☎ 01273 242 017
jane.blunden@southdowns.nhs.uk
ACAT

**BOTT**, David
**Family & Systemic Psychotherapist**
9 Marine Terrace Mews
Brighton
BN2 1AR
☎ 01273 696 108
D.P.Bott@bton.ac.uk
AFT

**BRADY**, Peter
**Cognitive Behavioural Psychotherapist**
♿ Cognitive Behaviour Therapy Department
Hove Polyclinic
Nevill Avenue
Hove
BN3 7HY
☎ 01273 242 018
☎ 01825 763 156
BABCP

**BRISTOW**, John
**Cognitive Analytic Therapist**
48 Norfolk Road
Brighton
Sussex
BN1 3AB
☎ 01273 820 543
john.bristow1@btopenworld.com
ACAT, BPS

**BUCK**, Carol
**Sexual and Relationship Psychotherapist**
Brighton and Hove
East Sussex
BN1
☎ 01273 552 205
Carol.Buck@btinternet.com
BASRT

**CARRITT**, Sally
**Psychoanalytic Psychotherapist**
145 Freshfield Road
Brighton
BN2 9YE
☎ 01273 690 162
carritt@ntlworld.com
AGIP

**CASARES**, Jonathan
**Transpersonal Psychotherapist**
♿ 34 Lower Market Street
Hove
East Sussex
BN2 2NX
CCPE

**CHAMBERLAIN**, Heather
**Lacanian Analyst**
♿ 17 Lewes Crescent
Brighton
BN2 1GB
☎ 01273 600 053
heather.chamberlain@mistral.co.uk
CFAR

**COULSON**, Christopher J
**Individual and Group Humanistic Psychotherapist, Integrative Psychotherapist**
4 Eaton Manor
The Drive
Hove
BN3 3PT
☎ 01273 749 636
cjcoulson@bigfoot.com
AHPP

**CULLUM**, Mike
**Integrative Psychotherapist**
155 Osbourne Road
Brighton
East Sussex
BN1 6LW
☎ 01273 561619
☎ 0777 333 0673
MET

**DENFORD**, Lindsey D.
**Cognitive Behavioural Psychotherapist**
248A Portland Road
Hove
BN3 5QT
☎ 020 7848 0505
l.denford@iop.kcl.ac.uk
BABCP

**DOLMAN**, Christine
**Systemic Psychotherapist**
72 Franklin Road
Brighton
BN2 3AD
☎ 01273 672 097
chrisdolm@yahoo.com
KCC

**DRIJVER**, Caroline
**Cognitive Behavioural Psychotherapist**
♿ 37 Princes Terrace
Brighton
E Sussex
BN2 5JS
☎ 01273 690 770
☎ 01273 242 018
Behavioural Psychotherapy Dept
Hove Polyclinic
Hove
BN3 7HY
BABCP

**EDMUNDS**, Howard
**Group Analytic Psychotherapist**
Montpelier Crescent Consulting Rooms
Flat 1
19 Montpellier Crescent
Brighton
BN1 3JF
☎ 01273 230 317
☎ 07905 941 944
howardedmunds@southvine.co.uk
FPC

**ELDRIDGE**, Melanie
**Psychodrama Psychotherapist**
7 Hartington Terrace
Brighton
East Sussex
BN2 3LT
☎ 01273 608 987
BPA

**FOSBURY**, Jacqueline Ann
**Cognitive Analytic Therapist**
29 Upper Abbey Road
Brighton
BN2 2AD
☎ 07710 215 617
ACAT

**GEESON**, Patricia
**Psychoanalytic Psychotherapist**
149 New Church Road
Hove
BN3 4DB
☎ 01273 419 481
AGIP

**GODDARD**, Lynne
**Transactional Analysis Psychotherapist**
♿ Hove
East Sussex
BN3
☎ 01273 202 721
lynnegoddard@beeb.net
ITA

**GOLDMAN**, Manya
**Integrative Psychotherapist**
The Dyke Road Natural Health Clinic
274 Dyke Road
Brighton
BN1 5AE
☎ 01273 561 844
manya@pobox.com
MC

**GRANT**, Alec John
**Cognitive Behavioural Psychotherapist**
John McKeown Associates
17 Prince Albert Street
Brighton
BN1 1HF
☎ 01273 821 402
☎ 01323 430 831
A.Grant@bton.ac.uk
BABCP

**GREEN**, Carolyn
**Existential Psychotherapist**
♿ 19E Sussex Heights
St Margaret's Place
Brighton
BN1 2FR
☎ 01273 738 998
greencm@dial.pipex.com
SPCRC

**JONES**, Helen
**Biodynamic Psychotherapist**
52 Newmarket Road
Brighton
Sussex
BN2 3QF
☎ 01273 621347
LSBP

**JOSEPH**, Jerome Devakumar
**Cognitive Psychotherapist**
Gilgal
17 Nyetimber Hill
Brighton
East Sussex
BN2 4TL
☎ 01273 278 632
☎ 07970 150 923
BABCP

**KATZ**, Shawn
**Transpersonal Psychotherapist**
55A Grantham Road
Brighton
East Sussex
BN1 6EF
☎ 01273 324790
ShawnhKatz@aol.com
CCPE

**LAMPLOUGH**, Alexis
**Transpersonal Psychotherapist**
29 Spring Street
Brighton
BN1 3EF
☎ 01273 779513
CCPE

**LIDSTER**, Wendy
**Sexual and Relationship Psychotherapist**
♿ 19 Shirley Drive
Hove
BN3 6NQ
☎ 01273 330 262
wendylid@tiscali.co.uk
BASRT

**LOVE**, Mollie
**Group Analytic Psychotherapist, Psychoanalytic Psychotherapist**
Larkswood
162 Warren Road
Woodingdean
Brighton
BN2 6DD
☎ 01273 607 529
molliel@larkswood.fslife.co.uk
AGIP, FIP

**MACKENZIE**, Nancy
**Group Analyst**
18 Wolstonbury Road
Hove
BN3 6EJ
☎ 020 7935 3103
IGA

**MANSFIELD-OSBORNE**, Lynne
**Existential Psychotherapist**
61b Beaconsfield Villas
Brighton
Sussex
BN1 6HB
☎ 01273 550188
Lynnemo39@aol.com
UPCA

**MCCLELLAND**, Sheila
**Psychodynamic Psychotherapist**
♿ 24 Leicester Villas
Hove
BN3 5SQ
☎ 01273 421 501
☎ 01444 441 881 x4515
bishopeliza@aol.com
UPCA

**PAGE**, Marcus
**Group Analyst**
61b Beaconsfield Villas
Brighton
BN1 6HB
☎ 01273 387 829
marcus@triangle-services.co.uk
IGA

**PARKINSON**, Jane
**Attachment-based Psychoanalytic Psychotherapist**
14 Westhill Street
Brighton
East Sussex
BN1 3RR
☎ 01273 739 281
CAPP

**POTHIG**, Elisabeth
**Transpersonal Psychotherapist**
♿ Albion Clinic
1 Albion Street
Brighton
BN2 2NE
☎ 01444 453 384
☎ 07870 967 179
elisabethpothig@hotmail.com
CCPE

**RICKMAN**, Christine
**Integrative Psychotherapist**
30A Canning Street
Brighton
East Sussex
BN2 0EF
☎ 07798 843 059
xxeena2@aol.com
MET

**ROSE**, Russell
**Body Psychotherapist, Integrative Psychotherapist**
7 Carlyle Street
Brighton
BN2 2XU
☎ 01273 684 831
russrose@btconnect.com
CCBP

**ROYCE**, Heather
**Educational Therapist**
133 Havelock Road
Brighton
BN1 6GN
☎ 01273 701 219
heatherroyce@hotmail.com
CFET

**RUBIN**, Ann
**Existential Psychotherapist**
14 Hove Park Way
Hove
East Sussex
BN3 6PT
☎ 01273 556 550
☎ 07729 510 300
annrubin@ntlworld.com
UPCA

**SAVINS**, Charlotte
**Integrative Arts Psychotherapist**
11 Hanover Street
Brighton
BN2 9ST
☎ 01273 691 166
IATE

**SECRETT**, David
**Family & Systemic Psychotherapist**
♿ 37 Princes Terrace
Brighton & Hove
BN2 5JS
☎ 01273 690 770
AFT

**SHAW**, Jason
**Hypno-Psychotherapist**
Dept. Clinical and Counselling Psychology
4 St Peters Place
Brighton
BN1 4SA
☎ 01273 624 885
jason.shaw@southdowns.nhs.uk
NSHAP

**SIM**, Edward
**Hypno-Psychotherapist**
28 Wilbury Road
Hove
BN3 3JP
☎ 01825 766 400
ridgewoodhouse@hotmail.com
NSHAP

**SINGER**, Rory
**Gestalt Psychotherapist**
22 Avondale Road
Brighton & Hove
BN3 6ER
☎ 07739 556 438
rory.singer@virgin.net
GCL

**STREETER**, Elaine
**Family & Systemic Psychotherapist**
♿ 54 Southover Street
Hanover
Brighton
BN2 9UF
☎ 01273 700 745
AFT

**VELARDE**, Dominique
**Integrative Arts Psychotherapist**
Stone Street Practice
6 Stone Street
Brighton
BN1
☎ 01273 208 525
domvelarde@yahoo.co.uk
IATE

**WALLER**, Diane E
**Group Analytic Psychotherapist**
11A Richmond Road
Brighton
Sussex
BN2 3RL
☎ 01273 685 852
diane.waller@virgin.net
UPCA

**WARLOW**, Steve
**Systemic Psychotherapist**
33 Hythe Road
Brighton
BN1 6JR
KCC

**WELLS**, Peter
**Sexual and Relationship Psychotherapist**
The Garden Flat
67 Lansdowne Street
Hove
East Sussex
BN3 1FT
☎ 01273 327 986
post@peterwells.org.uk
BASRT

**WEST**, Dr Elizabeth
**Sexual and Relationship Psychotherapist**
♿ Priory Clinic
14-18 New Church Road
Hove
East Sussex
BN3 4FH
☎ 01273 747 464
BASRT

**WHITE**, Jennifer Madeline
**Gestalt Psychotherapist**
6 The Dock
Firle
BN1 4NF
☎ 01273 858 950
GCL

## BRISTOL

**ARIS**, Sarajane
**Transpersonal Psychotherapist**
3 Branksome Road
Redland
Bristol
BS6 7LL
☎ 0117 944 6446
CTP

**ASH**, Robert
**Psychoanalytic Psychotherapist**
Top Flat
54 Cotham Road
Cotham
Bristol
BS6 6DW
☎ 0117 942 7079
r_c_ash@hotmail.com
SIP

**ATKINS**, Sue
**Integrative Psychotherapist**
20 Hatherley
Bishopston
Bristol
BS7 8QA
☎ 07958 565 244
sueatkins@blueyonder.co.uk
MET

**BABIKER**, Gloria
**Psychoanalytic Psychotherapist**
Psychology Dept.
Barrow Hospital
Barrow Gurney
North Somerset
BS48 3SG
☎ 01179 286 551
☎ 07976 745 788
gloria.babiker@awp.nhs.uk
WMIP

**BARRETT**, Julie
**Humanistic and Integrative Psychotherapist**
♿ St Augustine's Clinic
495 Bath Road
Saltford
Bristol
BS31 3HQ
☎ 01392 258 915
juliebarret@ukonline.co.uk
BCPC

**BARWELL**, Peter
**Psychoanalytic Psychotherapist**
51 Woodstock Road
Redland
Bristol
BS6 7EW
☎ 0117 9247 580
barwells@onetel.net.uk
GUILD

**BOWES**, Ann
**Psychoanalytic Psychotherapist**
21 Canowie Road
Bristol
BS6 7HR
☎ 0117 973 5844
ann@bowes.fsnet.co.uk
FIP

**BOX**, Sally
**Psychoanalytic Psychotherapist**
22 Clifton Wood Road
Clifton
Bristol
BS8 4TW
☎ 0117 926 2902
SIP

**BRAMWELL**, Valerie
**Psychoanalytic Psychotherapist**
Yew Tree Farm
Rolestone
Hewish
Weston Super Mare
BS24 6UG
☎ 01934 822 370
SIP

**BROWN**, Jill
**Psychoanalytic Psychotherapist**
2a Cotham Lawn Road
Cotham
Bristol
BS6 6DU
☎ 0117 973 9161
SIP

**BROWN**, Ray
**Psychoanalytic Psychotherapist**
15 Nottingham Road
Bishopston
Bristol
BS7 9DH
☎ 0117 942 6105
drraybrown@blueyonder.co.uk
SIP

**BROWN**, Robin Gordon
**Psychoanalytic Psychotherapist**
14 Ambra Vale West
Clifton Wood
Bristol
BS8 4RD
☎ 0117 926 2886
robingordonbrown@blueyonder.co.uk
SIP

**BUDDEN**, Mark
**Psychoanalytic Psychotherapist**
6 York Place
Clifton
Bristol
BS8 1AH
☎ 0117 974 2885
SIP

**CAMPBELL**, Jan
**Transpersonal Psychotherapist**
50 Banner Road
Montpelier
Bristol
BS6 5LZ
☎ 0117 955 2395
CTP

**CAMPS**, Thomas
**Psychoanalytic Psychotherapist**
8 Duchess Road
Bristol
BS8 2LA
☎ 01179 741 388
WMIP

**CASE**, Caroline
**Child Psychotherapist**
Knowle Child & Adolescent Services
Broadfield Road, Knowle
Bristol
BS4 2UH
☎ 01275 462 779
ACP

**CHALKLEY**, A.J.
**Cognitive Psychotherapist**
♿ Psychology Department
34 Oldfield Road
Bath
BA2 3ND
☎ 01225 359 904
BABCP

**CLACEY**, Robert
**Psychoanalytic Psychotherapist**
51 Devonshire Buildings
Bath
BA2 4SU
☎ 01225 313 742
SIP

**CLARK**, Andrew
**Group Analyst**
♿ Avon & Wiltshire Mental Health
Partnership NHS
Cedar House, Blackberry Hill Hospit
Manor Rd
Bristol
BS16 2EW
☎ 0117 918 6811
Andrew.clark@awp.nhs.uk
GASW, IGA

**COLLENS**, Louise
**Psychoanalytic Psychotherapist**
120 Chesterfield Road
St. Andrews
Bristol
BS6 5DU
☎ 0117 908 6849
coll.alex@blueyonder.co.uk
SIP

**COLLIN**, Charlie
**Integrative Psychotherapist**
93 Belomont Roa
St. Andrews
Bristol
BS6 5AR
☎ 0117 987 7124
78 Egerton Road
Bishopston
Bristol
BS7 8HP
MET

**COLLIS**, Whiz
**Humanistic and Integrative Psychotherapist**
♿ 74 York Road
Montpelier
Bristol
BS6 5QF
☎ 0117 955 9600
whizc@74york.freeserve.co.uk
AHPP, BCPC

**COOK**, Lynn
**Analytical Psychologist-Jungian Analyst**
Top Floor
64 Alma Road
Clifton
BS8 2DJ
☎ 01934 710 233
lynn.cook@ic24.net
2 New Cottages
Notting Hill Way
Stone Allerton
Axbridge
BS26 2NQ
IGAP

**COUCILL**, Judith
**Group Analyst**
12 Sydenham Road
Bristol
BS6 5SH
☎ 0117 944 1005
☎ 01453 884 403
GASW

**CROSTON**, Richard
**Hypno-Psychotherapist**
Abbotsleigh Coach House
Rosemary Lane
Freshford
Bath
BA2 7UD
☎ 01225 720 103
Richard@rcroston.freeserve.co.uk
CTIS

**CUBIE**, Paul
**Family & Systemic Psychotherapist**
Student Counselling Services
UWE
Coldharbour Lane
Frenchay, Bristol
BS16 1QY
☎ 0117 965 6261
paulcubie@hotmail.com
AFT

**CUTLER**, Jane
**Psychosynthesis Psychotherapist**
59 Quantock Road
Windmill Hill
Bristol
BS3 4PQ
☎ 01179 632 505
janecutler@freeuk.co
IPS

**DANIEL**, Liz
**Hypno-Psychotherapist**
♿ Orchard Cottage
Middle Lane
Kingston Seymour
North Somerset
BS21 6XP
☎ 01934 834 765
peoplepotential@aol.com
CTIS

**DAVIES**, Sheila
**Psychoanalytic Psychotherapist**
35 Bath Hill
Keynsham
Bristol
BS18 1HJ
☎ 0117 986 1020
sheila.davies@sheiladavies.fsnet.co.uk
SIP

**DAWKINS**, Sue
**Integrative Arts Psychotherapist**
♿ 6 Tyning Place
Combe Down
Bath
BA2 5HA
☎ 01225 833 315
☎ 01225 445013
IATE

**DEWEY**, George
**Humanistic and Integrative Psychotherapist**
♿ 22 Merioneth Street
Victoria Park
Bedminster
Bristol
BS3 4SL
☎ 01458 851 016
☎ 0117 977 2164
BCPC

**DIAZ**, Marie Claire
**Psychoanalytic Psychotherapist**
54 Devonshire Road
Bristol
Westbury Park
BS6 7NL
☎ 0117 914 6835
diazmc1@aol.com
SIP

**DIXON**, Marion Shirley
**Family & Systemic Psychotherapist**
♿ The Seasons
Clevedon Hospital
Old Street
Clevedon
BS21 6BS
☎ 01275 870 316
marion.dixon@awp.nhs.uk
AFT

**DOYLE**, Mary
**Analytical Psychotherapist**
36 Tudor Road
Easton
Bristol
BS5 6BW
☎ 01179 9514 828
WMIP

**DRESSER**, Iain
**Psychoanalytic Psychotherapist**
14 Cornwall Road
Bishopston
Bristol
BS7 8LH
☎ 0117 924 8735
SIP

**DUNCAN**, Fraser
**Hypno-Psychotherapist**
2 Monks Park Avenue
Horfield
Bristol
BS7 0UE
☎ 01179 692 989
fraser@fraserduncan.com
NSHAP

**ELLIOTT**, Hazel
**Gestalt Psychotherapist**
18 Elton road
Bishopston
Bristol
BS7 8DD
☎ 0117 924 1815
GPTI

**ESSEX**, Susanne
**Family & Systemic Psychotherapist**
♿ CAMHS Monks Park House
Southmead Hospital
Monks Park Road
Bristol
BS10 5NB
☎ 0117 959 5800
susanne.essex@north-bristol.swest.nhs.co.uk
AFT

**FAIRBAIRNS**, Sarah
**Humanistic and Integrative Psychotherapist,**
♿ 55 Dunkery Road
Windmill Hill
Bristol
BS3 4LD
☎ 0117 908 2282
fairbairns@blueyonder.co.uk
BCPC

**FERNANDEZ**, Nigel R.
**Cognitive Behavioural Psychotherapist**
The Priory Hospital - Bristol
Heath House Lane
Stapleton
Bristol
BS16 1EQ
☎ 01258 858 489
☎ 0117 952 5255
nigelfernandez@hotmail.com
BABCP

**GARDNER**, Fiona
**Psychoanalytic Psychotherapist**
Suite 3
4/5 Bridge Street
Bath
BA2 4AS
☎ 01225 319 121
SIP

**GARDNER**, Peter
**Integrative Psychotherapist**
Harpers Batch
Winford
Bristol
BS40 8AF
☎ 01275 472 598
SPCRC

**GASKELL**, Christine
**Family & Systemic Psychotherapist**
Riverside Adolescent Unit
Blackberry Hill Hospital
Manor Road
Bristol
BS16 2EW
☎ 0117 975 4878
c.gaskell@which.net
AFT

**GELL**, Eva
**Psychoanalytic Psychotherapist**
116 Redland Road
Bristol
BS6 6QT
☎ 0117 909 5730
evagell@blueyonder.co.uk
SIP

**GILL**, Douglas
**Psychoanalytic Psychotherapist**
144 Coronation Road
Southville
Bristol
BS3 1RE
☎ 07796 408 222
☎ 0117 902 0781
douglasgill@blueyonder.com
PA

**GRANEY**, Mike
**Systemic Psychotherapist**
5 Seymour Rd
Bishopston
Bristol
BS7 9HR
☎ 0117 942 2815
FIC

**GRESTY**, Julia
**Core Process Psychotherapist**
71 Mendip Road
Bedminster
Bristol
BS3 4BP
☎ 0117 9637 285
KI

**GUEST**, Nicola
**Child Psychotherapist**
The Bridge Foundation
12 Sydenham Road
Bristol
BS6 5SH
☎ 0117 942510
ACP

**HAASE-DERRETT**, Susan
**Humanistic and Integrative Psychotherapist**
♿ 2 Cliftonwood Terrace
Clifton
Bristol
BS8 4TZ
☎ 0117 922 6544
susan.haase-derrett@bigfoot.com
BCPC

**HAHN**, Herbert
**Psychoanalytic Psychotherapist**
45 Alma Vale Road
Clifton
Bristol
BS8 2HL
☎ 0117 974 5757
herbh@btconnect.com
SIP

**HAMILTON-JAMES**, Tina
**Transactional Analysis Psychotherapist**
Parkwood
42 Frenchay Close
Frenchay
Bristol
BS16 2QX
☎ 0117 939 1007
thamjam@aol.com
ITA, MET

**HARRIS**, Clare
**Psychoanalytic Psychotherapist**
24a Upper Cheltenham Place
Montpelier
Bristol
BS6 5HR
☎ 0117 949 2534
clare@harris.yates.fsnet.co.uk
SIP

**HART**, Ellen
**Humanistic and Integrative Psychotherapist**
6 Queens Parade
Brandon Hill
Bristol
BS1 5XJ
☎ 0117 927 2686
mikeb@foe.co.uk
BCPC

**HASKAYNE**, Amanda
**Integrative Psychotherapist**
♿ 10 Bluebell Road
Wick St Laurence
Weston-Super-Mare
BS22 9QJ
amanda@amandahaskayne.co.uk
SPCRC

**HASTINGS**, Jon
**Humanistic and Integrative Psychotherapist**
29 Cobourg Road
Montpelier
Bristol
BS6 5HT
☎ 0117 941 3746
jonrhastings@onetel.net.uk
BCPC

**HASTINGS**, Kim
**Humanistic and Integrative Psychotherapist, Psychodynamic Psychotherapist**
♿ 42A Upper Cheltenham Place
Montpelier
Bristol
BS6 5HR
☎ 0117 954 0649
BCPC

**HAYWOOD**, Carol
**Transpersonal Psychotherapist**
24 Royal York Crescent
Bristol
BS8 4JX
☎ 0117 974 3717
CTP

**HICKS**, Jan
**Humanistic and Integrative Psychotherapist**
16 Somerset Street
Kingsdown
Bristol
BS2 8NB
☎ 0117 944 5127
BCPC

**HIGGINS**, Judith
**Gestalt Psychotherapist**
86 Langton Court Road
St Annes
Bristol
BS4 4EQ
☎ 0117 985 0391
jahiggins@bigfoot.com
GPTI

**HILES**, Margaret
**Family & Systemic Psychotherapist**
22 Coombe Lane
Stoke Bishop
Bristol
BS9 2AA
☎ 07974 802 498
childandfamily@blueyonder.co.uk
AFT

**HORTON**, David
**Group Analyst**
♿ 21a Blethwin Close
Henbury
Bristol
BS10 7BH
☎ 01179 505 517
david@counselling-bristol.co.uk
GASW

**HORWOOD**, Tone
**Humanistic Psychotherapist, Psychoanalytic Psychotherapist**
41 St Luke's Crescent
Totterdown
Bristol
BS3 4RZ
☎ 0117 972 1077
ToneH@talk21.com
IPSS

**HUGHES**, Hatty
**Attachment-based Psychoanalytic Psychotherapist**
♿ 11 Orchard Street
Bristol
BS1 5EH
☎ 0117 954 1843
CAPP

**JONES**, Rhiannon Marie
**Cognitive Behavioural Psychotherapist**
39 Wellington Park
Bristol
BS8 2UW
☎ 0117 317 9014
☎ 07989 367 181
rhim.jones@virgin.net
BABCP

**KEVLIN**, Kunderke
**Psychosynthesis Psychotherapist**
♿ 12 Avon Vale
Stoke Bishop
Bristol
BS9 1TB
☎ 0117 968 7748
kunderke.kevlin@lineone.net
PET

**LAPWORTH**, Phil
**Integrative Psychotherapist, Transactional Analysis Psychotherapist**
Lilac Cottage
65 Murhill
Limpley Stoke
Bath
BA2 7FQ
☎ 01225 722 348
phil@murhill.com
ITA, MET

**MACKEWN**, Jennifer
**Gestalt Psychotherapist, Integrative Psychotherapist**
♿ Southstoke House
Packhorse Lane
Southstoke
Bath
BA2 7DJ
☎ 01225 836 090
jennymac@netgates.co.uk
GPTI, MET

**MALONE**, Judy
**Psychoanalytic Psychotherapist**
16 Sydenham Lane
Cotham
Bristol
BS6 5SQ
☎ 0117 907 0022
SIP

**MANSI**, Susan
**Core Process Psychotherapist**
♿ 16 Greenbank Road
Southville
Bristol
BS3 1RH
☎ 0117 9660973
KI

**MATTHEWS**, Shane
**Systemic Psychotherapist**
Dept. of Clinical Psychology
University of Bristol
29 Park Row
Bristol
BS1 5NB
☎ 0117 331 5020
shane.matthews@bristol.ac.uk
FIC

**MARKHAM**, Angela
**Family & Systemic Psychotherapist**
3 The Paragon
Clifton
Bristol
BS8 4LA
☎ 0117 923 9038
AFT

**MAYNE**, Rob
**Humanistic and Integrative Psychotherapist**
♿ 6 Redland Terrrace
Redland
Bristol
BS6 6TD
☎ 0117 974 1426
mayne.payne@blueyonder.co.uk
BCPC

**MCCLOSKEY**, Fiona
**Psychoanalytic Psychotherapist**
37 Stafford Road
St .Werburgh's
Bristol
BS2 9UR
☎ 07779 243 216
☎ 01173 732 409
fionamccloskey@blueyonder.co.uk
The Bridge Foundation
12 Sydenham Road
Cotham
BS6 5SH
SIP, WMIP

**MCCORKINDALE**, Jan
**Humanistic and Integrative Psychotherapist**
11 John Street
St Werburghs
Bristol
BS2 9UE
☎ 0117 373 2409
jan.mccorkindale@ukgateway.net
BCPC

**MCNAMARA**, Barbara
**Psychoanalytic Psychotherapist**
31 Sommerville Road
St. Andrews
Bristol
BS7 9AD
☎ 0117 944 4206
SIP

**MELROSE**, Hannya
**Core Process Psychotherapist**
28 Royal York Crescent
Clifton
Bristol
BS8 4JX
☎ 0117 973 1973
KI

**MILTON**, Thelma
**Humanistic and Integrative Psychotherapist**
26 Salisbury Road
Redland
Bristol
BS6 7AP
☎ 0117 9427 518
BCPC

**MITCHESON BROWN**, Muriel
**Psychoanalytic Psychotherapist**
16 Woodstock Road
Redland
Bristol
BS6 7EJ
☎ 0117 924 1676
mumitch@eggconnect.net
SIP

**MORGAN**, Leigh
**Psychoanalytic Psychotherapist**
♿ 11 Orchard Street
Bristol
BS1 5EH
☎ 0117 977 4396
leighmorgan@tantraweb.co.uk
FPC

**MOSER**, Marianne
**Humanistic and Integrative Psychotherapist**
159 Cotswold Road
Windmill Hill
Bristol
BS3 4PH
☎ 0117 983 1465
marianneeurope@yahoo.co.uk
BCPC

**MUNRO**, Carole
**Hypno-Psychotherapist**
♿ 7 Park Road
Congresbury
Bristol
BS49 5HJ
☎ 01934 834 169
carole@hypnohelp.com
♿ Boulevard Pharmacy
23 Waterloo Street
Weston Super-Mare
BS23 1LF
NRHP

**NAVIN**, Tony
**Psychoanalytic Psychotherapist**
The Bridge Foundation
12 Sydenham Road
Cotham
Bristol
BS6 5SH
☎ 01285 652 017
SIP

**NAYDLER**, Nick
**Integrative Psychotherapist**
♿ 4 Seddon Road
St. Werburghs
Bristol
BS2 9YA
☎ 0117 955 0752
BCPC

**NORMAN**, Harry
**Neurolinguistic Psychotherapist**
29 Wesley Place
Clifton
Bristol
BS8 4YD
☎ 01179 682 417
support@solutionsology.co.uk
NLPtCA

**NYE**, Georgiana
**Psychosynthesis Psychotherapist**
45 Canynge Road
Clifton
Bristol
BS8 3LH
☎ 0117 973 3769
georgiananye@blueyonder.co.uk
PET

**PADGETT**, Louise
**Core Process Psychotherapist**
6 Fenton Road
Bishopston
Bristol
BS7 8ND
☎ 01179 426 332
KI

**PARSONS**, Mick
**Humanistic and Integrative Psychotherapist**
14 Seymour Avenue
Bishopston
Bristol
BS7 9HJ
☎ 0117 942 6727
mick@dowling-parsons.demon.co.uk
BCPC

**PATOCCHI**, Matilde
**Family & Systemic Psychotherapist**
83 St Werburghs Park
Bristol
BS2 9YX
☎ 07771 766 080
matilde57@hotmail.com
AFT

**PERSSON**, Rose
**Group Analytic Psychotherapist**
495 Bath Road
Saltford
BS18 3HQ
☎ 01225 873 245
rosepersson@aol.com
FPC

**PREECE**, Rob
**Transpersonal Psychotherapist**
53 Balmain Street
Totterdown
Bristol
☎ 01364 654 044
CTP

**PULLEN**, Caroline
**Sexual and Relationship Psychotherapist**
The Coach House
40a Eastfield
Westbury on Trym
Bristol
BS9
☎ 01275 374 170
cj.pullen@virgin.net
BASRT

**PULLIN**, Andrew
**Group Analyst**
♿ Bath Practice for Group Analysis
1 Frome Road
Beckington
Nr Frome
BA3 6TD
☎ 01373 731 389
bpga@lineone.net
GASW, IGA

**PURKISS**, Jane
**Humanistic and Integrative Psychotherapist**
93 Stackpool Road
Southville
Bristol
BS3 1NX
☎ 0117 966 2957
janep93uk@yahoo.co.uk
BCPC

**RICHARDS**, Christopher
**Psychoanalytic Psychotherapist**
4 St. Ronan's Avenue
Redland
Bristol
BS6 6EP
☎ 0117 909 3474
cmrichards@blueyonder.co.uk
GUILD, SIP

**RICHARDSON**, Gillian
**Sexual and Relationship Psychotherapist**
Maycroft Cottage
Highbury Villas
Kingsdown
Bristol
BS2 8BY
☎ 0117 925 0115
BASRT

**ROSE**, Alivia
**Gestalt Psychotherapist**
22 Merioneth Street
Bristol
BS3 4SL
☎ 0117 977 2164
☎ 01458 851 016
GCL

**ROWE**, Jill
**Psychoanalytic Psychotherapist**
8 Somerset Street
Kingsdown
Bristol
BS2 8NB
☎ 0117 942 1016
SIP

**RUSSELL**, Marion
**Humanistic and Integrative Psychotherapist**
Alma Vale Centre
30 Alma Vale Road
Clifton
Bristol
BS8 2HY
☎ 0117 377 1186
SPEC

**RYALL**, Sue
**Integrative Psychosynthesis Psychotherapist**
Emmaus House
Clifton Hill
Bristol
BS8 1BN
☎ 0117 925 0041
susan.ryall@virgin.net
RE.V

**SAWERS**, Martin
**Humanistic and Integrative Psychotherapist**
♿ 24 Ambrose Road
Clifton Wood
Bristol
BS8 4RJ
☎ 0117 909 8196
☎ 01735 673 765
martinsawers@ukonline.co.uk
BCPC

**SHAW**, Adrian
**Core Process Psychotherapist**
5 Blackberry Hill
Stapleton
Bristol
BS16 1DB
☎ 01179 652880
KI

**SILMAN**, Chris
**Cognitive Behavioural Psychotherapist**
Doctors Surgery
2 Clifton Park
Bristol
BS8 3BS
☎ 0116 225 2613
☎ 0117 9060 4200
chris_silman@yahoo.co.uk
BABCP

**SIMMONS**, Alison R.
**Psychodrama Psychotherapist**
♿ Lower Hounsley Farm
Pool Lane
Ridgehill, Nr. Winford
Bristol
BS40 8BP
☎ 01275 472 264
BCPC, BPA

**SOOLE**, Trevor
**Cognitive Behavioural Psychotherapist**
♿ 13 Cornwallis Crescent
Clifton
Bristol
BS8 4PJ
☎ 011797 32080
tsoole@hotmail.com
BABCP

**SPROSTON**, Suzanne
**Psychoanalytic Psychotherapist**
7 Hampton Park
Redland
Bristol
BS6 6LG
☎ 0117 974 5682
bluemoon@suztom.freeserve.co.uk
SIP

**STEVENS**, Yvonne J
**Cognitive Analytic Therapist**
The Observatory
4 Archfield Road
Cotham
Bristol
BS6
☎ 01934 713 693
ACAT

**STRATFORD**, Jacqueline
**Family & Systemic Psychotherapist**
8 Owen Grove
Henleaze
Bristol
BS9 4ER
☎ 0117 962 8627
AFT

**SUTTON-SMITH**, Deirdre
**Group Analyst**
12 Sydenham Road
Cotham
Bristol
BS6 5SH
☎ 0117 944 1005
☎ 01392 434 441
gasw@ukonline.co.uk
GASW, IGA

**THOMAS**, Penny
**Humanistic and Integrative Psychotherapist**
16 Sydenham Lane
Cotham
Bristol
BS6 5FQ
☎ 01453 861 101
pen.thomas@virgin.net
BCPC

**TRAVIS**, Mary
**Analytical Psychologist-Jungian Analyst, Psychoanalytic Psychotherapist**
73 Alma Road
Clifton
Bristol
BS8 2DW
☎ 0117 973 0403
AJA, SIP

**VOSS**, Tony
**Gestalt Psychotherapist**
Connexions
Combe Down Branch Surgery
Sulis Manor Road
Odd Down, Bath
BA2 2 A
☎ 0845 458 8263
tv@antipole.co.uk
GPTI

**WALKER**, George
**Family & Systemic Psychotherapist**
♿ Gloucester House
Southmead Hospital
Westbury-on-Trym
Bristol
BS10 5NB
☎ 0117 959 5808
AFT

**WEBB**, Deborah
**Biodynamic Psychotherapist**
17 Rockliffe Road
Bath
BA2 6QN
☎ 01225 461 361
deborahw@fish.co.uk
LSBP

**WELLS**, Martin
**Transactional Analysis Psychotherapist**
11 Clare Road
Cotham
Bristol
BS6 5TB
☎ 01179 247 457
martin_wells@lineone.net
ITA

**WHEWAY**, John Kirti
**Humanistic and Integrative Psychotherapist**
86 Langton Court Road
St Annes
Bristol
BS4 4EQ
☎ 0117 985 0391
jkwheway@bigfoot.com
BCPC

**WILBRAHAM**, Daphne
**Humanistic and Integrative Psychotherapist**
1 Canynge Square
Clifton
Bristol
BS8 3LA
☎ 0117 973 3029
dapwill@ukonline.co.uk
BCPC

**WILLIAMS**, Chris
**Analytical Psychologist-Jungian Analyst**
8 Stuart Place
Bath
BA2 3RQ
☎ 01225 463 054
☎ 01225 427 705
chris.williamsuk@virgin.net
AJA

**WILLS**, Frank
**Cognitive Psychotherapist**
♿ 7 St. Matthews Road
Cotham
Bristol
BS6 5TS
☎ 0117 924 3574
f.wills@newport.ac.uk
BABCP

**WITT**, Erica
**Humanistic and Integrative Psychotherapist**
Alma Vale Centre
30 Alma Vale Road
Bristol
BS8 2HY
☎ 0117 377 1186
☎ 01275 818 580
johnwitt@dial.pipe.com
2 Fircliff Park
Portishead
Bristol
BS20 7HQ
SPEC

**WITT**, John
**Humanistic and Integrative Psychotherapist**
Alma Vale Centre
30 Alma Vale Road
Bristol
BS8 2HY
☎ 01275 818 580
☎ 0117 377 1186
johnwitt@dial.pipex.com
2 Fircliff Park
Portishead
Bristol
BS20 7HQ
SPEC

**WOODCOCK**, Jeremy
**Family & Systemic Psychotherapist**
Bridge Foundation
12 Sydenham Road
Bristol
BS6 5SH
☎ 01453 835 365
☎ 0117 954 6724
Jeremy.Woodcock@bristol.ac.uk
IFT

**YARIV**, Gail
**Psychoanalytic Psychotherapist**
121 York Road
Montpelier
BRISTOL
BS6 5QG
☎ 0117 955 1827
FPC, SIP

**YOUNG**, Jeremy
**Family & Systemic Psychotherapist**
Edie's Cottage
Hodshill
Southstocke
Bath
BA2 7ED
☎ 01225 832 806
jeremy_young@mac.com
AFT

## BUCKINGHAMSHIRE

**ADAMS**, Ghislaine
**Hypno-Psychotherapist**
41 London Road
Stony Stratford
Milton Keynes
MK11 1JQ
☎ 01908 566 362
NSHAP

**ALDER**, Helena
**Integrative Psychotherapist**
Woodside Corner
11 Baring Crescent
Beaconsfield
Bucks
HP9 2NG
☎ 01494 673557
MC

**ALDER**, Roger
**Integrative Psychotherapist**
Woodside Corner
11 Baring Crescent
Beaconsfield
Bucks
HP9 2NG
☎ 01494 673557
MC

**ALLISON**, Virginia
**Psychoanalytic Psychotherapist**
Woodcroft
Deanfield
Saunderton
High Wycombe, Bucks
HP14 4JR
☎ 01494 481 084
FPC

**AMIN**, Sheetal
**Integrative Arts Psychotherapist**
'Abishek'
Solesbridge Lane
Chorleywood
WD3 5SR
☎ 019233 283 213
sheetal_admin@hotmail.com
IATE

**AXSON**, Astrid
**Educational Therapist**
"Westways"
Milton Avenue
Gerrards Cross
Bucks
SL9 8QW
☎ 01753 886 928
CFET

**BENNETT**, Joy
**Integrative Psychotherapist**
Camelot
Penn Street Village
HP7 0PY
☎ 01494 717 702
ajbennett_us@hotmail.com
SPCRC

**BLOCH**, Linda
**Group Analyst**
Psychotherapy Service, Bucks Mental Health NHS Tru
Harlow House
Harlow Road
High Wycombe
HP13 6AA
☎ 01494 425 777
IGA

**BOLLINGHAUS**, Elaine
**Couple Psychoanalytic Psychotherapist**
'Loudhams'
Burtons Lane
Little Chalfont
Buckinghamshire
HP8 4RS
☎ 01494 765 947
elaine@bollinghaus.demon.co.uk
SCPP

**BROWNE**, Val
**Psychoanalytic Psychotherapist**
19 Hampden Hill
Beaconsfield
Bucks
HP9 1BP
☎ 01494 678 023
vbrowne@waitrose.com
FPC

**BURNS**, Elizabeth
**Family & Systemic Psychotherapist**
11 Green End Street
Aston Clinton
Aylesbury
Bucks
HP22 5JE
☎ 01296 630 048
lizburns@dial.pipex.com
IFT

**BUTCHER**, Barbara
**Hypno-Psychotherapist**
♿ 35 Lowfield Way
Hazlemere
Buckinghamshire
HP15 7RR
☎ 01494 814 306
bb@purpose.demon.co.uk
NSHAP

**CALVERT**, Harriet B.
**Child Psychotherapist**
Riemore
Bangors Road South
Iver, Bucks
SL0
☎ 01753 631021
harrietcalvert@compuserve
ACP

**CAPO-BIANCO**, Suzanne
**Integrative Psychotherapist**
Aberdeen House
46 Heronsgate Road
Chorleywood
WD3 5BB
☎ 01494 766 620
SPCRC

**CHAUNDY**, Jan
**Family & Systemic Psychotherapist**
♿ The Sue Nicholls Centre
Manor House, Bierton Road
Aylesbury
Bucks
HP20 1EG
☎ 01296 489 951
IFT

**CLOVER**, Gillian
**Psychosynthesis Psychotherapist**
51 Buckland Road
Near Aylesbury
Bucks
HP22 5LL
☎ 01296 630 626
gill@sophia99.fsnet.co.uk
IPS

**CROFT**, Janet
**Core Process Psychotherapist**
24 Long View
Berkhamsted
Hertfordshire
HP4 1BY
☎ 01442 872 822
KI

**DAMANI**, S
**Cognitive Behavioural Psychotherapist**
♿ Psychology Treatment Services
Campbell Centre, Hospital Campus
Standing Way, Eaglestone
Milton Keynes
MK6 5NG
BABCP

**DOBBIN**, Gloria
**Integrative Psychotherapist**
Wicklow Lodge
1 Boulters Lock
Giffard Park
Milton Keynes
MK14 5QR
☎ 01908 610 363
clover@dobbin552freeserve.co.uk
MC

**DOKTER**, Ditty
**Psychoanalytic Psychotherapist**
22 Trafalgar Avenue
Barleyhurst
Milton Keynes
MK3 7UL
☎ 01223 218 800
d.dokter@roehampton.ac.uk
FPC

**DOWNIE**, Andrew
**Group Analytic Psychotherapist**
21 Stacey Avenue
Wolverton
Milton Keynes
MK12 5DN
☎ 01296 770 301
☎ 01908 313 014
downie@ukonline.co.uk
HMP Grendon
Grendon Underwood
Bucks
HP18 0TL
UPCA

**DUNNE**, Paul
**Transpersonal Psychotherapist**
44 Woodlands Avenue
Berkhamsted
Herts
HP4 2JQ
☎ 01442 863 929
CTP

**EDGE**, Andrew
**Systemic Psychotherapist**
♿ 21 High St
Hanslope
MK19 7LQ
☎ 01908 510 723
andrew.edge@talk21.com
KCC

**EGAN**, Jude
**Systemic Psychotherapist**
33 North Road
Berkhamstead
Hertfordshire
HP4 3DU
☎ 01442 864 045
KCC

**FAITH**, Pat
**Hypno-Psychotherapist**
Butterfly Cottage
1 Huntsman Grove
Blakelands
Milton Keynes
MK14 5HS
☎ 01908 616 317
spirituality@btopenworld.com
NRHP

**FLANAGAN**, Eileen
**Psychoanalytic Psychotherapist**
56 Portfields Road
Newport Pagnall
MK16 8BU
☎ 01908 613 533
☎ 07710 411 765
FPC

**GOLLINS**, Joanna
**Transpersonal Psychotherapist**
Marsh Cottage
Bassetsbury Lane
High Wycombe
Bucks
HP11 1QZ
☎ 01494 529 418
CCPE

**GUNDRY**, Catherine
**Core Process Psychotherapist**
29 Drayton Road
Aylesbury
HP20 2EN
☎ 01296 334 832
KI

**GUSTAFSSON**, Birgitta
50A Lovel Road
Chalfont St Peter
Bucks
SL9 9NS
☎ 01753 880 664
gustafssonbirgitta@hotmail.com
AFT

**HAMILTON**, Jane
**Psychoanalytic Psychotherapist**
Low Farm
Hay Lane
Fulmer
Bucks
SL3 6HJ
WMIP

**HARBORNE**, Lynette
**Integrative Psychotherapist**
25 Elmdale Gardens
Princes Risborough
Bucks
HP27 0DL
☎ 01844 343 442
lynette@innpact.prestel.co.uk
MET

**HARDMAN**, Jacquie
**Psychoanalytic Psychotherapist**
Oak House
Botley Road
Chesham
Bucks
HP5 1XG
☎ 01494 783 402
jacquie_hardman@hotmail.com
FPC

**HARRIS**, Bob
**Group Analyst**
Norfolk House
Chesham
Bucks
☎ 01494 785 031
020 7431 7246
IGA

**HARRIS**, Jonathan
**Transpersonal Psychotherapist**
♿ 11 Gable Thorne
Milton Keynes
MK7 7RT
☎ 07000 Counsel
☎ 01908 282 427
CCPE

**HARRISON**, Susan
**Sexual and Relationship Psychotherapist**
Briar Patch
Little London Green
Oakley
Aylesbury
HP18 9QL
☎ 01844 238 313
susan.f.harrison@btconnect.com
BASRT

**HELEY**, Mary
**Integrative Psychotherapist**
♿ The Old Lamb
Potter Row
Great Missenden
HP16 9LT
☎ 01494 862860
mary.heley@ucl.ac.uk
MET

**HILL**, Finella
**Family & Systemic Psychotherapist**
♿ 10 Bowerdean Road
High Wycombe
Bucks
HP13 6AX
☎ 01494 471 739
☎ 020 8438 1770
IFT

**HOLLAND**, Ray
**Family & Systemic Psychotherapist**
10 Heath End Road
Great Kingshill
Nr High Wycombe
HP15 6HL
☎ 01494 714 624
rayholland67@hotmail.com
AFT

**HORNBY**, Jackie
**Integrative Psychotherapist**
11 Tripps Hill Close
Chalfont St Giles
HP8 4JZ
☎ 01494 871 698
jackie@liquidlife.freeserve.co.uk
SPCRC, SEA

**ISAACSON**, Hanna
**Family & Systemic Psychotherapist**
♿ New Horizons CMHT
Pursers Court
Elliman Ave
Slough
SL2 5BX
☎ 01753 690 950
hanna.isaacson@slough.gov.uk
AFT

**JENKINS**, Harry
**Psychosynthesis Psychotherapist**
28 Carter Walk
Penn
High Wycombe
Bucks
HP10 8ER
☎ 01494 814 164
harry@jenkinsh.clara.co.uk
IPS

**JOHNSTON**, Candace
**Sexual and Relationship Psychotherapist**
♿ Newport Pagnell Medical Centre
Queens Avenue
Newport Pagnell
MK16 8QT
☎ 01908 611 767
BASRT

**JORDAN**, Elizabeth
**Humanistic Psychotherapist**
Counselling Service
Bucks Chilterns University College
Queen Alexandra Road
High Wycombe
HP11 2JZ
☎ 01494 605 018
☎ 020 8998 5739
Elizabeth.jordan@bcuc.ac.uk
AHPP

**KANAKAM**, Jonathan
**Hypno-Psychotherapist**
50 Farnham Road
Slough
Berks
SL1 3TA
☎ 01753 552 976
NSHAP

**KAUR-LOVE**, Jasminder
**Psychoanalytic Psychotherapist**
Duncombe
Farmhouse
Barley End
Stocks Road, Aldbury, Her
HP23 5RZ
☎ 01763 838 510
jkl@jklove.com
NAFSI

**KEMPS**, Charmaine
**Family & Systemic Psychotherapist**
♿ Child & Adolescent Psychiatry
Eaglestone Health Centre
Standing Way, Eaglestone
Milton Keynes
MK6 5AZ
☎ 01908 607 501
AFT

**KENDALL**, Tricia
**Transpersonal Psychotherapist**
11 Rectory Road
Rickmansworth
WD3 1FH
☎ 01923 333 110
CCPE

**KNOWLES**, Valerie
**Psychoanalytic Psychotherapist**
19 Candlemas Lane
Beaconsfield
Bucks
HP9 1AF
☎ 01494 675 714
FPC

**KOWALSKI**, Reinhard
**Psychosynthesis Psychotherapist**
65 Eskdale Avenue
Chesham
Bucks
HP5 3AY
☎ 01494 785 761
reinhard@talk21.com
IPS

**LEON**, Barbara D.
**Psychoanalytic Psychotherapist**
10 Darlington Close
Amersham-on-the-Hill
Buckinghamshire
HP6 5AD
☎ 01494 729 903
FPC

**LEVITSKY**, Patricia D.
**Gestalt Psychotherapist**
Sportsman's Cottage
Beacon Hill
Penn
Bucks
HP10 8NJ
☎ 01494 812 219
jplevits@dial.pipex.com
GPTI

**LORENZ**, Bernice
**Autogenic Psychotherapist**
The Spinney
Magpie Lane
Coleshill
Amersham, Bucks
HP7 0LS
☎ 01494 722 618
bernicelorenz@hotmail.com
BAS

**MARSH**, Jane
**Attachment-based Psychoanalytic Psychotherapist**
The Barn
Princes Lane
Lee Common
Great Missenden, Bucks
HP16 9JW
☎ 01494 837 482
janemarsh@compuserve.com
CAPP

**MAY**, Suzanne
**Integrative Psychotherapist**
254 Littlebrook Avenue
Burnham
Slough
Berks
SL2 2PF
☎ 0870 787 5198
suz.may@virgin.net
SPCRC

**MCNAB**, Sue
**Family & Systemic Psychotherapist**
Dell House
Wash Hill
Wooburn Green
Bucks.
HP10 0JA
☎ 01628 526 275
sue@smcnab.fsnet.co.uk
AFT

**MORRIS**, Peter A.
**Cognitive Behavioural Psychotherapist**
Summers End
6 Park Road
Tring
Hertfordshire
HP23 6AT
☎ 01582 382 546
peter.morris@ntlworld.com
BABCP

**MOSCOSO DE RICHARDSON**, Gloria
**Existential Psychotherapist**
Tudor Lodge
The Pyghtle
Denham Village
UB9 5BD
☎ 01895 832 444
☎ 01895 831 697
gloriamoscoso@clara.co.uk
SEA

**NORMAN**, Gilllian
**Family & Systemic Psychotherapist**
The Rowans
Nairdwood Lane
Prestwood
HP16 0QQ
☎ 01494 868 280
gillnorman@onetel.net.uk
AFT

**NYE**, Ann
**Integrative Psychotherapist**
♿ Beech Cottage
Gorelands Lane
Chalfont St Giles
HP8 4HQ
☎ 01494 872 087
annmnye@aol.com
SPCRC

**O'SULLIVAN**, Sheila
**Body Psychotherapist, Integrative Psychotherapist**
12 Glenmore House
Brambleside
High Wycombe
Bucks
HP11 1JE
☎ 01494 459 517
Sheila.o'sullivan@virgin.net
CCBP

**ORME**, Patricia Joyce
**Personal Construct Psychotherapist**
49 Lowndes Avenue
Chesham
Bucks
HP5 2HH
☎ 01494 792 647
Pageormelowndes@tiscali.co.uk
PCP

**PANCHKOWRY**, Marion
**Group Analyst**
Psychotherapy Department
Tinoal Centre
Bierton Road
Alyesbury
HP20 1HU
☎ 01296 504 365
☎ 01525 240 083
IGA

**PAWSON**, Chris
**Biodynamic Psychotherapist**
10 Hunters Park
Berkhamstead
Herts
HP4 2PT
☎ 01442 862029
LSBP

**PHILPS**, Janet
**Child Psychotherapist**
Department of Child & Adolescent Psychiatry
Eaglestone Health Centre
Standing Way, Eaglestone
Milton Keynes
MK6 5NG
☎ 01908 607501
☎ 01234 881365
ACP

**POLLARD**, Cynthia
**Cognitive Analytic Therapist**
♿ Mill End
Mill Lane
Gerrards Cross
Bucks
SL9 8AZ
☎ 01753 885164
MILLEND@COMPUSERVE.COM
ACAT

**POOL**, Nicky
**Transpersonal Psychotherapist**
Purton House
Purton Lane
Farnham Royal
Bucks
SL2 3LY
☎ 01753 644 541
☎ 01494 485 952
NickyPool@aol.com
Penley Grange
Marlow Road
Stokenchurch
CTP

**REAY**, Ruth
**Family & Systemic Psychotherapist**
Greensleeves
Thorns Lane
Whiteleaf
HP27 0LT
☎ 01844 275 052
ruth@reay70.freeserve.co.uk
AFT

**REIDY**, Rachel
**Cognitive Analytic Therapist**
Woodbine Cottage
81 Totteridge Lane
High Wycombe
Bucks
HP13 7QA
☎ 01494 527 597
☎ 01494 512 903
Rhrcat1@aol.com
ACAT

**REYNOLDS**, Pat
**Group Analytic Psychotherapist**
Abbey Barn
Lavendon
Bucks
MK46 4HL
☎ 07770 952 999
☎ 01234 241 908
patreynolds@theabbeyloft.freeserve.co.u
k
UPCA

**ROBERTS**, Alison
**Systemic Psychotherapist**
Dormers
Buckland Village
Nr Aylesbury
HP22 5HY
☎ 01296 630 256
☎ 01628 667 881
robertsathome@yahoo.co.uk
KCC

**ROSSETER**, Bill
**Psychoanalytic Psychotherapist**
14 Lower Way
Great Brickhill
Milton Keynes
MK17 9AG
☎ 01525 261 839
☎ 01525 261 493
brosseter@aol.com
F P C

**ROY**, Jane
**Sexual and Relationship Psychotherapist**
♿ 10 Faraday Drive
Shenley Lodge
Milton Keynes
MK5 7DA
☎ 01908 674 118
☎ 07711 917 002
B A S R T

**SPENCER**, Jake
**Integrative Arts Psychotherapist**
4 Loakes House
Rutland Street
High Wycombe
HP11 2LL
☎ 01494 450 842
I A T E

**STEINER CELEBI**, Monika
**Psychoanalytic Psychotherapist**
Chalfont St Peter
Buckinghamshire
SL9 9SP
☎ 01753 882112
moni@ymte.co.uk
I P S S

**STRICKLAND**, Martin Decoury
**Integrative Psychotherapist**
Leafy Hollow
62 Dukes Wood Drive
Gerrards Cross
Bucks
SL9 7LF
☎ 01753 880 320
strickpsych@aol.com
M E T

**STRINGER**, Vivien
**Family & Systemic Psychotherapist**
♿ Child & Adolescent Psychiatric Service
Eaglestone Hospital
Standing Way
Milton Keynes
MK6 5AZ
☎ 01908 607 501
vivienstringer@aol.com
A F T

**VINCENT**, Christopher
**Psychoanalytic Psychotherapist, Couple Psychoanalytic Psychotherapist**
Wellington Cottage
18 Victoria Street
Slough
SL1 1PR
☎ 01753 774 558
☎ 01932 872 010
Christopher.Vincent@btinternet.com
S C P P

**WANLESS**, Anna
**Integrative Psychotherapist**
27 Seymour Road
Northchurch
Berkhamstead
Herts
HP4 3RQ
☎ 01442 864 708
☎ 02073 287 641
annawanless@hotmail.com
M C

**WANLESS**, Peter
**Integrative Psychotherapist**
27 Seymour Road
Northchurch
Berkhamstead
HP4 3RQ
☎ 01442 864 708
☎ 020 7328 7641
Peter.Wanless@ntlworld.com
M C

**WATKINS SEYMOUR**, Eileen
**Neurolinguistic Psychotherapist**
Ravenscroft
Ibstone
Bucks
HP14 3XY
☎ 01491 638 767
ravenscroft@easynet.co.uk
N L P t C A

**WICHENÉ**, Danièle
**Systemic Psychotherapist**
9 Capell Way
Chorleywood
WD3 5JA
K C C

**WILLIS**, Lynne
**Family & Systemic Psychotherapist**
♿ Amersham C&FCS
Amersham Health Centre
Chiltern Avenue
Amersham
HP6 5AY
☎ 01494 722 111
lynne.willis@bigfoot.com
A F T

**WORTH**, Piers
**Neurolinguistic Psychotherapist**
4 Hollow Rise
High Wycombe
Bucks.
HP13 5NU
☎ 01494 464 297
N L P t C A

**WRIGHT**, Susanna
**Analytical Psychologist-Jungian Analyst**
The Gables
HP17
☎ 01844 290 994
☎ 020 7435 8117
susanna@wright9899.fsnet.co.uk
C A P *

**YOUNG**, Diana
**Transpersonal Psychotherapist**
9 Hermitage
High Street
Great Missenden
HP16 0DA
☎ 01494 866 440
C C P E

**YOUNG**, Raymond
**Transpersonal Psychotherapist**
♿ The Royal Buckinghamshire Hospital
Buckingham Road
Aylesbury
Bucks
HP19 3AB
C C P E

**DE GROOT**, Marianne
**Sexual and Relationship Psychotherapist**
52 Longfield Drive
Amersham
HP6 5HE
☎ 01494 727 321
m.deGroot@btopenworld.com
B A S R T

## CAMBRIDGESHIRE

**ARRIENS**, Pamela
**Psychoanalytic Psychotherapist**
36 Alpha Terrace
Trumpington
Cambridge
CB2 2HT
☎ 01223 842 898
C S P

**ATKINSON**, Pamela
**Integrative Psychotherapist**
105 Coleridge Road
Cambridge
CB1 3PN
☎ 01223 520 578
pamela.atkinson@ntlworld.com
SPTI

**BACON**, Roger
**Psychoanalytic Psychotherapist**
Cambridge Psychotherapy Practice
26 Newnham Road
Cambridge
CB3 9EY
☎ 01223 369894
☎ 01223 560262
GUILD

**BATES**, Helen
**Family & Systemic Psychotherapist**
2 Ivy Court
Sleaford Street
Cambridge
CB1 2RX
☎ 01223 363 062
hrbates@aol.com
AFT

**BELL**, Mike
**Psychoanalytic Psychotherapist**
53 Narrow Lane
Histon
Cambridge
CB4 4HD
☎ 01223 513 531
CSP

**BRIANT**, Michael
**Psychoanalytic Psychotherapist**
Kingfisher Cottage
1 Church Rate Walk
Cambridge
CB3 9HJ
☎ 01223 332865
☎ 01223 464611
GUILD

**BRIANT**, Steve
**Psychoanalytic Psychotherapist**
57 Victoria Road
Cambridge
CB4 3BW
☎ 01223 327 165
CSP

**BROSAN**, Lee
**Cognitive Psychotherapist**
♿ Dept of Cognitive-Behaviour Therapy
Psychological Treatment Service
Box 190, Addenbrookes Hospital
Cambridge
CB2 2QQ
☎ 01223 217 960
BABCP

**BROWN**, Ulla
**Psychoanalytic Psychotherapist**
♿ 9 Stretton Avenue
Cambridge
CB4 3ES
☎ 01223 327 117
ulla.brown@virgin.net
CSP

**BYFORD**, Sally
**Biodynamic Psychotherapist**
♿ The Little Orchard
Long Lane
Linton
Cambs
CB1 6NS
☎ 01223 890779
☎ 01223 416166
The Cambridge Body Psychotherapy Centre
28 Ditton Walk
Cambridge
CB5 8QE
LSBP

**CAMERON**, Angela
**Integrative Psychotherapist**
The Old School House
Dullingham
Suffolk
CB8 9UJ
☎ 01638 507 884
angela.cameron@lineone.net
SPCRC

**CAMPBELL NYE**, Aileen
**Analytical Psychologist-Jungian Analyst, Analytical Psychotherapist (Jungian)**
6 Granham's Road
Great Shelford
Cambridge
CB2 5LQ
☎ 01223 844 218
IGAP, GAPS

**CARR**, Samantha
**Systemic Psychotherapist**
27 Meadow Way
Great Paxton
St Neots
Cambridgeshire
PE19 4RR
☎ 01480 211 001
KCC

**CHADWICK**, Mary
**Body Psychotherapist, Integrative Psychotherapist**
69 Eden Street
Cambridge
CB1 1EL
☎ 01223 322 819
mary.chadwick@ntlworld.com
CCBP

**CLARK**, Margaret
**Gestalt Psychotherapist**
8 Crauden Gardens
Ely
Cambridgeshire
CB7 4PR
☎ 01353 666 410
margic@waitrose.com
GPTI

**COCKETT**, Ann
**Psychoanalytic Psychotherapist**
Watermeadows
Kings Mill Lane
Great Shelford
Cambridge
CB2 5EN
☎ 01223 843 265
annted@ntlworld.com
CSP

**CORRIGALL**, Jenny
**Psychoanalytic Psychotherapist**
10 Willow Walk
Cambridge
CB1 1LA
☎ 01223 361 703
jenny.corrigall@usa.net
CSP

**COWELL**, Judy
**Body Psychotherapist, Integrative Psychotherapist**
11 Golding Road
Cambridge
CB1 3RN
☎ 01223 412 060
CCBP

**CUNLIFFE**, Rosemary Jean
**Family & Systemic Psychotherapist**
The Vicarage
6 Braggs Lane
Hemingford Grey
Cambs
PE28 9BW
☎ 01480 390 375
r.cunliffe@ukonline.co.uk
AFT

**D'ARCY**, Fiona
**Cognitive Behavioural Psychotherapist**
♿ Brookside Family Counsultation Clinic
18D Trumpington Road
Cambridge
CB2 2AH
☎ 01223 746 001
☎ 07900 520 999
psyandsw@ntlworld.com
BABCP

**DAMANI**, S
**Cognitive Behavioural Psychotherapist**
♿ 108-110 Burghley Road
Peterborough
PE1 2QE
BABCP

**DASGUPTA**, Carol
**Psychoanalytic Psychotherapist**
♿ 1 Dean Drive
Holbrook Road
Cambridge
CB1 4SW
☎ 01223 212 179
carol.dasgupta@econ.cam.ac.uk
CSP

**DAVIES**, Alison
**Psychoanalytic Psychotherapist**
♿ 27 Priory Road
Cambridge
CB5 8HT
☎ 01522 512 000
abdavies@hotmail.com
PA

**DAVIES**, Judy
**Psychoanalytic Psychotherapist**
87 Alpha Road
Cambridge
CB4 3DQ
☎ 01223 355 543
judy@jad.uklinux.net
71 Bridge Street
Cambridge
CB2 1UR
CSP

**DAVY**, Dr John
**Family & Systemic Psychotherapist**
♿ Brookside Family Consultation Service
Douglas House
18d Trumpington Road
Cambridge
CB2 2AH
☎ 01223 746 001
John.davy@dial.pipex.com
IFT

**DELL**, Jacqueline
**Humanistic Psychotherapist**
White Lodge
1 Comberton Road
Harlton
Cambs.
CB3 7EU
☎ 01223 262281
jacquelinedell@hotmail.com
AHPP

**DENMAN**, Chess
**Cognitive Analytic Therapist**
Dept of Psychological Treatments
Box 190
Addenbrookes Hospital
Hills Road, Cambridge
CB2 2QQ
☎ 01223 217 958
Chess.Denman@ntlworld.com
14 Cranmer Road
Cambridge
CB3 9BL
ACAT

**DYSON**, Margaret
**Integrative Psychotherapist**
4 Kimberley Road
Cambridge
CB4 1HH
☎ 01223 367311
m_dyson@ntlworld.com
MC

**ELIA**, Dr Irene
**Cognitive Analytic Therapist**
80 Highsett Hills Road
Cambridge
CB2 1NZ
☎ 01223 561 781
☎ 02380 220 034
me14@cam.ac.uk
ACAT

**FARRELL**, Margaret
**Psychoanalytic Psychotherapist**
The Old Stores
5 High Street
Grantchester
Cambridge
CB3 9NF
☎ 01223 369 894
marga.farrell@dial.pipex.com
CSP, GUILD

**FITZGERALD-KLEIN**, Marianne
**Transpersonal Psychotherapist**
178 Green End Road
Cambridge
CB4 1RN
☎ 01223 438 181
mariannefk@hotmail.com
CCPE

**FLANAGAN**, Diana
**Psychodynamic Psychotherapist**
16 Crawthorne Road
PETERBOROUGH
PE1 4AB
☎ 01733 563 060
☎ 01780 410 177
VAPP

**FLEMING**, Nicola G.
**Cognitive Behavioural Psychotherapist**
University of Cambridge Counselling
16-17 Trumpington Street
Cambridge
CB2 1QA
☎ 01223 332 865
reception@counselling.cam.uk
BABCP

**GARDINER**, Vicki
**Analytical Psychologist-Jungian Analyst**
35 Walcot Walk
Netherton
Peterborough
PE3 9QF
☎ 01733 266213
gardipysch@aol.com
CAP *

**GELSTHORPE**, Loraine
**Psychoanalytic Psychotherapist**
Pembroke College
Trumpington Street
Cambridge
CB2 1RF
☎ 01223 338 148
☎ 01233 314 684
ing10@cam.ac.uk
CSP

**GENTRY**, Valerie
**Psychoanalytic Psychotherapist**
30 Hinton Avenue
Cambridge
CB1 7AS
☎ 01223 212 821
CSP

**GOBBATO**, Wendy
**Gestalt Psychotherapist**
26 Barkston Drive
Peterborough
PE1 4LA
☎ 01733 569 609
☎ 01733 558 781
wendytg@hotmail.com
SPTI

**GOLD**, Bev
**Psychoanalytic Psychotherapist**
1 Damms Pastures
Caldecote
Cambridge
CB3 7ZA
☎ 07941760 463
GUILD

**GOODRICK**, Jean
**Psychoanalytic Psychotherapist**
155 Stanley Road
Cambridge
CB5 8LF
☎ 01223 513 480
jean.goodrick@btopenworld.com
CSP

**GORDON**, Leila
**Psychoanalytic Psychotherapist**
37 Herbert Street
Cambridge
CB4 1AQ
☏ 01223 367 912
leila.gordon@ntlworld.com
CSP

**GREAVES**, Sarah
**Psychoanalyst**
♿ 33 Eltisley Avenue
Newnham
Cambridge
CB3 9JQ
☏ 01223 354 526
sarah.greaves@virgin.net
CSP, GUILD

**GREENLAND**, Sue
**Group Analyst**
Myrtleberry Cottage
27a Pierce Lane
Fulbourn
Cambridge
CB1 5DJ
☏ 01223 880 287
sue.greenland@btinternet.com
IGA

**GUEST**, Hazel
**Humanistic Psychotherapist, Transpersonal Psychotherapist**
44 Beaufort Place
Thompson's Lane
Cambridge
CB5 8AG
☏ 01223 369 148
CTP

**GUILD**, Liz
**Psychoanalytic Psychotherapist**
♿ 198 Sturton Street
Cambridge
CB1 2QF
☏ 01223 339 166
☏ 01223 311 042
emg23@cam.ac.uk
SITE

**HALL**, David
**Psychoanalytic Psychotherapist**
47 Cavendish Avenue
Cambridge
CB1 7UR
☏ 01223 249 732
GUILD

**HARDY**, Liz
**Psychoanalytic Psychotherapist**
Cambridge
CB1
PA

**HARGRAVE**, Annie
**Psychoanalytic Psychotherapist**
192 Peverel Road
Cambridge
CB5 8RL
☏ 020 790 2900
annieh@interhealth.org.uk
CSP

**HARRILD**, Sandra M.
**Cognitive Psychotherapist**
♿ P.o. Box 190
Addenbrookes NHS Trust
Hills Road
Cambridge
CB2 2QQ
☏ 01223 217 960
BABCP

**HARRISON**, Gillian
**Family & Systemic Psychotherapist**
21 Millington Road
Cambridge
CB3 9HW
☏ 01223 357 778
☏ 01860 415 300
IFT

**HARRISON**, Jacqueline
**Psychoanalytic Psychotherapist**
Riverview
21 Back Lane
Ely
CB7 4AR
☏ 020 8541 1297
☏ 020 8974 6862
harrison.j@btopenworld.com
GUILD

**HARTLEY**, Althea
**Systemic Psychotherapist**
1 Newbold Close
Oundle
Peterborough
PE8 4QS
☏ 01733 875 954
Child & Adolescent Mental Health Services
The Cedars
16 Aldermans Drive
Peterborough
PE8
KCC

**HARVEY**, Paul
**Personal Construct Psychotherapist**
112 Lynn Road
Ely
Cambridge
CB6 1DE
☏ 07071 880 870
paulharvey@iname.com
PCP

**HARWARD**, Matthew
**Psychoanalytic Psychotherapist**
Studio 4
37 City Road
Cambridge
CB1 1DP
☏ 01223 720863
☏ 07808 612 777
matthew.harward@ntlworld.com
ARBS

**HAYNES**, Eric
**Hypno-Psychotherapist**
33A Brideswell Road
Cherry Hinton
Cambridge
CB1 9EN
☏ 01223 214 281
eric@haynes810.freeserve.co.uk
NSHAP

**HEATH**, Christine
**Child Psychotherapist, Family & Systemic Psychotherapist**
♿ 6 Baldwins Close
Bourne
Cambridge
CB3 7TH
☏ 01582 708140
☏ 01462 700021
ACP

**HILBER**, Charlotte
**Family & Systemic Psychotherapist**
♿ Cambridge University Counselling Service
13/14 Trumpington Street
Cambridge
CB2 1QA
☏ 01223 741 777
ch291@cam.ac.uk
AFT

**HIVERNEL**, Dr Francoise
**Psychoanalytic Psychotherapist**
40 High Street
Girton
CB3 0PU
☏ 01223 276 738
fh101@btclick.com
WMIP

**HOLLAND**, Louise
**Child Psychotherapist**
21 Richmond Road
Cambridge
CB4 3PP
☏ 01223 353029
ACP

**HOLLIDAY**, Carol
**Integrative Arts Psychotherapist**
55 Sturton Street
Cambridge
CB1 2QG
☏ 01223 511 183
☏ 07813 157 006
holliday_carol@hotmail.com
IATE

**HUGHES**, Ann
**Psychoanalytic Psychotherapist**
College Counselling Service
Emmanuel College
Cambridge
CB2 3AP
☏ 01394 380 100
☏ 01986 788 170
ah300@cam.co.uk
GUILD

**HUTCHISON**, Eric
**Analytical Psychologist-Jungian Analyst**
♿ 77 Long Road
Cambridge
CB2 2HE
☏ 01223 840 381
CAP *

**JOHANNSSON**, Cessie
**Family & Systemic Psychotherapist**
33 Oxford Road
Cambridge
CB4 3PH
☏ 01223 561 338
cessie.cole@virgin.net
AFT

**KILGOUR**, Mimi
**Neurolinguistic Psychotherapist**
332 Eastfield Road
Peterborough
Cambridgeshire
PE1 4RA
☏ 01733 312 900
NLPtCA

**KING**, Lucy
**Psychoanalytic Psychotherapist**
34 Chruch Street
Fen Ditton
CB5 8SU
☏ 01223 292 663
lucyking@onetel.net.uk
CSP, PA

**KINSEY**, Bruce
**Psychoanalytic Psychotherapist**
33 Montague Road
Cambridge
CB4 1BU
☏ 01223 301 080
bhk1@cam.ac.uk
CSP

**KLUG**, Liebe
**Psychoanalytic Psychotherapist**
70 Cavendish Avenue
Cambridge
CB1 4UT
☏ 01223 248 959
liebeklug@hotmail.com
CSP

**LEGGATT**, Jenny
**Analytical Psychotherapist**
158 Gwydir Street
Cambridge
CB1 2LW
☏ 01223 369 977
jennyleggatt@btopenworld.com
FIP

**LEW**, Clara
**Psychoanalytic Psychotherapist**
20 Owlstone Road
Cambridge
CB3 9JH
clew20@aol.com
CSP

**LEWINGTON**, Paul
**Family & Systemic Psychotherapist**
♿ 18d Trumpington Road
Cambridge
CB2 2AH
☏ 01223 746 001
IFT

**LINTOTT**, Bill
**Group Analyst**
Cambridge Psychotherapy Practice
26 Newman Road
Cambridge
CB3 9EY
☏ 01223 369 894
IGA

**MCDOUALL**, Veronica
**Psychoanalytic Psychotherapist**
119 Thornton Road
Cambridge
CB3 0NE
☏ 01223 313 515
veronica@mcdouall.co.uk
FPC

**MILLER**, Dr Michael
**Psychoanalytic Psychotherapist**
11 Bishops Road
Trumpington
Cambridge
CB2 2NQ
☏ 01223 217 960
☏ 01223 845 030
mmiller@cix.compulink.co.uk
Psychological Treatment Service
Addenbrookes Hospital
Box 190
Cambridge
CB2 2QQ
GUILD

**MILLS-POWELL**, Dana Sedgwick
**Systemic Psychotherapist**
The Rectory
Church Lane
Linton
Cambridge
CB1 6JX
☏ 07950 020 076
danamillspowell@aol.com
KCC

**MINNAAR**, Doris
**Psychoanalytic Psychotherapist**
4 Millington Road
Cambridge
CB3 9HP
☏ 01223 357 895
dormin2002@aol.com
CSP

**MORGAN**, Sian
**Psychoanalytic Psychotherapist**
The Cambridge Psychotherapy Practice
26 Newnham Road
Cambridge
CB3 9EY
☏ 01223 369 894
☏ 01638 741 390
mgrn222@hotmail.com
12 Lower End
Swaffham Prior
Cambridge
CB5 0HT
CSP, GUILD

**MORGAN**, Walter
**Psychoanalytic Psychotherapist**
12 Lower End
Swaffham
Prior
CB5 0HT
☏ 01638 741 390
mrgn22@hotmail.com
CSP

**MURDIN**, Lesley
**Psychoanalytic Psychotherapist**
32 Belvoir Road
Cambridge
Cambs
CB4 1JJ
☏ 020 7361 4853
☏ 01223 312 848
murdin@compuserve.com
FPC, SITE

**MURPHY**, Enda Patrick
**Systemic Psychotherapist**
♿ Douglas House
Adolescent Unit
Ida Darwin Fulbourn
Cambridge
CB1 5EE
☏ 01223 885 850
enda.murphy@cambsmh.nhs.uk
KCC

**PAIN**, Jean
**Hypno-Psychotherapist, Neurolinguistic Psychotherapist**
7 Way Lane
Waterbeach
Cambridgeshire
CB5 9NQ
☎ 01223 860 356
NLPtCA, NRHP

**PALMER**, Ben
**Systemic Psychotherapist**
The Cogwheel Trust, The Maltings
41 The High Street
Chesterton
Cambridge
CB4 1NQ
☎ 01223 464 385
cwt@btclick.com
KCC

**PARKINSON**, Dorn
**Psychoanalytic Psychotherapist**
Archway House
Town Street
Upwell
Wisbech
PE14 9AD
☎ 01945 773 941
The Health Centre
Townley Close
Upwell
Wisbech
PE14 9BT
CSP

**PEGLAR**, Graham
**Psychodynamic Psychotherapist**
26 Malta Road
Cambridge
CB1 3PZ
☎ 01223 242 029
☎ 01223 411 514
VAPP

**PEPPER**, Marie
**Psychoanalytic Psychotherapist**
1 Barrow Road
Cambridge
CB2 2AP
☎ 01223 352 800
CSP

**POLLARD**, James
**Attachment-based Psychoanalytic Psychotherapist**
♿ 60 Montague Road
Cambridge
CB4 1BX
☎ 01223 514 917
james@pollardj.fsnet.co.uk
CAPP

**PROCTER**, Sue
**Body Psychotherapist, Integrative Psychotherapist**
The Coach House
3 Queen Edith's Way
Cambridge
CB1 7PH
☎ 01223 413 098
cambs.sue@virgin.net
CCBP

**RAISBECK**, Linde
**Humanistic and Integrative Psychotherapist**
♿ 10 Leys Avenue
Cambridge
CB4 2AW
☎ 01223 352 811
linde@raisbeck.org
AHPP

**RANDALL**, Rosemary
**Psychoanalytic Psychotherapist**
113 Gwydir Street
Cambridge
CB1 2LG
☎ 01223 313 539
rer28@cam.ac.uk
CSP

**REYNOLDS**, Alun
**Body Psychotherapist, Gestalt Psychotherapist, Humanistic Psychotherapist**
12 Orchard Avenue
Cambridge
CB4 2AH
☎ 01223 461 744
alun@alunreynolds.co.uk
AHPP, CCBP

**ROBINSON**, Carole
**Psychoanalytic Psychotherapist**
♿ University of Cambridge Counselling Service
14 Trumpington Street
Cambridge
CB2 1QA
☎ 01223 332 865
CSP

**ROWE**, Frances
**Psychodynamic Psychotherapist**
The Old Rectory
2 Greatford Road
Liffington
Stamford
PE9 4SW
☎ 01780 785 103
☎ 01780 753 087
VAPP

**SERPELL**, Vivienne
**Sexual and Relationship Psychotherapist**
♿ Scotts
High Street
Whittlesford
Cambridge
CB2 4LT
☎ 01223 833 218
vivienne@serpell.com
BASRT

**SHIELDS**, Jill
**Psychoanalytic Psychotherapist**
36 Lyndewode Road
Cambridge
CB1 2HN
☎ 01223 359 246
jill.h.shields@ukgateway.net
CSP

**SIMMS**, Mandy
**Systemic Psychotherapist**
♿ 15 North Cottages
Trumpington Road
Cambridge
CB2 2EZ
☎ 01223 844 536
mandyj.franklin@virgin.net
IFT

**SINCLAIR**, Alison
**Psychoanalytic Psychotherapist**
99 Windsor Road
Cambridge
CB4 3JL
☎ 01223 369894
☎ 01223 565985
as49@cam.ac.uk
GUILD

**SINCLAIR**, Fiona
**Contemporary Psychoanalyst**
♿ 9 Emmanuel Road
Cambridge
CB1 1JW
☎ 01223 364 834
Fiona.Sinclair@lineone.net
SITE

**STAUFFER**, Kathrin
**Body Psychotherapist, Integrative Psychotherapist**
42 Catharine Street
Cambridge
CB1 3AW
☎ 01223 240 815
kathrin@ahbmt.org
CCBP

**STYLES**, Heather
**Gestalt Psychotherapist**
109 Vinery Road
Cambridge
CB1 3DW
☎ 01223 414 595
GCL

**TATE**, Patricia
**Psychoanalytic Psychotherapist**
♿ 109 Grantchester Meadows
Newnham
Cambridge
CB3 9JN
☎ 01223 357 905
pat34@cam.ac.uk
CSP

**TAUSSIG**, Hanna
**Psychoanalytic Psychotherapist**
296 Hills Road
Cambridge
CB2 2QG
☎ 01223 246643
☎ 01223 246643
hannataussig@hotmail.com
GUILD

**TODD**, Gillian
**Cognitive Behavioural Psychotherapist**
The University of Cambridge
Dept of Psychiatry, Douglas House
18b Trumpigton Road
Cambridge
CB2 2AH
☎ 01799 530 553
☎ 01223 746 045
gt235@cam.ac.uk
BABCP

**TOWNSEND**, Heather
**Psychoanalytic Psychotherapist**
♿ 12 Gwydir Road
Cambridge
CB1 2LL
☎ 01223 700 231
heather.townstead@ntlworld.com
SITE

**TREGEAR**, Barbara
**Psychodrama Psychotherapist**
79 Gough Way
Cambridge
CB3 9LN
☎ 01223 365 963
☎ 01223 357 221
barbara@tregearr.freeserve.co.uk
BPA

**URQUHART**, Isabel
**Psychoanalytic Psychotherapist**
26 Newnham Road
Cambridge
CB3 9EY
☎ 01223 369 894
☎ 01279 441 337
isobelurquhart@compuserve.com
CSP

**VOIKHANSKAYA**, Marina
**Psychoanalyst, Psychoanalytic Psychotherapist**
20 Garden Walk
Cambridge
CB4 3EN
☎ 01223 369 894
☎ 01223 367 747
Cambridge Psychotherapy Practice
26 Newham Road
Cambridge
CB3 9EY
GUILD, SITE

**WARWICK**, Heather
**Sexual and Relationship Psychotherapist**
♿ 31 Sedley Taylor Road
Cambridge
CB2 2PN
☎ 01223 245 380
warwick@uvitec.demon.co.uk
BASRT

**WATERSTON**, John
**Humanistic Psychotherapist, Integrative Psychotherapist**
22 Waverly Park
Orchard Road
Great Shelford
Cambridge
CB2 5BA
☎ 01223 843 894
john@johnwaterston.co.uk
AHPP, CCBP

**WATSON**, Sandra
**Gestalt Psychotherapist**
3 Tudor Place
London Road
Yaxley
Peterborough
PE7 3HU
☎ 01733 241 578
sandraewatson@aol.com
SPTI

**WESTLAND**, Gill
**Body Psychotherapist, Humanistic Psychotherapist**
8 Wetenhall Road
Cambridge
CB1 3AG
☎ 01223 214 658
☎ 01223 416 416
gillwestland@cbpc.org.uk
Cambridge Body Psychotherapy Centre
28 Ditton Walk
Cambridge
Cambs.
CB5 8QE
AHPP, CCBP

**WHITTLE**, Lorna
**Psychoanalytic Psychotherapist**
28 Missleton Court
Cambridge
CB1 8BL
☎ 01223 213969
ARBS

**WILDE**, Deborah
**Psychoanalytic Psychotherapist**
45 Riverside
Cambridge
CB5 8HN
☎ 01223 562 519
deborah.wilde@ntlworld.com
CSP

**WOOLLISCROFT**, Jenny
**Gestalt Psychotherapist, Humanistic Psychotherapist**
80 Andrew Road
Eynesbury
St. Neots
Huntingdon
PE19 2PP
☎ 01480 470 804
AHPP

## CHESHIRE

**ACKROYD**, Rosemary
**Sexual and Relationship Psychotherapist**
Marple Bridge
Stockport
SK6
☎ 0161 427 1568
BASRT

**ALDERTON**, Chris
**Cognitive Behavioural Psychotherapist**
70 Tarvin Road
Littleton
Chester
CH3 7DF
☎ 01244 355 417
BABCP

**ASHCROFT**, Jennifer
**Cognitive Behavioural Psychotherapist**
♿ The Chester Clinic
68 Heath Road
Upton
CHESTER
CH2 1HX
☎ 01244 390 411
BABCP

**BARSKY**, Sue
**Gestalt Psychotherapist**
2 Selkirk Drive
Curzon Park
Chester
CH4 8AQ
☎ 01244 683 321
barskyreid@aol.com
SPTI

**BERMAN**, Linda
**Psychoanalytic Psychotherapist**
The Moorings
Mereside Road
Mere
Knutsford
WA16 6QR
☎ 01565 830 874
linda.berman@talk21.com
NWIDP

**BERMAN**, Paul
**Group Analyst**
☎ 01565 830 075
paul.berman@talk21.com
IGA

**BIRD**, John
**Psychoanalytic Psychotherapist**
17 Macclesfield Road
Wilmslow
Cheshire
SK9 2AA
☎ 0161 445 2099
☎ 0162 552 3292
johnb458@aol.com
NWIDP

**BURROWS-WOOD**, Joanna
**Family & Systemic Psychotherapist**
3 Mount Pleasant
Rainow
Macclesfield
SK10 5TJ
☎ 01625 434 352
AFT

**BUTCHER**, Josie
**Sexual and Relationship Psychotherapist**
♿ Nantwich Health Centre
Beam Street
Nantwich
Cheshire
CW5 5NX
☎ 01270 610 181
☎ 01270 506 700
Eaton House
Eaton Street
Crewe
CW2 7EG
BASRT

**CLARKE**, Elaine
**Psychoanalytic Psychotherapist**
8 Windmill Lane
Preston-on-the-Hill
Warrington
Cheshire
WA4 4AZ
☎ 01928 713 811
LPDO

**COLBOURNE**, Graham
**Gestalt Psychotherapist**
♿ 11 Granby Road
Walton
Warrington
WA4 6PH
☎ 01925 861 924
☎ 07769 646 807
graham@colbourne.org
GPTI

**COLLINS**, Gloria
**Psychoanalytic Psychotherapist**
7 Victoria Road
Runcorn
Cheshire
WA7 5BH
☎ 01928 561453
LPDO

**COOPER**, Graham
**Psychoanalytic Psychotherapist**
♿ Denton House
Denton Drive
Northwich
Cheshire
CW9 7LU
☎ 01606 353 800
LPDO

**CROCKER**, Allen John
**Family & Systemic Psychotherapist**
♿ The Elms Child Mental Health
50 Crowley Hill Lane
St Helens
WA1 2AW
☎ 01744 454 368
allen.crocker@sthkhealth.nhs.uk
AFT

**DAVIES**, Joyce
**Psychoanalytic Psychotherapist**
♿ Webb House Therapeutic Community
Webb House
Victoria Avenue
Crewe
CW2 7SQ
☎ 01270 614 408
jdavies@webbhouse.bstmhp.nhs.uk
NWIDP

**DOSSETT**, Rosmary
**Hypno-Psychotherapist**
The Cross Clinic
20 The Cross
Lymm
Cheshire
WA13 0HU
☎ 01925 757 513
NRHP

**ELSON**, Monica
**Cognitive Behavioural Psychotherapist**
44 St Peters Way
Mickle Trafford
Chester
CH2 4EJ
☎ 01244 301 485
cmelson@btopenworld.com
BABCP

**GELDEARD**, Bryan W.J.
**Psychoanalytic Psychotherapist**
♿ The Brooker Centre
Psychology Dept
Halton General Hospital
Runcorn
WA7 2DA
LPDO

**GIBSON**, Mike
**Family & Systemic Psychotherapist**
19 Buckingham Road
Wilmslow
SK9 5JU
☎ 01625 522 321
gibson123@onetel.net.uk
AFT

**GILL**, Jennifer
**Cognitive Behavioural Psychotherapist**
4 Curzon Park North
Chester
Cheshire
CH4 8AR
☎ 01244 671 855
☎ 07718 316 417
jennifer.gill1@virgin.net
BABCP

**GOEPFERT**, Michael
**Group Analyst, Psychoanalytic Psychotherapist**
♿ Webb House DTC
Victoria Avenue
Crewe
Cheshire
CW2 7SQ
☎ 01270 614400
mjg@liv.ac.uk
IGA, LPDO

**HANDLEY**, Christine
**Cognitive Behavioural Psychotherapist**
Manor Farm
White Lane
Christleton
Chester
CH3 6AH
☎ 01244 330 008
christine.handley@btopenworld.com
BABCP

**HARDING-DAVIES**, Valerie
**Transpersonal Psychotherapist**
57 Wellington Road
Nantwich
Cheshire
CW5 7DA
☎ 01270 625 487
CTP

**HARTLEY**, Phil
**Group Analyst**
Webb House
Victoria Avenue
Crewe
CW2 7SQ
☎ 01270 614 408
IGA

**HAWORTH**, Ann
**Psychoanalytic Psychotherapist**
♿ 1 Gifford Mount
East Downs Road
Altrincham
Cheshire
WA14 2LG
☎ 0161 928 7101
bob-annhaworth@hotmail.com
NWIDP

**HELLIN**, Katherine
**Psychoanalytic Psychotherapist**
♿ Webb House
Therapeutic Community Service
Victoria Avenue
Crewe
CW2 7SQ
☎ 07880 501 256
NWIDP

**HOBBES**, Robin
**Transactional Analysis Psychotherapist**
2 Woodleigh
Bradgate Road
Altricham
WA15 4QU
☎ 01619 289 997
admin@elantraining.org
ITA

**HOLLAND**, Anthony R
**Sexual and Relationship Psychotherapist**
Roewood House
351 Hungerford Road
Crewe
CW1 5EZ
☎ 01270 583 554
☎ 01270 506 706
t_holland55@hotmail.com
Eaton House Resource Centre
Eaton Street
Crewe
CW2 7EG
BASRT

**HOLYOAK**, Patricia
**Cognitive Behavioural Psychotherapist**
8 Wicker Lane
Guilden Sutton
Chester
CH3 7EL
☎ 01244 300 513
holyoak@cwcom.net
BABCP

**HORROCKS**, Pam
**Psychodynamic Psychotherapist**
36 Station Road
Alsager
Stoke on Trent
ST7 2PD
☎ 01270 877 284
Pam.horrocks@btopenworld.com
VAPP

**HUNT**, Patricia
**Psychoanalytic Psychotherapist**
Rose Cottage
Foxwist Green
Whitegate, nr. Northwich
CW8 2BJ
☎ 01606 882170
NWIDP

**HYDE**, Keith
**Group Analyst, Psychodynamic Psychotherapist**
♿ Webb House Therapeutic Community
Webb House, Victoria Avenue
Crewe
Cheshire
CW2 7SQ
☎ 01270 614 400
keith47hyde@supanet.com
IGA, NWIDP

**JONES**, Janet
**Psychoanalytic Psychotherapist**
The Anchorite Cell
The Groves
Chester
Cheshire
CH1 1SD
☎ 01244 401 564
alpha.centre@zetnet.co.uk
FPC

**KAY**, Malcolm
**Psychodrama Psychotherapist**
♿ Halton Psychotherapy & Family Service
Thorn Road Clinic
Runcorn
Cheshire
WA7 5HQ
☎ 01606 75321
☎ 01928 575 073
BPA

**LAWRENCE**, Elisabeth
**Sexual and Relationship Psychotherapist**
Hay Barn
Ferry Lane
Thelwall
Cheshire
WA4 2SS
☎ 01925 861 862
ellaw@supanet.com
BASRT

**LAWTON**, Jane
**Transpersonal Psychotherapist**
Northwich
Cheshire
CW8
☎ 01606 882535
CCPE

**LE'SURF**, Anne
**Humanistic Psychotherapist**
Newton Cottage
Mile Bank
Whitchurch
Shropshire
SY13 4JY
☎ 01948 664 762
☎ 01948 352 717
AHPP

**LEE**, Denis
**Family & Systemic Psychotherapist**
♿ CAMHS Alderly Building
Macclesfield DGH
Victoria Road
Macclesfield
SK10 3BL
☎ 01625 663 772
densle@hotmail.com
AFT

**LEWIS**, Ken
**Cognitive Behavioural Psychotherapist**
♿ 7 Brown Heath Road
Waverton
Chester
CH3 7PP
☎ 01244 336 744
kenlewis@surfaid.org
BABCP

**LILLEY**, Diana
**Group Analyst**
Working with Conflict
P.O. Box 323
Altrincham
WA14 6YF
☎ 07813 085 953
diana.lilley@workingwithconflict.co.uk
IGA

**MAHON**, David
**Hypno-Psychotherapist**
7 Grammar School Road
Warrington
Cheshire
WA4 1JN
☎ 01925 635 662
tumble-trust@yahoo.co.uk
NRHP

**MARSHALL**, Lindsey
**Cognitive Behavioural Psychotherapist**
The Cottage
Corks Lane
Disley
Stockport
SK12 2DA
☎ 01663 766 950
pete.linz@btinternet.com
BABCP

**MCCORMICK**, Helen
**Psychoanalytic Psychotherapist**
13 Lyceum Way
Coppenhall
Crewe
Cheshire
CW1 3YF
☎ 01270 256397
WMIP

**MCINTEE**, Jeannie
**Psychoanalytic Psychotherapist**
Chester Therapy Centre
20 Walpole Street
Chester
CH1 4HG
☎ 01244 390 121
LPDO

**MCKAY**, Molly
**Cognitive Behavioural Psychotherapist**
♿ Dept. of Psychological Therapies
5 Boroughs Partnership Trust
Garven Place Clinic
Sankey St., Warrington
WA1 1RH
☎ 01925 653 295
☎ 01925 655 052 x3838
molly.mckay1@ntlworld.com
BABCP

**MCLOUGHLIN**, Una
**Group Analyst**
The Priory Hospital Altrincham
Rappox Road
Hale
Altrincham
WA15 ONX
unamcloughlin@prioryhealthcare.com
IGA

**MOORE**, Carol
**Cognitive Behavioural Psychotherapist**
Chester
CH2
☎ 01244 380 964
☎ 07710 222 413
carol.moore@lineone.net
BABCP

**NEILL**, Denis E.
**Family & Systemic Psychotherapist**
17 Sunnybank
Holly Road South
Wilmslow
Cheshire
SK9 1ND
☎ 01625 539 707
dennis.neill@btinternet.com
AFT

**NEVIN**, Jacqui
**Psychoanalytic Psychotherapist**
♿ Denton House CMHU
Denton Drive
Northwich
Cheshire
CW9 7LU
☎ 01606 353 809
LPDO

**NOWELL**, Valerie
**Gestalt Psychotherapist**
Old Shop Cottage
Swanley Lane
Nantwich
Cheshire
CW5 8QB
☎ 01270 524 455
GPTI

**OATES**, Stephanie
**Transactional Analysis Psychotherapist**
♿ Swallowfield
Slade Lane
Mobberley
WA16 7QN
☎ 01565 873 059
Hilltop Centre
Hale, Altrincham
Cheshire
WA15 9SZ
ITA

**OGLEY**, Julia
**Systemic Psychotherapist**
Broomwood Primary School
Mainwood Road
Timperley
WA15 7JU
☎ 0161 440 9296
☎ 0161 980 4968 or 0161 941 4011
KCC

**POLLET**, Sheena
**Psychoanalytic Psychotherapist**
Cherry Tree Farm
Bushells Lane
Kingswood
Frodsham
WA6 6HX
☎ 01928 740 973
☎ 01928 575 073
Thorn Road Clinic
Thorn Road
Runcorn
WA7 5HQ
LPDO

**POLLITT**, Mo
**Cognitive Behavioural Psychotherapist**
Lane End
1 Lache Lane
Chester
CH4 7LP
☎ 01244 681 130
☎ 07713 159 018
pollitmo@hotmail.com
BABCP

**PRICE JONES**, Daniel
**Behavioural Psychotherapist**
♿ 102 Sandy Lane
Lymm
WA13 9HR
☎ 01695 626 181
☎ 01925 752 768
daniel.jones@wiganlhs-tr.nwest.nhs.uk
BABCP

**PRINCE**, Tania
**Hypno-Psychotherapist**
20 Cumberland Street
Macclesfield
Cheshire
SK10 1DD
☎ 01625 520 016
☎ 01625 850 555
tania@nlp-hypnotherapy.com
NRHP

**READING**, Clive
**Cognitive Behavioural Psychotherapist**
♿ 5 Moorlands Close
Macclesfield
SK10 2TL
☎ 0161 419 5755
BABCP

**REDGRAVE**, Kenneth
**Hypno-Psychotherapist**
11 Parker Avenue
Hartford
Northwich
Cheshire
CW8 3AH
☎ 01606 74874
kenredgrave@welcare.fsnet.co.uk
CTIS

**ROSS**, Gill
**Cognitive Behavioural Psychotherapist**
♿ Nirvana
The Green
Higher Kinnerton
Chester
CH4 9BZ
☎ 01244 822 244
gill.ross@virgin.net
BABCP

**SHAH**, E.M.
**Cognitive Behavioural Psychotherapist**
♿ Plattbridge Farm
Platt Lane
Penyffordd
Nr Chester
CH4 0HX
☎ 01978 760 567
maryshah@hotmail.com
BABCP

**SHARPLES**, Geraldine M
**Psychoanalytic Psychotherapist**
9 Grove Court
West Hyde
LYMM
Cheshire
WA13 0HA
☎ 01925 751 589
☎ 0151 430 1321
geraldine-sharples@btopenworld.com
LPDO

**SMITHERS**, Martyn
**Group Analyst**
Department of Psychological Therapies
Garden Place Clinic
Sankey Street
Warrington
WA1 1RH
☎ 01925 655 052
martyn.smithers@5boroughspartnership.nhs.uk
IGA

**STRAWSON**, Anne
**Integrative Psychotherapist**
West Barn
Church House Farm
Austerson
Nantwich
CW5 8AB
☎ 01270 627 105
anne.strawson@virgin.net
SPTI

**TAYLOR**, Margaret
**Family & Systemic Psychotherapist**
10 Holly Grove
Tabley
Cheshire
WA16 0HR
☎ 01565 653041
margarettaylor@meighan.fsnet.co.uk
FIC

**THOBURN MBE**, Marj
**Sexual and Relationship Psychotherapist**
♿ White Gable
5 Vicarage Hill
Helsby
Frodsham
WA6 9AD
☎ 01928 727 990
marj@thoburn.clara.co.uk
BASRT

**WEBSTER**, Jeni
**Family & Systemic Psychotherapist**
♿ Dept of Psychological Therapies
Garven Place
Sankey St
Warrington
WA1 1RH
☎ 01925 655 052
jeni.webster@btinternet.com
AFT

**WETHERILL**, Julie
**Cognitive Analytic Therapist, Group Analyst**
♿ Halton Psychotherapy & Family Service
Thorn Road Clinic
Thorn Road
Runcorn
WA7 5HQ
☎ 01928 575 073
julie.wetherill@5boroughspartnership.nhs.uk
IGA

**WILSON**, Llynwen
**Sexual and Relationship Psychotherapist**
♿ Swythamley Chapel
Swythamley
Macclesfield
SK11 0SN
☎ 01260 227 302
llynwen.wilson@talk21.com
BASRT

**WOOLLISCROFT**, Jessica
**Humanistic Psychotherapist**
Psychology Department
Gawsworth Building, West Park
Victoria Road
Macclesfield
SK10 3BL
☎ 01625 663 547
☎ 01270 884 594
cjwoolliscroft@supanet.com
AHPP

## CLEVELAND

**ARCARI**, Stephen
**Group Analyst**
Pine Hills
Guisborough
TS14
stephen_arcari@hotmail.com
IGA

**ARUNDALE**, Rita
**Integrative Psychotherapist**
42 Cobble Carr
Guisborough
Cleveland
TS14 6NR
☎ 01287 610232
ritaarundale@aol.com
NGP

**DAVIES-HOUGH**, Karen
**Integrative Psychotherapist**
T.A.C.T.
294 Norton Road
Norton
Stockton-on-Tees
TS20 2BX
ScPTI

**DHAR**, Devika
**Integrative Psychotherapist**
Northern Guild for Psychotherapy
77 Acklan Road
Thornday
Stockton-on-Tees
TS17 7BD
☎ 01642 649 005
NGP

**HOMER**, Marjorie
**Integrative Psychotherapist**
2 Hebron Road
Linthorpe
Middlesbrough
TS5 6RD
☎ 01642 814270
☎ 01642 814270
NGP

**LISTER-FORD**, Christine
**Integrative Psychotherapist**
Northern Guild for Psychotherapy
77 Acklam Road
Stockton on Tees
TS17 7BD
☎ 01912 098 383
☎ 01642 649 004
NGP

**MARSHALL**, Howard
**Family & Systemic Psychotherapist**
1 Pennyman Close
Normanby
Middlesbrough
TS6 0JG
☎ 01642 466 471
howard@pennyman.freeserve.co.uk
AFT

**MCNAMARA**, Jennifer
**Integrative Psychotherapist**
The Northern Guild for Psychotherapy
77 Acklan Road
Thornday
Stockton-on-Tees
TS17 7BD
☎ 01642 649 004
☎ 01912 098 383
NGP

**PEARSON**, Beryl
**Integrative Psychotherapist**
The Giardini
Roxby Lane
Staithes
Saltburn-by-the-Sea
TS13 5DZ
☎ 01947 840 572
beryl@maypearson.freeserve.co.uk
SPTI

**PROUDLEY**, Helen G
**Sexual and Relationship Psychotherapist**
♿ Psychological Therapies Service
University Hospital of N Tees
Hardwick Road
Stockton-on-Tees
TS19 8PE
☎ 01845 523 238
☎ 01642 624 291
helenproudley@yahoo.co.uk
BASRT

**RICHARDSON**, Sue
**Attachment-based Psychoanalytic Psychotherapist**
22 Queens Road
Middlesbrough
TS5 6EE
☎ 01642 817 658
SueRichardson1@compuserve.com
CAPP

**STRANG WOOD**, Susi
**Neurolinguistic Psychotherapist**
♿ 29 High Street
Skelton
Saltburn by the Sea
Cleveland
TS12 2EF
☎ 01287 654 175
drsusistrang@aol.com
NLPtCA

**THACKER**, Rose
**Transactional Analysis Psychotherapist**
20 Hilda Place
Saltburn by the Sea
Cleveland
TS12 1BP
☎ 01287 622 947
ITA

**WILLIAMS**, Steve
**Cognitive Psychotherapist**
♿ The Spinney
Hutton Village
Guisborough
TS14 8EP
☎ 01287 637 416
stevemw@doctors.org.uk
The Garth Surgery
Rectory Lane
Guisborough
TS14 6DJ
BABCP

**WOOD**, Craig
**Neurolinguistic Psychotherapist**
♿ 29 High Street
Skelton
Saltburn by the Sea
Cleveland
TS12 2EF
☎ 01287 654 175
cwooduk@aol.com
NLPtCA

## CORNWALL

**ALLEN**, Cheryl
**Core Process Psychotherapist**
23 Holmbush Road
St.Austell
Cornwall
PL25 3LF
☎ 0172 669 486
KI

**BIRD**, Julia
**Gestalt Psychotherapist**
Collywell
Brownston
Nrlvybridge
Devon
PL12 0SQ
☎ 01548 821 192
sowelusAss@aol.com
MET

**BOWLBY-WEST**, Lorna
**Family & Systemic Psychotherapist**
Duchy Hospital
Treliske
Truro
TR1 3UP
☎ 01872 226 127
☎ 01326 250 806
cottage@cottage.go-plus.net
AFT

**COGAN**, Margaret
**Cognitive Behavioural Psychotherapist**
♿ Dept. of Clinical Psychology
Banham House
St.Lawrences Hospital
Bodmin
PL31 2QT
☎ 01208 251 460
BABCP

**COOMBS**, Suzanne
**Psychoanalytic Psychotherapist**
"Garth"
Steeple Lane
Trelyon Downs
Cornwall
TR26 2AP
☎ 01736 795032
GUILD

**DARGERT**, Guy
**Humanistic Psychotherapist**
Bellview House
18 Bellair Terrace
St Ives
Cornwall
TR26 1JR
☎ 01736 798 076
G.Dargert@btinternet.com
AHPP

**DONALD**, Philippa
**Transpersonal Psychotherapist**
The Old Dairy Barn
Pencuke
St Gennys
Bude
EX23 0BH
☎ 01840 230 070
CCPE

**FOWLES**, Ann
**Transpersonal Psychotherapist**
Rainbow's End
22 York Street
Penzance
Cornwall
TR18 2PW
☎ 01736 363 114
CTP

**FRENCH**, Jean
**Transactional Analysis Psychotherapist**
The Twelve Steps
Trenance
Mawgan Porth
Cornwall
TR8 4BX
☎ 01637 860 435
ITA

**GILL**, Ali
**Psychodrama Psychotherapist**
26 Bosorne Road
St Just
Cornwall
TR19 7JJ
☎ 01736 786 157
ali.gill@bluecarrots.com
BPA

**GIMBLETT**, Jeanne
**Cognitive Behavioural Psychotherapist**
BALLOO
14 Mount Crescent
PAR
Cornwall
PL24 2BU
☎ 01726 813 617
gimblepar@onetel.net.uk
BABCP

**GIRLING**, Gail
**Humanistic Psychotherapist**
Trevan House
8 Dolphin Street
Port Isaac
Cornwall
PL29 3RJ
☎ 01608 730812
AHPP

**GREEN**, Marian
**Gestalt Psychotherapist**
2 Gibbons Fields
Mullion
Helston
Conwall
TR12 7EA
☎ 01326 240 734
marianfgreen@btopenworld.com
SPTI

**GRIFFITHS**, Thelma
**Transpersonal Psychotherapist**
♿ Boswedden House
St Just
Cornwall
TR19 7NJ
☎ 01736 788733
thelma.g@btclick.com
CCPE

**HANNA**, Dorothy
**Psychosynthesis Psychotherapist**
Jems Cottage
Badgall
Launceston
Cornwall
PL15 8SZ
☎ 0156 686 476
IPS

**HAYWARD**, Mark
**Family & Systemic Psychotherapist**
♿ Little Clicker
Horningtops
Liskeard
Cornwall
PL14 3QA
☎ 01503 240 822
mark@hayward.flyer.co.uk
AFT

**HODD**, Amanda
**Family & Systemic Psychotherapist**
Child & Family Centre
Treliske
Truro
Cornwal
TR1 3LA
☎ 07974 802 498
childandfamily@blueyonder.co.uk
AFT

**HUDSON**, Peter
**Family & Systemic Psychotherapist**
♿ Child & Family Centre
Treliske Hospital
Truro
Cornwall
TR1 3LQ
☎ 01872 354 350
peter.hudson@cpt.cornwall.nhs.co.uk
AFT

**JACKSON**, Rosalind
**Family & Systemic Psychotherapist**
Landicla House
Gulval Churchtown
Penzance
TR18 3BG
☎ 01736 365 161
rosjack@tinyworld.co.uk
AFT

**KING**, Michael
**Family & Systemic Psychotherapist**
♿ Meneage Street Surgery
100 Meneage Street
Helston
Cornwall
TR13 8RF
AFT

**KIRKPATRICK**, M.J.
**Sexual and Relationship Psychotherapist**
♿ Nuffield Clinic
Lipson Road
Plymouth
PL17 8BJ
☎ 01752 660 281
Michael.Kirkpatrick@pcs-tr.swest.nhs.uk
BASRT

**LUCE**, Peter James
**Hypno-Psychotherapist**
269 New Road
Saltash
Cornwall
PL12 6HQ
☎ 01752 844 777
peterjluce@lineone.net
NRHP

**MANNING**, Helen
**Gestalt Psychotherapist**
Bounds Cottage
Cargreen
Saltash
Cornwall
PL12 6PA
☎ 01752 840 603
helenmanning50@hotmail.com
GPTI, MET

**MCQUAID**, Cathy
**Integrative Psychotherapist, Transactional Analysis Psychotherapist**
74 Boxwell Park
Bodmin
Cornwall
PL31 2BE
☎ 01208 74600
cathy.mcquaid@ntlworld.com
ITA, SPTI

**MIDDLETON**, Richard
**Family & Systemic Psychotherapist**
8 Lescudjack Road
Penzance
Cornwall
TR18 3AD
☎ 01736 362 196
middleton.pohl@virgin.net
AFT

**NICHOLSON**, David
**Integrative Psychotherapist**
Pillaton Cottage
The Row
Pillaton
Cornwall
PL12 6QS
☎ 01579 351 404
davidwnichols@lineone.net
MC

**PAYNE**, John
**Psychoanalytic Psychotherapist**
"Manor Cottage"
Trematon
Saltash
PL12 4RT
☎ 01752 848 893
drjohnpayne@hotmail.com
GUILD

**PRESTWOOD**, Christopher
**Family & Systemic Psychotherapist**
♿ Treludruss
Ruan Lanihorne
Truro
TR2 5NX
☎ 01872 501 982
chris.prestwood@cpt.cornwall.nhs.uk
AFT

**RETALLICK**, Malcolm
**Gestalt Psychotherapist**
48 Molesworth Street
Wadebridge
Cornwall
PL27 7DP
☎ 01208 812 048
malcretallestag@presence.co.uk
GPTI, MET

**RILEY**, Sue
**Analytical Psychologist-Jungian Analyst**
Pencoose
Tregony
Cornwall
TR2 5TR
☎ 01872 530 245
AJA

**RIMMER**, Lynn
**Psychoanalytic Psychotherapist**
4 Knill Cottages
Steeple Lane
St Ives
TR26 2AY
☎ 01736 799018
GUILD

**ROSE**, David
**Core Process Psychotherapist**
5 Beacon Road
Sancreed
Penzance
Cornwall
TR20 8QR
☎ 01736 810362
KI

**SALA**, Monica
**Integrative Psychotherapist**
27 Castle Meadows
St Agnes
Trurow
Cornwall
TR5 0UB
☎ 01872 554 338
monicasala@hotmail.com
MET

**SALAMANDER**, Jas Ananda
**Transpersonal Psychotherapist**
Bell View House
18 Bellair Terrace
St Ives
Cornwall
TR26 1JR
☎ 01736 798076
CCPE

**SEVER**, Michael
**Hypno-Psychotherapist**
'Veritas'
25 Polwithen Drive
Carbis Bay, St. Ives
Cornwall
TR26 2SP
☎ 01736 798 399
NRHP

**SPRENT**, Sue
**Group Analytic Psychotherapist**
Beagletodn
Towednack
Nr. St Ives
Cornwall
TR26 3AY
☎ 01736 794 304
beagletodn@aol.com
FIP

**STUART**, Gillian
**Analytical Psychologist-Jungian Analyst**
7 Bar Terrace
Bar Road
Falmouth
Cornwall
TR11 4BP
☎ 01326 316 384
AJA

**TREWHELLA**, John
**Hypno-Psychotherapist**
♿ Castle Gayer
Leys Lane
Marazion
Cornwall
TR17 0AQ
☎ 01736 711 548
john.trewhella@btinternet.com
NRHP

**WATSON**, Mike
**Group Analytic Psychotherapist**
5 West Porthmear Cottages
Duporth Road
Charlestown
Cornwall
PL25 3NT
☎ 07980 734 777
mikewatson@cornwall-psychotherapy.com
FPC

**WOOD**, Richard
**Integrative Psychotherapist**
♿ 1 Plough Court
Roskrow
Penryn
Cornwall
TR10 9AP
☎ 01326 378 298
☎ 01872 240 795
rmtwood@aol.com
1st Floor
57 Little Castle Street
Truro
Cornwall
TR1 3DL
MET

**YOUNG**, Margot
**Integrative Psychotherapist**
17 Regents Square
Penzance
Cornwall
TR18 4BG
☎ 01736 351 669
margotyoung@bigfoot.com
M C

**D'ARAGONA**, Una
**Integrative Psychosynthesis Psychotherapist**
"Hillsand"
Treskillard
Nr Redruth
Cornwall
TR16 6JY
☎ 01209 715 364
☎ 0771 338 1823
unadaragona@hotmail.com
RE.V

## COUNTY DURHAM

**BEM**, M
**Cognitive Behavioural Psychotherapist**
♿ Woodlands
Elemore Grange Farm
Littletown
DH6 1QF
☎ 0191 372 3759
☎ 07734 391 694
drbem@lineone.net
B A B C P

**BIRCHMORE**, Terry
**Group Analyst**
♿ North End House
42 North End
Durham City
DH1 4LW
birchmore@yahoo.com
I G A

**CATESBY**, Cynthia
**Integrative Psychotherapist**
5 Leazes Court
Leazes Place
Durham City
DH1 1XF
☎ 0191 386 6669
catesby@fsnet.co.uk
S P T I

**COOPER**, Margaret H
**Psychoanalytic Psychotherapist**
2 Manor Close
Shincliffe Village
County Durham
DH1 2NS
☎ 0191 386 5818
F I P

**DOUGLAS**, Angela
**Analytical Psychotherapist, Group Analyst**
♿ Dept. of Clinical Psychology & Psychotherapy
County Hospital
North Road
Durham
DH1 4ST
☎ 01943 333 3437/99
angela.douglas@cddps.northy.nhs.uk
I G A, Y A P P

**EKERS**, David
**Cognitive Behavioural Psychotherapist**
♿ Chester Le Street CMHT
Newcastle Road
Chester Le Street
DH3 3UR
☎ 0191 333 3866
David.Ekers@cddps.northy.nhs.uk
B A B C P

**ELLIS**, Susan Mary
**Family & Systemic Psychotherapist**
Whitwell Grange
Durham
DH1 2SJ
☎ 0191 372 0219
whitwell@lineone.net
A F T

**FOSTER**, Tonia
**Family & Systemic Psychotherapist**
36 The Parks
Chester le Street
Co. Durham
DH3 3QX
☎ 0191 388 3453
gdf.tf@virgin.net
A F T

**JOHNSON**, Janette
**Integrative Psychotherapist**
The Old Pit Practice
21 Front Street
Fromvellgate Moor
Durham
DH1 5EJ
☎ 01913 844 942
janette@doctorjohnson.demon.co.uk
N G P

**KENDRICK**, Lesley
**Psychodynamic Psychotherapist**
♿ Specialist Psychotherapy & Psychological Service f
County Hospital
North Road
Durham
DH1 4ST
☎ 0191 333 3499
lesley.kendrick@cddps.northy.nhs.uk
U P C A

**MILES**, Carolyn
**Psychoanalytic Psychotherapist**
8 Ornsby Hill
Lanchester
Co. Durham
DH7 0QL
☎ 01207 521 622
F I P

**THOMPSON**, Mandy
**Family & Systemic Psychotherapist**
♿ 18 Askerton Drive
Oakerside Park
Peterlee
SR8 1PW
☎ 0191 518 3437
mandy.thompson@stw.nhs.uk
A F T

**WATSON**, Pauline
**Psychoanalytic Psychotherapist**
27 Albert Street
Western Hill
Durham
DH1 4RL
☎ 0191 384 5716
p.e.watson@durham.ac.uk
F I P

**WILLIAMS**, Thomas
**Family & Systemic Psychotherapist**
15 Highsteads
Medomsley
Co. Durham
DH8 6QA
☎ 01207 563 895
tew@supanet.com
A F T

**WRAY**, Marie
**Family & Systemic Psychotherapist**
High Edge End
Aukside
Middleton in Teesdale
DL12 0QY
☎ 01325 743 076
marie.wray@sddpsnothry.nhs.uk
A F T

## CUMBRIA

**APPLEGARTH**, Janet
**Psychoanalytic Psychotherapist**
2 Tallows Whins
Lazonby
Penrith
Cumbria
CA10 1AR
☎ 01768 898 390
jan.applegarth@lineone.net
L P D O

**BARNES**, Pam
**Cognitive Behavioural Psychotherapist**
Perandale
Hornsby
Heads Nook
Brampton, Cumbria
CA8 9HF
☎ 01228 561 698
pam.dek.barnes@virgin.net
BABCP

**BURGESS**, Alison
**Family & Systemic Psychotherapist**
♿ The Hopegill Centre, CAMHS
Child & Adolescent Mental
Health Service, 25 Banklands
Workington, Cumbria
CA14 2UN
☎ 01900 324 200
alison.burgess@ncumbria.nhs.uk
AFT

**COLE**, Shanti
**Hypno-Psychotherapist**
♿ Rose Cottage
Colthouse Ambleside
Cumbria
LA22 0JT
☎ 01539 436 150
NSHAP

**COOK**, Jane
**Integrative Psychotherapist**
Alderbeck Castle Carrock
Brampton
CA8 9LT
☎ 01387 244 495
☎ 01228 670 646
butlercook2002@yahoo.ie
MC

**COX**, Mary
**Transactional Analysis Psychotherapist**
Cambrai House
Calderbridge
Seascale
Cumbria
CA20 1DH
☎ 01946 841 239
marycox@cambraihouse.demon.co.uk
ITA

**DAVIES**, Jennifer
**Group Analytic Psychotherapist**
♿ Fair View
Town End
Witherslack
Cumbria
LA11 6RN
☎ 01539 552 230
jennie@davies4328.freeserve.co.uk
UPCA

**DONOVAN**, Andrew
**Group Analyst**
♿ Dept. Clinical Psychology
13-14 Portland Square
Carlisle
CA1 3PT
☎ 01228 603 124
andrew.donovan@ncumbria.nhs.uk
IGA

**EGERTON**, Judi
**Psychoanalytic Psychotherapist**
♿ Beech Lodge
Psychotherapy Department
Carleton Clinic
Carlisle
CA1 3SU
☎ 01228 602 392
LPDO

**FORSYTH**, Angus
**Cognitive Behavioural Psychotherapist**
104 Greenacres
Wetheral
Carlisle
Cumbria
CA4 8LD
☎ 01228 561 786
angusforsyth@tiscali.co.uk
BABCP

**GILL**, Susan
**Neurolinguistic Psychotherapist**
Cameron Gill
Dykesfield House
Burgh-by-Sands
Carlisle, Cumbria
CA5 6AG
☎ 01228 576 631
camgill@lineone.net
NLPtCA

**GOSS**, Phil
**Analytical Psychologist-Jungian Analyst**
22 Ruskin Drive
Kirkby Lonsdale
Lanc.
Nr Carnforth
LA6 2DB
☎ 01524 273 581
AJA

**HEATH**, John
**Transactional Analysis Psychotherapist**
122 Highgate
Kendal
Cumbria
LA9 4HE
☎ 01539 723 356
jheath.highgate@virgin.net
ITA

**HEATH**, Lis
**Transactional Analysis Psychotherapist**
24 Wordsworth Street
Penrith
Cumbria
CA11 7QY
☎ 01768 899 941
lisandjohn@lineone.net
ITA

**JONES**, Judith
**Sexual and Relationship Psychotherapist**
Galley Cottage
Melling
Carnforth, Lancs
LA6 2RE
☎ 01524 221 321
☎ 07761 957 243
irbyfarm@supanet.com
BASRT

**KELLY**, Gillian
**Body Psychotherapist, Gestalt Psychotherapist**
Dillygarth
Loughrigg
Ambleside
Cumbria
LA22 9HF
☎ 01539 433 903
gilliankelly@onetel.net.uk
CCBP

**LOBEL**, Sandra
**Sexual and Relationship Psychotherapist**
♿ Low Lodge
Rockland Road
Grange-Over-Sands
Cumbria
LA11 7HR
☎ 01539 535 140
sanlobel@aol.com
BASRT

**LONGFORD**, Joan
**Psychoanalytic Psychotherapist**
6 Highbank Close
Carlisle
Cumbria
CA1 2QG
☎ 01228 544 853
☎ 01228 602 392
Beech Lodge Dept of Psychotherapy
Cumwhinten Drive
Carlisle
Cumbria
CA1 3SX
FIP

**MACDONALD**, Alasdair
**Family & Systemic Psychotherapist**
8 Wellgate Close
Scotby
Carlisle
CA4 8BA
☎ 01228 513 005
ajmacdon@psychsft.freeserve.co.uk
AFT

**MCNEIL**, Delcia
**Humanistic and Integrative Psychotherapist**
5 Woodlands Close
Storth
Milnthorpe
Cumbria
LA7 7JH
☎ 01539 562 420
☎ 020 8442 0391
delcia.mcneil@virgin.net
SPEC

**MCQUILLIN**, Jane
**Transactional Analysis Psychotherapist**
♿ 31 Prince's Street
Ulverston
Cumbria
LA12 7NQ
☎ 01229 588 404
janemcqui@aol.com
ITA

**PENNEFATHER**, Heather
**Hypno-Psychotherapist**
Hill House
Alston
Cumbria
CA9 3BS
☎ 01434 381 620
pennefather@cybermoor.org
CTIS

**RILEY**, Fran
**Integrative Arts Psychotherapist**
Ulverston
LA12
☎ 01229 588 853
☎ 07976 062 145
spiralfran@aol.com
IATE

**SCHMID-BORGSCHULTE**, Heide-Marie
**Family & Systemic Psychotherapist**
Psychological Services
13/14 Portland Square
Carlisle
CA1 1PT
☎ 01228 603 100
hmborgschulte@aol.com
AFT

**WILSON**, Maureen
**Psychoanalytic Psychotherapist**
♿ Banna Cottage
Hutton Park
New Hutton
Kendal
LA8 0AY
☎ 01539 737 766
AGIP

## DARLINGTON

**ELDRIDGE**, Alison
**Integrative Psychotherapist**
9 The Green
Aycliffe Village
Co Durham
DL5 6LX
☎ 01325 316 197
☎ 07947 640 104
alison@eldridge999.fslife.co.uk
NGP

**HAMILTON**, Kim (Mr)
**Psychoanalytic Psychotherapist**
♿ 1A Hawkswood Hurworth Place
Nr Darlington
Co Durham
Darlington
DL2 2HL
☎ 01325 722 505
khamilton@onetel.net
AGIP

**LOISEAU**, Kate
**Integrative Psychotherapist**
Cholet Cottage
Killerby
Darlington
DL2 3UQ
☎ 01325 374 994
plm@loiseau.freeserve.co.uk
SPTI

**MAY**, Mrs Jennifer
**Sexual and Relationship Psychotherapist**
27 Cleveland Terrace
Darlington
Co Durham
DL3 7HD
☎ 01325 489 394
☎ 07818 022 045
pathways.jmay@ntlworld.com
Woodlands Hospital
Morton Park
Darlington
Co Durham
DL1 4PL
BASRT

## DERBYSHIRE

**ANDERSON**, Naomi
**Gestalt Psychotherapist**
The White Lodge
The Hayes
Swanwick
Derbyshire
DE55 1AT
☎ 07931 557 939
☎ 01773 608 950
naomi1258@hotmail.com
ScPTI

**ARCHER**, Alan
**Humanistic Psychotherapist**
Old Hall Cottage
New Road
Alderwasley
Belper
DE56 2SQ
☎ 01629 825 005
☎ 07974 954 643
alangarcher@aol.com
SPTI

**ATKINSON**, Laura
**Gestalt Psychotherapist**
32 St John Street
Wirksworth
DE4 4DS
☎ 01629 823 760
GCL

**BARBER**, Julie
**Family & Systemic Psychotherapist**
♿ Rivermead CAMHS
Goods Road
Belper
Derbyshire
DE56 1UU
☎ 01773 880 554
juliebarber@talk21.com
AFT

**BOULTON**, Sylvia
Hurworth Cottage
1 Posey Lane
Aston on Trent
DE7 2DT
☎ 01332 792 203
gristock@posey.fsnet.co.uk
AFT

**BOX**, Kay
**Cognitive Behavioural Psychotherapist**
♿ CMHT Derby City North
Older Adult Teams Building
Kingsway Hospital, Kingsway
Derby
DE22 3LZ
☎ 01332 623 586
☎ 01332 624 594
kay.box@ntlworld.com
27 Sunny Grove
Chaddesden
Derby
DE21 6QP
BABCP

**CHALLIS**, Raymond Thomas
**Hypno-Psychotherapist**
♿ Adam House Medical Centre, 85-91
Derby Road
Sandieacre
Nottinghamshire
NG10 5HZ
☎ 01159 606 116
raychallis@tiscali.co.uk
NRHP

**COOPER**, Penny
**Sexual and Relationship Psychotherapist**
♿ Community Mental Health Team
Heatherdene Resource Centre
Mansfield
NG19 7AE
☎ 01623 626 147
☎ 0114 271 6671
BASRT

**DANIELS**, Frank
**Neurolinguistic Psychotherapist**
♿ 103 Hands Road
Heanor
Derbyshire
DE75 7HB
☎ 01773 532 195
info@FrankDanielsAssociates.co.uk
NLPtCA

**DENNESS**, Brian
**Psychoanalytic Psychotherapist**
♿ Psychotherapy Department
Temple House
Mill Hill Lane
Derby
DE23 6SA
☎ 01332 364 512
☎ 01332 553 658
briandenness@ntworld.com
314 Duffield Road
Darley Abbey
Derby
DE22 1EQ
FIP, STTDP

**DICKS**, Russell
**Psychodynamic Psychotherapist**
164 Church Street
Waingroves
Ripley
DE5 9TF
☎ 01773 570 682
russell@dicks297.freeserve.co.uk
UPCA

**DONOVAN**, Marlyn
**Psychosynthesis Psychotherapist**
16 Pikes Lane
Glossop
SK13 8EA
☎ 01457 857 588
marlfd@aol.com
PET

**DUFFY**, Gervase J.
**Transactional Analysis Psychotherapist**
19 Chapel Street
Measham
Swadlincote
Derbys
DE12 7JD
☎ 01530 272 772
jillandgerryd@aol.com
ITA

**DUNKS**, Kathryn
**Cognitive Behavioural Psychotherapist**
Community Mental Heath Team
Old Vicarage
30 High Street, Bolsover
Chesterfield
S44 6HF
☎ 01246 827 904
☎ 01246 452 863
Kathryndunks@aol.com
287 High Street
New Whittington
Chesterfield
Derbyshire
S43 2AP
BABCP

**FLETCHER**, John
**Psychoanalytic Psychotherapist**
♿ Department of Psychotherapy
Temple House
Mill Hill Lane
Derby
DE23 6SA
☎ 01332 364 512
STTDP

**FOXGOLD**, Sheila
**Psychodrama Psychotherapist**
Laburnum Farm
Main Road
Pentrich
DE5 3RE
☎ 01773 741 930
sheilafoxgold@totalserve.co.uk
BPA

**FRANCIS**, Denise
**Cognitive Behavioural Psychotherapist**
♿ 130 Kilbourne Road
Belper
Derby
DE56 1SA
☎ 01773 825 178
☎ 01629 57410/57176
denise_saintmonk@yahoo.com
Community Mental Health Team
Victoria Chambers
113 Dale Road
Matlock
DE4 3LU
BABCP

**GILBOY**, Carol A.
**Cognitive Behavioural Psychotherapist**
Valentine Cottage
19 Shepherd Street
Littleover
Derby
DE23 6GA
☎ 01332 774 729
optacag@aol.com
BABCP

**GILSON**, Jean
**Gestalt Psychotherapist**
♿ 34 The Green
Swanwick
Derbyshire
DE55 1AN
☎ 01733 607 926
jean.gilson@nottscc.gov.uk
SPTI

**GOODLIFFE**, Martin
**Existential Psychotherapist**
♿ 1 Rosecottages
Uppertown Bonsall
Matlock
DE4 2AW
☎ 01629 826 434
SEA

**GRAHAM**, Hilary
**Hypno-Psychotherapist**
Impact Physiotherapy
128 Derby Road
Long Eaton
Nottinghamshire
NG10 4LS
☎ 01159 455 290
NRHP

**GRANTHIER**, Miriam
**Gestalt Psychotherapist**
Flat 5
31 Hollies Road
Allestree
Derby
DE22 2EU
☎ 01332 559 668
SPTI

**GREVILLE**, Coral
**Gestalt Psychotherapist**
♿ The Willows
Main Road
Ellastone
Nr Ashbourne, Derby
DE6 2GZ
☎ 01335 324593
coralg@ntlworld.com
SPTI

**HACKETT**, Michelle
**Gestalt Psychotherapist**
47 Radbourne Street
Derby
Derbyshire
DE22 3HD
☎ 01332 728 852
SPTI

**HALFORD**, Ann
**Cognitive Behavioural Psychotherapist**
♿ The Gables
Poyser Lane
Kirk Langley
Ashbourne
DE6 4LR
☎ 01332 824 357
annhalford@aol.com
BABCP

**HIGHLEY**, John
**Integrative Psychotherapist**
♿ 6 Trent Lane
Newton Solney
Burton on Trent
Staffordshire
DE15 0LF
☎ 01283 702 054
johnhighley@aol.com
MET

**HOLLAND**, Hilary Elizabeth
**Transactional Analysis Psychotherapist**
♿ Peak Health Clinic
88 High Street
West Glossop
SK13 8BB
☎ 01457 766 866
hilary-holland@usa.net
ITA

**JOHNSON**, Michael
**Neurolinguistic Psychotherapist**
5 Glenthorne Close
Chesterfield
Derbyshire
S40 3AR
☎ 01246 273 002
NLPtCA

**JONES**, K R
**Cognitive Behavioural Psychotherapist**
♿ Four Gables
Hillcliff Lane
Turnditch
Belper
DE56 2EA
☎ 01773 550 224
peakcbt@hotmail.com
BABCP

**LAWES**, Ginny
**Integrative Psychotherapist**
36 Carrfield Avenue
Long Eaton
Nottingham
NG10 2BW
☎ 0115 849 3027
MET

**LEAKEY**, Peter
**Neurolinguistic Psychotherapist**
16 Cromwell Road
Chesterfield
Derbyshire
S40 4TH
☎ 01246 552 871
☎ 01246 232 765
peter.leakey@dsl.pipex.com
NLPtCA

**MANSALL**, Cordelia
**Integrative Psychotherapist**
30 Toadmoor Lane
Ambergate
DE56 2GN
☎ 01773 853 916
cordeliamansall@hotmail.com
SPCRC

**MITCHELL**, Paul Christoph
**Integrative Psychotherapist**
2 Springbank
Unstone
Dronfield
S18 4AD
☎ 01246 416 051
☎ 07815 956 251
SPTI

**MONROE**, Claire
**Psychodynamic Psychotherapist**
♿ Department of Psychotherapy
Temple House
Mill Hill Lane
Derby
DE23 6SA
☎ 01332 364 512
UPCA

**MOORE**, Meg
**Sexual and Relationship Psychotherapist**
♿ c/o Derwent Rural Counselling Service
New Holme Hospital
Baslow Road
Bakewell
DE45 1AD
☎ 01629 813 099
☎ 07976 607 554
megc.moore@virgin.net
BASRT

**MURRAY**, Valerie
**Integrative Psychotherapist**
75 Mount Pleasant Road
Swadlincote
DE11 9JE
☎ 01283 550 130
SPTI

**MUSCHAMP**, Maureen
**Transpersonal Psychotherapist**
Hillcroft
37 Summer Lane
Wirksworth
Derby
DE4 4EB
☎ 01629 823 146
CTP

**PARKINSON**, Jillian
**Transactional Analysis Psychotherapist**
19 Chapel Street
Measham
Swadlincote
Derbyshire
DE12 7JD
☎ 01530 272 772
JillandGerryD@aol.com
ITA

**PIZER**, Isaac
**Gestalt Psychotherapist**
5 Clifton Drive
Mickleover
Derby
DE3 9HS
☎ 01332 516 074
ipizer@ipizer.freeserve.co.uk
SPTI

**PRINCE**, Tania
**Hypno-Psychotherapist**
♿ The Poynton Natural Therapy Centre
95 Park Lane
Poynton
Cheshire
SK12 1RB
☎ 01625 520 016
☎ 01625 850 555
tania@nlp-hypnotherapy.com
NRHP

**PROCTER**, Sue
**Cognitive Psychotherapist**
Shirley Centre
16A South Street
Derby
DE1 1DS
☎ 01332 571 765
34 Coronation Avenue
Alvaston
Derby
DE24 0LQ
BABCP

**QUILTER**, Sally
**Integrative Psychotherapist**
Wisteria Cottage
45 Main Road
Watnall
Nottingham
NG16 1HE
☎ 0115 854 2519
sallyjquilter@ntlworld.com
SPTI

**RIDLEY**, Wendy
**Psychosynthesis Psychotherapist**
Rivendell
Top Lane
Whatstandwell, Matlock
Derbyshire
DE4 5EN
☎ 01773 852 491
IPS

**ROBINSON**, Gary
**Family & Systemic Psychotherapist**
Oaklands
103 Duffield Road
Derby
DE22 1AE
☎ 01332 365 221
gary.robinson@sderbys-cmhst.trent nhs .uk
FIC

**RYAN**, Angella M.J.
**Psychodynamic Psychotherapist**
253 Ladybank Road
Mickleover
Derby
DE3 ORS
☎ 01332 519 928
WMIP

**SCHRÖDER**, Thomas
**Psychoanalytic Psychotherapist**
♿ Psychotherapy Department
Temple House
Mill Hill Lane
Derby
DE23 6SA
☎ 01332 364 512
tom_schroder@derbysnhservices.nhs.uk
STTDP

**SEED**, Deborah
**Group Analyst**
Shirley Centre
16a South Street
Derby
DE1 1DS
☎ 01332 292 160
IGA

**SERIEYS**, Nicholas Michael
**Cognitive Behavioural Psychotherapist**
♿ 14 Balmoral Close
Littleover
Derby
DE23 6DY
☎ 07973 520 550
nick.serieys@ntlworld.com
BABCP

**SHAW**, Robert
**Integrative Psychotherapist**
41 St. John Street
Ashbourne
Derby
DE6 1GP
☎ 01335 300 440
☎ 01332 371 184
rest@psychost.fsnet.co.uk
Derven House
32 Friar Gate
Derby
DE1 1BX
SPTI

**SLANEY**, Ruth
**Cognitive Behavioural Psychotherapist**
48 Chesterfield Avenue
New Whittington
Chesterfield
S43 2DD
☎ 01246 456 963
roo-slaney@supaworld.com
BABCP

**SMITH**, David
**Psychoanalytic Psychotherapist**
♿ Derby Psychotherapy Unit (NHS)
Temple House
Mill Hill Lane
Derby
DE23 6SA
☎ 01332 364 512
STTDP

**TALBOT**, Mike
**Gestalt Psychotherapist**
63 Belper Lane
Belper
Derbyshire
DE56 2UQ
☎ 01773 829 700
mtalbot@globalnet.co.uk
SPTI

**TAYLOR**, Jon
**Cognitive Behavioural Psychotherapist**
55 Church Street
Littleover
Derby
DE23 6GF
☎ 01332 749 876
☎ 01283 505 330
pjt0007@currantbun.com
BABCP

**THOMAS**, Simon
**Psychoanalytic Psychotherapist**
♿ Department of Psychotherapy
Temple House
Mill Hill lane
Derby
DE23 6SA
☎ 01332 364 512
STTDP

**THOMPSON**, Jeannette
**Family & Systemic Psychotherapist**
Stubbins House
Stubbins Lane
Chinley
High Peak
SK23 6ED
☎ 01663 750 842
AFT

**TOWNEND**, Michael
**Cognitive Behavioural Psychotherapist**
♿ School Healty & Community Studies
UPPR, University of Derby
Western Road
Mickleover, Derby
DE3 9GX
☎ 0121 704 1451
☎ 01332 592 054
m.townend@Derby.ac.uk
BABCP

**WALLIS**, Gillian
**Family & Systemic Psychotherapist**
♿ The Old Chapel
Lodge Row
Mapperley Village
DE7 6BR
☎ 0115 944 0211
AFT

**WALSH**, Belinda
**Cognitive Behavioural Psychotherapist**
♿ Clinical Psychology Department
Walton Hospital
Whitecotes Lane
Chesterfield, Derbyshire
S40 3HN
☎ 01246 552 871
BABCP

**WALTERS**, Ian
**Psychodynamic Psychotherapist**
Glenwood House
159 Burton Road
Derby
DE23 6AB
☎ 01332 344 717
ianwalters@glenwoodpsychotherapy.co.uk
UPCA

**WATSON**, Clare
**Psychoanalytic Psychotherapist**
Derby Department of Psychotherapy (NHS)
Temple House
Mill Hill Lane
Derby
DE3 6SA
☎ 01332 364 512
☎ 01509 843 393
cqwatson@onetel.net.uk
STTDP

**WILSON**, Mary
**Cognitive Behavioural Psychotherapist**
3 Back Jodrell Street
New Mills
High Peak
SK22 3HL
☎ 01663 745 219
☎ 07850 297 276
mwilsonmtw@aol.com
BABCP

**DE HOOGH-ROWNTREE**, Patricia
**Analytical Psychologist-Jungian Analyst**
Rowan Cottage
Carsington
DE4 4DE
☎ 01629 540 936
pdehoogh@aol.com
CAP *

## DEVON

**ANJALI**, Yon
**Core Process Psychotherapist**
53 Denys Road
Totnes
S Devon
TQ9 5TL
☎ 01803 862 543
KI

**BENNUN**, Ian
**Family & Systemic Psychotherapist**
♿ Dept of Child Psychology
Hengrave House
Torbay Hospital
Torquay
TQ2 7AA
☎ 01803 654 572
ian.bennun@sdevonhc-tr.swest.nhs.uk
AFT

**BENOR**, Ruth
**Autogenic Psychotherapist**
May Cottage
19 Fore Street,
Bishopsteighton
South Devon
TQ14 9QR
☎ 01626 779 649
ruth@benor.eclipse.co.uk
BAS

**BIRD**, Lorna
**Core Process Psychotherapist**
4 Puddavine Terrace
Dartington
Totnes
TQ9 6EU
☎ 01803 862 722
KI

**BOND**, Christine
**Core Process Psychotherapist**
1 Rew Road
Ashburton
TQ13 7EJ
☎ 01364 652 140
KI

**BOOTH**, Nick
**Family & Systemic Psychotherapist**
♿ Department of Clinical Psychology
Church Lane
Heavitree
Exeter
EX2 5SH
☎ 01392 403 170
njbooth@exeter.ac.uk
AFT

**BREEZE**, Linda
**Sexual and Relationship Psychotherapist**
19 Richmond Road
Exeter
EX4 4JA
☎ 01363 77 6184
BASRT

**BROMLEY**, Joanne
**Family & Systemic Psychotherapist**
♿ Joint Agencies Child Abuse Team
Church Lane
Heavitree
Exeter
EX1 2TF
☎ 01392 403 271
AFT

**BROUGH**, Julie
**Family & Systemic Psychotherapist**
♿ 44 South Street
Torrington
EX38 8AB
☎ 01805 622 223
julie@brough2911.fsnet.co.uk
AFT

**BUCKLAND**, Richard
**Child Psychotherapist**
Plymouth Child & Family Consultation Service
Erme House
Mount Gould Hospital
Plymouth,Devon
PL4 7QD
☎ 01752 272360
ACP

**BUDGELL**, Rosemary
**Integrative Psychotherapist**
Winnowing Knapp
Ridge Lane
Stockland
Honiton
EX14 9EW
☎ 07952 886 625
rsmrybud@aol.com
SPCRC

**BURLAND**, Roger
**Cognitive Behavioural Psychotherapist**
Middle Yarnacott
Swimbridge
Barnstaple
Devon
EX32 0QY
☎ 01271 830 373
☎ 07741 010 071 mobile
MiddleYarnacot@Globalnet.co.uk
BABCP

**BUTTERFIELD**, Alison
**Family Therapist**
Wadlands
6 Higher Street
Hatherleigh
EX20 3JD
☎ 01837 810 560
alisonbutterfield66@hotmail.com
AFT

**CALLAWAY**, Hazel
**Attachment-based Psychoanalytic Psychotherapist**
8 Victoria Avenue
Millbridge
Plymouth
PL1 5NH
☎ 01752 509 535
CAPP

**CAMPBELL**, Kate
**Core Process Psychotherapist**
♿ Foxhole
Dartington
Totnes
Devon
TQ9 6EB
☎ 01548 821 466
KI

**CAMPBELL-BEATTIE**, John
**Hypno-Psychotherapist**
♿ Rosemary Hill
64A Underlane
Plymstock
Plymouth
PL9 9JZ
☎ 01752 484 265
campbellbeattie@supanet.com
NRHP

**CASE**, Karenza
**Core Process Psychotherapist**
3 Pilton House
Pilton Lane
Exeter
EX1 3RA
☎ 01392 467 118
KI

**CASSIDY**, Sheila Anne
**Cognitive Analytic Therapist**
7 The Esplanade
The Hoe
Plymouth
PL1 2PJ
☎ 01752 265 892
ACAT

**CLAYTON**, Valerie
**Core Process Psychotherapist**
Beaumont
Bridgetown
Totnes
Devon
TQ9 5BE
☎ 01803 866 294
KI

**CLEVELY**, Sarah
**Transactional Analysis Psychotherapist**
10 Bartholomew Terrace
Exeter
Devon
EX4 3BW
☎ 01392 432 952
clevely@ukgateway.net
MET

**COX**, Miranda
**Core Process Psychotherapist**
♿ 3 St Helens
Heywood Road
Bideford
Devon
EX39 3PQ
☎ 01237 473252
KI

**CRITTENDEN**, Juliet
**Core Process Psychotherapist**
Foxhole
Dartington
Totnes
Devon
TQ9 6EB
☎ 01364 653614
KI

**DALE**, Francis
**Child Psychotherapist**
Rockmead
Lustleigh
Newton Abbot
South Devon
TQ13 9TH
☎ 01647 277237
ACP

**DAVID**, Ann
**Transactional Analysis Psychotherapist**
Pullybanks Farm
Churchstow
Kingsbridge
Devon
TQ7 3QR
☎ 01548 855 730
ann.david@virgin.net
ITA, MET

**DAVID**, Julian
**Analytical Psychologist-Jungian Analyst**
Luscombe Farm
Buckfastleigh
Devon
TQ11 0LP
☎ 01364 642 373
julian.david@virgin.net
IGAP

**DAWSON**, Jenny
**Gestalt Psychotherapist**
36 Raleigh Road
Exmouth
Devon
EX8 2SB
☎ 01395 269 076
jenny@eldaw.freeserve.co.uk
GPTI

**DEAS**, Francis
**Core Process Psychotherapist**
Highgate House
Hennock
Nr Bovey Tracy
Newton Abbot, Devon
TQ13 9PZ
☎ 01626 833 654
KI

**DRUMMOND**, Mark
**Core Process Psychotherapist**
12 Somerset Place
Totnes
Devon
TQ9 5AX
☎ 01803 862220
KI

**DYEHOUSE**, Pat
**Psychoanalytic Psychotherapist**
Hazel Tor Barn, Lower Soar
Soar Mill Cove
Malborough, Kingsbridge
Devon
TQ7 3DS
☎ 01548 561 450
pdyehouse@aol.com
ARBS

**DYMOND**, Christina
**Core Process Psychotherapist**
♿ Maybelle Cottage
Sandford
Crediton
Devon
EX17 4LR
☎ 01363 775138
KI

**EASTMAN**, Rachel
**Cognitive Behavioural Psychotherapist**
April Cottage
Exeter Road
Honiton
Devon
EX14 1AL
☎ 01404 42350
rachel.eastman15@ukonline.co.uk
BABCP

**ETHERINGTON**, Mary
**Transactional Analysis Psychotherapist**
Piglet Cottqage Floods Lane
13 New Street
Cullompton
Devon
EX15 1HA
☎ 0188 434 610
ITA

**FERRIS**, Mary
**Core Process Psychotherapist**
27 Lawn Vista
Sidmouth
Devon
EX10 9BY
☎ 01395 577588
KI

**GERLACH**, Lynne
**Integrative Psychotherapist**
Arcturus Clinic
47 Fore Street
Totnes
Devon
TQ9 5NJ
☎ 01932 874902
☎ 01548 821192
soweluass@aol.com
MET

**GRAYSON**, Juliet
**Neurolinguistic Psychotherapist**
The Gatehouse
Middle Coombe Farm
Uplowman
Tiverton
EX16 7QQ
☎ 02089 745 573
☎ 07770 964 864
juliet.grayson@virgin.net
NLPtCA

**GREBOT**, Peter
**Core Process Psychotherapist**
Foxhole
Dartington
Totnes
TQ9 6EB
☎ 01364 72879
KI

**GÖLZ**, Angelika
**Group Analyst, Humanistic Psychotherapist**
♿ 19 Bridgetown
Totnes
TQ9 5BH
☎ 01803 867 413
☎ 01392 434 441
angelika@macunlimited.net
45 Queen Street
Exeter
EX4 3SR
GASW, AHPP

**HACKETT**, Jenny
**Integrative Psychotherapist**
Hillcross
Stockland
Honiton
Devon
EX14 9DA
☎ 01404 881 565
BCPC

**HANNAH**, Margaret
**Core Process Psychotherapist**
18 Bossell Park
Buckfastleigh
Devon
TQ11 0DX
☎ 01364 642165
KI

**HEWSON**, Julie Anne
**Transactional Analysis Psychotherapist**
♿ The Iron Mill Institute
Hems Studio
86 Longbrook Street
Exeter
EX4 6AP
☎ 01392 219 200
ironmill@ironmill.demon.co.uk
Julie Hewson Consultancy
1st Floor Hems Studio
86 Longbrook Street
Exeter
EX4 6AP
ITA, MET

**HOLMES**, Jeremy
**Psychoanalytic Psychotherapist**
Furze Farm
Brayford
Barnstaple
Devon
EX32 7PL
☎ 01271 830 085
j.a.holmes@btinternet.com
SIP

**HORTON**, Annie
**Transactional Analysis Psychotherapist**
28 Halyards
Topsham
Exeter
Devon
EX3 0JU
ITA

**IVES**, Caroline
**Core Process Psychotherapist**
♿ Appletree
Talaton Road
Feniton
Nr Honiton, Devon
EX14 3BU
☎ 01404 850414
KI

**JEFFERIES**, Barbara
**Integrative Psychotherapist**
5 Priory Park Road
Dawlish
Devon
EX7 9LX
☎ 01626 862 542
MC

**JENKINS**, Dinah
**Cognitive Behavioural Psychotherapist**
♿ Occupational Health &Safety Unit
Derriford Hospital
Plymouth
PL6 8DH
☎ 01752 763 586
☎ 01503 262 067
dinah.jenkins@phnt.swest.nhs.uk
BABCP

**JENSEN**, Greta
**Psychosynthesis Psychotherapist**
Pleases Passage
Star House
High Street
Totnes, Devon
TQ9 5QN
☎ 01803 865 954
greta@dircon.co.uk
IPS

**JONES**, Nicole
**Psychoanalytic Psychotherapist**
57 Thornton Hill
Exeter
Devon
EX4 4NR
☎ 01392 254 408
SIP

**JOSEPHS-SERRA**, Elisabeth
**Psychosynthesis Psychotherapist**
The Old Cider Barn
Stoke Road
Collaton St Mary
South Devon
TQ4 7DD
☎ 01803 552 609
balance@lineone.net
IPS

**KALISCH**, David
**Core Process Psychotherapist, Humanistic Psychotherapist**
Warrencroft
56 East Budleigh Road
Budleigh Salterton
Devon
EX9 6EJ
☎ 01395 446 307
AHPP, KI

**KERRIDGE**, Petra
**Psychosynthesis Psychotherapist**
'Carisma'
188 Victoria Road
Dartmouth
TQ6 8EL
☎ 01803 833 532
petra.kerridge@btopenworld.com
PET

**KINGHAM LANGTON**, Rosemary
**Family & Systemic Psychotherapist**
♿ Blue Waters
Holcombe Road
Teignmouth
TQ14 8UP
☎ 01626 779 992
safehouses@hotmail.com
AFT

**KNOWLES**, Gwen
**Group Analyst**
The Chalet
Trood Stables Trood Lane
Matford
Exeter
EX2 8XX
☎ 01392 215 430
GASW

**LABWORTH**, Yig
**Core Process Psychotherapist, Humanistic and Integrative Psychotherapist**
Chalice House
11 Howell Road
Exeter
Devon
EX4 4LG
☎ 01392 427 370
yigwill@aol.com
BCPC, KI

**LAITINEN**, Irmeli
**Psychoanalytic Psychotherapist**
Student Counselling Services
Academic and Information Services
University of Plymouth
40 Portland Square, Plymo
PL4 8AA
☎ 01752 232788
I.Laitinen@plymouth.ac.uk
irmelilaitinen@beeb.net
3 Commercial Place
Plymouth
PL4 OLS
SIP, WTC

**LAKE**, Moira
**Gestalt Psychotherapist**
Chalfont Cottage
Hallsands
Kingsbridge
TQ7 2EY
☎ 020 8943 5507
☎ 01548 511 188
moiralake@groundtruth.fslife.co.uk
GPTI, MET

**LANGLEY**, Dorothy
**Psychodrama Psychotherapist**
Hanningfields
Warborough Hill
Kenton, Exeter
Devon
EX6 8LR
☎ 01626 890 433
gdlangly@eclipse.co.uk
BPA

**LAYDON-WALTERS**, Katrina
**Family & Systemic Psychotherapist**
♿ Dept of Clinical & Community Psychology
Church Lane
Heavitree
Exeter
EX2 5SH
☎ 01392 403 170
AFT

**LLEWELLYN**, Alice
**Neurolinguistic Psychotherapist**
Bay Villa
Plymouth Road
Totnes
Devon
TQ9 5PQ
☎ 01803 866 706
alice.llewellyn@totalise.co.uk
NLPtCA

**LOBB**, David
**Cognitive Analytic Therapist**
Flat 3
5 The Esplanade
The Hoe
Plymouth
PL1 2PJ
☎ 01752 227 800
david.lobb@talk21.com
ACAT

**LOXTERKAMP**, Lorne
**Child Psychotherapist**
Family Consultancy
Health Centre
Vicarage Street
Barnstaple, North Devon
EX32 7BT
☎ 01271 371761
☎ 01271 814901
ACP

**M. PETRIE**, Julie
**Body Psychotherapist, Integrative Psychotherapist**
Grimstone Manor
Horrabridge
Yelverton
Devon
PL20 7QY
☎ 01822 854 358
☎ 01822 855 982
CCBP

**MALONEY**, Sean
**Core Process Psychotherapist**
Room D15
Foxhole
Dartington
Totnes
TQ9 6EB
☎ 01803 732185
KI

**MCGOURAN**, Gill
**Transpersonal Psychotherapist**
South West Counselling Centre
34 New Street
The Barbican
Plymouth
PL1 2ND
☎ 01752 250 621
CTP

**MILLS**, Judith
**Neurolinguistic Psychotherapist**
♿ Higher Thatch
Ebford Lane
Ebford
Exeter, Devon
EX3 0QX
☎ 01392 87984
NLPtCA

**MONTGOMERY**, Charles
**Group Analyst**
Wonford House Hospital
Dryden Road
Exeter
EX2 5AF
☎ 01392 403 483
c.d.montgomery@exeter.co.uk
GASW

**MOORE**, Jill
**Sexual and Relationship Psychotherapist**
♿ 3 Marlowe Close
Shiphay
Torquay
Devon
TQ2 6DQ
☎ 01803 409 940
☎ 07960 323 682
BASRT

**MUNSEY**, Jon
**Psychodrama Psychotherapist**
37 North View Avenue
Bideford
North Devon
EX39 3LJ
☎ 01237 472 379
jonfern@hotmail.com
BPA

**NICHOLSON**, Elizabeth
**Psychoanalytic Psychotherapist**
White Oaks
18 St. Brannocks Park Road
Ilfracombe
Devon
EX34 8HX
☎ 01271 864003
liznicholson43@hotmail.com
GUILD

**NIGHTINGALE**, Eileen
**Psychosynthesis Psychotherapist**
4 Sycamore Close
Honiton
EX14 2XP
☎ 01404 46451
☎ 01395 513 923
nightingale@blackmorehouse.fsnet.co.uk
PET

**NOACK**, Miké
**Individual and Group Humanistic Psychotherapist**
The Maisonette
50a Fore Street
Totnes
TQ9 5RP
☎ 01803 863 805
AHPP

**NORRIS**, Penny
**Analytical Psychologist-Jungian Analyst**
3 Moorview
The Square
Broadhempston
Devon
TQ9 6BL
☎ 01803 812 510
penerrol.norris@virgin.net
IGAP

**NORTH**, Joanna
**Core Process Psychotherapist**
♿ 5 Culm Valley Way
Uffculme
Cullompton
Devon
EX15 3XZ
☎ 01884 841 333
dwright@aol.com
KI

**OPENSHAW**, Sally
**Sexual and Relationship Psychotherapist**
North Down House
North Down Road
Bideford
EX39 3LT
☎ 01237 473 052
salopen@freeuk.com
BASRT

**OVERZEE**, Anne
**Core Process Psychotherapist**
c/o Karuna Institute
Natsworthy Manor
Widecombe in the Moor
Newton Abbot
TQ13 7TR
☎ 01647 221457
KI

**PEHRSSON-TATHAM**, Lena
**Psychoanalytic Psychotherapist**
Maynards
Cornworthy
Totnes
Devon
TQ9 7HR
☎ 01803 732 733
☎ 01803 864 466
SIP

**PERRY**, Belinda
**Family & Systemic Psychotherapist**
Clinical Psychology Service
Ladywell Unit
Raleigh Park
Barnstaple
EX31 4JB
☎ 01271 322 442
belindaperry@onetel.com
AFT

**PLANT**, Robert
**Group Analyst**
Group Analytic Network
45 Queen Street
Exeter
☎ 01392 434 441
robertcp@hotmail.com
GASW, IGA

**PREECE**, Rob
**Transpersonal Psychotherapist**
7 Holne Cross
Ashburton
Devon
TQ13 7QU
☎ 01364 654 044
CTP

**PRENTICE**, Hilary
**Integrative Psychotherapist**
7 Baker's Park
Holne
Buckfastleigh
TQ13 7SN
☎ 01364 631 033
☎ 07985 410229
hilarypr@gn.apc.org
MET

**RAWLINSON**, Lynn
**Psychodrama Psychotherapist**
Tinavor Cottage
Aish Lane
South Brent
Devon
TQ10 9JG
☎ 01364 73117
lynnrawlinson@btinternet.com
BPA

**REIBSTEIN**, Janet
**Family & Systemic Psychotherapist**
♿ 14 Howell Road
Exeter
EX4 4LG
☎ 01392 214 231
j.reibstein:exeter.ac.uk
AFT

**ROBERTSON**, Zuleika
**Psychoanalytic Psychotherapist**
♿ 6 Prospect Park
off Old Tiverton Road
St. James, Exeter
Devon
EX4 6NA
☎ 01392 430162
zlk.rbrtsn.@aol.com
GUILD

**RODDICK**, Mary
**Family & Systemic Psychotherapist**
Combe Farm
Christow
Exeter
EX6 7NR
☎ 01647 252 553
mary.roddick@bigfoot.com
AFT

**ROTAS**, Joanna
**Core Process Psychotherapist**
3 Western Villas
Collins Road
Totnes
Devon
TQ9 5PW
☎ 01803 864990
KI

**RUGEN**, Ellen
**Family & Systemic Psychotherapist**
6 The Old School
North Street
Totnes
TQ9 5NZ
☎ 01803 865 279
ellenrugen@hotmail.com
AFT

**RUSLING**, David Michael
**Family & Systemic Psychotherapist**
Plymouth Child & Family Service
Erme House
Mount Gould Hospital
Plymouth
PL4 7QD
☎ 01752 313 166
mrusling-keystone@hotmail.com
AFT

**SARRA**, Nicholas
**Group Analyst**
♿ Devon Partnership NHS Trust H.Q
Wonford House Hospital
Exeter
☎ 07815 815 202
nick.sarra@devonptnrs.nhs.uk
IGA

**SCOTT HAYWARD**, Anna
**Neurolinguistic Psychotherapist**
♿ 16 Brunswick Terrace
Torquay
Devon
TQ1 4AE
☎ 01803 323 885
ashayward@hotmail.com
NLPtCA

**SEYMOUR-CLARK**, Vivienne
**Psychoanalytic Psychotherapist**
25 Brooklands
Bridgetown
Totnes
Devon
TQ9 5AR
☎ 01803 864 976
vclark@eurobell.co.uk
CSP

**SHELDON**, Brian
**Cognitive Behavioural Psychotherapist**
♿ Centre for Evidence Based Soc Srvcs
Amory Building
University of Exeter
Exeter
EX4 4RJ
☎ 01392 263 323
B.Sheldon@exeter.ac.uk
BABCP

**SILLS**, Franklyn
**Core Process Psychotherapist**
♿ Kauruna Institute
Natsworthy Manor
Widecombe in the Moor
Devon
TQ13 7TR
☎ 01647 221 457
KI

**SILLS**, Maura
**Core Process Psychotherapist**
♿ Kauruna Institute
Natsworthy Manor
Widecombe in the Moor
Devon
TQ13 7TR
☎ 01647 221 457
KI

**SKEET**, Maggie
**Gestalt Psychotherapist**
Heavitree
Exeter
☎ 01392 218 783
maggie@magskeet.freeserve.co.uk
GPTI

**SPRAGUE**, Ken
**Psychodrama Psychotherapist**
Little Zephyr
Lydiate Lane
Lynton
North Devon
EX35 6AJ
☎ 01598 753 754
BPA

**STEWART**, Lindsey
**Humanistic Psychotherapist**
Burnside
Avonwick
South Brent
Devon
TQ10 9EZ
☎ 01364 73201
AHPP

**SUTTON-SMITH**, Deirdre
**Group Analyst**
♿ 45 Queen Street
Exeter
EX4 3SR
☎ 0117 944 1005
☎ 01392 434 441
gasw@ukonline.co.uk
GASW, IGA

**SWALLOW**, Reynold
**Transpersonal Psychotherapist**
Bridge House
Culmstock
Cullompton
Devon
EX15 3JJ
☎ 01884 840 513
CTP

**TATHAM**, Peter
**Analytical Psychologist-Jungian Analyst, Psychoanalytic Psychotherapist**
Maynards
Cornworthy
Totnes
South Devon
TQ9 7HR
☎ 01803 732 733
IGAP, SIP

**TAYLOR**, Crispin
**Family & Systemic Psychotherapist**
♿ 124 Pennsylvania Road
Exeter
EX4 6DW
☎ 07989 548 218
crispin.taylor@devonptnrs.nhs.uk
AFT

**TAYLOR**, Helen
**Personal Construct Psychotherapist**
56 Camperdown Terrace
Exmouth
Devon
EX8 1EQ
☎ 01395 267615
helen_seaside_taylor@btopenworld.com
PCP

**TAYLOR**, Susan
**Core Process Psychotherapist**
Kingston Cottage
Kingston
Dittisham
Dartmouth, S Devon
TQ6 0JB
☎ 01803 722 459
KI

**THOMAS**, Alyss
**Core Process Psychotherapist**
The Practice
One The Plains
Totnes Deven
TQ9 5DR
☎ 01803 862 300
KI

**TILLEY**, Alison
**Gestalt Psychotherapist**
1 Railway Cottages
Lapford
Nr. Crediton
Devon
EX17 6QU
☎ 01363 83057
alisontilley@onetel.net.uk
SPTI

**TOBLINI**, Roberta
**Core Process Psychotherapist**
12 Somerset Place
Totnes
TQ9 5AX
☎ 01803 862 220
KI

**TOMLINSON**, Catherine
**Transpersonal Psychotherapist**
Harnas Oak Centre
PL19 0LN
☎ 01822 810 389
harnesoak@yahoo.co.uk
CCPE

**URRY**, Amy
**Family & Systemic Psychotherapist**
64 Queen Elizabeth Drive
Crediton
Devon
EX17 2EJ
☎ 07710 216 828
☎ 01363 774 707
amy@systemic.fsnet.co.uk
AFT

**VERNON**, Bisi
**Transactional Analysis Psychotherapist**
♿ Taylors Cottage
Chittlehamholt
Umberleigh
N. Devon
EX37 9NT
☎ 01769 540 609
ITA

**WARD**, Barbara
**Psychosynthesis Psychotherapist**
The Retreat
3 Wheelwright Court
Walkhampton
Yelverton, Devon
PL20 6LA
☎ 01822 855 619
PET

**WARRICK**, Jilly
**Core Process Psychotherapist**
The Linhay House
Broadhempston
Nr Totnes
Devon
TQ9 6BJ
☎ 01803 812056
KI

**WATKINS**, Judy
**Psychoanalytic Psychotherapist**
Rose Cottage
Tedburn St. Mary
Exeter
EX6 6AY
☎ 01647 61 276
SIP

**WATSON**, Gay
**Core Process Psychotherapist**
Coombery
Tuckenhay
Totnes
Devon
TQ9 7EP
☎ 01803 732 272
KI

**WEIGHTMAN**, Elizabeth
**Psychoanalytic Psychotherapist**
146 Heavitree Road
Exeter
EX1 2LZ
☎ 01392 491 910
ecweight@aol.com
SIP

**WELLS**, Roger
**Psychoanalytic Psychotherapist**
Argyle House
New Buildings Lane
Gandy Street
Exeter
EX4 3LS
☎ 01823 323363
☎ 01392 494466
GUILD

**WHEADON**, Sylvia
**Psychodrama Psychotherapist**
Littlecroft, 16 Clampitt Road
Ipplepen
Newton Abbot
Devon
TQ12 5TE
sylvia.m.wheadon@btinternet.com
BPA

**WHEBA**, Raymond
**Family & Systemic Psychotherapist**
♿ Parkfield House
38 Esplanade Road
Paigton
TQ3 2NH
☎ 07779 573 968
AFT

**WHITTLE**, Peter
**Cognitive Analytic Therapist**
♿ Teign View
CMHC
16 Orchard Gardens
Teignmouth
TQ14 8DS
☎ 01626 775 951
Peter.whittle@nhs.net
ACAT

**WILLOW**, Angela
**Core Process Psychotherapist**
1 Orchard Terrace
Tuckenhay
Totnes
South Devon
TQ9 7EJ
☎ 01803 732185
KI

**WILSON**, Jancis
**Core Process Psychotherapist**
♿ Church Close
Shilstone Lane
Throwleigh
EX20 2HX
☎ 01647 231 264
KI

**WOODING**, Sandy
**Psychodrama Psychotherapist**
Tumblestones
3 Pinchaford Cottages
Haytor
Ilsington, Devon
TQ13 9XU
☎ 01364 661 541
sandy@tumblestones.freeserve.co.uk
BPA

**WOOLNER**, John
**Family & Systemic Psychotherapist**
16 Parkfield Road
Topsham
Exeter
EX3 0DR
☎ 01392 874 088
jwoolner@devon.gov.uk
16 Parkfield Road
Topsham
Exeter
Devon
EX3 ODR
IFT

**WORLEY**, Clive
**Family & Systemic Psychotherapist**
15 Lower Kings Avenue
Exeter
EX4 6JT
☎ 01392 412 492
cliveworley@blueyonder.co.uk
AFT

**WRIGHT**, Maureen
**Group Analyst, Psychodrama Psychotherapist**
Thornlea
Town Lane
Woodbury
Nr. Exeter, Devon
EX4 1NB
☎ 01395 232 001
GASW, BPA

## DORSET

**ARCHER**, Ruth
**Psychoanalytic Psychotherapist**
31 Wessex Road
Dorchester
Dorset
DT1 2NU
☎ 01305 751 965
ruthc.archer@virgin.net
FPC

**BARMES**, Sally
**Body Psychotherapist, Integrative Psychotherapist**
Cobwebs
Godmanstone
nr Dorchester
Dorset
DT2 7AQ
☎ 01300 341 547
☎ 07773 616 890
CCBP

**BARTLETT**, Mark
**Psychoanalytic Psychotherapist**
44 Alexandra Court
Bridport
Dorset
DT6 5QP
☎ 01308 459 440
SIP

**BOTTERILL**, Willie
**Personal Construct Psychotherapist**
Northleigh House
Northleigh Lane
Colehill, Wimbourne
Dorset
BH21 2PH
☎ 020 7530 4238
☎ 01202 884 835
willie.botterill 1 @virginnet.co.uk
PCP

**BRADLEY**, Linda
**Integrative Psychotherapist**
Kingston Farm
Kingston
Sturminster Newton
DT10 2AR
☎ 07775 665 702
SPCRC

**BRAMHAM**, Mick
**Existential Psychotherapist**
101 Sutton Road
Sutton Poyntz
Weymouth
DT3 6LW
☎ 01305 834 686
☎ 01305 787 940
mick.lantern@freenet.co.uk
SEA

**CARSLEY**, Carol
**Integrative Psychotherapist**
Old Smithy
Ibberton
Blandford Forum
DT11 0EN
☎ 01258 817 361
SPCRC

**DARE-BRYAN**, Arminal
**Psychoanalytic Psychotherapist**
Merle Cottage
Church Street
Yetminstet
Sherbourne
DT9 6LG
☎ 020 8874 3138
☎ 01935 872 111
FPC

**DENNIS**, Steve
**Transactional Analysis Psychotherapist**
♿ The Thatches
31 Dorchester Road
Maiden Newton
Dorset
DT2 0BD
☎ 01300 320 000
☎ 07905 917 435
ITA

**FERNANDEZ**, Nigel R.
**Cognitive Behavioural Psychotherapist**
The Farmhouse Therapy Centre
Sturminster Marshall
Wimborne
BH21 4AZ
☎ 01258 858 489
☎ 0117 952 5255
nigelfernandez@hotmail.com
BABCP

**FINCH**, Auberon
**Core Process Psychotherapist**
6 Bakers Paddock
Broadmayne
Dorchester
Dorset
DT2 8HD
☎ 01305 854501
GASW, KI

**FRESHWATER**, Dawn
**Integrative Psychosynthesis Psychotherapist**
Swanage
BH19
☎ 01202 504 126
RE.V

**GESSERT**, Astrid
**Lacanian Analyst**
♿ Consulting Rooms
1 Colliton Street
Dorchester
Dorset
DT1 1HX
☎ 01297 560 497
astnd@gessert.fsnet.co.uk
CFAR

**HARRIS**, Neil
**Gestalt Psychotherapist**
♿ Roundhay, Chapel Lane
Bransgore
Dorset
BH23 8BN
☎ 01425 673 652
neilph@aol.com
GPTI

**HEGAN**, Laurence
**Gestalt Psychotherapist**
72 Rempstone Road
Merley
Wimborne
Dorset
BH21 1RP
☎ 01202 848 978
laurencehegan@btinternet.com
MET

**JACOBS**, Michael
**Integrative Psychotherapist, Psychodynamic Psychotherapist**
♿ 18 Battlemead
Swanage
Dorset
BH19 1PH
☎ 01929 423 068
battlemead@aol.com
UPCA, VAPP

**KERRY**, Liz
**Gestalt Psychotherapist**
16 Barnsfield Road
St Leonards
Ringwood
BH24 2BX
☎ 01202 897 903
liz.kerry@tesco.net
MET

**KERSHAW**, Jennifer
**Humanistic and Integrative Psychotherapist**
Priestlands House
Priestlands
Sherborne
Dorset
DT9 4HN
☎ 01395 262 626
☎ 01935 814 525
JenKershaw@aol.com
Middlemarsh Clinic
Poundbury
Dorchester
DT1 3GX
AHPP

**LACY-SMITH**, Jo
**Humanistic and Integrative Psychotherapist**
♿ 2 Ackerman Road
Dorchester
Dorset
DT1 1NZ
☎ 0117 944 5127
JoLacySmith@aol.com
BCPC

**LOGUE**, Nancy
**Sexual and Relationship Psychotherapist**
Halves House
132 East Street
Corfe Castle
BH20 5EH
☎ 01929 481 163
nancy.logue@care4free.net
BASRT

**MARCH-SMITH**, Rosie
**Humanistic and Integrative Psychotherapist**
♿ Ellerslie
Cattistock
Dorchester
Dorset
DT2 0JL
☎ 01300 321355
rosie@ellersliedorset.co.uk
AHPP, BCPC

**MCNAIR**, Ann G
**Systemic Psychotherapist**
♿ 12 St Stephens Lane
Verwood
BH31 7BQ
☎ 01202 814 603
KCC

**MILLS**, Christopher
**Humanistic and Integrative Psychotherapist**
♿ Bute House Surgery
Wooton Grove
Sherbourne
Dorset
DT9 4DL
☎ 01225 445 237
c.a.mills@bath.ac.uk
BCPC

**MOWLAM**, Madeleine
**Core Process Psychotherapist**
6 Fleet Lane
Chickerell
Weymouth
Dorset
DT3 4DF
☎ 01305 839732
KI

**NEWBERY**, Christopher
**Humanistic and Integrative Psychotherapist**
12 St. Georges Avenue
Weymouth
Dorset
DT4 7TU
☎ 01305 786 172
AHPP, BCPC

**POOLE**, Carol Lynn
**Systemic Psychotherapist**
Lowdens
Frenchmoor Lane
East Dean
Wiltshire
SP5 1HA
☎ 01794 342 173
☎ 02380 586 154
carolrsa@msn.com
KCC

**PORTEOUS**, Trish
**Psychodynamic Psychotherapist**
Mayo Farm
Higher Slandford Road
Shaftesbury
Dorset
SP7 0EF
☎ 01747 852 051
trish_porteous@hotmail.com
FPC

**ROBINSON**, Christina
**Psychoanalytic Psychotherapist**
White Hill Farmhouse
Stoke Wake
Blandford Forum
Dorset
DT11 0HF
☎ 01258 817301
martinjrobinson@hotmail.com
GUILD

**ROBINSON**, Martin
**Analytical Psychologist-Jungian Analyst**
White Hill Farmhouse
Stoke Wake
Nr. Blandford Forum
Dorset
DT11 0HF
☎ 0208 459 5442
☎ 01258 817 301
AJA, SIP

**ROSE**, Stuart
**Cognitive Behavioural Psychotherapist**
♿ Highfield
Lee Lane
Bridport
DT6 4AJ
☎ 01308 458 600
stuartrose@psychealth.co.uk
BABCP

**ROSEN**, Mrs Judith
**Sexual and Relationship Psychotherapist**
Park Centre for Sexual Health
Weymouth
☎ 01202 670 627
☎ 01305 762 682
judyrosen@hotmail.com
BASRT

**ROSENTHAL**, Alison
**Transpersonal Psychotherapist**
♿ "Tiptoe"
Rockbourne Road
Sandleheath
Fordingbridge
SP6 1QF
☎ 01425 655 078
☎ 01722 411 998
alisonrose@supalife.com
CCPE

**RUBIE**, Val
**Attachment-based Psychoanalytic Psychotherapist**
5 Partway Lane
Hazelbury Bryan
Sturminster Newton
Dorset
DT10 2DP
☎ 01258 817 496
bmvcounselling@aol.com
CAPP

**SHARPE**, John
**Group Analyst**
♿ Clare Cottage
23 West Dean
Nr. Salisbury
SP5 1JB
☎ 01794 340 028
john@jlsharpe.freeserve.co.uk
IGA

**SINGLETON**, Kyrin
**Transpersonal Psychotherapist**
"Morningstar"
29 Richmond Road
Sherborne
Dorset
DT9 3HL
☎ 01935 812 791
CCPE

**SONES**, Joanne
**Child Psychotherapist**
West Dorset Childrens' Centre
Damers Road
Dorchester
Dorset
DT1 2LB
☎ 01305 254712
ACP

**TOMLINSON**, Andrew
**Hypno-Psychotherapist**
71 Wareham Road
Corfe Mullen
Wimborne
Dorset
BH21 3JX
☎ 01202 659 883
andy.tomlinson@virgin.net
NSHAP

**TRACY**, Colin
**Humanistic and Integrative Psychotherapist**
2 Ackerman Road
Dorchester
Dorset
DT1 1NZ
☎ 01305 266 721
BCPC

**WALKER**, Moira
**Integrative Psychotherapist, Psychodynamic Psychotherapist**
♿ 18 Battlermead
Swanage
Dorset
BH19 1PH
☎ 01929 423 068
mw2021@aol.com
UPCA, VAPP

**WATERFIELD**, Julia
**Integrative Arts Psychotherapist**
Ismene Cottage
3 Bridge View
Pimperne
Blandford, Dorset
DT11 8TX
☎ 01258 480 691
waterfield@ismene.freeserve.co.uk
IATE

**WATERFIELD**, Michael
**Integrative Psychosynthesis Psychotherapist**
Ismene Cottage
3 Bridge View
Pimperne
Blandford Forum
DT11 8TX
☎ 01258 480 691
waterfield@ismene.freeserve.co.uk
RE.V

**WERMIG-MORGAN**, Julia
**Hypno-Psychotherapist**
65a The Pound
Burton Bradstock
Bridport
Dorset
DT6 4QA
☎ 01308 897 031
jwermigmorgan@hotmail.com
Therapy Room
7 Barrack Street
Bridport
DT6 3LX
CTIS

**WILDASH**, Sheila
**Psychoanalytic Psychotherapist**
10 Fairway Drive
Northmoor Park
Wareham
Dorset
BH20 4SG
☎ 01929 553 097
AGIP

**WILLIAMS**, Rosamund
**Integrative Psychotherapist**
♿ 1 Vinney Cross
Dorchester Road
Bridport
Dorset
DT6 4PJ
☎ 01308 425 413
vinneycross@hotmail.com
MET

**WILLIAMS**, Sam
**Gestalt Psychotherapist**
1 Vinney Cross
Uploders
Bridport
Dorset
DT6 4PJ
☎ 01308 425 413
vinneycross@hotmail.com
MET

**WINTERBURN**, Ann
**Neurolinguistic Psychotherapist**
66 Williams Avenue
Wyke Regis
Weymouth
Dorset
DT4 9BP
☎ 01305 777 457
ann@winterburn29.freeserve.co.uk
NLPtCA

## ESSEX

**AHEARNE**, Jan
**Integrative Psychotherapist**
♿ Spectrum, N. Essex NHS Trust
C & E Centre
New London Road
Chelmsford
CM2 0QH
☎ 01245 318 614
SPCRC

**ARUNDELL**, Jane
**Group Analytic Psychotherapist**
49 Alfred Road
Brentwood
CM14 4BT
☎ 01245 345 345
FPC

**BARKER**, Janet
**Sexual and Relationship Psychotherapist**
Theydon End
Forest Side
Epping
CM16 4ED
☎ 01992 575 527
☎ 01922 570 116
janet.barker@btinternet.com
BASRT

**BARRETT**, Jenny
**Psychoanalytic Psychotherapist**
Lapis centre for Psychotherapy & Counselling
49 North Hill
Colchester
Essex
CO1 1PY
☎ 01206 572 205
☎ 01728 628 538
jennyagbarrett@any-mail.co.uk
CSP

**BAYLEY**, Sydney
**Core Process Psychotherapist**
44 Ernest Road
Wivenhoe
Colchester
CO7 9LQ
☎ 01206 822 406
KI

**BEVAN**, Judith Lesley
**Systemic Psychotherapist**
♿ Child & Family Consultation Service
Wych Elm House
Hamstell Road
Harlow
CM20 1QR
KCC

**BINGHAM**, Jane
**Psychoanalytic Psychotherapist**
Sycamore
Sadlers House
2 Legg Street
Chelmsford
CM1 1AH
☎ 01702 558 969
☎ 01245 359 353
binghamj@fish.co.uk
FPC

**BORTHWICK**, Rosemary
43 Forest Road
Loughton
Essex
IG10 1EE
☎ 020 8508 7292
ARBS

**BRANKIN**, Irene
**Psychosynthesis Psychotherapist**
14 Lynton Road
Hadleigh
Essex
SS7 2QQ
☎ 01702 555 420
irene.brankin14@virgin.net
PET

**BRIGGS**, Andrew
**Child Psychotherapist**
North Essex Mental Health Partnership NHS Trust
Child & Family Consultation Service
Stanwell House, Stanwell Stree
Colchester
CO2 7DL
☎ 01206 287321
☎ 01206 560934
ACP

**BROWN**, Diana
**Systemic Psychotherapist**
115 Gleber Crescent
Witham
CM8 2HZ
☎ 01376 501 696
☎ 01376 555 763
dianajdei@aol.com
The Gables
17 Bocking End
Braintree
CM7 9AE
KCC

**BROWN**, Iain
**Group Analytic Psychotherapist**
182 Upper Bridge Road
Chelmsford
Essex
CM2 0AY
iainbrown@madasafish.com
UPCA

**BUNCE**, Maureen
**Psychoanalytic Psychotherapist**
Tolleshunt Knights
Maldon, Essex
CM9
☎ 01621 816 415
bunces@btinternet.com
CCOPPP

**BURROWS**, Leslely
**Transpersonal Psychotherapist**
Southend
☎ 01702 589 793
☎ 07979 961 479
CCPE

**BURTON**, Jean
**Family & Systemic Psychotherapist**
The Hermitage
Constitution Hill
Sudbury
Suffolk
CO1 2PT
☎ 01787 374 121
chrisandjean@sief.freeserve.co.uk
AFT

**BWALYA**, Alf
**Systemic Psychotherapist**
♿ North Essex Mental Health Partnership NHS Trust
Chelmsford and Essex Centre
New London Road
Chelmsford
CM2 0QH
☎ 01245 318 614
alfbwalya@aol.com
KCC

**CAHILL**, Denise
**Systemic Psychotherapist**
♿ C/O Clover Ward
King George Hospital
Barley Lane
Goodmayes
IG3
KCC

**CAVISTON**, Paul
**Psychoanalytic Psychotherapist**
♿ The Priory
Stump Lane
Springfield Green
Chelmsford, Essex
CM1 7SJ
☎ 01245 345 345
PA

**CHANDLER**, Emma
**Systemic Psychotherapist**
Child and Family Consultation Service
24 Norton Road
Ingatestone
Essex
CM13
☎ 01227 350 610
☎ 01892 619 766
margaretbanfield@yahoo.co.uk
KCC

**CHAPMAN**, Maureen
**Psychoanalytic Psychotherapist**
The Old Rectory
Mount Road
Theydon Mount
Epping
CM16 7PW
☎ 01992 578 723
☎ 01992 572 283
mrchap@msn.com
FPC

**CHRISTY**, Jackie
**Cognitive Behavioural Psychotherapist**
Health & Fitness Centre
14 Chapel Road
Tiptree
Colchester
CO5 0RA
☎ 01621 788 113
jchristyandcbt@esprit.fslife.co.uk
BABCP

**CLARK**, Isobel
**Psychodynamic Psychotherapist**
♿ 5-6 School Barn Cottages
Pentlow
Sudbury
Suffolk
CO10 7JN
☎ 01206 768 211
☎ 01787 280 648
iaclark@waitrose.com
The Stockwell Centre
44 East Stockwell Street
Colchester
Essex
CO1 1SR
FIP

**CLEMENTS**, Iris
**Analytical Psychotherapist**
4 Pembroke Close
Colchester
CO2 8AF
☎ 01206 572 583
irisclem@aol.com
AIP

**CLEMENTS**, Sue
**Family & Systemic Psychotherapist**
♿ Early Intervention Project Coordinator
220 Stamford Road
Dagenham
Essex
RM9 4EL
☎ 020 8270 6572
earlyinterventionproject@rmplc.co.uk
AFT

**CLOWES**, Brenda
**Sexual and Relationship Psychotherapist**
176 Princes Road
Buckhurst Hill
Essex
IG9 5DJ
☎ 020 8505 8328
brendaclowes@therapia.co.uk or
Bclowestherapy@aol.com
BASRT

**COHN**, Nancy
**Child Psychotherapist, Psychoanalytic Psychotherapist**
Psychotherapy & Counselling Service
St Andrews Centre for Plastic Surge
Court Road, Broomfield,
Chelmsford, Essex
CM1 7ET
☎ 01245 516030
☎ 01206 396581
ACP, GUILD

**COLLINS**, Lynda
**Systemic Psychotherapist**
♿ 26 Guys Farm Road
South Woodham Ferrers
Chelmsford
Essex
CM3 5NE
☎ 01245 320 733
collins.Lynda@1stopenworld.com
IFT

**COLLINS**, Natalie
**Psychoanalytic Psychotherapist**
133 Larkshall Road
North Chingford
London
E4 6PE
☎ 020 8529 4986
☎ 07796 36 31 88
GUILD

**COLMER**, Enid
**Family & Systemic Psychotherapist**
♿ Child & Family Consultation Service
Wych Elm House
Hamstel Road
Harlow
CM20 1QR
☎ 01279 692 300
Enid@ecolmer.fsnet.co.uk
IFT

**COUSSENS**, Kay
**Integrative Psychotherapist**
42 Glenwood Drive
Gidea Park
Romford
Essex
RM2 5AS
☎ 01708 755384
MC

**CRAIB**, Ian
**Group Analytic Psychotherapist**
Millhouse
Bulmer Road
Sudbury
Suffolk
CO10 7EZ
☎ 01206 872638
☎ 01787 310210
icraib@essex.ac.uk
FIP

**CROUCH**, Carol
**Existential Psychotherapist**
Woodside
61 Russell Road
Buckhurst Hill
IG9 5QF
☎ 020 8504 0059
rgca@blcrouch.freeserve.co.uk
SPCRC

**DANIEL**, Karen
21 Oliver Road
Rainham
RM1 7UH
☎ 01708 522 067
AFT

**DARIVAKIS**, Dimitri
**Group Analytic Psychotherapist**
99 Kingswood Road
Goodmayes
Ilford
IG3 8UB
☎ 020 8599 2363
☎ 0794 105 4114
dimitridarivakis@hotmail.com
UPCA

**DAVY-BARNES**, Malcolm
**Analytical Psychotherapist**
'The Lilacs'
The Street
Steeple, near Southminster
Essex
CM0 7LF
☎ 01621 774 218
AIP

**DEEBLE**, Elizabeth A.
**Cognitive Behavioural Psychotherapist**
Psychology Dept.
Goodmayes Hospital
Barley Lane
Ilford
IG3 8XJ
☎ 020 8970 4039
BABCP

**EDEN**, Sharon
**Psychosynthesis Psychotherapist**
128 Meads Lane
Seven Kings
Ilford
Essex
IG3 8PE
☎ 020 8590 3850
☎ 020 8947 6059
sharon.eden@btopenworld.com
PET

**EDWARDS**, Brian
**Psychoanalytic Psychotherapist**
22 St Peters Road
West Mersea
Colchester
Essex
CO5 8LJ
☎ 01206 386 991
edwardsbr22@aol.com
AIP

**EDWARDS-POLLARD**, Astrid
**Family & Systemic Psychotherapist**
8 Sandford Close
Wivenhoe
Colchester
CO7 9NP
Astrid@btinternet.com
IFT

**ELDON**, Martin
**Neurolinguistic Psychotherapist**
♿ Marlin House
2 Coppice Close
The Street, Takely
Bishop's Stortford
CM22 6QB
☎ 01279 873 494
info@marlin-nlp.co.uk
NLPtCA

**ELLIS**, Sian
**Psychoanalytic Psychotherapist**
171 Theydon Grove
Epping
Essex
CM16 4QA
☎ 01992 574 018
sian.ellis@talk21.com
AGIP, FIP

**FABIAN**, Carole
**Psychoanalytic Psychotherapist**
21 St Albans Road
Colchester
Essex
CO3 3JQ
☎ 01206 541 499
The Trinity Centre
12 and 21 Trinity Street
Colchester
Essex
CO1 1JN
AGIP

**FORMAN**, Sally
**Attachment-based Psychoanalytic Psychotherapist**
25 Beechwood Drive
Woodford Green
IG8 9QY
☎ 020 8502 9076
sallyforman@btinternet.com
CAPP

**FOX**, Almuth-Maria
**Integrative Psychotherapist**
101 Hadleigh Road
Leigh-on-Sea
SS9 2LY
☎ 01702 472 634
mclean.fox@btinternet.com
SPCRC

**GALE**, Derek
**Humanistic Psychotherapist**
Stable Cottage
Whitakers Way
Loughton
Essex
IG10 1SQ
☎ 020 8508 9344
☎ 0958 578031
Derek@galecent.demon.co.uk
AHPP

**GANDA**, Matthew
**Family & Systemic Psychotherapist**
♿ 110 Beeches Road
Chelmsford
Essex
CM1 2RX
☎ 01245 603 564
Matthew.Ganda@nemht.nhs.uk
The Priory Hospital
Chelmsford
Stump Lane
Chelmsford
CM1 7SJ
IFT

**GOLDING**, Michelle A.
**Psychoanalytic Psychotherapist**
4 Sheredan Road
Highams Park
London
E4 9RW
☎ 020 8523 5518
michelleagolding@hotmail.com
FPC

**GOLDSTEIN**, Marc
**Integrative Psychotherapist**
106 Whitehall Road
North Chingford
London
E4 6DW
☎ 020 8524 6528
☎ 07876 520 129
marcgoldstein@goldserve.net
SPTI

**GRAINGER**, Eve
**Child Psychotherapist**
Barking & Dagenham Child & Family Consult. Service
31 Woodward Road
Dagenham
Essex
RM9 4SJ
☎ 020 8592 4445
☎ 020 8348 5457
ACP

**GREATREX**, Julian
**Psychosynthesis Psychotherapist**
15 Grange Avenue
Woodford Green
Essex
IG8 9JT
☎ 020 8504 0191
Julian.Greatrex@btinternet.com
PET

**GREENWOOD**, Angela
**Educational Therapist**
34 Sea View Road
Leigh on Sea
Essex
SS9 1AT
☎ 01702 431 540
angelaanddavidgreenwood@yahoo.co.uk
CFET

**GREGG**, Peter D
**Group Analytic Psychotherapist**
166 Warren Drive
Hornchurch
Essex
RM12 4PP
☎ 07967 362 597
jwroe@tesco.net
UPCA

**GROVER**, Miriam Ruth
**Cognitive Behavioural Psychotherapist**
7 Lyndhurst Drive
Bicknacre
Chelmsford
CM3 4XL
☎ 01245 227 538
☎ 07812 931 104
miriam.grover@virgin.net
BABCP

**HANDRICK**, Olaf
**Cognitive Behavioural Psychotherapist**
♿ Department of Psychology
Runwell Hospital
Runwell Chase, Runwell
Wickford
SS11 7XX
☎ 01268 366 011/013
☎ 01604 465 269
handrick@barclays.net
BABCP

**HASLAM**, Deirdre
**Humanistic Psychotherapist**
♿ Rivermead Campus
3rd Floor, Ashby House
Bishop Hall Lane
Chelmsford
CM1 1SQ
☎ 020 8986 3051
☎ 01245 493 131 x4982
deirdre@haslam1.co.uk
AHPP

**HOLLINGWORTH**, Amanda
**Sexual and Relationship Psychotherapist**
Old Fairfields
Hatfield Peverel
Chelmsford
Essex
CM3 2NT
☎ 01245 381 480
hollingworth@btclick.com
BASRT

**HOWARD**, Caroline Pui
**Cognitive Behavioural Psychotherapist**
10 Elms Farm Road
Hornchurch
RM12 5RD
☎ 01708 476 198
☎ 020 8594 4894
cats11@uk2.net
CATS (London) Ltd
Trocoll House
Wakering Road
Barking
IG11 8PD
BABCP

**HUDSON**, Rachel
**Psychoanalytic Psychotherapist**
30 Gordon Road
Ilford
Essex
IG1 1SP
☎ 020 8553 3089
FPC

**HUGHES**, Linda
**Humanistic Psychotherapist**
Fox Hall
The Croft
Bures
Suffolk
CO8 5JB
☎ 01787 227 195
linda@dragonland.demon.co.uk
AHPP

**HUMPHREYS**, David
**Systemic Psychotherapist**
♿ Whelby House Medical Centre
33 London Road
Old Harlow
CM17 0DB
☎ 01279 442 602
☎ 01279 757 751
Familyworks@btinternet.com
Family Works
Thorley Health Centre
Bishops Stortford
CM23 4EG
IFT

**JACOBS**, Linda
**Family & Systemic Psychotherapist**
101 Farmleigh Avenue
Clacton on Sea
Essex
CO15 4UL
☎ 01255 426 115
☎ 020 8700 8877
LINDA.JACOBS@slam.nhs.uk
IFT

**JONES**, Amanda
**Systemic Psychotherapist**
Infant Mental Health Project
Child & Family Consultation Service
Loxford Hall
Loxford Lane, Ilford
IG1 2PL
☎ 020 8478 7211
☎ 020 8970 8098
Paediatric LiaisonTeam
Peadiatric Department
King George Hospital
Barley Lane, Goodmayes
IG3 8YB
KCC

**JULIEN**, Michael
**Integrative Psychotherapist**
497 Aldborough Road North
Newbury Park
Ilford
IG2 7SY
☎ 020 8599 0625
SPCRC

**KWEI**, Caryl Lesley
**Cognitive Behavioural Psychotherapist**
♿ 6 Brentwood Place
Sawyers Hall Lane
Brentwood
Essex
CM15 9DN
☎ 01277 226 834
caryl_kwei@yahoo.co.uk
BABCP

**LEACH**, Mark J
**Sexual and Relationship Psychotherapist**
♿ 94 Station Lane
Hornchurch
RM12 6LX
☎ 01708 445 156
☎ 020 7346 4535
BASRT

**LEWIS**, Jo-Ann
**Psychoanalytic Psychotherapist**
6 Fairview Gardens
Woodford Green
Essex
IG8 7DJ
☎ 020 8559 1318
jo-ann-lewis@postmaster.co.uk
AGIP

**LLOYD**, Roger
**Group Analytic Psychotherapist**
♿ 494 Heathway
Dagenham
Essex
RM10 7SH
☎ 020 8984 9887
rogerblloyd@aol.com
FPC

**MATHEWS**, Trevor J.
**Cognitive Behavioural Psychotherapist, Rational Emotive Behaviour Therapist**
11 Arundel Mews
Billericay
CM12 0FW
☎ 01277 634 817
mathews@conflict.co.uk
BABCP, AREBT

**MCCANDLESS**, Lynn
**Family & Systemic Psychotherapist**
North East London Mental Health Trust
(seconded to L.B. Barking & Dagenha
Seabrook House
22 Shipton Close, Dagenha
RM8 3QR
☎ 020 8270 6900
lmccandl@hotmail.com
IFT

**MCCARRON**, Gerard
**Cognitive Psychotherapist**
111 Brackley Square
Woodford Green
Essex
IG8 7LN
☎ 020 8491 7756
☎ 077309 924 361
gmccarron@totalise.co.uk
The Priory Hospital
Springfield Green
CM1 7SJ
BABCP

**MCDERMOTT**, Ian
**Neurolinguistic Psychotherapist**
ITS House
Websters Court
Websters Way
Reyleigh
SS6 8JQ
☎ 01268 777 125
www.itsnlp.com
NLPtCA

**MILLAR**, David
**Psychoanalytic Psychotherapist**
North Essex Child & Family Consultation Service
Stanwell House
Stanwell Street
Colchester, Essex
CO2 7DL
☎ 01206 287 321
millad@essex.ac.uk
University of Essex
Wivenhoe Park
Colchester
Essex
CO4 3SQ
UPCA

**MOORE**, Ian
**Integrative Psychosynthesis Psychotherapist**
49 Honey Lane
Waltham Abbey
EN9 3AT
☎ 01992 787 307
ianrogermoore@lineone.net
RE.V

**MORO**, Julie Ann
**Family & Systemic Psychotherapist**
9 St James Mews
Billericay
Essex
CM1 9DH
☎ 07990 968 364
morojulie@hotmail.com
AFT

**MUMVURI-ELLIS**, Gladys
**Systemic Psychotherapist**
39 Percy Road
Seven Kings
Ilford
Essex
IG3 8SF
☎ 020 8597 0623
☎ 020 7919 3464
Gladys.Ellis@slam.nhs.uk
IFT

**NEENAN**, Michael
**Cognitive Behavioural Psychotherapist, Rational Emotive Behaviour Therapist**
36 Shearers Way
Boreham
Chelmsford
Essex
CM3 3AE
☎ 01245 468 262
BABCP, AREBT

**O'BRIAN**, Charles
**Family & Systemic Psychotherapist**
12 Farmadine
Saffron Walden
CB11 3HP
☎ 01799 526 589
charlesobrian@btinternet.com
IFT

**O'BRIEN**, Jackie
**Systemic Psychotherapist**
75 Windemere Avenue
Elm Park
Hornchurch
RM12 5ER
☎ 020 7445 7800
☎ 01708 453 665
KCC

**O'CALLAGHAN**, Annemarie
**Psychoanalytic Psychotherapist**
Greensleeves
Layer Breton Heath
Colchester
Essex
CO2 0PP
☎ 01206 331 705
AGIP

**O'LEARY**, Carmen
**Group Analyst**
North Chingford
E4
☎ 020 8529 3536
IGA

**PARMLEY**, Alison
**Gestalt Psychotherapist**
♿ 8 Orchard Close
Great Baddow
Chelmsford
Essex
CM2 9SL
☎ 01245 600 159
alison@rparmley.freeserve.co.uk
GPTI

**PLOWMAN**, Polly
**Integrative Psychosynthesis Psychotherapist**
71 South Street
Manningtree
Essex
CO11 1DT
☎ 0870 787 5131
plowmancolvin@supanet.com
Trinity Centre
12 & 21 Trinity Street
Colchester
CO1 1JN
RE.V

**PLUMMER**, Glenys
**Psychoanalytic Psychotherapist**
"Conifers" , Ravenstock Lane
Little Walden
Saffron Walden
Essex
CB10 1XG
☎ 01799 522 116
glenysplummer@hotmail.com
CSP

**RAICAR**, Alexandra Maeja
**Attachment-based Psychoanalytic Psychotherapist**
8 Feering Road
Billericay
Essex
CM11 2DR
☎ 01277 654 351
☎ 01268 770 990
Child-Centred Attachment Therapy
Review Chambers
39 Websters Way
Rayleigh, Essex
SS6 8JQ
CAPP

**RASHID**, Shila
**Family & Systemic Psychotherapist**
190 Balfour Road
Ilford
Essex
IG1 4JB
☎ 07958 405 216
shila.rashid@talk21.com
AFT

**REDFEARN**, Joseph
**Analytical Psychologist-Jungian Analyst, Psychoanalytic Psychotherapist**
90-92 High Street
Brightlingsea
CO7 0EG
☎ 01206 305 374
j.redfearn@virgin.net
CAP, GUILD *

**REYNOLDS**, Dorothy A
**Family & Systemic Psychotherapist**
♿ 6 Ruskin Dene
Billericay
Essex
CM12 0AN
☎ 01277 653 259
ian@reynolds-cm12.fsnet.co.uk
IFT

**RICE**, Paul
**Behavioural Psychotherapist**
♿ Blackwater House
81 Riverside Way
Kelvedon
Colchester
CO5 9LX
☎ 01376 571 515
☎ 01277 223 581
CMHT, 8 Lime Grove House
Highwood Hospital
Geary Drive
Brentwood
CM15 9DY
BABCP

**RIX**, Mrs Sandy
**Sexual and Relationship Psychotherapist**
Coopers
Coopers Hill
Ongar
CM5 9EG
☎ 01277 362 912
☎ 07050 162 912
SandyRix@aol.com
BASRT

**ROBSON**, Ian
**Hypno-Psychotherapist**
58 Arcadian Gardens
Hadleigh
Essex
SS7 2RP
☎ 01702 555 185
ian@robson63.freeserve.co.uk
NRHP

**ROWAN**, John
**Individual and Group Humanistic Psychotherapist**
70 Kings Head Hill
North Chingford
London
E4 7LY
☎ 020 8524 7381
JohnRowan@aol.com
AHPP

**RUGELEY**, Brenda
**Humanistic and Integrative Psychotherapist**
39 Woodland Way
Marden Ash
Ongar
Essex
CM5 9EP
☎ 01277 363 307
brenda.rugeley@lineone.net
AHPP

**SABAYINDA**, Michael
**Integrative Psychotherapist**
287 Prittlewell Chase
Westcliffe-on-Sea
Southend
SS0 0PL
☎ 01702 322 767
SPCRC

**SAGARAN**, Stephen
**Cognitive Behavioural Psychotherapist**
♿ 24 Wooldlands
Bishop's Strotford
CM23 5BS
☎ 01279 659 160
☎ 01279 635 670
stephensagaran@aol.com
Community Mental Health Centre
Latton Bush Centre
Southern Way
Harlow
CM18 7BL
BABCP

**SALMON**, Cindy
**Transpersonal Psychotherapist**
Friars Cottages
68/69 Castle Road
Colchester
Essex
CO1 1UN
☎ 01206 573 721
CTP

**SAUNDERS-WARD**, Pam
**Rational Emotive Behaviour Therapist**
♿ The Old Post Office
Harborough Hall Road
Messing
Colchester
CO5 9UA
☎ 01621 816 837
pam@fhr-services.co.uk
AREBT

**SCOTT**, Michael
**Group Analyst**
♿ The Psychotherapy Department
Oyster Court
St Helen's Lane
Colchester
CO1 1TY
☎ 01206 287 200
michael.scott@nemht.nhs.uk
IGA

**SHOOTER**, Lesley
**Psychoanalytic Psychotherapist**
38 Links Avenue
Gidea Park
Romford Essex
RM2 6ND
☎ 01708 760 286
lesleyshooter@aol.com
AIP

**SHRIMPTON**, David W
**Psychodynamic Psychotherapist**
CO9
☎ 01787 269 594
david.shrimpton@ukgateway.net
WMIP

**SMITH**, Richard
**Transpersonal Psychotherapist**
15 Squirrel's Field
Myland Gate
Mill Road
Colchester, Essex
CO4 5YA
CCPE

**STACEY-ONG**, Lesley
**Systemic Psychotherapist**
9 The Copse
Bannister Green
Felsted
nr Dunmow
CM6 3NP
☎ 01371 821 428
☎ 020 8276 7288
lesley.ong@lineone.net
Becontree Psychotherapy Service
508 Becontree Avenue
Dagenham
CM6 3NP
KCC

**STEEL**, Patricia
**Hypno-Psychotherapist**
56 Burnway
Emerson Park
Hornchurch
Essex
RM11 3SG
☎ 01708 472 573
NRHP

**STIFFELL**, Gilly
**Psychoanalytic Psychotherapist**
♿ 9 Baronia Croft
Colchester
Essex
CO4 9EE
☎ 01206 845 602
gilly.stiffell@ntlworld.com
FPC

**TAPANG**, Peter
**Family & Systemic Psychotherapist**
♿ 23 Joydon Drive
Chadwell Heath
Romford
Essex
RM6 4ST
☎ 020 8220 7757
☎ 020 8887 0606
P.Tapang@btopenworld.com
IFT

**TEMPEST**, Jeanette
**Psychosynthesis Psychotherapist**
11 Seaview Road
Shoeburyness
Essex
SS3 9DX
☎ 01702 294 754
PET

**TENG**, Christina
**Systemic Psychotherapist**
♿ 33 Furrowfelde
Basildon
SS16 5HA
☎ 01268 533 769
chris.teng@ic24.net
KCC

**THOMPSON**, Joan
**Neurolinguistic Psychotherapist, Personal Construct Psychotherapist**
31 Priory Crescent
Prittlewell
Southend-on-Sea
Essex
SS2 6JY
☎ 01702 613 828
NLPtCA, PCP

**TODD**, Gillian
**Cognitive Behavioural Psychotherapist**
The Old School Hall
4 Frogge Street
Ickleton
Saffron Walden
CB10 1SH
☎ 01799 530 553
☎ 01223 746 045
gt235@cam.ac.uk
BABCP

**TUNE**, David
**Body Psychotherapist, Humanistic Psychotherapist, Integrative Psychotherapist**
23 Rectory Road
Wivenhoe
Essex
CO7 9EP
☎ 01206 827 863
david.tune@virgin.net
The Stockwell Centre
44 East Stockwell Street
Colchester
Essex
CO1 1SR
AHPP, CCBP

**TURNER**, Diana
**Psychoanalytic Psychotherapist**
2 Parsonage Terrace
Vicarage Road
Finchingfield
Essex
CM7 4LD
☎ 01245 493622
☎ 01371 810727
ARBS

**URQUHART**, Isabel
**Psychoanalytic Psychotherapist**
67 Old Orchard
Harlow
Essex
CM18 6YQ
☎ 01223 369 894
☎ 01279 441 337
isobelurquhart@compuserve.com
CSP

**VAIZEY**, Philippa
**Transpersonal Psychotherapist**
Dragon Tye, Church Street
Belchamp St.Paul
Sudbury
CO10 7DJ
☎ 01787 278 704
CTP

**VIBHAKAR**, Lopa
**Systemic Psychotherapist**
24 Belgrave Road
Ilford
Essex
IG1 3AW
☎ 020 8514 7641
☎ 020 7377 7969
IFT

**WAINWRIGHT**, Claire Stephanie
**Systemic Psychotherapist**
♿ CAMHS
39 Woodward Road
Dagenham
RM9 4SJ
☎ 020 8488 4212
☎ 020 8592 4445
clairewainwright60@hotmail.com
KCC

**WALKER**, Clare
**Psychosynthesis Psychotherapist**
56 Hurst Green
Brightlingsea
Essex
CO7 0EH
☎ 01206 303 345
☎ 02083 404 874
IPS

**WALKER**, Steven
**Family & Systemic Psychotherapist**
School of Community Health Studies
Anglia Polytechnic University
Brook St
Chelmsford
CM1 1SQ
☎ 01245 493 131
s.walker@apu.ac.uk
AFT

**WEEDEN**, Ruth
**Psychoanalytic Psychotherapist**
♿ 60 High Beech Road
Loughton
Essex
IG10 4BL
☎ 020 8502 5198
AIP

**WELSH**, Anne
**Psychosynthesis Psychotherapist**
Blacksmith's Cottage
Middle Street
Clavering, Nr. Saffron Walden, Essex
CB11 4QL
☎ 01799 550 024
☎ 02082 024 525
hestia2000@hotmail.com
IPS

**WHEELEY**, Eleanor
**Sexual and Relationship Psychotherapist**
Cromwell House
7 Cromwell Avenue
Billericay
CM12 0AE
☎ 01277 624 961
eleanor@tsys.freeserve.co.uk
BASRT

**WILLIAMS**, Dorothee
**Cognitive Behavioural Psychotherapist, Rational Emotive Behaviour Therapist**
14 Pudsey Hall Lane
Canewdon
Rochford
Essex
SS4 3RY
☎ 01702 258 764
Doroatpudsey@aol.com
BABCP, AREBT

**WOOLF**, Tanya
**Integrative Psychotherapist**
Psychology Dept.
Goodmayes Hospital
Barley Lane
Goodmayes, Ilford
IG3 8XH
☎ 020 8970 4039
Tanya.Woolf@redbridge.gov.uk
SPCRC

**WRIGHT**, Kenneth
**Couple Psychoanalytic Psychotherapist**
The Oaks Hospital
Oaks Place
Colchester
Essex
CO4 5XR
☎ 01473 828 976
kenwright@doctors.org.uk
SCPP

**YUSEF**, Dori Fatma
**Transpersonal Psychotherapist**
♿ Dickens Lodge
High Road
Chigwell
Essex
IG7 6QB
☎ 020 8 502 7095
CCPE

## FLINTSHIRE

**BUTLER**, Linda
**Cognitive Behavioural Psychotherapist**
♿ Child and Adolescent Mental Health
31 Grosvenor Road
Wrexham
LL11 1BT
☎ 01978 350 050
BABCP

**KEANE**, Johanna
**Family & Systemic Psychotherapist**
1 St James Court
Friars Court
Hawarden
Flintshire
CH5 3QL
☎ 01244 532 199
AFT

## GLOUCESTERSHIRE

**ADAMS**, Eve
**Integrative Psychosynthesis Psychotherapist**
Lantern Cottage
Stockend
Edge
Stroud
GL6 6PN
☎ 01452 813 355
eve@adams9.free-online.co.uk
RE.V

**AGAR**, James
**Transactional Analysis Psychotherapist**
Spring Cottage
High Street
South Woodchester
Stroud, Glos.
GL5 5EL
☎ 01453 872 703
ward-taylorp@msn.com
ITA

**ALLAN**, Kay
**Psychoanalytic Psychotherapist**
111 The Promenade
Cheltenham
GL50 1NW
☎ 01242 252 902
FPC, SIP

**BAUM**, Stefanie
**Biodynamic Psychotherapist**
53 Boverton Drive
Brockworth
Gloucester
GL3 4DA
☎ 01452 623 966
☎ 01453 759 444
stefaniembaum@yahoo.co.uk
LSBP

**BENTLEY**, Elizabeth
**Gestalt Psychotherapist**
Upper Steanbridge Mill
Steanbridge Lane
Slad
Nr Stroud
GL6 7QE
☎ 01452 813 908
lizmbentley@aol.com
GPTI

**BIELENKY**, Marina
**Humanistic and Integrative Psychotherapist**
18 Watermoor Road
Cirencester
GL7
☎ 01285 651 221
marina@bielenky.freeserve.co.uk
BCPC

**BRUCE**, Sue
**Humanistic and Integrative Psychotherapist**
Suite f21b
The Old Convent
Beeches Green
Stroud
GL6 0RS
☎ 01453 836 823
pike.cottage@virgin.net
BCPC

**BURRITT**, William
**Analytical Psychologist-Jungian Analyst**
1 Merestones Drive
The Park
Cheltenham
Glos.
GL50 2SU
☎ 01242 244 744
the3sequoias@msn.com
IGAP

**CARTER**, Paula
**Sexual and Relationship Psychotherapist**
♿ Nethercot
Rissington Road
Bourton-on-the-Water
Cheltenham
GL54 2DT
☎ 01451 822 837
The Park Surgery
Old Tetbury Road
Cirencester
GL7 1US
BASRT

**CROSS**, John
**Psychoanalytic Psychotherapist**
The Old Coach House
Lye Lane
Cleeve Hill
Cheltenham, Glos.
GL52 3QD
☎ 01242 678 895
☎ 01242 620 125
trust@pettarchiv.org.uk
AGIP

**DAVIES**, Angela
**Cognitive Behavioural Psychotherapist, Rational Emotive Behaviour Therapist**
9 Davies Road
Moreton in Marsh
GL56 0HR
☎ 07979 656 909
☎ 01992 578 017
anglea@sms02.fsnet.co.uk
BABCP, AREBT

**DEVINE**, Amanda
**Integrative Psychotherapist, Transpersonal Psychotherapist**
71 Bisley Road
Stroud
Glos
GL5 1HF
☎ 01453 752 815
CTP

**ELLIOTT**, Lea
**Psychoanalytic Psychotherapist**
6 Halland Road
Leckhampton
Cheltenham
Gloucestershire
GL53 0DJ
☎ 01242 518 642
SIP

**EUSDEN**, Sue
**Transactional Analysis Psychotherapist**
Stone Cottage Harleywood
Nailsworth
Gloucestershire
GL6 0LB
☎ 01453 833 965
☎ 01179 745 084
sueeusden@blueyonder.co.uk
ITA

**FRENCH**, Jennifer
**Group Analytic Psychotherapist**
♿ East Herefordshire CMHT
Rose Cottage
Belle Orchard
Ledbury
HR8 1DD
☎ 01531 633 872
jjenfren@aol.com
UPCA

**FRYE**, Helen
**Psychoanalytic Psychotherapist**
Hazelwell
Undercliffe Terrace
Cheltenham
GL53 9AE
☎ 01242 518 113
SIP

**GERBRANDS**, Kardien
**Body Psychotherapist, Integrative Psychotherapist**
Off Licence Cottage
Westrip
Stroud
Glos.
GL6 6HA
☎ 01453 758 060
☎ 01453 755 388
CCBP

**GOODRICH**, Anne
**Psychoanalytic Psychotherapist**
♿ 6 Wychbury Close
Leckhampton
Cheltenham
Glos
GL53 0HT
☎ 01242 262 526
FPC

**GOWLING**, David
**Transactional Analysis Psychotherapist**
Red House Farm
Foxmoor Lane
Westrip
Gloucestershire
GL5 4PL
☎ 01453 750 716
ITA

**GRACIE**, Jane
**Psychoanalytic Psychotherapist**
10 Somerford Road
Cirencester
Gloucestershire
GL7 1TN
☎ 01285 650 143
janegracie@aol.com
SIP

**GROCOTT**, Annie
**Psychoanalytic Psychotherapist**
20 Moorend Crescent
Leckhampton
Cheltenham
Gloucestershire
GL53 0EL
☎ 01242 572 290
SIP

**HALL**, Kelvin
**Humanistic and Integrative Psychotherapist**
Cherry Tree Cottage
Shortwood
Nailsworth
Glos.
GL6 0SB
☎ 01453 833 861
BCPC

**HEDLEY**, Karen
**Psychosynthesis Psychotherapist**
42 Thompson Road
Stroud
GL5 1SY
☎ 01453 753 342
k.hedley@ukonline.co.uk
IPS

**HUBBARD**, Caroline
**Cognitive Analytic Therapist**
♿ Park House
Park Road
Stroud
GL5 2JG
☎ 08711 747 932
☎ 01453 562 090
Clevedon
Coronation Road
Rodborough
Stroud
GL5 3SB
ACAT

**HUMPHRIES**, Harold W A
**Psychoanalytic Psychotherapist**
Praha
11 Heazle Place
Stroud
Gloucestershire
GL5 1UW
☎ 01453 757 900
AGIP

**LINDEN**, Roger
**Psychoanalytic Psychotherapist**
The Old Convent
Beeches Green
Stroud
Glos
GL5 4AD
☎ 020 7485 2292
r.linden@virgin.net
FPC

**LLEWELYN**, Billie
**Humanistic and Integrative Psychotherapist**
11 Sandhurst Road
Gloucester
GL1 2SE
☎ 01452 537 313
BCPC

**LUTHY**, Barbara
**Humanistic Psychotherapist**
College Farm, Beacon Lane
Haresfield
Glos.
GL10 3ES
☎ 01452 720 934
bluthy@roughcast.demon.co.uk
AHPP, BCPC

**MASLEN**, Gill
**Humanistic and Integrative Psychotherapist**
17 Gloucester Street
Cirencester
Glos.
GL7 2DJ
☎ 01285 656 280
gmaslen@chelt.ac.uk
BCPC

**MCOSTRICH**, June
**Psychosynthesis Psychotherapist**
Forge House
Kemble
Gloucestershire
GL7 6AD
☎ 01285 770 538
IPS

**MILLAR**, Peter
**Analytical Psychologist-Jungian Analyst**
Thistledown
Down Ampney
Cirencester
Gloucestershire
GL7 5QU
☎ 01793 751 241
petersmillar@onetel.net.uk
AJA

**MILLER**, Sarah
**Psychodrama Psychotherapist**
Hazel Hill
Drybrook
GL17
☎ 01594 541 388
BPA

**MOORE**, Alan
**Humanistic and Integrative Psychotherapist**
The Avenue
Brownshill
Stroud
Glos.
GL6 8AH
☎ 01453 884 403
BCPC

**MORRIS**, Elizabeth
**Humanistic and Integrative Psychotherapist**
Buckholdt House
The Street
Frampton on Severn
Gloucestershire
GL7 7ED
☎ 01452 741106
liz@buckholdtassociates.com
AHPP

**MORRIS**, Steven
**Psychoanalytic Psychotherapist**
53 Slad Road
Stroud
Glos
GL7 1QT
☎ 01453 750 765
SIP

**NAVIN**, Tony
**Psychoanalytic Psychotherapist**
5 Cotswold Close
Cirencester
Gloucestershire
GL7 1XP
☎ 01285 652 017
SIP

**PETERS**, Maggie
**Transpersonal Psychotherapist**
Atcombe Court Wing
South Woodchester
Stroud
Glos
GL5 5ER
☎ 01453 872 709
CTP

**PRICE**, Sue
**Family & Systemic Psychotherapist**
♿ Countywide Specilaist Substance Misuse
44 London Road
Gloucester
GL1 3NZ
☎ 01452 891 260
AFT

**REYNAL**, Carmen
**Analytical Psychologist-Jungian Analyst, Analytical Psychotherapist (Jungian)**
Keyneton Hayes
Upper Slaughter
Gloucestershire
GL54 2JG
☎ 01865 511 063
☎ 01451 821 947
cqreynal@btinternet.com
IGAP, GAPS

**RITSON**, Louise
**Cognitive Behavioural Psychotherapist**
12 Alveston Grange
Mickleton
Chipping Campden
GL55 6RT
☎ 07050 663 553
Louise@costwoldcbt.co.uk
BABCP

**RODMAN**, Fiona
**Humanistic and Integrative Psychotherapist**
Bide Cottage
Newmarket
Nailsworth
GL6 0RJ
☎ 01453 835 191
BCPC

**SACKETT**, Kate
**Cognitive Analytic Therapist**
♿ Park House
Park Road
Stroud
Gloucester
GL6 8EL
☎ 01453 562 100
k.sackett@glospart.nhs.uk
ACAT

**SEIGAL**, Liz
**Psychoanalytic Psychotherapist**
Westbourne
43 Middle Street
Stroud
Glos
GL5 1DZ
☎ 01453 751 114
SIP

**SHAW**, Annie
**Humanistic and Integrative Psychotherapist**
17 The Wordens
Stroud
Glos
GL5 4RX
☎ 01453 752 484
annie_shaw@onetel.net.uk
BCPC

**SKAILES**, Claire
**Psychoanalytic Psychotherapist (Jungian)**
5 Fairview Terrace
Wallsquarry
Brimscombe
Stroud
GL5 2PB
☎ 01453 885 229
WMIP

**SLATTERY**, David
**Humanistic and Integrative Psychotherapist**
52 George Street
Nailsworth
Glos
GL6 0NP
☎ 01453 832 215
☎ 01225 445 237
dnslattery@blackbird6.freeserve.co.uk
BCPC

**SMITH**, Hilary Frances
**Humanistic and Integrative Psychotherapist**
☎ 07980 542 170
BCPC

**SNUDDEN**, Mike
**Psychoanalytic Psychotherapist**
Kimsbury House
Moor Street
Saul
Gloucestershire
GL2 7LQ
☎ 01452 740 389
SIP

**STAUNTON**, Tree
**Body Psychotherapist, Integrative Psychotherapist**
85 Sald Road
Stroud
Gloucestershire
GL5 1QY
☎ 07966 400 190
tree@presentmoment.freeserve.co.uk
CCBP

**STEPHENS**, Lyn
**Psychoanalytic Psychotherapist**
9 Montpellier Grove
Cheltenham
Gloucestershire
GL50 2XB
☎ 01242 521 945
lyn@montp.demon.co.uk
AGIP, FIP

**TAYLOR-DAVIES**, Mary
**Cognitive Behavioural Psychotherapist**
Newcog Cognitive Therapy Centre
Churchgate House
Cerney Wick
Cirencester
GL7 5QJ
☎ 01793 751 895
mary@newcog.co.uk
BABCP

**THOMAS**, Penny
**Humanistic and Integrative Psychotherapist**
4 Boxwood Close
Kingscote
Tetbury
GL8 8YR
☎ 01453 861 101
pen.thomas@virgin.net
BCPC

**WELLER**, Alison
**Core Process Psychotherapist**
Little Larkhill Cottage
Long Newton
Tetbury
Glos.
GL8 8RU
☎ 01666 503529
KI

**WHITWELL**, John
**Group Analytic Psychotherapist**
The Old Post Office
Somerford Keynes
Cirencester
Glos.
GL7 6DP
☎ 01795 428 097 / 436 085
☎ 01285 861 694
johnwhit@freenetname.co.uk
FIP

**WIGAN**, Rose
**Integrative Psychotherapist**
♿ Beckley House
Bleddington
Oxon
OX7 6XQ
☎ 01608 658 527
rose-wigan@bleddington.freeserve.co.uk
SPCRC

**WILLIAMS**, Jan
**Humanistic and Integrative Psychotherapist**
"The Centre"
5 London Road
Stroud
GL5 2AG
☎ 01453 821 018
☎ 07710 403 399
"The Centre"
5 London Road
Stroud
Glos
GL5 2AG
BCPC

**WOODCOCK**, Jeremy
**Family & Systemic Psychotherapist**
♿ Holman's Cottage
Windsoredge
Nailsworth
Glos
GL6 0NP
☎ 01453 835 365
☎ 0117 954 6724
Jeremy.Woodcock@bristol.ac.uk
IFT

**WRIGHT**, Sue
**Integrative Psychotherapist**
Huma Kusu
Coronation Road
Rodborough
Stroud
GL5 3SL
☎ 01452 309 026
MET

## GLOUCESTERSHIRE - SOUTH

**ELTON WILSON**, Jenifer
**Integrative Psychotherapist**
The Bakehouse
Thickwood Lane
Colerne
Nr Chippenham
SN14 8BN
☎ 07971 627 804
jenifer_bakehouse@lineone.net
MET

**GRAY**, Judith
**Family & Systemic Psychotherapist**
♿ Old Orchard House
Westerleigh
Bristol
BS37 8QH
☎ 01454 325 178
des-judy@gray6717.freeserve.co.uk
AFT

**GREGORY**, Judith
**Gestalt Psychotherapist**
'Fernlea'
Yate Road
Iron Acton
Bristol
BS37 9XY
☎ 01454 228 418
judithgregory@ukonline.co.uk
GPTI

**HADWIN**, Peter
**Integrative Psychotherapist**
27 Cloverdale Drive
Longwell Green
Bristol
BS30 9XZ
☎ 0117 932 5917
☎ 0794 1246959
MET

**HOLT**, Colin A
**Sexual and Relationship Psychotherapist**
20 London Road
Warmley
Bristol
BS30 5JB
☎ 0117 961 1229
☎ 07952 820 199
colinaholt1@ukgateway.net
BASRT

**HUDSON-ALLEZ**, Dr Glyn
**Sexual and Relationship Psychotherapist**
♿ 28 Brins Close
Stoke Gifford
Bristol
BS34 8XU
☎ 0117 969 9547
glyn@therapy4u.co.uk
BASRT

**KING**, Diana
**Group Analytic Psychotherapist**
East Foscote Farm
Grittleton
Chippenham
SN14 6AD
☎ 01249 782 448
☎ 01249 783 541
diking@efoscote.prestet.co.uk
FPC

**WARNER**, Kerri
**Transactional Analysis Psychotherapist**
4 Laburnum Road
Hanham
Bristol
BS15 3DU
☎ 01179 090 784
ITA

## GREATER MANCHESTER

**ADDERLEY**, Diane
**Psychodrama Psychotherapist**
6 Greengate Lane
Prestwich
Manchester
M25 3HW
☎ 0161 798 6044
adderley@dircon.co.uk
BPA

**AGARWALA**, Rosemary
**Family & Systemic Psychotherapist**
♿ 35 Edge Fold Road
Worsley
Manchester
M28 7GE
☎ 0161 790 5085
rosemary@argarwala.co.uk
AFT

**APPLEBY**, Joy
**Gestalt Psychotherapist**
3 The Beeches
West Didsbury
Manchester
M20 2BG
☎ 0161 445 0766
GPTI

**ASHWORTH**, Freda
**Hypno-Psychotherapist**
♿ Mulsanne
16 Harefield Drive
Heywood nr. Rochdale
Lancashire
OL10 1RN
☎ 01706 368 193
NRHP

**BACHA**, Claire
**Group Analyst, Psychoanalytic Psychotherapist**
20 Kersal Road
Prestwich
Manchester
M25 9SJ
☎ 01617 730 409
IGA, NWIDP

**BANNISTER**, Anne
**Psychodrama Psychotherapist**
Glebe Cottage
Church Road
Mellor
Stockport
SK6 5LX
☎ 0161 427 3307
Anne.Bannister@BTInternet.com
BPA

**BARKER**, Helen
**Psychoanalytic Psychotherapist**
♿ Hampden House Psychotherapy Centre
2 Palatine Road
Manchester
M20 3JA
☎ 0161 445 2099
hcbarker@tackaberrys.co.uk
NWIDP

**BARLEY**, Andrew
**Gestalt Psychotherapist**
18 Atwood Road
Didsbury
Manchester
M20 6TD
☎ 0161 446 2470
ab@shrinkwrapped.org
SPTI

**BARNETT**, Gillian
**Psychoanalytic Psychotherapist**
Hampden House Psychotherapy Centre
2 Palatine Road
Withington
Manchester
M20 3JA
☎ 0161 445 4399
NWIDP

**BIBBEY**, Judy
**Psychoanalytic Psychotherapist**
♿ Psychology Services Department
Stepping Hill Hospital
Stockport
SK2 7JE
☎ 01614 195 767
UPCA

**BIRD**, John
**Psychoanalytic Psychotherapist**
Hampden House
2 Palatine Road
Withington
Manchester
M20 3JA
☎ 0161 445 2099
☎ 0162 552 3292
johnb458@aol.com
NWIDP

**BLAMPIED**, Annette N
**Psychoanalytic Psychotherapist**
Dept Applied Community Studies
Manchester Metropolitan University
799 Wilmslow Road
Didsbury
M20 2RR
☎ 01782 751 509
☎ 01612 472 141
A.Blampied@mmu.ac.uk
UPCA

**BORONAT**, Dascha
**Group Analyst**
Hampden House
2 Palatine Road
Withington
M20 3JA
☎ 0161 282 2470
d.boronat@ntlworld.com
IGA

**BRADY**, Alec
**Cognitive Behavioural Psychotherapist**
Dept of Clinical Psychology
Stepping Hill Hospital
Stockport
Cheshire
SK2 7JE
☎ 0114 288 3276
☎ 07768 593 117
alec.brady@virgin.net
BABCP

**BRERETON**, June
**Transactional Analysis Psychotherapist**
116 Stocks Lane
Stalybridge
Cheshire
SK15 2TQ
☎ 01613 037 925
junebrereton@therapist65.freeserve.co.uk
ITA

**BROOKHOUSE**, Shaun
**Hypno-Psychotherapist**
Richmael House
25 Edge Lane
Chorlton
Manchester
M21 9JH
☎ 01618 811 677
drb@hypno-nlp.com
CTIS, UPCA

**BROWN**, Dee M
**Integrative Psychotherapist**
20 Everett Road
Withington
Manchester
M20 3DQ
☎ 01614 345 932
dmb@xenopsyche.com
NGP

**BUCKLEY**, Michael
**Psychoanalytic Psychotherapist**
♿ Macartney House
Psychotherapy Service
Beech Mount, Rochdale Road
Manchester
M9 1XS
☎ 0161 205 7555
mike.buckley@mhsc.manchester.nhs.uk
NWIDP

**BURMAN**, Erica
**Group Analyst**
Department of Psychology & Speech Pathology
The Manchester Metropolitan Univers
Hathersage Road
Manchester
M13 0JA
☎ 0161 247 6394
e.burman@mmu.ac.uk
IGA

**BUROW**, Birgit
**Neurolinguistic Psychotherapist**
114 Kingsbrook Road
Manchester
M16 8QX
☎ 01612 330 421
NLPtCA

**BURTON**, Tom
**Transactional Analysis Psychotherapist**
The Manchester Institute for Psychotherapy
454 Barlow Moor Road
Chorlton
Manchester
M21 1BQ
☎ 0161 862 9456
☎ 07930 243495
manningburton@hotmail.com
ITA

**BYRNE**, Elizabeth
**Psychoanalytic Psychotherapist**
Department of Clinical Psychology
Royal Bolton Hospital
Minerva Road, Farnworth
Bolton
BL4 0JR
☎ 01204 390 675
NWIDP

**CASSON**, John
**Psychodrama Psychotherapist**
♿ 62 Shaw Hall Bank Road
Greenfield
Saddleworth
OL3 7LE
☎ 01457 877 161
☎ 01457 877 659
joncassun@beeb.net
BPA

**CHARLTON**, Maureen
**Psychoanalytic Psychotherapist**
Hampden House Psychotherapy Centre
2 Palatine Road
Withington
Manchester
M20 3JA
☎ 0161 445 2099
maureencharlton@tiscali.co.uk
NWIDP

**CHURCHER**, John
**Psychoanalytic Psychotherapist**
4 Rippingham Road
Withington
Manchester
M20 3EX
☎ 0161 434 0952
churcher@psy.man.ac.uk
NWIDP

**COLDRIDGE**, Elizabeth
**Psychoanalytic Psychotherapist**
School Of Community Health
Science & Social Care
Directorate of Counselling and Psyc
Allerton Building
Frederick Road, Salford
M6 6PU
☎ 0161 295 2484
l.coldridge@salford.ac.uk
NWIDP

**COOKE**, Bob
**Transactional Analysis Psychotherapist**
454 Barlow Moor Road
Chorlton
Manchester
M21 1BQ
☎ 01618 629 456
bob@mcpt.co.uk
ITA

**COSTA**, Jan
**Psychodrama Psychotherapist**
Manchester
M35
☎ 0161 794 0875
jan.costa@whsmithnet.co.uk
The Red House
78 Manchester Road
Swinton
Manchester
M27 5FG
BPA

**COX**, Deborah A
**Cognitive Behavioural Psychotherapist**
♿ Primary Care Mental Health Team
Dept. of Psychology
Stepping Hill Hospital
Poplar Grove, Stockport
SK2 7JE
☎ 0161 419 5766
☎ 07929 733 509
BABCP

**CROPPER**, Josephine
**Integrative Psychotherapist**
62 Pennine Road
Howich
Bolton
BL6 7HR
☎ 01204 696 395
healthyhorizons@ukonline.co.uk
NGP

**DAVIS**, Jim
**Transactional Analysis Psychotherapist**
7 Talbot Road
Ladybarn
Manchester
M14 6TA
☎ 0161 225 2556
jedavis@onetel.net.uk
ITA

**DAVISON**, John
**Group Analytic Psychotherapist**
Red House Psychotherapy Service
78 Manchester Road
Swinton
Manchester
M27 5FG
☎ 01617 940 875
UPCA

**ELLIS**, Robin Margaret
**Family & Systemic Psychotherapist**
Bowness Administration
Prestwich Hospital
Bury New Road
Manchester
M25 3BL
☎ 0161 772 3664
rellis@hds.bstmhp.nhs.uk
AFT

**EMINSON**, Mary
**Family & Systemic Psychotherapist**
♿ CAMHS
Royal Bolton Hospital
Minerva Road
Bolton
BL4 0JR
☎ 01204 390 663
mary.eminson@boltonh-tr-nwest.nhs.uk
AFT

**EVANS**, Mark
**Cognitive Analytic Therapist**
♿ Gaskell House Psychotherapy
Department
Swinton Grove
Manchester
M13 0EU
☎ 0161 273 2762
ACAT, NWIDP

**FAGBADEGUN**, Rufus
**Group Analyst**
♿ Elton Grange Farm
Elton Vale Road
Bury
Lancs
BL8 2RZ
☎ 0161 764 3848
rufagb@talk21.com
IGA

**FEASEY**, Don
**Psychoanalytic Psychotherapist**
16 Raynham Avenue
Didsbury
Manchester
M20 6BW
☎ 01614 453 612
don@feasey.fsnet.co.uk
WMIP

**FIRTH**, Mr Malcolm Thomas
**Sexual and Relationship Psychotherapist**
♿ Manchester Mental Health & Social
Care NHS Trust
Rawnsley Building
Manchester Royal Infirmary
Oxford Road, Manchester
M13 9WL
☎ 0161 276 5365/5366
☎ 0161 882 1095
malcolm.firth@mhsc.manchester.nhs.uk
Manchester Mental Health & Social
Care NHS Trust
Chorlton House
70 Manchester Road
Chorlton-Cum-Hardy, Manch
M21 9UN
BASRT

**FOLLAND**, Mark
**Psychoanalytic Psychotherapist**
Hampden House Psychotherapy
Centre
2 Palatine Road
Withington
Manchester
M20 3JA
☎ 0161 445 2099
NWIDP

**FOX**, Hugh
**Family & Systemic Psychotherapist**
87 Denison Road
Victoria Park
Manchester
M14 5RN
☎ 0161 224 6282
narrativefox@aol.com
AFT

**FROGGETT**, Antony
**Group Analyst, Psychoanalytic Psychotherapist**
The Red House
Psychotherapy Service
78 Manchester Road
Swinton, Salford
M27 5FG
☎ 0845 456 1240
antony_froggett@yahoo.co.uk
IGA

**GALLAGHER**, Eileen
**Group Analyst**
45 York Street
Heywood
OL10 4NN
☎ 01706 622 755
☎ 01204 811 468
IGA

**GATRELL**, Jane
**Psychoanalytic Psychotherapist**
♿ Macartney House
Psychotherapy Centre
Beech Mount, Rochdale Road
Manchester
M9 1XS
☎ 0161 205 7555
macartneypsy@mhsc.manchester.nhs.uk
NWIDP

**GLENNIS**, Brierley
**Gestalt Psychotherapist**
21 Calf Hey Shore
Littleborough
Lancs
OL15 8HB
☎ 01706 373 132
MET

**GONSALKORALE**, Wendy
**Hypno-Psychotherapist**
Westward
Brooklands Crescent
Sale
Cheshire
M33 3NB
☎ 0161 976 1248
wgonsalkorale@compuserve.com
CTIS

**GOWRISUNKUR**, Jaya
**Psychoanalytic Psychotherapist**
♿ Thameside General Hospital
Fountain Street Mental Health Unit
Ashton Under Lyne
OL6 9RW
☎ 0161 331 5066
☎ 0161 904 0050
NWIDP

**GRAY**, Pat
**Family & Systemic Psychotherapist**
35 Springfield Road
Gatley
Cheadle
Cheshire
SK8 4PE
☎ 0161 428 2646
patsyg@nubian.freeserve.co.uk
AFT

**GREEN**, Pippa
**Sexual and Relationship Psychotherapist**
♿ Dept. of Sexual Health
Baillie Street Health Centre
Rochdale
OL16 1XS
☎ 01706 517 655
☎ 0161 778 2800
BASRT

**GREENFIELD**, Terence Aubrey
**Cognitive Behavioural Psychotherapist**
First Floor
157 Ashley Road
Hale, Altrincham
Cheshire
WA14 2UW
☎ 0161 928 3898
☎ 0161 929 0361
BABCP

**GUTHRIE**, Else
**Psychoanalytic Psychotherapist**
♿ Department of Psychiatry
Rawnsley Building
Manchester Royal Infirmary
Oxford Road, Manchester
M13 9BX
☎ 0161 276 5383
NWIDP

**HANNAH**, Francesca
**Transactional Analysis Psychotherapist**
12 Lawton Road
Heaton Chapel
Stockport
SK4 2RG
☎ 01616 100 927
☎ 07960 495 235
francesca@horizons.idps.co.uk
ITA

**HARDY**, Jennifer
**Transactional Analysis Psychotherapist**
♿ 21 Holland Green
Ashton-Under-Lyne
Lancs
OL6 8TN
☎ 01613 306 598
☎ 07966 198 665
jennihardy@onetel.net.uk
Flat 13 Kirkmanshulme Lane
3 Kirkmanshulme Lane
Longsight
Manchester
M12 4NA
ITA

**HARRIS**, John Bernard
**Gestalt Psychotherapist**
10 Devon Drive
Diggle
Oldham
OL3 5PP
☎ 01457 870 476
johnbernard@onetel.net.uk
GPTI

**HAYWARD**, Marjorie
**Hypno-Psychotherapist**
33 Ramsbottom Road
Horwich
Bolton
BL6 5NH
☎ 01257 411 983
☎ 01204 438 807
marjoriehayward12@hotmail.com
CTIS

**HORNE**, Alan
**Psychoanalytic Psychotherapist**
♿ Gaskell House Psychotherapy Service
Swinton Grove
Manchester
M13 0EU
☎ 0161 273 2762
hornea@psy.cmht.nwest.nhs.uk
NWIDP

**HOWDIN**, Jules
**Gestalt Psychotherapist**
18 Dawlish Road
Chorlton-cum-Hardy
Manchester
M21 8XR
☎ 0161 881 5738
jules-howdin@dawlish39.freeserve.co.uk
GPTI

**HUGHES**, Lynette
**Psychoanalytic Psychotherapist, Couple Psychoanalytic Psychotherapist**
Winnicott Centre
195-7 Hathersage Road
Manchester
M13 0JE
☎ 0161 248 9494
☎ 01824 702 656
NWIDP, SCPP

**ISAAC**, Toni-Lee
**Hypno-Psychotherapist**
♿ 81 Palatine Road
Didsbury
Manchester
M20 3LJ
☎ 07909 988 952
CTIS

**JACKSON**, Elizabeth
**Gestalt Psychotherapist**
Manchester Gestalt Centre
7 Norman Road
Rusholme
Manchester
M14 5LF
☎ 0161 257 2202
GPTI

**JOHNSON**, Shirley
**Integrative Psychotherapist**
86 Atwood Road
Didsbury
Manchester
M20 6JN
☎ 0161 434 1362
NGP

**KABERRY**, Susan
**Psychoanalytic Psychotherapist**
Grove Cottage
8 Grenfell Road
Didsbury
Manchester
M20 6TQ
☎ 01614 481 475
sekaberry@aol.com
NWIDP

**KIEMLE**, Gundi
**Psychoanalytic Psychotherapist**
♿ Bolton Centre For Sexual Health
Royal Bolton Hospital
Minerva Rd, Farnworth
Bolton
BL4 0JR
☎ 01204 390 775
☎ 01619 507 245
gundi.kiemle@bolton-tr.nwest.nhg.uk
LPDO

**KILGOUR**, Joyce
**Family & Systemic Psychotherapist**
8 Moss Lane
Bramhall
Stockport
SK7 1EH
☎ 0161 439 7982
joycekilgour@hotmail.com
AFT

**KINCEY**, John
**Cognitive Behavioural Psychotherapist**
♿ Dept Clinical & Health Psychology
Central Manchester Healthcare Trust
Gaskell House
Swinton Grove
M13 0EU
☎ 0161 273 3271
BABCP

**LAMB**, Kirsten
**Psychoanalytic Psychotherapist**
Tameside and Glossop Psychological Services
Haughton Mews
71-73 Stamford Street East
Ashton-under-Lyne
OL6 6QQ
☎ 0161 330 6947
Kirsten.Lamb@penninecare.nhs.uk
LPDO

**LEDWARD HOBBES**, Judi
**Integrative Psychotherapist**
2 Woodleigh
Bradgate Road
Artrincham
Cheshire
WA14 4QU
☎ 01619 289 997
judi@mantra.demon.co.uk
NGP

**LEWIS**, Mary
**Psychoanalytic Psychotherapist**
♿ Macartney House Psychotherapy Service
Beech Mount
Rochdale Road
Harpurhey, Manchester
M9 1XS
☎ 0161 205 7555
stemale@ntlworld.com
NWIDP

**LINDSAY**, Marion
**Psychoanalytic Psychotherapist**
The Red House Psychotherapy Service
78 Manchester Road
Swinton
Manchester
M27 5FG
☎ 0161 794 0875
marionlindsay@lineone.net
NWIDP

**LINFORD**, Richard J
**Sexual and Relationship Psychotherapist**
♿ Health Centre
Maxwell Building
University of Salford
Salford
M5 4WT
☎ 0161 295 4209
☎ 0161 434 3555
antricman@aol.com
Palatine Centre
63/65 Palatine Road
Manchester
M20 3LJ
BASRT

**LIPSEDGE**, Catherine
**Cognitive Behavioural Psychotherapist**
♿ Psychology Department
Prestwich Hospital
Bury New Road
Prestwich, Manchester
M25 3BL
☎ 07770 853 320
cbaptiste-cyrous@cwctv.net
BABCP

**LITTLEJOHN**, Sarah
**Integrative Psychotherapist**
♿ Manchester University and UMIST Counselling
Service, Crawford House
Oxford Road
Manchester
M13 9QS
☎ 0161 275 2868
sarah.littlejohn@man.ac.uk
MC

**LITTLEWOOD**, Ann
**Psychodynamic Psychotherapist**
69 Oldfield Road
Altrincham
Cheshire
WA14 4BH
☎ 0161 928 2792
HIP

**LUCAS**, Carol
**Transactional Analysis Psychotherapist**
338a, Wellington Road North
Heaton Chapel
Stockport
Cheshire
SK4 5DA
☎ 0161 432 9320
☎ 0161 4431 628
carol@therapeia-smcp.freeserve.co.uk
ITA

**MAGUIRE**, Claire
**Psychoanalytic Psychotherapist**
♿ Dept. of Clinical Psychology
Fairfield General Hospital
Rochdale Old Road
Bury
BL9 7TD
☎ 0161 778 3538
claire.maguire@penninecare.nhs.uk
LPDO

**MAKIN**, Anne
**Gestalt Psychotherapist**
27 Beeston Close
Bolton
BL1 7RT
☎ 01204 594 000
annemakin@btinternet.com
GPTI

**MARGISON**, Frank
**Cognitive Analytic Therapist, Psychoanalytic Psychotherapist**
♿ Gaskell House
Psychotherapy Service
Swinton Grove
Manchester
M13 0EU
☎ 01612 732 762
ACAT, NWIDP

**MARRIOT**, Alison
**Family & Systemic Psychotherapist**
♿ Clinical Psychology, Carisbrooke
Wenlock Way, West Gorton
Manchester
M12 5LF
☎ 0161 274 4173
marriottalison@talk21.com
AFT

**MARTIN**, Jane
**Psychoanalytic Psychotherapist**
♿ The Red House
Psychotherapy Service
78 Manchester Road
Manchester
M27 5FG
☎ 0161 794 0875
☎ 0161 772 3873
The Edenfield Medium Secure Unit
Bolton & Trafford
Mental Health Turst
Bur New Road
Prestwich, Manchester
M25 3BL
NWIDP

**MARTIN**, Tim
**Cognitive Behavioural Psychotherapist**
♿ Human Focus Return to Work
Fourth Floor Washbrook House
The Lancastrian Office Centre
Talbot Road, Stretford, M
M32 0FP
☎ 0161 875 0300
tmartin@returntowork.co.uk
BABCP

**MCDONNELL**, Fokkina
**Neurolinguistic Psychotherapist**
♿ 65 Norwood Road
Stretford
Manchester
M32 8PN
☎ 01618 653 193
fokkina.mcd@zen.co.uk
NLPtCA

**MCHUGH**, Branwen
**Family & Systemic Psychotherapist**
♿ 35 Parsonage Road
Withington
Manchester
M20 4PS
☎ 0161 445 2884
branwen.mchugh@smuht.nwest.nhs.uk
AFT

**MEEKUMS**, Bonnie
**Humanistic and Integrative Psychotherapist**
2 Meadow Close
Mossley
Ashton Under Lyne
Tameside
OL5 9DS
☎ 01457 839 013
☎ 0113 343 9414
bonniem@unisonfree.net
AHPP

**MEGRAM**, Patricia
**Transactional Analysis Psychotherapist**
35 The Crescent
Davenport
Stockport
SK3 8SL
☎ 01614 833 726
☎ 01613 554 452
contactswc@aol.com
Stockport Women's Centre
250 Wellington Road South
Stockport
SK2 6NW
ITA

**MEREDITH**, Joan
**Psychoanalytic Psychotherapist, Psychodynamic Psychotherapist**
11 Shaftesbury Road
Manchester
M8 0WL
☎ 0161 795 8365
HIP

**MILLER**, Edna
**Sexual and Relationship Psychotherapist**
5 Valley Road
Cheadle
Cheshire
SK8 1HY
☎ 0161 428 2964
a.miller@tinyworld.co.uk
BASRT

**MITCHELL**, Lesley
**Psychoanalytic Psychotherapist**
♿ Macartney House Psychotherapy Service
Beech Mount
Rochdale Road
Harpurhey, Manchester
M9 1XS
☎ 01612 057 555
macartney.psy@mhsc.manchester.nhs.uk
NWIDP

**MORLEY**, Michael
**Cognitive Behavioural Psychotherapist**
♿ Dept. Clinical & Health Psychology
Central Manchester Healthcare Trust
Swinton Grove
Manchester
M13 0EU
☎ 0161 276 5365
mmorley@psy.cmht.nwest.nhs.uk
BABCP

**NAUGHTON**, Marie
**Transactional Analysis Psychotherapist**
15 Ellesmere Road
Chorlton
Manchester
M21 0SG
☎ 01613 742 502
mandp@questmail.fsnet.co.uk
ITA

**NICHOLSON**, Jane
**Psychoanalytic Psychotherapist**
♿ Gaskell House
Psychotherapy Service
Swinton Grove
Manchester
M13 0EU
☎ 01612 732 762
jane.f.nicholson@man.ac.uk
NWIDP

**NOWELL**, Valerie
**Gestalt Psychotherapist**
Also works from South Manchester
☎ 01270 524 455
GPTI

**O'NEILL**, Thomas
**Family & Systemic Psychotherapist**
301 Brantingham Road
Chorlton cum Hardy
Manchester
M21 0GU
☎ 0161 881 5463
oneill301@aol.com
AFT

**OGLEY**, Julia
**Systemic Psychotherapist**
136 Meadway
Bramhall
Stockport
SK7 1NN
☏ 0161 440 9296
☏ 0161 980 4968
or 0161 941 4011
KCC

**PANTALL**, Marlis
**Integrative Psychotherapist**
7 Balmoral Avenue
Cheadle Hulme
Cheadle
Cheshire
SK8 5EG
☏ 0161 485 5274
SPTI

**PEDEN**, Alison
**Family & Systemic Psychotherapist**
♿ 28 Church St
Eccles
Manchester
M30 0DF
☏ 0161 789 4668
AFT

**PERRIOLLAT MUNRO**, Elisabeth
**Psychoanalytic Psychotherapist**
The Clarendon Clinic,
115 Chorley Road
Swinton,
Greater Manchester
M27 4AA
☏ 0797 049 9042
elisabeth.munro@ukonline.co.uk
ARBS

**PHILIPPSON**, Peter
**Gestalt Psychotherapist**
Manchester Gestalt Centre
7 Norman Road
Rusholme
Manchester
M14 5LF
☏ 01612 572 202
Peter@mgc.org.uk
GPTI, MET

**PIRQUET**, Caroline
**Psychoanalytic Psychotherapist**
13 Malsham Road
Northen Moor
Manchester
M23 0JB
☏ 0161 998 1516
Hampden House
2 Palatine Road
Withington
Manchester
M20 3JA
FPC

**POOLE**, David
**Hypno-Psychotherapist**
50 Bridgewater Road
Worsley
Manchester
M28 3AE
☏ 01204 306 618
Phoenix Personal Development Center
Phoenix House
2 South Grove
Sale
M33 3AU
NRHP

**POOLE**, Nick
**Neurolinguistic Psychotherapist**
♿ 386 Kingsway
Burnage
Manchester
M19 1PL
☏ 01614 328 624
nickpoole@tesco.net
NLPtCA

**PORTER**, Danny
**Gestalt Psychotherapist**
4 Zetland Road
Chorlton
Manchester
M21 8TH
☏ 0161 860 5108
☏ 07733 125 528
dannyporter@tesco.net
Manchester Therapy Centre
77 Russel Road
Manchester
M16 8AR
GPTI

**POTTER**, Steve
**Psychoanalytic Psychotherapist**
♿ Counselling Service, University of Manchester
5th Floor, Crawford House
Booth St East
Manchester
M13 9QS
☏ 0161 275 2854
Steve.Potter@man.ac.uk
21 Chatfield Road
Chorlton
Manchester
M21 8UR
LPDO

**PRICE JONES**, Daniel
**Behavioural Psychotherapist**
♿ Dept. of Clinical Psychology
Nurses Home 1, Billinge Hospital
Upholland Road, Billinge
Wigan
WN5 7ET
☏ 01695 626 181
☏ 01925 752 768
daniel.jones@wiganlhs-tr.nwest.nhs.uk
BABCP

**PRODGERS**, Alan
**Psychoanalytic Psychotherapist**
6 Mabel Avenue
Roe Green
Worsley
M28 2TT
☏ 01617 937 576
prodg@lineone.net
NWIDP

**QUARMBY**, David
**Psychoanalytic Psychotherapist**
30 College Avenue
Oldham
OL8 4DS
☏ 01616 262 771
therapy@dqnet.freeserve.co.uk
UPCA

**RAWSTHORNE**, Jean
**Psychoanalytic Psychotherapist**
The Red House Psychotherapy Service
78 Manchester Road
Swinton
Manchester
M27 5FG
☏ 0161 794 0875
NWIDP

**RHODES**, Adrian
**Psychoanalytic Psychotherapist**
58 Errwood Road
Burnage
Manchester
M19 2QH
☏ 01612 241 739
☏ 01614 194 773
adrian@rhodes.net
Mental Health Directorate
Stepping Hill Hospital
Stockport
SK2 7JE
NWIDP

**RIDGWAY**, Jane
**Cognitive Behavioural Psychotherapist**
♿ Department of Psychology
Stepping Hill Hospital
Poplar Grove
Stockport, Cheshire
SK2 7JE
☏ 0161 419 5766
☏ 07776 220 426
lts3060@hotmail.com
BABCP

**ROSS**, Julie
**Psychoanalytic Psychotherapist**
♿ Psychology Department
314 - 316 Oldham Road
Royton
Oldham
OL2 5AS
☎ 0161 909 8200
julieross77@aol.com
LPDO

**SAWYER**, Albert
**Hypno-Psychotherapist**
♿ 5 Lyndene Avenue
Roegreen
Worsley
Manchester
M28 2RJ
☎ 01617 995 537
albertsawyer@aol.com
NSHAP

**SCHAKEL**, Hildegard
**Cognitive Behavioural Psychotherapist**
Department of Clinical Psychology
Laurence Burns Unit
Birch Hill Hospital
Rochdale
OL12 9QB
☎ 01706 754 070
BABCP

**SCOTT**, Mary
**Gestalt Psychotherapist**
Earnsdale
3 Bamford Way
Rochdale
Lancs
OL11 5NA
☎ 01706 659 287
7 Norman Road
Rusholme
Manchester
M14 5LF
GPTI

**SELLERS**, Carolyn
**Cognitive Behavioural Psychotherapist**
♿ Salford Psychology Services
Bury New Road
Prestwich
Manchester
M25 3BL
☎ 01274 878 600
☎ 0161 772 3480
carolynsellers@usa.net
BABCP

**SHELDON**, Helen
**Psychoanalytic Psychotherapist**
♿ Department of Clinical Psychology
Royal Bolton Hospital
Minerva Road, Farnworth
Bolton
BL4 0JR
☎ 01204 390 675
helen@sheldon51.freeserve.co.uk
NWIDP

**SHIERS**, John
**Psychosynthesis Psychotherapist**
62 Atwood Road
Didsbury
Manchester
M20 6GQ
☎ 01614 489 048
john@discovery65.freeserve.co.uk
IPS

**SIDDLE**, Ronald
**Cognitive Behavioural Psychotherapist**
♿ Dept. of Clinical Psychology
North Manchester General Hospital
Delaunays Road
Manchester
M8 5RB
☎ 0161 720 2810
Ron.Siddle@mail.nmanhc-tr.nwest.nhs.uk
BABCP

**SMALLEY**, John
**Analytical Psychologist-Jungian Analyst**
835 Wilmslow Road
Didsbury
Manchester
M20 5WD
☎ 01535 665 362
☎ 07739 358 335
johsma@aol.com
IGAP

**STEIN**, Nathan Bernard
**Personal Construct Psychotherapist**
12 Ravensway
Prestwich
Manchester
M25 0EU
☎ 07984 012 365
dovstein@aol.com
PCP

**STUMMER**, Gudrun
**Transactional Analysis Psychotherapist**
274a Upper Chorlton Road
Manchester
M16 0BN
☎ 0161 232 7692
☎ 07947 380 070
ITA

**SUDBERY**, John
**Psychodynamic Psychotherapist**
University of Salford
Frederick Road
Salford
M6 6PU
☎ 0161 295 2053
j.sudbery@salford.ac.uk
HIP

**SUTTON**, Adrian
**Psychoanalytic Psychotherapist**
♿ The Winnicott Centre
195 Hathersage Road
Manchester
M13 0JE
☎ 01612 489 494
adrian.sutton@cmmc.nhs.uk
NWIDP

**SYKES**, Kathleen
**Psychoanalytic Psychotherapist**
♿ Macartney House
Psychotherapy Service
Beech Mount
Harpurhey
M9 1XS
☎ 01612 057 555
macartney.psy@mhsc.manchester.nhs.uk
NWIDP

**TATHAM**, Alan
**Cognitive Behavioural Psychotherapist**
Psychology Services
M.H.Services of Salford NHS Trust
Bury New Road
Prestwich, Manchester
M25 3BL
☎ 0161 772 3487
☎ 0161 834 4122
atatham@psychology.bstmhp.nhs.uk
11 St John Street
Manchester
M3 4DW
BABCP

**THOMAS**, Sandra
**Psychoanalytic Psychotherapist**
27 Heath Road
Stockport
SK2 6JJ
☎ 01614 199 001
sandravmthomas@aol.com
HIP, NWIDP

**THORNTON**, Maria A.
**Cognitive Behavioural Psychotherapist**
♿ Palliative Care Counselling Service
Ordsall Health Centre
Belfort Drive
Salford
M5 3PP
☎ 0161 212 4779
BABCP

**TINDLE**, Kate
**Psychoanalytic Psychotherapist**
♿ Manchester University & UMIST
Counselling Service
5th Floor, Crawford House
Precinct Centre
Oxford Road, Manchester
M13 9QS
☎ 01612 752 864
kate.tindle@man.ac.uk
NWIDP

**TOWSE**, Esme
**Psychoanalytic Psychotherapist**
Hampden House Psychotherapy
Centre
2 Palatine Road
Withington
Manchester
M20 3JA
☎ 01614 452 099
e.towse@hampdenhouse.co.uk
NWIDP

**TRYTHALL**, Patricia
**Psychoanalytic Psychotherapist**
1 Craigwell Avenue
Didsbury
Manchester
M20 6JQ
☎ 01616 137 593
☎ 01613 391 100
UPCA

**TUNWELL**, Ann
**Sexual and Relationship Psychotherapist**
Hampden House
Psychotherapy Centre
2 Palatine Road
Withington, Manchester
M20 3JA
☎ 0161 445 2099
BASRT

**VERDUYN**, Christine M.
**Cognitive Behavioural Psychotherapist, Family & Systemic Psychotherapist**
♿ Department of Clinical Psychology
Royal Manchester Childrens Hospital
Swinton
Manchester
M27 4HA
AFT, BABCP

**VORA**, Valerie
**Sexual and Relationship Psychotherapist**
♿ 196 Manchester Road
Westhoughton
Bolton
BL5 3LA
☎ 01942 813 647
BASRT

**WALKER**, Kanta
**Psychoanalytic Psychotherapist**
38 Victoria Avenue
Didsbury
Manchester
M20 2RA
☎ 01614 348 294
NWIDP

**WALKER**, Sundar Kanta
**Psychoanalytic Psychotherapist**
38 Victoria Avenue
Didsbury
Manchester
M20 2R
☎ 015395 32224
kantawalker@hotmail.com
NWIDP

**WATTS**, Susan
**Cognitive Behavioural Psychotherapist**
♿ Psychology Dept. Bolton
Saltford & Trafford MH Trust
Bury New Road, Prestwich
Manchester
M25 3BL
☎ 0161 772 3481
BABCP

**WELFORD**, Enid
**Transactional Analysis Psychotherapist**
41 Derby Road
Fallowfield
Manchester
M14 6UX
☎ 01614 290 010
enid-n-mike@welford01.fsnet.co.uk
ITA

**WESSON**, Peter M.J.
**Hypno-Psychotherapist**
Bury Complementary Health Centre
12 Tenterden Street
Bury
Lancashire
BL9 0EG
☎ 01617 631 660
NRHP

**WHITMORE**, Robert
**Psychoanalytic Psychotherapist**
15 Moorland Road
Didsbury
Manchester
M20 6BB
☎ 01614 452 941
bob.whitmore@bolton-tr.nwest.nhs.uk
NWIDP

**WIDDOWSON**, Erica Simone
**Family & Systemic Psychotherapist**
25 Melrose Road
Little Lever
Bolton
BL3 1DX
☎ 01204 791 157
TEKWiddowson@hotmail.com
AFT

**WILLMER**, Emma
**Gestalt Psychotherapist**
♿ 58 Danes Road
Rusholme
Manchester
M14 5JS
☎ 0161 225 4782
emmawillmer@lineone.net
GPTI

**WINDER**, Joy
**Integrative Psychotherapist**
11 Gildridge Road
Whalley Range
Manchester
M16 8PS
☎ 01618 813 639
joy@winder144.freeserve.co.uk
MC

**WOLF**, Runa
**Gestalt Psychotherapist**
312 City Road
Hulme
Manchester
M15 4FA
☎ 07866 693822 (M)
SPTI

**WOOLFE**, Ray
**Psychoanalytic Psychotherapist**
Hampden House Psychotherapy
Centre
2 Palatine Road, Withington
Manchester
M20 3JA
☎ 01614 452 099
raywoolfe@woodvale13.freeserve.co.uk
NWIDP

**WRIGHT**, Mary
**Transactional Analysis Psychotherapist**
The Genesis Centre
23 Mellor Road
Cheadle Hulme
Cheshire
SK8 5AT
☎ 01614 498 910
mary_wright@lineone.net
ITA

## GUERNSEY

**AYRES**, Gary
**Family & Systemic Psychotherapist**
"Le Coin", Petit Marais
Bordeaux, Vale
Guernsey
GY3 5DH
☎ 01481 246 196
Mishgar1@aol.com
IFT

**CRASKE**, Sarah
**Family & Systemic Psychotherapist**
3 Mount Row
St Peter Port
Guernsey
GY1 1NS
☎ 07781 127 243
SarahCraske1@aol.com
IFT

**FARMER**, Christopher
**Psychodrama Psychotherapist**
La Couture
Belval Road
Vale
Guernsey, Channel Islands
GY3 5LW
☎ 01481 245 334
☎ 01484 725 241 x 3369
cjimfarm@guernsey.net
BPA

**LE LIEVRE**, John
**Neurolinguistic Psychotherapist**
♿ Le Haut Pave
Rue de la Lande
Castel
Guernsey, Channel Islands
GY5 7PN
☎ 01481 259 222
☎ 01481 259 523
johnnlp@aol.com
NLPtCA

## HAMPSHIRE

**ANDERTON**, Michael
**Analytical Psychologist-Jungian Analyst, Analytical Psychotherapist (Jungian)**
61 Brassey Road
Winchester
Hampshire
SO22 6SB
☎ 01962 856 326
robin.anderton@lineone.net
IGAP, GAPS

**ARNOLD**, Julia
**Gestalt Psychotherapist**
♿ Springfield House
Swanmore Road
Swanmore
Southampton, Hants
SO32 2QH
☎ 01489 896 284
julia.arnold@virgin.net
GPTI

**ASHCROFT**, Dinah
**Gestalt Psychotherapist**
6-8 The Soke
Alresford
Hampshire
SO24 9DB
☎ 01962 733 219
dmashcroft@aol.com
GPTI, MET

**BARRINGER**, Jan
**Sexual and Relationship Psychotherapist**
21 Mercury Gardens
Hamble
Southampton
SO31 4NZ
☎ 023 80 561 792
jan.barringer@virgin.net
BASRT

**BEACH**, Jan D.
**Cognitive Behavioural Psychotherapist**
♿ G Block
Royal Hospital Haslar
Gosport
Hants
PO12 2AA
☎ 023 92 762178/762421
BABCP

**BEECH**, Trevor
**Transpersonal Psychotherapist**
The Retreat
229 Knowle Avenue
Knowle Village
Fareham, Hampshire
PO17 5DQ
☎ 01329 834 999
☎ 07802 824 699
trevor@workshopsandretreats
CCPE

**BELAS**, Patrick
**Family & Systemic Psychotherapist**
♿ Child & Family Therapy
2 Floor Osborne Clinic
Osborn Road
Fareham
PO16 7ES
☎ 01329 822 220
AFT

**BENNETT**, Ross
**Humanistic and Integrative Psychotherapist**
Kwanti
Jermyns Lane
Ampfield
Romsey, Hampshire
SO51 0QA
☎ 01794 368 012
rossbennett@which.net
SPEC

**BERRY**, Eileen
**Group Analyst**
4 Eastgate Street
Winchester
Hants
SO23 8EB
☎ 01962 854 439
IGA

**BLACK**, Nicholas J.
**Cognitive Behavioural Psychotherapist**
♿ Health Psychology Services
Royal Hampshire County Hospital
Romsey Road
Winchester, Hants
SO22 5DG
☎ 01962 824 351
☎ 01489 860 260
Nick.Black@weht.swest.nhs.uk
BABCP

**BORGHGRAEF**, Dr Guy
**Sexual and Relationship Psychotherapist**
c/o P Gregory
19 Chatsworth Road
Boyatt Wood
Eastleigh
SO50 4PE
☎ 0030 28250 32238
borghgraef@grecian.com
BASRT

**BOULD**, Jane
**Psychodrama Psychotherapist**
17 Tudor Avenue
Emsworth
Hampshire
PO10 7UG
☎ 01243 431 637
☎ 01243 623 404
jane.bould@ukonline.co.uk
BPA

**BOWEN**, Barry
**Family & Systemic Psychotherapist**
♿ Elson
Gosport
PO12
☎ 02392 439822
barrybowen1@aol.com
AFT

**BOWN**, Terry
**Sexual and Relationship Psychotherapist**
5 Beaumont Close
Bassett
Southampton
SO16 7NE
☎ 023 80 529 100
☎ 023 80 790 216
info@walkinthesun.com
28 Western Road
Chandler's Ford
Eastleigh
Southampton
SO53 5DB
BASRT

**BOYD**, Ann A.
**Humanistic Psychotherapist, Integrative Psychotherapist**
17 Kipling Close
Yateley
Hampshire
GU46 6YA
☎ 01252 871 731
ann.boyd@virgin.net
AHPP

**BRANDWOOD**, Pat
**Psychodrama Psychotherapist**
59 Bassett Green Road
Southampton
Hampshire
SO16 3DW
☎ 023 80 556 562
☎ 07977 564 170
patbrandwood@hotmail.com
BPA

**BROCK**, Sue
**Neurolinguistic Psychotherapist**
4 Paddock Fields
Old Basing
Hampshire
RG24 7DB
☎ 01256 354 688
☎ 01256 326 176
suebrock@basing.swinternet.co.uk
NLPtCA

**BUNDAY**, Christine
**Group Analyst**
Psychotherapy Department
Department of Psychiatry, Royal Sou
Brintons Lane
Southampton
☎ 02380 825 536
IGA

**BUTLER**, Graham
**Neurolinguistic Psychotherapist**
18 Cooper Court
Salisbury Road
Farnborough
GU14 7AZ
☎ 01252 377 787
graham@lifeskills4u.co.uk
NLPtCA

**CARTER**, Christine
**Sexual and Relationship Psychotherapist**
28 Western Road
Chandlers Ford
Eastleigh
Southampton
SO53 5DB
☎ 023 80 529 100
☎ 023 80 251 551
info@walkinthesun.com
5 Beaumont Close
Bassett
Southampton
Hants
SO16 7NE
BASRT

**CASSON**, Isabel
**Psychoanalytic Psychotherapist**
7 Archery Lane
Winchester
Hampshire
SO23 8GG
☎ 01962 878 065
AGIP

**CLARKE**, Wendela
**Hypno-Psychotherapist**
♿ The Laurels
10 Fairview Road
Headley Down
Hampshire
GU35 8JP
☎ 01428 717 413
wendelac@ntlworld.com
NRHP

**CLEMENT DE L'EPINE**, Karen
**Integrative Psychotherapist**
♿ Primrose Patch
Primrose Lane
Rake
Liss
GU33 7HG
☎ 017308940211
UPCA

**CLIFFORD-POSTON**, Andrea
**Educational Therapist**
Osborne House
Kingsley
Hampshire
GU35 9LW
☎ 01420 476 042
CFET

**CLIFTON**, Sandra
**Sexual and Relationship Psychotherapist**
3 Hermitage Gardens
Waterlooville
Hants
PO7 7PR
☎ 02392 253 370 or 0871 733 3585
☎ 07801 239 020
sandra.clifton@dsl.pipex.com
BASRT

**CLORIDOR-WOOD**, Madie
**Integrative Psychotherapist**
23 Lucas Close
Yateley
Camberley
GU46 6JD
☎ 01252-409722
☎ 01252-671488
madeleine_clowood@yahoo.com
SPCRC

**COPLEY**, Brian
**Cognitive Behavioural Psychotherapist**
♿ Marchwood Priory Hospital
Hythe Road
Marchwood
Southampton, Hants
SO40 4WU
☎ 023 8084 0044
BABCP

**COWDRILL**, Vivia A.
**Cognitive Behavioural Psychotherapist**
♿ Hawthorn Lodge
Moorgreen Hospital
Botley Road
West End, Southampton
SO30 3JB
☎ 023 8047 5130
viv.cowdrill@wht.nhs.uk
BABCP

**DAVIS**, Chris
**Family & Systemic Psychotherapist**
Lanes End
64 Abbots Ann
Andover
SP11 7BG
☎ 01264 710 289
cwrj.davis@lineone.net
AFT

**DOLAN**, Francis
**Existential Psychotherapist**
♿ 2 The Grove
London Road
Hartley Wintney
RG27 8RN
☎ 01252 842 467
UPCA

**DOLLERY**, Jayne
**Cognitive Behavioural Psychotherapist**
♿ Ravenswood House
Knowle Hospital
Fareham
PO17 5NA
☎ 01329 836 189
☎ 07900 932 024
Jayne.Dollery@wht.nhs.uk
BABCP

**DOULTON MA**, Caroline
**Transpersonal Psychotherapist**
c/o Ochre
Odiham Cottage Hospital
Buryfields, Odiham
Hook, Hampshire
RG29 1NF
☎ 07831 120119
☎ 01256 460745
CCPE

**DRAPER**, Rosalind
**Family & Systemic Psychotherapist**
37 Lower Wardown
Petersfield
Hants
GU31 4PA
☎ 01730 260 023
rosdraper@bigfoot.com
IFT

**DYER**, Paula
**Sexual and Relationship Psychotherapist**
♿ 6 Silverdale
Fleet
GU52 7TT
☎ 01252 628 744
☎ 07870 372 064
b.dyer@ntlworld.com
BASRT

**EVANS**, Peter L.
**Child Psychotherapist**
24 Chequers Road
Basingstoke
Hampshire
RG21 7PU
☎ 01256 422771
pllevans@aol.com
ACP

**FERNANDO - O'CONNOR**, Chandra
**Systemic Psychotherapist**
♿ 136 Alexandra Road
Farnborough
GU14 6RN
☎ 01252 515 053
chandra.oconnor@yahoo.com
KCC

**FOX**, Helen
**Integrative Psychotherapist**
♿ 7 Station Road
Liphook
GU35 7DW
☎ 01428 727 525
SPCRC

**FRY**, Richard
**Family & Systemic Psychotherapist**
The Mount
Roman Road
Twyford
SO21 1QW
☎ 01962 715 898
rfry@email.com
AFT

**GLASSPOOL**, Patricia
**Hypno-Psychotherapist**
The Southgate Natural Therapy Clinic
13 Southgate Street
Winchester
Hampshire
SO23 9DZ
☎ 01962 866 903
☎ 02380 255 678
12 Hocombe Drive
Chandlers Ford
Eastleigh
Hampshire
SO53 5QE
NRHP

**GRAY**, Gay
**Body Psychotherapist, Integrative Psychotherapist**
Providence Cottage
Gazing Lane
West Wellow
Romsey
SO51 6BS
☎ 01794 324 757
☎ 01489 576 168
gay.gray@btopenworld.com
CCBP

**GREGORY**, Peter
**Sexual and Relationship Psychotherapist**
19 Chatsworth Road
Eastleigh
Hampshire
SO50 4PE
☎ 023 80 617 990
☎ 01202 769 976
BASRT

**GURR**, Mrs R
**Sexual and Relationship Psychotherapist**
The Old Village Stores
Braishfield Road
Romsey
SO51 0PQ
☎ 01794 3683 15
rosalie@alan.gurr.com
BASRT

**GUTHRIE**, Barbara
**Integrative Psychotherapist**
44 Stanmore Lane
Winchester
SO22 4AJ
☎ 01962 868 990
barbara@guthrie.co.uk
SPCRC

**HATSWELL**, Valerie Elliot
**Psychoanalytic Psychotherapist**
♿ Stillions
3 Windmill Hill
Alton
Hampshire
GU34 2RY
☎ 01420 82385
FIP

**HOOPER**, Christine
**Family & Systemic Psychotherapist**
♿ Ellesmere
The Crescent
Romsey
Hampshire
SO51 7NG
☎ 01794 512 102
christinehooper@yahoo.co.uk
AFT

**HOPKINS**, Vera M.
**Psychodynamic Psychotherapist**
♿ "Oakwood"
4 The Grange
Everton
Lymington
SO41 0ZR
☎ 01590 643 335
vmhopkins@aol.com
HIP

**HOWDEN RICHARDS**, Barbara
**Integrative Psychotherapist**
The Spinney
25 Claremont Gardens
Purbrook
HAMPSHIRE
PO7 5LL
☎ 02392 240 607
brichards@dlaing.eurobell.co.uk
MET

**HUSBAND**, Chris
**Attachment-based Psychoanalytic Psychotherapist**
Ferney Close
Thackhams Lane
Hartley Witney
Hook
RG27 8JG
☎ 01252 849 937
CAPP

**ISAAC**, Vivien
**Cognitive Behavioural Psychotherapist**
♿ Western Community Hospital
Walnut grove
Millbrook
Southampton
SO16 4XE
☎ 07986 082 988
BABCP

**KIRKLAND**, Denise
**Sexual and Relationship Psychotherapist**
Winchester
☎ 01962 851 187
BASRT

**LINGARD**, Shirley Ruth
**Systemic Psychotherapist**
♿ Rosemead
Churt
Nr. Farnham
GU10 2NX
KCC

**MACE**, Barbara
**Integrative Arts Psychotherapist**
West Broom
Hempland Lane
Privett
Alton
GU34 3NT
☎ 01730 828 200
☎ 07798 764 899
IATE

**MAJOR**, Ammanda
**Sexual and Relationship Psychotherapist**
Copelands
Brightstone Lane
Lower Farringdon
GU34 3DP
☎ 01420 587 263
ammanda.major@btinternet.com
BASRT

**MALONE**, Sue Germaine
**Sexual and Relationship Psychotherapist**
♿ Tresco
Forest Road
Liss Forest
Hants
GU33 7BL
☎ 01730 893 034
☎ 07713 739 251
gmsuemalone@msn.com
BASRT

**MATTHEWS**, Helen P.
**Cognitive Behavioural Psychotherapist**
♿ Moorgreen Hospital
Botley Road
West End
Southampton
SO30 3JB
BABCP

**MAY**, Suzanne
**Integrative Psychotherapist**
♿ Bridleway House
Homestead Road
Medstead
Nr. Alton
GU34 5NA
☎ 0870 787 5198
suz.may@virgin.net
SPCRC

**NICHOLLS**, Hazel
**Cognitive Analytic Therapist**
♿ Consultant Clinical Psychologist
Eating Disorder Service, Eastleigh
Enterprise Centre, Unit 3
Barton Park
SO50 6RR
☎ 02380 626 262
ACAT

**O'CONNELL**, Patrick
**Group Analytic Psychotherapist**
♿ 33 beech Way
Basingstoke
RG23 8LR
☎ 01256 420 048
☎ 0118 956 1250
p.oconnell1@ntlworld.com
FPC

**O'CONNOR**, Michael
**Systemic Psychotherapist**
♿ 136 Alexandra Road
Farnborough
GU14 6RN
☎ 01252 515 053
☎ 01483 783 330
mike.oconnor@ntlworld.com
KCC

**O'TOOLE**, Andrew
**Family & Systemic Psychotherapist**
Eating Disorder Service
Eastleigh Community Centre
Barton Park
Eastleigh
SO50 6RR
☎ 023 80 626 262
AFT

**PARKER**, Michael
**Group Analyst**
Director of Therapy
HMP Winchester
West Hill, Romsey Road
Winchester
SO22 5DF
☎ 01962 854 494 x381
IGA

**PAYNE**, Adette
**Integrative Psychotherapist**
The Flat
Meadowlands
Bradley
Arlesford
SO24 9RY
SPCRC

**PERRY**, Pamela
**Cognitive Analytic Therapist**
♿ Psychological Services, West Hants NHS Trust
Waterford House
142 Station Road
New Milton
BH25 6LP
☎ 01425 622 922
☎ 023 80 671 558
ACAT

**PLATTS**, June Elizabeth
**Cognitive Behavioural Psychotherapist**
♿ 24 Telegraph Lane
Four Marks
Alton
Hampshire
GU34 5AX
☎ 01420 561 797
BABCP

**PRESTON**, Dr John
**Sexual and Relationship Psychotherapist**
29 Selsmore Road
Hayling Island
PO11 9JZ
☎ 023 92 461 980
john.preston@ukgateway.net
BASRT

**PUGH**, Anna
**Body Psychotherapist, Integrative Psychotherapist**
Old Place
91 Manor Way
Lee-on-the-Solent
Hants
PO13 9JQ
☎ 023 92 550 757
CCBP

**RENZ**, Johanna
**Systemic Psychotherapist**
Child & Family Consultation Service
Church Grange Health Centre
Brambly's Drie
Basingstoke
RG21 8QN
☎ 01344 875 095
info@upsticksandgo.com
KCC

**RIDDELL**, Caroline
**Hypno-Psychotherapist**
Henley House
Winchester House
King's Sombourne
Nr Winchester, Hants
SO20 6NY
☎ 01794 388 557
caroliner@mind-doctor.co.uk
NRHP

**RIDLEY**, Stella V
**Lacanian Analyst, Psychoanalytic Psychotherapist**
The Old Lloyds Bank
23 Pier Street
Lee on the Solent
Hants
PO13 9LD
☎ 023 9258 6889
svr2@tutor.opem.ac.uk
CFAR

**RILEY**, Jacqueline
**Sexual and Relationship Psychotherapist**
♿ Relate
The Orchard
White Hart Lane
London Road, Basingstoke
RG21 4AF
☎ 01256 324 364
BASRT

**SELBY**, Gina
**Personal Construct Psychotherapist**
Ships Cottage
Ashford Hill
Newbury
Berks
RG19 8BD
☎ 01189 811 793
Gina.Selby@hotmail.com
PCP

**SHELLEY**, Dr Trevor
**Sexual and Relationship Psychotherapist**
3 Tithe Mead
Romsey
Hampshire
SO51 7SD
☎ 01794 830 514
☎ 01962 824 608
trevorshelley@waitrose.com
Department of Sexual Health
Royal Hampshire County Hospital
Winchester
SO22 5DG
BASRT

**SMITH**, Peter
**Psychoanalytic Psychotherapist**
53 North Street
Pennington
Lymington
Hants
SO41 8GB
☎ 01590 688064
ARBS

**STANKO**, Alison
**Gestalt Psychotherapist**
27 Bereweeke Way
Winchester
Hampshire
SO22 6BJ
☎ 01962 864 070
alisonclare27@hotmail.com
MET

**STIMPSON**, Quentin
**Transpersonal Psychotherapist**
201c West Street
Fareham
Hants
PO16 0EN
☎ 01329 826 621
Quentin@qstimpson.fsnet.co.uk
CCPE

**STOTT**, Jackie
**Psychoanalytic Psychotherapist**
22 Wensley Gardens
Emsworth
Hants
PO10 7RA
☎ 01243 375421
jackiestott@hotmail.com
IPSS

**SWINDEN**, Penni
**Autogenic Psychotherapist**
'Twin Rowan'
Woodlands Road
Brockenhurst
Hampshire
SO42 7SF
☎ 01590 624 518
☎ 07775 500 849
penni@pswinden.freeserve.co.uk
BAS

**THORNTON**, Christine
**Group Analyst**
♿ Orchard House
43 Chilbolton Avnue
Winchester
SO22 5HJ
☎ 01962 620 573
thorntonco@ntlworld.com
IGA

**VODDEN**, Ann
**Integrative Psychotherapist**
38 West Street
Tadley
Hampshire
RG26 3SX
☎ 01189 821 587
annvodden@beeb.net
MC

**WALKER HAMPTON**, Joan
**Gestalt Psychotherapist**
'Harveston'
1 The Flats, Balckwater
Camberley
Surrey
GU17 0AN
☎ 01252 874 367
jwhampton@ukonline.co.uk
SPTI

**WILLIAMS**, Ann
**Hypno-Psychotherapist**
♿ Centre for Personal & Professional Development
The Brewery, Twyford
Nr Winchester
Hants
SO21 1RQ
☎ 01962 715 838
NRHP

**WILLIAMS**, Katherine
**Integrative Psychotherapist**
15 Laverstock Lane
Lavestock
Whitchurch
RG28 7NY
☎ 01256 895 126
SPCRC

**VON BUHLER**, J M A Herbert Pardo
**Sexual and Relationship Psychotherapist**
33 High Street
Farnborough
GU14 6ES
☎ 07973 442 143
☎ 01753 869 755
jvbuhler@buhler.demon.co.uk
BASRT

## HEREFORD AND WORCESTER

**ANSON**, Carol
**Systemic Psychotherapist**
The Sun Inn
St Margarets
HR2 0QW
☎ 01432 378 940
Child and Adolescent Mental Health Service
Gaol Street Health Centre
Gaol Street
Hereford
HR2
KCC

**ASTON**, John
**Integrative Psychotherapist**
♿ Community Mental Health
Rose Cottage
Belle Orchard, Ledbury
HR1 4SA
☎ 01531 633 872
SPCRC

**BALLANTYNE**, Jacki
**Humanistic and Integrative Psychotherapist**
Handley Cross House
Harenwood End
Herefordshire
HR2 8JT
☎ 01989 730 579
BCPC

**BRUNT**, Mervyn
**Transactional Analysis Psychotherapist**
19 Clive Street
Hereford
HR1 2SB
☎ 01432 342 789
mervynb@supanet.com
ITA

**BURSTON**, Helen
**Humanistic and Integrative Psychotherapist**
4 Veldt Barns
Much Marcle
nr Ledbury
HR8 2ND
☎ 01531 660 465
helen@helenburston.co.uk
BCPC

**CAMPBELL**, Duine
**Jungian Analytical Psychotherapist**
Home Farm
High Park
Droitwich
Worcestershire
WR9 0AG
☎ 01905 794 442
duinec@aol.com
WMIP

**CLAYTON**, Kate
**Sexual and Relationship Psychotherapist**
♿ Tranquil House
258 Old Birmingham Road
Lickey
Birmingham
B60 1NU
☎ 0121 605 0348
katec@pstnet.net
BASRT

**DENHAM-VAUGHAN**, Sally
**Gestalt Psychotherapist**
'Nash Dom'
28 Grundy's Lane
Malvern Wells
WR14 4HS
☎ 01905 760 305
☎ 01684 899 387
feelines@yahoo.co.uk
GPTI

**ELLIS**, June Blythe
**Jungian Analytical Psychotherapist**
♿ Shinns Croft
Bosbury Ledbury
Herefordshire
HR8 1QD
☎ 01531 640 552
blythe.ellis@talk21.com
WMIP

**FEARNSIDE**, Derek
**Cognitive Behavioural Psychotherapist**
Thomas & Fearnside Lifeskills
BD Business Centre
Blackpole Road
Worcester
WR3 8SQ
☎ 01905 754 334
drek@fearnside.evesham.net
BABCP

**FOSTER**, Lesley
**Humanistic and Integrative Psychotherapist**
♿ Keepers Cottage
67 Stoke Edith
Hereford
HR1 4HQ
☎ 01432 890 328
BCPC

**FOUQUE**, Patricia
**Integrative Psychotherapist**
Wold Cottage
Cradley
Malvern
WR13 5LF
☎ 01886 880 860
fouque@btinternet.com
SPCRC

**FRENCH**, Jennifer
**Group Analytic Psychotherapist**
Meadow Sweet
Mordiford
Hereford
HR1 4LN
☎ 01531 633 872
jjenfren@aol.com
UPCA

**GILLIGAN**, Toni
**Gestalt Psychotherapist**
♿ 22 Tilesford Cottages
Long Lane, Throckmorton
Nr. Pershore
Worcs
WR10 2LA
☎ 01386 561 528
toni.gilligan@which.net
GCL

**GROOM**, Nigel
**Psychoanalytic Psychotherapist (Jungian)**
♿ 7 Powick Mills
Old Road
Worcester
Worcestershire
WR2 4BU
☎ 01905 425 285
FPC

**HANDY**, Susan
**Humanistic and Integrative Psychotherapist**
62 Green Street
Hereford
HR1 2QH
☎ 01432 276 814
susanehandy@hotmail.com
Quay House
Quay Street
Hereford
BCPC

**HERINGTON**, Steve
**Family & Systemic Psychotherapist**
The Sun Inn
St Margarets
Herefordshire
HR2 0QW
☎ 01981 510 223
heringbone@tesco.net
IFT

**HILL**, Jenny
**Psychoanalytic Psychotherapist**
The Garden Flat
13 Broomy Hill
Hereford
HR4 0LJ
☎ 01432 264 947
Harpton Gardens
New Radnor
Presteigne
Powys
LD8 2RE
SIP

**JACOBS**, Paula
**Transpersonal Psychotherapist**
♿ The Wren's Nest
Brampton Road
Madley
Hereford
HR2 9LU
☎ 01981 250597
noorjacobs@hotmail.com
CCPE

**JOYNES**, Debbie
**Integrative Psychotherapist**
20 Marshfield Close
Church Hill North
Redditch
B98 8RW
☎ 01527 452 566
Debbiejoynes@blueyonder.co.uk
SPTI

**KENT**, Rachel
**Gestalt Psychotherapist**
147 High St
Pershore
Worcestershire
WR10 1EQ
☎ 01386 561 798
rach@kent4985.freeserve.co.uk
SPTI

**KIRKPATRICK**, Ian
**Psychodrama Psychotherapist**
87 Lichfield Avenue
Hereford
HR1 2RL
☎ 01432 272 275
ian@psychodramatist.com
BPA

**LACEY**, Tim
**Cognitive Behavioural Psychotherapist**
9 Tanglewood Close
Blackwell
Bromsgrove
B60 1BU
☎ 0121 447 7787
☎ 07900 916 857
laceypiglet@aol.com
BABCP

**LAW**, Gordon
**Transactional Analysis Psychotherapist**
♿ 5 Bawdey Avenue
Malvern
Worcester
WR14 2EW
☎ 01684 566 268
gordon.law1@btopenworld.com
ITA

**MONTEIRO**, Marian
**Family & Systemic Psychotherapist**
The Health Clinic CAMHS
Gaol Street
Hereford
HR1 2HU
☎ 01432 378 940
FIC

**MORGAN**, Linda
**Hypno-Psychotherapist**
♿ 11 Deane Close
Powick
Worcester
WR2 4QL
☎ 07773 167 647
☎ 01905 830 538
linda@morgan325.freeserve.co.uk
NSHAP

**O'LEARY**, Anne M.T.
**Group Analytic Psychotherapist**
14a Beoley Road West
Redditch
B98 8LT
☎ 0152 761 687
☎ 01527 501 565
FPC, WMIP

**OLIVER**, Jenny
**Psychosynthesis Psychotherapist**
♿ 3 Elgar Court
27 Hampton Park Road
Hereford
HR1 1TH
☎ 01432 267 822
jennyolipsysy@hotmail.com
IPS

**OWEN**, Angela
**Psychoanalytic Psychotherapist**
47 Reservoir Road
Coston Hackett
Nr Rednall
B45 8PJ
☎ 01214 454 516
FPC, WMIP

**PALMER BARNES**, Fiona
**Analytical Psychologist-Jungian Analyst**
Rock Cottage
Newton St. Margarets
Herefordshire
HR2 0QW
☎ 01981 510 613
Quay House
3 Quay Street
Hereford
HR1 2NH
AJA, SIP

**PETERS**, Sheena
**Family & Systemic Psychotherapist**
28 Station Road
Alvechurch
Bromsgrove
B48 7SD
☎ 0121 445 6973
steve.race@btopenworld.com
AFT

**PRICE**, Jeremy
**Transpersonal Psychotherapist**
Borderlands Transpersonal Centre
Whithe House
10 Broad Street
Preteigne, Powys
LD8 2AB
☎ 01544 260 028
CTP

**SHORE**, Barbara
**Family & Systemic Psychotherapist**
7 Hagley Orchard
Bartestree
Hereford
HR1 4BU
☎ 01432 850 161
barbara.shore@ btopenworld.com
FIC

**SMITH**, Lorraine
**Psychoanalytic Psychotherapist**
♿ Smallwood House
Church Green West
Redditch
Worcs
B97 4BD
☎ 01527 488 637
WMIP

**STERN**, Michele
**Child Psychotherapist**
Hereford Child & Adolescent Mental Health Service
Gaol Street
Hereford
HR1 2HU
☎ 01432 357351
ACP

**TAYLOR**, Jill
**Biodynamic Psychotherapist**
Rosebank
Lucton Leominister
Herefordshire
HR6 9PH
☎ 07881 957 597
jill.t@virgin.net
LSBP

**THOMPSON**, Hilary
**Psychosynthesis Psychotherapist**
Tanwick Cottage
Tanhouse Lane
Upper Wick
Worcester
WR2 5SZ
☎ 01905 420 187
IPS

**TURNER**, Mary
**Integrative Psychotherapist**
72 Lower Wyche Road
Malvern
Worcs.
WR14 4ET
☎ 01684 891548
maryturner.psychotherapist@ukonline.co.uk
MET

**TURNER**, Philip
**Psychoanalytic Psychotherapist**
Roundway House
48 Southbank Road
Hereford
HR1 2TL
☎ 01432 355 746
SIP

**VAN WARMELO**, Estelle
**Hypno-Psychotherapist**
Old School House
Abbey Dore,
Herefordshire
HR1 4AE
☎ 01981 240 727
☎ 01432 354 244
vanclan@tiscali.co.uk
CTIS

**VAN WARMELO**, Estelle
**Hypno-Psychotherapist**
Hereford Natural Therapy Centre
5a King Street
Hereford
HR4 9BW
☎ 01981 240 727
☎ 01432 354 244
vanclan@tiscali.co.uk

**VOGEL**, Karin
**Humanistic and Integrative Psychotherapist**
The Poplars
Ewyas Harold
Hereford
HR2 OHU
☎ 01981 240 516
BCPC

**WESTCOTT**, Rosemary
**Psychoanalytic Psychotherapist**
22 Geoffrey Avenue
Hereford
HR1 1BZ
☎ 01432 350226
GUILD

**WYNN**, Joan
**Systemic Psychotherapist**
♿ Bridges Counselling Service
12 Cedar Road
Redditch
B97 6HN
☎ 01527 452 121
joan.bridgestherapy1@btopenworld.com
KCC, CTIS

## HERTFORDSHIRE

**ALDRED**, Sue
**Transpersonal Psychotherapist**
18 Baldock Road
Letchworth
Hertfordshire
SG6 3JX
☎ 01462 480 336
CCPE

**ALLPORT**, Maggie
**Gestalt Psychotherapist**
65 Mymms Drive
Brookmans Park
Hatfield
AL9 7AE
☎ 01707 656 250
Natural Medicine Centre
11 Southgate Road
Potters Bar
EN6 5AR
GCL

**ANDERSON**, Eleanor
**Systemic Psychotherapist**
9 Moneyhill Road
Rickmansworth
WD3 7EE
☎ 01923 775 993
☎ 020 8962 4362
moneyhill@ntlworld.com
KCC

**ANDREWS**, Ulla
**Transpersonal Psychotherapist**
Watford
Herts
WD17 3HG
☎ 01923 229240
☎ 07787 511777
ulla@Andrews.uk.net
CCPE

**AZARKADEH**, Shoreh
**Existential Psychotherapist**
1 Waterworks Cottage
Redricks Lane
Sawbridgeworth
CM21 0RL
☎ 07932 976 827
shorehazarkadeh@yahoo.com
SPCRC

**BACTAWAR**, Charles D.
**Cognitive Behavioural Psychotherapist**
82 St Annes Road
London Colney
St.Albans
Herts
AL2 1NY
☎ 01727 823 675
☎ 07887 562 450
Charles@Bactawar.freeserve.co.uk
BABCP

**BAILEY**, David
**Systemic Psychotherapist**
♿ Peace Children's Centre
Peace Prospect
Watford
WD17 3EW
☎ 020 7607 8017
☎ 01923 470 610
david.bailey@hpt.nhs.uk
KCC

**BAKER**, Ewa
**Transpersonal Psychotherapist**
2A Grovelands Avenue
Hitchin
Herts
SG4 0QT
☎ 01462 458 245
CTP

**BALANCE**, Gillian
**Analytical Psychologist-Jungian Analyst**
30 Westminster Court
St. Albans
Hertfordshire
AL1 2DY
☎ 01727 858 361
CAP *

**BARRATT**, Sara
**Family & Systemic Psychotherapist**
♿ 26 Bushey Grove Road
Bushey
Hertfordshire
WD23 2JQ
☎ 01923 817 247
barratts@bushey-grove.demon.co.uk
IFT

**BEAUMONT**, Anne
**Integrative Psychotherapist**
♿ 2 Field Lane
Letchworth
Herts
SG6 3LE
☎ 01462 625674
ajbeaumont@ntlworld.com
MC

**BEIGHTON**, Chris
**Sexual and Relationship Psychotherapist**
♿ Sewell House
349 The Hides
Harlow
Essex
CM20 3QY
☎ 01279 450 285
cchrismcs@aol.com
BASRT

**BERRY**, Peter
**Psychoanalytic Psychotherapist**
9 Sandridgebury Lane
St. Albans
Hertfordshire
AL3 6DD
☎ 01727 761789
GUILD

**BLACKER**, Sandra Rosamond
**Systemic Psychotherapist**
7 Jill Grey Place
Queens Gate Mews
Hitchin
SG4 9YH
KCC

**BRIGGS**, Margarete
**Psychoanalytic Psychotherapist**
11 Home Close
Harlow
Essex
CM20 3PD
☎ 01279 423 093
margaretebriggs@hotmail.com
CSP

**BROCKWELL**, Badger
**Body Psychotherapist, Integrative Psychotherapist**
60 Cross Road
Oxhey
Watford
WD1 4DQ
☎ 01923 229 060
CCBP

**BUCHAN**, Ann
**Group Analytic Psychotherapist**
Watford Ind. Psychotherapy Practice
60a Market Street
Watford
WD18 0PX
☎ 01923 254 439
☎ 01923 676 278
annbuchan@moose.co.uk
FPC

**BUCKLEY**, Judy
**Psychoanalytic Psychotherapist**
20 Hanyards Lane
Cuffley
Herts
EN6 4AT
☎ 01707 879 513
IPSS

**BUDNICK**, Susan
**Psychoanalytic Psychotherapist**
17 Watling Mansions
Watling Road
Radlett
WD7 7NA
☎ 01923 854 600
☎ +1 860 371 2654
susanbudnick@hotmail.com
ARBS

**BUSOLINI**, Don
**Hypno-Psychotherapist**
45 Valley Road
Welwyn Garden City
Hertfordshire
AL8 7DH
☎ 01707 330 557
d.t.busolini@herts.ac.uk
NSHAP

**BUTCHER**, Marilyn
**Integrative Psychosynthesis Psychotherapist**
20 New Forge Place
Redbourn
St Albans
Herts
AL3 7NY
☎ 01582 794762
☎ 01707 895623/07790 436515(Mob)
merrlyn@ntlworld.com
RE.V

**BYNG**, Rosemary
**Sexual and Relationship Psychotherapist**
♿ Relate Dacorum
The Gables
3 St Mary's Road
Hemel Hempstead
HP2 5HG
☎ 01442 262 618
☎ 01442 214 768
relate@nildram.co.uk
BASRT

**CARRINGTON**, Linda
**Transpersonal Psychotherapist**
The Hadleigh Clinic
161 High Street
Barnet
Herts
EN5 5SU
☎ 020 8449 0413
CCPE

**CLULOW**, Christopher
**Couple Psychoanalytic Psychotherapist**
62 Clarence Road
St Albans
AL1 4NG
☎ 020 7435 7111
☎ 01727 868 108
TMSI, SCPP

**COBDEN**, Vivienne
**Group Analytic Psychotherapist**
53 Little Bushey Lane
Bushey
Herts
WD2 3SD
☎ 020 8950 4301
FPC

**COHEN**, Barbara
**Family & Systemic Psychotherapist**
♿ 57 Valley Road
Chorleywood
Hertfordshire
WD3 4DT
☎ 01923 773 984
dodoco1@aol.com
AFT

**COLLINGWOOD**, Katharine
**Systemic Psychotherapist**
♿ Hertfordshire Patnership NHS Trust
Harper Lane
Shenley
Nr. Radlett
WD7 9HQ
☎ 01923 427 311
katharine.collingwood@hpt.nhs.uk
KCC

**COLLINS**, Leila
**Integrative Psychotherapist**
2 King Edward Road
Barnet
EN5 5AP
☎ 020 8440 9776
l.collins@mdx.ac.uk
SPCRC

**CONNOLLY**, David
**Personal Construct Psychotherapist**
151 London Road
St Albans
AL1 1TA
PCP

**CROSSLEY**, Gillian
**Integrative Psychotherapist**
6 Cylers Thicket
Welwyn
Herts
AL6 9RS
☎ 01438 715580
Parkway Health Clinic
Birdcroft Road
Welwyn Garden City
Hertfordshire
AL8 6JE
MET

**CULLINAN**, Deborah
**Child Psychotherapist**
11 Morland Road
Hemel Hempstead
Herts
HP1 1NQ
☎ 01442 218478
DeborahLCullinan@netscape.net
ACP

**DAVEY**, Stephen
2, Cranbourne Road,
Hatfield,
Herts
AL10 8AP
ARBS

**DAVIES-SMITH**, Lorraine
**Family & Systemic Psychotherapist, Systemic Psychotherapist**
Ripley
1a Beechroft Road
Bushey
Herts
WD23 2JU
☎ 01923 243 443
☎ 020 8967 5988
lds3@mac.com
IFT

**DAVIS**, Gill
**Systemic Psychotherapist**
Double Two Consultancy
P O Box 251
Hatfield
AL10 8ZZ
☎ 07973 767 671
KCC

**DEVEREUX**, Dawn
**Psychoanalytic Psychotherapist**
47 Beaumont Avenue
St Albans
AL1 4TW
☎ 01727 842 868
dawn.devereux@ntlworld.com
CCOPPP

**DHILLON**, Manjit
**Cognitive Behavioural Psychotherapist**
Letchworth Centre for Healthy Living
Rosehill Hospital
Hitchin Road
Letchworth
SG6 3NA
☎ 01462 678 804
☎ 01462 646 921
dillonmd@msn.com
14 Uplands Avenue
Hitchin
SG4 9NH
BABCP

**DIMCOVIC**, Nada
**Personal Construct Psychotherapist**
27 Meadway Close
Barnet
Herts.
EN5 5LA
☎ 020 8440 2169
☎ 020 8952 2381 ext 3761
nada@dimcovic.fsnet.co.uk
PCP

**DORRELL-DAHL**, Tiffany
**Existential Psychotherapist**
66 Poynders Meadow
Cwaerds Lane
Codicote
Hertfordshire
SH4 8UJ
☎ 07778 659 393
tiffany.dorrelldahl@london.probation.gsx.gov.uk
SEA

**DUNSTAN**, Gina
**Analytical Psychologist-Jungian Analyst**
15 Old Garden Court
St Albans
AL3 4RQ
☎ 01727 838 952
gina@dunstan1515.freeserve.co.uk
CAP *

**EDWARDS**, Rachel
**Integrative Psychotherapist**
4 Meadstone Cottages
Chorleywood Bottom
Chorleywood
WD3 5JQ
☎ 01923 285 474
r.edwards80@ntlworld.com
SPCRC

**ELLIOTT**, Andrew
**Systemic Psychotherapist**
13 Coney Close
Hatfield
AL10 8PR
☎ 01707 258 562
☎ 01992 465 042
aelliott63@yahoo.co.uk
CAMHS
Health Centre
High Street
Haddesdon
EN11 8BE
KCC

**EVEREST**, Pauline
**Psychoanalytic Psychotherapist**
79 Whitney Drive
Stevenage
Herts
SG1 4BL
☎ 01438 357 151
everest@nildram.co.uk
AIP

**FEENEY**, Michael
**Group Analyst**
Rickmansworth
WD3
☎ 01923 718 718
☎ 020 8318 9023
mhfeeney@aol.com
IGA

**FERNANDEZ**, Florence
**Systemic Psychotherapist**
22 Firwood Avenue
St Albans
AL4 0TF
☎ 01727 851 575
KCC

**FISHMAN**, Doreen
**Couple Psychoanalytic Psychotherapist**
16 Hamblings Close
Shenley
Herts
WD7 9JJ
☎ 01923 858 131
SCPP

**FREE-PEARCE**, Carolyn
**Autogenic Psychotherapist**
P.O. Box 178
Hertford
Hertfordshire
SG14
☎ 01992 423 800
☎ 0870 751 8827
carolyn@freepearce.com
BAS

**FRIEND**, Sue
**Systemic Psychotherapist**
1 The Cottages
Bull Stag Green
Hatfield
AL9 5DE
☎ 01707 273 894
KCC

**GENT**, Sheila
**Group Analytic Psychotherapist**
Edinburgh House
Community Mental Health Service
82-90 London Road
St Albans
AL1 1NG
☎ 01727 830 031
sheila.gent@ntlworld.com
FPC

**GOLDSMITH**, Anna
**Psychoanalytic Psychotherapist**
32 St Peters Street
St Albans
Herts
AL1 3NA
☎ 01727 864663
GUILD

**GOURNAY**, Kevin
**Cognitive Behavioural Psychotherapist**
♿ 14 Cassandra Gate
Cheshunt
WALTHAM CROSS
EN8 0XE
☎ 01992 446 817
☎ 020 8882 8191
BABCP

**GRUBER**, Angela
**Transpersonal Psychotherapist**
204 Nevells Road
Letchworth
Herts
SG6 4TZ
☎ 020 7266 3006
☎ 01462 635027
CCPE

**HALE**, John
**Family & Systemic Psychotherapist**
9 Park Avenue
Watford
WD1 7HR
☎ 01923 461 553
johnhale9@aol.com
AFT

**HALLETT**, Caroline
**Psychoanalytic Psychotherapist**
111 Ware Road
Hertford
Herts
SG13 7EE
☎ 01992 504 662
horakhalett@onetel.net.uk
AGIP

**HARRIS**, Dianne
**Analytical Psychologist-Jungian Analyst**
6 Whitelands Avenue
Chorleywood
Rickmansworth
Herts
WD3 5RD
☎ 01923 283 600
☎ 01923 282 490
dianne.harris@dial.pipex.com
CAP *

**HARRISON MAYOR**, Susan
**Analytical Psychologist-Jungian Analyst**
♿ 86 Handside Lane
Welwyn Garden City
Herts
AL8 6SJ
☎ 01707 897 678
AJA

**HARVEY**, Linda M
**Cognitive Analytic Therapist**
♿ Norbrook
Eastwick
Nr. Harlow
CM20 2QX
☎ 01279 410 435
☎ 01279 600 282
linda-harvey@lineone.net
The Rivers Hospital
High Wych Road
Sawbridgeworth
CM21 0HH
ACAT

**HENDRY**, Devam
**Psychosynthesis Psychotherapist**
14 Home Close
Harlow
Essex
CM20 3PD
☎ 01279 414 470
devam@tesco.net
PET

**HONIG**, Peter
**Family & Systemic Psychotherapist**
Hope Cottage
77 Orchard Road
Melbourn
Hertfordshire
SG8 6BB
☎ 01763 262 906
peteh@arsenalfc.net
AFT

**HOWELL**, Raymond
**Group Analytic Psychotherapist**
5 Burghely Close
Stevenage
SG2 8SX
☎ 0131 313 0813
Rdc41@dialpipex.com
UPCA

**HOWELLS**, Megan
**Psychoanalytic Psychotherapist**
11 Broad Green Wood
Bayford
Herts
SG13 8PS
☎ 01992 511294
M.Howells@broadgreen.demon.co.uk
IPSS

**HUISH**, Margot
**Sexual and Relationship Psychotherapist**
96 Hadley Road
New Barnet
Herts
EN5 5QR
☎ 020 8440 4092
☎ 020 8216 4862
Talk2Huish@aol.com
Psychosexual Clinic
Psychology Department
Barnet Hospital
Wellhouse Lane, Barnet,
EN5 3DJ
BASRT

**HUSZCZA**, Anna K.
**Cognitive Behavioural Psychotherapist**
♿ The Elms
24 Hall Place Gardens
St Albans
Herts.
AL1 3SF
☎ 01582 757 765
anna_huszcza@hotmail.com
Marie Foster Home
Wood Street
Barnet
Herts
EN5 4BS
BABCP

**ILJON FOREMAN**, Elaine
**Cognitive Behavioural Psychotherapist**
DAS
1st Floor, Avenue Clinic
The Avenue
Watford
WD17 3NU
☎ 020 8459 3428
free2fly@dial.pipex.com
BABCP

**JACOBSON**, Rosemary
**Integrative Psychotherapist**
Dept. of Clinical Psychology
Mental Health Unit
Princess Alexandra Hospital
Harlow
CM20 1QX
☎ 020 8444 8009
romey@clin.demon.co.uk
BPS, SPCRC

**JENKINS**, Beverley
**Psychoanalytic Psychotherapist**
Oaks and Bushes
Sawbridgeworth Road
Little Hallingbury,
Bishop's Stortford,Herts
CM22 7QU
☎ 01279 723 608
beverley@oaksandbushes.freeserve.co.uk
FIP

**KANJI**, Nasim
**Autogenic Psychotherapist**
Carwood House
147 Hamernill Lane
Oxhey
Hertfordshire
WD1 4PF
☎ 01923 225402
nkanji@exeter.ac.uk
BAS

**KAUR-LOVE**, Jasminder
**Psychoanalytic Psychotherapist**
♿ 2 Abrams Lane
Chrishall
Hertfordshire
SG8 8QD
☎ 01763 838 510
jkl@jklove.com
NAFSI

**KELL**, Midge
**Psychoanalytic Psychotherapist**
6 Hall Grove
Welwyn Garden City
Herts
AL7 4PN
☎ 01707 334 552
FPC

**KORN**, Susan
**Transpersonal Psychotherapist**
4 The Maltings
Kings Langley
Herts
WD4 8QL
☎ 07985 129642
☎ 01923 263355
CCPE

**LAKEMAN FRASER**, Judith
**Analytical Psychotherapist**
3 Old London Road
St Albans
Herts
AL1 1QE
☎ 01727 752 711
judelf6@hotmail.com
AIP

**LAW**, Heather
**Psychoanalytic Psychotherapist**
22 Leggatts Close
Watford
Herts
WD24 5NG
☎ 01923 671 311
heatherlaw@freeuk.com
IPSS

**LEINSTER**, Carline
**Psychosynthesis Psychotherapist**
47 Herbert Street
Hemel Hempstead
HP2 5HP
☎ 0775 263 2629
carolineleinster@hotmail.com
IPS

**LETTS**, Muriel
**Psychoanalytic Psychotherapist**
67 Strafford Gate
Potters Bar
Herts
EN6 1PR
☎ 01707 665423
muriel@bletts.dircon.co.uk
IPSS

**LUCAS**, Pauline
**Humanistic and Integrative Psychotherapist**
♿ The Croft
Stevenage Road
Little Wymondley
Hitchin
SG4 7JA
☎ 020 8742 0982
SPEC

**LUCKOCK**, Brenda
**Gestalt Psychotherapist**
♿ 22 Durban Road East
Watford
Herts
WD18 ORN
☎ 01923 250 983
GPTI

**MACCHESNEY**, Kirsty
**Systemic Psychotherapist**
High Firs Lodge
Woodhall Lane
Hemel Hempstead
Herts
HP2 5PS
☎ 01442 258 088
☎ 01727 867 936
kirstyandken@kirken01.fsnet.co.uk
The Causway
26 King Harry Lane
St Albans
Herts
AL3 4AU
KCC

**MAUDLING**, Caroline
**Gestalt Psychotherapist**
7 Holwell Court
Hertford Road
Essendon, Nr. Hatfield
Hertfordshire
AL9 5RE
☎ 01707 257366
consult@LCG-First.demon.co.uk
GPTI, SPTI

**MAYHEW**, Richard
**Sexual and Relationship Psychotherapist**
♿ Relate
Watford Advice Centre
St Mary's Churchyard
High Street, Watford
WD17 2BE
☎ 01923 230 080
☎ 01442 262 618
richard.mayhew@ntlworld.com
Relate
The Gables
3 St Mary's Road
Hemel Hempstead
HP2 5HL
BASRT

**MCCANN**, Anita
**Child Psychotherapist**
Barnet Child & Family Consultation Service
Vale Drive Clinic
Vale Drive
Barnet
EN5 2ED
☎ 020 8440 8668
☎ 020 7538 3698
ACP

**MCCANN**, Damian
**Family & Systemic Psychotherapist, Systemic Psychotherapist**
♿ 35 Hart Road
St. Albans
Herts
AL1 1NF
☎ 01727 856 690
damian@dmccann.demon.co.uk
IFT

**MCCARTNEY**, Meryl
**Child Psychotherapist**
Marlowes Health Centre
Marlowes
Hemel Hempstead
Herts
HP1 1HE
☎ 01442 259132
ACP

**MCSHERRY**, Loraine
**Sexual and Relationship Psychotherapist**
♿ The Nap Surgery
Kings Langley
WD4 8ET
☎ 01923 261 035
loraine.mcsherry@lineone.net
BASRT

**MENCZER**, Wendy
**Analytical Psychotherapist**
♿ 3 Browning Road
Harpenden
AL5 4TS
☎ 015821 713 282
GUILD

**MENEZES**, Ray
**Transpersonal Psychotherapist**
St Albans
AL3
☎ 020 7 266 3006
CCPE

**MESSENGER**, Daren
**Existential Psychotherapist**
14 Cavalier Court
Stevenage
SG1 4RD
☎ 01438 749 374
☎ 07866 372 021
darel@dmessenger.fslife.co.uk
SEA

**MILANI**, Belinda
**Systemic Psychotherapist**
♿ Westfield Gardener's Cottage
Grubbs Lane
Nr. Hatfield
AL9 6EF
KCC

**MILLER**, Joanna
**Integrative Psychotherapist**
♿ 18 Partridge Close
Arkley Gate
Barnet
EN5 2DT
☎ 020 8449 0619
joannamiller31@mns.com
SPCRC

**MITCHELL**, Richard
**Individual and Group Humanistic Psychotherapist**
31 Chiswell Green Lane
St. Albans
Herts
AL2 3AJ
☎ 01727 861 468
☎ 020 7224 3387
richard-mitchell@ntlworld.com
AHPP

**MOORE**, Maureen
**Integrative Psychotherapist**
♿ 18 Albury Ride
Cheshunt
Hertfordshire
EN8 8XF
☎ 01992 633100
maureenmoore@livingrelaxed.com
MET

**MORRISON**, Barbara
**Integrative Psychotherapist**
35 Dury Road
Hadley Green
Barnet
EN5 5PU
☎ 020 8440 4584
MC

**MORRISON**, Paul
**Humanistic and Integrative Psychotherapist**
♿ 35 Dury Road
Hadley Green
Barnet
Herts
EN5 5PU
☎ 020 8440 4584
paul@aptfilms.com
SPEC

**MOUNTFORD**, Corinne
**Psychoanalytic Psychotherapist**
9 Milton Road
Ware
Herts
SG12 0QA

**NOLTE**, Lizette
♿ Hertfordshire Partnership NHS Trust
Edinburgh House
82-90 London Road
St Albans
AL1 1NG
p.nel@psychology.bbk.ac.uk
IFT

**NORTON**, Lynda
**Analytical Psychologist-Jungian Analyst**
4 The Shaws
Welwyn Garden City
Herts
AL7 2HR
☎ 01707 695 353
☎ 07973 463 315
lynda.norton@ntlworld.com
AJA

**NOTTINGHAM**, Sue
**Systemic Psychotherapist**
Melrose
Croft Lane
Chipperfield
Kings Langley
WD4 9DU
☎ 01923 267 907
KCC

**O'DONOGHUE**, Margot
**Lacanian Analyst**
3 The Drive
New Barnet
EN5 1DZ
☎ 020 8441 3127
☎ 07778 049 893
modonoghue3@hotmail.com
CFAR

**O'LEARY**, Brid
**Systemic Psychotherapist**
3 Langley Crescent
St Albans
AL3 5RS
☎ 01727 867 936
brid.o'l@virgin.net
The Causeway Mental Health
Rehabilitation Unit
(Herts Partnership NHS Trust)
26 King Harry Lane
St Albans
AL3 4AU
KCC

**OZAKI-OWEN**, Mariko
**Transpersonal Psychotherapist**
80 Harwood Hill
Welwyn Garden City
Herts
AL8 7AN
☎ 01707 371455
ozaki-owen@ntlworld.com
CCPE

**PALLENBERG**, Sue
**Sexual and Relationship Psychotherapist**
101 St. Albans Road
Sandridge
St. Albans
Hertfordshire
AL4 9LH
☎ 01727 832 403
BASRT

**PARR**, Meriel A
**Integrative Psychotherapist**
Stevenage Comm. Mental Health
Services
Southgate
Stevenage
SG1 1HW
mel.parr@virgin.net
SPCRC

**PATCHETT**, Angela
**Transpersonal Psychotherapist**
♿ Mimosa Cottage
9 Springhead
Ashwell
Hertfordshire
SG7 5LL
☎ 01462 743109
angela.patchett@btinternet.com
CCPE

**PAYNE**, Helen
**Integrative Psychotherapist**
1 The Wick
High Street
Kimpton
Herts
SG4 8SA
☎ 01438 833 440
☎ 01707 285 861
H.L.Payne@herts.ac.uk
AHPP

**PERREN**, Mary
**Psychodynamic Psychotherapist**
1 Graysfield
Welwyn Garden City
AL7 4BL
☎ 01707 327 289
mary.perren@ntworld.com
FIP

**POOLEY**, Jane
**Systemic Psychotherapist**
♿ Saw Mill Cottage
Water End Lane
Ayot Green
Welwyn, Herts
AL6 4BB
☎ 01707 376169
jane@pooley67.fsworld.co.uk
IFT

**POPPLE**, Gillian
**Integrative Psychotherapist**
27 St. John's Road
Watford
WD17 1PY
☎ 01923 247 567
g.l.popple@herts.ac.uk
SPCRC

**POZZI**, Maria E.
**Child Psychotherapist**
North Herts C.A.M.H.S.
Southgate Health Centre
Stevenage
Herts
SG1 1HB
☎ 01438 781406/7
☎ 020 8340 6167
maria@pozzi-monzo.freeserve.co.uk
ACP

**PRESS**, Joanne
**Transpersonal Psychotherapist**
15 Avenue Terrace
Oxhey
Watford
Herts
WD19 4AP
☎ 0786 799 6176
☎ 020 8866 5773
CCPE

**RADMALL**, Bill
**Systemic Psychotherapist**
11 Kenerne Drive
Barnet
EN5 2NW
☎ 020 8440 2138
KCC

**RENWICK**, John
**Transactional Analysis Psychotherapist**
101 St Albans Road
Sandridge
St Albans
AL4 9LH
☎ 01727 832 403
ITA, MET

**RICHARDSON**, Elizabeth
**Analytical Psychologist-Jungian Analyst**
43 Barleycroft Road
Welwyn Garden City
Hertfordshire
AL8 6JX
☎ 01707 336 696
e.m.richardson@ntlworld.com
CAP, FIP *

**RICHTER**, Nicola
**Transpersonal Psychotherapist**
♿ Doggetts Way
St Albans
AL1
☎ 01727 750 088
nicolarichter@email.com
CCPE

**RICKETT**, Marion
**Psychoanalytic Psychotherapist**
40 High Street
Old Town
Hemel Hampstead
Herts
HP1 3AE
☎ 01442 250294
GUILD

**ROBERTS**, Mary
**Psychoanalytic Psychotherapist**
♿ The Spinney
Hempstead Rd
Bovingdon
Hemel Hempstead
HP3 0DS
☎ 01442 833 154
bredon@aol.com
FIP, FPC

**ROSSOTTI**, Nicole
**Personal Construct Psychotherapist**
22 Church End
Redbourn
Nr. St Albans
Herts
AL3 7DU
☎ 020 8952 2381 ext 3578
☎ 01582 792 970
n.rossotti@mtlworld.com
PCP

**RUSSELL-WINTER**, Kym
Flat 4
150 St Albans Road
Sandridge
St Albans
AL4 9LP
☎ 01727 753 820
tk.russell-winter@ntl.world.com

**SAUNDERS**, Alton
**Transpersonal Psychotherapist**
13 Arnett Way
Rickmansworth
Herts
WD3 4DA
☎ 01923 447063
Bushey Therapy Centre
39 High Street
Bushey
Hertfordshire
WD23 1BD
CCPE

**SINGH**, Tony
**Psychodrama Psychotherapist**
52 Redwood Way
Barnet
Herts
EN5 2RT
☎ 020 8441 8149
BPA

**SMITH**, Lois
**Psychoanalytic Psychotherapist**
7 Aysgarth Road
Redbourn
AL3 7PJ
☎ 01582 791 962
lois@whsmith.co.uk
FPC

**SORENSEN**, Bernice
**Integrative Psychotherapist**
♿ 9 Selwyn Avenue
Hatfield
AL10 9NR
☎ 01707 273 457
bernicesorensen@yahoo.com
SPCRC

**SPENCER**, Mary
**Psychoanalytic Psychotherapist**
26 Lower Luton Road
Harpenden
Herts
AL5 5AQ
☎ 01582 766 024
spencer.com@virgin.net
AGIP, FIP

**SPENCER**, Vivienne
**Integrative Arts Psychotherapist**
27 Spencer Avenue
West Cheshunt
Herts
EN7 6RP
☎ 01992 309 284
☎ 07979 981 155
vivienne.spencer@virgin.net
IATE

**SPROUL-BOLTON**, Robin
**Group Analyst**
♿ Shrodells Unit
Watford General Hospital
Vicarage Road
Watford, Herts
WD1 8HB
☎ 01923 217 561
IGA

**SPYROPOULOS**, Nick
**Child Psychotherapist**
74 Normandy Road
St. Albans
Herts
AL3 5PW
☎ 01727 54402
nicospyro@hotmail.com
ACP

**STACEY**, Linda
**Psychosynthesis Psychotherapist**
218 Stansted Road
Bishops Stortford
Herts
CM23 2AR
☎ 01279 637 041
linda.stacey@tiscali.co.uk
PET

**STAINSBY**, Jacki
**Sexual and Relationship Psychotherapist**
The Hertford Natural Therapy Centre
4 Old Cross
Hertford
SG14 1RB
☎ 01992 582 550
BASRT

**STANNARD**, Marie
**Transpersonal Psychotherapist**
39 Haycroft Road
Stevenage
Herts
SG1 3JL
☎ 020 7266 3006
☎ 07767 698966
CCPE

**STEEL**, Sandra
**Integrative Psychotherapist**
10 Abbotts Park
London Road
St Albans
Herts
AL1 1TW
☎ 01727 830378
MC

**STEWARD**, Jennifer
**Existential Psychotherapist**
Kings Langley
Hertfordshire
WD4
☎ 01923 266 168
SPCRC

**STOLEAR**, Meir
**Rational Emotive Behaviour Therapist**
10 Hammond Close
Stevenage
SG1 3JQ
☎ 01438 364 638
☎ 07900 258 207
meir1@mac.com
BABCP

**THIEL**, Geoffrey
**Transpersonal Psychotherapist**
17 Browning Road
Harpenden
Herts
AL5 4TS
☎ 01582 764579
CCPE

**TIDY**, Deirdre
**Neurolinguistic Psychotherapist**
♿ 8 Herkomer Road
Bushey
Hertfordshire
WD23 3NL
☎ 02089 501 825
tidy@btinternet.com
NLPtCA, KCC

**TIMMANN**, S.
**Cognitive Behavioural Psychotherapist, Hypno-Psychotherapist, Transpersonal Psychotherapist**
16 Brackendene
Bricket Wood
St. Albans
Hertfordshire
AL2 3SX
☎ 01923 672 880
st@pamir.co.uk
BABCP, CCPE, NRHP

**TOMLINSON**, Sharn
**Systemic Psychotherapist**
♿ Croft Cottage
Great Wymondley
Hitchin
SG4 7ER
☎ 01438 355 215
sharntomlinson@compuserve.com
KCC

**VINE**, Mike
**Family & Systemic Psychotherapist**
30 Franklin Rose
Colney Heath
St Albans
AL4 0QL
☎ 01727 821 563
m.vine@cnwl.nhs.uk
AFT

**WALKER**, Jillian
**Integrative Psychotherapist**
209 Chambersbury Lane
Hemel Hempstead
HP3 8BQ
☎ 01442 256 738
jill@jillwalker.freeserve.co.uk
SPCRC

**WALLIS**, Jill Alexis
**Systemic Psychotherapist**
9 Old London Road
St. Albans
Hertfordshire
AL1 1QE
KCC

**WATSON**, Eve
**Systemic Psychotherapist**
68 Bulwer Road
New Barnet
London
EN5 5EY
☎ 020 8440 7106
evew.sysft@virgin.net
IFT

**WHAN**, Michael
**Analytical Psychologist-Jungian Analyst**
16 East Common
Redbourn
Hertfordshire
AL3 7NB
☎ 01582 792 102
☎ 01727 810 371
michael@whan.fslife.co.uk
16 Chequer Street
St Albans
AL1 3YD
AIP, IGAP

**WHEELER**, Maria
**Systemic Psychotherapist**
64 Gloucester Road
New Barnet
EN5 1NB
KCC

**WISEMAN**, Anna
**Integrative Psychotherapist**
Kettle Barn
Kettle Green
Much Hadham
Herts
SG10 6AE
☎ 01279 842739
MC

**WOODER**, Bernard
**Core Process Psychotherapist**
17 Farrant Way
Borehamwood
Hertfordshire
WD6 4TE
☎ 020 8386 4846
berniewooder@hotmail.com
AHPP, UPCA

**WOODWARD**, Jan
**Systemic Psychotherapist**
♿ 53a High Street
Whitwell
Hitchin
SG4 8AJ
☎ 01438 871 975
KCC

**VAN BILSEN**, Henck P.J.G.
**Cognitive Behavioural Psychotherapist**
Watton Place Clinic
60 High Street
Watton at Stone
SG14 3SY
☎ 01920 830 005
henckvb@msn.com
BABCP

**VAN BILSEN**, Lynne
**Cognitive Behavioural Psychotherapist**
Watton Place Clinic
60 High Street
Watton at Stone
SG14 3SY
☎ 01920 830 055
☎ 07786 118 147
lynnecbt@aol.com
BABCP

## ISLE OF MAN

**BANKES-JONES**, Elizabeth
**Hypno-Psychotherapist**
6 Brookfield Terrace
Foxdale
Isle of Man
IM4 3ED
☎ 01624 801 624
☎ 01624 665 675
bankesjones@tinyworld.co.uk
The Centre of Balance
114 Bucks Road
Douglas
Isle of Man
IM1 3AH
CTIS

**KIRK**, Catharine Rose
**Psychodrama Psychotherapist**
11 Thorny Road
Douglas
Isle of Man
IM5 2EF
☎ 01624 673 505
☎ 01624 642 875
kate_kirk@manx.net
BPA

## ISLE OF WIGHT

**BARNES-KILPATRICK**, Shirley
**Integrative Psychotherapist**
Hunny Lodge
7 The Bramleys
Newport
Isle of Wight
PO30 5XL
☎ 01983 527 139
☎ 02392 822 444 ext. 4063
shirley@hunnylodge.freeserve.co.uk
MET

**BROOKE-SMITH**, Chris
**Systemic Psychotherapist**
Bank Cottage
Hulverstone
Nr Newport
Isle of Wight
PO30 4EH
☎ 01983 740 950
KCC

**HAMER**, Neil
**Psychoanalytic Psychotherapist**
42 The Mall
Carisbrooke Road
Newport
PO30 1BU
☎ 01983 760 724
GUILD

**KENNEDY**, Fiona C
**Cognitive Behavioural Psychotherapist**
♿ Sevenacres
St Marys Hospital
Parkhurst Road
Newport
PO30 5TG
☎ 01983 534 052
fiona.kennedy@iow.nhs.uk
BABCP

**KILLPACK**, Louisa
**Psychoanalytic Psychotherapist**
Psychological Therapies Service
The Gables
Halberry Lane
Newport
PO30 2ER
☎ 01983 525 334
☎ 01983 521 427
AGIP

**ORCHIN**, Susan
**Group Analytic Psychotherapist**
Snaefell
Woodland Close
Ryde
Isle of Wight
PO33 1PW
☎ 01983 563 715
sorchin960@aol.com
UPCA

**RUSSELL**, Hilary Jane
**Psychoanalytic Psychotherapist**
♿ Psychological Therapies Service
The Gables
Halberry Lane
Newport
PO30 2ER
☎ 01983 525 334
AGIP

**STEELE**, Lesley
**Psychoanalytic Psychotherapist**
♿ Cherry Tree Cottage
Sandy Lane
Blackwater
Isle of Wight
PO30 3BS
☎ 01983 526 214
AGIP

## JERSEY

**DYER**, Ian P.
**Cognitive Behavioural Psychotherapist**
♿ Queens House
St Saviours Hospital
La Route de la Hougue Bie
St Saviour, Jersey
JE2 7UW
☎ 01534 623 220
☎ 01534 878 018
i.dyer@gov.je
No 1 Coastlands
Greve D'Azette
St Clement
Jersey
JE2 6PD
BABCP

**POINTON**, Jane
**Family & Systemic Psychotherapist**
Beech Vale House
Sion St John
Jersey
JE3 4FL
☎ 01534 864 224
janepointon@hotmail.com
AFT

**REEVES**, Sarah
**Family & Systemic Psychotherapist**
Dept. of Psychology
Lil Maude House
14 Byron Road
St Helier
JE2 4LQ
☎ 01534 716 060
IFT

**TUMELTY**, Patricia
8 Millais Park
Mont Millais
St Helier
Jersey
JE2 4RU
☎ 01534 509 495
☎ 01534 630 760
p.tumelty@gov.je
AFT

**WADE**, Tracy
**Cognitive Analytic Therapist**
♿ Overdale Westmount Hospital
St Helier
JE1 3UH
☎ 01534 623 003
ACAT

## KENT

**ALEXANDER**, Barbara
**Cognitive Psychotherapist**
70 Old Dover Road
Canterbury
Kent
CT1 3AY
barbara.alexander15@btopenworld.com
BABCP

**ALEXANDER**, Paul T.
**Cognitive Behavioural Psychotherapist**
♿ Chronic Pain Clinic
Kent & Canterbruy Hospital
Ethelbert Road
Canterbury
CT1 3NG
☎ 01823 343 770
Paul.Alexander@ekkht.nhs.uk
BABCP

**ALMOND**, Elaine
**Integrative Psychotherapist**
2 Dryland Road
Borough Green
Nr Sevenoaks
TN15 8SG
☎ 01732 886 440
etalmond@aol.com
SPCRC

**ANDERSON**, Paul
**Psychoanalytic Psychotherapist**
43 St Thomas Hill
Canterbury
CT2 8HW
☎ 01227 471 680
andersononthehill@btopenworld.com
AGIP

**ASHTON**, Carole
**Psychoanalytic Psychotherapist**
Hillview
8 Dunstan Road
Turnbridge Wells
TN14 9NE
☎ 01892 543 561
CCOPPP

**AVERBECK**, Jennifer
**Transpersonal Psychotherapist**
Oakwood Lodge
4 St Stephen's Hill
Canterbury
CT2 7AX
CCPE

**AVERBECK**, Marcus
**Family & Systemic Psychotherapist**
Orchard House
17 Church Street
St. Peters
Broadstairs, Kent
CT10 2TT
☎ 01843 604 777
AFT

**BAKER**, David
**Rational Emotive Behaviour Therapist**
Stirling House
Black Robin Lane
Kingston
Canterbury
CT4 6HR
☎ 01227 832 286
baker.100@virgin.net
BABCP

**BAMBER**, Nicola
**Psychoanalytic Psychotherapist**
Psychotherapy Dept.
East Kent Commnity Trust
2 Cossington Road
Canterbury
CT1 3HH
☎ 01227 597 100
FIP

**BANFIELD**, Margaret
**Systemic Psychotherapist**
Grove Villa
South Grove
Tunbridge Wells
Kent
TN1 1UR
KCC

**BASSAM**, Bruce
**Cognitive Behavioural Psychotherapist**
♿ Acorn Lodge
Bethlem Royal Hospital
Monks Orchard Road
Beckenham
BR3 3BX
☎ 020 8776 4516
☎ 020 7737 3527
bruce.bassam@exmachina.demon.co.uk
BABCP

**BEARD**, Dorrie
**Psychoanalytic Psychotherapist**
♿ 4 Groveland Road
Beckenham
Kent
BR3 3QA
☎ 020 8650 9057
dorriebeard@onetel.net.uk
FPC

**BENTLEY**, Jacqueline
**Gestalt Psychotherapist**
Highlands
The Droveway
St Margaret's Bay
Dover, Kent
CT15 6BZ
☎ 01304 851 721
GPTI

**BHAT**, Radha
**Group Analyst**
♿ The Priory Hospital
Hayes Grove
Prestons Road
Hayes, Bromley
BR2 7AS
☎ 01883 388 303
☎ 020 8462 7722
IGA

**BLAKE**, Adrian
**Hypno-Psychotherapist**
Centre for Counselling
67-69 Widmore Road
Bromley
Kent
BR1 3AA
☎ 01263 733 271
blake@couns.fslife.co.uk
NRHP

**BLAKE**, Penny
**Psychoanalytic Psychotherapist**
20 Lower Green Road
Pembury
Tunbridge Wells
TN2 4HB
☎ 01892 822 668
☎ 01622 723 144
penny.blake@icc.wkentmht.nhs.uk
Kent Forensic Psychiatry Service
Trevor Gibbens Unit
Hermitage Lane
Maidstone
CCOPPP

**BOTHA**, Dr Marie
**Group Analytic Psychotherapist**
♿ 70 Bradbourne Road
Sevenoaks
Kent
TN13 3QA
☎ 01732 455 903
FPC

**BOURNE**, Juliet
**Family & Systemic Psychotherapist**
Centre for Counselling Training and Therapy
67 - 69 Widmore Road
Bromley
Kent
BR1 3AA
☎ 020 8853 0642
IFT

**BOYD**, Suzanne
**Transactional Analysis Psychotherapist**
The Old Farmhouse
Biddenden Road
Frittenden
Cranbrook, Kent
TN17 2BE
☎ 01580 852 414
Suzanne@boyd98.freeserve.co.uk
ITA

**BRENNAN**, Marilyn
**Family & Systemic Psychotherapist**
♿ 32 Castle Avenue
Dover
CT16 1EZ
☎ 01304 330 573
AFT

**BROOKS**, Carole
**Gestalt Psychotherapist**
Wheelspin
The Street
Ulcombe, Nr Maidstone
Kent
ME17 1DR
☎ 01622 842 979
GestaltKe@aol.com
GPTI

**BRUCE**, Ann
**Analytical Psychologist-Jungian Analyst**
6 Huxley Court
King Street
Rochester
ME1 1BJ
☎ 01634 827 065
CAP *

**BUCKNALL**, Valerie
**Attachment-based Psychoanalytic Psychotherapist**
26 Burnt Ash Lane
Bromley
Kent
BR1 4DH
☎ 020 8290 6817
val@valbucknall.co.uk
CAPP

**BUFFERY**, Elli
**Systemic Psychotherapist**
♿ Barnardos, Chilston
The Lodge Project
Pembury Road
Tunbridge Wells
TN2 3QJ
☎ 01892 511 468
KCC

**BUNDHOO**, Devanand
**Group Analytic Psychotherapist**
♿ 8 Nelson Road
Dartford
Kent
DA1 3EJ
☎ 01322 273 165
dbundhoo@hotmail.com
UPCA

**BUNKER**, Carol
**Psychoanalytic Psychotherapist**
Ivy Cottage
The Lees
Boughton Aluph
Ashford, Kent
TN25 4JB
☎ 01233 620 000
CCOPPP

**BUNKER**, Nigel
**Psychoanalytic Psychotherapist**
Ivy Cottage
The Lees
Boughton Aluph
Ashford, Kent
TN25 4JB
☎ 01233 620 000
nigel.bunker@ekentmht.nhs.uk
CCOPPP

**BURGESS**, Mary
**Cognitive Behavioural Psychotherapist**
7 Pickhurst Lane
Hayes
Kent
BR2 7JE
☎ 07957 469 118
☎ 020 7346 3363
mary.burgess@slam.nhs.uk
BABCP

**CAIRNS**, Mary
**Psychoanalytic Psychotherapist**
39 Chapel Lane
Blean
Canterbury
Kent
CT2 9HE
☎ 01227 472 439
CCOPPP

**CANT**, Diana
**Child Psychotherapist**
Breeches Field Oast
Egerton
Kent
TN27 9HA
☎ 01233 756552
ACP

**CANTY**, Josephine
**Group Analyst**
Oxleas NHS Trust
4 Emerton Close
Bexleyheath
Kent
DA6 8DX
☎ 020 8301 9428
☎ 020 8318 9023
IGA

**CAREY**, Jean
**Psychoanalytic Psychotherapist**
1 The Close
Bridge
Canterbury
Kent
CT4 5NJ
☎ 01227 831 405
CCOPPP

**CARTER**, Sybil
**Family & Systemic Psychotherapist**
♿ The Beacon Therapy Centre
Beacon Hill, The Downs
Herne Bay
Kent
CT6 6JN
☎ 01227 742 880
IFT

**CHALLENDER**, David
**Family & Systemic Psychotherapist**
1 St Radigunds
Canterbury
Kent
CT1 2AA
☎ 01227 709 135
david@challender.fsnet.co.uk
AFT

**CHANDLER**, Emma
**Systemic Psychotherapist**
The Therapy Team
Grove Villa
South Grove
Tunbridge Wells
TN1 1UR
☎ 01227 350 610
☎ 01892 619 766
margaretbanfield@yahoo.co.uk
KCC

**CHESTERS**, Neil R
**Family & Systemic Psychotherapist**
♿ Seafaring
Kingsdown Hill
Kingsdown
Nr Deal
CT14 8EA
☎ 01304 363 112
IFT

**CLARK**, Christine
**Group Analytic Psychotherapist**
Lydens
28 Pembury Road
Tonbridge
Kent
TN9 2HX
☎ 01732 352 637
FPC

**CLIFT**, Lynda
**Psychoanalytic Psychotherapist**
2 Oaklands
Staines Hill
Sturry
Canterbury
CT2 0ER
☎ 01227 711 698
CCOPPP

**COLEBY**, Gillian
**Neurolinguistic Psychotherapist**
The Coleby Centre
91 Station Road
Sidcup
Kent
DA15 4DP
☎ 020 8300 4044
info@colebycentre.com
NLPtCA

**CONNOLLY**, Cath
**Family & Systemic Psychotherapist**
The Priory
Hayes Grove
Prestons Road
Hayes
BR2 7AS
☎ 020 8700 8800
☎ 020 8462 7722
Cath.connolly@slam-tr.nhs.uk
IFT

**COOPER**, Heather
**Cognitive Behavioural Psychotherapist**
40 Stone Road
Broadstairs
Kent
CT10 1DZ
☎ 01843 863 643
BABCP

**COURTNEY**, Jan
**Transpersonal Psychotherapist**
Faversham
Kent
ME13
☎ 01795 531 576
jpcm@onetel.net.uk
CCPE

**COUTTS**, Linda
**Hypno-Psychotherapist**
4 Ashleigh Gardens
Headcorn
Kent
TN27 9TW
☎ 01622 890 720
lbriminyton.@ukonline.co.uk
NSHAP

**CRONIN**, Jeremiah
**Psychoanalytic Psychotherapist**
The Canterbury Clinic
47 Castle Street
Canterbury
Kent
CT1 2PY
☎ 01303 267946
☎ 01303 770509
CCOPPP, GUILD

**CUNNINGHAM**, Diane J
**Psychoanalytic Psychotherapist**
Willow Farmhouse
Upper Harbledown
Canterbury
Kent
CT2 9AL
☎ 01227 768 131
☎ 01227 379 700
dianecunn@btopenworld.com
AGIP, CCOPPP

**CUNNINGHAM**, Valerie
**Transactional Analysis Psychotherapist**
19 Birling Road
Tunbridge Wells
Kent
TN2 5LX
☎ 01892 529 903
vc@valcunningham.co.uk
ITA

**CURWEN**, Bernadette
**Cognitive Behavioural Psychotherapist**
♿ Prim. Care Counselling & Psychology
St Saviours Walk
Dartford
DA1 1DH
☎ 01322 284 433
BABCP

**CUTHBERT**, V. M.
**Cognitive Behavioural Psychotherapist**
In Patient CBT Unit, Alexandra House
Royal Bethlehem Hospital
Monks Orchard Road
Beckenham
BR3 3BX
☎ 020 8776 4146
BABCP

**DALE**, Tim
**Transpersonal Psychotherapist**
79 Hartnup Street
Maidstone
Kent
ME16 8LT
☎ 01622 725 302
timothy_dale@hotmail.com
CCPE

**DANIELS**, Deborah
**Integrative Psychotherapist**
Canterbury Counselling & Psychotherapy Centre
35 Watling Street
Canterbury
CT1 2UD
☎ 01227 477 173
SPCRC

**DANIELS**, Kate
**Family & Systemic Psychotherapist**
♿ 15 Ashburnham Road
Tonbridge
Kent
TN10 3DU
☎ 01732 359120
katedaniels@eurobell.co.uk
AFT

**DARNLEY**, Hazel
**Psychoanalytic Psychotherapist**
♿ Dove Cot
Anvil Green
Waltham
Canterbury, Kent
CT4 7EU
☎ 01227 700 752
ghinja@aol.com
CCOPPP

**DAVIES**, Peggy
**Transactional Analysis Psychotherapist**
♿ 11 Oakhurst Close
Walderslade
Chatham
Kent
ME5 9AN
☎ 01634 861 262
ITA

**DAWSON**, Joyce
**Psychoanalytic Psychotherapist**
23 Mapledene
Kemnal Road
Chislehurst
Kent
BR7 6LX
☎ 020 8295 0286
joyce@kemnal.freeserve.co.uk
FPC

**DAY**, Elizabeth
**Systemic Psychotherapist**
♿ 8 Brampton Road
Bexleyheath
Kent
DA7 4EY
☎ 07801 854561
liz@the-graig.co.uk
KCC

**DOHERTY**, Jackie
**Transpersonal Psychotherapist**
Bank House
38 St Mildred's Road
Westgate-on-Sea
CT8 8RF
☎ 01843 834 843
☎ 07721 853 824
Jackie233@yahoo.co.uk
CCPE

**DOOLAN**, Moira
**Family & Systemic Psychotherapist**
27 Barnmead Road
Beckenham
Kent
BR3 2JF
☎ 020 8676 8495
moira.doolan@ntlworld.com
AFT

**DOUGLAS**, Mica
**Transactional Analysis Psychotherapist**
Admiralty House
36 Mill Road
Gillingham
ME7 1HN
☎ 01634 576 672
mica.douglas@btinternet.com
ITA

**DRAYCOTT**, Christine
**Cognitive Behavioural Psychotherapist**
Behavioural Psychotherapy Service
George Villa
Hermitage Lane
Maidstone
ME16 9PH
☎ 020 8857 7465
☎ 01622 723 813
chris.draycott@lineone.net
BABCP

**DUCK**, Dorothy
**Hypno-Psychotherapist**
Fairhaven
Station Road
Pluckley
Ashford, Kent
TN27 0Q2
☎ 01233 840 263
NSHAP

**EMMANS**, Noreen Philomena
**Rational Emotive Behaviour Therapist**
22 Fernlea Avenue
Herne Bay
CT6 8UG
☎ 01227 362 220
n-emmans@supanet.com
AREBT

**EUBA**, Rachel
**Integrative Psychotherapist**
Oakleigh Lodge
Summer Hill
Chislehurst
BR7 5NY
☎ 07957 232 739
SPCRC

**EVANS**, Dorice
**Transpersonal Psychotherapist**
Ralph & Evans
11 Best Lane
Canterbury
CT1 2JB
☎ 01227 478 283
dorice.evans@thebesttimeoflife.demon.co.uk
CCPE

**FENTON**, Brian
**Transactional Analysis Psychotherapist**
6 Acton Road
Whitstable
Kent
CT5 1JH
☎ 01227 266358
brianjfenton@yahoo.co.uk
ITA

**FLYNN**, Kevin
**Systemic Psychotherapist**
36 Vectis Drive
Sittingbourne
M10 2JQ
KCC

**FOFAH**, Ngozi
**Group Analytic Psychotherapist**
13 Ripley Road
Belvedere
Kent
DA17 5AH
☎ 020 8310 2169
☎ 020 7525 1508
ngozi.fofah@southwark.gov.uk
UPCA

**FRASER**, Daphne
**Transpersonal Psychotherapist**
Herne Bay
Kent
HOME VISITS
☎ 01227 740580
CCPE

**FREEMAN**, Rabbi David
**Analytical Psychologist-Jungian Analyst**
222 Mackenzie Road
Beckenham
Kent
BR3 4SJ
☎ 020 8659 0108
☎ 020 8325 8211
AJA

**FREEMAN**, Susan
**Hypno-Psychotherapist**
5 King Arthur's Drive
Strood
Rochester
Kent
ME2 3LZ
☎ 01634 715 141
suefreeman2000@aol.com
NSHAP

**GOODBAN**, Wendy
**Transactional Analysis Psychotherapist**
♿ 5 Caslocke Street
Faversham
Kent
ME13 7JU
☎ 01795 532 805
goodban@entweb.net
ITA

**GORDON**, Elizabeth
**Integrative Psychotherapist**
♿ West Kent NHS & Social Care Trust
Priority House
Hermitage Lane
Maidstone
ME16 9PH
davidw-lizg@tinyworld.co.uk
SPCRC

**GRAHAM**, Vera
**Cognitive Behavioural Psychotherapist**
♿ Oxleas NHS Trust Mental Health
CATT, Bexleyheath Centre
Bexley Hospital
4 Emerton Close, Bexley H
DA6 8DX
☎ 020 8301 9435
BABCP

**GREEN**, Eliott
**Transactional Analysis Psychotherapist**
St. Mary's Health Centre
Vicarage Road
Strood
Rochester, Kent
ME2 4DG
☎ 01634 868 809
☎ 07879 454 110
ITA

**HALL**, Deborah
**Cognitive Behavioural Psychotherapist**
Hayes Grove Priory Hospital
Prestons Road
Bromley
BR2 7AS
☎ 020 8315 8837
BABCP

**HARMAN**, Josephine
**Integrative Psychotherapist**
♿ Walmer
The High Street
Greenhithe
DA9 9NP
☎ 07808 295 191
SPCRC

**HAUKE**, Christopher
**Analytical Psychologist-Jungian Analyst**
46 The Drive
Bexley
Kent
DA5 3DE
☎ 0781 805 1571
☎ 020 8301 5886
chauke@blythehill.u-net.com
CAP *

**HEINITZ**, Karin
**Biodynamic Psychotherapist**
30 Manor Road
Whitstable
Kent
CT5 2JT
☎ 01227 273 580
k.heinitza@btopenworld.com
LSBP

**HEMINGWAY**, Paul
**Group Analytic Psychotherapist**
18 Beckford Drive
Petts Wood
Orpington
Kent
BR5 1SH
☎ 01689 836 437
paulhemingway@Goldserve.net
UPCA

**HEMMONS**, Judy
**Integrative Psychotherapist**
Oakwell Farmhouse
11 Calais Hill
Tyler Hill
Canterbury, Kent
CT2 9LT
☎ 01227 471 516
☎ 07816 051 806
peter4judy@rubicon/freeserve.co.uk
MC

**HETHERINGTON**, Hugh
**Existential Psychotherapist**
26 High Street
Sandwich
Kent
CT13 9EB
☎ 01304 620 467
☎ 01843 598 982
SEA

**HEWITT**, Philip
**Psychoanalytic Psychotherapist**
27 Barnmead Road
Beckenham
Kent
BR3 1JF
☎ 020 7963 1099
☎ 020 8402 2984
philipjhewitt@yahoo.co.uk
FIP

**HEYLIGER**, Veann
**Family & Systemic Psychotherapist**
CAMHS
Cherry Tree House
Cheriton Hight Street
Folkestone
CT18 8AN
☎ 01303 717 233
Veann@ukonline.co.uk
IFT

**HEYWARD**, Julie
**Sexual and Relationship Psychotherapist**
♿ The Priory Hospital
Hayes Grove
Prestons Road
Hayes, Kent
BR2 7AS
☎ 020 8462 7722
BASRT

**HILLS**, John
**Family & Systemic Psychotherapist**
47 St Augustines Road
Canterbury
Kent
CT1 1XR
☎ 01227 452 155
august@cathcity.demon.co.uk
AFT

**HIRONS**, Ruth
**Psychoanalytic Psychotherapist**
♿ 1 Lavender Bank
Beesfield Lane
Farningham
Kent
DA4 0DA
☎ 01322 862629
Consultant Psychotherapist
West Kent NHS and Social Care Trust
The Courtyard, Pudding Lane
Maidstone
ME14 1PA
CCOPPP

**HOBBS**, Kevin
**Sexual and Relationship Psychotherapist**
♿ Canterbury Psychological Clinic
198 Wincheap Road
Canterbury
CT1 3RY
☎ 01227 457 575
☎ 01303 222 460
kevin@hobbs52.fsnet.co.uk
BASRT

**HUGHES**, Deri
**Psychoanalytic Psychotherapist**
4 Tudor House
315-323 High Street
Chatham
Kent
ME4 4BN
☎ 01634 828 528
hughd106@aol.com
NAFSI

**HUGHES**, Jennifer
**Psychoanalytic Psychotherapist**
♿ 2 The Cheynes
Broad Street
Sutton Valence
Maidstone Kent
ME17 3AJ
☎ 01622 844 937
CCOPPP, FPC

**HUSSONG**, Barbara
**Biodynamic Psychotherapist**
26 Milford Close
Maidstone
ME16 0EY
☎ 01622 670 587
LSBP

**JONES**, Deborah
**Psychoanalytic Psychotherapist**
Woodlands
Smeeth
Kent
TN25 6QL
☎ 01303 813 031
CCOPPP

**JONES**, Margaret
**Psychoanalytic Psychotherapist**
Mill Cottage
120 Heathfield Road
Keston
Kent
BR2 6BA
☎ 01689 853881
GUILD

**JONES**, Pamela
**Hypno-Psychotherapist**
25 Harrow Way
Weavering
Maidstone
Kent
ME14 5TU
☎ 01622 739 266
NSHAP

**KELLY**, Bridget
**Psychoanalytic Psychotherapist**
54 Beacon Drive
Bean
Dartford
Kent
DA2 8BG
☎ 01474 705171
ARBS

**KENWARD**, Raymond P
**Existential Psychotherapist**
3 Mockford Alley
Tenderden
Kent
TN30 6AU
☎ 01580 762 881
kenward@madasafish.com
UPCA

**KING**, Johanna (Jo/Hannetjie)
**Integrative Psychotherapist**
Spring Bank House
13 Penbroke Road
Seven Oaks
TN13 1XR
☎ 01732 453 956
jo.king2@easynet.co.uk
SPTI

**KONTOSTERGIOU**, Theodora Nora
**Psychoanalytic Psychotherapist**
Mount Zeehan
St Martin's Hospital
Canterbury
CT1 1TD
☎ 01227 761 310
☎ 01227 463 254
CCOPPP

**LANCZI**, Katalin
**Psychoanalytic Psychotherapist**
♿ 37 Preston Lane
Faversham
Kent
ME13 8LG
☎ 01795 590 653
KLanczi@aol.com
ARBS, CCOPPP

**LAURENCE**, Lee
**Group Analytic Psychotherapist**
♿ 32 Woodbridge Drive
Tovil Mill
Maidstone
Kent
ME15 6FU
☎ 01622 661 167
leelaurence42@hotmail.com
UPCA

**LAWRENCE**, Sandra
**Psychoanalytic Psychotherapist**
26 Sandown Lees
Sandwich
Kent
CT13 9NZ
☎ 01304 615 118 (24 hour ansa phone)
westbrookbeach@lineone.net
CCOPPP

**LEIPER**, Rob
**Psychoanalytic Psychotherapist**
Huntley Cottage
122 Wateringbury Road
East Malling
Kent
ME19 6JD
☎ 01622 776 355
☎ 01732 842 349
Psychotherapy Service
The Courtyard
Pudding Lane, Maidstone
Kent
ME14 1PA
CCOPPP

**LENNOX**, Graham
**Neurolinguistic Psychotherapist**
72 Queens Road
Tankerton
Whistable
Kent
CT5 2JQ
☎ 01227 273 042
NLPtCA

**LEONARD**, Avril
**Psychoanalytic Psychotherapist**
17 Richmond Gardens
Canterbury
CT2 8ES
☎ 01227 471 885
CCOPPP

**LETTINGTON**, Liisa
**Cognitive Analytic Therapist**
9 Waldegrave Road
Bickley
Bromley
Kent
BR1 2JP
☎ 020 8852 1384
☎ 07930 618564
ACAT

**LEWIN**, Melanie
**Transactional Analysis Psychotherapist**
2 Railway Cottages
Railway Hill
Barham
Canterbury, Kent
CT4 6PZ
☎ 01227 831 757
ITA

**LEWIS**, Penny
**Psychoanalytic Psychotherapist**
♿ Mill View
Mill Lane
Eastry
Kent
CT13 0LD
☎ 01304 611 434
CCOPPP

**LOMAX**, Vivien
**Psychoanalytic Psychotherapist**
♿ 28 Fisher Street
Sandwich
Kent
CT13 9EJ
☎ 01304 613 041
CCOPPP

**LOVEL**, Mary
**Psychoanalytic Psychotherapist**
♿ 7c Spencer Road
Bromley
Kent
BR1 3SU
☎ 020 8325 1566
mary@lovel.fsnet.co.uk
IPSS

**MAGILL**, Bernadette
**Systemic Psychotherapist**
♿ Family Therapy Team
Psychology Dept. A Block Corridor
Medway Maritime Hospital
Gillingham, Kent
ME7 5NY
☎ 01634 830 000 x3083
IFT

**MANN**, David
**Psychoanalytic Psychotherapist**
78 Stephens Road
Tunbridge Wells
TN4 9QA
☎ 01892 541 917
CCOPPP

**MANN**, James
**Psychoanalyst, Psychoanalytic Psychotherapist**
18 Regent Street
Whitstable
Kent
CT5 1SF
☎ 020 7622 8700
☎ 01227 273 681
SITE

**MANSON**, Greg
**Cognitive Behavioural Psychotherapist**
♿ Cossington House Surgery
51 Crossington Road
Canterbury
CT1 3HX
☎ 01227 763 377
greg.manson@btopenworld.com
BABCP

**MARSHALL**, Nicky
**Integrative Psychosynthesis Psychotherapist**
Hope Cottage
28 High Street
Seal
Sevenoaks
TN15 0AP
☎ 01732 763 615
nickymarshall19@hotmail.com
RE.V

**MARTIN**, Suzanne
**Psychoanalytic Psychotherapist**
2 Beach Walk
Whitstable
Kent
CT5 2BP
☎ 01227 772 654
CCOPPP

**MARU**, Rashmi
**Psychoanalytic Psychotherapist**
39 Latham Road
Bexleyheath
Kent
DA6 7NW
☎ 01322 407 547
NAFSI

**MAY**, Kathryn
**Sexual and Relationship Psychotherapist**
♿ The Canterbury Psychological Clinic
198 Wincheap Road
Canterbury
CT1 3RY
☎ 01227 457 575
☎ 01303 222 460
kathmay@ukonline.co.uk
BASRT

**MCANDREW**, Brigitte
**Psychoanalytic Psychotherapist**
80 Shalloak Road
Broad Oak
Nr Canterbury
Kent
CT2 0QE
☎ 01227 713 911
ARBS, CCOPPP

**MCDERMOTT**, Cathy
**Transpersonal Psychotherapist**
46 Pelham Road
Beckenham
Kent
BR36 4SG
☎ 020 8776 9590
CCPE

**MCLEWIN**, Ali
**Psychoanalytic Psychotherapist**
6 Albion Place
Canterbury
Kent
CT1 1LH
☎ 01227 764 710
CCOPPP

**MENDELSSOHN**, Penelope Clare
**Family & Systemic Psychotherapist**
The Coach House
Uckfield Lane
Hever
Nr. Edenbridge, Kent
TN8 7LQ
☎ 01732 862 865
pmendel@netcomuk.co.uk
AFT

**MILLAIS**, Suzy
**Transpersonal Psychotherapist**
Old Tar Cottage
Sea Wall
Whitstable
Kent
CT5 1BX
☎ 01227 264 529
CTP

**MINIHANE**, Anna
**Integrative Psychotherapist**
22 Athelstan Road
Folkstone
Kent
CT19 6EU
☎ 020 8776 5946
☎ 01303 257 659
amvm@ukgateway.net
MET

**MORGAN**, Ruth
**Integrative Psychotherapist**
206 Croydon Road
Beckenham
Kent
BR3 4DE
☎ 020 8658 3791
ruth@morgan206.freeserve.co.uk
MC

**MURPHY**, Carole
**Cognitive Analytic Therapist**
1 Rudland Gate
Bromley
BR2 0TG
☎ 020 8290 0122
ACAT

**MURPHY**, Patricia A.M.
**Cognitive Behavioural Psychotherapist**
♿ 6 Magdalen Close
Hempstead
Gillingham
ME7 3TA
☎ 07789 902 404
☎ 01634 239 543
pamurph55@aol.com
The Dame Sybil Thorndike Centre
Longly Road
Rochester
ME1 2TH
BABCP

**MURRAY**, Anne
**Educational Therapist**
Fern Cottage
Old Ryarsh Lane
West Malling
Kent
ME19 5AQ
☎ 01732 843 502
annemurray64@hotmail.com
CFET

**NAZIF**, Mahin Golbandi
**Psychoanalytic Psychotherapist**
♿ 215 Hempstead Road
Hemstead
Gillingham
Kent
ME7 3QH
☎ 01634 373 015
CCOPPP

**NEAL**, James
**Transactional Analysis Psychotherapist**
16 West Cliff Drive
Herne Bay
Kent
CT6 8DA
☎ 01227 364 666
anni-jimneal@hotmail.com
ITA

**NELSON**, Denise
**Sexual and Relationship Psychotherapist**
♿ Maidstone
ME16
☎ 07885 427 659
dennel@psv4.fslife.co.uk
BASRT

**NEWMAN**, Alan
**Family & Systemic Psychotherapist**
♿ Child & Adolscent Mental Heatlh Service
Cherry Tree House
Cheriton High Street
Folkestone, Kent
CT18 8AN
☎ 01303 717 233
alan.newman@ekht.nhs.uk
IFT

**NEWNS**, Kerri
**Systemic Psychotherapist**
♿ Child & Adolescent Mental Health Service
Unit One, Twistleton Court
Priory Hill
Dartford
DA1 2EN
☎ 020 8305 9842
☎ 01322 299 900
kerri@globalnet.co.uk
KCC

**NICE**, Terence
**Psychoanalytic Psychotherapist**
38 Gibraltar Place
New Road
Chatham
Kent
ME4 4QR
☎ 01634 846 831
CCOPPP

**NIXON**, Jane
**Transactional Analysis Psychotherapist**
139 Hockers Lane
Weaving
Maidstone
ME14 5JY
☎ 01622 630 422
jnnxn@aol.com
ITA

**NUAIMI**, Christine
**Family & Systemic Psychotherapist**
♿ Bromley CAMHS
2 Newman Road
Bromley
Kent
BR1 1RJ
☎ 020 8315 4430
carlton.parade@bromley.gov.uk
AFT

**O'BRIEN**, Sally
**Psychoanalytic Psychotherapist**
Old Church Cottage
High Street
Marden
Kent
TN12 9HN
☎ 01622 831292
Psychology Department
Benenden Hospital
Benenden
Cranbrook, Kent
TN17 4AX
CCOPPP

**O'BRIEN**, Teddy
**Integrative Psychotherapist**
12 Range Road
Eastchurch
Sheerness
Kent
ME12 4DU
☎ 01795 880 423
teddy@obrien2000.freeserve.co.uk
MC

**O'LOUGHLIN**, Pauline A
**Group Analytic Psychotherapist**
Eden Lodge
121 South Eden Park Road
Beckenham
Kent
BR3 3AT
☎ 02086 636 050
☎ 07956 892 520
oloughlinpa@hotmail.com
UPCA

**O'REGAN**, Emma
**Cognitive Behavioural Psychotherapist**
Centre for Counselling & Therapy
67-69 Windmore Road
Bromley
BR1 3AA
☎ 07810 775841
phobiafree@yahoo.com
BABCP

**OWENS-WARD**, Lyn
**Integrative Psychotherapist**
58 Hayes Road
Bromley
Kent
BR2 9AA
☎ 020 8466 8802
SPCRC

**PALANISAMY**, Shan
**Cognitive Behavioural Psychotherapist**
6 Upper Abbey Road
Belvedere
DA17 5AJ
☎ 020 8921 3514
☎ 07950 916 166
shan@palanisamy.freeserve.co.uk
BABCP

**PANGRAZI**, Sue
**Family & Systemic Psychotherapist**
Flat 5
Ivy House
129 High Street
Rainham
ME8 8AN
IFT

**PASSMORE**, Pascale
**Integrative Psychosynthesis Psychotherapist**
Tunbridge Wells
Kent
TN2
☎ 0189 254 2610
☎ 07703 276 027
pascale_passmore@Yahoo.com
RE.V

**PENWARDEN**, Mary M.
**Child Psychotherapist**
Lenworth Clinic
Dept. of Child & Family Psychiatry
329 Hythe Road
Ashford, Kent
TN24 0QE
☎ 020 7351 9429
☎ 01233 204180
ACP

**PIANTA-MORRISH**, Susan L.
**Transactional Analysis Psychotherapist**
163 The Gateway
Marine Parade
Dover
Kent
CT16 1LJ
☎ 01304 219 723
susie-p@dover163.fslife.co.uk
ITA

**PILE**, Adele
Speach and Language Therapy Service
South West Kent PCT
Tornbridge Cottage Hospital
Vauxhall Lane, Tornbridge
TN11 0NE
PCP

**POVER**, Jane S E
**Group Analytic Psychotherapist**
1 St Mary's Close
St Mary's Platt
Sevenoaks
Kent
TN15 8NH
☎ 02078 483 582
☎ 01732 887 346
jane.pover@kcl.ac.uk
UPCA

**POWELL**, Helen
**Gestalt Psychotherapist**
22 Weald Close
Weald
Sevenoaks
Kent
TN14 6QH
☎ 01732 455 587
helencpowell@aol.com
GCL

**POWER**, Kevin
**Group Analytic Psychotherapist, Psychoanalytic Psychotherapist**
Spring Gardens Clinic
Simmonds Road
Canterbury
CT1 3RD
☎ 01227 453 010
☎ 07762 334 747
kevin.power@btopenworld.co.uk
197 Old Dover Road
Canterbury
Kent
CT1 3ER
FIP, UPCA

**PREMPEH ADU BOBI**, Henry K.
**Cognitive Behavioural Psychotherapist**
Flat 2
19 Upper Park Road
Bromley
BR1 3HN
☎ 020 8460 0547
☎ 07947 121 977
BABCP

**PURCELL**, Anna Marie
**Integrative Psychotherapist**
3 Rowan Road
Bexley Heath
Kent
DA7 4BW
☎ 02076 436 009
MET

**READING**, Bill
**Psychoanalytic Psychotherapist**
1 Denstead Oast
Chartham Hatch
Canterbury
Kent
CT4 7SH
☎ 01227 730 808
Oastbooks@aol.com
CCOPPP

**REILLY**, Anne
**Psychoanalytic Psychotherapist**
Flat 5 Burley Court
8 Castle Hill Avenue
Folkestone
Kent
CT20 2QT
☎ 01303 259 145
☎ 07941 173 716
lizanner45@hotmail.com
Laurel House
41 Old Dover Road
Canterbury
Kent
CT1 3HH
CCOPPP

**RICHARDS**, Mrs Maureen V
**Sexual and Relationship Psychotherapist**
5 Lapins Lane
Kings Hill
West Malling
ME19 4LA
☎ 01732 875 096
maureenvr@lineone.net
BASRT

**RIDING**, Ann
**Psychoanalytic Psychotherapist**
32 Cromwell Road
Canterbury
Kent
CT1 3LE
☎ 01227 462 511
CCOPPP

**RIDING**, Nick
**Psychoanalytic Psychotherapist**
Kent Institute of Medicine and Health Sciences
The University
Canterbury
Kent
CT2 7PD
☎ 01227 823 380
☎ 01227 462 511
n.c.riding@kent.ac.uk
32 Cromwell Road
Canterbury
Kent
CT1 3LE
CCOPPP

**RIGNEY**, Ann
**Transactional Analysis Psychotherapist**
12 The Close
Rochester
Kent
ME1 1SD
☎ 01634 812 531
amyrgny@aol.com
ITA

**RILEY**, Brenda
**Hypno-Psychotherapist**
The Round Room
Monks Meadows Oast
Appledore Road
Tenterden, Kent
TN30 7DB
☎ 07980 412 475
hypnotherapy@milady.fsbusiness.co.uk
NRHP

**RIMER**, Penelope Ann
**Cognitive Analytic Therapist**
17 Manor Way
Beckenham
BR3 2LH
ACAT

**ROBERTS**, Jane
**Psychoanalytic Psychotherapist**
61 Radnor Cliff
Sandgate
Kent
CT20 2JL
☎ 01227 761 310
☎ 01303 249 385
roberts@jane81.freeserve.co.uk
CCOPPP

**ROBINSON**, Jane
**Psychoanalytic Psychotherapist**
83 Frant Road
Tunbridge Wells
Kent
TN2 5LP
☎ 01892 549 525
☎ 01322 229 116
West Kent NHS Trust
St Saviour's Walk
Dartford
Kent
DA1 1DH
CCOPPP

**ROSEN**, Sacha
**Individual and Group Humanistic Psychotherapist**
Copper Beech
3 Herons Close
Chilham
CT4 8DN
☎ 01227 730 462
AHPP

**RUSSELL**, Tina
**Integrative Psychotherapist**
84 Thong Lane
Chalk
Gravesend
DA12 4LD
☎ 01322 299 900
trussell@invicta-tr.sthames.nhs.uk
SPCRC

**RYAN**, Corrine
**Transpersonal Psychotherapist**
Tudor Cottage
Poundsbridge
Penshurst, Tunbridge Wells
Kent
TN11 8AP
☎ 01892 863005
CCPE

**SCHAEDEL**, Maggie
**Psychoanalytic Psychotherapist, Psychodynamic Psychotherapist**
♿ The Spinney Cottage
Knockholt Road
Halstead
Sevenoaks, Kent
TN14 7EX
☎ 01959 532 510
☎ 01227 823 691
M.Schaedel@kent.ac.uk
Psychotherapy Group
Kent Institute of Medicine & Health
University of Kent
Canterbury
CT2 7PD
ARBS, CCOPPP

**SCHUEPPERT**, Deirdre
**Psychoanalytic Psychotherapist**
Wildwood
Seal
Nr Sevenoaks
Kent
TN15 0EH
☎ 01732 762 294
deirdrevsch@aol.com
FPC

**SCRIVENER**, Amanda E.
**Psychoanalytic Psychotherapist**
Psychology Department
A Block, Medway Hospital
Gillingham
Kent
ME7 5NY
CCOPPP

**SHARPE**, Tracey
**Rational Emotive Behaviour Therapist**
Child & Adolescent MH Services
Gatland House
Gatland Lane
Maidstone
ME16 8PF
☎ 01622 723 600
BABCP

**SHAW**, Maureen
**Psychoanalytic Psychotherapist**
56 Whitstable Road
Canterbury
Kent
CT2 8DJ
☎ 01227 767 741
moshaw@hotmail.com
Kent Institute of Medicine and Health Sciences
The University
Canterbury
Kent
CT2 7PD
CCOPPP

**SHELLEY MARTENS**, Karin
**Gestalt Psychotherapist**
1 Woodgate Cottages
Selling
Faversham
Kent
ME13 9PN
☎ 01227 750 889
SPTI

**SHILLING**, Tara
**Hypno-Psychotherapist**
♿ 74 Darland Avenue
Upper Gillingham
Kent
ME7 3AP
☎ 01634 353 353
tara@therapypages.com
NSHAP

**SHYAM-ANSARI**, Dr Shakir
**Cognitive Analytic Therapist**
♿ Bexleyheath Centre
4 Emerton Close
Bexleyheath
DA6 8DX
☎ 020 8301 9421
ACAT

**SMITH**, Susan Diane
**Hypno-Psychotherapist**
♿ The Bromley Stress Management Centre
67-69 Widmore Road
Bromley
BR1 3AA
☎ 02084 602 528
sue@bsmctr.demon.co.uk
NRHP

**SPALDING**, John
**Psychoanalytic Psychotherapist**
♿ Stepping Stones Clinic
38 Masons Hill
Bromley
Kent
BR2 9JG
☎ 020 8466 2500
☎ 020 8464 8292
jpespalding@yahoo.co.uk
AGIP

**SPARKS**, Mrs Rebecca
**Sexual and Relationship Psychotherapist**
♿ Relate
Community House
South Street
Bromley
BR1 1RH
☎ 020 8315 1999
BASRT

**STEVENSON**, Alice
**Transactional Analysis Psychotherapist**
Upper Green
Sandhurst
Hawkhurst
Kent
TN18 5JX
alice@training.south-east.co.uk
ITA

**THOMASON**, June
**Psychoanalytic Psychotherapist**
South Cottage
High Street
Staplehurst
Kent
TN12 0BH
☎ 01580 891 402
jt@scottagestap.fsnet.co.uk
CCOPPP

**TILL**, Patricia
**Rational Emotive Behaviour Therapist**
Day Hospital
Archery House
Bow Arrow Lane
Dartford
DA2 6PB
☎ 01474 833 379
BABCP

**TINKER**, Siobhan
**Psychosynthesis Psychotherapist**
10 Chipstead Park
Sevenoaks
TN13 2SN
☎ 01732 458 251
siobhantinker@10cpfreeserve.co.uk
PET

**TOMLINSON**, Moya
**Sexual and Relationship Psychotherapist**
Section of Affective Disorders
Alex House 2, Bethlem Hospital
Monks Orchard Road
Beckenham
BR3 3BX
BASRT

**TOTMAN**, Maria
**Psychosynthesis Psychotherapist**
61 Avenue Road
Lesney Park
Erith
Kent
DA8 3AT
☎ 01322 334139
IPS

**TOYNE**, Joy K.
**Hypno-Psychotherapist**
♿ Oast Meadow
Burrs Hill
Brenchley
Tonbridge, Kent
TN12 7AT
☎ 01892 723 799
NRHP

**TRAYLEN**, Hilary
**Attachment-based Psychoanalytic Psychotherapist**
c/o East Kent Community NHS Trust
Primary Care Counselling Service
Coleman House, Brookfield Ave.
Dover, Kent
CT16 2AH
☎ 01304 216 666
CAPP

**TRAYLING**, Laurie
**Psychoanalytic Psychotherapist**
2 Parkside
Greattong
Headcorn
TN27 9PN
☎ 01622 892 336
FPC

**TRUSCOTT**, Frances
**Child Psychotherapist**
9 Sandown Close
Sandown Park
Tunbridge Wells
Kent
TN2 4RL
☎ 01892 822093
ACP

**TSE**, Claude
**Behavioural Psychotherapist**
219 Lower Higham Road
Chalk
Gravesend
DA12 2NP
☎ 01474 335 251
BABCP

**TUBBS**, I.A.
**Cognitive Behavioural Psychotherapist**
Englewood
Farningham Hill Road
Farningham
DA4 0JR
☎ 01322 862 158
BABCP

**TWELVETREES**, Heidy
**Humanistic and Integrative Psychotherapist**
Park Lodge
Briarside
38 Longlands Road
Sidcup
DA15 7LT
☎ 020 8302 3800
heidytwelvetrees@aol.com
AHPP, GCL

**VAN LOO**, Douglas A
**Systemic Psychotherapist**
5 Foxdown Close
Canterbury
Kent
CT2 7RR
☎ 01227 781 045
dougvanloo@aol.com
IFT

**VIRGO**, Leslie
**Integrative Psychotherapist**
♿ The Rectory
Skibbs Lane
Chelsfield
Kent
BR6 7RH
☎ 01689 825 749
☎ 07792 085 809
leslie.virgo@tinyworld.co.uk
MC

**WALKER**, David
**Group Analyst**
Dairy Cottage
17 Dower House Crescent
Tunbridge Wells
TN4 0TT
☎ 01292 520 239
IGA

**WARREN**, Yvonne
**Integrative Psychotherapist**
1 Sandling Way
St Mary's Island
Chatham
ME4 3AZ
☎ 01634 891 363
yvonnewarren@mac.com
SPCRC

**WATTERS**, Tamara
**Integrative Psychotherapist**
♿ 26 Glen Iris Avenue
Canterbury
Kent
CT2 8HP
☎ 01227 463 342
MET

**WEATHERLEY**, Paul
**Systemic Psychotherapist**
11 Jackson Road
Bromley
BR2 8NL
☎ 020 8462 1453
pj.weatherley@ntlworld.com
KCC

**WEST**, Helen
**Psychoanalytic Psychotherapist**
5 Shepherdsgate
Roper Road
Canterbury
CT2 7RU
☎ 01227 760 344
helen@dunstan.u-net.com
CCOPPP

**WEST**, Linden
**Psychoanalytic Psychotherapist**
5 Sheperdsgate
Roper Road
Canterbury
CT2 7RU
☎ 01227 760 344
wests@dunstan.u-net.com
CCOPPP

**WESTPHAL**, Joy
**Sexual and Relationship Psychotherapist**
Littleshaw
The Lane
Fordcombe
TN3 0RP
☎ 01892 740 263
joywestphal@lineone.net
BASRT

**WHITE**, Anne
**Systemic Psychotherapist**
♿ Child & Family Mental Health Services
Homeopathic Hospital
41 Church Road
Tunbridge Wells
TN1 1JU
☎ 01580 860 355
☎ 01892 522 598
annewhiteuk@yahoo.co.uk
KCC

**WHITMORE**, Diana
**Psychosynthesis Psychotherapist**
Southfield
Leigh
Nr. Tonbridge
Kent
TN11 8PJ
☎ 020 7403 2100
psychosynthesis.eductrust@btinternet.com
PET

**WHITWELL**, John
**Group Analytic Psychotherapist**
10 Vaughan Drive
Sittingbourne
Kent
ME10 2UA
☎ 01795 428 097 / 436 085
☎ 01285 861 694
johnwhit@freenetname.co.uk
FIP

**WIGHAM**, Avril
**Psychosynthesis Psychotherapist**
Hythe
CT21
☎ 01303 263 118
☎ 07855 063 554
avrilw@btconnect.com
PET

**WILKINSON**, Susan
**Psychoanalytic Psychotherapist**
♿ Target Cottage
Greenway Court Road
Hollingbourne
Kent
ME17 1QE
☎ 01622 880 168
smw@kinuta.fsnet.co.uk
CCOPPP

**WILSON**, Ronni
**Integrative Arts Psychotherapist**
1 Hunts Hill
Moons Green
Wittersham
Kent
TN30 7PR
☎ 01797 270621
IATE

## LANCASHIRE

**ARKWRIGHT**, Lynda
**Psychoanalytic Psychotherapist**
♿ Calderstones NHS Trust
Chestnut Drive, Mitton Road
Whalley
Blackburn
BB7 9PE
☎ 01254 821 851
lynda.arkwright@cstone-tr.nwest.nhs.uk
NWIDP

**ARROWSMITH**, Margaret
**Hypno-Psychotherapist**
2 Meadowlands
Charnock Richard
Chorley
Lancs
PR7 5RX
☎ 01257 792 087
ma@nj-m-arrowsmith.freeserve.co.uk
CTIS

**BARTON**, Alan
**Psychodrama Psychotherapist**
18 Jubilee Street
Read
Burnley
Lancashire
BB12 7PR
☎ 01282 774 136
abarton@24.net
BPA

**BENTLEY**, Ros
**Gestalt Psychotherapist**
Preston Therapy Centre
57 Garstang Road
Preston
PR1 1LB
☎ 01772 886 994
☎ 01524 841 993
rosb@connectfree.co.uk
GPTI

**BILLINGHAM**, Joy
**Integrative Psychotherapist**
♿ Department of Psychological
Services
Burnley General Hospital
Casterton Avenue
Burnley
BB10 2PQ
☎ 01282 474 760
☎ 07880 511 717
NGP

**BLACK**, Margaret
**Hypno-Psychotherapist**
9 Greengate Close
Wardle
Rochdale
Lancs
OL12 9PX
☎ 01706 631 099
NSHAP

**BROWN**, Philip
**Psychoanalytic Psychotherapist**
Department of Psychotherapy
1 Albert Road
Off Watling St Road
Fulwood, Preston
PR2 8BQ
☎ 01772 401 370
phil.brown29@virgin.net
NWIDP

**CANNON**, Bennedict
**Hypno-Psychotherapist**
♿ The Lodge
1 Oakford Close
Southport
Merseyside
PR9 8BP
☎ 01704 214 713
☎ 07951 648 167
benn_cannon@yahoo.co.uk
CTIS

**CARTWRIGHT**, Tony
**Family & Systemic Psychotherapist, Systemic Psychotherapist**
The Psychotherapy Service
1 Albert Road
Fulwood
Preston
PR2 8PJ
☎ 01772 401 370
☎ 01772 882 871
adcw@globalnet.co.uk
FIC

**CHEVREAU**, Marc
**Personal Construct Psychotherapist**
4 Grange Road
St-Annes-on-Sea
Lancashire
FY8 2BN
PCP

**CLARKSON**, Tony
**Neurolinguistic Psychotherapist**
Withgill House
Withgill Fold
Clitheroe
Lancashire
BB7 3LW
☎ 01254 826 635
tony@tonyclarkson.com
NLPtCA

**COOPER**, Patricia
**Hypno-Psychotherapist**
♿ 16 Waterside Terrace
Waterside
Darwen
Lancashire
BB3 3PD
☎ 01254 773 754
CTIS

**CORNELL**, Maria
**Psychoanalytic Psychotherapist**
♿ Psychotherapy Clinic
St. Leonard's House
St. Leonard'd Gate
Lancaster
LA1 1NN
☎ 01524 687 381
Maria.Cornell@mhpct.nhs.uk
NWIDP

**CRICHTON**, N
**Cognitive Behavioural Psychotherapist**
16 Darwen Street
Blackburn
BB2 2BY
☎ 01254 706 604
☎ 07957 871 588
nick@awave.freeserve.co.uk
BABCP

**DAVIDOFF**, Leslie
**Psychoanalytic Psychotherapist**
12 Woodfield Terrace
Bierfield
Nelson
Lancashire
BB9 5BU
☎ 01282 690741
lcd0302@aol.com
IPSS

**DENVIR**, Hazel
**Transpersonal Psychotherapist**
Main Street
Bentham
LA2 7HY
☎ 020 8986 6344
☎ 01524 263 147
Hazeldenvir@mac.com
CCPE, RE.V

**DILLON**, Annot
**Psychodrama Psychotherapist**
3 The Shore
Bolton-le-Sands
Carnforth
Lancs
LA5 8JR
☎ 01524 822 045
annot@europe.com
BPA

**DUNN**, Michael
**Gestalt Psychotherapist**
49 Vale Road
Lancaster
LA1 2JN
☎ 01524 382 609
mickd@@totalise.co.uk
SPTI

**DWYER**, Teresa
**Hypno-Psychotherapist**
69 Freshfield Road
Formby
L37 7BG
☎ 01704 871 203
CTIS

**FERGUSON**, Mary
**Psychoanalytic Psychotherapist**
♿ Calderstones NHS Trust
Mitton Road
Whalley
Clitheroe
BB7 9PE
☎ 01254 822 121
LPDO

**FLANAGAN**, June D
**Cognitive Behavioural Psychotherapist**
Palmers Greave
Lovely Hall Lane
Salesbury
Blackburn
BB1 9EQ
☎ 0161 772 3490
☎ 07790 364 026
BABCP

**FOWLER**, Barry
**Cognitive Behavioural Psychotherapist**
♿ Clinical Psychology Department
Birch Hill Hospital
Union Road
Rochdale
OL12 9QB
☎ 01706 754 070
☎ 01422 824 872 Privt ref
barryfowler@onetel.net.uk
BABCP

**GAUTHIER**, Jean-Baptise
**Family & Systemic Psychotherapist**
♿ 10 Wicks Lane
Formby
L37 3JG
AFT

**GOODSON**, Christina
**Hypno-Psychotherapist**
♿ 29 Pilkington Road
Southport
Merseyside
PR8 6PD
☎ 01704 537 753
CTIS

**GORDON**, John Fredrick
**Psychoanalytic Psychotherapist**
19 Hall Park
Lancaster
LA1 4SH
PA

**GOULD**, Frank
**Hypno-Psychotherapist**
Derwenlas
5 Acorn Bank
Garstang
Preston
PR3 1LP
☎ 01995 605 895
☎ 01772 761 166
frankxgould@aol.com
Remedy Centre for Health
166 Tulketh Road
Preston
PR2 1ER
CTIS

**HARRINGTON**, Rufus
**Cognitive Behavioural Psychotherapist**
♿ The Lancaster & Lakeland Nuffield Hospital
Meadowside
Lancaster
LA1 3RH
☎ 07961 378 329
☎ 01539 535 607
AEMETH@COMPUSERVE.COM
BABCP

**HAYWARD**, Marjorie
**Hypno-Psychotherapist**
Mahogany, 38 Merefield
Astley Village
Chorley
Lancashire
PR7 1UR
☎ 01257 411 983
☎ 01204 438 807
marjoriehayward12@hotmail.com
CTIS

**HAZLEHURST**, Jean
**Hypno-Psychotherapist**
♿ 33 Regent Avenue
Lytham St Annes
FY8 4AG
☎ 01253 735 677
dandyandfan@aol.com
NRHP

**HEWITT**, Patricia
**Hypno-Psychotherapist**
Alston Old Hall
Alston Lane
Longridge
Preston
PR3 3BN
☎ 01772 783 828
m.hewitt@btinternet.com
CTIS

**HINDE**, Chrissie
**Gestalt Psychotherapist**
57 Windermere Road
Lancaster
LA1 3EZ
☎ 01524 383 784
chrissiehinde@onetel.com
GPTI

**HOYLE-WOOD**, John
**Hypno-Psychotherapist**
126 Whalley Road
Accrington
Lancashire
BB5 1BS
☎ 01254 395 443
CTIS

**HUNTINGTON**, Annie
**Psychodrama Psychotherapist**
37 Primrose Street
Lancaster
LA1 3BN
☎ 01524 66635
annie@circusgirl.freeserve.co.uk
BPA

**JONES**, Judith
**Sexual and Relationship Psychotherapist**
♿ GUM Dept.
Southport and Ormskirk Hospital
Town Lane
Kew, Southport
PR8
☎ 01524 221 321
☎ 07761 957 243
irbyfarm@supanet.com
BASRT

**JUDKINS**, Malcolm
**Psychoanalytic Psychotherapist**
♿ Adelphi House Psychotherapy Unit
20 Queen Street
Blackpool
Lancs.
FY1 1PD
☎ 01253 751 155
NWIDP

**LAMB**, Janice
**Sexual and Relationship Psychotherapist**
St Leonardsgate Centre
St Leonards House
St Leonardsgate
Lancaster
LA1 1NN
☎ 01524 68743
☎ 01772 524 733
Rebecca.Dowthwaite@mbpct.nhs.uk
Sexual Problems Service
c/o Gynaecology Out Patients Dept.
Sharoe Green Hospital
Sharoe Green Lane, Fulwoo
PR2 8DU
BASRT

**LEGGATT**, Claire
**Psychoanalytic Psychotherapist**
5 Portland Street
Lancaster
LA1 1SZ
☎ 01524 687 38
☎ 01524 383 822
Psychotherapy Clinic
St Leonard's House
St Leonard's Gate
Lancaster
LA1 1NN
AGIP

**LEWIS**, Steve
**Gestalt Psychotherapist**
56 Clarence Street
Lancaster
LA1 3BB
☎ 01524 35193
improv@btopenworld.com
SPTI

**LIDDLE**, Helen
**Psychoanalytic Psychotherapist**
♿ Adelphi House
20 Queen Street
Blackpool
FY1 1PD
☎ 01253 751 115
hellid@aol.com
NWIDP

**LUCKRAFT-VOGES**, Julie
**Integrative Psychotherapist**
7 Haighton Drive
Fulwood
Preston
PR2 9LU
☎ 01772 709 782
luckraftvoges@supanet.com
SPTI

**MACKIE**, Lynn
**Cognitive Behavioural Psychotherapist**
♿ 19 Anshaw Close
Belmont
Bolton
BL7 8BS
☎ 01204 811 116
DrLynnMackie@aol.com
BABCP

**MACNAB**, Celia
**Gestalt Psychotherapist**
11 Park Avenue
Lancaster
LA1 3DX
☎ 01524 63812
celiamac@lineone.net
GPTI, MET

**MAGUIRE**, Anne
**Analytical Psychologist-Jungian Analyst**
17 Wellington Street
St John's
Blackburn
BB1 8AF
☎ 020 7436 5262
☎ 01254 59910
IGAP

**MARKOVIC**, Olivera
**Family & Systemic Psychotherapist**
3 Hayhurst Road
Whalley
Lancs
BB7 9RL
☎ 01254 824 902
olivera@ukgateway.net
AFT

**MCALLISTER**, Susan
**Psychoanalytic Psychotherapist**
Psychotherapy Service
1 Albert Road
Fulwood
Preston
PR2 8PJ
☎ 01772 406 933
NWIDP

**MICHAELSON**, Jess
**Gestalt Psychotherapist**
30 Greaves St
Mossley
Lancs
OL5 0QH
☎ 01457 832 411
☎ 07790 637 849
jess@jmichaelson.freeserve.co.uk
GPTI

**MOON**, Barbara
**Hypno-Psychotherapist**
♿ 90 Watkin Road
Clayton-le-Woods
Chorley
Lancashire
PR6 7PX
☎ 01257 275169
CTIS

**PAMPHLETT**, Nick
**Transactional Analysis Psychotherapist**
17 Fairfield Drive
Clitheroe
BB7 2PE
☎ 07200 428 858
☎ 0798 386 130
nickpamphlette@phoenixgroup.co.uk
ITA

**RAWSON**, Wendy
**Psychoanalytic Psychotherapist**
♿ Clinical Psychology Service
St Leonard's House
St. Leonard's Gate
Lancaster
LA1 1NN
☎ 0152 468 738
NWIDP

**ROBINSON**, Isabel
**Transactional Analysis Psychotherapist**
♿ Bridge House
Whalley Banks
Blackburn
Lancashire
BB2 1NT
☎ 01254 695 698
isabell.robinson@communicare.nhs.uk
ITA

**RODRIQUEZ-SLAWINSKI**, Flavia
Clougha Cottage
Quernmore
Lancaster
LA2 9EG
☎ 01524 388 530
☎ 01524 64297
arete_clinhyp@yahoo.com
CTIS

**SANDERS**, Paul J
**Psychoanalytic Psychotherapist**
Department of Psychotherapy
1 Albert Road
Fulwood
Preston
PR2 8PJ
☎ 01772 401 370
paul@aardwolf.freeserve.co.uk
UPCA

**SAVAGE**, Peter J.D.
**Hypno-Psychotherapist**
National College of Hypnosis & Psychotherapy
12 Cross Street
Nelson
Lancs
BB9 7EN
☎ 01282 699 378
hypnosis_nchp@compuserve.com
NRHP

**SCOTT**, Catherine
**Hypno-Psychotherapist**
1 Deep Cutting Farm
Ashton Road
Lancaster
LA2 0AA
☎ 01524 388 788
NRHP

**STEPHENSON**, Keri P
**Psychodynamic Psychotherapist**
♿ Clinical Psychology Department
Burnley General Hospital
Casterton Avenue
Burnley
BB10 2PQ
☎ 01282 474 760
StephensonKeri@aol.com
UPCA

**STOKES**, Fergus
**Hypno-Psychotherapist**
♿ 6 Kensington Road
Lytham St. Annes
Lancashire
FY8 4ET
☎ 01253 730 588
Fergus@btclick.com
CTIS

**STUNDEN**, Patricia
**Core Process Psychotherapist**
6 Old Hay Croft
Penwortham
Preston
PR1 9ET
☎ 01772 740 522
KI

**SUMMERS**, Graeme
**Transactional Analysis Psychotherapist**
♿ "Langtree"
Hollins Lane
Arnside
Cumbria
LA5 0EG
☎ 01524 762 607
graeme@cc-creativity.com
ITA

**TAYLOR**, Theresa
**Psychoanalytic Psychotherapist**
♿ Department of Psychotherapy
Guild Community Healthcare Trust
1 Albert Road, Fulwood
Preston
PR2 8PJ
☎ 01772 401 370
NWIDP

**TURNER**, Mary
**Gestalt Psychotherapist**
80 Aldcliffe Road
Lancaster
LA1 5BB
☎ 01524 68332
turner.mary@tiscali.co.uk
GPTI

**VANNEN-HYLAND**, Joan
**Hypno-Psychotherapist**
♿ Centre for Health & Healing
2 Prescot Green
Ormskirk
Lancashire
L39 4US
☎ 01695 580 288
joan@dstraining.co.uk
CTIS

**WALLACE**, Daphne
**Psychoanalytic Psychotherapist**
The Vicarage
Skipton Road
Earby, Barnoldswick
Lancashire
BB18 6JC
☎ 01943 468 443
☎ 01282 841 608
LPDO

**WASHINGTON**, Sue
**Hypno-Psychotherapist**
♿ 145 Chapel Lane
Longton
Preston
PR4 5NA
☎ 01772 617 663
☎ 01704 549 555
peaceofmind@ukip.co.uk
CTIS

**WATSON**, Jane
86 Wateringpool Lane
Lostock Hall
Preston
PR5 5UA
☎ 01772 337 228
jane@bjwatson.co.uk
CTIS

**WESTLEY**, Andrew
**Cognitive Behavioural Psychotherapist**
♿ 8 Curzon Road
Southport
PR8 6PL
☎ 01704 380 789
☎ 07801 351 101
ajwestley@blueyonder.co.uk
BABCP

**WETHERELL**, Annette
**Family & Systemic Psychotherapist**
Moorgate Barn
Littledale Road
Brookhouse
Nr Lancaster
LA2 9PH
☎ 01524 771 363
wetherell2001@aol.com
AFT

**WHITAKER**, Kim
**Cognitive Behavioural Psychotherapist**
♿ Department of Clinical Pyschology
Birdch Hill Hospital
Union Road
Rochdale
OL12 9QB
☎ 01706 754 070
☎ 07813 437 276
drkimwhitaker@hotmail.com
BABCP

**WILLIAMS**, Les
**Hypno-Psychotherapist**
♿ 157 Manchester Road
Burnley
BB11 4HT
☎ 01282 414 820
a1leswill1@aol.com
CTIS

**YATES**, Alison
**Cognitive Behavioural Psychotherapist**
♿ 23 Union Street
Egerton
Bolton
BL7 9SP
☎ 01204 593 516
BABCP

## LEEDS

**BOSTON**, Paula
**Systemic Psychotherapist**
♿ School Of Psychology
University of Leeds
Leeds
LS9 9JT
☎ 01943 601 162
PaulaB@parishghyll.u-net.com
IFT

## LEICESTERSHIRE

**AMBROSE**, Laura
**Gestalt Psychotherapist**
Access to rooms in Oakham
Rutland
LE15
☎ 07759 775 111
lambrose@handbag.com
MET

**ANDERSON**, Maureen
**Integrative Psychotherapist**
♿ 139 Coleman Road
Leicester
LE5 4LG
☎ 0116 210 9524
maureenshapeshifter8@fsmail.net
SPTI

**ANTAO**, Ivor
**Group Analyst**
Francis Dixon Lodge
Gipsy Lane
Leicester
LE5 0TD
☎ 0116 225 6800
ivo.antao@leicspart.nhs.uk
IGA

**BAILEY**, James
**Psychoanalytic Psychotherapist**
♿ Dynamic Psychotherapy Service
Humberstone Grange Clinic
Thurmaston Lane
Leicester
LE5 0TA
☎ 01162 256 430/3778
james.bailey@leicspart.nhs.uk
Dynamic Psychotherapy Service
Main Lodge
Gipsy Lane
Leicester
LE5 0TA
STTDP

**BAKER**, Carol
**Psychodynamic Psychotherapist**
27 Church Road
Kibworth
Leicester
LE8 0NB
☎ 0116 2577602
☎ 0116 2792956
cbaker1@dmu.ac.uk
VAPP

**BALL**, Derek
**Sexual and Relationship Psychotherapist**
8 Barrow Crescent
Gaddersby
Leicester
LE7 4WA
☎ 01664 840 353
BASRT

**BARKER**, John F.
**Psychoanalytic Psychotherapist**
Highway
Main Street
Cold Newton
Leicestershire
LE7 9DA
☎ 0116 259 5205
WMIP

**BRADLEY**, Marie
**Psychoanalytic Psychotherapist**
♿ Dynamic Psychotherapy Service (NHS)
Humberstone Grange Clinic
Thurmaston Lane
Leicester
LE5 0TA
☎ 01162 252 606
Bradgate Unit
Glenfield Hospital
Groby Road
LE3 9EJ
STTDP

**BRINICOMBE**, Phyl
**Integrative Psychotherapist**
♿ Silverstone
84 Letchworth Road
Leicester
LE3 6FH
☎ 0116 225 7742
pbrinicombe@ntlworld.com
SPTI

**CARTER**, Nick
**Integrative Psychotherapist**
28 Loughborough Road
Thringstone
Coalville
Leicestershire
LE67 8LP
☎ 01530 223 241
SPTI

**DALEY**, Lema
**Transactional Analysis Psychotherapist**
♿ Eastgate CCMP Health Centre
Eastgate House
19 Humberstone Road
LE5 3GJ
☎ 01162 511 647
☎ 01162 628 158
ITA

**DAVIS**, Bob
**Gestalt Psychotherapist**
6 School Close
Burbage
Leicester
LE10 2FE
☎ 01455 612 314
GPTI

**DAVIS**, Christopher
**Transactional Analysis Psychotherapist**
182A London Road
Victoria Park
Leicester
LE2 1ND
☎ 01162 558 505
☎ 01536 770 883
christopherdavis.therapy@virgin.net
ITA

**DENT**, Peter
**Psychodynamic Psychotherapist**
♿ The Woodlands Unit
The Pastures
Narborough
Leicester
LE9 5DY
☎ 01162 255 850
☎ 01455 440 898
peterdent@leicspart.nhs.uk
VAPP

**DICKSON DUMMER**, Karine
**Psychodynamic Psychotherapist**
The Coach House
182A London Road
Leicester
LE2 1ND
☎ 07939 505 158
dummer@ukonline.co.uk
VAPP

**EVANS**, Jenny
**Cognitive Behavioural Psychotherapist**
♿ 25 Leicester Road
Shepshed
Loughborough
LE12 9DF
☎ 01509 650 602
jenny_evans_121@hotmail.com
BABCP

**FLANAGAN**, Diana
**Psychodynamic Psychotherapist**
♿ The Old Vicarage
Castle Bytham
Grantham
LINCOLNSHIRE
NG33 4SG
☎ 01733 563 060
☎ 01780 410 177
VAPP

**GARVEY**, Rachel
**Cognitive Behavioural Psychotherapist**
♿ CBT Department
Bradgate Mental Health Unit
Glenfield Hospital
Leicester
LE3 9EJ
rachel.ian@ntl.world.com
BABCP

**HEWITT-TAYLOR**, Joanna
**Gestalt Psychotherapist**
5 Lyndon Drive
Oadby
Leicester
LE2 5GA
☎ 0116 271 9482
☎ 0781 330 4884
ScPTI

**HILES**, David
**Transpersonal Psychotherapist**
Leicester
LE7
☎ 0116 212 8194
drhiles@ntlworld.com
CCPE

**HIRST**, Hazel
**Transactional Analysis Psychotherapist**
♿ Holly Cottage
26 Church Street
Billesdon
Leicestershire
LE7 9AE
☎ 01162 596 851
The Eastgate
Complementary Health Centre
Leicester
LE7 9AE
ITA

**HONEY**, Joanna
**Integrative Psychotherapist**
5 Winckley Close
Houghton-on-the-Hill
Leicestershire
LE7 9HS
☎ 0116 241 5969
joannah@btinternet.com
SPTI

**HOPCROFT**, Susan
**Psychoanalytic Psychotherapist**
♿ Dynamic Psychotherapy Service
Humberstone Grange Clinic
Thurmaston Lane
Leicester
LE5 0TA
STTDP

**HOTHAM**, Aine
**Gestalt Psychotherapist**
1 Warn Crescent
Oakham
Leicester
LE15 6LZ
☎ 01572 757 727
☎ 07951 242 135
aine@spudhotham.fsnet.co.uk
SPTI

**HOUSE**, Mrs Wyn
**Sexual and Relationship Psychotherapist**
♿ Relate Leicesteshire
83 Aylestone Road
Leicester
LE2 7LL
☎ 0116 254 3011
wynjimhouse@hotmail.com
4 Victoria Avenue
Market Harborough
LE16 7BQ
BASRT

**HUMPHREYS**, Nicholas
**Psychoanalytic Psychotherapist**
♿ Francis Dixon Lodge
Therapeutic Community
Gipsy Lane
Leicester
LE5 0TD
☎ 01162 256 800
Dynamic Psychotherapy Service
Humberstone Grange Clinic
Gipsy Lane
Leicester
LE5 0TA
STTDP

**JONES**, Richard
**Psychoanalytic Psychotherapist**
♿ Dynamic Psychotherapy Service(NHS)
Humberstone Grange Clinic
Thurmaston Lane
Leicester
LE5 0TA
☎ 01162 256 430
STTDP

**JUDSON**, Janice
**Psychodynamic Psychotherapist**
14 Balmoral Avenue
Shepshed
Loughborough
Leicestershire
LE12 9PX
☎ 01509 561 285
☎ 01509 829 303
janice.judson@nhworld.com
VAPP

**KEEN**, Caroline
**Gestalt Psychotherapist**
119 Ashby Road
Loughborough
Leicester
LE11 3AB
☎ 01509 235 338
caroline.keen@ntlworld.com
SPTI

**KING**, Gail
**Psychodynamic Psychotherapist**
♿ 4 Hillcrest Avenue
Market Harborough
Leicestershire
LE16 7AR
☎ 01858 461 570
gail.king@cwcom.net
University of Leicester
Institute of Life Long Learning
Vanghan College
St Nicholas
LE1 4LB
VAPP

**KINGSLEY-MILLS**, Christine
**Gestalt Psychotherapist**
Mayfield
26 West View Avenue
Glen Parva
Leicester
LE2 9JT
☎ 0116 278 9598
kingsleymills@rmplc.co.uk
SPTI

**LAHER**, Aftab
**Cognitive Behavioural Psychotherapist**
♿ BUPA Hospital Leicester
Gartree Road
Oadby
Leicester
LE2 2FF
☎ 0116 265 3685
☎ 07900 916 857
al@laheronline.com
BABCP

**LEE**, Adrienne
**Transactional Analysis Psychotherapist**
The Berne Institute
Berne House
29 Derby Road, Kegworth
Nottingham
DE74 2EN
☎ 01509 673 649
☎ 0115 9475 447
ta@theberne.com
ITA

**LINNELL**, Maxine
**Humanistic Psychotherapist**
63 Foxcroft Close
Rowley Fields
Leicester
LE3 2DZ
☎ 01237 441 691
AHPP, KI

**MACKENZIE**, Liz
**Gestalt Psychotherapist**
♿ Unit 02
Beaumont Enterprise Centre
Boston Road
Leicester
LE4 IHB
☎ 0116 229 3102
justandwhitehill@yahoo.com
GPTI

**MALIK**, Shehzad
**Hypno-Psychotherapist**
♿ Leicestershire Community Drug Team
Paget House
2 West Street
Leicester
LE1 6XP
☎ 01162 126 173
s.malik4@ntlworld.com
44 Ripon Street
Leicester
LE2 1LW
NSHAP

**MARSHALL**, Hazel
**Transpersonal Psychotherapist**
52 Station Road
Cropston
Leicester
LE7 7HD
☎ 0116 236 4256
CTP

**MARSHALL**, Pam
**Psychoanalytic Psychotherapist**
♿ Dynamic Psychotherapy Service (NHS)
Humberstone Grange Clinic
Thurmaston Lane
Leicester
LE5 0TA
☎ 01162 256 430
STTDP

**MCFARLAND**, Alf
**Analytical Psychotherapist**
♿ 16 Oakthorpe Avenue
Leicester
LE3 0UQ
☎ 01162 553 549
VAPP, WMIP

**MCKAY**, Carol
**Integrative Psychotherapist**
3-5 Hurley Common
Hurley
Nr Atherstone
CV9 2LS
☎ 01827 874 644
carol.mckay@virgin.net
SPTI

**MONK-STEEL**, Barbara
**Transactional Analysis Psychotherapist**
43, Stoneygate Road
Leicester
LE2 2BP
☎ 01162 700 290
monksteel@hotmail.com
ITA

**MONK-STEEL**, John Michael
**Transactional Analysis Psychotherapist**
43 Stoneygate Road
Leicester
LE2 2BP
☎ 01162 700 290
monksteel@eidosnet.co.uk
ITA

**MOUNTAIN**, Anita
**Transactional Analysis Psychotherapist**
♿ Beechwoods
56 Main Street
Desford
Leicester
LE9 9GR
☎ 01455 824 475
anita@mountassoc.demon.co.uk
ITA

**PARNELL**, Mike
**Personal Construct Psychotherapist**
63 Beacon Road
Loughborough
LE11 2BE
☎ 01509 269 254
mpgam58@hotmail.com
PCP

**PAYNE**, Katherine Elizabeth
**Systemic Psychotherapist**
17 Barkby Road
Queniborough
Leicester
LE7 3FE
☎ 01162 695 580
IFT

**PELZ**, Doris
**Psychodynamic Psychotherapist**
Leicester
East Midlands
LE2 2DB
☎ 01162 231 780
☎ 01162 109 874
dorispelz@ntlworld.com
VAPP

**PERRY**, Janet
**Sexual and Relationship Psychotherapist**
Knighton Church Road
Knighton
Leicester
☎ 0116 244 8182
camsgil@btinternet.com
BASRT

**POOLEY**, Steve
**Gestalt Psychotherapist**
21 Wreake Drive
Rearsby
Leicestershire
LE7 4YZ
☎ 01664 424 483
pooley@beeb.net
SPTI

**PORTER**, Jim
**Hypno-Psychotherapist**
♿ 97 Sanvey Lane
Leicester
LE2 8NG
☎ 01509 415 184
NSHAP

**RATIGAN**, Bernard
**Psychoanalytic Psychotherapist**
36 Arthur Street
Loughborough
Leicestershire
LE11 3AY
☎ 01509 213 779
bjr@dircon.co.uk
FIP, STTDP, UPCA

**RICHARDSON**, Sacha
**Transpersonal Psychotherapist**
The Laura Centre
4 Tower Street
Leicester
Leicestershire
LE1 6WS
☎ 0116 254 4341
☎ 01858 463211
sacha@thelauracentre.org
19 Kettering Road
Market Harborough
Leicestershire
LE16 8AY
CCPE

**RIDGEWELL**, Margaret
**Gestalt Psychotherapist**
68 Elms Road
Leicester
LE2 3JB
☎ 0116 270 7197
ridgewellm@aol.com
GPTI

**RYDER**, John
**Psychoanalytic Psychotherapist**
♿ Dynamic Psychotherapy Service
Humberstone Grange Clinic
Thurmaston Lane
Leicester
LE5 0TA
☎ 01162 256 430
johnryder@doctors.net.uk
STTDP

**SCHNEEWEISS**, Rose
**Psychodynamic Psychotherapist**
98 Highway Road
LEICESTER
LE5 5RF
☎ 01162 490 208
rose.s@totalise.co.uk
VAPP

**SILMAN**, Chris
**Cognitive Behavioural Psychotherapist**
Dept. Cognitive Behavioural Therapy
Bradgate Mental Health Unit
Groby Road
Leicester
LE3 93J
☎ 0116 225 2613
☎ 0117 9060 4200
chris_silman@yahoo.co.uk
BABCP

**SPARE**, Elaine
**Psychodynamic Psychotherapist**
♿ 182 London Road
Leicester
LE2 1ND
☎ 07752 977 193
☎ 01530 460 984
spare_elaine@hotmail.com
The Pebbles
201 Thornborough Road
Coalville
Leicester
LE67 3TN
VAPP

**STEWART**, Ian
**Transactional Analysis Psychotherapist**
The Berne Institute
29 Derby Road
Kegworth
DE74 2EN
☎ 01509 673 649
☎ 01664 444 652
ta@theberne.com
New Barn
Wycomb
Melton Mowbray
LE14 4QG
ITA

**STEWART**, Naomi
**Psychoanalytic Psychotherapist**
♿ Dynamic Psychotherapy Service
Humberstone Grange Clinic
Thurmaston Lane
Leicester
LE5 0TA
☎ 0116 225 6430
☎ 01949 836 691
naomi.stewart@lineone.net
FIP, STTDP

**STRANG**, Jenny
**Psychodynamic Psychotherapist**
♿ University Counselling Service
161 Welford Road
Leicester
LE2 6BF
VAPP

**THORNLEY**, John
**Hypno-Psychotherapist**
Mind and Body
70 Ashby Road
Loughborough
Leicestershire
LE11 3AE
☎ 08712 300 039
j.k.thornley@btopenworld.com
NRHP

**TURNER**, Judith C
**Sexual and Relationship Psychotherapist**
♿ 16 Church Lane
Dingley
Market Harborough
LE16 8PG
☎ 01858 535 319
☎ 07780 697 120
dcturner2@aol.com
BASRT

**TWIST**, Graham
**Cognitive Analytic Therapist**
9 Wellesbourne Drive
Glenfield
Leicester
LE3 8ER
Gtwist@hotmail.com
ACAT

**TYNAN**, Imelda
**Gestalt Psychotherapist**
♿ 23 Charnwood Avenue
Sutton Bonington
Loughborough
LE12 5NA
☎ 01509 672 234
imelda@grindlay.freeserve.co.uk
SPTI

**WALKER**, Catriona
**Psychoanalytic Psychotherapist**
♿ Dynamic Psychotherapy Service
Humberstone Grange Clinic
Thurmaston Road
Leicester
LE5 0TA
☎ 01162 556 430
STTDP

**WATSON**, Clare
**Psychoanalytic Psychotherapist**
9a Turrey Lane
Long Whatton
Loughborough
LE12 5DN
☎ 01332 364 512
☎ 01509 843 393
cqwatson@onetel.net.uk
STTDP

**WEEKS**, Mary
**Transactional Analysis Psychotherapist**
4 High Street
Desford
Leics
LE9 9JF
☎ 01455 822 277
mweeks@supanet.com
ITA

**WRIGHT**, Marilyn
**Transactional Analysis Psychotherapist**
26 Ludlam Close
Countesthorpe
LE8 5BY
☎ 0116 278 8894
www.willwright@ludlam26.freeserve.co.uk
ACAT, ITA

**ZICO**, Junaid
**Hypno-Psychotherapist**
22 Ripon Street
Leicester
LE2 1LW
☎ 01162 471 977
NSHAP

## LINCOLNSHIRE

**ALDINGTON**, kay
**Integrative Psychotherapist**
Fonaby Lodge
Brigg Road
Caister
Lincolnshire
LN7 6RU
☎ 01472 852 105
kaldinton@aol.com
MET

**BIRCH**, Carol
**Gestalt Psychotherapist**
Warrawee
Welton Road
Nettleham Heath
Lincoln
LN2 2LU
☎ 01522 753 995
Carol@warrawee.freeserve.co.uk
SPTI

**BLYTH**, Douglas
**Integrative Psychotherapist**
Brook Cottage
Magna Mile
Ludford
Market Rasen
LN8 6AJ
☎ 01507 313 549
SPCRC

**BOWERMAN**, Elaine
**Psychodynamic Psychotherapist**
Southdene
44 Low Street
Collingham
Newark-on-Trent
NG23 7LS
☎ 01636 892 386
☎ 01636 893 270
elaine.bowerman@talk21.com
VAPP

**BRADY**, Carol
**Cognitive Behavioural Psychotherapist**
Peter Hodgkinosn Centre
Greetwell Road
Lincoln
LN2 5UA
☎ 01522 573 553
Carol.Brady@lht.nhs.uk
BABCP

**BRIDGE**, Sheila
**Psychoanalytic Psychotherapist**
♿ The Granary
Westgate
Louth
Lincolnshire
LN11 9YH
☎ 01507 604 940
UPCA

**CLEGG**, Ian
**Hypno-Psychotherapist**
♿ 5 Richards Avenue
Lincoln
Lincolnshire
LN6 8SJ
☎ 01522 688 142
ianclegg@caduceas.freeserve.co.uk
NSHAP

**CRABTREE**, Lyn
**Psychoanalytic Psychotherapist**
♿ Department of Psychotherapy
1, St Annes Road
Lincoln
LN2 5RA
☎ 01522 512 000
lyncrabtree@yahoo.co.uk
STTDP

**DIXON**, Linda
**Psychoanalytic Psychotherapist**
44 High Street
Nettleham
Lincoln
LN2 2PL
☎ 01522 809 315
HIP, UPCA

**DOLAN**, Bernadette
**Gestalt Psychotherapist**
8 Bridge St
Saxilby
Lincoln
LN1 2PZ
☎ 01522 704 000
higgins842@aol.com
SPTI

**ELLIS**, Roger
**Psychodynamic Psychotherapist**
Frogs Leap
615 Newark Road
LINCOLN
LN6 8SA
☎ 01522 681 510
frogs.leap@virgin.net
VAPP

**FISK**, Geoffrey
**Psychoanalytic Psychotherapist**
♿ Department of Psychotherapy
1, St Anne's Road
Lincoln
LN2 5RA
☎ 01522 512 000
FIP, STTDP

**FLANNERY**, Jean
**Psychoanalytic Psychotherapist**
8 Church Drive
Lincoln
LN6 7AX
☎ 01522 514 453
UPCA

**GAGNERE**, Maryline
**Biodynamic Psychotherapist**
23 Dewent Street
Lincoln
LN1 1SL
☎ 01522 807 099
LSBP

**GERAGHTY**, Nadine
**Psychodynamic Psychotherapist**
Grantham
NG31
☎ 01476 579 524
ngerag@aol.com
VAPP

**HASSALL**, Alan
**Integrative Psychotherapist**
34 High Street
Navenby
Lincoln
LN5 0DZ
☎ 01522 810 940
☎ 07733 004 458
alan@nscpc.co.uk
SPTI

**HENDERSON**, Stuart R.
**Integrative Psychotherapist**
6 Park Close
Sudbrooke
Lincoln
LN2 2RE
☎ 01522 595 826
Stromarie@freenetname.co.uk
SPTI

**JANICKYJ**, John
**Psychodynamic Psychotherapist**
♿ 22 Main Street
Ewerby
Sleaford
Lincolnshire
NG34 9PH
☎ 01529 301 845
VAPP

**KERR**, Julie
**Gestalt Psychotherapist**
177a Belton Lane
Grantham
NG31 9PL
☎ 01476 591 422
kerr.julie@talk21.com
SPTI

**LOHMAN**, Frans
**Psychoanalytic Psychotherapist**
♿ 35 Linden Walk
Louth
Lincs.
LN11 9HT
☎ 01507 605 407
fl@daflincs.demon.co.uk
UPCA

**MAYHO**, Rosalyn
**Group Analyst, Psychoanalytic Psychotherapist**
Department of Psychotherapy
1, St Anne's Road
Lincoln
LN2 5RA
☏ 01522 512 000
IGA

**SCOTT-COMBES**, Jacqueline
**Gestalt Psychotherapist**
♿ 11 Main Street
Wilsford
Grantham
NG32 3NS
☏ 01400 231 062
Jacky@scott-combes.freeserve.co.uk
SPTI

**SUTHERLAND**, Janet
**Biodynamic Psychotherapist**
♿ 4 St Andrews Street
Heckington
Sleaford
Lincs
NG34 9RA
☏ 01529 461571
janetsutherland0@talk21.com
LSBP

**THOMSON**, Alan
**Personal Construct Psychotherapist**
8 Welby Gardens
Grantham
NG31 8BN
☏ 01476 562 362
EAThomson@aol.com
PCP

**WALDRAM**, Roger
**Integrative Psychotherapist**
138 Tattershall Drive
Market Deeping
Peterborough
PE6 8BZ
☏ 01778 348 448
ScPTI

**WALLIS**, Valerie
**Sexual and Relationship Psychotherapist**
♿ 9 Chestnut Close
Sudbrooke
Lincoln
LN2 2RD
☏ 01522 751 211
BASRT

**WALTON**, Michael
**Integrative Psychotherapist**
53 West Road
Pointon
NG34 0NA
michael.walton@btinternet.com
SPCRC

## LINCOLNSHIRE - NORTH

**COLLETT**, Gail
**Family & Systemic Psychotherapist**
♿ Child, Adolescent and Family Unit
St Nicholas House
Shelford Street
Scunthorpe
DN15 6NU
☏ 01724 290 080
gail.collett@virgin.net
AFT

**WRIGHT**, Christine M.J.
**Cognitive Behavioural Psychotherapist**
2 Handley Square
The Finningley Estate
Doncaster
DN9 3GH
☏ 01302 802 139
BABCP

## LINCOLNSHIRE - NORTH EAST

**EMM**, Susan
**Transpersonal Psychotherapist**
The Rectory
Church Lane
North Thoresby
Lincs
DN36 5QG
☏ 01472 840029
CCPE

## MERSEYSIDE

**AINSWORTH**, Eileen
**Integrative Psychotherapist**
18 Deysbrook Lane
West Derby
Liverpool
L12 8RF
☏ 0151 228 7248
eileen.ainsworth@btinternet.com
SPTI

**BENDE**, Brigitta
**Cognitive Analytic Therapist**
LPCS Mossley
Hill Hospital Park Avenue
Liverpool
L18 8BU
ACAT

**BERRY**, Margaret
**Hypno-Psychotherapist**
♿ 37 Orton Road
Liverpool
L16 6AR
☏ 0151 280 1021
CTIS

**BEST**, Aileen
**Psychoanalytic Psychotherapist**
7 Oakwood Road
Halewood
Liverpool
L26 1KD
☏ 0151 280 6531
LPDO

**BIGGINS**, Toby
**Family & Systemic Psychotherapist**
Rosta Project
Poplar Cottage
New Halls Campus, Longmoor Lan
Liverpool
L10 1LD
☏ 0151 523 5979
toby.biggins@rlch-tr.nwest.nhs.uk
AFT

**BRYSON**, Sandra
**Family & Systemic Psychotherapist, Psychoanalytic Psychotherapist**
59 Vaughan Road
Wallasey
CH45 1LJ
☏ 0151 639 7830
sbryson@globalnet.co.uk
AFT, LPDO

**CAWLEY**, Tony
**Hypno-Psychotherapist**
44 Wellesley Road
Liverpool
Merseyside
L8 3SU
☏ 01517 271 485
NRHP

**DAVENPORT**, Sarah
**Psychoanalytic Psychotherapist**
♿ East Admin Building
Ashworth Hospital
Parkbourn,Maghull
Liverpool
L31 1HW
☏ 01514 712 353
COYLE-K@ashworth.nwest.nhs.uk
NWIDP

**DAVIES**, Ann Dorothy Maitland
**Cognitive Behavioural Psychotherapist**
Department of Psychology
Eleanor Rathbone Building
University of Liverpool
Liverpool
L69 7ZA
☎ 0151 794 2961
☎ 0151 529 3249
Oakdale Unit
University Hospital
Aintree
Liverpool
L9 7AL
BABCP

**DICKINSON**, Paul
**Psychoanalytic Psychotherapist**
Liverpool Psychotherapy &
Consultation Service
Mossley House
Mossley Hill Hospital
Liverpool
L18 8BU
☎ 01512 506 128
pauls.pad@virgin.net
LPDO

**DOYLE**, Elizabeth
**Psychoanalytic Psychotherapist**
18 Dunraven Road
Little Neston
South Wirral
CH64 9QU
LPDO

**DRAPER**, J
**Cognitive Behavioural Psychotherapist**
♿ 3 Cheshire Grove
Moreton
Wirral
CH46 0TB
☎ 0151 605 0144
ajkdprospsol@euphony.net
BABCP

**ESSEX**, Delia
**Psychoanalytic Psychotherapist**
18 Garth Drive
Liverpool
L18 6HW
☎ 0151 724 3033
deliaessex@hotmail.com
LPDO

**FAIRBANKS**, Arthur
**Cognitive Behavioural Psychotherapist**
Dir. of Psychological Therapies
Hamilton Centre
St Catherine Hospital
Church Road, Birkenhead
CH42 0LQ
☎ 0151 604 7276
☎ 07931 311 895
fogbarks@aol.com
BABCP

**FAIRHURST**, Pat
**Hypno-Psychotherapist**
♿ 55 Wyndham Avenue
Liverpool
L14 0LA
☎ 0151 449 2399
CTIS

**FINLAYSON**, Sara
**Cognitive Behavioural Psychotherapist**
Department of Clinical Psychology
Rathbone Hospital
Mill Lane
Liverpool
L9 7JP
☎ 0151 250 3035
BABCP

**FOSTER**, Paul
**Psychoanalytic Psychotherapist**
♿ Child & Family Services
Royal Liverpool Childrens NHS Trust
Empire Hs, 138-148 Linacre Rd
Litherland
L21 8JU
☎ 0151 285 6500
pfoster23@yahoo.co.uk
LPDO

**FYNE**, Jo
**Group Analyst**
Child & Family Services
North West CAMHS Team SureStart
West Everton & Breckfield Chil
Spencer Street, Liverpool
L6 2WS
☎ 0151 222 5862
IGA

**GABBAY**, Mark
**Psychoanalytic Psychotherapist**
♿ Department of Primary Care
University of Liverpool
Whelan Building Quadrangle
Liverpool
L69 3GB
☎ 0151 794 5610
LPDO

**GEORGE**, Stephen David
**Gestalt Psychotherapist**
Liverpool Centre for Counselling &
Psychotherapy
55 Rodney St
Liverpool
L1 9ER
☎ 0151 651 0114
☎ 07941 149 486
stegeodragon@hotmail.com
SPTI

**GLASSCOE**, Claire
**Systemic Psychotherapist**
♿ University Child Mental Health Unit
Royal Liverpool Childrens Hospital,
1st Floor, Mulberry House
Eaton Road, Liverpool
L12 2AP
☎ 0151 252 5509
glassc@liv.ac.uk
IFT

**HAMILTON**, Sheila L.L.
**Psychoanalytic Psychotherapist**
Department of Psychological
Services
Oakdale Unit
University Hospital Aintree
Lower Lane, Liverpool
L9 7AL
☎ 0151 529 3249
LPDO

**HANNAH**, Audrey
**Hypno-Psychotherapist**
15 Brocklebank Road
Hesketh Park
Southport
PR9 9LL
☎ 01704 546 956
☎ 01704 512 130
warren4633@aol.com
CTIS

**HARDMAN**, Anne
**Hypno-Psychotherapist**
22 Lawton Road
Rainhill
Merseyside
L35 0PP
☎ 0151 426 1795
☎ 07876 337 689
CTIS

**HARMSWORTH**, Pete
**Family & Systemic Psychotherapist**
33 Sydenham Avenue
Liverpool
L17 3AU
☎ 0151 734 3832
randpharmsworth@aol.com
AFT

**HOOPER**, Molly
**Cognitive Behavioural Psychotherapist**
"Panache"
Venables Close
Spital
Bebington, Wirral
CH63 9HS
☎ 0151 334 6619
ron@hooper76.Fsnet.co.uk
BABCP

**HUMPHREYS**, A-L.
**Cognitive Behavioural Psychotherapist**
Dept.of Allied Health Professions
School of Health Sciences
Johnston Building
Brownlow Hill, LIVERPOOL
L69 3GB
☎ 0151 794 4916
☎ 07720 289 050
lhumph@liv.ac.uk
Lifespan Therapy Consultants
The Cottage, Little Lane
Parkgate
Wirral, Cheshire
CH64 6SD
BABCP

**JONES**, Dr Caroline M
**Sexual and Relationship Psychotherapist**
♿ Parkfield Medical Centre
Sefton Road
New Ferry
Wirral
CH62 5HS
☎ 0151 644 0055
caroline.jones@gp-N85057.nhs.uk
BASRT

**KEENAN**, Paul Stephen
**Cognitive Behavioural Psychotherapist**
Department of Phychological Therapies
St Catherines Hospital
Church Road
Birkenhead
CH42 0LQ
☎ 07899 085 2830
paul.keenan@cwpnt.nhs.uk
BABCP

**KENNEDY**, Des
**Gestalt Psychotherapist**
Shalom
36 Hillside Road
West Kirby
Wirral
CH48 8BB
☎ 0151 625 9839
DesKennedy@freezone.co.uk
GPTI

**LEWIS**, Kate A
**Group Analytic Psychotherapist, Psychoanalytic Psychotherapist**
37 Prospect Vale
Fairfield
Liverpool
L6 8PE
☎ 01512 280 166
UPCA

**MARTIN**, Susan
**Hypno-Psychotherapist**
♿ 10 Moss Lane
Orrell Park
Liverpool
L9 8AJ
☎ 0151 286 5650
hilbilsue@blueyonder.co.uk
CTIS

**MATTISON**, Sheila
**Psychoanalytic Psychotherapist**
♿ Wellcroft Centre
Wellcroft Road
Huyton
Liverpool
L36 7RT
☎ 0151 489 6136
Sheila.Mattison@Bigfoot.com
LPDO

**MCALEER**, Eileen
**Integrative Psychotherapist**
21 Beach Grove
Wallasey
CH45 7QY
☎ 0151 637 0219
SPCRC

**MCCLATCHEY**, E.P.(Toni)
**Hypno-Psychotherapist**
20 Cromer Road
Liverpool
L17 0AD
☎ 0151 727 3448
CTIS

**MCGRATH**, Adrian
**Cognitive Behavioural Psychotherapist**
♿ Forensic Psychol & Psychotherapy
82 St Georges Road
Wallasey
CH45 6TX
☎ 07773 382 895
fmspsychol@aol.com
BABCP

**MCGRATH**, Carol
**Hypno-Psychotherapist**
82 St. George's Road
Wallasey
Wirral
Merseyside
CH45 6TX
☎ 0151 639 6660
CTIS

**MCNAB**, Stuart
**Psychoanalytic Psychotherapist**
♿ Bridge House Clinic
73 Village Road
Higher Bebington
Wirral
CH63 8PS
☎ 0151 608 1991
stuart_mcnab@hotmail.com
LPDO

**MERCER**, Annie
**Psychoanalytic Psychotherapist**
♿ Dept. of Paediatric Liaison, Mulberry House
Royal Liverpool Childrens NHS Trust
Eaton Rd.
Liverpool
L12 2AP
☎ 0151 252 5586
LPDO

**MOON**, Penny
**Hypno-Psychotherapist**
1-2 Normans Cottages
Newton
Wirral
CH64 6BP
☎ 0151 333 3602
CTIS

**MOORE**, Lena Rosaria
**Integrative Psychotherapist**
4 Redvers Avenue
Hooton
South Wirral
CH66 6AJ
☎ 0151 327 6491
SPTI

**NEWTON**, Brian Samuel
**Cognitive Behavioural Psychotherapist**
♿ Newton-le-Willows & Haydock CMHT
New Vista Locality Centre
Vista Road
Newton-le-Willows
WA12 9ED
☎ 01925 291 094
linda.jones@5boroughspartnership.nhs.uk
BABCP

**PROFFITT**, Dorothea
**Hypno-Psychotherapist**
1 Whitham Avenue
Great Crosby
Liverpool
L23 0RD
☎ 0151 928 4442 (t/f)
CTIS

**RICHMAN**, Sheila
**Psychodrama Psychotherapist**
19 Halkyn Avenue
Liverpool
L17 2AH
☎ 0151 733 0983
stuthesp@aol.com
BPA

**RIMMER**, Linda M.
**Cognitive Behavioural Psychotherapist**
Greasby
Wirral
CH49
☎ 07813 635 833
lynrimmer@uk2.net
BABCP

**ROFF**, Hermione
**Family & Systemic Psychotherapist**
♿ Child Mental Health Unit
Mulberry House, Alder Hey
Eaton Road
Liverpool
L12 2AP
☎ 0151 252 5509
hroff@liverpool.ac.uk
AFT

**ROGERS**, Jonathan
**Cognitive Behavioural Psychotherapist**
Dept. of Forensic Psychology
Ashworth Hospital
Parkbourn
Liverpool
L31 1HW
☎ 07976 212 744
☎ 0151 472 4516
jonathan_rogers@lycos.co.uk
BABCP

**SALTER**, Audrey J
**Cognitive Behavioural Psychotherapist**
30 The Ridgeway
Meols
Hoylake
Wirral
CH47 9SA
☎ 0151 632 6968
☎ 07771 624 042
BABCP

**SAVAGE**, Patrick
**Family & Systemic Psychotherapist**
♿ CAMHS
The Wellcroft Centre
Wellcroft Road
Huyton
L36 7TA
☎ 0151 489 6137
AFT

**SCOTT**, Michael
**Cognitive Behavioural Psychotherapist**
39 Hayles Green
Liverpool
L25 4SG
☎ 0151 428 6846
scott@carpeday.u-net.com
BABCP

**SHARP**, Frank
**Integrative Psychotherapist**
♿ Psychological Services
Ashworth Hospital,
N.Administration
Parkbourn, Maghull
Liverpool
L31 IHW
☎ 0151 472 4509
fsharp7777@aol.com
SPTI

**SMITH**, Barbara
**Transactional Analysis Psychotherapist**
55 Rodney Street
Liverpool
L1 9ER
☎ 07957 208 698
big.fish@virgin.net
ITA

**SMITH**, Flo
**Psychoanalytic Psychotherapist**
♿ Directorate of Psychological Services
2nd Floor Hamilton Centre, St Cathe
Church Road
Birkenhead
CH42 0LQ
☎ 0151 604 7276
fmfsmith@aol.com
LPDO

**STEWART**, June
**Psychoanalytic Psychotherapist**
♿ Child Guidance Centre, Wellcroft Centre
Wellcroft Road
Huyton
Liverpool
L36 7RT
☎ 0151 489 6136
LPDO

**STOWELL-SMITH**, Mark
**Cognitive Analytic Therapist**
10 Gerard Road
Wallasey
Merseyside
CH45 6UY
☎ 07711 921946
Mark@Stowell-Smith.fsgusiness.co.uk
ACAT

**TAYLOR**, Patsy
**Psychoanalytic Psychotherapist**
8 Victoria Mount
Oxton
Birkenhead
Merseyside
CH43 5TH
☎ 0151 651 0558
taylor_patsy@hotmail.com
LPDO

**TRANTER**, Paul
**Family & Systemic Psychotherapist**
♿ Royal Liverpool Children's Hospital
NHST
Alder Hey
Eaton Road
Liverpool
L12 2AP
☎ 0151 724 6872
AFT

**VAN DER EIJK**, Mike
**Systemic Psychotherapist**
♿ CFS
138-148 Linacre Road
Litherland
S. Sefton
L21 8JU
☎ 01824 703 883
mikevde@whsmithnet.co.uk
KCC

**WEEKS**, Mark
**Family & Systemic Psychotherapist, Systemic Psychotherapist**
12 Moel Famau View
Liverpool
L17 7ET
☎ 0151 7268465
FIC

**WHARMBY**, Ian
**Hypno-Psychotherapist**
14 Government Road
Hoylake
Wirral
CH47 2DB
☎ 0151 632 0389
iwharmby@hoylakewirral.fsnet.co.uk
CTIS

**WOODS**, Angie
**Psychoanalytic Psychotherapist**
♿ Locality Counselling Service
Whiston Hospital, Warrington Road
Prescot
Merseyside
L35 5DR
☎ 0151 430 1407
LPDO

**WOODWARD**, Raie
**Psychoanalytic Psychotherapist**
♿ Directorate Psychological Therapy
St. Catherine's Hospital
Derby Road
Birkenhead
CH42 0LQ
☎ 0151 604 7276
LPDO

**WYNN**, Michelle
**Cognitive Behavioural Psychotherapist**
17B Park Road
West Kirby
Wirral
CH48 4DN
☎ 0151 625 4091
BABCP

## MIDDLESEX

**AKAN**, Semra
**Systemic Psychotherapist**
Children & Families Consultation Services
West London Mental Health NHS Trust
Windmill Lodge, Uxbridge Road
Southall, London
UB1 3EU
☎ 0796 183 7507
KCC

**ALLSOP**, Wendy
**Group Analyst**
Twickenham
TW1
☎ 020 8891 1614
wendy.allsop@btopenworld.com
IGA

**ARDEMAN**, Jacqueline
**Family & Systemic Psychotherapist**
♿ 44 Stanmore Hill
Stanmore
Middlesex
HA7 3BN
☎ 020 8954 1462
AFT

**ASMALL**, Ismail
**Existential Psychotherapist**
134 Priory Road
Hampton
Middlesex
TW12 2PS
☎ 020 7381 8778 x22
☎ 020 8941 1460
ismail.asmall@virgin.net
SEA

**BAILEY**, Catalena
**Integrative Psychotherapist**
♿ 41 Eastbury Road
Northwood
Middlesex
HA6 3AN
☎ 01923 822 209
SPCRC

**BAILLIE**, Karen
**Psychosynthesis Psychotherapist**
37 Newton Road
Isleworth
TW7 6QD
☎ 020 850 3707
karen@kbaille.fsnet.co.uk
PET

**BANKS**, Jan
**Transactional Analysis Psychotherapist**
116 Thornbury Road
Osterley
Isleworth
Middlesex
TW7 4NH
☎ 02085 605 989
janbanks@blueyonder.co.uk
ITA

**BARFRED-DIXON**, Ameyo Katharina
**Integrative Psychosynthesis Psychotherapist**
1 Fairfax Road
Teddington
Middlesex
TW11 9DJ
☎ 07905 034 101
☎ 020 8943 3163
RE.V

**BARNARD**, Leo
**Hypno-Psychotherapist**
Flat 2
129 Cambridge Park
Twickenham
TW1 2JL
☎ 02088 926 712
leobarnard@gogmagog.freeserve.co.uk
NRHP

**BELLAMY**, Malka
**Psychodrama Psychotherapist**
24 Gordon Road
Enfield
Middlesex
EN2 0PX
☎ 020 8366 7974
BPA

**BENTLEY**, Patrick
**Systemic Psychotherapist**
♿ West London Mental Health NHS Trust
Ealing C.A.M.H.S
Windmill Lodge, Uxbridge Road
Southall
UB1 3EJ
☎ 020 8883 9943
☎ 020 8354 8030
KCC

**BERGER**, Iris
**Sexual and Relationship Psychotherapist**
♿ Cockfosters
Barnet
EN4
☎ 020 8449 5973
BASRT

**BOA**, Cherry
**Cognitive Analytic Therapist**
♿ 3 Holmesdale Road
Kew
Richmond
TW9 3JZ
☎ 020 8940 1501
cherryboa@aol.com
ACAT

**BRENNAN**, Joady
**Personal Construct Psychotherapist**
Dept. of Education
Brunel University
300 St Margaret's Road
Twickenham
TW1 1PT
☎ 020 7341 9974
☎ 07966 976 213
joady.brennan@brunel.ac.uk
PCP

**BROOKS**, Irene
**Integrative Psychotherapist**
6 Cunningham Park
Harrow
Middlesex
HA1 4QL
☎ 020 8427 2519
irene.brooks@tiscali.co.uk
MET

**BRUNT**, Clare
**Integrative Psychotherapist**
97 Warren Road
Whitton
Twickenham
Middlesex
TW2 7DJ
☎ 020 8755 0353
clarebrunt@lineone.net
AHPP

**BURNS**, Paul
**Neurolinguistic Psychotherapist**
98 West Hill
Wembley Park
Middlesex
HA9 9RR
☎ 02083 852 900
☎ 02089 046 433
paul.burns@btinternet.com
NLPtCA

**CERNER**, Ruth
**Integrative Psychotherapist**
65 Green Lane
Edgware
Middlesex
HA8 7PZ
☎ 020 8958 9758
Communicare Counselling Service
Redford Way
Uxbridge
UB8 1SZ
MET

**CHILDS-CLARKE**, Adrian
**Cognitive Behavioural Psychotherapist**
♿ Psychology Department
Northwick Park Hospital
Watford Road
Harrow, Middlesex
HA1 3UJ
☎ 020 8728 1778
BABCP

**COHEN**, Pat
**Attachment-based Psychoanalytic Psychotherapist**
♿ Noah's Ark
6 Spring Lane
Stanmore
Middlesex
HA7 3BX
☎ 020 8954 9366
CAPP

**COHEN**, Ruth
**Cognitive Behavioural Psychotherapist**
6 Regent Close
Kenton
Harrow
HA3 0SF
☎ 020 8907 3928
☎ 07931 881 770
ruth_cohen@hotmail.com
BABCP

**CONNOLLY**, Patricia
**Core Process Psychotherapist**
219 Tentelow Lane
Norwood Green
Middlesex
UB2 4LP
☎ 020 8571 9362
KI

**COONEY**, Joanne Elaine
**Systemic Psychotherapist**
♿ Sherbourne House
3 St Martin's
Northwood
Middlesex
HA6 2BP
KCC

**COOPER**, Suzanne
**Body Psychotherapist, Integrative Psychotherapist**
5 Lawrence Road
Pinner
Middlesex
HA5 1LH
☎ 020 8866 1521
CCBP

**COURTMAN**, Anita
**Psychosynthesis Psychotherapist**
252 St. Margarets Road
Twickenham
Middlesex
TW1 1PR
☎ 020 8892 2324
courtman@lineone.net
PET

**CRICK**, Verena
**Child Psychotherapist**
Barnet Child & Family Consultation Service
Edgware Community Hospital
Edgware
Middlesex
HA8 OAD
☎ 020 8905 6679
☎ 020 7431 1761
ACP

**CROFTON**, Sue
**Humanistic Psychotherapist, Integrative Psychotherapist**
98 West Hill
Wembley Park
Middlesex
HA9 9RR
☎ 020 8904 6433
sue.crofton@btinternet.com
SPEC

**CUSSINS**, Anne
**Psychoanalytic Psychotherapist**
55a Pope's Avenue
Strawberry Hill
Twickenham
Middlesex
TW2 5TD
☎ 020 8 898 1366
acussins@aol.com
IPSS

**DALEY**, Morica
**Integrative Psychotherapist**
169 Arundel Drive
South Harrow
Middlesex
HA2 8PW
☎ 0207 534 6697
☎ 07833 593 876
moricad@aol.com
MET

**DARCY**, Gillian
**Psychoanalytic Psychotherapist**
Willow Court Surgery
Stone Grove
Stanmore
Middlesex
HA8 8AG
☎ 01553 773 776 (t/f)
darcy-hamilton@budhinternet.com
FIP

**DAVIES-SMITH**, Lorraine
**Family & Systemic Psychotherapist, Systemic Psychotherapist**
♿ Barnet Enfield & Haringey Mental Health NHS Trust
Couple & Family Consultation Servic
Mental Health Unit, Chase Farm
The Ridgeway, Enfield
EN2 8JL
☎ 01923 243 443
☎ 020 8967 5988
lds3@mac.com
IFT

**DAWSON**, Alison
**Group Analytic Psychotherapist**
84 Chhurch Road
Richmond
TW10 6LW
☎ 020 8940 9790
alidawso@aol.com
FPC

**DAY**, Lesley
**Integrative Psychotherapist**
41 Ailsa Avenue
St. Margarets
Twickenham
Middlesex
TW1 1NF
☎ 020 8892 2076
MET

**DAY**, Michael
**Family & Systemic Psychotherapist**
♿ 1 Burtons Road
Hampton Hill
Middlesex
TW1 1DB
☎ 020 8977 7280
AFT

**DAY**, Sally
**Psychoanalytic Psychotherapist**
27 Trafalgar Road
Twickenham
Middlesex
TW2 5EJ
☎ 020 8894 1609
FPC

**DEAN**, Sally
**Group Analyst, Psychoanalytic Psychotherapist**
74 Lincoln Avenue
Twickenham
Middlesex
TW2 6NP
☎ 020 8898 2522
sallydean@blueyonder.co.uk
FPC, IGA

**DESAI**, Asha
**Systemic Psychotherapist**
♿ The Berkley Centre
C.T.P.L.D
27 Cranford Lane
Heston
TW5 9EP
☎ 02085 833 529/3530
ashadesai@compuserve.com
IFT

**DONALDSON**, Gill
**Integrative Psychotherapist**
81 Osterley Views
West Park Road
Middlesex
UB2 4UB
☎ 02085 748 189
106355.2415@compuserve.com
MET

**DREWNOWSKA**, Alicja
**Body Psychotherapist, Integrative Psychotherapist**
72 Hindes Road
Harrow
Middlesex
HA1 1SL
☎ 020 8427 9516
adrewnowska@hotmail.com
CCBP

**DUBINSKY**, Alexandre
**Child Psychotherapist**
Richmond Royal
Kew Foot Road
Richmond
TW9 2TE
☎ 020 8940 4775
☎ 020 7794 5047
ACP

**EISEN**, Mrs Shelley
**Sexual and Relationship Psychotherapist**
♿ The Kings Oak Hospital
Chase Farm (N Side)
The Ridgeway
Enfield
EN2 8SD
☎ 07973 502 657
☎ 08700 555 500 ask 878 650
skeisen@aol.com
BASRT

**EVANS**, Ray
**Personal Construct Psychotherapist**
6 Fabyc House
8 -14 Cumberland Road
Kew
Richmond, Surrey
TW9 3HH
☎ 020 8940 1597
ray@kewpcp.junglelink.co.uk
PCP

**GALLIERS**, Mary
**Psychoanalytic Psychotherapist**
185 Rochester Avenue
Feltham
Middlesex
TW13 4EH
☎ 020 8893 2351
AGIP

**GEDDES**, Heather
**Educational Therapist**
8 Blagdon Walk
Teddington
TW11 9LN
☎ 020 8 977 2418
angel@hgeddes.fsnet.co.uk
CFET

**GILLMAN-SMITH**, Ian
**Personal Construct Psychotherapist**
Clinical Psychology Dept
6th Floor, Premier House
112 Station Road
Edgware, Middlesex
HA8 7BJ
☎ 020 8951 2010
☎ 020 8907 3676
ian@gillman-smith.freeserve.co.uk
5 Aston Avenue
Kenton
Middlesex
HA3 0DB
PCP

**GOLDSTEIN**, Pam
**Systemic Psychotherapist**
18 Hazeldene Drive
Pinner
HA5 3NJ
KCC

**GOLTEN**, Carole
**Transpersonal Psychotherapist**
♿ Harrow Health Care Centre
84-88 Pinner Road
Harrow
HA1 1LF
☎ 020 8861 1221
CCPE

**GORDON**, Deidre
**Core Process Psychotherapist**
16 Pasture Close
North Wembley
HA0 3JE
☎ 020 8904 6488
KI

**GRAFF-PERRON**, Avril
**Group Analytic Psychotherapist**
♿ 12 Evelyn Road
Cockfosters
Herts
EN4 9ST
☎ 020 8441 6905
agptherapy@hotmail.com
FPC

**GRAHAM**, Marilyn
29 Court Close
Twickenham
Middlesex
TW2 5JH
☎ 020 8755 1029
MET

**GREEN**, June
**Psychoanalytic Psychotherapist**
'Redholme'
15 Ducks Hill Road
Northwood
Middx
HA6 2NW
☎ 01923 824858
IPSS

**GRIFFITHS**, Mark
**Educational Therapist**
♿ 10 Argyle Road
Hounslow
Middlesex
TW3 2BE
☎ 020 8572 5144
griffiths.napierbrown@virgin.net
CFET

**GUNTON**, Gaye
**Integrative Psychotherapist**
♿ Northwood Consulting Rooms
7 Greenhill Court
25b Green Lane
Northwood
HA6 2UZ
☎ 01923 241 626
gaye.gunton@ntlworld.com
SPCRC

**HAILEY**, Peg
**Hypno-Psychotherapist**
Elizabeth Cottages
Kew
Richmond
Surrey
TW9 3NJ
☎ 02089 487 496
☎ 02084 878 292
peghailey@btinternet.com
Kew Medical Practice
14 High Park Road
Kew
Richmond, Surrey
TW9 3BH
NRHP

**HARTLAND**, Marilyn Jean
**Systemic Psychotherapist**
147 Burtons Road
Hampton Hill
TW12 1DX
marilynhartland@hotmail.com
KCC

**HARVEY**, Ann
**Transactional Analysis Psychotherapist**
44 Clifden Road
Twickenham
Middlesex
TW1 4LX
☎ 02087 442 069
☎ 020 8892 6136
annharvey6@hotmail.com
ITA

**HAYDEN**, Martina
**Psychosynthesis Psychotherapist**
267 Hale Lane
Edgware
Middlesex
HA8
☎ 02089 585 622
m.hayden@amserve.com
IPS

**HILL**, Jenny
**Neurolinguistic Psychotherapist**
30 Wakehams Hill
Pinner
Middlesex
HA5 3BQ
☎ 02088 666 729
jenny@star-rise.demon.co.uk
NLPtCA

**HILTON**, Anni
**Systemic Psychotherapist**
♿ CAMHS, West London Mental Health Trust
Windmill Lodge
Uxbridge Road
Southall
UB1 3EU
☎ 020 8354 8170
Anni.hilton@wlmht.nhs.uk
IFT

**HIREMATH**, Paramita
**Transactional Analysis Psychotherapist**
30 Boundary Rd
Eastcote
Pinner
Middlesex
HA5 1PN
☎ 02084 291 064
mitahiremath1@btopenworld.com
ITA

**HOBBS**, Anita
**Sexual and Relationship Psychotherapist**
89 Syon Park Gardens
Isleworth
Middlesex
TW7 5NF
☎ 020 8568 4967
anita.hobbs@olcs.net
BASRT

**HUGHES**, Jacqui
**Gestalt Psychotherapist**
39 Crane Road
Twickenham
TW2 6RX
☎ 020 8755 0992
jacqui_hughes@hotmail.com
GPTI

**HUSSAIN**, Nasima
**Systemic Psychotherapist**
273 Carr Road
Northolt
Middlesex
UB5 4RN
☎ 020 7912 9529
Nasima.Hussain@ukgateway.net
IFT

**ISAACS**, Glenys
**Cognitive Behavioural Psychotherapist**
♿ Psychology Dept.
Northwick park Hospital
Watford Road
Harrow
HA1 3UJ
☎ 020 8869 2326
glenys.isaacs@harrowpct.nhs.uk
BABCP

**JAFFE**, Alyson
**Integrative Psychotherapist**
27 Canon's Park
Donnefield Avenue
Edgware
HA8 6RL
☎ 0208 905 7323
MC

**JEFFS**, Graeme
**Family & Systemic Psychotherapist**
41 Lower Road
Harrow
HA2 0DE
☎ 020 8423 1935
graeme.jeffs@wlmht.nhs.uk
AFT

**JOHNSON**, Deirdre
**Analytical Psychologist-Jungian Analyst**
16 Barrow Point Avenue
Pinner
Middlesex
HA5 3HF
☎ 020 8866 9006
AJA

**JOHNSON**, Geoffrey
**Core Process Psychotherapist**
♿ 99 Elms Lane
North Wembley
London
HA0 2NS
☎ 02089046037
KI

**JONES**, Eileen
**Hypno-Psychotherapist**
The Mapple Leaf Clinic
20 The Green
Twickenham
TW2 5AB
☎ 02082 559 666
☎ 01932 351 120
eileen@jayvant.fsnet.co.uk
NRHP

**KINGSNORTH**, Wendy
**Psychoanalytic Psychotherapist**
10 Second Avenue
Bush Hill Park
Enfield
EN1 1BT
☎ 020 8245 8680
wendykings@tinyonline.co.uk
FPC

**KOKOTT**, Claudius
**Body Psychotherapist, Integrative Psychotherapist**
19 Clitherow Road
Brentford
Middlesex
TW8 9JT
☎ 020 8568 0589
c.kokott@clara.co.uk
CCBP

**KRAUS**, Frances
**Integrative Psychotherapist**
♿ 125 Sandycombe Road
Kew
Surrey
TW9 2EN
☎ 0208 255 3681
gun@blueyonder.co.uk
MET

**LASCHINGER**, Bernice
**Attachment-based Psychoanalytic Psychotherapist**
27 Chalkhill Road
Wembley Park
London
HA9 9DS
☎ 020 8904 2176
bernice@laschinger.force9.co.uk
CAPP

**LAW**, Susan
**Body Psychotherapist, Integrative Psychotherapist**
9 Cambrian Road
Richmond upon Thames
TW10 6JQ
☎ 020 8332 1727
Sue@SusanLaw.freeserve.co.uk
CCBP

**LEVIN**, Barbara
**Integrative Psychotherapist**
☎ 020 8958 6850
☎ 020 8958 5378
94 Hartland Drive
Edgware
Middlesex
HA8 8RH
SPTI

**LEVY**, Gillian
**Cognitive Behavioural Psychotherapist**
10 Rofant Road
Northwood
Middlesex
HA6 3BE
☎ 01923 824 338
☎ 07958 770 827
gillian@levy1937.fsnet.co.uk
BABCP

**LONDON**, Elizabeth
**Attachment-based Psychoanalytic Psychotherapist**
22 Ivybridge Close
Twickenham
Middlesex
TW1 1EA
☎ 020 8892 1833
CAPP

**LUCAS**, Tina
**Group Analyst**
♿ 60 Lebanon Park
Twickenham
Middlesex
TW1 3DQ
☎ 020 8892 6584
IGA

**LYNCH**, Maria
**Analytical Psychologist-Jungian Analyst**
34 Abbottsmede Close
Strawberry Hill
Twickenham
Middlesex
TW1 4RL
☎ 020 8891 4242
mlynch@fslife.co.uk
CAP *

**MACDONALD**, Pat
**Group Analytic Psychotherapist**
16 Allbrook Close
Teddington
Middlesex
TW11 8TY
☎ 020 8977 6934
FPC

**MAGAN**, Bhagya
**Integrative Arts Psychotherapist**
Middlesex
HA3
☎ 07880 574 166
bhagymagan@hotmail.com
IATE

**MANOJLOVIC**, Jelena
**Systemic Psychotherapist**
♿ Richmond Royal Hospital
Kew Foot Road
Richmond
TW9 2TE
☎ 020 8940 3331
jelenamanojlovic@onetel.net.uk or
jelena.manojlovic@swlstg-tr.nhs.uk
KCC

**MARTIN**, Gloria
**Systemic Psychotherapist**
♿ CFCC
Richmond Royal
Kew Toot Road
Richmond
TW9 2TE
☎ 020 8546 8317
☎ 020 8355 1984
KCC

**MCCAFFERTY**, Stewart
**Systemic Psychotherapist**
♿ Keats Complimentary Practice
18a London Road
Enfield
EN2 6EB
☎ 020 8366 2300
info@keatshealth.co.uk
KCC

**MCCANDLESS**, Robert
**Family & Systemic Psychotherapist**
♿ Child & Family Consultation Centre
Richmond Royal
Kew Foot Road
Richmond
TW9 2TE
☎ 020 8355 1984
☎ 020 8949 7289
robert.mccandless@swlstg-tr.nhs.uk
IFT

**MCGRATH**, Rita E.
**Family & Systemic Psychotherapist**
♿ Enfield Child Guidance Service
8 Dryden Road
Bush Hill Park
Enfield
EN1 2PP
☎ 020 8360 6771
IFT

**MCNULTY**, Annie
**Body Psychotherapist, Integrative Psychotherapist**
95 Willow Road
Enfield
Middlesex
EN1 3BP
☏ 020 8367 5930
ann.mcnulty@bt.com
CCBP

**MEINRATH**, Monica
**Group Analyst**
Psychotherapy Department
Lakeside Mental Health Unit NHS Tru
West Middlesex Hospital
Twickenham Road, Islewort
TW7 6AF
☏ 020 8321 5058
monica.meinrath@wlmht.nhs.uk
IGA

**MICHAUD-LENNOX**, Suzanne
**Psychoanalytic Psychotherapist**
20 Heming Road
Edgware
London
HA8 9AE
☏ 020 8 952 2418
suzanne.michaud@virgin.net
IPSS

**MILLINGTON**, Malcolm
**Couple Psychoanalytic Psychotherapist**
Bowden House Clinic
St Andrew's at Harrow
London Road
Harrow on the Hill, Middx
HA1 3JL
☏ 020 7435 7111
TMSI, SCPP

**MILLS**, Ted
**Integrative Psychotherapist**
86 Waverley Avenue
Twickenham
Middlesex
TW2 6DN
☏ 020 8894 1651
tedmills@hotmail.com
MET

**MONAGHAN**, Catherine
**Integrative Psychotherapist**
Flat G, The Stable Block
Boston Manor House
Boston Manor Road
Brentford
TW8 9JX
☏ 020 8568 6147
kaymona@ukonline.co.uk
SPCRC

**MULDOON**, Nuala
**Integrative Psychotherapist**
11 Flemming Avenue
Ruislip
HA4 9LE
☏ 020 8429 2893
nuala.muldoon@wlmht.nhs.uk
SPCRC

**MYERS**, Marsha
**Family & Systemic Psychotherapist**
Pathways
Wellington Avenue
Pinner
HA5 4NG
☏ 07966 455 539
IFT

**NEELD**, Rebecca
**Group Analyst**
The Cassel Hospital
1 Ham Common
Richmond upon Thames
TW10 7JF
☏ 020 8940 8181
IGA

**NEWNS**, David
**Transpersonal Psychotherapist**
110 Waterloo Road
Uxbridge
Middlesex
UB8 2QY
☏ 01895 467046
CCPE

**NOBLE**, Susi
**Integrative Psychotherapist**
♿ 93 Clarence Road
Teddington
Middlesex
TW11 0BN
☏ 020 8408 1930
suto.noble@virgin.net
MET

**NORSA**, Giuliana
**Child Psychotherapist**
Enfield Child & Family Service
8 Dryden Road
Bush Hill Park
Enfield, Middlesex
EN1 2PP
☏ 020 8360 6771
☏ 020 8455 7290
ACP

**O'CONNELL RIBET**, Oonagh
**Analytical Psychologist-Jungian Analyst**
22 Redesdale Gardens
Isleworth
Middlesex
TW7 5JB
☏ 020 8568 0110
oonagh.ribet@blueyonder.co.uk
IGAP

**PEACOCK**, Katrina
**Systemic Psychotherapist**
35 Stags Way
Osterley
Middlesex
TW7 5PG
KCC

**PERRY**, Christopher
**Analytical Psychologist-Jungian Analyst**
Flat 3
208 St Margarets Road
Twickenham
TW1 1NP
☏ 020 8892 3126
CAP *

**POLDEN**, Anne
**Psychoanalytic Psychotherapist**
23 Lulworth Drive
Pinner
Middlesex
HA5 1NF
☏ 020 8868 9429
IPSS

**POPLE**, Sue
**Group Analytic Psychotherapist**
Enfield Counselling Service
St Paul's Centre
102A Church Street
Enfield
EN2 6AR
☏ 020 8367 2333
bselpop@aol.com
FPC

**POTSIDES**, Penny
**Integrative Psychotherapist**
6 East Walk
East Barnet
EN4 8JX
ppotsides@hotmail.com
SPCRC

**RAWSON-JONES**, Elizabeth
**Hypno-Psychotherapist**
96 Highland Road
Northwood Hills
Middlesex
HA6 1JU
☏ 01923 824 755
NRHP

**REES-ROBERTS**, Diane
**Psychoanalytic Psychotherapist**
♿ 12 Cambridge Crescent
Teddington
Middlesex
TW11 8DY
☎ 020 8287 7417
☎ 020 8977 7282
diane@reesroberts.demon.co.uk
FPC

**RENN**, Paul
**Attachment-based Psychoanalytic Psychotherapist**
13 Seaton Road
Twickenham
Middlesex
TW2 7AT
☎ 020 8894 3696
Paul_renn2003@yahoo.co.uk
CAPP

**RISHIRAJ**, Narinder S
**Cognitive Behavioural Psychotherapist**
♿ 321 Lady Margaret Road
Southall
UB1 2PY
☎ 020 8575 7896
BABCP

**ROBERTS**, Sylvia Marguerite
**Systemic Psychotherapist**
Keats Complimentary Practice
18a London Road
Enfield
EN2 6EB
☎ 020 8340 6336 or 020 8366 2300
☎ 07900 891 412
KCC

**ROBSON**, Christine
**Child Psychotherapist**
The Lancaster Centre
26 Bennetts Yard
Off Lancaster Road
Uxbridge, Middlesex
UB8 1JH
☎ 01895 256521
ACP

**ROSS**, Suzanne
**Transpersonal Psychotherapist**
Maple Leaf Clinic
20 The Green
Twickenham
Middx
TW1
☎ 020 8891 3234
CCPE

**ROUHIFAR**, Zhila
**Cognitive Behavioural Psychotherapist**
Ealing Hammersmith and Fulham MH NHS
Local Secure Directorate,
St Bernards' Wing, C Block
Uxbridge Rd, Southall
UB1 3EU
☎ 020 8354 8640
BABCP

**RUTHERFORD**, Penelope Anne
**Family & Systemic Psychotherapist**
9 College Drive
Ruislip
Middlesex
HA4 8SD
☎ 01895 636 193
AFT

**SABATELLI**, Peter John
**Cognitive Behavioural Psychotherapist**
♿ Psychology Department
Northwick Park Hospital
Watford Road
Harrow, Middlesex
HA1 3UJ
☎ 07949 47288
petersabatelli@aol.com
BABCP

**SARWAR**, Iwona
**Existential Psychotherapist**
10 Wordsworth Way
West Drayton
UB7 9HT
☎ 01895 421 846
☎ 07932 541 437
ls0572@aol.com or ls0575@hotmail.com
UPCA

**SEEBARUN**, Dev
**Psychoanalytic Psychotherapist**
61 Oakley Close
Isleworth
Nuttworth
Midlesex
TW7 4HY
☎ 07939 553 737
☎ 01932 872 010 x2458
devseebarun@hotmail.com
FIP, NAFSI

**SHORTALL**, Thomas R.
**Cognitive Psychotherapist**
♿ Bowden House clinic
London Road
Harrow-on-the-Hill
Middlesex
HA1 3JL
☎ 020 8966 7000
☎ 020 8864 1482
pysch@shortall.demon.co.uk
BABCP

**SHUTTLEWORTH**, Judy
**Child Psychotherapist**
Enfield Child & Family Service
Avenue House
8 Byculla h Avenue
Enfield
EN2 8DW
☎ 020 8367 8844
☎ 020 8883 7908
ACP

**STANIER**, Graham
**Hypno-Psychotherapist**
21 St Albans Gardens
Teddington
Middlesex
TW11 8AE
☎ 02089 775 638
saunier@lineone.net
NRHP

**STEWART**, Elizabeth
**Integrative Psychotherapist**
♿ 509 Kenton Lane
Harrow
Middlesex
HA3 7JW
☎ 02089 300 892
Lizstewart@fsmail.net
MET

**STOCKLEY**, Rosalind
**Integrative Psychotherapist**
♿ 7 Greenhill Court
25B Green Lane
Northwood
HA6 2UZ
☎ 01923 842 351
roz@copsewood.org.uk
SPCRC

**STRANG**, Emily
**Systemic Psychotherapist**
48 Cecil Avenue
Enfield
EN1 1PP
emilystrang@blueyonder.co.uk
KCC

**SUSSMAN**, Susan
**Transpersonal Psychotherapist**
♿ Ruislip
Middlesex
☎ 01895 622202
CCPE

**SWIFT**, Joanna
**Psychoanalyst, Psychoanalytic Psychotherapist**
♿ 5 Beresford Avenue
Twickenham
Middlesex
TW1 2PY
☎ 020 8892 4722
PA, SITE

**THOMAS**, Carmel
**Cognitive Behavioural Psychotherapist**
152 Somervell Road
South Harrow
Middlesex
HA2 8TS
☎ 020 8248 7422
☎ 01344 773 111 x4661
BABCP

**TIMBER**, Jennifer
**Psychoanalytic Psychotherapist**
7 Grovewood
345 Sandycombe Road
Kew
Surrey
TW9 3NF
☎ 020 8948 6741
jennytimber1@aol.com
GUILD

**TRAYNOR**, Barbara
**Transactional Analysis Psychotherapist**
♿ 24 Bristow Road
Hounslow
Middlesex
TW3 1UP
☎ 02085 720 650
btraynor2003@hotmail.com
ITA

**TRELEASE**, P.
**Cognitive Behavioural Psychotherapist**
♿ 85 Twickenham Road
Teddington
TW11 8AL
☎ 020 8943 1543
nels.trelease@tesco.net
11 Spring Road
Feltham
TW13 7JA
BABCP

**VALE**, Elissa
**Integrative Psychotherapist**
45a Barchester Road
Harrow Weald
HA5 5HH
☎ 020 8868 5059
evale@talk21.com
SPCRC

**VENTHAM**, Brian
**Integrative Psychotherapist**
68 Gloucester Road
Hampton
TW12 2UJ
☎ 07802 764 119
bve@globalnet.co.uk
SPCRC

**WAINWRIGHT**, Margaret
**Psychosynthesis Psychotherapist**
52 Sweetcroft Lane
Hillingdon
UB10 9LF
☎ 01895 234 207
margaretwainwright@supanet.com
IPS

**WARD**, John
**Psychoanalytic Psychotherapist**
123 Amyand Park Road
Twickenham
TW1 3HN
☎ 020 8744 2780
j.ward8@blueyonder.co.uk
AGIP

**WHINES**, Jonathan
**Gestalt Psychotherapist**
39 Crane Road
Twickenham Green
Twickenham
TW2 6RX
☎ 020 8755 0992
☎ 01603 663 186
jonathan@dialogueconsultancy.com
GPTI

**WINTER**, David
**Personal Construct Psychotherapist**
Clinical Psychology Depart.
6th Floor, Premier House
112 Station Road
Edgware
HA8 7B
☎ 020 8951 2000
d.winter@herts.ac.uk
PCP

**WISE**, Anne
**Group Analyst**
West London Mental Health Nhs Trust
Psychotherapy Department
John Conolly Wing
Uxbridge Road, Southall
UB1 3EJ
☎ 020 8354 8935
anne.wise@wlmht.nhs.uk
IGA

**WISHART**, Marion
**Transpersonal Psychotherapist**
197 Jersey Road
Osterley
Isleworth
Middlesex
TW7 4QJ
☎ 020 8560 5363
CTP

**WOLFE**, Pamela
**Psychosynthesis Psychotherapist**
33B Edwards Avenue
South Ruslip
Middlesex
HA4 6UP
warrendenwolfe@aol.com
IPS

**WOOTTON**, Jenny
**Attachment-based Psychoanalytic Psychotherapist**
15 Merton Road
Enfield
EN2 0LS
☎ 020 8350 0056
CAPP

**DE SERDICI**, Simona
**Transpersonal Psychotherapist**
146 Windmill Road
The Garden Flat
Brentford
Middlesex
TW8 9NQ
☎ 020 8560 0663
CTP

## NORFOLK

**AQUARONE**, Luc-Remy
**Psychoanalytic Psychotherapist**
The Pottergate Centre for Dissociation & Trauma
26 Princess Street
Norwich
NR3 1AE
☎ 01603 872 236
☎ 01603 469 888
remyaquarone@btconnect.com
FIP

**ARNOLD**, Rosemary
**Psychoanalytic Psychotherapist**
48 Freeman Street
Wells-Next-The-Sea
Norfolk
NR23 1BA
☎ 020 8 889 7335
GUILD

**BAKER**, Jackie
**Cognitive Analytic Therapist**
Red Brick House
14 Hurn Road
Drayton
Norwich
NR8 6DA
☎ 01603 406 941
jackiebaker1@hotmail.com
ACAT

**BLAKE**, Adrian
**Hypno-Psychotherapist**
Birchdale
Blickling Road
Aylsham
Norfolk
NR11 6ND
☎ 01263 733 271
blake@couns.fslife.co.uk
NRHP

**BROWN**, Robert
**Integrative Psychotherapist**
119 Elvington
King's Lynn
Norfolk
PE30 4TB
☎ 01553 776 915
SPTI

**BURTON**, Simon
**Systemic Psychotherapist**
17 Eade Road
Norwich
NR3 3EH
☎ 01603 667 072
☎ 01603 421 950
simonb.syst@virgin.net
Bethel Child & Family Centre
Mary Chapman House
Norwich
NR2 4HN
KCC

**CHRISTIANSON**, Donna
**Cognitive Behavioural Psychotherapist**
♿ Blanchflower House
23 Wells Road
Fakenham
NR21 9EG
☎ 07905 698 364
D.Christianson@uea.ac.uk
The Health Centre
University of east Anglia
Earlham Road
Norwich
NR4 7TJ
BABCP

**CLARK**, Dr Julia
**Cognitive Analytic Therapist**
36 Christchurch Road
Norwich
NR2 2AE
☎ 01603 457 726
ACAT

**CLARKE**, Simon
**Gestalt Psychotherapist, Humanistic Psychotherapist**
4 St Peters Close
West Lynn
Kings Lynn
Norfolk
PE34 3JX
☎ 07881 620 253
sclarkenp@aol.com
AHPP

**CULME-SEYMOUR**, Joanna
**Systemic Psychotherapist**
♿ 14 Park Lane
Norwich
NR2 3EE
☎ 01603 631 741
jcs@thesite.demon.co.uk
KCC

**DARCY**, Gillian
**Psychoanalytic Psychotherapist**
Hamilton House
64 Goodwins Road
Kings Lynn
Norfolk
PE30 5PD
☎ 01553 773 776 (t/f)
darcy-hamilton@budhinternet.com
FIP

**DAVISON**, Charles
**Humanistic Psychotherapist**
Crowgate Cottage
Stone Lane
Ashmanhaugh
Norwich
NR12 8YW
☎ 01603 783 033
charles.davison@btinternet.com
SPTI

**DAYKIN**, Amanda
**Group Analyst**
♿ GAIN
6 Elveden Close
Norwich
Norfolk
NR4 6AS
☎ 01603 458 620
IGA

**DOCKING**, Raymond Fredrick
**Systemic Psychotherapist**
♿ 1 Kettlewell Lane
King's Lynn
Norfolk
PE30 1PW
☎ 01553 767 520
KCC

**ENDER**, Christine
**Psychosynthesis Psychotherapist**
♿ 8 Russell Terrace
Trowse
Norwich
NR14 8TQ
☎ 01603 626 831
IPS

**HARBEN**, Ursula Mary Ann
**Systemic Psychotherapist**
♿ The Bethel
Hotblack Road
Norwich
NR2 4HN
☎ 01603 421 950
KCC

**HART**, Sally
**Humanistic Psychotherapist**
26 Grant Street
Norwich
NR2 4HA
☎ 01603 623 795
AHPP

**HAYWOOD**, Jill
**Existential Psychotherapist**
Gowers Farm Cottage
Fressingfield
Eye
Suffolk
IP21 5RL
☎ 01379 586 614
UPCA

**HENDERSON**, Ned
**Integrative Psychotherapist**
Sawmill Cottage
The Street
Aylmerton Norfolk
NR11 8AA
☎ 01263 837 489
ned.henderson@virgin.net
CCBP

**HUGHES**, William
**Analytical Psychologist-Jungian Analyst, Analytical Psychotherapist, Analytical Psychotherapist (Jungian)**
The Coach House
2c Church Avenue
Norwich
NR2 2AQ
☎ 01603 503 845
hughesw@globalnet.co.uk
CAP, GAPS *

**IRVING**, Nicholas
**Transactional Analysis Psychotherapist**
22 Lynn Road
Hillington
Kings Lynn
Norfolk
PE31 6DD
☎ 01485 600 987
ITA

**JESS**, Carrie
**Sexual and Relationship Psychotherapist**
8 Britannia Road
Norwich
NR1 4HP
☎ 01603 661 150
carrie@jess1.fsbusiness.co.uk
BASRT

**JOHNSON**, Paul
**Group Analytic Psychotherapist**
44 Firs Road
Hethersett
Norwich
NR9 3EH
☎ 01603 811 674
pauljohnson@btinternet.com
UPCA

**JONES**, Sue
**Integrative Psychotherapist**
Stubbs Cottage
Stubbs Green
Loddon
Norwich
NR14 6EA
☎ 01508 528800
susiemjones@yahoo.co.uk
MET

**KENNEDY**, Caroline
**Psychoanalytic Psychotherapist**
The Pottergate Psychotherapy Practice
11 Pottergate
Norwich
NR2 1DS
☎ 01603 629 576
☎ 01603 612 178
caroline@kennedyc.fsbusiness.co.uk
10 Heigham Grove
Norwich
NR2 3DQ
GUILD

**KERKHAM**, Patricia
**Psychoanalytic Psychotherapist**
15 Tuesday Market Place
King's Lynn
Norfolk
PE30 1JN
☎ 01553 773854
IPSS

**KIRBY**, Phillipa
**Integrative Psychotherapist**
16 Bardolph Road
Bungay
Suffolk
NR35 1BN
☎ 01986 893 759
lucy.collie@ukonline.co.uk
MET

**LITTLE**, Jon
**Integrative Psychotherapist**
♿ 14 Central Close
Hethersett
Norwich
NR9 3ER
☎ 01603 810 946
SPCRC, UPCA

**LLOYD**, Annie
**Transpersonal Psychotherapist**
The Turning Point
Silver Fox Farm
Sheringwood, Beeston Regis
Norfolk
NR26 8TS
☎ 01263 820 054
☎ 020 7266 3006
ALloyd702@aol.com
CCPE

**LODRICK**, Michael
**Group Analyst, Psychoanalytic Psychotherapist**
Willow Fen
Castle Lane
Bungay
NR35 1DE
☎ 020 7609 9112
☎ 01986 896 419
lodrick@ukonline.co.uk
FPC, IGA

**MACGREGOR**, Wynne
**Integrative Psychotherapist**
20 Neville Street
Norwich
NR2 2PR
☎ 01603 461864
MET

**MAK-PEARCE**, George
**Psychoanalytic Psychotherapist**
♿ Rose Court
1 Rockland Drive
Thorpe St. Andrew
Norwich
NR7 0BL
☎ 01603 300 701
makpearce@btopenworld.com
ARBS

**MARSH**, Colin
**Autogenic Psychotherapist**
♿ 25 Daseleys Close
Kings Lynn
Norfolk
PE30 3SL
☎ 01553 674 790
BAS

**MASON**, Christina
**Integrative Psychotherapist**
♿ 1 The Coppice
Attleborough
Norfolk
NR17 2PY
☎ 0208 980 4124
cmason@stjh.org.uk
MET

**MAYO**, Rosalind
**Psychoanalytic Psychotherapist**
15 Tuesday Market Place
King's Lynn
PE30 1JN
☎ 01553 760 978
☎ 07811 480 310
rosalindmayo@aol.com
PA

**MIDDLECOAT**, Andrew
**Family & Systemic Psychotherapist**
♿ Grange Cottage
Chapel Road
Dilham
NR28 9PZ
☎ 01692 536 558
☎ 01493 337 601
The Silverwood Child & Family Centre
Northgate Street
Great Yarmouth
Norfolk
NR30 1BL
IFT

**MOLLAHAN**, L. G.
**Cognitive Behavioural Psychotherapist**
190 Drayton High Road
Drayton
Norwich
NR8 6BE
☎ 01603 864 305
laimollahan@msn.com
BABCP

**MUNDY**, Jean
**Biodynamic Psychotherapist**
7 Caystreward
Great Yarmouth
Norfolk
NR30 4AS
☎ 01493 850867
LSBP

**PITTMAN**, Karen
**Behavioural Psychotherapist**
♿ Northgate MH Resource Centre
Northgate Hospital
Northgate Street
Great Yarmouth
NR30 1BU
☎ 01493 337 677
☎ 01692 581 755
kp@cognitivebehaviourtherapy.org
The Costal Clinic
Gorleston
Great Yarmouth
Norfolk
NR31 6EJ
BABCP

**POLDEN**, Jane
**Psychoanalytic Psychotherapist**
♿ 16 Catton Grove Road
Norwich
NR3 3NH
☎ 01603 404 363
jane.polden@ntlworld.com
AGIP

**POSTON**, Frances
**Psychodynamic Psychotherapist**
Hill Farm
Flixton
Nr Bungay
Suffolk
NR35 1NZ
☎ 07966 505 166
☎ 01986 895 333
VAPP

**PURCHASE-WALKER**, Anne
**Rational Emotive Behaviour Therapist**
Elements of Health Ltd
64 Bethel Street Road
Norwich
NR2 1NR
☎ 01603 666 546
☎ 07931 556 712
annepurchase-walker@ukonline.co.uk
Complementary Health Care Clinic
34 Exchange Street
Norwich
NR2 1AX
BABCP

**RAND**, Judith Ann
**Psychosynthesis Psychotherapist**
Great Barn
Bacton
Norwich
NR12 0EY
☎ 07780 672 734
judith@jrand.freeserve.co.uk
PET

**RUSSELL**, Doug
**Integrative Psychotherapist**
♿ 35 Beech Road
Beetley
East Dereham
NR20 4EZ
☎ 01362 861 194
doug.russell@virgin.net
SPCRC

**SHARMAN**, Sally
**Cognitive Behavioural Psychotherapist**
Community Menthal Health Team
'Carrobreck' Hellesdon Hospital
Drayton High Road
Norwich
NR6 5BE
☎ 01603 421 258
BABCP

**SHAW**, Lynda
**Psychoanalytic Psychotherapist**
2 Shrublands
Polka Road
Wells-Next-The-Sea
NR23 1PU
☎ 01328 711 691
lyndashaw_7@hotmail.com
FIP, STTDP

**SHEPPARD**, Jan
**Existential Psychotherapist**
83 College Road
Norwich
NR2 3JP
☎ 07742 423 222
shebaddi@yahoo.co.uk
SEA

**SHETTY**, Girish
**Psychoanalytic Psychotherapist**
Norvic Clinic
St Andrews Business Park
Thorpe
Norwich
NR7 0HT
☎ 01603 701 954
LPDO

**SLUCKIN**, Andy
**Systemic Psychotherapist**
♿ 77 Gipsy Lane
Norwich
NR5 8AX
☎ 01603 507 934
☎ 01502 533 500
asluckin@aol.com
KCC

**SPRINGWOOD**, Bee
**Body Psychotherapist, Humanistic and Integrative Psychotherapist**
9 Squires Haven
Thorpe Hamlet
Norwich
NR1 1HQ
☎ 01603 434 400
☎ 07944 694 854
springwood@onetel.net.uk
The Studio
32 Chapel Lane
Norwich
NR7 0EX
AHPP

**TAGUE**, Jackie
**Systemic Psychotherapist**
51 Hollow Lane
West Raynham
Near Fakenham
Norfolk
NR1 7ET
☎ 01328 838 321
☎ 01553 815 161
West Norfolk CAMHS Clinic
Thurlow House
Goodwins Road
Kings Lynn
PE30 5PD
KCC

**WALLACE**, Edward
**Rational Emotive Behaviour Therapist**
Wenspur
The Green
Aldborough
Norwich
NR11 7AA
☎ 01263 761 667
AREBT

**WHINES**, Jonathan
**Gestalt Psychotherapist**
62 Unthank Road
Norwich
Norfolk
NR2 2RN
☎ 020 8755 0992
☎ 01603 663 186
jonathan@dialogueconsultancy.com
GPTI

**WILKINSON**, Mary Elaine
**Family & Systemic Psychotherapist**
♿ Yew Tree Cottage
Stocks Hill
Bawburgh
Norwich
NR9 3LL
☎ 014603 811 456
mary01@clara.co.uk
AFT

**WYMBS**, Patrick
**Cognitive Behavioural Psychotherapist**
♿ 9 Pelham Road
Norwich
NR3 3NG
☎ 01603 418 792
ptwymbs@aol.com
BABCP

## NORTHAMPTONSHIRE

**BEAUMONT**, Caroline
**Psychodynamic Psychotherapist**
Church House
High Street
Hardingstone
Northampton
NN4 6BZ
☎ 01604 765 513
caroline.beaumont@northampton.ac.uk
VAPP

**BEECH**, Julie C.
**Cognitive Psychotherapist**
Psychology Department
Campbell House
Campbell Square
Northampton
NN1 3AA
☎ 01604 658 917
BABCP

**BRIDGMENT**, Julia
**Psychoanalytic Psychotherapist**
36 Blackmile Lane
Grendon
Northampton
NN7 1JR
☎ 01933 663034
julia.bridgment@tesco.net
GUILD

**CHESSUM**, Lucy
**Group Analytic Psychotherapist**
21 Milton Street
Kingsley
Northampton
NN2 7JG
☎ 01604 710 909
lachessum@tiscali.co.uk
UPCA

**CLARK**, Alec
**Family & Systemic Psychotherapist**
♿ 280 Wellingborough Road
Rushden
Northants
NN10 9XP
☎ 01933 386 354
a.clark9@ntlworld.com
AFT

**DAVIS**, Bob
**Gestalt Psychotherapist**
Oundle Medical Centre
Glpthurn Road
Oundle
Nr Peterborough, Northant
☎ 01455 612 314
GPTI

**DAVIS**, Christopher
**Transactional Analysis Psychotherapist**
5 School Lane
Cottingham
Market Harborough
Leics
LE16 8XT
☎ 01162 558 505
☎ 01536 770 883
christopherdavis.therapy@virgin.net
ITA

**ESPEY**, Andrew
**Group Analytic Psychotherapist**
1 Kent Close
Northampton
NN5 4UQ
☎ 01604 588 529
andy-espey@supanet.com
UPCA

**FISHER**, Paul
**Integrative Psychotherapist**
27 High St
Kingsthorpe
Northampton
NN2 6QF
☎ 01604 719 923
paulmfisher@paulmfisher.demon.co.uk
SPTI

**GARDNER**, Damian
**Integrative Psychotherapist**
9 The Square
Thorpe Malson
Kettering
NN14 1JP
☎ 01536 494146
☎ 01536 411004
damian.nien@virgin.net
SPTI

**HANDRICK**, Olaf
**Cognitive Behavioural Psychotherapist**
♿ Flat 7
113 Overstone Road
Northampton
NN1 3JW
☎ 01268 366 011/013
☎ 01604 465 269
handrick@barclays.net
BABCP

**HARRIS**, Debra
**Jungian Analytical Psychotherapist**
51 Berry Lane
Wootton
Northampton
NN4 6JU
☎ 01604 761 882
WMIP

**HOLMES**, Janice
**Hypno-Psychotherapist**
11a Station Road
Long Buckby
Northampton
NN6 7QB
☎ 01327 843 115
☎ 01327 844 646
CTIS

**KEITH**, Irene
**Psychoanalytic Psychotherapist**
15 Hamlet Green
Northampton
NN5 7AR
☎ 01604 589 429
iekkeith@yahoo.co.uk
IPSS

**LEE-EVANS**, Michael
**Cognitive Behavioural Psychotherapist**
Department of Psychology
St Andrews Hospital
Billing Road
Northampton
NN1 5DG
☎ 01604 629 696 x6420
BABCP

**LONG**, Clive G.
**Cognitive Behavioural Psychotherapist**
♿ St. Andrews Hospital
Billing Road
Northampton
NN1 5DG
☎ 01604 629 696
BABCP

**MACPHERSON**, David
**Hypno-Psychotherapist**
24 Coldstreamm Close
Daventry
Northampton
NN11 5HL
☎ 01327 704 500
dmacp@compuserve.com
CTIS

**MARSDEN-ALLEN**, Peter Harry
**Family & Systemic Psychotherapist**
0-12 Team Wellingborough Social Services Dept.
Oxford House
West Villa Road
Wellingborough
NN8 4JR
☎ 01933 220 700
AFT

**MARSHALL**, Clare
**Integrative Psychotherapist**
Lavender Cottage
2 Bettycroft Close
Ravensthorpe
Northampton
NN6 8EL
☎ 01604 770 435
SPTI

**O'NEILL**, Helen M.
**Cognitive Behavioural Psychotherapist**
♿ Occupational Therapy Dept
St. Andrews Hospital
Kemsley Division, Billing Road
Northampton
NN1 5DG
☎ 01604 616 444
BABCP

**PHILLIPS**, Marianne
**Psychoanalytic Psychotherapist**
Cattleshed Cottage
1 Bakers Lane
Shutlanger
Nr. Towcester, Northants
NN12 7RT
☎ 01604 863313
phillips.marianne@talk21.com
ARBS

**PIRIE**, Linda Ellen
**Hypno-Psychotherapist**
Farriers House
35 Main Street
Middleton, Market Harborough
Leicestershire
LE16 8YU
☎ 01536 204 154
☎ 01536 771 140
Hypno-Psychotherapy Clinic
Lakeside Surgery
Cottingham Road
Corby, Northamptonshire
NN17 2UR
NRHP

**REES**, Myfanwy
**Analytical Psychologist-Jungian Analyst**
Ford Cottage
1 High Street
Denford
Northants
NN14 4EQ
☎ 01832 733 502
mrees@denford34.freeserve.co.uk
IGAP

**ROBERTS**, Julie
**Group Analyst**
♿ Department of Psychotherapy
Campbell House
Campbell Square
NN1 3EB
☎ 01604 658 925
IGA

**SAMPSON**, Gill
**Integrative Psychotherapist**
♿ 28 Lodge Road
Little Houghton
Northamptonshire
NN7 1AE
☎ 07931 868 972
samsongill@hotmail.com
MET

**SHADRACH-LONG**, Philippa
**Psychoanalytic Psychotherapist**
31 Church Street
Rothersthorpe
Northhants
NN7 3JD
☎ 020 8546 4082
☎ 020 8541 3436
FIP

**SMITH**, Nicola
**Cognitive Behavioural Psychotherapist**
Chandos Pole Division
St Andrews Hospital
Billing Road
Northampton
NN1 5DG
☎ 01604 616 620
nsmith@standrew.co.uk
BABCP

**SPRINCE**, Jenny
**Child Psychotherapist**
Thornby Hall
Peper Harow Foundation
Northampton
NN6 8SW
☎ 01604 740001
☎ 020 8800 5735
ACP

**STEVENS**, Penny
**Cognitive Behavioural Psychotherapist**
♿ 40 Kingsley Road
Northampton
NN2 7BL
☎ 01604 711 133
nipc@ic24.net
BABCP

**THOMPSON**, Patricia
**Integrative Psychotherapist**
♿ The Dovecote
Slade Farm
Evenley
Brackley
NN13 5SB
☎ 01869 811 241
SPCRC

**TOWNSEND**, Frances
**Transactional Analysis Psychotherapist**
♿ The Trundle
Ringstead Road
Gt. Addington
NN14 4BW
☎ 01536 330 648
frances@thetrundle.demon.co.uk
ITA

**WEAVER**, Carol
**Integrative Psychotherapist**
♿ Nene Cottage
10 Fotheringhay
Peterborough
PE8 5HZ
☎ 01832 226 329
CaroleWeaver@compuserve.com
SPCRC

**WHEATLEY**, Malcolm
**Cognitive Behavioural Psychotherapist**
♿ St Andrews Hospital
Billing Road
Northampton
NN1 5DG
☎ 01604 629 696
mwheatley@standrew.co.uk
BABCP

## NORTHERN IRELAND

**ADAMS**, Clare E A
**Psychoanalytic Psychotherapist**
Department of Psychotherapy
Woodstock Lodge
1 Woodstock Link
Belfast
BT6 8DD
☎ 02890 737 531
☎ 02890 655 056
clare.adams@sebt.n-i.nhs.uk
UPCA

**BENSON**, Jarlath
**Group Analytic Psychotherapist, Psychosynthesis Psychotherapist**
♿ 10 Mill Road
Drumaness
Ballynahinch
Co.Down
BT24 8SF
☎ 02897 564 420
jarlath.f.benson@btinternet.com
IPS, UPCA

**BLACK**, Alastair R J
**Cognitive Behavioural Psychotherapist**
♿ P R R T Ltd
100 Belfast Road
Holywood
County Down
BT18 9QY
☎ 028 9042 7788
a.black@btclick.com
BABCP

**BRANAGAN**, Noelle
**Psychodrama Psychotherapist**
47 Jameson Street
Ormeau Road
Belfast
BT2 2GU
☎ 07980 607 658
☎ 028 90 649 557
nbranagan@yahoo.com
BPA

**BROWN**, Avril
**Sexual and Relationship Psychotherapist**
♿ 113 University Street
Belfast
Northern Ireland
BT7 1HP
☎ 028 90 312942
avril.brown@dnet.co.uk
BASRT

**BUET GONZALEZ**, Silvia
**Rational Emotive Behaviour Therapist**
♿ 118 Ardenlee Avenue
Belfast
BT6 0AD
☎ 028 9058 6361
silvia@anapsys.co.uk
BABCP

**BURNS**, Maura
**Psychosynthesis Psychotherapist**
35 St James's Road
Belfast
BT12 6EA
☎ 02890 247 363
☎ 02890 779 922
mauraburns@hotmail.com
Wade Trauma Centre
5 Chichester Pk. Sth
Belfast
BT15 5DW
IPS

**CAIRNS**, Mary
**Psychoanalytic Psychotherapist**
171 Barnett's Road
Belfast
N. Ireland
BT5 7BG
☎ 028 90 877936
mary@cairns19.freeserve.co.uk
ARBS

**COULTER**, Stephen
**Family & Systemic Psychotherapist**
Family Trauma Centre
1 Wellington Park
Belfast
BT9 6DJ
stephen.coulte@sebt.n-i.nhs.uk
AFT

**CRESSWELL**, Maxine
**Cognitive Behavioural Psychotherapist**
♿ 11 Sans Souci Park
Belfast
Northern Ireland
BT9 5BZ
☎ 028 9020 9684
☎ 028 9266 5141 x2523
maxine_cresswell@DLTrust.n-i.nhs.uk
BABCP

**CROMEY**, Terry
**Cognitive Behavioural Psychotherapist**
♿ 'Brakken'
43 Sheridan Drive
Helens Bay, Bangor
Co. Down
BT19 1LB
☎ 07710 470 570
TCromey@cs.com
BABCP

**CUNNINGHAM**, Gerry
**Family & Systemic Psychotherapist**
c/o Child & Family Team, Woodlea House
Gransha Park
Londonderry
Northern Ireland
BT47 6TF
☎ 028 7186 5238
gcunningham@foylebv.n-i.nhs.uk
AFT

**DAVIS**, Patrick
**Psychoanalytic Psychotherapist**
28 Brookvale Avenue
Belfast
BT14 6BW
☎ 02890 744 676
☎ 02890 757 615
peter.faber248@hotmail.com
WMIP

**DAVREN**, Moira
**Family & Systemic Psychotherapist**
1 Laurel Grove
Newry
Co Down
N. Ireland
BT34 1TP
☎ 028 302 60095
moira.davren@rcw.org.uk
AFT

**DEVINE**, Rosaleen
20 Brookview Glen
Eglinton
Co. Londonderry
BT47 3GW
☎ 02871 810 060
CTIS

**GALLAGHER**, Monica
**Hypno-Psychotherapist**
Convent of Mercy
Enniskillen
Co. Fermanagh
BT74 6AB
☎ 028 322 561
☎ 0035312 837 176
m.gallagher@st-vincents.ie
NSHAP

**GILLESPIE**, Kate
**Cognitive Psychotherapist**
♿ Cognitive Therapy Centre
Erne House
Tyrone & Fermanagh Hospital
Omagh
BT79 0NS
☎ 028 8283 5456
kategillespie@nictt.org
BABCP

**GRANT**, Mary
**Transpersonal Psychotherapist**
111 Cliftonville Road
Belfast
Northern Ireland
BT14 6JQ
☎ 028 90 753 658
CTP

**HANLEY**, Ian G.
**Cognitive Behavioural Psychotherapist**
♿ 7 Lynnehurst Drive
Comber, Newtownards
Co. Down
BT23 5LN
☎ 028 9187 3644
☎ 028 9061 4650
32 Malone View Road
Belfast
BT9 5PH
BABCP

**HAVERN**, Eileen
**Hypno-Psychotherapist**
♿ 1 Drumserk Place
Warren Point
Newry
Co Down
BT34 3NL
☎ 02830 252 935 (after 7pm)
☎ 07713 112 871
E-haverne@nkifhe.ac.uk
CTIS

**KENNY**, Brigid
**Psychosynthesis Psychotherapist**
Drumshancorick
Roslea
Fermanagh
N. Ireland
BT92 7HP
☎ 028 677 51465
bkenny@freenetname.co.uk
PET

**KENNY**, Marie
**Family & Systemic Psychotherapist**
16 Broughton Gardens
Belfast
BT6 0BB
☎ 028 90 641 268
AFT

**LAFARGUE-MEENAN**, Martine
**Integrative Psychotherapist, Primal Psychotherapist**
♿ Lifeways, 2nd Floor
10 Clarendon Street
Derry City
N. Ireland
BT48 7ET
☎ 0044 2871 279 545
lifeways@nireland.com
LAPP

**LAWSON**, Ruth
**Cognitive Behavioural Psychotherapist**
♿ Psychology Dept
McQueen Home
Ards Hospital, Regent Street
Newtownards. Co Down
BT23 4AD
☎ 028 9151 0193
☎ 028 9042 5102
Martello House
228 Bangor Road
Craigavad
Holywood, Co.Down
BT18 0JH
BABCP

**MCGOWAN**, Dominica
**Gestalt Psychotherapist**
30 North Parade Road
Belfast
Northern Ireland
BT7 2GG
☎ 0289 064 7410
☎ 0289 032 6803
dominicamcgowan@hotmail.com
GPTI, MET

**MCGREEVY**, Edith
**Hypno-Psychotherapist**
238 Townhill Road
Portglenone
Ballymena. Co Antrim
N.Ireland
BT44 8HA
☎ 02829 571 625
NSHAP

**MCKENNY**, Anne
**Cognitive Behavioural Psychotherapist**
♿ P R R T Ltd
100 Belfast Road
Hollywood
Co. Down
BT18 9QY
☎ 028 9042 7788
333 Ravenhill Road
Belfast
BT6 0BT
BABCP

**MCKEOWN**, Patricia I.
**Transpersonal Psychotherapist**
2 Beechvale Court
Banbridge
Co. Down
N. Ireland
BT32 3YB
☎ 028 406 24806
CCPE

**MCMAHON**, Eamon
**Family & Systemic Psychotherapist**
♿ 13 Cardigan Drive
Belfast
BT14 6LX
☎ 028 90 593 115
eamon-mcmahon@dltrust.n-i.nhs.uk
AFT

**MCMURRAY**, Marjorie C.
**Cognitive Behavioural Psychotherapist**
♿ 33 Woodford Drive
Armagh
BT60 2AY
☎ 028 3752 4501
☎ 07815 902 717
marjoriemcmurray@hotmail.com
BABCP

**MULLOWNEY**, Mandy
**Psychoanalytic Psychotherapist**
30 Springvale Road
Ballywater
Co.Down
Northern Ireland
BT2 2RS
☎ 02842 758 320
magrruru@aol.com
NAFSI

**O'NEILL**, Arthur Joseph
**Family & Systemic Psychotherapist**
Whitefield House
2 The Hawthorns
Belfast
Northern Ireland
BT10 0NR
☎ 028 9030 1611
artieo@jjbni-whitefield.org
AFT

**QUIGLEY**, Hugh M.
**Hypno-Psychotherapist**
♿ 109 Fergleen Park
Galliagh Estate
Derry City
N. Ireland
BT48 8LF
☎ 028 71 292 259
hugh@hughm.freeserve.co.uk
CTIS

**QUINN**, Paul
**Cognitive Behavioural Psychotherapist**
♿ 38 Garland Hill
Belfast
BT8 6YL
☎ 028 9079 7139
Paul@pquinn38.fsnet.co.uk
110A University Street
Belfast
Northern Ireland
BT7 1HH
BABCP

**REILLY**, Isobel
**Family & Systemic Psychotherapist**
♿ 21 Wellington Park
Belfast
BT9 6DL
☎ 028 90 292 656
I.reilly@qub.ac.uk
AFT

**WALSH**, Ken
**Cognitive Behavioural Psychotherapist**
♿ 75 Wynchurch Road
Rosetta
Belfast
BT6 0JJ
☎ 028 9079 7210
☎ 07740 861 113
BABCP

## NORTHUMBERLAND

**BLACK**, Patricia Anne
**Psychoanalytic Psychotherapist**
Seatsides Farmhouse
Once Brewed
Northumberland
NE47 7HE
☎ 0191 282 4087
☎ 0143 4344 4639
stanegatepb@aol.com
FIP

**DIJKMAN**, Theo
**Psychosynthesis Psychotherapist**
Hirsel Lodge
Kelso Road
Coldstream
TD12 4LH
☎ 01890 882 977
theo@dijkman.freeserve.co.uk
IPS

**JANSEN**, Diana
**Psychoanalytic Psychotherapist**
The Cottage
Dalton Northumberland
Newcastle upon Tyne
NE18 0AA
☎ 01661 886 200
diana.jansen@btinternet.com
FIP

**LUND**, Charles
**Psychoanalytic Psychotherapist, Psychodynamic Psychotherapist**
92 Errington Road
Darras Hall
Ponteland
Newcastle upon Tyne
NE20 9LA
☎ 01661 872 018
charles@cplund.freeserve.co.uk
UPCA

**MORGAN**, Shirley P.
**Psychoanalytic Psychotherapist**
High Rawgreen Cottage
Steel
Hexham
Northumberland
NE47 0HL
☎ 0191 569 9026
☎ 01434 673 090
FIP

**NADKARNI**, Joanne
**Integrative Psychotherapist**
17 Vernon Drive
Monkseaton
Tyne & Wear
NE25 8JN
☎ 0191 451 6293
SPTI

**REED**, Alexander
**Family & Systemic Psychotherapist**
1a Leazes Terrace
Hexham
Northumberland
NE46 3DL
☎ 01434 601 928
alex.reed@virgin.net
AFT

## NOTTINGHAMSHIRE

**ACKROYD**, Elaine
**Sexual and Relationship Psychotherapist**
The Hollies
Bleasby Road
Thurgarton
NG14 7FW
☎ 01636 830 871
☎ 07900 004 593
eandmackroyd@ukonline.co.uk
BASRT

**ADLINGTON**, Jethro
**Neurolinguistic Psychotherapist**
12 Nelson Road
Daybrook
Nottingham
NG5 6JE
☎ 07003 999 666
jethro_adlington@yahoo.com
NLPtCA

**AITKEN**, Fiona
**Integrative Psychotherapist**
12 Rufford Road
Sherwood
Nottingham
NG5 2NR
☎ 0115 847 8090
SPTI

**ARMSTRONG**, Marie Ann
**Family & Systemic Psychotherapist**
c/o Thorneywood CAMHS
Porchester Road
Nottingham
NG3 6LF
☎ 0115 844 0505
marie.armstrong@nottshc.nhs.uk
AFT

**AUSTIN**, Catherine
**Integrative Psychotherapist**
14 Oundle Drive
Wollaton Park
Nottingham
NG8 1BN
☎ 0115 978 3874
☎ 07765 406 699
c.austin2@ntlworld.com
SPTI

**AVERY**, Anna
**Gestalt Psychotherapist**
Clovers
Little Lane
Clarborough
Retford, Nottingham
DN22 9LR
☎ 01777 869 913
anna@avery100.freeserve.co.uk
SPTI

**BASSETT**, George
**Gestalt Psychotherapist**
4 Fullmonty House
27 Orlando Dr, Gedling
Nottingham
NG4 3FN
☎ 0115 961 7911
G.S.Bassett@Derby.ac.uk
SPTI

**BATTEN**, Francis
**Psychodrama Psychotherapist**
16 Milner Road
Sherwood
Nottingham
NG5 2ES
☎ 0115 847 9281
☎ 0115 847 9280
batten-howell@ntlworld.com
BPA

**BEECHCROFT**, Diane
**Transactional Analysis Psychotherapist**
178 Harrington Drive
Lenton
Nottingham
NG7 1JH
☎ 01159 414 378
diane.beechcroft@ntlworld.com
ITA

**BELL-BOULÉ**, Annabell
**Gestalt Psychotherapist**
Alternatives
170 Derby Road
Nottingham
NG7 1LR
☎ 0115 978 1006/953 4754
☎ 07900 671 44
annabellbb@hotmail.com
SPTI

**BROCK**, Martin J
**Cognitive Behavioural Psychotherapist**
♿ Nottingham Psychotherapy Unit
St Annes House
114 Thorneywood Mount
Thorneywood, Nottingham
NG3 2PZ
☎ 0115 956 4911
sevenofnine@ukonline.co.uk
BABCP

**BRYANT**, Pat
**Gestalt Psychotherapist, Integrative Psychotherapist**
25 Park Wharf
Haslam St
Nottingham
NG7 1FA
☎ 0115 9240762
patbryantempa@aol.com
SPTI

**BULLEN-SPICER**, Robert
**Gestalt Psychotherapist**
♿ 76 Hallam Road
Nottingham
NG3 6HR
☎ 0115 9504336
robertspicer@hotmail.com
SPTI

**CARRETTE**, Timothy
**Gestalt Psychotherapist**
21 Percival Road
Sherwood
Nottingham
NG5 2FA
☎ 0115 8449270
tim.carrette@ntlworld.com
SPTI

**CHAN-WILLIAMS**, Molly
**Group Analyst**
The Garden House
May Lodge Drive
Rufford
Notts
NG22 9DE
☎ 01623 823 421
FPC, IGA

**CLARKE**, Ann Marie
**Gestalt Psychotherapist**
♿ 64 Latimer Drive
Bramcove Hills
Nottingham
NG9 3HT
☎ 0115 928 4920
SPTI

**CLEGG**, Jennifer Anne
**Family & Systemic Psychotherapist**
Dept. Of LD
Highbury Hospital
Bulwell
Nottingham
NG6 9DR
☎ 00115 952 9462
jenifer.clegg@nottshc.nhs.uk
AFT

**CLEMENTS**, Wendy
**Integrative Psychotherapist**
21 Walcote Drive
West Brigford
Nottingham
NG2 7JQ
☎ 0115 984 4647
wendy.clements@btinternet.com
SPTI

**CODMAN**, Chris
**Gestalt Psychotherapist**
♿ 3 Bramcote Avenue
Beeston
Nottingham
NG9 4DG
☎ 0115 849 7795
chris.codman@ntlworld.com
SPTI

**CODMAN**, Sarah
**Gestalt Psychotherapist**
♿ 3 Bramcote Avenue
Beeston
Nottingham
NG9 4DG
☎ 0115 849 7795
sarah.codman@ntlworld.com
SPTI

**COLLS**, Jennifer
**Gestalt Psychotherapist**
75 Park Lane
Sutton Bonington
Loughborough
LE12 5NQ
☎ 01509 673 204
GCL

**COOPER**, Virginia
**Cognitive Behavioural Psychotherapist**
♿ Stonebridge Centre
Cardiff Street
Carlton Road
Nottingham
NG3 2FH
☎ 07890 478 782
virginia.cooper@talk21.com
BABCP

**COUPE**, Aileen
**Integrative Psychotherapist**
13 Banbury Drive
Shepshed
Loughborough
LE12 9PL
☎ 01509 503 635
aileencoupe@care4free.net
SPTI

**DYCE**, James
**Gestalt Psychotherapist**
50 William Road
Stapleford
Nottingham
NG9 8ES
☎ 0115 877 2033
SPTI

**EINARSSON**, Pall
**Integrative Psychotherapist**
18B Monsall Street
New Brasford
Nottingham
NG7 7HD
palleinarsson@visir.is - www.psychotherapy-nottingham.co.uk
SPTI

**EVANS**, Chris
**Group Analyst**
Rampton Hospital
Retford
Nottinghamshire
DN22 OPD
☎ 01777 247 242
chris@psyctc.org
IGA

**EVANS**, Kenneth
**Gestalt Psychotherapist, Integrative Psychotherapist**
26 Radford Grove Lane
Radford
Nottingham
NG7 5QB
☎ 07855 323 305
ken@kenevans.fsnet.co.uk
ScPTI

**FILE**, Sharon
**Cognitive Behavioural Psychotherapist**
♿ E19 Fleming Drive
Rampton Hospital
Beeston
Retford
DN22 0PD
☎ 0115 943 0456
BABCP

**FLETCHER**, Paul
**Family & Systemic Psychotherapist**
♿ 152 Huthwaite Road
Sutton in Ashfield
Notts
NG1 2GX
☎ 01623 550 141
paul.fletcher@nottsc.nhs.uk
AFT

**FOOKES**, Andrew
**Gestalt Psychotherapist**
c/o SPTI
2 St James's Terrace
Nottingham
NG1 6FW
☎ 0115 924 3994
therapy@spti.net
SPTI

**GILL**, Eileen
**Gestalt Psychotherapist**
Tower Croft
19 Richmond Drive
Mapperley Park
Nottingham
NG3 5EL
☎ 0115 962 3154
SPTI

**GRAHAM**, Hilary
**Hypno-Psychotherapist**
25 George Road
West Bridgford
Nottingham
NG2 7PT
☎ 01159 455 290
NRHP

**GREENWAY**, Ian
**Gestalt Psychotherapist**
♿ 11 Shirley Road
Mapperley Park
Nottingham
NG3 5DA
☎ 0115 940 6081
i.greenway@btinternet.com
GPTI

**HADDON**, Neale
**Gestalt Psychotherapist**
7 Rise Court
Hamilton Road
Nottingham
NG5 1EU
☎ 0115 985 6684
neale.haddon@uktherapists.net
SPTI

**HARLEY**, Maxine
**Integrative Psychotherapist**
2 Glendale Gardens
Arnold
Nottingham
NG5 6NS
☎ 01522 532 164
SPTI

**HELPS**, Davina
**Sexual and Relationship Psychotherapist**
♿ Grove Farm
Main Street
Epperstone
NG14 6AU
☎ 0115 966 3919
BASRT

**HILLS**, Janet
**Body Psychotherapist, Integrative Psychotherapist**
105 North Street
Barrow-on-Soar
Leicester
LE12 8PZ
☎ 01509 621 376
janethills@tiscali.co.uk
CCBP

**HINDLE**, Deborah
**Child Psychotherapist**
Thornywood Child & Adolescent Psychiatry Unit
Porchester Road
Mapperley
Nottingham
NG3 6LF
☎ 0115 9529479 (t/f)
ACP

**HOLT GARNER**, Lydia
**Psychoanalytic Psychotherapist**
♿ Nottingham Psychotherapy Unit
St. Annes House
114, Thorneywood Mount
Nottingham
NG3 2PZ
☎ 01158 440 544
STTDP

**HOWELL**, Julia
**Psychodrama Psychotherapist**
♿ 16 Milner Road
Sherwood
Nottingham
NG5 2ES
☎ 0115 847 9281
☎ 0115 847 9280
batten-howell@ntlworld.com
BPA

**JACKSON**, Christopher
**Cognitive Behavioural Psychotherapist**
♿ Clinical Psychology Services
Nottinghamshire Healthcare NHS
Southwell Road West
Mansfield
NG18 4HH
☎ 07905 759 535
cb-therapy@ntlworld.com
PO Box 7780
Nottingham
NG2 4WU
BABCP

**JOHNSON-HILL**, Heather
**Gestalt Psychotherapist**
5 Pelham Crescent
The Park
Nottingham
NG7 1AR
☎ 0115 941 7250
heather.johnsonhill@ntlworld.com
SPTI

**JONES**, Helen
**Gestalt Psychotherapist**
60 Selby Road
West Bridgford
Nottingham
NG2 7BL
☎ 0115 981 6465
SPTI

**JUGGINS**, Kate
**Humanistic Psychotherapist**
SPTI Clinical Annexe
30 Park Row
Nottingham
NG1 6GR
☎ 0115 929 1470
SPTI

**KERRY**, Helen
**Gestalt Psychotherapist**
♿ 3 Dagmar Grove
Alexandra Park
Mapperley
Nottingham
NG3 4JE
☎ 0115 962 1107
helen.kerry@nottingham.ac.uk
GPTI

**KIRTLEY**, Jane
**Gestalt Psychotherapist**
♿ 50 Fosse Road
Farndon
Newark
Notts
NG24 4ST
☎ 01636 651 937
SPTI

**LAKE**, Dorry
**Integrative Psychotherapist**
8 Fourth Avenue
Sherwood Rise
Nottingham
NG7 6JB
☎ 0115 962 5092
SPTI

**LANGFORD BELLABY**, Rosemary
**Integrative Psychotherapist**
Thiskney House
2 St James' Terrace
Nottingham
NG1 6FW
☎ 0115 844 7875
2 St James Terrace
Nottingham
NG1 6FW
SPTI

**LAVENDER**, Peter
**Gestalt Psychotherapist**
30 Park Row
Nottingham
NG1 6GR
☎ 0115 920 0186
☎ 07930 371 369
peterlavender@onetel.net.uk
SPTI

**LAW**, Anne M
**Sexual and Relationship Psychotherapist**
Church Meadow
Calverton
NG14
☎ 0115 845 7841
anne.lawcllg@virgin.net
BASRT

**LEE**, Adrienne
**Transactional Analysis Psychotherapist**
2 Castle Grove
The Park
Nottingham
NG7 1DN
☎ 01509 673 649
☎ 0115 9475 447
ta@theberne.com
ITA

**LEE**, Helen
**Psychoanalytic Psychotherapist**
♿ Nottingham Psychotherapy Unit (NHS)
St. Ann's House
114 Thorneywood Mount
Nottingham
NG3 2PZ
☎ 01158 440 545
Helen.A.Lee@btinternet.com
STTDP

**LUX**, Julius
**Cognitive Behavioural Psychotherapist**
Lifetime Training & Counselling
Gresham Gardens
Woodthrope
Nottingham
NG5 4LU
☎ 0115 967 3060
☎ 07768 961 349
BABCP

**MANN**, David
**Gestalt Psychotherapist**
1 Ashtree Cottage
Maythorne
Southwell
Notts
NG25 0RS
☎ 01636 816 939
☎ 07940 590 662
dp.mann@virgin.net
30 Park Road
Nottingham
NG1 6GR
GPTI, SPTI

**MANN**, Sarah
**Integrative Psychotherapist**
61 Caledon Road
Sherwood
Nottingham
NG5 5NF
☎ 0115 841 1206
SPTI

**MCGUINNESS**, Maureen
**Psychosynthesis Psychotherapist**
21 Girton Road
Sherwood
Nottingham
NG5 1FY
☎ 0115 911 21 26 (t/f)
IPS

**MCKAY**, Lynn
**Psychodynamic Psychotherapist**
Kirkland House
58 Church Street
Southwell
Notts
NG25 0HQ
☎ 01636 815 509
LynnMckay50@aol.com
VAPP

**MORLEY**, Ann
**Jungian Analytical Psychotherapist**
36 Crosby Road
West Bridgford
Nottingham
NG2 5GH
☎ 01159 140 256
WMIP

**MOULDING**, Jacqueline
**Integrative Psychotherapist**
♿ CLADDAGH HOUSE
High St
East Markham
Newark
NG22 0GL
☎ 01777 872 172
☎ 01777 711 150
SPTI

**O'REILLY**, Tom
**Psychoanalytic Psychotherapist**
♿ Nottingham Psychotherapy Unit
St.Anne's House
114, Thorneywood Mount
Nottingham
NG3 2PZ
☎ 01158 440 546
STTDP

**ORLANDI-FANTINI**, Claire
**Gestalt Psychotherapist**
c/o SPTI
2 St James's Terrace
Nottingham
NG1 6FW
☎ 0115 924 3994
SPTI

**ORLANDI-FANTINI**, Peter
**Gestalt Psychotherapist**
c/o SPTI
2 St James's Terrace
Nottingham
NG1 6FW
☎ 0115 9313023
peterof@btinternet.com
SPTI

**PEARSON**, Mark Alan
**Family & Systemic Psychotherapist**
70 Holme Road
West Bridgeford
Nottingham
NG2 5AD
☎ 0115 982 0633
mark.pearson@nottshc.nhs.uk
AFT

**PECKITT**, R.G.
**Cognitive Behavioural Psychotherapist**
♿ Personality Disorder Service
Rampton Hospital
Retford
DN22 0PD
☎ 01777 248 321
BABCP

**PHILLIPS**, Sue
**Transactional Analysis Psychotherapist**
Woodbury
Parklands Close
Coddington
Newark
NG24 2RE
sue@susanphillips.demon.co.uk
ITA, MET

**PIGOTT**, Sheila
**Integrative Psychotherapist**
♿ St. Paul's House
Boundary Road
West Bridgeford
Nottingham
NG2 7DB
☎ 0115 923 3998
sheila.pigott@virgin.net
SPTI

**PITT**, Daniel
**Gestalt Psychotherapist**
Flat1
50 Forest Road West
Nottingham
NG7 4EQ
Suite 12
Clarendon Chambers
32 Clarendon Street
Nottingham
NG1 5JD
SPTI

**PUGSLEY**, Stephanie
**Gestalt Psychotherapist**
48 Tavistock Drive
Mapperley Park
Nottingham
NG3 5DW
☎ 0115 960 6489
☎ 07074 814 582
steph_pugsley_2@hotmail.com
GPTI, SPTI

**REGEL**, Stephen
**Cognitive Behavioural Psychotherapist**
♿ Centre for Trauma Studies
Notts Healthcare NHS Trust
Westminster House
598 The Wells Road, Notti
NG3 6AA
☎ 0115 952 9436
stephen.regel@nhc-tr.trent.nhs.uk
BABCP

**RICHARDS**, Paul
**Neurolinguistic Psychotherapist**
Flat 2
12a Alexandra Street
Sherwood Rise
Nottingham
NG5 1AY
☎ 01159 857 372
NLPtCA

**RICHARDS**, Simon
**Gestalt Psychotherapist**
♿ Dept. of Psychology
Nottinghamshire Health Care Trust
H
Southwell Road
Mansfield
NG18 4HH
☎ 01623 784 911
ScPTI

**ROLAND-SMITH**, Mandy
**Integrative Psychotherapist**
3 Weston Avenue
Mount Hooton Road
Nottingham
NG7 4BA
☎ 0115 970 804
mandyjrs@aol.com
SPTI

**RYAN**, Sandra
169 Kenrick Road
Mapperley
Nottingham
NG3 6EY
☎ 0115 955 3514
AFT

**SAHNI**, Jadean
**Gestalt Psychotherapist**
24 Meadow Close
Turneys Quay
Nottingham
NG2 3HZ
☎ 0115 986 8451
j.sahni@virgin.net
SPTI

**SALISBURY**, Jonathan F. H.
**Psychodrama Psychotherapist**
♿ 148 Coppice Road
Arnold
Nottingham
NG5 7GZ
☎ 0115 9200470
jeanniejonathan@aol.com
BPA

**SENIOR**, Maggie
**Integrative Psychotherapist**
♿ c/o SPTI
Thiskney House
2 St James Terrace
Nottingham
NG1 6FW
☎ 0115 844 7876
therapy@spti.net
SPTI

**SHARP**, Rob
**Integrative Psychotherapist**
84 Victoria Road
Sherwood
Nottingham
NG5 2ND
☎ 0115 962 2252
SPTI

**SHORT**, Deborah
**Gestalt Psychotherapist**
♿ 20 Langton Hollow
Selston
Nottinghamshire
NG16 6DU
☎ 01773 778 380
deborahesshort@yahoo.co.uk
SPTI

**SHOTTER**, Ann
**Integrative Psychotherapist**
♿ 5 Second Avenue
Sherwwod Rise
Nottingham
NG7 6JJ
☎ 0115 962 5418
SPTI

**SPICER**, Rob
**Gestalt Psychotherapist**
76 Hallam Road
Nottingham
NG3 6HR
☎ 0115 950 4336
robertospicer@hotmail.com
SPTI

**STAINES**, Jillian
**Psychoanalytic Psychotherapist**
♿ Nottingham Psychotherapy Unit
(NHS)
St. Ann's House
114 Thorneywood Mount
Nottingham
NG3 2PZ
☎ 01158 440 546
STTDP

**STALMEISTERS**, Dzintra
**Gestalt Psychotherapist**
The Moorings
Main Street
Bleasby
Nottingham
NG14 7GH
☎ 01636 831 062
BABCP

**STAVELEY**, Susan
**Gestalt Psychotherapist**
4 Thorpe Crescent
Mapperley
Nottingham
NG3 6BY
☎ 0115 960 5026
susan.staveley@ic24.net
SPTI

**STEVENS**, Christine
**Gestalt Psychotherapist**
Malvern House
41 Mapperley Road
Nottingham
NG3 5AQ
☎ 0115 841 2006
therapy@mappmed.co.uk
SPTI

**STEWART**, Naomi
**Psychoanalytic Psychotherapist**
5 Primrose Bank
Bingham
Notts
NG13 8TU
☎ 0116 225 6430
☎ 01949 836 691
naomi.stewart@lineone.net
FIP, STTDP

**SWAN PARENTE**, Alison
**Child Psychotherapist**
Thorneywood CAMHS
Porchester Road
Mapperley, Notts.
NG3 6LF
☎ 0115 8440500
☎ 01909 500263
swanparent@aol.com
ACP

**TATHAM**, Elizabeth
**Family & Systemic Psychotherapist**
♿ Tree Tops
Forest Hill
Mansfield
NG1 5BQ
☎ 01623 407 640
liz.tatham@ntlworld.com
AFT

**THOMPSON**, Jean Mary
**Psychodrama Psychotherapist**
148 Coppice Road
Arnold
Nottingham
NG5 7GZ
☎ 01159 200 470
jeanniejonathan@aol.com
BPA

**TOMS**, David A.
**Psychodynamic Psychotherapist**
♿ 2 Regent Street
Nottingham
NG1 5BQ
☎ 01159 474 755
WMIP

**WARD**, Keltie
**Sexual and Relationship Psychotherapist**
64 Musters Road
West Bridgford
Nottingham
NG2 7PR
☎ 0115 981 3338
☎ 07759 360 676
keltie.ward@talk21.com
BASRT

**WATERSTONE**, Carolyn
**Gestalt Psychotherapist**
10 Hampden Grove
Beeston
Nottingham
NG9 1FG
☎ 0115 925 9083
GPTI

**WHITWORTH**, Patricia
**Integrative Psychotherapist**
Wisteria Cottage
93 Melton Road
Barrow-on-Soar
Leicester
LE12 8NT
☎ 01509 413 327
piewhit@jubilate.fsnet.co.uk
SPTI

**WOLF**, Runa
**Gestalt Psychotherapist**
c/o The Sherwood Psychotherapy
Training Institute
Thiskney House
2 St James Terrace
Nottingham
NG1 6FW
☎ 07866 693822 (M)
SPTI

**WOOD**, Christine D.J.
**Transactional Analysis Psychotherapist**
64 Henry Road
West Bridgford
Nottingham
NG2 7ND
☎ 01159 825 498
ITA

**WOOD**, Sally
**Family & Systemic Psychotherapist**
♿ Long Eaton
NG10
☎ 0115 9725 621
AFT

**WRIGHT**, Norman
**Integrative Psychotherapist**
109 Prospect Road
Carlton
Nottingham
NG4 1LU
☎ 0115 987 3756
normankem@hotmail.com
SPTI

**WYATT**, Gill
**Transactional Analysis Psychotherapist**
17 Denison Street
Beeston
Nottingham
NG9 1AY
☎ 01159 177 287
gw@earthsky.demon.co.uk
MET

**YOUNG**, Raymond
**Psychoanalytic Psychotherapist**
♿ Nottingham Psychotherapy Unit
St. Ann's House
114 Thorneywood Mount
Nottingham
NG3 2PZ
☎ 01158 440 547
ray.young@nttshc.nhs.uk
STTDP

## OXFORDSHIRE

**ALLEN**, Patricia
**Transactional Analysis Psychotherapist**
♿ 142 Gidley Way
Horspath
Oxford
OX33 1TD
☎ 01865 872 388
Patricia.Allen.oxcpt@ukgateway.net
ITA

**AMEY**, Sue
**Integrative Arts Psychotherapist**
Oxford
OX2
☎ 01865 554 961
amey@macunlimited.net
University of Oxford
Dept. of Psychiatry
Warneford Hospital
Oxford
OX3 7JX
IATE

**AMIES**, Peter
**Cognitive Psychotherapist**
77 Victoria Road
Summertown
Oxford
OX2 7QG
☎ 01865 556 322
☎ 01793 491 917
100422.624@compuserve.com
BABCP

**ANDREWS**, Gill
**Group Analyst**
Oxford
OX4
☎ 01865 724 190
gillandrews@care4free.net
IGA

**ARMITAGE**, Pamela
**Psychoanalytic Psychotherapist**
94 Wytham Street
Oxford
OX1 4TW
☎ 01865 424 699
pamarmitage@totalise.co.uk
GUILD

**BARLOW**, Linda
**Transpersonal Psychotherapist**
Little Barn
Bitterell
Eynsham
Oxon
OX29 4JL
☎ 01865 880 578
CTP

**BLOW**, Kirsten
**Family & Systemic Psychotherapist**
♿ Oxford Family Institute
2 Woodlands , Mill End
Kidlington
Oxon
OX5 2ER
☎ 01865 842 407
kirstenblow@ofi.org.uk
AFT

**BLYTH**, Fiona
**Transactional Analysis Psychotherapist**
1 Ayrton Plac
Wallingford
Oxfordshire
OX10 0DG
☎ 07779 103 798
blythfiona@hotmail.com
MET

**BRADLEY**, Lorne-Natalie
**Psychoanalytic Psychotherapist**
29 Boulter Street
St. Clements
Oxford
OX4 1AX
☎ 01873 812 387
☎ 01865 246 879
xqx29@Dial.Pipex.com
CPP, FIP

**BRAMLEY**, Wyn
**Psychodynamic Psychotherapist**
Dar Farhan
Woodstock Road
Stonesfield, witney
Oxon
OX29 8QA
☎ 01993 89151
FIP

**BREWER**, Madelyn
**Psychoanalytic Psychotherapist**
38 Rectory Road
St Clements
Oxford
OX4 1BU
☎ 01865 725 588
madelynbrewer@hotmail.com
FIP, SITE

**BROSNAN**, Judi
**Psychoanalytic Psychotherapist**
2 Wootten Drive
Iffley
Oxford
OX4 4DS
☎ 01865 716 771
judi.v.brosnan@ntlworld.com
SIP

**BROWNER**, Nancy
**Integrative Psychotherapist**
47 Castle Mill House
Juxton Street
Oxford
OX2 6DR
☎ 01865 316 004
nancy@browner.freeserve.co.uk
MC

**BRYANT**, Roger
**Transpersonal Psychotherapist**
♿ 10 Foxburrow Lane
Hailey
Witney
Oxon
OX29 9UN
☎ 01993 704345
CCPE

**BURNS-LUNDGREN**, Eva
**Cognitive Analytic Therapist**
♿ Oxfordshire Mental HealthCare NHS Trust
Psychotherapy Dept,
Warneford Hospital,
Warneford Lane Headington
OX3 7JX
☎ 01865 226 330
Eva.Burns-Lundgren@oxmhc-tr.nhs.uk
ACAT

**BUTLER**, Gillian
**Cognitive Behavioural Psychotherapist**
♿ Department of Psychology
The Warneford Hospital
Headington
Oxford
OX3 7JX
☎ 01869 226 430
Gillian.Butler@Psychiatry.ox.ac.uk
BABCP

**CAMPBELL**, Jane
**Group Analyst**
227 Kennington Road
Kennington
Oxford
OX1 5PG
☎ 01865 735 519
☎ 01865 730 347
jane.d.campbell@ukgateway.net
IGA, UPCA

**CARNEY**, Joanne
**Family & Systemic Psychotherapist**
66 Crescent Road
Cowley
Oxford
OX4 2PB
☎ 01865 770 725
AFT

**CARR**, Jean
**Analytical Psychologist-Jungian Analyst**
12 Windsor Street
Headington
Oxford
OX3 7AP
☎ 01865 750 796
CAP *

**CHRISTOPHAS**, Sheelagh
**Humanistic Psychotherapist**
70 West Way
Botley
Oxford
OX2 9JT
☎ 01865 790 687
sheelagh.christophas@ntlworld.com
AHPP

**CLANCY**, Ian
**Hypno-Psychotherapist**
Orchard Counselling Practice
Orchard Holding
The Croft
East Hagbourne
OX11 9LS
☎ 01235 813 370
i.clancy@virgin.net
NSHAP

**COREN**, Alex B
**Psychoanalytic Psychotherapist**
86 Church Way
Iffley
Oxford
OX4 4EF
☎ 01865 435 321
alex.coren@conted.ox.ac.uk
Director of Counselling Courses
Psychotherapeutic Studies
University of Oxford, Rewley House, 1 Wellington Sq.
OX1 2JA
UPCA

**CRANE**, Kanta
**Integrative Psychotherapist**
73 Bullington Road
Oxford
OX4 1QL
☎ 01865 244 366
AHPP

**CREIGHTON**, Janet
**Family & Systemic Psychotherapist**
93 Mill Street
Steventon
Oxon
OX13 6SP
☎ 01235 831 331
janet@g-jcreighton.demon.co.uk
AFT

**CULLINGTON**, Anne
**Cognitive Behavioural Psychotherapist**
The Lodge
51A High Street
Wallingford
OX10 0DB
☎ 01491 825 199
anne.cullington@virgin.net
BABCP

**CUNNINGHAM**, Gordon
**Group Analyst**
Oxford University Counselling Service
11 Wellington Square
OX1 2ES
☎ 01865 270 300
reception@counserv.ox.ac.uk
IGA

**DODD**, Harry
**Cognitive Behavioural Psychotherapist**
♿ Dept. of Psychotherapy
Warneford Hospital
Headington
Oxford
OX3 7JX
☎ 01865 226 330
☎ 07801 387 599
harry.dodd@oxmhc-tr.anglox.nhs.uk
BABCP

**DOUGLAS**, Sue
**Humanistic and Integrative Psychotherapist**
♿ Fawler Barn
Kingston Lisle
Nr. Wantage
Oxon
OX12 9QJ
☎ 01367 820 562
BCPC

**DOWNES**, Vanessa Susan
**Cognitive Behavioural Psychotherapist**
♿ Cotswold House
Warneford Hospital
Headington
Oxford
OX3 7JX
☎ 01856 226 248
☎ 01865 451 632
BABCP

**DUFFIN**, Lorna
**Psychodynamic Psychotherapist**
♿ 16 Southmoor Road
Oxford
OX2 6RD
☎ 01865 512 915
VAPP

**ELWELL**, Louise
**Cognitive Analytic Therapist**
57 Western Road
Grandpont
Oxford
OX1 4LF
☎ 01865 202 546
ACAT

**FINAR**, Ruth
**Gestalt Psychotherapist**
16 Mill Street
Oxford
OX2 0AJ
☎ 01865 727 572
ruthfinar@lodestar.charitydays.co.uk
GPTI

**FORD**, Jane Lucy
**Family & Systemic Psychotherapist**
11 Bickerton Road
Headington
Oxford
OX3 7LT
☎ 01865 766 165
jane@oxfordprojects.co.uk
AFT

**FRISVOLD**, Tove
**Psychoanalytic Psychotherapist**
5 Dyers Hill
Charlbury
Oxon
OX7 3QD
☎ 01608 810412
tove@amberbridge.co.uk
IPSS

**GAGE**, Mike
**Sexual and Relationship Psychotherapist**
♿ West Street Surgery
12 West Street
Chipping Norton
Oxon
OX7 5AA
☎ 01295 258 452
☎ 01295 680 506
oxgage@aol.com
BASRT

**GALLOP**, Margaret
**Group Analytic Psychotherapist**
The Asbury Medical Centre
Trent Road
Didcot
Oxon
OX11
IGA

**GERHARDT**, Sue
**Psychoanalytic Psychotherapist**
Flat 1
4 Crick Road
Oxford
OX2 6QJ
☎ 01865 311 772
AIP

**GILLIE**, Marion
**Gestalt Psychotherapist**
Field End House
53 Ramsay Road
Headington
Oxford
OX3 8AY
☎ 01865 751 282
GCL

**GOSS**, Thomas
**Psychosynthesis Psychotherapist**
Rose Cottage
Pound Lane
Stanton St. John
Oxon
OX33 1HF
☎ 01865 351765
PET

**GUGENHEIM**, Camilla
**Humanistic Psychotherapist**
38 Cherwell Street
Oxford
OX4 1BG
☎ 01865 246 5890
camilla@doublespiral.clara.co.uk
AHPP

**GUY**, Liana
**Psychoanalytic Psychotherapist**
33 Marlborough Road
Oxford
OX1 4LW
☎ 07773 092707
GUILD

**HALMARACK**, Philip
**Psychodrama Psychotherapist**
Church Cottage
The Square
Eynsham
Oxon
OX29 4HW
☎ 01865 731 102
phalmarack@hotmail.com
BPA

**HANAWAY**, Monica
**Integrative Psychotherapist**
79 Fairacres Road
Iffley Fields
Oxford
OX4 1TQ
☎ 01865 436 538
monica.hanaway@ntlworld.com
SPCRC

**HANNA**, Gilli
**Transpersonal Psychotherapist**
49 Freehold Street
Lower Heyford
Oxon
OX25 5NT
☎ 07771 766 055
gilli@lifework.org.uk
CCPE

**HARRIS**, Gordon
**Analytical Psychologist-Jungian Analyst**
Hillside, 72 Honey Lane
Cholsey
Wallingford
Oxon
OX10 9NJ
☎ 01491 651 271
SIP

**HAWORTH**, Peter
**Psychodrama Psychotherapist**
♿ 8 Rahere Road
Cowley
Oxford
OX4 3QC
☎ 01865 747 604
☎ 01865 226 404
peter.haworth@oxmhc-tr.anglox.nhs.uk
Dept. of Psychotherapy
Warneford Hospital
Oxford
OX3 7JP
BPA

**HAWXWELL**, Frances
**Integrative Psychotherapist**
♿ 87 Victoria Road
Oxford
OX2 7QG
☎ 01865 439 123
fmhawxwell@ntl.world.com
MET

**HAYES**, Lesley
**Humanistic and Integrative Psychotherapist**
Celastrina Cottage
26 Cherwell Street
Oxford
OX4 1BG
☎ 01865 249 975
sky@lesleyhayes.fsworld.co.uk
AHPP

**HAYHURST**, Sohani
**Integrative Psychotherapist**
1 Upper Fisher Row
Oxford
OX1 2EZ
☎ 01865 727351
Sohanihayhurst@aol.com
MC

**HEITZLER**, Morit
**Body Psychotherapist, Integrative Psychotherapist**
14 Hawthorn Close
Oxford
OX2 9DY
☎ 01865 725 205
CCBP

**HERBERT**, Claudia
**Cognitive Behavioural Psychotherapist**
The Oxford Development Centre Ltd
The Oxford Stress & Trauma Centre
8a Market Square
Witney, Oxon
OX28 6BB
☎ 01993 779 994
claudia.herbert@oxdev.co.uk
BABCP

**HILL**, Penny
**Psychoanalytic Psychotherapist**
17 Norreys Avenue
Oxford
OX1 4ST
☎ 01865 429 284
☎ 01865 429 285
SITE

**HOBBS**, Michael
**Group Analyst**
Psychotherapy Department
Warneford Hospital
Headington
Oxford
OX3 7JX
☎ 01865 226 331
mike.hobbs@axmhc-tr.nhs.uk
IGA

**HOCK**, Gaby
**Psychodynamic Psychotherapist, Transpersonal Psychotherapist**
59 Warwick Street
Oxford
OX4 1SZ
☎ 01865 247 851
CTP

**HODSON**, Pauline
**Couple Psychoanalytic Psychotherapist**
14 Brookside
Headington
Oxford
OX3 7PJ
☎ 01865 762 991
Paulinehodson@supanet.com
SCPP

**HUGHES**, Eleanor
**Family & Systemic Psychotherapist**
5 Chaucer Court
Ewlme
Wallingford
Oxon
OX10 6HW
☎ 01491 835 617
elliemhughes@btopenworld.com
AFT

**HUISH**, I.P.
**Psychoanalytic Psychotherapist**
Hilary's
Shenington
Banbury
Oxon
OX15 6NH
☎ 01295 670 387
AGIP

**HUTCHINSON**, Peter
**Psychodrama Psychotherapist**
95 Sunningwell Road
Oxford
OX1 4SY
☎ 01865 454 246
peter@somuch.info
BPA

**JAQUES**, Penny
**Psychoanalytic Psychotherapist**
7 Stanley Road
Oxford
OX4 1QY
☎ 01865 724141
p-jaques@dircon.co.uk
FIP

**JOHNSTON**, Linda Ann May
**Family & Systemic Psychotherapist**
62 Sadlers Court
Abingdon
Oxon
OX14 2PA
☎ 01235 530 274
lindajohnston@tinyworld.co.uk
AFT

**KEATING**, Jacqueline
**Analytical Psychologist-Jungian Analyst**
Abbots Place
Church Lane
Islip
OX5 2TA
☎ 01865 376 162
jackie.keating@ntlworld.com
IGAP

**KUCHEMANN**, Christine
**Psychoanalytic Psychotherapist**
62 Victoria Road
Oxford
OX2 6QD
☎ 01865 512 410
AGIP

**LAMONT-HOFFMAN**, Elisabeth
**Family & Systemic Psychotherapist**
72 Westfield Way
Wantage
Oxon
OX12 7EP
☎ 01235 760 387
elisabeth.lamhoff@talk21.com
AFT

**LANDALE**, Margaret
**Body Psychotherapist, Integrative Psychotherapist, Transpersonal Psychotherapist**
Mill House
Mill Lane
Dyers Hill
Charlbury, Oxon
OX7 3QG
☎ 01608 810 485
margaret.landale@evenlode.org.uk
CCBP

**LEA**, Tan
**Psychodrama Psychotherapist**
54 St Mary's Road
Oxford
OX4 1PY
☎ 01865 437 039
☎ 01865 716 739
tanlea@sure-start.org.uk
BPA

**LEE**, Debbie
**Psychodrama Psychotherapist**
52 Witney Road
Eynsham
Witney
Oxon
OX29 4PQ
☎ 01865 880 076
BPA

**LEVICK**, Barbara
**Psychoanalytic Psychotherapist**
12 Frenchay Road
Oxford
OX2 6TG
☎ 01865 512 683
barbaralevick@yahoo.co.uk
FPC

**LEWIS**, Sue
**Gestalt Psychotherapist**
7 South Street
Middle Barton
Oxfordshire
OX7 7BU
☎ 01869 347 721
suelewis@dircon.co.uk
GPTI

**LINDLEY-JONES**, Kerstin
**Transpersonal Psychotherapist**
15 Warwick Street
Oxford
OX4 1SZ
☎ 01865 243 351
CTP

**LOCKETT**, Arthur
**Psychoanalytic Psychotherapist**
Redwing
Kingsgrove Orchard
Main Street, Grove
Wantage, Oxon
OX12 7HT
☎ 01235 762 733
ArthurALockett@Redwing99.freeserve.co.uk
AIP

**LUTYENS**, Marianna
**Psychoanalytic Psychotherapist**
31 Warnborough Road
Oxford
OX2 6JA
☎ 01865 553 130
lutyens@freeuk.com
FPC

**LUXMOORE**, Nick
**Psychodrama Psychotherapist**
176 Divinity Road
Oxford
OX4 1LR
☎ 01865 245 510
nickluxmoore@lineone.net
BPA

**MACK SMITH**, Catharine
**Child Psychotherapist**
23 Alexandra Road
Oxford
OX2 0DD
☎ 01865 242400
ACP

**MACKINTOSH MILLARD**, Sheila
**Group Analyst**
78 Cumner Hill
Oxon
Oxford
OX2 9HU
☎ 01865 862 224
dwmillard@compuserve.com
IGA

**MILLER**, John
**Analytical Psychologist-Jungian Analyst**
19 Stanley Road
Cowley
Oxford
OX4 1QY
☎ 01865 725 203
AJA

**MILLS BURTON**, M.
**Psychoanalytic Psychotherapist**
The Old Rectory
Childrey
OX12 9UP
WMIP

**MORRIS**, Lesley Anne
**Humanistic Psychotherapist**
3 Church Green
Witney
Oxon
OX8 6AZ
☎ 01993 776 445
ed_morris@lineone.net
AHPP

**MORRIS**, Petrina
**Analytical Psychologist-Jungian Analyst, Analytical Psychotherapist (Jungian)**
Flat 17
Ponsonby House
Osburton Road
Oxford
OX2 7PQ
☎ 01865 557 253
IGAP, GAPS

**MORRISON**, Philippa
**Existential Psychotherapist**
Church Wing, The Old Rectory
Church Street
Somerton
Oxton
OX25 6NB
pmorrison@london.edu
SPCRC, SEA

**MYERS**, Liora
**Family & Systemic Psychotherapist**
♿ Educational Psychology Service
Farringdon Road
Off Wooton Road
Abbingdon
OX14 1BA
☎ 01235 554 554
liora.myers@oxfordshire.gov.uk
AFT

**NATHAN**, (Jennifer) Ruth
**Gestalt Psychotherapist, Integrative Psychotherapist**
The Old School House
Merton
Bicester
Oxon
OX25 2NF
☎ 01865 331 899
rntherapy@aol.com
GPTI, MET

**NELSON**, Helen
**Psychoanalytic Psychotherapist**
Oxfordshire Mental Healthcare NHS Trust
Psychotherapy Dept., Warneford Hosp
Warneford Lane
Headington, Oxford
OX3 7JX
☎ 01865 226 330
hminelson@tiscali.co.uk
FIP

**NISSIM**, Ruth
**Family & Systemic Psychotherapist**
♿ Dores Cottage
17 High Street
Finstock
Oxon
OX7 3DA
☎ 01993 868 147
AFT

**O'BRIEN**, Maja
**Psychoanalytic Psychotherapist**
♿ 28 Wytham Street
Oxford
OX1 4TS
☎ 01865 728 111
majaob@aol.com
FIP, UPCA

**OFFER**, Leah
**Humanistic Psychotherapist**
♿ 15 Hamilton Road
Summertown
Oxford
OX2 7PY
☎ 01865 553 380
AHPP

**ORTON**, Jane
**Humanistic and Integrative Psychotherapist**
♿ 28 Bloxham Road
Banbury
Oxfordshire
OX16 9JN
☎ 01295 262 626
janeorton.psychotherapy@btopenworld.com
BCPC

**PEGORARO**, Carla
**Transpersonal Psychotherapist**
♿ 89 Islip Road
Oxford
OX2 7SP
☎ 01865 556053
CCPE

**PORTER**, Barbara
**Transactional Analysis Psychotherapist**
Silver Birches
Peppard Common
Henley
RG9 5LR
☎ 01491 628 609
ITA, MET

**PREGNALL**, Sheila
**Psychodrama Psychotherapist**
71 Eastrop
Highworth
Swindon
Wiltshire
SN6 7AT
☎ 01793 766 862
☎ 01793 766 863
s.pregnall@ukonline.co.uk
BPA

**PROUD**, Roger
**Transpersonal Psychotherapist**
The Old School
Northmoor
Witney
Oxon
OX29 5SX
☎ 01865 303048
CCPE

**PUGHE**, Billy
**Group Analyst**
Cotswold Community
Spine Road West
Ashton Keynes
Swindon, Wilts
SN6 6QU
☎ 01285 861 239
IGA

**PYE**, Jim
**Integrative Psychotherapist**
18 Bickerton Road
Headington
Oxford
OX3 7LS
☎ 07810 785 636
MET

**REDINGTON**, Heather
**Humanistic and Integrative Psychotherapist**
18 Trenlhard Road
Stanton Fitzwarren
Nr Highworth
Wiltshire
SN6 7R2
☎ 01793 428 800
BCPC

**RENDALL**, Davina
**Sexual and Relationship Psychotherapist**
5 Abberbury Avenue
Iffley Village
Oxford
OX4 4EU
☎ 01865 717 994
davina_rendall@talk21.com
BASRT

**REYNAL**, Carmen
**Analytical Psychologist-Jungian Analyst, Analytical Psychotherapist (Jungian)**
31 Warnborough Road
Oxford
OX2 6JA
☎ 01865 511 063
☎ 01451 821 947
cqreynal@btinternet.com
IGAP, GAPS

**ROWLAND**, Catherine
**Group Analytic Psychotherapist**
522 Banbury Road
Oxford
Oxon
OX2 8LG
☎ 01865 558 190
catherine.rowland@counselling-service.ox.co.uk
UPCA

**RUGGIERI**, Gloria
**Integrative Psychotherapist**
40 Cavendish Road
Summertown
Oxford
Oxon
OX2 7TW
☎ 01865 513 363
g.ruggieri@ntlworld.com
SPCRC

**RUSCOMBE-KING**, Gillie
**Psychodrama Psychotherapist**
12 The Green
Cuddesdon
Oxford
OX44 9JZ
☎ 01865 873 721
BPA

**RYAN**, Dr Elizabeth
**Sexual and Relationship Psychotherapist**
White Cottage
Church Lane
Harwell
OX11 0HD
drlizryan@hotmail.com
BASRT

**SCULLY**, Dee
**Cognitive Behavioural Psychotherapist**
40 Lizmans Court
Silkdale Close
Oxford
OX4 2HF
☎ 07771 532 273
BABCP

**SHADBOLT**, Carole
**Transactional Analysis Psychotherapist**
Chipping Norton Psychotherapy Centre
Hawthorn, Horseshoe Lane
Chadlington
Oxon
OX7 3NB
☎ 01608 676 298
carole@hawthornesc.freeserve.co.uk
ITA

**SHAW**, Sue
**Sexual and Relationship Psychotherapist**
♿ 8 Stoke Place
Headington
Oxford
OX3 9BX
☎ 01865 763 821
BASRT

**SHEAF**, Tessa
**Cognitive Analytic Therapist**
♿ Waveney House
Radley Road
Abingdon
Oxon
OX14 3PP
sheaftessa@hotmail.com
ACAT

**SHEWAN**, Doreen
**Psychoanalytic Psychotherapist**
19 Stanley Road
Oxford
OX4 1QY
☎ 01865 725 203
SIP

**SMITH**, Eva
**Cognitive Analytic Therapist**
9 Western Road
Oxford
OX1 4LF
☎ 01865 724 351
ACAT

**SOTH**, Michael
**Body Psychotherapist, Integrative Psychotherapist**
14 Hawthorn Close
Oxford
OX2 9DY
☎ 01865 725 205
michael@soth.co.uk
C C B P

**SPARKES**, Frances
**Personal Construct Psychotherapist**
Finches
Hill Top Lane
Chinnor
Oxfordshire
OX9 4BH
☎ 020 7530 4238
kit.sparkes@lineone.net
P C P

**SPILIOS**, Joanne
**Analytical Psychologist-Jungian Analyst**
Consulting Room
Delawarr Clinic
Raleigh Park Road
Botley, Oxford
OX2 9BB
☎ 07050 261 908
☎ 01865 396 453
jmspilios@onetel.net.uk
A J A

**SPRENT**, Nigel
**Hypno-Psychotherapist**
145 Iffley Road
Oxford
OX4 1EJ
☎ 01865 281 055
nigelsprent@hotmail.com
N R H P

**STANDISH**, Elizabeth
**Psychoanalytic Psychotherapist**
46 Park Street
Abingdon
Oxon
OX14 1DG
☎ 01235 528 806
lizstandish@supanet.com
S I P

**STEVENSON**, Beaumont
**Group Analyst**
♿ School House
School Lane
Stanton St John
Oxford
OX33 1ET
☎ 01865 351 635
101531.3264@compuserve.com
I G A

**STEWARD**, Jill
**Psychoanalytic Psychotherapist**
Kenricks
Hambleden
Henley-on-Thames
Oxon
RG9 6RP
☎ 01491 576 799
F P C

**SWABEY**, ffiona
**Analytical Psychologist-Jungian Analyst**
Ivy Cottage
Chilson
Chipping Norton
West Oxfordshire
OX7 3HU
☎ 01608 676 928
☎ 020 7794 5061
ffiona@chilson.freeserve.co.uk
I G A P

**TAYLOR**, Susie
**Psychodrama Psychotherapist**
St. Brelades
15 Swinbourne Road
Littlemore
Oxford
OX4 4PQ
☎ 01865 454 932
dikkta@aol.com
B P A

**TAYLOR-BROOK**, Delia
**Transpersonal Psychotherapist**
Dartford House
Two Rivers
Station Lane
Witney
OX28 4BL
☎ 01993 778 882
☎ 07899 891 992
delia@taylor-brook.fslife.co.uk
C C P E

**THOMSON**, Simon
**Psychodrama Psychotherapist**
13 Harcourt Road
Wantage
Oxon
OX12 7DQ
☎ 01235 221 344
☎ 07715 806 606
simonlisa@ntlworld.com
B P A

**THRASHER**, Sian
**Cognitive Behavioural Psychotherapist**
Symnel
High Street
Hook Norton
Banbury, Oxfordshire
OX15 5NH
☎ 01608 737 614
sian.thrasher@iname.com
B A B C P

**TOYE**, Janet
**Cognitive Analytic Therapist**
♿ 10 Great Mead
Rewley Park
Oxford
OX1 2RB
☎ 01865 246 170
A C A T

**TUCKER**, Joanna
**Psychoanalytic Psychotherapist**
♿ 71 Headley Way
Headington
Oxford
OX3 7SR
☎ 01865 760 547
jtucker71@ntlworld.com
W M I P

**WAINER**, Hilary
**Transpersonal Psychotherapist**
19 Florence Park Road
Oxford
OX4 3PN
☎ 01865 772213
C C P E

**WATSON**, Andrea
**Child Psychotherapist**
12 Rectory Road
St. Clements
Oxford
OX4 1BW
☎ 01865 243491
andreawatson@ecosse.net
A C P

**WAYGOOD**, Rob
**Transpersonal Psychotherapist**
59 Warwick Street
Oxford
OX4 1SZ
☎ 01865 247 851
C T P

**WILSON**, Gina
**Humanistic and Integrative Psychotherapist**
24 Beaumont Street
Oxford
OX1 2NP
A H P P

**WOODS**, Eleanor
**Family & Systemic Psychotherapist**
19 Rowland Close
Wolverton
Oxford
OX2 8PW
☎ 01865 557 630
eleanorwoods@btopenworld.com
AFT

**YATES**, Helen
**Integrative Psychotherapist**
♿ The Rectory
Water Stratford Road
Finmere
Buckingham
MK18 4AT
☎ 01280 848 012
MET

## POOLE

**ANDREWS**, Stuart
**Group Analyst**
♿ 1 Caesars Way
Broadstone
Dorset
BH18 9DP
☎ 01202 695 796
stuart.andrews1@btinternet.com
IGA

**BURKE**, Erylene
**Existential Psychotherapist**
♿ 1 Caesars Way
Broadstone
Dorset
BH18 9DP
☎ 01202 695 796
erylene.burke@btinternet.com
UPCA

**FAWKES**, Liz
**Cognitive Analytic Therapist**
♿ IPTS Branksome Clinic
Layton Road
Parkstone
Poole
BH12 2BJ
☎ 01202 584 120
ACAT

**LIPSITH**, Josie
**Sexual and Relationship Psychotherapist**
Heronsmore
4 Martello Road
Poole
Dorset
BH13 7DH
☎ 01202 709 155
☎ 020 7722 9397
josie.lipsith@virgin.net
BASRT

**ROSEN**, Mrs Judith
**Sexual and Relationship Psychotherapist**
15 Barbers Gate
The Quay
Poole
BH15 1ZA
☎ 01202 670 627
☎ 01305 762 682
judyrosen@hotmail.com
BASRT

**SONES**, Michael
**Child Psychotherapist**
Child, Adolescent & Family Mental Health Service
Poole General Hospital
Longfleet Road
Poole, Dorset
BH15 2JB
☎ 01202 442741
ACP

**WEBSTER**, Mark
**Cognitive Analytic Therapist**
♿ IPTS Branksome Clinic
51a Layton Road
Poole
Dorset
BH12 2BJ
☎ 01202 298 344
ACAT

**WHITE**, Eve
**Psychodrama Psychotherapist**
Flat 1
27 Spur Hill Avenue
Poole
BH14 9PH
☎ 07789 680 571
BPA

## PORTSMOUTH

**ATTRIDGE**, Brian
**Core Process Psychotherapist**
♿ 16 Victoria Grove
Southsea
Hampshire
PO5 1NE
☎ 02392 863 266
KI

**BARDEN**, Nicola
**Analytical Psychotherapist, Psychoanalytic Psychotherapist**
♿ 9b Worsley Road
Southsea
Portsmouth
Hants
PO5 3DY
☎ 02392 843 157
nicola.barden@port.ac.uk
University of Portsmouth
Counselling Service
Nuffiels Centre St Michaels Road
Portsmouth
Hants
PO1 2ED
WMIP

**BENNETT**, Ross
**Humanistic and Integrative Psychotherapist**
The Centre in Portsmouth
20 Landport Terrace
Portsmouth
Hants
PO1 2RG
☎ 01794 368 012
rossbennett@which.net
SPEC

**BRADLEY**, Rex
**Integrative Psychotherapist**
Walden
28 Down End Road
Drayton
Portsmouth
PO6 1HU
☎ 0239 264 9266
rex@rexbradley.com
SPTI

**CARRUTHERS**, Dianna
**Humanistic and Integrative Psychotherapist**
The Centre in Portsmouth
20 Landport Terrace
Portsmouth
Hampshire
PO1 2RG
☎ 02392 830 558
☎ 02392 828 129
Dianna@thecentreinportsmouth.co.uk
Centre Psychotherapy Practice
14 Landport Terrace
Portsmouth
PO1 2RG
SPEC

**GOSS**, Diana
**Sexual and Relationship Psychotherapist**
♿ Consulting Rooms
Suite M1
Venture Tower
57-61 Fratton Road, Port
PO1 2DL
☎ 023 92 296 962
☎ 07770 453 693
diana@caretotalk.co.uk
BASRT

**HENDRA**, Theresa
**Family & Systemic Psychotherapist**
♿ Child & Family Therapy Service
The Merlin Centre
19 Villiers Road
Southsea
PO5 2NR
☎ 023 9282 1912
thendra@compuserve.com
AFT

**HOWARTH**, Kay
**Sexual and Relationship Psychotherapist**
♿ Contraception & Sexual Health Service
Ella Gordon Unit
St Mary's Hospital
Portsmouth, Hants
PO3 6AD
☎ 023 92 866 301
☎ 07803 178 571
kay.howarth@ports.nhs.uk
BASRT

**LEVER**, Maureen
**Integrative Psychotherapist**
Nelson House
15 High Street
Old Portsmouth
PO1 2LP
☎ 023 92 838 625
maureenlever@hotmail.com
SPCRC

**LYONS**, Heather
**Group Analyst**
University Counselling Service
University of Portsmouth
The Nuffield Centre
St Michael's Road
PO1 2ED
☎ 023 92 843 157
heather.lyons@port.ac.uk
IGA

**METCALF**, Jenni
**Psychodrama Psychotherapist**
♿ 35 Godwit Road
Southsea
Portsmouth
Hants
PO4 8XR
☎ 023 92 752 247
☎ 023 80 840 044
jennimetcalf@aol.com
BPA

**MILLHAM**, Alexander
**Family & Systemic Psychotherapist**
17 Harold Road
Southsea
Hants
PO4 0LR
☎ 02392 837 309
☎ 02392 653 433
alex.millham@virgin.net
Portsmouth City NHS Primary Care Trust
Battenburg Avenue Clinic
Battenburg Avenue
North End Portsmouth
PO2 0TA
IFT

**MOORE**, Terry
**Neurolinguistic Psychotherapist**
♿ 58 Northern Parade
Portsmouth
Hants.
PO2 8NE
☎ 02392 365 311
nlp.therapist@ntworld.com
NLPtCA

**QUIN**, Barbara
**Family & Systemic Psychotherapist, Psychodrama Psychotherapist**
♿ 9 Campbell Road
Southsea
Hampshire
PO5 1RH
☎ 023 92 294 818
barbaraquin@email.com
AFT, BPA

**ROSE-SMITH**, Gillian
**Humanistic and Integrative Psychotherapist**
Centre Psychotherapy Practice
14 Landport Terrace
Portsmouth
PO1 2RG
☎ 02392 830 558
10 Andover Road
Southsea
Portsmouth
PO4 9QG
SPEC

**SPILLER**, Beverly
**Body Psychotherapist, Integrative Psychotherapist**
76 Dover Road
Copnor
Portsmouth
Hants
PO3 6JX
☎ 023 92 669 595
bspiller@southdowns.ac.uk
CCBP

**STOLTE**, Eva
**Psychoanalytic Psychotherapist**
34 St. David's Road
Southsea
Portsmouth
Hants
PO5 1QN
☎ 023 9279 3983
e.stolte@ntlworld.com
AGIP

## RUTLAND

**SCHAVERIEN**, Joy
**Analytical Psychologist-Jungian Analyst**
♿ 1 The Square
South Luffenham
Oakham
Leicestershire
LE15 8NS
☎ 01780 720 117
joyschaverien@aol.com
CAP, SAP, WMIP *

## SHEFFIELD

**SHEPPARD**, Caren
**Sexual and Relationship Psychotherapist**
♿ c/o Porterbrook Clinic
Lyndhurst Road
Sheffield
☎ 0114 271 6671
caren@sheppard35.freeserve.co.uk
BASRT

## SHROPSHIRE

**BLAMPIED**, Annette N
**Psychoanalytic Psychotherapist**
30 Wharf Terrace
Madeley Heath
Nr Crewe
Cheshire
CW3 9LP
☎ 01782 751 509
☎ 01612 472 141
A.Blampied@mmu.ac.uk
UPCA

**DENHAM**, Juliet
**Gestalt Psychotherapist**
♿ Orchard House
Prescott, Nr Cleobury Mortimer
Worcs.
DY14 8RR
☎ 01746 718 231
julietdenham@synergynet.co.uk
GPTI

**FARRELL**, Derek P.
**Cognitive Behavioural Psychotherapist**
♿ 18 Danesbrook
Claverley
Wolverhampton
WV5 7BB
☎ 01746 710 052
derek.farrell@uce.ac.uk
BABCP

**FOX**, Sheila Margaret
**Family & Systemic Psychotherapist**
83 King Street
Cherry Orchard
Shrewsbury
SY2 5ET
☎ 01743 367 114
AFT

**GILLINGHAM**, Michael
**Cognitive Behavioural Psychotherapist**
21 Wigeon Grove
Leegomery
TELFORD
Shropshire
TF1 6GZ
☎ 01952 244 425
BABCP

**GOODWILLIE**, Gill
**Systemic Psychotherapist**
♿ 15 North Hermitage
Shrewsbury
SY3 7JW
☎ 01743 249 194
☎ 01902 444 021
gill@grg.enta.net
KCC

**GRIFFITHS**, Tina Carole
**Cognitive Analytic Therapist**
♿ Chaddeslode House
130 Abbey Forelate
Shrewsbury
SY2 6AX
☎ 01743 361 295
ACAT

**HARVEY**, Sandra
**Integrative Psychotherapist**
The Old Grammar School House
School Gardens
Shrewsbury
SY1 2AJ
☎ 01743 241 155
sandraharvey@talk21.com
SPCRC

**JONES**, Sue
**Family & Systemic Psychotherapist**
Bourne House
Radbrook College Complex
Radbrook Rd
Shrewsbury
SY3 9BL
☎ 01743 254 800
suejones@shropcomm.wmids.nhs.uk
FIC

**LOUMIDIS**, K
**Cognitive Behavioural Psychotherapist**
♿ The Carriages
Kemberton
Shifnal
TF11 9LH
☎ 01952 588 889
kloumidis@yahoo.co.uk
BABCP

**MCDONALD**, James T
**Psychoanalytic Psychotherapist**
20 Greenfields Road
Wombourne
Staffs
WV5 0HP
☎ 01902 893 512
WMIP

**MORGAN**, Elizabeth
**Sexual and Relationship Psychotherapist**
♿ 70 Kingston Drive
London Road
Shrewsbury
SY2
☎ 01743 354 007
BASRT

**PENCAVEL**, Ursula
**Gestalt Psychotherapist**
Bridge House
Hereford Road
Shrewsbury
SY3 7RB
☎ 01743 235 092
SPTI

**PRINGLE**, Diana
**Transactional Analysis Psychotherapist**
Brough House
The Keep
Ironbridge Road
Telford
TF7 5NN
☎ 01952 583 260
dianapringle@cix.co.uk
ITA

**PURNELL**, Christopher
**Attachment-based Psychoanalytic Psychotherapist**
Fern Cottage
5 St Luke's Road
Doseley
Telford, Shropshire
TF4 3BE
☎ 01952 503 523
☎ 07721 039 151
CAPP

**RATOFF**, Tammy
**Psychoanalytic Psychotherapist**
♿ 1 Greyfriars,
Bridgnorth
Shropshire
WV16 4JX
☎ 01746 768 675
tammy.ratoff@ukgateway.net
WMIP

**RENTOUL**, Robert W.
**Psychoanalytic Psychotherapist**
♿ 3 The Orchard
Wolverhampton
West Midlands
WV6 9PF
☎ 01902 758 504
☎
WMIP

**ROONEY**, Helen
**Cognitive Behavioural Psychotherapist**
The Oswald Centre
11-13 Church Street
Oswestry
SY11 2SU
☎ 07974 725 594
helenrooney@counsellor-uk.net
BABCP

**SPENCER**, Margaret
**Psychoanalytic Psychotherapist**
44 Underdale Road
Shrewsbury
Shropshire
SY2 5DT
☎ 01743 236 696
WMIP

**STOCKWELL**, Rose
**Psychoanalytic Psychotherapist**
P.O.Box 196
Shrewsbury
SY1 2XF
☎ 01743 240 455
rnstockwell@lycos.com
WMIP

**THORLEY**, Helen
**Psychoanalytic Psychotherapist**
Black Firs
Birks Drive, Ashley Heath
Near Market Drayton
Shropshire
TF9 4PQ
☎ 01782 427 650
LPDO

**WARD**, Dawn
**Hypno-Psychotherapist**
2 Fairfields
Chapel Lane
Yorton Heath, Shrewsbury
Shropshire
SY4 3HA
☎ 01939 210 953
NSHAP

## SOMERSET

**ASH**, Jennifer
**Core Process Psychotherapist**
23 Cleveland Street
Taunton
Somerset
TA1 1XB
☎ 1803 324 077
KI

**BICKNELL**, Sara
**Psychosynthesis Psychotherapist**
'Openings'
Bluecoat House
Sawclose
Bath
BA11 1EY
☎ 01225 858 647
☎ 01225 445 013
IPS

**BODDAERT**, Michael
**Transpersonal Psychotherapist**
22 Hexton Road
Glastonbury
Somerset
BA6 8HL
☎ 01458 830 063
CTP

**BROUGHTON**, Vivian
**Gestalt Psychotherapist**
Fox Cottage, Witham Friary
Near Frome
Somerset
BA11 5HF
☎ 01749 850 661
☎ 07813 812 852
vivian@ordinarypeople.org.uk
GPTI

**BURBACH**, Frank
**Cognitive Behavioural Psychotherapist**
♿ Psychology Department
Rosebank
Priory Parks
Wells
BA5 1TH
☎ 01749 683 300
BABCP

**BYGOTT**, Catherine
**Analytical Psychologist-Jungian Analyst**
59 High Street
Bruton
Somerset
BA10 0AW
☎ 01749 812 362
AJA

**CASHFORD**, Jules
**Analytical Psychologist-Jungian Analyst**
Woolmington Farmhouse
Ilford
Ilminster
Somerset
TA19 9EB
☎ 01460 53280
AJA

**CHURCHILL-MOSS**, Duncan
**Cognitive Behavioural Psychotherapist**
♿ High Street
Glastonbury
BA6 8UB
☎ 01458 851 654
☎ 07815 563 832
dcm@tesco.net
1 Holm Oaks
Butleigh
Glastonbury
BA6 8UB
BABCP

**COLE**, Laurence E
**Group Analytic Psychotherapist**
38 Westbrook Road
Evercreech
Shepton Mallet
Somerset
BA4 6LR
☎ 01749 830 174
laurieedwardcole@hotmail.com/laurence
cole.coleuk@virgin.net
UPCA

**DEWEY**, George
**Humanistic and Integrative Psychotherapist**
♿ 14 Northload Street
Glastonbury
Somerset
BA6 9JJ
☎ 01458 851 016
☎ 0117 977 2164
BCPC

**FORSSANDER**, Jennifer
**Analytical Psychologist-Jungian Analyst, Transpersonal Psychotherapist**
Robin Cottage
Folly Road
Kingsbury Episcopi
Somerset
TA2 6AT
☎ 020 7402 0290
☎ 01935 825 869
jenniforssander@aol.com
AJA, CCPE

**GOSLING**, Patricia
**Psychoanalytic Psychotherapist**
25 High Street
Rode
Bath
BA3 6PA
☎ 01373 8309 01
gospat@aol.com
White Hart Cottage
38 High Street
Rode
Somerset
BA3 6PA
GUILD, SIP

**GOTTO**, Jane
**Humanistic and Integrative Psychotherapist**
♿ The Terrace Psychotherapy and Natural Health Centre
35 Staplegrove Road
Taunton
TA1 1DU
☎ 01823 338 968
post@the-terrace.co.uk
SPEC

**GREENAN**, Maria
**Cognitive Behavioural Psychotherapist**
The Old Smithy
Bath Road
Oakhill
Bath
BA3 5AF
☎ 01749 841 334
BABCP

**GREGORY**, Kirby
**Cognitive Analytic Therapist**
2 Exeter Close
Burnham on Sea
Somerset
TA8 1JF
☎ 01278 795 406
ACAT

**HART**, Kate
**Cognitive Behavioural Psychotherapist**
2 Burton Place
Taunton
Somerset
TA1 4HD
☎ 01823 324 419
☎ 07074 518 169
BABCP

**HILLIER**, Anna Clare
**Psychoanalytic Psychotherapist**
Elbow Corner
Pylle
Shepton Mallet
Somerset
BA4 6SY
☎ 01749 830 983
SIP

**HOPKINS**, Jill
**Psychoanalytic Psychotherapist**
Badgers Hay, Lodes Lane
Kingston St. Mary
Taunton
Somerset
TA2 8HU
☎ 01823 451 656
GUILD, SIP

**HOWE**, Patti
**Psychosynthesis Psychotherapist**
♿ 27 Roman Way
Glastonbury
Somerset
BA6 8AB
☎ 01458 833 864
pattihowe@dial.pipex.com
PET

**JAMES**, Pat
**Psychoanalytic Psychotherapist**
♿ 2 The Dymboro
Midsomer Norton
Bath
BA3 2QU
☎ 01761 415 538
SIP, WMIP

**LOCKIE**, Gisela
**Integrative Psychotherapist**
215 Greenway Road
Taunton
Somerset
TA2 6LN
☎ 01823 323 240
CCBP

**MATHER**, Janine
**Body Psychotherapist, Integrative Psychotherapist**
The Studio at Sunny Glen
Upper New Road
Cheddar
Somerset
BS27 3DL
☎ 01934 741 097
☎ 07957 330 009
CCBP

**MCKEOWN**, Andy
**Integrative Psychotherapist**
Fairleigh House
Leigh Street
Leigh on Mendip
Somerset
BA3 5QQ
☎ 01373 812237
☎ 020 8202 1023
andy.mckeown@talk21.com
MET

**MITCHELL**, John
**Gestalt Psychotherapist**
Fox Cottage
Witham Friary
Nr. Frome
BA11 5HF
☎ 01749 850 661
GPTI

**NOWLAN**, Kate
**Psychoanalytic Psychotherapist**
Westhill House
Westend
Frome
Somerset
BA11
☎ 01373 471 172
☎ 07889 979 686
k.nowlan@macunlimited.net
FPC

**O'HAGAN**, Judith
**Transpersonal Psychotherapist**
Middlethorpe House
Curry Rivel
Nr Taunton
TA10 0JF
☎ 01458 252 236
☎ 020 8995 2250
johagan@dircon.co.uk
CTP

**PARFITT**, Will
**Psychosynthesis Psychotherapist**
27 Roman Way
Glastonbury
Somerset
BA6 8AB
☎ 01458 833 864
willparfitt@dial.pipex.com
PET

**PARKER**, Niki
**Child Psychotherapist**
Child and Adolescent Mental Health Service
18 Crook Log
Bexley Heath
Kent
BA6 8BT
☎ 020 8303 4786
☎ 020 8693 3805
parkers@dircon.co.uk
ACP

**PROCTER**, Ann
**Transpersonal Psychotherapist**
Coombe Quarry
Keinton Mandeville
Nr Somerton
Somerset
TA11 6DQ
☎ 01458 223 215
CTP

**PROCTER**, Harry
**Family & Systemic Psychotherapist, Personal Construct Psychotherapist**
♿ Petrel House
Barclay Square
Bridgewater
Somerset
TA6 5YA
☎ 01278 446 909
harry.proctor@sompar.nhs.uk
AFT, PCP

**QUARRY**, Andrew
**Cognitive Behavioural Psychotherapist**
♿ Beech Court
Southgate Park
Taunton Road
Bridgwater
TA6 3LS
☎ 01278 444 737
andrew.quarry@sompar.nhs.uk
BABCP

**REEVES**, David
**Group Analyst**
♿ 3 Hayes Cottages
Stocklinch
Nr Ilminster
TA19 9JG
☎ 0146 057 976
dreeves@hayescott.freeserve
GASW, LCP

**ROSE**, Alivia
**Gestalt Psychotherapist**
♿ The Terrace
35 Staplegrove Road
Taunton
TA1 1DG
☎ 0117 977 2164
☎ 01458 851 016
GCL

**SANDERS**, Jane
**Core Process Psychotherapist**
93 Roman Way
Glastonbury
Somerset
BA6 8AD
☎ 01458 833 382
KI

**SCOTT**, Judy
**Integrative Psychotherapist**
The Old School House
Church Street
Croscombe
Near Wells
BA5 3QS
☎ 01749 343 069
judyscott22@hotmail.com
MET

**SCOVELL**, Michael
**Psychoanalytic Psychotherapist**
1 Hawkington Cottages
Wheddon Cross
Minehead
Somerset
TA24 7AT
☎ 01643 831 164
SIP

**STEVENS**, Yvonne J
**Cognitive Analytic Therapist**
The Annexe
Blackford
Wemore
BS28
☎ 01934 713 693
ACAT

**TAIT**, Adrian
**Psychoanalytic Psychotherapist**
7 Elm Grove
Taunton
Somerset
TA1 1EG
☎ 01823 321588
aectait@hotmail.com
GUILD

**TATE**, Shan
**Family & Systemic Psychotherapist**
The Market House
Market Square
South Petherton
TA13 5BT
☎ 01460 241 339
shan.tate@btinternet.com
AFT

**VOSS**, Tony
**Gestalt Psychotherapist**
Cedar Cottage
Barrow Lane
Pilton
Somerset
BA4 4BH
☎ 0845 458 8263
tv@antipole.co.uk
GPTI

**WALKER**, Jan
**Humanistic and Integrative Psychotherapist**
15 Eastwick Road
Taunton
TA2 7HU
☎ 01823 270 480
janwalker88@hotmail.com
BCPC

**WATTS**, Paul
**Group Analyst**
♿ Somerset Partnership NHS Trust
c/o Broadway House, Broadway Park
Barclay Street
Bridgwater
TA6 5YA
☎ 01373 473 905
paul.watts@sompar.nhs.uk
GASW, IGA

**WEDDERKOPP**, Abigail
**Psychoanalytic Psychotherapist**
St Michael's
3 Upper High Street
Tauton
Somerset
TA1 3PX
☎ 01823 353 409
SIP

**WELLS**, Roger
**Psychoanalytic Psychotherapist**
Prioryfield House
20 Canon Street
Taunton
Somerset
TA1 1SW
☎ 01823 323363
☎ 01392 494466
GUILD

**WHITE**, Janet Mary
**Family & Systemic Psychotherapist**
♿ Child & Family Therapeutic Service
Somerset Partnership NHS
Petrel House, Broadway Park
Bridgwater
TA6 5LY
☎ 01278 446 909
janwhite@sompar.nhs.uk
AFT

**WILLIAMS**, Nigel
**Integrative Psychotherapist**
♿ 38 Belvedere Road
Taunton
Somerset
TA1 1HD
☎ 01823 353 009
nigel@scctaunton.plus.com
MC

**WILSON**, Jim
**Humanistic and Integrative Psychotherapist**
4 Millcross Cottages
Kingston St Mary
Taunton
TA2 8HH
☎ 01823 451 125
☎ 07890 165 431
BCPC

**WINDLE**, Ruth
**Analytical Psychologist-Jungian Analyst**
25 Vallis Way
Frome
Somerset
BA11 3BH
☎ 020 8459 5442
☎ 01373 467 661
AJA

**ZEAL**, Paul
**Psychoanalytic Psychotherapist**
♿ 12 Elm Grove
Taunton
Somerset
TA1 1EG
☎ 01823 323 099
paul.zeal@btopenworld.com
SIP

## SOUTHAMPTON

**ATWELL**, Rosemary Anne
**Sexual and Relationship Psychotherapist**
♿ Contraception & Sexual Health Service
The Quay to Health, The Quays
27 Harbour Parade
Southampton
SO15 1BA
☎ 023 80 388 916
BASRT

**CLARKE**, Isabel
**Cognitive Behavioural Psychotherapist**
♿ Psychological Therapies Service
Department of Psychiatry
Royal South Hants Hospital
Southampton
SO14 0YG
☎ 023 80 825 531
BABCP

**DAHLE**, Josephine
**Humanistic and Integrative Psychotherapist**
♿ 88 Gordon Avenue
Portswood
Southampton
SO14 6WD
☎ 02380 320 097
phinedahle@spectrumtherapy.co.uk
SPEC

**DANIELS**, Mo
**Psychodrama Psychotherapist**
♿ 14 Sir Georges Road
Southampton
Hampshire
SO15 3AT
☎ 023 80 227 778
☎ 023 80 475 130
modaniels@hotmail.com
BPA

**ELIA**, Dr Irene
**Cognitive Analytic Therapist**
1 Solent House
Cuckoo Lane
Southampton
SO14 2AN
☎ 01223 561 781
☎ 02380 220 034
me14@cam.ac.uk
ACAT

**ELLIOTT**, John
**Neurolinguistic Psychotherapist**
♿ Woolston Lodge Surgery
66 Portsmouth Road
Woolston
Southampton
SO19 9AL
☎ 02380 363 566
☎ 01489 786 621
ellojohn@hotmail.com
NLPtCA

**ELLIOTT**, Peter
**Cognitive Behavioural Psychotherapist**
♿ Dept. of Psychology
Shackleton Building
University of Southampton
Highfield, Southampton
SO17 1BJ
☎ 023 8059 5321
☎ 07889 658 295
pae@soton.ac.uk
BABCP

**FULFORD**, Ann
**Cognitive Behavioural Psychotherapist**
♿ Psychological Therapies Service
Department of Psychiatry
Royal South Hants Hospital
Southampton
SO14 0YG
☎ 023 8082 5336
BABCP

**GADSDEN**, Rosswell
**Core Process Psychotherapist**
26 Treeside Close
Shirley
Southampton
SO15 5FZ
☎ 023 8077 8978
KI

**GRAY**, Sally
**Cognitive Analytic Therapist**
♿ Psychotherapy Department,
Department of Psychiatry
Royal Sourth Hants Hospital
Brintons Terrace
Southampton
SO14 0YG
☎ 023 80 82 55 36
☎ 023 80 82 56 91
sally.gray@nhs.uk
ACAT

**HOOK**, Beatrice
**Group Analyst**
1 Henstead Road
Bedford Place
Southampton
SO15 2DE
☎ 023 80 332 182
IGA

**HOOK**, John
**Group Analyst**
♿ 1 Henstead Road
Bedford Place
Southampton
SO15 2DE
☎ 023 80 332 182
johnhook@boltblue.com
IGA

**ISAAC**, Vivien
**Cognitive Behavioural Psychotherapist**
♿ 23 Mayflower Road
Shirley
Southampton
SO15 3LU
☎ 07986 082 988
BABCP

**JACKSON**, Dr Paul
**Sexual and Relationship Psychotherapist**
♿ Psychosexual Clinic
Southampton Primary Care NHS Trust
The Quay to Health, The Quay C
27 Harbour Parade, Soton
SO15 1BA
☎ 02380 388 900
pauljackson@which.net
BASRT

**LANE**, Jeff
**Humanistic and Integrative Psychotherapist**
♿ The Grove Centre
22 Grosvenor Road
Southampton
SO17 1RT
☎ 02392 782 987
jeff@jeffreylane.co.uk
SPEC, UPCA

**LOVETT-DARBY**, Linda
**Transpersonal Psychotherapist**
9 Atlantic Close
Ocean Village
Southampton
SO14 3TA
☎ 02380 235110
CCPE

**LUNT**, Aidan
**Cognitive Analytic Therapist, Psychoanalytic Psychotherapist**
1 Henstead Road
Bedford Place
Southampton
SO15 2DE
adrian.lunt@btinternet.com
ACAT, NWIDP

**MELDRUM**, Ron
**Rational Emotive Behaviour Therapist**
12 Atherley Road
Upper Shirley
Southampton
Hants
SO15 5DQ
☎ 023 8063 1308
☎ 07970 336 471
BABCP

**MERRIOTT**, Peter
**Transpersonal Psychotherapist**
13 Evelyn Crescent
Upper Shirley
Southampton
Hampshire
SO15 5JF
☎ 02380 513 166
CTP

**PARRACK**, Norma
**Rational Emotive Behaviour Therapist**
Central Hall
St Mary Street
Southampton
SO14 1NF
☎ 023 8023 7230
BABCP

**PERRY**, Pamela
**Cognitive Analytic Therapist**
♿ The Psychotherapy Practice
2 Univesity Road
Southampton
SO17 1TJ
☎ 01425 622 922
☎ 023 80 671 558
ACAT

**ROSS**, Susan M.
**Cognitive Behavioural Psychotherapist**
Clinical Psychology Department
Department of Psychiatry
Royal South Hants Hospital
Southampton
SO14 0YG
☎ 023 8082 5531
BABCP

**SALTER**, Gill
**Humanistic and Integrative Psychotherapist**
♿ The Grove Centre
22 Grosvenor Road
Portswood
Southampton
SO17 1RT
☎ 02380 582 245
☎ 01489 893 105
gillsalter@starlands.freeserve.co.uk
UPCA

**SCOTT**, Brigitte
**Biodynamic Psychotherapist**
♿ Centre for the study of Complementary Medicine
51 Bedford Place
Southhampton
SO1 2GD
☎ 01425 652577
brigitte@flor12.freeserve.co.uk
LSBP

**THOMPSON**, Fiona
**Integrative Psychotherapist**
69 Roselands Gardens
Highfield
Southampton
SO17 1QJ
☎ 023 80 581 109
SPCRC

## STAFFORDSHIRE

**ADAMS**, Megan
**Hypno-Psychotherapist**
Hawthorn Cottage
Church Farm
Church Road, Dosthill
Tamworth, Staffs
B77 1PU
☎ 01827 281 233
megan.adams@virgin.net
NSHAP

**ANEES**, Nabil
**Psychoanalytic Psychotherapist**
3 Cooke Close
Penkridge
Stafford
ST19 5SL
nabilanees@hotmail.com
WMIP

**APERGUIS**, Caroline
**Family & Systemic Psychotherapist**
34 James Street
Stoke on Trent
ST4 5HD
☎ 01782 411 856
AFT

**BIRLEY**, Paul
**Hypno-Psychotherapist**
♿ 15 Lee Road
Hollywood
Wythall
West Midlands
B74 5NY
☎ 01564 822 967
CTIS

**BONNEBAIGT**, Andre
**Hypno-Psychotherapist**
♿ 17 Spruce Park
Rode Heath
Alsager
Cheshire
ST7 3SQ
☎ 01270 876 672
☎ 01270 763 926
andrebonnebaigt@aol.com
CTIS

**BREEZE**, Graham
**Integrative Psychotherapist**
87 Basford Bridge Lane
Cheddleton
NR Leek
Staffordshire
ST13 7EQ
☎ 01538 361 193
graham@gbreeze.freeserve.co.uk
SPTI

**BROCKLEY**, Sally
**Psychoanalytic Psychotherapist**
♿ 14 Elmsdale
Wightwick
Wolverhampton
WV6 8ED
☎ 01902 380 408
WMIP

**BROWN**, Kate
**Integrative Psychotherapist**
38 Ashbrook Close
Uttoxeter
ST14 8UL
☎ 01889 566 460
SPTI

**BULL**, Graham E
**Lacanian Analyst, Psychoanalytic Psychotherapist**
♿ 84 Main Road
Milford
Stafford
ST17 0UW
☎ 01785 660 173
tianlung003@hotmail.com
CFAR

**BUNCE**, Jillian
**Educational Therapist**
28 The Crescent
Eccleshall
ST21 6AZ
☎ 01785 850 195
jmb@bunceeccleshall.freeserve.co.uk
CFET

**BURGESS**, Tony
**Hypno-Psychotherapist**
8 Prescott Drive
Penkridge
Stafford
ST19 5EQ
☎ 01785 716 683
☎ 07989 469 570
tony@coaching-and-training.com
CTIS

**CARPENTER**, David
**Neurolinguistic Psychotherapist**
136 Lichfield Road
Walsall Wood
Walsall
West Midlands
WS9 9PD
☎ 01543 820 092
david@helpishere.co.uk
NLPtCA

**CHALLIS**, Suzy
**Psychoanalytic Psychotherapist**
Rosemead
7 The Village
Keele
Staffordshire
ST5 5AD
☎ 01782 635 807
LPDO

**CHEVINS**, Lynda
**Analytical Psychotherapist**
The Stables
Tamhorn Park Farm
Fisherwick Road
Whittington, Lichfield
WS14 9JJ
☎ 01543 433 335
WMIP

**CORKER**, Enid
**Psychoanalytic Psychotherapist**
55 The Avenue
Harpfields
Stoke-on-Trent
ST4 6BT
☎ 01782 662 655
enidcorker@aol.com
AGIP

**COX**, Margaret
**Analytical Psychotherapist**
♿ 18, The Charters
Lichfield
WS13 7LX
☎ 01543 263 916
WMIP

**CRISP**, Jennifer
**Psychodynamic Psychotherapist**
♿ Harplands Hospital
Psychotherapy Department
Hilton Road,
Stoke on Trent
ST4 6TH
☎ 01782 441 674
WMIP

**CROSS**, Susan
**Cognitive Behavioural Psychotherapist**
1 Nab Hill Court
Leek
Staffordshire
ST13 8BZ
☎ 01583 387 486
sandscross@hotmail.com
BABCP

**DARONGKAMAS**, Jurai
**Cognitive Behavioural Psychotherapist**
♿ Adult Psychology Service
1st floor, 12 Park Road
Cannock
WS11 1JN
☎ 01543 431 564
BABCP

**DUNN**, Elizabeth
**Psychodynamic Psychotherapist**
♿ The Mount
Longton Road
Barlaston
Stoke on Trent
ST12 9AA
☎ 01782 372 911
☎ 01782 372 424
VAPP

**FELTON**, Mo
**Transactional Analysis Psychotherapist**
Hynch Cottage
34 Church Road
Dordon
Tamworth
B78 1RW
☎ 01827 897 733
☎ 01922 639 680
c.felton@ntlworld.com
ITA

**GHENT**, Rita
**Integrative Psychotherapist**
♿ 17 Willotts Hill Road
Newcastle under Lyme
Staffordshire
ST5 7TF
☎ 01782 560 360
SPTI

**GRAY**, Peter
**Family & Systemic Psychotherapist**
♿ 33 Church Lane
Oulton
Nr. Stone
Staffs
ST15 8UB
☎ 01785 819 217
jameg@lineone.net
AFT

**GREGORY**, Kayt
**Integrative Psychotherapist**
28 Lichfield Drive
Great Haywood
Stafford
ST18 0SX
☎ 01889 882 435
SPTI

**GRIFFITHS**, E. Anne
**Psychoanalytic Psychotherapist**
59 Stockwood Road
Seabridge
Newcastle-under-Lyme
ST5 3LQ
☎ 01782 871 909
annegriffiths@doctors.org.uk
St Chad's House
The Foundation NHS Trust
Corporation Street
Stafford
ST16 3AG
UPCA

**HALLARD**, Sharon
**Group Analyst**
31A St Edward Street
Leek
Staffordshire
ST13 5DN
☎ 07831 295 599
sharon@hallard.com
IGA

**HARRINGTON**, Leslie
**Psychoanalytic Psychotherapist**
♿ The Spires Practice
St Chad's Health Centre
Dimbles Lane
Lichfield, Staffordshire
WS13 7HT
☎ 01543 258987
leslie.harrington@sshawebmail.nhs.uk
WMIP

**HARRIS**, Gerald A.
**Hypno-Psychotherapist**
♿ 78 Park View Road
Streetly
Sutton Coldfield
West Midlands
B74 4PS
☎ 01213 533 131
geraldharris@hypnosis9.freeserve.co.uk
NRHP

**HOWARD TAYLER**, Jaqueline
**Gestalt Psychotherapist**
12 Munro Street
Stoke on Trent
ST4 5HA
☎ 01782 412 841
SPTI

**HOWELL**, Hilary
**Systemic Psychotherapist**
Learning Disabilities Team
Margaret Stanhope Centre
Belvidere Rd
Burton-on- Trent
DE13 ORB
☎ 01283 505 330
Hillary.howell@ssh-tr.nhs.uk
FIC

**HOWELL**, Judy
**Hypno-Psychotherapist**
41 Badgers Bank Road
Four Oaks
Sutton Coldfield
West Midlands
B74 4ER
☎ 0121 308 7566
☎ 07761 242 834
j.e.howell@talk21.com
CTIS

**KUNDU**, Dr Arabinda
**Sexual and Relationship Psychotherapist**
♿ South Staffordshire NHS Healthcare Trust
Sexual Health Service
St Michael's Hospital
Trent Valley, Lichfield
WS13 6EF
☎ 01543 414 555
☎ 07803 668 023
BASRT

**LINN**, Iris
**Hypno-Psychotherapist**
♿ 52 Clive Road
Pattingham
Wolverhampton
WV6 7BY
☎ 01902 701 023
NRHP

**MOLONEY**, Paul
**Cognitive Behavioural Psychotherapist**
29 Main Street
Alrewas
Burton on Trent
DE13 7AA
☎ 0121 685 6685
☎ 01283 791 754
BABCP

**NEWELL**, Adrian
**Cognitive Psychotherapist**
♿ South Staffs NHS Trust
St. Georges Hospital
Corporation Street
Stafford
ST16 3AG
☎ 01785 221 429
BABCP

**OSBORN**, James
**Family & Systemic Psychotherapist**
South Staffordshire Healthcare NHS Trust
Swiftbrook House
Corporation Street
Stafford
ST16 3LU
☎ 01785 221 375
james.osborn@ssh-tr.nhs.uk
FIC

**OVERS**, Nicola
**Personal Construct Psychotherapist**
98 Westwood Road
Leek
Staffs
ST13 8DL
☎ 01827 308 820
☎ 01538 386 681
mnonjo@aol.com
PCP

**PHELPS**, Gwyneth
**Transactional Analysis Psychotherapist**
Beacon Cottage
69 Beacon Street
Lichfield
WS13 7AS
☎ 01543 415 651
☎ 07930 367 330
gwynphelps@aol.com
ITA

**PRESTON**, Margaret
**Integrative Arts Psychotherapist**
Seefeld
Trent Road
Stone
Stafford
ST15 8LE
☎ 01785 851 3399
SPTI

**QUEENING**, Vanessa
**Psychodrama Psychotherapist**
16 Newcastle Road
Leek
Staffs
ST13 5RW
☎ 01538 383 592
☎ 01270 614 400
v.queening@webhousebstm.hp.nhs.uk
BPA

**REGAN**, Catherine
**Integrative Psychotherapist**
18 Hartington Street
Wolstanton
Newcastle-under-Lyme
Staffordshire
☎ 01782 866973
SPTI

**SCHREIBER**, Kaye
**Systemic Psychotherapist**
♿ 3 Inglewood Drive
Porthill
Newcastle-under-Lyme
ST5 0DY
KCC

**SHUBINSKY**, Kath
**Integrative Psychotherapist**
53 Cedar Way
Stafford
ST17 0NB
☎ 01922 416 223
☎ 01902 444 036
kathshubinsky@btopenworld.com
SPTI

**SUTTON**, Elizabeth
**Cognitive Behavioural Psychotherapist**
Dove Clinic
Brookside
Rolleston-on-Dove
Burton-on-Trent
DE13 9BD
☎ 01283 812 362
dove.clinic@graegmoor.co.uk
BABCP

**TAYLOR**, Jon
**Cognitive Behavioural Psychotherapist**
Margaret Stanhope Centre
Outwoods
Belvedere Road
Burton on Trent, Staffs
DE13 0RB
☎ 01332 749 876
☎ 01283 505 330
pjt0007@currantbun.com
BABCP

**THOMPSON**, Geoffrey
**Gestalt Psychotherapist**
The Pines
9 Greenhill Gardens
Wombourne
Staffordshire
WV5 0JB
☎ 01902 898 160
thr@talk21.com
SPTI

**WALLACE**, Norma
**Integrative Psychotherapist**
"Two Hoots"
Audmore
Gnosall
Stafford
ST20 0HF
☎ 01785 824 033
norma@wallaceclan.freeserve.co.uk
MET

**WARD**, Rachel
**Personal Construct Psychotherapist**
1, The Meadows
Uttoxeter Road
Kingstone
Nr. Uttoxeter
ST14 8QE
☎ 01889 500 410
PCP

**WILES**, Margaret
**Integrative Psychotherapist**
18 Cornwall Avenue
Clayton
Newcastle under Lyme
Staffordshire
ST5 3DJ
☎ 01782 614 222
SPTI

**WOOLLISCROFT**, Jessica
**Humanistic Psychotherapist**
72 Station Road
Alsager
Stoke on Trent
ST7 2PD
☎ 01625 663 547
☎ 01270 884 594
cjwoolliscroft@supanet.com
AHPP

## SUFFOLK

**ALLEN**, Tessa
**Psychoanalytic Psychotherapist**
63 Victoria Road
Woodbridge
Suffolk
IP12 1EL
☎ 01394 388 654
NWIDP

**ASKIN**, Pauline
**Systemic Psychotherapist**
♿ Meridian House
62 Alexandra Road
Lowestoft
Suffolk
NR32 1NR
☎ 01502 533 500
IFT

**BARCLAY**, Bridget (Biddy)
**Integrative Arts Psychotherapist**
Aldeburgh
IP15
☎ 01728 454 007
biddybarclay@btconnect.com
IATE

**BARNARD**, Conrad
**Cognitive Analytic Therapist**
♿ St Clements Hospital
Foxhall Road
Ipswich
IP3 8LS
☎ 01473 329 038
☎ 01473 329 000
Conrad.barnard@lhp.nhs.uk
ACAT

**BARRETT**, Jenny
**Psychoanalytic Psychotherapist**
"Mardle"
The Green
Monk Soham
Woodbridge
IP13 7EZ
☎ 01206 572 205
☎ 01728 628 538
jennyagbarrett@any-mail.co.uk
CSP

**BELL**, Lydia J.
**Cognitive Behavioural Psychotherapist**
Ivry House
23 Henley Road
Ipswich
IP1 3TF
☎ 01473 214 811
BABCP

**BUCKLER**, Jackie
**Sexual and Relationship Psychotherapist**
♿ 19 Brookhill Way
Rushmere St Andrew
Ipswich
Suffolk
IP4 5UL
☎ 01473 716 212
☎ 07979 906 848
jackie@buckler2.fsnet.co.uk
BASRT

**CROSS**, Jacqueline
**Integrative Psychotherapist**
♿ 12 Bowthorpe Close
Ipswich
Suffolk
IP1 3PZ
☎ 01473 438 426
jacuelinecross@yahoo.com
MET

**CULLUM**, Sylvia
**Sexual and Relationship Psychotherapist**
♿ Briar Hill
Aldringham
Suffolk
IP16
☎ 01728 452 442
BASRT

**DAVISON**, Susan
**Psychoanalytic Psychotherapist**
♿ 30 Seckford Street
Woodbridge
Suffolk
IP12 4LY
☎ 01394 389 574
sueinwoodbridge@hotmail.com
GUILD

**EASTON**, Margaret
**Psychoanalytic Psychotherapist**
79 College Road
Farmlingham
Suffolk
IP13 9EU
☎ 01728 724 882
margaret.easton@ukonline.co.uk
AGIP

**EDWARDS**, Harry
**Integrative Psychotherapist**
The Rectory
Marlesford
Woodbridge
Suffolk
IP13 0AT
☎ 01728 746 747
harry@psalm23.demon.co.uk
MET

**FAULL**, Keith
**Family & Systemic Psychotherapist**
76 Oxford Street
Ipswich
Suffolk
IP1 3PE
☎ 01473 420 762
keithandvickyfaull@tinyworld.co.uk
AFT

**FRANCES**, Jane
**Humanistic Psychotherapist**
Juniper Cottage
The Common
Ashfield Road
Norton, Bury St Edmunds
IP31 3NF
☎ 01359 241 498
☎ 01223 416 166
janefrances@beeb.net
AHPP

**GRAHAM**, Hilary
**Family & Systemic Psychotherapist**
♿ 29 Benhall Green
Benhall
Saxmundham
Suffolk
IP17 1HL
☎ 01728 602 563
hilaryhg@aol.com
AFT

**GRIFFITHS**, Sheila
**Systemic Psychotherapist**
♿ Wyndham House
Wickham Market
Woodbridge
Suffolk
IP13 0QU
KCC

**HOARE**, Elizabeth
**Systemic Psychotherapist**
St Nicholas Yard
Diss
Norfolk
IP22
☎ 01379 651 762
KCC

**HUGHES**, Ann
**Psychoanalytic Psychotherapist**
Lindos Psychotherapy Centre
Saddlemarker's Lane
Melton, Woodbridge
Suffolk
IP12 1PP
☎ 01394 380 100
☎ 01986 788 170
ah300@cam.co.uk
GUILD

**JOHNSTON**, Di
**Sexual and Relationship Psychotherapist**
29 Rosebery Road
Ipswich
IP4 1PS
☎ 01473 420 550
☎ 07903 624 524
dijohnston@ntlworld.com
BASRT

**JONES**, Sue
**Integrative Psychotherapist**
♿ Southwold Hospital
Fieldstyle Road
Suffolk
IP18 6LD
☎ 01508 528800
susiemjones@yahoo.co.uk
MET

**LEA**, Ian
**Family & Systemic Psychotherapist**
2 Coucy Close
Framlingham
Woodbridge
IP13 9AX
☎ 01728 724 502
ianlea@suffolkonline.net
AFT

**MACHON**, Adrian
**Psychosynthesis Psychotherapist**
The Mill House
The Green
Beyton
IP30 9AF
☎ 01359 271 930
☎ 0208 047 5274
adrian.j.macho@gsk.com
IPS

**MCCABE**, Ruth
**Group Analyst**
♿ Wenhaston
Halesworth
IP19
☎ 01502 478 295
☎ 07710 275 738
ruth.mccabe@ntlworld.com
IGA

**MCCORMICK**, Elizabeth
**Cognitive Analytic Therapist, Transpersonal Psychotherapist**
The Old Woodyard
Dunwich
Suffolk
IP17 3DW
☎ 01728 648 672
ACAT, CTP

**MOHAN**, Terry
**Neurolinguistic Psychotherapist**
20 Nelson Road
Bury St. Edmunds
Suffolk
IP33 3AG
☎ 01284 701 505
zen33060@zen.co.uk
NLPtCA

**POOLE**, Robert
**Group Analytic Psychotherapist**
♿ 6 East Lane
Bawdsey
Suffolk
IP12 3AP
☎ 01394 411 696
amabuthu@hotmail.com
FIP

**READER**, Fran
**Sexual and Relationship Psychotherapist**
♿ Ipswich Hospital NHS Trust
Heath Road
Ipswich
Suffolk
IP4 5PD
☎ 01473 703 016
BASRT

**RIDGEWAY**, Nicola Louise
**Cognitive Behavioural Psychotherapist**
2 Dalham Road
Ousden
Newmarket
CB8 8UA
☎ 01638 500 182
NicolaRidgeway@aol.com
BABCP

**SHINGLER**, Christopher
**Psychosynthesis Psychotherapist**
Vanessa Villa
4 Snape Road
Tunstall
Suffolk
IP12 2JL
☎ 01728 688 898
IPS

**SINEY**, Sky
**Psychoanalytic Psychotherapist**
Tandem House
The Hill, Hartest
Bury St Edmunds
Suffolk
IP29 4ES
☎ 01284 830 203
sky.siney@macunlimited.net
AGIP

**SLUCKIN**, Andy
**Systemic Psychotherapist**
♿ Child & Adolescent Mental Health Service
Meridian House
62 Alexandra Road
Lowestoft
NR32 1NR
☎ 01603 507 934
☎ 01502 533 500
asluckin@aol.com
KCC

**SUCHER**, Ingeborg A.
**Psychoanalytic Psychotherapist**
♿ 33 Sussex Road
Woodfield Park
Bury St. Edmunds
IP32 6TE
☎ 01284 702932
Ingeborg.Sucher@ukgateway.net
IPSS

**WALLER**, Rosa
**Integrative Psychotherapist**
Novocastria, Sandy Lane
Waldring Field
Woodbridge
IP12 4QY
☎ 01473 736 224
rosawaller@hotmail.com
SPCRC

**WESTCOTT**, Emma
**Integrative Arts Psychotherapist**
11 Haven
Thorpeness
Leiston
IP16 4NN
☎ 01728 452 321
IATE

**WIGHTWICK**, Helen
**Psychodynamic Psychotherapist**
Chapel House
Lindsey
Nr Hadleigh
Suffolk
IP7 6QA
☎ 01787 211 120
helen.wightwick@tiscali.co.uk
VAPP

**WRIGHT**, James
**Psychoanalytic Psychotherapist**
Three Chimneys
Crown Lane
Orford, Woodbridge
Suffolk
IP12 2NB
☎ 01394 450 497
☎ 020 7385 6279
FPC

**WRIGHT**, Kenneth
**Couple Psychoanalytic Psychotherapist**
♿ 6 Queen Street
Hadleigh
Ipswich
Suffolk
IP7 5DZ
☎ 01473 828 976
kenwright@doctors.org.uk
SCPP

## SURREY

**ADDENBROOKE**, Mary
**Analytical Psychologist, Psychoanalytic Psychotherapist**
Oaks
Forest Road
Colgate, Horsham
West Sussex
RH12 4SZ
☎ 01293 851 826
mary.addenbrooke@lineone.net
GUILD

**AGGLETON**, Sue
**Integrative Psychotherapist**
Noel Cottage
7 Tekels Park
Camberley
Surrey
GU15 2LE
☎ 01276 676367
saggleton@hotmail.com
MET

**ALLEN**, Valerie
**Transpersonal Psychotherapist**
36 Arethusa Way
Bisley
Woking
GU24 9BX
☎ 01483 853 896
Valallen36@yahoo.co.uk
CCPE

**ASHLEY**, Anne
**Analytical Psychologist-Jungian Analyst**
Timmynoggy House
49 Godstone Road
Purley
Surrey
CR8 2AN
☎ 020 8660 9544
☎ 020 8660 3099
CAP *

**AUSTIN**, Bill
**Psychoanalytic Psychotherapist**
12 Glebelands
West Molesey
Surrey
KT8 2PY
☎ 020 8979 2768
bilaustin@aol.com
IPSS

**BAKER**, Moke
**Psychoanalytic Psychotherapist**
59 Hillside Road
Ashtead
Surrey
KT21 1RZ
☎ 01372 275 885
Mokeuk@aol.com
FPC

**BARKER**, Jocelyn
**Integrative Psychotherapist**
1 Valley View
Godalming
Surrey
GU7 1RD
☎ 01483 414 517
jocelyn.barker@ukgateway.net
The Holistic Centre
The Barn, Wiggins Yard
Bridge Street
Godalming
GU7
MET

**BARNETT**, Laura M E
**Existential Psychotherapist**
♿ Haling House
38 Haling Park Road
South Croydon
CR2 6NE
☎ 02086 868 525
UPCA

**BATCHELOR**, Carol
**Humanistic Psychotherapist**
♿ 46 Westville Road
Thames Ditton
Surrey
KT7 0UJ
☎ 020 8398 5990
AHPP

**BAYLEY**, Eva
**Psychosynthesis Psychotherapist**
125 Addison Road
Guildford
Surrey
GU1 3QE
☎ 01483 531 552
evabaley@aol.com
PET

**BEER**, Margaret E
**Psychoanalytic Psychotherapist**
♿ 7 Fabyc House
Cumberland Road
Kew Gardens
Surrey
TW9 3HH
☎ 020 8940 7353
FPC

**BENJAMIN**, Joan
**Psychoanalytic Psychotherapist**
The Roses
Farnham Lane
Haslemere
Surrey
GU27 1HA
☎ 01428 644 605
AGIP

**BENNETT**, Margaret
**Family & Systemic Psychotherapist**
♿ Kingston Gate Therapy
285 Kings Road
Kingston upon Thames
KT2 5JJ
☎ 020 8546 9785
☎ 020 8296 1381
margaret@kseltd.fsnet.co.uk
IFT

**BENTO-THIEME**, Maria
**Transpersonal Psychotherapist**
62 Ellerton Road
Surbiton
KT6 7TX
☎ 020 8286 4399
CTP

**BETON**, Linda
**Transpersonal Psychotherapist**
'Sandycrest'
Millfield Lane
Tadworth
KT2 6RP
☎ 01737 832 563
CCPE

**BHAT**, Radha
**Group Analyst**
♿ Child & Adolescent Mental Health Service
Langley House
Church Lane
Oxted
RH8 9LN
☎ 01883 388 303
☎ 020 8462 7722
IGA

**BLACKWOOD**, Renate
**Psychoanalytic Psychotherapist**
♿ 7 Esher Park Avenue
Esher
Surrey
KT10 9NP
☎ 01372 462 852
01372 462 852
FPC

**BOA**, Quint
**Integrative Psychotherapist**
300 Kings Road
Kingston
KT2 5JL
☎ 020 8546 5190
mail@shootyou.co.uk
SPCRC

**BOFF**, Roger
**Hypno-Psychotherapist**
88 Ingleboro Drive
Purley
Surrey
CR8 1EF
☎ 02086 681 128
rjboff@hotmail.com
NSHAP

**BRENNAN**, Catherine
**Integrative Psychotherapist**
20 Brokes Crescent
Reigate
Surrey
RH2 9PS
☎ 01737 213 170
☎ 07811 347 752
MET

**BRIDGE**, Jenny
**Transactional Analysis Psychotherapist**
569 Upper Richmond Road West
Richmond
Surrey
TW10 5DU
☎ 02088 782 658
☎ 07766 563 959
jenny@jenny-b.co.uk
ITA

**BROADBENT**, Sara
**Psychoanalytic Psychotherapist**
♿ 4 Dynevor Road
Richmond
Surrey
TW10 6PF
☎ 020 8 940 2228
Sara.peregrine@zoom.co.uk
IPSS

**BROWN**, Gillian Anne
**Family & Systemic Psychotherapist**
May Bank
29 Mountside
Guildford
Surrey
GU2 5JD
☎ 01483 504 360
ggabrown@29mountside.freeserve.co.uk
AFT

**BROWN**, Lesley
**Gestalt Psychotherapist, Integrative Psychotherapist, Integrative Psychosynthesis Psychotherapist**
Bright Water
Dunally Park
Shepperton
TW17 8LJ
☎ 01932 220 590
GPTI, MET, RE.V

**BURNS**, Serena
**Group Analytic Psychotherapist**
♿ Surrey Hampshire Border Trust
Child & Family Consultation Service
Buryfields Clinic
61 Buryfields, Guildford
GU2 4AX
☎ 01483 418 103
FPC

**BYRON**, Geraldine
**Family & Systemic Psychotherapist**
10 Upper West Street
Reigate
RH2 9HX
☎ 01737 225 631
AFT

**CARR**, Brede
**Psychoanalytic Psychotherapist**
9 Chepstow Rise
Croydon
Surrey
CR0 5LX
☎ 020 8667 0970
brede.carr@virgin.net
FPC

**CARROLL**, Helen
**Humanistic Psychotherapist**
42 Ross Road
Wallington
Surrey
SM6 8QR
☎ 020 8669 4474
helencarroll77@hotmail.com
AHPP

**CASSIDY**, Mandy
**Integrative Psychotherapist**
♿ 13 Victoria Road
Guildford
Surrey
GU1 4DJ
☎ 01483 566 928
MET

**CHALFONT**, Alexandra
**Neurolinguistic Psychotherapist**
19 Rosewood Court
Alexandra Road
Kingston upon Thames
Surrey
KT2 6SJ
☎ 02085 464 178
ac@integralfocus.co.uk
NLPtCA

**CHANDLER**, Diana
**Psychosynthesis Psychotherapist**
9 Basil Gardens
Shirley Oaks Village
Croydon
CR0 8XD
☎ 02086 569 209
IPS

**CHATTERJEE**, Sherna Ghyara
**Psychoanalytic Psychotherapist**
♿ 40 Couchmore Avenue
Esher
Surrey
KT10 9AU
☎ 02083 390 061
chatterjee@enterprise.net
NAFSI

**CHILCOTT**, Diana
**Family & Systemic Psychotherapist**
55 Wolsey Road
East Molesy
Surrey
KT8 9EW
☎ 020 8979 9036
dianachilcott@btinternet.com
AFT

**CHIMERA**, Kathleen
**Systemic Psychotherapist**
P. O. Box 230
Leatherhead
Surrey
KT22 8WZ
☎ 01372 376 577
chipchimera@aol.com
IFT

**CHRISTIE**, Rose
**Psychoanalytic Psychotherapist**
17 Woodside Road
New Malden
Surrey
KT3 3AW
☎ 020 8942 3835
rose@christie.intonet.co.uk
FPC

**CHURCH**, John
**Cognitive Behavioural Psychotherapist**
♿ The Counselling Concern
66 Avenue Road
Belmont
Sutton
SM2 6JB
☎ 020 8715 4547
☎ 07958 651322
johnchurch@thecounsellingconcern.freeserve.co.uk
BABCP

**CLARK**, Margaret
**Psychoanalytic Psychotherapist**
11 The Broadway
Manor Lane
Sutton
Surrey
SM1 4BU
☎ 020 8661 0007
FPC

**CLAYTON**, Gillian
**Lacanian Analyst, Psychoanalytic Psychotherapist**
92 Clyde Road
Croydon
CR0 6SW
☎ 020 8656 7864
gillclayton@blueyonder.co.uk
CFAR

**CLEAVELY**, Evelyn
**Couple Psychoanalytic Psychotherapist**
8 Cox's Avenue
Grange Farm
Upper Halliford
Shepperton, Middlesex
TW17 8TF
☎ 01932 789 088
SCPP

**COLDICOTT**, Tim
**Family & Systemic Psychotherapist**
♿ The White Cottage
Hamlash Lane
Frensham
Surrey
GU1 3AU
☎ 01252 792 609
coldicott@onetel.net.uk
AFT

**COLLINS**, John
**Hypno-Psychotherapist**
Farm Cottage
Lockner Holt
Chilworth
Guildford
GU4 8RG
☎ 01483 898 913
NRHP

**CONNOLLY**, Cath
**Family & Systemic Psychotherapist**
♿ Croydon CAMHS
South London & Maudsley NHS Trust
3 Lennard Road
Croydon
CR0 2UL
☎ 020 8700 8800
☎ 020 8462 7722
Cath.connolly@slam-tr.nhs.uk
IFT

**COOMBES**, Clare
**Integrative Psychotherapist, Primal Psychotherapist**
64 Montacute Road
Morden
Surrey
SM4 6RL
☎ 02086 407 665
clare.pam@btinternet.com
LAPP

**COOPER**, Jane
**Gestalt Psychotherapist**
67 Southdown Road
Hersham
Walton-on-Thames
Surrey
KT12 4PJ
☎ 01932 246 407
jane.doc@virgin.net
SPTI

**COTTRELL**, Teresa
**Integrative Psychotherapist**
7 Delmey Close
Croydon
CR0 5QD
☎ 020 8680 9282
trees@seven78.freeserve.co.uk
SPCRC

**CREASE**, Jennifer
**Psychodynamic Psychotherapist**
Row Town
Addlestone
KT15
☎ 01932 855 420
FPC

**CRIPPS**, Suzanne
**Family & Systemic Psychotherapist**
♿ 8 Dornton Road
South Croydon
CR2 7DP
☎ 020 8686 4679
ccripps@supanet.com
AFT

**CUTTING**, Penny
**Integrative Psychotherapist**
158 Foxley Lane
Purley
CR8 3NF
☎ 020 8660 8676
SPCRC

**DARRELL**, Linda
**Analytical Psychologist-Jungian Analyst, Psychoanalytic Psychotherapist**
9 Burghley Avenue
New Malden
Surrey
KT3 4SW
CAP, FPC *

**DAVENPORT**, Hilary
**Psychodrama Psychotherapist**
♿ 4 Bradstone Brook Cottages
New Road
Chilworth
GU4 8LS
☎ 01483 504 882
BPA

**DAVIDSON**, Jill
**Existential Psychotherapist**
31 Bearfield Road
Kingston-Upon-Thames
KT2 5ET
☎ 020 8549 7938
Davidsonjill@bearfield.freeserve.co.uk
UPCA

**DAVIES**, Ann
**Psychoanalytic Psychotherapist**
The Old Dog Kennel Hill House
Woodside Road
Chiddingfold
Nr. Godalming
GU8 4RF
☎ 01428 683 102
AGIP

**DAY**, Laurie
**Integrative Psychotherapist**
4 Squirrels Way
Epsom
Surrey
KT18 8AQ
☎ 01372 747 616
MET

**DE BERKER**, Patricia
**Analytical Psychotherapist**
Ferndown Cottage
3 Hillier Road
Guildford
Surrey
GU1 2JG
☎ 01483 504 554
FIP

**DE BERKER**, Paul
**Psychoanalytic Psychotherapist**
Ferndown Cottage
3 Hillier Road
Guildford
Surrey
GU1 2JG
☎ 01483 504 554
FIP

**DELPORT**, Juan
**Transactional Analysis Psychotherapist**
♿ Farnham Road Hospital
Farnham Road
Guildford
Surrey
GU2 7LX
☎ 01483 223949
juan.delport@which.net
ITA

**DENINGTON**, Julia
**Integrative Psychotherapist**
Consulting Room in Richmond
Surrey
☎ 07770 467187
jdeningtonpsychotherapy@hotmail.com
MC

**DHILLON STEVENS**, Harbrinder
**Integrative Psychotherapist**
Corner Cottage
Guildford Road
Chertsey
KT16 9RU
☎ 01932 874902
harbrinder.dhillonstevens@virgin.net
MET

**DINNING**, Penelope J
**Systemic Psychotherapist**
96 Gordon Road
Camberley
GU15 2JE
☎ 0127 629 273
☎ 01784 248 666 ext 241
Spelthorne College
Church Road
Ashford
TW15 2XD
KCC

**DODSWORTH**, Evelyn
**Sexual and Relationship Psychotherapist**
8 Croham Close
South Croydon
Surrey
CR2 0DA
☎ 020 8688 1468
evelyn.dodsworth@btopenworld.com
BASRT

**DOOR**, Annette
**Existential Psychotherapist**
29 Templemere
Weybridge
Surrey
KT13 9PA
☎ 01932 830 682
ad@arbor-ltd.demon.co.uk
UPCA

**DOUBLE**, Veronica
**Psychodynamic Psychotherapist**
52 Selcroft Road
Purley
CR8 1AS
☎ 020 8660 7466
CCOPPP

**DOWLING**, Deirdre
**Child Psychotherapist**
10 Dowlans Road
Great Bookham
Surrey
KT23 4LE
☎ 01372 453 451
ACP

**DUCKHAM**, Jennifer
**Analytical Psychologist-Jungian Analyst, Analytical Psychotherapist, Group Analyst**
♿ 7 Upper Park Road
Kingston-upon-Thames
Surrey
KT2 5LB
☎ 020 8546 4173
jenny@sevduck.fsnet.co.uk
CAP, IGA *

**DUDLEY**, Jane M
**Group Analytic Psychotherapist**
21 Downsway
Whyteleafe
Surrey
CR3 0EW
☎ 02086 601 402
Jane.Dudley@down21.freeuk.net
UPCA

**DUFFIELD**, Ruth
**Transpersonal Psychotherapist**
3 Albany Place
Egham
Surrey
TW20 9HG
☎ 01784 472069 (t/f)
matt.duffield@virgin.net
CCPE

**DURBAN**, Ann
**Transpersonal Psychotherapist**
Omega, Shaftesbury Road
Bisley
Woking
Surrey
GU24 9ER
☎ 01483 799277
CCPE

**EDELEANU**, Andrea K
**Cognitive Behavioural Psychotherapist**
♿ The Horizon Centre
Farnham Road Hospital
Farnham Road
Guildford
GU2 7LX
☎ 01483 443 704
andy.edeleanu@shb-tr.sthames.nhs.uk
BABCP

**ERTELT**, Sylvia
**Psychoanalytic Psychotherapist**
15 Hedgeway
Onslow Village
Guildford
SURREY
GU2 7RB
☎ 01483 566940
sylvia@analyst.force9.co.uk
ARBS

**ESTERHUYZEN**, Alex
**Analytical Psychotherapist (Jungian)**
Leylands Farm
West Park Road
Newchapel
Surrey
RH7 6HT
☎ 01342 836 588
☎ 07770 471 975
alexe@btinternet.com
IGAP

**EVANS**, Tricia
**Sexual and Relationship Psychotherapist**
♿ 38 Blackborough Road
Reigate
Surrey
RH2 7BX
☎ 01737 240 952
tricia@asdellevans.co.uk
BASRT

**EYRES**, Robert
**Group Analyst**
Surrey Oaklands Pyschotherapy Service
2 Whitepost Hill
Redhill
RH1 6BD
☎ 01737 277 706
rob.eyres@surreyoaklands.nhs.uk
IGA

**EZEKIEL**, Lyn
**Psychoanalytic Psychotherapist**
Flat 1, June Rose House
23 Havelock Road
Croydon
CR0 6QQ
☎ 020 8348 4125
GUILD

**FERNANDO - O'CONNOR**, Chandra
**Systemic Psychotherapist**
♿ Family Thearpy Service
Surrey Hampshire Borders NHS Trust
Horizon Centre, Farnham Road H
Farnham Road, Guildford
☎ 01252 515 053
chandra.oconnor@yahoo.com
KCC

**FIELD**, Kate
**Psychoanalytic Psychotherapist**
31 Havelock Road
Addiscombe
Croydon
Surrey
CR0 6QQ
☎ 020 8 656 3666
GUILD

**FISHER NORTON**, Jane
**Psychoanalytic Psychotherapist**
Park Clinic
Park Road
Kingston
KT2
☎ 020 8549 3233
ARBS

**FRANCIS**, Anne M
**Psychoanalytic Psychotherapist**
1 Orchard Close
Epsom Road
Guildford
Surrey
GU1 2PR
☎ 01483 567 688
AGIP

**FREEMAN**, Patricia Ann
**Family & Systemic Psychotherapist**
5 Shaftesbury Road
Richmond upon Thames
Surrey
TW9 2TD
☎ 020 8948 7197
P1Freeman@aol.com
AFT

**FRY**, Julie
**Gestalt Psychotherapist**
59 Eastwood Road
Bramley
Guildford
Surrey
GU5 0DY
☎ 01483 892 599
julie@fry.net
GPTI, MET

**GALLAGHER**, Rose
**Lacanian Analyst, Psychoanalytic Psychotherapist**
♿ 66 Hookefield
Epsom
KT19 8JG
☎ 01372 741 178
rosgallagher@btconnect.com
CFAR

**GANZLEBEN**, Jacqueline
**Family & Systemic Psychotherapist**
36 Manor Road
Cheam
SM2 7AG
☎ 020 8642 0415
jackie@ganzleben.com
AFT

**GARNER**, Joanne
**Transactional Analysis Psychotherapist**
193 Three Bridges Road
Three Bridges
Crawley
RH10 1LG
☎ 01293 419 894
info@coachingandcounselling.co.uk
ITA

**GAUVAIN**, Tony
**Hypno-Psychotherapist**
♿ Near Cranleigh
Surrey
GU6 7RR
☎ 01483 267 027
tony.gauvain@btopenworld.com
NRHP

**GLAISTER**, Brian
**Cognitive Psychotherapist**
135 Foxley Lane
Purley
CR8 3HR
☎ 020 8660 7465
brian@glaister0.freeserve.co.uk
BABCP

**GOALEN**, Rosalinde
**Existential Psychotherapist**
♿ April Cottage
79 Cranbrook Drive
Esher
Surrey
KT10 8DN
☎ 02083 987 906
☎ 02083 981 574
Rgoalen@aol.com
UPCA

**GOWER**, Myrna
**Family & Systemic Psychotherapist**
♿ 14 The Crest
Surbiton
Surrey
KT5 8JZ
☎ 020 8399 2012
Gower@cig.ftech.co.uk
AFT

**GREENAWAY**, Jennifer
**Transactional Analysis Psychotherapist**
Sutton
SM2
☎ 020 8395 4951
ITA

**GREGORY**, Josie
**Transactional Analysis Psychotherapist**
14 Buff Avenue
Banstead
Surrey
SM7 2DW
☎ 01737 373 629
josie.gregory@tiscali.co.uk
ITA

**GRIMSHAW**, Francoise
**Personal Construct Psychotherapist**
8 Cosdach Avenue
Wallington
Surrey
SM6 9RA
☎ 020 8255 2464
☎ 020 8288 2796
fran@alter.demon.co.uk
PCP

**HALL**, Joan
**Integrative Psychotherapist**
1 Poyle Road
Guildford
Surrey
GU1 3SL
☎ 01483 533 829
joan.hall@onepoyle.net
BPS, MET

**HAMM**, Alexandra
**Integrative Psychotherapist**
12 The Orangery
Ham Street
Richmond
TW10 7HJ
☎ 020 8940 7266
SPCRC

**HAMMOND**, Margaret
**Analytical Psychologist-Jungian Analyst**
Fulford
Sandhills Meadow
Shepperton
Middlesex
TW17 9HY
☎ 01932 222 712
mhammond@macunlimited.net
CAP *

**HARRINGTON**, Rufus
**Cognitive Behavioural Psychotherapist**
♿ The Runnymede Hospital
Guildford Road
Chertsey
Surrey
KT16 0RQ
☎ 07961 378 329
☎ 01539 535 607
AEMETH@COMPUSERVE.COM
BABCP

**HARRISON**, Jacqueline
**Psychoanalytic Psychotherapist**
Flat 2 (Lower Ground)
4 Surbiton Crescent
Kingston Upon Thames
Surrey
KT1 2JP
☎ 020 8541 1297
☎ 020 8974 6862
harrison.j@btopenworld.com
GUILD

**HART**, Azina
**Systemic Psychotherapist**
55 Aveley Lane
Farnham
Surrey
GU9 8PS
KCC

**HART**, Robert
**Analytical Psychologist-Jungian Analyst**
39 Orchard Way
Dorking
Surrey
RH4 2JJ
☎ 01306 875 521
robert1864hart@tiscali.co.uk
CAP *

**HASHEMI**, Beth
**Psychoanalytic Psychotherapist**
♿ 7 Nightingale Road
Guildford
Surrey
GU1 1ER
☎ 01483 563 135
FPC

**HASLER-WINTER**, Susan
**Group Analyst**
Coniston
25 Bodley Road
New Malden
KT3 5QD
haslerwinter@blueyonder.co.uk
IGA

**HEDINGER-FARRELL**, Korinna
**Integrative Psychotherapist**
36 Woodbines Avenue
Kingston-upon-Thames
Surrey
KT1 2AY
☎ 020 8255 3468
hedinger-farrell@ukgateway.net
CCBP

**HEILLER**, Birgitta R.
**Humanistic Psychotherapist, Transactional Analysis Psychotherapist**
More House
13 Warwicks Bench
Guildford
Surrey
GU1 3SZ
☎ 01483 574 304
BirgitBH@aol.com
AHPP, ITA

**HEIMANN**, Michael
**Group Analyst**
♿ Psychotherapy Department
Abraham Cowley Unit
St Peter's hospital
Chertsey
KT16 OAE
☎ 01932 723 787
IGA

**HELM**, Caroline
**Child Psychotherapist**
40 Park Road
Hampton Wick
Surrey
KT1 4AS
☎ 020 8977 2950
ACP

**HETHERTON**, Jacquie
**Cognitive Behavioural Psychotherapist**
Dept. of Psychology
Royal Holloway College
Egham Hill
Egham
TW20 0EX
☏ 01784 444 049
☏ 07976 621 020
jacquiehetherton@hotmail.com
BABCP

**HEWETT**, Rachel
**Transactional Analysis Psychotherapist**
13 Cambrian Road
Richmond
Surrey
TW10 6JQ
☏ 02089 408 010
rachaelhewett@aol.com
ITA

**HOLLAND**, Nicki
**Integrative Psychosynthesis Psychotherapist**
Overton
Weston Green
Thames Ditton
Surrey
KT7 0JX
☏ 020 8398 8401
nicki.holland@btopenworld.com
RE.V

**HOPWOOD**, Jean
**Psychoanalytic Psychotherapist**
Waverley
Somerswey
Shalford
Guildford
GU4 8EQ
☏ 01483 568 669
jeanhopwood@freeuk.com
FIP

**HOPWOOD**, Michael
**Psychoanalytic Psychotherapist**
Waverley
Somerswey
Shalford
Guildford
GU4 8EQ
☏ 01483 568 669
FIP

**HORTON**, Mary
**Psychoanalytic Psychotherapist**
42 Station Road East
Oxted
Surrey
RH8 0PG
☏ 01883 723 651
maryhorton@mhpost.freeserve.co.uk
FPC

**HOUGHTON**, Christine
**Gestalt Psychotherapist**
3 Locke King Road
Weybridge Road
Surrey
KT13 0SY
☏ 01932 844478
MET

**HUET**, Valerie
**Group Analytic Psychotherapist**
5 Vicarage Garden
Mitcham
Surrey
CR4 3BL
☏ 02082 874 116
valeriehuet@aol.com
UPCA

**HUGHES**, Janet
**Integrative Psychotherapist**
39 Mosslea Road
Whyteleafe
CR3 0DR
☏ 020 8668 1186
janet_hughes@blueyonder.co.uk
SPCRC

**HUGHES-BRUDERLIN**, Silvia
**Transpersonal Psychotherapist**
♿ 53 Crosby Hill Drive
Camberley
Surrey
GU15 3TZ
☏ 01276 28133
silviabrud@aol.com
CCPE

**HUSSAIN**, Fakhir
**Integrative Psychotherapist**
7 Kingswood Court
Marchmont Road
Richmond
Surrey
TW10 6EU
☏ 02089 484 551
hussain_fakir@hotmail.com
MC

**HYDE**, Dennis H
**Integrative Psychotherapist**
32 Amis Avenue
New Haw
Addlestone
Surrey
KT15 3ET
☏ 01932 345526
MC

**INGHAM**, Nida
**Autogenic Psychotherapist, Transpersonal Psychotherapist**
Heath Cottage
Pitch Hill
Ewhurst
Nr. Cranleigh, Surrey
GU6 7NP
☏ 01483 277 333
nida_ingham@onetel.net.uk
BAS, CCPE

**JACOBS**, Linda
**Family & Systemic Psychotherapist**
♿ ACMHT
78 London Road
Croydon
CR0 2TB
☏ 01255 426 115
☏ 020 8700 8877
LINDA.JACOBS@slam.nhs.uk
IFT

**JEFFERIES**, J.I.
**Psychodrama Psychotherapist**
15 Audley Road
Richmond
Surrey
TW10 6EY
☏ 020 8948 5595
jefferies@jinnie.freeserve.co.uk
BPA

**JEFFRIES**, V. Kiki
**Psychoanalytic Psychotherapist**
Stratton Cottage
Tilburstow Hill Road
Godstone
RH9 8LX
☏ 01883 745 025
kiki@vjeffries.freeserve.co.uk
CCOPPP

**JESSON**, Alison
**Transactional Analysis Psychotherapist**
85 Fairfield Drive
Dorking
Surrey
RH4 1JG
☏ 01306 882357
ITA, MET

**JIGGINS**, Mary
**Transpersonal Psychotherapist**
30 Buckingham Avenue
Hurst Park
West Molesey
Surrey
KT8 1SY
☏ 020 8941 5904
☏ 01737 814 488
CTP

**JOHN**, Beverlyn
**Systemic Psychotherapist**
16 Compton Road
Croydon
CR0 7JA
KCC

**JONATHAN**, Arthur
**Existential Psychotherapist**
'The Jays'
27 Aultone Way
Sutton
SM1 3LD
☎ 020 8641 1601
arthurj@blueyonder.co.uk
SPCRC

**JONES**, Alan
**Existential Psychotherapist, Humanistic Psychotherapist**
3 Bushey Road
Sutton
Surrey
SM1 1QR
☎ 020 8641 1792
elliff@blueyonder.co.uk
AHPP

**JONES**, Eileen
**Hypno-Psychotherapist**
The New Haw Therapy Clinic
189 Woodham Land
New Haw
Surrey
KT15 3NN
☎ 02082 559 666
☎ 01932 351 120
eileen@jayvant.fsnet.co.uk
NRHP

**KARTER**, John
**Integrative Psychotherapist**
20 Albany Mews
Kingston upon Thames
KT2 5SL
☎ 020 8541 1438
albany.co@virgin.net
SPCRC

**KIRKLAND-HANDLEY**, Nicholas
**Existential Psychotherapist, Psychoanalytic Psychotherapist**
♿ 20 Ham Common
Richmond
Surrey
TW10 7JB
☎ 020 8940 5583
LPDO, SPCRC

**KISSACK**, Debbie
**Family & Systemic Psychotherapist**
♿ Mole Valley CAMHS The Dene Centre
Dorking General Hospital
Horsham Road
Dorking
RH4 2AA
☎ 01306 502 708
debie.kissack@surreyoaklands.nhs.uk
AFT

**KNIGHTS**, Jean
**Integrative Psychotherapist**
♿ Barn Close
Portsmouth Road
Milford
Surrey
GU8 5HP
☎ 01483 424 024
jeanlksoul@aol.com
SPTI

**LAFON**, Robert
**Systemic Psychotherapist**
251 Richmond Road
Kingston
Surrey
KT2 5DJ
☎ 020 8549 1922
☎ 020 8949 0727
Kingston Gate Therapy
Glenlyn Medical Centre
115 Molesey Park Road
East Molesey
KT8
IFT

**LAKE**, Moira
**Gestalt Psychotherapist**
11 St. John's Road
Kingston-on-Thames
Surrey
KT1 4AN
☎ 020 8943 5507
☎ 01548 511 188
moiralake@groundtruth.fslife.co.uk
GPTI, MET

**LAUCHLAN**, Sheila
**Systemic Psychotherapist**
Heathmere
Stoke Close
Stoke D'abernan
KT7 0NB
☎ 01932 866 171
sheilalauchlan@waitrose.com
Kent Clinic
104 Walton Road
East Molesey
KT8 0DL
KCC

**LEES**, Fiona Elizabeth
**Family & Systemic Psychotherapist**
12 Dickerage Road
Kingston upon Thames
KT1 3SP
☎ 020 8949 0727
lizlees100@aol.com
AFT

**LESLEY**, Alison
**Psychoanalytic Psychotherapist**
11 Links Road
Ashford
Middlesex
TW15 3RA
☎ 01784 255197
IPSS

**LINGARD**, Shirley Ruth
**Systemic Psychotherapist**
Child & Family Consultation Service
The Health Centre
Brightwells
Farnham
KCC

**LINTERN**, Fran
**Psychoanalytic Psychotherapist**
128 Osward
Courtwood Lane
Forestdale
Croydon, Surrey
CR0 9HE
☎ 020 8657 0429
fran.lin@btopenworld.com
GUILD

**LLEWELLYN**, Martha
**Biodynamic Psychotherapist**
103 Richmond Hill Court
Richmond
Surrey
TW10 6BG
☎ 020 8940 4726
r.llewellyn@virgin.net
LSBP

**LOEWENTHAL**, Del
**Psychoanalytic Psychotherapist**
Centre for Therapeutic Education
School of Educational Studies
University of Surrey
Guildford
GU2 5XH
☎ 01483 683 143
☎ 02089 477 085
D.Loewenthal@surrey.ac.uk
PA, UPCA

**LOOMS**, Suzanne
**Neurolinguistic Psychotherapist**
Pinehurst
18 Southcote Road
Croydon
Surrey
CR2 OEQ
☎ 02086 515 898
heart@medicine.co.uk
NLPtCA

**LUDEN**, Maureen
**Transactional Analysis Psychotherapist**
17 Chester Close
Kings Road
Richmond
Surrey
TW10 6NR
☎ 02089 403 366
maureen.luden@europe.com
ITA

**LUND**, Leslie Ann
**Integrative Psychotherapist**
"Suncroft"
3 Norrels Ride
East Horsley
KT24 5EH
☎ 01483 281 435
SPCRC

**LYNCH**, Valerie
**Psychoanalytic Psychotherapist**
♿ 2 Church Court
Foxenden Road
Guildford
Surrey
GU1 4DY
☎ 01483 562 204
Valcanbefound@AOL.com
FIP

**MAGUIRE**, Roisin
**Cognitive Analytic Therapist**
Tamworth Road Resource Centre
37 Tamworth Road
Croydon
CR0 1XT
☎ 020 8700 8728
rmgu@supanet.com
ACAT

**MANICOM**, Hilary
**Systemic Psychotherapist**
A.T.S. Kingsdown
112 Orchard Road
Sanderstead
CR2 9LQ
☎ 020 8651 5611
KCC

**MANN**, Angela
**Psychoanalytic Psychotherapist**
Beresford Road
Cheam
SM2
☎ 020 8770 0303
amann@fsmail.net
FPC

**MAPLE**, Norma Anderson
**Cognitive Analytic Therapist, Group Analyst**
♿ Weir View
Towpath
Shepperton
Middlesex
TW17 9LL
☎ 01932 224 717
m.maple@virgin.net
ACAT, IGA

**MARSDEN**, Lee
**Educational Therapist**
♿ 57 Gloucester Road
Kingston Upon Thames
KT1 3QZ
☎ 020 8241 2749
leemarsden@blueyonder.co.uk
CFET

**MARSHALL**, Janet
**Autogenic Psychotherapist**
12 Churchfields Avenue
Weybridge
Surrey
KT13 9YA
☎ 01932 849 513
janmarshall@supanet.com
BAS

**MARSHALL**, Jill
**Hypno-Psychotherapist**
♿ Kingston Natural Healing Centre
40 Eastbury Road
Kingston Upon Thames
Surrey
KT2 5AN
☎ 02085 465 793
☎ 02087 892 548
jill.marshall@virgin.net
NRHP

**MARSHALL**, Vivien
**Psychoanalytic Psychotherapist**
Chart Cottage
Nutfield Road
Redhill
Surrey
RH1 4BA
☎ 01737 780 015
viv@cleevej.freeserve.co.uk
FPC

**MARTIN**, Gloria
**Systemic Psychotherapist**
89 Durlston Road
Kingston upon Thames
Surrey
KT2 5RS
☎ 020 8546 8317
☎ 020 8355 1984
KCC

**MATHEWS**, Micheal
**Body Psychotherapist, Integrative Psychotherapist**
48 Norbiton Hall
Birkenhead Avenue
Kingston upon Thames
Surrey
KT2 6RB
☎ 020 8549 6235
michaelamathews@hotmail.com
CCBP

**MAXWELL**, Brian
**Group Analyst**
60 Chiltern Drive
Surbiton
KT5 8LW
☎ 020 8399 3964
IGA

**MAYNERD**, Cynthia
**Family & Systemic Psychotherapist**
15 Smoke Lane
Reigate
Surrey
RH2 7HJ
☎ 01737 242 051
clm@cmaynerd.fsnet.co.uk
AFT

**MCCANDLESS**, Robert
**Family & Systemic Psychotherapist**
87 Coombe Gardens
New Malden
KT3 4AB
☎ 020 8355 1984
☎ 020 8949 7289
robert.mccandless@swlstg-tr.nhs.uk
IFT

**MCCARRY**, Nicola
**Systemic Psychotherapist**
180 Acre Road
Kingston upon Thames
KT2 6EU
☎ 020 8682 6195
nicolamccarry@blueyonder.co.uk
KCC

**MCKENNA**, Clare
**Integrative Psychotherapist**
Joseph Palmer Centre
319a Walton Road
East Molesey
KT8 2QG
☎ 020 8873 4338
SPCRC

**MCKEOWN**, Jane
**Group Analytic Psychotherapist**
Verdley
Portsmouth Road
Milford
Surrey
GU8 5DS
☎ 01483 424 973
jane@jmckeown.demon.co.uk
FPC

**MCMINN**, Les
**Integrative Psychotherapist**
Pilgrim Cottage
31A Warren Road
Guildford
Surrey
GU1 2HQ
☎ 01483 302 171
☎ 01483 689 498
p.mcminn@surrey.ac.uk
Student Counselling Centre
University of Surrey
Guildford
Surrey
GU2 7XH
AHPP

**MILTON**, Martin
**Integrative Psychotherapist**
Department of Psychology
School of Human Sciences
University of Surrey
Guildford
GU2 7XH
☎ 01483 689 176
m.milton@surrey.ac.uk
SPCRC

**MITCHELL**, Diana
**Existential Psychotherapist**
32 Cambridge Road
Walton-on-Thames
Surrey
KT12 2DP
☎ 01932 225 599
Dianavmitchell@aol.com
SEA, UPCA

**MORCOM**, Caroline
**Psychoanalytic Psychotherapist**
24 Lawn Crescent
Kew
Richmond
Surrey
TW9 3NS
☎ 020 8940 3151
csmorcom@hotmail.com
FPC

**MORRISON**, Lesley
**Psychoanalytic Psychotherapist**
The Cottage
27 Burghley Avenue
New Malden
Surrey
KT3 4SW
☎ 020 8949 5628
Lmorrison@saqnet.co.uk
FPC

**NATH**, Krish
**Cognitive Behavioural Psychotherapist**
72 Chaffers Mead
Ashtead
KT21 1NH
☎ 01372 278 831
☎ 07831 425 712
BABCP

**NEILL**, Christopher
**Psychosynthesis Psychotherapist**
9 Park Avenue
Peper Harow
Godalming
Surrey
GU8 6BA
☎ 02082 024 525
☎ 01483 423560
chris.neill@talk21.com
IPS

**NEWBERY**, Christine
**Integrative Psychotherapist**
16 Lancaster Avenue
Farnham
Surrey
GU9 8JY
☎ 01252 723 589
chris_newbery@yahoo.co.uk
SPTI

**NEWNHAM**, Elizabeth
**Transpersonal Psychotherapist**
Lawn Cottage
Portsmouth Road
Milford
Surrey
GU8 5HZ
☎ 01483 417 789
CTP

**O'BRIEN**, John
**Integrative Psychotherapist**
♿ Great Frenches Park
Snow Hill
Crawley Down
RH10 3EE
john.obrien@hanoverexecutive.com
SPCRC

**O'CONNOR**, Michael
**Systemic Psychotherapist**
SW Surrey CAMHS Buryfields Clinic
61 Buryfields
Guilford
GU2 4AX
☎ 01252 515 053
☎ 01483 783 330
mike.oconnor@ntlworld.com
KCC

**O'DELL**, Tricia
**Psychoanalytic Psychotherapist**
♿ Lichfield
161 New Haw Road
Addlestone
Weybridge, Surrey
KT15 2DP
☎ 01932 857 818
FIP, FPC

**O'NEILL**, Christopher
**Hypno-Psychotherapist**
14 Chapelfields
Charterhouse Road
Godalming
Surrey
GU7 2BS
☎ 01483 414 443
NSHAP, UPCA

**O'SULLIVAN**, Geraldine
**Integrative Psychotherapist**
♿ Lilliput Cottage
Cramhurst Lane
Witley
Surrey
GU8 5QZ
☎ 01428 685086
geraldine@lillyput.co.uk
MET

**OLDMAN**, David
**Couple Psychoanalytic Psychotherapist**
5 Buckland Court
Buckland
Betchworth
Surrey
RH3 7EA
☎ 020 7487 3766
☎ 01737 844 079
david@oldmanonline.me.uk
SCPP

**OSBORNE**, Lynda
**Gestalt Psychotherapist**
Crossways
8 Lancaster Avenue
Farnham
Surrey
GU9 8JY
☎ 01252 724 403
lynda@osborneuk.co.uk
GPTI, MET

**OUTRAM**, Jo
**Analytical Psychotherapist**
Willow House
Vicarage Road
Bagshot
Surrey
GU19 5EJ
☎ 01276 476 279
jo.o@outrams.com
AIP

**OWTRAM**, Peter
**Psychoanalytic Psychotherapist**
♿ 14 Busbridge Lane
Godalming
Surrey
GU7 1PU
☎ 01483 417 443
peter.owtram@btopenworld.com
FIP

**PARTRIDGE**, Karen
**Systemic Psychotherapist**
1 Woodside Road
Kingston Upon Thames
KT2 5AT
☎ 020 8549 1815
☎ 020 8846 6051
karenpartridge@blueyonder.co.uk
KCC

**PATIENCE**, Elizabeth
**Analytical Psychologist-Jungian Analyst**
27 Atwood Avenue
Richmond
Surrey
TW9 4HF
☎ 020 8876 9857
☎ 020 8876 5590
CAP *

**PEARMAN**, Cathy
**Attachment-based Psychoanalytic Psychotherapist, Psychosynthesis Psychotherapist, Transpersonal Psychotherapist**
♿ 'Tzaneen'
Blackhorse Road
Woking
Surrey
GU22 0RE
☎ 01483 232 030
cathypearman@btconnect.com
CAPP, CTP, IPS

**PEET**, Sandra
**Transpersonal Psychotherapist**
Chestnuts
31 Firfield Road
Addlestone
Surrey
KT15 1QU
☎ 01932 853 667
CTP

**PERERA**, Ajit
**Cognitive Behavioural Psychotherapist**
Sandy Ridge
2 Park Lane East
Reigate
RH2 8HN
☎ 01737 222 246
☎ 07775 857 504
info@cognitivetherapist.com
BABCP

**PHILLIPS**, Mary
**Sexual and Relationship Psychotherapist**
♿ Camberley
GU15 3LZ
☎ 01252 723 522
Guildford
GU1 4RP
BASRT

**PLATT**, Hilary
**Integrative Psychotherapist**
14 Waterloo Close
Wellington Park
Camberley
Surrey
GU15 1PY
☎ 01276 505 382
☎ 07971 054 859
MET

**PLATT**, Monique
**Integrative Psychotherapist**
Flat 3
28 Knights Park
Kingston Upon Thames
KT1 2QN
☎ 020 8541 4631
moniq.platt@accorservices.co.uk
SPCRC

**PORTER**, Dorothy
**Systemic Psychotherapist**
11 The Avenue
Coulsdon
CR5 2BN
☎ 020 8660 3377
☎ 020 8651 6045
dorothy.porter@barnardos.org.uk
Peepul Family Resource Centre
170 Sanderstead Road
Croydon
CR2 0DB
KCC

**POUTEAUX (MRS)**, Diana
**Sexual and Relationship Psychotherapist**
Thorsby
26 Crownpits Lane
Godalming
Surrey
GU7 1PB
☎ 01483 416 984
BASRT

**PRATT**, Sheila
**Psychoanalytic Psychotherapist**
44 East Meads
Onslow Village
Guildford
Surrey
GU2 7SP
☎ 01483 572093
GUILD

**PREEDY**, Jan
**Integrative Psychotherapist**
12 Hurst Close
Headley
Epsom
KT18 6DZ
☎ 01372 361 151
janpreedy@hotmail.com
SPCRC

**PYLE**, Magdalena
**Integrative Psychotherapist**
31 Earle Gardens
Kingston
Surrey
KT2 5TB
☎ 02082 875 067
☎ 07973 370 702
magadelan.pyle@blueyonder.co.uk
MET

**RABE**, Marie-Louise
**Group Analyst, Psychoanalytic Psychotherapist, Psychodynamic Psychotherapist**
23 Addiscombe Court Road
Croydon
CR0 6TT
☎ 020 8656 7954
rabeml@clara.co.uk
ARBS, IGA

**RANDALL-VINING**, Morgan
**Cognitive Behavioural Psychotherapist**
♿ Twin Elms
Green Lane
Chessington
KT9 2DS
☎ 020 8397 6820
☎ 020 7489 9292
BABCP

**REDMOND**, Jayne
**Integrative Psychotherapist**
15 Mayfield Road
Walton-on-Thames
Surrey
KT12 5PL
☎ 01932 222 789
j.redmond99@merseymail.com
U P C A

**REYNOLDS**, Hilary
**Psychoanalytic Psychotherapist**
11 The Waldrons
Oxted
Surrey
RH8 9DY
☎ 01883 722 190
☎ 01883 712 783
F P C

**RICHARDSON**, Magda Hafez
**Integrative Psychotherapist**
5 Wessex Close
Thames Ditton
Surrey
KT7 0EJ
☎ 02083 390 060
M C

**RIDLEY**, Jane
**Sexual and Relationship Psychotherapist**
77 Church Road
Richmond
TW10 6LX
☎ 020 8940 7678
janeridley@tandj77.demon.co.uk
B A S R T

**ROBERTSON**, Judith
**Integrative Psychotherapist**
9 Banks Way
Guildford
Surrey
GU4 7NL
☎ 01483 536 054
M C

**ROBERTSON**, Judith
**Psychoanalytic Psychotherapist**
♿ 1 Avebury Park
Lovelace Gardens
Surbiton
Surrey
KT6 6SQ
☎ 020 8399 6419
G U I L D

**SAGE**, Nigel A.
**Cognitive Behavioural Psychotherapist**
Primary Care Psychol & Counselling
2 Barossa Road
Camberley
Surrey
GU15 4JE
☎ 01276 66772
nigel.sage@ntlworld.com
B A B C P

**SAGOE**, Pauline
**Transpersonal Psychotherapist**
Surbiton
Surrey
☎ 020 8399 9973
C C P E

**SANDBANK**, Audrey
**Family & Systemic Psychotherapist**
♿ Winterfold, 30 Beech Road
Reigate
Surrey
RH2 9NA
☎ 01737 221 347
A F T

**SAROFF**, Rahel
**Integrative Psychotherapist**
"Westside"
142 Nutfield Road
Merstham
RH1 3HG
☎ 01737 646 068
rk.saroff@ntlworld.com
S P C R C

**SCHOFIELD**, Peter
**Psychosynthesis Psychotherapist**
12 Springfield Road
Kingston-upon-Thames
KT1 2SA
☎ 020 8549 2334
perter.schofield@theseed.net
P E T

**SHADRACH-LONG**, Philippa
**Psychoanalytic Psychotherapist**
The Lodge
233 Richmond Road
Kinston-upon-Thames
Surrey
KT2 5DH
☎ 020 8546 4082
☎ 020 8541 3436
F I P

**SHAWE-TAYLOR**, Metka
**Cognitive Behavioural Psychotherapist**
South Tanbridge CMHT
Langley House
Church Lane
Oxted
RH8 9LH
☎ 01882 388 301
B A B C P

**SHEPPARD FIDLER**, Angela
**Family & Systemic Psychotherapist**
♿ 3 Sunnybank
Epsom
Surrey
KT18 7DY
☎ 01372 727 200
angela@sheppardfidler.freeserve.co.uk
A F T

**SIMMONS**, Linda
**Psychosynthesis Psychotherapist**
12 Rydens Park
Walton on Thames
Surrey
KT12 3DP
☎ 01932 228 582
P E T

**SIPOS**, Zsuzsa
**Group Analyst**
SW London & St George's Mental Health NHS Trust
Psychotherapy Dept, Villiers House
Tolworth Hospital
Red Lion Road
KT6 7QU
☎ 020 8390 0102
I G A

**SKILLICORN**, Ingrid
**Family & Systemic Psychotherapist**
♿ Buryfield Clinic
Lawn Road
Guildford
GU2 4AX
☎ 01444 482 924
☎ 01483 783 330
I F T

**SPENDER**, Quentin Wynn
**Family & Systemic Psychotherapist**
♿ 16 Hemingford Road
Cheam
Surrey
SM3 8HG
☎ 01243 815 514
quentin.spender@btinternet.com
A F T

**STAMMERS**, Sigrid
**Neurolinguistic Psychotherapist**
6 Providence Place
Pyford Road
Woking
Surrey
GU22 8UN
☎ 01932 348 890
siggi@astammers.fsbusiness.co.uk
NLPtCA

**STANLEY**, Annie
**Humanistic and Integrative Psychotherapist**
12 Trodds Lane
Merrow
Guildford
Surrey
GU1 2XR
AHPP

**STEWART**, Lisa
**Cognitive Behavioural Psychotherapist**
♿ Practise 2
York House Medical Centre
Heathside Road
Woking
GU22 7XL
☎ 01483 486 583
BABCP

**STREBEL**, Silvia
**Integrative Psychotherapist**
Cornerways
Bute Avenue
Petersham
Richmond
TW10 7AX
☎ 020 8940 0194
MC

**SUTTON**, Bobbie
**Psychoanalytic Psychotherapist**
17 Sheen Park
Richmond
Surrey
TW9 1UN
☎ 020 8940 7628
bobbiesuttonuk@hotmail.com
FPC

**TABAK**, Carolyn
**Integrative Psychotherapist**
15 Melvin Court
High Park Avenue
Kew
Surrey
TW9 4BW
☎ 020 8876 0858
carolyntabak@hotmail.com
MET

**TARSH**, Helen
**Couple Psychoanalytic Psychotherapist**
Wentworth House
The Green
Richmond upon Thames
Surrey
TW9 1PB
htarsh@talk21.com
SCPP

**TAYLOR**, Marsha
**Integrative Psychotherapist**
NW Surrey Mental Health P. NHS Trust
Abraham Cowley Unit
Holloway Hill
Chertsey
KT16 0AE
☎ 01932 723 787
marsha.taylor@nwsurrey.nhs.uk
SPCRC

**TAYLOR**, Maureen
**Integrative Psychotherapist**
21 Horne Road
Shepperton
Middlesex
TW17 0DJ
☎ 01932 564 198
maureen.a.taylor@ntlworld.com
UPCA

**TESTA**, Rita
**Child Psychotherapist**
5 Ascent House
2 Ellesmere Road
Weybridge
KT13 0HZ
☎ 01932 842633
☎ 020 7830 2931
ritatesta@hotmail.com
Sutton Hospital
Cotswold House
Cotswold Road
Sutton
SM2 5MF
ACP

**THORNTON**, Susanne
**Integrative Psychotherapist**
♿ Ivy Cottage
Clockhouse Lane East
Egham
TW20 8PF
☎ 01784 433 480
susi.thornton@ukgateway.net
SPCRC

**TOMLIN**, Minoo
**Group Analytic Psychotherapist**
Oaktrees
Bishopswalk
Shirley Hills
Surrey
CR0 5BA
☎ 02086 545 335
☎ 07900 845 334
mamosh@aol.com
UPCA

**TOMS**, Moira
**Family & Systemic Psychotherapist**
♿ Bramblewood
Guildford Road
Cranleigh
Surrey
GU6 8PR
☎ 01483 274 183
moiratom@btopenworld.com
AFT

**TOYER**, Malcolm
**Cognitive Behavioural Psychotherapist**
♿ Horizon Centre
Farnham Road Hospital
Farnham Road
Guildford
GU2 7LX
☎ 01483 443 620
☎ 07808 123 723
malcolmtoyer@hotmail.com
BABCP

**TURNER**, Elizabeth
**Integrative Psychotherapist**
62 Rothes Road
Dorking
RH4 1LB
☎ 01306 880 089
eliztrnr@aol.com
SPCRC

**UNSWORTH**, Gisela
**Integrative Psychotherapist**
♿ Occupational Health Department
Kingston Hospital
Galsworthy Road
Kingston
KT2 7QB
☎ 01932 267 108
gunswort@kingstonhospital.nhs.uk
SPCRC

**VALLINS**, Yvonne
**Psychoanalytic Psychotherapist**
21 Hardwicke Road
Reigate
Surrey
RH2 9HJ
☎ 01737 247 608
GUILD

**VEASEY**, Helen
**Psychoanalytic Psychotherapist**
8 Hilgay Close
Guildford
Surrey
GU1 2EN
☎ 01483 689498
☎ 01483 538077
h.veasey@surrey.ac.uk
Student Counselling Centre
University of Surrey
Guildford
GU2 7XH
GUILD

**VINCENT**, Christopher
**Psychoanalytic Psychotherapist, Couple Psychoanalytic Psychotherapist**
Dept. of Psychotherapy
NW Surrey Mental Health Partnership
Abraham Cowley Unit, Holloway Lyne, Chertsey
KT16 0AE
☎ 01753 774 558
☎ 01932 872 010
Christopher.Vincent@btinternet.com
SCPP

**WALKER**, Mary J.
**Child Psychotherapist**
Merton Child, Adolescent & Family Service
Birches Close
Cricket Green Polyclinic
Mitcham Surrey
CR4 4LQ
☎ 020 8770 8828
walkeruk@netscapeonline.com
ACP

**WALSH**, Eileen
**Neurolinguistic Psychotherapist**
239 Sandycombe Road
Kew
London
TW9 2EW
☎ 020 7385 8914
☎ 07776 237852
E.Walsh@btinternet.com,
www.ewalsh.co.uk
NLPtCA

**WHEELER**, Judith
**Cognitive Behavioural Psychotherapist**
Wickets
71 Highlands Road
Leatherhead
KT22 8NW
☎ 01372 373 791
BABCP

**WHITAKER**, Christine
**Transpersonal Psychotherapist**
Home Farmhouse
The Street
Puttenham
Guildford, Surrey
GU3 1AR
☎ 01483 810632
CCPE

**WHITELEY**, Stuart
**Group Analyst**
Wheelwrights Cottage
33 Wheelers Lane
Brockham
RH3 7LA
☎ 01737 843 446
stuart.whiteley@virgin.net
IGA

**WIDDICOMBE**, Howard
**Humanistic and Integrative Psychotherapist**
32 Armadale Road
Goldsworth Park
Woking
Surrey
GU21 3LB
☎ 01483 721 458
tpp@globalnet.co.uk
SPEC

**WILFORD**, Gerti
**Family & Systemic Psychotherapist**
♿ 30 Spencer Road
East Moseley
Surrey
KT8 0SR
☎ 020 8979 3003
wilfordg@aol.com
AFT

**WILKINS**, David
**Hypno-Psychotherapist**
9 Burbidge Road
Shepperton
Middlesex
TW17 0ED
☎ 01932 232 401
NRHP

**WILLIAMS**, Heather
**Psychosynthesis Psychotherapist**
76 Deerings Road
Reigate
Surrey
RH2 0PN
☎ 01737 240 638
PET

**WILLIAMS**, Jill
**Integrative Psychotherapist**
98 Waleton Acres
Carew Road
SM6 8PU
SPCRC

**WILLIS**, Sally
**Group Analyst**
50d Maple Road
Surbiton
Surrey
KT6 4AE
☎ 020 8399 3334
sallywillis@themutual.net
IGA

**WILSON**, James
**Group Analyst**
Department of Psychiatry
Epsom General Hospital
Dorking Road
Epsom
KT17 4JL
☎ 01372 204 195
IGA

**WITTER**, Judith
**Integrative Psychotherapist**
34 Aragon Avenue
Ewell
Epsom
Surrey
KT17 2QG
☎ 02083 932 512
MET

**WODDIS**, Helena
**Sexual and Relationship Psychotherapist**
Flat A
Heatherfield
181 Queens Road
Weybridge
KT13 0AH
☎ 01932 851 561
☎ 07884 312 965
helena.woddis@dial.pipex.com
BASRT

**WOOD**, Margarita
**Child Psychotherapist**
13 Uxbridge Road
Kingston-upon-Thames
Surrey
KT1 2LH
☎ 020 8546 4668
ACP

**WYSE**, Gill
**Family & Systemic Psychotherapist**
47 Ashcombe Road
Carshalton Park
Surrey
SM5 3ET
☎ 020 8647 8568
gillwyse@hotmail.com
AFT

**WYSE**, Hymie
**Group Analyst**
47 Ashcombe Road
Carshalton
Surrey
SM5 3ET
☎ 020 8647 8568
IGA

**YALLOP**, Melanie
**Psychoanalytic Psychotherapist**
11 Mount Pleasant
Weybridge
Surrey
KT13 8EP
☎ 01932 844 688
FIP, FPC

**ZIMINSKI**, Jeanne Marguerite
**Family & Systemic Psychotherapist**
♿ Sutton CAMHS Cotswold House
Sutton Hospital
Cotswold Road
Sutton
SM2 5NF
☎ 020 8652 7900
jziminski@blueyonder.co.uk
AFT

## SUSSEX - EAST

**ADAMSON**, Niki
**Psychosynthesis Psychotherapist**
Weald cottage
Coggins Mill Lane
Mayfield
TN20 6UL
☎ 01435 872 789
☎ 07799 866 640
niki@solutions-inc.co.uk
PET

**ALLARD**, Alain
**Transpersonal Psychotherapist**
The Haven
Berwick
East Sussex
BN26 6TF
☎ 01323 871 057
CTP

**ANDERSON**, Tony
**Psychoanalytic Psychotherapist**
4 Elmstead Road
Bexhill on Sea
Sussex
TN40 5HP
☎ 01424 734 027
CCOPPP

**ARTHUR**, Andrew R.
**Psychoanalytic Psychotherapist**
1 Langton Close
Battle
East Sussex
TN33 0XH
☎ 01424 772 740
andrew@aarthur.fsnet.co.uk
FIP

**BAKER**, Kevin
**Core Process Psychotherapist**
The Cottage Clinic
Howard Cottage
Broomans Lane
Lewes
BN7 2LT
☎ 01273 475 556
KI

**BARGH**, Julie
**Group Analytic Psychotherapist**
4 Temple Gardens
Brighton
BN1 3AE
☎ 01273 380 374
j.bargh@ntlworld.com
FPC

**BEAZLEY RICHARDS**, Joanna
**Transactional Analysis Psychotherapist**
♿ 2 Quarry View
Whitehill Road
Crowborough
East Sussex
TN6 1JT
☎ 01892 655 195
jbrich@dircon.co.uk
ITA

**BECK**, Rose
**Group Analytic Psychotherapist**
Sea Rose
Channel Way
Fairlght
TN35 4BP
☎ 01424 812 183
FPC

**BLOWERS**, Colin M.
**Cognitive Behavioural Psychotherapist**
Glenside
Wincombe Road
Brighton
East Sussex
BN1 5AR
☎ 020 8876 8261
☎ 01273 504 980
BABCP

**BOBSIN**, Mica
**Integrative Psychosynthesis Psychotherapist**
14 Maldon Road
Brighton
East Sussex
BN1 5BE
☎ 01273 505 521
RE.V

**BODIAM**, Rosemary J
**Group Analytic Psychotherapist**
3 Mill Drove
Uckfield
East Sussex
TN22 5AB
☎ 01825 766 280
rosmary@bodiam.fslife.co.uk
UPCA

**BONHAM**, Elizabeth
**Cognitive Behavioural Psychotherapist**
Mortains
Station Road
MAYFIELD
East Sussex
TN20 6BN
☎ 01273 821 402
BABCP

**BRADY**, Peter
**Cognitive Behavioural Psychotherapist**
♿ 16 Roman Way
Hempstead Fields
Uckfield
TN22 1UY
☎ 01273 242 018
☎ 01825 763 156
BABCP

**BRENNAN**, Clare
**Group Analyst, Group Analytic Psychotherapist, Psychoanalytic Psychotherapist**
♿ The Merchant House
English Passage
Cliffe High Street
Lewes, East Sussex
BN7 2AP
☎ 01273 479 157
WTC

**BROSSKAMP**, Cornelia
**Biodynamic Psychotherapist**
94 Graham Avenue
Brighton
East Suusex
BN1 8HD
☎ 01273 385228
cbroesskamp@onetel.net.uk
LSBP

**BURTON**, Michael
**Psychoanalytic Psychotherapist**
♿ Brackley
11A Harrington Road
Brighton
Sussex
BN1 9RE
☎ 01273 502923
mjburton56@hotmail.com
GUILD

**BUTTON**, Rachel
**Transpersonal Psychotherapist**
Old End Cottage
Priory Road
Forest Row
Sussex
RH18 5HS
☎ 01342 822871
CCPE

**BYRNE**, Dorothy
**Jungian Analytical Psychotherapist**
St Leonard's House
35 Sutton Road
Seaford
BN25 1SG
☎ 01323 894 008
WMIP

**CANNAN**, Philippa
**Integrative Psychotherapist**
21 St Swithuns Terrace
Lewes
BN7 1UJ
☎ 01273 476 063
philippa@cannan.fsnet.co.uk
SPCRC

**CHARLTON**, Patricia S.
**Group Analytic Psychotherapist**
14 Pelham Terrace
Lewes
East Sussex
BN7 2DR
☎ 01273 472 393
pat/robin@virgin.net
UPCA

**CHISWELL-JONES**, Sue
**Transpersonal Psychotherapist**
205 Osbourne Road
Brighton
East Sussex
BN1 6LT
☎ 01273 541 985
CTP

**CLEMINSON**, Richard
**Biodynamic Psychotherapist**
8 Harrington Villas
Brighton
East Sussex
BN1 6RG
☎ 01273 500797
richard@bodywisdom.co.uk
LSBP

**COTTRELL**, Sue
**Integrative Psychotherapist**
50 Waldegrave Road
Brighton
Sussex
BN1 6GE
☎ 01273 507 776
MET

**COX**, Christine Sarah
**Hypno-Psychotherapist**
28 Fern Road
St Leonards on Sea
East Sussex
TN38 0UH
☎ 01424 424 797
NRHP

**CRELLIN**, Clare
**Psychoanalyst**
♿ 10 Oldlands Hall
Heron's Ghyll
Uckfield
East Sussex
TN22 3DA
☎ 01825 712 139
☎ 01444 416 606
clare@crellins.org.uk
PA, SITE

**CROSBY**, Simon
**Personal Construct Psychotherapist**
Hindleap Corner
Priory Road
Forest Row
East Sussex
RH18 5JF
☎ 01342 824 545
Simon@scapegoat.demon.co.uk
PCP

**DANIEL**, Ishbel
**Sexual and Relationship Psychotherapist**
♿ 61B Beaconsfield Villas
Brighton
BN1 6HB
☎ 01273 846 832
☎ 07710 948 952
ishbeldaniel@btopenworld.com
BASRT

**DESMOND**, Hanora
**Transpersonal Psychotherapist**
♿ Seaford
BN25 1JJ
☎ 01323 490 721
CCPE

**EASTHAM**, Peter
**Cognitive Behavioural Psychotherapist**
School Hill Surgery
School Hill House
33 High Street
Lewes
BN7 2LU
☎ 01273 480 888
mr.e@btinternet.com
BABCP

**EDWARDS**, Ben
**Autogenic Psychotherapist**
3 Place Farm Cottages
Fairlight Place Farm
Hastings
TN35 5DT
☎ 01424 812 761
benedwards@tinyworld.co.uk
BAS

**EISENBARTH**, Heiner
**Biodynamic Psychotherapist**
Holistic Health Centre
Beaconsfield Road
Brighton
BN1 8HD
☎ 01273 382 878
☎ 01273 696 295
heinereisenbarth@onetel.net.uk
LSBP

**FELLOWS**, Ron
**Family & Systemic Psychotherapist**
Lavender Cottage
90 Turkey Road
Bexhill on Sea
East Sussex
TN39 5HE
☎ 01424 213200
ronfellows@mac.com
AFT

**FELLOWS**, Ronald Edward
**Family & Systemic Psychotherapist**
Lavender Cottage
90 Turkey Toad
Bexhill on Sea
TN39 5HE
☎ 01424 213 200
ronff@tiscali.co.uk
AFT

**FIELD**, Rosalind
**Integrative Psychotherapist**
The Pines
Spithurst Road
Barcombe
East Sussex
BN8 5ED
☎ 01273 401163
MC

**FLOWER**, Charles
**Transpersonal Psychotherapist**
2 Poppyfield Cottages, Houghton
Green Lane
Playden
Rye
East Sussex
TN31 7PJ
☏ 020 7266 3006
CCPE

**GORDON**, Inger
**Systemic Psychotherapist**
♿ East Sussex Community Healthcare
NHS Trust Community Mental
Health
Grove House, The Grove
South View Road Crowborou
TN6 1HB
☏ 01892 771 225
inger.gordon@virgin.net
KCC

**GOULD**, Vreni
**Psychoanalytic Psychotherapist**
Forge Cottage
Cobbarn
Eridge,
Tunbridge Wells
TN3 9LA
☏ 01892 860 582
vreni.gould@virgin.net
AGIP

**GRANT**, Alec John
**Cognitive Behavioural Psychotherapist**
The Eastbourne Clinic
21 Grange Road
Eastbourne
BN21 4HE
☏ 01273 821 402
☏ 01323 430 831
A.Grant@bton.ac.uk
BABCP

**GREEN**, Prue
**Psychoanalytic Psychotherapist**
♿ The Therapy Rooms
St. Andrew's Lane
East Sussex
BN7 1UW
☏ 01273 471 422
PA

**HALL**, Jill
**Gestalt Psychotherapist**
22 Collier Road
Hastings
East Sussex
TN34 3JR
☏ 01424 436 497
GCL

**HALPIN**, Jill
**Psychoanalytic Psychotherapist**
♿ Stonerunner Cottage
Rye Harbour
East Sussex
TN31 7TT
☏ 01797 224351
GUILD

**HAYNES**, Tanya
**Systemic Psychotherapist**
5 Bolsover Road
Eastbourne
BN20 7JF
CAMHS, The Scott Unit
Eastbourne District General Hospita
Kings Drive
Eastbourne
BN21 2UD
KCC

**HEMMINGS**, Adrian
**Humanistic Psychotherapist**
The Pines
Spithurst Road
Barcombe
East Sussex
BN8 5ED
☏ 01273 401 163
☏ 01273 678 156
a.j.hemmings@sussex.ac.uk
Psychological & Counselling Services
University of Sussex
Brighton
BN1 9RW
AHPP

**HOLLAND**, Sue
**Psychosynthesis Psychotherapist**
16 Bavant Road
Preston Park
Brighton
BN1 6RD
☏ 07939 111 062
☏ 01273 563 098
IPS

**HUETING**, Margaret
**Neurolinguistic Psychotherapist**
31 Elm Grove
Hampden Park
Eastbourne
East Sussex
BN22 9NN
☏ 01323 511150
NLPtCA

**HUTTON**, Francoise
**Analytical Psychologist-Jungian Analyst**
10 Albion Street
Lewes
East Sussex
BN7 2ND
☏ 01273 473 850
CAP *

**IREMONGER**, Sue
**Hypno-Psychotherapist**
PO Box 2764
Lewes
East Sussex
BN8 4WB
☏ 01825 723017
sue.iremonger@add-support-clinic.co.uk
NRHP

**IRONSIDE**, Leslie
**Child Psychotherapist**
35 Clermont Terrace
Brighton
East Sussex
BN1 6SJ
☏ 01273 327221
☏ 01273 540642
ACP

**JACQUES**, Glenys
**Humanistic Psychotherapist**
Flat 4
87 Pevensey Road
St Leonards on Sea
East Sussex
TN38 0LR
☏ 01424 427 836
☏ 07766 082 272
gj@gjacques.fsnet.co.uk
AHPP

**JENNINGS-NICOL**, Sara
**Sexual and Relationship Psychotherapist**
♿ Little Bernhurst
77 London Road
Hurst Green
Etchingham
TN19 7PN
☏ 01580 860345
sarajennings32@hotmail.com
BASRT, IFT

**JONES**, Ros
**Transpersonal Psychotherapist**
Brighton
BN1
☏ 01273 540875
CCPE

**JUPP**, Elizabeth
**Group Analytic Psychotherapist**
33 Beechwood Avenue
Brighton
East Sussex
BN1 8ED
☏ 01273 559 306
UPCA

**KATZ**, Shawn
**Transpersonal Psychotherapist**
c/o Dolphin House Clinic
14 New Road
Brighton
East Sussex
BN1 1UF
☎ 01273 324790
ShawnhKatz@aol.com
CCPE

**LATTIMER**, Carol
**Integrative Psychotherapist**
♿ Florance Cottage
Withyham Road
Groombridge
East Sussex
TN3 9QR
☎ 01892 860 599
☎ 07778 815 279
carol.lattimer@virgin.net
MET

**LEEBURN**, Jennifer
**Psychoanalytic Psychotherapist**
12 Priory Crescent
Lewes
East Sussex
BN7 1HP
☎ 01273 476 444
jennyleeburn@hotmail.com
FIP

**LESSEM**, Pauline Joey
**Cognitive Analytic Therapist**
♿ 7 Michael Fields
Forest Row
East Sussex
RH18 5BM
☎ 01342 823 291
☎ 07050 098 785
jlessem@btopenworld.com
ACAT

**LLOYD**, Elizabeth
**Psychoanalytic Psychotherapist**
12 Preston Park Avenue
Brighton
East Sussex
BN1 6HJ
☎ 01273 555 017
GUILD, SITE

**LOWN**, Judy
**Core Process Psychotherapist**
♿ Flat 1
8 Preston Park Avenue
Brighton
Sussex
BN1 6HJ
☎ 01273 500193
KI

**LYNN**, Kay
**Gestalt Psychotherapist**
156 Osborne Road
Brighton
BN1 6LS
☎ 01273 558 197
GCL

**MALTBY**, Michael
**Group Analyst**
Salomons:Canterbury Christ Church Uni. College
Broomhill Road,
Tunbridge Wells
Kent
TN3 0TG
☎ 01892 507 674
m.maltby@salomons.org.uk
IGA

**MARSHALL**, Susan
**Integrative Psychotherapist**
Moat Mill Farm
Newick Lane
Mayfield
TN20 6RF
☎ 01435 873 483
ssm@moatmill.fsnet.co.uk
SPCRC

**MASANI**, Peter
**Analytical Psychologist-Jungian Analyst**
7 Clare Road
Lewes
East Sussex
BN7 1PN
☎ 01273 474 800
CAP *

**MASTERSON**, Karen
**Existential Psychotherapist**
6 The Acorns
Stonegate
TN5 7EY
☎ 01580 201 742
Karen.masterson@dial.pipex.com
UPCA

**MAXWELL**, Hugh
**Psychodrama Psychotherapist**
Dept. of Psychological Services
Braybrook House
9 Holmesdale Gardens
Hastings
TN34 1LY
☎ 01424 710 070
yesitshugh@yahoo.co.uk
BPA

**MCALPINE**, A M
**Cognitive Behavioural Psychotherapist**
Flat 3
16 Quarry Road
Hastings
TN34 3SE
☎ 01424 721 017
ammca65@hotmail.com
BABCP

**MCLEOD**, Paula
**Biodynamic Psychotherapist**
68 Stanley Road
Brighton
East Sussex
BN1 4NH
☎ 01273 383429
LSBP

**MEDHAT**, Katayoun Tamara
**Psychoanalytic Psychotherapist**
50 Compton Avenue
Brighton
East Sussex
BN1 3PS
☎ 01273 204 527
ktmedhat-@hotmail.com
NAFSI

**MENSINGA**, Vera
**Transpersonal Psychotherapist**
Shepherds Corner
Tompsets Bank
Forest Row
East Sussex
RH18 5U
☎ 01342 823006
veramensinga@compuserve.com
CCPE

**MEREDITH**, Judith
**Transpersonal Psychotherapist**
♿ 58 North Trade Road
Battle
East Sussex
Hants
TN33 0HU
☎ 01424 777 985
☎ 01252 628 428
CCPE

**MICHAELSON**, Sue
**Transpersonal Psychotherapist**
34 St Mary's Terrace
Hastings
East Sussex
TN34 3LR
☎ 01424 429 858
CTP

**MITCHELL**, Leilani
**Transactional Analysis Psychotherapist**
Forest Dell
Green Lane
Crowborough
Sussex
TN6 2DG
☎ 01892 668 079
leilanimitchell@yahoo.co.uk
ITA

**MORGAN-JONES**, Richard
**Psychoanalytic Psychotherapist**
♿ 25 Lewes Road
Eastbourne
East Sussex
BN1 2BY
☎ 01323 647 531
richard.morganjones@btopenworld.com
FIP

**MURRAY**, Linda
**Sexual and Relationship Psychotherapist**
22 Church Street
Old Town
Eastbourne
East Sussex
BN21 1HS
☎ 01323 410 001
☎ 01323 416 552
Linda_murray71@hotmail.com
BASRT

**MYERS**, Janet
**Integrative Psychotherapist**
21 Temple Street
Brighton
BN1 3BH
☎ 01273 775 157
janekeston@hotmail.com
SPCRC

**NORMAN**, Caroline
**Group Analytic Psychotherapist**
36 Buxton Road
Brighton
East Sussex
BN1 5DE
☎ 01273 542 208
carolinmnorman@hotmail.com
UPCA

**PRICE**, Mark
**Transpersonal Psychotherapist**
52 Clyde Road
Brighton
East Sussex
BN1 4NP
☎ 01273 600 534
CTP

**RAE**, Frances
**Systemic Psychotherapist**
♿ Reynards Brook House
Hawkenbury Road
Tunbridge Wells
TN3 9AD
☎ 01892 543 025
KCC

**REEVES**, Alan
**Transpersonal Psychotherapist**
213b Ditchling Road
Brighton
East Sussex
BN1 6JD
☎ 01273 541 194
CCPE

**RICHARDS**, Michael
**Psychoanalytic Psychotherapist**
64 Southover High Street
Lewes
East Sussex
BN7 1JA
☎ 01273 488 250
richards@solutions-inc.co.uk
FPC

**RICHARDSON**, Madeleine
**Sexual and Relationship Psychotherapist**
133 Preston Drove
Brighton
BN1 6LE
☎ 01273 504 385
myr@thebeechgroup.com
BASRT

**RIGNELL**, John
**Psychoanalytic Psychotherapist**
4 Temple Gardens
Brighton
BN1 3AE
☎ 01273 204314
john.rignell@amserve.net
FPC

**RILEY**, Brenda
**Hypno-Psychotherapist**
♿ Hailsham Clinic
2 North Street
Hailsham
East Sussex
BN27 1DQ
☎ 07980 412 475
hypnotherapy@milady.fsbusiness.co.uk
NRHP

**ROBINSON**, Judy
**Psychoanalytic Psychotherapist**
St Laurence House
Park Street, Falmer
Brighton
BN1 9PG
☎ 01273 685937
☎ 01273 606928
GUILD

**RUBIN**, Ann
**Existential Psychotherapist**
Flat 1
19 Montpelier Crescent
Brighton
East Sussex
BN1 3JF
☎ 01273 556 550
☎ 07729 510 300
annrubin@ntlworld.com
UPCA

**SANDERS**, Peter
**Transactional Analysis Psychotherapist**
"Midsummer House"
66 St Helens Park Road
Hastings
East Sussex
TN34 2JJ
☎ 01424 420615
ph.sanders@talk21.com
ITA

**SELLERS**, Duncan
**Integrative Psychotherapist**
18 Shepherds Croft
Withdean
Brighton
BN1 5JF
☎ 01273 552747
duncananddiane@btinternet.com
MC

**SIDHU**, Frankie
**Psychosynthesis Psychotherapist**
4 Gerard Street
Brighton
Sussex
BN1 4NW
☎ 01273 603 896
frankiesidhu@hotmail.com
PET

**SIESE**, Andrew
**Systemic Psychotherapist**
1 Cleve Terrace
Lewes
East Sussex
BN7 1JJ
☎ 01273 478 971
☎ 01323 847 619/01323 414 953
C.A.M.H.S.
Sturton Place
Station Road
Hailsham, East Sussex
BN27 2AU
KCC

**SIM**, Edward
**Hypno-Psychotherapist**
♿ Ridgewood House
Lewes Road
Uckfield
Sussex
TN22 5SN
☎ 01825 766 400
ridgewoodhouse@hotmail.com
NSHAP

**SKYE**, Emily
**Gestalt Psychotherapist**
The Cottage
Maurice Road
Seaford
BN25 1BG
☎ 01323 899 787
GPTI

**SNELL**, Robert C
**Existential Psychotherapist**
19 Montpelier Crescent
Brighton
Sussex
BN1 3JF
☎ 01273 328 355
r.snell@sussex.ac.uk
UPCA

**SNOWDEN**, Patricia
**Sexual and Relationship Psychotherapist**
South Edge
5 Lincoln Close
Meads
Eastbourne
BN20 7TZ
☎ 01323 645 140
BASRT

**SOUTAR**, Sarah
**Psychoanalytic Psychotherapist**
Star Breweries Workshops and Studios
Castle Ditch Lane
Lewes
East Sussex
BN7 1YJ
☎ 01273 486 782
s.soutar@sussex.ac.uk
AGIP

**STEHLE**, Peter
**Existential Psychotherapist**
86b High Street
Rye
TN31 7JN
☎ 01797 225 306
fp.stehle@talk21.com
SPCRC

**SUSS**, Lawrence
**Psychoanalytic Psychotherapist**
♿ 61b Beaconsfield Villas
Brighton
East Sussex
BN1 6HB
☎ 01273 502 900
☎ 01273 508 688
lawrence@suss.org.uk
AGIP

**THOMAS**, Christina
**Psychosynthesis Psychotherapist**
'Quorndon'
Tompsets Bank
Forest Row
East Sussex
RH18 5BE
☎ 01342 822973
PET

**TIERNEY**, Sue
**Hypno-Psychotherapist**
♿ PO Box 69
Heathfield
East Sussex
NRHP

**VALLELY**, Patricia M.
**Transpersonal Psychotherapist**
9 Blatchington Hill
Seaford
East Sussex
BN25 2AH
☎ 01323 893 917
CCPE

**VAN HALM**, Corrie
**Transactional Analysis Psychotherapist**
St. John's Lodge
Burgh Hill
Etchingham
East Sussex
TN19 7PE
☎ 01580 860 891
ITA

**WEAVER**, David
**Group Analytic Psychotherapist**
17 Lauriston Road
Preston Park
Brighton
East Sussex
BN1 6SN
☎ 01273 566 551
synaptics@ntlworld.com.
UPCA

**WHITE**, Anne
**Systemic Psychotherapist**
33 Ridgeway
Hurst Green
Etchingham
TN19 7PJ
☎ 01580 860 355
☎ 01892 522 598
annewhiteuk@yahoo.co.uk
KCC

**WHITE**, Lela Ljiljana
**Psychoanalytic Psychotherapist**
37 Surrenden Road
Brighton
Sussex
BN1 6PQ
☎ 01273 554 543
lelabela@solutions-inc.co.uk
FPC

**WHITE**, Ruth
**Transpersonal Psychotherapist**
9 Telscombe Grange
407 S. Coast Road
Telscombe Cliffs
East Sussex
BN10 7AF
☎ 01273 584 542
☎ 07808 610 386
CTP

**WIGGLESWORTH**, Julia
**Family & Systemic Psychotherapist**
♿ High Combe
Chitcombe Road
Broadoak Brede
Rye
TN31 6EX
☎ 01424 882 881
juliewigs@aol.com
AFT

**YOUNG**, Anna
**Transactional Analysis Psychotherapist**
♿ 13 Abbots Close
Battle
East Sussex
TN33 0BZ
☎ 01424 774 137
anna.young@classicfm.net
ITA *

## SUSSEX - WEST

**ALDRIDGE**, Janet
**Integrative Psychotherapist**
64 Stocks Lane
East Wittering
PO20 8NJ
☎ 01243 670 924
J.Aldridge@ucc.ac.uk
SPCRC

**ANDERSON**, Jette
**Transpersonal Psychotherapist**
10 Mercer Close
Maidenbower
Crawley
West Sussex
RH10 7HZ
☎ 01293 884450
☎ 0775 184 3056
CCPE

**ANSTICE**, Christine
**Psychoanalytic Psychotherapist, Sexual and Relationship Psychotherapist**
10 Selham Close
Ifield
Crawley
West Sussex
RH11 0EH
☎ 01293 535654
canstice@onetel.net.uk
GUILD

**APPS**, Jean
**Hypno-Psychotherapist**
♿ 4 East Court Villas
Cranston Road
East Grinstead
West Sussex
RH19 3HQ
☎ 01342 321 547
NRHP

**ASHWIN**, Mary
**Psychoanalytic Psychotherapist**
31 Wellington Road
Chichester
West Sussex
PO19 6BB
☎ 01243 786 501
Mashwin@waitrose.com
AIP, FPC

**BARDELLE-CARRIER**, Rosemary
**Psychoanalytic Psychotherapist**
27a Goring Road
Goring-by-Sea
West Sussex
BN12 4AR
☎ 01903 856 964
CCOPPP

**BAYNE**, Brenda
**Transpersonal Psychotherapist**
5 The Gatehouse
Edinburgh Square
Midhurst
West Sussex
GU29 9NL
☎ 01730 812 063
CTP

**BEACH**, Roger
**Family & Systemic Psychotherapist**
♿ Cherry Trees
The Ridgway, Beach Estate
Felpham
PO22 7JQ
☎ 01243 869 984
rogerbeach1@hotmail.com
AFT

**BODDINGTON**, Daphne
**Sexual and Relationship Psychotherapist**
♿ 28 Heathfield Park
Midhurst
West Sussex
GU29 9HN
☎ 01730 814 767
djbod@bigfoot.com
BASRT

**BURLTON**, Katherine
**Group Analyst**
Psychotherapy Service
Chapel Street Clinic
Chichester
PO19 1BX
☎ 01243 623 404
IGA

**CATO**, Jane
**Integrative Psychotherapist**
17 Buckingham Road
Shoreham-by-Sea
West Sussex
BN43 5UA
☎ 01273 454865
janecato@clear1britishLibrary.net
MC

**CHARLEY**, Geoff
**Transpersonal Psychotherapist**
2 Northend Farm Cottages
Milland
Near Liphook
Hampshire
GU30 7LT
☎ 01428 741533
☎ 07961 891259
geoffcharley@mac.com
CCPE

**CHRISTIE**, Patricia A.
**Transpersonal Psychotherapist**
♿ Acorn Centre for Natural Health
57A Railway Approach
East Grinstead
West Sussex
RH19 1BT
☎ 01342 317620
basirachristie@hotmail.com
CCPE

**COLE**, Barbara
**Humanistic Psychotherapist, Transpersonal Psychotherapist**
6 Cowper Road
Worthing
West Sussex
BN11 4PD
☎ 01903 209 554
barbaraskycole@tinyworld.co.uk
AHPP

**COLEMAN**, Eva
**Integrative Psychotherapist, Psychoanalytic Psychotherapist**
Lattenbells
Farm Lane
Ditching, Hassocks
West Sussex
BN6 8UR
☎ 01273 844142
evacoleman@yahoo.co.uk
GUILD, SPCRC

**CONNOLLY**, Holly
**Neurolinguistic Psychotherapist**
38 Neville Road
Bognor Regis
West Sussex
PO22 8BJ
☎ 01243 827 411
holly.connolly@ukonline.co.uk
NLPtCA

**COTTAM**, Angela
**Integrative Psychotherapist**
Park House Farm
Vann Road
Fernhurst
GU27 3JP
☎ 01428 658 547
angelacottam@aol.com
SPCRC

**DAVIDSON**, John
**Cognitive Behavioural Psychotherapist**
Greenwoods
Selsey Road
Sidlesham
Chichester, W. Sussex
PO20 7LR
☎ 01243 641 436
☎ 01444 416 778
Cuckfield Surgery
Glebe Road
Cuckfield
RH17 5BQ
BABCP

**DUNCAN**, Sally B
**Sexual and Relationship Psychotherapist**
♿ The Coach House
Elsted
Nr Midhurst
West Sussex
GU29 0JY
☎ 01730 825 789
BASRT

**DUNFORD**, Kathy
**Psychoanalytic Psychotherapist**
22 Juxon Close
Chichester
PO19 7AA
☎ 01243 771 548
IPSS

**DUNLOP**, Joan
**Body Psychotherapist, Integrative Psychotherapist**
10 Balliol Close
Bognor Regis
West Sussex
PO21 5QE
☎ 01243 863 720
CCBP

**DUPONT-JOSHUA**, Aisha
**Psychoanalytic Psychotherapist**
62 Lion Lane
Haslemere
Surrey
GU27 1JD
☎ 01428 651 262
aisha@dupjosh1.demon.co.uk
NAFSI

**ESPOSITO**, Claude
**Family & Systemic Psychotherapist**
♿ Smiles Cottage
47 High Street
Ardingly
West Sussex
RH17 6TB
☎ 01444 892 497
champini@cfesposito.freeserve.co.uk
IFT

**EVANS**, Richard
**Gestalt Psychotherapist**
Brook House
Quay Meadow
Bosham
West Sussex
PO18 8LY
☎ 01243 573 475
RichE@Metanoia.ac.uk
GPTI

**FIELD**, John Cranston
**Cognitive Analytic Therapist**
♿ 64 Wickham Hill
Hurstpierpoint
West Sussex
BN6 9NP
☎ 01273 843 012
☎ 01273 834 716
ACAT

**FISHER**, Maggie
**Transpersonal Psychotherapist**
38 Perryfields
Burgess Hill
West Sussex
RH15 8TU
☎ 01444 257 326
CTP

**GOILLON**, Margaret
**Gestalt Psychotherapist**
Oak Tree Cottage
Chase Lane
Haslemere
Surrey
GU27 3AG
☎ 01428 645 292
margaret@4psychotherapy.co.uk
GCL

**GOTTESMANN**, Ewa
**Group Analyst**
Midhurst
West Sussex
GU29
☎ 01730 815 200
IGA

**GRAY**, Rebecca
**Sexual and Relationship Psychotherapist**
78 Maltravers Street
Arundel
BN18
☎ 01903 884 251
☎ 020 8694 0189
rg.ds.doz@virgin.net
BASRT

**HAGENBACH**, Keith
**Transpersonal Psychotherapist**
Nenthorne West
Hammerwood Road
Ashurst Wood
West Sussex
RH19 3RU
☎ 01342 823461
kk.hagenbach@virgin.net
CCPE

**HAGENBACH**, Kitty
**Transpersonal Psychotherapist**
Nenthorne West
Hammerwood Road
Ashurst Wood
West Sussex
RH19 3BU
☎ 020 7483 3788
☎ 01342 823461
kitty@kittyh.demon.co.uk
CCPE

**HALTER**, Kathy
**Integrative Arts Psychotherapist**
"Sunflowers"
Kimbridge Road
Bracklesham Bay
West Sussex
PO20 8PE
☎ 01243 672 126
☎ 01243 775 302 x153
IATE

**HAMMOND**, Liz
**Existential Psychotherapist**
Catherine Russel Center
Avenue House
Southgate
Chichester
PO19 1ES
☎ 01903 779 037
hamfam@mistral.co.uk
UPCA

**HERDMAN**, Linda
**Cognitive Behavioural Psychotherapist**
♿ Bedale Mental Health Centre
1 Glencathara Road
Bognor Regis
West Sussex
PO21 2SF
☎ 01243 623 732
BABCP

**HOSBURN**, Tania
**Integrative Psychosynthesis Psychotherapist**
Hayling Pond Cottage
Church Street
West Chittington
Pulborough
RH20 2JW
☎ 0771 464 8877
☎ 01798 815 446
tania@time2relate.fsnet.co.uk
Steyning Health Centre
Tanyard Lane
Steyning
West Sussex
BN44 3RJ
RE.V

**JAMES**, Clare
**Integrative Psychotherapist**
♿ Lilac Cottage
Roundstreet Common
Wisborough Green
West Sussex
RH14 0AN
clarelilac@aol.com
MET

**JENNINGS**, Lyn C.
**Educational Therapist**
27 Woodmancote Road
Worthing
West Sussex
BN14 7HT
☎ 01903 237 395
CFET

**KANE**, Janine
**Integrative Psychotherapist**
♿ Whyke Bakery House
Whyke Lane
Chichester
West Sussex
PO19 8AS
☎ 01243 776489
MC

**LAMB**, Geoff
**Humanistic Psychotherapist**
♿ 119 Lingfield Road
East Grinstead
West Sussex
RH19 2EL
☎ 01342 315 640
☎ 07949 153 431
G.C.Lamb@btinternet.com
AHPP

**LANE**, Jeff
**Humanistic and Integrative Psychotherapist**
1 Brooklands Road
Havant
PO9 3NS
☎ 02392 782 987
jeff@jeffreylane.co.uk
SPEC, UPCA

**LITTLE**, Marie
**Psychoanalytic Psychotherapist**
Spindrift
24 Warner Road, Selsey
Chichester
West Sussex
PO20 9DD
☎ 01243 601073
IPSS

**MARIEN**, Brian
**Cognitive Behavioural Psychotherapist**
♿ King Edward VII Hospital
Midhurst
GU29 0BL
☎ 01730 812 341
☎ 01243 530 600
brianmarien@aol.com
The Chichester Nuffield Hospital
78 Broyle Road
Chichester
PO19 4BE
BABCP

**MARTIN**, Linda
**Gestalt Psychotherapist**
♿ 14 Garden House Lane
East Grinstead
W Sussex
RH19 4JT
☎ 01342 312 974
lmart@tinyworld.co.uk
GCL

**MCCLELLAND**, Sheila
**Psychodynamic Psychotherapist**
Princess Royal Hospital
c/o Villa Reception, Psychotherapy
Lewes Road
Haywards Heath
RH16 4EX
☎ 01273 421 501
☎ 01444 441 881 x4515
bishopeliza@aol.com
UPCA

**MCMINNIES**, Patricia
**Psychoanalytic Psychotherapist**
149 Western Road
Hurstpierpoint
Hassocks
West Sussex
BN6 9SZ
☎ 01273 834 454
AGIP

**MIDDLEHURST**, Daniel
**Cognitive Behavioural Psychotherapist**
♿ Child & Family Service for MH
Orchard House
9 College Lane
Chichester
PO19 4PQ
☎ 01243 815 514
BABCP

**MILLER**, Bob
**Attachment-based Psychoanalytic Psychotherapist**
11 Arthur Road
Horsham
West Sussex
RH13 5BG
☎ 01403 255 387
CAPP

**MONTANARO**, Caroline F B
**Existential Psychotherapist**
118 Congreve Road
Broadwater
Worthing
W. Sussex
BN14 8EW
☎ 01903 235 191
caroline.montanaro@ukgateway.net
UPCA

**MURPHY**, Derry
**Personal Construct Psychotherapist**
1 Splashpoint House
2 Marine Parade
Worthing
West Sussex
BN11
☎ 07930 361 736
derry@derry2001.co.uk
PCP

**PARKER**, Caroline
**Attachment-based Psychoanalytic Psychotherapist**
6 St Mary's Close
Lavant
Chichester
West Sussex
PO18 0DL
☎ 01243 533 227
CAPP

**PELISSIER**, Kate
**Family & Systemic Psychotherapist**
♿ 3 Farmleigh Close
Pound Hill
Crawley
RH10 3AH
☎ 01293 426 267
kate.pelissier@surreyoaklands.nhs.uk
AFT

**PERRY**, Philip
**Transactional Analysis Psychotherapist**
Calthorpe House
Brighton
BN12
☎ 01273 626 040
philip@maximizepeople.com
ITA

**POTHIG**, Elisabeth
**Transpersonal Psychotherapist**
♿ 83 Penland Road
Haywards Heath
RH16 1PJ
☎ 01444 453 384
☎ 07870 967 179
elisabethpothig@hotmail.com
CCPE

**PRUE**, Janet
**Psychoanalytic Psychotherapist**
37 Balcombe Road
Haywards Heath
RH16 1PA
☎ 01444 455 502
Janet.prue@talk21.com
GUILD

**PYPER**, Julia
**Psychoanalytic Psychotherapist**
West Sussex Health and Social Care, NHS Trust
The Psychotherapy Service
Chapel Street
Chichester
PO19 1BX
☎ 01243 623 400
CSP

**QUINN**, Susan
**Transpersonal Psychotherapist**
The Psychology Service for Sexual Health
16 Liverpool Gardens
Worthing
West Sussex
BN11 1RY
☎ 01903 843 543
CTP

**REILLY**, Nicole S.
**Transpersonal Psychotherapist**
♿ 28 St. George's Road
Worthing
West Sussex
BN11 2DR
☎ 01903 203533
CCPE

**ROSE**, Theresa
**Integrative Psychotherapist**
48 Burleigh Way
Crawley Down
West Sussex
RH10 4UQ
☎ 01342 717 095
t.rose@surrey.ac.uk
UPCA

**RUIJTERMAN**, Caroline
**Psychoanalytic Psychotherapist**
♿ Acorns
Coldharbour Lane
Patching
Worthing
BN13 3XE
☎ 01903 871 469
AIP

**RUSSEL**, Pat
**Hypno-Psychotherapist**
♿ Chichester Natural Health Centre
5 City Business Centre
Basin Road
Chichester
PO19 8DU
☎ 01243 786 946
☎ 01243 816 679
patrussel@messages.co.uk
16 Oving Road
Chichester
West Sussex
PO19 7EH
NRHP

**SCOTT**, Liz
**Sexual and Relationship Psychotherapist**
♿ York Lodge
Haywards Heath
West Sussex
RH16
☎ 01444 410 715
liz@scottej.freeserve.co.uk
BASRT

**SHUTTLEWORTH**, John
**Gestalt Psychotherapist**
Crawley College Counselling Dept.
Crawley College, West Green Centre
West Green Drive
Crawley
RH11 7EL
☎ 01293 442 290
☎ 020 8749 3792
john@jshuttleworth.fsnet.co.uk
GPTI

**SKEGG**, Roz
**Integrative Psychotherapist**
20 Furnace Farm Road
Furnace Green
Crawley
West Sussex
RH10 6QA
☎ 01293 516 212
MET

**SKILLICORN**, Ingrid
**Family & Systemic Psychotherapist**
IONA
Great Walstead School
Eat Mascalls Lane
Lindfield
RH16 2QL
☎ 01444 482 924
☎ 01483 783 330
IFT

**STRATTON-WOODWARD**, Edward
**Transpersonal Psychotherapist**
1 Old Warehouse
Mews
Littlehampton
West Sussex
BN17 5GE
☎ 01903 725100
CCPE

**SYNNOTT**, Annie
**Existential Psychotherapist**
Mill Farm
Mill Road
Slindon Common
Arundel
BN18 0LY
☎ 01243 814 169
hilsynn@aol.com
UPCA

**THOMAS**, Jenny
**Sexual and Relationship Psychotherapist**
PO20
BASRT

**THORPE**, Ivan
**Integrative Psychotherapist**
♿ Counselling and Welfare Unit
North Brook College
Worthing
BN14 8HJ
☎ 01903 606 440
SPCRC

**WALKER**, Jim
**Psychoanalytic Psychotherapist**
Westlake
Broad Street
Cuckfield
West Sussex
RH17 5LL
☎ 01444 440204 (t/f)
jimawalker@hotmail.com
IPSS

**WALKER**, Rosalind
**Family & Systemic Psychotherapist**
Westlake
Broad Street
Cuckfield, Haywards Heath
West Sussex
RH17 5LL
☎ 01444 440 204
roalsind.w@virgin.net
AFT

**WARREN**, Tony
**Neurolinguistic Psychotherapist**
16 Noel Green
Burgess Hill
West Sussex
RH15 8BS
☎ 01444 246 660
tonybalance@aol.com
NLPtCA

**WEST**, Marcus
**Analytical Psychologist-Jungian Analyst**
Highbank
45 Cross Lane Findon
Findon
West Sussex
BN14 0UB
☎ 01903 877039
marcusaswest@aol.com
CAP *

**WILMOT**, Vivienne
**Psychoanalytic Psychotherapist**
♿ "Ithaca"
62 Petworth Road
Haslemere
Surrey
GU27 3AU
☎ 01428 643 912
pandorascatalyst@yahoo.co.uk
FIP

**VAN RIJN**, Biljana
**Transactional Analysis Psychotherapist**
21 Kingsham Avenue
Chichester
West Sussex
PO19 8AW
☎ 07960 180 284
biljanavanrijn@yahoo.co.uk
ITA, MET

## SWINDON

**AMIES**, Peter
**Cognitive Psychotherapist**
Kingshill House
Kingshill Road
Swindon
SN1 4LG
☎ 01865 556 322
☎ 01793 491 917
100422.624@compuserve.com
BABCP

**DE SOUZA**, Janice
**Cognitive Psychotherapist**
♿ Kingshill House
Kingshill Road
Swindon
Wiltshire
SN1 4LG
☎ 01793 491 917
BABCP

**HOLLOWAY**, Elizabeth
**Gestalt Psychotherapist**
Lantern Cottage
Elcombe
Swindon
Wilts
SN4 9QL
☎ 01793 845 909
lizholloway@uk-consultants.co.uk
GPTI

**LAW**, Annie
**Sexual and Relationship Psychotherapist**
♿ C P Counselling
Park House
Church Place
Swindon
SN1 5ED
☎ 01793 339 482
☎ 07971 627 478
cpcounselling@i12.com
BASRT

**MACGREGOR**, Alan M
**Cognitive Behavioural Psychotherapist**
♿ Ease Management Centre
7 Newport Street
Old Town
Swindon
SN1 3DX
☎ 01793 433 422
alan.macgregor@virgin.net
BABCP

**POCOCK**, David
**Family & Systemic Psychotherapist**
♿ Child and Family Consultation Service
Marlborough House
Princess Margaret Hospital
Okus Road, Swindon
SN1 4JS
☎ 01793 428 800
dpocock@poey.demon.co.uk
AFT, SIP

**PREGNALL**, Sheila
**Psychodrama Psychotherapist**
Wroughton Health Centre
Barret Way
Wroughton
Swindon
SN4 9LW
☎ 01793 766 862
☎ 01793 766 863
s.pregnall@ukonline.co.uk
BPA

**ROBB**, Melissa
**Family & Systemic Psychotherapist**
Wat Tyler House
Euclid Street
Swindon
SN1 2JH
☎ 01793 466 927
AFT

**WESTMAN**, Stephen
**Cognitive Behavioural Psychotherapist**
♿ Kingshill House
Kingshill Road
Swindon
Wiltshire
SN1 4LG
☎ 01793 491 917
steve.westman@awp.nhs.uk
BABCP

**WORTHING-DAVIES**, Richard
**Systemic Psychotherapist**
♿ 11 Grovelands Avenue
Swindon
SN1 4ET
☎ 01793 642 702
richard@kcsswift.fsnet.co.uk
KCC

**WORTHING-DAVIES**, Sally
**Systemic Psychotherapist**
♿ 11 Grovelands Avenue
Swindon
SN1 4ET
☎ 01793 612 702
sally@kingswayconsult.co.uk
KCC

## TYNE AND WEAR

**ALLISON**, Janet
**Analytical Psychologist, Psychoanalytic Psychotherapist**
9 Lilac Gardens
Low Fell
Gateshead
NE9 5TL
☎ 0191 487 6807
allibags@care4free.co.uk
FIP

**BATCHELOR (MRS)**, Henrietta
**Sexual and Relationship Psychotherapist**
♿ Dept. of Health Psychology
North Tyneside General Hospital
Rake Lane
North Shields
☎ 0191 259 6660
☎ 0191 226 8508
profjonbat@aol.com
8 The Drive
Gosforth
Newcastle-upon-Tyne
NE3 4AH
BASRT

**BIANCARDI**, Jenny
**Psychodrama Psychotherapist**
9 Stratford Grove
Heaton
Newcastle Upon Tyne
NE6 5AT
☎ 0191 281 6243
☎ 0191 265 9664
jenny.biancardi@dial.pipex.com
BPA

**BIRD**, Margaret
**Psychodrama Psychotherapist**
Student Counselling Service
University of Newcastle
Barras Buildings
Eldon Place
NE1 7RU
☎ 0191 222 7699
margaret.bird@ncl.ac.uk
BPA

**BLACK**, Patricia Anne
**Psychoanalytic Psychotherapist**
Psychotherapy Dept.
Off Framlington Place
Newcastle-upon-Tyne
NE2 4AA
☎ 0191 282 4087
☎ 0143 4344 4639
stanegatepb@aol.com
FIP

**BLACKBURN**, Ivy-Marie
**Cognitive Behavioural Psychotherapist**
♿ Newcastle Cognitive Therapy Centre
Plummer Court
Carliol Place
Newcastle upon Tyne
NE1 6UR
☎ 0191 219 6284
☎ 0191 236 4808
ivyblackburn@tiscali.co.uk
48 Westwood Road
Brunton Park
Newcastle upon Tyne
NE3 5NN
BABCP

**CHANDRA**, Ish
**Hypno-Psychotherapist**
13 Montrose Drive
Gateshead
Tyne & Wear
NE10 8BP
☎ 01914 694 667
ish@victoriaclinic.co.uk
NRHP

**CLARKE**, Stephen Lawrence
**Cognitive Psychotherapist**
♿ Denethorpe
Stockton Road
Ryhope
SUNDERLAND
SR2 0NE
☎ 0191 569 9408
BABCP

**CROMARTY**, Paul
**Cognitive Behavioural Psychotherapist**
♿ Newcastle Cognitive Therapy Centre
Plummer Court
Carliol Place
Newcastle upon Tyne
NE1 6UR
☎ 0191 219 6288
BABCP

**DAVIDSON**, Eileen
**Psychosynthesis Psychotherapist**
♿ 9 Highbury
Jesmond
Newcastle upon Tyne
NE2 3DX
☎ 01912 812 511
eileen@globalnet.co.uk
IPS

**DAVIS**, Edna
**Psychodrama Psychotherapist**
60 Northumberland Avenue
Gosforth
Newcastle upon Tyne
Tyneside
NE3 4AQ
☎ 0191 213 5274
☎ 0191 121 0237
matrix.therpay@virgin.net
BPA

**DOBSON**, Mary
**Psychoanalytic Psychotherapist**
10 Meadway
Forest Hall
Newcastle upon Tyne
NE12 9RB
☎ 0191 261 7643
☎ 0191 266 6501
Lindisfarne Centre
71 Westgate Road
Newcastle-upon-Tyne
NE1 1SG
FIP

**ENNIS**, Sally-Anne
**Cognitive Analytic Therapist**
♿ Dept. of Adult Psychology
Cherry Knowle Hospital
Denethorpe Stockton Road
Ryhope, Sunderland
SR2 0NE
☎ 07931 618 029
☎ 0191 569 9427
ACAT

**FRASER**, Julie
**Family & Systemic Psychotherapist**
Child & Family Dept.
Sunderland Royal Hospital
Kaylle Road
Sunderland
☎ 0191 569 9026
AFT

**GARRETT**, Pat
**Integrative Psychotherapist**
83 Jesmond Road
Jesmond
Newcastle
NE2 1NH
☎ 01912 098 383
NGP

**GILBERT**, Barbara
**Psychoanalytic Psychotherapist**
1st Floor, St Nicholas House
St Nicholas Hospital
Jubilee Road
Newcastle upon Tyne
NE3 3XT
☎ 0191 223 2226
barbara.gilbert@eggconnect.net
FIP

**HIRSCH**, Regina
**Cognitive Behavioural Psychotherapist**
♿ 7 Oxford Terrace
Gateshead
Tyne & Wear
NE8 1RQ
☎ 0191 477 5677
☎ 0191 477 3294
BABCP

**JACKSON**, Paul
**Family & Systemic Psychotherapist**
63 Park Avenue
Seaburn
Sunderland
SR6 9DJ
☎ 0191 548 5417
paul@4glenthorpe.fsnet.co.uk
AFT

**JELLEMA**, Anna
**Cognitive Analytic Therapist**
♿ "Denethorpe"
Stockton Road
Ryhope
Sunderland
SR2 0NE
☎ 0191 569 9408
ACAT

**KENDAL**, Jo Reed
**Psychoanalytic Psychotherapist**
Southern Wood
2 Ridgeway Fenham
Newcastle
NE4 9UL
☎ 0191 275 0612
jo.kendal@tiscali.co.uk
FIP

**LEMON**, Marcia
**Psychosynthesis Psychotherapist**
53 Jesmond Vale
Newcastle upon Tyne
NE2 1PH
☎ 01912 300 878
IPS

**LISTER-FORD**, Christine
**Integrative Psychotherapist**
83 Jesmond Road
Jesmond
Newcastle Upon Tyne
NE2 1HH
☎ 01912 098 383
☎ 01642 649 004
NGP

**MCNAMARA**, Jennifer
**Integrative Psychotherapist**
83 Jesmond Road
Jesmond
Newcastle
NE2 1HH
☎ 01642 649 004
☎ 01912 098 383
NGP

**MITCHISON**, Sally
**Group Analyst**
Upper Poplars
Cherry Knowle Hospital
Ryhope
Sunderland
SR2 0NB
☎ 0191 569 9477
sally.mitchison@stw.nhs.uk
IGA

**MOORHEAD**, Steve
**Cognitive Behavioural Psychotherapist**
♿ Newcastle CBT Centre
Plummer Court
Carliol Place
Newcastle Upon Tyne
NE1 6UR
steve.moorhead@nmht.nhs.uk
BABCP

**MORGAN**, Shirley P.
**Psychoanalytic Psychotherapist**
Child & Family Unit
Sunderland Royal Hospital
Kayll Road
Sunderland
SR4 7TP
☎ 0191 569 9026
☎ 01434 673 090
FIP

**NEDEN**, Jeanette
**Family & Systemic Psychotherapist**
C/O The Lindisfarne Centre
71 Westgate Rd
Newcastle Upon Tyne
NE1 1SG
☎ 0191 261 7643
neden@haggbank.freeserve.co.uk
AFT

**O'NEILL**, Shelagh
**Family & Systemic Psychotherapist**
♿ The Child and Family Dept.
Sunderland Royal Hospital
Kayll Road
Sunderland
SR4 7TP
☎ 0191 569 9026
AFT

**PHOENIX**, Ashleigh
**Psychoanalytic Psychotherapist**
Claremont House
Off Framlington Place
Newcastle upon Tyne
NE2 4AA
☎ 0191 420 0198
☎ 0191 282 4547
Daisy Cottage
Ivy Lane
Lawfell
Gateshead
FIP

**QUINN**, Jacqueline
**Psychosynthesis Psychotherapist**
11 The Gardens
Monkseaton
Whitley Bay
Tyne and Wear
NE25 8BG
☎ 01912 510 487
quinnjacqueline@aol.com
IPS

**REEVES**, Thomas
**Cognitive Behavioural Psychotherapist**
♿ Department of Clinical Psychology
Denethorpe
Stockton Road
Ryhope, Sunderland
SR2 0NE
☎ 0191 569 9408
☎ 07761 120 280
BABCP

**STANDART**, Sally H
**Cognitive Psychotherapist**
2a Holly Avenue
Jesmond
Newscastle Upon Tyne
NE2 2PY
☎ 0191 281 9468
sallystandart@doctors.org.uk
BABCP

**TURKINGTON**, Douglas
**Cognitive Psychotherapist**
♿ Royal Victoria Infirmary
Leazes Wing, Dept of Psychiatry
Richardson Road
Newcastle-upon-Tyne
NE1 4LP
☎ 0191 282 4842
BABCP

**WHEELER**, John
**Family & Systemic Psychotherapist**
5 Runhead Gardens
Ryton
Tyne & Wear
NE40 3HH
☎ 0191 413 8568
john@jwheeler.freeserve.co.uk
AFT

**WILSON**, Sandy
**Integrative Psychotherapist**
The Northern Guild for Psychotherapy
83 Jesmond Road
Jesmond
Newcastle
NE2
☎ 01912 402 850
NGP

## WARWICKSHIRE

**ABBERLEY**, Colette
**Analytical Psychotherapist, Psychodynamic Psychotherapist**
5 Highcroft Crescent
Avonside, Milverton
Leamington Spa
Warwickshire
CV32 6BZ
WMIP

**ANDERSON**, Judith
48 Grove Street
Leamington Spa
CV32 5AG
☎ 01926 421 524
WMIP

**BARRETT**, James
**Psychoanalytic Psychotherapist (Jungian)**
48 Grove Street
Leamington Spa
Warwickshire
CV32 5AG
☎ 01926 316 178
james.barrett1@btinternet.com
WMIP

**BEEDIE**, Margaret
**Psychodynamic Psychotherapist**
St Michael's Hospital
St Michael's Road
Warwick
CV34 5QW
WMIP

**BENNETT**, John
**Group Analytic Psychotherapist**
1, Eastlands Road
Rugby
Warwicks
CV21 3RP
☎ 01788 571 508
john.bennett@bigfoot.com
UPCA

**BREWSTER**, Marnie
**Sexual and Relationship Psychotherapist**
The Brooke Centre
58 Regent Street
Rugby
CV21 2PS
☎ 0800 587 8080
☎ 07796 445 588
marniebrewster@thebrookecentre.co.uk
BASRT

**BURNS**, Alex
**Psychoanalytic Psychotherapist**
30 Langton Road
Rugby
Warwicks
CV21 3UA
☎ 020 7 586 7076
☎ 01788 536446
alexburns@nwlpc.co.uk
IPSS

**CERFONTYNE**, Suzanne
**Systemic Psychotherapist**
65 Marfield Close
Sutton Coldfield
B76 1YD
☎ 0121 351 6495
rkc@cerfon.fresserve.co.uk
KCC

**CHAPMAN**, Jane
**Rational Emotive Behaviour Therapist**
109 Lower Hillmorton Road
Rugby
Warwickshire
CV21 3TN
☎ 01788 551 626
BABCP

**DAVIS**, John D
**Integrative Psychotherapist**
20 Beauchamp Avenue
Leamington Spa
Warwickshire
CV32 5TA
☎ 01926 336 668
UPCA

**DAVIS**, Marcia L
**Integrative Psychotherapist**
20 Beauchamp Avenue
Leamington Spa
Warwickshire
CV32 5TA
☎ 01926 336 668
marcialeedavis@aol.com
UPCA

**DAY**, Melanie
**Cognitive Behavioural Psychotherapist**
Clinical Psychology Department
St. Michaels Hospital
St. Michaels Road
Warwick
CV34 5QW
☎ 01926 406 714
☎ 01926 410 281
melanie.day@swarkpct.nhs.uk
Clinical Psychology
The Woodleigh Beeches Centre
Lakin Road
Warwick
CV34 5BW
BABCP

**DAZELEY**, Jen Fiona
**Psychodrama Psychotherapist**
Westwinds
Brookside Close
Rugby
Warwickshire
CV22 6AH
☎ 01788 560 941
BPA

**DEEBLE**, Elizabeth A.
**Cognitive Behavioural Psychotherapist**
Clinical Psychology
The Woodlegih Beeches Centre
Lakin Road
Warwick
CV34 5BW
☎ 020 8970 4039
BABCP

**ENSER**, Nigel
**Family & Systemic Psychotherapist**
♿ Department for Children, Young People & Families
Tiddington Fields
Main Road
Tiddington
CV34 7AY
☎ 01789 414 643
nigel.enser@swarkpct.nhs.uk
AFT

**FOKIAS**, Dene
**Cognitive Behavioural Psychotherapist**
♿ Royal Lemmington Spa Rehabilitation
Heathcote Lane
Heathcote
Warwick
CV34 6SR
☎ 0121 459 6364
dene@denebritig.glowinternet.com
BABCP

**HALL**, Paula
**Sexual and Relationship Psychotherapist**
1 Williams Road
Radford Semele
Nr Leamington Spa
CV31 1UR
☎ 01926 885 129
paulaahall@aol.com
BASRT

**HARRIS**, Richard
**Gestalt Psychotherapist**
41 Weston Lane
Bulkington, Nr Nuneaton
Warwickshire
CV12 9RS
☎ 024 76 319 872
rharris@doctors.org.uk
SPTI

**HILL**, Brenda
**Sexual and Relationship Psychotherapist**
♿ 93 High Street
Bidford on Avon
☎ 01789 773 192
topic@btinternet.com
BASRT

**HOLMES**, Dorothy
**Jungian Analytical Psychotherapist**
1 Quarry Lane
Nuneaton
Warwickshire
CV11 6QB
WMIP

**HOPE**, David
**Gestalt Psychotherapist**
59 Red Lane
Kenilworth
Warwickshire
CV8 1PA
☎ 07939 085 326
enquiries@david-hope.co.uk
SPTI

**HUDSON**, Rachel
**Integrative Psychotherapist**
14 Windyridge Road
Sutton Coldfield
B76 1HB
☎ 0121 351 3193
☎ 07974 410 409
rachel.hudson@tinyonline.co.uk
SPTI

**JANE**, Susan
**Psychodynamic Psychotherapist**
♿ 17 Weedon Lane
Norton
Nr Daventry
Northampton
NN11 5NQ
☎ 07887 903 109
☎ 01327 312 535
sue@suej.fsbusiness.co.uk
VAPP

**LACEY**, Irene
**Family & Systemic Psychotherapist**
16 Keytes Lane
Barford
Warwick
CV35 8EP
☎ 01926 624 543
AFT

**LLOYD**, Patricia
**Psychoanalytic Psychotherapist**
Fernvilla, Daventry Road
Newnham
Northants
NN11 3HF
☎ 01327 879524
Trish.Lloyd@btopenworld.com
IPSS

**MACE**, Chris
**Group Analyst**
Dept. of Psychology
University of Warwick
Coventry
CV4 7AL
☎ 024 76 524 225
c.mace@warwick.ac.uk
IGA

**MCNAUGHT**, Janet
**Sexual and Relationship Psychotherapist**
♿ Coach House Counselling
The Coach House
1 Russell Street
Leamington Spa
CV32 5QA
☎ 01926 882 521
☎ 01926 881 355
info@thecoachhouse.uk.com
BASRT

**MCNICHOLL**, Declan
**Personal Construct Psychotherapist**
Tamworth Adult Mental Health Service
c/o Cherry Orchard House
Tamworth
Staffs
B79 7EE
☎ 01827 308 820
declan21@hotmail.com
PCP

**MEREDITH-OWEN**, William
**Analytical Psychotherapist**
♿ Boscobel
Hatton Rock
Stratford-upon-Avon
CV37 0NU
WMIP

**MOREBY**, Patricia Joyce
**Hypno-Psychotherapist**
12 Heycroft, Gibbet Hill
Coventry
West Midlands
CV4 7HE
☎ 02476 418 202
patricia.mga-coatings@virgin.net
NRHP

**MYERS**, Marion
**Jungian Analytical Psychotherapist**
44 St. Mary's Road
Leamington Spa
Warks.
CV31 1JP
☎ 01926 425403
Mmyers4544@aol.com
WMIP

**NICHOLAS**, John
**Jungian Analytical Psychotherapist**
41 Portland Street
Leamington Spa
CV32 5EY
☎ 01926 452 891
john.nicholas@btinternet.com
WMIP

**PAYMAN**, Barbara
**Transactional Analysis Psychotherapist**
Creative Health Centre
39a Regent Street
Leamington Spa
Warwickshire
CV32 5JX
☎ 01926 316 500
☎ 01926 859 924
ITA

**ROY**, Geraldine
**Psychoanalytic Psychotherapist**
174 Walmley Road
Sutton Coldfield
West Midlands
B76 2PY
☎ 01213 511 651
WMIP

**SAMSON**, Anne
**Psychoanalytic Psychotherapist**
19 St. Marys Crescent
Leamington Spa
Warks.
CV31 1JL
☎ 01926 883 115
anne.samson@virgin.net
WMIP

**SIMPSON**, Elizabeth
**Jungian Analytical Psychotherapist**
49 Holly Street
Leamington Spa
Warwickshire
CV32 4TT
☎ 01926 773 215
lizson@ntlworld.com
WMIP

**SMITH**, Robert
**Neurolinguistic Psychotherapist**
5 Hall Close
Kilsby
Nr. Rugby
Warwickshire
CV23 8XZ
☎ 01788 822 141
robert-smith@freeuk.com
NLPtCA

**TAYLOR**, Vivienne
**Analytical Psychotherapist**
♿ 146 Malt House Lane
Earlswood
Solihull
West Midlands
B94 5SD
☎ 01564 702 992
viviennetaylorwm@aol.com
WMIP

**WEIGHT**, Pam
**Neurolinguistic Psychotherapist**
4 Chetwynd Drive
Whitestone
Nuneaton
Warwickshire
CV11 4TE
☎ 02476 743 139
pamweight@ntlworld.com
NLPtCA

**WILLIAMS**, Tina
**Integrative Psychotherapist**
31 Glenfield Avenue
Weddington
Nuneaton
CV10 0DZ
☎ 0124 7638 3670
tintintkw@supanet.com
SPTI

**WREN**, Pauline
**Hypno-Psychotherapist**
2 Paddox House
25 Dunsmore Avenue
Rugby
Warwickshire
CV22 5HD
☎ 01788 560793
paulinewren@amserve.net
NRHP

## WEST MIDLANDS

**ALEXANDER**, Erica
**Family & Systemic Psychotherapist**
Barnford Placement support Unit
Causeway Green Rd
Oldbury
B68 8LA
☎ 0121 544 6203
FIC

**ALLEN**, Diane
**Personal Construct Psychotherapist**
Sage Ward, Gulson Hospital
Gulson Road
Coventry
CV5
☎ 02476 246268
PCP

**ANDREWS**, Ruth
**Psychoanalytic Psychotherapist**
The Birmingham Nuffield Hospital
22 Somerset Road
Edgbaston
Birmingham
B15 2QQ
☎ 0121 456 2000
CCOPPP

**ANSTEY**, John
**Hypno-Psychotherapist**
7 Primrose Croft
Hall Green
Birmingham
B28 0JP
☎ 0121 733 7726
☎ 07966 475 036
ansteyj@blueyonder.co.uk
CTIS

**APPEL-OPPER**, Julianne
**Gestalt Psychotherapist, Integrative Psychotherapist**
Selly Park
Birmingham
B29
☎ 0121 472 3633
AHPP

**BAIM**, Clark
**Psychodrama Psychotherapist**
c/o Change Point
44 Daisy Road
Edgbaston
Birmingham
B16 9DZ
☎ 0121 454 2739
☎ 07961 517 135
cbaim@hotmail.com
BPA

**BEER**, Charmian
**Sexual and Relationship Psychotherapist**
11a Salisbury Road
Moseley
Birmingham
B13 8JS
☎ 0121 449 4343
cjbeer@hotmail.com
BASRT

**BENNETT**, Robert
28 Ufton Close
Shirley
Solihull
B90 3SB
☎ 0121 603 5280
bob@bobbennett.freeserve.co.uk
AFT

**BIRTLE**, Janice
**Psychoanalytic Psychotherapist**
Bridger House
22 Summer Road
Acocks Green
Birmingham
B27 7UT
☎ 0121 678 3244
WMIP

**BISCONTI**, Maria
**Hypno-Psychotherapist**
2D Hilaries Road
Birmingham
B23 7QP
☎ 0121 350 3762
CTIS

**BLACK**, Teresa
**Psychoanalytic Psychotherapist**
♿ Clevelands House
10/12 Tetten Hall Road
Wolverhampton
WV1 4SA
☎ 01902 445 937
NWIDP

**BLAKEY**, Angela
**Psychoanalytic Psychotherapist**
39 Carlyle Road
Edgbaston
Birmingham
B16 9BH
☎ 01214 545 440
WMIP

**BOND**, Ann R.
**Psychodynamic Psychotherapist**
Devon House
Adult Psychotherapy Service
Mindelsohn Way, Edgbaston
Birmingham
B15 2QR
WMIP

**BRADISH**, Hazel
**Sexual and Relationship Psychotherapist**
♿ 22 Westfield Road
Edgbaston
Birmingham
B15 3QG
☎ 0121 246 4768
☎ 0121 507 4375
hbradish@blueyonder.co.uk
BASRT

**BRINSDON**, Nicholas William
**Family & Systemic Psychotherapist**
♿ Child and Family Unit
93 Northbrook Road
Shirley
Solihull
B90 3LX
☎ 0121 744 0449
nick.brinsdon@solihull-pct.nhs.uk
AFT

**BROCK**, Susan
**Hypno-Psychotherapist**
♿ 83 Clarke Road
Woverhampton
WV3 9PA
☎ 01902 659 887
s.brock@wlv.ac.uk
NRHP

**BROOKS**, John
**Cognitive Behavioural Psychotherapist**
♿ CBP Services
Sycamore House Medical Centre
111 Birmingham Road
Walsall
WS1 2NL
☎ 01922 644 661
brookspsych@aol.com
BABCP

**BRUCE**, John
**Integrative Psychotherapist**
108 Poplar Road
Dorridge
Solihull
B93 8DG
☎ 01564 730 250
☎ 0121 627 1627
MC

**BURKE**, Robina
**Analytical Psychotherapist**
39 Beaumont Road
Bournville
Birmingham
B30 2EA
☎ 01216 285 124
WMIP

**BURNHAM**, John
**Systemic Psychotherapist**
♿ Parkview Clinic
Queensbridge Road
Moseley
Birmingham
B13 8DS
☎ 0121 243 2000
☎ 020 7720 7301
burnham1@aol.com
KCC

**CALVERT**, Jane
**Psychoanalytic Psychotherapist**
48 Hartopp Road
Four Oaks
Sutton Coldfield
Birmingham
B74 2QR
WMIP

**CARLISH**, Sonia
**Psychoanalytic Psychotherapist**
8 Moor Green Lane
Moseley
Birmingham
B13 8ND
☎ 0121 449 0544
WMIP

**CERFONTYNE**, Suzanne
**Systemic Psychotherapist**
♿ Parkview Clinic
60 Queensbridge Road
Moseley
Birmingham
B13 8QE
☎ 0121 351 6495
rkc@cerfon.fresserve.co.uk
KCC

**COOPER**, Grahame F.
**Psychoanalytic Psychotherapist, Sexual and Relationship Psychotherapist**
6 Clarence Road
Moseley
Birmingham
B13 9SX
☎ 0121 449 2308
BASRT, WMIP

**COUPE**, Alyson
**Psychodrama Psychotherapist**
119 Murdock Road
Handsworth
Birmingham
B21 9JR
☎ 0121 685 7232
alysoncoupe@aol.com
BPA

**CULL**, Rose
**Child Psychotherapist**
B.T.P.P.
Queen's College, Somerset Road
Edgbaston
Birmingham
B15 2QH
☎ 0121-455 9393
ACP

**CUMMINS**, Peter
**Personal Construct Psychotherapist**
Psychological Services
Sage Ward, Gulson Hospital
Gulson Road
Coventry
CV1 2HR
☎ 02476 246 268
petercummins@dial.pipex.com
PCP

**DAVIS**, Richard
**Integrative Psychotherapist**
66 Rosslyn Avenue
Coundon
Coventry
CV6 1GN
☎ 02476 335 668
r.davis@coventry.ac.uk
MET

**DENHAM**, Juliet
**Gestalt Psychotherapist**
Birmingham Counselling Centre
131 Pottery Road
Worley Woods
Oldbury, Birmingham
B29 9HE
☎ 01746 718 231
julietdenham@synergynet.co.uk
GPTI

**DENNIS**, Elisabeth
**Psychoanalytic Psychotherapist, Psychoanalytic Psychotherapist (Jungian)**
47 Carlyle road
Edgbaston
Birmingham
B16 9BH
WMIP

**DOGGART**, Elizabeth Anne
**Cognitive Behavioural Psychotherapist**
97 Wood Lane
Harborne
Birmingham
B17 9AY
☎ 0121 427 7292
☎ 07850 990 711
BABCP

**DOVEY**, Alan
**Cognitive Behavioural Psychotherapist**
♿ 44 Coles Lane
Sutton Coldfield
B72 1NE
☎ 0121 355 7510
☎ 07941 196 379
alan@adovey.fsnet.co.uk
BABCP

**EDGINGTON**, Paula
**Systemic Psychotherapist**
Primary Care Team Crescent House
Broad Street
Bilston
Wolverhampton
WV14 0BZ
☎ 01902 444 809
☎ 01902 444 819
paula.edgington@wolvespct.nhs.uk
KCC

**FALLOWES**, Diana
**Child Psychotherapist**
Craig Croft Clinic
Craig Croft
Chelmsley Wood
Birmingham
B37 7TR
☎ 0121-788-8852
diana.fallowes@solihull-pct.nhs.uk
ACP

**FELTON**, Mo
**Transactional Analysis Psychotherapist**
♿ Walsall Psycotherapy and Counselling Centre
The Unicorn
19 Lowerhall Lane
Walsall
WS1 1RN
☎ 01827 897 733
☎ 01922 639 680
c.felton@ntlworld.com
ITA

**FITZGERALD**, Pen
**Psychodrama Psychotherapist**
♿ Therapeutic Community Service
Main House
201 Hollymoor Way, Northfield
Birmingham
B31 5HE
☎ 0121 460 1423
penn.fitzgerals@bsmht.nhs.uk
Rednal
Birmingham
B45
BPA

**FLANAGAN**, Helen
**Psychoanalytic Psychotherapist**
38 Radbourne Road
Shirley
Solihull
B90 3RT
☎ 0121 744 7839
WMIP

**FOKIAS**, Dene
**Cognitive Behavioural Psychotherapist**
♿ 18 Hazelbank
Kings Norton
Birmingham
B38 8BT
☎ 0121 459 6364
dene@denebritig.glowinternet.com
BABCP

**GEORGE**, Elizabeth
**Child Psychotherapist**
Beech House
Hewell Lane
Barnt Green
Worcestershire
B45 8NZ
☎ 0121 445 1338
ACP

**GILBERT**, Anne
92 Springfield Road
Kings Heath
Birmingham
B14 7D
☎ 0121 443 4787
anne.gilbert2@btopenworld.com
SPTI

**GLADWELL**, Stephen
**Psychodynamic Psychotherapist**
♿ Devon House SBMHT
Mindelsohn Way
Edgbaston
Birmingham
B15 2QR
☎ 01216 782 471
stephen.gladwell@bsmht.nhs.uk
UPCA

**GOODWILLIE**, Gill
**Systemic Psychotherapist**
♿ City PCT Child & Family Service
Pennfields Health Centre
Upper Zoar Street
Wolverhampton
WV3 0JH
☎ 01743 249 194
☎ 01902 444 021
gill@grg.enta.net
KCC

**GOODYEAR**, P A J
**Psychoanalytic Psychotherapist**
139 Knightlow Road
Harborne
Birmingham
B17 8PY
☎ 01214 292 364
WMIP

**HANDY**, S.
**Cognitive Behavioural Psychotherapist**
♿ Birmingham Children's Hospital
Steelhouse Lane
Birmingham
B4 6NH
☎ 0121 333 9180
BABCP

**HARRIS**, Nina
**Child Psychotherapist**
B1
☎ 0121 427 9546
ACP

**HARVEY**, Tricia A.
**Child Psychotherapist, Psychoanalytic Psychotherapist**
6 Clarence Road
Moseley
Birmingham
B13 9SX
☎ 01214 492 308
ACP, WMIP

**HEATH**, Suzanne
**Sexual and Relationship Psychotherapist**
♿ c/o Davis & Samuels Ltd
Opticians and Health Therapy Centre
Darwall Street
Walsall
WS1 1DA
☎ 01922 626 500
info@davisandsamuels.co.uk
BASRT

**HILL**, Val
**Psychodynamic Psychotherapist**
♿ BAC Centre
26 Wake Green Road
Moseley
Birmingham
B13 9PA
☎ 01214 499 515
WMIP

**HOAG**, Linda M.
**Jungian Analytical Psychotherapist**
Flat 4
36A Wake Green Road
Moseley
Birmingham
B13 9PE
☎ 01214 496 443
☎ 01214 511 479
GUILD, WMIP

**HOGG**, Rosemary
**Psychoanalytic Psychotherapist**
131a Alcester Road
Moseley
Birmingham
B13 8JP
☎ 01214 753 912
WMIP

**ILES**, David
**Hypno-Psychotherapist**
46 Marsh End
Kings Norton
Birmingham
B38 9BB
☎ 0121 459 6719
☎ 0777 353 721
ilesdavid@aol.com
CTIS

**INGHAM**, Rosie
**Integrative Arts Psychotherapist**
35 Holmfield Road
Coventry
CV2 4DD
☎ 02476 265 668
rosieingham@ntlworld.com
IATE

**JOHNSON**, Judy
**Psychoanalytic Psychotherapist**
♿ 173 Beaumont Road
Bournville
Birmingham
B30 1NT
☎ 01214 861 057
WMIP

**KING**, David
**Psychoanalytic Psychotherapist**
131A Alcester Road
Moseley
Birmingham
B13 8JP
☎ 0121 449 8122
☎ 07966 504 180
davidh.king@btinternet.com
WMIP

**KINGSLEY**, Laurence
**Psychoanalytic Psychotherapist**
131a Alcester Road
Moseley
Birmingham
B13 8JP
☎ 01214 498 122
l.kingsley@blueyonder.co.uk
WMIP

**KUETTNER**, Enno
**Family & Systemic Psychotherapist**
♿ Child & Family Service
Pennfields Health Centre
Upper Zoar Street
Penfold, Wolverhampton
WV3 0JH
☎ 01902 444 021
enno.kuttner@wolvespct.nhs.uk
AFT

**KYPRIDEMOS**, Petros
**Hypno-Psychotherapist**
254 Bristol Road
Edgbaston
Birmingham
B5 7SL
☎ 0121 415 5660
☎ 07831 109 859
pkypridemos@another.com
CTIS

**LIEBLING**, Angela J.
**Psychoanalytic Psychotherapist**
6 Cherry Hill Avenue
Barnt Green
Birmingham
B45 8LA
angelacarmalt@aol.com
WMIP

**LLOYD**, Helen
**Psychoanalytic Psychotherapist**
65 Blakedown Road
Halesowen
West Midlands
B63 4NG
☎ 01215 013 194
hlloyd@blueyonder.co.uk
WMIP

**LOGAN**, Ailsa
**Gestalt Psychotherapist**
60 Mickleton Road
Earlsdon
Coventry
CV5 6PQ
☎ 024 7667 6736
ailsalogan@synergynet.co.uk
SPTI

**LYNTON**, Joseph A
**Psychoanalytic Psychotherapist**
22 Colebourne Road
Billesley
Birmingham
B13 0EY
☎ 0121 772 449
joelynton@blueyonder.co.uk
UPCA

**MACKLIN**, Glen
**Cognitive Behavioural Psychotherapist**
♿ Sycamore House Medical Centre
111 Birmingham Road
Walsall
WS1 2NL
☎ 07880 745 375
☎ 01922 644 661
glen@gmtherapy.freeserve.co.uk
BABCP

**MALE**, David F.
**Psychoanalytic Psychotherapist**
81 Belle Vue
Wordsley
Nr. Stourbridge
W. Midlands
DY8 5DB
☎ 01384 278 761
☎ 01384 402 735
WMIP

**MARSTON**, Maureen
**Integrative Arts Psychotherapist**
160 Uplands Road
Handsworth
Birmingham
B21 8BS
☎ 0121 515 2798
☎ 0212 551 7041
IATE

**MATE**, Helen
**Psychoanalytic Psychotherapist**
♿ 177 Pineapple Road
Kings Norton
Birmingham
B30 2SY
☎ 01214 411 330
WMIP

**MCLEOD**, Terry
**Cognitive Behavioural Psychotherapist**
♿ Early Interventions Service
Harry Watton House
97 Church Lane
Aston, Birmingham
B6 5UG
terrymcleod5563@aol.com
BABCP

**MINHINNICK**, Frances
**Family & Systemic Psychotherapist**
56 Orchard Road
Birmingham
B24 9JA
☎ 0121 581 0288
francesminhinick@hotmail.com
AFT

**MOLONEY**, Paul
**Cognitive Behavioural Psychotherapist**
Sutton CMHT
Patrick House
5 Maney Corner
Sutton, Coldfield
B72 1QL
☎ 0121 685 6685
☎ 01283 791 754
BABCP

**MOUKAM**, Rameri Reshkhi
**Group Analytic Psychotherapist**
56 Denham Road
Birmingham
B27 6JD
☎ 01217 062 442
AUSET9@aol.com
UPCA

**MOULIN**, Laurence
**Family & Systemic Psychotherapist**
47 Prospect Road
Moseley
Birmingham
B13 9TD
☎ 0121 449 2817
lawrencemoulin@waitrose.com
AFT

**PARAVA**, Anna
**Gestalt Psychotherapist**
20 Moorland Court
42 Melville Road
Edgbaston
Birmingham
B16 9JR
☎ 0121 452 1682
GPTI, MET

**PEREZ-DE-ALBENIZ**, Alberto
**Group Analyst**
♿ Cauldon Centre
Clifford Bridge Road
Walsgrave
Coventry
CV2 2TE
☎ 024 76 602 020 x7226
alberto.albeniz@coventrypct.nhs.uk
IGA

**PITT**, Christine
**Psychoanalytic Psychotherapist**
67 St Denis Road
Selly Oak
Birmingham
B29 4JU
☎ 0121 476 3804
WMIP

**PYE**, Amaryllis
**Transpersonal Psychotherapist**
Birmingham
B13
☎ 07880 716 481
eduserve@tcp.co.uk
CCPE

**RAWSON**, David
**Transactional Analysis Psychotherapist**
Connect Therapeutic Community
19 Park Road
Moseley
Birmingham
B13 8AB
☎ 01214 492 204
☎ 01564 777 998
slowdown@btinternet.com
42 Kixley Lane
Knowle
Solihull
B93 0JG
ITA

**REYNOLDS**, Michael
**Psychoanalytic Psychotherapist**
16 Bantock Court
Broad Lane
Bradmore
Wolverhampton
WV3 9DA
WMIP

**ROBINSON**, Jenny
**Transactional Analysis Psychotherapist**
19 Park Road
Moseley
Birmingham
B13 8AB
☎ 01214 492 204
connect@therap.fsnet.co.uk
ITA

**ROPER HALL**, Alison
**Family & Systemic Psychotherapist**
♿ 208 Monyhull Hall Road
Kings Norton
Birmingham
B30 3QJ
☎ 0121 678 3400
☎ 0121 678 3401
Alison.Roper-Hall@bsmht.nhs.uk
AFT

**ROSE**, Chris
**Group Analytic Psychotherapist**
62 Huntingdon Road
Coventry
Warks
CV5 6PU
☎ 07976 299 989
☎ 02476 713 908
chrisrose@freezone.co.uk
UPCA

**SMITH**, Baden Bob
**Gestalt Psychotherapist**
62 Lightwoods Hill
Bearwood
Warley Woods
West Midlands
B67 5EB
☎ 0121 429 1758
bob@counselling-direct.co.uk
SPTI

**SMITH**, Di
**Transpersonal Psychotherapist**
'Pentire'
34 Marsh Lane
Hampton in Arden
Solihull, West Midlands
B92 0AJ
☎ 01675 442422
CCPE

**STOKES**, Jenny
**Jungian Analytical Psychotherapist**
51 Greenhill Road
Moseley
Birmingham
B13 9SU
☎ 01214 491 247
GUILD, WMIP

**STOKOE**, Wendy
**Integrative Psychotherapist**
207 Sherborne Lofts
33 Grosvenor Street West
Birmingham
B16 8HW
☎ 0121 246 7100
SPCRC

**STOTT**, Nicki
**Integrative Arts Psychotherapist**
35 Holmfield Road
Stoke
Coventry
CV2 4DD
☎ 02476 265 668
nicki.stott1@ntlworld.com
IATE

**TILNEY**, Tony
**Transactional Analysis Psychotherapist**
63 Victoria Road
Sutton Coldfield
West Midlands
B72 1SN
☎ 01213 544 042
aatilney@aol.com
ITA

**TOOLE**, Stuart
**Cognitive Behavioural Psychotherapist**
24 Herondale Crescent
Stourbridge
DY8 3LH
☎ 01384 829 124
stuarttoole@compuserve.com
BABCP

**TOWNEND**, Michael
**Cognitive Behavioural Psychotherapist**
♿ BUPA
Parkway Hospital
Damson Parkway
Solihull
B91 2PP
☎ 0121 704 1451
☎ 01332 592 054
m.townend@Derby.ac.uk
BABCP

**TRUCKLE**, Brian
**Child Psychotherapist, Psychoanalytic Psychotherapist**
♿ Oaklands Centre
Raddlebarn Road
Selly Oak
Birmingham
B29 6JB
☎ 01216 278 231
ACP, WMIP

**TRUCKLE**, Shirley
**Child Psychotherapist, Psychoanalytic Psychotherapist (Jungian)**
Qeens College
Summerset Road
Edgbaston
Birmingham
B15 2QH
☎ 01214 559 393
ACP, WMIP

**VALLANCE**, Fiona
**Psychodynamic Psychotherapist**
94 Selly Park Road
Selly Park
Birmingham
B29 7LL
WMIP

**VAN MARLE**, Susanna J
**Psychodynamic Psychotherapist**
Devon House
Uffculme Psychotherapy Service
Mindelsohn Way
Edgbaston
B15 2OR
WMIP

**VILLIA-GOSLING**, Athina
**Jungian Analytical Psychotherapist**
1075 Bristol Road
Selly Oak
Birmingham
B29 6LX
☎ 01214 726 587
AT.Villia@btinternet.com
WMIP

**WAKE**, Elaine
**Psychoanalytic Psychotherapist**
78 Pereira Road
Harborne
Birmingham
B17 9JN
☎ 01214 263 882
WMIP

**WHEELER**, Sue
**Psychodynamic Psychotherapist**
♿ 42 Grove Avenue
Moseley
Birmingham
B13 9RY
☎ 0121 449 6791
☎ 0121 449 5834
sw103@le.ac.uk
VAPP

**WILDE**, Paul
**Integrative Psychotherapist**
30 Abbey Road
Erdington
Birmingham
B23 7QG
☎ 0121 240 7273
paul@centralcounselling.co.uk
SPTI

**WILLIAMS**, Debra
**Psychoanalytic Psychotherapist**
Devon House
Uffaulme Psychotherapy Service
Mindeljohn Way
Edgbaston, Birmingham
B15 2QR
☎ 0121 678 2450
WMIP

**WINKLEY**, Linda
**Psychoanalytic Psychotherapist**
♿ Oaklands Centre
Selly Oak
Raddlebarn Road
Birmingham
B29 6JB
☎ 01216 278 231
ACP, WMIP

**WOODWARD**, Joan
**Attachment-based Psychoanalytic Psychotherapist**
♿ 61 Selly Wick Drive
Selly Park
Birmingham
B29 7JR
☎ 0121 472 3055
CAPP

**WYNN**, Joan
**Systemic Psychotherapist**
♿ CAMHS
Parkview Clinic
60 Queensbridge Road
Moseley, Birmingham
B13 8QE
☎ 01527 452 121
joan.bridgestherapy1@btopenworld.com
KCC

## WILTSHIRE

**BARKER**, Elizabeth
**Biodynamic Psychotherapist**
47 Kingsbury Street
Marlborough
Wilts
SN8 4JE
☎ 01672 551051
☎ 020 8995 7031
liz.barker@amservice.net
LSBP

**CHALK**, Caroline
**Psychosynthesis Psychotherapist**
The Granary
Hazelbury Manor
Box
Wiltshire
SN13 8HX
☎ 01225 810 861
caroline.chalk@btopenworld.com
Church Street Practise
15a Church Street
Bradford on Avon
Wiltshire
BA15 1LN
GASW, PET

**CROSTON**, Richard
**Hypno-Psychotherapist**
The Bridge Street Centre for Complementary Medicin
12 Bridge Street
Bradford On Avon
BA15 1BY
☎ 01225 720 103
Richard@rcroston.freeserve.co.uk
CTIS

**FOX**, Fiona
**Psychodynamic Psychotherapist**
Mand R Cottage
Hanging
Langford
SP3 4NW
☏ 01722 790 174
WMIP

**GARDNER**, Philippa
**Cognitive Analytic Therapist**
Watersmeet
Mill Lane
Ramsbury
Murlborough
SN8 2RE
☏ 01672 520 316
gardner@12mayfieldrd.freeserve.co.uk
ACAT

**GOOLD**, Peter
**Personal Construct Psychotherapist**
Aepelford Acre
Woodborough
Pewsey Wilts
SN9 5P
☏ 01672 851 942
PCP

**GRIFFITHS**, C A
**Sexual and Relationship Psychotherapist**
Wiltshire/Dorset/Hampshire
Avonbourne Chiropractice
51 Salt Lane
Salisbury
d.griffiths@freenet.co.uk
BASRT

**HANCOCK**, Patricia
**Psychoanalytic Psychotherapist**
1 Hockett's Close
Lyneham
Chippenham
Wilts
SN15 4QX
☏ 01249 890 254
SIP

**HILDER**, Sonia
**Cognitive Analytic Therapist**
♿ 50 Avenue Road
Trowbridge
BA14 0AQ
☏ 01225 763 598
sonia@cavesoft.net
ACAT

**HUTCHINSON**, Garry
**Integrative Psychosynthesis Psychotherapist**
Rudloe
Corsham
SN13
☏ 01225 812 851
garry.hutchinson2@btopenworld.com
RE.V

**JOHNSON SMITH**, Camilla
**Humanistic Psychotherapist**
St. Giles
Poulton Hill
Marlborough
Wiltshire
SN8 1AZ
☏ 01672 519 347
☏ 07973 110 029
camillajohnsonsmith@hotmail.com
AHPP, LCP

**KELLY**, Peter
**Integrative Psychotherapist**
27 Ancient Way
Salisbury
Wilts
SP2 8TE
☏ 01722 506 727
ptk@ntlworld.com
NGP

**KERRY**, Sue
**Transpersonal Psychotherapist**
1 Water Street
Mere
Warminster
Wiltshire
BA12 6DZ
☏ 07815 532045
☏ 020 8 672 6573
apairoftrainers@fsbdial.co.uk
CCPE

**KING**, Rosalind Ann
**Cognitive Analytic Therapist**
Salisbury Alcohol & Drug Advisory Service
139 Fisherton Street
Salisbury
SP2 7DT
☏ 01722 412 632
☏ 01722 429 401
Avon & Wilt Mental Health Partnerships NHS Trust
Psychological Therapy Service, Cent
52-54 Endless Street
Salisbury
SP1 3UH
ACAT

**LEACH**, Kathy
**Transactional Analysis Psychotherapist**
♿ Townsend House
Ogbourne St. Andrew
Marlborough
Wiltshire
SN8 1SE
ITA, MET

**LEGH-SMITH**, Andrea
**Core Process Psychotherapist**
Garden Cottage
Mount Scylla
Ford
Near Chippenham,Wiltshire
SN14 8RR
☏ 01249 782516
KI

**LEIGHTON**, Tim
**Cognitive Analytic Therapist**
Clouds House
East Knoyle
nr Salisbury
Wiltshire
SP3 6BE
☏ 01747 830 733
tim.leighton@clouds.org.uk
ACAT

**MELLETT**, Jane
**Humanistic and Integrative Psychotherapist**
16 Tutton Hill
Colerne
Chippenham
Wilts
SN14 8DN
☏ 01225 742 163
AHPP, BCPC

**MIDDLETON-SMITH**, Virginia
**Systemic Psychotherapist**
1 Queensberry Road
Salisbury
SP1 3PH
KCC

**MOJSA**, Jan
**Transpersonal Psychotherapist**
36 Prospect Square
Westbury
BA13 3ET
☏ 01373 824 314
☏ 07940 937 267
CTP

**O'CONNOR**, Nadia
**Transpersonal Psychotherapist**
13 The College
Froxfield
Marlborough
Wilts
SN8 3LA
CCPE

**POCOCK**, Olga
**Psychoanalytic Psychotherapist**
32 Elizabeth Court
Cranebridge Road
Salisbury
Wiltshire
SP2 7UX
☎ 01722 320 093
SIP

**REES**, Ian
**Core Process Psychotherapist**
60 Bristol Street
Malmesbury
Wiltshire
SN16 0AX
☎ 01666 823471
KI

**REIMERS**, Sigurd
**Family & Systemic Psychotherapist**
Child & Family Therapy Service
Family Health Centre
The Halve
Trowbridge, Wiltshire
BA14 8SE
☎ 01225 352 281
sigurd.reimers@awp.nhs.uk
FIC

**RHEINSCHMIEDT**, Otto
**Group Analyst**
Madron Well Cottage
78 Farleigh Road
Trowbridge
Wilts
BA14 9LG
☎ 01225 763 531
IGA

**ROSENTHAL**, Alison
**Transpersonal Psychotherapist**
31 Salt Lane
Salisbury
SP1 1EG
☎ 01425 655 078
☎ 01722 411 998
alisonrose@supalife.com
CCPE

**ROYS**, Clare
**Family & Systemic Psychotherapist**
Child & Family Therapy Service
Chippenham Family Health Centre
Goldney Avenue
Chippenham
SN15 1ND
☎ 01249 656 321
clare.roys@awp.nhs.uk
FIC

**SYKES**, Margaret
**Family & Systemic Psychotherapist**
♿ Child and Family Therapy Service
Chippenham Health Centre
Goldney Avenue
Chippenham
SN15 1ND
☎ 01249 656 321
margaret.sykes@awp.nhs.uk
AFT

**TADMAN**, Fenella
**Group Analytic Psychotherapist**
♿ Alma Cottage
Lottage Road
Aldbourne
Marlborough
SN8 2EB
☎ 0787 623 2782
FPC

**TYLER**, Peter
**Integrative Psychotherapist**
The Cottage
25 The Close
Salisbury
SP1 2EH
☎ 01722 321 277
☎ 01722 424 801
petermtyler@hotmail.com
MC

**VOELCKER**, Cara
**Humanistic and Integrative Psychotherapist**
♿ Avils Farm
Lower Stanton
Quinton
Chippenham, Wilts
SN14 6DA
☎ 01249 720 202
caravoelckeravils@lineone.net
BCPC

## WORCESTERSHIRE

**NOYES**, Elizabeth
**Cognitive Behavioural Psychotherapist**
4 High Street
Badsey
Evesham
WR11 5EW
☎ 01386 831 112
lizzi@badsey.net
BABCP

## WREXHAM

**ARNOLD**, Sue
**Psychosynthesis Psychotherapist**
Willow Cottage
Tallarn Green
Nr. Malpas
Cheshire
SY14 7LJ
☎ 01948 770 697
IPS

**CHIPMAN**, Tina Louise
**Cognitive Behavioural Psychotherapist**
♿ Psychological Therapies Department
Wrexham Maelor Hospital
Croesnewydd Road
Clwyd
LL13 7TD
☎ 01978 725 349
tina.chipman@new-tr.wales.nhs.uk
BABCP

**CROSSLEY**, David
**Cognitive Behavioural Psychotherapist**
♿ Psychological Treatment Service
Wrexham Maelor Hospital
Croesnewydd Road
Wrexham
LL13 7TD
☎ 01978 291 100
BABCP

**FORD**, Vicki
**Sexual and Relationship Psychotherapist**
Orme Lodge
High Street
Bangor on Dee
LL13 0AU
☎ 01978 312 982
☎ 01978 780 479
clients@vickiford.co.uk
BASRT

**PRUSSIA**, Celia
**Psychoanalytic Psychotherapist**
♿ BUPA Yale Hospital
Wrexham Technology Park
Croesnwydd Road
Wrexham
LL13 7YP
☎ 01978 291306
celiaprussia@yahoo.co.uk
LPDO

## YORK

**ASHTON**, Carole
**Gestalt Psychotherapist**
9 Park Street
The Mount
York
YO24 1BQ
☎ 01904 643 073
caroleashton@aol.com
SPTI

**BAILEY**, Russell
**Integrative Psychotherapist**
♿ 29 Askham Lane
York
YO24 3HB
☎ 07950 000 335
☎ 01904 798 756
russ.jen@freeuk.com
NGP

**BINGLEY MILLER**, Liza
**Family & Systemic Psychotherapist**
10 St. Oswald's Road
Fulford
York
YO1 4PF
☎ 01904 633 417
liza.miller@Intlworld.com
AFT

**GALLOWAY**, Betsy
**Transactional Analysis Psychotherapist**
10 Gray Street
Scarcroft Green
York
YO23 1BN
☎ 01904 647 893
betsygalloway@zephrine.freeserve.co.uk
ITA

**JONES**, Helen
**Personal Construct Psychotherapist**
2 Heslington Court
School Lane
Heslington
York
YO1 5EX
☎ 01904 438 757
helenjo@tinyworld.co.uk
PCP

**KELLETT**, Rachael
**Gestalt Psychotherapist**
Flat 3
27 St Saviourgate
York
YO1 8NQ
☎ 01904 639 918
SPTI

**KENNETT**, Christine
**Gestalt Psychotherapist**
38 Millfield Road
York
YO23 1NQ
☎ 01904 638 623
ckennett45@aol.com
GPTI

**TURTON**, Michael
**Gestalt Psychotherapist**
38 Millfield Road
York
YO23 1NQ
☎ 01904 638 623
miketurtonyork@aol.com
GPTI

**WARING**, Judith
**Gestalt Psychotherapist**
6 Norfolk Street
York
YO23 1JY
☎ 01904 641 996
judith@warings.freeserve.co.uk
SPTI

## YORKSHIRE - EAST

**ALI**, Saadi
**Psychoanalytic Psychotherapist**
♿ CMHT
Manor Road
Beverley
East Riding
☎ 01482 886 441
☎ 01964 550 953
saadiali@hotmail.com
18 Highcroft
Cherry Burton
Beverley
Hull
HU17 7SG
HIP

**BOLSOVER**, Nick
**Psychoanalytic Psychotherapist**
6a Station Road
Brough
Nr Hull
HU15 1DY
☎ 01482 665 412
☎ 01482 641 579
nkbolsover@aol.com
22 Station Road
Hessle
Hull
HU13 0BB
HIP, IFT, YAPP

**DENT-BROWN**, Tracey
**Gestalt Psychotherapist**
♿ 6 Station Road
Hessle
East Yorkshire
HU13 0BB
☎ 01482 640 578
tracey@dent-brown.co.uk
MET

**DERRICK**, Stephen
**Gestalt Psychotherapist**
7 Highfield
Sutton
Hull
HU7 4TW
☎ 01482 712 283
steve@smep.freeserve.co.uk
SPTI

**FISHER**, Paul
**Integrative Psychotherapist**
9 Stephensen Close
Cleeve Road
Hedon
Hull
HU12 8RB
☎ 01482 891 453
Paul.Fisher@telinco.co.uk
SPTI

**GREEN**, Lynette
**Psychodrama Psychotherapist**
25 Salisbury Street
Hull
Yorks
HU5 3HA
☎ 01482 343 664
☎ 01482 214 118
BPA

**GUERNINA**, Zoubida
**Psychoanalytic Psychotherapist**
33 Beech Dale
Cottingham
North Humberside
HU16 4RH
☎ 01482 875 712
guerzon@hotmail.com
NAFSI

**HAMLIN**, Cynthia Diana
**Family & Systemic Psychotherapist**
♿ Coltman Avenue Clinic
Coltman Avenue
Beverley
HU17 4LP
☎ 01482 869 200
cynthia_hamlin@yahoo.co.uk
IFT

**HOSTICK**, Kathie
**Transactional Analysis Psychotherapist**
735 Holderness Road
Hull
East Yorkshire
HU8 9AR
☎ 01482 701 268
☎ 07957 209 270
kathie@hostick.fsnet.co.uk
ITA

**HUBBARD**, Leslie
**Family & Systemic Psychotherapist**
242 Great Thornton Street
Hull
HU3 2LS
☎ 01482 321 470
IFT

**KUROWSKA**, Irena
**Integrative Psychotherapist**
138 Marlborough Avenue
Hull
HU5 3JX
☎ 01482 447 665
☎ 07944 986 665
renak@renak.karoo.co.uk
ScPTI

**LEHAIN**, Daniel
**Gestalt Psychotherapist**
34 Beverley Parklands
Beverley
HU17 0RA
☎ 01482 870 458
☎ 07791 128 351
danlehain@danlehain.karoo.co.uk
GPTI, SPTI

**LITTLEDALE**, Nadine
**Psychodrama Psychotherapist**
2 Westbourne Grove
Hessle
East Yorkshire
HU13 0QL
☎ 01482 649 237
☎ 01482 642 223
nadine@nlittledale.freeserve.co.uk
BPA

**MARONITIS**, Maggie
**Gestalt Psychotherapist**
5 Victoria Gardens
Victoria Avenue
Hull
HU5 3ED
☎ 01482 341 525
maggiemaronitis@hotmail.com
SPTI

**MARTIN**, Gill
**Psychodynamic Psychotherapist**
♿ 15 Grammar School Yard
Fish Street
Hull
HU1 1SE
☎ 01347 848 376
☎ 01482 325 422
ycpn@mulberry4.fsnet.co.uk
YAPP

**MEAD**, Jannie
**Cognitive Analytic Therapist**
♿ Psychotherapy Department
Herch Trust
Miranda House, Gladstone Stree
Hull
HU3 2RT
☎ 01482 617 527
ACAT

**PEARCE**, Liz
**Integrative Psychotherapist**
♿ West End Child Adolescent Family Service
2062-2068 Hessle Road
Hessle
Hull
HU13 9NW
☎ 01482 872554
NGP

**PETTY**, Susan P.H.
**Family & Systemic Psychotherapist**
40 Lowfield Road
Beverley
East Yorkshire
HU17 9RE
☎ 01482 864 461
sue-pettypetwzg@supanet.com
IFT

**URQUHART**, Peta A
**Psychoanalytic Psychotherapist**
Middle Farm
Walkington
Beverley
East Yorkshire
HU17 8SZ
☎ 01430 828 139
UPCA

**WANG**, Michael
**Cognitive Behavioural Psychotherapist**
♿ Dept of Clinical Psychology
School of Medicine
University of Hull
Hull
HU6 7RX
☎ 01482 465 416
M.Wang@medschool.hull.ac.uk
BABCP

**WILLETTS**, Dean
**Cognitive Behavioural Psychotherapist**
♿ Nuffield Hospital
Castle Hill
Cottingham
HU16 5FQ
☎ 01472 595 655
☎ 01302 736 761
d.willets@talk21.com
BABCP

**WILLINGHAM**, Christine
**Family & Systemic Psychotherapist**
♿ 220 Park Avenue
Hull
HU5 3EY
☎ 01482 342 033
chrisitne@park.karoo.co.uk
AFT

## YORKSHIRE - NORTH

**ANDREWS**, Carol
**Integrative Psychotherapist**
1 Columbus Way
Brompton on Swale
Richmond
DL10 7TW
☎ 01748 818 717
NGP

**ARCARI**, Sallie R
**Group Analytic Psychotherapist**
The Penthouse
Airy Hill Manor
Whiby
North Yorkshire
YO21 1QB
☎ 01947 821 091
UPCA

**BOSTON**, Paula
**Systemic Psychotherapist**
68 Parish Ghyll Drive
Ilkley
LS29 9PR
☎ 01943 601 162
PaulaB@parishghyll.u-net.com
IFT

**BRADBURY**, Susan Elizabeth
**Group Analyst**
York Medical Society
23 Stonegate
York
YO26 6PB
☎ 07092 248 471
sebrad@doctors.org.uk
IGA

**BRADSHAW**, Lynn E
**Psychodynamic Psychotherapist**
Rose Villa
15 Bellevue Terrace
York
YO10 5AZ
☎ 01904 651 036
lynn@rosevilla757.freeserve.co.uk
St Andrews Counselling &
Psychotherapy Unit
59 Huntingdon Road
York
YO31 8RL
UPCA, YAPP

**BRAY**, Malcolm
**Neurolinguistic Psychotherapist**
7 George Street
Carleton
Nr Skipton
North Yorks
BD23 3HQ
☎ 01756 791 110
NLPtCA

**BROWN**, Antony
**Cognitive Behavioural Psychotherapist**
♿ York Cognitive Behavioural
Psychotherapy Clinic
36 Scarcroft Road
York
YO23 1NF
☎ 01904 621 648
☎ 07775 603 853
antonybrowncbt@hotmail.com
BABCP

**BULMER**, E.A
**Integrative Psychotherapist, Transactional Analysis Psychotherapist**
♿ The Oakdale Centre
49 Valley Drive
Harrogate
N Yorks
HG2 0JH
☎ 01423 503 080
NGP

**BUTTERWORTH**, Lorna
**Family & Systemic Psychotherapist**
26 St Marygate
Ripon
HG4 1LX
☎ 01765 607 827
foreverwindswept@yahoo.co.uk
AFT

**CHAMIER**, Suzanne
**Hypno-Psychotherapist**
Broadway West
York
YO10
☎ 01904 621 866
NRHP

**CROSBY**, Dianne
**Psychodynamic Psychotherapist**
1 Stonefall Cottages
Hookstone Chase
Harrogate
HG2 7DN
FPC

**CULLWICK**, Joy
**Gestalt Psychotherapist**
64 Strensall Road
Huntington
York
YO32 9SH
☎ 01904 764 608
jcullwick@lineone.net
SPTI

**DAVIS**, Mrs Rosemary
**Sexual and Relationship Psychotherapist**
♿ Department of Psychological
Therapies
The Old Chapel
Bootham Park
York
YO30 7BY
☎ 01904 725 353
BASRT

**DUNCAN**, Ursula
**Integrative Psychotherapist**
♿ c/o Harrogate Clinid
23 Ripon Road
Harrogate
HG1 2JL
☎ 01423 500 599
☎ 07000 788 222
ursula.duncan@virgin.net
ITA, NGP

**EASBY**, Barbara
**Psychodynamic Psychotherapist**
♿ Acomb Health Centre
1 Beech Grove
Acomb
York
YO26 5LD
☎ 01904 787 174
UPCA

**ELLENOR**, Deby
**Integrative Psychotherapist**
13 Strathmore Drive
Kirklevington
Yarm
TS15 9NS
☎ 01642 789 860
☎ 07801 431 720
deby.ellenor@sclearning.fsbusiness.co.uk
NGP

**EMERY**, Judith
**Cognitive Behavioural Psychotherapist**
♿ The Retreat
107 Heslington Road
York
YO10 5BN
☎ 01904 412 551
BABCP

**EPSTEIN**, Melanie Lynn
**Integrative Psychotherapist**
The Iris Centre
307 Harrogate Road
Leeds
LS17 6PA
☎ 01132 662 402
NGP

**EVANS**, Kenneth
**Gestalt Psychotherapist, Integrative Psychotherapist**
Scarbrough Psychotherapy Training
Institute
117 Colombus Ravine
Scarbrough
YO12 7QU
☎ 07855 323 305
ken@kenevans.fsnet.co.uk
ScPTI

**EVETTS-SECKER**, Josephine
**Analytical Psychologist-Jungian Analyst**
Lidgate
Victoria Square
Lythe
Whitby, N.Yorks
YO21 3RW
☎ 01947 893 338
j.evettssecker@btopenworld.com
IGAP

**GILLJAM**, Annika
**Psychoanalytic Psychotherapist**
24 Eaton Road
Ilkley
West Yorkshire
LS29 9PU
☎ 01943 602 449
GUILD, YAPP

**GREENING**, Sarah
**Integrative Psychotherapist**
Blue Cottage
38 South End
Osmotherley
DL6 3BL
☎ 01609 883 748
ITA, NGP

**HESTER**, Bridget
**Psychoanalytic Psychotherapist**
The Old Rectory
Crayke
York
YO61 4TA
☎ 01347 821 593
LPDO

**KENNARD**, David
**Group Analyst, Psychodynamic Psychotherapist**
♿ The Retreat
Heslington Road
York
YO10 5BN
☎ 01904 412 551
dkennard@retreat-hospital.org
IGA, YAPP

**LAWRENCE**, Yvonne
**Integrative Psychotherapist, Transactional Analysis Psychotherapist**
Shannon House
13 York Terrace
Whitby
North Yorkshire
YO21 1QT
☎ 01947 603496
☎ 01947 603496
ITA, NGP

**LEVINE**, Peter
**Integrative Psychotherapist, Transactional Analysis Psychotherapist**
♿ Shannon House
13 York Terrace
Whitby
North Yorkshire
YO21
☎ 01947 603 496
ITA, NGP

**LEWIS**, Sheila
**Psychoanalytic Psychotherapist**
17 Princess Road
Ilkley
West Yorkshire
LS29 9NP
☎ 01943 601 948
☎ 01484 343 480
GUILD, YAPP

**MARTIN**, Gill
**Psychodynamic Psychotherapist**
♿ Mulberry House
4 Beechfield
Newton-on-Ouse
York
YO10 3HH
☎ 01347 848 376
☎ 01482 325 422
ycpn@mulberry4.fsnet.co.uk
YAPP

**MASTERS**, Sue
**Transpersonal Psychotherapist**
137 Haxby Road
York
YO31 8JW
☎ 01904 612069
sue@totalise.co.uk
CCPE

**MCCLUSKEY**, Una
**Psychoanalytic Psychotherapist**
Department Social Policy and Social Work
University of York
York
YO10 5DD
☎ 01759 302 104
AFT, YAPP

**MCCROHAN**, Denise
**Integrative Psychotherapist**
25 Romanby Road
North Allerton
N Yorkshire
DL7 8NE
☎ 01609 773 841
Patden.McCrohan@care4free.net
CCBP

**MEAD**, Jannie
**Cognitive Analytic Therapist**
13 Belle Vue Terrace
York
YO10 5AZ
☎ 01482 617 527
ACAT

**MILLAR**, Elizabeth M
**Psychodynamic Psychotherapist**
9 Foxthorn Paddock
Badger Hill
York
YO10 5HJ
☎ 01924 327 499
elizabeth.millar@swyt.nhs.uk
UPCA

**MORGAN-WILLIAMS**, Susan
**Existential Psychotherapist**
Garthfoot
Preston-Under-Scar
Leyburn
DL8 4AH
☎ 01969 625 072
SPCRC, SEA

**MORRIS**, Jane
**Psychoanalytic Psychotherapist**
♿ Psychotherapy Department
Moor Lane Centre
Burley in Wharfedale
West Yorkshire
LS29 7AJ
☎ 01422 845 314
☎ 01943 862 031
janemorris@jmch.co.uk
NWIDP, YAPP

**PAGE**, Annabel
**Psychoanalytic Psychotherapist**
18 Crossbeck Road
Ilkley
W. Yorks
LS29 9JN
☎ 01943 601 184
YAPP

**PARKER**, John
**Psychoanalytic Psychotherapist**
18 Eaton Road
Ilkley
West Yorkshire
LS29 9PU
☎ 01943 604 085
john@trauma-response.co.uk
LPDO

**PAYNE**, Graham
**Psychoanalytic Psychotherapist**
Dept. of Mental Health
Friarage Hospital
Northallerton
DL6 1JG
☎ 01609 763 435
☎ 01609 774 198
graham.payne@hrpct.nhs.uk
FIP

**PROUDLEY**, Helen G
**Sexual and Relationship Psychotherapist**
♿ Doxford House
73 Front Street
Sowerby
Thirsk
YO7 1JP
☎ 01845 523 238
☎ 01642 624 291
helenproudley@yahoo.co.uk
BASRT

**READ**, Nicholas
**Psychoanalytic Psychotherapist, Psychodynamic Psychotherapist**
35 Lister Street
Ilkley
LS29 9ET
☎ 01943 608 623
n.w.read@sheffield.ac.uk
HIP

**REILLY**, Stephen
**Psychodynamic Psychotherapist**
♿ Bootham Park Hospital
York
YO30 7BY
☎ 01904 610 777
stephen.reilly@yorknhs.uk
UPCA, YAPP

**RICHARDSON**, Caroline
**Sexual and Relationship Psychotherapist**
♿ The Oakdale Centre
49 Valley Drive
Harrogate
N Yorks
HG2 0JH
☎ 01423 503 080
caroline@theoakdalecentre.co.uk
BASRT

**RICHARDSON**, Sylvia
**Sexual and Relationship Psychotherapist**
♿ York NHS Psychological Therapies
The Old Chapel
Bootham Park
York
YO30 7BY
☎ 07885 375 521
SrichardsonYork@aol.com
BASRT

**SIMON**, Gail
**Systemic Psychotherapist**
♿ Hillbrook Bradford CAMHS
Mayfield Road
Spring Gardens Lane
Keighley
BD20 6LD
☎ 07020 955 512
☎ 01535 661 531
KCC

**TENNISON**, John F.S.
**Cognitive Behavioural Psychotherapist**
♿ 179 King Edwards Drive
Harrogate
HG1 4HB
☎ 01302 734 050
☎ 01423 701 116
john@tenison.org
BABCP

**TYSON**, Robert
**Gestalt Psychotherapist**
Forge House
65 High Street
Snainton, Scarborough
North Yorkshire
YO13 9AL
☎ 01723 859 265
tysonmcmahon@supanet.com
GPTI

**WAKE**, Lisa
**Neurolinguistic Psychotherapist**
♿ Villa Farm Cottage
Newby
North Yorkshire
TS9 0AE
☎ 01642 310 022
lwakestok@aol.com
NLPtCA

**WATSON**, Caroline
**Gestalt Psychotherapist**
Horn End Cottage East
Low Mill
Farndale
York YO62 7XA
YO62 7XA
☎ 01751 431 293
caro@hornmed.fsnet.co.uk
SPTI

**WILKINSON**, Kathleen
**Gestalt Psychotherapist, Integrative Psychotherapist**
Vere House
117 Columbus Ravine
Scarborough
YO12 7QU
☎ 01723 374 585
kate.scpti@online.co.uk
ScPTI

**WOJCIECHOWSKA**, Ewa
**Group Analyst**
The Oakdale Centre
49 Valley Drive
Harrogate
North Yorkshire
HG2 0JH
☎ 01423 503 080
IGA

**WRIGHT**, Nina
**Transactional Analysis Psychotherapist**
37 Ramsey Terrace
Wharfe Street
Otley
Leeds
LS21 1AW
☎ 01943 464 366
ninaejwright@yahoo.com
ITA

## YORKSHIRE - SOUTH

**ALLEN**, Penny
**Integrative Psychotherapist**
415 Fulwood Road
Sheffield
S10 3GF
☎ 0114 230 5702
pennyallen@madasafish.com
SPTI

**ALLEN-BROWN**, Jane
**Psychodynamic Psychotherapist**
223 Highcliffe Road
Sheffield
S11 7LQ
☎ 0114 230 9194
FPC

**ARNESEN**, Elizabeth
**Educational Therapist**
21 Horndean Road
Sheffield
S5 6UJ
☎ 07960 523 911
liz@arnies.org.uk
CFET

**ARNESEN**, Paul
**Psychoanalytic Psychotherapist**
21 Horndean Road
Sheffield
S5 6UJ
☎ 07974 837 342
paul@arnies.org.uk
HIP, UPCA

**ATHERTON**, Alistair N
**Psychodynamic Psychotherapist**
c/o Head Injury Rehabilitation Centre
Albert Terrace Road
Sheffield
S6 3EB
☎ 01142 737 451
alistair.atherton@sth.nhs.uk or
anatherton@yahoo.co.uk
UPCA

**BEARD**, Hilary
**Psychodynamic Psychotherapist**
177 Rustlings Road
Sheffield
S11 7AD
☎ 0114 268 5884
☎ 0114 258 4489
hilarybeard@onetel.net.uk
HIP

**BLACKBURN**, John
**Rational Emotive Behaviour Therapist**
♿ Behavioural Psychotherapy
Michael Carlisle Centre
75 Osborne Road
Sheffield
S11 9BF
☎ 0114 271 8699
john.blackburn@chs.nhs.uk
Claremont Hospital
104 Sandygate Road
Sheffield
S10 5UB
AREBT

**BLOOM**, Jane
**Group Analyst**
Dpt. of Midwifery & Child Health
The University of Sheffield
Winter Street
Sheffield
S3 7ND
☎ 0114 222 9820
j.c.bloom@sheffield.ac.uk
IGA

**BOJANIC-WRIGHT**, Stoya
**Psychoanalytic Psychotherapist, Psychodynamic Psychotherapist**
103 Carterknowle Road
Sheffield
S7 2DY
☎ 0114 258 6700
HIP

**BRADY**, Alec
**Cognitive Behavioural Psychotherapist**
25 Hunshelf Park
Stocksbridge
Sheffield
S36 2BT
☎ 0114 288 3276
☎ 07768 593 117
alec.brady@virgin.net
BABCP

**BRYANT**, Anne
32 The Quadrant
Sheffield
S17 4DB
anne.c.bryant@virgin.net
SPTI

**CAIN**, Christine
**Psychosynthesis Psychotherapist**
5 Grove Road
Totley Rise
Sheffield
S17 4DJ
☎ 0114 236 3204
candpcain@aol.com
IPS

**CARIAPA**, Illana
**Cognitive Behavioural Psychotherapist**
♿ 25 Cortworth Road
Sheffield
S11 9LN
illana@cariapa.fsnet.co.uk
BABCP

**CAW**, Jeanette
**Gestalt Psychotherapist**
♿ 18 Empire Road
Nether Edge
Sheffield
S7 1GL
☎ 0114 255 0645
stancaw@aol.com
SPTI

**CLESHAM**, Lilian
**Transpersonal Psychotherapist**
Nether Edge
Sheffield
S7
☎ 0114 255 4373
CCPE

**COAN**, Anita
**Psychoanalytic Psychotherapist**
29 Frickley Road
Nethergreen
Sheffield
S11 7EX
☎ 0114 263 0945
UPCA

**COOPER**, Penny
**Sexual and Relationship Psychotherapist**
♿ Porterbrook Clinic
75 Osborne Road
Never Edge
Sheffield
S11 9BF
☎ 01623 626 147
☎ 0114 271 6671
BASRT

**DAINES**, Brian
**Sexual and Relationship Psychotherapist**
Ferndale
61 Fern Road
Sheffield
S6 5AX
☎ 0114 233 5641
☎ 0114 268 2883
b.daines@sheffield.ac.uk
Share Psychotherapy
176 Crookesmoor Road
Sheffield
S6 3FS
BASRT

**DALE**, Carole
**Psychodrama Psychotherapist**
99 Meersbrook Park Road
Sheffield
Yorkshire
S8 9FP
☎ 01142 588 088
carole@mixim.freeserve.co.uk
BPA

**DAVIES**, John
**Cognitive Behavioural Psychotherapist**
Specialist Psychotherapy Services
Brunswick House
299 Glossop Road
Sheffield
S10 2HL
☎ 0114 271 8140
☎ 07973 305 578
BABCP

**DORNDORF-TURNER**, Rhoda
**Psychoanalytic Psychotherapist**
22 Queensway
Moorgate
Rotherham
South Yorkshire
S60 3EE
☎ 01709 362 544
rhodorf@yahoo.co.uk
LPDO

**DRUCQUER**, Helen
**Psychodynamic Psychotherapist**
84 Southgrove Road
Sheffield
S10 2NQ
☎ 0114 268 5240
galen.helen@ukonline.co.uk
HIP

**EDWARDS**, David
**Psychodynamic Psychotherapist**
93 Fraser Road
Woodseats
Sheffield
S8 0JH
☎ 07946 458 367
d.g.edwards@sheffield.ac.uk
HIP

**ELLINGWORTH**, Janice
**Family & Systemic Psychotherapist**
♿ Oakwood Young People's Centre
Longley Centre
Norwood Grange Drive
Sheffield
S5 7JT
☎ 0114 226 1601
jan.ellingworth@sct.nhs.uk
AFT

**ELLIOT**, Mary
**Integrative Psychotherapist**
Barnsley Primary Care NHS Trust
11/12 Keresforth Close
Off Braodway
Barnsley
S70 6RS
☎ 01226 341 374
mary.elliot@onetel.net
NGP

**ELLIS**, Lynda
**Psychoanalytic Psychotherapist**
Sheffield
S11 7PZ
☎ 0114 236 1533
HIP

**EMBLETON TUDOR**, Louise
**Integrative Psychotherapist**
13 Penrhyn Road
Sheffield
S11 8UL
☎ 0114 267 8277
louiseembletontudor@temenos.ac.uk
MC

**EVANS**, Gail
**Sexual and Relationship Psychotherapist**
♿ Counselling Studies Unit, School of Education
Sheffield Hallam University
Collegiate Crescent Campus
Sheffield
S10 2BP
☎ 0114 225 2576
g.e.evans@shu.ac.uk
BASRT

**FITZGERALD**, Gearoid
**Psychoanalytic Psychotherapist**
♿ Sheffield Care Trust
Brunswick House
299 Glossop Road
Sheffield
S10 2HL
☎ 07718 894 811
gearoid@fitzhawk.solis.co.uk
HIP

**GARLOVSKY**, Rita
**Psychoanalytic Psychotherapist**
41 Oak Hill Road
Nether Edge
Sheffield
S7 1SJ
☎ 0114 258 7910
ritagarlovsky@btopenworld.com
GUILD, HIP

**GIBBONS**, Sandra
**Psychodynamic Psychotherapist**
9 Crookesmoor Drive
Walkley
Sheffield
S6 2FX
☎ 0114 267 9474
HIP

**GODDARD**, Kay
**Psychoanalytic Psychotherapist**
11b Wilsic Road
Tickhill
Doncaster
DN11 9JG
☎ 01302 744 983
kay_goddard@pgen.net
FIP, HIP

**GORNEY**, Carry
**Systemic Psychotherapist**
26 Westwood Road
Sheffield
S11 7EY
☎ 01142 295 792
carrygorney@btopenworld.com
KCC

**GUDJONSSON**, Ingolfur A
**Psychoanalytic Psychotherapist, Psychodynamic Psychotherapist**
69 Nether Edge Road
Sheffield
S7 1RW
☎ 0114 255 3516
susingo@lineone.net
HIP, YAPP

**GUITON**, Anita
**Psychoanalytic Psychotherapist, Psychodynamic Psychotherapist**
88 Upperthorpe
Sheffield
S6 3NE
☎ 07973 426 786
☎ 0114 268 2883
anita.guiton@blueyonder.co.uk
Share Psychotherapy
176 Crookesmoor Road
Sheffield
S6 3FS
HIP

**HADDOCK**, Ray
**Group Analyst**
♿ Specialist Psychotherapy Services
Brunswick House
299 Glossop Road
S10 2HL
☎ 0114 271 6894
IGA

**HALLAM-JONES**, Ruth
**Sexual and Relationship Psychotherapist**
c/o Porterbrook Cllinic
75 Osborne Road
Nether Edge Hospital
Sheffield
S11 9BF
☎ 0114 271 6671
☎ 0114 237 4377
ruth.hallamjones@sct.nhs.uk
BASRT

**HALLY**, Dianne
**Psychoanalytic Psychotherapist**
61 Crescent Road
Nether Edge
Sheffield
S7 1HN
☎ 0114 255 3780
diannehally@onetel.net.uk
HIP

**HARDWICK**, Barbara
**Psychoanalytic Psychotherapist**
1 Hesley Mews
Scholes
Rotherham
S7 1HN
☎ 01709 554 795
☎ 07790 540 409
barbara.hardwick@virgin.net
HIP

**HARRIES**, Rashida
**Body Psychotherapist, Integrative Psychotherapist**
86 Sandford Grove Road
Sheffield
S7 1RR
☎ 0845 456 3898
☎ 0798 445 2525
rashida@aswab.co.uk
CCBP

**HART**, Carolyn
**Child Psychotherapist**
Shirle Hill Hospital
6A Cherry Tree Road
Sheffield
S11 9AA
☎ 0114 271 6860
☎ 0114 268 4480
ACP

**HAWKSWORTH**, Janet
**Gestalt Psychotherapist**
90 Brincliffe Edge Road
Sheffield
Sout Yorkshire
S11 9BW
☎ 0114 258 6192
janet@brincliffe.plus.com
SPTI

**HOWLETT**, Stephanie
**Psychoanalytic Psychotherapist, Psychodynamic Psychotherapist**
66 Psalter Lane
Sheffield
S11 8YQ
☎ 0114 268 2483
steph@howlett66.fsnet.co.uk
HIP

**HUNT**, Pat
**Psychoanalytic Psychotherapist**
Share Psychotherapy
176 Crookesmoor Road
Sheffield
S6 3FS
☎ 0114 268 2883
☎ 0114 285 1473
pat.share@virgin.net
Spring Cottage
High Bradfield
Sheffield
S6 6LG
HIP

**HUWS**, Rhodri
**Sexual and Relationship Psychotherapist**
♿ St George's CHC
Winter Street
Sheffield
S3 7ND
☎ 0114 271 8930
☎ 0114 271 6671
r.huws@Sheffield.ac.uk
Porterbrook Clinic
75 Osborne Road
Sheffield
S11 9BF
BASRT

**KATIS**, Elisabeth
**Psychoanalytic Psychotherapist**
35 Oakhill Road
Sheffield
S7 1SJ
☎ 01142 554 013
CLROakhill@aol.com
UPCA

**KENDALL**, Tim
**Psychoanalytic Psychotherapist**
Fulwood House
Old Fulwood Road
Sheffield
S10 3TH
☎ 0114 271 8710
☎ 0114 271 6715
tim.kendall@sct.nhs.uk
UPCA

**KERR**, Libby
**Integrative Psychotherapist**
39 Pinner Road
Sheffield
S11 8UG
☎ 0114 268 2420
libby@libby.fsnet.co.uk
SPCRC

**KITCHIN**, Paul Duncan
**Gestalt Psychotherapist**
Flat 8
18 Endcliffe Crescent
Sheffield
S10 3ED
☎ 0114 267 0118
res133@aol.com
SPTI

**KNOWLES**, Louise
**Gestalt Psychotherapist**
127 Alexandra Road
Heeley
Sheffield
S2 3EH
☎ 0114 250 1148
alexrd@freeuk.com
SPTI

**LEESON**, Julie
**Psychodrama Psychotherapist**
93 Fraser Road
Woodseats
Sheffield
S8 0JH
☎ 01142 749 117
☎ 01142 271 8754
julie@dajoc.freeserve.co.uk
BPA

**LIDMILA**, Alan
**Psychoanalytic Psychotherapist**
Broomhill Medical Centre
183 Whitham Road
Sheffield
S10 2SN
☎ 0114 230 9163
HIP

**LOBATTO**, Wendy
**Family & Systemic Psychotherapist**
Child and Family Therapy Team
Beighton Community Hospital
Sevenairs Road
Sheffield
S20 6NZ
☎ 0114 271 6542
wendy.lobatto@sct.nhs.uk
The Coach House
9 Mackon Bank
Sheffield
S7 1GQ
IFT

**LOFTUS**, Patrick A.
**Psychoanalytic Psychotherapist**
♿ 114 Industry Street
Walkley
Sheffield
S6 2WX
☎ 0114 233 6570
patrick.a.loftus@btinternet.com
HIP

**LONGMAN**, R L
**Cognitive Behavioural Psychotherapist**
10 Argyle Close
Sheffield
S8 9HL
☎ 07971 786 797
bobbylongman@btconnect.com
BABCP

**LOVEMAN**, Judith
**Family & Systemic Psychotherapist**
♿ The Yews
Worrall Road
Sheffield
S35 0AU
☎ 0114 271 6107
AFT

**MACNEILL**, Enid
**Psychodrama Psychotherapist, Psychodynamic Psychotherapist**
21 Knaresborough Road
Sheffield
S7 2TA
☎ 0114 236 4349
macneill@legend.co.uk
BPA, HIP

**MACHON**, Andrew
**Psychosynthesis Psychotherapist**
1 Hall Mews
Ravenfield
Near Rotherham
South Yorks
S65 4PW
☎ 07812 148 699
andrew@machon.fsnet.co.uk
IPS

**MAITLIS**, Marion
**Psychoanalytic Psychotherapist, Psychodynamic Psychotherapist**
♿ 13 Park Avenue
Sheffield
S10 3EY
☎ 0114 266 0888
smaitlis@compuserve.com
HIP

**MARSHALL**, Myra
**Psychoanalytic Psychotherapist**
11 Rutland Park
Broomhill
Sheffield
S10 2PB
HIP

**MASON**, Peter J.
**Cognitive Behavioural Psychotherapist**
♿ The Burns Medical Practice
46 Albion Place
Doncaster
DN1 2EG
☎ 01302 812 888
BABCP

**MATTHEWS**, Linda
**Cognitive Behavioural Psychotherapist**
Department of Psychological Health Care
11/12 Keresforth Close
Barnsley
South Yorkshire
S70 6RS
☎ 01709 876 995
☎ 07970 189 496
LindAMatthews@aol.com
57 Fitzwilliam Street
Wath upon Deane
Rotherham
South Yorkshire
S63 7HG
BABCP

**MCAULEY**, John
**Psychoanalytic Psychotherapist**
Share Psychotherapy
176 Crookesmoor Road
Sheffield
S6 3FS
HIP

**MCDONALD**, James
**Integrative Psychotherapist**
The Spring Dale Practice
27 Sparken Dale
Worksop
Nottinghamshire
S80 1BL
☎ 01909 477 862
james.mcd@lineone.net
SPTI

**MERCER**, Shirley
**Gestalt Psychotherapist**
164A Psalter Lane
Sheffield
Yorkshire
S11 8UR
☎ 01142 665 328
MET

**METTAM**, Lisa
**Cognitive Behavioural Psychotherapist**
♿ Specialist Psychotherapy Service
Brunswick House
299 Glosop Road
Sheffield
S10 2HL
☎ 0114 271 8688
lisa@mettam.fsbusiness.co.uk
67A Clarence Road
Sheffield
S6 4QE
BABCP

**MOHAMED**, Carol G M
**Psychoanalytic Psychotherapist**
♿ 16 Hoober Avenue
Ecclesall
Sheffield
South Yorkshire
S11 9SG
☎ 01142 363 271
☎ 07710 768 935
cazmohamed@aol.com
UPCA

**MOORE**, Meg
**Sexual and Relationship Psychotherapist**
♿ c/o Porterbrook Clinic
Nether Edge Hospital
75 Osbourne Road
Sheffield
S11 9BF
☎ 01629 813 099
☎ 07976 607 554
megc.moore@virgin.net
BASRT

**OCHYRA**, Krysia
**Gestalt Psychotherapist**
72 Portsea Road
Hillsborough
Sheffield
S6 4QB
☎ 0114 231 0220
SPTI

**ORAM**, Gill
**Psychoanalytic Psychotherapist**
29 Ben Bank Road
Silkstone Common
Barnsley
S75 4PB
☎ 01226 790 541
g.m.oram@shu.ac.uk
UPCA

**ORAM**, John E.D.
**Psychodynamic Psychotherapist**
John Oram & Associates
Psychotherapy Centre
13 Rustlings Road
Sheffield
S11 7AA
☎ 0114 266 3910
☎ 0114 221 4982
oramj@argonet.co.uk
12 Montgomery Road
Sheffield
S7 1LQ
HIP

**OWEN**, Lynne M.
**Cognitive Behavioural Psychotherapist**
1A Worry Goose Lane
Whiston Hospital
Adwick Road
Rotherham
S60 4AA
☎ 01709 305 105
☎ 07985 049 760
BABCP

**PARDOE**, Kathleen A
**Psychoanalytic Psychotherapist**
14 Steade Road
Nether Edge
Sheffield
S7 1DS
☎ 01142 589 123
UPCA

**PARRY**, Glenys
**Cognitive Analytic Therapist**
♿ University of Sheffield School of Health & Related
Sheffield NHS Trust
30 Regent Street
Sheffield
S1 4DA
ACAT

**PETHEN**, Susan
**Psychodynamic Psychotherapist**
62 Brincliffe Edge Road
Sheffield
S11 9BW
☎ 0114 255 1576
Pethen@aol.com
HIP

**PICKVANCE**, Deborah
**Psychodynamic Psychotherapist**
108 Carr Road
Sheffield
S6 2WZ
☎ 0114 233 6020
dpickvance@onetel.net.uk
HIP

**PORTEOUS**, Louise
**Psychodynamic Psychotherapist**
151 Chelsea Road
Sheffield
S11 9BQ
☎ 0114 2581 644
louiseporteous@ukonline.co.uk
HIP, UPCA

**RAYNER**, Beryl A
**Psychoanalytic Psychotherapist, Psychodynamic Psychotherapist**
5 Sherwood Chase
Totley Brook Road
Sheffield
S17 3QT
☎ 0114 236 2825
☎ 0114 236 0890
Greenways Natural Health Centre
180 Baslow Road
Totley
Sheffield
S17 4DS
HIP

**REJAIE**, Carol
**Psychoanalytic Psychotherapist**
12 Lawson Road
Broomhill
Sheffield
S.Yorkshire
S10 5BW
☎ 01142 686 965
crejaie@aol.com
UPCA

**RICKETTS**, Thomas N.
**Cognitive Behavioural Psychotherapist**
♿ Behavioural Psychotherapy
Michael Carlisle Centre
75 Osborne Road
Sheffield
S11 9BF
☎ 0114 271 8676
BABCP

**ROBERTSON**, Judith Ann
**Cognitive Psychotherapist**
♿ 52 Grove Road
Sheffield
S7 2GZ
☎ 0114 235 2883
judian.robertson@virgin.net
BABCP

**ROBINSON**, Felicity
**Psychoanalytic Psychotherapist, Psychodynamic Psychotherapist**
12 Brincliffe Edge Road
Sheffield
S11 9BW
☎ 0114 255 2989
HIP

**ROSEMARY**, Margaret
**Gestalt Psychotherapist**
♿ 3 Strathtay Road
Sheffield
S11 7GU
☎ 01142 660 229
margaret@rosemary1943.fsnet.co.uk
GPTI

**ROSENFELD**, Angela
**Group Analyst**
♿ Specialist Psychotherapy Service
Brunswock House
299 Glossop Road
Sheffield
S10
☎ 0114 271 6890
IGA

**SHEEHAN**, Maureen
**Gestalt Psychotherapist**
♿ 37 Norborough Road
Doncaster
DN2 4AT
☎ 01302 349 450
msheehan@dynamitechicken.com
GPTI

**SHIPTON**, Geraldine
**Psychoanalytic Psychotherapist**
The Coach House
25 Lyndhurst Road
Sheffield
S11 9BJ
☎ 0114 2554 326
☎ 0114 2222 980
Centre for Psychotherapeutic Studies
University of Sheffield
Former Jessop Hospital
Levygreave Road, Sheffiel
S10 2TA
HIP, UPCA

**SLANEY**, Ruth
**Cognitive Behavioural Psychotherapist**
Summer Lane South CMHT
Summer Lane
Wombwell
Barnsley
S73 8QH
☎ 01246 456 963
roo-slaney@supaworld.com
BABCP

**SMITH**, Valerie
**Group Analyst**
Flat 2
27 Collegiate Crescent
Sheffield
S10 2BT
☎ 0114 268 6924
IGA

**STANBURY**, Christine
**Psychoanalytic Psychotherapist**
CDDPS Trust Headquarters, Central Resources
Earls House Hospital
Lanchester Road
Durham
DN1 5RD
☎ 07971 020 257
☎ 0191 333 6533
chris.stanbury@cddps.northy.nhs.uk
FIP

**TANTAM**, Digby
**Group Analyst, Psychodynamic Psychotherapist**
Dilemma
3 Hollow Meadow Mews
Sheffield
S6 6GB
☎ 0114 230 9990
dilemma@dial.pipex.com
IGA, NWIDP, SEA, UPCA

**TENNISON**, John F.S.
**Cognitive Behavioural Psychotherapist**
♿ Dept. Cognitive Behavioural Therapy
East Dene Centre
Landsdowne Road
Doncaster
DN2 6QN
☎ 01302 734 050
☎ 01423 701 116
john@tenison.org
BABCP

**THOMSON**, Pat
**Psychodynamic Psychotherapist**
35 Slayleigh Avenue
Sheffield
S10 3RA
☎ 0114 230 7471
HIP

**TUDOR**, Keith
**Group Humanistic Psychotherapist, Transactional Analysis Psychotherapist**
13A Penrhyn Road
Hunter's Bar
Sheffield
S11 8UL
☎ 0114 267 8277
keith.tudor@temenos.ac.uk
AHPP, ITA, MET

**TWEED**, Mary
**Transactional Analysis Psychotherapist**
Alison Centre
Alison Crescent
Sheffield
S2 1AS
☎ 01142 416 228
☎ 01142 656 613
ITA

**VASSILIADIS**, Helena
**Psychoanalytic Psychotherapist**
4 Fulney Road
Nethergreen
Sheffield
S11 7EW
☎ 0114 230 7002
helena.vassiliadis@virgin.net
HIP

**WIDDOWSON**, Mark
**Transactional Analysis Psychotherapist**
Flat 1
217-219 London Road
Sheffield
S2 4L
☎ 01142 586 480
☎ 01142 201 665
mark.widdowson1@btopenworld.com
Sheffield Natural Health Centre
289 Abbeydale Road
Sheffield
S7 1FJ
ITA

**WILLETTS**, Dean
**Cognitive Behavioural Psychotherapist**
♿ Department of Behavioural Psychology
Doncaster Royal Infirmary
Doncaster
DN2 5LT
☎ 01472 595 655
☎ 01302 736 761
d.willets@talk21.com
BABCP

**WILLIAMS**, Steve
**Body Psychotherapist, Integrative Psychotherapist**
86 Sandford Grove
Sheffield
S7 1RR
☎ 0114 255 7565 / 0845 456 3898
☎ 07958 977 630
Steve@aswab.co.uk
CCBP

**WILSON**, Janet Lynn
**Integrative Psychotherapist**
8 Milton Road
Sheffield
S7 1HP
☎ 0114 221 4402
☎ 07814 515 381
SPTI

**WRATTEN**, Stephen
**Family & Systemic Psychotherapist**
♿ 177 Rushfield Road
Sheffield
S8 9QD
☎ 0114 258 8298
stephen.wratten@sheffield-tr.trent.nhs.uk
Child & Family Therapy Team (North Centenary House
55 Albert Terrace Road
Sheffield
S6 3BR
AFT

**WRIGHT**, Christine M.J.
**Cognitive Behavioural Psychotherapist**
Wathwood Hospital
Gipsy Green Lane
Wath-upon-Dearne
Rotherham
S63 7TQ
☎ 01302 802 139
BABCP

**WYLIE**, Dr Kevan
**Sexual and Relationship Psychotherapist**
♿ Porterbrook Clinic
75 Osborne Road
Sheffield
S11 9BF
☎ 0114 271 8674
☎ 0114 271 3334
k.r.wylie@sheffield.ac.uk
BASRT

**YOUNG**, Robert
**Psychoanalytic Psychotherapist**
Centre for Psychotherapeutic Studies
University of Sheffield
16 Claremont Crescent
Sheffield
S10 2TA
☎ 020 7607 8306
robert@rmy1.demon.co.uk
FIP, UPCA

**VAN DEURZEN**, Emmy
**Existential Psychotherapist**
♿ Dilemma Consultancy, 3 Hollow Meadows Mews
Hollow Meadows
Peak National Park
Sheffield
S6 6GJ
☎ 01142 309 990
dilemma@dial.pipex.com or emmy@dilemmas.org
27 Brocco Bank
Sheffield
S11 8RQ
SEA, UPCA

## YORKSHIRE - WEST

**ADDISON**, Susan
**Psychodynamic Psychotherapist**
8 Blackhill
Pecket Well
Hebden Bridge
HX7 8QS
☎ 01422 847 076
UPCA

**ASHTON**, Anthony
**Group Analyst**
Specialist Psychotherapy Team APTS
S.W. Yorks NHS Mental Health Trust
Horbury Health Centre
2A Westfield Road, Horbur
WF4 6LL
☎ 01924 327 721
tony.ashton@swyt.nhs.uk
IGA

**ASHTON**, John
**Psychoanalytic Psychotherapist, Psychodynamic Psychotherapist**
19 Kirkwood Gardens
Leeds
LS16 7EB
☎ 0113 230 1156
HIP, YAPP

**BALLS**, Margaret A
**Psychodynamic Psychotherapist**
♿ 33 Moseley Wood Avenue
Leeds
LS16 7HL
☎ 01132 817 011
margaret.balls@ntlworld.com
UPCA

**BEESE**, Angela G.
**Cognitive Behavioural Psychotherapist**
♿ Academic Unit of Psychiatry
15 Hyde Terrace
University of Leeds
Leeds
LS2 9LT
☎ 0113 343 2731
a.beese@leeds.ac.uk
Dept. of Psychotherapy
40 Clarendon Road
Leeds
LS2 9LT
BABCP

**BERGIN**, Stella
**Transactional Analysis Psychotherapist**
Leeds Counselling & Psychotherapy Services
Victoria Buildings, 14 Weetwood Lan
Far Headingley
Leeds
LS16 5LX
☎ 01422 847 793
ITA

**BONNER**, Kate
**Psychodynamic Psychotherapist**
17 Rochdale Road
Golcar
Huddersfield
HD7 4NN
☎ 01484 654 508
randkbonner@btopenworld.com
YAPP

**BRADLEY**, Anne Marie
**Transactional Analysis Psychotherapist**
♿ The Stables
10c Henshaw Lane
Yeadon
Leeds
LS19 7RW
☎ 01133 910 024
☎ 07831 262 977
jbamb@supanet.com
ITA

**BRAMALL**, Keith
**Jungian Analytical Psychotherapist**
'The Cottage'
8 Kingswood Gardens
Leeds
LS8 2BT
☎ 01132 667 549
earlswood_k@onetel.net.uk
WMIP, YAPP

**BRESLOFF**, Valerie
**Transactional Analysis Psychotherapist**
Leeds Counselling & Psychotherapy Services
Victoria Buildings
14 Weetwood Lane
Leeds
LS16 5LX
☎ 01132 754 616 ext 8
valbresloff@bigfoot.com
ITA

**BROOKE**, Paul
**Cognitive Behavioural Psychotherapist**
♿ Dept. of Clinical Psychology
SW Yorkshire Mental Health Trust
Halifax Road
Dewsbury
WF13 4HS
☎ 01924 816 056
paul.brooke@dhc-tr.northy.nhs.uk
BABCP

**BROWN**, Antony
**Cognitive Behavioural Psychotherapist**
♿ Cognitive Behavioural Psych Clinic
suite 290
57 Great George Clinic
Leeds
LS1 3AY
☎ 01904 621 648
☎ 07775 603 853
antonybrowncbt@hotmail.com
BABCP

**BROWN**, Helen
**Transactional Analysis Psychotherapist**
8 YorkTerrace
Akroydon
Halifax
HX3 6LZ
☎ 04122 368 068
ITA

**BUDDEN**, Mark
**Gestalt Psychotherapist**
Matomo
7 Redhouse Lane
Chapel Allerton
Leeds
LS7 4RA
☎ 0113 294 4993
juliadavies@matomo.com
ScPTI

**BURTON**, Tom
**Transactional Analysis Psychotherapist**
9 Osborne Place
Todmorden
West Yorkshire
OL14 5BQ
☎ 0161 862 9456
☎ 07930 243495
manningburton@hotmail.com
ITA

**BUTLIN**, Lesley
**Transactional Analysis Psychotherapist**
♿ Leeds Counselling & Psychotherapy Services
Victoria Buildings
14 Weetwood Lane
Leeds
LS16 5LX
☎ 01132 754 616 ext5
lesley@butlinsirrs.freeserv.co.uk
ITA

**CANON**, Rob
**Humanistic Psychotherapist**
♿ The Hebden Bridge Centre for Counselling & Psychot
Machpelah Works
Burney Road
Hebden Bridge
HX7 8AU
☎ 01422 823 828
rob-canon@beeb.net
SPTI

**CANON**, Sue
**Gestalt Psychotherapist**
♿ The Hebden Bridge Centre for Counselling & Psychotherapy
Hebden Bridge
West Yorkshire
HX7 8AU
☎ 01422 823828
sue-canon@beeb.net
Burnley Road
Hebden Bridge
West Yorks
HX7 8AU
SPTI

**CLARKSON**, Barbara
**Transactional Analysis Psychotherapist**
♿ 14 Weetwood Lane
Leeds
LS16 5LX
☎ 01132 754 616 ext 2
☎ 01132 643 994
ITA

**CLEMENTS-JEWERY**, Sue
**Sexual and Relationship Psychotherapist**
41 Spinkfield Road
Birkby
Huddersfield
HD2 2AY
☎ 01484 318 132
☎ 07980 117 684
pandscj@fish.co.uk
BASRT

**CONLON**, Isobel
**Group Analyst, Psychoanalytic Psychotherapist**
1 Ancaster Road
West Park
Leeds
LS16 5HH
☎ 01132 751 958
smallconlon@clara.co.uk
IGA, NWIDP

**CONWAY**, Mary
**Transactional Analysis Psychotherapist**
92 Thornhill Avenue
Lindley
Huddersfield
HD3 3DG
☎ 01484 300 687
ITA

**CONWAY**, Sally
**Group Analyst, Psychodynamic Psychotherapist**
Tuke House
60 Sholebrook Avenue
Leeds
LS7 3HB
☎ 01132 952 790
IGA, UPCA

**COTTRELL**, David
**Family & Systemic Psychotherapist**
Academic Unit of Child & Adolescent Mental Health
12A Clarendon Road
Leeds
LS2 9NN
☎ 0113 295 1760
d.j.cottrell@leeds.ac.uk
AFT

**COULE**, Jaqueline
**Integrative Psychotherapist**
♿ Adult Psychological Therapies
H.Elwynne Jones Centre
Pinderfields South Site
Aberford Road, Wakefield
WF1 4DE
☎ 01924 814641
BPS, MET

**COWARD**, Malcolm
**Gestalt Psychotherapist**
19 Whitebeam Park
Birkby
Huddersfield
HD2 2GZ
☎ 01484 430 995
mcowardtherapy@clara.co.uk
Leeds Counselling and
Psychotherapy Services
Victoria Buildings
14 Weetwood Lane
Far Headingly
LS16
GPTI, SPTI

**DUMMETT**, Nicola J.
**Cognitive Behavioural Psychotherapist**
The Child & Family unit
St. James's University Hospital
Beckett Street
Leeds
LS9 7TF
☎ 0113 206 4068/4292
BABCP

**EADIE**, Yvonne
**Cognitive Analytic Therapist**
4 Alberta Avenue
Leeds
LS7 4LX
ACAT, YAPP

**EDWARDS**, Jennifer
**Psychoanalytic Psychotherapist**
5 Farrar Drive
Mirfield
West Yorkshire
WF14 9DX
☎ 01924 492 811
LPDO

**GARTLAND**, Michael
**Psychodynamic Psychotherapist**
Fall Hall
Waterside
Marsden
Huddersfield
HD7 6BU
☎ 01484 845 851
☎
mike.gartland@swyt.nhs.uk
HIP

**GAUNTLETT**, Tim
**Psychoanalytic Psychotherapist**
♿ "Waske Hall"
50 Skircoat Green
Halifax
HX3 0SA
☎ 01422 341391
timgauntlett@totalise.co.uk
IPSS

**GIBBS**, Catherine
**Group Analyst**
♿ Child & Adolescent Mental Health
West Team Leeds, Gringlebar Clinic
415 Bradford Road
Leeds
LS28
IGA

**HAMLYN**, Sarah
**Integrative Psychotherapist**
307 Harrogate Road
Leeds
LS17 6PA
☎ 01132 682 665
sjhamlyn@agnes.cix.co.uk
NGP

**HANKS**, Helga
**Psychodynamic Psychotherapist**
♿ Leeds Family Therapy & Research Centre
Department of Psychology
Leeds University
Leeds
LS2 9JT
☎ 01133 436 686
☎ 01133 926 796/01132 667 378
helga@dial.pipex.com
Department of Psychological Medicine
(Children) Clarendon Wing
Leeds General Infirmary
Leeds
LS2 9DE
KCC, YAPP

**HARDEN**, Bev
**Psychoanalytic Psychotherapist**
5 Well Street
Todmorden
OL14 6LW
☎ 01706 819 607
bharden@dsl.pipex.com
NWIDP

**HARDY**, Joanne
**Cognitive Behavioural Psychotherapist**
♿ Dept. Psychol & Counselling Services
The Calderdale Royal Hospital
Salterhebble, Halifax
West Yorks
HX3 0PW
☎ 01422 222 731
psychology@calderdale.nhs.uk
BABCP

**HARROW**, Anne
**Group Analyst, Psychoanalytic Psychotherapist**
Dept Psychotherapy
40 Clarendon Road
Leeds
anne@anneharrow.force9.co.uk
IGA, YAPP

**HEENAN**, Colleen
**Psychodynamic Psychotherapist**
♿ Heathroyd Garden Practice
4 Toller Drive
Bradford
W York
BD9 5NU
☎ 01274 493 125
colleenheenan@onetel.net.uk
YAPP

**JACKSON**, Sherin
**Personal Construct Psychotherapist**
Highdale Cottage
217 Barnsley Road
Denby Dale
Huddersfield
HD8 8TS
☎ 01484 864 824
sherin@IC24.net
PCP

**JARRETT**, Betty
**Psychodynamic Psychotherapist**
3 North Lane
Roundhay
Leeds
LS8 2QJ
☎ 01132 329 227
bjarrettpsych.@yahoo.co.uk
VAPP

**JOHNSTON**, James
**Psychoanalytic Psychotherapist**
Southfield House
40 Clarendon Road
Leeds
LS2 9PJ
☎ 0113 295 5430
HIP

**JONES**, Maggy
**Family & Systemic Psychotherapist**
♿ 1st Floor
100 Wellington Street
Leeds
LS1 4LT
☎ 01535 637 202
☎ 07773 332 297
AFT

**KEEN**, John
**Cognitive Behavioural Psychotherapist**
♿ CBT Centre for West Yorkshire
The Barn, Ing House
350 Bradford Road
Liversedge
WF15 6BY
☎ 01924 235 822
cbtwestyorkshire@btconnect.com
BABCP

**KERRY**, Richard
**Cognitive Behavioural Psychotherapist**
♿ Department of Psychology
St. Lukes Hospital
Blackmoorfoot Road
Huddersfield
HD4 5RQ
☎ 01484 343 480
richard.kerry@virgin.net
BABCP

**KOHLER**, Christiane
**Hypno-Psychotherapist**
6 Shire Close
Rein Park. Morley
Leeds
LS27 0QU
☎ 01132 523 690
NSHAP

**LANCELOT**, Maggie
**Psychoanalytic Psychotherapist**
5c Chapel Lane
Bingley
West Yorks
BD16 2NG
☎ 01274 531 607
isgralot@aol.com
NWIDP

**LAWTON**, Derek
**Humanistic Psychotherapist**
♿ Specialist Psychotherapy Services
Southfield House
40 Clarendon Road
Leeds
LS2 9PJ
☎ 01132 955 430
dellawton@aol.com
AHPP, UPCA

**LEWIS**, Sheila
**Psychoanalytic Psychotherapist**
♿ Department of Clinical Psychology
St Luke's Hospital
Blackmoorfoot Road
Crosland Moor
HD4 5RQ
☎ 01943 601 948
☎ 01484 343 480
GUILD, YAPP

**LUDOLF**, Monica
**Hypno-Psychotherapist**
4 Riviera Gardens
Chapel Allerton
Leeds
Yorkshire
LS7 3DW
☎ 01132 622 355
NRHP

**MACASKIE**, Jane
**Psychodynamic Psychotherapist**
♿ The Orchard
Town Street
Horsforth
Leeds
LS18 5BN
☎ 0113 258 6450
jane@macaskie.fsnet.co.uk
FPC

**MARTIN**, Carol
**Psychodynamic Psychotherapist**
Unit of Psychiatry
University of Leeds
15 Hyde Terrace
Leeds
LS2 9JT
☎ 01132 332 723
FIP, YAPP

**MASON**, Christine
**Psychodynamic Psychotherapist**
16 East Moor Road
Leeds
LS8 1AE
☎ 01132 661 273
cm.gh@ukgateway.net
UPCA

**MCCARTHY-HOFFBAUER**, Iris
**Cognitive Behavioural Psychotherapist**
♿ St Lukes Hospital
Psychological Services
Blackmoorfoot Road
Huddersfield
HD4 5RQ
☎ 01484 343 481
BABCP

**MCFARLANE**, Kay
**Gestalt Psychotherapist**
Leeds Counselling & Psychotherapy Services
Victoria Buildings
14 Weetwood Lane
Headingley, Leeds
LS16 5LX
☎ 01423 734 140
mcliu8@hotmail.com
SPTI

**MEEKUMS**, Bonnie
**Humanistic and Integrative Psychotherapist**
♿ Univeristy of Leeds
Manygates Campus
Barnsley
Wakefield
WF1 5NS
☎ 01457 839 013
☎ 0113 343 9414
bonniem@unisonfree.net
AHPP

**MERTZANAKIS**, Christos
**Group Analytic Psychotherapist**
39 Riviera Gardens
Leeds
LS7 3DW
☎ 0113 262 7040
cmertzanakis@yahoo.co.uk
UPCA

**MIDGLEY**, Karen
**Transactional Analysis Psychotherapist**
3 King Street
Mirfield
West Yorks
WF14 8AW
☎ 01924 499 758
☎ 01132 754 616
14 Westwood Lane
Far Headingley
Leeds
LS16
ITA

**MILLAR**, Elizabeth M
**Psychodynamic Psychotherapist**
♿ Aberford Centre
Fieldhead
Ouchthorpe Lane
Wakefield
WF1 3SP
☎ 01924 327 499
elizabeth.millar@swyt.nhs.uk
UPCA

**MORRIS**, Jane
**Psychoanalytic Psychotherapist**
♿ The Birchcliffe Centre
Birchcliffe Road
Hebden Bridge
West Yorkshire
HX7 8DG
☎ 01422 845 314
☎ 01943 862 031
janemorris@jmch.co.uk
NWIDP, YAPP

**MOYES**, Theresa
**Cognitive Behavioural Psychotherapist**
♿ Leeds Psychology & Therapies Group
Leeds CMHS Teaching NHS Trust
17 Blenheim Terrace
Leeds
LS2 9HN
☎ 0113 343 1942
theresa.moyes@leeds.nhs.uk
BABCP

**NOLAN**, Philip
**Neurolinguistic Psychotherapist**
67 Kaye Lane
Almondbury
Huddersfield
West Yorkshire
HD5 8XT
☎ 01484 432847
pjo8@ntlworld.com
NLPtCA

**OWEN**, Ian
**Integrative Psychotherapist**
25 Hyde Terrace
Leeds
LS2 9LN
ian@daisyspoon.fsnet.co.uk
SPCRC

**PALEY**, Graham
**Psychodynamic Psychotherapist**
♿ Southfield House
40 Clarendon Road
Leeds
LS2 9PJ
☎ 0113 295 5435
grahampaley@yahoo.co.uk
UPCA

**PARTINGTON-UTTLEY**, Paula
**Transactional Analysis Psychotherapist**
c/o The Guiseley Osteopathic Centre
113 Otley Road
Leeds
LS20 8AF
☎ 01943 872 278
☎ 01132 754 616
Paula-partingtonuttley@hotmail.com
Leeds Counselling and Psychotherapy services
Victoria Building
14 weetwood lane
Leeds
LS16 5LX
ITA

**PATTINSON**, Philip
**Cognitive Behavioural Psychotherapist**
Dept. Psychological Services
The Calderdale Royal Hospital
Halifax
HX3 0PW
☎ 01422 222 733
☎ 01706 766 600
101516.2474@compuserve.com
BABCP

**PELTIER**, Judy
**Psychoanalytic Psychotherapist, Psychodynamic Psychotherapist**
♿ c/o Manningham Project
203 Lumb Lane
Bradford
BD8 7SG
☎ 01234 502 604
☎ 01274 502 604
47 Hutton Road
Bradford
BD5 9DT
HIP

**PHILLIPS**, Pauline
**Psychodynamic Psychotherapist**
27 Gledhow Avenue
Leeds
LS8 1LD
☎ 01132 667 175
phillips@gledhow2000.fsnet.co.uk
School of Health Care Studies
Baines Wing
University of Leeds
PO Box 214
LS2 9UT
UPCA

**PHILLIPS**, Thomas Lambton
**Cognitive Behavioural Psychotherapist**
♿ 90 Redwood Drive
Bradley Manor
Huddersfield
HD2 1PW
☎ 01484 455 150
☎ 01484 347 725
lambton@redwoodpsychotherapy.fsnet.co.uk
Dept Behavioural Psychotherapy
6A Greenhead Road
Huddersfield
HD1 4EN
BABCP

**PITTOCK**, Frances
**Psychoanalytic Psychotherapist, Psychodynamic Psychotherapist**
4 Huntsmans Close
Eldwick
Bingley
BD16 3NX
☎ 01274 560 178
☎ 0113 295 2402
fpittock@aol.com
Clinical Psychology & Therapies Service
St Mary's House
St Mary's Road
Leeds
LS7 3JX
HIP

**RADCLIFFE**, Mark
**Psychodynamic Psychotherapist**
20 Eastcourt Avenue
Headingly
Leeds
LS6 3ES
☎ 01132 785 991
UPCA

**REID**, Errol
**Psychoanalytic Psychotherapist**
63 Shaftesbury Avenue
Roundhay
Leeds
LS8 1DR
☎ 01132 955 430
☎ 01132 933 446
Day-Reid@roundhay86.freeserve.co.uk
Psychotherapy Department
40 Clarendon Road
Leeds
LS2 9PJ
UPCA

**ROBINSON**, Lesley
**Gestalt Psychotherapist**
23 De Lacies Road
Woodlesford
Leeds
LS26 8WH
☎ 01132 823 491
MET

**ROMAINE**, Stephanie
**Psychodynamic Psychotherapist**
♿ The Orchard
Town Street
Horsforth
Leeds
LS18 5BN
☎ 0113 226 2407
saromaine@aol.com
FPC

**ROSE**, Sally
**Psychoanalytic Psychotherapist**
♿ Mill House
Valley Farm
Parkside Road
Leeds
LS16 8EZ
☎ 01132 612 949
sallyrose@mac.com
ARBS, YAPP

**ROSENTHAL**, Hat A
**Group Analytic Psychotherapist**
Fairview
Primrose Bank
Gilstead
Bingley, W Yorkshire
BD16 4RG
☎ 01274 562 903
UPCA

**ROWAN**, Chris
**Gestalt Psychotherapist,**
**Integrative Arts Psychotherapist**
25 Hollin Lane
Westwood
Leeds
LS16 5NB
☎ 0113 274 3065
GCL, IATE

**ROWE**, Celly
**Psychoanalytic Psychotherapist,**
**Psychodynamic Psychotherapist**
♿ Southfield House Specialist
Psychotherapy Services
40 Clarendon Road
Leeds
LS2 9PJ
☎ 0113 295 5430
dr.cellyrowe@talk21.com
UPCA, YAPP

**SANDERS**, Paul J
**Psychoanalytic Psychotherapist**
94 Shipley Fields Road
Shipley
W Yorks
BD18 2DL
☎ 01772 401 370
paul@aardwolf.freeserve.co.uk
UPCA

**SCOTT**, John B
**Systemic Psychotherapist**
♿ Child & Adolescent Service
Fieldhead House
2-8 St Martin's Avenue
Fieldhead Business Centre
Bradford
BD7 1LG
☎ 01274 723 241
john.scott@bdct.nhs.uk/johnbscott58@
hotmail.com
KCC

**SELLERS**, Carolyn
**Cognitive Behavioural**
**Psychotherapist**
♿ The Grange Consulting Rooms
92 Whitcliffe Road
Cleckheaton
BD19 3DR
☎ 01274 878 600
☎ 0161 772 3480
carolynsellers@usa.net
BABCP

**SIDEY**, Brian
**Psychoanalytic Psychotherapist,**
**Psychodynamic Psychotherapist**
38 Wellington Crescent
Shipley
W. Yorks
BD18 3PH
☎ 01943 862 031 ext 3105
☎ 01274 599327
briansidey@blueyonder.co.uk
FIP, YAPP

**SMITH**, Gail P
**Psychodrama Psychotherapist**
Room 15
20 Clarendon Road
Leeds
LS2 9NZ
☎ 07753 218 996
☎ 0113 206 4495
gailphillipasmith@hotmail.com
BPA

**SPENCELEY**, Dave
**Transactional Analysis**
**Psychotherapist**
161a Kings Cross Road
Halifax
West Yorkshire
HX3 3LW
☎ 01422 366 356
☎ 07710 419 378
dave@ta_psychotherapy.co.uk
ITA

**STEWART**, Kate
**Family & Systemic**
**Psychotherapist**
8 Selbourne Villas
St Mary's Road
Bradford
BD9 4NN
☎ 01274 493 308
lkate.stewart@blueyonder.co.uk
AFT

**STEWART**, Phil
**Cognitive Behavioural**
**Psychotherapist**
59 Hill Top Road
Paddock
Huddersfield
HD1 4SQ
☎ 01484 510 892
BABCP

**STOKELD**, Alasdair
**Psychoanalytic Psychotherapist,**
**Psychodynamic Psychotherapist**
♿ Mill House
Valley Farm
Parkside Road
Leeds
LS16 8EZ
☎ 01132 612 949
alstokeld@mac.com
ARBS, YAPP

**STRATTON**, Peter M
**Systemic Psychotherapist**
♿ Leeds Family Therapy and Research
Centre
School of Psychology
University of Leeds
Leeds
LS2 9JT
☎ 01132 335 728
KCC

**SYME**, Gabrielle
**Psychoanalytic Psychotherapist**
♿ Mount Farm House
Town Street
Rawdon
Leeds
LS19 6QJ
☎ 01132 505 700
YAPP

**TAYLOR**, James
**Integrative Psychotherapist**
15 Broomfield Crescent
Leeds
LS6 3DD
☎ 01132 268 481
james.taylor@ntlworld.com
SPTI

**THARRATT**, Penny
**Gestalt Psychotherapist**
Flat 3, Moorbank House
31 Shire Oak Road
Headingley
Leeds
LS6 2DD
☎ 0113 275 5593
p.a.tharratt@leeds.ac.uk
GCL

**TOWNSEND**, Pat
**Cognitive Behavioural**
**Psychotherapist**
♿ Day Treatment Service
Baghill House
Walkergate
Pontefract
WF8 1QS
☎ 01977 465 493
BABCP

**TURNER**, Avril
**Cognitive Behavioural Psychotherapist**
♿ CBT Centre for West Yorkshire
The Barn, Ings House
350 Bradford Road
Liversedge
WF15 6BY
☎ 01924 235 822
cbtwestyorkshire@btconnect.com
BABCP

**VINCENT**, Jane
**Psychodynamic Psychotherapist**
16 Pasture Terrace
Leeds
LS7 4QR
☎ 01132 951 770
☎ 01132 289 885
jvincent30@hotmail.com
HIP, UPCA

**WADDINGTON**, Ann
**Psychoanalytic Psychotherapist**
6 Lambert Drive
Leeds
LS8 1NL
☎ 01274 531536
☎ 0113 3930438
GUILD

**WALFORD**, Jane
**Transactional Analysis Psychotherapist**
♿ L.P.T.I.
2a Weetwood Lane
Far Headingley
Leeds
LS16 5LS
☎ 01132 789 953
walford@leedstherapy.fsnet.co.uk
ITA

**WALFORD**, Robin
**Transactional Analysis Psychotherapist**
♿ Leeds Psychotherapy Training Institute
2a Weetwood Lane
Leeds
LS16 5LS
☎ 01132 789 953
walford@leedstherapy.fsnet.co.uk
ITA

**WALKER**, Dawn
**Family & Systemic Psychotherapist**
♿ Therapeutic Social Work Team
Osmond Thorpe Centre
81a Wykebeck Mount
Leeds
LS9 0DW
☎ 0113 247 7652
dawn.m.walker@leeds.gov.uk
AFT

**WALLACE**, Daphne
**Psychoanalytic Psychotherapist**
♿ Wharfedale Psychology and Psychotherapy Centre
5a Westgate
Otley
LS20 3AT
☎ 01943 468 443
☎ 01282 841 608
LPDO

**WALSH**, Stuart
**Family & Systemic Psychotherapist, Psychodrama Psychotherapist**
4 Wood Lea
Church Road
Todmorden
West Yorkshire
OL14 8EZ
☎ 01706 819 873
☎ 0161 276 5370
salsastuart@aol.com
AFT, BPA

**WARD**, Bernard
**Group Analytic Psychotherapist**
100 North Park Avenue
Leeds
Yorkshire
LS8 1HP
☎ 01132 933 262
UPCA, YAPP

**WARDEN**, Jennifer
**Family & Systemic Psychotherapist**
♿ 1 Manor Place
Horbury
Wakefield
WF4 6JB
☎ 01924 260 831
jennifer.warden@virgin.net
AFT

**WATSON**, Jean
144 Harrogate Road
Leeds
LS7 4NZ
☎ 0113 237 0700
☎ 0113 269 4448
JeanWatsonLifeskills@hotmail.com
CTIS

**WATTIS**, Libby
**Integrative Psychotherapist, Psychoanalytic Psychotherapist, Psychodynamic Psychotherapist**
8 Compton Mount
Leeds
LS9 7BT
☎ 0113 240 8611
Libbywattis@aol.com
LPDO, WMIP, YAPP

**WEBB**, Joan
**Psychoanalytic Psychotherapist**
23 Henconner Lane
Chapel Allerton
Leeds
LS27 3NX
☎ 0113 262 3766
FIP, YAPP

**WELCH**, Lawrence
**Cognitive Analytic Therapist**
♿ Psychology & Psychotherapy Service
Malham House
25 Hyde Terrace
Leeds
LS2 9LN
☎ 0113 295 3402
ACAT

**WELSH**, Catherine
**Psychoanalytic Psychotherapist**
36 Priesthorpe Road
Farsley
Leeds
LS28 5JX
☎ 01132 293 761
YAPP

**WYATT**, Katherine
**Psychodynamic Psychotherapist**
35 The Drive
Roundhay
Leeds
LS8 1JQ
☎ 0113 225 0275
wyattleeds@supanet.com
FPC

**YATES**, Andrew F.J.
**Sexual and Relationship Psychotherapist**
♿ Psychosexual Medicine
Liaison Psychiatry
Leeds General Infirmary
Great George Street, Lee
LS1 3EX
☎ 07901 825 634
☎ 0113 392 5706
andrew.Yates@leedsth.nhs.uk
BASRT

## ABERDEENSHIRE

**EDWARDS**, Kareen
**Sexual and Relationship Psychotherapist**
39 Desswood Place
Aberdeen
AB25 2EE
☎ 01224 642 947
BASRT

**HOWIE**, David D.
**Hypno-Psychotherapist**
9B Millburn Street
Aberdeen
Grampian
AB11 6SS
☎ 01224 574 190
ddhowie@aol.com
NRHP

**LOUGH**, Mark
**Integrative Psychotherapist**
35 Huntly Street
Aberdeen
AB10 1TJ
☎ 01224 640 725
☎ 01224 572 295
NGP

**LOUGH**, Ruth
**Integrative Psychotherapist**
12 Ellerslie Road
Bucksburn
Aberdeen
AB21 9EJ
☎ 01224 713 332
ken@lough430.freeserve.co.uk
NGP

**MILNE**, Frances
**Analytical Psychologist-Jungian Analyst**
3 Northcote Hill
Aberdeen
AB15 7TW
☎ 01224 311 468
frances.milne@btopenworld.com
IGAP

**MORRISON**, Sandra
**Sexual and Relationship Psychotherapist**
Prye
Forest Road
Kintore
AB51 0YX
☎ 01467 633 257
sandrakintore@aol.com
BASRT

**RENNIE**, Belinda
**Cognitive Behavioural Psychotherapist**
♿ Shampher Cottage
Strachan
Banchory
AB31 6NN
☎ 01330 850 316
☎ 01244 636 378
belrennie@hotmail.com
The Rosemount Centre
1C Mount Street
Aberdeen
AB25 2RA
BABCP

**ROBINSON**, J.G.
**Child Psychotherapist**
South Leylodge Farmhouse
Leylodge
Kintore
Aberdeenshire
AB5 0XY
☎ 01330 860333
ACP

**SAWYER**, Ken
**Hypno-Psychotherapist**
31 Cairngrassie Circle
Portlethen
Aberdeen
AB1 4TZ
☎ 01224 781 452
sawyerkand@aol.com
CTIS

**STOCKS**, Samantha
**Systemic Psychotherapist**
Craigstone Lodge
Broadiach
Kingswells
Aberdeen
AB15 8RJ
☎ 01224 747 804
☎ 01224 552 234
Royal Aberdeen Childrens Hospital
Child Clinic Psychology
Cornhill Road
AB25 2ZG
KCC

**TAYLOR**, Carolyn D W
**Cognitive Behavioural Psychotherapist**
♿ Activating Better Choices Ltd
Thainstone Business Centre
Inverurie
AB51 5TB
☎ 01467 629 531
carolyn@abchoices.com
20 Maitland Crescent
Inverurie
Aberdeenshire
AB51 4HG
BABCP

**THOMPSON**, Rosalind
**Core Process Psychotherapist**
♿ 'Bundanoon'
Pitbee, Pitcaple
Inverurie
Aberdeenshire
AB51 5HJ
☎ 01467 681 639
KI

**WOOLLARD**, Diana
**Integrative Psychotherapist, Transpersonal Psychotherapist**
36 Watson Street
Aberdeen
AB25 2QL
☎ 01224 633 104
dianawoollard@bigfoot.com
CTP

**WRIGHT**, Harry
**Group Analyst, Psychoanalytic Psychotherapist**
Psychotherapy Department
Upper Garden Villa
Royal Cornhill Hospital
Aberdeen
AB25 2ZH
☎ 01224 557 397
IGA, WMIP

## ANGUS

**MORTON**, Richard Victor
**Cognitive Behavioural Psychotherapist**
40 Carlogie Road
Carnoustie
Angus
Scotland
DD7 6EY
☎ 01382 632 410
☎ 01241 853 002
BABCP

**NESS**, Thomas William
**Family & Systemic Psychotherapist**
♿ St. Helens
29 Mount Road
Montrose
Angus, Scotland
DD10 8SP
☎ 01674 674 659
bill@nesses.fsnet.co.uk
AFT

**PYE**, Robina
**Transpersonal Psychotherapist**
Hawksgrove
16 Grove Road
Broughty Ferry
Dundee
DD5 1JL
☎ 01567 830 210
CTP

**STEWART**, Henry B.
**Cognitive Behavioural Psychotherapist**
♿ 2 Erskine Street
Montrose
Angus
DD10 8HL
☎ 01674 676 011
☎ 01356 624 411
henry@adastra42.fsnet.co.uk
BABCP

## ARGYLL AND BUTE

**MACDONALD**, Ross
**Hypno-Psychotherapist**
17 Carrochan Crescent
Balloch
Alexandria
G83 8PX
☎ 01389 721 873
NRHP

## AYRSHIRE - SOUTH

**SLOAN**, Graham
**Cognitive Behavioural Psychotherapist**
♿ CCPS
Strathdoon House
50 Racecourse Road
AYR
KA7 2UZ
☎ 01292 285 607
BABCP

**SMITH**, Alicia
**Hypno-Psychotherapist**
17 Fotheringham Road
Ayr, Scotland
KA8 0EY
☎ 01292 281 793
aliciasmith@supanet.com
NRHP

## AYRSHIRE - NORTH

**COIT**, Frank James
**Cognitive Behavioural Psychotherapist**
♿ Clinical & Consulting Psychology Services
Pavillion Seven
Ayrshire Central Hospital
Irvine, Ayrshire
KA12 8SS
☎ 01294 323 566
BABCP

## DUMFRIES AND GALLOWAY

**CAMPBELL**, Colin
**Hypno-Psychotherapist**
Scaleridge Cottage
Waterbeck
Lockerbie
DG11 3EU
☎ 01461 204 022
col.cam@virgin.net
NRHP

**CARDILE**, Pietro
**Transactional Analysis Psychotherapist**
Duncree House
Kings Street
Newton Stewart
DG8 6DL
☎ 01671 402 792
pietro@duncreehouse.fslife.co.uk
ITA

**COOK**, Jane
**Integrative Psychotherapist**
♿ The Department of Psychological Services and Resea
Nithbank
Dumfries
DG1 2SA
☎ 01387 244 495
☎ 01228 670 646
butlercook2002@yahoo.ie
MC

**HEPPEL**, Valerie
**Transactional Analysis Psychotherapist**
♿ Smithy Cottage
Kirkpatrick Durham
Castle Douglas
DG7 3HT
☎ 01556 650 437
cropwalker@cwcom.net
ITA

**ISLES**, Rosaleen
**Cognitive Psychotherapist**
Glebe House
Kirkmahoe
Dumfries
DG1 1SY
☎ 01387 710 202
BABCP

**MACALISTER**, Eileen
**Group Analyst**
'Kames'
20 Drumlanrig Street
Thornhill
DG3 5LL
☎ 01848 331 862
eileenmacalister@lineone.net
IGA

**MACKIE**, James
**Psychodynamic Psychotherapist**
♿ Consultant Psychotherapist
The Ailsa Hospital
Dalmellington Road
Ayr
KA6 6AB
☎ 01292 513 954
mackieclan@beeb.net
UPCA

## EAST DUNBARTONSHIRE

**FOXLEY**, Richard
4a Dumgoyne Avenue
Milngavie
Glasgow
G62 7AL
☎ 01698 426 753
☎ 0141 563 8313
r.foxley@ntlworld.com
AFT

**HOGG**, Christine Retson
**Hypno-Psychotherapist**
26 Westbourne Crescent
Bearsden
Glasgow
G61 4HD
☎ 01415 701 426
sinep1@msn.com
NRHP

## EAST LOTHIAN

**FINLAY**, Rosalind
**Analytical Psychologist-Jungian Analyst**
15 High Street
East Linton
East Lothian
EH40 3AA
☎ 01620 860 228
AJA

**MACFADYEN**, John
**Core Process Psychotherapist**
♿ 'Morham-Loanhead'
Morham
by Haddington
East Lothian, Scotland
EH41 4LH
☎ 0162 082 5300
KI

**MACFADYEN**, Susan
**Core Process Psychotherapist**
♿ 'Morham-Loanhead'
Morham by Haddington
East Lothian
EH41 4LH
☎ 01620 825300
KI

**MCDONALD**, Christina
**Transpersonal Psychotherapist**
39 West Crescent
East Saltoun
Pencaitland
East Lothian
EH34 5EF
☎ 01875 341 191
CTP

**ROSS**, Ian
**Autogenic Psychotherapist**
52 Hopetoun Terrace
Gullane
East Lothian
EH31 2DD
☎ 01620 844 321
☎ 0131 554 1274
rossat52@waitrose.com
BAS

## EDINBURGH

**AYRES**, Alison
**Transactional Analysis Psychotherapist**
Edinburgh Institute for Counselling and Psychother
86 Causewayside
Edinburgh
EH9 1PY
☎ 01316 676 173
alisonayres@eicp.org
ITA

**BENNETT**, Rosanagh
**Transpersonal Psychotherapist**
59 Ashley Terrace
Edinburgh
EH11 1RX
☎ 0131 337 1579
CTP

**BRAID**, Rosemary
**Gestalt Psychotherapist, Humanistic Psychotherapist**
♿ 8 Clarendon Crescent
Edinburgh
Scotland
EH4 1DT
☎ 0131 332 1449
☎ 01592 840 442
rosiebraid@aol.com
AHPP

**CAMPBELL**, Caroline
**Hypno-Psychotherapist**
17 Pittville Street Lane
Portobello
Edinburgh
EH15 2BU
☎ 0131 657 1050
cc@skirnir.com
CTIS

**CHILD**, Nicolas John
**Family & Systemic Psychotherapist**
8 Lee Crescent
Edinburgh
EH15 1LW
☎ 0131 669 2184
nick.child@virgin.net
AFT

**CROMBIE**, Clare
**Gestalt Psychotherapist**
136 Constitution Street
Edinburgh
EH6 6AJ
☎ 0131 555 3615
☎ 07906 680 397
GCL

**ELSDALE**, Bethan
**Core Process Psychotherapist**
8/8 Pitt Street
Edinburgh
EH6 4BU
☎ 0131 555 1836
KI

**FRASER**, Mrs Bobbie
**Sexual and Relationship Psychotherapist**
21 Warriston Crescent
Edinburgh
Scotland
EH3 5LB
☎ 0131 557 2252
BASRT

**FREEDEN**, Mairi
**Core Process Psychotherapist**
The Whole Works
Jackson's Close
High Street
Edinburgh
EH1 1PZ
☎ 0131 225 8092
KI

**FYVEL**, Susan
**Family & Systemic Psychotherapist**
♿ 9 Warriston Crescent
Edinburgh
EH3 5LA
☎ 0131 556 7774
sue.fyvel@amserve.net
AFT

**GIBSON**, Miles
**Integrative Psychotherapist**
3 Thornville Terrace
Edinburgh
EH3 8DB
☎ 07968 102 230
MET

**GRAY**, Maggie
**Cognitive Behavioural Psychotherapist**
Cullen Rivers Centre
Tipperlin HOuse
Tipperlin Road
Edinburgh
EH10 5HF
☎ 0131 537 6874
☎ 07980 852 723
3 Sciennes Road
Edinburgh
EH9 1LE
BABCP

**GREIG**, Edward
**Existential Psychotherapist**
21 Glencairn Crescent
Edinburgh
EH12 5BT
UPCA

**HART**, Mary
**Hypno-Psychotherapist**
Edinburgh
EH9 1LE
☎ 01316 683 051
maryamhart@aol.com
NRHP

**HERRMANN**, Joan
**Child Psychotherapist**
Scottish Institute of Human Relations
56 Albany Street
Edinburgh
EH1 3QR
☎ 0131 556 0924
☎ 0141 2119069
ACP

**HIGGS**, Jody
**Core Process Psychotherapist**
♿ 12 Saxe Coburg Street
Edinburgh
EH3 5BN
☎ 0131 332 7987
KI

**KENNEDY**, Helen
**Gestalt Psychotherapist**
Edinburgh Gestalt Institute
51 Lothian Road
Edinburgh
EH1 2DJ
☎ 0131 228 3841
edinburgh.gestalt.inst@totalise.co.uk
GPTI

**KJELLSTROM**, Laila
**Psychodrama Psychotherapist**
16 Roseneath Place
Edinburgh
EH9 1JB
☎ 0131 553 6660
☎ 0131 229 3310
BPA

**KUNKLER**, Jane
**Cognitive Behavioural Psychotherapist**
♿ Department of Health Psychology
Astley Ainslie Hospital
133 Grange Loan
Edinburgh
EH9 2HL
☎ 0131 537 9128
☎ 0131 667 3454
BABCP

**LENDRUM**, Susan
**Psychoanalytic Psychotherapist**
9 Randolph Cliff
Edinburgh
EH3 7TE
☎ 01312 252 848
slendrum@dircon.co.uk
NWIDP

**LONIE**, Dorothy
**Hypno-Psychotherapist**
15 Warriston Terrace
Edinburgh
EH3 5LZ
☎ 0131 552 5247
CTIS

**MACNICOL**, Annie
**Cognitive Behavioural Psychotherapist**
♿ Dept. of Psychological Medicine
Royal Infirmary
1 Lauriston Place
Edinburgh
EH3 9YW
☎ 0131 536 2875
BABCP

**MAXWELL**, Sue
**Sexual and Relationship Psychotherapist**
Southside Centre
86 Causewayside
Edinburgh
Scotland
EH9 1YP
☎ 0131 667 5251
☎ 07813 915 533
BASRT

**MCKINNON**, Sophia
**Sexual and Relationship Psychotherapist**
18 York Place
Edinburgh
EH1 3EP
☎ 0131 558 9669
phia@couplecounselling.org
BASRT

**OSBORN**, Madeline
**Psychoanalytic Psychotherapist**
Mental Welfare Commission for Scotland
Argyle House
Lady Lawson Street
Edinburgh
EH3 95H
☎ 01312 226 111
NWIDP

**RANDALL**, Peter
**Systemic Psychotherapist**
♿ 28 Lauriston Street
Edinburgh
EH3 9DJ
☎ 0131 229 9821
peterarandall@aol.com
Royal Edinburgh Children's Hospital
Child & Family
Mental Health Department
3 Rillbank Terrace
EH9 1LL
KCC

**RITCHIE**, Robert
**Hypno-Psychotherapist**
♿ The Whole Works, Complementary Therapy & Counselli
Jacksons Close
209 Royal Mile
Edinburgh
EH1 1PZ
☎ 0131 225 8092
CTIS

**RUSSELL**, Wilson J
**Group Analyst**
Psychotherapy Department
40 Colinton Road
Edinburgh
EH10 5BT
☎ 0131 537 6926
IGA

**SHEWAN**, Alistair
**Hypno-Psychotherapist**
3 Castle Wynd North
Edinburgh
EH1 2NQ
☎ 01312 256 537
NRHP

**SHORTER**, Bani
**Analytical Psychologist-Jungian Analyst**
69B Cumberland Street
Edinburgh
Scotland
EH3 6RD
☎ 0131 556 6654
IGAP

**SMITH**, Norah
**Analytical Psychologist-Jungian Analyst**
2 Shaw's Street
Edinburgh
EH7 4PH
☎ 0131 225 2990
☎ 0131 554 9144
norahsmith@aol.com
CAP *

**STRUTHERS**, Cassandra
**Psychoanalytic Psychotherapist**
35 Royal Terrace
Edinburgh
EH7 5AH
☎ 0131 556 2786
cassandra@struthersi.freeserve.co.uk
AGIP

**SUTHERLAND**, James
**Core Process Psychotherapist**
37a Thistle Street
Edinburgh Road
Biggar
EH2 1DY
☎ 01312 258 044
KI

**VICKERS**, Linda
**Integrative Psychotherapist**
145 Drum Street
Gilmerton
Edinburgh
EH17 8RX
☎ 07966 449 667
lindavickers@utvinternet.com
SPCRC

**WILLIAMS**, Guinevere
**Gestalt Psychotherapist**
Edinburgh Gestalt Institute
Teamwork
51 Lothian Road
Edinburgh
EH1 2DJ
☎ 0131 228 3841
burywill@globalnet.co.uk
GPTI

**WRIGHT**, Cathie
Whole Works
Jackson's Close
209 Royal Mile
Edinburgh
EH1
KI

**YOUNG**, Courtenay
**Humanistic Psychotherapist**
7 Alnick Hill Raod
Liberton
Edinburgh
Scotland
EH16 6LG
☎ 0131 666 2605
☎ 0773 042 2800
cyoung@findhorn.org
AHPP

## FALKIRK

**CROSS**, Richard
**Hypno-Psychotherapist**
53 Livingstone Drive
Bo'ness
West Lothian
EH51 0BQ
☎ 0772 1757 927
hypno-psych@yahoo.com
CTIS

**HENDERSON**, Anne
**Sexual and Relationship Psychotherapist**
22 Sunart Place
Grangemouth
FK3 0HN
☎ 01324 872 568
☎ 0141 248 2662
anne_3258@hotmail.com
BASRT

**KENNEDY**, Kay
**Individual and Group Humanistic Psychotherapist**
Dalmore
15 High Station Road
Falkirk
C. Lothian
FK1 5LP
☎ 01324 621 930
KayKennedy@connectfree.co.uk
AHPP

**MORTON**, Mary
**Psychoanalytic Psychotherapist**
♿ Department of Dynamic Psychotherapy
Bungalow 3
RSNH
Stirling Road
FK5 4SD
☎ 01324 574 322
STTDP

**YOUNG**, Katherine
**Cognitive Behavioural Psychotherapist**
20 Kellie Place
Alloa
FK10 2DW
☎ 01259 214 623
☎ 01786 434 000 x78413
BABCP

## FIFE

**AGNEW**, Joyce
**Personal Construct Psychotherapist**
Cintra
Cupar Road
Ceres
Fife, Scotland
KY15 5LP
☎ 01334 828340
jodocaagnew@aol.com
PCP

**BRAID**, Rosemary
**Gestalt Psychotherapist, Humanistic Psychotherapist**
♿ Nether Birniehouse
Pittendreich
Kinross
KY13 9HD
☎ 0131 332 1449
☎ 01592 840 442
rosiebraid@aol.com
AHPP

**LANZA**, Pamela
**Cognitive Behavioural Psychotherapist**
♿ Dept. of Clinical Psychology
Stratheden Hospital
Stratheden
Cupar
KY15 5RR
☎ 01334 652 611
BABCP

**MALCOM**, Hanne
**Hypno-Psychotherapist**
29 Bell Street
Tayport
Fife
DD6 9AP
☎ 01382 553 596
hannemalcom@supanet.com
NRHP

**MIDDLETON**, Margaret
**Hypno-Psychotherapist**
♿ Glenesk
26 Lade Braes
St. Andrews
Fife
KY16 9DA
☎ 01334 475 270
mail@clanlands.sol.co.uk
CTIS

**STROBOS**, Carolyn
**Integrative Psychotherapist**
Sylvan House
12 Woodbine Terrace
Newport-on-Tay
Scotland
DD6 8EB
☎ 01382 542 957
☎ 07984 100 703
c.strobos@virgin.net
MC

**SWITZER**, Fiona
**Cognitive Behavioural Psychotherapist**
♿ Psychology Dept.
Stratheden Hospital
Stratheden, Cupar
Fife
KY15 5RR
☎ 01334 652 611
psychology@fife-pct.scot.nhs.uk
BABCP

## GLASGOW

**ADAMS**, John
**Cognitive Behavioural Psychotherapist**
Centre of Therapy & Counselling
402 Sauchieall Street
Glasgow
G2 3JD
☎ 0141 331 0750
☎ 07905 298 962
jadams@primex.co.uk
BABCP

**ANDREW**, Alison
**Family & Systemic Psychotherapist**
♿ 10 Belhaven Terrace
Great Western Road
Glasgow
G12 0TG
☎ 0141 357 6404
AFT

**BEGG**, Ean
**Analytical Psychologist-Jungian Analyst**
30 Westbourne Gardens
Glasgow
G12 9PF
☎ 0141 334 8391
IGAP

**BROWN DOUGLAS**, Lucinda
**Psychodrama Psychotherapist**
561 Clarkson Road
Neverlee
Glasgow
G44 3TR
☎ 0141 637 2046
BPA

**BROWN**, Teresa
**Psychodrama Psychotherapist**
Stoneleigh
48 Cleveden Drive
Kelvinside
Glasgow
G12 0NU
☎ 0141 334 8908
☎ 0141 334 9299
iaingbrown@aol.com
BPA

**BRYANS**, Sally
**Sexual and Relationship Psychotherapist**
The Consulting Rooms
34 West George Street
Glasgow
G2 1DA
☎ 01292 571 391
s.bryans@btopenworld.com
BASRT

**CALLAGHAN**, Phillip
**Core Process Psychotherapist**
467 Shields Road
Pollockshields
Glasgow
G41 2RG
☎ 0141 429 0411
KI

**CARRIGG**, Gerrard
**Family & Systemic Psychotherapist**
23 Markdow Avenue
Crookston
Glasgow
G53 7GA
☎ 0141 891 5742
gerrardcarigg@aol.com
AFT

**CHRISTIE**, Jim
**Group Analyst**
The Garnethill Centre
28 Rose Street
Glasgow
G3 6RE
☎ 0141 333 0730
christiejim@btopenworld.com
IGA

**CHRISTIE**, Marilyn
**Cognitive Behavioural Psychotherapist**
Centre for Cuonselling Services
3rd Floor, Ashfield House
402 Sauchiehall Street
Glasgow
G2 3JD
☎ 0141 331 0750
MCHRISTIEB@AOL.COM
BABCP

**COIA**, Grace
**Hypno-Psychotherapist**
10 Carment Drive
Glasgow
G41 3PP
☎ 01416 326 663
grace.coia@talk21.com
NRHP

**CONNOLLY**, Moira
**Cognitive Behavioural Psychotherapist**
♿ Intensive Community Treatment Team
2 Whittingehame Gardens
1091 Great Western Road
Glasgow
G12 0AA
noira.connolly@scot.nhs.uk
BABCP

**COOPER**, Michael
**Existential Psychotherapist**
Senior Lecturer in Counselling
University of Strathclyde
76 Southbrae Drive
Glasgow
G13 1PP
mick.cooper@strath.ac.uk
SPCRC

**CRUTHERS**, Helen
**Integrative Arts Psychotherapist**
16 austen Road
Jordanhill
Glasgow
G13 1SJ
☎ 0141 959 9192
helencruthers@freeuk.com
IATE

**DAVIDSON**, Dorothy
**Cognitive Behavioural Psychotherapist**
♿ R.N.I.D.
Crowngate Business Centre
115-127 Brook Street
Glasgow
G40 3AP
☎ 0141 550 5756
BABCP

**DUNCAN**, Sheila
**Family & Systemic Psychotherapist**
♿ Department of Child & Family Psychiatry
Caledonia House
Yorkhill Hospital
Glasgow
G3 8SJ
☎ 0141 201 0213
sheila.duncan@yorkhill.scot.nhs.uk
AFT

**ELLWOOD**, Jane
**Child Psychotherapist**
Department of Child & Family Psychiatry
Royal Hospital for Sick Children
Glasgow
G3 8SJ
☎ 0141 201 0228
☎ 01560 485828
ACP

**FINNERTY**, Margaret E
**Cognitive Behavioural Psychotherapist**
Glasgow
G15
☎ 0141 589 2254
mfinnerty@ntlworld.com
BABCP

**FRASER**, Douglas A.
**Psychoanalytic Psychotherapist**
5 Hampden Terrace
Mount Florida
Glasgow
Scotland
G42 9XG
☎ 01698 266 717
rdm.fraser@ukgateway.net
WMIP

**GRIFFITHS**, John
**Integrative Psychotherapist**
17 Woodside Terrace
Glasgow
G3 7HX
☎ 0141 331 0165
MET

**HAMILTON**, Angela
**Psychoanalytic Psychotherapist**
4 Park Quadrant
Glasgow
G3 6BS
LPDO

**HAY**, Patricia
**Core Process Psychotherapist**
♿ 13 North Gardner Street
Glasgow
G11 5BU
☎ 0141 334 3700
KI

**HOLLYWOOD**, Helena
**Cognitive Behavioural Psychotherapist**
♿ c/o SCOTACS
3rd Floor, Ashfield House
402 Sauchiehall Street
Glasgow
G2 3JD
☎ 07092 042 855
helenahollywood@armserve.com
BABCP

**LINDSAY**, Robert
**Family & Systemic Psychotherapist**
♿ DCFP
90 Kerr St
Glasgow
G40 2QP
☎ 0141 531 3301
rlindsay@doctors.org.uk
AFT

**MACCALLUM SULLIVAN**, Mary
**Integrative Psychotherapist**
2nd Floor Flat
68 Montague Street
Glasgow
G4 9EY
☎ 0141 337 2171
eoie.sullivan@virgin.net
SPCRC

**MCCONNOCHIE**, Charlie
**Cognitive Behavioural Psychotherapist**
Centre for counselling Studies
3rd floor, ashfield House
402 Sauchiehall Street
Glasgow
G2 3JD
☎ 0141 331 0750
BABCP

**MCMASTER**, Catherine
**Cognitive Psychotherapist**
Centre for Therapy & Counselling Studies
Ashfield House
402 Sauchiehall Street
Glasgow
G2 3JD
☎ 0141 226 4373
☎ 07740 913 055
catherine.mcmaster@counillors.glasgow.gov.uk
2 Manse Road
Mount Vernon
Glasgow
G32 0RA
BABCP

**MOLLESON**, John Ivitsky
**Cognitive Psychotherapist**
Centre of Consellling Studies
3rd floor, Ashfield House
402 Sauchiehall Street
Glasgow
G2 3JD
☎ 0141 331 0750
SCOTACS@AOL.COM
BABCP

**MOODIE**, Alastair
**Transactional Analysis Psychotherapist**
5 Buckingham Terrace
Glasgow
Scotland
G12 8EB
☎ 01413 576 790
amoodie@glasta.co.uk
ITA

**PATERSON**, Anne
**Psychosynthesis Psychotherapist**
470 Anniesland Road
Scotstounhill
Glasgow
G13 1YH
☎ 0141 434 1371
annepat@lineone.net
PET

**PETRIE**, Clare
**Transpersonal Psychotherapist**
Glasgow
☎ 0141 644 0880
CCPE

**PUSZTAI**, Edit E.
**Cognitive Behavioural Psychotherapist**
♿ Department of Psychiatry
Southern General Hospital
1345 Govan Road
Glasgow
G51 4TF
☎ 0141 201 1906
BABCP

**ROSS**, Michael Killoran
**Cognitive Behavioural Psychotherapist**
Nuffield House
1000 Great Western Road
Glasgow
G12 0NR
☎ 01355 265 936
☎ 0141 576 2900
Michael.Ross@gghb.scot.nhs.uk
BABCP

**SCANLAN**, Celia
**Psychodrama Psychotherapist**
Flat 1/1
105 Hyndland Road
Glasgow
G12 9JD
☎ 0141 339 1077
cscan@nspd.co.uk
BPA

**SELLARS**, Val
**Group Analyst**
♿ Psychotherapy Dept
Stobhill Hospital
133 Balornock
Glasgow
G21 3UW
☎ 01415 313 150
valerie.sellars@glacoment.scot.nhs.uk
IGA

**SHEARER**, Anne
**Hypno-Psychotherapist**
The Pheonix Centre
201 St James Road
Glasgow
G4 0NT
☎ 01721 730 289
☎ 01415 532 353
NRHP

**SMITH**, Alicia
**Hypno-Psychotherapist**
107 Crown Road North
Hyndland
Glasgow
G12 9HS
☎ 01292 281 793
aliciasmith@supanet.com
NRHP

**SMITH**, Hilda C.
**Cognitive Behavioural Psychotherapist**
♿ Centre of Therapy
Ashfield House
402 Sauchiehall Street
Glasgow
G2 3JD
☎ 0141 331 0750
☎ 07773 539 324
BABCP

**STRUTHERS**, Morag
**Sexual and Relationship Psychotherapist**
Couple Counselling Glasgow (GMCS)
27 Sandyford Place
Glasgow
G3 7NB
☎ 0141 248 5249
☎ 0141 211 8600
Morag.Struthers@glacomen.scot.nhs.uk
Greater Glasgow Primary Care Health Trust (NHS)
Sandyford Clinic
6 Sandy Ford Place
Glasgow
G3 7NB
BASRT

**WHITFIELD**, Graeme
**Cognitive Behavioural Psychotherapist**
♿ Dept. Psychological Medicine
Trust HQ, Garnavel Royal Hospital
1055 Great Western Road
Glasgow
G12 0XH
☎ 0141 211 3775
gwhitfield@clinmed.gla.ac.uk
BABCP

**WILLIAMS**, Christopher John
**Cognitive Behavioural Psychotherapist**
Dept of Psychological Medicine
Gartnavel Royal Hospital
1055 Great Western Road
Glasgow
G12 0XH
☎ 0141 211 0685
chris.williams@clinmed.gla.ac.uk
BABCP

## HIGHLAND

**EDMONSTONE**, Yvonne G.
**Cognitive Behavioural Psychotherapist**
♿ New Craigs Hospital
Leachin Road
Inverness
IV3 8NP
☎ 01463 242 860
BABCP

**ELDRID**, Sarah
**Systemic Psychotherapist**
Chlinaig
The Knoll
Roy Bridge
Inverness-shire
PH31 4AQ
☎ 01397 712 639
saeldrid@aol.com
KCC

**GERRY**, Marian
**Family & Systemic Psychotherapist**
Maple cottage
St Ronguald's Street
Kirkwall
Orkney
KW1 1LS
☎ 01856 872 741
mgerry@fambusiness.idps.co.uk
AFT

**WILLIAMS MACKENZIE**, Kate
**Humanistic and Integrative Psychotherapist**
Forest Lodge
4 Forest Drive
Balloh
Inverness
IV2 7HT
☎ 01463 794 828
☎ 07903 411 534
info@katewilliamsmackenzie.com
SPEC

## LANARKSHIRE - NORTH

**FRASER**, Douglas A.
**Psychoanalytic Psychotherapist**
♿ Lanarkshire Primary Care NHS Trust
Department of Psychotherapy
504 Windmill Street
Motherwell
ML1 2AF
☎ 01698 266 717
rdm.fraser@ukgateway.net
WMIP

**HAMILL**, Dan
**Hypno-Psychotherapist**
Ashcraig
12a Grahamshill Street
Airdrie
ML6 7EN
☎ 01236 764 353
☎ 0776 231 211
hamilldan@hotmail.com
CTIS

## LANARKSHIRE - SOUTH

**GRIEVE**, Sandra
**Psychodrama Psychotherapist**
4 Gilroy Close
Lanark
ML11 7JN
☎ 01555 661 522
☎ 01698 376 387
sanron@globalnet.co.uk
BPA

**HUME**, Anne J.A.
**Cognitive Behavioural Psychotherapist**
The Coach House
67a Carlisle Road
Crawford
Biggar, Lanarkshire
ML12 6TP
☎ 01864 502 224
BABCP

**LOGAN**, Jean
**Family & Systemic Psychotherapist**
30 Glen Gairn
St Leonards
East Kilbride
Scotland
G74 2JG
FIC

**ROSS**, Michael Killoran
**Cognitive Behavioural Psychotherapist**
68 Keswick Road
East Kilbride
Glasgow
G75 8QX
☎ 01355 265 936
☎ 0141 576 2900
Michael.Ross@gghb.scot.nhs.uk
BABCP

**ROY**, Margaret
**Core Process Psychotherapist**
17 Edinburgh Road
Biggar
S. Lanarkshire
ML12 6AX
☎ 01899 220931
KI

## MIDLOTHIAN

**ANGOLD**, Mrs Monica
**Sexual and Relationship Psychotherapist**
17 Morningside Park
Edinburgh
EH10 5HD
☎ 0131 447 4342
monica.angold@btopenworld.com
BASRT

**BIENKOWSKI**, Geraldine
**Cognitive Behavioural Psychotherapist**
Department of Clinical Psychology
40 Colinton Road
Edinburgh
EH10 5BT
☎ 0131 537 6905
BABCP

**FEE**, Angie
**Humanistic and Integrative Psychotherapist**
4 Wester Millerhill
Dalkeith
Midlothian
Scotland
EH22 1RY
☎ 0131 660 6852
angiefee@beeb.net
AHPP

**FREEMAN**, Christopher
**Cognitive Behavioural Psychotherapist**
Department of Psychotherapy
Cullen Centre, Tipperlin House
Royal Edinburgh Hospital
Morningside Pk, Edinburgh
EH10 5HF
☎ 0131 537 6708
c.freeman@which.net
BABCP

**MCFARLANE**, Alison M.
**Cognitive Behavioural Psychotherapist**
The Cullen Centre, Tipperlin House
Royal Edinburgh Hospital
Tipperlin Road
Edinburgh
EH10 5HF
☎ 0131 537 6874
BABCP

**PERKS**, Alison
**Gestalt Psychotherapist**
13 Glebe Street
Dalkeith
Midlothian
EH22 1JG
☎ 0131 663 1173
alisonperks@freeuk.com
GPTI

**ROBINSON**, Peter
**Cognitive Behavioural Psychotherapist, Family & Systemic Psychotherapist**
The Young People's Unit
Royal Edinburgh Hospital
Tipperlinn Road
Edinburgh
EH10 5HF
☎ 0795 104 4549
peterwrobinson@insyt.org
AFT, BABCP

## MORAY

**HARTE**, Vivienne
**Integrative Psychotherapist**
12 Adam Drive
Forres
Scotland
IV36 2JN
☎ 01309 676 013
vivharte@talk21.com
SPCRC

**SHERIFFS**, Alison
**Psychosynthesis Psychotherapist**
Fishermans Bothies
The Mains of Sluie
Dunphail
Forres, Moray
IV36 2QG
☎ 01309 611 263
alison.sluie@virgin.net
PET

## ORKNEY ISLANDS

**MILLER**, Lynda R
**Psychoanalytic Psychotherapist**
1 Manse Road
Stromness
Orkney Isles
Scotland
KW16 3BX
☎ 01856 851 209
orkneylrmiller@aol.com
UPCA

## PERTH AND KINROSS

**DOLAN**, Lesley Catherine
**Cognitive Behavioural Psychotherapist**
Murray Royal Hospital
Perth
Scotland
PH2 7BH
☎ 01738 621 151
BABCP

**LIEBING-WILSON**, Marianne
**Cognitive Behavioural Psychotherapist**
North West CMHT
29 Barosa Place
Perth
PH1 5HH
☎ 01738 494 926
☎ 01738 631 333
Perth Centre for Counselling
17 Hospital Street
Perth
PH2 8HN
BABCP

**PYE**, Robina
**Transpersonal Psychotherapist**
Rowan Consultancy
49 Scott Street
Perth
PH2 8JN
☎ 01567 830 210
CTP

**WICKS**, Carole Ann
**Integrative Psychotherapist**
Complementary Health Centre
5-7 Springfield Tce
Dunblance
Perthshire, Scotland
FK15 9AA
☎ 01786 825 900
NGP

## SCOTTISH BORDERS

**SHEARER**, Anne
**Hypno-Psychotherapist**
St Mungo's Rest
5/7 Station Road
Eddleston
Peebleshire
EH45 8QN
☎ 01721 730 289
☎ 01415 532 353
NRHP

**SMITH**, Gerry
**Transpersonal Psychotherapist**
The Angels
Crookston
Heriot
Midlothian
EH38 5YS
☎ 01578 760 265
CTP

**STARK**, Lynda
**Core Process Psychotherapist**
Old Schoolhouse
Nenthorn
Kelso
Scotland
TD5 7RY
☎ 01573 225 567
KI

**STILL**, Arthur
**Rational Emotive Behaviour Therapist**
♿ 6 - 7 Hadden Farm Cottages
Sprouston
Kelso
TD5 8HU
☎ 01890 830 364
BABCP

**WILSON**, Nirved
**Neurolinguistic Psychotherapist**
Sorrowlessfield Cottage
Earlston
Berwickshire
Scotland
TD4 6AG
☎ 01896 848 863
nirved@euphony.net
NLPtCA

## STIRLING

**COATS**, Elizabeth
**Sexual and Relationship Psychotherapist**
♿ c/o Couple Counselling Central Scotland
Drummond House
Well Green Place
Stirling
FK8 2ET
☎ 01786 443 757
☎ 01786 479 424
libby@coats1954.fsnet.co.uk
28 Snowdon Place
Stirling
FK8 2JN
BASRT

**TURNER**, Senga
**Transpersonal Psychotherapist**
7 Allan Park
Stirling
FK8 2QG
☎ 01786 465 211
CTP

## WEST LOTHIAN

**BROWN**, Thomas M.
**Cognitive Behavioural Psychotherapist**
♿ St Johns Hospital at Howden
Livingston
EH54 6PP
☎ 01506 419 666
BABCP

**MACGILLIVRAY**, J. Lorna
**Cognitive Behavioural Psychotherapist**
♿ 17 Craigs Court
Torphichen
Bathgate
EH48 4NU
☎ 01506 634 538
lorna@connectfree.co.uk
BABCP

**TENNANT**, Duncan
**Family & Systemic Psychotherapist**
♿ 66 Easterbankton
Livingston
West Lothian
EH54 9BE
☎ 01506 438 153
duncantennant@msn.com
AFT

## BRIDGEND

**VIVAN-BYRNE**, Kieran
**Systemic Psychotherapist**
♿ Bridgend Clinic
83 Towerbridge Road
Bridgend
CF31 3DH
☎ 01656 728 021
☎ 01792 644 442
veebees2@aol.com
FIC

**VIVIAN BYRNE**, Sue
**Systemic Psychotherapist**
Caswell Clinic
Glanryhd Hospital
Bridgend
CF31 4LN
☎ 01656 662 179
sue.vivian-byrne@bromor-tr.nhs.wales.uk
FIC

## CAERPHILLY

**ROBERTS**, Susan
**Core Process Psychotherapist**
♿ Brynawel
5 Mountain Road
Caerphilly
CF83 1HG
☎ 029 2088 155
KI

## CARDIFF

**BRAZIER**, Anna
**Family & Systemic Psychotherapist**
♿ Department of Child & Clinical Psychology
University Hospital of Wales
Heath Park
Cardiff
CF5 1GF
ana.brazier@cardiffandvale.wales.nhs.uk
AFT

**BRITTEN**, Hilary
**Psychoanalytic Psychotherapist**
45 Fairleigh Road
Pontcanna
Cardiff
CF1 9JW
☎ 029 20 387 173
SIP

**CHATHAM**, Jon
**Family & Systemic Psychotherapist**
♿ CAMHS
St David's Hospital
Cowbridge Road East
Cardiff
CF5 1GN
☎ 029 205 36730
AFT

**DAVIES**, Mairlis
**Family & Systemic Psychotherapist**
♿ Harvey Jones Adolescent Unit
Felindre Road
Whitchurch
Cardiff
CF14 2TG
☎ 029 2033 6302
mairlis@hotmail.com
AFT

**DRYDEN**, Jan
**Humanistic Psychotherapist**
22 Talbot Street
Cardiff
CF11 9BW
☎ 029 2030 2881
jandryden@ntlworld.com
SPEC

**EDWARDS**, Lorna
**Family & Systemic Psychotherapist**
12 Clos y Wiver
Thornhill
Cardiff
CF14 9ET
☎ 02920 752 724
FIC

**EVANS**, Christine
**Attachment-based Psychoanalytic Psychotherapist**
Mulberry Lodge
3 Pencisely Road
Llandaff
Cardiff
CF5 1DG
☎ 0292 022 6029
CAPP

**GRAF**, Fern
**Family & Systemic Psychotherapist**
♿ Preswylfa Child and Family Service
St David's Hospital
Cowbridge Rd East, Canton
Cardiff
CF11 9XB
☎ 029 2053 6673
AFT

**JONES**, Elsa
**Family & Systemic Psychotherapist**
♿ The Natural Health Clinic
98 Cathedral Road
Cardiff
CF11 9LP
☎ 029 2022 2221
AFT

**JONES**, Fiona
**Family & Systemic Psychotherapist**
CAMHS
Cardiff and Vale NHS Trust
St Davids Hospital,Cowbridge R
Cardiff
CF11 9XB
☎ 029 20 536 730
FIC

**MORRIS**, Mary
**Family & Systemic Psychotherapist**
Child & Adolescent Mental Health Service
St David's Hospital
Cowbridge Road East
Cardiff
CF11 9XB
☎ 029 20 536 769
☎ 029 20 536 762
FIC

**MYLAN**, Trish
**Family & Systemic Psychotherapist**
Caehir House
Peterston-Super-Ely
Cardiff
CF5 6LH
☎ [65] 354 8102
patricia_mylan@mcds.gov.sg
FIC

**PARSONS**, Barbara
**Family & Systemic Psychotherapist**
♿ St David's Hospital
Children's Centre Preswylfa
Cowbridge Rd East, Canton
Cardiff
CF11 9XB
☎ 029 2053 6730
AFT

**PENNY**, Sarah
**Integrative Psychotherapist**
Many Trees Clinic
Bruton Place
Llandaff
Cardiff
CF5 2ER
☎ 02920 226 967
sarah.penny1@btinternet.com
MET

**RICHARDS**, Alyson
**Integrative Psychotherapist**
Many Trees
Bruton Place
Llandaff
Cardiff
CF5 2ER
☎ 02920 226 967
alyson.richards@bt-openworld.com
MET

**RIVETT**, Mark
**Family & Systemic Psychotherapist**
♿ 3 Pitman Street
Pontcanna
Cardiff
CF11 9DJ
☎ 029 203 82266
markrivett@beeb.net
AFT

**ROUTLEDGE**, Derek
**Family & Systemic Psychotherapist**
♿ Preswylfa Child and Family Service
St David's Hospital
Cowbridge Rd East, Canton
Cardiff
CF11 9XB
☎ 029 2053 6730
AFT

**SELIGMAN**, Philippa
**Family & Systemic Psychotherapist**
♿ 22 West Orchard Crescent
Llandaff
Cardiff
CF5 1AR
☎ 029 2056 1491
p.seligman@freeuk.com
AFT

**TELDERS**, Martina
**Psychoanalytic Psychotherapist**
25 Pontcanna Street
Cardiff
CF11 9HQ
☎ 029 20 371 391
SIP

**WILSON**, James
**Systemic Psychotherapist**
86 Donald Street
Roath
Cardiff
CF24 4TR
☎ 02920 317 878
IFT

## CARMARTHENSHIRE

**APPLETON**, Richard Lonsdale
**Family & Systemic Psychotherapist**
♿ 47 Cilddewi Park
Johnstown
Carmarthen
SA31 3HP
☎ 01267 237 136
AFT

**DAVIES**, Dilys
**Cognitive Analytic Therapist**
1 Morley Street
Carmarthen
South Wales
SA31 1RB
☎ 0777 571 3876
dilysdavies@hotmail.com
ACAT, BPS

**GAGG**, Susan
**Family & Systemic Psychotherapist**
13 Gardde
Llwynhendy
Llanelli
SA14 9NH
☏ 01554 771 885
Carl.p.turner@btinternet.com
FIC

**GAUNT**, Pamela
**Transpersonal Psychotherapist**
♿ Bach Y Gwyddel
Cwmpengraig
Drefach Felindre
Llandysul,Carmarthenshire
SA44 5HX
☏ 01559 371954
CCPE

**HARRIS**, Paul David Gwyn
**Cognitive Behavioural Psychotherapist**
109 Bolgoed Road
Pontarddulais
Swansea
SA4 8JP
☏ 01792 884 952
paulharris109@talk21.com
BABCP

**HARRISON**, Jane
**Psychosynthesis Psychotherapist**
♿ The Reading Rooms
Station Road
Clynderwen
Pembrokeshire
SA66 7NF
☏ 01437 563 212
janieharri@hotmail.com
IPS

**HEATHERSPRITE**, Gina
**Hypno-Psychotherapist**
Cwrt y Cylchau
Llanfair Clydogau
Lampeter
Ceredigion
SA48 8LT
☏ 01570 493 526
info@courtofcircles.org.uk
NSHAP

**JONES**, Christopher S
**Cognitive Behavioural Psychotherapist**
♿ Myddfai Psychotherapy Centre
West Wales General Hospital
Carmarthen
SA31 2AF
☏ 01267 235 151 ext 2085
BABCP

**LISTER**, Ian
**Family & Systemic Psychotherapist**
♿ Child & Family Consultation Service
West Wales Hospital
Carmarthen
SA31 2AF
☏ 01267 221 225
AFT

**THOMPSON**, Jenny
**Gestalt Psychotherapist**
♿ 34 Pntarddulais Road
Garnswilt
Ammanford
Dyfed
SA18 2RR
☏ 01269 592 694
GPTI

## CEREDIGION

**BISGOOD**, Bill
**Transactional Analysis Psychotherapist**
♿ 6 Ebens Lane
Cardigan
Ceredigion
SA43 1HN
☏ 01239 613 996
bill@bisgood.co.uk
ITA

**DONNAI**, Andrew
**Integrative Psychotherapist**
♿ Llwyn
Brynowen Lane
Borth
Ceredigion
SY24 5LR
☏ 01970 871 591
andrew@andamt.freeserve.co.uk
SPTI

**STRAUSS**, Judith
**Hypno-Psychotherapist**
♿ Dan-y-Coed
Port Rhryd-y-Groes
Ystrad Meurig
Ceredigion
SY25 6DQ
☏ 01974 282 599
judith.strauss@btclick.com
NSHAP

## CONWY

**BOARDMAN**, Ian
**Group Analyst**
♿ Park Street Clinic
Park Street
Denbigh
LL16 3DE
☏ 01745 815 332
user@gardenhouse.u-net.com
IGA

**CAMPBELL DAVIES**, Maureen
**Gestalt Psychotherapist**
3 Grosvenor Avenue
Rhyl
Denbighshire
N. Wales
LL18 4HA
☏ 01745 343 600
maureendavies@ntlworld.com
SPTI

**CAMPBELL HUGHES**, Patricia
**Cognitive Behavioural Psychotherapist**
31 Kings Way
Liddell Park
Craig-y-Don
llandudno
LL30 1YQ
☏ 01244 364 046
pcampbellHughes@btinternet.com
BABCP

**LANGLEY**, Allen
**Hypno-Psychotherapist**
♿ Leaf Health Centre
2 Nant Terrace
Menai Bridge
Anglesey
LL57 5EW
☏ 01248 717 744
☏ 01407 861 258
allenlangley@hotmail.com
NRHP

**MARDULA**, Jody
**Transactional Analysis Psychotherapist**
30 Seiriol Road
Penmaenmawr
Conwy
LL34 6HB
☏ 01492 622 488
jody.m@mountaintherapy.org.uk
ITA

**RICKARD**, Ian
**Cognitive Behavioural Psychotherapist**
♿ Green Oak
1 Dolydd Terrace
Pentre Du
Betws y Coed
LL24 0BU
☎ 01690 710 647
ianr@zoom.co.uk
BABCP

**UDEN**, Christine
**Transactional Analysis Psychotherapist**
BRANAS ISAF Personal Development Centre
Llan Drillo
near Corwen
Norht Wales
LL21 0TA
☎ 01490 413 176
☎ 01824 704 668
christine@udenbusiness.fsnet.co.uk
ITA

## DENBIGHSHIRE

**EMBLETON**, Joan
**Psychoanalytic Psychotherapist**
Cwm Hardd
Nantyr
Nr. Llangollen
Clywd
LL20 7DD
☎ 01691 718 450
jovaem@aol.com
SITE

**HUGHES**, Lynette
**Psychoanalytic Psychotherapist, Couple Psychoanalytic Psychotherapist**
Cartrefle
149 Mwrog Street
Ruthin
Denbighshire
LL15 1LE
☎ 0161 248 9494
☎ 01824 702 656
NWIDP, SCPP

**SCHEMBRI**, Veronica
**Humanistic and Integrative Psychotherapist**
1 Walton House
Queen Street
Llangollen
LL20 8LF
☎ 01978 860 337
BCTA@vschembri.demon.co.uk
Woodcroft
Abbey Road
Llangollen
North Wales
LL20 8SS
AHPP

**UDEN**, Christine
**Transactional Analysis Psychotherapist**
7 Upper Clwyd Street
Ruthin
Denbighshire
N. Wales
LL15 1HY
☎ 01490 413 176
☎ 01824 704 668
christine@udenbusiness.fsnet.co.uk
ITA

**VAN DER EIJK**, Mike
**Systemic Psychotherapist**
♿ Tyn Y Caeau Farmhouse
Llandrhydd Ruthin
North Wales
LL15 2US
☎ 01824 703 883
mikevde@whsmithnet.co.uk
KCC

## GWENT

**ALFORD**, Sue
**Humanistic Psychotherapist**
Half Moon Cottage
Old Chepstow Road
Penhow
Gwent
NP6 3AD
☎ 01633 400 829
salford@supanet.com
AHPP

**DAVID**, Johanna Turcan
**Analytical Psychologist-Jungian Analyst**
The Callow
Welsh Newton
Monmouth
Gwent
NP25 5RL
☎ 01600 716 634
☎ 01600 713 233
johanna.david@virgin.net
IGAP

**FISHER**, Clare
**Cognitive Analytic Therapist**
♿ Lyndhurst House
Eureka Place
Ebbw Vale
NP23 6PN
☎ 01495 353 700
Clare.fisher@gwent.wales.nhs.uk
ACAT

**HILLMAN**, Jan
**Sexual and Relationship Psychotherapist**
♿ Gwent Counselling Centre
St Mary Street
Monmouth
☎ 01600 715 717
Gwentcounselling@aol.com
BASRT

**PLOWMAN**, John
**Hypno-Psychotherapist**
Newport Clinic, 4 Llanethewy Road
Newport South
Gwent
NP20 4JA
☎ 01633 211 586
☎ 01633 843333
john@plowman68.freeserve.co.uk
NRHP

## GWYNEDD

**ASHTON**, Peter
**Cognitive Behavioural Psychotherapist**
♿ School of Nursing
University of Wales
Ffriddoedd Road
Bangor
LL57 2EF
☎ 01248 383 116
p.r.j.ashton@bangor.ac.uk
BABCP

**FEARNS**, Keith
**Cognitive Behavioural Psychotherapist**
C.M.H.T.
26 College Road
BANGOR
LL57 2AN
☎ 01248 364 215
BABCP

**HICKMOTT**, Barbara
**Psychodrama Psychotherapist**
Cynefin
Glan Gors
Coed y Parc Bethesda
Gwynedd
LL57 4YW
☎ 01248 602 342
barbara@psychodrama.fsnet.co.uk
BPA

**NIESSER**, Arthur
**Analytical Psychologist-Jungian Analyst**
♿ Fron Olau
Mersey Street
Borth Y Gest
Porthmadog
LL49 9UF
☎ 01766 514 191
☎ 01766 513 041
arthur.niesser@doctors.org.uk
AJA

## ISLE OF ANGLESEY

**GILL**, Martin
**Psychodrama Psychotherapist**
Rhuddgaer Bach
Dwyran
Llanfairpwllgwyn etc
North Wales
LL61 6BJ
☎ 01248 430 445
martin@artslinc.org
BPA

**LANGLEY**, Allen
**Hypno-Psychotherapist**
♿ Bryn Hyfryd
Lon St Ffraid
Trearddur Bay
Holyhead, Anglesey
LL65 2UD
☎ 01248 717 744
☎ 01407 861 258
allenlangley@hotmail.com
NRHP

**MAY**, Adam
**Cognitive Behavioural Psychotherapist, Hypno-Psychotherapist**
♿ 2 Fron Heulog
Llanddaniel Fab
Gaerwen, Sir Fon
LL60 6EF
☎ 01248 421 015
therapy@adammay.co.uk
BABCP, NRHP

## MONMOUTHSHIRE

**BARRY**, Keith
**Cognitive Behavioural Psychotherapist**
♿ Partnerships in Care Ltd
Llanarth Court Hospital
Llanarth, Raglan
USK
NP15 2YD
☎ 01873 840 555
BABCP

**HARRIS**, Judith
**Psychoanalytic Psychotherapist**
Glebe Cottage
Skenfrith
Abergavenny
Gwent
NP7 8UH
☎ 01600 750 608
SIP

**KIRWIN**, Mark
**Psychosynthesis Psychotherapist**
♿ Old Church Cottage
Birches Road
Penallt
Monmouth
NP5 4AW
☎ 01600 712 857
☎ 01291 627 722
PET

**MILLS**, Nigel
**Cognitive Behavioural Psychotherapist**
♿ The Holistic Clinic
Henton House
28 Monk Street
Abergavenny
NP7 5NP
☎ 01873 858 020
nigel@chigung.fsnet.co.uk
BABCP

**WAINWRIGHT**, Pauline
**Transactional Analysis Psychotherapist**
91 Sunnybank Road
Griffithstown
Pontypool
NP4 5LN
☎ 04195 752 386
jim.florance@tiscali.co.uk
ITA

## NEATH PORT TALBOT

**HUGHES**, Geraldine
**Gestalt Psychotherapist**
Ty'n-y-Coed
17 Graig Gellinudd
Pontardawe
SA8 3HP
☎ 01792 862 916
☎ 029 2045 4001
gerriehughes@hotmail.com
GPTI

**SHERLOCK**, Teresa
**Neurolinguistic Psychotherapist**
The Cherry House
141 Brecon Road
Ystradgynlais
Swansea
SA9 1QL
☎ 01639 843 477
tereska@macunlimited.net
NLPtCA

## PEMBROKESHIRE

**EVANS**, Noeleen
**Sexual and Relationship Psychotherapist**
Tinkersfold
Cosheston
Pembroke
SA72 4UG
☎ 01646 686 758
noeleen.evans@btopenworld.com
BASRT

**SCOTT CHINNERY**, Jean M
**Cognitive Behavioural Psychotherapist**
Rose Cottage
Dredgeman Hill
Haverfordwest
SA61 1XL
☎ 01437 760 978
BABCP

## POWYS

**BRADLEY**, Lorne-Natalie
**Psychoanalytic Psychotherapist**
Ffawyddog Barn
Ffawyddog
Crickhowell
Powys, Wales
NP8 1PY
☎ 01873 812 387
☎ 01865 246 879
xqx29@Dial.Pipex.com
CPP, FIP

**COWARD**, Roger
**Transpersonal Psychotherapist**
cwm Bedw
Abbeycwmhir
Llandrindod Wells
Powys
LD1 6PH
☎ 01597 851 929
☎ 020 7603 9692
roger.coward@dial.pipex.com
CTP

**CURRAN**, Maureen
**Psychoanalytic Psychotherapist**
Penarth
Cregrina
Nr. Llandrindod Wells
Powys
LD1 5SF
☎ 01982 570 212
The Old Surgery
Cambrian House
West Street
Rhayader, Powys
LD6 5AD
WMIP

**EDWARDS**, Linda Mary
**Group Analyst**
♿ The Melangell Centre
Pennant Melangell
Llangynog Via Oswestry
Powys
SY10 0HQ
☎ 01691 860 455
lme1@fish.co.uk
IGA

**FRASER**, Mary Elizabeth
**Psychoanalytic Psychotherapist**
29 Harley Road
Cressage
Shrewsbury
Shropshire
SY5 6DF
maryfraser@ic24.net
WMIP

**GORDON CLARK**, Thalia
**Core Process Psychotherapist**
4 Danyrallt
Llaneglwys
Builth Wells
Powys
LD2 3BJ
☎ 01982 560735
KI

**JAMESON MILNER**, Jane
**Gestalt Psychotherapist**
The Waen
Bettws Cedewain
Newtown
Powys
SY16 3LF
☎ 01686 625 170
kejane@freenetname.co.uk
GPTI

**KOSTORIS**, Laura
**Integrative Psychotherapist**
♿ 1 Tower Street
Crickhowell
Powys
NP8 1EL
☎ 01874 676 498
kosto@ukonline.co.uk
SPCRC

**MACKENZIE**, Ian D.
**Psychoanalytic Psychotherapist**
Penarth
Cregrina
Nr. Llandrindod Wells
Powys
LD1 5SF
☎ 01982 570 212
WMIP

**MIDDLESTONE-LOWE**, Carole
**Transactional Analysis Psychotherapist**
"Southerndown"
9 Pontywal Lane
Bronllys
Brecon Powys
LD3 0HU
☎ 01874 712 335
carole_lowe@talk21.com
ITA

**PARLETT**, Malcolm
**Gestalt Psychotherapist**
The Coach House
Nether Skyborry
Knighton, Powys
LD7 1TW
☎ 01547 528 132
malcolm.parlett@virgin.net
GPTI

**PEACE**, Susan
**Hypno-Psychotherapist**
♿ Cwm Meillion
Llangammarch Wells
Powys
LD4 4EN
☎ 01591 620 339
susan.peace@btinternet.com
NRHP

**SCLATER**, Michael
**Transpersonal Psychotherapist**
Geufron
Llansilin
Shropshire
SY10 7JW
☎ 01691 691 289
sclater@sclater.co.uk
CCPE

## RHONDDA CYNON TAFF

**DAVIES**, Michael
**Family & Systemic Psychotherapist**
♿ Bryn Ffrwd
17 Rock Terrace
Old Ynysybwl
Pontypridd Mid
CF37 3NT
☎ 01443 791 419
mgdavies1@hotmail.com
AFT

**FARIS**, Jeff
**Family & Systemic Psychotherapist**
University of Glamorgan
Pontypridd
CF37
☎ 01443 483 821
☎ 029 20 486 553
jfaris@glam.ac.uk
FIC

**HARDY**, William
**Family & Systemic Psychotherapist**
The Family Institute
School of Care Sciences
University of Glamorgan
Pontypridd
CF37 1DL
☎ 01443 483 820
FIC

**JONES**, Teresa
**Systemic Psychotherapist**
4 Tollgate Close
Caerphilly
CF38 3AY
☎ 02920 888 240
FIC

**THOMAS**, Jenny
**Transactional Analysis Psychotherapist**
♿ "The Highlands"
Old Llantrisant Road
Tonyrefail Porth
CF39 8YU
☎ 01443 676 579
jlthom@globalnet.co.uk
ITA

## SWANSEA

**BRETT**, John David
**Systemic Psychotherapist**
11 Church Park
Mumbles
Swansea
SA3 4DE
☎ 01792 582 338
☎ 01792 520 139
John.brett@swansea-tr-wales.nhs.uk
FIC

**GIBBIN**, Jane
**Sexual and Relationship Psychotherapist**
♿ The Grove Medical Centre
6 Uplands Terrace
Uplands
SA2 0GU
☎ 01994 427 644
janegibbin@btinternet.com
BASRT

**GREGG**, Annzella
**Transpersonal Psychotherapist**
♿ Swansea
SA1
☎ 01792 536 748
CCPE

**HALE**, Sue
**Integrative Psychotherapist**
♿ 51 Linkside Drive
Southgate
Pennard
Swansea
SA3 2BS
☎ 01792 234 176
sue@ashera.co.uk
SPTI

**LOMOND**, Marsha
**Transactional Analysis Psychotherapist**
♿ 22 Howells Road
Dunvant
Swansea
SA2 7SX
☎ 01792 296 528
marsha_lomond@hotmail.com
ITA, MET

**REGAN JONES**, Columba
**Child Psychotherapist**
Swansea Child & Family Clinic
"Trehafad"
Waunarlwydd Road
Sketty, Swansea
SA2 0GP
☎ 01792 582 139
jonespenllt@aol.com
ACP

**VIVAN-BYRNE**, Kieran
**Systemic Psychotherapist**
Foster Care Associate Cwmru
57 Walter Road
Swansea
SA1 5PZ
☎ 01656 728 021
☎ 01792 644 442
veebees2@aol.com
FIC

**WOOD-BEVAN**, Rosy
**Integrative Psychotherapist**
48 Hazel Road
Uplands
Swansea
SA2 OLX
☎ 01792 201 257
MC

## VALE OF GLAMORGAN

**BLACKBURN**, Annie
**Gestalt Psychotherapist**
Kymin Cottage
7 Beach Lane
Penarth
Cardiff
CF64 1AN
☎ 029 2071 1789
dreamtimekurrajong@hotmail.com
GPTI

**ROWLANDS**, Helen
**Integrative Psychotherapist**
110 Heol Hir
Llanishen
Cardiff
South Glamorgan
CF14 5AD
☎ 02920 756 784
hrowlands@tiscali.co.uk
MET

**SIMPSON**, Elaine
**Family & Systemic Psychotherapist**
♿ 9 Elm Grove Place
Dinas Powys
Cardiff
CF64 4DJ
☎ 029 20 512 717
AFT

**SZARY**, Gerard
**Neurolinguistic Psychotherapist**
76 Cosmeston Drive
Penarth
Vale of Glamorgan
CF64 5FA
☎ 02920 701 493
☎ 07753 620 777
gerard@szary2.fsnet.co.uk
NLPtCA

**TOMSETT**, Jean
**Family & Systemic Psychotherapist**
62 Althorp Drive
Penarth
Vale of Glamorgan
CF64 5JF
☎ 02920 707 549
AFT

## OVERSEAS - AUSTRALIA

**ASKEW-WALINDA**, Margaret
**Psychoanalytic Psychotherapist**
♿ 53 Ocean Boulevard
Jan Juc
Victoria, 3228
Australia
☎ + 61 3 5261 2795
☎ 0439 712 795
margaw1@bigpond.com
FPC

**AVERY**, Trisha
**Transpersonal Psychotherapist**
PO Box 6566
Melbourne
3004 Victoria
Australia
trishavery@bpca.com.au
CCPE

**CADE**, Brian
**Family & Systemic Psychotherapist**
PO Box 386
Eastwood
New South Wales 2122
Australia
☎ 612 9868 2606
bcade@netspace.net.au
AFT

**CEBON**, Ann
**Child Psychotherapist**
8 Coombs Avenue
Kew
Victoria 3101
Australia
☎ 0061 398 533 114
ACP

**CLARK**, Giles
**Analytical Psychologist-Jungian Analyst**
1 Russell Street
Woollahra
Sydney
NSW 2025, Australia
☎ 02 9386 0648
gijaclar@ozemail.com.au
IGAP

**DAVID**, Anna-Kristin
**Integrative Psychotherapist**
E301
26 Pont Street
Pyrmont
NSW 2009 Australia
☎ +61 438 215 110
adavid@mteliza.com.au
SPCRC

**DURLACH**, Stefan
**Integrative Psychotherapist**
242a Oxford Street
Paddington
Sydney NSW
Australia 2021
☎ 0061 2 9990 0772
sdurlach@bigpond.net.au
SPCRC

**HARLAP**, Nahum
**Integrative Psychotherapist**
19a Salvado Street
Cottesloe
WA
Australia 6011
☎ 0061 8938 33360
☎ 0061 4397 34313
nharlap@bigpond.net.au
SPCRC

**HENRY**, Rachel M.
**Child Psychotherapist**
4 Wigram Road
Austinmer
NSW 2515
Australia
☎ 00612 42674531
ACP

**HOLMES**, Carol
**Integrative Psychotherapist**
Warehouse 3
5. Mouat Street
Western Australia 6160
Australia
☎ 0061 93 36 15 64
carol@cavh.fsnet.co.uk
SPCRC

**KALITOWSKI**, Matthew
**Hypno-Psychotherapist**
♿ c/o Balmain Osteopaths
2 Booth Street
Balmain, Sydney
NSW, Australia 2041
☎ 00612 9665 8284
NSHAP

**KING**, Madeleine
**Systemic Psychotherapist**
328 Gulpha Street
North Albury
New South Wales 2640
Australia
☎ 00 61 260 402 188
KCC

**KONDOS**, Sandy
**Integrative Psychotherapist**
242a Oxford Street
Paddington
Sydney NSW
Australia 2021
SPCRC

**LEIGH**, Elana
**Integrative Psychotherapist, Transactional Analysis Psychotherapist**
158 Wellington Street
Bondi 2026
Sydney
Australia
☎ 00 612 9300 9907
eleigh@ozemail.com.au
MET

**MALKIN**, Julius
**Cognitive Behavioural Psychotherapist**
♿ 18 Harris Street
Balmain
2041 NSW Australia
☎ 020 7591 7793
☎ 0061 9810 6586
BABCP

**MORRISSEY**, Shirley A
**Cognitive Behavioural Psychotherapist**
PO BOX U62
Casuarina Campus Post Office
Northern Territory University
Darwin, NT Australia 0815
shirleym7@bigpond.com
BABCP

**OATEN**, Gae
**Integrative Psychotherapist**
3/5 Mouat Street
Freemantle
W.A. 6160
Australia
☎ 0061 933 61564
dgae@fsmail.net
Warehouse 3
5. Mouat Street
W.A 6160
Australia
SPCRC

**OGILVIE**, Renate
**Existential Psychotherapist**
P.O. Box 5434
West Chatswood (10/854)
Pacific Highway
NSW 1515 (2067) Australia
☎ 0061 2 9411 1184
renateog@pnc.com.au
SPCRC

**PHILLIPS**, Helen
**Analytical Psychotherapist (Jungian)**
Box 123
TANUNDA
SA 5352
S Australia
☎ 00 61 8 8563 0207
helen.phillips@internode.on.net
GAPS

**SCHMIDT-NEVEN**, Ruth
**Child Psychotherapist**
Centre for Child & Family Development
721A Riversdale Road
Camberwell, Victoria 3124
Australia
☎ 00 618 300422
ccfdau@ozemail.com.au
ACP

**STRAKER**, Gillian
**Integrative Psychotherapist**
23 Liguria Street
Coogee
2034 Sydney
Australia
☎ 00612 93 444 184
MET

**STRASSER**, Alison
**Integrative Psychotherapist**
31 Regent Street
Paddington
NSW 2021
Australia
☎ (02) 9357 1505
raws@forge.com.au
SPCRC

**TOLCHARD**, Barry
**Cognitive Behavioural Psychotherapist**
♿ Department of Psychiatry
Flinders Medical Centre
Bedford Park, Adelaide
S Australia 5042
☎ 08 8204 4779
barry.tolchard@flinders.edu.au
BABCP

**VINEY**, Linda
**Personal Construct Psychotherapist**
Department of Psychology
University of Wollongong
Northfields Avenue, Wollongong
NSW 2522, Australia
☎ +61 02 4221 3693
linda_viney@uow.edu.au
PCP

**WALKER**, Lorraine
**Analytical Psychotherapist (Jungian)**
PO Box 7020
Shepparton
VIC 3632
Australia
☎ 00 613 5821 6232
lwalker5@vtown.co.au
GAPS

**WILLIAMS**, Graham
**Family & Systemic Psychotherapist**
745 Gembrook Road
Hoddes Creek
Victoria 3139
Australia
☎ 03 5967 4210
dihamtess@aol.com.au
A F T

## OVERSEAS - AUSTRIA

**AL RUBAIE**, Talal
**Hypno-Psychotherapist**
Schlossgasse 14/12
1050 Vienna
Austria
☎ (00431) 545 1832
N S H A P

## OVERSEAS - CANADA

**BATE**, Dolores
**Gestalt Psychotherapist**
2360 Waterloo Street
Vancouver
B.C.
V6R 4M6
☎ 001 604 737 7099
G P T I

**FISH**, Deborah M.
**Hypno-Psychotherapist**
2 - 4 Prince Albert Street
Ottowa
Ontario
Canada
K1K 2A4
☎ (613) 8 420 542
deb_m_fish@hotmail.com
N R H P

## OVERSEAS - CARIBBEAN

**CROWLEY-SCHWEITZER**, Brigitte
**Integrative Psychotherapist**
P.O. Box 10039 APO
Grand Cayman
Cayman Islands BW1
British West Indies
☎ (001 345) 946 48 60
crowleys@candw.ky
S P T I

## OVERSEAS - CYPRUS

**KLEANTHOUS**, Dina
**Psychoanalytic Psychotherapist**
Leoforos Eleftherias 52
Larnaca
Cyprus
☎ 0035724 624017
dina.k@cytanet.com.cy
A R B S

## OVERSEAS - DENMARK

**BURKHARDT**, Tansen I
**Transpersonal Psychotherapist**
c/o Edelberg
Holtestationsvej 22, 1
2840 HOLTE
Denmark
☎ 0045 454 11068
tansenburkhardt@hotmail.com
C C P E

**VEJE**, Margit
**Psychoanalytic Psychotherapist**
♿ Skt. Pauls Gade 8b St.
DK-8000
Arhus C.
DENMARK
☎ 00 45 86 128530
margit.veje@get2net.dk
A R B S

## OVERSEAS - EGYPT

**NAFIE**, Omar Ibrahim
**Systemic Psychotherapist**
Behman Hospital
32 El Marsad Street
Helwan
Cairo
☎ 002025 557 551
omar.i@btinternet.com
K C C

## OVERSEAS - FINLAND

**SÖDERSTRÖM**, Anne-Charlotte
**Psychoanalytic Psychotherapist**
♿ Villa Enhagen
Hyddans Vag 37
10600 Ekenas
Finland
☎ 00358 19 241 2151
☎ 00358 40 726 0273
anne-charlotte.soderstrom@pp.inet.fi
I P S S

## OVERSEAS - FRANCE

**DAUDY**, Isabelle
**Psychoanalytic Psychotherapist**
♿ 4 Rue Job
31000 Toulouse
France
☎ +33 (0) 561 62 74 63 [t/f]
daudy.Isabelle@libertysurf.fr
I P S S

**DAWSON**, Roger
**Cognitive Psychotherapist**
Communaute Jesuite Centre-Sevres
35bis rue de Sevres
75006 Paris
France
☎ 0033 1 44 39 56 15
rogerdawsonsj@yahoo.co.uk
B A B C P

**GAVIN**, Verity J
**Integrative Psychotherapist**
♿ Le Bastidon
Hameau de St Pierre
84750 St Martin de Castillon
France
☎ 0033 04 90 75 25 71
S P C R C

**HAMILTON-DUCKETT**, Paule
**Psychoanalytic Psychotherapist**
Rue Ravel
84240 La Motte d'Aigues
Vaucluse
France
☎ 020 8444 3577
☎ 0033 04 90 77 60 43
F P C

**WEIXEL-DIXON**, Karen
**Existential Psychotherapist**
Chateau de Cambes
Pont du Casse
47480 Agen
France
☎ +33 5 53 87 46 37
☎ +33 6 70 56 45 76
karenweixeldixon@aol.com
S E A

## OVERSEAS - GERMANY

**CATINA**, Ana
**Personal Construct Psychotherapist**
Langestr 54
70174 Stuttgart
Germany
☎ 0049 711 3000 440 (t/f)
catina@psyres-stuttgart.de
P C P

**PERVÖLTZ**, Rainer
**Body Psychotherapist, Integrative Psychotherapist**
Oberan 49
79102 - Freiburg
Germany
☏ 07668 94532
r.pervoeltz@t-online.de
CCBP

**POLLAK**, Angela
**Integrative Psychotherapist, Primal Psychotherapist**
Gaden 28
93326 Abensberg
Germany
☏ 0049 9443 992 480
LAPP

**ROBERTSON**, Isobelle
**Cognitive Behavioural Psychotherapist**
Community Mental Health
M.R.S. Hohne
Haig Barracks
B.F.P.O. 30
☏ 0049 5051962 740
☏ 0049 5051 970 885
rbuster8@yahoo.co.uk
Community Psychiatry
M.R.S. Hohne
Haig Barracks
B.F.P.O. 30
BABCP

## OVERSEAS - GREECE

**LAYIOU-LIGNOS**, Effie
**Child Psychotherapist**
54 Aimonos Street
Colonos
10442
Athens, Greece
☏ 00 301 514 8123
cel-lignos@otenet.gr
ACP

**MOUTZOUKIS**, Chris
**Cognitive Behavioural Psychotherapist**
P O Box 117
57013 Oreokastro
Thessalonikis
Greece
☏ 0030 2 310 288 380
☏ 0030 2 310 692 271
mjcm@otenet.gr
BABCP

**PLOUMAKI**, Sophia
**Group Analytic Psychotherapist**
12 Kiras Tis Ro Street
Kipoupoli
Heraklion
Crete 71306
☏ 07718 914 296
☏ 01344 452 519
ploumaki@aol.com
UPCA

**POULOPOULOS**, Katerina
**Existential Psychotherapist**
♿ Didotou 25 & Asklipiou
Athens 10680
Greece
☏ 0030 1036 02190
katipgr@yahoo.com
SPCRC

**SPILIOPOULOS**, Valentine Andrikopoulos
**Psychoanalytic Psychotherapist**
11 Nikolakopoulou Street
Neo Psychiko
154 51 Athens
Greece
☏ +30 10 67 76 280
CCOPPP

**ZIDIANAKI**, Rania Argyro
Megalou Alexandrou
75 Heraklion
Crete 71305
Greece
☏ 6942 5959 88
☏ 6944 5869 88
gmagio@eap.gr
G. Georgiadou 64
Heraklion
71305
Greece
CCPE

## OVERSEAS - HONG KONG

**LAU**, Bernard Wai Kai
**Cognitive Behavioural Psychotherapist**
♿ Nicholson Tower, Block A1, 5/F
8 Wong Nai Chung Gap Road
Happy Valley
Hong Kong
☏ 00 852 2577 6045
bwklau00@hotmail.com
BABCP

**PRYDE**, Nia
**Sexual and Relationship Psychotherapist**
14A Block 1
Tam Towers
25 Sha Wan Drive
Victoria Road, Hong Kong
☏ 00852 2855 8435
BASRT

**SHUEN**, Dorcas
**Group Analytic Psychotherapist**
42 River North, 8th Street
Fairview Park
Yuen Long
N.T., Hong Kong
☏ 2369 2101
☏ 248 20308 (t/f)
dorcas@hkstar.com
FIP

## OVERSEAS - HUNGARY

**ORMAY**, Tom
**Group Analyst**
Nagydiofa U.3
1072
Budapest
Hungary

☏ +361 343 1179
tomormay@axeleno.hu
IGA

## OVERSEAS - ICELAND

**SVEINSDÓTTIR**, Björg
**Psychoanalytic Psychotherapist**
Stigahlid 8,
105 Reykjavik,
ICELAND
☏ (00 354) 568 6404
☏ mob: (00 354) 846 1042
bjorgsv@landspitali.is
ARBS

## OVERSEAS - INDIA

**BHARUCHA**, Aiveen
**Child Psychotherapist**
125 Wodehouse Road
Colaba
Bombay 400005
India
☏ 009122 2151 260
ACP

**BHARUCHA**, Manek P E
**Child Psychotherapist**
125 Wodehouse Road
Colaba
Bombay 400005
India
☎ 009122 215 1257
ACP

## OVERSEAS - IRELAND

**BARTLETT**, Olivia
**Transpersonal Psychotherapist**
102 Sorrento Road
Dalkey
Republic of Ireland
☎ (00353 1) 284 7786
jrbartlett@eircom.net
CCPE

**BRITTON**, N.C.
**Hypno-Psychotherapist**
♿ Durnesh Lake
Rossnowlagh
Co Donegal
Ireland
☎ 00353 72 52220
nc@barrybritton.com
CTIS

**BUTCHER**, Gerard
**Cognitive Behavioural Psychotherapist**
69 Baggot Street Lower
Baggot Street Bridge
Dublin 2
☎ 00 353 1 662 5148
GBUTCHER@IOL.IE
BABCP

**BYRNE**, Philomena Kearney
**Integrative Psychosynthesis Psychotherapist**
Main Street
Carrick-on-Shannon
Co. Leitrim
Ireland
☎ +353 87 64 32 907
philfbyrne@eircom.net
RE.V

**CAIRD**, Elizabeth
**Hypno-Psychotherapist**
♿ 22 Cherrymount Park
Dublin 7
Irish Republic
☎ 00353 1 938 767
NSHAP

**COAKLEY**, Una
**Integrative Psychotherapist**
♿ 17 Inchvale Drive
Shamrock Lawn
Douglas
Cork, Ireland
☎ 021 4361 798
MET

**CONROY**, Kay
**Psychosynthesis Psychotherapist**
White House
Templeogue
Dublin 6W
Ireland
☎ 00 353 1 2807888
☎ 00 353 1 4906615
kay@turningpoint.ie(w/e)

**CRONE**, Ms Joni
**Psychodrama Psychotherapist**
1 Arnott Street
Dublin 8
Ireland
☎ 00353 879 178 189
jccrone@eircom.net
BPA

**CULLEN**, Anne M.
**Cognitive Behavioural Psychotherapist**
Department of Psychiatry
Roscommon General Hospital
Roscommon
Ireland
☎ 00 353 903 26255
BABCP

**DAVIES**, Debra
**Core Process Psychotherapist**
Flat 2, 8 McCurtain Hill
Clonakilly
West Cork
Eire
☎ 00 353 23 35782
KI

**DONNELLY**, Clare
**Integrative Psychotherapist**
63 Annamore
Philsboro
Dublin 7
Ireland
☎ 00 353 8 385 541
donncmc@hotmail.com
MET

**DOOLEY**, Patricia
**Psychoanalytic Psychotherapist**
Unit 3 Gleneask
Dublin Road
Castletroy
Limerick
☎ 00353 61 34907
☎ 00353 86 839 0885
patdool@eircom.net
**Psychoanalytic Psychotherapist**
Riverview House
Cahara
Glin
County Limerick
FPC

**DUFFY**, Kathleen
**Integrative Psychotherapist**
♿ 14 Lower Main Street
Ballymahon
Co. Longford
Ireland
☎ 00353 902 32762
SPCRC

**FITZGERALD**, Pamela
**Hypno-Psychotherapist**
12 Mount Eagle Drive
Leopardstown Heights
Dublin 18
☎ 012 957 991
pfitz2002@eiscon.net
NSHAP

**FLACKE**, Theresa
**Group Analytic Psychotherapist**
29 Monivea Park
Galway
Eire
☎ 00353 9153 9902
☎ 00353 9156 1174
theresa.flacke@bsi.ie
UPCA

**FOLEY**, Dermot
**Integrative Psychotherapist**
21 Leeson Park
Dublin 6
Ireland
☎ 00353 1 497 7897
dfoleysps@eircom.net
SPCRC

**GAVIN**, Bea
**Psychoanalytic Psychotherapist**
Furrymelia West
Barna
Galway
Ireland
☎ 00353 915 90900
☎ 00353 876 697800
beagavin@gofree.indigo.ie
ARBS, FPC

**GAYNOR**, Donal F
**Sexual and Relationship Psychotherapist**
82 Lorcan Crescent
Santry
Dublin 9
Ireland
☎ +353 1 842 0919
☎ 087 2095 943
dfgaynor@eircom.net
BASRT

**GILMORE**, Jane
**Body Psychotherapist, Integrative Psychotherapist**
87 Devon Park
Salthill
Gallway
Ireland
☎ 00353 91 521 398
jmgilmore@eircom.net
CCBP

**HANRAHAN**, Josephine
**Sexual and Relationship Psychotherapist**
♿ Carrowmoneen
Tuam
Co. Galway
Ireland
☎ +353 (0) 93 24619
☎ +353 (0) 93 26239
shanrah@indigo.ie
BASRT

**HARRISON**, Caroline M
**Sexual and Relationship Psychotherapist**
HARI Unit
Rotunda Hospital
Parnell Square
DUBLIN 1
☎ +353 1 807 2732
BASRT

**LAWLOR**, Elizabeth
**Cognitive Behavioural Psychotherapist**
♿ Cluain Mhuire
St John of God Service
Newtownpark Avenue, Blackrock
Dublin
☎ +353 1 217 2144
☎ +353 8723 99379
elizabeth.lawlor@sjog.ie
BABCP

**LEONARD**, Mary E
**Sexual and Relationship Psychotherapist**
♿ Newtown Surgery
Athlone
Co Westmeath
☎ 086 823 3376
☎ 078 35201
♿ Kilmacumsey
Elphin
Co Roscommon
Eire
BASRT

**LONG**, Angela
**Sexual and Relationship Psychotherapist**
Rose Cottage
Foxrock Close
Dublin 18
Ireland
☎ 01 289 7138
☎ 087 294 1127
angelahl@gofree.indigo.ie
BASRT

**MASTERSON**, Ingrid
**Psychoanalytic Psychotherapist**
♿ "Alberta"
Ardtona Avenue
Lower Churchtown
Dublin 14, Ireland
☎ 003531 2988 288
IPSS

**MAUGER**, Benig
**Psychoanalytic Psychotherapist**
69 Cowper Road
Rathmines
Dublin 6
Ireland
☎ 00353 1 497 0501
benmau@iol.ie
AGIP

**MCBURNIE**, Dolores
**Psychosynthesis Psychotherapist**
Glensted
Murroe
County Limerick
Irish Republic
☎ 061 386 923
IPS

**MCCARTHY**, Rita
**Analytical Psychologist-Jungian Analyst**
Tarrea House
Tarrea Pier
Kilcolgan
Co. Galway
☎ 00353 (0) 91 637 580
AJA

**MCEVOY**, Liz
**Body Psychotherapist, Integrative Psychotherapist**
GAP
29 Lower Abbey Street
Dublin 1
Ireland
☎ 00353 1 667 3171
☎ 00353 1 672 8086
lizmcevoy@eircom.net
CCBP

**MCFADDEN**, Hugh E.
**Cognitive Behavioural Psychotherapist**
"Sancta Maria"
Gortlee
Letterkenny
Co. Donegal
☎ 00 353 74 21919
☎ 00 353 74 88405
hemcfadden@eircom.net
**Cognitive Behavioural Psychotherapist**
19 Solomon's Court
Letterkenny
Co Donegal
BABCP

**MCGOLDRICK**, Mary
**Cognitive Behavioural Psychotherapist**
♿ St. Patrick's Hospital
James's Street
Dublin 8
Ireland
☎ 00 3531 677 5423
BABCP

**MCGROARY-MEEHAN**, Maureen
**Cognitive Behavioural Psychotherapist, Sexual and Relationship Psychotherapist**
East End House
Clar Road
Donegal Town
County Donegal
☎ 00353 73 21933
mcgroarymeehan@iol.ie
BABCP, BASRT

**MCKENNA**, Jacqueline
**Cognitive Behavioural Psychotherapist**
Dernalusett House
Emyvale
Co. Monaghan
IRELAND
☎ +353 47 876 646
☎ 028 375 22381
BABCP

**MURRAY**, Catherine
**Psychodrama Psychotherapist**
Newtown House
Doneraile
Co.Cork
Eire, Ireland
☎ 00353 22 24117
☎ 00353 21 4861 360
catherinemurray@eircom.net
BPA

**O'CALLAGHAN**, Mary
**Humanistic Psychotherapist**
61 St Albans Road
SCR
Dublin 8
Rep. of Ireland
☎ 00 353 1453 2620
☎ 00 353 86600 1935
ocallaghanmar4@hotmail.com
AHPP

**O'CONNOR**, Aine
**Integrative Psychotherapist, Primal Psychotherapist**
♿ 45 Huntsdown Court
Clonsilla
Dublin 15
Ireland
☎ 0035318 216 163
LAPP

**O'KEEFFE**, Mary
**Integrative Psychotherapist**
The Old Parochial House
Church Street
Miltown Malbay
Co Clare
☎ 087 226 4196
mvokeeffe@eircom.net
MET

**O'KELLY**, Jackie
**Cognitive Behavioural Psychotherapist**
♿ Heather Edge
Llullymore
Rathangan
Co Kildare
☎ 00353 45 870 423
☎ 00353 1 677 5423 x428
St Patrick's Hospital
P O Box 136
James' Street
Dublin 8
BABCP

**O'MAHONY**, Angela
**Sexual and Relationship Psychotherapist**
The Kilkenny Clinic
Norebank House
Greens Hill
Kilkenny, Ireland
☎ 00 353 56 51420
OMahonnyAngela@eircom.net
BASRT

**O'NEILL**, Julia
**Biodynamic Psychotherapist**
Auginish
Kinvarra
Co. Galway
Eire
☎ 065 70 78252
LSBP

**O'SCANLAIN**, Peadar
**Humanistic Psychotherapist**
31 Larchfield
Kilkenny City
Rep. of Ireland
AHPP

**O'SULLIVAN**, Bernadette
**Personal Construct Psychotherapist**
VICO Consultation Centre
2 Dungar Terrace
Dun Laoghaire
Co. Dublin, Ireland
☎ 01 284 3336
clanaodh@indigo.ie
PCP

**RAWAT**, Shenaz
**Personal Construct Psychotherapist**
57 Dollymount Avenue
Clontarf
Dublin 3
Ireland
☎ 00 353 1 853 2147
shenaz@indigo.ie
PCP

**REYNOLDS**, Malcolm
**Psychosynthesis Psychotherapist**
Clonmore
Glebryan
Enniscorthy
Co. Wexford
☎ +353 1 294 2239
☎ +353 054 34572
10 Greenlands
Sandyford
Dublin 16
Ireland
PET

**SHIELDS**, Ellen Attracta
**Existential Psychotherapist**
♿ 16 University Road
Galway
Ireland
☎ 020 767 140
ashields@eircom.net
SPCRC

**SULLIVAN**, Gerald
**Lacanian Analyst**
14 The Belfry
Inchicore Road
Dublin 8
Ireland
☎ 00353 1454 4304
CFAR

**THORP**, Terry
**Hypno-Psychotherapist**
♿ Greystones
Co. Wicklow
☎ 0872 730 395
☎ 012 871 620
terrythorp@hypnopsychotherapy.net
NRHP

**TONE**, Yvonne
**Cognitive Behavioural Psychotherapist**
♿ St. Patrick's Hospital
PO Box No. 136
Jame's Street
Dublin 8
☎ 00 353 1 677 5423
ytone@stpatsmail.com
BABCP

**WALSH**, Deirdre
**Core Process Psychotherapist**
Harbour
Penrose Wharf
Penrose Quay
Cork, Ireland
☎ 00353 21 4876103
KI

**YOUNG**, Anne
**Analytical Psychologist-Jungian Analyst**
"Chertsey"
27 Rostrevor Road
Rathgar
Dublin 6, Ireland
☎ 003531 497 0331
CAP *

**WARD**, Shirley
**Humanistic and Integrative Psychotherapist**
♿ Amethyst
Ballyvalley Fort
Ballvalley, Killaloe
Co. Clare
☎ 00353 61 374 926
☎ 00353 61 376 331
shirleyward@eircom.net
Amethyst
Balbrogham
Killaloe
County Clare
AHPP

## OVERSEAS - ISRAEL

**DANA**, Mira
**Psychoanalytic Psychotherapist**
♿ 22 Shimshon Street
Haifa 34615
Israel
☎ (04) 834 3242
WTC

**GREEN**, Dror
**Integrative Psychotherapist**
♿ Kibbutz Ramat Yohanan
Israel
30050
☎ 00972 4 843 6301
drorgreen@psychom.com
SPCRC

**MANIELEVITCH**, Edna
**Gestalt Psychotherapist**
♿ 50 Yitzhar Street
Giv'at Canada
Jersualem 93892
Israel
☎ 972 2 676 1101
ednam@bezeqint.net
GPTI, MET

**MAZLIACH**, Yaron
**Child Psychotherapist**
PO Box 195
Ramat Tiron 36531
Israel
☎ 09 648213
ACP

## OVERSEAS - ITALY

**BENVENUTO**, Bice
**Lacanian Analyst**
Via Giulia di Gallese 23
00151 Roma
Italy
☎ 00 390 653 43615
Bice.Benvenuto@inwind.it
CFAR

**COSKERAN**, Helena
**Systemic Psychotherapist**
Suore Mariste
Via Aurelia 292
00165 Roma
☎ (06) 39 36 65 32
burgensm@suoremariste.191.it
KCC

**GRAZIOSI**, Mariolina
**Analytical Psychotherapist (Jungian)**
Viale Montenero 20
I-20135 Milano
Italy
☎ 025 468 401
☎ 3391 796 131
mariolina.graziosi@unimi.it
IGAP

**KENNY**, Vincent
**Personal Construct Psychotherapist**
Via Benedetto Croce 68
(Scala A:12)
Roma 00142
Italy
☎ 06 541 4774
vincent.kenny@flashnet.it
PCP

**MOLINO**, Anthony
**Psychoanalyst, Psychoanalytic Psychotherapist**
Via del Porto 10A
Vasto (CH) 66054
Italy
☎ 0039 (0)873 60386
anmoli@tin.it
SITE

**PIONTELLI**, Alessandra
**Child Psychotherapist**
Largo Richini 1
20122 Milan
Italy
☎ 00 392 583 07193
ACP

## OVERSEAS - LEBANON

**JAROUDI**, Leila
**Systemic Psychotherapist**
♿ Specialty Voice Centre
Specialty Clinics BDG-
Suites 12C and 12D, Maamari St
Hamra, Beirut
é Po Box 13-5154
Chourane
Beirut
Lebanon
☎ +00 961 1 360 326
☎ +00 961 3 729 551
lamiajar@cyberia.net.lb
KCC

## OVERSEAS - NETHERLANDS

**CARTON**, Roy
**Integrative Psychotherapist**
♿ Anton Constandsestraat 44
1095EM Amsterdam
The Netherlands
☎ 020 693 4075
☎ 06 55 188737
roycarton@hotmail.com
SPTI

**TENGELIN**, Hans
**Systemic Psychotherapist**
Projektcentrum Karlaskolan
Master Johansgatan 16
S-416 62 Goteborg
Sweden
☎ 0046 313 309 102
☎ 0046 31 847 267
hanstengelin@projektcentrum.com
KCC

**TJEPKEMA**, Froukje
**Psychoanalytic Psychotherapist**
Johan De Wittstraat 7 bis
3581XX Utrecht
The Netherlands
☎ 0031 30 233 3715
f.tjepkema@hetnet.nl
FPC

**VAN ROSSUM**, Diederik
**Psychosynthesis Psychotherapist**
Bilstraat 200
3572 BS
Utrecht
Netherlands
☎ 00302 714 634
info@psychosynthese.nl
IPS

## OVERSEAS - NEW ZEALAND

**ELDERTON**, Tan Shen
**Gestalt Psychotherapist**
37 Tiri View Road
Palm Beach
Waikeke Island
New Zealand 1240
☎ (0) 9372 3333
shen47_@hotmail.com
GPTI

**MADENHOLT-TITLEY**, Steph
**Psychosynthesis Psychotherapist**
30 Fairview Avenue
Waterview
Auckland
New Zealand
☎ 09-3074949 ext 7002
☎ +64 9820 3137
stephmt@quicksilver.net.nz
IPS

**MAILLARD**, Annie M
**Cognitive Behavioural Psychotherapist**
148 Hackthorne Road
Cashmere
Christchurch 8002
maillard@paradise.net.nz
BABCP

**PETERS**, Anthony
**Personal Construct Psychotherapist**
117 Waitoki Road, RDI
Kaukapakapa
Auckland
New Zealand
☎ 00 64 (0)9 420 4018
☎ 00 64 (0)9 377 2602
tonyp@adhb.gout.n2
PCP

## OVERSEAS - NORWAY

**GIBBS**, John
**Psychosynthesis Psychotherapist**
Asta Kongshorsgate 7
4044 Hafrsfjord
Norway
☎ 00 47 51 893 337
johnandchristek@hotmail.com
PET

**MOHN ENGEBRETSEN**, Karin
**Gestalt Psychotherapist**
St Olavsgt 27
0166 Oslo
Norway
☎ 0047 456 08 726
kme@interdevelop.no
SPTI

## OVERSEAS - PERU

**MONTALBETTI**, M.L.
**Child Psychotherapist**
Santander 147
Miraflores
Lima 18
Peru
☎ 00511 2543491
ACP

## OVERSEAS - SINGAPORE

**LEONG**, Jessica
**Transactional Analysis Psychotherapist**
55 Siglap Road
02-06/07 Siglap Centre
Singapore
455871
☎ 62440108
p3jcjessica@pacific.net.sg
ITA

## OVERSEAS - SLOVENIA

**KOTNIK**, Rudi
**Gestalt Psychotherapist**
Studenca 4
1241 Kamnik
Slovenia
☎ 00 386 1 831 7227
rudi.kotnik@guest.arnes.si
GPTI

## OVERSEAS - SOUTH AFRICA

**CASSIDY**, Allison Christine
**Integrative Psychotherapist**
5 Caledon Road
Emmarentia Gauteng
2195 South Africa
☎ 0027 11 782 0420
SPTI

**GREEN**, Margaret
**Psychoanalytic Psychotherapist**
♿ 7 Buckingham Road
Plumstead 7800
CAPE TOWN
South Africa
☎ 0027 217 613 027
mgreen@mweb.co.za
ARBS, WTC

**JANKS**, Ann
**Integrative Psychotherapist**
21 Illoof Street
Fairwood
2192 Johannesburg
South Africa
☎ 027 11 728 6756
dejan@mweb.co.za
SPTI

**KALINKO**, Sharon
**Integrative Psychotherapist**
P.O. Box 783459
2146 Sandton
South Africa
☎ 27 11 802 3000
skalinko@global.co.za
SPTI

**ROSENBAUM**, Linda Ann
**Integrative Psychotherapist**
PO Box 650229
Benmore
Johannesburg 2010
South Africa
☎ (011) 783 0696
linda@iafrica.com
SPTI

**SALTERS**, Diane
**Transactional Analysis Psychotherapist**
15 Disa Road
Murdock Valley
Simon's Town 7975
South Africa
☎ +27 21 786 1910
dsalters@iafrica.com
ITA

**SEARLE**, Joanne
**Humanistic Psychotherapist**
19 Belgrave Street
Bryanston 2021
South Africa
☎ +27 11 463 4332
josearle@telkomsa.net
P.O. Box 4
Rivonia 2128
South Africa
SPEC

## OVERSEAS - SOUTH AMERICA

**SALAZAR**, Maria Idalid Carreno
**Systemic Psychotherapist**
♿ Carrera 15 #27-82
Apto 601
Bogota
Colombia
☎ 0057 (1) 288 2436
☎ 0057 (1) 333 4850 ext 604
mariadalid@hotmail.com
KCC

## OVERSEAS - SPAIN

**ASHLEY**, Stephen
**Attachment-based Psychoanalytic Psychotherapist**
1b Calle Honda
Finestrat 03509
Allicante
☎ 0034 965 878 789
steveashley@btclick.com
CAPP

**BOTELLA**, Luis
**Personal Construct Psychotherapist**
Department of Psychology
Ramon Llull University
Cister 24-34
08022 Barcelona
☎ +34 93 253 3000
lluisbg@blanquerna.url.es
PCP

**CAMPOS**, Hanne
**Group Analyst**
Paseo San Gervasio 30
08022 Barcelona
Spain
☎ 34 93 417 56 39
hannecam@copc.es
IGA

**DRURY**, Gitta
**Gestalt Psychotherapist**
Casa Media Luna
Calle Xopena
03790 Orba
Alicante, Spain
☎ 00 34 96 5583884
SPTI

**FEBRER-BOWEN**, Ines
**Psychoanalytic Psychotherapist**
Bonavista 63 Primero
08960 Sant Just Desvern
Barcelona
Spain
☎ +34 9347 00384
inesfebrer@hotmail.com
ARBS

**GREAVES**, Thomas
**Core Process Psychotherapist**
Gran de Garcia 100, 3, 1
Barcelona 00812
Spain
☎ 0034 93 218 1792
KI

**HANNANT**, Fiona
**Hypno-Psychotherapist**
Carrer D'Espicio 36
Escalera A 2 / 2
Lesseps
08023 Barcelona
☎ 0034 661 2920
davefiona15@hotmail.com
CTIS

**IBANEZ**, Julian
**Psychoanalytic Psychotherapist**
Alameda de Urquijo 94
lero DCHA
48013 Bilbao
Spain
☎ 00 344 4277340
j.opacua@correo.cop.es
ARBS

**LEYGRAF**, Bernd C
**Humanistic and Integrative Psychotherapist, Sexual and Relationship Psychotherapist**
C/Patio de la Acequia
Urb Garmenes, San Miguel
Sacromonte No 4
18010 Granada
☎ 020 7281 5324
☎ +34 958 270 334
leygraf@aol.com

**TURNER**, Carole
**Transactional Analysis Psychotherapist**
♿ La Galera de Las Palmeras 119
03590 Altea
Alicante
Spain
☎ 0034 965 846 191
carojim@ctv.es
ITA, MET

## OVERSEAS - SWEDEN

**BENGTSSON**, Lars-Erik
**Systemic Psychotherapist**
BUP-mottagningen/VC
Glasgatan 27
S-731 81 Köping
Sweden
KCC

**BERARDI**, Chris
**Gestalt Psychotherapist**
Sandhamnsgatan 62
S-11528 Stockholm
Sweden
☎ +46 866 04 008
☎ +46 704 933 311
chris.berardi@telia.com
SPTI

**BRAGÉE**, Britt
**Gestalt Psychotherapist**
Banérgatan 25
S-11522 Stockholm
Sweden
☎ 0046 810 8055
☎ 0046 708 185781
britt@bragee.se
SPTI

**BRITT**, Bragee
**Gestalt Psychotherapist**
Banergatan 25
S-11522
Stockholm
Sweden
☎ +46 810 8055
☎ +46 708 185 781
britt@bragee.se
SPTI

**CARLSSON**, Lena
**Systemic Psychotherapist**
Degelugnsvägen 3
S-732 33 Arboga
Sweden
☎ 0046 589 16448
lena-carlsson@telia.com
KCC

**CURMAN**, Barbro
**Gestalt Psychotherapist**
Erstavilas Krarnvag 13
S-13336 Saltsjobaden
Sweden
☎ +46 8717 2784
☎ +46 707 23 23 16
barbara.curman@perlan.com
SPTI

**DEWHIRST**, Elisabeth
**Psychoanalytic Psychotherapist**
Bjersundsragen 27
237 36 Bjarred
SWEDEN
☎ 0046 46 141213
☎ 0046 46 295733
Skt Lukas
Mollegatan 17
222 29 LUND
SWEDEN
CCOPPP

**ELIASON**, Bertil L
**Systemic Psychotherapist**
♿ PO Box 104
S-430 33 Fjärås
Sweden
☎ +46 300 54 08 20
frivolten@telia.com
KCC

**ERIKSSON**, Anders
**Gestalt Psychotherapist**
Carl Skottsbergs gata 46
413 19 Goteborg
Sweden
SPTI

**ERIKSSON**, Tina
**Gestalt Psychotherapist**
Ljusstoparcgatan 7
41261 Gothenburg
Sweden
☎ +46 31 812530
tina.eriksson@humanresource.se
SPTI

**FRISCHER**, Livia
**Integrative Psychosynthesis Psychotherapist**
Antilopgatan 7
412 38 Molndal
Sweden
☎ +46 31 205 602
☎ +46 31 711 0430
livia.frischer@hotmail.com
RE.V

**HAGELTHORN**, Christina
**Psychodrama Psychotherapist**
Foreningsgatan 4
411 27 Goteborg
Sweden
☎ 0046 (0) 31 711 8732
☎ 07074 10268
christinahagelthorn@swipnet.se
BPA

**SULLIVAN**, Christopher
**Psychosynthesis Psychotherapist**
Skeppar Ka rls Grand 4nb
11130 Stockholm
☎ 020 8830 5662
☎ +46 820 0054
christophersullivan@compuserve.com
PET

**SÖDERQVIST**, Ingrid
**Systemic Psychotherapist**
Dalvägen 2
640 45 Kvicksund
Sweden
☎ 0046 16 34 21 81
☎ 0046 221 26 436
ingrid.soderqvist@itvastmanland
BUP mottagningen värdcentralen
Galsgatan27
731 81 Köping
Sweden
KCC

**THRANE**, Susanne
**Gestalt Psychotherapist**
♿ Sankt Goransgatan 102
112 45 Stockholm
Sweden
☎ 08 652 7675
thrane@telia.com
SPTI

## OVERSEAS - SWITZERLAND

**ITTEN**, Theodor
**Psychoanalytic Psychotherapist**
♿ Psychotherapeutische Praxis
Magnihalden 14
CH-9000 St Gallen
Switzerland
☎ +41 71 244 2121
info@ittentheodor.ch
PA

**OHNESORG**, Johanna
**Biodynamic Psychotherapist**
Badenerstrasse 332
8004
☎ 0041 13 717 647
☎ 0041 14 927 465
♿ Bachlerstrasse 62/1
CH-8046 Zurich
Switzerland
LSBP

## OVERSEAS - USA

**CEDRO**, Karin
**Integrative Psychotherapist**
8905 Battery Road
Alexandria
VA 22308
USA
☎ 001 (703) 575 5148
karincedro@cox.net
SPCRC

**ERSKINE**, Richard
**Integrative Psychotherapist**
500 East 85th Street
New York
NY 10028
USA
☎ +212 734 5291
integpsych@cs.com
SPTI

**HAMILTON**, Victoria
**Child Psychotherapist**
244 W. 72nd Street
Apt. 14C
New York, NY 10023
USA
☎ 001212 724 1470
ACP

**HERMON**, Deborah
**Child Psychotherapist**
7120 Via Marbella
Boca
Raton, Florida
33433
☎ 00561 4173300
ACP

**HILL**, Jude G
**Analytical Psychotherapist (Jungian)**
573 Dolores Street
San Francisco
CA 94110-1564
USA
☎ 001 415 861 7951
judehillssf@aol.com
GAPS

**HOOK**, Susan
**Cognitive Behavioural Psychotherapist**
10403 SE 98th Court
Portland
OR 97266
USA
☎ 00 1 503 771 3371
cognitiv@hevanet.com
BABCP

**JONES-DUBE**, Elvyn
**Psychoanalytic Psychotherapist**
7 Sheldrake Road
Scarsdale
New York
USA 10583 3507
☎ 001 914 723 2675
ejonesdube1@yahoo.com
FIP

**SUTCLIFFE**, Pauline
**Family & Systemic Psychotherapist**
P.O. Box 803
Wainscott
New York 11975-0803
USA
IFT

**THOMPSON**, Michael Guy
**Psychoanalytic Psychotherapist**
684 Colusa Avenue
Berkeley
CA 94707
USA
☎ 020 7794 2652
michaelguy@aol.com
PA

**TYRRELL**, Susannah
**Transpersonal Psychotherapist**
2219 Paseo de los Chamisos
Santa Fe
New Mexico 87505
☎ 001 505 954 4156
CTP

**VIBERT**, Eva
**Integrative Psychosynthesis Psychotherapist, Transpersonal Psychotherapist**
1014 22nd St. NW
Washington DC 20037
☎ 020 7486 8747
evavibert@aol.com
CTP, RE.V

## OVERSEAS - YUGOSLAVIA

**STOJNOV**, Dusan
**Personal Construct Psychotherapist**
Gracanicka 9
1100 Belgrade
Yugoslavia
PCP

# Organisational Contact Information

## Analytical Psychology Section

### Association of Jungian Analysts
7 Eton Avenue
LONDON
NW3 3EL
Tel: 020 7794 8711
aja@dircon.co.uk
www.aja.dircon.co.uk

### Confederation of Analytical Psychologists
Consulting Room, Flat 1
62 Rosslyn Hill
Hampstead
LONDON
NW3 8GP
marstone@dircon.co.uk

### The Independent Group of Analytical Psychologists
PO Box 22343
LONDON
W13 8GP
Tel: 020 8933 0353
office@igap.co.uk
www.igap.co.uk

## Behavioural and Cognitive Psychotherapies

### Association of Rational Emotive Behaviour Therapists
Behavioural Psychotherapy
Michael Carlisle Centre
75 Osborne Road
SHEFFIELD
S11 9BF
Tel: 0114 271 8699
rebtadmin@managingstress.com
http://rebt.bizland.com

### British Association of Behavioural and Cognitive Psychotherapies
The Globe
PO Box 9
ACCRINGTON
Lancashire
BB5 2GD
Tel: 01254 875 277
babcp@babcp.org.uk
www.babcp.org.uk

## Experiential Constructivist Therapies

### British Autogenic Society
Royal London Homeopathic Hospital
Greenwell Street
LONDON
W1W 5BP
Tel: 020 7383 5108
Fax: 020 7383 5108
admin@autogenic-therapy.org.uk
www.autogenic-therapy.org.uk

### Neuro Linguistic Psychotherapy Counselling Association
13 Chisick Village
LONDON
W4 3BY
Tel: 0870 241 3276
administration@nlptca.com
www.anlp-pcs.co.uk

### PCP Education and Training
20 Cleveland Avenue
Chiswick
LONDON
W4 1SN
Tel: 020 8994 7959
daltonpcp@talk21.com
www.pcpet.org.uk

### Society for Existential Analysis
BM Existential
LONDON
WC1N 3XX
Tel: 07000 473 337
info@existentialanalysis.co.uk
www.existentialanalysis.co.uk

## Family, Couple, Sexual & Systemic Therapy

### The Association for Family Therapy
12A Executive Suite
St James Court
Wilderspool Causeway
WARRINGTON
WA4 6PS
Tel: 01925 444 414
s.kennedy@aft.org.uk
www.aft.org.uk

### British Association for Sexual and Relationship Therapy
PO Box 13686
LONDON
SW20 9ZH
Tel: 020 8543 2707
info@basrt.org.uk
www.basrt.org.uk

### Family Institute Cardiff
School of Care Sciences
University of Glamorgan
PONTYPRIDD
CF37 1DL
Tel: 01443 483 820
bcox@glam.ac.uk

### Institute of Family Therapy
24-32 Stephenson Way
LONDON
NW1 2HX
Tel: 020 7391 9150
ift@psyc.bbk.ac.uk
www.instituteoffamilytherapy.org.uk

### Kensington Consultation Centre
2 Wyvil Court
Trenchold Street
LONDON
SW8 2TG
Tel: 020 7720 7301
enquiries@kcc-international.com
www.kcc-international.com

## Humanistic and Integrative Psychotherapy

### Association for Cognitive Analytic Therapists
ACAT 3rd Floor, South Wing
Division of Academic Psychiatry
St. Thomas' Hospital
Lambeth Palace Road,
LONDON
SE1 7EH
Tel: 020 7928 9292 Ext 3769
AofCat@aol.com
www.acat.org.uk

### UK Association of Humanistic Psychology Practitioners
Box BCM AHPP
LONDON
WC1N 3XX
Tel: 08457 660 326
Fax: 01348 840 845
admin.ahpp@talk21.com
www.ahpp.org

### Bath Centre for Psychotherapy and Counselling
1 Walcot Terrace
London Road
BATH
BA1 6AB
Tel: 01225 429 720 (t/f)
bcpc@ukonline.co.uk

### British Psychodrama Association
The Administrator
Flat 1/1 105 Hyndland Road
GLASGOW
G12 9JD
Tel: 0141 339 0141
jscan@bpad.freeserve.co.uk
www.psychodrama.org.uk

**Centre for Counselling and Psychotherapy Education**
Beauchamp Lodge
2 Warwick Crescent
LONDON
W2 6NE
Tel: 020 7266 3006
Fax: 020 7266 3691
info@ccpe.org.uk
www.ccpe.org.uk

**Centre for Transpersonal Psychology**
101 Crawford Street
LONDON
W1H 2HP
Tel: 020 7724 9842
Fax: 020 7724 9243
enquiries@transpersonalcentre.co.uk
www.transpersonalcentre.co.uk

**Chiron Centre for Body Psychotherapy**
26 Eaton Rise
LONDON
W5 2ER
Tel: 020 8997 5219
chiron@chiron.org
www.chiron.org

**The Gestalt Centre, London**
First Floor
62 Paul Street
LONDON
EC2A 4NA
Tel: 020 7613 4480
mail@gestaltcentre.co.uk
www.dspace.dial.pipex.com/gestaltc

**Gestalt Psychotherapy Training Institute**
PO Box 2555
BATH
BA1 6XR
Tel: 01225 482 35 (t/f)
admin@gpti.org.uk
www.gestaltcentre.co.uk

**Guild of Analytical Psychology and Spirituality**
122 Lupus Street
LONDON
SW1V 4AN
Tel: 020 7834 1708 (t/f)
info@gaps.co.uk
www.gaps.co.uk

**Institute for Arts in Therapy and Education**
2-18 Brittania Row
LONDON
N1 8PA
Tel: 020 7704 2534
info@arts-therapy.demon.co.uk
www.arts-therapy.demon.co.uk

**Institute for Psychosynthesis**
65a Watford Way
Hendon
LONDON
NW4 3AQ
Tel: 020 8202 4525
institute@psychosynthesis.org
www.dircon.co.uk/uk/contents

**Institute of Transactional Analysis**
P.O. Box 1101
Wigton
Cumbria
CA7 9YH
Tel: 0845 0099 101
admin@ita.org.uk
www.ita.org.uk

**Karuna Institute**
Natsworthy Manor
Widecombe in the Moor
NEWTON ABBOT
TQ13 7TR
Tel: 01647 221 457
karuna@eurobell.co.uk
www.karuna-institute.co.uk

**London Association of Primal Psychotherapists**
West Hill House
6 Swains Lane
LONDON
N6 6QU
Tel: 020 7267 9616
info@lapp.org
www.lapp.org

**London School of Biodynamic Psychotherapy**
Admin Office:
Willow Cottage
Off Wokingham Road
HURST RG10 0RU
(Training Centre, London N19)
Tel: 07000 794 725
enquiries@lsbp.org.uk
www.lsbp.org.uk

**The Metanoia Institute**
13 North Common Road
LONDON
W5 2QB
Tel: 020 8579 2505
mail@metanoia.ac.uk
www.metanoia.ac.uk

**The Minster Centre**
Mapesbury Lodge
17 Mapesbury Road
LONDON
NW2 4HU
Tel: 020 8450 3311
minster@dial.pipex.com
www.os94.dial.pipex.com

**Northern Guild for Psychotherapy**
77 Acklan Road
Thornday
Stockton-on-Tees
CLEVELAND
TS17 7BD
Tel: 01642 649 004
stockton@northern-guild.co.uk or
newcastle@northern-guild.co.uk
www.northern-guild.co.uk

**Psychosynthesis and Education Trust**
92-94 Tooley Street
LONDON
SE1 2TH
Tel: 020 7403 2100
petrust@btinternet.com
www.essential-life.org

**School of Psychotherapy and Counselling at Regents College**
Regent's College
Inner Circle
Regent's Park
LONDON
NW1 4NS
Tel: 020 7487 7406
pccc@regents.ac.uk or
spc@regents.ac.uk
www.spc.ac.uk

**Re-Vision**
97 Brondesbury Road
LONDON
NW6 6RY
Tel: 020 8357 8881
re-vision@cwcom.net
www.re-vision.org.uk

**Scarbrough Psychotherapy Training Institute**
Vere House
117 Columbus Ravine
Scarbrough
YO12 7QU
Tel: 01723 376 246
Kate.scpti@ukonline.co.uk

**The Sherwood Psychotherapy Training Institute**
Thiskney House
2 St James Terrace
NOTTINGHAM
NG1 6FW
Tel: 0115 924 3994
therapy@spti.net
www.spti.net

**Spectrum**
7 Endymion Road
LONDON
N4 1EE
Tel: 020 8341 2277
www.spectrumtherapy.co.uk

## Hypno-Psychotherapy

**Centre Training International School for Hypnotherapy and Psychotherapy**
145 Chapel Lane
Longton
PRESTON
PR4 5NA
Tel: 01772 617 663
peaceofmind@ukip.co.uk
www.hypnotherapy-training.com

**National College of Hypnosis and Psychotherapy**
12 Cross Street
NELSON
Lancashire
BB9 7EN
Tel: 01282 699378
hypnosis_nchp@compuserve.com
www.hypnotherapyuk.net

**National Register of Hypnotherapists and Psychotherapists**
Room B, 12 Cross Street
NELSON
Lancashire
BB9 7EN
Tel: 020 7359 6991 / 01282 716 839
Fax : 01282 698 633
nrhp@btconnect.com
www.nrhp.co.uk

**National School of Hypnosis and Psychotherapy**
28 Finsbury Park Road
LONDON
N4 2JX
Tel: 020 7354 9938 (answerphone only)
Fax: 020 7226 6963
www.n-shap-eriksonian.co.uk

## Psychoanalytic & Psychodynamic Section

**Arbours Association**
6 Church Lane
LONDON
N8 7BU
Tel: 020 8340 7646
arbours@dircon.co.uk

**Association for Group and Individual Psychotherapy**
1 Fairbridge Road
LONDON
N19 3EW
Tel: 020 7272 7013
Fax: 020 7272 6945
office@agip.org.uk
www.agip.org.uk

**Association of Independent Psychotherapists**
PO Box 1194
LONDON
N6 5PW
Tel: 020 7700 1911
referrals@aip.org.uk

**British Association of Psychoanalytic and Psychodynamic Supervision**
PO Box 419
Redhill
RH9 8DL
bapad@adbapps.freeserve.co.uk
www.supervision.org.uk

**Cambridge Society for Psychotherapy**
41 Beaulands Close
CAMBRIDGE
CB3 1JL
Tel: 01223 510 229
info@cambridge-psychotherapy.org.uk
www.cambridge-psychotherapy.org.uk

**Centre for Attachment Based Psychoanalytic Psychotherapy**
Claremont Building
24-27 White Lion Street
LONDON
N1 9PD
Tel: 020 7689 3672
capp@dial.pipex.com
www.attachment.org.uk

**Centre for Freudian Analysis and Research**
60 Ivydale Road
LONDON
SE15 3BS
Tel: 020 7640 0277
admin@cfar.demon.co.uk

**Canterbury Consortium of Psychoanalytic & Psychodynamic Psychotherapists**
Coleman House
Brookefield Avenue
DOVER
CT16 2AH
Tel: 01304 216 666
Nigel.bunker@ekentc-tr.sthames.nhs.uk

**Forum for Independent Psychotherapists**
35 Alexander Road
LONDON
N19 3PF
Tel: 020 7359 2282
info@fip.org.uk
www.fip.org.uk

**Foundation for Psychotherapy and Counselling**
607 The Chandlery
50 Westminster Bridge Road
LONDON
SE1 7QY
Tel: 020 7721 7660
office@psychotherapy-counselling.org
www.psychotherapy-councelling.org

**Group Analysis South West**
12 Sydenham Road
Bristol BS6 5SH
Tel : 0117 942 3343
Fax : 0117 942 4510
gasw@ukonline.co.uk

**Guild of Psychotherapists**
47 Nelson Square
LONDON
SE1 0QA
Tel: 020 7401 3260
Fax: 020 7401 3472
adminguild@btopenworld.com
www.guildofpsychotherapists.org.uk

**Hallam Institute of Psychotherapy**
PO Box 1098
SHEFFIELD
S20 7YQ
Hallam-institute.psychotherapy@virgin.net

**Institute of Group Analysis**
1 Daleham Gardens
LONDON
NW3 5BY
Tel: 020 7431 2693
Fax: 020 7431 7246
iga@igalondon.org.uk
www.igalondon.org.uk

**Institute of Psychotherapy and Social Studies**
76-80 Isledon Road
LONDON
N7 7LB
Tel: 020 7284 4762
Fax: 020 7281 5193
Psychotherapy Referal Service: 020 8314 1686
ipss@ipss-psychotherapy.org
www.ipss-psychotherapy.org

**Liverpool Psychotherapy Diploma Organisation**
8 Victoria Mount
Oxton
BIRKENHEAD
CH43 5TH
Tel: 0151 651 0558

**NAFSIYAT**
Anotnia House
262 Holloway Road
LONDON
N7 6NE
Tel: 020 7686 8666
Fax: 020 7686 8667
nafsiyat-therapy@supanet.com
www.nafsiyat-therapy.supanet.com

**North West Institute for Dynamic Psychotherapy**
MacCartney House, Psychotherapy Service
Beech Mount
Rochdale Road
Harpurhey
MANCHESTER
M9 1XS
Tel: 0161 203 5968
www.geocities.com/~nwidp

**Philadelphia Association**
4 Marty's Yard
17 Hampstead High Street
LONDON
N17 0BN
Tel: 020 7794 2652
paoffice@globalnet.co.uk
www.philadelphia-association.co.uk

**Severnside Institute for Psychotherapy**
11 Orchard Street
BRISTOL
BS1 5EH
Tel: 01275 333 266
Fionamcginn.sip@virgin.net
www.sipsychotherapy.org.uk

**The Site for Contemporary Psychoanalysis**
5 Russell Road
Bowes Park
LONDON
N13 4RS
Tel: 020 8482 1247
the-site@the-site.org.uk
www.the-site.org.uk

**Society of Couple Psychoanalytic Psychotherapists**
103 Tottenham Road
LONDON
N1 4EA
Tel: 020 7254 3581
Fax: 020 7249 7816
Paul.pengelly@virgin.net
www.couplepsychotherapy.co.uk

**South Trent Training in Dynamic Psychotherapy**
c/o Department of Psychotherapy
1 St Anns Road
LINCOLN
LN2 5RA
Tel: 01522 512 000
Fax: 01522 532 445

**Tavistock Marital Studies Institute**
Tavistock Clinic
120 Belsize Lane
LONDON
NW3 5BA
Tel: 020 7435 7111
Fax: 020 7435 1080
tmsi@tmsi.org.uk
www.tmsi.org.uk

**Vaughan Association of Psychodynamic Psychotherapists**
Dept of Adult Education
Vaughan College
St Nicholas Circle
LEICESTER
LE1 4LB
Tel: 01522 512 000
gail.king@cwcom.net

**West Midlands Institute of Psychotherapy**
Rooms 123-124
First Floor Gazette Buildings
168 Corporation Street
BIRMINGHAM
B4 6TF
Tel: 0121 248 4450
Fax: 0121 248 4451
admin@wmip.org
www.wmip.org

**Westminster Pastoral Foundation**
23 Kensington Square
LONDON
W8 5HN
Tel: 020 7361 4853
training@wpf.org.uk
www.wpf.org.uk

**Women's Therapy Centre**
10 Manor Gardens
LONDON
N7 6JS
Tel: 020 7263 6200
info@womenstherapycentre.co.uk
www.womenstherapycentre.co.uk

**Yorkshire Association for Psychodynamic Psychotherapy**
c/o Leeds Mind Counselling and Therapy Service
Grove Villa
82 Cardigan Road
LEEDS
LS6 3BJ
Tel: 0113 278 7300
Yapp.admin@ukonline.co.uk
www.yapp.org.uk

## Psychoanalytically Based Therapy with Children

**Association of Child Psychotherapists**
120 West Heath Street
LONDON
NW3 7TU
Tel: 020 8458 1609
Fax: 020 8458 1482
acp@dial.pipex.com

**The Caspari Foundation (Formerly FAETT)**
Caspari House
1 Noel Road
Islington
LONDON
N1 8HQ
Tel: 020 7704 1977
administrator@casparihouse.fsnet.co.uk

## Institutional Members

**Association of Counsellors and Psychotherapists in Primary Care**
Queensway House
Queensway
BOGNOR REGIS
PO21 1QT
Tel: 01243 870 701
cpc@cpc-online.co.uk
www.cpc-online.co.uk

**Tavistock Clinic**
120 Belsize Lane
LONDON
NW3 5BA
Tel: 020 7435 7111
www.tavi-port.org

**Universities Psychotherapy and Counselling Association**
PO Box 84
LOUTH
Lincs
LN11 9ND
Tel: 01507 610 746
upca@daflincs.demon.co.uk

## Special Members

**British Psychological Society**
St Andrews House
48 Princess Road East
LEICESTER
LE1 7DR
Tel: 0116 254 9568
www.bps.org.uk

**Royal College of Psychiatrists**
17 Belgrave Square
LONDON
SW1X 8PG
Tel: 020 7235 2351
rcpsych@rcpsych.ac.uk
www.rcpsych.ac.uk

## Friend of the Council

**British Association for Counselling and Psychotherapy**
BACP House
35-37 Albert Street
RUGBY
CV21 2SG
Tel: 0870 443 5252
Fax: 0870 443 5160
bacp@bacp.co.uk
www.counselling.org.uk

# Organisation Membership List

### ACAT - Association of Cognitive Analytic Therapists

Akgun, Shirley
Armson, Simon
Baker, Jackie
Barnard, Conrad
Beard, Hilary
Bende, Brigitta
Blunden, Jane
Boa, Cherry
Bristow, John
Brooks, Beverly
Buckley, Miranda
Burns-Lundgren, Eva
Calvert, Michelle
Cassidy, Sheila Anne
Choudree, Sangamithra U.D.
Clark, Dr Julia
Clarke, Susan Elizabeth
Cluley, Sarah
Cowmeadow, Pauline
Crowley, Valerie
Curran, Anna Lee
Davies, Dilys
Denman, Chess
Dunn, Mark
Dunn, Sophia
Eadie, Yvonne
Eleftheriou-Barwell, Despina
Elia, Dr Irene
Elwell, Louise
Ennis, Sally-Anne
Evans, Mark
Fawkes, Liz
Field, John Cranston
Fisher, Clare
Fosbury, Jacqueline Ann
Gardner, Philippa
Gray, Sally
Gregory, Kirby
Griffiths, Tina Carole
Harvey, Linda M
Haupts, Brigitta
Hilder, Sonia
Hubbard, Caroline
Hughes, Rose
Jellema, Anna
King, Rosalind Ann
Knight, Michael
Kuhn, Sue
Leighton, Tim
Lessem, Pauline Joey
Lettington, Liisa
Lobb, David
Low, James
Lunt, Aidan
Lynsey, Paul
Maguire, Roisin
Maple, Norma Anderson
Margison, Frank
Marlowe, Martin
McCormick, Elizabeth
Mead, Jannie
Melton, Jane
Merz, Juliet
Murphy, Carole
Nehmad, Annie
Nicholls, Hazel
Nield, Carolyn
Nuttall, Serena
O'Brien, Celia
Palgrave, Lesley
Parry, Glenys
Perry, Pamela
Plant, Victoria
Pollard, Cynthia
Reidy, Rachel
Rimer, Penelope Ann
Sackett, Kate
Scott Stewart, Mog
Sharman, Geoffrey
Sheaf, Tessa
Shyam-Ansari, Dr Shakir
Singham, Stephanie
Smith, Eva
Stevens, Yvonne J
Stowell-Smith, Mark
Tanner, Claire
Toye, Janet
Turner, Vivien
Twist, Graham
Wade, Tracy
Webster, Mark
Welch, Lawrence
West, Virginia
Whittle, Peter
Wilson, Dawn
Withers, Jacqueline M.J.
Wright, Marilyn

### ACP - Association of Child Psychotherapists

Acquarone, Stella
Akinboro-Cooper, Bobbie
Alvarez, Anne
Antonis, Phyllis
Arnold, Katherine
Balogh Henghes, Tessa
Barter, Ruth
Bender, Helen
Benjamin, Haydene
Bergese, Rebecca
Bharucha, Aiveen
Bharucha, Manek P E
Blandy, Evanthe M
Bradley, Catrin
Bradley, Jonathan
Briggs, Andrew
Britton, Julia
Brough, Sue
Buckingham, Linda
Buckland, Richard
Bungener, Janet
Calvert, Harriet B.
Cant, Diana
Case, Caroline
Cebon, Ann
Cohen, Maggie
Cohn, Nancy
Cousins, Jan
Cregeen, Simon
Crick, Verena
Crockatt, Gabrielle
Cudmore, Lynne
Cull, Rose
Cullinan, Deborah
Cummings, Celia
Dale, Francis
Davids, Jennifer
Domb, Yair
Dowling, Deirdre
Dubinsky, Alexandre
Dubinsky, Helene
Eichelberger Cleese, Alyce Faye
Elliott, Victoria
Ellwood, Jane
Emanuel, Louise
Emanuel, Ricky
Essenhigh, Caroline
Evans, Peter L.
Fallowes, Diana
Feldman, Wendy
Fleming, Robert W.K.
Gavshon, Audrey
George, Elizabeth
Grainger, Eve
Green, Viviane
Guest, Nicola
Gurion, Michal
Hadary, Gideon
Halton, William
Hamilton, Victoria
Harris, Nina
Hart, Carolyn
Harvey, Tricia A.
Heath, Christine
Helm, Caroline
Henderson, John
Henry, Rachel M.
Hering-Josefowitz, Pauline
Hermon, Deborah
Herrmann, Joan
Hilder, Alison
Hindle, Deborah
Hodges, Jill
Holland, Louise
Horne, Ann
Hunter, Margaret
Hurry, Anne
Ironside, Leslie
Jacobs, Joe
Jarvis, Charlotte
Kegerreis, Susan
Kerbekian, Rosalie
Kohon, Valli
Lanyado, Monica
Laport-Steuerman, M.
Layiou-Lignos, Effie
Likierman, Meira
Loose, Judith Green
Loxterkamp, Lorne
Luciani, Dorothy
Mack Smith, Catharine
Magagna, Jeanne
Marks, Susannah
Martin, Christine
Martin, Stephen
Mazliach, Yaron
McCann, Anita
McCartney, Meryl
McCutcheon, Moira
Mendelsohn, Annette
Miller, Lisa
Montalbetti, M.L.
Music, Graham
Netzer-Stein, Antje
Ngah, Zah
Norsa, Giuliana
Orford, Eileen
Parker, Christopher
Parker, Niki
Pecotic, Branka
Penwarden, Mary M.
Phillips, Adam
Phillips, Asha
Philps, Janet
Pick, Rachel
Piontelli, Alessandra
Porter, Christine
Power, Teresa
Pozzi, Maria E.
Proner, Barry D
Regan Jones, Columba
Reid, Susan
Renton, Mirjana
Robinson, J.G.
Robson, Christine
Roth, Priscilla
Ryz, Patsy
Schmidt-Neven, Ruth
Schnurmann, Anneliese
Segal, Barbara
Seglow, Ruth M.
Selwyn, Ruth
Shapiro, Philip
Shine, Sharon
Shuttleworth, Alan
Shuttleworth, Judy

Sinason, Valerie
Sones, Joanne
Sones, Michael
Sprince, Jenny
Spyropoulos, Nick
Steele, Miriam
Stern, Michele
Stiasny, Jennifer
Stone, Sandra
Swan Parente, Alison
Syz, Ann
Testa, Rita
Townley, Judy Rifkin
Trevatt, David
Truckle, Brian
Truckle, Shirley
Truscott, Frances
Urwin, Catherine
Usiskin, Judith
Van Heeswyk, Paul
Vas Dias, Susan
Walker, Mary J.
Warwick, Kate
Watson, Andrea
Williams, Gianna
Wilson, Jilian
Wilson, Peter
Winkley, Linda
Wood, Margarita
Woodcock, Therese
Zaphiriou Woods, Marie

**AFT - Association for Family Therapy**

Agarwala, Rosemary
Alabaster, Nigel
Allan, Brenda
Altschuler, Jenny
Andrew, Alison
Aperguis, Caroline
Appleton, Richard Lonsdale
Ardeman, Jacqueline
Armstrong, Marie Ann
Atkins, Lorna
Averbeck, Marcus
Bailey-Smith, Yvonne A
Barber, Julie
Bartlett, Andy
Bates, Helen
Beach, Roger
Belas, Patrick
Bennett, Robert
Bennun, Ian
Bentley, Radhe
Best, Richard
Biggins, Toby
Bingley Miller, Liza
Blow, Kirsten
Booth, Nick
Bott, David
Boulton, Sylvia
Bowen, Barry
Bowlby-West, Lorna
Bratley, Mary
Brazier, Anna
Brennan, Marilyn
Brinsdon, Nicholas William
Bromiley, Elspeth
Bromley, Joanne
Brough, Julie
Brown, Gillian Anne
Bryson, Sandra
Burgess, Alison
Burroughes, Christopher Henry
Burrows-Wood, Joanna
Burton, Jean
Butterfield, Alison
Butterworth, Lorna
Byng-Hall, John
Byron, Geraldine
Cade, Brian
Carney, Joanne
Carrigg, Gerrard
Challender, David
Chatham, Jon
Chilcott, Diana
Child, Melanie
Child, Nicolas John
Clark, Alec
Clegg, Jennifer Anne
Clements, Sue
Clery, Cairns
Cohen, Barbara
Colahan, Mireille
Coldicott, Tim
Collett, Gail
Cooper, Janette
Cottrell, David
Coulter, Stephen
Cox, Keith Frederick
Creedy, Katherine
Creighton, Janet
Cripps, Suzanne
Crocker, Allen John
Crowe, Michael
Cubie, Paul
Cunliffe, Rosemary Jean
Cunningham, Gerry
Curti-Gialdino, Francesca
Daniel, Karen
Daniels, Kate
Daum, Minna
Davies, Mairlis
Davies, Michael
Davis, Chris
Davren, Moira
Day, Michael
Delve, Stuart
Dixon, Marion Shirley
Donaldson, Kathy
Doolan, Moira
Duncan, Sheila
Ellingworth, Janice
Ellis, Robin Margaret
Ellis, Susan Mary
Eminson, Mary
Enser, Nigel
Eslava, Carlota
Essex, Susanne
Faull, Keith
Fellows, Ron
Fellows, Ronald Edward
Fenwick, John
Finnigan, Cathy
Fletcher, Paul
Flower, Annie
Ford, Jane Lucy
Foster, Tonia
Fox, Hugh
Fox, Sheila Margaret
Foxley, Richard
Fraser, Julie
Freeman, Patricia Ann
Fry, Richard
Fyvel, Susan
Gairdner, Wendy
Ganzleben, Jacqueline
Gaskell, Christine
Gauthier, Jean-Baptise
Geraghty, Wendy
Gerry, Marian
Gibson, Mike
Glendinning, Laura
Goldberg, Henia
Gower, Myrna
Graf, Fern
Graham, Hilary
Gray, Elizabeth
Gray, Judith
Gray, Pat
Gray, Peter
Gregory, Marilyn
Griffin, Susanne
Gustafsson, Birgitta
Hale, John
Halpin, Julia
Harmsworth, Pete
Harris, Rita
Hayward, Mark
Healey, Arlene
Hendra, Theresa
Hewitt, Amanda
Hilber, Charlotte
Hiles, Margaret
Hills, John
Hodd, Amanda
Holland, Ray
Holt, Joan
Honig, Peter
Hooper, Christine
Hudson, Peter
Hughes, Eleanor
Isaacson, Hanna
Jackson, Paul
Jackson, Rosalind
Jeffs, Graeme
Johannsson, Cessie
Johnston, Linda Ann May
Jones, Elsa
Jones, Maggy
Keane, Johanna
Kemps, Charmaine
Kenny, Marie
Kilgour, Joyce
King, Michael
Kingham Langton, Rosemary
Kissack, Debbie
Klein, Wendy T
Krause, Inga-Britt
Kuettner, Enno
Lacey, Irene
Lamont-Hoffman, Elisabeth
Lask, Judith
Launer, John
Laydon-Walters, Katrina
Lazarus, Myrna
Lea, Ian
Lee, Denis
Lees, Fiona Elizabeth
Lindsay, Robert
Lister, Ian
Loveman, Judith
Macdonald, Alasdair
Markham, Angela
Markovic, Olivera
Marriot, Alison
Marsden-Allen, Peter Harry
Marshall, Howard
Maynerd, Cynthia
McCluskey, Una
McHugh, Branwen
McMahon, Eamon
McNab, Sue
Mendelssohn, Penelope Clare
Middleton, Richard
Milton, Alison
Minhinnick, Frances
Morino, Yuriko
Moro, Julie Ann
Moulin, Laurence
Mouratoglou, Vassilis
Myers, Liora
Myers, Philip
Neden, Jeanette
Neill, Denis E.
Ness, Thomas William
Nissim, Ruth
Norman, Gilllian
Nuaimi, Christine
O'Neill, Arthur Joseph
O'Neill, Shelagh
O'Neill, Thomas
O'Toole, Andrew
Oakley, Madeleine
Owen, Mike
Papadopoulos, Renos K
Parikh, Prakash
Parsons, Barbara
Patocchi, Matilde
Patterson, Sharon
Pearson, Mark Alan
Peden, Alison
Pelissier, Kate
Pentecost, David
Perry, Belinda
Peters, Sheena
Petkova, Petia
Pocock, David
Pointon, Jane
Prestwood, Christopher

Price, Sue
Procter, Harry
Quin, Barbara
Raeside, Dominic
Rashid, Shila
Reay, Ruth
Reed, Alexander
Reibstein, Janet
Reilly, Isobel
Rivett, Mark
Robb, Melissa
Roberts, Philip
Roberts, Rosemarie
Robinson, Peter
Robinson, Sue
Roddick, Mary
Roff, Hermione
Roper Hall, Alison
Rosenwould Smith, Joanne
Routledge, Derek
Rudgley, Lisa
Rugen, Ellen
Rusling, David Michael
Rutherford, Penelope Anne
Ryan, Sandra
Sandbank, Audrey
Savage, Patrick
Sawyerr, Alice A A
Schmid-Borgschulte, Heide-Marie
Secrett, David
Seligman, Philippa
Seymour, Charlotte
Sheppard Fidler, Angela
Simmons, Gloria
Simpson, Elaine
Singh, Reenee
Smolira, David
Spender, Quentin Wynn
Stein, Yvonne
Stewart, Kate
Stratford, Jacqueline
Streeter, Elaine
Stringer, Vivien
Sykes, Margaret
Tate, Shan
Tatham, Elizabeth
Taylor, Crispin
Tennant, Duncan
Thompson, Jeannette
Thompson, Mandy
Tibbles, Paul
Toms, Moira
Tomsett, Jean
Totsuka, Yoko
Tranter, Paul
Trombaccia, Francesca R
Tumelty, Patricia
Urry, Amy
Usher, Margaret Christine
Verduyn, Christine M.
Vetere, Arlene
Vine, Mike
Wadland, Elisabeth
Wagstaff, Susan
Walker, Dawn
Walker, George
Walker, Rosalind
Walker, Steven
Wallis, Gillian
Walsh, Stuart
Warden, Jennifer
Warner, Barbara
Webster, Jeni
Weeramanthri, Tara
Weider, Bilha
Wetherell, Annette
Wheba, Raymond
Wheeler, John
White, Janet Mary
Widdowson, Erica Simone
Wigglesworth, Julia
Wilford, Gerti
Wilkinson, Mary Elaine
Williams, Graham
Williams, Thomas
Willingham, Christine
Willis, Lynne
Wood, Sally
Woods, Eleanor
Worley, Clive
Wratten, Stephen
Wray, Marie
Wright, Shelagh
Wyse, Gill
Young, Jeremy
Ziminski, Jeanne Marguerite
Zimmerman, Frankie
Zin, Shoshi

### AGIP - Association for Group and Individual Psychotherapy

Anderson, Liz
Anderson, Paul
Ariel, Seema
Astor, Bronwen
Barry, Anne
Benjamin, Joan
Breathnach, Eibhlin (Eileen)
Brown, Sara
Carritt, Sally
Caruana, Charles Victor
Casson, Isabel
Codd, Anne Marie
Cooper, Howard
Corker, Enid
Corneck, Sue
Cross, John
Cunningham, Diane J
Dacre, Winnie
Davies, Ann
Dobbs, Wendy
Doe, Anthony J
Easton, Margaret
Ellis, Sian
Fabian, Carole
Fagin, Dee
Francis, Anne M
Franke, Christine
Frazer, Diane
Freeman, Catherine
Galliers, Mary
Gardiner, Margaret
Geeson, Patricia
Good, Elizabeth
Gould, Vreni
Haine, Stephen R
Hallett, Caroline
Hamilton, Dorothy
Hamilton, Kim (Mr)
Hirst, Sue
Huish, I.P.
Humphries, Harold W A
Inlander, Antonia
Kaplan, Myron R
Kennett-Brown, Wendy
Kenny, Angela
Killpack, Louisa
Kloepfer, Irene
Kuchemann, Christine
Langdon, Monica
Leader Maynard, Carol
Lee, Graham
Leggatt, Claire
Lewis, Jo-Ann
Longley, Joan
Love, Mollie
Lyndon, Barbara
Malkin, Marion
Mauger, Benig
McAteer, Catherine
McKenzie-Smith, Bryce
McMinnies, Patricia
Mead, Betty
Miller, John Andrew
Neiva, Judith
Nesbit, Judith
Neumann, Anton
O'Callaghan, Annemarie
O'Callaghan, Diane
O'Grady, Margaret
O'Keeffe, Mandy
O'Keeffe, Tim
Pike, Joanna
Polden, Jane
Raphael-Lincoln, Francesca
Richards, Val
Ritchie, Sheila
Rogers, Anne
Ross, Mo
Rozenberg, Rosette
Russell, Hilary Jane
Sills, Ros
Silver, Anna-Mae
Siney, Sky
Soutar, Sarah
Spalding, John
Spencer, Mary
Steele, Lesley
Stephens, Lyn
Stolte, Eva
Struthers, Cassandra
Suss, Lawrence
Symons, Judith Jane
Taylor, Harvey
Thorpe, Carola
Trustam, Gillian
Ward, John
Wellings, Nigel
Wells, Lindsay James
West, Virginia
Wieland, Christina
Wildash, Sheila
Wilson, Maureen
Winter, Rachel

### AHPP - Association of Humanistic Psychology Practitioners

Abram, Vicky
Aldridge, Felicity
Alford, Sue
Antonas, Vassilis
Appel-Opper, Julianne
Batchelor, Carol
Becker, Amely
Beecher-Moore, Naona
Bell, Christine
Bowdery, Sally
Boyd, Ann A.
Braid, Rosemary
Brunt, Clare
Cahill, Pauline
Callea, Tamara
Carroll, Helen
Christophas, Sheelagh
Clarke, Simon
Cole, Barbara
Collings, Sarah
Collis, Whiz
Cooper, Rebecca
Copsey, Nigel
Coronas, Ita
Coulson, Christopher J
Crane, Kanta
Dargert, Guy
Davis, Wendy
Dell, Jacqueline
Dennison, Nishah
Eiden, Bernd
Encke, Jochen
Fee, Angie
Forster, Sally
Fox, Su
Frances, Jane
Gale, Derek
Girling, Gail
Gladstone, Guy
Glynn, Paul
Gomez, Lavinia
Graham, Judith
Gugenheim, Camilla
Gölz, Angelika
Hart, Sally
Haslam, Deirdre
Hayes, Lesley
Heiller, Birgitta R.
Hemmings, Adrian
Henriques, Marika

Hollings, Avril
Horrocks, Roger
Hughes, Linda
Jacques, Glenys
Jelfs, Martin
Johnson Smith, Camilla
Jones, Alan
Jones, Dave
Jones, David
Jordan, Elizabeth
Kalisch, David
Kennedy, Kay
Kershaw, Jennifer
Keshet-Orr, Judi
Kirby, Babs
Kowszun, Graz
Laffy, Cabby
Lamb, Geoff
Lawton, Derek
Le'Surf, Anne
Leder, Catherine
Leygraf, Bernd C
Linnell, Maxine
Lude, Jochen
Luthy, Barbara
March-Smith, Rosie
McMinn, Les
Meekums, Bonnie
Mellett, Jane
Mitchell, Richard
Morris, Elizabeth
Morris, Lesley Anne
Newbery, Christopher
Nippoda, Yuko
Noack, Miké
O'Callaghan, Mary
O'Scanlain, Peadar
Offer, Leah
Owens, Patti
Parker, Mary
Payne, Helen
Pimentel, Edna Barreto
Preisinger, Kristiane
Raisbeck, Linde
Reynolds, Alun
Rosen, Sacha
Rowan, John
Rugeley, Brenda
Ryley, Brigitte
Salisbury, Claire
Schembri, Veronica
Scott, Tricia
Sell, Patrick
Smith, Jonathan
Soloway, Clare
Speyer, Josefine
Springwood, Bee
Stanley, Annie
Stewart, Lindsey
Stow, Doug
Sullivan, Anita
Taylor, Louise
Tudor, Keith
Tune, David
Twelvetrees, Heidy
Veale, Maurice
Ward, Shirley
Waterston, John
Westland, Gill
Whitton, Eric
Wilson, Gina
Wooder, Bernard
Woolliscroft, Jenny
Woolliscroft, Jessica
Young, Courtenay

**AIP - The Association of Independent Psychotherapists**

Ashwin, Mary
Chisholm, Lisa
Clements, Iris
Crace, Gay
Davy-Barnes, Malcolm
Debenham, Jane
Edwards, Brian
Everest, Pauline
Friedrich, Stephen
Gerhardt, Sue
Goodman, Diana
Gross, Stephen
Henderson, David
Lakeman Fraser, Judith
Lockett, Arthur
McKenzie-Smith, Bryce
Muller, Nina
Myers, Dania
Newbigin, Alison
Outram, Jo
Panetta-Crean, Simona
Pearson, Jenny
Perry, Ann
Richards, Val
Ruijterman, Caroline
Shearer, Ann
Sherman, Arthur
Shivakumar, H.
Shooter, Lesley
Stadlen, Anthony
Taylor, Alan
Weeden, Ruth
Wellings, Nigel
Wells, Lindsay James
Whan, Michael
Wright, Jason

**AJA - Association of Jungian Analysts**

Bamber, James
Bell, Frances
Bierschenk, John Henry
Boll, Antonia
ByGott, Catherine
Casement, Ann
Cashford, Jules
Culliford, Penny
Davide, Adele
Doorley, Damien
Duckworth, Moira
Falk, Helen
Finlay, Rosalind
Forssander, Jennifer
Freeman, Rabbi David
Goss, Phil
Hall, Keven
Harrison Mayor, Susan
Heuer, Gottfried
Johnson, Deirdre
Maitra, Begum
Mathers, Dale
McCarthy, Rita
McLean, Julienne
Millar, Peter
Miller, John
Miller, Juliet
Mulhern, Alan
Niesser, Arthur
Noack, Amelie
Norton, Lynda
Palmer Barnes, Fiona
Riley, Sue
Robinson, Martin
Silverman, Carl M.
Spilios, Joanne
Spitzer, Shayne
Stokes, Jean
Stone, Martin
Stuart, Gillian
Syrett, Karin
Travis, Mary
Wainwright, Richard
Williams, Chris
Windle, Ruth

**ARBS - Arbours Association**

Bartlett, Neill
Berke, Joseph H
Berry, Sally
Borthwick, Rosemary
Bradshaw, Thomas Owen
Buckley, Nicky
Budnick, Susan
Burch, Nigel
Cairns, Mary
Cameron, Anna
Cameron, Roderick
Cave, Prue
Child, Rachel
Clancy, Pauline
Davey, Stephen
Dewsbery, Sarah
Dianin, Gianni
Dyehouse, Pat
Ehlers, Hella
Elliott, Lois
Ertelt, Sylvia
Fagan, Margaret
Febrer-Bowen, Ines
Fisher Norton, Jane
Forti, Laura
Gavin, Bea
Ginkell, Andreas
Goodes, Deborah
Grant, Bob
Grant, Iona
Green, Margaret
Greenwood, John
Haberlin, Jane
Hacker, Roger
Harward, Matthew
Holt, Alexandra
Ibanez, Julian
Kelly, Bridget
Kelly, Michael
Kleanthous, Dina
Kleinot, Pamela
Lanczi, Katalin
Letley, Emma
Mak-Pearce, George
Masoliver, Chandra
McAndrew, Brigitte
Milroy, Rachel
Montero, Isabel
Navarro, Trinidad
Nevill, Stuart
Oley, Mary
Pavincich, Lesley
Payne, Lizzi
Pericleous, Christine
Perriollat Munro, Elisabeth
Phillips, Marianne
Pick, Geoffrey
Powell, Angela
Rabe, Marie-Louise
Ravensdale, Verity
Reguis, Marie-Christine
Rose, Sally
Ryan, Geraldine
Ryan, Tom
Sabath, Martin Edmund Francis
Sabbadini, Andrea
Schaedel, Maggie
Schatzman, Morton
Schonfield, Tamar
Seu, Bruna Irene
Smith, Peter
Solemani, Hannah
Stokeld, Alasdair
Sveinsdóttir, Björg
Swan, Adrienne
Turner, Diana
Valea, Ana
Valentine, Marguerite
Veje, Margit
Wach, Karin Marie
Waddy, Melanie
Waterfield, Hilary
Whittle, Lorna
Whittle, Sonia J

**AREBT - Association for Rational and Emotive Behaviour**

Blackburn, John
Dabor, Thelma
Davies, Angela
Dryden, Windy
Emmans, Noreen

Philomena
Mathews, Trevor J.
Neenan, Michael
Palmer, Stephen
Ruddell, Peter
Saunders-Ward, Pam
Wallace, Edward
Williams, Dorothee

**BABCP - British Association for Behavioural & Cognitive Psychotherapies**

Adams, John
Alderton, Chris
Alexander, Barbara
Alexander, Paul T.
Altman, Michelle M
Amies, Peter
Ashcroft, Jennifer
Ashton, Peter
Bactawar, Charles D.
Baker, David
Barnes, Pam
Barry, Keith
Bassam, Bruce
Beach, Jan D.
Beech, Julie C.
Beese, Angela G.
Bell, Lydia J.
Bem, M
Bennett, Gerald A.
Bienkowski, Geraldine
Black, Alastair R J
Black, Nicholas J.
Blackburn, Ivy-Marie
Blowers, Colin M.
Bond, Frank W
Bonham, Elizabeth
Box, Kay
Brady, Alec
Brady, Carol
Brady, Peter
Breninek, Andrea
Bright, Jenifer A
Brock, Martin J
Brooke, Paul
Brooks, John
Brosan, Lee
Brown, Antony
Brown, Thomas M.
Buet Gonzalez, Silvia
Burbach, Frank
Burgess, Mary
Burland, Roger
Bury, Dennis R.
Butcher, Gerard
Butler, Gillian
Butler, Linda
Cameron, Michael John
Campbell Hughes, Patricia
Capuzzo, Nicoletta
Cariapa, Illana
Chalkley, A.J.
Chapman, Jane
Childs-Clarke, Adrian
Chipman, Tina Louise
Christianson, Donna
Christie, Marilyn
Christy, Jackie
Church, John
Churchill-Moss, Duncan
Clarke, Isabel
Clarke, Stephen Lawrence
Clarke, Susan Elizabeth
Cogan, Margaret
Cohen, Ruth
Coit, Frank James
Collard, Patrizia C
Connolly, Moira
Constantinou, Daniel
Cooper, Heather
Cooper, Virginia
Copley, Brian
Cowdrill, Vivia A.
Cox, Deborah A
Cresswell, Maxine
Crichton, N
Cromarty, Paul
Cromey, Terry
Cross, Susan
Crossley, David
Crowe, Michael
Cullen, Anne M.
Cullington, Anne
Curwen, Bernadette
Cuthbert, V. M.
D'Arcy, Fiona
Dabor, Thelma
Daly, Kevin
Damani, S
Dardenne, Patricia
Darongkamas, Jurai
Davidson, Dorothy
Davidson, John
Davies, Angela
Davies, Ann Dorothy Maitland
Davies, John
Davies, Stephen
Davis, Brenda
Davis, Paul E.
Dawson, Roger
Day, Melanie
De Souza, Janice
Deeble, Elizabeth A.
Denford, Lindsey D.
Dhillon, Manjit
Dodd, Harry
Doggart, Elizabeth Anne
Dolan, Lesley Catherine
Dollery, Jayne
Dovey, Alan
Downes, Vanessa Susan
Draper, J
Draycott, Christine
Drijver, Caroline
Drummond, Lynne M
Dryden, Windy
Dummett, Nicola J.
Dunks, Kathryn
Dyer, Ian P.
Eastham, Peter
Eastman, Rachel
Edeleanu, Andrea K
Edmonstone, Yvonne G.
Ekers, David
Elliott, Peter
Elliott, Sandra A.
Elson, Monica
Emery, Judith
Evans, Jenny
Fairbanks, Arthur
Farley, Nancy M.
Farrell, Derek P.
Fearns, Keith
Fearnside, Derek
Fernandez, Nigel R.
Fieldman, George
File, Sharon
Findley, Patricia
Finlayson, Sara
Finnerty, Margaret E
Fisher, Linda
Fitzsimmons, Michele Anne
Flanagan, June D
Fleming, Nicola G.
Fokias, Dene
Forsyth, Angus
Fowler, Barry
Francis, Denise
Freeman, Christopher
Frize, Graham
Fulford, Ann
Garcia-Llavona, Cristina M
Gardiner, Brenda
Garvey, Rachel
Gilboy, Carol A.
Gill, Jennifer
Gillespie, Kate
Gillingham, Michael
Gimblett, Jeanne
Glaister, Brian
Gournay, Kevin
Graham, Vera
Grant, Alec John
Gray, Maggie
Greenan, Maria
Greenfield, Terence Aubrey
Griffiths, John
Grover, Miriam Ruth
Halford, Ann
Hall, Deborah
Handley, Christine
Handrick, Olaf
Handy, S.
Hanley, Ian G.
Hardy, Joanne
Harrild, Sandra M.
Harrington, Finola
Harrington, Rufus
Harris, Paul David Gwyn
Hart, Kate
Hart, Robin
Hendry, Evelyn R.
Herbert, Claudia
Herdman, Linda
Hetherton, Jacquie
Hirsch, Regina
Hollywood, Helena
Holyoak, Patricia
Hook, Susan
Hooper, Molly
Howard, Caroline Pui
Hume, Anne J.A.
Humphreys, A-L.
Huszcza, Anna K.
Ibison, Janet M.
Iljon Foreman, Elaine
Isaac, Vivien
Isaacs, Glenys
Isles, Rosaleen
Jackson, Christopher
Jenkins, Dinah
Jiah, Hildah
Jones, Christopher S
Jones, K R
Jones, Rhiannon Marie
Joseph, Jerome Devakumar
Keen, John
Keenan, Paul Stephen
Kendal, Susan J.
Kennedy, Fiona C
Kerry, Richard
Kincey, John
Kolb, Peter John
Kunkler, Jane
Kwei, Caryl Lesley
Lacey, Tim
Laher, Aftab
Lanza, Pamela
Lau, Bernard Wai Kai
Lawlor, Elizabeth
Lawson, Ruth
Lee-Evans, Michael
Levy, Gillian
Lewis, Ken
Liebing-Wilson, Marianne
Lillie, Francis
Lipsedge, Catherine
Lister, Patricia Anne
Livanou, M.
Long, Clive G.
Long, Jennifer
Longman, R L
Loumidis, K
Lux, Julius
MacGillivray, J. Lorna
MacGregor, Alan M
Mackie, Lynn
Macklin, Glen
Macnicol, Annie
Maillard, Annie M
Malkin, Julius
Manson, Greg
Marien, Brian
Marshall, Lindsey
Martin, Tim
Mason, Peter J.
Mathews, Trevor J.
Matthews, Helen P.
Matthews, Linda

May, Adam
McAllister, Christopher
McAlpine, A M
McCarron, Gerard
McCarthy-Hoffbauer, Iris
McConnochie, Charlie
McFadden, Hugh E.
McFarlane, Alison M.
McGoldrick, Mary
McGrath, Adrian
McGroary-Meehan, Maureen
McKay, Molly
McKenna, Jacqueline
McKenny, Anne
McLeod, Terry
McMahon, Gladeana
McMaster, Catherine
McMurray, Marjorie C.
Meldrum, Ron
Mettam, Lisa
Middlehurst, Daniel
Millard, Maureen
Mills, Nigel
Mollahan, L. G.
Molleson, John Ivitsky
Moloney, Paul
Moore, Carol
Moorey, Stirling
Moorhead, Steve
Morgan, Guy
Morley, Michael
Morris, Gillian
Morris, Peter A.
Morrissey, Shirley A
Morton, Richard Victor
Moutzoukis, Chris
Moyes, Theresa
Munro, Angela
Murphy, Patricia A.M.
Nadirshaw, Zenobia
Nath, Krish
Neenan, Michael
Newell, Adrian
Newton, Brian Samuel
Noyes, Elizabeth
Ntarili, Kassandra-Maria
O'Carroll, Madeline
O'Kelly, Jackie
O'Neill, Helen M.
O'Regan, Emma
Owen, Lynne M.
Palanisamy, Shan
Palmer, Stephen
Parrack, Norma
Pattinson, Philip
Peckitt, R.G.
Perera, Ajit
Phillips, Thomas Lambton
Pickelin, Ulrike
Pidd, Gregory
Pittman, Karen
Plant, Barbara
Platts, June Elizabeth
Pollitt, Mo
Prempeh Adu Bobi, Henry K.
Price Jones, Daniel
Procter, Sue
Purchase-Walker, Anne
Pusztai, Edit E.
Quarry, Andrew
Quinn, Paul
Randall-Vining, Morgan
Rani, R S
Reading, Clive
Reeves, Thomas
Regel, Stephen
Rennie, Belinda
Renshaw, Julia
Rice, Paul
Rickard, Ian
Ricketts, Thomas N.
Ridgeway, Nicola Louise
Ridgway, Jane
Rimmer, Linda M.
Rishiraj, Narinder S
Ritson, Louise
Robertson, Isobelle
Robertson, Judith Ann
Robinson, Ferga
Robinson, Peter
Rogers, Jonathan
Rooney, Helen
Rose, Stuart
Ross, Gill
Ross, Michael Killoran
Ross, Susan M.
Rouhifar, Zhila
Ruddell, Peter
Ryan, Frank
Sabatelli, Peter John
Sagaran, Stephen
Sage, Nigel A.
Salter, Audrey J
Schakel, Hildegard
Scott, Michael
Scott Chinnery, Jean M
Scully, Dee
Sellers, Carolyn
Serfaty, Marc A.
Serieys, Nicholas Michael
Shah, E.M.
Sharman, Sally
Sharpe, Tracey
Shaw, Elizabeth
Shawe-Taylor, Metka
Sheldon, Brian
Shortall, Thomas R.
Siddle, Ronald
Silman, Chris
Simpson, Peter
Slaney, Ruth
Sloan, Graham
Smail, Richard
Smith, Hilda C.
Smith, Nicola
Smith, R.L
Smith, Trevor E.L.
Soole, Trevor
Spada, Marcantonio
Stallard, Paul
Stalmeisters, Dzintra
Standart, Sally H
Stevens, Penny
Stewart, Henry B.
Stewart, Lisa
Stewart, Phil
Still, Arthur
Stolear, Meir
Stromberg, Marla J
Sutton, Elizabeth
Switzer, Fiona
Szymanska, Kasia (Y.L.C)
Tatham, Alan
Taylor, Carolyn D W
Taylor, Jon
Taylor-Davies, Mary
Tennison, John F.S.
Thomas, Carmel
Thornton, Maria A.
Thrasher, Sian
Till, Patricia
Timmann, S.
Todd, Gillian
Tolchard, Barry
Tone, Yvonne
Toole, Stuart
Townend, Michael
Townsend, Pat
Toyer, Malcolm
Trelease, P.
Tse, Claude
Tubbs, I.A.
Turkington, Douglas
Turnbull, Dheeresh Charles
Turner, Avril
Venki, Malathi
Verduyn, Christine M.
Waddington, Louise
Walsh, Belinda
Walsh, Ken
Wang, Michael
Wardley, Jean
Watts, Susan
Westley, Andrew
Westman, Stephen
Wheatley, Malcolm
Wheeler, Judith
Whitaker, Kim
Whiteley, Christopher M.
Whitfield, Graeme
Wilday, Sharon
Willetts, Dean
Williams, Christopher John
Williams, Dorothee
Williams, K.A.
Williams, Ruth M.
Williams, Steve
Wills, Frank
Wilson, Mary
Wiltshire, Gill
Withers, Jacqueline M.J.
Wright, Christine M.J.
Wymbs, Patrick
Wynn, Michelle
Yates, Alison
Young, Katherine
Zagorska, Joan Krystyna
van Bilsen, Henck P.J.G.
van Bilsen, Lynne

## BAS - British Autogenic Society

Benor, Ruth
Bird, Jane
Butler, John
Callea, Tamara
Cuff, Jenny
Diamond, Vera
Edwards, Ben
Free-Pearce, Carolyn
Greene, Alice
Ingham, Nida
Kanji, Nasim
Lorenz, Bernice
Marsh, Colin
Marshall, Janet
Reuvid, Jennie
Ross, Ian
Saunders, Sonia
Swinden, Penni

## BASRT - British Association for Sexual and Relationship Therapy

A Whelan, The Rev'd FR P Warwick
Ackroyd, Elaine
Ackroyd, Rosemary
Angold, Mrs Monica
Arnold, Brian
Atwell, Rosemary Anne
Ball, Derek
Barker, Janet
Barnes, Tricia
Barringer, Jan
Batchelor (Mrs), Henrietta
Beer, Charmian
Beighton, Chris
Berger, Iris
Birchard, Thaddeus
Blum, Anita
Boddington, Daphne
Borghgraef, Dr Guy
Bown, Terry
Bradish, Hazel
Breeze, Linda
Brewster, Marnie
Brown, Avril
Bryans, Sally
Buchan, Ian
Buck, Carol
Buckler, Jackie
Burch, Jean
Butcher, Josie
Byng, Rosemary
Carter, Christine
Carter, Paula
Chalcraft, Helen
Chopin, Mathias

Clark, Diane
Clayton, Kate
Clements-Jewery, Sue
Clifton, Sandra
Clowes, Brenda
Coats, Elizabeth
Collings, Sarah
Collins, Jane
Cooper, Grahame F.
Cooper, Penny
Crowe, Michael
Cullum, Sylvia
Curtis, Debra
Cybulska, Dr Beata Adriana
Daines, Brian
Daniel, Ishbel
Dardenne, Patricia
Davis, Mrs Rosemary
Dighton, Rosemary
Dixon, John
Dodsworth, Evelyn
Duncan, Sally B
Dyer, Paula
Edwards, Kareen
Eisen, Mrs Shelley
Eisler, Z
Emeleus, Frances
Evans, Gail
Evans, Noeleen
Evans, Tricia
Firth, Mr Malcolm Thomas
Ford, Vicki
Fraser, Mrs Bobbie
Gage, Mike
Gann, Sandra Y
Gaynor, Donal F
Gibbin, Jane
Goldman, John
Goss, Diana
Gower, Barry
Grant, Núala
Gray, Rebecca
Green, Pippa
Gregory, Peter
Griffin, Dr M
Griffiths, C A
Guilfoyle, John Francis
Gurr, Mrs R
Hall, Paula
Hallam-Jones, Ruth
Hanrahan, Josephine
Harris, Frances
Harrison, Caroline M
Harrison, Susan
Hayes, Cheryl
Headon (PH D), Christopher F
Heath, Suzanne
Helps, Davina
Henderson, Anne
Hendrickse, Begum
Hewitt, Rosalind
Heyward, Julie
Hill, Brenda
Hillman, Jan
Hobbs, Anita
Hobbs, Kevin
Holland, Anthony R
Hollingworth, Amanda
Holt, Colin A
House, Mrs Wyn
Howarth, Kay
Hudson-Allez, Dr Glyn
Huish, Margot
Huws, Rhodri
Jackson, Dr Paul
Jennings-Nicol, Sara
Jess, Carrie
Johnston, Candace
Johnston, Di
Jones, Dr Caroline M
Jones, Judith
Keshet-Orr, Judi
Kirkland, Denise
Kirkpatrick, M.J.
Kundu, Dr Arabinda
Lamb, Janice
Law, Anne M
Law, Annie
Lawrence, Elisabeth
Leach, Mark J
Leonard, Mary E
Leygraf, Bernd C
Lidster, Wendy
Linford, Richard J
Lipsith, Josie
Lobb-Rossini, Karen
Lobel, Sandra
Logue, Nancy
Long, Angela
Loudon, Mrs Julia B
Low, James
Major, Ammanda
Malone, Sue Germaine
Martin, Angela
Massil, Dr Helen
Maxwell, Sue
May, Kathryn
May, Mrs Jennifer
Mayhew, Richard
McGroary-Meehan, Maureen
McKinnon, Sophia
McNaught, Janet
McSherry, Loraine
Miller, Edna
Miller, Jean
Milton MSc, Sylvia
Mitchell, Ruth
Moncur, Pamela
Moore, Jill
Moore, Meg
Morgan, Elizabeth
Morrison, Sandra
Mulvey, Josephine
Murray, Linda
Nelson, Denise
O'Mahony, Angela
Openshaw, Sally
Pacey, Susan
Pallenberg, Sue
Papé, Maureen
Perring, Dr Michael
Perry, Janet
Phillips, Mary
Pollock, Jo
Pouteaux (Mrs), Diana
Preston, Dr John
Proudley, Helen G
Pryde, Nia
Pullen, Caroline
Ramage, Margaret
Read, Jane
Read, Linda
Reader, Fran
Rendall, Davina
Richards, Mrs Maureen V
Richardson, Caroline
Richardson, Gillian
Richardson, Madeleine
Richardson, Sylvia
Ridley, Jane
Riley, Jacqueline
Rix, Mrs Sandy
Rosen, Mrs Judith
Roy, Jane
Ryan, Dr Elizabeth
Sandelson, Jennifer
Sanders, Gill
Scott, Liz
Serpell, Vivienne
Seymour, Jane
Shaw, Sue
Shelley, Dr Trevor
Sheppard, Caren
Simpson, Richard
Sliw, Mrs Regina
Snowden, Patricia
Soultani, Effie
Sparks, Mrs Rebecca
Stainsby, Jacki
Stow, Doug
Struthers, Morag
Symes, Jan
Taylor, Mrs Jane
Tharp, David
Thoburn MBE, Marj
Thomas, Jenny
Tomlinson, Moya
Tunwell, Ann
Turner, Judith C
Vora, Valerie
Wallace-Smith, Nigel
Wallis, Valerie
Ward, Keltie
Warwick, Heather
Wells, Peter
West, Dr Elizabeth
Westphal, Joy
Wheeley, Eleanor
Wilson, Llynwen
Wilson, Norman
Woddis, Helena
Wood, Mrs L M
Wylie, Dr Kevan
Yates, Andrew F.J.
Yawetz, Mrs Christine
de Groot, Marianne
de Marquiegui, Dr Asun
von Buhler, J M A Herbert Pardo

**BCPC - Bath Centre for Psychotherapy and Counselling**

Adams, Sue
Ballantyne, Jacki
Barrett, Julie
Bielenky, Marina
Bruce, Sue
Burston, Helen
Catton, Derek
Collis, Whiz
Dewey, George
Douglas, Sue
Fairbairns, Sarah
Feilden, Tish
Foster, Lesley
Graham, Margaret
Groves, Stephanie
Haase-Derrett, Susan
Hackett, Jenny
Hall, Kelvin
Handy, Susan
Hart, Ellen
Hastings, Jon
Hastings, Kim
Hicks, Jan
Labworth, Yig
Lacy-Smith, Jo
Llewelyn, Billie
Luthy, Barbara
March-Smith, Rosie
Maslen, Gill
Mayne, Rob
McCorkindale, Jan
Mellett, Jane
Mills, Christopher
Milton, Thelma
Moore, Alan
Moravia Kessel, Inge
Moser, Marianne
Naydler, Nick
Newbery, Christopher
Orton, Jane
Parsons, Mick
Purkiss, Jane
Redington, Heather
Rodman, Fiona
Roth, Ruth
Sawers, Martin
Scholefield, Miranda
Selby, Anne
Shaw, Annie
Simmons, Alison R.
Slattery, David
Smith, Hilary Frances
Thomas, Penny
Tracy, Colin
Valentine, Christine
Vaughan, Victoria
Voelcker, Cara
Vogel, Karin
Walker, Jan

Wheway, John Kirti
Wilbraham, Daphne
Williams, Jan
Wilson, Jim

**BPA - British Psychodrama Association**

Adderley, Diane
Aguirregabiria, Ana
Baim, Clark
Bannister, Anne
Barton, Alan
Batten, Francis
Bellamy, Malka
Biancardi, Jenny
Bird, Margaret
Bould, Jane
Branagan, Noelle
Brandwood, Pat
Brown, Teresa
Brown Douglas, Lucinda
Casson, John
Chesner, Anna
Costa, Beverley
Costa, Jan
Coupe, Alyson
Crone, Ms Joni
Dale, Carole
Daniels, Mo
Davenport, Hilary
Davis, Edna
Dazeley, Jen Fiona
Dillon, Annot
Eldridge, Melanie
Farmer, Christopher
FitzGerald, Pen
Foxgold, Sheila
Gill, Ali
Gill, Martin
Green, Lynette
Grieve, Sandra
Hagelthorn, Christina
Halmarack, Philip
Haworth, Peter
Hickmott, Barbara
Howell, Julia
Huntington, Annie
Hutchinson, Peter
Jefferies, J.I.
Karp, Marcia
Kay, Malcolm
Kirk, Catharine Rose
Kirkpatrick, Ian
Kjellstrom, Laila
Langley, Dorothy
Lea, Tan
Lee, Debbie
Leeson, Julie
Levens, Mary
Littledale, Nadine
Lousada, Olivia
Luxmoore, Nick
MacNeill, Enid
Maxwell, Hugh
Metcalf, Jenni
Miller, Sarah
Munsey, Jon
Murray, Catherine
Pregnall, Sheila
Queening, Vanessa
Quin, Barbara
Rawlinson, Lynn
Richman, Sheila
Ruscombe-King, Gillie
Salisbury, Jonathan F. H.
Scanlan, Celia
Simmons, Alison R.
Singh, Tony
Smith, Gail P
Sprague, Ken
Taylor, Susie
Thompson, Jean Mary
Thomson, Simon
Tregear, Barbara
Turkié, Janine
Walsh, Stuart
Wheadon, Sylvia
White, Eve
Widlake, Bernard C.
Wooding, Sandy
Wright, Maureen

**BPS - British Psychological Society**

Boysan, Zehra
Bristow, John
Coule, Jaqueline
Dardenne, Patricia
Davies, Dilys
Hall, Joan
Jacobson, Rosemary
Sharman, Geoffrey

**CAP - The Confederation of Analytical Psychologists**

Addison, Ann
Ashley, Anne
Balance, Gillian
Beddington, Jenny
Benwell, Jennifer
Blackie, Suzanne
Bravesmith, Anna
Bruce, Ann
Carr, Jean
Chapman, Sandy
Comins, Jayne
Crowther, Catherine
Darrell, Linda
Dennison, Paul
Duckham, Jennifer
Dunbar, Gill
Dunstan, Gina
Fell, Angela
Gardiner, Vicki
Goodman, Susan
Hammond, Margaret
Harris, Dianne
Hart, Robert
Hauke, Christopher
Herst, Edward
Hewison, David
Hughes, William
Hutchison, Eric
Hutton, Francoise
Katzman, Stewart
Lee, Joan Mary
Lynch, Maria
MacKenna, Christopher
Marcus, Marietta
Marshallsay, Nicholas
Masani, Peter
Masters, Alison
Mathers, Carola
Muffet, Ruth
Newman, Adam
Panetta-Crean, Simona
Patience, Elizabeth
Perry, Christopher
Philo, Judith
Pickles, Penny
Priestley, John
Redfearn, Joseph
Reed, Keith
Richardson, Elizabeth
Samuels, Andrew
Schaverien, Joy
Schmidt, Martin
Sharifi, Pury
Shivakumar, H.
Smith, Norah
Steffens, Dorothy
Thackray, Dayle
Thomas, Kerry
Thomson, Jean
Walline, Sandra
West, Marcus
Williams, Averil
Wilson, Catherine
Woodhead, Judith M
Wright, Susanna
Young, Anne
de Hoogh-Rowntree, Patricia

**CAPP - Centre for Attachment - Based Psychoanalytic Psychotherapy**

Adams, Janet
Aleksic, Sonya
Ashley, Stephen
Ashton, Barbara
Ball, Rebekah
Barker, Gina
Berger, Sue
Beveridge, John
Bucknall, Valerie
Callaway, Hazel
Carter, Clare
Christopher, Elphis
Cohen, Pat
Colvin, Naomi
Cundy, Linda
Davies, Judy
Davis, Cascia
Davis, Emerald
Enever, Andrew
Erskine, Judith
Evans, Christine
Forman, Sally
Gill, Richard
Henry, John
Hertzmann, Leezah
Holland, Stevie
Hughes, Hatty
Hurst, Hannah
Husband, Chris
Jack, Sarah
Jolliffe, John
Kahr, Brett
Kenny, Miranda H.
Landaw, John
Landi, Donatella
Laschinger, Bernice
Leach, Victoria
Linington, Mark
London, Elizabeth
MacAdam, Gregor
Marsh, Jane
McBride, Nigel
McMillan, Penny
Michael, Jess
Miller, Bob
Miller, Penny
Mitson, Catherine
Odgers, Andrew
Park, James
Parker, Caroline
Parkinson, Jane
Pearman, Cathy
Pollard, James
Power, Anne
Purnell, Christopher
Raicar, Alexandra Maeja
Rao, Ms Varija
Renn, Paul
Richardson, Sue
Riddell, Jenny
Robertson, Jo
Rubie, Val
Ryan, Jane
Sachs, Adah
Schwartz, Joseph
Simmonds-Jones, Arlene
Singer, Iris
Southgate, John
Straupmanis, Helen
Thompson, Thea
Traylen, Hilary
Vas Dias, Susan
White, Kate
Wingfield, Rachel
Woodward, Joan
Wootton, Jenny
Wright, Laurie Jo

**CCBP - Chiron Centre for Body Psychotherapy**

Ablack, Joanne
Asheri, Shoshi
Barmes, Sally
Blair, George
Boening, Joachim
Boening, Michaela
Brockwell, Badger
Browne, Maureen
Carroll, Roz
Chadwick, Mary
Chipperfield, Dianne
Cooper, Suzanne
Cowell, Judy
Coxwell-White, Jenny
Cusack, Anne
Dosanjh, Charanjit
Drewnowska, Alicja
Dunlop, Joan
Eiden, Bernd
Elliott, Dena
Gaster, Yishai
Gerbrands, Kardien
Gilmore, Jane
Gray, Gay
Harries, Rashida
Hedinger-Farrell, Korinna
Heitzler, Morit
Henderson, Ned
Hills, Janet
Holland, Ray
Holmes, Lynne
Kelly, Gillian
Kidd, Vicky
Kokott, Claudius
Landale, Margaret
Law, Susan
Lockie, Gisela
Lude, Jochen
M. Petrie, Julie
Macnicol, Fred
Magriel, Nicolas
Mather, Janine
Mathews, Micheal
McCrohan, Denise
McEvoy, Liz
McNulty, Annie
Millar, Wilma
O'Sullivan, Sheila
Pervöltz, Rainer
Preisinger, Kristiane
Procter, Sue
Pugh, Anna
Reynolds, Alun
Roberts, Jennifer
Rose, Russell
Schaible, Monika
Sell, Patrick
Sood, Punam
Soth, Michael
Speyer, Josefine
Spiller, Beverly
Stauffer, Kathrin
Staunton, Tree
Stevenson, Bruce
Stracey, Amarilla
Tristram, Sue
Tune, David
Waterston, John
Weaver, Ziva
Westland, Gill
Williams, Steve

**CCOPPP - Canterbury Consortium of Psychoanalytic and Psychodynamic Psychotherapists**

Anderson, Tony
Andrews, Ruth
Ashton, Carole
Bardelle-Carrier, Rosemary
Blake, Penny
Bunce, Maureen
Bunker, Carol
Bunker, Nigel
Cairns, Mary
Carey, Jean
Casey, Aideen
Clift, Lynda
Cronin, Jeremiah
Cunningham, Diane J
Darnley, Hazel
Devereux, Dawn
Dewhirst, Elisabeth
Double, Veronica
Hirons, Ruth
Hughes, Jennifer
Jeffries, V. Kiki
Jones, Deborah
Kontostergiou, Theodora Nora
Lanczi, Katalin
Lawrence, Sandra
Leeper, Rob
Leonard, Avril
Lepper, Georgia
Lewis, Penny
Lomax, Vivien
Mann, David
Martin, Suzanne
Matadeen, Dev' Yasdeo
McAndrew, Brigitte
McLewin, Ali
Nazif, Mahin Golbandi
Nice, Terence
O'Brien, Sally
Pannell, Penelope
Reading, Bill
Reilly, Anne
Riding, Ann
Riding, Nick
Roberts, Jane
Robinson, Jane
Robson, Annie
Schaedel, Maggie
Scrivener, Amanda E.
Shaw, Maureen
Spiliopoulos, Valentine Andrikopoulos
Thomason, June
West, Helen
West, Linden
Wilkinson, Susan

**CCPE - Centre for Counselling & Psychotherapy Education**

Aldred, Sue
Alferoff, Tamara
Allen, Valerie
Anderson, Jette
Andrews, Ulla
Arbia, G. Nicoletta
Archutowska, Jane
Askew, Mary
Atkinson, Debbee
Attias, Sandra
Averbeck, Jennifer
Avery, Trisha
Bartlett, Olivia
Basharan, Harika
Beech, Trevor
Bennis, Jackie
Bernard, Beverley
Beton, Linda
Bhatia, Pushan
Bilder, Tessa
Blockley, Kate
Bond, Lesley
Brayne, Mark
Brittain, Charlie
Broughton, Helen
Bryant, Roger
Buirski, Diana
Burkhardt, Tansen I
Burrows, Leslely
Button, Rachel
Byrne, Patricia
Cain, Dennis
Cantelo, Frances
Carlson, Theresa
Carrington, Linda
Casares, Jonathan
Casey, Jan
Charles MA, Debbie
Charley, Geoff
Christie, Patricia A.
Clark, Corah
Clesham, Lilian
Clifford MA, Barry
Collins, Ann
Courtney, Jan
Creamer, Mary
Cummins MA, Kate
D'Costa, Fjona
Dale, Tim
Dann, Lois
Dawson, Peter
Deaville, Debra
Dennehy, Carmel
Denvir, Hazel
Desmond, Hanora
Dobb, Cornelia
Doherty, Jackie
Donald, Philippa
Doulton MA, Caroline
Duffield, Ruth
Durban, Ann
Economidou, Nitsa
Emm, Susan
Evans, Dorice
Fentiman, John
Ferguson, Joyce
Ferguson MA, Peter
Fitzgerald-Klein, Marianne
Flower, Charles
Forssander, Jennifer
Fraser, Daphne
Fraser, Sonia
Gaunt, Pamela
Gollins, Joanna
Golten, Carole
Gregg, Annzella
Griffiths, Pamela
Griffiths, Thelma
Gruber, Angela
Hagenbach, Keith
Hagenbach, Kitty
Hamilton, Nigel
Hamilton, Susan
Hanman, Elke
Hanna, Gilli
Harber-Kelly, Andrea
Harper, Anita
Harrel, Julia
Harris, Jonathan
Harvey, Angelia
Haskins, Nicola
Hassain, Alan
Hay-Burns, Jean
Hayes, Susan
Heap, Maggie
Hearn, Julie
Hiles, David
Hodgson, Phillip A. J.
Howell, Carolyn
Howell, Sylvia
Hughes-Bruderlin, Silvia
Ingham, Nida
Jacobs, Paula
Jones, Ros
Kafton, Maggie
Katz, Shawn
Keane, Agnes
Keane, Pamela
Kendall, Tricia
Kerry, Sue
Korn, Susan
L'Estrange, Jeanette
Lamplough, Alexis
Latham, Valerie
Laut, Susan
Lavender, Lesley
Lawton, Jane
Livingston, Christine
Lloyd, Annie
Lovett-Darby, Linda

Lowden, Barbara
Margrie, Paul
Marsh, Jeanette
Martin, Sheila
Masters, Sue
May, Ian
McDermott, Cathy
McDermott, Paul
McKeown, Patricia I.
Medice, Pauline
Menezes, Ray
Mensinga, Vera
Meredith, Judith
Merrick, Bozena
Meza, Ann L.
Millard, Lorraine
Millward, Christopher
Morley, Myriel
Murphy, Alan
Nappez, Sue
Newns, David
Nieboer, Sarah
O Ruairc, Micheál
O'Connor, Nadia
Opik, Urve
Ozaki-Owen, Mariko
Parkinson, Phil
Patchett, Angela
Pegoraro, Carla
Petrie, Bill
Petrie, Clare
Petrie, Julie
Pimentel, Allan
Pothig, Elisabeth
Press, Joanne
Proud, Roger
Pye, Amaryllis
Quinn, Asher
Reeves, Alan
Reilly, Nicole S.
Richardson, Ann
Richardson, Sacha
Richter, Nicola
Rose, Wendy
Rosenthal, Alison
Ross, Suzanne
Rowan, Cathy
Ryan, Corrine
Sagoe, Pauline
Salamander, Jas Ananda
Sanders, Julie
Sanders, Susie
Saunders, Alton
Sclater, Michael
Sharma, Meera
Sheridan, Dolores
Signora, Susanna Jamila
Silver-Leigh, Vivienne
Singleton, Kyrin
Smith, Di
Smith, Richard
Smyly, Penelope
Somerfield, Lynn
Souta, Marie Ludmila
Stannard, Marie
Stewart, Richard
Stimpson, Quentin
Stobezki, Yael
Stone, Marie Clare
Stratton-Woodward, Edward
Sussman, Susan
Swatton, Richard
Szopa, Miriam
Taylor, Alison
Taylor, Jackie
Taylor, Sajada Katalin
Taylor-Brook, Delia
Thiel, Geoffrey
Timmann, S.
Tomlinson, Catherine
Trowbridge, Louise
Tufnell, Jane
Turner, Jenny
Vallely, Patricia M.
Wainer, Hilary
Waller, MA, Charlotte
Ward, Hilary
Ward, Sharron
Wastell MA, Karen
Waterman, Zak
Weaver, Stephen
Whitaker, Christine
Woods, William
Young, Diana
Young, Raymond
Young, Sabine
Yusef, Dori Fatma
Zidianaki, Rania Argyro

**CFAR - Centre for Freudian Analysis and Research**

Benvenuto, Bice
Bull, Graham E
Burgoyne, Bernard
Burgoyne, Vivien
Chamberlain, Heather
Clayton, Gillian
Conolly, John
Corti, Lucia
Dachy, Vincent
Du Ry, Marc
Farquhar-Stanton, Kate
Gallagher, Rose
Gessert, Astrid
Hill, Philip
Hodgkiss, Andrew
Jaax, Stepahnie
Johnson, Kay
Kennedy, Michael
Leader, Darian
Machado, Danuza
O'Donoghue, Margot
Pepeli, Hara
Ridley, Stella V
Rowan, Alan J
Sullivan, Gerald
Watson, Lindsay
Wine, Noga

**CFET - The Caspari Foundation for Educational Therapy**

Arnesen, Elizabeth
Axson, Astrid
Barney, Lesley
Beaumont, Mia
Blakelock, Pamela
Bunce, Jillian
Casimir, Anne
Chappell, Claire
Clifford-Poston, Andrea
Coles, Walter
Daniel, Catherine
Dover, Jennifer
Geddes, Heather
Greenwood, Angela
Griffiths, Mark
Hannon, Letizia M
Haussman, Rochelle
High, Helen
Jennings, Lyn C.
Lyndon, Barbara
Marsden, Lee
McWilliam, Jill
Morton, Gillian
Murray, Anne
Richards-Gray, Susan
Robertson, Ruth
Royce, Heather
Salmon, Gillian
Selby, Marilyn
Taube, Idonea
Tillett, Penny

**CPP - Centre for Psychoanalytical Psychotherapy**

Bradley, Lorne-Natalie
Kinder, Diana

**CSP - Cambridge Society for Psychotherapy**

Arriens, Pamela
Barrett, Jenny
Bell, Mike
Briant, Steve
Briggs, Margarete
Brown, Ulla
Cockett, Ann
Corrigall, Jenny
Dasgupta, Carol
Davies, Judy
Farrell, Margaret
Gelsthorpe, Loraine
Gentry, Valerie
Goodrick, Jean
Gordon, Leila
Greaves, Sarah
Hargrave, Annie
King, Lucy
Kinsey, Bruce
Klug, Liebe
Lew, Clara
Minnaar, Doris
Morgan, Sian
Morgan, Walter
Paramour, Annabelle
Parkinson, Dorn
Pepper, Marie
Plummer, Glenys
Pyper, Julia
Randall, Rosemary
Robinson, Carole
Seymour-Clark, Vivienne
Shields, Jill
Tate, Patricia
Taylor, Hilary
Urquhart, Isabel
Wilde, Deborah

**CTIS - Centre Training International School of Hypnotherapy and Psychotherapy**

Anstey, John
Arrowsmith, Margaret
Bankes-Jones, Elizabeth
Berry, Margaret
Birley, Paul
Bisconti, Maria
Bonnebaigt, Andre
Britton, N.C.
Brookhouse, Shaun
Burgess, Tony
Campbell, Caroline
Cannon, Bennedict
Cooper, Patricia
Cross, Richard
Croston, Richard
Daniel, Liz
Devine, Rosaleen
Dwyer, Teresa
Fairhurst, Pat
Gonsalkorale, Wendy
Goodson, Christina
Gould, Frank
Hamill, Dan
Hannah, Audrey
Hannant, Fiona
Hardman, Anne
Havern, Eileen
Hayward, Marjorie
Hewitt, Patricia
Holmes, Janice
Howell, Judy
Hoyle-Wood, John
Iles, David
Isaac, Toni-Lee
Kypridemos, Petros
Lonie, Dorothy
MacPherson, David
Martin, Susan
McClatchey, E.P.(Toni)
McGrath, Carol
Middleton, Margaret
Moon, Barbara

Moon, Penny
Pennefather, Heather
Proffitt, Dorothea
Quigley, Hugh M.
Redgrave, Kenneth
Renwick, Fran
Ritchie, Robert
Rodriquez-Slawinski, Flavia
Sawyer, Ken
Stokes, Fergus
Van Warmelo, Estelle
Vannen-Hyland, Joan
Washington, Sue
Watson, Jane
Watson, Jean
Wermig-Morgan, Julia
Wharmby, Ian
Williams, Les

### CTP - Centre for Transpersonal Psychology

Allard, Alain
Allen, Dorothy
Allsop, Pamela
Anthony, Monica
Aris, Sarajane
Baker, Ewa
Barclay, Elizabeth
Barlow, Linda
Bayne, Brenda
Bazzard, Helen
Bennett, Rosanagh
Bento-Thieme, Maria
Bishop, Beata
Boddaert, Michael
Campbell, Jan
Chappell, Claire
Chiswell-Jones, Sue
Connell, Anne
Coward, Roger
Denman, Dido
Devine, Amanda
Dunne, Paul
Fisher, Maggie
Fletcher, Karyn
Fowles, Ann
Friedrich, Stephen
Grant, Mary
Guest, Hazel
Harding-Davies, Valerie
Haywood, Carol
Hock, Gaby
Holden, Maxine
Jiggins, Mary
Knight, Elaine
Lindley-Jones, Kerstin
Lynn-Evans, Julie
Marshall, Hazel
McCormick, Elizabeth
McDonald, Christina
McGouran, Gill
McKenzie, Thomas
Merriott, Peter
Michaelson, Sue
Millais, Suzy
Mojsa, Jan
Muschamp, Maureen
Newnham, Elizabeth
Nimenko, Wasyl
O'Hagan, Judith
Pearman, Cathy
Peet, Sandra
Peters, Maggie
Pool, Nicky
Preece, Rob
Price, Jeremy
Price, Mark
Procter, Ann
Pye, Robina
Quinn, Susan
Saabor, Geraldine
Salmon, Cindy
Smith, Gerry
Swallow, Reynold
Tower, Rupert
Turner, Senga
Tyrrell, Susannah
Vaizey, Philippa
Vibert, Eva
Vick, Philippa
Waygood, Rob
West, Alison
White, Ruth
Whyte, Miranda
Williams, Diana
Wishart, Marion
Wood, Mary
Woollard, Diana
Wright, Jason
de Serdici, Simona

### FIC - The Family Institute, Cardiff

Alexander, Erica
Booth, Philip
Brett, John David
Cartwright, Tony
Cox, Brenda
Edwards, Lorna
Faris, Jeff
Gagg, Susan
Graney, Mike
Hardy, William
Howell, Hilary
Jones, Fiona
Jones, Sue
Jones, Teresa
Logan, Jean
Matthews, Shane
Monteiro, Marian
Morris, Mary
Mylan, Trish
Osborn, James
Ostler, Dorothy
Reimers, Sigurd
Robinson, Gary
Roys, Clare
Sayers, Jacqui
Shore, Barbara
Speed, Bebe
Tanner, Gareth
Taylor, Margaret
Vivan-Byrne, Kieran
Vivian Byrne, Sue
Weeks, Mark
Williams, Richard

### FIP - The Forum for Independent Psychotherapist

Adema, Rachel
Alexander, Gail
Alleyne, Aileen
Allison, Janet
Aquarone, Luc-Remy
Arthur, Andrew R.
Bamber, Nicola
Barlow, Sanchia
Barnett, Ruth
Bathai, Parizad
Birkett, Diana
Black, Patricia Anne
Bowes, Ann
Bradley, Lorne-Natalie
Bramley, Wyn
Brewer, Madelyn
Chapman, Sandy
Christopher, Elphis
Clark, Isobel
Cooper, Margaret H
Craib, Ian
Darcy, Gillian
Dell, Judith
Denness, Brian
Dianin, Gianni
Dobbs, Wendy
Dobson, Mary
Downes, Celia
Eiles, Clive
El-Hadi, Ali
Ellis, Sian
Fanning, Alexandra
Farquhar-Stanton, Kate
Ferguson, Geoffrey
Fisk, Geoffrey
Freeman, Martin
Froshaug, Ann
Gardiner, Margaret
Gilbert, Barbara
Goddard, Kay
Gomez, Lavinia
Griffiths, Anne-Megan
Guppy, Madeleine
Haddington, Janet
Hall, Guy
Harris, Tirril
Hatswell, Valerie Elliot
Hewitt, Philip
Hopwood, Jean
Hopwood, Michael
Irving, Susan
Jansen, Diana
Jaques, Penny
Jenkins, Beverley
Jones-Dube, Elvyn
Katz, Janice
Kendal, Jo Reed
Kenny, Miranda H.
Kramer, Claudia
Le Quesne, Susan
Leeburn, Jennifer
Leggatt, Jenny
Levitsky, Jackie
Longford, Joan
Love, Mollie
Lynch, Valerie
Maloney, Chris
Martin, Carol
McCreanor, Teresa
Mellows, David
Mellows, Hilary
Miles, Carolyn
Mordecai, Aslan
Mordecai, Kay
Morgan, Shirley P.
Morgan-Jones, Richard
Morley, Elspeth
Morley, Robert
Nelson, Helen
O'Brien, Maja
O'Dell, Tricia
Owtram, Peter
Payne, Graham
Pearson, Eileen
Perren, Mary
Phoenix, Ashleigh
Poole, Robert
Power, Kevin
Ratigan, Bernard
Reeves, Richard
Richardson, Elizabeth
Roberts, Mary
Rogers, Anne
Samuels, Andrew
Scarlett, Jean
Seebarun, Dev
Shadrach-Long, Philippa
Shaw, Lynda
Shuen, Dorcas
Sidey, Brian
Spencer, Mary
Sprent, Sue
Stafford, Amanda
Stanbury, Christine
Stephens, Lyn
Stewart, Naomi
Stone, Miriam
Sueke, Minoo
Thomas, Kerry
Thomson, Jean
Tytel, Laurie
Vernon, Paul
Watson, Pauline
Webb, Joan
Whitwell, John
Wigram, Penny
Wilkinson, Linda
Wilmot, Vivienne
Winter, Rachel
Yallop, Melanie

Young, Robert
Zane, Helen
de Berker, Patricia
de Berker, Paul

**FPC - Foundation for Psychotherapy and Counselling**

Albrecht, Gisela
Allan, Kay
Allen-Brown, Jane
Allison, Virginia
Archer, Ruth
Arundell, Jane
Ashwin, Mary
Askew-Walinda, Margaret
Aylward, Peter
Baker, Moke
Bannister, Gill
Bargh, Julie
Bartlett, Beatrice
Beard, Dorrie
Beck, Rose
Beer, Margaret E
Benwell, Jennifer
Bingham, Jane
Black, David
Blackwood, Renate
Botha, Dr Marie
Browne, Val
Buchan, Ann
Buckley, Marie-Noël (aka Billie)
Burch, Rosemary
Burns, Serena
Carr, Brede
Cathie, Sean
Chan-Williams, Molly
Chapman, Maureen
Christie, Rose
Clancy, Catherine
Clark, Christine
Clark, Margaret
Clifford, Jennifer
Clutterbuck, Annie
Cobden, Vivienne
Combes, Ann
Costello, Marie
Coutts, Melody
Crawford, Stephen
Crease, Jennifer
Crosby, Dianne
Crowley, Julia
Culliford, Penny
Czubinska, Grazyna
Danks, Alan
Dare-Bryan, Arminal
Darrell, Linda
Dawson, Alison
Dawson, Joyce
Day, Sally
Dean, Sally
Dokter, Ditty
Dooley, Patricia
Driver, Christine
Duckworth, Moira
Dunbar, Gill
Edmunds, Howard
Errington, Meg
Flanagan, Eileen
Flatt, Raymond
Freeman, Sue
Gavin, Bea
Gent, Sheila
Gibson, Melanie
Golding, Michelle A.
Goodrich, Anne
Goodrich, Diana
Graff-Perron, Avril
Gray, Dennis
Greally, Brid
Green, Brian
Greensmith, Katherine
Greenwood, John
Groom, Nigel
Gundry, Caroline
Hamilton-Duckett, Paule
Harding, C.
Hardman, Jacquie
Hartman, Wendy
Harvey, Natasha
Hashemi, Beth
Henny, Lindy
Hoang, Astrid
Holden, John
Horton, Mary
Howard, Gloria
Hudson, Rachel
Hughes, Jennifer
Humphry, Alexis
Hutton, Margaret
Jones, Janet
Jones, Merryn
Keane, Barry
Kell, Midge
Kidd, Lee
King, Diana
Kingsnorth, Wendy
Kisch, Marlies
Knowles, Valerie
Lallah, Regine
Le Quesne, Susan
Leeming, Gareth
Leon, Barbara D.
Levick, Barbara
Levy, Colette
Linden, Roger
Lloyd, Roger
Lodrick, Michael
Lutyens, Marianna
MacDonald, Pat
Macaskie, Jane
Mander, Gertrud
Mann, Angela
Marsden, Patricia
Marshall, Vivien
Marx, Philippa
Matthews, Carol
Maunder, Brian
McDouall, Veronica
McKeon, Mary
McKeown, Jane
McLoughlin, Brendan
Meaden, Rosaleen
Millier, Sylvia
Milner-Jones, Cassandra
Monticelli, Wendy
Morcom, Caroline
Morgan, Leigh
Morrison, Lesley
Murdin, Lesley
Neal, (Ms) Lalage
North, Bindy
Nowlan, Kate
O'Connell, Patrick
O'Dell, Tricia
O'Leary, Anne M.T.
Owen, Angela
Parker, Rosie
Parkinson, Judy
Parks, Val
Pawsey, Jack
Pearson, Jenny
Persson, Rose
Peters, Linda
Pirquet, Caroline
Plows, Barbara
Pople, Sue
Porteous, Trish
Preston, Kay
Quaine, Mary
Raphaely, Mary
Rees-Roberts, Diane
Renouf, Johanna
Reynolds, Hilary
Richards, Michael
Rignell, John
Roberts, Mary
Romaine, Stephanie
Rosseter, Bill
Saville, Sue
Schueppert, Deirdre
Sharman, Juliet
Sharp, Belinda
Shuttleworth, Caroline
Smith, Lois
Snow, Randa
Somerville, Gwynnedd
Stang, Pamela
Steffens, Dorothy
Steward, Jill
Stewart, John
Steyn, Angela
Stiffell, Gilly
Stone, Miriam
Sutton, Bobbie
Tadman, Fenella
Taggart, John
Taylor-Thomas, Caroline
Thomas, Mary R.
Thorndycraft, Bill
Tjepkema, Froukje
Trayling, Laurie
Vanesse, Connie
Walsh, Aine (Anne)
Walters, Cheryl
Watson, Mike
Webster, Anne
Weisz, Janet
Wenham, Jane
White, Lela Ljiljana
Whyte, Prue
Wigram, Penny
Wilding, Vicky
Williams, Sherly
Winders, Suzanne
Wood, Rob
Wright, James
Wyatt, Katherine
Yallop, Melanie
Yariv, Gail
Yates, Tony
del Strother, Sybil

**GAPS - The Guild of Analytical Psychology and Spirituality**

Aksoy Robins, A. Asu
Anderton, Michael
Blair, Margaret
Campbell Nye, Aileen
Cantwell, Maureen
Costello, John J
Cotter, Angela
Fitzgerald, Jim
Gordon, Elizabeth
Hill, Jude G
Hirst, Diane Zervas
Hughes, William
Morris, Petrina
Phillips, Helen
Pictet, Dariane
Reynal, Carmen
Russell, Olivia
Walker, Lorraine
Walsh, Aine (Anne)

**GASW - Group Analysis South West**

Chalk, Caroline
Clark, Andrew
Coucill, Judith
Finch, Auberon
Gölz, Angelika
Horton, David
Knowles, Gwen
Montgomery, Charles
Plant, Robert
Pullin, Andrew
Reeves, David
Sutton-Smith, Deirdre
Watts, Paul
Wright, Maureen

**GCL - The Gestalt Centre, London**

Allport, Maggie
Ambrose, Tony
Amundsen, Paul

Atkinson, Laura
Becker, Amely
Bryan, Agnes
Colls, Jennifer
Crombie, Clare
Davidge, Maggie
Ellis, Michael
Gillie, Marion
Gilligan, Toni
Goillon, Margaret
Hall, Jill
Hancock, Maureen
Houston, Gaie
Jaynes, Eddie
John-Wilson, Deb'bora
Lynn, Kay
Martin, Linda
Morgan, Barbara
Patton, Jane
Powell, Helen
Puddy, Jane
Rigby, Yvonne
Rose, Alivia
Rowan, Chris
Sherno, Peggy
Siederer, Carol
Singer, Rory
Smith, Jonathan
Stacey, Jenny
Styles, Heather
Tharratt, Penny
Twelvetrees, Heidy
Veale, Maurice
Weinstein, Jeremy
White, Jennifer Madeline
White, Nuala

**GPTI - Gestalt Psychotherapy Training Institute**

Appleby, Joy
Aram, Eliat
Arnold, Julia
Ashcroft, Dinah
Barty, Alison
Bate, Dolores
Bentley, Elizabeth
Bentley, Jacqueline
Bentley, Ros
Blackburn, Annie
Brooks, Carole
Broughton, Vivian
Brown, Lesley
Clark, Margaret
Colbourne, Graham
Coward, Malcolm
Critchley, Bill
Daintry, Penelope
Davis, Bob
Dawson, Jenny
Denham, Juliet
Denham-Vaughan, Sally
Elderton, Tan Shen
Elliott, Hazel
Evans, Richard
Finar, Ruth
Fry, Julie
Gilbert, Maria
Glanville, Tony
Greenway, Ian
Gregory, Judith
Harris, John Bernard
Harris, Neil
Hemming, Judith
Higgins, Judith
Hinde, Chrissie
Hodgson, Diane
Holloway, Elizabeth
Howdin, Jules
Hughes, Geraldine
Hughes, Jacqui
Jackson, Elizabeth
Jameson Milner, Jane
Joyce, Philip
Kearns, Anne
Kelly, Caro
Kennedy, Des
Kennedy, Helen
Kennett, Christine
Kerry, Helen
Kotnik, Rudi
Lake, Moira
Lehain, Daniel
Levitsky, Patricia D.
Lewis, Sue
Luckock, Brenda
MacKenzie, Liz
Mackewn, Jennifer
Mackintosh, Peri
Macnab, Celia
Makin, Anne
Manielevitch, Edna
Mann, David
Manning, Helen
Marshall, Eamonn
Maudling, Caroline
McGowan, Dominica
Michaelson, Jess
Mitchell, John
Morgan, Natasha
Mukuma, Diana
Nathan, (Jennifer) Ruth
Nowell, Valerie
Opienski, Jacek
Orchard, Caroline
Orlans, Vanja
Osborne, Lynda
Parava, Anna
Parlett, Malcolm
Parmley, Alison
Perks, Alison
Philippson, Peter
Porter, Danny
Pugsley, Stephanie
Retallick, Malcolm
Ridgewell, Margaret
Romero, Maria Jose
Rosemary, Margaret
Scott, Janice
Scott, Mary
Shearman, Christine
Sheehan, Maureen
Shuttleworth, John
Skeet, Maggie
Skye, Emily
Thomas, Mark
Thompson, Jenny
Turner, Mary
Turton, Michael
Tyson, Robert
Voss, Tony
Wallstein, Richard S
Waterstone, Carolyn
Whines, Jonathan
Williams, Chris
Williams, Guinevere
Willmer, Emma

**GUILD - Guild of Psychotherapists**

Adams, Kathryn
Adams, Tessa
Addenbrooke, Mary
Amiel, Olivia
Anstice, Christine
Armitage, Pamela
Arnold, Rosemary
Atkinson, Paul
Ayres, Anthony
Bacon, Roger
Barker, Sally
Barnett, Mary
Barrett, Jean
Barwell, Peter
Battersby, Audrey
Beard, Hilary
Beaumont, Mia
Berry, Peter
Bhatt, Vibha
Bickerton, Tricia
Blandy, Evanthe M
Brennan, Sue
Briant, Michael
Bridgment, Julia
Buckingham, Linda
Buckroyd, Julia
Burgoyne, Vivien
Burton, Michael
Campbell, Elizabeth
Chancer, Anne
Chandler, Philip
Chapman, Trudy
China, Jacques
Clackson, Suzanne
Clare, Louise
Cohen, Sylvia
Cohn, Nancy
Coleman, Eva
Collins, Natalie
Coombs, Suzanne
Cooper, Sara
Couzyn, Jeni
Cronin, Jeremiah
Daniel, Barbara
Davison, Susan
Defries, Nicky
Draney, Sue
Dutton, Andrew
Easter, Judith
Edge, Jon
Egert, Susan
Eisen, Susan
Ezekiel, Lyn
Farhi, Nina
Farrell, Margaret
Ficarra, Berthe
Field, Kate
Finn, Walter
Fisher, Jinny
Friedrich, Michael
Fry, Caroline
Gal, Oshrat
Garlovsky, Rita
Gilljam, Annika
Glynn, Tania
Gold, Bev
Goldsmith, Anna
Good, Simon
Goodrich, Diana
Gosling, Patricia
Gow, Marion
Grant, Rosamund
Gray, Anne
Gray, Kati
Greaves, Sarah
Griffiths, Anne-Megan
Guy, Liana
Hall, David
Halpin, Jill
Hamer, Neil
Harrison, Jacqueline
Harvard-Watts, Olivia
Henriques, Marika
Hoag, Linda M.
Hopkins, Jill
Horsman, Val
Howard, Angela
Hughes, Ann
Johansson, Birgitta
Jones, Margaret
Kane, Ros
Karan, Alexandra
Kennedy, Caroline
Kerr, Anna
Kerridge, Jack
Krzowski, Sue
Lee, Jan
Lewis, Sheila
Lintern, Fran
Lloyd, Elizabeth
Maguire, Marie
Marsh, Jennifer
Meakins, Elizabeth
Menczer, Wendy
Miller, Dr Michael
Moore, Rosemary
Morgan, Sian
Morris, Monique
Morris, Shosh
Nabarro, Elizabeth
Nicholson, Elizabeth
Noble, Jane

O'Connor, Noreen
Oakley, Haya
Payne, John
Pearmain, Dr Rosalind
Phillips, Adam
Pratt, Sheila
Prendeville, William
Price, Susan
Prue, Janet
Rea, Judith
Redfearn, Joseph
Richards, Christopher
Richards, Janet
Richards, Val
Rickett, Marion
Rimmer, Lynn
Roberts, Laurence
Robertson, Judith
Robertson, Zuleika
Robinson, Christina
Robinson, Judy
Robinson, Sue
Rumney, Boris
Schofield, Lynn-Ella
Simmons, Ruth
Sinclair, Alison
Slade, Laurie
Smith, Anne
Spurling, Laurence
Stokes, Jenny
Tait, Adrian
Taussig, Hanna
Timber, Jennifer
Townsend, Anne
Vallins, Yvonne
Veasey, Helen
Voikhanskaya, Marina
Waddington, Ann
Wells, Roger
Westcott, Rosemary
White, Jean
Wilce, Gillian
Woodhead, Louise
Wooster, Frances
Worrall, Chrysoula
Worthington, Anne
Zeff, Paula

**HIP - The Hallam Institute of Psychotherapy**

Ali, Saadi
Arnesen, Paul
Ashton, John
Beard, Hilary
Bojanic-Wright, Stoya
Bolsover, Nick
Boysan, Zehra
Dixon, Linda
Drucquer, Helen
Edwards, David
Ellis, Lynda
FitzGerald, Gearoid
Garlovsky, Rita
Gartland, Michael
Gibbons, Sandra
Goddard, Kay
Gudjonsson, Ingolfur A
Guiton, Anita
Hally, Dianne
Hardwick, Barbara
Hopkins, Vera M.
Howlett, Stephanie
Hunt, Pat
Johnston, James
Lidmila, Alan
Littlewood, Ann
Loftus, Patrick A.
MacNeill, Enid
Maitlis, Marion
Marshall, Myra
McAuley, John
Meredith, Joan
Oram, John E.D.
Peltier, Judy
Pethen, Susan
Pickvance, Deborah
Pittock, Frances
Porteous, Louise
Rayner, Beryl A
Read, Nicholas
Robinson, Felicity
Sadgrove, Jenny
Shipton, Geraldine
Sudbery, John
Thomas, Sandra
Thomson, Pat
Vassiliadis, Helena
Vincent, Jane

**IATE - Institute for Arts in Therapy and Education**

Amey, Sue
Amin, Sheetal
Ball, Jo
Barclay, Bridget (Biddy)
Berry, Julia
Blench, Graeme
Craster, Helen
Cree, Anni
Cruthers, Helen
Dar, Limor
Dawkins, Sue
Edington, Jane
Efstratiou, Alida
Farleigh, Laura
Hadfield, Chris
Hall, Francesca
Halter, Kathy
Harris, Sue
Holliday, Carol
Ingham, Rosie
Katz, Andy
Leon, Sara
Leslie, Tina
Low, James
Mace, Barbara
Magan, Bhagya
Marston, Maureen
Mendoza, Hilda
Naor, Lillie
Plunkett, Eileen
Riley, Fran
Roemmele, Caroline
Rowan, Chris
Samuels, Jocelyne
Savins, Charlotte
Smosarski, Lizzie
Spencer, Jake
Spencer, Vivienne
Stott, Nicki
Sunderland, Margot
Velarde, Dominique
Walker, Bridget
Waterfield, Julia
Westcott, Emma
Wilson, Ronni

**IFT - Institute of Family Therapy**

Aggett, Percy
Ali-Khan, Farra
Amias, David
Askin, Pauline
Attwood, Peter
Aust, Frank
Ayres, Gary
Barratt, Sara
Bennett, Margaret
Bentovim, Dr Arnon
Berdasco, Lourdes
Bianco, Vicky
Bolsover, Nick
Bor, Prof. Robert
Boston, Paula
Bourne, Juliet
Burck, Charlotte
Burns, Elizabeth
Campbell, David
Carter, Mary Hope
Carter, Sybil
Chaundy, Jan
Chesters, Neil R
Chimera, Kathleen
Collins, Lynda
Colmer, Enid
Connolly, Cath
Cornish, Ursula
Craske, Sarah
Crowe, Michael
Dale, Barbara Janet
Daniel, Gwyn
Davies, Hilary
Davies-Smith, Lorraine
Davy, Dr John
Dawson, Neil K
Desai, Asha
Dodge, Elizabeth
Dowling, Emilia
Down, Gwynneth
Draper, Rosalind
Dutton, Jane
Edwards-Pollard, Astrid
Egert, Stella
Eisler, Ivan
Esposito, Claude
Farah, Paula
Farzim, Pari
Foskett, Julia
Ganda, Matthew
George, Evan A H
Glasscoe, Claire
Gorrell Barnes, Gill
Graham, Nancy H
Granville, Julia
Gross, Erwin
Gross, Vivienne
Hamlin, Cynthia Diana
Harrison, Gillian
Herington, Steve
Heyliger, Veann
Hildebrand, Judy
Hill, Finella
Hilton, Anni
Hubbard, Leslie
Hudson, Alan
Humphreys, David
Hussain, Nasima
Iveson, Chris
Iveson, Diana
Jacobs, Dr Brian William
Jacobs, Linda
Jenkins, Hugh
Jennings-Nicol, Sara
Kavner, Ellie
Kelly, Ann
Kelly, Ann
Lafon, Robert
Lau, Annie
Lewington, Paul
Lindsey, Dr Caroline
Lobatto, Wendy
Lynch, Monica
Magill, Bernadette
Malik, Rabia
Malley, Maeve
Mandin, Philippe
Markovic, Desa
Mason, Dr Barry
Mayer, Robert
McBride, Marie
McCandless, Lynn
McCandless, Robert
McCann, Damian
McCann, Linda
McGrath, Rita E.
Messent, Philip
Middlecoat, Andrew
Miller, Ann
Miller, Riva
Millham, Alexander
Morris, Allan
Mumvuri-Ellis, Gladys
Myers, Marsha
Newman, Alan
Nolte, Lizette
O'Brian, Charles
Pangrazi, Sue
Paulson, Diana
Payne, Katherine Elizabeth

Petty, Susan P.H.
Pooley, Jane
Rapley, Catherine
Ratner, Harvey
Read, Elizabeth J.
Reeves, Sarah
Reynolds, Dorothy A
Rodger, Catherine
Simmons, Kevin
Simms, Mandy
Skillicorn, Ingrid
Smith, Gerrilyn
St John, Frances
Staines, John
Stedman, Maire
Stephens, Sally
Stogdon, Mark
Summer, Jennifer
Sutcliffe, Pauline
Tapang, Peter
Taylor, Dee
Topliss, Nick
Turner, Annie
Van Loo, Douglas A
Vibhakar, Lopa
Virtanen, Helena
Watson, Eve
Wieselberg, Huguette
Wilson, James
Woodcock, Jeremy
Woolner, John
Yandoli, Dennis
Yousry, Menis

**IGA - Institute of Group Analysis**

Adshead, Gwen
Allsop, Wendy
Anderson, Linda
Andrews, Gill
Andrews, Stuart
Andry, Robert
Antao, Ivor
Arcari, Stephen
Ashton, Anthony
Bacha, Claire
Bamber, James
Behr, Harold
Berman, Paul
Berry, Eileen
Bhat, Radha
Birchmore, Terry
Bledin, Kenneth
Bloch, Linda
Bloom, Jane
Boakes, Janet
Boardman, Ian
Boronat, Dascha
Boswood, Bryan
Bozovic, Zoran
Bradbury, Susan Elizabeth
Bunday, Christine
Burlton, Katherine
Burman, Erica
Campbell, Jane
Campos, Hanne
Canete, Maria
Canty, Josephine
Carter, David
Chan-Williams, Molly
Chilton, Maggie
Christie, Jim
Clark, Andrew
Conlon, Isobel
Conway, Sally
Corbett, Martyn
Cunningham, Gordon
Dalal, Farhad
Daykin, Amanda
De Mare, Patrick
De Zulueta, Felicity
Dean, Sally
Deco, Sarah
Dillon Weston, Marisa
Donovan, Andrew
Doran, Monica
Douglas, Angela
Duckham, Jennifer
Eagles, Marje
Edwards, Linda Mary
Einhorn, Sue
Ernst, Sheila
Evans, Chris
Evans, Sandra
Eyres, Robert
Fagbadegun, Rufus
Feeney, Michael
Festenstein, Geraldine
Firn, Peter
Fischer, Michael
Freudenberg, Susan
Froggett, Antony
Fyne, Jo
Gallagher, Eileen
Gallop, Margaret
Gibbs, Catherine
Glenn, Liza
Goepfert, Michael
Gold, Bonnie
Gorman, Susan
Gottesmann, Ewa
Graham Fuller, Victoria
Green, Roberta
Greenberg, Maurice
Greenland, Sue
Haddock, Ray
Haigh, Rex
Hallard, Sharon
Hamrogue, Tom
Harris, Bob
Harrow, Anne
Hartley, Phil
Hasler-Winter, Susan
Hearst, Liesel
Heimann, Michael
Hindmarch, Dorothea
Hobbs, Michael
Holden, Sarah
Holmes, Anne
Hook, Beatrice
Hook, John
Hopper, Earl
Hudson, Inge
Hughes, Patrick
Hutchinson, Sylvia
Hyde, Keith
Ikkos, George
Ingram, Sonia
James, Jessica
Jones, Dan
Jukes, Adam
Keggereis, Duncan
Kelly, Michael
Kennard, David
Kinder, Diana
Knowles, Jane
Krajnovic, Valentina J
Lee, John
Lilley, Diana
Lintott, Bill
Lodrick, Michael
Love, Derek
Lucas, Tina
Lyons, Heather
MacAlister, Eileen
MacKenzie, Nancy
Mace, Chris
Mackintosh Millard, Sheila
Maltby, Michael
Manzi, Christine
Maple, Norma Anderson
Maratos, Jason
Mars, Percival
Maxwell, Brian
Mayer-Johnson, Jessica
Mayho, Rosalyn
McCabe, Ruth
McGrath, Patrick
McLoughlin, Una
McNeilly, Gerald
Meinrath, Monica
Mitchison, Sally
Mittwoch, Adele
Murphy, Dennis
Neeld, Rebecca
Nitsun, Morris
Noack, Amelie
O'Leary, Carmen
Ormay, Tom
Page, Marcus
Panchkowry, Marion
Parker, Michael
Parkes, John
Perez-De-Albeniz, Alberto
Pines, Malcolm
Plant, Robert
Pughe, Billy
Pullin, Andrew
Rabe, Marie-Louise
Rance, Christopher
Rheinschmiedt, Otto
Roberts, Jeff
Roberts, Julie
Robinson, Mardi
Rogers, Cynthia
Rosenfeld, Angela
Russell, Wilson J
Salm, Anne Marie
Sanders, Susie
Sarra, Nicholas
Schiemann, Margot
Schneider, Evelyne
Scott, Michael
Seed, Deborah
Sellars, Val
Sengun, Seda
Sevitt, Michael
Sharpe, John
Simpson, Ian
Singh Sehmi, Harjinder
Sipos, Zsuzsa
Smith, Margaret
Smith, Valerie
Smithers, Martyn
Sproul-Bolton, Robin
Stacey, Ralph
Stevenson, Beaumont
Strich, Sabina
Sullivan, Jill
Sutton-Smith, Deirdre
Tait, Michael
Tanna, Nick
Tantam, Digby
Thomas, Tim
Thornton, Christine
Thummel, Uwe
Trevor Davies, Helen
Turner, Morag Conway
Vincent, David
Walker, David
Watts, Paul
Wetherill, Julie
White, Jeremy
Whiteley, Stuart
Wilke, Gerhard
Willis, Sally
Willis, Susan
Wilson, James
Wilson, Peter
Wise, Anne
Wojciechowska, Ewa
Woolmer, Tim
Wright, Harry
Wyse, Hymie

**IGAP - The Independent Group of Analytical Psychologists**

Anderton, Michael
Begg, Ean
Blass, David
Burritt, William
Campbell Nye, Aileen
Cantwell, Maureen
Clark, Giles
Cook, Lynn
Costello, John J
David, Johanna Turcan
David, Julian
Davis, Joyce
Denman, Cara

Esterhuyzen, Alex
Evetts-Secker, Josephine
Fitzgerald, Jim
Freeman, Linda
Ginsborg, Robby
Gordon, Elizabeth
Graziosi, Mariolina
Harwood, Matthew
Hirst, Diane Zervas
Jackson, Eve
Keating, Jacqueline
Kind, Gillian
Kujawski, Pedro
Maguire, Anne
Milne, Frances
Morris, Petrina
Newman, Bracha
Norris, Penny
O'Connell Ribet, Oonagh
Rees, Myfanwy
Reynal, Carmen
Sayama, Kinko
Shearer, Ann
Shorter, Bani
Smalley, John
Spencer, Janet W
Swabey, ffiona
Tatham, Peter
Tuby, Molly
Weinrich, Hildegard
Whan, Michael

**IPS - Institute of Psychosynthesis**

Acket, Marijke
Anker, Ofra
Arnold, Sue
Benson, Jarlath
Beresford, Marie
Bickers, Adrian
Bicknell, Sara
Bondi, Alice
Boyle, Alexander
Burns, Maura
Cain, Christine
Cairns, Samantha
Carroll, Pennie
Chandler, Diana
Clough, Andrea
Clover, Gillian
Cutler, Jane
Davidson, Eileen
Dijkman, Theo
Dyczkowska, Ania
Ender, Beckett
Ender, Christine
Ender, Dorry
England, David
Evans, Joan
Evans, Roger
Friedman, Debbie
Gerra, Stephanie
Gibson, Glen
Hacker, Margaret
Hanna, Dorothy
Harrison, Jane
Hayden, Martina
Hedley, Karen
Hickey, Alaco
Holland, Sue
Hope, Francis
Hunneybell, Darrel
Huson, Richard
Jenkins, Harry
Jensen, Greta
Josephs-Serra, Elisabeth
Kaufmann, Mickey
Kirkland, Margot
Kowalski, Reinhard
Landman, Angus
Leinster, Carline
Lemon, Marcia
MacGregor, Catherine
Machon, Adrian
Machon, Andrew
Madenholt-Titley, Steph
Marcus-Jedamzik, Deena
McBurnie, Dolores
McGuinness, Maureen
McOstrich, June
Mead, Christine
Millar, Gerry
Neill, Christopher
Oliver, Jenny
Pearman, Cathy
Peart, Mary
Philbin, Mairead
Quinn, Jacqueline
Rhind, Sue
Ridley, Wendy
Schild, Maureen
Seddon, Hester
Shiers, John
Shingler, Christopher
Silvester, Keith
Simpson, Steve
Thompson, Hilary
Totman, Maria
Toubkin, Rita
Wainwright, Margaret
Walker, Clare
Welsh, Anne
Wolfe, Pamela
Wren, Gillian
van Rossum, Diederik

**IPSS - Institute of Psychotherapy and Social Studies**

Aizenberg, Eldad
Allawi, Nadia
Antrican, James Gray
Austin, Bill
Baker, Kathy
Beck, Orit
Bennett, Lesley
Bensimon, Marlene
Bishop, Patricia
Black, Sandra
Blackwell, Frances
Blair, Dana-Jane
Broadbent, Sara
Brown, Ian B
Buckley, Judy
Burns, Alex
Canning, Miles
Chandwani, Lilian
Charley, Lydia
Chessell, Karen
China, Giselle
Clare, John
Cotten, Naomi
Cullis, Andrew
Cussins, Anne
Daniels, Susan
Daudy, Isabelle
Davidoff, Leslie
Davidson, Steve
Davis, Diana
Davy, Rosalind
Dogmetchi, Geri
Dowber, Hilary
Duckworth, Rosemary
Dunford, Kathy
Evans, Caron
Franklyn, Frank
Frisvold, Tove
Gauntlett, Tim
Gladstone, Guy
Glantz, Robert
Goslett, Kate
Gracie, Judith
Green, June
Greengrass, Carol
Grey, David
Harriot, Juanita
Hawkes, Bernadette
Horwood, Tone
Howard, Heather
Howells, Megan
Ielitro, Denise
Joffe, Riva
John-Baptiste, Louisa
Johnson, Avril
Jones, Kevin
Kaur, Manshant Rani
Keith, Irene
Kerkham, Patricia
Knott, Louise
Law, Heather
Lehrer, Pam
Lesadd, Jenny
Lesley, Alison
Letts, Muriel
Little, Marie
Lloyd, Patricia
Lovel, Mary
Manglani, Dona
Martello, Liza
Masterson, Ingrid
McEldowney, Dennis
McGee, Colin
Michaud-Lennox, Suzanne
Morante, Flavia
Mycroft, Jessica
Nash, Sue
Norburn, Veronica
Oakley, Madeleine
Palmer, Ede
Polden, Anne
Rapp, Hilde
Richards, Val
Robertson, Judith
Rogers, Maggie
Rose, Kevin
Shampan, Linda
Shetland, Ilrich
Silver, Claire
Smith, Carole
Smith, Jonathan
Spyer, Natalie
Steiner Celebi, Monika
Stott, Jackie
Sucher, Ingeborg A.
Sünkel, Sue
Söderström, Anne-Charlotte
Turp, Maggie
Utting, Julia
Walker, Jim
Ward, Elaine
Whitby, Susan
Williams, Gwen
Wise, Penny
Woodley, Ermine
Yazar, Jale
Zarbafi, Ali

**ITA - Institute of Transactional Analysis**

Agar, James
Allen, Patricia
Arredondo, Beverly
Ayres, Alison
Banks, Jan
Baskerville, Victoria
Beazley Richards, Joanna
Beechcroft, Diane
Bergin, Stella
Bisgood, Bill
Boyd, Suzanne
Bradley, Anne Marie
Brauner, Rita
Brereton, June
Bresloff, Valerie
Bridge, Jenny
Brown, Helen
Brunt, Mervyn
Burton, Tom
Butlin, Lesley
Cardile, Pietro
Cheetham, Brian
Clarkson, Barbara
Conway, Mary
Cooke, Bob
Cox, Mary
Cunningham, Valerie
Daley, Lema
David, Ann
Davies, Peggy
Davis, Christopher

Davis, Jim
Delport, Juan
Dennis, Steve
Douglas, Mica
Duffy, Gervase J.
Duncan, Ursula
Etherington, Mary
Eusden, Sue
Felton, Mo
Fenton, Brian
Flatt, Deborah
Fowlie, Heather
Franses, Adena
French, Jean
Galloway, Betsy
Garner, Joanne
Gibson, Jenny
Gilbert, Maria
Gildebrand, Katarina
Goddard, Lynne
Goodban, Wendy
Gowling, David
Green, Eliott
Greenaway, Jennifer
Greening, Sarah
Gregory, Josie
Hamilton-James, Tina
Hannah, Francesca
Hardy, Jennifer
Hargaden, Helena
Harley, Ki
Harvey, Ann
Heath, John
Heath, Lis
Heiller, Birgitta R.
Heppel, Valerie
Hewett, Rachel
Hewson, Julie Anne
Hiremath, Paramita
Hirst, Hazel
Hobbes, Robin
Holland, Hilary Elizabeth
Hooker, Dennis
Hopping, Geoff
Horton, Annie
Hostick, Kathie
Hunt, Jill
Irving, Nicholas
Jesson, Alison
Kelley, Linda
Lapworth, Phil
Law, Gordon
Lawrence, Yvonne
Leach, Kathy
Lee, Adrienne
Leong, Jessica
Levine, Peter
Lewin, Melanie
Little, Ray
Lomond, Marsha
Lucas, Carol
Luden, Maureen
Mardula, Jody
McQuaid, Cathy
McQuillin, Jane
Megram, Patricia
Middlestone-Lowe, Carole
Midgley, Karen
Mitchell, Leilani
Monk-Steel, Barbara
Monk-Steel, John Michael
Moodie, Alastair
Moore, Joan
Mountain, Anita
Murphy, Katherine
Naughton, Marie
Neal, James
Nixon, Jane
Oates, Stephanie
Pamphlett, Nick
Parkinson, Jillian
Partington-Uttley, Paula
Payman, Barbara
Perry, Philip
Phelps, Gwyneth
Phillips, Sue
Pianta-Morrish, Susan L.
Politzer, Juliette
Porter, Barbara
Pringle, Diana
Rawson, David
Renwick, John
Rigney, Ann
Rimmer, Annie
Ring, Brendan
Robinson, Isabel
Robinson, Jenny
Salters, Diane
Sanders, Peter
Shadbolt, Carole
Shearman, Christine
Shmukler, Diana
Sills, Charlotte
Sless, Deborah
Smith, Barbara
Spenceley, Dave
Stevenson, Alice
Stewart, Ian
Stummer, Gudrun
Summers, Graeme
Thacker, Rose
Thomas, Jenny
Tilney, Tony
Townsend, Frances
Traynor, Barbara
Tudor, Keith
Turner, Carole
Tweed, Mary
Ucen, Christine
Van Halm, Corrie
Vernon, Bisi
Wainwright, Pauline
Walford, Jane
Walford, Robin
Warner, Kerri
Weeks, Mary
Welford, Enid
Wells, Martin
Widdowson, Mark
Wood, Christine D.J.
Wright, Marilyn
Wright, Mary
Wright, Nina
Young, Anna
van Rijn, Biljana

## KCC - Kensington Consultation Centre

Abeles, Margi (Margaret)
Akan, Semra
Allen, Lesley
Alphonse, Jenny
Anderson, Eleanor
Anson, Carol
Anthony, Paul
Arora, Alka
Ashmore, Tom
Aufflick, Julia
Ayo, Yvonne
Bailey, David
Banfield, Margaret
Bengtsson, Lars-Erik
Bentley, Patrick
Bevan, Judith Lesley
Blacker, Sandra Rosamond
Bond, Sharon
Bownas, Jo
Briner, Wendy
Brooke-Smith, Chris
Brown, Diana
Brown, Mavis
Buffery, Elli
Burnham, John
Burton, Simon
Bwalya, Alf
Cahill, Denise
Cardelle Martinez, Raquel
Cardwell, Amynta
Carlsson, Lena
Carr, Samantha
Cerfontyne, Suzanne
Chadwick, Philip
Chandler, Emma
Chataway, Carola
Childs, Margaret
Cohen, Nomy
Collingwood, Katharine
Cooney, Joanne Elaine
Corrales, Iris
Coskeran, Helena
Culme-Seymour, Joanna
Cumberbatch, Andrea
Cutteridge, Simon
Dalal, Caroline
Davis, Gill
Day, Elizabeth
Deres, Mebrat
Dighton, Rosemary
Dinning, Penelope J
Divac, Aleksandra Sanya
Docking, Raymond Fredrick
Dolman, Christine
Drew, Philippa
Edge, Andrew
Edgington, Paula
Egan, Jude
Ekdawi, Isabelle
Eldrid, Sarah
Eliason, Bertil L
Elliott, Andrew
Fausset, Ann
Fernandez, Florence
Fernando - O'Connor, Chandra
Flower, Michael
Flynn, Kevin
Francis, Gabriela
Fredman, Glenda
Friend, Sue
Georgopoulou, Victoria
Godinho, Bernadette
Goldstein, Pam
Goodwillie, Gill
Gordon, Inger
Gorney, Carry
Graham, Anthony
Griffiths, Sheila
Groocock, Pamela
Hamilton, Doreen
Hanks, Helga
Hannah, Chris
Hannah, Clare
Harben, Ursula Mary Ann
Hart, Azina
Hartland, Marilyn Jean
Hartley, Althea
Haynes, Tanya
Heaphy, Grace
Hedges, Fran
Heismann, Elisabeth
Heseltine, Lynne
Hickman, Sue
Hoare, Elizabeth
Hogarth, Susy
Hudson, Pauline
Hughes, Gillian
James, Christopher
Jaroudi, Leila
Jarvis, Eileen
John, Beverlyn
Jones, Amanda
Jones, Annvirginia
Kardouche, Amanda
Kemmis Betty, Sally
King, Madeleine
Lang, Peter
Lang, Susan
Lauchlan, Sheila
Layfield, Elly
Lema, Juan Carlos
Levitt, Olga
Lewis, Joan
Lingard, Shirley Ruth
Little, Martin
Longhurst, Martin
Louden, Penny
MacChesney, Kirsty
Mahaffey, Helen
Makgoba, Sindi
Manicom, Hilary
Manojlovic, Jelena
Martin, Gloria
Masters, David

McAdam, Elspeth
McCafferty, Stewart
McCarry, Nicola
McEvoy, Patricia Elaine
McKay, Barbara
McManus, Gaynor
McNair, Ann G
Mendenhall, Marybeth
Micciarelli, Felicia
Middleton-Smith, Virginia
Milani, Belinda
Mills-Powell, Dana Sedgwick
Moorhead, Michael
Moriarty, Leigh
Moulding, Sara
Murphy, Enda Patrick
Nafie, Omar Ibrahim
Neate, Patricia
Newns, Kerri
Noonan, Mairead
Nottingham, Sue
O'Brien, Jackie
O'Connor, Michael
O'Leary, Brid
O'Loughlin, Brenda
Ogley, Julia
Ohene, Margaret D.
Oliver, Christine
Palmer, Ben
Partridge, Karen
Peacock, Katrina
Penalosa-Clarke, Adriana Lucia
Philip, Debra
Poole, Carol Lynn
Porter, Dorothy
Priest, Caroline
Pugh, Gabrielle
Qualtrough, Heather
Radmall, Bill
Rae, Frances
Randall, Peter
Rebuck, Alexandra Jane
Renz, Johanna
Richardson, Miriam Ann
Roberts, Alison
Roberts, Sylvia Marguerite
Rushforth, Catherine
Salazar, Maria Idalid Carreno
Schreiber, Kaye
Scott, John B
Short, Patricia
Siese, Andrew
Simon, Gail
Sluckin, Andy
Smart, Tanya
Smiljanic, Slobadanka
Smith, Maggie
Spence, Mary
Stacey-Ong, Lesley
Stevenson, Kate
Stocks, Samantha
Strang, Emily
Stratton, Peter M
Sweet, Patricia
Sykes, Ann
Söderqvist, Ingrid
Tague, Jackie
Taylor, Mary
Teng, Christina
Tengelin, Hans
Tenwick, Stephanie
Tidy, Deirdre
Tomlinson, Sharn
Tugendhat, Julia
Van Der Eijk, Mike
Vincent, Christopher R
Wainwright, Claire Stephanie
Wallis, Jill Alexis
Warlow, Steve
Way, Patsy
Weatherley, Paul
Webb, Ann
Wheeler, Maria
White, Anne
Whitfield, Gwyn
Wichené, Danièle
Wilson, Teresa
Woodward, Jan
Worthing-Davies, Richard
Worthing-Davies, Sally
Worthington, Rory
Wynn, Joan
de Laszlo, Alexandra

**KI - Karuna Institute**

Allen, Cheryl
Anjali, Yon
Ash, Jennifer
Attridge, Brian
Baker, Kevin
Bayley, Sydney
Bird, Lorna
Bond, Christine
Callaghan, Phillip
Campbell, Kate
Case, Karenza
Clayton, Valerie
Collins, Andrew
Connolly, Patricia
Cox, Miranda
Crittenden, Juliet
Croft, Janet
Davies, Debra
Deas, Francis
Donington, Laura
Drummond, Mark
Dymond, Christina
Elsdale, Bethan
Ferris, Mary
Finch, Auberon
Freeden, Mairi
Gadsden, Rosswell
Gordon, Deidre
Gordon Clark, Thalia
Greaves, Thomas
Grebot, Peter
Gresty, Julia
Gundry, Catherine
Hannah, Margaret
Hardy, Jo
Hay, Patricia
Higgs, Jody
Ives, Caroline
Johnson, Geoffrey
Jordan, Susan
Kalisch, David
Labworth, Yig
Layton, Clare
Legh-Smith, Andrea
Linnell, Maxine
Lown, Judy
MacFadyen, John
MacFadyen, Susan
Maloney, Sean
Mansi, Susan
Melrose, Hannya
Mowlam, Madeleine
Nancarrow, Kiya
North, Joanna
Oliver, Rosamund
Overzee, Anne
Padgett, Louise
Parkins, Yvonne
Rees, Ian
Roberts, Susan
Rose, David
Rotas, Joanna
Roy, Margaret
Sanders, Jane
Shaw, Adrian
Sills, Franklyn
Sills, Maura
Silverton, Stephen
Stark, Lynda
Stunden, Patricia
Sutherland, James
Taylor, Susan
Thomas, Alyss
Thompson, Rosalind
Toblini, Roberta
Walsh, Deirdre
Warrick, Jilly
Watson, Gay
Weller, Alison
Whitfield, Erica
Willow, Angela
Wilson, Jancis
Wright, Cathie

**LAPP - The London Association of Primal Psychotherapists**

Coombes, Clare
Cowan-Jenssen, Susan
Jenssen, Einar D.
Kostic, Jasna
Lafargue-Meenan, Martine
Nodelman, Marsha
O'Connor, Aine
Pollak, Angela

**LCP - London Centre for Psychotherapy**

Johnson Smith, Camilla
Reeves, David

**LPDO - Liverpool Psychotherapy Diploma Organisation (University of Liverpool)**

Applegarth, Janet
Bergel, Edith
Best, Aileen
Bryson, Sandra
Challis, Suzy
Clarke, Elaine
Collins, Gloria
Cooper, Graham
Dickinson, Paul
Dorndorf-Turner, Rhoda
Doyle, Elizabeth
Edwards, Jennifer
Egerton, Judi
Essex, Delia
Ferguson, Mary
Foster, Paul
Gabbay, Mark
Geldeard, Bryan W.J.
Glynn, Julie
Goepfert, Michael
Hamilton, Angela
Hamilton, Sheila L.L.
Hester, Bridget
Kiemle, Gundi
Kirkland-Handley, Nicholas
Lamb, Kirsten
Maguire, Claire
Mattison, Sheila
McIntee, Jeannie
McNab, Stuart
Mercer, Annie
Nevin, Jacqui
Parker, John
Pollet, Sheena
Potter, Steve
Prussia, Celia
Ross, Julie
Sharples, Geraldine M
Shetty, Girish
Smith, Flo
Smith, Margaret
Stewart, June
Taylor, Patsy
Thorley, Helen
Wallace, Daphne
Wattis, Libby
Woods, Angie
Woodward, Raie

**LSBP - London School of Biodynamic Psychotherapy**

Allen, Lynne

Armstrong, Caroline
Barker, Elizabeth
Baum, Stefanie
Boyesen, Gerda
Brosskamp, Cornelia
Byford, Sally
Byring, Carola
Cleminson, Richard
Deniflee, Ursula
Eisenbarth, Heiner
Evans-Stickland, Deborah
Gad, Gabriele
Gagnere, Maryline
Gandy, Rus
Gilbert, Gillie
Hauser, Susan
Heinitz, Karin
Hussong, Barbara
Jones, Helen
Lederman, Tsafi
Liebling, Lauren
Llewellyn, Martha
McLeod, Paula
Mundy, Jean
O'Neill, Julia
Ohnesorg, Johanna
Pawson, Chris
Quoilin, Michelle
Salles, Miriam
Scott, Brigitte
Southwell, Clover
Sutherland, Janet
Tanguay, Daniel
Taylor, Jill
Webb, Deborah
Wuebbeler, Hartmut
de Samaio Campos, Claudia
van Heel, Carlien

**MC - Minster Centre**

Abrahams, Elizabeth M
Alder, Helena
Alder, Roger
Arnold, Lynn
Baker, Jan
Barnett, Madeleine
Batchelor, Sue
Beaumont, Anne
Borges, Sheila
Bowman, Heather
Browner, Nancy
Bruce, John
Cato, Jane
Cherry, Chris
Cohen, Clare
Cook, Alice
Cook, Jane
Coumont Graubart, Valerie
Coussens, Kay
Davis, Helen
Denington, Julia
Dobbin, Gloria
Dunn, Nicola
Dunstan, Julie Leger
Dyson, Margaret
Embleton Tudor, Louise
Field, Rosalind
Fitzpatrick, Marion
Forster, Sally
Gelberg, Gilla
Gibson, Walter
Goldman, Manya
Gottschalk, Margaret
Granowski, Margaret
Guillemot, Yves
Hayhurst, Sohani
Hemmons, Judy
Humphrey, Anna
Hussain, Fakhir
Hyde, Dennis H
Jaffe, Alyson
Jefferies, Alison
Jefferies, Barbara
Jordan, Ruth
Kane, Janine
Kolbuszewski, Marianne
Lang, Richard
Lewis, Richard
Littlejohn, Sarah
Lock, Josephine
May, Caroline
Mazure, David
Moore, Julia
Morgan, Ruth
Morrison, Barbara
Music, Graham
Nelson, Sandy
Newbigin, Alison
Nicholson, David
Norton, Prue
O'Brien, Teddy
O'Callaghan, Lesley
O'Gorman, Mary Pat
Palmer, Jane
Pixner, Stefanie
Platt, Sue
Presant, Fern
Randle, Alan
Reilly, Philip
Renoux, Martine
Richardson, Magda Hafez
Robertson, Eileen
Robertson, Judith
Schiemann, Margot
Scovell, Janet
Sellers, Duncan
Shapiro, Adella
Sichel, David
Simmonds, Tina
Slade, John
Smith, Gill
Smith, Sue
Staplehurst, Carron
Steel, Sandra
Strebel, Silvia
Strobos, Carolyn
Sutters, Amabel
Tyler, Peter
Virgo, Leslie
Vodden, Ann
Walsh, Carys
Wanless, Anna
Wanless, Peter
Wilkinson, Gill
Wilkinson, Joan
Williams, Nigel
Williams, Pat
Williams, Ruth
Winder, Joy
Wiseman, Anna
Wood, Philip
Wood-Bevan, Rosy
Wootton, Julie
Young, Margot

**MET - Metanoia Institute**

Adams, Marie
Aggleton, Sue
Aldington, kay
Ambrose, Laura
Aram, Eliat
Ashcroft, Dinah
Atkins, Sue
Atkinson, Francis
Barker, Jocelyn
Barnes-Kilpatrick, Shirley
Bird, Julia
Blyth, Fiona
Bodgener, Sue
Borsig, Su
Boyle, John
Brauner, Rita
Breitenstein, Dorrit
Brennan, Catherine
Brooks, Irene
Brown, Lesley
Casatello, Giovanna
Cassidy, Mandy
Cerner, Ruth
Cheetham, Brian
Clevely, Sarah
Clifton, Elaine
Coakley, Una
Collin, Charlie
Coppens, Arnoldus
Cottrell, Sue
Coule, Jaqueline
Critchley, Bill
Cross, Jacqueline
Crossley, Gillian
Cullum, Mike
Daintry, Penelope
Daley, Morica
David, Ann
Davidge, Maggie
Davis, Richard
Dawson, Liz
Day, Laurie
Day, Lesley
Dent-Brown, Tracey
Dhillon Stevens, Harbrinder
Donaldson, Gill
Donnelly, Clare
Dove, Rabbi Jonathan
Edwards, Dagmar
Edwards, Harry
Elton Wilson, Jenifer
Flatt, Deborah
Fowlie, Heather
Fry, Julie
Gerlach, Lynne
Gibson, Jenny
Gibson, Miles
Gilbert, Maria
Glennis, Brierley
Graham, Marilyn
Griffiths, John
Hadwin, Peter
Hall, Joan
Hamilton-James, Tina
Harborne, Lynette
Hargaden, Helena
Harley, Ki
Harris, Lynn
Harrison, Lin
Hawxwell, Frances
Hegan, Laurence
Heley, Mary
Henderson, Andrew
Hewson, Julie Anne
Highley, John
Hipps, Hilary
Hitchings, Paul
Hodgson, Diane
Hopping, Geoff
Houghton, Christine
Howden Richards, Barbara
Hughes, Janet
Isaksson-Hurst, Gun I.E.
James, Clare
Jesson, Alison
Jones, Sue
Jordan, Hazel
Joyce, Philip
Kearns, Anne
Kerry, Liz
Kirby, Phillipa
Kowszun, Graz
Kraus, Frances
Lake, Moira
Lapworth, Phil
Lattimer, Carol
Lawes, Ginny
Lawley, Mike
Leach, Kathy
Leigh, Elana
Lomond, Marsha
MacLean, Annie
Macgregor, Wynne
Mackewn, Jennifer
Mackintosh, Peri
Macnab, Celia
Manielevitch, Edna
Manning, Helen
Mason, Christina
McGlashan, Judy
McGowan, Dominica
McKeown, Andy
Mercer, Shirley
Michaels, Ruth

Miller, John Andrew
Mills, Ted
Minihane, Anna
Moore, Maureen
Morin (Ms), Terry
Mukuma, Diana
Murphy, Katherine
Murray, Christine
Murray, Jane
Nathan, (Jennifer) Ruth
Noble, Susi
O'Brien, Gillian
O'Callaghan, Jean
O'Dwyer, Annegret
O'Keeffe, Mary
O'Sullivan, Geraldine
Omodiagbe, Kemi
Opienski, Jacek
Orlans, Vanja
Osborne, Lynda
Parava, Anna
Pearce, Gerald
Pearce, Peter
Penny, Sarah
Perkins, Kevin
Perring, Dr Michael
Philippson, Peter
Phillips, Amanda
Phillips, Sue
Pinto, Luca
Platt, Hilary
Plissart, Liesbet
Porter, Barbara
Prall, Werner
Prentice, Hilary
Proffitt, Sue
Prokayeva-Ross, Tatiana
Purcell, Anna Marie
Pye, Jim
Pyle, Magdalena
Ransley, Cynthia
Rapp, Hilde
Rattigan, Bridget
Rauf, Rozen
Razzaq-Bains, Saira
Renwick, John
Retallick, Malcolm
Richards, Alyson
Rickman, Christine
Rimmer, Annie
Robinson, Lesley
Romero, Maria Jose
Rowlands, Helen
Sala, Monica
Sampson, Gill
Samuel, Irene
Scott, Janice
Scott, Judy
Selwyn-Smith, Jacky
Shearman, Christine
Shivanath, Suhith
Shmukler, Diana
Sills, Charlotte
Skegg, Roz
Smethurst, Philippa
Smith, Amanda
Smith, Juliet
Smith, Steven
Stanko, Alison
Stevenson, Bruce
Stewart, Elizabeth
Straker, Gillian
Strickland, Martin Decourcy
Sunderland, Margot
Tabak, Carolyn
Tampin, Jill
Taussig, Maggie
Taylor, Diana
Taylor, Sheena
Tholstrup, Margaret
Thomas, Marcia
Tillman, Linda
Tudor, Keith
Turner, Carole
Turner, Mary
Valentine, Victoria
Vollum, Dorothy
Wallace, Norma
Wallstein, Richard S
Warburton, Geoff
Watters, Tamara
Wela Nkumanda, Rachel
Williams, Rosamund
Williams, Sam
Witter, Judith
Wood, Jane
Wood, Richard
Wright, Sue
Wyatt, Gill
Yates, Helen
van Rijn, Biljana

**NAFSI - Nafsiyat**

Ababio, Baffour Senkyere
Al-Jarrah, Nadina
Alayarian, Aida
Allen, Anita
Alleyne, Aileen
Bartels-Ellis, Phillida
Brauner, Rita
Brown, Mo
Chatterjee, Sherna Ghyara
Chavunduka, Gladys
Cockersell, Peter
Dupont-Joshua, Aisha
Eleftheriadou, Zack
Green, Rosita
Guernina, Zoubida
Güngör, Dilek
Harding, Valentine
Hoque, Rumman
Hughes, Deri
Kaur-Love, Jasminder
Laville, Vicki
Maru, Rashmi
McKenzie-Mavinga, I
Medhat, Katayoun Tamara
Morris, Patricia
Muir, Adeola
Mullowney, Mandy
Nippoda, Yuko
Owusu-Hirsch, Mary
Patel, Gita
Railton, Ja'far
Rao, Ms Varija
Richards, Diana
Seebarun, Dev
Shackle, Shahrukh Husain
Sheng, Rosemary Hui
Sheriff, Farida
Sigalas, Anthony
Thomas, Kim
Thomas, Lennox
Torey, Sharon
Wela Nkumanda, Rachel
Yazar, Jale

**NGP - The Northern Guild for Psychotherapy**

Andrews, Carol
Arundale, Rita
Bailey, Russell
Billingham, Joy
Brown, Dee M
Bulmer, E.A
Cropper, Josephine
Dhar, Devika
Duncan, Ursula
Eldridge, Alison
Ellenor, Deby
Elliot, Mary
Epstein, Melanie Lynn
Garrett, Pat
Greening, Sarah
Hamlyn, Sarah
Homer, Marjorie
Johnson, Janette
Johnson, Shirley
Kelly, Peter
Lawrence, Yvonne
Ledward Hobbes, Judi
Levine, Peter
Lister-Ford, Christine
Lough, Mark
Lough, Ruth
McNamara, Jennifer
Pearce, Liz
Wicks, Carole Ann
Wilson, Sandy

**NLPtCA - Neuro Linguistic Psychotherapy Counselling Association**

Abdulezer, Tania
Adlington, Jethro
Asseily, Alexandra
Blake, Nancy
Boyden, Tina
Bray, Malcolm
Brion, Marion
Brock, Sue
Burns, Paul
Burow, Birgit
Burtt, Lucy
Butler, Graham
Carpenter, David
Chalfont, Alexandra
Chamlee-Cole, Laurena
Clarkson, Tony
Coleby, Gillian
Connolly, Holly
Daniels, Frank
Deahl, Kieron
Dinwoodie, John
Eldon, Martin
Elliott, John
Gawler-Wright, Pamela
Gill, Susan
Grayson, Juliet
Hanchen, Tomasz
Hill, Jenny
Hueting, Margaret
Johnson, Michael
Kilgour, Mimi
La Tourelle, Maggie
Lampshire, Julia
Lawley, James
Le Lievre, John
Leakey, Peter
Lennox, Graham
Llewellyn, Alice
Looms, Suzanne
Lovegrove, Sherine
Macdonald, Laurie
McDermott, Ian
McDonnell, Fokkina
McEwan, Geraldine
Mills, Judith
Mohan, Terry
Moore, Terry
Morton, Valerie
Nolan, Philip
Norman, Harry
Pain, Jean
Poole, Nick
Reynolds, Francois
Richards, Paul
Russell, Julian
Scott Hayward, Anna
Sherlock, Teresa
Smith, Robert
Stammers, Sigrid
Strang Wood, Susi
Szary, Gerard
Thompson, Joan
Tidy, Deirdre
Tompkins, Penny
Vogel, Ludwig
Wake, Lisa
Walsh, Eileen
Warren, Tony
Watkins Seymour, Eileen
Weaver, Martin
Weight, Pam
Wilson, Nirved
Winterburn, Ann
Wood, Craig
Worth, Piers

**NRHP - The National Register of Hypnotherapists and Psychotherapists**

Apps, Jean
Ashworth, Freda
Barnard, Leo
Blake, Adrian
Bonner, David C
Brock, Susan
Butler, John
Campbell, Colin
Campbell-Beattie, John
Cawley, Tony
Challis, Raymond Thomas
Chamier, Suzanne
Chandra, Ish
Clarke, Simon
Clarke, Wendela
Coia, Grace
Collins, John
Cox, Christine Sarah
Diyaljee, Angeli
Dossett, Rosmary
Faith, Pat
Fish, Deborah M.
Gauvain, Tony
Glasspool, Patricia
Graham, Hilary
Grew, Lesley
Hailey, Peg
Harris, Gerald A.
Hart, Mary
Hazlehurst, Jean
Hogg, Christine Retson
Hormasji, Faridoon
Howie, David D.
Iremonger, Sue
Jackson, Maureen
Jones, Eileen
Khan, Sacha
King, Christine
Kulyk, Michael
Langley, Allen
Linn, Iris
Luce, Peter James
Ludolf, Monica
MacDonald, Ross
Mahon, David
Malcom, Hanne
Marshall, Jill
May, Adam
McGregor, Tony
Moreby, Patricia Joyce
Munro, Carole
Pain, Jean
Peace, Susan
Peters, Sheila
Pirie, Linda Ellen
Plotel, Angela
Plowman, John
Podolska, Sue
Poole, David
Prasad, Vijaya
Prince, Tania
Puckett, Jane
Rawson-Jones, Elizabeth
Riddell, Caroline
Riley, Brenda
Robertson, Donald
Robson, Ian
Russel, Pat
Savage, Peter J.D.
Scott, Catherine
Sever, Michael
Shearer, Anne
Shewan, Alistair
Smith, Alicia
Smith, Debra
Smith, Susan Diane
Sprent, Nigel
Stanier, Graham
Steel, Patricia
Tenn, Linda
Thornley, John
Thorp, Terry
Tierney, Sue
Timmann, S.
Tcyne, Joy K.
Trewhella, John
Wesson, Peter M.J.
Wilkins, David
Williams, Ann
Wren, Pauline

**NSHAP - National School of Hypnosis and Psychotherapy**

Adams, Ghislaine
Adams, Megan
Al Rubaie, Talal
Barwick, Kay
Bibby, Keith
Black, Judith
Black, Margaret
Boff, Roger
Boyden, Tina
Braterman, Eleanor
Burgess, Shanti
Busolini, Don
Butcher, Barbara
Caird, Elizabeth
Clancy, Ian
Clegg, Ian
Cole, Shanti
Coutts, Linda
Duck, Dorothy
Duncan, Fraser
Eaton, John
Economakis, Tara
Fitzgerald, Pamela
Freeman, Susan
Gallagher, Monica
Gawler-Wright, Pamela
Haynes, Eric
Heathersprite, Gina
Holm, Kirsti
Jones, Pamela
Kalitowski, Matthew
Kanakam, Jonathan
Keedy-Lilley, Ray
Kohler, Christiane
Lyon, Josephine
Malik, Shehzad
McGreevy, Edith
McGuinness, Mark
Morgan, Linda
O'Neill, Christopher
Peacock, Anne
Porter, Jim
Ratcliffe, Susan
Ridley, Elizabeth
Sawyer, Albert
Shaw, Jason
Shilling, Tara
Sim, Edward
Smolira, David
Strauss, Judith
Thomas, Graham
Tomlinson, Andrew
Ward, Dawn
Wilson, Janet
Zico, Junaid

**NWIDP - North West Institute for Dynamic Psychotherapy**

Allen, Tessa
Arkwright, Lynda
Bacha, Claire
Barker, Helen
Barnett, Gillian
Berman, Linda
Bird, John
Black, Teresa
Brown, Philip
Buckley, Michael
Byrne, Elizabeth
Charlton, Maureen
Churcher, John
Coldridge, Elizabeth
Conlon, Isobel
Cornell, Maria
Davenport, Sarah
Davies, Joyce
Evans, Mark
Fischer, Michael
Folland, Mark
Gatrell, Jane
Gowrisunkur, Jaya
Guthrie, Else
Harden, Bev
Haworth, Ann
Hellin, Katherine
Horne, Alan
Hughes, Lynette
Hunt, Patricia
Hyde, Keith
Judkins, Malcolm
Kaberry, Susan
Lancelot, Maggie
Lendrum, Susan
Lewis, Mary
Liddle, Helen
Lindsay, Marion
Lunt, Aidan
Margison, Frank
Martin, Jane
McAllister, Susan
Mitchell, Lesley
Morris, Jane
Nicholson, Jane
Osborn, Madeline
Prodgers, Alan
Rawson, Wendy
Rawsthorne, Jean
Rhodes, Adrian
Sheldon, Helen
Sutton, Adrian
Sykes, Kathleen
Tantam, Digby
Taylor, Theresa
Thomas, Sandra
Tindle, Kate
Towse, Esme
Walker, Kanta
Walker, Sundar Kanta
Whitmore, Robert
Woolfe, Ray

**PA - Philadelphia Association**

Ball, Kevin
Caviston, Paul
Clapham, Miles
Cooper, Hilary
Crellin, Clare
Davenport, Marie-Laure
Davies, Alison
Esterhuyse Falck, Sonja
Fielder, Michael
Friedman, Joe
Gilbert, Kate
Gill, Douglas
Glossop, Miranda
Gordon, John Fredrick
Gordon, Paul
Green, Prue
Gurney, Paul
Hardy, Liz
Itten, Theodor
King, Lucy
Loewenthal, Del
Low, James
Mayo, Rosalind
Moutsou, Christina
Nevins, Peter
O'Neill, James
Redler, Leon
Swift, Joanna
Thompson, Michael Guy
Touton-Victor, Patricia
de Leon, Heather

**PCP - PCP Education and Training**

Agnew, Joyce
Allen, Diane
Botella, Luis

Botterill, Willie
Brennan, Damian
Brennan, Joady
Bury, Dennis R.
Butler Smith, Catherine
Catina, Ana
Chevreau, Marc
Connolly, David
Crosby, Simon
Cross, Malcolm C
Cummins, Peter
Dalton, Peggy
Dimcovic, Nada
Dupuy, Alan
Evans, Ray
Gillman-Smith, Ian
Goold, Peter
Grimshaw, Francoise
Harvey, Paul
Jackson, Sherin
Jones, Helen
Kenny, Vincent
McNicholl, Declan
Morris, Clare
Murphy, Derry
O'Sullivan, Bernadette
Orme, Patricia Joyce
Overs, Nicola
Parnell, Mike
Peters, Anthony
Pile, Adele
Procter, Harry
Rawat, Shenaz
Rossotti, Nicole
Rowe, Dorothy
Selby, Gina
Smith, Alison
Sparkes, Frances
Stein, Nathan Bernard
Stojnov, Dusan
Taylor, Helen
Thompson, Joan
Thomson, Alan
Thorman, Chris
Townsend, Hugo
Viney, Linda
Ward, Rachel
Winter, David

**PET - Psychosynthesis & Education Trust**

Adamson, Niki
Afford, Peter
Audley, Matthew
Baillie, Karen
Bateson, Fiona
Bayley, Eva
Beecher-Moore, Naona
Bennett, Barbara
Blomfield, Valerie
Brankin, Irene
Burlington, Maggie
Chalk, Caroline
Clay, Lorna
Courtman, Anita
Crawley, Barbara
Davis, Susan
Donovan, Marlyn
Dormandy, Ruth
Eden, Sharon
Elliot, Patricia
Fogel, Vivienne
Fox, Catherine
Fox, Loretta
Genova, Jacqueline
Gibbs, John
Goss, Thomas
Greatrex, Julian
Hancock, Pauline
Harrison, Simon
Hendry, Devam
Hopkins, Kathleen
Howe, Patti
Jarvis, Cecilia
Jury, Lorraine
Kenny, Brigid
Kernoff, Marilyn
Kerridge, Petra
Kevlin, Kunderke
Kirwin, Mark
Koeppelmann, Marianna
Lyons, Kathleen
Marling, Frances
McAulay, Ruth
Millichamp, Stacey
Muir, Kate
Mutti, Derek
Nightingale, Eileen
Nye, Georgiana
O'Kelly, Marie
Parfitt, Will
Paterson, Anne
Pickstock, Keith
Rand, Judith Ann
Reynolds, Malcolm
Schofield, Peter
Sheriffs, Alison
Shorrock, Andrew
Sidhu, Frankie
Simmons, Linda
Smith, Heather
Specterman, Liz
Stacey, Linda
Strauli, Ursula
Sullivan, Christopher
Sutherland, Elisabeth
Tandy (Pilbrow), Alannah
Tempest, Jeanette
Thomas, Christina
Tinker, Siobhan
Todd, Janet
Ward, Barbara
Whitmore, Diana
Wigham, Avril
Williams, Heather
Williams, Timothy

**RE.V - Re.Vision**

Adams, Eve
Barber, Keith
Barfred-Dixon, Ameyo Katharina
Bartlett, Sheila
Bobsin, Mica
Brady, Kate
Brown, Lesley
Butcher, Marilyn
Byrne, Philomena Kearney
Crawford, Joan
Dennis, Suzanne
Denvir, Hazel
Findlay, David Alistair
Fisher, Anstice
Freshwater, Dawn
Frischer, Livia
Holland, Nicki
Hooper, Rosanne
Hosburn, Tania
Hutchinson, Garry
Marshall, Nicky
Moore, Ian
Nicolaus, Georg
O'Connor, Ann
Passmore, Pascale
Payne, Christopher
Plowman, Polly
Robertson, Chris
Robertson, Ewa
Ryall, Sue
Smail, Mary
Taylor, Shirley
Tutton, Catherine
Van Gogh, Mark
Vibert, Eva
Waterfield, Michael
Weinberg, Jane
Woodroffe, Roe
d'Aragona, Una

**SAP - Society of Analytical Psychology**

Schaverien, Joy

**SCPP - Soceity of Couple Psychoanalytical Psychotherapists**

Abse, Susanna
Bollinghaus, Elaine
Buss-Twachtmann, Christel
Cleavely, Evelyn
Clulow, Christopher
Cudmore, Lynne
Daniels, Orpa
Fishman, Doreen
Hewison, David
Hodson, Pauline
Hughes, Lynette
Koppelman, Liora
Millington, Malcolm
Morgan, Mary
Morley, Elspeth
Morley, Robert
Oldman, David
Pengelly, Paul
Rosenthall, Joanna
Shand, Belinda
Tarsh, Helen
Vincent, Christopher
Wright, Kenneth
Yass, Marion

**SEA - Society for Existential Analysis**

Asmall, Ismail
Bramham, Mick
Clary, George
Cooper, Jill
Corso, Teresa
Dorrell-Dahl, Tiffany
Frawley, Thomas Oliver
Goldberger, Danny
Goodliffe, Martin
Harding, Michael
Hetherington, Hugh
Hornby, Jackie
Lee, Simone
Leveque, Brigitte
Lewis, Jacqueline
Messenger, Daren
Mitchell, Diana
Morgan-Williams, Susan
Morrison, Philippa
Moscoso de Richardson, Gloria
Moss, Valerie
Myers, Carole
O'Sullivan, Elizabeth
Rabin, Judith
Ribeiro-Nelson, Caroline
Sheppard, Jan
Smith, Alexander
Tantam, Digby
Thomas, Tinu
Weisensel, Karin
Weixel-Dixon, Karen
Worrell, Michael
van Deurzen, Emmy

**SIP - Severnside Institute for Psychotherapy**

Allan, Kay
Ash, Robert
Bartlett, Mark
Bebber, Gillian
Box, Sally
Bramwell, Valerie
Britten, Hilary
Brosnan, Judi
Brown, Jill
Brown, Ray
Brown, Robin Gordon
Budden, Mark
Cheshire, Jane
Clacey, Robert
Collens, Louise
Cottman, Barbara

Davies, Sheila
Diaz, Marie Claire
Dresser, Iain
Elliott, Lea
Frye, Helen
Gardner, Fiona
Gell, Eva
Gosling, Patricia
Gracie, Jane
Green, Sylvia
Grocott, Annie
Hahn, Herbert
Hancock, Patricia
Harris, Clare
Harris, Gordon
Harris, Judith
Hawdon, Sheila
Hill, Jenny
Hillier, Anna Clare
Holmes, Jeremy
Hopkins, Jill
James, Glenys
James, Pat
Jones, Nicole
Kingston, Breda
Laitinen, Irmeli
Malone, Judy
Matthews, Carol
McCloskey, Fiona
McNamara, Barbara
Mitcheson Brown, Muriel
Morris, Steven
Navin, Tony
Palmer Barnes, Fiona
Patterson, Linda
Pehrsson-Tatham, Lena
Pocock, David
Pocock, Olga
Richards, Christopher
Robinson, Martin
Rowe, Jill
Scovell, Michael
Seigal, Liz
Shewan, Doreen
Snudden, Mike
Sproston, Suzanne
Standish, Elizabeth
Tatham, Peter
Telders, Martina
Travis, Mary
Turner, Philip
Watkins, Judy
Wedderkopp, Abigail
Weightman, Elizabeth
Wilson, Alexandra
Yariv, Gail
Zeal, Paul

**SITE - The SITE for Contemporary Psychoanalysis**

Adams, Tessa
Azgad, Racheli
Berry, Sally
Brewer, Madelyn
Cohen, Sylvia
Crellin, Clare
Defries, Nicky
Einhorn, Sue
Ellis, Mary Lynne
Embleton, Joan
Gee, Stephen
Gow, Marion
Gray, Kati
Guild, Liz
Gurney, Paul
Hall, Kirsty
Harper, Eric
Hill, Penny
Kreeger, Angela
Lebon, Marsha
Lloyd, Elizabeth
Mann, James
Molino, Anthony
Murdin, Lesley
Nevins, Peter
O'Connor, Noreen
O'Mally, Gerry
Oakley, Haya
Parker, Rosie
Pope, Alan
Reid, Elizabeth
Revelli, Simona
Roberts, Laurence
Ryan, Joanna
Ryan, Tom
Sales, Sally
Shetland, Ilrich
Sinclair, Fiona
Swift, Joanna
Townsend, Heather
Valea, Ana
Voikhanskaya, Marina
Worthington, Anne
de Leon, Heather

**SPCRC - School of Psychotherapy and Counselling Regent's College**

Adams, Martin
Adams-Langley, Stephen
Adler, Phyllis
Ahearne, Jan
Ahern, Geoffrey
Aldridge, Janet
Alexander, Zelda
Almond, Elaine
Alward, Susanna
Arzoumanides, Yiannis
Ashwin, Mary
Aston, John
Austin, Lesley
Azarkadeh, Shoreh
Babarik, Anthony
Bailey, Catalena
Baker, Adrienne
Barry, Ruth
Bennett, Joy
Beresford, Lucy
Berger, Jocelyn
Blyth, Douglas
Boa, Quint
Bowers, Petina
Bradley, Linda
Brown, Malcolm
Browne, Margaret
Budgell, Rosemary
Burnard, Linda
Caleb, Ruth
Cameron, Angela
Campbell, Christine
Campher, Rosemary
Cannan, Philippa
Capo-Bianco, Suzanne
Carroll, Victoria
Carsley, Carol
Cedro, Karin
Cloridor-Wood, Madie
Coetzee, Kotie
Coleman, Eva
Collins, Leila
Cooper, Michael
Corbett, Gemma
Cottam, Angela
Cottrell, Teresa
Crouch, Carol
Cutting, Penny
Daniels, Deborah
David, Anna-Kristin
Davies, Valentine
Dent, Carey
Dolphin, Eve
Dorrian, Maeve
Dove, Rabbi Jonathan
Du Plock, Simon
Duffy, Kathleen
Durlach, Stefan
Edwards, Rachel
Eglin, Patricia
Eisenhauer, Gary
Eleftheriadou, Zack
Epstein, Bunny ( F.C)
Epstein, June
Euba, Rachel
Farell, Em
Farrell, Em
Ferraiolo, Stefano
Foley, Dermot
Fouque, Patricia
Fox, Almuth-Maria
Fox, Helen
French, Anne
Friedrich, Brigitte
Gallagher, Teresa
Gardner, Peter
Gavin, Verity J
George, Dorothy
Goldberger, Danny
Goldenberg, Harriet
Gooding, Kim
Gordon, Elizabeth
Gorodensky, Arlene
Grace, Carole
Green, Carolyn
Green, Dror
Greenwood, Lynn
Gunton, Gaye
Guthrie, Barbara
Hall, Albyn
Hamm, Alexandra
Hammond, Tania
Hanaway, Monica
Harding, Michael
Harlap, Nahum
Harman, Josephine
Harris, Mary
Harte, Vivienne
Harvey, Sandra
Haskayne, Amanda
Haugh, Sheila
Hazelton, Sally
Heralall, Ellen
Hirigoyen, Sarah
Holmes, Carol
Hornby, Jackie
Horne, David C
Hudson, David
Hughes, Janet
Jacobson, Rosemary
Jennings, Peter
Jolles, Pamela
Jonathan, Arthur
Jones, Alan
Julien, Michael
Kahr, Brett
Karban, Barbara
Karter, John
Keal, Susan
Kerr, Libby
Kingsley, Joan
Kirkland-Handley, Nicholas
Kondos, Sandy
Kostoris, Laura
Kristal, Barbie
Lawlor, Virginia
Le Brun, Christine
Lee, Simone
Leveque, Brigitte
Lever, Maureen
Lipman, Amanda
Little, Jon
Lock, Gillian
Luca, Maria
Lumbis, Gerald
Lund, Leslie Ann
MacCallum Sullivan, Mary
Madison, Gregory
Malkin, Marion
Mansall, Cordelia
Marriott, Marcia
Marshall, Susan
Massara, Catharina
Massil, Ros
May, Catriona
May, Suzanne
McAleer, Eileen
McKenna, Clare
Miles, Natalie
Miller, Joanna
Milton, Martin
Miqueu-Baz, Christine

Moja-Strasser, Lucia
Monaghan, Catherine
Morgan-Williams, Susan
Morrison, Philippa
Muldoon, Nuala
Murphy, Sue
Myers, Janet
Ngone, Mary
Nielsen, Claudia
Nuttall, Caryn
Nye, Ann
O'Brien, John
O'Driscoll, David
Oaten, Gae
Ogilvie, Renate
Oliver, Mandy
Owen, Ian
Owens-Ward, Lyn
Palamountain, Alan
Parissis, Maria
Parkin, Gwendolyn
Parr, Meriel A
Payne, Adette
Pearmain, Dr Rosalind
Pictet, Dariane
Platt, Monique
Ponomareva, Nadejda
Popple, Gillian
Potsides, Penny
Poulopoulos, Katerina
Preedy, Jan
Purpura, Davide
Rabin, Judith
Radlett, Marty
Radziszewicz, Tina
Rayner, Mark
Reardon, Paula
Reinisch, Lili
Revelli, Simona
Riddy, Paula
Romisch-Clay, Liza
Royle, Anthony
Ruggieri, Gloria
Russell, Doug
Russell, Tina
Sabayinda, Michael
Sachs, Adah
Saroff, Rahel
Sayyah, Shahrzad
Scherzer, Andrea
Schmitt-Castilla, Maria
Shields, Ellen Attracta
Sim, Camilla
Simpson, Catherine
Singer, Dani
Slater, Joan
Smallwood, Imogen
Smolar, Monika
Sorensen, Bernice
Spinelli, Ernesto
Stadlen, Anthony
Steeds, Leila
Steel, Marion
Stehle, Peter
Stein, Yvonne
Steward, Jennifer
Stockley, Rosalind
Stokoe, Wendy
Strasser, Alison
Strasser, Freddie
Swynnerton, Richard
Taylor, Jennifer
Taylor, Marsha
Thompson, Fiona
Thompson, Patricia
Thornton, Susanne
Thorpe, Ivan
Ticktin, Stephen
Turner, Elizabeth
Unsworth, Gisela
Uphoff-Chmielnik, Andrea
Vale, Elissa
Ventham, Brian
Vickers, Linda
Walker, Jillian
Wallace, Patti
Waller, Rosa
Walton, Michael
Warren, Yvonne
Weaver, Carol
Weisensel, Karin
Whitney, Glenn
Wigan, Rose
Williams, Jill
Williams, Katherine
Wilson, Carol
Wilson, Shula
Wolf, Darren
Wood, Morag
Woolf, Tanya
Yentob, Linda
Young, Dianne
Young, Sarah
Zinovieff, Nicholas
de Botton, Susan
von Britzke, Michaela

## SPEC - Spectrum

Allsop, Paul
Bennett, Ross
Carruthers, Dianna
Cooper, Terry
Crofton, Sue
Dahle, Josephine
Doust, Gill
Dryden, Jan
Fletcher, Joan
Freedman, Jax
Gabriel, Jill
Gotto, Jane
Hargreaves, Judy
Lane, Jeff
Lucas, Pauline
McKenzie, Maggie
McNeil, Delcia
Methuen, Oriel
Morrison, Paul
Naish, Julia
Neal, Charles
Patterson, Anna
Rose-Smith, Gillian
Roth, Jenner
Russell, Marion
Searle, Joanne
Shreeves, Rosa
Stone, Anthony
Widdicombe, Howard
Williams MacKenzie, Kate
Willmott, Susan
Witt, Erica
Witt, John

## SPTI - The Sherwood Psychotherapy Training Institute

Ainsworth, Eileen
Aitken, Fiona
Allen, Penny
Anderson, Maureen
Archer, Alan
Ashton, Carole
Atkinson, Pamela
Austin, Catherine
Avery, Anna
Balick, Aaron
Barley, Andrew
Barsky, Sue
Bassett, George
Beacham, Sonja
Bell-Boulé, Annabell
Berardi, Chris
Birch, Carol
Bradley, Rex
Bragée, Britt
Breeze, Graham
Brinicombe, Phyl
Britt, Bragee
Brown, Kate
Brown, Robert
Browning, Peter
Bryant, Anne
Bryant, Pat
Bullen-Spicer, Robert
Campbell Davies, Maureen
Canon, Rob
Canon, Sue
Carrette, Timothy
Carter, Nick
Carton, Roy
Cassidy, Allison Christine
Catesby, Cynthia
Caw, Jeanette
Clarke, Ann Marie
Clements, Wendy
Codman, Chris
Codman, Sarah
Cooper, Jane
Coupe, Aileen
Coward, Malcolm
Crowley-Schweitzer, Brigitte
Cullwick, Joy
Curman, Barbro
Davison, Charles
Derrick, Stephen
Diamond, Dawn Lorraine
Dolan, Bernadette
Donnai, Andrew
Drury, Gitta
Dunn, Michael
Dyce, James
Edelman, Barbara
Einarsson, Pall
Eriksson, Anders
Eriksson, Tina
Erskine, Richard
Fisher, Paul
Fisher, Paul
Fookes, Andrew
Gardner, Damian
George, Stephen David
Ghent, Rita
Gilbert, Anne
Gill, Eileen
Gilson, Jean
Gobbato, Wendy
Goldstein, Marc
Granthier, Miriam
Green, Marian
Gregory, Kayt
Greville, Coral
Hackett, Michelle
Haddon, Neale
Hale, Sue
Harley, Maxine
Harris, Richard
Hassall, Alan
Hawksworth, Janet
Henderson, Stuart R.
Honey, Joanna
Hope, David
Hotham, Aine
Howard Tayler, Jaqueline
Hudson, Rachel
Jackson, Diana
Janks, Ann
Johnson-Hill, Heather
Jones, Helen
Joynes, Debbie
Juggins, Kate
Kalinko, Sharon
Keen, Caroline
Kellett, Rachael
Kent, Rachel
Kerr, Julie
King, Johanna (Jo/Hannetjie)
Kingsley-Mills, Christine
Kirtley, Jane
Kitchin, Paul Duncan
Knights, Jean
Knowles, Louise
Lake, Dorry
Langford Bellaby, Rosemary
Lavender, Peter
Lehain, Daniel
Levin, Barbara
Lewis, Steve
Logan, Ailsa
Loiseau, Kate
Louw, Francois
Luckraft-Voges, Julie
Mann, David

Mann, Sarah
Maronitis, Maggie
Marshall, Clare
Maudling, Caroline
McDonald, James
McFarlane, Kay
McKay, Carol
McQuaid, Cathy
Mitchell, Paul Christoph
Mohn Engebretsen, Karin
Moore, Lena Rosaria
Moore, Maria
Moulding, Jacqueline
Murray, Valerie
Nadkarni, Joanne
Newbery, Christine
Ochyra, Krysia
Orlandi-Fantini, Claire
Orlandi-Fantini, Peter
Pantall, Marlis
Paris, Jan
Pearson, Beryl
Pencavel, Ursula
Pigott, Sheila
Pitt, Daniel
Pizer, Isaac
Pooley, Steve
Preston, Margaret
Pugsley, Stephanie
Quilter, Sally
Regan, Catherine
Roland-Smith, Mandy
Rosenbaum, Linda Ann
Sahni, Jadean
Scott-Combes, Jacqueline
Senior, Maggie
Sharp, Frank
Sharp, Rob
Shaw, Robert
Shelley Martens, Karin
Shmukler, Diana
Short, Deborah
Shotter, Ann
Shubinsky, Kath
Sless, Deborah
Smith, Angie
Smith, Baden Bob
Spicer, Rob
Spitz, Shirley
Staveley, Susan
Stevens, Christine
Stevens, Lynda
Stratton-Woodward, Sally
Strawson, Anne
Talbot, Mike
Taylor, James
Thompson, Geoffrey
Thrane, Susanne
Tilley, Alison
Turner, Susie
Tynan, Imelda
Walker Hampton, Joan
Waring, Judith
Watson, Caroline
Watson, Sandra
Whitworth, Patricia
Wilde, Paul
Wiles, Margaret
Williams, Tina
Wilson, Janet Lynn
Wolf, Runa
Wright, Norman

**STTDP - South Trent Training in Dynamic Psychotherapy**

Bailey, James
Bradley, Marie
Crabtree, Lyn
Denness, Brian
Fisk, Geoffrey
Fletcher, John
Holt Garner, Lydia
Hopcroft, Susan
Humphreys, Nicholas
Jones, Richard
Lee, Helen
Marshall, Pam
Morton, Mary
O'Reilly, Tom
Ratigan, Bernard
Ryder, John
Schröder, Thomas
Shaw, Lynda
Smith, David
Staines, Jillian
Stewart, Naomi
Thomas, Simon
Walker, Catriona
Watson, Clare
Young, Raymond

**ScPTI - Scarbrough Psychotherapy Training Institute**

Anderson, Naomi
Budden, Mark
Davies-Hough, Karen
Evans, Kenneth
Hewitt-Taylor, Joanna
Kurowska, Irena
Richards, Simon
Waldram, Roger
Wilkinson, Heward
Wilkinson, Kathleen

**TMSI - Tavistock Marital Studies Institute**

Abse, Susanna
Buss-Twachtmann, Christel
Clulow, Christopher
Cudmore, Lynne
Hewison, David
Millington, Malcolm
Morgan, Mary
Rosenthall, Joanna

**UPCA - Universities Psychotherapy & Counselling Association**

Adams, Clare E A
Addison, Susan
Aksoy Robins, A Asu
Arcari, Sallie R
Arnesen, Paul
Arnold-Baker, Claire
Atherton, Alistair N
Bajer, Maryse
Balls, Margaret A
Barnett, Laura M E
Beber, Ray
Bennett, John
Benson, Jarlath
Bibbey, Judy
Bishop, Elizabeth
Blampied, Annette N
Bodiam, Rosemary J
Boronska, Teresa .W
Bradshaw, Lynn E
Bridge, Sheila
Brittain, Charlie
Brookhouse, Shaun
Brooks, Cynthia M
Brown, Iain
Bundhoo, Devanand
Burden, Michele A
Burke, Erylene
Butler, John
Byers, Angela
Campbell, Jane
Chandler, Philip
Charlton, Patricia S.
Chessum, Lucy
Clarke, Colin
Clement de L'Epine, Karen
Coan, Anita
Cole, Laurence E
Collings, Sarah
Conway, Sally
Coren, Alex B
Coverdale, Sally
D, Niki
Darivakis, Dimitri
Davidson, Jill
Davies, Jennifer
Davis, John D
Davis, Marcia L
Davison, John
Dicks, Russell
Dixon, Linda
Dolan, Francis
Donaghy, Miriam
Door, Annette
Downie, Andrew
Dudley, Jane M
Dunn, Mark
Easby, Barbara
Elvin, Gill R
Espey, Andrew
Fairweather, Cassandra
Fanning, Alexandra
Finch, Helen
Fisher, Jonathan
Fisher, Kim
Fitzgerald-Pool, Zoe
Flacke, Theresa
Flannery, Jean
Fofah, Ngozi
French, Jennifer
Gladwell, Stephen
Glyn, David R
Goalen, Rosalinde
Goti, Itsaso
Gower, Barry
Greenwood, Anthony
Gregg, Peter D
Greig, Edward
Griffiths, E. Anne
Güngör, Dilek
Haigh, Rex
Hammond, Liz
Haywood, Jill
Heller, Fawkia
Hemingway, Paul
Henderson, David
Hershkowitz, Annie
Hobart, Angela
Hodgkiss, Andrew
Hollows, Belinda
Hotchkies, Lynsey
Howell, Raymond
Hudson, Inge
Huet, Valerie
Jacobs, Michael
Jefford, Adam
Johnson, Paul
Jude, Julia
Jupp, Elizabeth
Katis, Elisabeth
Kendall, Tim
Kendrick, Lesley
Kenward, Raymond P
Keshet-Orr, Judi
Kirby, Steve
Lane, Jeff
Laurence, Lee
Lawton, Derek
Lewis, Kate A
Leygraf, Bernd C
Little, Jon
Loewenthal, Del
Lohman, Frans
Lund, Charles
Lynton, Joseph A
MacLaren, Ian
Macaro, Antonia
Mackie, James
Maddox, Chris
Maglo, Dorothy
Maloney, Chris
Mansfield-Osborne, Lynne
Mason, Christine
Masterson, Karen
McCabe, Jennifer
McClelland, Sheila
McCombe, Brian
McLure, Elizabeth

Mertzanakis, Christos
Millar, David
Millar, Elizabeth M
Miller, Lynda R
Mitchell, Diana
Mohamed, Carol G M
Monroe, Claire
Montanaro, Caroline F B
Morley, Jane
Moukam, Rameri Reshkhi
Nicholls, John
Nolan, Michael A
Norman, Caroline
O'Brien, Maja
O'Loughlin, Pauline A
O'Neill, Christopher
Oakley, Sanja
Oram, Gill
Orchin, Susan
Page-Hanson, Paul
Paley, Graham
Pardoe, Kathleen A
Parsons, Kathy
Phillips, Pauline
Ploumaki, Sophia
Porteous, Louise
Pover, Jane S E
Power, Kevin
Quarmby, David
Radcliffe, Mark
Ragiadakos, Nikolas
Raimes, Peter
Rainsford, Helena
Rapp, Hilde
Ratigan, Bernard
Rawlinson, David
Redmond, Jayne
Reid, Errol
Reilly, Stephen
Rejaie, Carol
Reynolds, Pat
Ritchie, Sheila
Rose, Chris
Rose, Theresa
Rosenthal, Hat A
Rowe, Celly
Rowland, Catherine
Rubin, Ann
Salter, Gill
Sanders, Paul J
Sarwar, Iwona
Scott, Tricia
Shipton, Geraldine
Simpson, David
Siret, Rachel E
Smith-Pickard, Paul J
Snell, Robert C
Stadlen, Naomi
Stephenson, Keri P
Stone, Judith H
Synnott, Annie
Tantam, Digby
Taylor, Karen
Taylor, Maureen
Tomlin, Minoo
Trythall, Patricia
Urquhart, Peta A
Vincent, Jane
Walker, Moira
Waller, Diane E
Walters, Ian
Ward, Bernard
Weaver, David
Wells, Charles
Winship, Gary
Wooder, Bernard
Wynter-Philp, Lloyd
Yare, Brinley
Young, Robert
van Deurzen, Emmy

**VAPP - Vaughan Association of Psychodynamic Psychotherapists**

Baker, Carol
Beaumont, Caroline
Bowerman, Elaine
Dent, Peter
Dickson Dummer, Karine
Duffin, Lorna
Dunn, Elizabeth
Ellis, Roger
Flanagan, Diana
Geraghty, Nadine
Horrocks, Pam
Jacobs, Michael
Jane, Susan
Janickyj, John
Jarrett, Betty
Judson, Janice
King, Gail
Madden, Felicity W.
McFarland, Alf
McKay, Lynn
Peglar, Graham
Pelz, Doris
Poston, Frances
Rowe, Frances
Schneeweiss, Rose
Spare, Elaine
Strang, Jenny
Walker, Moira
Wheeler, Sue
Wightwick, Helen
Williams, Sherly

**WMIP - West Midlands Institute of Psychotherapy**

Abberley, Colette
Anderson, Judith
Anees, Nabil
Atkinson, Paul
Babiker, Gloria
Barden, Nicola
Barker, John F.
Barrett, James
Beedie, Margaret
Birtle, Janice
Blakey, Angela
Bond, Ann R.
Bramall, Keith
Brockley, Sally
Burke, Robina
Byrne, Dorothy
Calvert, Jane
Campbell, Duine
Camps, Thomas
Carlish, Sonia
Cheshire, Jane
Chevins, Lynda
Cooper, Grahame F.
Cox, Margaret
Crisp, Jennifer
Curran, Maureen
Davis, Patrick
Dennis, Elisabeth
Doyle, Mary
Ellis, June Blythe
Feasey, Don
Flanagan, Helen
Fox, Fiona
Fraser, Douglas A.
Fraser, Mary Elizabeth
Gilliver, Catherine
Goodyear, P A J
Hamilton, Jane
Harrington, Leslie
Harris, Debra
Harvey, Tricia A.
Hill, Val
Hivernel, Dr Françoise
Hoag, Linda M.
Hogg, Rosemary
Holmes, Dorothy
James, Pat
Johnson, Judy
King, David
Kingsley, Laurence
Liebling, Angela J.
Lloyd, Helen
Mackenzie, Ian D.
Madden, Felicity W.
Male, David F.
Maté, Helen
McCloskey, Fiona
McCormick, Helen
McDonald, James T
McFarland, Alf
Meredith-Owen, William
Mills Burton, M.
Morley, Ann
Myers, Marion
Nicholas, John
O'Leary, Anne M.T.
Owen, Angela
Pitt, Christine
Ratoff, Tammy
Rentoul, Robert W.
Reynolds, Michael
Roy, Geraldine
Ryan, Angella M.J.
Sadgrove, Jenny
Samson, Anne
Schaverien, Joy
Shrimpton, David W
Simpson, Elizabeth
Skailes, Claire
Smith, Lorraine
Speed, Bebe
Spencer, Margaret
Stockwell, Rose
Stokes, Jenny
Taylor, Vivienne
Toms, David A.
Truckle, Brian
Truckle, Shirley
Tucker, Joanna
Vallance, Fiona
Van Marle, Susanna J
Villia-Gosling, Athina
Wake, Elaine
Wattis, Libby
Williams, Debra
Williams, Sherly
Winkley, Linda
Wright, Harry
Yates, Kathleen

**WPF - Westminster Pastoral Foundation**

Goodrich, Diana
Neal, (Ms) Lalage

**WTC - The Women's Therapy Centre**

Aird, Eileen
Austin, Susan
Beck, Orit
Berry, Sally
Brennan, Clare
Burgoyne, Vivien
Chisholm, Lisa
Crace, Gay
Dana, Mira
Davenport, Marie-Laure
Fisher, Jinny
Gorman, Susan
Gow, Marion
Green, Margaret
Haberlin, Jane
Harvey, Trudy
Hudson, Inge
James, Jessica
Kleinot, Pamela
Laitinen, Irmeli
Maguire, Marie
Millier, Sylvia
Montero, Isabel
Mycroft, Jessica
Orbach, Susie
Patel, Gita
Platt, Sue
Powell, Angela
Price, Susan
Ritchie, Sheila
Ryan, Geraldine
Sengun, Seda
Smith, Ruthie

Williams, Gwen
Yazar, Jale

**YAPP - Yorkshire Association for Psychodynamic Psychotherapy**

Ashton, John
Bolsover, Nick
Bonner, Kate
Bradshaw, Lynn E
Bramall, Keith
Douglas, Angela
Eadie, Yvonne
Gilljam, Annika
Gudjonsson, Ingolfur A
Hanks, Helga
Harrow, Anne
Heenan, Colleen
Kennard, David
Kitsen, Jane
Lewis, Sheila
Martin, Carol
Martin, Gill
McCluskey, Una
Morris, Jane
Page, Annabel
Reilly, Stephen
Rose, Sally
Rowe, Celly
Sidey, Brian
Stokeld, Alasdair
Syme, Gabrielle
Tanna, Nick
Ward, Bernard
Wattis, Libby
Webb, Joan
Welsh, Catherine

# Multilingual Practitioners

### Afrikaans

Anderson, Maureen
KENT

Botha, Dr Marie
LONDON NORTH WEST

Campher, Rosemary
OVERSEAS-SOUTH AFRICA

Cassidy, Allison Christine
LONDON NORTH WEST

Davids, Jennifer
OVERSEAS-SOUTH AFRICA

Kalinko, Sharon
KENT

King, Johanna (Jo/Hannetjie)
LONDON NORTH

Louw, Francois
LONDON CENTRAL

Mayer-Johnson, Jessica
BERKSHIRE

Renz, Johanna
DORSET

Rosenthal, Alison
OVERSEAS-SOUTH AFRICA

Salters, Diane
LONDON SOUTH EAST

Wela Nkumanda, Rachel
LONDON SOUTH EAST

### Akan

Prempeh Adu Bobi, Henry K.
KENT

### Amharic

Deres, Mebrat
LONDON SOUTH EAST

### Arabic

Al Rubaie, Talal
EAST YORKSHIRE

Ali, Saadi
LONDON SOUTH WEST

Allawi, Nadia
NORTH SOMERSET

Babiker, Gloria
CHESHIRE

Burrows-Wood, Joanna
LONDON EAST

El-Hadi, Ali
EAST YORKSHIRE

Guernina, Zoubida
LONDON SOUTH WEST

Heller, Fawkia
OVERSEAS - LEBANON

Jaroudi, Leila
EGYPT - OVERSEAS

Nafie, Omar Ibrahim
LONDON NORTH

Yousry, Menis
LONDON NORTH

### Assyrian

Allen, Anita
LONDON NORTH WEST

### Azarbija

Rouhifar, Zhila
MIDDLESEX

### Balineese

Hobart, Angela
LONDON WEST

### BAS-Basque

Goti, Itsaso
LONDON EAST

### BEN-Bengali

Damani, S
LONDON NORTH

Hoque, Rumman
MIDDLESEX

Hussain, Nasima
STAFFORDSHIRE

Kundu, Dr Arabinda
ESSEX

Rashid, Shila
LONDON WEST

Sharma, Meera
ESSEX

Vibhakar, Lopa
ESSEX

### Brazillian

Nielsen, Claudia
LONDON NORTH WEST

### British Sign Language

Daniel, Liz
NOTTINGHAMSHIRE

Law, Anne M
NOTTINGHAMSHIRE

### Bulgarian

Pepper, Marie
LONDON NORTH

Petkova, Petia
BRIGHTON AND HOVE

Waller, Diane E
BRIGHTON AND HOVE

### Burmese

Wallis, Jill Alexis
HERTFORDSHIRE

### Cantonese

Howard, Caroline Pui
LONDON NORTH WEST

Lau, Annie
OVERSEAS-SINGAPORE

Leong, Jessica
NORFOLK

Mollahan, L. G.
LONDON EAST

Sheng, Rosemary Hui
ESSEX

Teng, Christina
ESSEX

### Catalan

Campos, Hanne
OVERSEAS-SPAIN

### Chinese

Lau, Bernard Wai Kai
LONDON EAST

Sheng, Rosemary Hui
OVERSEAS-HONG KONG

Shuen, Dorcas
KENT

Tse, Claude
KENT

### Creole

Alleyne, Aileen
LONDON NORTH WEST

Sawyerr, Alice A A
LONDON NORTH WEST

### Croatia

Oakley, Sanja
LONDON NORTH

### Czech

Boronat, Dascha
LONDON SOUTH EAST

Eisler, Z
SURREY

Pyle, Magdalena
LONDON SOUTH EAST

Souta, Marie Ludmila
LONDON SOUTH EAST

### Danish

Barfred-Dixon, Ameyo Katharina
LONDON CENTRAL

Bhatia, Pushan
OXFORDSHIRE

Blow, Kirsten
OVERSEAS-DENMARK

Burkhardt, Tansen I
SOUTHAMPTON

Dahle, Josephine
OXFORDSHIRE

Frisvold, Tove
LONDON EAST

Griffin, Susanne
BUCKINGHAMSHIRE

Gustafsson, Birgitta
NORTH SOMERSET

Haase-Derrett, Susan
DEVON

Jensen, Greta
LONDON NORTH

Johansson, Birgitta
BEDFORDSHIRE

Krause, Inga-Britt
CHESHIRE

Lawrence, Elisabeth
CHESHIRE

Lee, Denis
SURREY

Looms, Suzanne
FIFE

Malcom, Hanne
OVERSEAS - NORWAY

Mohn Engebretsen, Karin
LONDON SOUTH WEST

Priestley, John
OVERSEAS-DENMARK

Veje, Margit
OVERSEAS-DENMARK

### Deri

Alayarian, Aida
LONDON NORTH WEST

### Dutch

Anderson, Maureen
HAMPSHIRE

Borghgraef, Dr Guy
SOMERSET

Burbach, Frank
LONDON NORTH WEST

Burck, Charlotte
OVERSEAS-NETHERLANDS

Carton, Roy
LONDON NORTH WEST

Coppens, Arnoldus
NORTHUMBERLAND

Dijkman, Theo
BUCKINGHAMSHIRE

Dokter, Ditty
LONDON NORTH WEST

Du Ry, Marc
ESSEX

Edwards-Pollard, Astrid
OVERSEAS-NORWAY

Gibbs, John

Griffiths, Anne-Megan
SURREY

Heiller, Birgitta R.
LONDON WEST

Kaufmann, Mickey
BRISTOL

Kevlin, Kunderke
LINCOLNSHIRE

Lohman, Frans
GREATER MANCHESTER

McDonnell, Fokkina
CAMBRIDGESHIRE

Minnaar, Doris

Plissart, Liesbet
GREATER MANCHESTER

Schakel, Hildegard
NORFOLK

Sluckin, Andy
LONDON SOUTH WEST

Strauli, Ursula
CARDIFF

Telders, Martina
OVERSEAS-NETHERLANDS

Tjepkema, Froukje
MIDDLESEX

Trelease, P.
EAST SUSSEX

Van Halm, Corrie
BUCKINGHAMSHIRE

Wanless, Anna
GREATER MANCHESTER

Widdowson, Erica Simone
HERTFORDSHIRE

van Bilsen, Henck P.J.G.
SOUTH YORKSHIRE

van Deurzen, Emmy
LONDON NORTH WEST

van Heel, Carlien
OVERSEAS-NETHERLANDS

van Rossum, Diederik
OVERSEAS-NETHERLANDS

### Farsi

Alayarian, Aida
LONDON NORTH WEST

Allen, Anita
LONDON NORTH WEST

Bathai, Parizad
LONDON NORTH WEST

Farzim, Pari
MIDDLESEX

Rouhifar, Zhila
LONDON SOUTH WEST

Sayyah, Shahrzad
LONDON NORTH

Sharifi, Pury
LONDON NORTH WEST

Sueke, Minoo
LONDON WEST

Zarbafi, Ali
LONDON WEST

### Finnish

Brown, Ulla
LONDON NORTH

Byring, Carola
OXFORDSHIRE

Frisvold, Tove
CAMBRIDGESHIRE

Gordon, Leila
DEVON

Laitinen, Irmeli
KENT

Lettington, Liisa
OVERSEAS-FINLAND

Söderström, Anne-Charlotte
OVERSEAS-FINLAND

### French

Adams, Ghislaine
LONDON WEST

Addison, Ann
LONDON NORTH

Adema, Rachel
LONDON SOUTH EAST

Alabaster, Nigel
WEST SUSSEX

Aldridge, Janet
WEST MIDLANDS

Alexander, Erica
LONDON NORTH

Alferoff, Tamara
EAST SUSSEX

Allard, Alain
POOLE

Andrews, Stuart
NORFOLK

Aquarone, Luc-Remy
LONDON WEST

Armstrong, Caroline
LONDON WEST

Asseily, Alexandra
LONDON NORTH WEST

Austin, Susan
GUERNSEY

Ayres, Gary
NORTH SOMERSET

Babiker, Gloria
MIDDLESEX

Bailey, Catalena
LONDON WEST

Baker, Jan
SURREY

Barnett, Laura M E
GLASGOW

Begg, Ean
LONDON SOUTH EAST

Bell, Christine
NOTTINGHAMSHIRE

Bell-Boulé, Annabell
LONDON SOUTH WEST

Bennis, Jackie
LONDON NORTH WEST

Bensimon, Marlene
LONDON NORTH WEST

Bentovim, Dr Arnon
OVERSEAS-ITALY

Benvenuto, Bice
LONDON SOUTH WEST

Bibby, Keith
ESSEX

Bingham, Jane
LONDON SOUTH WEST

Birkett, Diana
WEST MIDLANDS

Black, Teresa
TYNE AND WEAR

Blackburn, Ivy-Marie
SOUTH YORKSHIRE

Bojanic-Wright, Stoya
LONDON SOUTH WEST

Boll, Antonia
BERKSHIRE

Booth, Philip
HAMPSHIRE

Borghgraef, Dr Guy
LONDON WEST

Boyesen, Gerda
LONDON NORTH WEST

Bradley, Jonathan
STAFFORDSHIRE

Brown, Kate
LONDON WEST

Browne, Maureen
LONDON SOUTH WEST

Buckley, Marie-Noël (aka Billie)
KENT

Bundhoo, Devanand
LONDON NORTH WEST

Burck, Charlotte
LONDON EAST

Burlington, Maggie
LONDON SOUTH EAST

Cahill, Pauline
BERKSHIRE

Callea, Tamara
DEVON

Campbell, Kate
OVERSEAS-SPAIN

Campos, Hanne
SURREY

Carr, Brede
SOMERSET

Cashford, Jules
HAMPSHIRE

Casson, Isabel
SURREY

Chalfont, Alexandra
BRISTOL

Chalkley, A.J.
BRIGHTON AND HOVE

Chamberlain, Heather
LONDON NORTH WEST

China, Giselle
LONDON NORTH

China, Jacques
LONDON NORTH

Chopin, Mathias
GLASGOW

Christie, Jim
BEDFORDSHIRE

Clare, Louise
SURREY

Clayton, Gillian
HAMPSHIRE

Clement de L'Epine, Karen
LONDON SOUTH WEST

Clifton, Elaine
HAMPSHIRE

Cloridor-Wood, Madie
LONDON SOUTH WEST

Cockersell, Peter
GLASGOW

Coia, Grace
LONDON NORTH WEST

Colahan, Mireille
LONDON SOUTH WEST

Coles, Walter
LONDON NORTH

Conolly, John
BERKSHIRE

Coxwell-White, Jenny
GUERNSEY

Craske, Sarah
LONDON SOUTH WEST

Crawley, Barbara
DEVON

Crittenden, Juliet
LONDON CENTRAL

Crowe, Michael
LONDON CENTRAL

Dachy, Vincent
OVERSEAS-ISRAEL

Dana, Mira

Daniel, Gwyn
LONDON EAST CENTRAL

Dardenne, Patricia
OVERSEAS-FRANCE

Daudy, Isabelle
LONDON NORTH

Davenport, Marie-Laure

De Zulueta, Felicity
WEST MIDLANDS

Dennis, Elisabeth
LONDON NORTH WEST

Dent, Carey
LEICESTERSHIRE

Dickson Dummer, Karine
LONDON CENTRAL

Dillon Weston, Marisa
LONDON SOUTH EAST

Dobb, Cornelia
LONDON WEST

Dolphin, Eve
LONDON NORTH

Domb, Yair
HAMPSHIRE

Doulton MA, Caroline
HAMPSHIRE

Draper, Rosalind
LONDON NORTH WEST

Du Ry, Marc
MIDDLESEX

Dubinsky, Alexandre
LONDON NORTH WEST

Dubinsky, Helene
KENT

Duck, Dorothy
STAFFORDSHIRE

Dunn, Elizabeth
WEST SUSSEX

Dupont-Joshua, Aisha
BERKSHIRE

Economakis, Tara
LONDON NORTH

Ellis, Mary Lynne
LONDON CENTRAL

Evans, Sandra
LONDON NORTH WEST

Farhi, Nina
LONDON NORTH WEST

Ficarra, Berthe

Fletcher, Karyn
LONDON NORTH

Forti, Laura
BERKSHIRE

Foskett, Julia
LONDON NORTH WEST

Freudenberg, Susan
OXFORDSHIRE

Frisvold, Tove
LINCOLNSHIRE

Gagnere, Maryline
ESSEX

Gale, Derek
LANCASHIRE

Gauthier, Jean-Baptise
OVERSEAS-FRANCE

Gavin, Verity J
LONDON NORTH WEST

Gilbert, Kate
OVERSEAS-IRELAND

Gilmore, Jane
LONDON NORTH WEST

Gorodensky, Arlene
LONDON NORTH

Gorrell Barnes, Gill
GREATER MANCHESTER

Gowrisunkur, Jaya
LONDON NORTH

Graham, Judith
LONDON NORTH

Granville, Julia
LONDON SOUTH WEST

Green, Roberta
LONDON NORTH WEST

Green, Viviane
LONDON SOUTH WEST

Greenwood, John

Griffiths, Anne-Megan
SURREY

Grimshaw, Francoise
EAST YORKSHIRE

Guernina, Zoubida
CAMBRIDGESHIRE

Guild, Liz
LONDON NORTH WEST

Guillemot, Yves
LONDON NORTH WEST

Haine, Stephen R
LONDON NORTH

Hall, Guy
WEST SUSSEX

Halter, Kathy
LONDON WEST

Hamilton, Susan
OVERSEAS-FRANCE

Hamilton-Duckett, Paule
OXFORDSHIRE

Hanna, Gilli
BUCKINGHAMSHIRE

Harris, Bob
LONDON NORTH

Harris, Tirril
LONDON NORTH WEST

Hay-Burns, Jean
MIDDLESEX

Hayden, Martina
LONDON EAST

Hayes, Cheryl
LONDON WEST

Heap, Maggie
LONDON SOUTH WEST

Heller, Fawkia
LONDON SOUTH WEST

Henny, Lindy
LONDON NORTH WEST

Hering-Josefowitz, Pauline
LONDON SOUTH WEST

Hershkowitz, Annie
KENT

Hetherington, Hugh
CAMBRIDGESHIRE

Hivernel, Dr Francoise
LONDON EAST

Hoang, Astrid
LONDON WEST

Hobart, Angela
LONDON CENTRAL

Hodges, Jill
EAST SUSSEX

Holland, Sue
ESSEX

Hollingworth, Amanda
DEVON

Holmes, Jeremy
LONDON NORTH WEST

Houston, Gaie
SOMERSET

Howe, Patti
OXFORDSHIRE

Hughes, Eleanor
SURREY

Hughes-Bruderlin, Silvia
OXFORDSHIRE

Huish, I.P.
LONDON WEST

Humphry, Alexis
SURREY

Hussain, Fakhir
EAST SUSSEX

Hutton, Francoise
LONDON CENTRAL

Ingram, Sonia
OVERSEAS - SWITZERLAND

Itten, Theodor
LONDON NORTH WEST

Jaax, Stepahnie
OVERSEAS-SOUTH AFRICA

Janks, Ann
OVERSEAS - LEBANON

Jaroudi, Leila
LONDON SOUTH EAST

Jenkins, Hugh
DEVON

Jones, Nicole
DEVON

Josephs-Serra, Elisabeth
NOTTINGHAMSHIRE

Juggins, Kate
ESSEX

Julien, Michael
LONDON CENTRAL

Kerr, Anna
DEVON

Kerridge, Petra
DORSET

Kerry, Liz
ISLE OF MAN

Kirk, Catharine Rose
LONDON NORTH WEST

Kohon, Valli
LONDON SOUTH WEST

Kolbuszewski, Marianne
NORTHERN IRELAND

Lafargue-Meenan, Martine
LONDON NORTH

Lallah, Regine
GREATER MANCHESTER

Lamb, Kirsten
OXFORDSHIRE

Lamont-Hoffman, Elisabeth
LONDON NORTH

Latham, Valerie
LONDON CENTRAL

Leader, Darian
EDINBURGH

Lendrum, Susan
LONDON WEST

Leveque, Brigitte
LONDON NORTH

Lewis, Jacqueline
LANCASHIRE

Liddle, Helen
EAST SUSSEX

Lloyd, Elizabeth
DARLINGTON

Loiseau, Kate
LONDON NORTH

Lousada, Olivia
SURREY

Luden, Maureen
LANCASHIRE

Macnab, Celia
LONDON CENTRAL

Maguire, Anne
SOUTH YORKSHIRE

Maitlis, Marion
LONDON NORTH WEST

Mandin, Philippe
LONDON SOUTH WEST

Marling, Frances
LONDON WEST

Masoliver, Chandra
LONDON SOUTH EAST

Massara, Catharina
HERTFORDSHIRE

Maudling, Caroline
OVERSEAS-IRELAND

Mauger, Benig
KENT

McAndrew, Brigitte
LONDON WEST

McEldowney, Dennis
BATH

McLoughlin, Brendan
NORFOLK

Middlecoat, Andrew
KENT

Millais, Suzy
LONDON NORTH

Miller, Jean
OXFORDSHIRE

Mills Burton, M.
LONDON NORTH

Milroy, Rachel
LONDON WEST

Miqueu-Baz, Christine
TYNE AND WEAR

Mitchison, Sally
LONDON NORTH WEST

Moja-Strasser, Lucia
GLASGOW

Molleson, John Ivitsky
BEDFORDSHIRE

Morgan, Barbara
LONDON SOUTH EAST

Morin (Ms), Terry

Morris, Monique
BUCKINGHAMSHIRE

Moscoso de Richardson, Gloria
LONDON CENTRAL

Muir, Kate
LONDON EAST

Muller, Nina
LONDON NORTH WEST

Nabarro, Elizabeth
LONDON SOUTH WEST

Nappez, Sue
LONDON SOUTH WEST

Neal, (Ms) Lalage
LONDON NORTH

Nehmad, Annie
LONDON EAST

Nesbit, Judith
SURREY

Newbery, Christine
OXFORDSHIRE

Nissim, Ruth
BUCKINGHAMSHIRE

Nye, Ann
OVERSEAS-IRELAND

O'Connor, Aine

O'Dwyer, Annegret
LONDON SOUTH EAST

O'Grady, Margaret
HEREFORD AND WORCESTER

Oliver, Jenny
LONDON CENTRAL

Pacey, Susan
KENT

Passmore, Pascale
WEST SUSSEX

Pelissier, Kate
WEST YORKSHIRE

Peltier, Judy
LONDON NORTH

Pepeli, Hara
GREATER MANCHESTER

Perriollat Munro, Elisabeth
LONDON NORTH WEST

Phillips, Asha
LONDON SOUTH WEST

Pickles, Penny

Plissart, Liesbet
WILTSHIRE

Pocock, Olga
CHESHIRE

Pollet, Sheena
LONDON SOUTH WEST

Pollitzer, Juliette
HERTFORDSHIRE

Pooley, Jane
OXFORDSHIRE

Porter, Barbara
OXFORDSHIRE

Pregnall, Sheila
LONDON WEST

Proner, Barry D
BRISTOL

Purkiss, Jane
LONDON NORTH

Quoilin, Michelle
LONDON WEST

Raphaely, Mary
LONDON NORTH WEST

Rapp, Hilde
LONDON NORTH

Reguis, Marie-Christine

Reid, Elizabeth
WEST SUSSEX

Reilly, Nicole S.
LONDON NORTH

Renoux, Martine
OXFORDSHIRE

Reynal, Carmen
LONDON NORTH

Richards, Val
LEICESTERSHIRE

Ridgewell, Margaret
DEVON

Robertson, Zuleika
SOUTH YORKSHIRE

Robinson, Felicity
DEVON

Roddick, Mary
LANCASHIRE

Rodriquez-Slawinski, Flavia
SOUTH YORKSHIRE

Rosemary, Margaret
DORSET

Rosenthal, Alison
LONDON NORTH

Rozenberg, Rosette
LONDON SOUTH EAST

Ryley, Brigitte
SURREY

Sandbank, Audrey
LONDON SOUTH WEST

Sanders, Gill
LONDON NORTH WEST

Scarlett, Jean
MIDDLESEX

Seebarun, Dev
LONDON WEST

Shand, Belinda
LONDON EAST

Shearman, Christine
SURREY

Sheppard Fidler, Angela
SOUTH YORKSHIRE

Shipton, Geraldine
LONDON WEST

Sills, Charlotte
DEVON

Sills, Maura
LONDON SOUTH EAST

Silverton, Stephen
LONDON CENTRAL

Simpson, David
CAMBRIDGESHIRE

Sinclair, Alison
CAMBRIDGESHIRE

Sinclair, Fiona
LONDON EAST

Slade, John
LONDON SOUTH WEST

Smail, Richard
EAST SUSSEX

Snell, Robert C
EAST SUSSEX

Soutar, Sarah
LONDON CENTRAL

Southwell, Clover
LEICESTERSHIRE

Spare, Elaine
OVERSEAS-GREECE

Spiliopoulos, Valentine Andrikopoulos
HERTFORDSHIRE

Sproul-Bolton, Robin
LONDON SOUTH EAST

Stedman, Maire
ISLE OF WIGHT

Steele, Lesley
HEREFORD AND WORCESTER

Stern, Michele
LEICESTERSHIRE

Stewart, Ian
LONDON NORTH WEST

Stone, Martin
LONDON NORTH

Symons, Judith Jane
SURREY

Tabak, Carolyn
LONDON SOUTH WEST

Tanguay, Daniel
HEREFORD AND WORCESTER

Taylor, Jill
LONDON SOUTH WEST

Taylor, Louise
LONDON WEST

Thomas, Lennox
LONDON NORTH WEST

Touton-Victor, Patricia
LONDON SOUTH WEST

Tuby, Molly
LONDON NORTH WEST

Turp, Maggie
LONDON NORTH

Tutton, Catherine
BRIGHTON AND HOVE

Velarde, Dominique
LONDON SOUTH WEST

Wallace, Patti
BRIGHTON AND HOVE

Waller, Diane E
KENT

Watters, Tamara
CAMBRIDGESHIRE

Whittle, Lorna
LONDON NORTH

Wieselberg, Huguette
LONDON CENTRAL

Wigram, Penny
SURREY

Wilford, Gerti
DEVON

Wilson, Jancis
LONDON NORTH WEST

Wine, Noga
WARWICKSHIRE

Wren, Pauline
LONDON SOUTH WEST

Young, Sabine
SURREY

de Berker, Patricia
MIDDLESEX

de Serdici, Simona
SOUTH YORKSHIRE

van Deurzen, Emmy
SOUTH YORKSHIRE

**Gaelic**

McGrath, Patrick
LONDON CENTRAL

O Ruairc, Micheál
LONDON CENTRAL

**German**

Al Rubaie, Talal
LONDON NORTH

Albrecht, Gisela
POOLE

Andrews, Stuart
WEST MIDLANDS

Appel-Opper, Julianne
LONDON SOUTH EAST

Aust, Frank
KENT

Averbeck, Marcus
GLOUCESTERSHIRE

Baum, Stefanie
SURREY

Bayley, Eva
BATH

Bebber, Gillian
LONDON NORTH

Becker, Amely
GLASGOW

Begg, Ean
MERSEYSIDE

Bende, Brigitta
KENT

Bentley, Jacqueline
LONDON NORTH

Bierschenk, John Henry
LONDON WEST

Bishop, Beata
LONDON WEST

Boening, Joachim
LONDON WEST

Boening, Michaela
LONDON WEST

Boyesen, Gerda
LONDON NORTH

Brauner, Rita
LONDON CENTRAL

Brayne, Mark
LONDON WEST

Breninek, Andrea
HERTFORDSHIRE

Briggs, Margarete
EAST SUSSEX

Brosskamp, Cornelia
LONDON NORTH WEST

Buss-Twachtmann, Christel
BERKSHIRE

Callea, Tamara
OVERSEAS-SPAIN

Campos, Hanne
OVERSEAS-NETHERLANDS

Carton, Roy
OVERSEAS-GERMANY

Catina, Ana
SURREY

Chalfont, Alexandra
LONDON EAST

Chesner, Anna
LONDON NORTH WEST

China, Giselle
LONDON SOUTH EAST

Collard, Patrizia C
SURREY

Coombes, Clare
LONDON SOUTH WEST

Coronas, Ita
BERKSHIRE

Coxwell-White, Jenny
MIDDLESEX

Crick, Verena
MIDDLESEX

Crofton, Sue
OVERSEAS-CARIBBEAN

Crowley-Schweitzer, Brigitte
SOUTHAMPTON

Daniels, Mo
OVERSEAS-AUSTRALIA

David, Anna-Kristin
LONDON WEST

Deniflee, Ursula
HAMPSHIRE

Draper, Rosalind
OVERSEAS-SPAIN

Drury, Gitta
OVERSEAS-AUSTRALIA

Durlach, Stefan
LONDON CENTRAL

Ehlers, Hella
LONDON WEST

Eiden, Bernd
EAST SUSSEX

Eisenbarth, Heiner
OVERSEAS-SWEDEN

Eriksson, Tina
SURREY

Ertelt, Sylvia
OVERSEAS-SPAIN

Febrer-Bowen, Ines
LONDON SOUTH WEST

Fischer, Michael
CAMBRIDGESHIRE

Fitzgerald-Klein, Marianne
ESSEX

Fox, Almuth-Maria
LONDON WEST

Friedrich, Brigitte
LONDON SOUTH WEST

Gad, Gabriele
SURREY

Ganzleben, Jacqueline
DORSET

Gessert, Astrid
LONDON CENTRAL

Ginkell, Andreas
CHESHIRE

Goepfert, Michael
EAST SUSSEX

Gould, Vreni
LONDON NORTH WEST

Gross, Erwin
BUCKINGHAMSHIRE

Gustafsson, Birgitta
DEVON

Gölz, Angelika
SURREY

Hamm, Alexandra
ESSEX

Handrick, Olaf
WEST YORKSHIRE

Hanks, Helga
LONDON CENTRAL

Hanman, Elke
OXFORDSHIRE

Harris, Gordon
LONDON CENTRAL

Haupts, Brigitta
LONDON WEST

Hauser, Susan
OXFORDSHIRE

Hawxwell, Frances
LONDON NORTH

Hearst, Liesel
SURREY

Hedinger-Farrell, Korinna
GLOUCESTERSHIRE

Hedley, Karen
SURREY

Heiller, Birgitta R.
SURREY

Heimann, Michael
KENT

Heinitz, Karin
LONDON NORTH

Heismann, Elisabeth
LONDON SOUTH WEST

Heller, Fawkia
OXFORDSHIRE

Herbert, Claudia
LONDON NORTH WEST

Herst, Edward
LONDON WEST

Heuer, Gottfried
LONDON EAST

Hoang, Astrid
LONDON WEST

Hobart, Angela
OXFORDSHIRE

Hock, Gaby
LONDON NORTH

Hudson, Inge
SURREY

Hughes-Bruderlin, Silvia
OXFORDSHIRE

Huish, I.P.
OVERSEAS - SWITZERLAND

Itten, Theodor
LONDON NORTH WEST

Jaax, Stepahnie
OVERSEAS-SOUTH AFRICA

Janks, Ann
LONDON WEST

Karan, Alexandra
LONDON NORTH WEST

Karban, Barbara
LONDON WEST

Kaufmann, Mickey
DEVON

Kerridge, Petra
GREATER MANCHESTER

Kiemle, Gundi
LONDON NORTH WEST

Kisch, Marlies
LONDON NORTH WEST

Kloepfer, Irene
LONDON SOUTH EAST

Koeppelmann, Marianna
WEST YORKSHIRE

Kohler, Christiane
MIDDLESEX

Kokott, Claudius
BUCKINGHAMSHIRE

Kowalski, Reinhard
WEST MIDLANDS

Kuettner, Enno
OXFORDSHIRE

Landale, Margaret
EDINBURGH

Lendrum, Susan
LONDON NORTH

Leygraf, Bernd C
LANCASHIRE

Liddle, Helen
PERTH AND KINROSS

Liebing-Wilson, Marianne
LONDON WEST

Lude, Jochen
OXFORDSHIRE

Lutyens, Marianna
LONDON NORTH WEST

Mander, Gertrud
LONDON SOUTH WEST

Marcus, Marietta
OVERSEAS-IRELAND

Masterson, Ingrid
WEST YORKSHIRE

McCarthy-Hoffbauer, Iris
EAST SUSSEX

Medhat, Katayoun Tamara
ABERDEENSHIRE

Milne, Frances
CAMBRIDGESHIRE

Minnaar, Doris
DERBYSHIRE

Mitchell, Paul Christoph
LONDON CENTRAL

Mittwoch, Adele
LONDON NORTH

Moravia Kessel, Inge
BRISTOL

Moser, Marianne
LONDON EAST

Muller, Nina

Munro, Angela
LONDON SOUTH WEST

Netzer-Stein, Antje
GWYNEDD

Niesser, Arthur
LONDON NORTH

Noack, Amelie
DEVON

Noack, Miké
LONDON NORTH WEST

Norburn, Veronica
HERTFORDSHIRE

O'Donoghue, Margot

O'Dwyer, Annegret
OVERSEAS-AUSTRALIA

Ogilvie, Renate
OVERSEAS-SWITZERLAND

Ohnesorg, Johanna
GREATER MANCHESTER

Pantall, Marlis
SOMERSET

Parker, Niki
OVERSEAS-GERMANY

Pervöltz, Rainer
LONDON SOUTH WEST

Pickelin, Ulrike
GREATER MANCHESTER

Pirquet, Caroline
OVERSEAS-GERMANY

Pollak, Angela
WEST SUSSEX

Pothig, Elisabeth
OVERSEAS-GREECE

Poulopoulos, Katerina
LONDON NORTH WEST

Prall, Werner
SURREY

Rabe, Marie-Louise
LONDON NORTH WEST

Rapp, Hilde

Reid, Elizabeth
WILTSHIRE

Rheinschmiedt, Otto
LONDON NORTH

Richards, Val
HERTFORDSHIRE

Richter, Nicola
DERBYSHIRE

Ridley, Wendy
DORSET

Rosenthal, Alison
LONDON SOUTH WEST

Salm, Anne Marie
LONDON WEST

Schaible, Monika
LONDON NORTH WEST

Schiemann, Margot
CUMBRIA

Schmid-Borgschulte, Heide-Marie
SOUTHAMPTON

Scott, Brigitte
LONDON WEST

Shand, Belinda
LONDON EAST

Shearman, Christine
LONDON WEST

Smith, Jonathan
OXFORDSHIRE

Soth, Michael
LONDON CENTRAL

Southwell, Clover
LONDON CENTRAL

Speyer, Josefine
CAMBRIDGESHIRE

Stauffer, Kathrin
LONDON SOUTH WEST

Steffens, Dorothy
EAST SUSSEX

Stehle, Peter
BUCKINGHAMSHIRE

Steiner Celebi, Monika
LEICESTERSHIRE

Stewart, Ian
PORTSMOUTH

Stolte, Eva
LONDON SOUTH WEST

Strauli, Ursula

Strich, Sabina
GREATER MANCHESTER

Stummer, Gudrun
SUFFOLK

Sucher, Ingeborg A.
LONDON WEST

Syrett, Karin
LONDON NORTH

Sünkel, Sue
LONDON EAST

Thummel, Uwe
LONDON NORTH WEST

Turp, Maggie
KENT

Twelvetrees, Heidy
LONDON WEST

Uphoff-Chmielnik, Andrea
HEREFORD AND WORCESTER

Vogel, Karin
LONDON SOUTH EAST

Wach, Karin Marie
BERKSHIRE

Ward, Hilary
LONDON NORTH WEST

Weinrich, Hildegard
LONDON WEST

Weisensel, Karin
SURREY

Wilford, Gerti
LONDON NORTH WEST

Wilke, Gerhard
ESSEX

Williams, Dorothee
SURREY

Willis, Sally
LONDON NORTH WEST

Wolf, Darren
SURREY

Wyse, Hymie
SURREY

Yallop, Melanie
LONDON SOUTH WEST

Young, Sabine
HERTFORDSHIRE

van Bilsen, Henck P.J.G.
LONDON CENTRAL

von Britzke, Michaela
LONDON CENTRAL

## Ghanaian

Sawyerr, Alice A A
LONDON NORTH WEST

## Greek

Antonas, Vassilis
LONDON WEST

Arzoumanides, Yiannis
OVERSEAS-IRELAND

Bartlett, Olivia
LONDON NORTH

Cameron, Anna
ESSEX

Darivakis, Dimitri
LONDON SOUTH EAST

Dobb, Cornelia
BERKSHIRE

Economakis, Tara
LONDON SOUTH EAST

Economidou, Nitsa
LONDON NORTH

Eleftheriadou, Zack
LONDON SOUTH WEST

Eleftheriou-Barwell, Despina
LONDON CENTRAL

Ikkos, George
SURREY

Jeffries, V. Kiki
WEST MIDLANDS

Kypridemos, Petros
OVERSEAS-GREECE

Layiou-Lignos, Effie
LONDON SOUTH EAST

Livanou, M.
SHROPSHIRE

Loumidis, K
LONDON EAST

Luca, Maria
LONDON CENTRAL

Maratos, Jason
WEST YORKSHIRE

Mertzanakis, Christos
GLOUCESTERSHIRE

Morris, Elizabeth
LONDON NORTH WEST

Mouratoglou, Vassilis
LONDON NORTH WEST

Moutsou, Christina
OVERSEAS-GREECE

Moutzoukis, Chris
LONDON SOUTH WEST

Ntarili, Kassandra-Maria
LONDON EAST

Papadopoulos, Renos K
LONDON NORTH WEST

Parissis, Maria
LONDON NORTH

Pepeli, Hara
LONDON NORTH

Pericleous, Christine
LONDON NORTH

Petkova, Petia
BERKSHIRE

Ploumaki, Sophia
OVERSEAS-GREECE

Poulopoulos, Katerina
LONDON SOUTH WEST

Ragiadakos, Nikolas
LONDON SOUTH EAST

Sigalas, Anthony
LONDON NORTH WEST

Soultani, Effie
OVERSEAS-GREECE

Spiliopoulos, Valentine Andrikopoulos
HERTFORDSHIRE

Spyropoulos, Nick
LANCASHIRE

Vannen-Hyland, Joan
WEST MIDLANDS

Villia-Gosling, Athina
LONDON NORTH

Wieland, Christina
LONDON NORTH

Worrall, Chrysoula
OVERSEAS - GREECE

Zidianaki, Rania Argyro
OVERSEAS - GREECE

### Gujurati

Bhat, Radha
BUCKINGHAMSHIRE

Damani, S
MIDDLESEX

Desai, Asha

Hormasji, Faridoon
HEREFORD AND WORCESTER

Lacey, Tim
LEICESTERSHIRE

Laher, Aftab
MIDDLESEX

Magan, Bhagya
KENT

Maru, Rashmi
LONDON WEST

Nadirshaw, Zenobia
LONDON SOUTH WEST

Parikh, Prakash
LONDON NORTH

Patel, Gita
LONDON WEST

Sharma, Meera
LONDON NORTH WEST

Sheriff, Farida
ESSEX

Vibhakar, Lopa
ESSEX

### Hebrew

Alferoff, Tamara
LONDON EAST CENTRAL

Altman, Michelle M
LONDON NORTH

Amias, David
LONDON NORTH WEST

Anker, Ofra
LONDON NORTH WEST

Aram, Eliat
LONDON NORTH

Asheri, Shoshi
LONDON NORTH

Azgad, Racheli
LONDON EAST

Bender, Helen
LONDON NORTH

Berke, Joseph H
LONDON NORTH WEST

Cohen, Nomy
MIDDLESEX

Cohen, Ruth
OVERSEAS-ISRAEL

Dana, Mira
LONDON NORTH

Daniels, Orpa
LONDON NORTH

Dar, Limor
WEST MIDLANDS

Dennis, Elisabeth
LONDON CENTRAL

Dove, Rabbi Jonathan
OVERSEAS-SWEDEN

Frischer, Livia
LONDON NORTH WEST

Gal, Oshrat
LONDON NORTH WEST

Gaster, Yishai
LONDON EAST

Glendinning, Laura
LONDON EAST

Goldberg, Henia
OVERSEAS-ISRAEL

Green, Dror
LONDON NORTH WEST

Gross, Erwin
LONDON NORTH

Gurion, Michal
LONDON NORTH

Hadary, Gideon
OVERSEAS-AUSTRALIA

Harlap, Nahum
OXFORDSHIRE

Heitzler, Morit
LONDON NORTH

Koppelman, Liora
LONDON NORTH

Lederman, Tsafi
BUCKINGHAMSHIRE

Levitsky, Patricia D.
OVERSEAS-ISRAEL

Manielevitch, Edna
OXFORDSHIRE

Myers, Liora
LONDON EAST

Naor, Lillie
LONDON NORTH WEST

Oakley, Haya
OXFORDSHIRE

Offer, Leah
LONDON NORTH WEST

Rabin, Judith
LONDON NORTH

Rebuck, Alexandra Jane
LONDON NORTH

Rozenberg, Rosette
LONDON NORTH WEST

Sachs, Adah
LONDON NORTH

Schonfield, Tamar
LONDON NORTH WEST

Selwyn, Ruth
LONDON NORTH

Shapiro, Adella
LONDON NORTH

Singer, Iris
LONDON NORTH

Spitzer, Shayne
LONDON NORTH WEST

Spyer, Natalie
BUCKINGHAMSHIRE

Steiner Celebi, Monika
LONDON NORTH WEST

Stobezki, Yael
HERTFORDSHIRE

Stolear, Meir
LONDON NORTH

Weaver, Ziva
LONDON NORTH WEST

Weider, Bilha
LONDON NORTH

Wilson, Shula
LONDON NORTH WEST

Wine, Noga
LONDON WEST

Zin, Shoshi
LONDON WEST

### Heldakiew

Teng, Christina
ESSEX

### Hindi

Arora, Alka
SURREY

Bhat, Radha
KENT

Bundhoo, Devanand
SOUTH YORKSHIRE

Cariapa, Illana
SURREY

Chatterjee, Sherna Ghyara
MIDDLESEX

Desai, Asha
CLEVELAND

Dhar, Devika
HERTFORDSHIRE

Dhillon, Manjit

Hormasji, Faridoon
SURREY

Hussain, Fakhir
MIDDLESEX

Hussain, Nasima
LONDON NORTH WEST

Magriel, Nicolas
ESSEX

O'Brian, Charles
LONDON SOUTH WEST

Parikh, Prakash
LONDON EAST

Rao, Ms Varija
LONDON SOUTH WEST

Razzaq-Bains, Saira
MIDDLESEX

Rishiraj, Narinder S
MIDDLESEX

Seebarun, Dev
LONDON NORTH WEST

Shackle, Shahrukh Husain
LONDON WEST

Sharma, Meera
LONDON NORTH WEST

Singh, Reenee
ESSEX

Vibhakar, Lopa
GREATER MANCHESTER

Walker, Kanta
GREATER MANCHESTER

Walker, Sundar Kanta
GREATER MANCHESTER

## Hokkiew

Teng, Christina
ESSEX

## Hungarian

Bailey, Catalena
LONDON WEST

Bishop, Beata
KENT

Lanczi, Katalin
LONDON NORTH

Macnicol, Fred
LONDON SOUTH WEST

Marcus, Marietta
LONDON NORTH WEST

Moja-Strasser, Lucia
OVERSEAS-HUNGARY

Ormay, Tom
SURREY

Sipos, Zsuzsa
LONDON CENTRAL

Vibert, Eva
BERKSHIRE

Williams, K.A.
BERKSHIRE

## Icelandic

Einarsson, Pall
SOUTH YORKSHIRE

Gudjonsson, Ingolfur A
OVERSEAS-ICELAND

Sveinsdóttir, Björg
OVERSEAS-ICELAND

## Indonesian

Hobart, Angela
LONDON WEST

## Irish

Duffy, Kathleen
OVERSEAS-IRELAND

Gilmore, Jane
OVERSEAS-IRELAND

## Isreali

## Italian

Adema, Rachel
LONDON WEST

Arbia, G. Nicoletta
LONDON SOUTH WEST

Bennis, Jackie
OVERSEAS-ITALY

Benvenuto, Bice
OVERSEAS-SWEDEN

Berardi, Chris
SOMERSET

Bicknell, Sara
WEST MIDLANDS

Bisconti, Maria
LONDON SOUTH WEST

Boll, Antonia
LONDON SOUTH WEST

Buckley, Marie-Noël (aka Billie)
BERKSHIRE

Callea, Tamara
DUMFRIES AND GALLOWAY

Cardile, Pietro
LONDON WEST

Casatello, Giovanna
SURREY

Clayton, Gillian
LONDON WEST

Clifford MA, Barry
LONDON SOUTH WEST

Coronas, Ita
LONDON NORTH

Corso, Teresa
LONDON NORTH

Curti-Gialdino, Francesca
CAMBRIDGESHIRE

Davies, Judy

De Zulueta, Felicity
LONDON SOUTH EAST

Deres, Mebrat
LONDON NORTH

Dianin, Gianni
LONDON CENTRAL

Dillon Weston, Marisa
LONDON NORTH WEST

Du Ry, Marc
LONDON NORTH

Forti, Laura
LONDON WEST

Garcia-Llavona, Cristina M
LONDON CENTRAL

Gerra, Stephanie
CAMBRIDGESHIRE

Gobbato, Wendy
OVERSEAS - ITALY

Graziosi, Mariolina
SURREY

Hamm, Alexandra
LONDON NORTH

Hannon, Letizia M
LONDON NORTH

Harris, Tirril
LONDON NORTH WEST

Hay-Burns, Jean
LONDON WEST

Heap, Maggie
LONDON WEST

Hirst, Diane Zervas
LANCASHIRE

Hoyle-Wood, John

Ielitro, Denise
LONDON CENTRAL

Ingram, Sonia
LONDON NORTH

Inlander, Antonia
OVERSEAS-ITALY

Kenny, Vincent
DEVON

Kerridge, Petra
LONDON NORTH

Landi, Donatella
LONDON CENTRAL

Livingston, Christine

Macaro, Antonia
SOUTH YORKSHIRE

Maitlis, Marion
LONDON WEST

Masoliver, Chandra
LONDON NORTH

Mellows, David
LONDON NORTH WEST

Mendelsohn, Annette
LONDON SOUTH WEST

Micciarelli, Felicia
MIDDLESEX

Mills, Ted
OVERSEAS-ITALY

Molino, Anthony
LONDON SOUTH WEST

Morante, Flavia
LONDON NORTH

Nehmad, Annie

O'Dwyer, Annegret
LONDON NORTH

Panetta-Crean, Simona
BRISTOL

Patocchi, Matilde
LONDON SOUTH WEST

Pavincich, Lesley
OXFORDSHIRE

Pegoraro, Carla
LONDON SOUTH WEST

Pinto, Luca
HERTFORDSHIRE

Pozzi, Maria E.
LONDON NORTH WEST

Purpura, Davide
CAMBRIDGESHIRE

Reynolds, Alun
LANCASHIRE

Rodriquez-Slawinski, Flavia
OXFORDSHIRE

Ruggieri, Gloria
LONDON NORTH

Sabbadini, Andrea
LONDON NORTH WEST

Seu, Bruna Irene
LONDON NORTH

Spada, Marcantonio
LONDON SOUTH EAST

Spinelli, Ernesto
SURREY

Tabak, Carolyn
LONDON EAST

Thummel, Uwe
DEVON

Toblini, Roberta
WEST MIDLANDS

Toole, Stuart
LONDON NORTH

Usiskin, Judith
BRIGHTON AND HOVE

Waller, Diane E
LONDON SOUTH WEST

Wilson, Teresa
LONDON SOUTH WEST

## Japanese

Morino, Yuriko
LONDON CENTRAL

Nippoda, Yuko
HERTFORDSHIRE

Ozaki-Owen, Mariko
LONDON NORTH WEST

Sayama, Kinko

Tharp, David
LONDON CENTRAL

Totsuka, Yoko
KENT

Wilkinson, Susan
KENT

## Kannada

Rao, Ms Varija
LONDON NORTH WEST

Shivakumar, H.
LONDON NORTH WEST

## Kikuyu

Barry, Ruth

Ngone, Mary

## Luganda

Sabayinda, Michael
ESSEX

## Makaton

Linington, Mark
LONDON NORTH WEST

## Malay

Kaur, Manshant Rani
LONDON NORTH

Ngah, Zah
LONDON NORTH

## Maltese

Caruana, Charles Victor
LONDON NORTH

## Mandarin

Daum, Minna
LONDON NORTH WEST

Lau, Annie
OVERSEAS-SINGAPORE

Leong, Jessica
LONDON EAST

Sheng, Rosemary Hui
LONDON EAST

## Marati

Vibhakar, Lopa
ESSEX

## Norwegian

Boyesen, Gerda
SOUTHAMPTON

Dahle, Josephine
OXFORDSHIRE

Frisvold, Tove
SURREY

Heiller, Birgitta R.
LONDON NORTH WEST

Holm, Kirsti
LONDON NORTH

Jenssen, Einar D.
OVERSEAS - NORWAY

Mohn Engebretsen, Karin
WILTSHIRE

Reimers, Sigurd
POWYS

Sclater, Michael
POWYS

## Persian

Alayarian, Aida
HERTFORDSHIRE

Azarkadeh, Shoreh
HERTFORDSHIRE

Collins, Leila
SURREY

Hussain, Fakhir
SURREY

## Polish

Bem, M
SURREY

Chalfont, Alexandra
LONDON SOUTH EAST

Czubinska, Grazyna
MIDDLESEX

Drewnowska, Alicja
LONDON WEST

Dyczkowska, Ania
WEST SUSSEX

Gottesmann, Ewa
LONDON SOUTH EAST

Hanchen, Tomasz
LONDON SOUTH WEST

Kolbuszewski, Marianne
LONDON SOUTH EAST

Kowszun, Graz
LONDON SOUTH WEST

Maglo, Dorothy
LONDON WEST

Szymanska, Kasia (Y.L.C)
NORTH YORKSHIRE

Wojciechowska, Ewa
NORTH YORKSHIRE

## Portuguese

Bacha, Claire
LONDON NORTH WEST

Beck, Orit
LONDON SOUTH EAST

Draycott, Christine
GLOUCESTERSHIRE

Elliott, Lea
LONDON SOUTH WEST

Kujawski, Pedro
LONDON NORTH WEST

Machado, Danuza
LONDON NORTH

Mazure, David
SOUTH YORKSHIRE

McDonald, James
LONDON WEST

Mensinga, Vera
LONDON WEST

Miqueu-Baz, Christine
LONDON SOUTH WEST

Morante, Flavia
BUCKINGHAMSHIRE

Moscoso de Richardson, Gloria
LONDON NORTH

Nehmad, Annie
LONDON NORTH WEST

Nielsen, Claudia
LONDON NORTH WEST

Pearson, Jenny
LONDON NORTH

Pimentel, Edna Barreto
LONDON NORTH

Salles, Miriam
LONDON WEST

Sell, Patrick
LINCOLNSHIRE

Sutherland, Janet
LONDON NORTH WEST

Wine, Noga
LONDON NORTH WEST

de Samaio Campos, Claudia
LONDON NORTH WEST

## Punjabi

Arora, Alka
HERTFORDSHIRE

Dhillon, Manjit
SURREY

Dhillon Stevens, Harbrinder
LONDON EAST

Dosanjh, Charanjit
SOUTH YORKSHIRE

Harries, Rashida
LONDON NORTH

Kaur, Manshant Rani
BEDFORDSHIRE

Krause, Inga-Britt
LONDON NORTH WEST

Malik, Rabia
LONDON CENTRAL

Martin, Sheila
MIDDLESEX

Rishiraj, Narinder S
LONDON NORTH WEST

Shackle, Shahrukh Husain
LONDON WEST

Sharma, Meera
LONDON SOUTH WEST

Singh Sehmi, Harjinder
GREATER MANCHESTER

Walker, Kanta
GREATER MANCHESTER

Walker, Sundar Kanta
GREATER MANCHESTER

## Romanian

Bailey, Catalena
OVERSEAS-GERMANY

Catina, Ana
LONDON CENTRAL

Francis, Gabriela
LONDON NORTH WEST

Moja-Strasser, Lucia
MIDDLESEX

de Serdici, Simona
MIDDLESEX

## Russian

Bem, M
LONDON CENTRAL

Brayne, Mark
WEST MIDLANDS

Dennis, Elisabeth
LONDON EAST

Muller, Nina
WILTSHIRE

Pocock, Olga
LONDON WEST

Ponomareva, Nadejda
LONDON NORTH WEST

Prokayeva-Ross, Tatiana
CAMBRIDGESHIRE

Voikhanskaya, Marina
CAMBRIDGESHIRE

**Serbo-Croat**

Bojanic-Wright, Stoya
LONDON CENTRAL

Bozovic, Zoran
HERTFORDSHIRE

Dimcovic, Nada
LONDON WEST

Divac, Aleksandra Sanya
LONDON NORTH

Kostic, Jasna
LONDON NORTH

Krajnovic, Valentina J
LONDON WEST

Manojlovic, Jelena
LONDON CENTRAL

Markovic, Desa
LANCASHIRE

Markovic, Olivera
LONDON EAST

Papadopoulos, Renos K
LONDON NORTH WEST

Pecotic, Branka
LONDON NORTH WEST

Renton, Mirjana
LONDON WEST

Smiljanic, Slobadanka
WEST SUSSEX

van Rijn, Biljana
WEST SUSSEX

**Shona**

Ganda, Matthew
ESSEX

Mumvuri-Ellis, Gladys
ESSEX

**Sinhalese**

Fernando - O'Connor, Chandra
HAMPSHIRE

**Slovenian**

Kotnik, Rudi
HAMPSHIRE

Pugh, Anna
SURREY

Shawe-Taylor, Metka
SURREY

**Spanish**

Acquarone, Stella
LONDON SOUTH WEST

Aguirregabiria, Ana
KENT

Almond, Elaine
LONDON NORTH

Amias, David

Arredondo, Beverly
LONDON SOUTH EAST

Attias, Sandra
GREATER MANCHESTER

Bacha, Claire
LONDON WEST

Baker, Jan

Ball, Kevin
LONDON NORTH WEST

Beck, Orit
GLASGOW

Begg, Ean
LONDON NORTH WEST

Berdasco, Lourdes
LONDON NORTH

Blair, Dana-Jane
OVERSEAS-SPAIN

Botella, Luis
NORTHERN IRELAND

Buet Gonzalez, Silvia
LONDON SOUTH EAST

Cahill, Pauline
BERKSHIRE

Callea, Tamara
DEVON

Campbell, Kate
OVERSEAS-SPAIN

Campos, Hanne
LONDON CENTRAL

Canete, Maria
LONDON NORTH WEST

Cardelle Martinez, Raquel
LONDON SOUTH EAST

Carter, Mary Hope
BATH

Catton, Derek
LONDON NORTH

Chopin, Mathias
LONDON SOUTH WEST

Cockersell, Peter
LONDON SOUTH WEST

Coronas, Ita
LONDON SOUTH WEST

Corrales, Iris
LONDON NORTH

Corti, Lucia
OVERSEAS-ITALY

Coskeran, Helena
BERKSHIRE

Costa, Beverley
LONDON SOUTH WEST

Crawley, Barbara
LONDON SOUTH EAST

Cumberbatch, Andrea

De Zulueta, Felicity
LONDON NORTH

Dianin, Gianni
BRISTOL

Diaz, Marie Claire
LONDON SOUTH EAST

Dobb, Cornelia
LONDON NORTH

Dowling, Emilia
OVERSEAS-SPAIN

Drury, Gitta
NORTH YORKSHIRE

Ellenor, Deby
LONDON NORTH WEST

Eslava, Carlota
OVERSEAS-SPAIN

Febrer-Bowen, Ines

Franses, Adena
LONDON SOUTH WEST

Friedrich, Michael
SURREY

Ganzleben, Jacqueline
LONDON WEST

Garcia-Llavona, Cristina M
LONDON WEST

Glyn, David R

Glynn, Julie
LONDON NORTH

Glynn, Tania
LONDON EAST

Goti, Itsaso
LONDON NORTH

Graham, Judith
KENT

Green, Eliott
EAST YORKSHIRE

Guernina, Zoubida
LONDON NORTH WEST

Guillemot, Yves
EAST YORKSHIRE

Hamlin, Cynthia Diana
LONDON CENTRAL

Hanman, Elke
GREATER MANCHESTER

Hardy, Jennifer
MIDDLESEX

Hayden, Martina
LANCASHIRE

Hayward, Marjorie
LONDON SOUTH WEST

Howard, Gloria
KENT

Hughes, Deri
BRISTOL

Hughes, Hatty
OVERSEAS-SPAIN

Ibanez, Julian
DEVON

Josephs-Serra, Elisabeth
GREATER MANCHESTER

Ledward Hobbes, Judi
LONDON SOUTH WEST

Lema, Juan Carlos
CAMBRIDGESHIRE

Lew, Clara
LONDON NORTH

Leygraf, Bernd C
SURREY

Llewellyn, Martha
LINCOLNSHIRE

Lohman, Frans
SURREY

Looms, Suzanne
SURREY

Luden, Maureen
SOUTH YORKSHIRE

Maitlis, Marion
LONDON SOUTH WEST

Marling, Frances
LONDON WEST

Masoliver, Chandra
BATH

McLoughlin, Brendan
LONDON WEST

Mendoza, Hilda
KENT

Millais, Suzy
GLOUCESTERSHIRE

Miller, Sarah
LONDON WEST

Miqueu-Baz, Christine
OVERSEAS-PERU

Montalbetti, M.L.
LONDON NORTH

Montero, Isabel
BUCKINGHAMSHIRE

Moscoso de Richardson, Gloria
LONDON NORTH

Mulhern, Alan
LONDON NORTH

Nehmad, Annie
LONDON CENTRAL

O Ruairc, Micheál
ESSEX

O'Leary, Carmen
CAMBRIDGESHIRE

Pain, Jean
LONDON NORTH

Penalosa-Clarke, Adriana Lucia
WEST MIDLANDS

Perez-De-Albeniz, Alberto
LONDON NORTH WEST

Purpura, Davide
EAST SUSSEX

Rae, Frances
LONDON SOUTH EAST

Renouf, Johanna
OXFORDSHIRE

Reynal, Carmen
LONDON SOUTH EAST

Robinson, Ferga

Robinson, Mardi
LANCASHIRE

Rodriquez-Slawinski, Flavia
LONDON NORTH

Ryz, Patsy
OVERSEAS-SOUTH AMERICA

Salazar, Maria Idalid Carreno
LONDON NORTH

Schmitt-Castilla, Maria
CAMBRIDGESHIRE

Sinclair, Alison
LONDON SOUTH EAST

Stedman, Maire
LONDON NORTH WEST

Stone, Martin
SURREY

Taylor, Marsha
SURREY

Testa, Rita
LONDON NORTH WEST

Touton-Victor, Patricia

Valea, Ana
LONDON NORTH

Valentine, Victoria
SUFFOLK

Westcott, Emma
HERTFORDSHIRE

Wheeler, Maria
LONDON EAST CENTRAL

Whitney, Glenn
SURREY

Woddis, Helena
LONDON SOUTH WEST

Young, Sabine
LONDON SOUTH WEST

de Marquiegui, Dr Asun
HAMPSHIRE

von Buhler, J M A Herbert Pardo
HAMPSHIRE

**Swahili**

Barry, Ruth

Ngone, Mary
ESSEX

Sabayinda, Michael
ESSEX

**Swedish**

Bengtsson, Lars-Erik
OVERSEAS-SWEDEN

Berardi, Chris
OVERSEAS-SWEDEN

Bragée, Britt
LONDON SOUTH WEST

Breitenstein, Dorrit
OVERSEAS - SWEDEN

Britt, Bragee
OXFORDSHIRE

Burns-Lundgren, Eva
LONDON NORTH

Byring, Carola
OVERSEAS - SWEDEN

Carlsson, Lena
OVERSEAS-SWEDEN

Curman, Barbro
OVERSEAS-SWEDEN

Dewhirst, Elisabeth
OVERSEAS-SWEDEN

Eliason, Bertil L
OVERSEAS-SWEDEN

Eriksson, Anders
OVERSEAS-SWEDEN

Eriksson, Tina
OVERSEAS-SWEDEN

Frischer, Livia
OXFORDSHIRE

Frisvold, Tove
LONDON NORTH WEST

Gildebrand, Katarina
BUCKINGHAMSHIRE

Gustafsson, Birgitta
OVERSEAS-SWEDEN

Hagelthorn, Christina

Harley, Ki
LONDON NORTH

Isaksson-Hurst, Gun I.E.
LONDON NORTH

Johansson, Birgitta
EDINBURGH

Kjellstrom, Laila
BEDFORDSHIRE

Krause, Inga-Britt
DEVON

Laitinen, Irmeli
OXFORDSHIRE

Lindley-Jones, Kerstin
LONDON SOUTH EAST

Massara, Catharina
OVERSEAS - NORWAY

Mohn Engebretsen, Karin
DEVON

Pehrsson-Tatham, Lena
SURREY

Perera, Ajit
LONDON NORTH

Seymour, Charlotte
OXFORDSHIRE

Smith, Eva
LONDON NORTH WEST

Sullivan, Anita
OVERSEAS - SWEDEN

Söderqvist, Ingrid
OVERSEAS-FINLAND

Söderström, Anne-Charlotte

Tengelin, Hans
OVERSEAS-SWEDEN

Thrane, Susanne
MIDDLESEX

de Serdici, Simona
MIDDLESEX

**Swiss German**

Itten, Theodor
LONDON NORTH WEST

Kisch, Marlies
KENT

Twelvetrees, Heidy
KENT

**Tamil**

Palanisamy, Shan
BOURNEMOUTH

Venki, Malathi
BOURNEMOUTH

**Tigrigna**

Deres, Mebrat
LONDON SOUTH EAST

**Turkish**

Akan, Semra
LONDON EAST

Aksoy Robins, A Asu
LONDON NORTH WEST

Boysan, Zehra
LONDON NORTH

Güngör, Dilek
LONDON NORTH

Sengun, Seda
LONDON SOUTH WEST

Yazar, Jale
ESSEX

Yusef, Dori Fatma
ESSEX

**Urdu**

Arora, Alka
SURREY

Bhat, Radha
SOUTH YORKSHIRE

Harries, Rashida

Hormasji, Faridoon
SURREY

Hussain, Fakhir
MIDDLESEX

Hussain, Nasima
LONDON NORTH WEST

Magriel, Nicolas
LONDON NORTH WEST

Malik, Rabia
ESSEX

O'Brian, Charles
LONDON SOUTH WEST

Razzaq-Bains, Saira
LONDON NORTH WEST

Shackle, Shahrukh Husain
LONDON WEST

Sharma, Meera
LONDON NORTH WEST

Sheriff, Farida
GREATER MANCHESTER

Walker, Kanta
GREATER MANCHESTER

Walker, Sundar Kanta
GREATER MANCHESTER

**Welsh**

Bisgood, Bill
CARMARTHENSHIRE

Davies, Dilys
CARDIFF

Davies, Mairlis
ESSEX

Ellis, Sian
ISLE OF ANGLESEY

Gill, Martin
DENBIGHSHIRE

Hughes, Lynette
EAST SUSSEX

Lloyd, Elizabeth
CAMBRIDGESHIRE

Morgan, Sian
RHONDDA CYNON TAFF

Thomas, Jenny
RHONDDA CYNON TAFF

**Xhoga**

Wela Nkumanda, Rachel
LONDON SOUTH EAST

**Yiddish**

Rozenberg, Rosette
LONDON NORTH

**Yoruba**

Fagbadegun, Rufus
GREATER MANCHESTER

**Zimbabwean**

Jiah, Hildah
LONDON SOUTH EAST

# Alphabetical Listing

## C

**E**

**F**

## G

**H**

## I



## J

**M**

**N**



**O**

**P**

## Q

**R**

**S**

**T**

**U**



**V**



**W**

**Y**



**Z**

For Product Safety Concerns and Information please contact our EU representative GPSR@taylorandfrancis.com Taylor & Francis Verlag GmbH, Kaufingerstraße 24, 80331 München, Germany

**Batch number: 10723886**

Printed by Printforce, the Netherlands